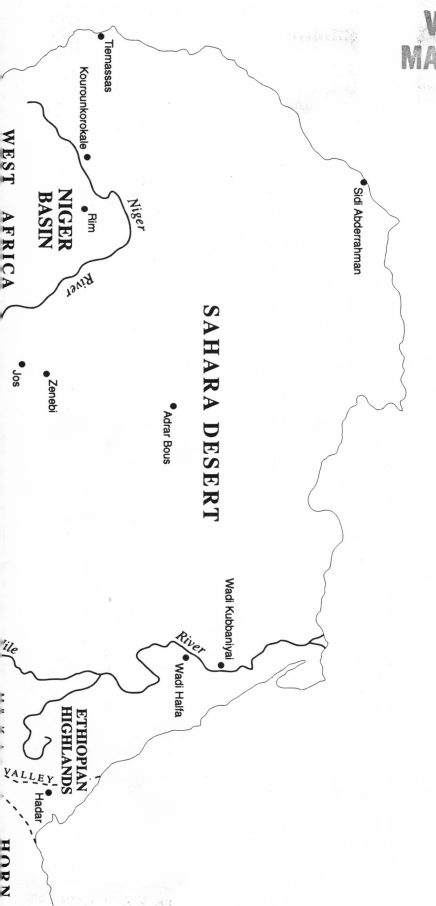

STONE AGE AFRICA

SAHARA DESERT

WEST AFRICA

NIGER BASIN

Temassas

Kourounkorokale

Rim

Niger

River

Jos

Zenebi

Adrar Bous

Sidi Abderrahman

Wadi Kubbaniya

River

Wadi Halfa

ETHIOPIAN HIGHLANDS

VALLEY

Hadar

HORN

Encyclopedia of

PRECOLONIAL AFRICA

Editor

JOSEPH O. VOGEL
University of Alabama
Department of Anthropology
Tuscalosa, Alabama

Editorial Advisors

BASSEY W. ANDAH
Department of Archaeology and Anthropology
University of Ibadan
Ibadan, Nigeria

FEKRI A. HASSAN
Petrie Professor of Archaeology
Institute of Archaeology
University College London
London, United Kingdom

FRANCIS B. MUSONDA
The Lusaka National Museum Project
Lusaka, Zambia

INNOCENT PIKIRAYI
History Department
University of Zimbabwe
Harari, Zimbabwe

PETER ROBERTSHAW
Department of Anthropology
California State University
San Bernardino, California

Encyclopedia of
PRECOLONIAL AFRICA

Archaeology, History, Languages,
Cultures, and Environments

JOSEPH O. VOGEL
Editor

JEAN VOGEL
Editorial Manager

A Division of Sage Publications, Inc.

Walnut Creek • London • New Delhi

For information contact:

AltaMira Press
A Division of Sage Publications, Inc.
1630 North Main Street, Suite 367
Walnut Creek, California 94596 U.S.A.

Sage Publications Ltd.
6 Bonhill Street
London EC2A 4PU United Kingdom

Sage Publications India Pvt. Ltd.
M-32 Market
Greater Katlash 1 New Delhi 110 048 India

Printed in the United States of America

Library of Congress Cataloging-in-Publication Data

Encyclopedia of precolonial Africa : archaeology, history,
    languages, cultures, and environments / editor, Joseph O. Vogel
            p. cm.
        Includes bibliographical references and index.
        ISBN 0-7619-8902-1 (alk. paper)
        1. Africa—Encyclopedias. I. Vogel, Joseph O.
        DT. E53 1996
        960'.2—dc21
96-51227
CIP

97 98 99 00 01 02 7 6 5 4 3 2 1

Produced by Zenda, Inc.
Interior and Cover Design by Gore Studio, Inc.
Editorial Management by Denise M. Santoro

CONTENTS

PEOPLE AND CULTURE

PREHISTORY OF AFRICA

LIST OF FIGURES

LIST OF TABLES

ABOUT THE EDITOR

The editor, Joseph O. Vogel, was born in the South Bronx, in New York City, in 1936. He received his undergraduate training in anthropology at Hunter College in New York City. While still an undergraduate, he traveled first to southern Illinois, to excavate at the Modoc rock shelter with the Illinois State Museum, and South Dakota, to dig at a number of prehistoric villages, with the Smithsonian Institution River Basin Survey. He pursued graduate studies at the University of California–Berkeley, while working as a preparator in the R. H. Lowie Museum of Anthropology and revisiting the Midwest to excavate a number of prehistoric sites for the Kansas State Historical Society. In 1961, he dug at the great Mississippian site of Cahokia and then spent the next three years revisiting Cahokia and analyzing the large collection of ceramics excavated there. Following his years at Cahokia, he spent a year and a half exploring the French fortress of Louisbourg on Cape Breton Island, Nova Scotia, with the National Parks Service, Canada. In 1964, he was appointed Keeper of Prehistory at the Livingstone Museum, Livingstone, Zambia.

Over the next decade, he, and his wife, explored the regions around Lake Bangweulu in northeastern Zambia, traveled to eastern Zambia, and conducted excavations at Late Stone Age caves in the Mumbwa district of central Zambia, as well as extensive stratigraphic excavations in the Upper Zambezi Valley, buLozi, and the Victoria Falls region. The outcome of these latter investigations was a comprehensive reconstruction of the settlement history of southwestern Zambia. He conducted an ethnographic survey of traditional African farming, which influenced his ideas on the history of farming in southeastern Africa, the development of small-scale polities, and their evolution into statelike formations.

In 1974, he earned his doctorate from Balliol College, University of Oxford, for a dissertation synthesizing his many years of archaeological fieldwork in the Victoria Falls region. He has published widely in scientific and popular journals on the archaeology of south central Africa and Victorian period exploration of southern Africa. He has taught at Northern Illinois University, where he was director of the Museum of Anthropology, and the University of Alabama, where he was director of the Alabama Museum of Natural History.

LIST OF CONTRIBUTORS

Alexander, John, St. John's College, Cambridge, U.K.

Ambrose, Stanley H., University of Illinois, U.S.A.

Barham, Lawrence S., University of Bristol, U.K.

Barich, Barbara, University of Rome, Italy

Bartram, Laurence, Jr., Franklin and Marshall College, U.S.A.

Bisson, Michael S., McGill University, Canada

Blench, Roger, Independent Researcher, Cambridge, U.K.

Blumenschine, Robert J., Rutgers University, U.S.A.

Bousman, C. Britt, University of Texas–San Antonio, U.S.A.

Bower, John R. F., University of Minnesota, U.S.A.

Brandt, Steven A., University of Florida, U.S.A.

Bunn, Henry T., University of Wisconsin, U.S.A.

Clutton-Brock, Juliet, The Natural History Museum, U.K.

Connah, Graham, The Australian National University, Australia

Cornelissen, Els, Koninklijk Museum voor Midden-Afrika, Belgium

de Barros, Philip, Palomar College, U.S.A.

de Maret, Pierre, Université Libre de Bruxelles, Belgium

Deacon, Hilary John, University of Stellenbosch, South Africa

DeCorse, Christopher, Syracuse University, U.S.A.

Dowson, Thomas A., University of Southampton, U.K.

Driskell, Boyce, Alabama Museum of Natural History, U.S.A.

Eggert, Manfred K. H., Eberhard-Karls-Universität Tüebingen, Germany

Ehret, Christopher, University of California–Los Angeles, U.S.A.

Fagan, Brian, University of California–Santa Barbara, U.S.A.

Fattovich, Rodolfo, Instituto Universitario Orientale, Italy

Grove, A. T., Downing College, U.K.

Guenther, Mathias G., Wilfrid Laurier University, Canada

Hakansson, N. Thomas, University of Kentucky, U.S.A.

Hall, Martin, University of Cape Town, South Africa

Harlan, Jack R., University of Illinois, U.S.A.

Hassan, Fekri A., Institute of Archaeology, U.K.

Holl, Augustin F. C., Université de Paris X, France

Horton, Mark, University of Bristol, U.K.

Huffman, Thomas N., University of the Witwatersrand, South Africa

Huysecom, Eric, Université de Genève, Switzerland

Inskeep, R. R., Pitt-Rivers Museum and University of Oxford, U.K.

Karega-Munene, I., National Museums of Kenya, Kenya

Kelly, Kenneth G., Northern Arizona University, U.S.A.

Krause, Richard A., University of Alabama, U.S.A

Kusimba, Chapurukha M., Field Museum of Natural History, U.S.A.

Levy, Thomas E., University of California–San Diego, U.S.A

Lim, Imogene L., Malaspina University-College, Canada

Lubell, David, University of Alberta, Canada

MacDonald, Kevin, The Institute of Archaeology, U.K.

MacEachern, Scott, Bowdoin College, U.S.A

Maggs, T. M. O'C., Constantia, South Africa

Marchi, Séverine, Université de Genève, Switzerland

McBrearty, Sally, University of Connecticut, U.S.A.

McIntosh, Roderick J., Rice University, U.S.A.

McIntosh, Susan Keech, Rice University, U.S.A.

Michael, Barbara J., American Institute for Yemeni Studies, U.S.A.

Miller, Duncan, University of Cape Town, South Africa

Mitchell, Peter J., Pitt-Rivers Museum, Oxford, U.K.

Motz, Jeffrey C., Alabama Museum of Natural History, U.S.A.

Musonda, Francis, Lusaka Museum, Zambia

Muzzolini, Alfred, Laboratoire d'Archaeozoologie, France

Negash, Agazi, University of Florida, U.S.A., and National Museums of Ethiopia, Ethiopia

Nurse, Derek, Memorial University of Newfoundland, Canada

Nyamweru, Celia, St. Lawrence University, U.S.A.

Parker, Sue Taylor, Sonoma State University, U.S.A

Paterson, James D., University of Calgary, Canada

Pennington, Renee L., Pennsylvania State University, U.S.A.

Pikirayi, Innocent, University of Zimbabwe, Zimbabwe

Pwiti, Gilbert, University of Zimbabwe, Zimbabwe

Reid, Andrew, University of Botswana, Botswana

Robbins, Lawrence H., Michigan State University, U.S.A.

Scott, Louis, University of the Free State, South Africa

Sheppard, Peter J., University of Auckland, New Zealand

Sillen, Andrew, University of Cape Town, South Africa

Smith, Andrew B., University of Cape Town, South Africa

Smith, Fred, Northern Illinois University, U.S.A.

Soper, Robert, University of Zimbabwe, Zimbabwe

Swan, Lorraine, Museum of Human Sciences, Zimbabwe

Thornton, John, Millersville University, U.S.A.

Vaum, Patricia A., University of Alabama, U.S.A.

Vogel, Joseph O., University of Alabama, U.S.A.

Werz, Bruno E. J. S., University of Cape Town, South Africa

Wetterstrom, Wilma, Harvard University, U.S.A.

Whitelaw, Gavin, Natal Museum, South Africa

Williams, Bruce, University of Chicago, U.S.A.

Williamson, Kay, University of Port Harcourt, Nigeria

PREFACE

Africa, the Dark Continent. Darkest Africa. Sub-Saharan Africa! The classical world knew the lands beyond the deserts of northern Africa as a source of rare and valuable commodities. Carthaginian mariners were said to have traded along the western and eastern coasts. Medieval Europe knew it only as a remote place of mystery: the abode of Prester John, griffins, and unicorns. Only Islam spreading south through the Sahara and settling along the east coast came into direct contact with the great kingdoms in the interior. Then in the 16th century, the Portuguese rounded the Cape venturing inland to trade with Monomatapa. European entrepreneurs near the end of the 18th century looked toward sub-Saharan Africa as a potential source of raw materials and new markets. By the mid-19th century, European adventurers were searching for the fabled cities of Tombouctou and Ophir (Great Zimbabwe) as well as exploring the headwaters of the Nile and other geological wonders of the continent.

By the end of the 19th century, tropical Africa had been divided up among the European powers. The enduring images of the continent were of the "white hunter" of Quatermain ilk, or colonial administrators, like Sanders of the River. Vaguely, the general culture comprehended East Africa as a source of interesting fossils of early kinds of human. Popular magazines even depicted the "South African missing link" in life and death conflict with baboons. Otherwise, the picture of a dark continent, of interest only as a curiosity, still remains a dominant literary (and cinematic) convention for depicting the history or cultures of the continent.

Slightly more than 100 years ago, the archaeologist J. Theodore Bent conducted one of the earliest archaeological expeditions to sub-Saharan Africa, seeking to explain the origins of the ruins of the Great Zimbabwe. He decided that the monumental architecture was the product of an ancient race of settlers from the Near East. His methods, with a heavy reliance on literary sources and late Victorian conventional wisdom, derived a solution to this "mystery" suited to his time and his contemporaries, who perceived tropical Africa as the home of naive tribal people barely subsisting on horticulture and simple technologies.

A decade later, the introduction of a more enlightened and scientific kind of archaeology by David Randall-McIver derived a quite different solution to the problem, ceding construction of these massive works to an unknown African people of relatively recent times. During the next half century, science sought to reconcile the invention of complex societies in tropical Africa with the fabrication of a fictional people—the Hamites—derived from Europe or India to whom monumental construction could be safely assigned without involving any Africans then under colonial administration.

Nearly 40 years ago, the rise of independent African states began to alter the world's perception of Africa, its people, and their history. Archaeologists, increasingly Africans themselves or non-Africans trained as anthropologists, began to explore once parochial subjects, such as the autochthonous origins and development of local chiefdoms, as well as the indigenous birth, development, and florescence of great states on the continent. Archaeology was in the process of returning to tropical Africa its history. As the numbers of investigators increased, so too did worldwide interest in the people of Africa.

At the same time, this increased number of researchers, no longer bound by the constraints of colonial governments and administrators, explored the myriad cultural byways of the continent describing a cultural diversity adapted to the varied environments of a complex continent. New inroads were made toward answering questions about the physical origins of humanity and of the properties of early culture, which facilitated the spread of humans throughout the continent and to the greater world beyond. New research technologies were tested, dating human fossils to distant eras or exploring trace elements absorbed from ancient diets. Investigators sought the earliest signs of human habitation, while elsewhere they looked for early evidence of cultivation or tested theories about the spread of herding or farming technologies.

If Africa had a relevance as the stage upon which the first acts of the human drama were played out, it has a further relevance as a continent of finely textured cultures and multilayered historical development belying the "Dark Continent" sobriquet.

Reflecting upon the changing attitudes within science toward Africa, its history, and its people and the growing body of new information published in journals and research monographs and presented at meetings worldwide, it seemed timely to assemble a select group of syntheses, representing an up-to-date appraisal of our comprehension of Africa's precolonial past. At the same time, for the general reader to understand the elements of past African culture, it was reasonable to supply entry into the many worlds of Africa, with ethnographic context and a discussion of the changing environments of the continent.

The African Experience

The editor derived his prime directive from the fact that not only would many readers have no previous experience of Africa, but that they could use an introduction to the lifeways there

and the varied technologies used. It was important to explain that humans once lived in Olduvai Gorge, how they manufactured their tools, and how the craft of working with stone was perfected into increasingly more efficient tools through time. It was also necessary to establish the credentials of the Stone Age as a time of experimentation and subtle adaptation. It seemed reasonable to assume, as well, that one can not fully appreciate the craft of African smiths without some introduction to the metallurgy they mastered. As one who long observed African farmers, I thought it essential to explain the mechanics of their agriculture and the slender margins for error created by the temperaments of Africa's dodgy climates.

And so, with the various aspects of African life and culture, we sought to distill our present knowledge of the field, synthesizing a vast and complex literature. The rule for creating the *Encyclopedia* was that it should offer anyone desiring a comprehensive knowledge of African culture and history the necessary syntheses, along with short bibliographies sufficient to pass the reader on to the more specialized literature. In so doing, we had in mind university undergraduates, the general reader interested in archaeology and anthropology, and teaching professionals needing insight into peripheral fields beyond their own research specialties.

Tales of the *Encyclopedia*

This project originally began as a suggestion from an editor at Garland Publishing, who posited an encyclopedia with information about African archaeology. As originally proposed, it would been a compilation of short notes defining significant sites, cultures, and personalities. That editor was replaced, and while we were still in the process of organizing the board of advisors, the project was redefined a couple of times into its present form as a series of essays. While we were in the process of collecting the entries, Garland decided to get out of the encyclopedia business and the project was, fortunately, picked up by Mitch Allen and AltaMira Press and given its present shape.

In the midst of arranging details with AltaMira, some authors, thinking the project terminated by Garland, had to be reassured that it was still ongoing and that their entries would still be needed.

This was a minor distraction to me and my wife, Jean, organizing what became a worldwide network, soliciting manuscripts, and working with the authors until they had completed them. More than one author became absorbed in a new university position, while others went into the field. Some, I am sure, hoped that we would stop pestering them. At one point, the only way we could communicate with a colleague in central Africa was through a Lusaka newspaper that happened to have a Web page on the Internet. Another, unable to mail or fax a manuscript directly to us, gave letters to friends who mailed them from a third country. When I tried to contact another colleague through a third party, I discovered that the Internet had been severed by the local government.

One thing I believe many of our authors discovered was how difficult it is to create short summaries, synthesizing a significant body of data. The editor discovered a fresh pleasure in drawing forth these entries and the information contained in them.

Others with experience in assembling similar volumes warned us of the possible frustrations attendant on late or delinquent authors. I believe that we were fortunate and have had a very cooperative cohort of collaborators. The experience has been a very pleasant one.

Organization of This Volume

As originally conceived, the volume was to be alphabetically arranged in such a way that geographically coincident entries would naturally fall together. Subsequently, it was decided to organize the entries according to an outline we had created to check that we had adequate coverage of specific subjects—that all the material on the Ceramic Late Stone Age or the Iron Age, for example, was assigned and completed. Early in the process, Nick David at Calgary critiqued an outline I had created and suggested a more logical construct. In time, the outline developed in various ways, but the basic format was to offer a more-or-less chronological, or developmental, progression.

The first part of the volume consists of material that may be considered context: the presentation of environmental information, research histories, and background to the technologies, languages, and lifeways of sub-Saharan Africa. The remainder of the volume carries the narrative from the physical development of humanity through the adaptive stages of stone-using foragers, food producers, and complex societies leading to the residues of historically recorded times and the investigation of sites identifiable in the historical record.

Creation of the *Encyclopedia*

Having set as our goal a comprehensive survey of African culture through time, having made a preliminary outline of the topics to be covered, and working with the Advisors Fekri Hassan, Peter Robertshaw, Bassey Andah, Innocent Pikirayi, and Francis Musonda, we sought out a group of prospective authors. Many of these people were already working on the problems we wanted synthesized. This brought us into contact with a broad spectrum of our immediate colleagues as well as with individuals engaged in research far afield from the editor's primary interest in the development of agriculture in south-central Africa.

One unspoken goal was to find colleagues willing to write essays on subjects that had intrigued me from time to time, since I felt that these discussions would appeal to others as well. The histories of research and the discussions of technology and palaeoanthropology, among others, like Phil de Barros' study of the social significance of iron workers, are prime examples of this approach. Over a period of a year (though the process was a continuing and evolving one), authors were contacted. The response was very heartening. Most interesting were the individuals who, having accepted our charge, suggested others who could expand or supplement their own work. This cross-fertilization helped increase the range and relevancy of the final offering, while establishing logical relationships between essays, as authors corresponded and complemented one another.

The feedback to and from the authors was always pleasant, as the drafts were perused, commented upon, and processed on our trusty computers. The people involved, at one time or another, lived in several countries on five continents and Oceania. Contact was maintained by telephone, air mail, E-mail, and fax as people living in awkward distant time zones moved from place to place and the different deadlines approached. As should be expected, during a nearly four-year period, involving nearly 100 individuals active in their research or teaching, beset with a myriad of small (and not so small) personal problems, we suffered through delays, missed communications, and prolonged silences, which made us doubt that the project would ever be completed as planned. In the end, our authors fulfilled their commitments to the project, and the volume appears pretty much as we envisioned it.

Reading the *Encyclopedia*

Having said that our intention was to cover as comprehensively as possible the varied information available on African culture and history, I must, at this juncture, explain certain limitations, if that is what they truly are. When the project was first discussed, it was suggested that a comprehensive archaeology of Africa be compiled. Although this was a worthy goal, I felt that to expand our geographical limits beyond sub-Saharan Africa would involve digressions into interaction between the European and northern African Stone Ages, or Phoenician, Roman, Byzantine and Islamic northern Africa and explorations of the wonders of Egypt, any of which could easily produce a volume equal to the present one. Rather than dwarf the substance of sub-Saharan African culture, I was determined to highlight it. Nevertheless, we pushed our geographical limits into the Sahara and beyond in the sections on rock art and the Neolithic and the discussions of the reciprocities among Egypt, the Upper Nile Valley, and the people of sub-Saharan Africa. We describe the interaction of the ancient Near East with eastern Africa but do not fully explore western Africa and its interaction with Europe or the Mediterranean world, generally, for lack of an author.

The question of the African Diaspora is hinted at in our essay on the slave trade. A more serious discussion, comprehending the migrations—forced and otherwise—of Africans into North and South America, the Middle East, Europe, and the Indian subcontinent, is an interesting and unfolding story necessary to be told, but one which severely overstepped our bounds.

Nevertheless, the success of this work rests ultimately on its utility. It is our hope that the *Encyclopedia* performs this primary function as a summary of the current state of Africanist archaeology and a benchmark helping to define and shape future opinion.

ACKNOWLEDGMENTS

The individual authors devoted considerable time and effort to their difficult task of digesting large complex bodies of data into useful bits of information. The board of advisors—Professor Fekri Hassan, Dr. Peter Robertshaw, Dr. Innocent Pikirayi, Professor Bassey Andah, and Dr. Francis Musonda—aided the preliminary planning of the volume, defining its scope and identifying the proper author for each article.

In addition, we wish to show our appreciation to Professor J. R. Bindon, anthropology chair, University of Alabama, for understanding our complete distraction with this ongoing project and to the department's clerical staff, Mrs. Pam Chesnutt and Mrs. Ruby Howard, for their aid in ensuring that our communication lines of faxes, phone calls, and mail operated without hitch.

My wife, Jean, kept tabs on the process of compiling the *Encyclopedia*. It was she who daily recorded our progress, maintained the record of our contacts and responses, did a great deal of editing, and oversaw a myriad of other details.

Professor Nick David commented on our earliest outline and offered many useful suggestions reminiscent of advice he gave me when we first met many years ago in Oxford.

During the organization of this project, we contacted many prospective authors who, though unable to take up our invitation, were interested enough to suggest an alternate or propose other topics to include. These include Dr. John Hinnant, who wrote from Bali, and Dr. Garth Sampson, who wrote from the field in South Africa. Others whose advice or suggestions of prospective authors we acknowledge were Professor Paul Baxter, Dr. Janette Deacon, Dr. Charles Bonnet, Dr. Erik Trinkaus, Professor John Fage, Dr. Harry Langworthy, Dr. Tim Kendall, Dr. Megan Biesele, Dr. David Schoebrun, Dr. Rashdi Said, Dr. Alan Almquist, Dr. John Speth, and Dr. Nick van der Merwe.

We wish especially to express our appreciation to Professor Jack R. Harlan.

Figures 1 and 2, Stone Age Africa and Iron Age Africa, were drawn by W. Craig Remington, Supervisor, Cartography Research Laboratory, University of Alabama, Tuscaloosa.

We wish also to thank the folks at Zenda, Inc.—Charles Phillips, Patricia Hogan, copy editor and layout artist Candace Floyd, and proofreader Tracey Linton Craig—and Bruce Gore of Gore Studio, Inc., for his wonderful book and cover design.

Lastly, the project might have faltered but for Mitch Allen, our publisher, and Denise Santoro, our editor at AltaMira.

INTRODUCTION

Before identifying some themes implicit to the history of precolonial Africa, we should set the stage.

The continent of Africa may be likened to an inverted soup bowl with steep escarpments along much of southeastern Africa separating the coastal plains from the plateau lands of the interior. The peneplain plateau surface reaches great heights in the southeast and dips into lowland rain forests in western Africa. The northern and southwestern limits of sub-Saharan Africa are formed by the great deserts of the Sahara, the Kalahari, and the Namib.

Of the great rivers, only the Zambezi flows to the east. It begins in a broad floodplain in western Zambia, before entering a deep gorge for much of the middle part of its course, cascading over the Victoria Falls as well as lesser cataracts before it descends in rapids to the coastal plain along the Indian Ocean. The Nile, in the northeast, begins its journey to the sea in highlands at Lake Victoria carrying the seasonal rains of eastern African northward through the Sudanese swamps, watering desert Egypt before spilling into the Mediterranean. The great rivers of the west—the Niger and the Zaire—flow through heavy rain forests formed in an oppressively hot, humid environment on their way to the Atlantic.

Running parallel to the Nile Valley, but extending south along the Luangwa Valley to the Zambezi are the Rift Valleys: long, narrow cracks in the surface of the plateau forming deep valleys and the basins of the Great Lakes of eastern Africa. To their west is the alluvial valley of the Zaire, while to the east and southwest of the lakes are highland savannas in eastern and southern Africa.

Straddling the equator, the African continent has hot, humid climates in the river valleys and drier, cooler ones on the highlands. Rainfall patterns are monsoonal in that there is an alternation of dry and wet seasons throughout the year. Rainfalls may be heavy but concentrated in a few months. The tropical soils tend to be thin and of marginal fertility, and game tends to follow the shifting curtain of rainfall, seeking the fields of florescent grasses. As the rains shifted, so did the foragers, who exploited African environments for more than a million years, and pastoralists, who moved their herds from depleted pasturages to fresh ones. The quality of the soils and the unpredictability of the rainfall severely affected farmers and constrained their productivity.

Themes in African History

In this introduction, I suggest a set of themes perceivable in the historical record of sub-Saharan Africa. I do not suggest these as an evolutionary process, because history is more complex than that. Foragers continued to persist long after farmers moved onto the southern savanna, and subsistence farmers remained outside the thrall of the continent's complex chiefdoms and states. The population of sub-Saharan Africa was, and remains, engaged in a process of adaptation, fitting people onto bits of the landscape by means of social ordering, ideological rationale, and material invention.

Human Origins and the Invention, Development, and Adaptation of the Forager Lifeway

That the first humans appeared nearly 2 million years ago in eastern Africa is an established fact. There is an extensive body of information describing the evolution of modern kinds of humanity. At the same time that they evolved physically, a variety of adaptations of a social or cultural kind took place by which early humans modified their behavior, or diet, or tool kits.

The progress of human physical evolution in eastern Africa was matched by the development of human ingenuity. Throughout the period of the Pleistocene, humans tested their ability to exploit their environment, inventing the social means to divide labor by sex and age, create new tools, and more efficiently use the raw materials available to them. The development of stoneworking techniques was one exploring means to extract a maximum amount of cutting edge from a given quantity of stone: a progression from tools based on blocks of stone to finely honed ones based on tiny slivers. The predominantly stone-based technologies of these times were supplemented by a variety of wooden and bone implements as well.

The early foragers of eastern Africa observed the seasonal movement of game and the annual progression of useful plants. Over long periods of time, this information was refined, taught to succeeding generations, and used to fit groups of people into specific ecological niches.

At the same time, the emergent forager lifeway engaged humans in several sets of social involvement: within families by birth, between families by marriage, and between individuals engaged in mutual enterprises. The recurrence of seasonal camps suggests annual rounds exploiting specific opportunities on an regular basis, the size of camps and the distribution of remains in them suggests the social order of the occupying group, and the number of simultaneous camps suggests the size of interacting groups.

Through the later stages of the Pleistocene, people began to explore environments outside the open grasslands. For the first time, we find people moving into heavily wooded zones of the west, inventing a new tool kit of woodworking tools and apparently implements of wood as well.

Invention of Food Production and the Establishment of the Agriculturist Lifeway

The long period of the Stone Age culminated in well-adapted bands of people able to exploit landscapes that they knew and understood. This way of life persisted where it remained viable, unstressed by changes in climate or environment and unchallenged by other lifeways that used the countryside differently or significantly altered the ecological ordering of man and beasts or plants.

Sometime late in the Pleistocene as conditions became drier and well-known economic opportunities altered, some people began adaptive processes by which they efficiently husbanded groups of animals they had preyed upon. Elsewhere, foragers experimented with increasing the availability of useful plants, either to encourage the presence of game near their camps or to consume themselves.

This time of regional experimentation created new sets of ecological arrangement, as well as new technologies and social organizations. These people became less involved with annual rounds of migratory transhumance, transferring their camps from place to place as economic opportunities presented themselves. They became more concerned with investments in permanent facilities—residences, fields, or storage—that they expected to use on an exclusive basis through future cycles.

As we shall see, the food-producing community also gave rise to groups of pastoralists tending flocks or herds. Investing in portable food sources, they sought to ameliorate monsoonal conditions by progressively shifting their residence within a traditional compass to more lush pastures. The pastoralist lifeway, in a general way, was an evolved form of the annual round perfected by the foragers. Managing herds rather than stalking them, most pastoralist communities created a complex set of ideological and social mechanisms emphasizing their symbiotic relationship to their animals.

On the other hand, some groups sought to compensate for seasonal shortfalls by cropping highly productive plants, which they stored against the inevitable dry season. The means to store, as well as to process plant foods, became essential. These people founded permanent settlements and explored new technologies.

Pottery and the products of metallurgy became prominent features of new communities that established themselves along the fringes of the Sahel. Farming communities required relatively large populations to manage them: clearing fields, cultivating the growing plants, and reaping and storing the crop among other activities necessary to sustain village life. As a result, farming populations burgeoned and found it useful to invest in social ties with related communities to compensate for shortfalls in one place or another.

In forested regions, fields were cleared to accommodate root crops. In highland regions, cereals were emphasized.

Advent of Southern Savanna Agriculturists

The growth of farming populations, based on cereal cultivation, had another effect. Not only did they come to dominate most landscapes, but they possessed the means to segment themselves, searching out belts of arable land, settling and interacting with the communities that spawned them, ensuring access to food stuffs and labor during times of stress.

The complex linguistic map of western Africa seems to be one long-term result of such segmentation: small groups of related people intermingled with segmented kinsmen. On the other hand, the uniform carpeting of Bantu-speakers on the southern savanna is the result of Iron Age agriculturists rapidly colonizing a terrain in which their only competition were bands of foragers.

Two streams of Iron Age settlers are now identified: one passed to the west of the Zaire Basin into regions in the Upper Zambezi Valley and Angola and then moved southwards into Botswana. The other stream, moving out of western Africa, consolidating north of Lake Victoria, and then establishing and spawning new daughter settlements, moved south along the Great Lakes until it penetrated south-central Africa, crossed the Middle Zambezi, spread across Zimbabwe, and populated southern Africa.

In these two movements of Bantu-speaking people, we find the origins of the present-day populations of the subcontinent. For nearly 2,000 years, these groups organized a complex cultural life based on small communities tied into intricate social networks meant to ameliorate environmental risk, delegate political authority, ensure land tenure, manage the labor requirements of agricultural systems, and ensure access to necessities through trade.

Development of the State

People everywhere needed to obtain commodities not readily available close at hand. Even foragers manage to gain access to such necessities by social or other means. Social management recognizes the obligation of kin or client to participate in exchanges or gift giving. Other means include the sale, barter, or exchange of things between individuals who may have no obligation beyond some agreed upon transaction.

The ability to manage invested some individuals, their clients, and their suppliers with authority. As a result, trade alliances enhanced the status of some strategically placed individuals able to attract goods to their towns, who then regulated the terms of exchange and managed internal distribution. From these indigenous trading combines developed a number of powerful lineages able to control production for exchange as well as the commerce, itself. As a result, trade and statelike entities were a fixture of the African landscape up into the 19th century. The flow of foreign goods might affect one region or another, or the balance of power might shift from one center to another, but common achievement of regional trade remained constant. The city-states of the interior—Harar, Songhai, Ghana, Kongo, and Angola—the states along the Great Lakes, Monomatapa and so forth, as part of world economy, interacted with the outside world long before there was substantial penetration by non-African nations.

The Historic Period

The term *historic period* is misleading. Foraging people, nomadic herdsmen, subsistence farmers, and even the African city-states all persisted into a time when they were observable to travelers, geographers, and anthropologists among others, who produced (or write today) a written record of their lifeway.

The field observations of anthropologists are of living cultures, adapting to present conditions, not the fossilized remnants of some earlier kind of human existence. Nonetheless, we may distinguish a kind of archaeology that explores the remains of foreign contact or colonization whether it be the first Dutch settlements on the Cape or the establishment of the Swahili city-states of eastern Africa or the historic cities of the southern Sahara periphery. Thus this historic period may be deemed to encompass the past 500 years or more.

The world of precolonial Africa, with its diverse geography, maze of languages, long cultural history, and complex of indigenous societies, was multilayered and elaborately textured: its story is little different from that of the rest of the preindustrial world. In sub-Saharan Africa, we have the first stirring of humankind—physically evolving in eastern Africa and developing new technologies and behaviors unique to humans. Successfully adapting to the open grasslands of the highlands in East Africa, these early humans explored new environments elsewhere and began the long trek to the involved ecological arrangements humans engage in today. Throughout the history of the subcontinent we can trace a pattern of successful adaptation to changing conditions, of people reacting to challenges. Over time, the people of sub-Saharan Africa exploited the rain forests of the west, the grasslands of both the northern and southern savannas, as well as deserts and high mountainous regions. They used every kind of society known to mankind: from the hunter-forager band to the formation of elaborate states. Their art and technologies have left a permanent archaeological record, and products created on the African continent made their way into world markets through the efforts of indigenous entrepreneurs. Shorn of unnecessary exaggeration or undue prejudice, we may safely conclude that precolonial Africa produced an exciting and significant record of achievement.

Joseph O. Vogel

AFRICAN ENVIRONMENTS

GEOGRAPHY AND GEOLOGY

The geology of Africa ranges from crystalline rocks of the Precambrian western, central, and southeastern cratons (the earth's stable crusts) to recent marine and lake sediments and volcanic lavas and tuffs (fused volcanic debris). During the Lower Paleozoic era (200 million to 500 million years ago), Africa was part of the supercontinent of Gondwanaland, and many aspects of its geology and topography can be interpreted in terms of events associated with the breakup of the supercontinent and subsequent continental uplift.

A major sedimentary system in southern Africa is the Karroo, composed of glacial tillites, marine clays, sandstones, and the coal-bearing deposits that contribute to the mineral wealth of South Africa and Zimbabwe.

In northern Africa, the Continental Intercalary is a major sedimentary system formed from the Triassic to Cretaceous ages of the Mesozoic era. The sandstones of this geologic feature underlie much of the Sahara Desert and provide groundwater resources in many arid areas.

Other sedimentary rocks have yielded the petroleum resources that have contributed significantly to the economies of Algeria, Libya, Nigeria, Gabon, and Angola. The majority of the young volcanic rocks are of the Miocene age (Cenozoic era) and later dates and are associated with the East African Rift System, while large areas of unconsolidated sediments occur in the Zaire Basin and in the sedimentary basins of the Sahara.

The distribution of mineral resources in Africa has influenced human activities on the continent over several thousand years. In prehistoric times, certain rocks were selected as the raw materials for stone tools. About 2 million years ago, early hominids, such as *Homo habilis,* selected fine-grained quartzites from which to shape the hand axes found at Olduvai Gorge, and beginning at least 3,000 years ago, obsidian from the central Kenya Rift Valley was carried west to Gogo Falls in the Lake Victoria Basin to manufacture scrapers and blades.

As metallurgy developed over the last 3,000 to 4,000 years, the distribution of copper, iron, gold, and other minerals became a major influence on patterns of trade and power relations. The earliest evidence of the use of iron in sub-Saharan Africa is at Nok, near the confluence of the Niger and Benue Rivers. Another mineral much sought after was salt. Trade in gold, iron, salt, and other products was probably widespread in West Africa before the establishment of trans-Saharan trade. West African trade developed from about the 7th century and was a key element in the emergence of West African empires such as Ghana, Mali, Songhai, and Kanem-Bornu. Gold from Senegambia and the Akan region (modern-day Ghana) was traded across the Sahara by Arabs and Berbers and attracted the interest of Portuguese traders in the Mediterranean Sea. By the 14th century, European cartographers were drawing detailed maps depicting the sources of gold in West Africa, and the exploration along the west coast of Africa during the 15th century was, in part, an attempt to find a more direct route to African gold and cut out the numerous middlemen of the trans-Saharan trade.

On the east coast of Africa, traders from Persia, Arabia, and the Asian mainland were attracted by a variety of plant, animal, and mineral resources that included the gold of Zimbabwe. During the 19th century, mineral resources, including gold, diamonds, and copper, attracted European powers and provided impetus for the establishment of colonial rule. The history of southern Africa is closely interwoven with the exploitation of its minerals.

The geology of Africa, especially the distribution of groundwater, has also influenced human activities. In the semiarid and arid regions, migration patterns and political power have been closely linked to the control of wells and water holes. Collapse of Swahili cities, such as Gedi on the Kenya coast, has been linked with invasion of saltwater into overused freshwater aquifers.

Topography

Africa's topography is dominated by areas of plateau. Most of the eastern and southern parts of the continent are more than 1,000 meters above sea level ("High Africa"), while lower land predominates in the north and west ("Low Africa"). Much of eastern and southern Africa is surrounded by steep escarpments that presented a significant barrier to movement inland, at first on foot and later by road and railway. Africa has little true coastal plain, and this probably reduced the ease with which outsiders penetrated the continent.

Much of the tropical East African coast is surrounded by coral reefs that prevent access to all but very shallow-draft vessels. Even where reefs are absent, smooth, straight sandy shorelines lacking deep sheltered inlets have provided a serious barrier to access from the sea. Most African rivers cross waterfalls and rapids in their path to the sea. Today these water features hold the potential for the generation of electric power, but in the past, they were barriers to transportation.

Many of the plateaus are underlain by Precambrian crystalline rocks, high in silica content and resistant to erosion, from which rise rocky hills known as *inselbergs*. African plateaus did not experience the Pleistocene glaciations that spread fertile rock flour over areas such as the North American prairies and Great Plains, so the plateau soils are often old, deeply leached, sandy, and infertile. In addition, many of these regions suffer from lack of surface water and do not support large human populations. Countries with large areas of plateau include Ethiopia, Kenya, Tanzania, Uganda, Mozambique, Zambia, Zimbabwe, and South Africa.

The landscape of western and northern Africa is dominated by plains, some of which lie close to the coastline. The coastal plains of Somalia and northeastern Kenya, for example, formerly the floor of the sea, were exposed as the level of the continental block rose.

The floodplains of major rivers, including the Nile, the Zaire, and the Niger, have fertile, fine-grained soils and an abundant water supply. The rise of dynastic power in Egypt more than 5,000 years ago was based on a farming system that made use of the annual floods generated by seasonal rains in the Blue Nile headwaters on the Ethiopian Highlands.

Less well known are the regions along the River Niger. Its "inland delta" upstream of Tombouctou in present-day Mali and its confluence with the Benue River were centers of early population concentration. Early agricultural experimentation in this region may have led to the domestication of indigenous food crops such as millet and sorghum.

Other African river basins remained undeveloped and sparsely populated. In some regions, technology and social organization did not develop to permit control of seasonal floods on major streams, though small irrigation systems are known from several areas of tropical Africa, for example on the slopes of Kilimanjaro (the Chagga) and on the walls of the eastern Rift Valley (the Pokot in Kenya and the prehistoric site at Engaruka in Tanzania).

Many African rivers are the home of crocodiles and hippopotamuses, both of them very dangerous to humans. Dwellers in river valleys are at high risk of contracting malaria, sleeping sickness, river blindness, and bilharziasis through bites of tsetse flies, mosquitoes, and various parasites.

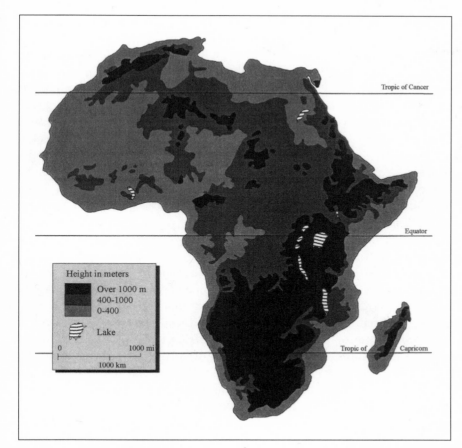

Fig. 3 *Relief map of Africa*

The highlands of Africa fall into three main categories based on their geological origin. Tectonic highlands have been formed by folding or faulting, endogenic processes originating from below the surface of the earth. Movements within the partly fluid rocks of the earth's upper mantle cause the rocks of the crust to bend or break. Large-scale bending of crystal rocks creates fold mountains, of which the Atlas Mountains in northwestern Africa (highest peak is Jebel Toubkal at 4,195 meters) are the only example on the continent. Another kind of tectonic mountain is formed by faulting, when subsurface forces cause rocks to break and slide against each other. This process creates block mountains, such as the Ruwenzori Range, which rises to 5,111 meters on the Uganda-Zaire border. Other block mountains are the Usambara and Pare Mountains of northeastern Tanzania. Faulting over the last

30 million years has also produced a major graven (a long trough bounded by faults), the East African Rift System.

Sediments laid down in the lake basins of the Rift Valley during the last 4 million years have yielded much evidence of human evolution. It appears that the Rift Valley region provided very favorable environments for the ancestors of modern humans. Freshwater was available in the lakes or from springs that emerged at the base of the rift scarps. Contrasts in altitude within a short distance provided varying ecosystems within which to hunt and forage at different seasons. The disproportionate quantity of hominid and other remains found here may be due to the preservation qualities of the lake sediments and volcanic ash characteristic of the region.

A second category of highland is the volcanic highlands formed by the outpouring of large volumes of volcanic rock. Like the creation of tectonic highlands, the formation of volcanic highlands is the result of crystal instability. Most of these areas are located within or on the margins of rift systems, including the East African Rift System and the much older Benue Trough in West Africa.

The major volcanic highlands of Africa are less than 50 million years old and include several active ranges, notably the Virunga Range north of Lake Kivu on the borders of Zaire, Rwanda, and Uganda. Here two centers, Nyamulagira and Nyiragongo, erupted large volumes of highly fluid basalt lava several times in the 20th century. Active volcanoes are also present in the Afar or Danakil Depression of northern Ethiopia, on Mount Cameroon, including the area of Lake Nyos (a carbon-dioxide-filled crater lake), and at Oldoinyo Lengai, a carbonatite cone in northern Tanzania. Oldoinyo Lengai and its neighbor Kerimasi were active during the period of lacustrine (lake) deposition in the Olduvai Gorge, and their ash forms a significant component of the sediments in which fossil bones are preserved at this locality.

Africa's two highest mountains are young volcanoes: Kilimanjaro (Tanzania) at 5,896 meters and Mount Kenya (Kenya) at 5,200 meters. Less than 1 million years old, Kilimanjaro may be described as dormant rather than extinct. It has steam jets, sulfur deposits, and young ash cones in its summit crater. Mount Kenya (2 million to 3 million years old) has a summit area deeply eroded by glaciers that are now very small and restricted to elevations above 4,600 meters but once extended to below 3,600 meters.

Other volcanic highlands consist of ridges and deeply eroded plateaus. Most of Africa's highlands have high ecological potential due to large amounts of annual rainfall. This is particularly true of the volcanic highlands, whose rocks weather into highly fertile soils. For several thousand years, these highlands, whose natural vegetation was forest, were occupied by small communities of hunter-foragers who had little effect on plant and animal populations and left little physical evidence of their occupation. The development and spread of iron tools made it possible to clear forested land for cultivation, and as population densities at lower altitudes increased, people made more intensive use of highland forest, with significant impacts on vegetation, soils, and animal life.

Examples of volcanic highlands are in Ethiopia, Kenya, Tanzania, Uganda, the Cameroon Highlands, eastern Zaire, Rwanda, Burundi, and the Ahaggar (Hoggar) and Tibesti Mountains in the Sahara. During the latest Pleistocene wet period, the Ahaggar and Tibesti Mountains formed oases of cool moist conditions that supported numerous animal species. Many of these species became extinct during the subsequent desiccation of the region.

The third category of highlands is the residual mountains, eroded masses of very hard rock left standing as the surrounding lowlands have been worn down. Many of these are rounded hills of bare, crystalline rock, domes, sugar loafs, and piles of boulders. Examples are the Jos Plateau (Nigeria), the Matopos (Zimbabwe), Mount Zomba and Mount Mulanje (Malawi), and the Machakos and Taita Hills (Kenya).

Soils on these crystalline-rock formations are not as fertile as those on young volcanic highlands. The higher rainfall these rocky regions receive, however, provides a more favorable environment for permanent settlement than the surrounding dry plateau, and these areas have tended to support large human populations.

Climatic Regions and Natural Vegetation

Africa's climatic regions, and the corresponding distribution of natural vegetation, are largely controlled by the amount and distribution of rainfall. Due to its equatorial position (77 percent of the land area of Africa lies between the tropics of Cancer and Capricorn), most of the continent experiences high solar radiation and temperatures, with consequent high evaporation rates. Lack of solar energy does not limit plant or animal life, but lack of moisture frequently does. Rainfall distribution in Africa can be explained largely in terms of latitude and altitude. Latitude explains the four major rainfall regimes of Africa.

Equatorial Climates

The equatorial climate owes its existence to the presence of the Inter-tropical Convergence Zone, a low-pressure belt along which warm air from the Northern and Southern Hemispheres converges, producing rainfall. The equatorial rainfall regime is bimodal, though no really dry months are experienced. The two rainy seasons mark the passage of the Inter-tropical Convergence Zone northward and southward across the equator.

Natural vegetation in the equatorial region is hardwood forest. The trees are mostly broadleaf evergreens. Their dense wood made them difficult to cut with stone or bronze tools, and the high moisture content made the wood not good for burning. Thus these forests, occupied only by small groups of hunter-foragers, remained largely untouched during much of the past. The development and spread of iron tools over the last 2,000 to 3,000 years enabled many African

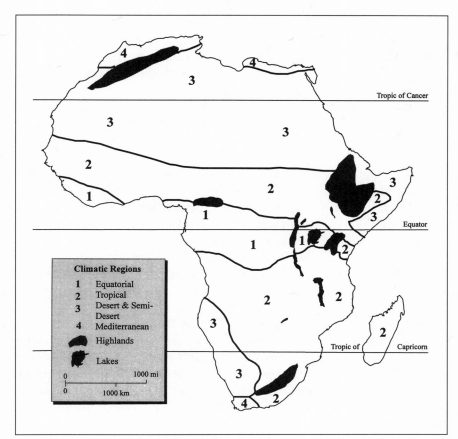

Fig. 4 *Simplified climatic regions of Africa*

cattle and small livestock. The presence of the tsetse fly, the carrier of trypanosomiasis, has been suggested as a factor limiting agriculture in equatorial Africa. Trypanosomiasis, a disease that affects cattle, reduces the viability of herds and prevents the use of oxen-drawn plows and animal manure in farming systems.

Tropical Climates

Tropical climates occur north and south of the equator. These regions are influenced, for part of the year, by the Inter-tropical Convergence Zone, which creates a unimodal rainfall pattern (one rainy season). For the rest of the year, the regions are influenced by dry air originating from the subtropical high-pressure cells.

Like the Inter-tropical Convergence Zone, the high-pressure cells move latitudinally according to season. In June and July when the Northern Hemisphere is tilted toward the sun, the Inter-tropical Convergence Zone and the moist equatorial air shift northward and bring rain to the tropical regions north of the equator. In these latitudes, the intense dry season is from November to April, when the Inter-tropical Convergence Zone moves southward and the region is influenced by the subtropical high-pressure cells. In December and January when the Southern Hemisphere is tilted toward the sun, the Inter-tropical Convergence Zone and the moist equatorial air shift southward and bring rain to the tropical regions south of the equator.

A general term for the vegetation of these areas is *savanna,* denoting a wide variety of trees, shrubs, and grasses. Savanna woodland has an open growth of trees with light grass cover beneath them. Savanna bushland is composed largely of thorny bushes and shrubs. Savanna grassland may include scattered trees on a sur-

peoples to make more intensive use of these forests. The spread of the Bantu from their homeland in western equatorial Africa has been linked to their acquisition of iron technology.

In the modern era, rapid population growth has increased the demand for cultivable land in many African countries. This, coupled with the demand of the world market for tropical hardwood, has contributed to an accelerated rate of deforestation.

Farming systems in equatorial regions are based on perennial crops (root and tree crops), as conditions are not favorable for the maturing of most cereals. Several indigenous African trees were significant in precolonial economies, such as the kola tree and oil palm, while tree crops such as cocoa, coffee, and rubber formed the basis of plantation industries in western and central Africa.

High humidity and the year-long presence of insect pests create conditions hostile to domestic livestock, though many communities keep a few face of tall or short grasses, depending on local rainfall, soil, and grazing pressure. Many savanna plants, adapted to the long dry season, have characteristics to reduce water loss—deep roots, thick bark, small leaves, and thorns.

Some savanna trees and shrubs produce aromatic resins, important commodities in early trade between Arabia and eastern Africa. Other plant products traded from eastern Africa, especially from the coastal forests, were mangrove poles, valued for building purposes in timber-deficient Arabia. Savannas have also been the home of large concentrations of wild game, including the huge elephant populations, whose ivory was one of Africa's major exports for many centuries.

Savanna soils tend to be low in organic material. They are vulnerable to wind erosion toward the end of the dry season and to erosion by running water during the heavy downpours at the onset of the rains. However, the moister savannas are able to support a variety of annual crops as well as domestic livestock. The domestication of millet and sorghum on the savannas south of the Sahara can be traced to 3,000 years ago. Groundnuts, sisal, tobacco, and cotton are among the other crops that have been grown by African and immigrant communities for local use and trade.

Desert and Semidesert Climates

Desert and semidesert climates lie farther from the equator to the north and the south, where the influence of the Inter-tropical Convergence Zone gives way to that of the subtropical high-pressure cells. Annual rainfall decreases from the tropical climate through the semidesert into the true desert, with less than 256 millimeters of rain a year.

The transitional zone is the Sahel in West Africa. In North Africa, the Sahara Desert stretches across the continent from west to east and continues across the Red Sea into the Arabian Desert. In the east, it is interrupted by the highlands of Ethiopia, but desert conditions continue to the eastern coast of Africa in the Somali Republic. In South Africa, the Namib Desert lies on the Atlantic Coast and continues inland as the Kalahari Desert.

Low annual rainfall figures are combined with extreme irregularity in seasonal distribution. There may be no rain at all for several years, and then a violent storm might bring several millimeters in a few hours. Intense solar radiation causes high evaporation rates. High daytime temperatures (over 38° C) rapidly drop at nightfall due to the clear skies.

Desert vegetation has many drought-resistant properties: deep roots, thick bark, small waxy or hairy leaves, thorns instead of leaves, and rapid growth after rain.

Soils are shallow and stony or sandy, frequently with layers of deposited salts in their upper horizons. Animal and human populations in deserts are generally low and concentrated in areas where groundwater or surface water is available. Control of surface water in desert regions has led to the development of centralized states such as the dynasties of ancient Egypt and the empires of the western Sahara such as Mali, Songhai, and Kanem-Bornu.

Many African desert regions contain evidence of more humid conditions during the Pleistocene and Early Holocene in the form of old lake sediments, archaeological sites, and rock paintings as seen in the Ahaggar and Tibesti Mountains.

Mediterranean Climates

Mediterranean climates lie to the extreme north and south of Africa, where the influence of the westerly wind systems is felt part of the year. The unimodal rainfall pattern brings winter rains and hot, dry summers.

In the northern summer, the Mediterranean regions are influenced by the subtropical high-pressure cells. As these cells shift southward, northwestern Africa is influenced by the moist air of the westerlies, bringing rain to Algiers between October and March. The reverse is true of the Mediterranean region of South Africa.

Vegetation in the Mediterranean regions has many drought-resistant properties. The trees have thick bark and small waxy or furry leaves to survive the long, hot summer, and aromatic shrubs are common. Agriculture in the Mediterranean regions has been based on cereals (mainly wheat), tree crops (olives and vines), and small livestock.

In North Africa, intensive land use during the last millennia B.C. resulted in environmental degradation and the collapse of states based on unsustainable resource-use systems.

Highland Climates

The highland climates of Africa are most widespread on the regions above about 1,525 meters in the southern and eastern parts of the continent. Increased altitude causes temperatures to be lower and rainfall higher than in the surrounding lowlands.

In East Africa, rainfall increases with altitude to between 1,150 and 1,530 millimeters a year at elevations of 1,830 to 3,050 meters. The natural vegetation at these elevations is montane forest. Increasing altitude brings conditions that are too cold and dry to support tree growth, and the forest gives way to tussock grassland and woodland. Forest soils are highly fertile, especially on the young volcanic highlands where the organic input from the vegetation is supplemented by the high nutrient status of the parent rock.

Thus these regions are productive farmlands and have long supported high concentrations of people. As population densities increase, cultivation extends to the steeper slopes and creates a serious risk of soil erosion.

African countries located almost entirely within the highlands are Rwanda, Burundi, Lesotho, and Swaziland. Countries that have significant areas of highlands are Ethiopia, Kenya, Uganda, Tanzania, Malawi, and South Africa. During the late 19th and early 20th centuries, the highland regions were particularly attractive to European immigrants, who created several "colonies of settlement" where land-tenure and farming systems of the Western world were imposed on indigenous systems. Several of these areas became centers of highly developed commercial farming, but beginning in the mid-20th century, the return of land ownership and political rights to Africans was associated with varying levels of political turmoil and loss of life.

BIBLIOGRAPHY

Adams, W. M., A. S. Goudie, and A. R. Orme. 1996. *The Physical Geography of Africa.* Oxford: Oxford University Press.

McEvedy, C. 1980. *Atlas of African history.* New York: Facts on File.

Parker, S. P. 1995. *World geographical encyclopedia, vol. 1, Africa.* New York: McGraw Hill.

Stock, R. 1995. *Africa south of the Sahara: A Geographical interpretation.* New York: Guilford Press.

Celia Nyamweru

PLEISTOCENE AND HOLOCENE CLIMATES AND VEGETATION ZONES

The Quaternary period, the geological era in which we are living, has so far lasted about 2 million years. It has been characterized by the repeated expansion and contraction of ice caps over much of North America and northern Eurasia. Oxygen-isotope analyses of long cores extracted from deep-sea sediments and from the Greenland and Antarctic ice caps have revealed much about the geological past. Much more is known about climates and vegetation in the last 10,000 years, the Holocene, than about the much longer preceding period, the Pleistocene, which constitutes the rest of the Quaternary. In sub-Saharan Africa, the most important climatic changes have involved rainfall and temperature. Rainfall changes have altered the extent of the rain forest, savanna, and desert. Temperature changes have affected the extent of montane vegetation.

Toward the end of the 19th century, moraines (accumulations of earth and stones carried and deposited by glaciers) were recognized on Mount Kenya lying more than 1,000 meters below its glaciers. They had evidently been formed when the climate was colder and the glaciers larger than they are now. Similar features were discovered on the Ruwenzori Range, Mount Elgon, and Kilimanjaro in East Africa and on the Semien Mountains of Ethiopia. They pointed to mean annual temperatures in intertropical Africa having been lower than now by about 6° C on more than one occasion in the past. The glacier advances presumably coincided in time with the expansions of ice caps in middle and high latitudes.

Former strandlines (shorelines) high above existing lakes were also recognized, and lacustrine (lake) sediments containing fish bones and other faunal remains were found in desert depressions where today there are no lakes and scarcely any rain. Evidently much of Africa had been wetter than it is now in the not-too-distant past. The paleo-lakes were attributed to wetter, pluvial periods and were generally assumed to have been contemporaneous with the glacial periods that had been distinguished in the Alps of central Europe and on the Great Plains of North America. It had been shown toward the end of 19th century that paleo-lakes Lahonian and Bonneville in the western United States had been contemporaneous with glacier expansion in the Sierra Nevada and Wasatch Mountains, so it was generally assumed that the pluvial periods in Africa had also been coincident with the glacial periods.

Ancient sand dunes, similar to desert dunes but covered with grass and even trees, ran long distances across the continent and were found well outside the borders of the Sahara and Kalahari in country where the mean annual rainfall today is much as 800 millimeters. In some of the ancient dune fields, the sand ridges are low and rounded as if they are very old. In others, the ridges are sharper and apparently younger. Evidently, during one or more periods in the past, the climate of Africa had been much drier than at present. During other periods, it was wetter.

If the pluvial periods in Africa coincided with midlatitude glaciations, the intervening periods must have coincided with interglacials. However, from time to time, scientists have expressed uncertainty about the validity of this glacio-pluvial hypothesis. They had noticed that the ancient dunes in Senegal appeared to stretch below present sea level, indicating that they had been formed in glacial periods when great volumes of water had been extracted from the oceans and incorporated in the continental ice caps.

In what terms were such climatic oscillations to be explained? In the 1920s, M. I. Milankovitch, a Serbian mathematician, determined that changes in the distribution of incoming radiation to the earth's surface were significant. These changes were caused by the regular variations, over thousands of years, in the relative positions of the sun and the earth, variations that result from the gravitational attraction exerted on the earth by the other planets orbiting the

sun. The Milankovitch orbital variations are of three kinds:

1. The earth's orbit varies from being almost circular to being more elliptical (eccentricity), the cycle lasting about 100,000 years.
2. The inclination of the earth's axis to the plane of the orbit (obliquity) varies through 2° 45', with a periodicity of about 41,000 years.
3. The direction of tilt of the axis varies through time (precession) so as to sweep out a cone about every 19,000 to 23,000 years.

Currently, the eccentricity of the orbit is marked, the obliquity at 23° 35' is intermediate between its extreme positions, and the earth's axis is aligned so that our planet in its annual circuit is farthest from the sun (at aphelion) in the Northern Hemisphere summer (when the North Pole is inclined toward the sun) and closest to the sun (at perihelion) in the Southern Hemisphere summer (when the South Pole is inclined toward the sun).

About 100,000 years ago, the northern tropic was at 24° 30', and because of precession, the earth was at perihelion in the Northern Hemisphere summer. As a result, tropical northern Africa received about 7 percent more solar radiation in June, July, and August than it does now (and 7 percent less in December, January, and February). Consequently, summer temperatures in Africa north of the equator would have been higher than now, and the monsoonal inflow of moist air would have been correspondingly greater. This monsoonal inflow created more rain than at present and caused lake levels to rise. On the other hand, between 13,000 and 20,000 years ago at the height of the last glaciation, carbon-dioxide concentrations in the atmosphere were lower than they are now, and the surface of the tropical Atlantic was 3° or 4° C cooler. Evaporation from the oceans and the moisture load of the monsoon were reduced, thereby causing greater aridity north of equator.

In the 1960s, radiocarbon dating of carbonates and shells from lake deposits in the Lake Chad Basin, the valley of the White Nile upstream of Khartoum, and in the Kenya Rift Valley showed that at the end of the Pleistocene and in the Early Holocene, lakes in closed basins in these regions had been larger than at present. The largest of all was Lake Chad, which today fluctuates between 2,000 and 26,000 square kilometers. Between about 6,000 and 12,000 years ago, it spread over 320,000 square kilometers. By then, the pluvial lakes in North America had dried up, and the continental ice caps of the last glaciation were rapidly disappearing. The glacio-pluvial hypothesis could not apply to Africa and the Tropics.

Further field research showed that lakes in the Sahara and the Ethiopia Rift Valley as well as in the Chad Basin and the East African Rift Valley had reached their highest levels, sometimes 100 meters or even 200 meters above their present levels, between 8,500 and 9,500 years ago. By that time, global temperatures were similar to those at the present day, and sea level had risen almost to its present level.

Scientists then made attempts to calculate, from geomorphological evidence, how much mean annual rainfall differed from that of the present day, in both the drier periods and the wetter ones. The present distribution of mobile desert dunes, not fixed by trees or grass, is limited to regions with a mean annual rainfall of 150 millimeters or less. Where the rainfall exceeds this amount, dunes are fixed by grass and trees, though they may be reactivated in times of prolonged drought when annual rainfall totals are much reduced for several successive years. The fixed dunes extend more than 500 kilometers toward the equator from the Kalahari into the Zaire Basin and from the Saharan into the Sahelian and Sudanian vegetation zones into areas where the mean annual rainfall now reaches 800 millimeters. Hence during the arid periods of the Pleistocene, extensive tracts of these regions received as much as 650 millimeters less rainfall than they do at the present. The discharge of great rivers, notably the Senegal and the Upper Niger, was diminished so much that they were blocked by dunes and failed to reach the sea, and the latitudinal vegetation zones to the south of the Sahara— namely the Sahelian, Sudanian, and Sudano-Guinean savanna—shifted about 500 kilometers toward the equator.

Calculations were made of the increase in rainfall required to sustain the enlarged lakes of the Early Holocene. At first, scientists calculated the water balance of two pluvial lakes, Nakuru-Elmenteita in Kenya and Ziway-Shala in Ethiopia, and made assumptions about past temperatures and evaporation. The results indicated that rainfall in these lake basins had been about 400 to 500 millimeters greater than at the present. Later on, computer models of the energy balance took into account the partitioning of the incident radiation (the Bowen ratio) and the effects of changing plant cover on the reflectivity of the surface and evapo-transpiration losses. The results suggested that mean annual rainfall over the Chad Basin was 350 millimeters greater than at the present and over the Kenyan Basin—Lakes Nakuru-Elmenteita, Naivasha, Turkana, and Victoria—between 140 and 300 millimeters greater than it is now. Neither kind of calculation took into account the water that overflowed from all these lakes at maximum levels: from Lake Chad to the Atlantic via the Benue River, from Lake Nakuru-Elmenteita into the Menengal Caldera, from Lake Ziway-Shala down the Awash River and into the Afar Depression, from Lake Naivasha through Hell's Gate Canyon toward Lake Magadi, and from Lakes Turkana and Victoria to the Nile. So the rainfall increase in the Early Holocene was greater than those calculated, but by how much is not known.

Analysis of the pollen in a core from Lake Bosumtwi in eastern Ghana indicates the disappearance of the forest between 15,000 and 20,000 years ago. The equatorial rain forests are believed to have been reduced to refuge areas, the largest of which were in Cameroon, Gabon, and eastern Zaire, with gallery forest extending along the lower courses of the Zaire River and the great tributaries and with other refuge areas near the coasts of West Africa and East Africa.

With the great increase in rainfall at the end of the Pleistocene, rain forests expanded from these refuges. Montane forests, which included the olive, *Olea hochstetter,* appeared in West Cameroon and near Lake Bosumtwi. The Sahelian and savanna vegetation belts began advancing 1,000 kilometers northward into the Sahara. All of Africa from the Sahara as far south as Lake Rukwa in Tanzania was affected by this "greening." Southernmost Africa and the KwaZulu-Natal region, which had been drier during the Last Glacial Maximum, became significantly wetter than at present. However, the Kalahari region of southern Africa, with great lakes occupying the Makgadikgadi Depression between 10,000 and 26,000 years ago and a shallow lake at the Tsodilo Hills between 15,000 and 17,500 years ago, was even drier than now.

Further studies have shown Quaternary climatic history in Africa south of the Sahara to have been more complicated than had at first appeared. The Late Pleistocene–Early Holocene pluvial period of Africa north of the equator was interrupted by dry phases lasting several centuries, notably about 10,500 years ago and again about 7,500 years ago, for reasons that are unknown but that may be associated with a cool North Atlantic and warmer southern oceans. The onset of drier climates, which have persisted into the present, can be placed at 4,500 years ago, about the time of the early pharaohs. These drier climates have been somewhat ameliorated from time to time, for instance in the centuries around 2,000 years ago in Ethiopia, Sudan, Egypt, and Libya. At other times, there have been continued droughts.

Analysis of the chemical composition and the pollen and diatom (a form of planktonic algae) content of cores from various African lake and from the deep sea fans of the Niger and Zaire Rivers has confirmed the conclusions reached by studies of ancient moraines and lake strandlines. Cores from Sacred Lake, high on Mount Kenya, and from other elevated sites in East Africa show that the upper limit of forests was 1,000 meters lower at times during the last glacial period. The upper limit rose again toward the end of the Pleistocene. Montane forests and grassland replaced lowland rain forest in western and central Africa. Cores from Lake Victoria show it dried up almost completely about 13,000 years ago. As it refilled, the region to the north of the lake, which had been mainly grassland for thousands of years, began to be reoccupied by forest. The rain forest now bordering Lake Bosumtwi in southern Ghana disappeared between 15,000 and 20,000 years ago but was completely restored by 9,000 years ago. The Dahomey Gap, an interruption of the West African rain-forest belt in Togo and Benin,

may not have existed in the Early Holocene. It probably formed with the drying that took place after 4,500 years ago.

Alternations of climatic conditions between drier and wetter periods extended far back into the Pleistocene. There were probably as many as 50 such oscillations. As precession is probably the dominant driving force, at least when orbital eccentricity is marked, one might expect the climate changes to have been in opposite directions in northern and southern Africa. There is, in fact, great uncertainty about what actually happened to climates in these remote times.

A cool, wet phase about 25,000 to 30,000 years ago raised the lakes in the East African and Ethiopian Rift Valleys, flooded parts of the Chad, Shati, and Taoudenni Depressions in the Sahara, and increased the discharge of rivers in Sierra Leone. Palynological (pollen and spore) evidence from Lake Albert indicates cooler and drier conditions in that region. The Namib and Kalahari seem to have been wetter than now, but the rest of southern Africa was drier.

There are indications that climates between 30,000 and 40,000 years ago were drier in the Sahara and East Africa and wetter in west-central and southern Africa. Carbonates precipitated by algae (stromatalites) mark high strandlines formed early in the last interstadial (glacial retreat), about 130,000 years ago, around Lake Natron in northwest Tanzania. A very shelly strandline 40 to 50 meters above the floor of the Shati Depression has given ^{22}Th/U dates (thorium/uranium dates) that range between 90,000 and 173,000 years ago. Speleothems (stalactites, stalagmites, and flowstone in caves) from Botswana and the former province of Transvaal, dated by ^{230}Th/^{234}U, indicate, about 200,000 years ago, a pluvial period that was more humid than any other period until the Holocene.

There are various obstacles in the way of tracing the climatic and vegetation record far back into the Pleistocene. Vertical displacements associated with faulting distort lake strandlines, and dating is nearly always uncertain. Thick accumulations of sediment on the floors of Rift Valley lakes, such as Lakes Malawi and Tanganyika, offer opportunities for future research, but it is very expensive to drill and extract deep cores from such remote places, and analyzing them takes much time and skill.

Marine cores are currently more readily available and provide useful information about the long-term history of climates and vegetation cover of the nearby continental areas. Cores extracted off northwestern Africa contain pollen from the Sahara and its borderlands. A high influx of *Artemisia* and pine pollen in glacial periods indicates a great strengthening of trade winds at such times. The varying relative contributions of Sahelian pollen *(Graminae)* and Saharan pollen *(Chenopodiaceae)* are believed to indicate changes to the southern limits of the Sahara. The Saharan-Sahelian boundary seems to have moved far to the south not only at about the time of the Last Glacial Maximum but also on five earlier occasions in the last half million years.

Early Pleistocene lake and river sediments at Koobi Fora, on the northeast side of Lake Turkana, contain pollen in beds interstratified with hominid fossils. Almost half the pollen grains counted in a sample believed to be 1.5 million years old were from grasses. Pollen from montane species was much more prominent than in recent pollen assemblages from the same area, and it has been concluded that the climate must have been cooler or wetter, though not excessively so. Such conclusions are based on relatively few pollen samples from special environmental settings, and future studies may call for revision of current ideas.

BIBLIOGRAPHY

Deacon, J., and N. Lancaster. 1988. *Late Quaternary palaeo-environments of southern Africa.* Oxford: Oxford University Press.

Grove, A. T. 1993. Africa's climate in the Holocene. In *The archaeology of Africa: Food, metals and towns,* eds. T. Shaw, P. Sinclair, B. Andah, and A. Okpoko, 32–42. London: Routledge.

Hamilton, A. C. 1982. *Environmental history of East Africa.* London: Academic Press.

Hastenrath, S. 1985. *Climate and circulation of the Tropics.* Dordrecht: Kluwer Academic Publishers.

Street-Perrott, P. A., and R. A. Perrott. 1993. Holocene vegetation: Lake levels and climate in Africa. In *Global climates since the Last Glacial Maximum,* eds. H. E. Wright, J. E. Kutzbach, T. Webb, III, W. F. Ruddiman, P. A. Street-Perrott, and P. J.

Bartlein, 318–356. Minneapolis: University of Minneapolis Press.

Vogel, J. C., ed. 1984. *Late Cainozoic palaeoclimates of the Southern Hemisphere.* Rotterdam: Balkema.

Williams, M. A. J., and H. Faure, eds. 1980. *The Sahara and the Nile.* Rotterdam: Balkema.

A. T. Grove

MODERN CLIMATES AND VEGETATION ZONES

Climate

Climate is probably the most important feature of the physical environment. It affects soil conditions, plant growth, water availability, and living conditions. Africa lies within 35° of the equator. Temperatures at low altitudes are consequently high throughout the year except in the extreme north and south of the continent, where there are cold spells in winter, and in the northern Sahara, where night temperatures can fall well below freezing. Shade temperatures decrease with altitude at a rate of about 6° C every 1,000 meters of ascent so that the highlands are much cooler than the lowlands. It is too cold for most trees above about 3,600 meters, and the snow line is reached at about 4,500 meters. The highest mountains in Africa—Mount Kenya, Kilimanjaro, and the Ruwenzori Range—rise above this level. They support small glaciers, which have been shrinking rapidly over the last 100 years.

Water loss to the atmosphere is high because of the high temperatures and abundant incident solar radiation. Evaporation loss from the surfaces of lakes ranges between 750 millimeters annually in the wetter regions of the Zaire Basin and more than 2,000 millimeters annually at the desert margins. Soils become desiccated to considerable depths in the course of the dry season.

Rainfall over intertropical Africa is essentially monsoonal, being associated with strong heating of the continent north of the equator in the northern summer, from June to August, and heating of the continent south of the equator in the southern summers, from December to February. The high temperatures create low-pressure areas into which humid air is drawn from high-pressure cells over the tropical Atlantic and Indian Oceans.

Between humid air over the oceans and dry, descending air in the easterlies of the continental high-pressure cells, a rather diffuse boundary surface, the Inter-tropical Convergence Zone, slopes up toward the equator with a gradient of between about 1:100 and 1:400. It moves north from February until August, when it coincides approximately with the southern side of the Sahara, about 15° to 20° north latitude. It then moves south over the next six months to reach as far south as the west coast, about 8° north latitude, and the Kalahari, about 16° south latitude. Disturbances move from east to west along the Inter-tropical Convergence Zone, and clouds build up in the moist, unstable air on its side facing the equator. Surface heating accentuates the vertical development of the clouds, causing thunderstorms. Rainfall is especially heavy where deep masses of moist air are forced to ascend over mountain ranges.

The north-south oscillation of the Inter-tropical Convergence Zone creates rainy seasons of various lengths. The regions near the tropics of Cancer and Capricorn have a single rainy season lasting only about three months each year, whereas regions close to the equator have two rainy seasons annually. In East Africa, the "long rains" fall between March and May, and the less widespread and less reliable "short rains," between September and December. Along the coast of West Africa, between Ivory Coast and the Niger Delta, the break between the two rainfall peaks is short and variable. On either side of the Volta Delta, the second peak is very subdued, creating a dry coastal zone.

The driest regions in Africa are the Sahara, the Namib, and the Kalahari Deserts. Scarcely reached by the Inter-tropical Convergence Zone, they remain under the influence of dry, descending air throughout the year. Rift valley floors in the lee of highlands have low rainfall totals. Eastern equatorial Africa is drier than western, in part because of the presence of the Asian land mass and the Tibetan Plateau to the northeast.

Aridity is accentuated along the west coast on either side of the tropics by cold ocean currents offshore—the Canaries current off Morocco and the Benguela current off Namibia. The Somali current off the Horn of Africa flows northeast in the northern summer and southwest in the winter months. In all these cases, upwelling cold water chills the lower layers of air moving onshore, increases air stability, and prevents upward convectional activity that might give rain. These arid coastal strips are often shrouded by fog in the early morning.

The Cape of South Africa at the southwestern extremity of the continent is peculiar in that most of the rain there falls in winter, May to August. It is brought by northwesterly air in midlatitude atmospheric depressions moving from west to east along tracks that lie farther north in winter than in summer.

Of special importance in Africa is the variability of the rainfall from year to year. Instrumental records show that dry years cluster together. In the Sahel-Sudan zones, a region about 500 kilometers wide stretching across Africa on the south side of the Sahara, rainfall between 1968 and 1993 was on average 30 to 40 percent less than it was between 1943 and 1967. Drought conditions were especially severe in the early 1970s and early 1980s. Even the rain-forest areas of West Africa, in Ghana for instance, suffered from drought in 1983. In southern Africa, droughts occurred in the early 1980s and early 1990s, but rainfall was above average in the 1970s. In the 20th century at least, successions of dry years in southern Africa have been less prolonged than in the Sahel-Sudan zone. The droughts experienced in Africa during the 20th century could conceivably be related to global warming, but evidence is accumulating that similar variability has been a feature of the climate for many centuries, if not millenia.

Wet years occurred in the Sahel-Sudan region in late 1950s and early 1960s. Exceptionally heavy rains fell over central and eastern Africa in the later months of 1961, and above-average rains were experienced there over the next three or four years. These rainfall amounts created high lake levels and river discharges.

Vegetation Zones

Vegetation cover depends primarily on the mean annual rainfall and the length of the dry season. Consequently, the vegetation zones are arranged across the continent in latitudinal bands, although these are distorted in East Africa by the complicated pattern of the rainfall associated with the topography of the rift valleys.

The floral composition of the plant cover in the Sudan zone and the Sahara is similar to that of southwestern Asia. The species characteristic of the southernmost part of the continent in the southwestern Cape have evolved in much greater isolation than have those on the Eurasian land mass and are much more distinctive. The flora of Madagascar, which has been separated from the rest of Africa for tens of millions of years, has its own peculiar features and shows some similarities to the flora of Southeast Asia. The African rain forest is poorer in species than the rain forests of South America and Southeast Asia and is especially poor in bamboo, ferns, and palms. Species richness is greatest in the areas with the highest rainfall, areas that acted as refugia (areas that can sustain viability during droughts) in times of Pleistocene aridity.

Deciduous high forest and montane forest occupy about 2 million square kilometers where mean annual rainfall exceeds about 1,500 millimeters and the dry season is not severe. Montane forest extends from 1,500 meters to about 3,000 meters above sea level. Above 3,000 meters, specialized Afro-alpine plants, which include giant species, extend to the snow line.

Savanna woodland, consisting of tall perennial grassland with thick-barked, fire-resistant trees forming an incomplete canopy, is extensively developed where mean annual rainfall is between about 400 and 1,500 millimeters. Typical of the great planation surfaces at about 1,000 to 1,500 meters above sea level in south-central Africa, the savanna woodland runs in a latitudinal belt from the Atlantic to Ethiopia at an altitude of about 500 meters. In regions with between 150 and 400 millimeters of rainfall in the Sahel zone south of the Sahara and in the Kalahari, the proportion of annual grasses increases, fires are uncommon, and the shrubs and trees are sclerophyllous (able to resist drought, thorny, and widely spaced or in clumps). With less than 150 millimeters of rain, the plant cover is very sparse, too sparse to prevent the formation of sand dunes.

Hydrological conditions are important. Mangroves colonize the tidal swamps along low coasts in low latitudes. Forest trees stand on stilt roots in freshwater swamps. Tall reeds and grasses occupy clay plains, floodplains, and deltas where trees may be confined to better drained sites, such as large termite mounds. Floodplains alongside rivers flowing across savanna plains are bordered by gallery forests, which depend on seasonal inundation.

The nature of the soil affects root penetration and water availability to plants. On the plains of Sudan grows *Acacia seyal,* from which gum arabic is obtained. The tree extends farther north, toward the desert, in sandy soils. It does not thrive in clay soils, from which tree roots have more difficulty in extracting water in the dry season.

Much depends on the density of the population and the ways in which people use the land—clearing, cultivating, herding, hunting, cutting firewood, and lighting fires. Vast areas of savanna grassland are burned every year, as result of either lightning strikes or, more often, fires set deliberately to clear the land for cultivation, to improve the grazing, or to drive game. Populations have quadrupled in many areas over the last half century, and although some of the extra numbers have moved into towns, the majority of the population is still rural and depends on cultivation and grazing.

Little rain forest remains in West Africa. It has either been cleared for cultivation or replaced by oil palm, coconut, rubber, cocoa, and other useful trees. Even in the Zaire Basin, though most of the rain forest remains, much of it has been cleared at some time in the past. Montane forests have suffered from cultivators clearing hillsides and transforming them into open woodland or coffee plantations. For most people, the main source of fuel is wood, and wide areas of savanna have been depleted of trees to serve urban, as well as rural, populations.

Small-scale vegetation maps conceal great variability in the nature and density of the plant cover. Furthermore, the boundary lines on the map between one region and another are deceptively simple. On the ground, they are commonly patchworks of the vegetation types on either side.

BIBLIOGRAPHY

Adams, W. M., A. S. Goudie, and A. R. Orme. 1996. *The physical geography of Africa.* Oxford: Oxford University Press.

Griffith, J. P. 1972. *Climates of Africa: World survey of climatology.* Oxford: Elsevier.

Hastenrath, S. 1985. *Climate and circulation of the Tropics.* Dordrecht: Kluwer Academic Publishers.

A. T. Grove

QUATERNARY ENVIRONMENT

The Quaternary period is represented by sediments from the last nearly 1.8 million years. Fluctuating climatic conditions, which were also noticeable in previous times like the Pliocene (the last epoch of the preceding Tertiary period), occurred during the Quaternary. They were mainly the result of different cyclical patterns of the earth's orbital movements and can be identified in sediment records as so-called glacial-interglacial patterns. The orbital changes had different climatic results, which are superimposed on each other, resulting in a complex, long-term climatic pattern. During Quaternary times, populations of plants, animals, and people in Africa were affected by physical changes in habitats, driven by climate. Past conditions must have influenced the evolution and distribution of modern species, and their study sheds light on the history of biomes (ecological communities) and human cultures leading to the establishment of the present environmental regime. The nature and scale of change can be inferred from biological and cultural remains in sediments.

Quaternary Environmental Cycles

During the late Tertiary period and the Quaternary period, hominid species and new faunal assemblages evolved in Africa and eventually gave rise to modern humans and their associated fauna through processes of speciation and extinction. This evolution occurred under continually changing environmental conditions.

Quaternary environments are recorded in marine and continental records. Long, continuous marine records, which are usually dated by the stable oxygen-isotope stratigraphy and magnetostratigraphy, consist of biological assemblages and geological data like dust layers. These records can be correlated globally with other long marine and ice-core records (for example, the Vostoc Ice Core in Antarctica) and give indications for ocean temperatures and global paleoenvironmental conditions. On the other hand, continental sediment records with fossils are fragmentary and are often difficult to date because of erosion, weathering, and decomposition.

Continental and marine records occur in different contexts and are usually difficult to correlate. Correlation is necessary, however, in order to understand the Quaternary environment in Africa. In these attempts, complexities like long-term tectonic movements, which influenced environmental conditions, should further be taken into account.

According to the work of M. I. Milankovitch, three kinds of orbital changes occur. Over a period of 100,000 years, the earth's orbit varies from almost circular to elliptical. Over a period of 41,000 years, the inclination of the earth's axis to the orbital plane varies 2° 45'. And over a period of 19,000 to 23,000 years, the direction of the tilt of the earth's axis varies (precession). Climatic changes associated with these orbital variations include glacial phenomena in temperate continental regions like Europe, but such changes are difficult to trace on the African continent, which is tropical and virtually ice-free except for isolated high mountain peaks in East Africa. However, deep-sea sediment and oxygen-isotope records from several sites, including sites in the West African and Arabian regions, show a consistent history of cyclical climatic oscillations during the Quaternary and Tertiary periods. Offshore records produced by Peter B. de Menocal and coworkers suggest that precession cycles, associated with wet-dry monsoonal fluctuations, dominated in the Pliocene, but that a 40,000-year glacial-interglacial cycle was more visible from about 2.8 million years ago onward. A 100,000-year glacial-interglacial periodicity prevailed since about 1 million years ago. The changing patterns, documented by marine records compiled close to the African coasts, must have affected environmental conditions on the continent markedly, and numerous glacial-interglacial cycles must have occurred during the Quaternary period. Orbital factors, however, have not necessarily affected different regions of the African continent uniformly.

From ocean sediments in the Atlantic and from relatively recent geological events, there is evidence for much shorter events, of hundreds to a few thousand years duration. The so-called Younger Dryas event, a cool period between 10,000 and 11,000 years ago, was first recognized in Europe. Recent research suggests that this cooling affected Africa at least in its northern regions. Together the effects of superimposed cycles result in a complex climatic pattern of shifts in long-term temperature and moisture conditions as well as shifts in the seasonal patterns of both rainfall and temperature. The terrestrial fossil records associated with these changes on the African continent are spatially and temporally fragmentary and often not well dated, complicating efforts to trace Quaternary changes of environment in detail.

The Development of Cultures in the Changing Environment

The effects of cyclical environmental change on the process of evolution of species is not fully understood, but it is likely that most speciation occurred in allopatry (that is, in species whose geographical ranges do not overlap). This suggests that physical factors like climate play a role in the process. Over the last few million years, climatic patterns must have influenced the spatial distribution, extinction, and evolution of species, including the hominid family.

The End of the Pliocene and the Early Pleistocene (750,000 to 2 Million Years Ago)

A sequence of progressively cooler glacial-interglacial cycles coincided with the beginning of the Quaternary period and the development of typical Quaternary environments. Around this time, the first of several species of hominids

emerged. Biological evidence, like R. Bonnefille's pollen data from the Plio-Pleistocene, confirm that vegetation changed cyclically in East Africa during the time when critical events in faunal and hominid evolution were taking place. These events coincided with the establishment of the first Early Stone Age cultures. The vegetation changes included alternations of *Acacia, Alchornea* woodland, and *Podocarpus* forests and expansions of salt-flat vegetation, all of which suggest strong temperature and moisture fluctuations. As part of this pattern, relatively arid conditions developed at the beginning of the Quaternary. Thure E. Cerling showed that early during the Quaternary, C_4 plants, typically tropical grasses adapted to optimal productivity during summer growth seasons, became established. In southern Africa, the Pliocene Makapanian faunal complex was replaced by the Lower Pleistocene Cornelian assemblages, probably as adaptations to more intense, and possibly drier, glacial-interglacial cycles. Botanical data on environments associated with Early Stone Age cultures from the rest of Africa are scarce.

The Middle Pleistocene (125,000 to 750,000 Years Ago)

Pollen data on Middle Pleistocene environments are very limited, but data compiled from sites like Florisbad and the Tswaing Crater (the Pretoria Saltpan) in South Africa shed light on the cyclical nature of environmental change during this phase. The Middle Pleistocene faunal site of Florisbad in the *highveld* grassland biome shows the development of the so-called Florisian fauna, which can be associated with Middle Stone Age cultures. Fauna and pollen studies suggest that periods with relatively good moisture availability can be associated with these finds.

However, occupation at Florisbad was not continuous. A pattern emerges from several South African Middle and Late Pleistocene archaeological sites: some regions, especially those with lower moisture availability, were unoccupied for tens of thousands of years.

The Tswaing Crater lies in the current *bushveld* savanna biome and yielded Middle Pleistocene polleniferous sediments between

150,000 and 200,000 years old. Assemblages of fossil pollen from the Middle Pleistocene indicate four cyclical stages during this time in the area: from (1) relatively dry, open savanna grassland to (2) cool, relatively wet grassland with small shrubs and *Podocarpus* forest in mountain valleys, to (3) dry, moderately warm, open savanna grassland, and then to (4) moderately cool, wet grassland and *Podocarpus* forest. High frequencies of microscopic charcoal ash suggest that fires occurred frequently. This is possibly an indication of human presence.

The Late Pleistocene
(10,000 to 125,000 Years Ago)

During the Late Pleistocene, Middle Stone Age people persisted in southern Africa and were replaced by Late Stone Age cultures only shortly before the end of the epoch. Biological evidence for the environmental conditions in which Middle Stone Age people lived is available in the form of macro- and micromammal faunas from the Border Cave site. It is suggested that woodlands became prominent about 125,000 years ago at the beginning of the last interglacial period. Pollen data are not available for this period, but it can be assumed that conditions resembled those of the Holocene period (the last 10,000 years). A pollen zone that can possibly be related to the end of the last interglacial period (about 80,000 years ago), from sediments in the Tswaing Crater sequence, indicates relatively warm *bushveld* conditions comparable to those of the Holocene.

A palynological (pollen and spore) reconstruction from different sites in South Africa, for the period between roughly 40,000 and 75,000 years ago, suggests that moderately cool conditions returned and that montane forests covered wide areas in the interior and along the east coast.

Although sharp oscillations in environmental conditions occurred during this phase, they were generally favorable, with moderately cool temperatures and good moisture availability. People of the Middle Stone Age cultures still persisted in the interior and along the southern coast in South Africa. In contrast, in central Africa, the Middle Stone Age environment was relatively dry, which resulted in a deforestation that prevailed during the Maluekian industrial phase between 40,000 and 70,000 years ago.

Between about 10,000 and 40,000 years ago in South Africa, further strong variations in vegetation composition took place under generally cool conditions. This is suggested by pollen data from the current *bushveld* savanna region. Grasslands with cool upland elements were more widespread. Pollen data from north of the Limpopo River in East Africa (for example, at Sacred Lake) suggest that the vast region lost some of its tropical characteristics with downward altitudinal shifts of vegetation zones.

Moisture availability in the region was not constant, however, during this long phase, as is suggested by evidence for fluctuations of water levels in several large East African lakes. Although good forest cover returned to central Africa during the Njilian phase between 30,000 and 40,000 years ago, drier conditions in the Leopoldian phase caused the retreat of forest into refugia (protected areas), culminating in wide extensions of open savanna vegetation around 18,000 years ago.

During the Late Pleistocene after 40,000 years ago, the fauna in the current savanna regions of southern Africa was characteristic of assemblages related to open, cooler grassland vegetation. Late Stone Age people were replacing the last Middle Stone Age people, who persisted as late as the Last Glacial Maximum in the inhospitable high Drakensberg Mountains. Parts of the interior *highveld,* semiarid regions, and the southern coasts were unoccupied for a long periods of time, however, probably due to unfavorably dry and cool conditions.

Biological data from several sites in South Africa suggest that 13,000 years ago, at the end of the Pleistocene, temperatures were rising and favorable moisture conditions developed. This change coincided with a change in Late Stone Age manifestations. In the Cape region, fauna included mainly grazers until about 12,000 years ago, when some large mammals became extinct and the faunal composition began to shift in favor of browsers and mixed feeders. Both climatic and cultural factors may have played a role in these developments.

The Holocene (The Last 10,000 Years)

At the beginning of the Holocene period in Africa, Late Stone Age occupation was well established, but during the last 2,500 years, Iron Age people moved from the north to the south. While temperatures gradually rose during the Early Holocene, the moisture pattern in sub-Saharan Africa showed a marked dichotomy from north to south. In the north, favorable moisture conditions resulted in high lake levels, increased biological productivity, and human settlement. In South Africa, fossil-pollen data suggest that arid conditions occurred. This kind of dichotomy finds support in global-model simulations of climates, which bring into account the 19,000-year pattern of monsoonal fluctuations based on orbital precession.

Pollen and spore evidence from South Africa suggests that a more even seasonal moisture distribution may have occurred during the early arid phases of the Holocene but that this was gradually replaced from the north by a stronger summer-rainfall pattern. As in the rest of Africa, the archaeological record in South Africa becomes more visible throughout the Holocene, but it is difficult to know exactly how climatic evolution influenced Late Stone Age occupation and if climatic factors played a role in the apparent lack of occupation in part of the interior plateaus during the Middle Holocene. However, the development of a stronger summer-rainfall pattern and good moisture availability in the Late Holocene might have favored the southward spread of Iron Age people. Thomas N. Huffman suggests that occupation patterns of these people in the marginal areas of South Africa is probably related to climatic conditions. Wet phases and favorable temperatures likely determined the southward limits of their expansion during the last 2,000 years.

BIBLIOGRAPHY

Deacon, J., and N. Lancaster. 1988. *Late Quaternary palaeo-environments of southern Africa.* Oxford: Oxford University Press.

Coetzee, J. A. 1967. Pollen analytical studies in East and southern Africa. *Palaeoecology of Africa* 3: 1–146.

Hamilton, A. C. 1982. *Environmental history of East Africa: A study of the Quaternary.* London: Academic Press.

Imbrie J., and K. P. Imbrie. 1979. *Ice ages: Solving the mystery.* London: The Macmillan Press, Ltd.

Klein, R. G. 1984. *Southern African prehistory and palaeoenvironments.* Rotterdam: A. A. Balkema.

Maley, J. 1993. The climate and vegetational history of the equatorial regions of Africa during the Upper Quaternary. In *The archaeology of Africa: Food, metals and towns,* eds. T. Shaw, P. Sinclair, B. Andah, and A. Okpoko, 43–52. London: Routledge.

Partridge, T. C., and M. A. J. Williams. 1993. Quaternary palaeo-climates of the Southern Hemisphere. *Palaeogeography, Palaeoclimatology and Palaeoecology* 101: 185–337.

Scott, L., and P. B. Beaumont. 1996. Quaternary environments: A southern African perspective. *Quaternary International* 33: 1–95.

Vrba, E. S., G. H. Denton, T. C. Partridge, and L. H. Burckle. 1995. *Paleoclimate and evolution with emphasis on human origins.* New Haven: Yale University Press.

Wright, H. E., J. E. Kutzbach, T. Webb, III, W. F. Ruddiman, F. A. Street-Perrot, and P. J. Bartlein. 1993. *Global climates since the Last Glacial Maximum.* Minneapolis: University of Minnesota Press.

Louis Scott

DISEASE AS A FACTOR IN AFRICAN HISTORY

Throughout much of sub-Saharan Africa, nearly one-half of all children die before reaching their fifth birthdays. Health professionals attribute many of these deaths to nutritional deficiencies exacerbated by parasitic infections. While diseases such as trypanosomiasis (sleeping sickness), malaria, and, less frequently, yellow fever may cause death directly, chronic infections caused by filariasis, schistosomiasis, yaws, and dracunculiasis are more likely to cause death indirectly by competing with their victims for body nutrients or by debilitating their hosts. Highly virulent pathogens are typically those that reproduce rapidly, savagely exploiting their hosts' body cells for their own use. So-called benign infections result when infectious agents prey on cellular and other natural body wastes. For decades, health professionals mistakenly believed that well-adapted pathogens and hosts eventually evolved into a system of benign coexistence, lending hope to modern Africans decimated by the same suite of diseases plaguing that continent since antiquity. Paul Ewald has shown, however, that natural selection can favor virulence in pathogens, especially when they are transmitted to new hosts by intermediates. Nearly all of the diseases identified above rely on nonhuman vectors for transmission. The exception, yaws, produces long-lasting skin lesions that may transmit infections to new hosts opportunistically for many years. Throughout history, most Africans have lived in rural areas of relatively low population densities. In these conditions, acute virulent infections die out while "waiting" for new hosts. Pathogens that reproduce more slowly, but kill just as surely, can survive indefinitely. Other pathogens can be carried great distances by insect vectors, uninfected carriers, and water. Some of the most lethal diseases to humans are zoonotic (communicable from animals to humans) infections with natural and abundant reservoirs in other animals, including domestic livestock.

Sleeping Sickness and Nagana

Trypanosomes, which cause sleeping sickness in humans and nagana in livestock, produce infections using several tactics. The parasitic disease trypanosomiasis is transmitted to animals through the bite of various tsetse flies of the genus *Glossina.* A fossilized tsetse fly in Colorado dates to 35 million years ago, suggesting a very ancient origin of trypanosomiasis. Five trypanosome species produce fatal infections in humans and cattle. Many species of wild ungulates are also susceptible to all but one of these trypanosomes but appear to suffer very few ill effects from them. Although trypanosomiasis is currently treatable, the wild-animal reservoir hampers control of the disease today. Two forms of sleeping sickness occur in humans. *Trypanosoma brucei gambiense* causes a chronic form of the disease in which death ensues several years after infection. Species of tsetse flies inhabiting riverine brush of the tropical forest areas of western and central Africa typically transmit this protozoan.

It primarily infects only humans. The second strain, *T. b. rhodesiense,* produces a more acute form of sleeping sickness, typically causing death within two or three months. Tsetse flies occupying savannas of eastern and southern Africa transmit this more virulent form. Humans appear to be only incidental hosts of *T. b. rhodesiense.* It produces benign infections in both wild ungulates and cattle. However, *T. b. vivax, T. b. congolense,* and *T. b. brucei,* which produce apparently benign infections in many of these same species of wildlife, are fatal to cattle. The tsetse belt, lying roughly between 20° north and south of the equator, has hindered the occupation and movement of peoples throughout much of tropical Africa. The impact of trypanosomiasis is hard to exaggerate. Untreated, it is always fatal to humans and often to cattle. Forests infested with trypanosome-infected tsetse flies prohibit stock raising there, and much of the savanna land is uninhabitable to humans, who are susceptible to the Rhodesian form. Frank Lambrecht has argued that tsetse flies have been a deterrent to human occupation of the East African savannas and that the flies promoted the survival of large-bodied mammals since big-game hunters apparently exterminated them elsewhere during the Upper Paleolithic. Today a fly-free corridor along the Rift Valley of East Africa permits occupation and movement of peoples and livestock between the north and south of the continent without danger of trypanosome infection. The impact of trypanosomiasis in Africa has no doubt varied historically due to climatic fluctuations affecting the ranges of tsetse flies.

Malaria

Like the African trypanosomes, malarial parasites have both virulent and less virulent forms. The disease is widespread throughout Africa. The most virulent form, *Plasmodium falciparum,* has affected Africans so severely that a second potentially lethal disease, sickle-cell anemia, has evolved to high frequencies because it mitigates the effects of *P. falciparum. P. vicar, P. malarial,* and *P. ovals* produce less virulent but longer-lasting infections in humans. Infected *Anopheles* mosquitoes transmit all four protozoa. Malarial parasites undergo portions of their life cycle in the red blood cells of their hosts. *P. falciparum* more ruthlessly exploits the red blood cells than the other forms of malaria during this phase, resulting in a faster reproductive rate and higher virulence. Ewald's work has also shown that when opportunities for transmission increase, we should expect more virulent strains to replace variants that reproduce more slowly. It is not surprising, then, that *P. falciparum* is more common in densely populated areas than the less virulent strains. In larger populations, where infections are more readily transmitted to new hosts, the less virulent forms lose out in competition with *P. falciparum*. Malaria is an ancient disease, possibly dating to the Middle Pleistocene. Areas endemic with *P. falciparum* are associated with higher frequencies of the sickle-cell allele (one of a group of genes that occur alternatively at a given locus). Producing the variant hemoglobin S, the allele causes sickling of the red blood cells, resulting in impaired oxygenation of tissues. Homozygotes for the hemoglobin S allele are afflicted with sickle-cell anemia, a severe disease that most often results in early death among Africans. Heterozygotes, who have sickle-cell traits, are typically only moderately anemic, since the majority of red blood cells are otherwise normal. Malarial parasites reproduce poorly in individuals with hemoglobin S, affording heterozygotes survival advantages over individuals with normal hemoglobin in regions where *P. falciparum* is endemic. The survival advantages against this form of malaria apparently outweigh the strong selection against the sickle-cell allele, since its frequency exceeds 40 percent in many regions endemic with *P. falciparum*. Other hemoglobin and blood-group variants also provide protection against other forms of malaria.

Other Diseases

Few individual diseases have affected Africans as severely and for as long as trypanosomiasis and malaria. Others have undoubtedly influenced, at least moderately, the distribution of humans and their economic systems. The best recognized of these is filariasis, which refers to several diseases caused by various parasitic filarial nematodes (worms), also transmitted through the bite of numerous arthropod insects. Female flies of genus *Simulium* infected with the roundworm *Onchocerca volvulus* transmit onchocerciasis (river blindness). Presently onchocerciasis is most common in West Africa and is less widely distributed but more debilitating than other filarial infections, such as *Wuchereria bancrofti,* the usual cause of elephantiasis (infection of the lymphatics). Onchocerciasis causes extreme itching and progressive deterioration of sight. Since the onchocerciasis vector prefers to breed near rapidly flowing water, fly infestations have caused abandonment of prime agricultural land and depopulation of river valleys in modern times. Another disease transmitted by mosquitoes, yellow fever, is most commonly associated with high population densities. Only rarely does it cause death. Recovery is fast and produces virtually lifelong immunity. Chronic diseases with long incubation periods (the time between inoculation and infection) have less noticeable effects on population distributions, since the links between sources of pathogens and their effects are harder for inhabitants to recognize. Like malaria, schistosomiasis (or bilharziasis) is widely distributed throughout Africa, but it takes years for serious effects to appear. Worms of the genus *Schistosoma,* which undergo part of their life cycle in certain species of freshwater snails, cause the infection. In Africa, the *Schistosoma* eggs are passed to the snails through shedding of human feces *(S. haematobium)* and urine *(S. mansoni)* near water sources occupied by the snails. Larvae later released by the snails bore through skin in contact with the water. Another waterborne infection, dracunculiasis (guinea-worm infection) is caused by ingesting crustaceans of the genus *Cyclops* infected with the parasitic worm *Dracunculus medinensis* in water. Since humans can easily avoid infections by boiling water and because infections are only sporadically debilitating, the disease probably has not significantly influenced the settlement of people across the Tropics.

The impact of yaws on human settlement patterns in Africa is harder to assess. Yaws is a childhood disease spread through skin contact in the moist Tropics. It is caused by the bacterium *Treponema pertenue* and is associated with poor hygiene. Although yaws may produce debilitating skin and bone lesions, it is most interesting because of its relationship to the other treponemal diseases. *T. carateum* causes pinto, a skin disease similar to yaws in the New World. A third yawslike disease, endemic syphilis, occurs in arid regions of Africa. It is caused by *T. pallidum,* which also causes venereal syphilis. Since treponemal infections cause cross-immunity, yaws and endemic syphilis inoculate children against the more deadly venereal syphilis prior to adulthood. Though the origin and antiquity of the treponemal bacteria is disputed, yaws has occurred in sub-Saharan Africa since at least the 16th century. This childhood disease probably spared many Africans from the epidemics of venereal syphilis that ravaged the rest of the Old World in the post-Columbian era.

BIBLIOGRAPHY

Baker, B. J., and G. J. Armelagos. 1988. The origin and antiquity of syphilis. *Current Anthropology* 29: 703–737.

Burned, Sir MacF., and D. O. White. 1940. *Natural history of infectious disease.* Cambridge: Cambridge University Press.

Ewald, P. W. 1994. *Evolution of infectious disease.* Oxford: Oxford University Press.

Lambrecht, F. L. Trypanosomiasis in prehistoric and later human populations: A tentative reconstruction. In *Diseases in antiquity: A survey of the diseases, injuries and surgery of early populations,* eds. D. Brothwell and A. T. Sandison, 132–151. Springfield: Charles C. Thomas.

Kiple, K. F., ed. 1993. *The Cambridge world history of human disease.* Cambridge: Cambridge University Press.

Nesse, R. M., and G. C. Williams. 1994. *Why we get sick.* New York: Random House.

Renee L. Pennington

HISTORIES OF RESEARCH

ARCHAEOLOGY IN AFRICA: ITS INFLUENCE

Archaeology has played an influential role in formulating ideas about African history since the mid-19th century. Africa's archaeological record, extending from modern times back for nearly 2.5 million years, is the longest in the world. Since archaeology is unique in its ability to describe and explain human cultural change over enormous periods of time, archaeologists have a vital role to play in the study and interpretation of ancient Africa not only for specialist scholars but also for much wider audiences both within and without the continent.

The Origins of Humankind

When the Victorian biologist Thomas Henry Huxley compared the newly discovered Neanderthal skull from Germany with the bones of an African chimpanzee, he firmly placed Africa and its diverse primate populations at the very core of what he called "the question of questions" for science, the relationship between humans and their closest living ancestors, the apes. His *Man's Place in Nature,* published in 1863, was a ringing endorsement of Charles Darwin's theories of evolution and natural selection, published only four years before. Darwin himself speculated in 1871 in his *Descent of Man* that tropical Africa would prove to be the cradle of humankind. But Africa's central role in human evolution was largely ignored until the late 1940s, despite the discovery of *Australopithecus africanus* by Raymond Dart in 1924 and archaeologists' establishment of long Stone Age cultural sequences in eastern and southern Africa well before World War II. European paleontologists were mesmerized by the Piltdown forgery, an attempt to create a missing link between man and ape by fabricating a fossil from a human skull and an altered, artificially weathered fragment of an ape's jaw. They did not finally accept the australopithecines as being close to the human ancestral line until the "Piltdown man" was discredited and they examined the fossils firsthand.

The modern science of paleoanthropology was effectively born with Mary Leakey's finding of *Zinjanthropus boisei* at Olduvai Gorge in 1959. The Olduvai discoveries and the appealing personalities of Mary and Louis Leakey brought the National Geographic Society into play. The society's articles, films, and television specials made the Leakeys international celebrities and firmly established Africa as the cradle of humanity in the popular mind. And as "big American science" brought substantial research funds and major field expeditions to such areas as Ethiopia's Hadar and Kenya's East Turkana, the major researchers, with their sometimes ambitious and abrasive personalities, became household names. Today, every major fossil discovery makes international headlines and keeps African archaeology in the news, but much of the most significant research, on tool technologies and subsistence, for example, takes place far from the limelight. To a large extent, paleoanthropology is still the province of foreign scholars, although systematic attempts have been made to train African researchers, some of whom are becoming prominent in the field. But it is fair to say that the greatest impact of early African prehistory has been outside Africa rather than within it.

The Origins of Modern Humans

The origins of *Homo sapiens sapiens* modern humanity is one of the great controversies of contemporary science, pitting those who believe that anatomically modern humans originated in Africa against those who argue for a multiregional origin. The evidence of both mitochondrial DNA and archaeology point reasonably convincingly to sub-Saharan Africa as the homeland of the first modern humans, but the pace of field research lags far behind the speculation. Some of the key sites, like Klasies River Mouth, have been known to African specialists for many years, but the influence of their thinking on modern human origins has been negligible until about a decade ago. Again, the impact of the controversy within Africa itself has been small, as, indeed, is the case with most Stone Age archaeology, which is historically remote to modern-day Africans and little-taught in African schools or universities, except at a somewhat specialized level.

Archaeology and Sub-Saharan African History

Africa was the cradle of humanity and of modern humans. It was also the home of one of the world's first civilizations, that of the ancient Egyptians. Today, we know that Egyptian civilization was a creation of the Nile Valley, an indigenous development with close ties to the Near Eastern world and, apparently, only fleeting connections with tropical Africa beyond its frontiers. But this distinctive civilization has had a profound influence on thinking about African history and about world history as well. Hardly surprisingly, the first theories of sub-Saharan African history looked toward Egypt for inspiration. The ancient Egyptians were considered Caucasian Hamitic speakers, light-skinned foreigners who brought the institutions of Hamitic civilization to tropical Africa long before modern Europeans arrived. And when huge iron-slag heaps came to light at

the ancient city of Meroë in Sudan, British philologist A. J. Sayce proclaimed it the "Birmingham of ancient Africa." Again, the implication was that everything "civilized" came from Egypt and the north. These racist theories reached their climax in the hands of British anthropologist Charles Gabriel Seligman, who was obsessed with the notion of divine kingship, epitomized by the ancient Egyptian pharaohs. In his *Races of Africa* published in 1930, Seligman proclaimed that the tall, light-skinned Hamites had migrated southward into the primitive wilderness that was Africa.

Seligman's Hamitic myth had the attraction of being a convenient explanation of complex historical events, an explanation that filled a historical vacuum and served as a rationale for colonial rule. Both the Hamitic theory and the assumption that ancient Egypt had a profound influence on African history were products of an era when Africa was not only a remote and little-known continent but was also thought of as a savage land to be exploited for its human and material riches.

Half a century before the publication of *The Races of Africa,* the German geologist Carl Mauch visited Great Zimbabwe far north of the Limpopo River in 1871 and claimed it was the long-lost Land of Ophir. The imperially minded magnate Cecil Rhodes seized on Zimbabwe with alacrity as his settlers crowded north of the Limpopo in 1890. Proclaiming it was a Phoenician palace, he commissioned archaeologist J. Theodore Bent to excavate the ruins. Bent reported that Zimbabwe was built by a "northern race coming from Arabia . . . a race closely akin to the Phoenician and the Egyptian." His conclusions dovetailed comfortably with prevailing beliefs that Africans were incapable of governing a state or building in stone. Despite important excavations by Egyptologist David Randall-MacIver in 1905, by Gertrude Caton-Thompson in 1929, and again in 1956 by a team of Rhodesian scholars, who showed the ruins to be of African construction and inspiration and to date to the early 2nd millennium B.C., until the 1980s, the interests of white settlers continued to propagate theories that Zimbabwe was an ancient Phoenician temple.

The colonial powers, especially the British, encouraged anthropological research as a means of achieving greater understanding of African society. These successful studies also coincided with a growing interest in the preservation of what was called "traditional African culture," sparked in part by an increasing consciousness of African art in Europe. Archaeologist Bernard Fagg expanded archaeological research throughout Nigeria in the 1950s, founded museums, and brought traditional art and culture closer to the mainstream of emerging African nationalism. His excavations placed the study of African art and metallurgy on a new footing.

Until the 1950s, most people assumed that farming and ironworking had come to tropical Africa very recently, perhaps within the past 1,000 years. This was partly because of theories that derived ironworking, and indeed civilization, from the Nile Valley, and because there were no reliable ways of dating archaeological sites in tropical Africa. Caton-Thompson dated Great Zimbabwe with imported glass beads and Chinese porcelain to about the 14th century, but most sites did not yield datable foreign artifacts. For their part, almost no historians took pre-European African history seriously. Even highly respected scholars argued there was no such history to write. Then came the radiocarbon-dating revolution of the mid-1950s. The new method of geophysical dating not only confirmed the accuracy of Caton-Thompson's medieval chronology for Great Zimbabwe but also showed that iron-using farmers had been living in most parts of tropical Africa for at least 2,000 years.

Radiocarbon dating came into use at a time when a rising tide of African nationalism had provoked a new and urgent interest in precolonial African history. Even as late as 1963, many textbooks used in African schools began with the Victorian explorers. South African Blacks were taught that Bantu-speaking peoples had crossed the Limpopo River at exactly the same moment that Dutchman Jan van Riebeck had settled at the Cape of Good Hope in 1652, despite abundant archaeological evidence for much earlier human occupation. The late 1950s and 1960s not only brought British Prime Minister Harold Macmillan's "winds of change" to Africa but also saw the upsurge of the civil rights movement in the United States. During this time, a deep and often passionate interest in African history was engendered among both African-American and African intellectuals. Many of them reacted violently against the ethnocentrism and racism of the Hamitic myth, against assumptions that Africa had no history. Out of these reactions developed Afrocentrism, a distinctive school of history that flourishes mainly in the United States and asserts the primacy of what Afrocentrists consider long-neglected African civilizations. Afrocentrists point to Ghana, an ancient West African empire that flourished while Europe was in the Middle Ages, and to Black Nubian pharaohs, who ruled ancient Egypt. They claim that Zairians invented mathematics using marked bones and that ancient Malians crossed the Atlantic to the Americas nearly two centuries before Christopher Columbus. At the same time, they assert that Western civilization and its institutions were derived from Black Africa. Egypt, they say, brought the institutions and technology of Africa to Western civilization.

African-American scholar Henry Louis Gates, Jr., of Harvard University theorizes that Afrocentrism is born of a superstitious faith in the power of race as a way of forging one's destiny. It is a revolt against European cultural arrogance that, with one hand, downgrades the importance of Western civilization yet, with the other, claims that the Africans of ancient Egypt were its parent.

During the 1960s and 1970s, a new African history came into being, one based on multidisciplinary inquiry. Archaeology was a primary source, and for the first time, historians applied rigorous critique to centuries-old oral histories, narrative histories passed verbally from generation to generation. Archaeology and oral history drew heavily on data derived from both ancient and contemporary sources, from biological and cultural anthropology. Comparative linguistics, the study of ancient languages, gave invaluable, if sometimes controversial, clues to the African past, especially into the origins of the Bantu-speaking peoples. The writings of Egyptian scribes, Arab geographers, and European travelers provided priceless information on ancient African societies.

At first, the new generation of multidisciplinary historians was concerned with broad issues, with sweeping theories of the Bantu expansion based on linguistics and archaeology, with the spread of institutions like divine kingship, with Sudanic states formed by the ideas of ancient Egypt percolating through the Meroitic filter. Now the focus has shifted, for the sheer complexity of Africa's myriad ancient societies makes such broad-based theories untenable. At the same time, historians have come to realize that one of the most powerful tools at their disposal is archaeology, for it allows one to study long-term cultural change and to trace the development of new technologies, cultural and social institutions, and even individual cultures.

Sub-Saharan Africa is unique among continents in that archaeology plays a central role not only in writing history but also in education. The results of archaeological research into West African kingdoms, East African kingdoms, Great Zimbabwe, and other topics figure prominently in school and university curricula. At the same time, new generations of African-born archaeologists are expanding their research on a regional basis and adding new chapters to an emerging story. In Africa, archaeology is a vital intellectual component in fostering national identity and historical consciousness.

BIBLIOGRAPHY
Garlake, P. L. 1973. *Great Zimbabwe.* London: Thames and Hudson.
Lewin, R. 1987. *Bones of contention.* New York: Simon and Schuster.
Oliver, R. 1991. *The African experience.* London: Weidenfeld and Nicholson.
Posnansky, M. 1966. Kingship, archaeology, and historical myth. *Uganda Journal* 1: 1–12.
Robertshaw, P., ed. 1990. *A history of African archaeology.* London and Portsmouth: James Currey Ltd. and Heinemann.
Sanders, R. S. 1969. The Hamitic hypothesis: Its origin and functions in time perspective. *Journal of African History* 10 (4): 521–532.
Seligman, C. G. 1930. *Races of Africa.* Oxford: Oxford University Press.

Brian Fagan

HISTORIOGRAPHY IN AFRICA

Archaeology in Africa has taken shape only quite recently and faces serious barriers to its rapid development. This is in spite of the strong demands for archaeological information in a continent where written records are scanty and incomplete, often of foreign origin, and frequently of fairly recent composition.

Serious professional archaeology began slowly in Africa as a result of social and historical circumstances. The imposition of colonial rule in the late 19th century, at the time when academic archaeology was coming into its own as a discipline, consigned Africa to a marginal area for study. Colonial governments had little money for such frivolities, and in most places, it was government policy not to support institutions of higher learning, where a cadre of professional archaeologists with local interests might find work and train students.

Generally, in the colonial period, archaeological research was promoted in Africa when it promised to provide an insight into what was perceived in Europe or North America as general human history rather than regional or local issues. European or North American archaeologists, with their own sources of funding, might investigate areas that seemed to promise such insights. The Nile Valley was therefore fully explored, as it was perceived as playing a role in the antiquity of Europe, while ancient hominid sites were investigated in East Africa and South Africa because they shed light on human origins. In only a few places, such as the Great Zimbabwe ruins, where dramatic remains and the possibility of ancient foreign connections got international attention, were professionals called in to examine a site in the historic period.

Elsewhere, what is known as *historic archaeology* (generally covering the period after about 1000 B.C.) was neglected by professionals and taken up in a sporadic way by amateurs. In much of sub-Saharan Africa (outside the Upper Nile Valley and Ethiopia), there were few written records. Those that exist were written by outsiders after A.D. 1000. Likewise, there were few dramatic remains and ruins that might draw attention on their own as the ruins of Zimbabwe had done. Ironically, while the shortage of visible sites and written records made the collection of archaeological data more important as a historical source, it also rendered archaeological research seemingly less promising and more difficult. A general sense that there were no really important archaeological discoveries to be made in sub-Saharan Africa, therefore, played a role in its underinvestigation by professionals.

Surface collection of stone tools or an occasional dig produced relatively little information about Africa outside the Nile Valley and in time periods later than the Early Stone Age. There was, of course, some fairly good work done in this limited way, such as French archaeology in the Middle Niger region, but such work was never sufficiently followed up to establish regional relationships or clear historical sequences outside of target sites. Even some of the more dramatic visible ruins, such as the site of Surame in Niger, large earthwork enclosures in Zaire and Angola, or various ruined cities in Chad, were never explored very fully, though their existence was noted by historically minded visitors.

In the absence of good field archaeology, much of the interpretation of the deeper African past relied on those elements of research that were well developed. Ethnography, linguistic findings, and the study of material culture had proceeded further than archaeology, in large measure because the colonial governments had been required by administrative necessity to study African law and social structure. Prehistorians used this material to create speculative schemes for early African history, which was heavily charged by the ideology of the period before World War II.

A cluster of interpretative schemes focused, for example, on what might be called the "Hamitic hypothesis." According to this generalization, developed through linguistics and the study of the distribution of cultural items, much of African history in ancient times was dominated by the notion of racially superior people who, along with various artifacts and civilization itself, migrated from the Nile Valley or North Africa into the land of the less intelligent sub-Saharan Africans. Some of the documented African history, such as that of the empires of the western Sudan, was explained in these terms as well, as the long-term interaction between civilizing outsiders and the indigenous people.

The birth of modern archaeology in Africa coincided in many ways with the development of nationalist movements and independence. The newly independent governments were anxious to create an educational infrastructure (including universities) as a part of their drive for development and thus provided a base for serious archaeological work to begin. Between 1960 and 1975, universities mushroomed in Africa. Many offered courses in archaeology and hired trained professional expatriates to teach in them and conduct research in the country. Soon a small cadre of professionally trained African archaeologists developed.

Several countries, such as Senegal, Nigeria, Ghana, and Zambia, started what would become effective archaeological services, cataloging sites, providing museums, and following up on leads exposed by private citizens (especially schoolchildren). Unfortunately, the severe financial restraints created by the recession that followed the mid-1970s, from which Africa has yet to recover, curtailed and then set back the growth of such services as well as the universities. As a result, Africa is still dependent upon foreign archaeologists and funding to pursue the archaeological investigation of its past. Fortunately, a growth of interest in the African past outside of the continent accompanied the nationalist period. Africa specialists, including some of the African trained archaeologists unable to work at home, have carried out research on the continent.

The nationalist governments that provided for the infrastructure of education and research also took an interest in supporting archaeological research that would serve its needs. In postcolonial Africa, leaders as well as many intellectuals, both within Africa and outside, were anxious to locate and document a precolonial history for the continent. At the same time, a new phase of the civil rights movement in the United States awakened strong interests in the development of a history for Americans of African descent, a history, that is, that preceded their enslavement. Some scholars and government leaders claimed that Africa was the "cradle of humanity" as they incorporated the Nile Valley civilizations, which had already been investigated during the colonial period, as a part of the African heritage, turned the Hamitic hypothesis on its head, and retained the idea of an African history driven by diffusion from the Nile Valley. Such views were a minority, and for most, the result of the new climate was a push for archaeologists to explore historic archaeology, which required the investigation of new areas and new time periods that had not been researched in the colonial period.

The issues and questions pursued in the 1960s and early 1970s were generally driven by the ideological demands of African nationalism and North American racial politics. Among these were searches for the origins for agriculture and metalworking (especially ironworking) and for the origin of the state as a way of asserting the equality of Africans and their descendants and affirming their right to rule themselves. Most of these issues were pursued at a continental level or at least a supranational level. The archaeologists who posed these questions were often less concerned about the origins of a specific state or the development of a particular region than about the general occurrence of these traits in the continent as a whole. Only in the case of the archaeological explorations of the spread of agriculture and metalworking in subequatorial Africa, and its possible connections with the so-called Bantu migrations, was a theme that did not touch directly on the nationalist concerns pursued systematically.

Given the ideological interests of the nationalist movement, research was focused especially on the origins of agriculture, ironworking, or the state rather than their development or regional chronology (save for the Bantu question). One result of this obsession with origins was a failure to connect archaeological investigation with time periods that could be documented through oral or written evidence, perhaps because too much concentration on regional history might promote ethnic particularism or "tribalism," a concern that made nationalists uncomfortable.

Scholarly interpretation and debates in the 1960s and 1970s also reflected the concerns of African nationalism and its American counter-

part. With a heightened nationalist pride, some scholars and leaders hoped that archaeology could prove that Africans had developed agriculture, ironworking, and states in ancient times and independently of influences from outside the continent. The development in the 1950s of radiocarbon dating, which allowed sites with organic remains to be securely dated in the absence of stratified sites or pottery sequences, promised sure answers to many of these questions, which turned, as it happened, on chronology. A few scholars, usually working with nonarchaeological sources, had posited such ancient developments, especially in the domestication of plants and the development of agriculture.

Archaeologists, however, were wary of ideological claims and conservative in their interpretation of the material remains they uncovered. With relatively little material to work with and acutely aware of the shortfalls of the colonial regime's speculative schemes that had led to the Hamitic hypothesis, archaeologists were reluctant to assert that they had found proof of the developments that nationalists wished for. Nevertheless, the demands for knowledge were so strong that almost any new evidence was seized upon, sometimes prematurely, to comment on the pressing questions of the field. On more than one occasion, a poorly reported site or an insecure date was rushed into print as evidence either to prove or disprove the issues under debate.

On the whole, however, both discussion and support for archaeological work accepted scientific cannons of proof. Nationalist leadership did not press the archaeologists and accepted their wariness. As a result, by the mid-1970s, the mainstream archaeological interpretation of the African past, in Africa as well as outside the continent, was that, in spite of the hopes of nationalists, agriculture had been first developed outside of Africa and diffused there (albeit, at a much earlier date than hitherto imagined), that ironworking had traveled from the Middle East to Africa through one or another route (though, again, at an early date), and that African states were largely started as a result of external stimuli, especially trade and contact with non-Africans.

It was only after the mid-1970s that archaeologists published results of research that might have satisfied nationalist demands, although by that time, the fervor as well as the support for systematic archaeology had wavered. Historians had provided African leaders with a "usable African past," and the first generation of archaeological research, while not providing the revelations some had hoped for, had still pushed back the origins of African economy and society to ancient times.

In the mid-1970s, J. E. G. Sutton pulled together evidence of very ancient (pre-7000 B.C.) pottery working at a variety of eastern and central African sites ("Middle Africa") to demonstrate that while this region had not developed agriculture at an early date, it had developed a settled lifestyle and pottery and had created a culture akin to the early agricultural settlements, through the intensive exploitation of aquatic resources in rivers, lakes, and seashores. At about the same time, Fred Wendorf announced that he had discovered remains of the earliest deliberate planting of crops (though not of domestic species) along the Nile near the border between Egypt and Sudan.

A few years earlier, Patrick Munson announced that his own explorations at Dhar Tichitt, in modern Mauritania, showed that the roots of the great empires of the western Sudan, long held to be the oldest sub-Saharan state systems, lay as far back at 600 B.C. and developed independently of the trans-Saharan trade or other outside influences. These views were subsequently supported by work done by Susan and Roderick McIntosh at Jenne. This, in turn, was followed by Peter Schmidt's announcements that his archaeological work in the Buhaya district of Tanzania suggested that African metalworking might be an indigenous development, could reach back as far as 700 B.C., and resulted in a product of very high quality. While some of the interpretative statements associated with these discoveries have been controversial and there is still debate about some of the conclusions, these results have gone a long way toward demonstrating the reality of African originality and antiquity, an agenda that nationalists had desired.

Even as these discoveries, and others modifying or extending them, were announced, however, the field of archaeology had changed directions.

The interest in the development of agriculture, ironworking, and state formation that had dominated discussion in the 1960s had been shaped by the widespread diffusionist conception, advanced by V. Gordon Childe in the 1930s and widely accepted by working archaeologists as late as 1970. According to Childe, agriculture, metalworking, and state formation defined a great transitional period of human history and established the creativity and intelligence of the people who made them.

In archaeological theory after 1970, agriculture was increasingly viewed not as a discovery of talented people (Childe had called them "proto-scientists") but as a response of desperate people to climatic change. Food production through agriculture did not necessarily make life easier for its practitioners but only allowed them to survive. In fact, it was increasingly argued that foraging was easier and more healthful than farming. The discovery of ironworking, likewise, was viewed as a response to the scarcity of bronze in the ancient Middle East, and its diffusion was explained in economic rather than technical terms. Finally, work by archaeologists with a social bent had suggested that early states and civilizations were as much instruments of exploitation as breakthroughs of human inventiveness that made life better for all. In shattering the equality of earlier societies, the state makers had created a small, wealthy, but highly visible elite and a larger group of poor, whose standard of living was no better than, and perhaps worse than, that of people living in stateless societies.

However, if the original program for African archaeology has been superseded by financial and political exigencies, the work has continued. The study of site relationships and the social and gender relationships manifested in these settlement patterns along with a closely controlled study of change in these relationships over time—all known as the *new archaeology*—have arrived in those parts of Africa where research is being done on an active basis. The newest work is more conscious of regional relationships, less concerned with origins and ideological implications (though these are still evoked where appropriate), and prepared to work to illuminate documentary and oral sources.

The greatest difficulty facing African archaeology at the present comes from the indifferent funding that it receives, the collapse of much of the intellectual and even physical infrastructure in Africa, and the increasing violence and civil war that make whole regions completely inaccessible to archaeologists. These problems dwarf the intellectual debates about the proper emphasis of survey versus extensive exploration of single sites, the interpretation of the remains uncovered, or the overall formation of research hypotheses that govern a project.

BIBLIOGRAPHY

Connah, G. 1987. *African civilizations: Precolonial cities and states in tropical Africa: An archaeological perspective.* Cambridge: Cambridge University Press.

Robertshaw, P., ed. 1990. *A history of African archaeology.* London and Portsmouth: James Currey Ltd. and Heinemann.

UNESCO. 1981–1993. *General history of Africa,* 8 vols. Berkeley: University of California Press.

John Thornton

PAN-AFRICANISM, DIFFUSIONISM, AND THE AFROCENTRIC IDEA

Archaeology is inherently political. It possesses a capability of shaping how the past is viewed, for the past is not only a foreign country we endlessly explore to discover new meanings, but a land of imagination malleable to the ebb and flow of fashionable theory and methodology and to the needs of the present to find justification in the idea of its history.

When the colonial military forces crushed African resistance and colonial administrative and economic systems were put in place, new encroachments on African land quickly generated serious conflicts. Out of these conflicts emerged native political activists and intellectuals who argued in defense of African's traditional rights to their ancestral lands and for respect of their traditional customs and social organization. During the colonial period, there were no indigenous archaeologists. However, not all of the professional archaeologists working in western Africa agreed consistently with the dominant diffusionist paradigm, which posited the spread of significant aspects of culture from ancient Egypt. In 1952, for instance, in a debate over the emergence of iron technology in West Africa with Raymond Mauny, Henri Lhote considered it the outcome of local developments.

Nevertheless, what may be considered a revisionist conception of archaeological, ethnological, and historical information was initiated by other scholars who were not themselves archaeologists, historians, or social scientists, but intellectuals and political thinkers, novelists, and poets. Some gathered as students in universities in France, Great Britain, and the United States. Most were political activists, fighting for the dignity of African peoples and for the freedom of Africa and protesting colonial paternalism, cultural alienation, and manipulation of knowledge.

The slogan "Africa for Africans" was adopted during the first Pan-African Congress, a political conference held in Paris in 1919. These pioneers sought to escape cultural alienation and restore African dignity by regaining control of their unique African heritage. Different ways of achieving this were explored, including attempts to construct an alternative African history, separate from the biases of a Eurocentric science, which they felt imbued so much of colonial scholarship. This process is still at work today.

H. Sylvestre-Williams, E. W. Blyden, Marcus Garvey, and W. E. B. DuBois were among the most important figures in this earliest stage, and their writings and activities were important milestones in Black peoples' first attempts at cultural and political revival.

After the abolition of slavery, people of African descent in the Americas began a long and difficult struggle for the recognition of their civil rights. The idea of active solidarity with Africans who had to combat economic exploitation and colonialism emerged during the 19th century. Sylvestre-Williams, born in Trinidad, worked as a barrister in London and acted as adviser to African political leaders from British colonies in England for discussions with the Colonial Office.

He organized the first African conference in London in 1900. The term *Pan-Africanism* was used for the first time there. Pan-Africanism was a set of political and philosophical ideas that aimed to guide African peoples in their quest for liberation, independence, and unity of the continent.

Blyden was a Liberian from Tobago. He tried to put African history in perspective, considering it as a process in which colonialism was only a painful episode to be superseded by a grander destiny for Black Africa. From this perspective, Blyden viewed colonialism as a logical step after the slave trade. His ideas revolved around two axes: (1) the importance of pharaonic Egypt to the history of Africa and its peoples and (2) the project for the unification of West Africa into a political entity.

Blyden was fascinated by the history of pharaonic Egypt and considered it to be part of Black Africa's heritage: the great cultural achievement of African-derived peoples. The Bible, Homer, and Herodotus, along with representations of the great Sphinx, were used as proof of direct historical connections. He believed that the peopling of West Africa resulted from migrations from the Nile heartland. He was also interested in Islam, especially in West African Moslem communities, and advocated cooperation between Christians and Moslems in a future West African state.

He held a quasi-mystical conception of the contribution of Black Africa to future world civilization:

> Each race is endowed with particular talents, and watchful at the least degree is the Creator over the individuality, the freedom, and independence of each. In the music of the universe each gives a different sound, but all were necessary to the grand symphony. There are several sounds not yet brought on and the feeblest of all is that hither to be produced by the Negro, but only he can furnish it. And when he does furnish it, in its fullness and perfection, it will be welcomed with delight by the world.

Blyden's Pan-Negrism was essentially cultural and intellectual. Garvey's Pan-Negrism, on the other hand, was more radical and politically active. Garvey advocated the return of African-Americans to Africa. His were overtly racist positions, but his radical political activity did not last long. However, he was instrumental in popularizing the ideas of Pan-Africanism in Africa and among African elites and students at European universities.

These early attempts at African cultural and political revival formed the milieu that nurtured the grand program of Cheikh Anta Diop. He attended university in France in the late 1940s, and by 1952, he was general secretary of the student organization Rassemblement Démocratique Africain (RDA), a confederation of political parties and workers' organizations of the French colonies of West Africa, which had important relations with the permanent secretariat of the Pan-African Congress in London.

The Program of Cheikh Anta Diop

The Senegalese scholar Cheikh Anta Diop was a proponent of the use of archaeological, historical, and anthropological data to produce a coherent body of theory supporting African radical nationalism. He never published any details about his formative years or his education in Paris, but it seems that his first book, written between 1948 and 1953—a period he presented as a very difficult time in the struggle against colonialism—was probably intended as a doctoral thesis. For some unknown reason, it was not accepted by his professors, even though its theoretical argument based on Egyptian diffusionism was not in itself all that radical. As Thurstan Shaw has pointed out, Egyptian diffusionism was advocated by colonial administrators and espoused by many African writers. But Diop's program of historical research was more than the simple restatement of earlier ideas.

He believed that Africans should study their past not for intellectual pleasure but as a charter for action in the present. The major purpose of his work was to fight against the diminution of the worth of one's heritage, a diminution that led to cultural alienation. He saw the whole body of *scientific* interpretation of Africa's past as a tool used to enforce colonial dominance, since it deprived Africans of an aptitude for cultural achievement. In order to create national self-consciousness, Africans had to study their past critically. Diop saw knowledge of the African past as a strategic tool in the fight against colonialism and as a crucial instrument in the competition for power and legitimacy.

At the time of its inception in the 1950s, Diop's worldview was rooted in three main ideas: (1) the struggle for the independence of Africa, (2) the creation of a federal and continental African state, and (3) the African and *Negroid* origin of mankind and civilization. He proceeded in three steps. The first was to establish ancient Egypt firmly as the cradle of most Black African people. The second was to demonstrate the true links between pharaonic Egypt and some African peoples and linguistic groups, while ascertaining the Negro identity of the Egyptians. Third, he wished to establish pharaonic Egypt as the center of civilization, influencing ancient Greece and the whole Western world.

Diop's Political Program

Diop's first book, *Nations Nègres et Culture,* emphasizes his idea of an African historical continuum from ancient Black Egypt to the present-day cultural problems of colonialized Africa. Published in 1955, it captures the essence and scope of his political and scientific program. The book is programmatic, with an admixture of political manifesto and descriptions of different African systems of values, past and present, as well as discussions of a well-stocked catalog of scientific issues. His wide-ranging conclusions, though well founded in the science of the times, are, he freely admitted, but a sketch lacking many details. He held it to be impossible for a single individual to get a total grasp of them all. This could only be achieved through the effort of many generations of African scholars.

The preface is a masterpiece of the political rhetoric of African revolutionaries and radicals. It singles out three kinds of African intellectuals as threats to the African struggle for independence and cultural revival. First were the "cosmopolitans-scientists-modernists," who neglected the study of the African past considering it useless in the modern world. Then came the "intellectual-who-has-forgotten-to-improve-his-Marxist-training," who disconnected revolutionary ideas from political practice. Finally, there were the "formalists-antinationalists," who considered independence of African countries undesirable because of the increasing interdependence of the world's economy. He mentioned no one by name, but by reading between the lines, it is possible to recognize some future African statesmen: L. S. Senghor of Senegal in the first category, many young African Marxists such as Mahmoud Diop and Abdoulaye Wade in the second, and Houphouet Boigny of Ivory Coast in the third.

Beyond the question of Africa's political independence, there were debates about the political nature of independent Africa. For some, such as Anta Diop, Kwame Nkrumah, Sekou Toure, and Modibo Keita, who may be called "progressives"—that is, revolutionaries and radicals—the future Africa should be a continental federal state, united against any attempt at neocolonial domination. Diop devoted three books to the cultural unity of Black Africa, precolonial history, and the economic and cultural foundations of an African federation. For these progressives, the African past had to be regained. Subsequently, Gold Coast was renamed Ghana, after the famous Ghana Empire (ca. A.D. 800 to 1200), and French Sudan recaptured the glory of the Mali Empire (ca. A.D. 1200 to 1500).

For others, such as Houphouet Boigny, L. S. Senghor, and A. Ahidjo, who considered themselves moderate, or pragmatic, but were called "conservative" or "reactionary" by the left wing, independent Africa would have to be built step-by-step according to the particularities of each country. Together the various nations could move toward greater political and economic integration at regional levels and then, if successful, at subcontinental and continental levels. It was this second position that was favored by African heads of states, who created the Organization for African Unity (OAU) at Addis-Ababa in 1963.

In Senegal in 1974, with the end of the "one-party system" characterizing post-independence politics throughout Africa, Diop created a new party, the Rassemblement National Démocratique, to continue the political struggle and popularize his ideas on cultural revival and self-reliance.

Diop's Research Program

Diop's research agenda was also established in his first book. All his life he labored to elaborate the details of his main arguments: dating the past by reliable scientific methods, establishing Egypt, a nation of Black people, as an antecedent civilization, and exploring historical linguistics, African migrations, the emergence of iron technology in Egypt, and physical and biological anthropology for clues toward confirming his theory of the African past and the African role in world history.

He considered ancient Egypt as the cradle of Black African culture. The idea was not really new. It was the scope that was different. Ancient Egypt was a part of Africa that had seen a glorious and great civilization. Thus, as noted by Shaw, it gave added luster to Africans' pride to trace their cultural and even physical ancestry to this source. During the colonial period, this argument had been used in a different way, to support the idea of African inability to achieve a high degree of "civilization" without external influence.

Diop used five categories of data to argue that ancient Egypt was, in fact, the cradle of Black Africa. First, he employed ethnological data to show similarities between the structure of pharaonic society and most Black African societies. Second, he used data from classical Greek authors, travelers, historians, and the later writings of the travelers of the 18th and 19th centuries to demonstrate a close connection between Egypt and Meroitic Sudan, the very early achievement of civilization in the Nilotic Sudan, the rise in power of the Meroitic dynasty of Piankhi, Shabaka, and Sabataka in Upper Egypt, and the color of the skin and the Negroid identity of the Egyptians. Third, he used data on the racial identity of Egyptian burials to show the overwhelming presence of Negroid racial traits in these populations, and he attempted to translate the proportions of racial traits into meaningful population figures. He also tested samples of skin from mummies to evaluate their proportions of melanin. Fourth, he investigated Egyptian hieroglyphic writing to uncover the ancient Egyptians' name for themselves, *kmt,* meaning "black" or "Negro." He analyzed artwork, both paintings and sculpture, to display Negroid traits, and he presented the Sphinx as a typical Negroid type. Finally, he employed linguistic data, comparing pharaonic Egyptian vocabulary and sub-Saharan African languages, to demonstrate close genetic relationships.

To Diop, this large body of data was sufficient to ascertain beyond any doubt that ancient Egypt was the cradle of the African peoples. He further considered that lack of scientific integrity, distortion of facts, manipulation of evidence, and even its purposeful destruction had led Egyptologists to different conclusions. He supported his arguments with quotations about the racial traits of the Sphinx from C. Volney, a French scholar and traveler who visited Egypt during the second half of the 18th century. Volney described the Egyptians in the following terms:

> They all have puffy faces, swollen eyes, flat noses, thick lips: in short, a real mulatto face. I was tempted to attribute it to the climate, but upon my visit to the Sphinx, its aspect suggested the final words of the story. Seeing this characteristic Negro head in all its traits reminded me of a remarkable passage in Herodotus, where he said: "I think that the Colches are an Egyptian colony because they have, like them, black skin and woolly hair."

This meant to Diop that ancient Egyptians were really like all the other natives of sub-Saharan Africa.

In 1837, however, Jean François Champollion-Figeac, one of the founders of Egyptology, replied that "black skin and woolly hair, these two physical qualities are not sufficient to characterize the Negro race, and Volney's conclusion relative to the Negro origin of the ancient peoples of Egypt is obviously extreme and unacceptable." Diop saw this kind of refutation as a fundamental deception implicit in modern colonial history and Egyptology.

The process of the peopling of sub-Saharan Africa was another theme of Diop's research. As the cradle of almost all Africans, ancient Egypt and the Nile Valley witnessed several waves of outward migration that radiated throughout the continent. According to Diop, the Kara of southern Sudan and Upper Oubangui, the Kare-Kare of northeastern Nigeria, the Yoruba of southwestern Nigeria, the Fulani, the Poular (ancient Toucoulleurs), the Serer, the Wolof, the Zulu, and others all originated in the Nile Valley. He analyzed archaeological evidence to trace their migration routes and interpreted the burial mounds of the Inland Niger Delta as West African versions of the pyramids of the Nile Valley. He considered the megaliths (roughly hewn stones standing on end) in Senegal, Gambia, and Mali to be markers of the migrations of the Serer from the Nile Valley to the Atlantic Coast of West Africa.

In this regard, the Malian site of Tondi-Daro became the subject of debate. It is an great field of megaliths located at the base of a red sandstone hill. It is thought to be part of a local agrarian ritual. For Jean Maes, though, in the 1920s, these stones were erected by Carthaginians:

> For he who knows the psychology of Negroes, one can surely ascertain that this undertaking was not executed by the representatives of the Negro race because it represents such a considerable amount of effort, without any immediate utility and bearing no relation to the regular requirements of feeding and reproduction, the only functions which are really appealing to the Negro.

For Diop, however, this field of megaliths was further support for his reconstruction of the migration route of the Serer people of Senegal, who still worship such megaliths.

According to Diop, the antecedents of present-day Black Africans left the Nile Valley because of overpopulation and social crisis and penetrated deeper into the continent. Subsequent adaptation to different ecological conditions met on the way brought about changes in material culture and technology. Some characteristics vital to life along the Nile were abandoned and forgotten. Later, he published, in detail, his identification of the Nilotic cradle of some Senegalese people. He compared the vocabulary and grammar of Egyptian and Coptic dialect, on one hand, and Nuer, Dinka, Fulani, Serer, and Wolof, on the other. He further suggested a development of matriarchy, in explanation of the matrilines so frequently found in Africa, in three main stages: (1) early strict matriarchy (represented by the Nuba Tullushi in the core area), (2) matrilocal postmarital residence, and (3) bilateral descent with patterns of social division of labor and castelike systems.

He confidently concluded that the Nilotic cradle of the Senegalese is located between the Bahr el Ghazzal and the Nile, an area inhabited today by the Nuba, Nuer, Dinka, and Shilluk. He further stated that at a relatively recent date a migratory movement started from the shores of Lake Albert and the Nuba Hills and reached Senegal via a corridor situated between 10° and 20° north latitude, while another migration starting from the same area of the Great Lakes may have followed the course of the Zaire River to its watershed and from there expanded along the coast, but not farther than Cameroon and the Niger Delta. People along the Gulf of Benin, from southern Nigeria to southern Ivory Coast (Ibo, Yoruba, Oyo, Ewe, Asante, Agni, and Baoule, among others), may belong to an earlier migratory wave, also from the east.

According to "Diop's syllogism," ancient Egypt brought civilization to the entire world. Because ancient Egypt was inhabited by dark-skinned people, it was the Black Africans who brought civilization to humankind. He considered ancient Egypt to have been the earliest great civilization. Once civilization developed there, it spread throughout the ancient world. This great achievement was realized by Africans who invented complex social systems, iron metallurgy, kingship, monotheism, mathematics, science, writing, monumental art and architecture, and sophisticated techniques of mummification. Many of the great philosophers and scientists of ancient Greece were trained partly by Egyptians: Pythagoras, Thales, Solon, Archimedes, Eratosthenes, and many others traveled to Egypt. Diop asserted that Black people must honor this glorious past, accept it as an unmistakable fact, and in continuity with ancient Egypt, revive their pride to regain their rightful place in the modern world.

In summary, Diop's thesis is the most radically revisionist and complete system of thought ever proposed by an Africanist concerning the past of Black Africa. It emerged out of the struggle against colonialism and the fight for independence and liberation of the African continent in the 1950s. In this context, he succeeded in demonstrating the weaknesses of colonialist rhetoric and the self-serving nature of their accounts of African history. Paradoxically, instead of destroying the methodological and theoretical foundations of colonialist theories of history, he helped to reinforce then current racial and diffusionist models, though he succeeded in reversing the flow inherent in the diffusionist model. Instead of being mere recipients of culture from some advanced civilization, Black Africa was said to have played, via Egypt, an important—if not the most important—role in the development of civilization and its dissemination to Europe. In this way, he set forth the basic tenets of the Afrocentric theory of history.

A new kind of dogmatism, resulting from uncritical, oversimplified presentations of Diop's ideas has now become fashionable. According to this new dogma, the data demonstrate a dominance of Black Africans and their culture from the most remote times and the maintenance of this cultural dominance all through the millennia of history.

Evaluating Diop's Work

Alternative histories emerge in response to circumstances and the need to reinforce political arguments and conflicts over "true" legitimacy. The alternative history is a political tool aiming to redress situations of imbalance, attempting to select the most relevant ideas to guide society in socioeconomic and cultural confrontation, and drawing strength from the past. This method may result in mythical and dogmatic histories, but such histories may be ideologically or psychologically satisfying, but not otherwise justifiable.

Diop's attempt to make an alternative history of Black Africa may have caused some Egyptologists and European Africanists to reconsider several ideas they had previously taken for granted. For example, the population of Egypt was logically dark or brown skinned, but whether this denoted a Negroid type, as characterized by the physical anthropology of the time, is open to

question and trapped in a simplistic concept of races. At the same time, Diop was handicapped not only by such simplistic notions of race, but also by the scientific methods of his time and difficulties in obtaining the materials needed to carry out his research.

Diop had great difficulty carrying out his research, in part because authorities of the Egyptian Antiquity Service systematically refused to answer his questions. He once wrote:

> Among the funerary furniture of Toutankhamon exhibited at the Cairo museum, I have noticed a few objects which, if they are authenticated, may show that the use of iron was already well integrated in daily life; such is the case with the metal hinges of Toutankhamon's bed. According to Dr. Ryad, the curator of the museum who was acting as our guide during the visit in November 1971, these metal hinges were made with iron. Back at Dakar, I wrote two letters asking him to check in his records whether these iron hinges do not result from recent restoration of the bed. Unfortunately, I did not receive any answer.

The same thing happened when he requested samples of mummified skin for analysis. However, when he succeeded in getting samples from the Department of Egyptology of the Musée de l'Homme in Paris, he unfortunately misreported the results of his analysis on melanin and raised even more skepticism.

Diop's discussion of bioanthropology is, on the whole, somewhat weak, but he shares such weakness with many others who studied the physical anthropology of Africa. According to D. P. Van Gerven, D. S. Carlson, and G. J. Armelagos in 1973, some physical anthropologists, in order to get archaeologists to collect skeletal materials, incorrectly proposed that the analysis and classification of those materials could provide information about the historical reconstruction of cultural traditions. Van Gerven, Carlson, and Armelagos add that such analyses consistently used similarities in skeletal morphology and hypothetical racial affinities to establish biological relationships between skeletal series. Such relationships, once established, were assumed to reflect the degree to which populations were culturally related. As Wyatt MacGaffey observed, the racial approach was retained in studying the physical anthropology of northeastern Africa, in spite of significant biological inconsistencies, because of ideas that were deeply rooted in Western culture and which sanctioned a "natural" polarization between rulers and the ruled or the bearers and receivers of culture. Diop, as well, was trapped within the inconsistencies of then current population biology and its scientific models of natural selection and variations of genotypes and phenotypes and such purely social constructs as the hierarchy of races, racism, ethnocentrism, and imperialism. When considered this way, the biological attributes resulting from natural processes were complemented by social processes such as domination, alienation, exploitation, and divide-and-rule. In this regard, the basic question was not about the existence of race, but the politics of race: Who needed the concept of race? What is its meaning?

The major problems in evaluating Diop's conclusions were not only lack of cooperation and the racial paradigm he was forced to use, but also that up until his death in 1986, he behaved as if nothing new had occurred in African studies, in general, and in West Africa, in particular.

His argument about a relatively recent migration of the Serer from their Nilotic homeland could have been modified, if not completely abandoned, had he but paid attention to recent research. There was no need to have all the aspects of Black African societies come from a single place, even if that place were the glorious ancient Egypt he posited.

Until recently, the archaeology of the western Cameroon Grassfields was known only from some 1950's surface finds of stone tools. Even if some researchers suspected the occurrence of very ancient settlements, the consensus, based partly on literal interpretations of oral accounts, was that this area was settled quite recently by immigrants from the northeast. Recent work, beginning in 1974, has shown, however, that the area was inhabited for the last 9,000 years and that iron technology was in use from about the 3rd or 4th century. Furthermore, it appears that the high-altitude savanna of the Cameroon Grassfields is a by-product of long-term human interference with the natural environment.

Archaeological surveys and test excavations have shown that the production of iron artifacts in the grassfields took place within the context of a long-distance trade network controlled by regional centers. Iron tools were exchanged for palm oil from the south and cotton and textiles from northern Nigeria. The nature of the ironworking sites, the technologies used, and the scale of production achieved all contradict the colonial stereotype, according to which African peoples lacked any kind of technological skill and initiative, a stereotype given credibility by the fact that the first Europeans to travel there observed highly dispersed, small-scale smelting operations.

In fact, three different types of smelting furnaces were used: a low cylindrical furnace, which appears to have been the earliest and most widespread form in use from the 3rd to the 17th century, a larger "clump" furnace in use from the 17th to the 19th century, and another form of small bowl furnace similar to the first, which survived in use until the 1940s. The development of clump furnaces was a response to the intensification of long-distance trade, the emergence of stratified and competing polities, and an energy crisis. This period of intensive production of iron implements resulted in deforestation, which in turn encouraged further technological advances in order to produce more iron with less fuel. This highly labor-intensive system required sustained consumer demand. The introduction of mass-produced European iron implements during the 18th and 19th centuries, combined with the effects of the slave trade, caused the whole socioeconomic system to collapse. Clump furnaces were replaced by small bowl furnaces in which iron and slag from an earlier period were recycled and smelted. Competing polities turned to warfare. The failure of the local economic system resulted from the increased flow of imported European ingots and hoe blanks during the late 19th century.

The archaeology of the western Cameroon Grassfields suggests that the encroachment and expansion of European trading networks served to break the complexity of existing local exchange networks and social relations of production and also to move local communities into more self-sufficient strategies of resource procurement and consumption. More importantly, it appears that it was the larger regional systems that were destabilized, resulting in increased warfare at the end of the 19th century, when colonial powers began to take control of Africa. Therefore, it is not surprising that Europeans found disturbed social and economic systems in the continent.

This case is important because it demonstrates how a long-standing autochthonous cultural history developed without Egyptian influence and how, in some situations, what was presented as African "backwardness" may be an artifact of exploitation and unequal exchanges initiated by the colonial powers.

Diop's attempts to produce a scientifically relevant history of sub-Saharan Africa were met by resistance by some in the scientific and political communities, and he was obliged to work in a kind of splendid isolation, suspicious of all who did not share his views. Breaking away from established scientific norms, he used the methodologies of archaeology, history, and biological and social anthropology and created a new paradigm for evaluating the results. The Afrocentric theory of history he created is such a paradigm and, like other such ideas, is testable.

Archaeology may yet play an even more significant role in revising African history. It has, as we said earlier, a political and cultural role. Sometimes these roles are played out overtly— as in the colonialist view of an Africa of scant cultural accomplishment or the Afrocentric one of paramount achievement. Archaeology has already played a significant role in discrediting the colonial myths about Africans and their past. But it will also have to deal with the well-intentioned but highly imaginative claims of some African researchers and intellectuals. Archaeological findings, to paraphrase the words of Bruce Trigger, have the power to restrain fantasy, if sufficient data are collected and analyzed in a rigorous fashion.

The colonial regimens attempted to populate the African past with examples of African backwardness. Other models sought to redress this travesty. The African intellectuals who created

the Afrocentric idea of history had political goals of their own. Both models of the African past may be challenged in favor of one emphasizing the genius of local cultural tradition.

In the end, the past remains a foreign land, which we experience vicariously, satisfying our present needs, yet, hopefully, honoring the spirit of those who live there.

BIBLIOGRAPHY

Andah, B. W. 1988. *African anthropology.* Ibadan: Shaneson Ltd.

Asante, M. K. 1987. *The Afrocentric idea.* Philadelphia: Temple University Press.

Diop, C. A.1955. *Nations nègres et culture.* Paris: Présence Africaine.

———. 1960. *L'Afrique noire précoloniale.* Paris: Présence Africaine.

Holl, A. F. C. 1990. West African archaeology: Colonialism and nationalism. In *A history of African archaeology,* ed. P. Robertshaw, 296–308. London and Portsmouth: James Currey Ltd. and Heinemann.

Schmidt, P. R., and T. C. Patterson, eds. 1995. *Making alternative histories.* Santa Fe: School of American Research.

Augustin F. C. Holl

WESTERN AFRICA: HISTORY OF ARCHAEOLOGY

1850–1935: Antiquarianism, Evolutionism, and Diffusionism

European interest in the antiquities of West Africa began in the colonial coastal outposts just as the great "scramble for Africa" began. At that time, the "scientific antiquarians" of Britain and France were casting their nets widely to find comparative material for the growing body of prehistoric materials unearthed in Europe. Already in 1851, a paper was published by de Beaufort concerning ancient artifacts from Senegal, while the explorer Sir Richard Burton copublished an article in 1883 on stone axes from Ghana. A growing body of African artifacts without context, collected by and for dilettantes, became known in Europe, but the notion of African prehistory was of only marginal interest. Instead, artifacts were valued as confirmation of the universal stages of cultural and material evolution throughout humanity, as defined by John Lubbock, Edward B. Tylor, Henry Lewis Morgan, and others.

By the turn of the 20th century, however, the colonization of the West African interior and imperial curiosity about new colonial holdings led to some substantial excavations. In method, most of these were akin to earlier European "barrow parties" with little attention to the meticulous horizontal or vertical recording of features and objects. Such excavations include Lieutenant L. Desplagnes's opening of the vast "tumuli" of El Qualedji and Killi (Mali) in 1904 and Serge Christoforoff and Clausel's trenching of the settlement mounds of Kolima and Péhé (Mali) in 1930. In the latter case, corvée labor from the Office du Niger hydraulic project was transferred to the excavation to allow a suitable accumulation of artifacts for a colonial exposition of African antiquities in Paris. One notable exception to this trend was an amateur excavation of the Kakimbon rock shelter in Guinea between 1893 and 1899. The stratigraphic excavation of this shelter allowed its lithic (stone) finds to be usefully analyzed by the French prehistorian Ernest T. Hamy, who reconstructed this evidence into a three-phase sequence of two "Neolithic" and one "recent" cultural facies (a temporally discrete assemblage). This was perhaps the first true prehistoric sequence derived in West Africa.

The early part of the 20th century was also a time of facile diffusionistic explanations for the advent of civilizations and cultural change. Leo Frobenius, part of the Germanic Kulturkreis movement and first popularizer of the naturalistic bronze busts of Ife, was to assert in *Und Afrika Sprach,* in 1912, that the ancient arts of Ife stemmed from a 9th-century B.C. Greek colony in Nigeria! Likewise, Maurice Delafosse was to assert in his three-volume tome *Haut-Senegal-Niger,* also published in 1912, that the founders of the empire of Ghana were Judeo-Syrians. The doctrine of *ex oriente lux* (out of the East light) was even to find its way into Stone Age archaeology, where Raymond Vaufrey and others sought North African (Capsian) or Egyptian origins for the lithic industries of "Neolithic" West Africa.

1935–1975: Cultural History and the First Syntheses

In the late 1930s began three key developments that were to alter profoundly future directions in research: the founding of the Institut Français d'Afrique Noire (now the Institut Fondamental d'Afrique Noire) in Dakar (Senegal) in 1938 and the respective arrivals on the continent of the Francophone and Anglophone fathers of West African archaeology, Raymond Mauny to Senegal in 1938 and Thurstan Shaw to Ghana in 1937. Mauny and Shaw were, in their own individual ways, to instruct coming generations of African and expatriate archaeologists, to write the initial syntheses of their regions, and to perform fieldwork that would lay the foundations of regional prehistories. Both were to leave as a lasting legacy key African university archaeological departments of which they were the organizers (Department Prehistoire et Protohistoire, L'Institut Français d'Afrique Noire, and the Department of Archaeology, University of Ibadan). The founding of such local research institutions from the 1940s onward had the effect of keeping artifact collections in West Africa, sustaining fieldwork programs, and training local archaeologists.

Theoretically speaking, archaeological efforts early in this period dealt mainly with cultural history and attempted to establish local cultural and economic successions, with researchers in the Sahel occasionally embarking on textually aided archaeology of the empires of Ghana and Songhai. This latter approach, the combination of texts (and eventually oral traditions) in the search for the histories of polities and peoples, gained an increasing importance over time. Mauny was at the forefront of such investigations, excavating at both Gao Ancien in Mali and Koumbi-Saleh in Mauritania during the 1950s and publishing his synthetic *Tableau Geographique de l'Ouest Africain au Moyen Age* in 1961.

However, most Francophone work at this time suffered from a lack of stratigraphic and horizontal control and a paucity of quantitatively presented data (including particularly the numerous excavations of Mauny and Georges Szumowski), and this lack ultimately limited the comparative utility of their data today. In contrast, Anglophone work was more methodologically concerned, if still imperfect. Shaw, in the early 1940s, used arbitrary spits (which use a predetermined depth of excavation, rather than attempting to follow soil layering) at the Bosumpra rock shelter (Ghana) and later correlated them with the site's stratigraphy with a thorough quantitative presentation of artifacts within this sequence. Consequently, the Bosumpra report of 1944 is still useful to us today, particularly with the radiocarbon dates from Andrew Smith's excavation in the early 1970s.

Stone Age archaeology, beyond what is conventionally termed the *Late Stone Age,* has historically been limited in West Africa due more to regional geology than to a lack of early occupations. More than any other researcher, Oliver Davies of the Department of Archaeology in Legon, Ghana, in the 1950s and 1960s, tried to come to an understanding of the West African Stone Age. His substantial survey work in Ghana left a rich database, which is still being drawn upon. However, his attempts to apply a strict typological template on the succession of ancient stone industries in West Africa forced him into many errors regarding the age of these objects and industries.

From the l950s through the early 1970s, the sites that remain the central data points of West African archaeology were initially excavated or surface-collected (with many being more recently reinvestigated): Karkarichinkat in Mali (originally investigated by Raymond Mauny), Kobadi in Mali (originally studied by Mauny and Theodore Monod), Korounkorokalé in Mali (surveyed by Georges Szumowski), Begho in Ghana investigated by Merrick Posnansky), Ntereso in Ghana (studied by Oliver Davies), Kintampo in Ghana (first investigated by Colin Flight), Iwo Eleru and Igbo Ukwu in Nigeria (surveyed by Thurstan Shaw), and Benin City and Daima in Nigeria (investigated by Graham Connah), among many others. Interestingly, much of the research first carried out at these sites was more thematic than cultural history. The research focused on issues such as the origins of food production, the origins of human occupations in forest environments, and the development of urbanism.

It would be difficult to omit from any discussion of this period the complex figure of the Senegalese radiocarbon physicist and archaeologist Cheikh Anta Diop. Diop could rightly be called the first indigenous synthesist of African prehistory. Notable among his work were *Nations Nègres et Culture* (1955) and *L'Afrique Noire Précoloniale* (1960). However, the conclusions he draws were more in line with the hyper-diffusionism of G. Elliot Smith and William Perry of the 1930s than with the theories of researchers of the time in which he lived. Augustin F. C. Holl has characterized the three major steps of Diop's thought as being: the establishment of dynastic Egypt as a Black African civilization, the assertion of cultural and linguistic links between dynastic Egypt and sub-Saharan Africa, and the placement of a Black pharaonic Egypt as the cultural centerpoint of the ancient world. This diffusionistic viewpoint, currently propagated within the Afrocentrist movement, remains a touchstone in Francophone West African academia. Its unfortunate consequence has been the comparative neglect by its followers of the early civilizations of West Africa.

1975–1995: New Approaches and the Growth of Local Cultural Heritage Programs

From 1975 onward, three major trends have had a decisive impact on the practice of West African archaeology: greater involvement with theoretical developments in America and Europe, the dissolution of old colonial alignments with a diversity of international teams working throughout the region, and the establishment of strong, locally led programs of research and cultural-heritage management.

Perhaps the greatest harbinger of theoretical change was Roderick and Susan Keech McIntosh's excavations and survey around Jenne (Mali) in 1977 and 1981. Inspired by the earlier work of Graham Connah at Daima (Nigeria) and Merrick Posnansky at Begho (Ghana), the McIntoshes created a new method of dealing with West

Africa's ubiquitous tell sites (stratified middens produced by successive occupations). This work applied many of the principles of the "new archaeology" to the archaeology of African urban origins: sampling strategies, regional (hinterland) archaeology, the application of central-place theory, and statistical (attribute-based) analysis of pottery assemblages, among other methodologies. Their work would set new standards for data analysis and presentation in West Africa.

Indeed, after a long history of site-centric archaeology in West Africa, broad regional surveys, with their later temporal integration through excavation programs, became the major research approach of the 1980s. Such programs included the work of Nicole Petit-Maire and her team in the Malian Sahara, the work of Scott MacEachern in the Mandara Highlands project, conducted in Nigeria and Cameroon, the research of Térésa Togola and Kevin C. MacDonald in Mali's Méma region, and the survey by J. D. Van der Waals and Peter Schmidt of the Inland Niger Delta.

Ethnoarchaeology, particularly that of ceramic production, was also to gain importance in the 1980s. In particular, notions of the equation of ceramics and ethnicity were scrutinized. Such work has placed West Africa in the forefront of ethnoarchaeological research. Prominent fieldworkers have included A. Adande in Benin; Leonard B. Crossland in Ghana; A. Gallay, Eric Huysecom, and Anne Mayer in Mali; and Nicholas J. David, J. Sterner, and Oliver Gosselain in Nigeria and Cameroon.

Most importantly, the 1970s saw the scholars of West Africa taking their archaeology into their own hands. Research and cultural-heritage institutions evolved rapidly during this period, particularly in Senegal, Mali, Niger, Ghana, and Nigeria. Important locally led research projects include: T. Togola's work on the Iron Age of the Méma and on the Bambuk gold fields in Mali, Bassey Andah's excavations at Rim in Burkina Faso, Hamadi Bocoum's excavations of Middle Senegal Valley settlement mounds, A. Camara's Stone Age research in eastern Senegal, James Anquandah's investigation of tumuli (grave sites) in Komaland, Ghana, and B. Gado's excavation of the cemeteries of Bura in Niger.

Museums, both national and local, have also grown, bringing West Africa's history and prehistory to the people. Local museums, as a means of involving the inhabitants of archaeologically rich areas in their own heritage, are particularly important since materials from local excavations are no longer seen as being the exclusive property of "the capital" or foreign investigators after being placed in a local museum's collections.

One particularly pressing concern in recent years has been the accelerating pace of organized looting, particularly from ancient settlement sites and cemeteries in Mali, Niger, and Nigeria. Artifacts from the great West African civilizations are now fetching high prices on the international art market. Efforts to curtail this looting have focused both at the local level and at the international level of art dealers and museums. Local programs have been particularly effective in Mali, where villagers are becoming increasingly proud and protective of their archaeological heritage. Additionally, recent legislative successes in the United States have banned the importation or sale of Malian antiquities without exportation permits. Unfortunately, such regulations do not yet exist in Europe. Unless the traffic in antiquities can be significantly reduced, the future of West African archaeology may be shorter than we think.

BIBLIOGRAPHY
Robertshaw, P., ed. 1990. *A history of African archaeology.* London and Portsmouth: James Currey Ltd. and Heinemann.
Dembélé, M., and J. D. Van der Waals. 1991. Looting the antiquities of Mali. *Antiquity* 65: 904–905.
MacDonald, K. C., H. Crawford, and F. Y. C. Hung. 1995. Prehistory as propaganda. *Papers from the Institute of Archaeology* 6: 1–10.
McIntosh, R. J., and S. K. McIntosh. 1988. From *siècles obscurs* to revolutionary centuries on the Middle Niger. *World Archaeology* 20: 141–165.
Shaw, T. 1989. African archaeology: Looking back and looking forward. *African Archaeological Review* 7: 3–31.
Shaw, T., and K. C. MacDonald. 1995. Out of Africa and out of context. *Antiquity* 69: 1,036–1,039.
Willet, F. 1960. Ife and its archaeology. *Journal of African History* 1: 231–248.

Kevin MacDonald

HORN OF AFRICA: HISTORY OF ARCHAEOLOGY

The Horn of Africa (Djibouti, Eritrea, Ethiopia, and Somalia) is composed of a diverse array of physiographic features that range from Africa's third highest mountain (Ras Dashan at 4,620 meters above sea level) to the continent's lowest point (the Afar Rift of Djibouti at 150 meters below sea level). The Horn is also the most mountainous region of Africa, it incorporates the continent's longest coastline and largest area of geological rifting (the Ethiopian and Afar Rifts), and it has extensive areas of extreme aridity and some of Africa's most arable soils. This environmental diversity has stimulated the development of a wide range of socioeconomic adaptations from ancient and contemporary urban centers to diverse farming and nomadic pastoral systems, all being operated by people who speak some of the most disparate languages in the world.

Perhaps it is not surprising then that the Horn of Africa encompasses the longest and possibly most diverse archaeological record in Africa, beginning some 2.5 million years ago and continuing to the ethnoarchaeological present. Nevertheless, when compared to what we know about surrounding regions, our knowledge of the archaeological record is poor. In part, this is due to the lack of roads and other logistical difficulties, which until recently have restricted archaeological research to areas of greater accessibility and resulted in a geographical patchwork of archaeological information. But it is also due to a complex series of political, social, academic, and ideological factors that have combined to shape the history of archaeological research in this region.

What follows is a survey of the major developments in the history of archaeology in the Horn. This survey is by no means comprehensive but instead tries to identify the major sites, players, and ideas. The chronological narrative is divided into two parts—prehistoric archaeology (that is, the Stone Age) and historical archaeology (including "protohistory")—because of the different theoretical, method-ological, topical, and historical trajectories these temporal subfields have taken.

Prehistoric Archaeology

The French explorer G. Revoil, who in 1882 described and illustrated bifacial points and other stone tools surface-collected from northeastern Somalia, is generally credited with the first documented report of a prehistoric site in the Horn. Over the next 40 years, Italian, British, and French scientists, military personnel, colonial administrators, travelers, and explorers surface-collected and described a wide range of stone artifacts from throughout the Horn. However, it was not until 1929 that P. Tielhard de Chardin and H. de Monfried conducted the first professional archaeological excavation of a Stone Age site in the Horn when they put in a test trench at Porc Epic Cave in eastern Ethiopia. This was soon followed by the first excavations of Stone Age sites in Somalia, as reported by P. Graziosi in 1940.

Comparing their material with European and southern and eastern African Paleolithic sequences, Tielhard and Graziosi established the first Stone Age cultural sequences for the Horn. Whereas Tielhard used European terms such as *Mousterian* to describe and classify his finds, Graziosi concluded that the Stone Age cultures of Somalia were similar technologically to other southern and eastern African industries known at that time but were local in origin. Consequently, Graziosi constructed his cultural-historical sequence by using already defined eastern and southern African "cultures" (for example, Stillbay and Magosian) as well as new local entities having no foreign equivalent (for example, Eibian).

Graziosi's excavations also yielded the first evidence of food production in the Horn (domesticated cattle and ovicaprids—sheep and goats), but he showed little interest in pursuing questions related to a Neolithic period in the Horn. This was in spite of the fact that the Russian agronomist N. Vavilov had already proposed Ethiopia to be one of the eight world centers of the origin of cultivated plants.

During and immediately after World War II, British military personnel were responsible for the majority of Stone Age archaeological investigations in the Horn. This included J. Desmond Clark who, in 1954, published the pioneering *Prehistoric Cultures of the Horn of Africa,* the first (and still the only) major attempt to place the Stone Age of the Horn of Africa into a regional and pan-African framework of culture, history, and climate. Drawing upon his 1940's fieldwork in Somalia and Ethiopia as well as upon his knowledge of the southern and eastern African Stone Age, he applied technological and topological criteria to divide the prehistory of the Horn into three Stone Ages: Early Stone Age, Middle Stone Age, and Late Stone Age. He further divided each age into a series of "culture complexes." Some of these owed their origins to southern or eastern Africa (for example, Somaliland Stillbay and Somaliland Magosian), while others were unique to the region (for example, Hargeisan and Doian). He also developed a stylistic sequence for the numerous rock-art sites depicting humped and humpless cattle, camels, and ovicaprids.

Clark emphasized both the migration of hominid populations and localized adaptations as the most likely explanatory factors for prehistoric cultural change in the Horn. In 1954, he characterised the Somaliland Stillbay, for example, as probably "indicative of a northward migration of Stillbay stock into the Horn," while he posited that the Hargeisan culture owed its origin to the "existence of a similar ecology and . . . a similar form of raw material rather than to any cultural connections." Pointing to stylistic similarities between the pastoral rock art of the Horn and Neolithic rock art of the Sahara and Nile Valley, he also argued for the migration of pastoral peoples into the Horn from northeastern Africa, bringing with them Neolithic "traits."

For reasons that remain unclear, the 1950s and 1960s witnessed surprisingly little prehistoric fieldwork, although there were significant developments in theoretical approaches to an understanding of the evolution of food production. In 1959, G. P. Murdock published *Africa: Its Peoples and Culture History.* Drawing essentially upon ethnographic and linguistic data, he hypothesized that more than 5,000 years ago "pre-Nilotes" from the Sudan introduced agricultural practices to the "Bushmanoid" and "Caucasoid Cushite" hunter-foragers of western Ethiopia, the latter of whom domesticated indigenous Ethiopian cultigens (domestic varieties of species for which wild ancestors are unknown). Although he regarded migration as the primary source of food production in the Horn (as Clark had done), Murdock was the first scholar to put forward the idea of independent invention and to realize that the diversity and complexity of contemporaneous food production in the Horn required equally diverse and complex prehistoric origins.

Three years later, Clark finally addressed the issue of agricultural origins in the Horn. Elaborating upon his pastoral migration model, he argued that "Nubian C-Group" pastoralists, driven by drought, moved south into the temperate Ethiopian Highlands, where they introduced cattle ranging and possibly wheat and barley cultivation to the indigenous Ethiopian foragers. Clearly influenced by Murdock, Clark further proposed, in 1967, that "pre-Nilote" populations from the Sudan, escaping the increasingly arid conditions of the Middle Holocene, introduced farming to the highlands of western Ethiopia.

In the late 1960s, two very important projects put Ethiopia firmly on the map as an area of great paleoanthropological potential. Beginning in 1966 and continuing into the late 1970s, J. Chavaillon and a team of scientists excavated numerous sites along the banks of the Awash River at Melka Kunture in highland central Ethiopia. The Melka Kunture sites have revealed one of the longest cultural sequences in the world, spanning more than 1 million years from the Early Pleistocene to the Holocene. Of particular significance was the discovery of late Olduwan and early Acheulian sites in association with fossils (both animal and hominid).

In 1967, the Omo Research Expedition began its first of many seasons of research at exposures dating to the Plio-Pleistocene north of Lake Turkana in southern Ethiopia. This multinational project rapidly became the model for virtually all future paleoanthropological projects in eastern Africa. Excavating at Omo in deposits now dated to between 2 million and 2.3 million years ago, Chavaillon, in 1971, and H. Merrick, in 1976, uncovered the world's earliest securely dated archaeological sites, characterized by the simple flake and core technology of the Oldu-wan complex.

Soon after the 1971 meeting of the Pan-African Congress of Prehistory and Related Studies in Addis Ababa, Ethiopia, the tempo of paleo-anthropological research in Ethiopia increased dramatically. Paleoanthropology projects were now all multidisciplinary and problem-oriented, with particular emphasis being placed upon spatial distributions, diet, and paleo-ecology rather than just technology and cultural history. Also established were projects on the Middle Stone Age, Late Stone Age, and Neolithic, as well as the first projects devoted exclusively to the origins of food production and ethnoarchaeology.

The 1970s also saw the development of new models for understanding the evolution of food production. Drawing largely upon historical linguistic data, Christopher Ehret proposed that the origins of Ethiopian agriculture owed little to the migration of populations from outside the Horn. Instead, he argued that the cultivation of such Ethiopian domesticates as teff and ensete by indigenous populations was already under way before the diffusion of livestock into the Horn by the Middle Holocene. Approaching the issue from a different perspective, Steven A. Brandt, in 1984, criticized previously constructed models as being too culture-historically oriented and difficult to test. He suggested that a more profitable avenue of research was to develop research programs designed to investigate the processes involved in the transition from hunting and gathering to food production and the concomitant social, demographic, and ecological effects of such a major economic change. As an example, Brandt constructed a testable model for the evolution of ensete agriculture, today one of the most economically important domesticates of southern Ethiopia. Unfortunately, evidence necessary to support or refute these models was (and still is) surprisingly poor due to the lack of fieldwork focused on these issues.

In 1982, all paleoanthropological and archaeological projects in Ethiopia came to an abrupt halt as the Ethiopian government suspended permits to foreign expeditions pending the establishment of new policies and laws governing research. That all research was stopped is a testimony to the fact that up to the early 1980s not a single project was led by a native Ethiopian, as none had been professionally trained in archaeology or paleoanthropology. However, by 1988, this situation had changed to the extent that the Paleo-anthropology Inventory of Ethiopia, a field-survey project designed to assess systematically Ethiopia's antiquities base, was initiated by professional Ethiopian researchers with immediate results. Using remote-sensing as well traditional survey methods, the inventory discovered five new paleoanthropological research areas rich in archaeological sites of all ages.

In 1982, archaeological fieldwork in neighboring Somalia resumed after almost a 20-year hiatus. Over the next decade, rapid reconnaissances and small test excavations characterized the majority of research in Somalia and Djibouti. However, in 1983, Brandt initiated the Buur Ecological and Archaeological Project, a long-term investigation of late Pleistocene-Holocene human adaptations in the region between the rivers in southern Somalia. His research represented a significant departure from previous projects in the Horn, as it represented the first attempt to apply a "processual," hypothesis-testing approach to understanding prehistoric cultural change. The education and training of professional Somali archaeologists were also important initiatives during this decade.

Historical Archaeology

In 1805, the British explorer Henry Salt conducted the earliest documented archaeological investigation of a historical site in the Horn when he undertook a reconnaissance of Aksum and cleared the rubble away from a stela (a carved or engraved stone slab) in order to document its inscriptions. The first actual "excavation" of a historical site took place in 1868 when troops of General Robert Napier's British military expedition, working under the auspices of the British Museum, put in trenches at the Aksumite port of Adulis along the Red Sea Coast of Eritrea. It remained for J. Theodore Bent to undertake the first professional excavations in the Horn when he excavated at Adulis, Yeha, and Aksum in 1893. Bent argued, in 1896, that the Sabaean-like ruins and inscriptions revealed by his excavations predated Aksumite levels, thereby suggesting a South Arabian colonization of northern Ethiopia in the 1st millennium B.C. Bent also proposed that the South Arabian immigrants joined, physically and culturally, with the indigenous populations of northern Ethiopia to form the Habashat people of ancient Aksum. These two theories were to dominate scholarly thought on the origins of Aksum for more than 50 years.

At the beginning of the 20th century, professionally trained European archaeologists introduced systematic excavations and surveys to the study of the Aksumite kingdom. Italian archaeologists concentrated upon further excavations at Adulis and a detailed geological, geographical, and archaeological reconnaissance of the Eritrean Plateau, the latter of which resulted in the documentation and description of virtually all surface monuments by G. Danielli and O. Marinelli in 1912. Placing particular emphasis upon detailed description and classification of finds, the German Deutsche Aksum-Expedition concentrated on systematic studies of sites along the route from Asmara to Aksum and undertook the first complete archaeological survey of the city of Aksum and surrounding regions. The masterful 1913 four-volume publication of the expedition's results provided a firm foundation for all future research at Aksum.

Four major syntheses of ancient Eritrean and Ethiopian history appeared in the 1920s, the most influential of which was C. Conti Rossini's *Storia d'Ethiopia*. Drawing upon linguistic, philological, epigraphic, historical, and archaeological data, Conti Rossini continued to support the theory, which was rapidly becoming dogma, that ancient South Arabians introduced state forms of political organization into the Horn. The 1920s also witnessed the extensive archaeological investigations of R. P. Azais and P. Chambard. Over a period of five years, the French team, exploring southern and eastern Ethiopia, discovered and documented thousands of megaliths in the form of stone dolmens (prehistoric monuments consisting of two upright stones supporting a horizontal stone slab), tombs, and stelae. The team's surveys and excavations formed

the foundation of all future archaeological research on these monuments.

In the early 1930s, A. J. Curle discovered a series of ruined Islamic towns in the plains of northwestern Somalia and eastern Ethiopia, thereby substantiating earlier claims of the existence of ruined Islamic urban centers in northern Somalia. Curle's test excavations at some of these towns revealed extensive material remains suggesting a date in the 15th century.

In spite of the promising finds in Ethiopia and Somalia, World War II effectively prevented any serious historical archaeological research in the Horn. However, the pace and quality of historical archaeological research in Ethiopia changed dramatically in the 1950s and 1960s with the establishment in Addis Ababa of the Ethiopian Institute of Archaeology. The institute and its longtime director, F. Anfray of the French Archaeological Mission, undertook a series of excavations in Eritrea and northeastern Ethiopia in an attempt to construct a detailed cultural history of the Aksumite period. From excavations at Matara, Yeha, Adulis, Aksum, and other sites, Anfray distinguished two main periods corresponding to different stages of state formation: (1) the pre-Aksumite period (from about 500 B.C. to A.D. 100), characterized by the appearance of the earliest urban settlements, and (2) the Aksumite period (from about A.D. 100 to 1000) representing the florescence of the Aksumite kingdom. Anfray argued that the Aksumite kingdom owed its origins to interactions between small groups of immigrants from South Arabia and indigenous northern Ethiopians and Eritreans.

In contrast to Ethiopia, Somalia witnessed few historical archaeological projects in the 1950s and 1960s or for that matter in the 1970s. One major exception was H. N. Chittick's rapid archaeological reconnaissance of the southern Somali coast in 1968. Surveying from Mogadishu south to Buur Gaabo as well as the Bajuni Islands, he found numerous remains of early Islamic ruins varying in size, preservation, and age. Returning to Somalia in 1975, he continued his survey of the coast and interior by heading north to Cape Guardafui and then east all the way to the Djibouti border. Once again, he found extensive remains of ruined early Islamic settlements, cairns, and tombs, similar to those first reported by G. Revoil in 1882, and a possible port at Ras Hafun dating to Ptolemaic or Roman times. Returning to Ras Hafun in 1976, Chittick conducted major excavations at what he proposed was the ancient port of Opone but unfortunately died before completing and publishing this research.

In the early 1970s, Anfray and the Ethiopian Institute of Archaeology continued to excavate pre-Aksumite and Aksumite sites, but archaeological research at Aksum itself took on a distinctly Anglo-American perspective. In 1973 and 1974, Chittick, representing the British Institute in Eastern Africa, directed excavations at Aksum to shed light on the age and functions of the monumental architecture. J. Michels also worked at Aksum in 1974 and focused upon a systematic surface survey of the Aksum region as a way of reconstructing settlement patterns. Preliminary analyses revealed eight distinct phases of cultural history dating (by obsidian hydration) from 700 B.C. to A.D. 1000. These phases reflected changes in the sociopolitical processes of state formation from the initial appearance of farming villages to the development of complex urban centers.

Drawing upon a preliminary analysis of the alluvial process (the depositing of clay, silt, sand, or gravel by running water) and soil erosion in the Aksum area, K. W. Butzer approached the archaeology of Aksum from a geomorphological and environmental perspective. He argued that improved climatic conditions in the 1st century A.D. resulted in increased agricultural productivity, thereby supporting the demographic base necessary for state formation. He also suggested that a return to more arid conditions in the 8th century A.D., combined with sociopolitical and economic changes, led to environmental degradation and the collapse of the Aksumite kingdom.

Michels's and Butzer's approaches to Aksumite archaeology represented a radical departure from previous Aksumite studies, virtually all of which owed their methodological allegiance to classical archaeology. The publication of Y. Kobishchanov's *Axum* was also a radical departure, but for other reasons. Originally published in Russian in 1966 and based essentially on epigraphic and other historical sources, *Axum* took a wide-ranging Marxist approach to Aksumite economic and sociopolitical systems and provided a series of archaeologically testable hypotheses on the political, economic, social, and ideological organization of the Aksumite state.

After 1974, fieldwork in northern Ethiopia and Eritrea became impossible due to political and military conflicts. Anfray and the Ethiopian Institute of Archaeology moved their field interests to southern Ethiopia and focused upon describing and stylistically classifying the stelae and other megaliths first documented by Azais and Chambard in the 1920s. Also following in the footsteps of Azais and Chambard was R. Joussaume who, from the late 1960s through the 1970s, mapped, excavated, and stylistically classified the megaliths of highland eastern Ethiopia.

During the 1980s, when foreign research in Ethiopia was suspended, Aksumite research shifted to refinements, reassessments, and syntheses of previously excavated data. The research included efforts to better understand the significant role of indigenous Ethiopian societies in the establishment of the pre-Aksumite and Aksumite kingdoms and the publication of book-length general syntheses by F. Anfray in 1990 and S. C. H. Munro Hay in 1991. This period also witnessed the untimely death of H. N. Chittick, but fortunately the results of his 1970's fieldwork at Aksum were later published by the British Institute.

More historical archaeological research was conducted in Somalia during the 1980s than during all of the previous century. This was due to a number of factors: (1) changes in Somali government policies toward foreign research, (2) the establishment of a government organization responsible for archaeological research (the Somali Academy of Sciences), (3) renewed interest by the archaeological community in Somalia's archaeological potential, and (4) the training of Somalia's first professional historical archaeologists. Of particular interest were the significant increase in research related to the evolution of urbanism in early Islamic Somalia and the confirmation of Chittick's hypothesis that the ancient port of Ras Hafun was involved in transoceanic trade with the classical world from at least the 1st century B.C. to the 5th century A.D.

Toward the 21st Century

The 1990s has been a period of both depression and excitement for archaeology in the Horn. Somalia's slide into anarchy in the early 1990s cut short the brief florescence archaeological research enjoyed there in the 1980s, while large areas of Djibouti have become inaccessible due to heightened political tension. However, Ethiopia has once again opened itself up for foreign- and Ethiopian-led archaeological investigations. Some of the projects initiated there in the 1970s have started again (by J. Desmond Clark and his associates, as well as by D. W. Phillipson), while others (by B. Asfaw, A. Beyene, G. Suwa, R. C. Walter, Tim White, A. Wolde Gabnel, and T. Yemane, Katherine Bard, Rudolfo Fattovich, Steven A. Brandt, and R. Joussaume) are new. Still others remain to be developed on topics that remain poorly researched (for example, the transition from the Middle to Late Stone Age, the evolution of food production, and post-Aksumite historical archaeology) or have never been explored (for example, the recognition and role of gender and ethnicity in the archaeological record, symbolic and ideological approaches to historical archaeology, the development of a comprehensive cultural-heritage management program, and non-Western approaches to archaeological method and theory).

Finally, newly independent Eritrea faces the challenge of developing an archaeological and cultural-heritage program almost from scratch, while Somalia can only hope it will soon have the opportunity to do so.

BIBLIOGRAPHY

Anfray, F. 1990. *Les anciens Ethiopiens*. Paris: Armand Colin.

Azais, R. P., and R. Chambard. 1931. *Cinq années de recherches archeologiques en Ethiopie*. Paris: Librarie Orientaliste Paul Gunther.

Begashaw, K. 1994. Archaeological research in Ethiopia: Progress and current situation. In *Etudes Ethiopiennes*, vol. 1., ed. C. Lepage, 95–103. Paris: Société Français pour les Etudes Ethiopiennes.

Bent, J. T. 1893. *The sacred city of the Ethiopians*. London: Longmans, Green.

Bishop, W. W., and J. D. Clark. 1967. *Background to evolution in Africa*. Chicago: University of Chicago Press.

Brandt, S. A. 1984. New perspectives on the origins of food production in Ethiopia. In *From hunters to farmers: The causes and consequences of food production in Africa,* eds. J. D. Clark and S. A. Brandt, 173–190. Berkeley: University of California Press.

Brandt, S. A., and G. A. Brook. 1984. Archaeological and paleoenvironmental research in northern Somalia. *Current Anthropology* 25: 119–121.

Brandt, S. A., and R. Fattovich. 1990. Late Quaternary archaeological research in the Horn of Africa. In *A history of African archaeology,* ed. P. Robertshaw, 95–108. London and Portsmouth: James Currey Ltd. and Heinemann.

Butzer, K. W. 1981. Rise and fall of Axum, Ethiopia: A geo-archaeological interpretation. *American Antiquity* 40: 471–495.

Chavaillon, J., N. Chavaillon, F. Hours, and M. Piperno. 1979. From the Oldowan to the Middle Stone Age at Melka-Kunture (Ethiopia): Understanding cultural changes. *Quaternaria* 21: 87–114.

Clark, J. D. l954. *The prehistoric cultures of the Horn of Africa*. Cambridge: Cambridge University Press.

Conti Rossini, C. 1928. *Storia d'Etiopia*. Bergamo: Istituto Italiano d'Arti Grafiche.

Curle, A. T. 1937. The ruined towns of Somaliland. *Antiquity* 11: 315–327.

Danielli, G., and O. Marinelli. 1912. *Risultati di un viaggio scientifico nella colonia Eritrea*. Firenze: Galletti e Cocci.

Ehret, C. 1979. On the antiquity of agriculture in Ethiopia. *Journal of African History* 20: 161–177.

Gallagher, J. 1977. Contemporary stone tools in Ethiopia: Implications for archaeology. *Journal of Field Archaeology* 4: 408–414.

Graziosi, P. 1940. *L'Eta della Pietra in Somalia*. Firenze: Centro di Studi Coloniali.

Howell, F. C. 1968. Omo Research Expedition. *Nature* 219: 567–572.

Isaac, G. L., and L. McCown. 1976. *Human origins: Louis Leakey and the East African evidence*. Menlo Park: W. A. Benjamin.

Littman, E., S. Krencker, and T. von Lupke. 1913. *Deutsche Aksum-Expedition,* vol. 1-4. Berlin: Reimer Verlag.

Munro-Hay, S. C. H. 1989. *Excavations at Aksum*. Nairobi: British Institute in Eastern Africa Memoir 10.

———. 1991. *Aksum: An African civilization of late antiquity*. Edinburgh: Edinburgh University Press.

Paribeni, R. 1907. Ricerche sul luogo dell'Antia Adulis. *Monumenti Antichi* 1907: 437–572.

Revoil, G. 1882. *La vallée du Darror.* Paris.

Shaw, T., P. Sinclair, B. Andah, and A. Okpoko. 1993. *The archaeology of Africa: Food, metals and towns.* London: Routledge.

Tielhard de Chardin, P. 1930. Le Paleolithique en Somali Française et en Abyssinie. *L'Anthropologie* 40: 331–334.

Vavilov, N. I. 1926. *Studies on the origin of cultivated plants.* Leningrad: Institute of Applied Botanical Plant Breeding.

Wendorf, F., and R. Schild. 1974. *A Middle Stone Age sequence from the Central Rift Valley, Ethiopia.* Warsaw: Ossolineum.

Steven A. Brandt

SOUTHERN AND EASTERN AFRICA: HISTORY OF ARCHAEOLOGY

The earlier stages of archaeological research in Africa are best understood against the background of what was known of European prehistory to about 1920. The year 1858 saw the recognition of the true association of human artifacts (hand axes) with extinct animals in the gravels of the Somme at St. Acheul (hence the term *Acheulian* for hand-ax industries). The following year, Charles Darwin published his framework for the theory of evolution, encouraging the expectation that evolution would be found in material culture as well as in nature. By the end of the century, geology had demonstrated the former existence of a great glacial epoch, and by 1920, four stages of glaciation, separated by interglacial periods, were recognized in the Alps. Chronology was problematical. In 1911, the Oxford geologist William J. Sollas thought Acheulian industries were associated with the third glacial stage, for which he suggested a date of 34,000 years ago. In 1920, Miles Burkitt associated the Acheulian with the onset of the first glaciation but refrained from suggesting any sort of date for the event. In France and some localities in England, simple stone artifacts, termed *eoliths,* were thought to predate the Acheulian industries. Much of this must have rubbed off on two of Burkitt's students at Cambridge—Africa's first professional archaeologists, A. J. H. (John) Goodwin and L. S. B. (Louis) Leakey, who graduated in 1922 and 1926, respectively.

There was the hope, and apparently the expectation, that some comparable climatic framework might be found in Africa—a framework that would permit at least the establishment of a relative chronology for African cultures and perhaps even a correlation of these cultures with events in Europe. The first hint of this came in 1901 from a German, Blankenhorn, who suggested that glacial stages in northern latitudes should have been accompanied in lower latitudes by periods of increased rainfall, which he termed *pluvials.* By 1904, L. Passarge, working in the Kalahari, had found field evidence that seemed to support the theory. In 1914, C. E. P. Brooks made the theory more accessible by introducing it to English readers, so that by the 1920s, when systematic work was just getting under way in southern Africa, and was to begin soon afterward in eastern Africa, the ground was already fertile for the growth of a pluvial scheme that might match the glacial framework taking shape in Europe.

Already the geologist J. W. Gregory, who first described the East African Rift Valley System in 1896, had linked the former extension of glaciers on Mount Kenya to the greater extent of some lakes in the Rift Valley. He was also, incidentally, the first person known to have collected stone artifacts in East Africa. He described these artifacts in 1921.

Stone tools were abundant in all areas and were sufficiently similar to those associated with the Lower and Middle Paleolithic ages of Europe to be recognizable by those who knew the latter. If there was no close parallel to the Upper Paleolithic period, what was to become known as the *Late Stone Age* in Africa bore some similarity to the European Mesolithic age and could safely be assumed to be of relatively recent date. Stratigraphic sequences to confirm the ordering and associated climatic indications were needed to provide the link with the Ice Ages. Obtaining these was the paramount concern of much of the earliest systematic archaeology.

The early 1920s could be said to be the starting point for systematic research in both eastern and southern Africa. Before then, very few discoveries had been reported in eastern Africa, the most significant being a burial site reported in 1923, excavated by Louis Leakey in 1926, and now recognized as an early Pastoral Neolithic site. In southern Africa, the situation was somewhat different. Sporadic references to the use of stone for tools go back to the 18th century, and the first recorded collection of stone tools was donated to the South African Museum in 1855 by T. H. Bowker. In 1837, Sir James Alexander published three color plates of rock paintings from the southern Cape. From around 1870, C. J. Busk and Langham Dale were collecting stone tools in the western Cape, and in the *Cape Monthly Magazine,* Dale initiated a series of articles that served to stimulate interest and involve enthusiasts further afield. Both sent artifacts to London for expert assessment, which tended to introduce egocentric ideas and terminology to South Africa but also had the effect of arousing interest in Britain in the potential of South African archaeology. When the British Association for the Advancement of Science visited South Africa in 1905, archaeology was among the topics for discussion. A number of papers on archaeology were presented, and A. C. Haddon offered some sound advice on methodology and the desirability of replacing imported European terminology with local terms. In fact, from the 1870s on, a surprising number of people were reporting sites, donating collections to museums, and experimenting with ideas. In 1881, C. J. Richard proposed a three-stage sequence of stone-tool use in South Africa—Paleolithic, Neolithic, and historic—in a talk to the Cambridge Antiquarian Society. In 1921, John Hewitt, director of the Albany Museum in Grahamstown, reported on his excavation of a cave on a farm in Wilton (hence the term *Wilton culture)* and was actively investigating other sites in the eastern Cape. When John Goodwin was appointed research assistant to Professor A. R. Radcliffe-Brown at the University of Cape Town in 1923, he found a wealth of material in the South African Museum and the literature to use as a starting point in a remarkably influential career in archaeology.

But work on establishing a sequence had already begun in eastern Africa. E. J. Wayland had been appointed director of the Uganda Geological Survey in 1919 and evidently saw even the most recent geology as part of his responsibility. In 1923, he published a paper on paleoliths in relation to Pleistocene deposits. Other papers were to follow. In 1929, he wrote a note on African pluvials and, by 1934, had gathered sufficient data to publish a detailed account of the Stone Age in Uganda tied to a framework of two two-stage pluvials and two postpluvial wet phases. He identified at the beginning of his sequence a simple pebble culture to which he gave the name *Kafuan* (from high-level gravels of the Kafu River). He gave the name *Sangoan* to specimens with Acheulian affinities but including heavy elements, such as picks, push planes, and core scrapers, found on the surface of the Sango Hills west of Lake Victoria. He also named a new industry, the *Magosian* (published in 1932 with Miles Burkitt) from the filling of a natural rock cistern, which displayed a combination of Middle and Late Stone Age characteristics. But in more recent years, many of Wayland's discoveries were to come to grief. Another geologist, W. W. Bishop, demonstrated in 1954 that the Kafuan "artifacts" were the products of geological forces. Reexcavation of the Magosi type site by G. Cole, in 1967, showed that the Magosian was the product of mixing of distinct Middle and Late Stone Age levels. Most recently, J. L. Cormack, in a 1994 study of the heavy elements of the Sangoan, has shown that there is no real distinction between these and similar artifacts associated with typical Acheulian in a number of sites. She recommends that the term *Sangoan* be dropped.

The search for long sequences was pursued in other parts of Africa. On the basis of comparison with procedures in Europe, river valleys and their terraces, together with overlying sediments, were seen as the key. In South Africa, P. G. Sohnge, D. J. L. Visser, and C. van Riet Lowe set out the sequence for industries in the Vaal River Basin in 1937: a pre-Stellenbosch, four stages of Stellenbosch (Acheulian), two stages of Fauresmith (late Acheulian variant), Middle Stone Age, and "Neolithic Elements" composed of Wilton and Smithfield. These were all set alongside evidence for wetter and drier phases, which were correlated with the pluvial scheme as established at that time in eastern Africa. Much the same was achieved in the Zambezi Valley by J. Desmond Clark between 1938 and 1949. Wayland's evidence for pluvials was developed by J. D. Solomon in Louis Leakey's *Stone Age Cultures of Kenya Colony* (1931), and in the same place, Brooks clearly demonstrated the correlation of the pluvials with the four glacial episodes in Europe. In the 1951 publication of his first series of investigations at Olduvai Gorge, Leakey, using the same kind of climatological interpretation tied to European glacial episodes, saw the evolution of the hand-ax culture there as extending from the beginning of the Mindel to the end of the Riss glaciation. But in all this, there was no indication of the absolute chronology of events beyond the uncertain extrapolations and guesses about the ages of the European glacial sequence.

Almost without exception, the evidence for former climates was geological: downcutting and aggravation of river valleys, old high-level strandlines (shorelines) around lakes in the Rift Valley, and colluvial and windblown sand bodies. In 1955, geologist H. B. S. Cooke issued a warning about the assumed universal equivalence of glacial and pluvial episodes, and in 1958, he published a critical review of the geological basis for the pluvials. A year later, R. F. Flint published a similarly critical review of the evidence. While the two papers did not propose that Africa had not experienced fluctuations of temperature and rainfall during the Pleistocene, they did explain that much of the evidence used to illustrate such changes was unreliable and that climatic evidence was not, in itself, an acceptable basis for interregional, far less intercontinental, correlation. From this moment, the fourfold pluvial scheme effectively ceased to be mentioned, and the emphasis is now much more on local evidence for former climatic regimes. This effectively undermined the basis for correlating Stone Age occurrences from different parts of the continent or with Europe. Fortunately, at the very time when

this desperately needed framework was being demolished, physical methods of dating, in particular potassium-argon dating, developed in the context of geological studies, began to be applied to deposits of Pleistocene age.

In 1961, Bed I at Olduvai Gorge was dated to 1.75 million years ago by the potassium-argon method, and this, combined with developing techniques in the excavation of Early Stone Age archaeological sites, ushered in a new era of thinking with regard to the Early Stone Age in particular. In subsequent years, artifact occurrences in the Omo River Valley (excavated from 1966 to 1974) have been dated to 2.35 million years ago (and less certainly to 2.9 million ago), and artifacts at Kada Gona in the Hadar (excavated between 1976 and 1977) have been dated to 2.6 million years ago.

The discovery and excavation of the Olorgesailie site in Kenya by Louis and Mary Leakey in the mid-1940s demonstrated the potential of lacustrine (lake) sediments (and related low-energy environments) for the preservation of intact occupation sites in which fauna and artifacts might lie virtually undisturbed since their abandonment. Delegates to the first Pan-African Congress on Prehistory, convened by Louis Leakey in Nairobi in 1947, visited the site, and it is hard to dissociate the event from the entirely new direction taken by Early Stone Age studies from that time onward. Archaeologists' interest in river gravels, with their often rich content of artifacts and fossils, dwindled with the realization of the infinitely greater potential of "archaeological context" sites.

The importance of context, as compared with succession, was reflected in the new series of excavations initiated by the Leakeys at Olduvai in 1951, where one of the first priorities was uncovering the "living floor" at the BKII locality. Between 1954 and 1959, Clark devoted enormous energy to uncovering and plotting in situ artifacts and plant remains (including the first Acheulian artifacts of wood found in Africa) at Kalambo Falls. Other sites followed: Isimilia, investigated by F. Clark Howell in the late 1950s; renewed excavations at Olorgesailie by Glynn Isaac in 1966; Kilombe, investigated by John A. J. Gowlett from 1973 to 1974; Melka Kunture, investigated by J. Chavaillon in 1974; the international series of investigations initiated by Howell in the Omo River Valley between 1966 and 1974; and the parallel investigations by Richard F. Leakey and Isaac at Koobi Fora, east of Lake Turkana from 1968 to 1974. For often differing reasons, all are important in the history of Early Stone Age studies—some for the light they have shed on early hominid behavior, some for their fossil content, including early hominid remains and some for the radiometric dates they have yielded from associated volcanic deposits.

The discovery of *Zinjanthropus* on a living floor in Bed I at Olduvai in 1959 and of *Homo habilis* at a lower level in the following year played a major role in stimulating interest and attracting funding in the years that followed.

While Olduvai was important for its long succession, chronology, fossils, and evidence of early hominid behavior, the value of the Isimilia site lay in its demonstration of the previously unsuspected variability in Acheulian assemblages in a number of sites closely grouped in time and space. Thus, it became apparent that the "Hope Fountain," which lacked larged cutting tools and was long thought of as a flake-tool tradition separate from the Acheulian, was no more than an activity variant of the Acheulian. Kilombe, a 700,000-year-old complex of Acheulian sites separated laterally, but with a limited chronological span, also demonstrated variability, this time leading the excavator, Gowlett, to question the validity of the Olduvai Developed Olduwan B as a tradition separate from the Acheulian and to consider whether the term *Olduwan* should be used for any assemblage younger than 1 million years.

The 1960s and 1970s were remarkable not only for the ferment of fieldwork on early hominid sites in East Africa, but also for the imaginative thinking, experimentation, and questioning that accompanied the work. Maxine R. Kleindienst had sought, in 1961, on the evidence from Isimilia, Kalambo, and Olorgesailie, to introduce more clarity and objectivity into the analysis and description of Acheulian assemblages, as a first step toward assessing the meaning of variability. Glynn Isaac carried this work a step further in his 1977 monograph on Olorgesailie with the

introduction of metrical data and statistical testing and with a critical review of the factors influencing site formation and clear distinctions between what was fact and what was hypothesis. His searching approach to the problems of Olorgesailie was sharpened still further by the challenges of the Koobi Fora sites, leading to his seminal models of food sharing and the home base. What Isaac had done, and others after him have persisted with, was to shift the primary focus of attention from artifacts to hypotheses about behavior—hypotheses that should be tested against the field data. Experiment was part of the process, and worrying problems of technology at Olduvai Gorge were elucidated by P. Jones's demonstration of the influence of raw material on stone-implement manufacture. Similarly, the extensive experiments of Nicholas Toth in 1985 in replicating excavated assemblages at Koobi Fora have radically challenged previously accepted views of Olduwan technology.

Ultimately this extraordinary surge of research into the Early Stone Age of East Africa is explicable in terms of phenomena associated with the geological history of the Rift Valley—its inland drainage basins, low-energy environments, favorable conditions for fossilization, and datable volcanic sediments. South of Isimilia and Kalambo, the Rift Valley has hardly figured in the history of research, but the mid-Pleistocene butchery site discovered at Mwanganda's Village (1965 and 1966) and the recent discovery (1993) of a very early *Homo* specimen at Uraha suggest that the Malawi arm of the rift may have more to offer.

Before the 1920s, South Africa had an active tradition of dilettante archaeology. Easily accessible cave sites, often the more attractive for the rock paintings they contained, and highly visible shell middens along the coast had attracted excavators and collectors, with the result that artifacts of the Late Stone Age were well known by the 1920s. In the interior, collectors had been equally busy from the later decades of the 19th century. The discovery of diamonds in the Vaal River gravels led to the discovery of fossils and artifacts, and while the earliest papers were primarily geological, the 1920s saw a greater interest in stratigraphy, leading, ultimately, to the detailed study by P. G. Sohnge, D. J. L. Visser, and C. van Riet Lowe, already referred to.

John Goodwin's self-appointed task, on taking up his post at the University of Cape Town in 1923, was to try to bring some sort of order to the welter of collections available to him at Cape Town and the many views expressed about them in print. He was convinced of "the absolute necessity for evolving an entirely new cultural terminology for South Africa." In 1925, he presented a scheme of Early Stone Age, containing three expressions of hand-ax industries and a Late Stone Age comprising the Eastern culture, D. R. Kannermeyer's Smithfield, and "Pygmy" industries, the latter based on John Hewitt's 1921 excavation of the Wilton rock shelter. Acceptance of the scheme was delayed for a later meeting of the South African Association for the Advancement of Science to be held in Pretoria in 1926. In the meantime, Goodwin had published a guide to the stone implements in the South African Museum in which he formally substituted the term *Stillbay* for the old *Eastern culture,* and the term *Wilton* to replace *Pygmy implements.* In a paper in 1928, he introduced the term *Middle Stone Age* to accommodate the Stillbay and other South African industries that showed "a strong Middle Paleolithic [European] influence." He believed that the final stage of the Stellenbosch (Acheulian) had been affected by Mousterian influences, spreading into South Africa, to produce the Fauresmith (the latter part of his Early Stone Age), and ultimately "the greater part of the Middle Stone Age."

In 1929, Goodwin and C. van Riet Lowe published *The Stone Age Cultures of South Africa,* setting out a justified terminology that survived with very few modifications until very recently. But despite their clear thinking and objectivity in so many respects, and in the absence of any basis for chronological correlation, both writers were committed to the concept that everything in the south owed its presence to diffusion from the north. Evolutionary stages of the Early Stone Age were due to successive "invasions" or "suggestions and impacts" from more northerly peoples. The Fauresmith and Middle Stone Age reflected Mousterian influences emanating, ultimately, out of Europe, while the bifacial points

of the Stillbay indicated a relatively late date, with "Neoanthropic" (Solutrean) techniques blending with the Mousterian (a view introduced by Miles Burkitt on his visit to South Africa in 1927). The same explanation was adopted to account for the apparent blending of Stillbay and Neoanthropic types in the assemblage recovered by John Hewitt from the Howieson's Poort cave in 1925. The Late Stone Age was also thought to be due to immigrants from the north—in this case, the North African Capsian.

In *The Stone Age Cultures of South Africa,* van Riet Lowe had divided D. R. Kannemeyer's Smithfield into three phases: A, B, and C. Smithfield A and B occurred on open sites in the interior of South Africa and both employed lydianite as the principal raw material. Smithfield A was characterized by large circular and concavo-convex scrapers. These were absent in Smithfield B, which included divergent ("duckbill") end scrapers, bored stones, and spokeshaves. Smithfield C generally occurred farther east in caves in the Drakensberg Mountains and was composed of "Pygmy implements" most frequently made of agate, chalcedony, and quartz. Smithfield B and C were said to show marked affinities with the Wilton industry. On the basis of Hewitt's 1921 report on the Wilton rock shelter, it is evident that the chief characteristic of his Wilton industry was the presence of numerous small crescents (now termed *segments).* Apart from the absence of crescents, the similarity between the Smithfield C and Wilton was such that many writers, in more recent years, have referred to the former as a *crescentless Wilton,* and it is interesting, in view of later developments, to note that Hewitt, though uncertain, thought there might have been a Smithfield C industry overlying the Wilton in the Wilton rock shelter.

In their 1929 publication, Goodwin and van Riet Lowe defined clearly the content and distribution of the Early Stone Age (Stellenbosch, Victoria West, and Fauresmith), the Middle Stone Age (Stillbay and Glen Grey industries and Pietersburg and Howieson's Poort "variations"), and the Late Stone Age (Smithfield A, B, and C and Wilton). The next 30 years, in South Africa and elsewhere, were marked by the expansion of their basic database but with virtually no new thinking about the meaning of the data. The term *Wilton* had been extended to Zimbabwe already by 1928 and, with the prefix *Kenya,* was adopted by Louis Leakey in 1931. Although the term was used widely, regional differences were recognized and were distinguished by appropriate prefixes: thus, in 1959, J. Desmond Clark described no less than eight regional variants of the Wilton and five of the Smithfield in southern Africa. The term *Stillbay* was similarly used throughout southern and eastern Africa, though occasional new names were added, such as *Bambata* for a Middle Stone Age industry with "Neoanthropic" elements overlying Mousterian in the Bambata Cave (Zimbabwe) in 1931. But essentially the work of these three decades, from 1929 to 1959, was additive, descriptive, and classificatory. A tiny handful of radiocarbon dates provided the first indications of absolute chronology.

The first advance in thinking came in the context of the Late Stone Age with Janette Deacon's reinvestigation of the Wilton type site, excavated from 1966 to 1967 and published in 1972. She described the chronological variation in the content of the assemblage in terms of David L. Clark's recently published ontogenetic model, and she explored the metrical attributes of several artifact types within this framework. Below the Wilton, as defined by shifts in raw-material preferences and associated scraper dimensions, was an industry of large quartzite flakes, associated with a large alcelaphine antelope indicative of an open grassland environment, in contrast to the closed environment of *bushveld* and woodland indicated by the fauna for the Wilton levels. Changes in style, or norms, of scraper manufacture were taken to reflect change within a unitary culture, while fluctuations in tool assemblages were seen to reflect the needs of varying activities. Most significantly, Deacon found that segments (crescents) were abundant in the climax phase of the culture but rare or absent in the formative and postclimax phases—effectively, they were "crescentless Wilton." In a 1974 paper, with the larger number of radiocarbon dates then available, she combined the evidence of the secular variation in the relative frequencies of segments, other backed pieces, and small scrapers as observed at Wilton, similar observations on the content of the old classic Smithfield A, B, and C, and geographical observations to demonstrate that there was no sensible basis for distinguishing Smithfield B and C from the Late Holocene Wilton, whose chronology they shared. The distinction between B and C was attributable to regional variation in the availability of raw materials, reflected primarily in scraper forms and dimensions.

Assemblages of the Smithfield A artifacts were shown to belong to the time period between 8,000 and 12,000 years ago and were assigned to the Albany industry, newly identified at such sites as Melkhoutboom and Boomplaas in the Cape Folded Mountains and Nelson Bay Cave on the south coast and including the pre-Wilton at the Wilton type site.

The reassessment of the Wilton type site heralded dramatic changes in research priorities in Late Stone Age studies in South Africa. The discovery of the macrolithic Albany industry and the recognition in effectively the same sites of another new industry, the microblade-based Robberg industry (12,000 to 20,000 years ago), were incidental. The new approach was, by design, ecological and behavioral, and the faunal studies by Robert G. Klein were a key element underpinning the behavioral and demographic hypotheses developed at this time. John E. Parkington's project in the western Cape, initiated in 1968, was designed expressly to test the hypothesis of seasonal transhumance (the seasonal moving from one region to another) between the Cape Fold Mountains and the coast, with their seasonally contrasting resources. Janette Deacon's project in the eastern Cape, and subsequently farther west, at Boomplaas, ranged widely over matters of plant-food exploitation, hunting patterns, and demography. While postulating transhumance between the mountains and the coast, Deacon remained uncommitted, allowing that intensification of the food quest could have permitted year-round residence by the hypothesized small groups of the Holocene. In 1984, Judith C. Sealy, employing stable carbon-isotope analysis, demonstrated that at least some of the groups described by Parkington had lived all year at the coast.

For all the richness of Early Stone Age sites in eastern Africa, none is particularly helpful in the study of the final stages of the Acheulian or the transition to the Middle Stone Age. The first series of potassium-argon dates released in 1965 contained dates greater than 200,000 and 400,000 years ago for two industries classified as Middle Stone Age in Kenya, while in 1975, a Middle Stone Age industry at Gadamotta was dated to between 150,000 and 180,000 years ago. More recently (1989), an early stage of the Middle Stone Age in South Africa has been assigned a comparable age at Klasies River Mouth Cave 1, for which uranium-series dating provides substantial support. At Border Cave, electron-spin resonance and amino-acid racemization indicate a date of around 130,000 years ago for the early Middle Stone Age. At the South African site of Rooidam, uranium-series dating indicates an age of around 200,000 years ago for an assumed late expression of the Acheulian. The Howieson's Poort industry, at one time thought to be a southern equivalent of the Magosian and to be transitional between the Middle and Late Stone Ages, was reported by A. H. J. (John) Goodwin, as long ago as 1935, to occur intercalated between Stillbay industries at the Cape St. Blaize Cave. In 1948, K. Jolly reported a similar occurrence at Skildergat Cave near Cape Town. But both sites were beset with problems, and uncertainty surrounded the chronology of the industry. In the 1980s, at both Klasies River Mouth and Border Cave, the Howieson's Poort industry was shown to appear as an episode, probably of a few thousand years duration at around 70,000 years ago, preceded and succeeded by "normal" Middle Stone Age industries. Both sites have proved important for the specimens of anatomically modern humans they have yielded and for critical environmental and behavioral evidence. This is in contrast to almost all other occurrences of Middle Stone Age industries in southern, central, and eastern Africa, where little information other than artifact content and relative chronology has been secured. In 1990, a late Middle Stone Age occupation dated to 22,000 years ago at Strathalan Cave in South Africa displayed dietary features and internal spatial organization reminiscent of Late Stone Age sites, and in the same year, Jonathan Kaplan, at the Umhlatuzana rock shelter in KwaZulu-Natal, demonstrated that microblades,

characteristic of the earliest Late Stone Age, made their appearance well down to the later stages of the Middle Stone Age.

By the late 1930s, in the field of rock-art studies, a sufficient number of reports and reproductions of the art had appeared to indicate distinct regional differences. While naturalistic paintings of animals, with variations in style, content, and abundance occur throughout, a very different corpus of schematic art and of crude, white, possibly finger-executed drawings existed in Kenya, Uganda, Tanzania, Zambia, Malawi, and part of Zimbabwe. This latter group became the subject of interpretative inquiry rather earlier than the naturalistic art. In 1931, A. T. Culwick reported evidence for ethnohistoric links with former pastoralist peoples for paintings at Bahi in central Tanzania. J. Desmond Clark, in 1959, thought the art ritualistic or magical in origin and proposed links with Bantu initiation rites and the suppressed Butwa society in northern Zambia. In a major survey posthumously published in summary in 1974, J. H. Chaplin presented the first wide-ranging survey of the schematic art, suggesting an origin among late hunter-foragers and early pastoralists. The most recent statement, by M. Lingren and M. Schoffeleers in 1970, convincingly links the red schematic art in Malawi with Chewa rain shrines, and the crude white paintings with the hiding places of paraphernalia associated with the *nyau* society, the Chewa boy's *rite de passage*.

The naturalistic paintings have, over the years, attracted a far greater amount of attention, but until recently it has been almost exclusively descriptive and speculative. Earlier surveys (for example, Miles Burkitt's in 1928 and Louis Leakey's in 1950) reflect the concern of many scholars of the day to establish, through style, color, and superposition, sequences in the art that might relate to sequences in the prehistoric record. A brief debate in 1959 and 1960 occurred between J. Rudner and A. Willcox on the authorship of the South African art. Down to the 1960s, numerous papers and monographs appeared, documenting context and distribution. Neville Jones, in 1949, thought the art arrived with the first "Neoanthropic invaders," and Willcox, in 1984, still espoused the view that the art derived, ultimately, from Europe via North Africa. Some thought the art related to hunting magic, while others believed it was merely decorative. J. Desmond Clark, in 1959, used the art as a source to illustrate dress, weapons, and daily life in the Late Stone Age. At the Kisese II rock shelter in Tanzania in 1957, Ray R. Inskeep obtained the first archaeological evidence that schematic red paintings were contemporaneous with, or later than, a late stage of the local Late Stone Age.

In 1967, T. M. O'C. Maggs published the first quantitative analysis of the content of a group of paintings in the southwest Cape. This study indicated that the art was neither representative of the diet of Late Stone Age hunters nor reflective of the fauna in their environment. Peter Vinnicombe, in a much larger survey in 1976, found the same to be true in the Drakensberg Mountains and, making wide use of Bushman mythology, argued for a basis in myth and religious belief. In a series of papers in the 1980s, D. Lewis-Williams demonstrated firmly and clearly the link between the art and San shamanism—a concept that he and others have continued to elaborate in subsequent years. His proposition that a representation on one of the slabs dated to 26,000 years ago at the Apollo 11 shelter in Namibia may represent the same shamanistic basis implies that the roots of the Late Stone Age and modern San ideology may lie within the later stages of the Middle Stone Age.

Leaving aside the question of early colonial settlements, which have recently attracted interest in South Africa, the most recent period of archaeology, and most recent in terms of research interest, is that of agro-pastoralism. The validity of the term *Iron Age* attracted some debate in the 1950s but became widely accepted after then. The term implies a package of mixed farming, ceramics, and metallurgy, primarily iron but including copper and gold. The term *agro-pastoralism* has recently been suggested to provide inclusion of nonmetal-using pastoralists, some of whom predate the appearance of metallurgical knowledge. The apparent neglect of this field, until recently, is not because archaeologists are antipathetic toward the prehistory of the subjects of colonialism, as has recently been suggested, but because stone implements lying around in the country-

side were more immediately recognizable as "archaeological" than broken potsherds. The apparent neglect may also have been due to the fact that the great pioneer professional archaeologists, John Goodwin, Louis Leakey, and J. Desmond Clark, all studied at Cambridge under the influential Paleolithic archaeologist Miles Burkitt. In a sense, their careers and therefore the early history of African archaeology were an extension of the relatively new and exciting discoveries in European Paleolithic to the continent of Africa.

Zimbabwe was an exception to this and serves to emphasize the point. Carl Mauch's discovery in 1871 of the dramatic ruins of Great Zimbabwe, reinforced soon after by J. Theodore Bent's discovery of gold there, and of numerous other ruins sites tipped the balance from the beginning in favor of the Iron Age. The discovery was unfortunately linked by Mauch to the 16th-century reports of gold mines in the region and hence to King Solomon and the Queen of Sheba. This link and the refusal to admit the possibility of an African origin were the views of fanciful men and bigots, whereas David Randall-MacIver, the first trained archaeologist to investigate the problem, concluded, in 1905, without doubt that the buildings were of African origin and were medieval in date. His results were amplified and confirmed by Gertrude Caton-Thompson in 1932. Gold was found the following year by farmers exploring the summit of Mapungubwe Hill in the middle Limpopo Valley. This led, in 1933, to the first of a series of field investigations by the University of Pretoria, the most recent of which, reported in summary in 1981, has provided good dating and substance for the sequence of occupations at this very large site complex.

The publications of John F. Schofield, in 1942 and 1948, on the pottery from Zimbabwe, Mapungubwe, and numerous other sites in southern Africa, including recent ethnographic pottery, sent a clear signal that the key to the Iron Age lay in the study of its pottery. His successor at the Queen Victoria Museum in Zimbabwe, Roger Summers, continued the Iron Age tradition, and with his colleagues K. R. Robinson and Anthony Whitty in 1958, refined the sequence of ceramics and architecture at Great Zimbabwe. The same year saw the publication of Summers's monograph on the Inyanga ruins, to be followed in 1959 by Robinson's volume on the Khami ruins.

Systematic research into the Iron Age in Zambia began in 1957 with Ray Inskeep's excavation of the Kalundu mound and was continued by Brian M. Fagan from 1959 to 1961 mainly on the plateau, by Joseph O. Vogel from 1966 to 1976 in the Zambezi Valley (followed more recently by Nicholas Katanekwa), by David W. Phillipson, working widely throughout the country, and by Michael S. Bisson investigating the early history of metallurgy on the Copperbelt of northern Zambia and southern Zaire.

In the mid-1960s, the African historian Roland Oliver made a bold attempt to synthesize emerging archaeological evidence, radiocarbon dates, and linguistic evidence to study the origin and spread of Bantu-speaking peoples. At the same time Jan Vansina (1965) was exploring oral tradition as a path into the past, and Christopher Ehret (1967) contributed the first of a series of papers specifically designed to explore later prehistory through linguistics. The British Institute in Eastern Africa set up its Bantu Studies Research Project in 1965 under the initial direction of Fagan, to investigate "the origins and early migrations of the Bantu." The upshot of all this activity is that, today, we have a vastly improved picture of the nature and chronology of regional ceramic traditions, while the diffusion of agriculture and metallurgy are set within a reasonably good chronological framework. But the question of "Bantu origins and dispersal" is still very much an open debate.

South of the Limpopo, perhaps because of the greater distance from the supposed source, Iron Age archaeology has been less concerned with the question of Bantu origins. In the north, investigations into the Mapungubwe complex continued, from 1935 to 1940 by Guy A. Gardner, in 1953 and 1954 by P. J. Coertze and H. F. Sentker, and from 1971 to 1979 by J. F. Eloff and A. Meyer. These investigations resulted in a good understanding of both the prehistoric sequence and the sociopolitical organization. In 1979, E. O. M. Hanisch uncovered at Schroda evidence of 9th-century trade in ivory, probably with east coast Arab traders.

Farther south, R. J. Mason in 1968 pioneered the use of aerial photographs in the exploration of widespread ruined stone structures in the southern part of the former province of Transvaal and KwaZulu-Natal, and T. M. O'C. Maggs in 1976 used the same device, supported by extensive excavation, to shed light on settlement types in the Free State and establish relationships with historically documented groups of the 14th to the 18th centuries. In Mozambique, in the 1970s and 1980s, T. da Cruz y Silva, J. M. Morais, and Paul Sinclair were tracing the spread of the Early Iron Age southward along the coast. Morais summarized this study in *The Early Farming Communities of Southern Mozambique* in 1988. Farther south, Maggs and his colleagues, in the 1980s, traced the southerly phases of Early Iron Age settlement and provided the first explanations for the absence of contemporaneous penetration of the southern *highveld*.

John Goodwin, in 1929, made a few brief comments on "Neolithic elements" in South Africa, and Louis Leakey, in 1931, much more emphatically recognized Neolithic culture in East Africa. But in both cases identification was on the basis of artifacts that would reflect the Neolithic in Europe or the Near East. No domestic plants or animals were associated, though Leakey assumed that stone bowls and pestles must reflect the presence of agriculture. Greater precision was given to the archaeological evidence by Mary Leakey's reports on Hyrax Hill and the Njoro River Cave in 1945 and 1950, respectively. Louis Leakey had excavated Late Stone Age industries with associated pottery at Nasera Rock (Apis Rock) in 1932, but details only appeared in print in 1977 with M. Mehlman's reexcavation of the site. The recognition of a Pastoral Neolithic phase really owes its origin to the combination of increasing fieldwork in the 1960s and 1970s in eastern Africa and the greater availability of radiocarbon dates. By the late 1960s, the ceramic content of the Early Iron Age was well known, and attention could be more effectively directed toward ceramic wares different from known Iron Age wares found with increasing frequency with Late Stone Age stone-tool assemblages. The equation "Stone Bowls equals Neolithic" actually persisted until the mid-1970s, when the emphasis was shifted to the presence or absence of domestic livestock. Intensification of field research in the 1970s produced a bewildering variety of pottery styles, not always clearly dated, which S. Wandibba, in 1977, assigned to six more-or-less well-defined groups. In the early 1980s, Peter Robertshaw attempted, for a limited area of southwestern Kenya, to shift the debate from concern with cultural content and succession to a more explicitly ecological approach, venturing reconstructions of economy, settlement patterns, and sociopolitical structure.

South of Kenya, there is less evidence for pre-Iron Age pastoralism. In 1968, Christopher Ehret had suggested the possibility on linguistic grounds, and in 1965, C. K. Cooke had used the distribution of representations of sheep in the rock art to suggest a route by which sheep might have been introduced into the south from East Africa. James K. Denbow and Edward N. Wilmsen, in 1986, suggested that pastoralists were present in the northern Kalahari 2,000 years ago, which, on current evidence would imply a pre-Iron Age occurrence. L. Webley, in 1993, reported sheep remains dated to 2,100 years ago in Namaqualand, and Christopher S. Henshilwood, in 1995, recorded sheep remains 200 kilometers east of Cape Town at 1,960 years ago. But the question of the precise origins of these southern African sheep, and the pottery generally associated with them, is far from solved.

Since the 1960s, the questions addressed in all periods of African prehistory are concerned less with the typology of artifacts and the sequence of archaeological "cultures" and more with the discovery of the social processes that sustained society.

BIBLIOGRAPHY
Clark, J. D. 1986. Archaeological retrospect 10. *Antiquity* 60: 179–188.
———. 1991. Louis Seymour Bazett Leakey, 1903–1972. *Proceedings of the British Academy* 59.
Dowson, T. A., and D. Lewis-Williams, eds. 1994. *Contested images: Diversity in southern African rock art research.* Johannesburg: Witwatersrand University Press.
Goodwin, A. J. H. 1935. A commentary on the history and present position of South African prehistory with full bibliography. *Bantu Studies* 9: 292–417.
Isaac, B., ed. 1989. *The archaeology of human origins: Papers by Glynn Issac.* Cambridge: Cambridge University Press.
Robertshaw, P., ed. 1990. *A history of African archaeology.* London and Portsmouth: James Currey Ltd. and Heinemann.

R. R. Inskeep

SEARCH FOR HUMAN ORIGINS IN AFRICA: A HISTORICAL NOTE

Over the past 90 years, an abundant variety of human fossils representing the various stages of mankind's development in Africa has been discovered. The description of the fossils and their interpretation is the subject of other entries in this volume. Here we shall only attempt to outline the sequence of their discovery and mention some of the more significant individuals involved in sorting through the geological and archaeological record for the origin of mankind.

The First Discoveries of Early Man

Before science's attention was drawn exclusively to the fossil-bearing deposits of Africa, other finds in Europe and the Far East significantly changed our view of human evolution and advanced our comprehension of mankind's physical development. This is a decidedly simplistic view, but one that will allow us to see the importance of Africa to humanity's beginnings.

The discoveries of the German Neanderthal remains in the 1850s, though resisted at first, spurred European scienctists to accept the idea, as well as the physical evidence, of an ancestral human who manufactured stone tools and hunted now extinct fauna during the distant period of the Ice Ages.

In 1891 at Trinil in Java, Eugene Dubois found the first remains of *Homo erectus,* a smaller-brained, primitive kind of man. Dubois called his find *Pithecanthropus erectus,* in the mistaken belief that he had discovered a "missing link" between humans and an apelike ancestor. These remains offered the first look at a fossil man palpably human, though distinctly different from the range of variation known to occur in more recent populations.

First Significant Finds in Africa

Though Victorian Europe had an inordinate interest in the economic potential of the African continent, only in the 20th century would its role in tracing the origins of early humans be demonstrated. By the end of the 19th century, the only importance attributed to the continent was Charles Darwin's intuitive suggestion that mankind first arose there. As the new century began, much of Africa, recently colonialized by the European powers, was a "frontier" community, with few of the facilities necessary to conduct serious research. Here and there, the occasional visiting scientific expedition explored the rich geological fabric of the continent for evidence of early man.

Little was known of the early history of mankind on the continent. The 1920s and the discovery and publication, by Raymond Dart, of the Taung infant skull, the first evidence of the australopithecines, changed that. After quite strong initial resistance in the academic community, paleoanthropology came to accept this and the other fossils found in breccia-filled caves (in the concretion formed from collapsed and fragmentary materials from walls and ceilings of caves) of South Africa as representative of early mankind—very different physically from the other early populations of *H. erectus* and *neanderthalensis* and very much more ancient.

The next discovery of equal significance was Louis and Mary Leakey's find of the late 1960s of *Homo habilis,* a relative of the australopithecines, equally ancient—nearly 2 million years old—but definitely a toolmaking hominid. As such, *H. habilis* fit neatly into mankind's physical heritage as an ancestor to *H. erectus,* as well as into our cultural heritage as the first acknowledged toolmaker.

Early Toolmakers?

Though in the 1950s Dart had attempted to attribute toolmaking abilities to the classic aus-

tralopithecines, based on his interpretations of oddly broken and altered bone and tooth fragments at Makapansgat, an *Australopithecus* locality in the former Transvaal province in the north of South Africa, there was little acceptance outside the popular press of the "osteodontokeratic" culture he proposed.

The idea of a osteodontokeratic culture, based on an early technology using slightly modified animal bone, teeth, and bits of horn, like E. J. Wayland's earlier idea of a "Kafuan" culture of simply flaked stone, has a certain attraction, explaining the earliest attempts to fashion tools. In the 1950s, an archaeologist well versed in sorting through the water-lain deposits of the Vaal Valley, C. van Riet Lowe went on to recognize a series of stages of the Kafuan. Eventually, geologist Walter W. Bishop demonstrated that many of Wayland's Kafuan artifacts were in fact the product of chance natural flaking created in water-lain deposits or the effect of gravity and that the stratigraphy of Wayland's Kafuan sequence was often misconstrued.

In the 1950s, C. K. Brain suggested that some stone artifacts from Sterkfontein, in South Africa, associated with *Australopithecus africanus* deposits, were similar to those found at the Tanzanian site Olduvai. It was therefore posited that Olduwan culture was attributable to the australopithecines. But in a discussion of the validity of the osteodontokeratic proposal, C. G. Sampson granted some appearance of consistent manufacture but stressed that the only evidence of true industrial activity, similar in its makeup to the Olduwan tradition of eastern Africa, occurs in South African caves where there is a coincident occurrence of a form of *Homo,* suggesting that they, rather than the australopithecines, were the toolmakers.

The debate over the earliest toolmakers, like that over the earliest evidence of humanity, is still ongoing, though it has clarified in recent years as investigators explore old localities and delve into new ones, thus adding fresh bits of information and fleshing out the general picture of human evolution.

These early discoveries in Africa and elsewhere outline the course of humanity's career on the continent and throughout the inhabited world.

Subsequent finds, though anticlimactic, should not be underrated since they have helped to expand our understanding of when these physical forms came about, how change in physical structure was integrated, and how these early members of mankind influenced cultural development, generally.

By 1924, when the Taung infant was discovered and identified as *Australopithecus africanus,* only three other African finds were known. The all-but-forgotten Boskop skull of dubious antiquity was discovered in South Africa in 1913 and published by S. H. Haughton in 1918. Though it has been variously attributed over the years, it is now considered an early representative of modern *H. sapiens.* It, along with OH1—the "Olduway Man" skeleton—found the following year at Olduvai Gorge in Tanzania by Hans Reck of the Berlin University, vividly suggested the potential of the Pleistocene deposits of the continent.

For some time, though, in the 1920s and 1930s, this "Olduway Man" was championed as a representative of the earliest kind of man who made stone tools of an intermediate Olduvai type and hunted now extinct animals found in the adjacent geological deposit. The Olduvai skeleton was subsequently shown to have been intrusive into the horizons in which it was found, and the extravagant claims made about its significance were discounted. Though its discussion, along with Louis Leakey's misreading of the age and significance of the Kanam mandible and a pair of skeletons from Kanjera, cast an early cloud on Leakey's career and professional judgment, he would ultimately spend many years working with his wife Mary at Olduvai Gorge. It was there that *H. habilis* and abundant evidence of a florescent Pleistocene environment would one day be discovered.

Meanwhile, mining operations during 1921 at a lead mine near Kabwe—then called Broken Hill—in central Zambia uncovered portions of a skull and skeleton of an archaic *H. sapiens.* This find, along with the Boskop skull, was considered to be an African representative of the Neanderthal race and was labeled *H. rhodesiensis,* "Rhodesian Man." Some flaked-stone tools were located along with the skeletal fragments, but not until the site was systematically examined in the late 1950s by J. Desmond Clark and representatives of the British Museum could these artifacts be accurately associated with a local Middle Stone Age culture. Nevertheless, "Broken Hill Man," as it was popularly called, as the first physical evidence of early man in the interior of the continent, offered an idea of the antiquity and technology of some early men in Africa.

Australopithecines Vindicated

More important was the equally accidental 1924 discovery, in lime-quarrying operations, of the Taung infant. This skull fragment brought to the fore not only a new form of early human, but also its champion, Raymond Dart, an Australian who had recently assumed the new post of professor of anatomy at Witwatersrand University. As in the later controversy over osteodontokeratic culture or his insistence that ancient travelers from the Near East were depicted in Bushman rock art, Dart displayed an active tendency to reach for conclusions not immediately warranted by the evidence. Given the immature individual represented by the Taung fragment and the case being made by Louis Leakey for his discoveries in East Africa for less radically different forms of early humanity, many foreign critics cautioned against an overeager introduction of the South African fossils into the human genealogy. Many wished to relegate this new material to some kind of fossil ape, possibly a chimpanzee. In 1929, having pried open the jaws of the Taung skull, Dart demonstrated that the teeth, though immature, displayed a pattern more usual to human dentition than to that of other apelike forms. Nevertheless, when Leakey published his landmark discussion of African prehistory "Adam's Ancestors" in 1934, he omitted all reference to *Australopithecus africanus.*

Given the quality of the evidence available at the time and a science still attempting to cope with the position of *Pithecanthropus* and to find a solution to the Piltdown quandary, posed by a fabricated "ape-man" found in England, many of these controversies should be viewed as a reflection of the academic culture of the time. It is fair to say that in the 1920s and 1930s, the presentation of the evidence, for all its precision, depended more on inspired speculation than reasoned analysis. Acceptance of scholarly opinions was still as much a function of social networks as of the value of new information bought into the debate.

As a result, for more than a quarter of a century, the status of the australopithecines languished, unaccepted by paleoanthropologists outside of South Africa. Finally their status was vindicated by the successful field investigations of Dart's colleague, Robert Broom, and his student, Philip Tobias. Throughout the 1920s and 1930s, Dart and more importantly Broom (who of the two was the more energetic field investigator) presented the case for the accepting the hominid status of the australopithecines. Broom returned to reinvestigate the initial find spot at Taung and eventually located an adult specimen of *Australopithecus africanus* at Sterkfontein. In 1938, at Kromdraai, a cave to which Broom was guided by a local schoolboy, he found the first adult specimens of the robust form of *Australopithecus*, originally termed *Paranthropus robustus.*

Like the Taung skull, an accidental discovery by a workman who brought it to the attention of someone who could appreciate its significance, the first fossils from Kromdraai were found in a schoolboy's pocket. Given this history of precarious discovery, one can only wonder at the numbers of fossils that found their way into the lime kilns or onto homeowners' mantles rather than to the laboratories in Johannesburg.

Finally, after World War II, Dart developed his idea of associating the osteodontokeratic culture with a type of *Australopithecus,* which he termed *A. prometheus* in the mistaken belief that there was concurrent evidence of fire making in the associated deposits. The controversies, side issues, and missteps aside, Dart and Broom had accomplished a great deal. In 1946 when Broom and his colleague G. W. H. Schepers published their definitive description of the evidence of the South African australopithecines, a general consensus was reached, and *Australopithecus* was finally accorded a niche in the ancestry of modern man and their discoverers a place in the history of science. As John A. J. Gowlett has pointed out, Broom, who died in 1951, though confirmed in his opinion, remained understandably bitter toward the British scientists who had rejected his and Dart's findings for so long.

Discoveries after World War II

NORTHERN AFRICA. The period following the Second World War also saw a new discovery of *Homo erectus* at Sidi Abderrahmen, by C. Arambourg, near Casablanca, Morocco, and another, during the field season of 1954 to 1955, at Tighenrif, Algeria. The former was found with an Acheulian assemblage, once again establishing evidence of a fairly developed form of *Homo* associated with a well-defined kind of stoneworking technology that facilitated the emergence of foraging humans from the African continent and throughout the greater part of the Old World.

OLDUVAI GORGE. Though Louis Leakey never accepted the conclusions of Dart and Broom that the australopithecines were more than a failed experiment of nature, a dead branch that evolved to extinction, his field investigations and syntheses in East Africa established the foundation for interpreting the prehistoric sequence. The main thrust of Leakey's later field investigations, along with the research of Mary Leakey, were at Olduvai Gorge in Tanzania. Located in a now quite desiccated area southeast of the Serengeti Plains, the site represents the deposits laid down in and along the fluctuating shores of a Pleistocene lake. The lake itself had a long, complicated hydrological history, as its outlets were from time to time blocked by volcanic debris from the nearby Ngorongoro Crater. Nevertheless, as a vital water source, the lake was attractive to a variety of game and, over time, bands of those who hunted. Like Kalambo Falls, to the southwest, Olduvai was a natural choke point that concentrated migrating herds responsive to the annual rainfall and vegetational patterns of equatorial Africa. Though a long sequence of occupations has been discovered and an 11-stage succession of the Olduwan pebble culture proposed, the main research interest has always been concentrated on the lowest portions of the deposit—Bed I, the location of interesting early forms of hominids and the type site of the Olduwan culture.

Leakey's research at the gorge began in earnest in the early 1950s when he obtained continuing financial support from Charles Boise. The

Kenyan-born son of British missionaries, Leakey had returned to East Africa with his second wife, Mary, in the early 1930s. His position as director of the Codrington Museum in Nairobi had given him ample access to the fossil resources of eastern Africa. Though actively involved in field research over the next two decades, his opportunities to exploit the research potential of many sites had been limited by the expense of mounting large-scale expeditions and a lack of the resources available to human paleontology in a small British colony. The financial support of Boise and later the National Geographic Society changed all that.

The Olduvai site was now visited almost annually, and the Leakeys uncovered a wide variety of interesting hominid and other mammalian fossils of Pleistocene age. In 1959, they began a period of truly significant discoveries. They uncovered evidence of a new form of robust *Australopithecus,* which they immediately termed a new genus, *Zinjanthropus,* and named *boisei* in honor of their sponsor. In keeping with a by now long-standing tradition, *Zinjanthropus* was at first represented as a toolmaker. This claim was subsequently replaced with the first definite association of a fossil hominid with toolmaking abilities—*H. habilis.*

The development of dating associated volcanic deposits through the potassium-argon method allowed the age of these very ancient contexts to be estimated for the first time. They were dated to a time easily preceding the earliest of Europe's glacial periods. The history of humanity was extended to a time predating the Pleistocene Ice Ages.

OMO AND EAST TURKANA. Since Louis Leakey's pioneering work at Olduvai in the 1950s and 1960s, much attention has been paid to investigation of "early man," the study not only of the earliest physical forms of humanity but of the culture and activities of the earliest hominids. The early 1960s saw attention pass to the fossil beds of the Omo Valley, a tributary valley north of Lake Turkana between Kenya and Ethiopia. Unlike the somewhat solitary exercises of an earlier generation of Africanist archaeologists, these endeavors, funded by major institutions, were intentionally multidisciplinary, involving a variety of investigators from several different countries. One result was the opportunity to explore beyond the primary find spot in order to describe the context of the early humans' immediate surroundings and to reveal how early humans used the resources found around and between their camps. As paleoanthropology came to recognize the complexities of human physical evolution, archaeology explored the range of behaviors that defined these early people.

The French and American groups led by F. C. Clark and Yves Coppens explored fossil beds deemed to be between 1 and 3 million years old and uncovered stone artifacts and numerous remains of *A. africanus, A. boisei, H. habilis,* and *H. erectus,* thereby extending both the geographical and temporal range of these types. In 1969, working in the Lake Turkana vicinity, Richard F. Leakey discovered a complete skeleton of *A. robustus,* extending its range from the the former Transvaal province to southern Ethiopia.

These and subsequent expeditions uncovered a great many dated examples of the fossil hominids while creating a new debate over their place in the human genealogy. In its simplest form, the argument revolves around questions first stated some time earlier: Were australopithecines the direct ancestors of more modern forms of man or had they separated from the human line at some distant point in the past and become extinct without further contributing to the evolution of humanity?

The answers to these questions depended on the evaluation of adequately dated fossils excavated under controlled conditions and on a scientific community united in its description and interpretation of the signs of humanity associated with the these fossilized bits of the past. The conditions for working in Africa can be extreme. Dart and his colleagues were required to search quarry debris reduced by mining processes by using explosives. Louis and Mary Leakey worked for many years on the deposits at Olduvai Gorge, an extremely barren region, without adequate financial support, a situation experienced by many of an older generation of Africanists. Even though outside interest has been stimulated in paleoanthropology and as J. Reader suggests the search shifted from an apocryphal "missing link" to the "oldest man," the opportunities for such research are still limited.

For the past few decades, scientific interest has been directed to the fossil beds of the Omo River and the terraces east of Lake Turkana. These are difficult places in which to work, beset with periodic warfare and lawlessness, as well as a barren environment requiring a degree of logistical support unavailable to earlier investigators. Nevertheless, the interdisciplinary efforts headed by Donald Johanson, in southern Ethiopia, and Richard F. Leakey, in East Turkana, have dramatically increased the numbers of fossil specimens.

In the early 1970s, Richard Leakey's activities in East Turkana uncovered a mass of hominid and other mammalian fossils. In the near vicinity of a tool-bearing locality, estimated be nearly 2.5 million years old, his party located a distorted cranium of a robust australopithecine of the *Zinjanthropus* type and a second skull—ER 3733—which Leakey suggested was an early form of *H. erectus,* living in eastern Africa and manufacturing tools nearly 2 million years before its first appearance in Java or China. A third hominid skull—1470—found during work in East Turkana and meticulously reconstructed from hundreds of pieces extracted from the lakeshore deposit, launched a vigorous debate about its designation as *Homo,* as Leakey posited, or *Australopithecus,* as the anatomist Alan Walker and others suggested. This larger-brained hominid skull dated to nearly 2.5 million years ago. Ultimately, the crosscorrelation of dated fossils of pigs from across the continent suggested that the 1470 skull was somewhat younger than first supposed—in the vicinity of 1.8 million years old—but still quite ancient. The research, though, established that both *Homo* and *Australopithecus* and a kind of toolmaking *H. erectus* were near contemporaries and living in the vicinity of Lake Turkana nearly 2 million years ago.

AFAR TRIANGLE. In the mid- to late 1970s, Johanson, as a serious diversion from his own research in the Omo Valley, began an important series of expeditions to the Hadar River Valley in the Afar region of northeastern Ethiopia. The Afar Depression has many similarities to other significant fossil-producing areas. In past times,

it acted as an internal catchment forming lakes and concentrating resources attractive to human communities. As a result, the consolidated sediments offered a signal opportunity to locate both the living surfaces of early man—lakeshore camps—as well as fossilized physical remains.

Johanson's first expedition, though significant in its findings, led to some extravagant claims based on scant physical evidence. Though the first expedition did not necessarily support his claims of having found the "oldest man" walking, eating meat, and using tools within organized societies 3 to 4 million years ago, subsequent work did offer an abundance of interesting and significant fossils.

Of the new fossils found in the Afar Depression, "Lucy," the relatively complete skeleton of a female, attributed, after much controversy, to a new species *Australopithecus afarensis,* has achieved a popular renown. Equally important was the find in another locality of 13 adults and juveniles of the same species. Whimsically named the "First Family" by their discoverers, these remains have the distinction of representing the first discovery of what might be termed a *population*—a group of obviously contemporary and associated individuals. Besides *A. afarensis,* Johanson and his colleagues found specimens identifiable as an *A. africanus,* the robust *Australopithecus,* and a 3-million-year-old representative of *Homo.* The field research, though interrupted by civil disturbances in Ethiopia, was exceedingly productive, uncovering more than 250 hominid fossils.

LAETOLI. At the same time, Mary Leakey and her son, Philip, were uncovering new fossil material at Laetoli, Tanzania. Johanson thought the new fossils resembled *A. afarensis.* Mary Leakey, Philip Tobias, and others thought they were more likely a kind of *Homo.*

In 1925, Raymond Dart had posited the australopithecines as erect walkers. He had no evidence of this, but he was engaged in a long-standing debate centered on whether the earliest forms of humanity first developed the capacity to walk upright and, as a consequence, adapted in ways requiring larger brains, or whether the development of large brains preceded the ability to free the hands, enhancing the capacities of a upright hominid. Important evidence of early bipedalism was discovered by the associates of Mary Leakey at Laetoli in the late 1970s. Through the fortunate occurrence of ash falls from a nearby volcano upon the soft muddy surfaces near the Laetoli water hole, a series of foot trails remained. As a result, eight sets of tracks made by hominids, living more than 3.6 million years ago, were preserved. In the welter of animal tracks making their way down to the lakeshore may be clearly seen the imprint of an upright, bipedal gait similar to that of modern man.

The Search Continues

Whether the Laetoli footprints were left by an early *Homo* or a representative of the australopithecines is less important than the realization that 3.5 million years ago there were individuals, with physical attributes and a rudimentary foraging lifeway, drawn to the shore of this lake and identifiable as the precursors of modern humans.

The history of palaeoanthropology in Africa is replete with colorful tales of the eccentricities of the searchers—Dart's willingness to demonstrate brachiation by swinging over the heads of undergraduates, Broom's habit of surveying the African bush in the nude, and Louis Leakey's illnesses at the time of important discoveries by his associates or the playful tossing of elephant dung, which led to the discovery of the first footprints at Laetoli. These many anecdotes lend color to, but do not detract from, the quality of the evidence found or the conclusions reached.

Some time in the past, humans began to use tools, and identifying these early tools is a difficult endeavor. As one proceeds back through the archaeological record, tools become more primitive and are more difficult to distinguish from randomly procured and used objects. By the same token, when we push back the curtain of time to uncover the oldest kinds of mankind, we also draw closer to the point where the earliest human most resembles its nearest "nonhuman" relative. As a result, we reach a point where convenient differentiation between the various lineages of hominids is both difficult and the cause of new debate.

BIBLIOGRAPHY

Gowlett, J. A. J. 1990. Archaeological studies of human origins and early prehistory in Africa. In *A history of African archaeology,* ed. P. Robertshaw, 13–38. London and Portsmouth: James Currey Ltd. and Heinemann.

Johanson, D., and M. Edey. 1981. *Lucy: The beginnings of mankind.* New York: Simon and Schuster.

Leakey, R. F., and R. Lewin. 1992. *Origins reconsidered: In search of what makes us human.* New York: Doubleday.

Lewin, R. 1987. *Bones of contention: Controversies in the search for human origins.* New York: Simon and Schuster.

Reader, J. 1988. *Missing links: The hunt for earliest man.* London: Penguin Books.

Sampson, C. G. 1974. *The Stone Age archaeology of southern Africa.* New York: Academic Press.

Joseph O. Vogel

LANGUAGE STUDIES IN AFRICA

Prehistorians of Africa who use linguistics to interpret archaeological data are generally dependent on the work of J. H. Greenberg. It is certainly true that his publications represent a sort of fulcrum of the century's research and a truly continental synthesis. However, recent research on the principal language phyla (groups of languages related more remotely than those of a family of stock) of Africa has modified his conclusions, in some cases quite dramatically. This article presents a historical overview of the research that led to Greenberg's results and summarizes developments since the 1960s. The phylum names he established are used to simplify the presentation.

Changing Methodologies in the Genetic Classification of African Languages

To understand the conclusions of individual researchers, some knowledge of their methods is essential. Early scholars tended to rely on simply identifying words that seemed alike and were

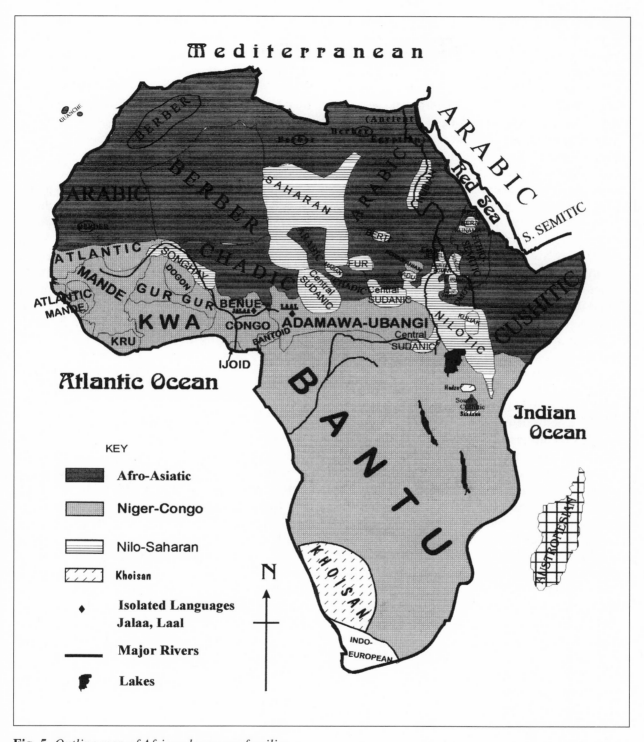

Fig. 5 *Outline map of African language families*

generally unable to distinguish borrowed words from basic vocabulary. In his studies, Greenberg used mass-comparison, the alignment of compa- rable lexical and grammatical elements in numbers thought to be convincing. In the 1960s, however, lexico-statistics was a more common technique to assign individual languages to families or phyla. Lexico-statistics proposed to establish the relationship between languages through counting cognates on a standard 100-word list, often known as a *Swadesh list*. With its sister-discipline, glotto-chronology, which converted these cognate percentages into estimates of historical time depth, lexico-statistics seemed to provide a scientific, quantifiable methodology for developing genetic classifications.

Although lexico-statistics has not been entirely discarded, linguists now add so many restrictions and qualifications as to limit its usefulness. Glotto-chronology has almost entirely disappeared, at least in Africa. The tighter correspondences that are available between lexico-statistics and archaeological data in the Pacific have highlighted the problems of uneven decay in particular items on the Swadesh list.

Although the situation at present is far from a consensus, most scholars prefer some version of "shared innovations" to determine subgroupings. Once borrowed phenomena have been eliminated, shared lexical, phonological, or morphological elements can be used to define subgroups. Even this technique is not easy to apply as such innovations often appear to crosscut one another.

More promising for the prehistorian is the technique pioneered by Christopher Ehret in the 1960s, the cross-comparison of words of cultural significance. N. Skinner has used this technique to reconstruct names for mammals in Chadic and Afro-Asiatic languages to situate their possible centers of origin. The hypothesis is similar to that adopted by scholars of Indo-European: the reconstruction of specific lexical items to various levels of protolanguage is taken as evidence that speakers of that language had the item in their cultural repertoire. Similarly, loanwords between subgroups or phyla can be taken as evidence for contact between speakers of the languages in question.

Negative evidence, the inability to reconstruct particular lexical sets, can also be used for historical purposes. For example, if no words associated with cultivation can be securely reconstructed, we can infer that the primary divisions of the phylum were in the preagricultural phase.

The classic problem of the origin and expansion of the Bantu was one of the earliest arenas

in which archaeologists, prehistorians, and linguists attempted to reconcile their findings. The fruitless debates that followed M. Guthrie's wayward interpretations of his data and consequent disagreement with Greenberg were poor prehistory but acted to throw the area of methodology into sharp relief. Syntheses such as those of L. Bouquiaux and J. T. Vansina have presented the linguistics-archaeology interface in a more focused way, but the debate continues. Others, for example John Sutton, Kay Williamson, and Roger Blench, have attempted to mesh archaeological and linguistic data in the reconstruction of broader aspects of African prehistory.

The most recent trend has been the exploration of links between genetic findings, especially mitochondrial DNA, and linguistic groupings. The agenda for this "emerging synthesis" has been set out on a global basis by Colin Renfrew and for Africa by L. P. Excoffier, B. Sanchez-Mazas, A. Simon, and C. and A. Langaney and by L. Cavalli-Sforza, P. Menozzi, and A. Piazza.

The Language Phyla of Africa

Figure 5 shows the present-day distribution of the language families of Africa. It is essentially a "homeland" map—that is, it shows languages in their core areas. Pastoralists with long-distance grazing orbits, such as the Fulɓe, Tamachek, or Teda, have undergone major simplification. Similarly, a family such as Afro-Asiatic with an extinct branch (Ancient Egyptian) and major regions of distribution outside Africa inevitably appear foreshortened.

Niger-Congo

Niger-Congo is the most widespread of Africa's language phyla and includes the majority of its languages—in excess of 1,500. The concept of Niger-Congo has its roots in D. Westermann's *Sudan-Sprachen,* and many of the families recognized today were first established there. Westermann was the first to illustrate the strong links between the Bantu languages and those spoken in West Africa, and later scholars have generally accepted his demonstrations. Greenberg's original analysis of Niger-Congo set up six coordinate branches:

West Atlantic (Fulfulde, Wolof, Temne, etc.)
Mande (Bambara, Vai, Kpelle, Busa, etc.)
Gur (Dogon, Mossi, Dagari, Bariba, etc.)
Kwa (Kru, Ewe, Akan, Yoruba, Igbo, Ijo, etc.)
Benue-Congo (Kamberi, Birom, Jukun, Efik, and Bantu)
Adamawa-Eastern (Mumuye, Chamba, Gbaya, Zande, Banda, etc.)

In the same volume, Greenberg also argued the case for including the Kordofanian languages, renaming the phylum *Niger-Kordofanian*. This name has not been retained, and the whole phylum, including Kordofanian, is now called *Niger-Congo*. Historically speaking, it is unlikely that a language family would have such a large number of coordinate branches, implying that a single

Table 1 *Subclassifications of the Niger-Congo language family*

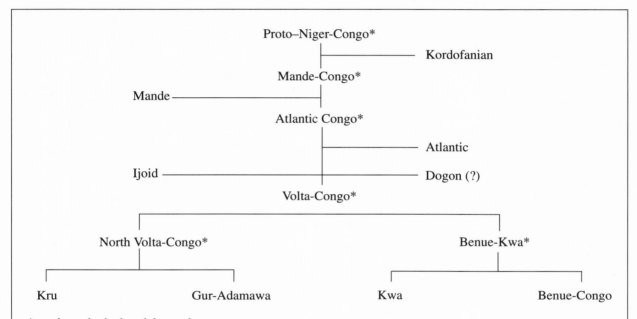

* = a hypothetical nodal protolanguage

Notes:

1. Greenberg included Kadugli (Tumtum) in the Kordofanian languages, but it is now regarded as Nilo-Saharan.
2. Dogon is distinct from Gur, and its position remains uncertain.

In comparison with Greenberg, the most important developments are:

1. Mande is the second principal division of Niger-Congo, confirming its status as the most separate of the West African branches.
2. Atlantic (formerly West Atlantic) has been promoted to an almost comparable level of distinctiveness.
3. Ijoid (originally part of Greenberg's Kwa) has been expanded to include the divergent Defaka and assigned to a separate branch.

4. Bennett and Sterk first proposed in 1977 that Gur, Adamawa, and Kru be treated as a coherent unit, which they called *North-Central Niger-Congo*. Although the lexical evidence is not conclusive for this grouping, the close relationship between Gur and Adamawa is generally accepted.
5. The terms *Kwa* and *Benue-Congo* have been retained, but their application has been radically revised. Kru and Ijo have been expelled from Kwa, and many of the language branches of western Nigeria, in particular, Yoruba, Nupe, Idoma, Edo, and Igbo, have been transferred to Benue-Congo.
6. Benue-Congo has consequently taken on a new appearance and now occupies virtually the whole of present-day southern Nigeria (see table 2).

Table 2 *Subclassifications of the Benue-Congo language family showing the place of Bantu according to Blench*

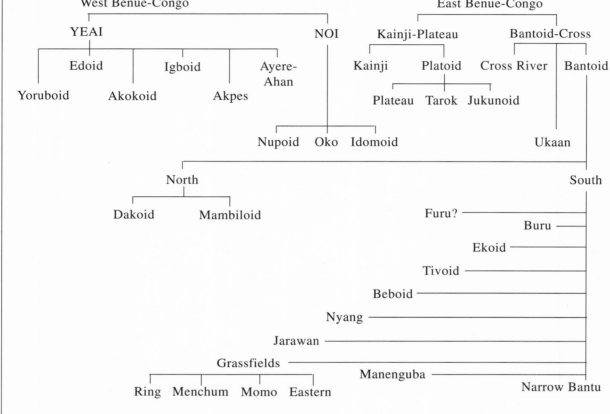

Notes: The main features of this new classification are:

1. A number of "remnant" languages existing in Nigeria, such as Ukaan-Akpes and Oko, have been recognized as distinct branches of Benue-Congo.
2. The distinction between East and West Benue-Congo is a practical reversal to Greenberg's original scheme. East Benue-Congo corresponds to his original Benue-Congo and West Benue-Congo to his Eastern Kwa (excluding Ijo).
3. Bantu is given clear definition and a relationship to the large number of Bantu-like languages, here called *Bantoid*.

protolanguage split into six distinct groups at one time. P. R. Bennett and J. P. Sterk undertook a complete revision of the internal structure of Niger-Congo to suggest the sequence of language splits. Although not all their suggestions have been retained, current models reflect their innovative approach. Table 1 shows the subclassifications of Niger-Congo developed from Kay Williamson's work on the basis of a consensus among the contributing linguists. Table 2 shows the further subclassification of Benue-Congo.

Nilo-Saharan

Although Nilo-Saharan comprises only a relatively low number of languages, it is generally

Table 3 *Subgroupings of the Nilo-Saharan language family according to Bender*

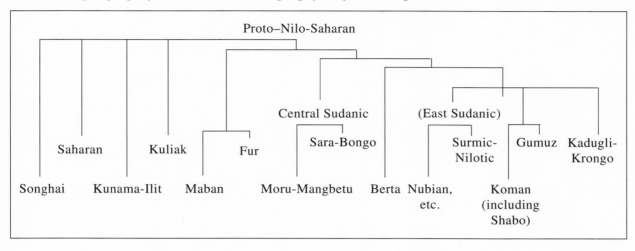

agreed that, with the exception of Khoisan, it is the most internally diversified of the African language phyla. Before Greenberg's work, the classification of many of the languages of Sudan and adjacent regions of central Africa was in doubt. The major handbook of A. N. Tucker and M. A. Bryan, published in 1956, simply left many speech forms in isolated groups. Nilo-Saharan was first characterized by Greenberg, and recent work by M. L. Bender and Ehret has confirmed Greenberg's basic hypothesis as to its overall unity. Greenberg treated Nilo-Saharan as having six coordinate branches:

Songhai
Saharan
Maban
Fur
Chari-Nile
Koman

Many more languages have been described since Greenberg's work, and the exact membership of the phylum is still in doubt. Table 3 shows the subgroupings of Nilo-Saharan languages according to Bender.

The membership of Kadu (also known as *Kadugli-Krongo),* Kuliak, and Shabo in the Nilo-Saharan language phylum is not accepted by all researchers. Moreover, the relationship between the members is still uncertain, and no overall "tree" is yet agreed upon by scholars.

Afro-Asiatic

Afro-Asiatic (also known as *Hamito-Semitic, Afrasian,* and *Lislakh)* is almost certainly the earliest African language phylum to be the subject of genetic hypotheses. The kinship of Hebrew, Arabic, and Aramaic was recognized as early as the 1530s, and Hiob Ludolf pointed out the affinity of Ethiosemitic with the Near Eastern languages in 1702. The name *Semitic* was proposed in 1781 by Ludwig von Schlözer. Berber and some of the Chadic languages, notably Hausa, were added during the course of the 19th century. The earliest version of Afro-Asiatic as presently understood probably appears in the work of F. Max Müller, who linked Egyptian, Semitic, Berber, Cushitic, and Hausa, the only known Chadic language at the time.

Greenberg's work "dethroned" Semitic from its formerly central position and emphasized its relations with the languages of Black Africa. He proposed the term *Afro-Asiatic* to replace the term *Hamito-Semitic* with its slightly bizarre, racist undertone. His original classification included five coordinate branches:

Semitic
Berber
Ancient Egyptian
Cushitic
Chad(ic)

The most significant development since Greenberg's work has been the establishment of

HISTORIES OF RESEARCH

96HISTORIES OF RESEARCH

Table 4 *Internal classifications of the Afro-Asiatic language family according to Fleming*

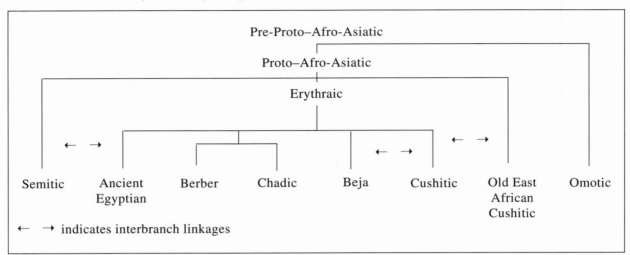

Table 5 *Proposed revision of the Afro-Asiatic language-family classification*

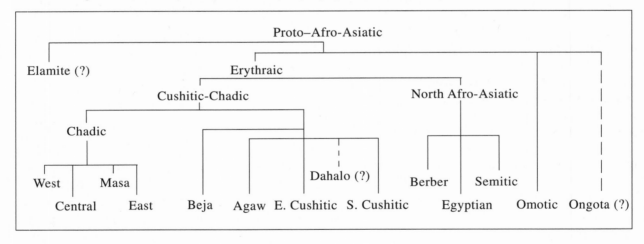

a sixth branch of the Afro-Asiatic languages: Omotic, a family confined to Ethiopia and consisting of little-known languages such as Nao, Ghimira, Hamar, and Dizi. There has also been considerable discussion about whether Cushitic really constitutes a family, and Beja, Ethiopian Cushitic, and Southern Cushitic are now often treated as distinct branches.

More recently, V. Blazek has proposed that Elamite, an extinct language of the ancient Near East, either constitutes a seventh branch of Afro-Asiatic or is a coordinate with it. Elamite is usually classified with Dravidian, spoken in southern India, but does show clear cognates with Afro-Asiatic.

The structure of Afro-Asiatic languages proposed by H. C. Fleming is shown in table 4.

Afro-Asiatic has been the subject of a number of overviews. Historically, the most important of these were done by M. Cohen and I. M. Diakonoff. Most recently, Christopher Ehret has proposed both reconstructions and an internal structure for Afro-Asiatic. His schema is fairly similar to the models proposed formally or informally by other researchers. Table 5 shows a composite view of Afro-Asiatic incorporating my own views and some recent proposals concerning Elamite and Ongota.

The composite in table 5 adopts the similar names for nodes (points from which subsidiary branches depend) proposed by Ehret, Erythraic and North Afro-Asiatic. Ehret does not claim a special relation between Cushitic and Chadic but does have Chadic branching off directly after Cushitic. A radically different view is taken in the *Hamito-Semitic Etymological Dictionary* by

Table 6 *Khoisan speech forms*

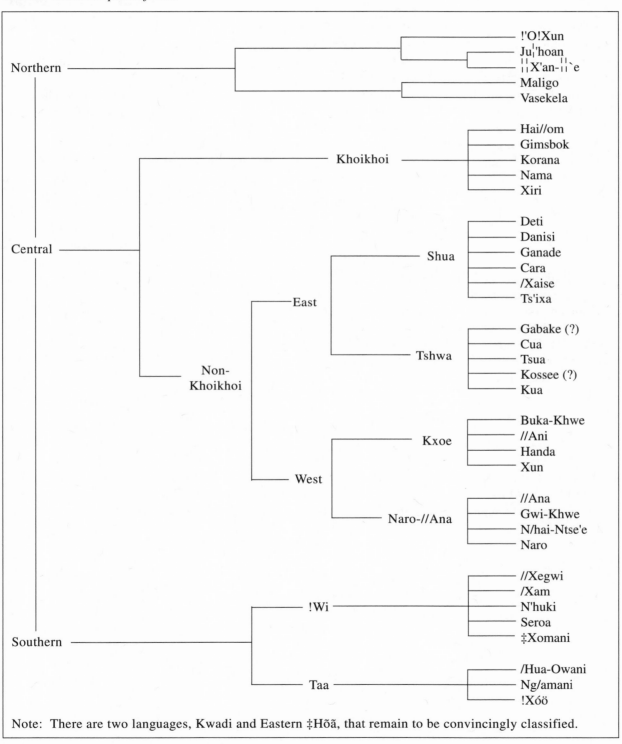

Note: There are two languages, Kwadi and Eastern ‡Hõã, that remain to be convincingly classified.

V. Orel and O. Stolbova, who consider that Cushitic and Omotic are not genetic groupings at all but an ancient *Sprachbund* (unrelated languages in a region).

Khoisan

Khoisan languages are primarily defined by a phonological feature, clicks, rather than by an evident common lexicon. Although the Khoisan languages, properly speaking, are confined to southern Africa, two isolates, Hadza and Sandawe in Tanzania, also have clicks. Various authors have advanced arguments for links between all the Khoisan languages, but no one schema is generally accepted. Research into Khoisan began in the mid-19th century with the work of Wilhelm and Dorothea Bleek, who also advanced the hypothesis of the unity of all Khoisan languages. Most recent classifications follow the extended study of O. Köhler who proposed a series of isoglosses (divisions separating different languages) linking the major Khoisan families.

The classification and, indeed, the inventory of Khoisan speech forms remain in doubt. One recently published classification was done by J. E. and B. F. Grimes. This has been combined and corrected in consultation with Rainer Vossen to produce the tree shown in table 6.

Isolated Languages

The existence and classification of language isolates in Africa remain controversial. Table 7 shows some of the languages proposed as isolates.

In addition, Malagasy should be mentioned, since it is isolated on the African continent. Malagasy is an Austronesian language, brought to East Africa from insular Southeast Asia less than 2,000 years ago.

Macrophylum Proposals and External Links for African Language Phyla

More speculative proposals have recently been advanced for "deep-level" relationships of African language phyla.

THE LOST LANGUAGE OF THE PYGMIES. The question of the origin of the Pygmies of the African rain forest and their relative antiquity has remained controversial. The Pygmies appear to be the ancient inhabitants of the forest, partly displaced by the incoming Bantu, but they speak no distinctive languages comparable to Khoisan. S. Bahuchet has recently presented a challenging view of the history of the Pygmy populations, in particular the Aka and the Baka. Despite speaking languages of quite different genetic affiliation, these groups prove to have a number of words in common, concerned especially with food gathering in the rain forest. If Bahuchet is right, then this vocabulary constitutes a trace of the lost language of the Pygmies.

AFRO-ASIATIC AND PROPOSALS FOR EXTRA-AFRICAN LINKS. Afro-Asiatic is the African language phylum that has been most commonly proposed as being related to the phyla of Eurasia. Afro-Asiatic is frequently connected to Indo-European and more broadly to Nostratic, a broad and variable grouping including most of the major language phyla of Eurasia. M. Ruhlen provides a useful summary of these debates in *A Guide to the World's Languages*.

Table 7 *African language isolates*

Language Name	Location	Source	Comments
Jalaa (=CuN Tuum)	Nigeria	Kleinwillinghöfer (1996)	
Hadza	Tanzania	Elderkin (1983)	Perhaps Khoisan
Kujarke	Sudan	Doornbos and Bender (1983)	Perhaps Chadic
Laal	Chad	Boyeldieu (n.d.)	
Ongota	Ethiopia	Fleming et al. (1992)	
Oropom	Uganda	Wilson (1970)	Existence unconfirmed
Sandawe	Tanzania	Elderkin (1983)	Perhaps Khoisan

Table 8 *Niger-Saharan language-family classifications*

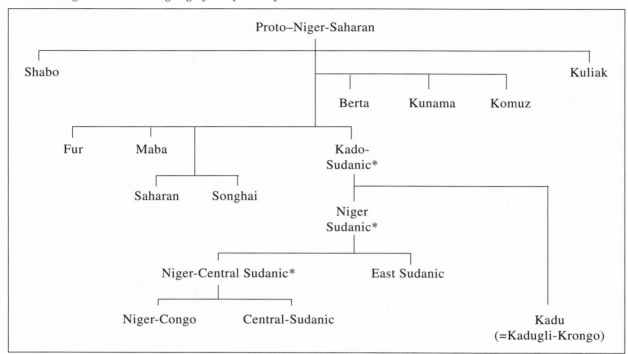

NIGER-SAHARAN. Although Greenberg considered Nilo-Saharan to be a wholly distinct phylum, several scholars have put forth evidence for its close link with Niger-Congo. A. Gregersen originally proposed a Kongo-Saharan superfamily, and Roger Blench has presented a detailed case for a unification of Nilo-Saharan and Niger-Congo, suggesting that Niger-Congo is most closely related to the central Sudanic languages. The proposed macrophylum would be named *Niger-Saharan,* of which Niger-Congo would then become one branch. A minimal "tree" of Niger-Saharan in provided in table 8.

———~~~~~~~~———

Substantial advances have been made in both the genetic classification and characterization of African language phyla since the 1960s. A problematic aspect of much of this work for prehistorians has always been the fluidity of linguists' classifications. The availability of improved data has historically been responsible for changes in both the internal classification and external relations of such families. Prehistorians can therefore legitimately question linguists concerning the reliability of their results. If there have been such major revisions since the 1960s, will not future revisions render present interpretations void?

The only realistic response that can be made is that although further changes may well occur, they are more likely to be matters of detail rather than broad continent-spanning revisions. It is more practical for prehistorians to work with smaller-scale groupings. Every phylum is divided into manageable units, most of which are commonly accepted by the linguistic community. Examples of these would be Mande, Bantu, Nilotic, Omotic, and Central Khoisan. Although a satisfactory model of the expansion of these families is yet to be worked out, they are neither so ancient nor so vast that such a task is, in principle, unachievable.

Macrophylum hypotheses are stimulating. They extend debate on broad connections and similarities between languages at a very great time depth. However, at a certain level, they are only linguistic hypotheses, and their conclusions cannot be easily extended to other disciplines. The results of this type of inquiry are much less well founded than the low-level reconstructions and classifications. They are more tools to help linguists think than representations of the past.

The question of the genetic classification of the language phyla of the world, from being a marginal study outside mainstream linguistics, has again begun to command considerable attention from both professional linguists and researchers in related disciplines. In Africa, where the density of archaeological sites of all periods remains low, linguistics has been a fruitful source of both testable hypotheses and explanatory models. The potential for correlation with genetics, notably mitochondrial DNA, combined with the expansion of field data and the shaking off of underlying currents of racial theories formerly attached to this type of speculation, has been important in returning credibility to this area.

BIBLIOGRAPHY

Bender, M. L. 1975. *Omotic: A new Afroasiatic language family.* Carbondale: University Museum, Southern Illinois University.

———, ed. 1983. *Nilo-Saharan language studies.* East Lansing: Michigan State University Press.

———, ed. 1991. *Proceedings of the Fourth Nilo-Saharan conference, Bayreuth, 1989.* Hamburg: Helmut Buske Verlag.

Bendor, S. J., ed. 1989. *The Niger-Congo languages.* Lanham: University Press of America.

Blench, R. M. 1993. Recent developments in African language classification and their implications for prehistory. In *The archaeology of Africa: Food, metals and towns,* eds. T. Shaw, P. Sinclair, B. Andah, and A. Okpoko, 126–138. London: Routledge.

Diakonoff, I. M. 1988. *Afrasian languages.* Moscow: Nauka.

Ehret, C. 1993. Nilo-Saharans and the Saharo-Sudanese Neolithic. In *The archaeology of Africa: Food, metals and towns,* eds. T. Shaw, P. Sinclair, B. Andah, and A. Okpoko, 104–125. London: Routledge.

Ehret, C., and M. Posnansky, eds. 1982. *The archaeological and linguistic reconstruction of African history.* Berkeley: University of California Press.

Fleming, H. C. 1983. Chadic external relations. In *Studies in Chadic and Afroasiatic linguistics,* eds. E. Wolff and H. Meyer-Bahlburg, 17–31. Hamburg: Helmut Buske.

Greenberg, J. H. 1963. *The languages of Africa.* The Hague: Published for Indiana University by Mouton.

Grimes, J. E., and B. F. Grimes. 1993. *Ethnologue language family index.* Dallas: SIL.

Guthrie, M. 1967-1971. *Comparative Bantu.* 4 vols. Farnborough: Gregg International Publishers.

Köhler, O. 1981. Les langues Khoisan. In *Les langues de l'Afrique subsaharienne,* ed. G. Manessy, 455–615. Paris: CNRS.

Nicolai, R., and F. Rottland, eds. 1996. *Proceedings of the Fifth Nilo-Saharan Linguistics Colloquium, Nice, 1992.* Köln: Rudiger Köppe.

Orel, V., and O. Stolbova. 1995. *Hamito-Semitic etymological dictionary.* Leiden: Brill.

Perrot, J., ed. 1988. *Les langues chamito-sémitiques.* Vol. 3 of *Les langues dans le monde ancien et moderne.* Paris: CNRS.

Ruhlen, M. 1991. *Classification.* Vol. 1 of *A guide to the world's languages.* London: Edwin Arnold.

Skinner, N. 1984. Afroasiatic vocabulary: Evidence for some culturally important items. *Africana Marburgensia,* Special Issue.

Tucker, A. N., and M. A. Bryan. 1956. *The non-Bantu languages of north-eastern Africa.* Vol. 3 of *Handbook of African languages.* London: IAI.

Westermann, D. 1927. *Die Westlichen Sudansprachen und ihre Beziehungen zum Bantu.* Berlin: De Gruyter, Berlin.

Williamson, K. 1989. Linguistic evidence for the prehistory of the Niger Delta. In *The early history of the Niger Delta,* eds. E. J. Alagoa, N. Anozie, and N. Nzewunwa, 65–119. Hamburg: Helmut Buske Verlag.

Roger Blench

TECHNOLOGY

STONEWORKING TECHNOLOGY

Making and using stone tools is one of the hallmarks of the emergence of humanity in Africa, and this technology has served various needs for strong, sharp, and durable tools for most of African history. Only within the last few millennia have metal technologies competed with stone-based technology in the Old World. The replacement of stone technologies with metal technologies is an even more recent development in sub-Saharan Africa. Stone tools were so important in the lifeways of preindustrial man that there is hardly an instance worldwide in which broken, used, and discarded stone tools and debris from their manufacture do not play a significant role in the cultural and historical demarcation and delineation of extinct societies. Archaeologists often categorize major segments of prehistory with terms such as *Paleolithic, Mesolithic,* and *Neolithic,* which suggest the important role of stone tools and stone-toolmaking.

Reports on preindustrial sites in sub-Saharan Africa (as elsewhere) usually contain sizable discussions of stone tools and manufacturing debris because of their prominence as an artifact category. Regional chronologies are very dependent on stone tools as indices of cultural developments. Kenneth P. Oakley's small book, *Man the Tool-maker,* provided a readable, popular introduction to the subject of early stone technology, but since its publication in 1959, archaeologists have refined regional chronologies considerably and have found several new ways to extract information on the manufacture and use of stone tools.

New understanding of traditional stone-tool technologies has been gained through ethnographic examination of living toolmakers in remote areas of Africa, South America, and Australia. With the translation into English of S. A. Semenov's *Prehistoric Technology* in 1964, archaeologists began to recognize that experimental replication, microscopic analysis of wear patterns, and chemical analysis of residues could provide important new information on methods of manufacture and uses of stone tools in prehistoric lifeways.

In spite of the importance of stone tools in prehistoric lifeways and their longevity in human history, the technology for their production and maintenance is fairly simple and has changed relatively little in the several thousand millennia since the invention of the first stone tools.

Principles of Stone Toolmaking

Manufacture of a stone tool is strictly a reduction technology, which involves shaping the object through the removal of unwanted material from a parent lithic (stone) source either by flaking or abrasion or some combination of these two techniques. Some stone tools, containers, and ornaments are simply pecked into shape by using a hard hammer stone to pulverize and remove grains from the parent rock carefully. Other procedures, such as incising, smoothing, drilling, and polishing sometimes employed to finish or re-

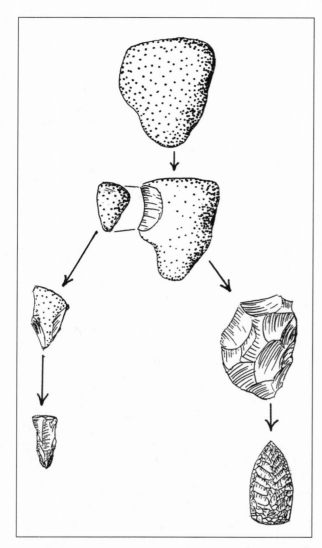

Fig. 6 *Reduction sequence*

rock's surface. When this point is near the intersection of two (or more) of the stone's facets whose surfaces form an acute angle, the fracture cone will attenuate along the surface and appear as a dish-shaped divot or flake scar. The stone thus removed is a flake. Shaping begins with strategic removal of the first flake and proceeds through planned, sequential removal of additional flakes.

Stones that have the characteristic of conchoidal fracture include siliceous solids like natural glass (obsidian) and fine-grained cryptocrystallines like flint or chert. They share several physical properties. They are homogeneous, meaning that internal structure varies little and lacks internal flaws, inclusions, or cracks that would affect the predictability of conchoidal fracture. They are brittle, meaning that they break relatively easily when a sudden force is applied. And, they are elastic, meaning that, if not deformed to the breaking point, the material will return to its original shape. When flint knappers speak of a high-quality material, they are referring to a combination of these properties that allows for highly predictable but relatively easy flaking. Incidentally, flint knappers have found that these properties can sometimes be altered somewhat through pretreatment such as soaking the raw material in water or heating it.

After some experimentation with strike angles and the sequencing of blows, anyone can produce a simple, usable tool from rock with the above characteristics using another stone as a percussor. However, to become an expert flint knapper requires much practice to acquire requisite hand-eye coordination and some considerable knowledge of flaking techniques and characteristics of parent materials. The experienced knapper also employs a mental recipe of steps to produce a particular type of object. This pattern of steps (sometimes called a *reductive strategy*) is to some extent determined by the nature of the reduction involved, but the knapper can exercise options along the way.

Options include: (1) which material will be further reduced or shaped to form a tool and (2) which knapping technique will be used. Flakes are struck from the parent rock (which is called a *core),* and initially, the knapper must choose either to shape the object from the core

fine the shape of a stone object further, also use the abrasion technique.

In the flaking, or knapping, technique, the parent stone is reduced and shaped through the use of natural fracture characteristics of certain types of stone under pressure. Flaked- or chipped-stone objects are produced from stones that possess the characteristic of conchoidal fracture. Conchoidal fractures are produced by application of requisite force with a blunt indentor. Like the impact of a BB or bullet on a glass windowpane, a fracture cone radiates from the point of percussion into and sometimes through the rock mass when enough force is applied to a specific point on the or to select a flake for further reduction. Obviously, shaping tools from flakes is a more economical use of material, a factor that may or may not be important to the knapper. As discussed later, several special technologies have been developed in the past to produce flakes or blades (long, narrow flakes) that require little additional shaping. These technologies are very efficient in regards to the amount of material wasted. Archaeologists often refer to waste materials as *debitage*.

Knapping techniques include hard-hammer percussion, soft-hammer percussion, indirect percussion, bipolar percussion, and pressure flaking. Hard-hammer percussion involves the use of another rock (a hammer stone) as a percussor, while soft-hammer percussion usually involves the use of a piece of bone, antler, ivory, or hardwood as a percussor. Hard-hammer percussion is possibly the most efficient way to reduce a core quickly, but too much force can easily collapse the edges or result in unwanted and unpredicted outcomes. Soft-hammer percussion diffuses the shock of impact, and most knappers feel more in control of the outcomes using this technique. Indirect percussion involves the use of an intermediate tool, such as an antler punch, to transfer the force of a hammer to the point of percussion. The technique is particularly advantageous when exact placement and direction of force is demanded. Bipolar percussion is a modification of this technique where the workpiece is placed on an anvil of hard material and then struck with a percussor. This technique is often used when the parent materials are small pieces that are difficult to flake freehandedly. Flakes and flake scars may show points of percussion at each end. Pressure flaking usually involves the use of a handheld tool of relatively hard material to apply pressure to the point of percussion, although there are accounts of pressure flaking using one's own teeth or fingernails. Pressure flaking is often the technique of choice for final shaping, applying finishing touches to stone-tool edges, or refurbishing an edge. Pressure-flaking tools are usually made of antler, bone, or hardwood.

Understanding the options and limitations of toolmaking technology gives the archaeologist a point of departure for examining the work executed by prehistoric flint knappers. It is clear that some options are motivated by a concern for the functional characteristics demanded in the tool, while others are driven by concerns for conformity of style. Each flint knapper not only wanted to produce a useful tool but knew exactly what the tool should look like when finished. Thus, all chipped-stone tools share some technological characteristics, tools intended for specific tasks share some morphological characteristics, and tools produced by knappers of the same culture share some stylistic characteristics. Modern researchers may seek to understand any one or any combination of these characteristics.

Industries, Assemblages, Tools, and Culture

Researchers use the term *industry* to refer to a technology (methods of tool production and use) and its associated tools and characteristic debitage. The term *assemblage* is usually applied to a group of tools and associated debitage found at a particular site and related to a specific time period and culture. It seems that the first stone tools were produced on the African continent sometime between 2 million and 3 million years ago. Before the first manufactured stone tools, African hominids may have relied on unmodified stone tools for extractive tasks in food procurement. The earliest toolmaking industry, the Olduwan industry (named for the area of East Africa where these tools were first associated with early hominid remains), is characterized by crude pebble tools or choppers. These were formed by the removal of a few flakes from the edges of an appropriately sized and shaped cobble to produce a sharp, chopperlike tool.

By about 1.9 million years ago in Africa, more technologically complex hand axes were produced by our *Homo erectus* ancestors. This artifact type has become the hallmark of the Acheulian industry characterized by retouched flake tools as well as by the famous hand ax, which was probably not an ax at all in the sense of an ax for felling trees, but rather a general-use, strong, sharp tool for butchering, grubbing, or shaping wooden artifacts. These hand axes were shaped over most or all of their surfaces through the removal of large, broad flakes. Many of the

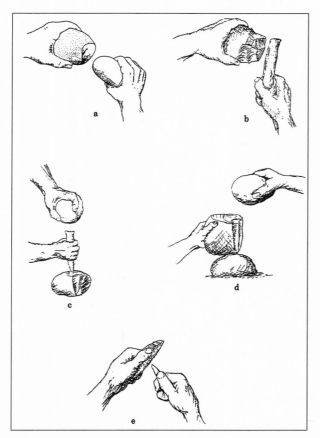

Fig. 7 *Reduction techniques: (a) direct percussion, (b) hard-hammer percussion, (c) indirect percussion, (d) bipolar percussion, and (e) pressure flaking*

ers and related tools found in Mousterian assemblages and the quantitative differences evident when comparing some assemblages. Although the precise meaning of this phenomenon remains a point of scientific debate, possibilities include the development of different forms for various tasks or differentiation of styles representing ethnic, social, or cultural differences. Possibly, the explanation lies somewhere in between, but assemblage differences may be the earliest archaeological evidence for cultural differentiation (or the development of specific traditions) yet recognized. An archaeological tradition is a set of material-culture traits and contextual associations that are usually found together and are assumed to identify related peoples or cultures.

Some Mousterian toolmakers employed the Levallois technique (a tool-making process first identified in the prehistory of France) to detach flakes approximating the size, shape, and thick-

earliest examples were produced using hard-hammer techniques. Soft-hammer techniques, which produce larger, flatter, and thinner flakes and flatter, thinner hand axes, were more prevalent later in the development of the Acheulian industry. Hand axes are bifaces—that is, they were produced through relatively symmetrical detachment of flakes from both faces of the artifact, while other Acheulian tools were usually made on large flakes by unifacial, or single face, flaking of an edge. This technique for producing a sharp cutting or scraping edge is often referred to as *retouching*.

The Mousterian industry, a later stone-tool industry characterized by large numbers and varieties of flake tools, is strongly associated with early *Homo sapiens*. Hand axes are still found in some assemblages, but most intriguing is the number of different shapes (types) of flake scrap-

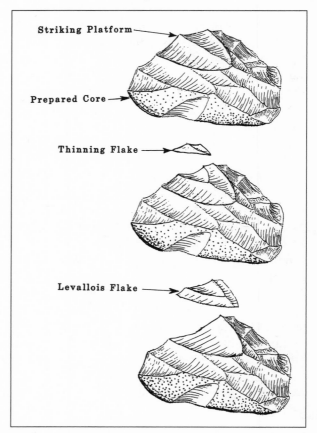

Fig. 8 *Levallois technique*

ness of the intended tool. The core was prepared by flaking a large, flat area with a good platform at one end. Then, one well-placed blow detached a large, thin flake with sharp edges all around except in the immediate area of the platform. Some triangular Levallois flakes have been referred to as *Levallois points,* implying their function as spear tips, but there is no good evidence that these artifacts were hafted (set into handles) or used in this way.

By about 40,000 years ago, some groups of people of essentially modern physical type had begun using techniques to produce blades, a specialized flake that is thin, long, and straight and usually exhibits a medial ridge (produced by the intersection of two older blade scars). Blade production is often based on the careful preparation of the core so that blades can be removed sequentially. The technique requires high-quality material and careful application of force, but there is relatively little wastage of material. The easiest and surest way to produce long, thin, reasonably flat blades is by using the punch (indirect percussion) technique. Even when blade technology is adopted, flakes are usually still present if not

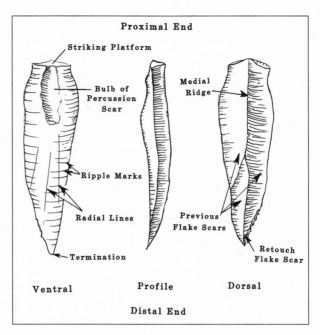

Fig. 10 *Morphological characteristics of flakes*

always dominant in the assemblage. Like earlier tools, flakes provide ready tools for cutting and scraping demands.

Blade industries have been touted by archaeologists as more efficient than more generalized technologies. While probably true, it is not necessarily clear that more efficient use of stone in toolmaking was particularly advantageous except in areas of severe resource scarcity. Equally important might be certain aesthetic qualities of blades, blade tools, and preferred materials. After all, showing off is a human quality of unknown antiquity and is often indulged in by modern flint knappers. For whatever reason, it is during this stage of cultural development in Africa, often referred to as the *Upper Paleolithic,* that cultural differentiation is clearly seen in development of regional, and sometimes local, seemingly competing technological traditions.

During the last 20,000 years or so, numerous regional and local traditions occupy places in the time-space continuum of African prehistory. In addition to blade industries, a new specialized technological innovation, production of microblades, emerged in some areas. Microblades are small versions of blades, and the technology for their production often relies on smaller pieces of

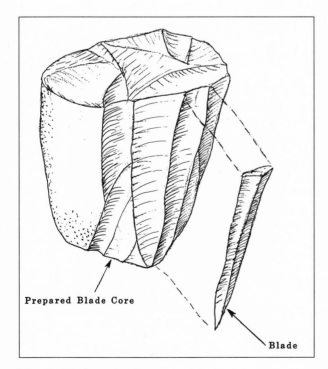

Fig. 9 *Blade technology*

raw material than would be acceptable for full-sized blades. Techniques of bipolar percussion are sometimes employed to render small pieces of raw material. Microblade tools are, of course, an extremely efficient use of raw materials but generally require some type of hafting or mounting because of their small size. Thus, composite tools are clearly suggested in some areas.

Reading Stone Tools

Early archaeologists and paleoanthropologists simply considered ancient stone tools to be analogs or older versions of modern hand tools. Functional connotations like *chopper, scraper,* and *knife* were applied without much critical thought. However, during the decades of the 1960s and 1970s, commonly held suppositions about stone tools were examined more critically through analogy to present-day or ethnographically documented stone-tool technologies, through experimental replication of various tool forms and technologies, and through analysis of wear and residue patterns on tool edges.

When archaeologists critically examined ethnographic accounts of stone-tool manufacture and use, distinctions between modern-day or industrial-tool technologies and traditional stone-tool technologies were recognized. Some archaeologists even implemented their own ethnographic research in order to record in minute detail the behaviors and processes associated with stone-toolmaking and use.

Other studies addressed the process of stone-toolmaking through experimentation. Some archaeologists learned to make stone tools, and through their attempts to replicate the steps and procedures in the production of various tools, they began to understand more fully the details of stone-tool production and their relationships with other aspects of behavior. Importantly, through their experiments with stone-tool manufacture and use, archaeologists also learned to recognize classes of artifacts that were unfinished or damaged beyond repair during manufacture.

An important result of experimental flint knapping was the recognition of classes of manufacturing and refurbishing debris (debitage) and their potential as a source of information on pre-

historic behavior and activities. Often referred to as *flake* or *debitage analysis,* this information is gleaned from careful inspection of morphological characteristics of flakes and other manufacturing debris. Flakes, like other artifacts resulting from the reduction sequence, exhibit morphological characteristics suggestive of their production. For instance, the size and shape of the bulb of percussion, the innermost remnant of the Hertzian (or fracture) cone, is often indicative of the type of pressure (hard hammer or soft hammer, for example) exerted to produce the flake. Such characteristics as the type of platform, thickness of the flake, overall size of the flake, and type of exterior or dorsal surface of the flake are often useful indicators of the stage of reduction at which the flake was detached.

Flakes, along with other lithic artifacts, have also played an important role in recent studies of raw-material origins. Archaeologists now employ a number of techniques ranging from simple mineralogical comparisons to sophisticated chemical analyses to investigate geographic and geological origins of lithic materials found at archaeological sites.

Ethnographic investigations and experimental flint knapping have provided models and comparisons useful in the interpretation of prehistoric activities. Often, information gleaned from experimental replication of tools can be used to identify components of the manufacture of stone tools and to infer more precisely the associated prehistoric behaviors and behavior patterns. Sometimes, even in the absence of formal tools, important elements of a technology can be reconstructed from characteristics of manufacturing debris alone. These new methods of investigation now allow archaeologists to examine economic patterns, at least those in which stone-toolmaking and use are significant components, within and between areas of a site and compare these activities from one site to another.

Unsatisfied with traditional assumptions about the function of stone tools, several archaeologists explored methods to interpret tool use from traces remaining on tool edges. Pioneering research in this area in the past 20 years now provides an established methodology to observe microscopically, record, and interpret tool use from micro-scarring, abrasion, and polish on tool edges. Usually, experimental protocols are employed to replicate patterns of stone-tool use and serve as comparative indices for identification. Other investigations into the potential for functional interpretation from chemical residues adhering to tool edges are in their infancy but show some promise. Both microwear analysis and residue analysis are still in the early stages of development, and their full potential as analytical tools are yet to be determined.

———〜〜〜〜〜———

Making and using stone tools is possibly the oldest technology, and because of their usual durability, stone tools and other artifacts resulting from their manufacture are most ubiquitously preserved in the archaeological record in Africa as elsewhere. The technology for producing stone tools is rather simple and has changed little in the course of human history although several hallmark innovations in manufacturing approach and tool design probably attest to important changes in economic and social organization through time. As the result of basic research into stone-toolmaking and use through ethnographic analogy, experimental replication, and use or wear analysis, archaeologists have become quite sophisticated in their attempts to generate information on prehistoric behavior from stone tools and manufacturing debris.

BIBLIOGRAPHY

Gould, R. A. 1988. *Living archaeology.* Cambridge: Cambridge University Press.

Keeley, L. H. 1988. *Experimental determination of stone tool uses.* Chicago: University of Chicago Press.

Lewin, R. 1988. *In the age of mankind.* Washington, D.C.: Smithsonian Books.

Oakley, K. P. 1959. *Man the tool-maker.* Chicago: University of Chicago Press.

Semenov, S. A. 1964. *Prehistoric technology.* London: Adams and Dart.

Swanson, E. 1975. *Lithic technology: Making and using stone tools.* New York: Mouton.

Vaughan. P. 1985. *Use-wear analysis of flaked stone tools.* Tucson: University of Arizona Press.

Whittaker, J. C. 1994. *Flintknapping, making and understanding stone tools.* Austin: University of Texas Press.

Boyce Driskell and Jeffrey C. Motz

STONEWORKING TECHNOLOGY: ITS EVOLUTION

Human behavioral evolution can be traced through the development of the cutting flake, the bifacial tool, and the emergence of composite-tool technology. Three major innovations punctuate the evolution of stone-tool working technology: the flake, the biface, and the composite tool. The earliest technology, the Olduwan industry, comprises a deceptively simple assemblage of flakes and cores. By 2.6 million years ago, some human ancestors, probably early *Homo,* understood the practical mechanics of working stone including the spatial concept of an acute-angled edge as the basis of flaking. Showing considerable forethought and organization, human ancestors selected stone and transported it for future use. A sharp cutting edge, used for butchering, increased *Homo*'s access to protein and fat in animals. Flakes and cores could also be used to work wood, bark, and skins into useful carrying tools. The use of tools to make other tools marks a threshold in human evolution achieved by Olduwan makers between 1.5 and 2.6 million years ago. The possibility that most toolmakers were predominantly right-handed suggests a neurological potential for the development of language in concert with tool use and living in cooperative social groups.

By 1.4 million years ago, experimentation with bifacially flaked cutting edges resulted in the Acheulian hand ax. The hand ax had its roots in Olduwan technology but differed in its deliberate symmetry and by being made on a flake blank produced by core preparation. Elaborate core preparation was a feature of the later Acheulian industry and an integral technology of many later flake industries. Experiments show the hand ax to be an effective tool for butchering large game. *Homo erectus,* the likely maker of early Acheulian tools, had the physical, intellectual, and social capabilities to colonize the Old World from temperate to tropical latitudes. The use of fire and living in more cooperative social groups may have been important aspects in the spread of *Homo*. After 1 million years ago, hand-ax technology reached a level of refinement that suggests an aesthetic sense and a long apprenticeship. Archaic *Homo sapiens* or *Homo heidelbergensis* is associated with the later Acheulian industries in Africa and Europe.

A gradual shift took place between 200,000 and 300,000 years ago away from bifaces to tools with handles and shafts with stone inserts as working edges. Composite-tool technology offered greater flexibility and economy and supported a wider range of economic strategies, including hunting at a distance and processing plant foods. Areas with poor stone resources, such as parts of the central Zaire Basin, were settled for the first time. In Middle Stone Age industries, patterns of regional adaptations to differing environments emerged. The development of composite-tool technology coincided with the gradual evolution of anatomically modern humans in sub-Saharan Africa and may have contributed to their success outside the continent. The Howieson's Poort and other southern African assemblages with standardized inserts represent a further development of hafting technology probably between 60,000 and 75,000 years ago. After 40,000 years ago, a transition to composite tools based on microlithic components occurred across sub-Saharan Africa. By 20,000 years ago, microlithic technology was found in most regions with local differences emerging in the types and frequencies of tools. Modern behaviors—such as the use of symbols in ritual, extended networks of social alliances, and bone-working technology—evolved in the post-Acheulian period and were fully expressed in the Late Stone Age.

The Oluwan Industry

Stone tools first appear in the archaeological record of sub-Saharan Africa about 2.6 million years ago. They provide the most durable and widespread evidence of past human behavior until the advent of pottery less than 10,000 years ago. Bone- and woodworking may be equally ancient, but the more perishable nature of their raw materials leaves an archaeological record biased toward stone.

The earliest tools are sharp flakes and the cores from which they were struck. The cores, generally called *choppers,* may show the scars of just a few flake removals or multiple scars, which radiate toward the center of the stone forming a disc shape, or if less regular, a polyhedron. Cores may themselves have been tools, and experiments with replicas show that their strong edges are useful for breaking open bones for marrow. Some flakes were also retouched to produce blunt scraping edges. This basic assemblage of flakes and cores is called the *Olduwan industry* after finds in Bed I at Olduvai Gorge in Tanzania.

The earliest Olduwan assemblages date to between 2.4 and 2.6 million years ago and are found in northern Ethiopia along the Gona River. Similar tools occur farther south in Ethiopia in the Shungura Formation of the Omo River Valley in deposits between 2 and 2.2 million years old. Other Olduwan sites in the range of 1.6 to 2 million years old are found throughout the East African Rift Valley System, in Ethiopia (Melka Kunture), Kenya (Chesowanja, Koobi Fora), Tanzania (Olduvai Gorge), eastern Zaire (Senga), and possibly in Malawi (Chiwondo Beds). In southern Africa, the Olduwan occurs in cave deposits at Sterkfontein and Swartkrans (South Africa) and in undated river gravels in Swaziland and the South African interior. Olduwan-like assemblages have been reported from West Africa, particularly in northeastern Nigeria, but

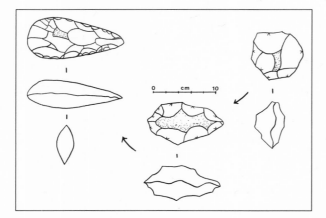

Fig. 11 *Development of bifacial flaking from an Olduwan disc core to the irregularly shaped Developed Olduwan hand ax to the symmetrical Acheulian hand ax*

they come from disturbed contexts and cannot be reliably dated.

A report of early Olduwan artifacts outside Africa comes from Pakistan where cores have been found in river-terrace deposits dated to 2 million years ago. The context and the dating have both been questioned, but the possibility remains of an early dispersal of tool-using hominines (humans and human ancestors) out of Africa.

The makers of these early tools were almost certainly members of the genus *Homo* (for example, *H. habilis* and *H. rudolfensis),* but other hominines such as the robust australopithicines *(Paranthropus robustus* and *P. boisei)* may also have been occasional tool users. After 1.8 million years ago, *Homo* was the only regular maker of stone tools. Olduwan assemblages continued to be made until 1.5 million years ago, when tools with more extensively flaked surfaces appear. These early bifacially flaked implements with nonstandardized shapes distinguish the Developed Olduwan industry at Olduvai and the Karari industry at Koobi Fora. This experimentation with bifacial flaking precedes Acheulian technology with its larger and more standardized implements.

Olduwan Behavior:
Planning and Perception

What do Olduwan flakes and cores tell us about the intelligence of their makers? Analysis of artifacts from Koobi Fora and Olduvai Gorge, combined with experimental replication studies, provides some answers. Evidence of planning comes from the transport of raw materials across the Koobi Fora landscape. Volcanic rocks were selected for flaking and carried in some cases more than 10 kilometers from a highland source toward sites on the margins of ancient Lake Turkana. The flakes show that some of the raw material was transported as partially flaked cores, perhaps having been tested first for its homogeneity. Experiments with refitting also show that some cores and flakes were carried away to other sites and kept for later use. The storage of these implements and the carrying of stone over long distances for later use reflect a degree of foresight that exceeds that of modern great apes. Olduwan implements are simple, but the organi-

zation of time and space involved in their creation and use reflects something more than an opportunistic technology.

The cores and flakes show a basic understanding of the mechanics of flaking and the physical properties of stone. To remove a flake from a nodule, a knapper must locate an acute-edge angle on the core face and strike away from the core with a glancing blow using a hammer stone of equal or greater hardness than the core. Olduwan makers mastered the geometry of flaking—something modern apes and students have difficulty in understanding—and from experience knew which types of stone were best. Most Olduwan cores bear the scars of a few well-directed hammer blows with little concern for the resulting shape. The production of flakes with sharp cutting edges was the primary objective. A few flakes were retouched to create sturdy scraping edges, but these implements show little standardization in their shape. Symmetry as an indicator of working to a preconceived design is lacking in Olduwan assemblages. Some symmetrical cores do occur from flaking both faces around the periphery and using acute angles created by previous flake scars as striking platforms. These radial or disc cores have biconical shapes, which presage later bifacial technologies, but their symmetry is incidental to the objective of making flakes.

Language

About 90 percent of modern humans are right-handed, a figure unique among primates. The operations of the right hand are controlled by the left hemisphere of the brain, which also governs the production and comprehension of speech. This hemispheric association suggests that language and technology share a common origin. If archaeological evidence exists of a clear preference for right-handed tool use, then an indirect link can be made to emerging language. Just such a link may exist in the production of Olduwan flakes. Experimental flaking of cobbles by inexperienced knappers shows that right-handed individuals tend to turn a core clockwise as they remove flakes in succession. The resulting flakes have a distinctive right-hand pattern of surface scars, which is reversed among left-handers who tend to turn cores in a counterclockwise direction. The scar patterns on Olduwan flakes from Koobi Fora show a predominantly right-handed population of toolmakers 1.9 million years ago. This suggests an early hemispheric specialization of the brain and an enhanced ability to communicate compared with contemporary apes. It does not suggest, however, that the toolmakers communicated through a complex, rule-governed language like our own.

The simplicity of Olduwan artifacts argues against the need for complex language. The selection of stone and the production of flakes could be learned through observation and imitation, as nut cracking and probing for termites are learned among modern chimpanzees. Given that tool use among modern humans takes place in a social context of which language is an integral part, we cannot expect to learn much about the intelligence of early *Homo* from flakes and cores alone. We need to know if *H. habilis* lived in groups where the integration of technology with communication and social living was minimal, like that of modern apes, or developed to the extent that food sharing and divisions of labor defined behaviors as they do for modern humans. The implements of Olduwan assemblages gave *Homo* access to meat and marrow, opening a new adaptive niche. How these foods were obtained and distributed remains a fundamental issue in the study of human origins.

The Acheulian Industry

About 1.4 million years ago, new forms of large bifacially flaked tools enter the archaeological record with features distinctive of Acheulian technology (named after the site of St. Acheul in northern France). The appearance of thin, symmetrical bifaces follows an interval of experimentation between 1.4 and 1.6 million years ago with thick, irregular bifaces made on cobbles in the Developed Olduwan and the Karari industries. The Acheulian industry, for much of its duration, is associated with a large-brained hominid, *Homo erectus,* which had evolved by 1.9 million years ago. The maker of later Acheulian assemblages, from 250,000 to 400,000 years ago, is a descendant of *H. erectus,* known

in Africa and Europe as *Homo heidelbergensis* or as archaic *Homo sapiens.*

Hand axes, picks, and cleavers are the characteristic implements of the Acheulian industry in Africa. Hand axes are generally pear-shaped and flaked on both surfaces to a tapering tip. Cleavers, also made on large flakes, are retouched to a *U*-shaped outline with a naturally sharp cutting end. Picks are thick implements flaked to create a stout triangular tip. They tend to be less regular in form than either hand axes or cleavers. The standardized shape of hand axes distinguishes Acheulian tools from Olduwan implements. For the first time in the archaeological record, we find an implement designed to a predetermined plan. The large flake blanks used to make bifaces also represent a significant technological innovation. Thinning a biface and creating a straight cutting edge is difficult, especially if the blank is a thick cobble. Starting with a thin flake automatically minimizes the amount of thinning needed. Acheulian knappers struck large flake blanks from cores deliberately prepared for the purpose. Core preparation has its origin in the Acheulian industry and becomes a hallmark of later flake industries, showing continuity across a continuum of technological development.

Experiments with replica hand axes and cleavers suggest that they are excellent tools for butchering large animals and are suitable implements for chopping wood. Bifaces are also portable and can be a source of sharp flakes to begin the butchering process. Other uses have been suggested, such as digging tools for finding bulbs and corms. The versatility of the hand ax may in part account for the success of the Acheulian as a long-lived and widespread technology.

Hand axes are found throughout Africa, with the exception of the Zaire River Basin and the highest mountain ranges. *H. erectus* expanded its range by settling in highland areas (higher than 2,000 meters), such as parts of Ethiopia, but the greatest expansion of the species took place with its movement outside Africa. Reports of early dates for *H. erectus* in Java and perhaps China at 1.6 to 1.8 million years ago and in Georgia at 1.5 million years ago suggest an early pre-Acheulian dispersal. Hand axes appear later in Europe as far north as Britain, in western Asia, and as far east as India. The rarity of Acheulian technology in eastern Asia may reflect the lack of suitable raw materials for making large bifaces, the use of other materials such as bamboo, or ecological conditions that favored a different stoneworking technology.

The Acheulian period was not a time of stasis. More standardized and finely retouched bifaces develop later, after 1 million years ago, reflecting more elaborate core preparation and the use of softer hammers of stone, wood, and bone for thinning. The range of small flake tools found in Acheulian assemblages, such as scrapers, awls, and denticulates (sawtooth-edged tools), also shows a trend toward more standardization. Retouched flake tools, becoming more prominent late in the Acheulian period, heralded a gradual transition to purely flake-based industries.

Perception, Planning, and Language

The symmetrical hand ax represents a significant departure from the informal tools of the Olduwan industry. The roots of bifacial symmetry lie in the radial cores of Olduwan tools, but the hand ax differs in the complexity of its symmetry in relation to the tool's long axis. Hand axes are symmetrical in plan view, in cross-section to the long axis, and perpendicular to the long axis. Such an unusual shape involves careful planning at each stage in the reduction process: from selecting the raw material, to preparing the core and producing a large blank, through the final steps of shaping and thinning. The complexity of the hand ax reflects a preconceived image of the final shape and an ability to anticipate the consequences of each flake's removal. Occasionally, raw materials permitting, the refinement of flaking surpasses the need for symmetry, suggesting an emerging aesthetic sense. Learning to make a hand ax takes time, and for *H. erectus*, this implies a period of apprenticeship with teaching by verbal instruction or learning by observation and imitation.

The long adolescence that modern humans experience may have its origins with *H. erectus* as a result of the interplay of increasingly complex tool technology, language, and social behavior. The hand ax opened opportunities for exploiting the carcasses of large game—with implications

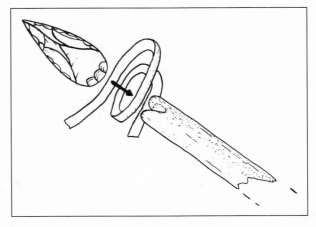

Fig. 12 *Elements of a composite tool: notched wooden shaft, stone point, and sinew binding combined to make a spear*

for food sharing—and as a portable and versatile technology, it enabled *H. erectus* to expand its range. The colonization of the temperate zones of Europe and Asia reflects a highly adaptable species, one that may have made use of fire and stone technology to suit local conditions, and one that may have lived in more cooperative social groups than did early *Homo*. Language in some basic form would have been integral to the success of Acheulian toolmakers.

The Composite Tool Revolution: The Middle and Late Stone Age

Between 200,000 and 300,000 years ago, a gradual shift in emphasis took place in stoneworking technology. Handheld bifaces gave way to small cutting edges inserted into handles of wood, bone, or ivory. Hafting involves positioning an insert that cuts, scrapes, or pierces onto a handle or shaft and securing the insert either with a binding or mastic. The result is a composite tool. As well as protecting the hand, a handle adds leverage to the processes of cutting, scraping, and drilling. Hunters can throw a shaft tipped with a light stone point at their prey from a safe distance, and if the animal is wounded, hunters can then follow a blood trail. A throwing spear places fewer physical demands on the body than a stabbing spear, and this innovation may underlie the gradual reduction in human robustness beginning

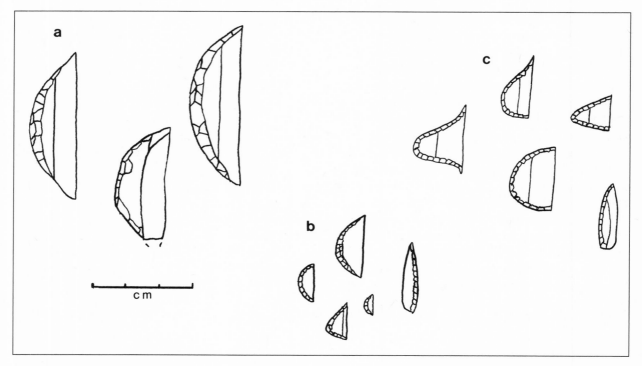

Fig. 13 *Post-Acheulian backed insets used as cutting edges: (a) Middle Stone Age of southern Africa, (b) Late Stone Age of southern Africa, and (c) Late Stone Age of south-central Africa*

about 200,000 years ago. Composite tools are also well suited to the efficient processing of plant and animal foods. Task-specific tools with standardized working edges can save time and effort and enable foragers to respond to changing or new environments. Standardized inserts also use less stone than a handheld version so that a wider range of raw materials, such as pebbles, can be used. Regions with poor supplies of stone, such as parts of equatorial Africa, were successfully exploited for the first time.

The transition to composite technology began in Acheulian industries with the development of core-preparation techniques for striking thin flakes of a desired size and shape. The Levallois technique, named after a site in northern France, is an elaborate means of shaping a core, a technique that may have originated in African Acheulian industries about 300,000 years ago. Some post-Acheulian industries in central Africa retain bifacial tools, like picks, but are otherwise flaked-tool assemblages. The new retouched elements marking post-Acheulian tools are small points, borers, scrapers made on blades, and later

the development of standardized blade inserts shaped by blunting to minimize damage to the haft. Points are distinctive tools of the period and may be bifacially or unifacially retouched with some thinned for hafting as spear tips or knives.

In sub-Saharan Africa, post-Acheulian assemblages are classified as Middle Stone Age and Late Stone Age. They represent divisions of a technological continuum in which the Late Stone Age is distinguished by an emphasis on small stone inserts or microliths as well as a more diverse material culture, alliance networks, and a strong ritual life with a focus on painting and engraving. The earliest dates for the Middle Stone Age (from Ethiopia, Kenya, and Zambia) suggest the transition to composite technology took place in some areas 230,000 years ago. The archaeological record is poor for the period between 100,000 and 200,000 years ago, during which anatomically modern humans, *Homo sapiens sapiens,* evolved. Beginning 100,000 years ago, differences in tool assemblages reflect broad regional adaptations. The Middle Stone Age sequence south of the Limpopo River differs from that of central and eastern Africa. Two technological developments cut across regions: the early use of blade technology and the appearance of standardized backed inserts. Blades, or long narrow flakes, provide a useful blank for retouching into a range of tool types and are an efficient use of stone. They form part of the technological repertoire of eastern and southern Africa beginning 100,000 years ago. The backing of blades to make crescent-shaped inserts for composite tools distinguishes the Howieson's Poort industry of southern Africa, probably between 60,000 and 75,000 years ago. Similarly shaped inserts occur in Middle Stone Age contexts as far north as central Zambia and to the east in Tanzania. In eastern Africa, the making of backed tools persisted to the end of the Middle Stone Age.

In southern Africa, the later phases of the Middle Stone Age show a trend toward smaller flakes and blades between 25,000 and 35,000 years ago, followed by fully microlithic industries by 20,000 years ago. Early experimentation with small inserts occurred in west-central and central Africa with fully microlithic assemblages developing between 30,000 and 40,000 years ago. In eastern Africa, microlithic assemblages with backed bladelets appeared 22,000 years ago and became widespread 10,000 years ago. Regional variations north and south of the Limpopo River occurred in the use of backed bladelets, plain bladelets, and backed flakes and in the shapes of backed inserts. The wide distribution and diversity of microlithic technology may reflect the adoption of bow-and-arrow technology and the use of composite technology by groups to express their identity through tool styles.

Elements of modern behavior—fully developed language, division of labor, food sharing, complex composite technology, controlled use of fire, ritual, and networks of social exchange—may all have developed at differing times during post-Acheulian periods. The antiquity of each of these behaviors bears on the debate about whether modern behavior originated in Africa and contributed to the success of *H. sapiens* in dispersing through the Old and New Worlds. The composite technology of the Middle Stone Age played an integral role in the evolution of our species.

BIBLIOGRAPHY

Clark, J. D. 1988. The Middle Stone Age of East Africa and the beginnings of regional identity. *Journal of World Prehistory* 2: 235–303.

Deacon, H. J. 1992. Southern Africa and modern human origins. *Philosophical Transactions of the Royal Society of London, Series B* 337: 177–183.

Deacon, J. 1984. Later Stone Age people and their descendants in southern Africa. In *Southern African prehistory and paleoenvironments,* ed. R. G. Klein, 221–328. Rotterdam: A. A. Balkema.

Gibson, K., and T. Ingold. 1993. *Tools, language and cognition in human evolution.* Cambridge: Cambridge University Press.

Gowlett, J. A. J. 1984. Mental abilities of early man: A look at some hard evidence. In *Hominid evolution and community ecology,* ed. R. Foley, 167–192. London: Academic Press.

Thackeray, A. I. 1992. The Middle Stone Age south of the Limpopo. *Journal of World Prehistory* 6: 385–440.

Toth, N. 1985. The Oldowan reassessed: A close look at early stone artifacts. *Journal of Archaeological Science* 12: 101–120.

Van Noten, F., ed. 1982. *The archaeology of central Africa.* Graz: Akademische Druck und Verlagsanstalt.

Volman, T. P. 1984. Early prehistory of southern Africa. In *Southern African prehistory and paleoenvironments,* ed. R. G. Klein, 169–220. Rotterdam: A. A. Balkema.

Wynn, T. 1989. *The evolution of spatial competence.* Urbana: University of Illinois Press.

Lawrence S. Barham

POTTERY MANUFACTURE

The capacity to confine liquids and dispersible solids—coupled with the ability to generate and direct the flow of heat to, around, and through them—is an important aspect of many of mankind's social and economic institutions. Before the advent of pottery making, liquids and dispersible solids were stored and transported in skin or fiber containers. These may also have served as measuring and mixing devices, but neither skin nor fiber can efficiently absorb and transfer the flow of directly applied heat. Those peoples lacking ceramic or stone vessels prepared and preserved food and other perishables by drying, salting, marinating, or roasting them or by time-consuming and cumbersome indirect methods of heat application. Some foods and other perishables were prepared or preserved through stone boiling or steaming. The former required the immersion of heated stones in water, while the latter needed the application of water to a bed of hot rocks. Both methods were inefficient techniques. Stone vessels were more effective than their skin or fiber counterparts, and their use often preceded the use of pottery. But stone vessels had drawbacks. Deposits of easily carved stone were not widely distributed, and stone vessels took a good deal of time to make. Once made, if large, they were difficult to transport. Carved-stone vessels light enough for easy transport lacked capacity. The raw materials for the manufacture of pottery, on the other hand, were widely distributed, and ceramic vessels were less time-consuming to produce. Once they were made and fired, they were reasonably light and durable. Thus, pottery vessels, however simple, were the earliest of mankind's efficient means for confining, storing, transporting, and especially heating substances.

Perhaps the strongest prima facie evidence for pottery's utilitarian value is the fact that once the ceramic art had been invented or introduced in one place, it spread rapidly to regions nearby. Japan and China were early centers of pottery production in the Far East, and from there the ceramic art spread rapidly throughout insular and peninsular Southeast Asia. Pottery making is also quite old in the Near East. From there, it spread around the Mediterranean, then eastward to the Indian subcontinent, northward into central Europe, westward into northwestern Europe, and southward throughout Africa. Although the evidence is less than satisfying, it now seems that the potter's craft was spread through sub-Saharan Africa during the Early Iron Age via a rather dramatic series of Bantu migrations.

Pottery vessels were prehistoric humans' earliest efficient means for confining, storing, measuring, mixing, transporting, heating, and cooling dispersible substances. However, these uses depend first on the ability of humans to enclose space with baked clay—that is, on the role of pottery vessels as containers. Herein, too, lies the key to their geometry. Because most vessels are symmetrical radially and asymmetrical from top to bottom, they are relatively easily divided into systematically related parts. Imagine a simple pot, a single-orifice form without appendages. Now mentally examine its topological properties, especially the number of its sides and edges. A simple pot will always have two sides (the inside and the outside) and one edge (the lip). This will be the case despite the highly variable appearance that bending, stretching, twisting, or adding appendages might produce. Since the lip of this vessel is circular, and since all points along it, and all points systematically related to it, will be topological invariants, we use the lip as a reference for dividing the rest of the container into parts.

All nonlip portions of such a vessel are its body. The pot's shoulder is the maximum circumference of the body. The bottom is the minimum circumference of the body (which may be a point), and portions adjacent to the bottom form the base. All portions of the pot below the shoulder are the lower body. Parts above the shoulder are the upper body. The minimal circumference of the upper body is the pot's mouth. If the mouth and lip are not the same, the portion between the lip and mouth is the rim. Shoulderless forms may be accounted for by stipulating that, if the vessel has no shoulder, its mouth is the circumference nearest the lip and its bottom is the circumference farthest from the lip. Then too, since most vessels approximate this ideal form, departures from it, additions to it, or transformations of it may, and should, be treated as special cases. Differently put, we may consider the ideal form as of primary morphological import and the expanded, contracted, or otherwise modified portions of the ideal form as important but not primary morphological elaborations. Thus we may treat handles, spouts, lugs, legs, annular bases, and feet, effigies that depict animals, gods, humans, or plants, vases and flowerpots, wine, oil, and water bottles, and so on as special cases—namely, as addenda to or appendages on a more fundamental morphological theme.

Production Steps and Stages

Baked-clay containers, of all shapes and sizes and regardless of any appendages, require a multi-stage, multistep construction effort. A general production sequence might, for instance, run as follows: (1) obtain clay, (2) prepare clay, (3) build the vessel, (4) decorate the vessel, (5) dry the vessel, and (6) fire the vessel. We may expect variations in the order of vessel-part fabrication and in the results obtained from different production techniques. If, for instance, we use the way the performance of a specific action in a sequence of actions affects the finished product, then not all actions need be considered equally essential. Some actions will be noncommutative, for they must occur in a fixed order if a reasonably uniform result is to be achieved. These noncommutative actions are listed above and numbered one through six. Other actions, however, may be commutative in the sense that the order of their occurrence may vary and such variation will not markedly affect the end product. The third production stage, building the vessel, may be a case in point. It may be easily and consistently subdivided into the following parts: build the bottom, build the lower vessel walls, build the shoulder (if the vessel is shouldered), build the upper-vessel walls, build the rim (if the mouth and lip are separate orifices), and build the lip. The potter might indeed start at the bottom and then build the lower body, shoulder, upper body, rim, and lip in that order. The potter could also start at the shoulder and build the upper body, the lip, the lower body, and then the bottom, or he or she could start at the shoulder and build the lower body, the upper body, the rim, and then the lip. Then again, the potter might begin forming the vessel near the lip, build the upper body, the shoulder, the lower body and bottom, and then finish by forming the lip. In short, the fabrication of vessel parts may be, and often is, commutative. Thus the order of the actions is an important aspect of a given tradition of potting.

Still other actions may be optional, and others may be alternatives. Optional actions are those that, at the discretion of the maker, may be deleted. Alternatives are those actions that may be rendered with different tools or hand movements at different times. The fourth production stage, decorating the vessel, is frequently optional, and if the option to decorate is adopted, the steps within it are quite often the subject of alternative means to virtually identical or at least very similar ends. Similar decorations may be rendered, for instance, by incising, trailing, or impressing, depending on the kind of tool used. The general stages of production and decoration can be easily detailed and conveniently subdivided.

Raw Material Acquisition

No matter when, where, or how pottery was made, the potter's first task was to find and collect suitable clay. Pots may be made from either primary or secondary clays. Igneous granites, decomposed by hot gasses into softer feldspar-containing rocks, provide the parent materials for both. The decomposition of feldspar-containing rocks by sun, rain, wind, or ice produces primary clays, all of which are found where they were formed. Primary clays tend to be light-colored (usually white, gray, or light pink), restricted in distribution, large in particle size, and relatively aplastic (with the exception of bentonite). They require high temperatures in firing ($1,200°$ C or higher). When properly treated, primary clays, insofar as they are refractory (capable of enduring high heat) or vitrifiable (capable of being made into a glasslike substance), may be used to produce light-colored earthenwares, stonewares, chinas, or porcelains. Although the ethnographic record contains evidence of a South African potter using primary clay from colluvial deposits near the base of a kopje (small hill), the majority of ethnographic observations and archaeological specimens available for most of Africa indicate the widespread, if not universal, use of secondary clays.

Beds of primary clay are the ultimate parent source for secondary clays. When primaries are moved from their source by wind, water, or ice, they pick up inorganic (iron and other minerals) and organic impurities and are modified in texture and particle size. Hence secondary clays are more widely distributed than primaries, and because of the impurities they contain, they tend to be shades of gray, brown, or red. Secondary clays are also smaller in particle size, have greater plasticity, and are more fusible—that is, they require lower firing temperatures (600° to 1,200° C) than primaries require. Since most fusible secondary clays will melt at firing temperatures much higher than 1,300° C, they are most suitable for the production of low-fired and porous earthenwares. If they are fired in oxygen-rich environments, secondary clays produce porous red, gray, tan, or buff wares. If they are fired in oxygen-poor surroundings (a process known as *reducing),* they yield earthenwares in black or various shades thereof. By far the greater number of Africa's native potters (those of both ethnographic and archaeological record) used secondary clays dug most frequently from alluvial deposits (river or pond banks and beds), some of them ancient but most of relatively recent origin.

Clay Preparation

Once the potter collected the clay and removed it to the place of manufacture, it was processed and prepared. During processing, the potter removed extraneous organic or inorganic matter, crushed, dried, sifted, or winnowed the raw clay, added water, and then set the clay aside to age (sour) or immediately kneaded or wedged it, with or without the addition of a tempering agent. Some clays require a tempering agent (an aplastic substance added to the clay body) to allow it to expand or contract without cracking during the drying process or spalling during the firing process. Sand (either purposefully added or intentionally included during clay selection), ground-up pottery fragments (grog), ground-up stone of various kinds (grit), and plant fibers are the most commonly reported tempering agents added to clay in wares from sub-Saharan Africa. The Ila of northern Zimbabwe, the Baronga of southern Mozambique, and the Ndebele of the south-central part of the former Transvaal province add ground-up pottery. Bechuana and Hottentot potters add pounded quartz. Baronga and southern Bantu potters add sand. BaVenda artisans in the northern part of the former Transvaal province select clays that contain enough sand so that more need not be added, and Tswana potters in the south-central part of the Transvaal collect primary clays that contain decomposing rock fragment sufficient to temper the clay body. The Bahurutsi of the southeastern

Transvaal add powdered asbestos. Grass was commonly used as a tempering and binding agent by South African Bushmen. D. A. Adamson, J. D. Clark, and M. A. J. Williams report the used of burned and crushed sponge spicules (minute calcareous or siliceous bodies that support the soft tissues of sponges) as tempering agents in prehistoric pottery at archaeological sites flanking the White Nile in central Sudan. Aplastic inclusions are, however, infrequently mentioned in descriptions of wares found to the north and west of the Zambezi, a gap in our knowledge that needs attention.

Vessel Building

TECHNIQUES OF MANUFACTURE. After preparing and processing, the clay may be formed into a vessel. If the vessel was to be hand built, as were all wares in prehistoric sub-Saharan Africa, the potter had three basic techniques at his or her disposal: modeling, coiling, or molding. If the vessel was modeled, it was pulled, pinched, punched, pounded, and scraped into the desired shape and size from a lump of prepared clay, which itself was of a size that would supply most, if not all, of the raw material. If the vessel was to be coiled, the prepared clay mass was divided into segments, each of which was subsequently rolled into coils that were then laid one upon the other, joined together, and then pinched, pulled, paddled, and scraped to form a pot of the desired size and shape. If the vessel was to be molded, the prepared clay was spread over or within a vertical or horizontal partial or half-mold made of wood, stone, or ceramic material. The pieces thus formed were joined together or were joined to coiled or mass-modeled sections to finish the job. These three basic building techniques were not, of course, mutually exclusive. Each may have been combined with others to manufacture separate parts of the same pot, but one of them was usually primary, in the sense that it was used to build the greater part of the vessel. Patch modeling may be considered a form of coiling. In fact, rolls, pinches, or patches of clay may be added during molding, modeling, or coiling, but these additions, insofar as they are ad hoc or are a part of rim and lip formation, do not change the basic characteristics of the three major body-forming techniques.

THE ORDER OF VESSEL-PART FABRICATION. When mass-modeling or coiling a vessel, the artisan may begin by forming the base, the shoulder, or the area near the lip. With shouldered vessels, it would have been difficult (but not impossible) for the potter to start near or at the lip when mass-modeling. The major difficulty would come during shoulder manufacture when the weight of the clay between lip (or near lip) and the shoulder rested on the near lip and the circumference of the shoulder exceeded the circumference of the near lip. While experiments in mass-modeling indicate that building from the lip down is feasible, using this order of fabrication results in vessels in which the shoulders and bases are markedly thinner than the lips and necks. Beginning near or at the lip is easier to accomplish if the potter is coiling, and both shouldered and shoulderless forms may be constructed in this manner. If the potter begins coiling at or near the lip, those portions of the pot are significantly thicker than those near the bottom. In such cases, the lower-vessel walls are thinner than their near-lip counterparts, and the base (which is usually formed from a pancakelike pad laid on and over the body coil most distant from the lip) is typically thinner than the lower portion of the vessel to which it is attached. Some archaeological specimens from the Caribbean show evidence of being formed by coiling from the near lip to the base, but this method has not been reported ethnographically or inferred archaeologically for African materials.

If the artisan begins modeling at the shoulder, the clay mass is rolled into a solid cylinder and then mashed into a flat rectangular strap. The free ends of this strap are mated and welded together to produce a hollow cylinder starter strap, from which both the top and the base are pulled. However, if the potter begins mass-modeling at the shoulder, then the shoulder is usually significantly thicker than the near-lip portions of the upper body and the base. P. W. Laidler and F. S. A. Scot report mass-modeled vessel building beginning with the "neck" (most probably the shoulder in our terms), proceeding to the lip, and then terminating with the base for the Ila (of northern Zimbabwe), the Mashona (of eastern Zimbabwe and adjacent Mozambique), the Baghatla (of the *highveld* of the former Transvaal province), and the Pondo (of KwaZulu-Natal). Richard A. Krause documents the use of a starter strap from which first the upper body and lip are formed and then the bottom is pulled for the Ndebele (of the south-central part of the former Transvaal province), the baVenda (of the northern Transvaal), and the Eastern Tswana (of the south-central Transvaal). He infers a similar production technique for 8th- to 19th-century archaeological specimens from the Phalaborwa district of the northeastern Transvaal. In those cases in which coiling begins at or near the shoulder, the bottom has usually been molded. Joseph O. Vogel infers bottom molding with coiling immediately below, at, and above the shoulder for Iron Age specimens in the Zambezi Valley of Zambia. For the Hide of Cameroon, N. J. David illustrates potting practices that feature mold-assisted, mass-modeled, bottom and lower-body construction followed by coiled upper-body, rim, and lip formation.

If the artisan begins at the bottom, he or she either excavates a clay mass or molds, models, or coils a base. If coiled, a long cylinder wound about itself on a flat surface or spiraled slightly upward and outward forms the base. Such bases, if examined under proper light and magnification, exhibit an ammonite- or nautiluslike spiral. William Saul describes a long cylinder of clay coiled on a flat surface for base construction among the Namaqua Hottentot. If the potter excavates a clay mass to form the bottom, we may expect a base that is thicker than the vessel walls in general and significantly thicker than the shoulder and upper body in particular. An excavated base is less uniform than one that is coiled, molded, or modeled and will not show the attachment seam of the latter two. A coiled base will be unlikely if the vessel body is mass-modeled. Although Laidler and Scot report modeled bases added to previously modeled bodies by the Pondo of KwaZulu-Natal, a molded or modeled base appears less frequently on mass-modeled bodies than on coiled bodies.

Laidler and Scot cite ethnographic reports of mass-modeled vessels formed from the bottom up among the Baronga (of southern Mozambique), the Bechuana (of the central and western parts of the former Transvaal province), and all Bushmen who produce pottery. H. Kuper reports coiled-body formation from the bottom up among Swazi potters (in Swaziland and Mozambique). In a videotape detailing the practices of Somalia's Buur Heybe potters, T. Belklin illustrates the production of coiled wares whose base shape determines the artisan's starting point. If the pot is to have a round bottom, coiled-body production begins with the lower-vessel walls. The upper-vessel walls and lip are formed next, and the bottom last. If the pot is to have a flat bottom, however, the bottom is coiled first, and the walls are built up of coils starting at the bottom and working upward to the lip.

Vessel Part Morphology

BASE SHAPE. The previously discussed techniques of vessel fabrication were, of course, used at different times and in different places to produce pots of various sizes and shapes. To assess this variability properly, we must further divide our units of description. All three production techniques (coiling, molding, and modeling) may be used to produce bases that are convex, concave, or flat. Then too, four customary descriptions may be given to convex bases: round, ellipsoidal, pointed, and conoidal. Transvaal Ndebele, Eastern Tswana, and baVenda potters mass-model a flat-bottomed ware by pulling, pinching, and stretching the lower portion of a starter strap to a point and then gently patting the point with the flat side of a bean pod or gourd scraper to flatten it. The Namaqua Hottentot coil flat bases. While mold-assisted flat bases are not reported in the literature, David illustrates their production in a videotape of Hide potting. Whether coiled, molded, or mass-modeled, flat bottoms are the hallmark of wares classified as belonging to the Zaire Basin's Batalimo-Maluba, Imbonga, and Lingonda horizons, carbon-dated to the last half of the 1st millennium B.C., and the earliest-known pottery in sub-Saharan Africa. Mass-modeled, concave bases are reported among the Ila (of southern Zambia), and although the literature is unclear about the technique of manufacture, concave bases are characteristic of the Early Iron Age dimple-based wares of the Sandawe and Kwale in the interior of East Africa during the middle years of the 1st millennium A.D., as suggested by P. L. Shinnie in 1971 and by R. Oliver and B. M.

Fagan in 1975. Round-bottomed wares were produced throughout the 1st millennium A.D. in the Zaire Basin (Bondongo and Nkile horizons) and are typical of the Early, Middle and Late Iron Age in the Zambezi Valley. Conical- or pointed-base wares were produced by Bushmen in the Kalahari and are found on Hottentot vessels from Little Namaqualand.

SHOULDER SHAPE. We must also distinguish between shouldered and shoulderless vessels. We have described the shoulder as the maximum circumference of the body. Shoulderless forms achieve their maximum diameter at the mouth, at the base, or, in the case of cylindrical pots, at both, but not in between. Shouldered forms (vessels whose maximum body circumference lies between mouth and base) may be divided into pots whose maximum circumference lies midway between mouth and base and those that do not. With respect to the latter, we may describe those whose maximum circumference lies above the mouth-base midpoint as *high-shouldered* and those whose maximum circumference lies below the midpoint as *low-shouldered. Midshouldered* is the term used to designate vessels whose maximum circumference lies at or near the midpoint between base and mouth.

Shoulderless vessels may have curved or straight walls. Those with curved walls assume the form of hemispherical or subhemispherical bowls. Those with straight walls may be cylindrical or may expand or contract from base to mouth. In the former, the walls may be described as *out-sloping,* while walls in the latter are referred to as *in-sloping.* Shoulderless vessels with flat or gently rounded bases and in-sloping, straight walls are relatively rare but were reported at Late Stone Age sites in the Kenya Highlands and were made on occasion by Bushman potters, who also produced cylindrical vessels. Shoulderless, out-sloping, straight-walled vessels were made in the Zaire Basin as early as 200 B.C. by potters producing wares identified as part of the Lingonda horizon. They occur sporadically, if at all, in later ceramic assemblages of eastern and southern Africa. In assemblages from the Zaire Basin, curved-walled, shoulderless vessels expressed as hemispherical or subhemispherical bowls formed part of an even earlier Imbonga horizon (from 500 B.C. to A.D. 100). Bowls of similar size and shape are found in most Iron Age ceramic assemblages in central, eastern, and southern Africa.

Shouldered vessels, whether high-, mid-, or low-shouldered, may be rounded or angular. Rounded vessels usually predominate in ceramic inventories of the Iron Age. Both angular and rounded, high- and midshouldered vessels are components of the Zaire Basin's Imbonga, Bondongo, and Nkile horizons. Rounded, high- and midshouldered specimens are the hallmark of Early, Middle, and Late Iron Age ceramic traditions in the Zambezi Valley, and although angular, shouldered wares occur, rounded, high- and midshouldered forms dominate the Iron Age ceramic assemblages to the north, east, and south of the Zambezi. Both angular and rounded, low-shouldered specimens have been found in Bondongo horizon deposits in the Zaire Basin, and low-shouldered, rounded forms are an integral part of the succeeding Botendo horizon. In Iron Age deposits elsewhere, rounded or angular, low-shouldered vessels are relatively rare.

RIM FORM. When the artisan reached the desired minimal circumference of the upper body, he or she could form a lip or continue to build and, in so doing, form a rim. On rimless vessels, the mouth and lip are coterminous. They are separate orifices in vessels with rims. Rims may be descibed as *high* or *low. High rim* is used to describe rims that are as tall as or taller than one-half the distance between mouth and bottom. By *low rim,* we mean those that are shorter than one-half the distance between mouth and bottom. Then too, both high and low rims may rise directly from the mouth, slope outward, or slope inward from the mouth. Rims with virtually identical lip and mouth circumferences are customarily called *straight* or *direct*. A rim whose circumference at the lip is greater than the circumference at the mouth is described as *out-flaring*. A rim whose circumference at the mouth is greater than the circumference at the lip is described as *in-flaring*. Thus, when the artisan reached the desired minimal circumference of the upper body, he or she could stop or proceed with one of several steps: (1) build straight upward, (2) build upward and outward—that is, form an

out-flaring rim, (3) build upward and outward and then brace the rim by adding a fillet of clay to the rim's outer and upper edge, (4) build upward and then brace the upper and outer edge, (5) build upward and inward—that is, form an in-flaring rim, (6) build upward and inward and then brace the upper and outer edge, (7) build upward and then outward and back again to form an *S*-shape, or (8) build upward, outward, and then upward to form a collar. Each of these practices may be executed in several different ways. All rim types may be formed by pulling, thinning, and scraping the clay used in upper-body formation. This procedure is, however, time-consuming and tedious and produces a thin and, in its greenware state, often brittle rim especially in those cases in which the rim is high, collared, or *S*-shaped. Telma Makwe, a Tswana potter did, however, use this procedure to produce a *nkgo*—a typical BaKxatla vessel with a low, out-flaring rim and flat lip.

All rim forms may also be built by adding a roll or strap of clay to the upper and outer surface of the mouth and then manipulating, scraping, and thinning it to the desired shape. Emma Rabalago, a Transvaal Ndebele potter, added a roll of clay to form a low, out-flaring rim, and Mutshekwa Litshira, a Venda potter, added a strap of clay to produce a rim of the same size and shape. The designation *unthickened* has been used for this single-roll or single-strap approach to rim manufacture. While *S*-shaped and collared rims may also be made from a single roll or strap, they are most easily fashioned by using two rolls or two straps. The first is welded to the upper and outer surface of the mouth, the second to the upper and outer surface of the roll or strap. Mutshekwa Litshira, for example, made both low- and high-collared *S*-shaped rims by using two straps. This two-roll or two-strap approach to manufacturing collared or *S*-shaped rims has been described as producing *thickened* rims. Thus rims may be unthickened or thickened; out-flared, direct, or in-flared; braced, collared, or *S*-shaped. All have been described or illustrated in the African ethnographic or archaeological literature.

LIP FORM. The lip may also be a highly variable part of a vessel on both rim-bearing and rimless forms. The lip itself may be flattened, rounded, beveled to the inside, beveled to the outside, beveled to both the inside and the outside (that is, tapered or triangular-shaped), shaped like an inverted *L*, or *T*-shaped. All but the *T*-shaped form have been reported for ceramic samples from sub-Saharan Africa. Most of the variability noted in the African literature has, however, been produced by manipulating a lip coil that has been laid over and joined to the upper edge of the rim or, if the vessel is rimless, to the upper edge of the upper body. The appearance of even greater variability is introduced by varying the diameter of the lip coil or forcing the upper-vessel wall or upper rim outward or inward.

APPENDAGES. Appendages added to African ceramics include spouts (usually springing from the shoulder or affixed to a drastically narrowed mouth), loop and strap handles (usually joining the lip and the shoulder), lugs (tab-shaped or oval, perforated or unperforated, affixed to the shoulder or the lip), and annular pedestals (supports or cone-shaped legs appended to vessel bases).

Decoration

In a general sense, African vessel decorations may be easily and systematically divided into (1) those that require a substance addition, such as painting, slipping, or filleting, (2) those that require the use of a tool, such as incising, trailing, forming punctations (minute spots or depressions), and impressing, (3) those that require only the use of the fingers such as pinching, finger and fingernail impressing, lip flattening, and rim bending, and (4) those that combine some or perhaps all of the above. The consequences of such actions, insofar as they are displayed as redundant surface alterations, may be termed *decorative elements*. By studying them, an analyst should be able to describe the manipulations of the artisan and the kind of tools or substances he or she used in these manipulations. Thus any redundant surface alteration that can be systematically linked to the artisan's use of tools, fingers, or extraneous substances is a decorative element. Both Iron Age and modern African potters seem to decorate most frequently by incising, trailing, impressing, forming punctations, polishing, painting, and adding appliqué work to the vessels.

INCISING. To incise, the artisan drew a pointed and edged tool over the clay at a high oblique angle, leaving an incision with a *V*-shaped trough and a marked wake. In some cases, a multipointed carved wood or bone tool (often called a *comb*) seems to have been used to incise parallel lines. In other instances, commonly described as *stab-and-drag incising*, the flat side of a single-edged, pointed tool was held against the clay surface, the point of the tool was pushed forward into the clay at about a 10° angle and then pulled back, and the flat side of the tool was dragged over the clay surface.

TRAILING. Trailing, both broad and narrow gauge (the former frequently decribed as *channeling* or *grooving*), is a common element of many Iron Age ceramic decorations. Trailing was done with a flat-sided, roughly rectangular tool drawn over the pliable clay at a very low, oblique angle, producing an even-bottomed, *U*-shaped trough and a shallow wake. A broader tool produced a broader trough or channel and a shallower wake. A narrower tool produced a narrower trough and a more substantial wake.

IMPRESSING AND FORMING PUNCTATIONS. Tool-impressed designs were most commonly produced by pressing the cut and shaped curved edge of a flat-sided, semilunar tool down into the clay with a rocking motion starting near the artisan's body. The impressing tool could be made of wood, calabash, bone, or metal. Tool impressing produced an uneven-bottomed, *U*-shaped trough with no perceivable wake. If notches had been cut from the curved edge of the impressing tool, its use produced a linear series of holes frequently described as *rouletting*. Fabric impressing, with either a single cord or a matlike woven fabric repeatedly pressed into the clay, is evident on wares from the Zaire Basin. Finger and fingernail impressing occurred but was rare. To accomplish the former, the artisan pressed a fingertip into the clay at an acute angle and then withdrew it. To form the latter, the artisan's finger was pressed into the clay at an oblique angle leaving only the impression of the fingernail. To produce punctations, the artisan pressed the square, triangular, or round end of a tool (made of wood, bone, or iron) into the clay and then withdrew it, leaving a hole.

POLISHING, PAINTING, AND APPLIQUÉ. Polishing was accomplished by rubbing a smooth-surfaced, oval or round stone back and forth across the clay until a shiny, compacted vessel surface was produced. It should be noted that polishing after impressing, punctating, incising, or trailing produced cantilevered edges where clean edges or wakes once stood. Polishing after painting produced an attractive lustrous painted surface. Crushed graphite, hematite, or magnetite were commonly mixed with water or animal fat to produce paint. The graphite paint was black, while the magnetite and hematite paints were red. The African artisan commonly applied paint to vessel surfaces with his or her fingertip by rubbing it on with a back-and-forth movement. The use of a slip (a colloidal suspension of coloring agent and clay), either scrubbed on with a rag or hide or applied as a dip, while rare, has been reported in South African assemblages. To produce appliqué work, the potter affixed a roll, strap, or a blob of moist clay to the pliable vessel surface and then pushed, pulled, pinched, or smoothed it into desired final shape. Appliqué work and paint or slip were usually applied before firing. Paint was often applied after stamping, trailing, or incising. If, for instance, the vessel was to be incised, painted, and polished, then the constituent operations would be performed in the following order: (1) incising, (2) painting, and (3) polishing. In sum, the decorative elements produced by the use of a tool usually precede those requiring the addition of a substance. Then too, decorative elements made by the use of a tool may be applied either before or after the vessel is completely formed. Modern baVenda, Transvaal Ndebele, and Tswana potters, for instance, impress, incise, or trail the shoulder and upper portions of their wares before the bottom is pulled.

DECORATIVE ENVIRONMENT, DESIGN, AND DESIGN STRUCTURE. If we exclude monochrome painting (because if a single color is used paint is usually applied to the whole of the vessel exterior) and polishing the exterior of the vessel, then any part of a vessel bearing a single decorative element may be termed a *decorative environment*. The most common decorative environments in the Iron Age and modern times are the lip, the rim exterior, the rim interior (on vessels with rims), the upper-body exterior, and the shoulder. In the Zaire Basin, the lower-body exterior and base are frequently decorated, but this practice is less evident elsewhere. In fact, if the descriptions rendered and the pieces illustrated in the literature are representative, then a greater number of decorative environments were used in the Zaire Basin than elsewhere, and earlier wares both in the Zaire Basin and beyond tend to bear decorative elements in a greater number of environments than their later counterparts.

Sets of decorative elements that contrast with all others in the same or complementary decorative environments may be considered *designs*. For the most part, both Iron Age and modern Bantu designs were composed of multiple rectilinear or curvilinear line sets rendered by incising, trailing, impressing, or forming punctations. These line sets were typically brought into opposition at a 45° or 90° angle or intersected at a 45° or 90° angle. The appearance of variability was achieved by using differing combinations of design elements in a single or complementary decorative environments or by enclosing one set of design elements within another in the same or in complementary decorative environments. The arrangement of decorative elements in a design is called *structure*. Thus the complexity of Bantu designs was realized through structural means—that is, the Bantu potters counterpoised design elements or nested one element within another.

Drying and Firing the Vessel

After pottery vessels are shaped and decorated, they must be dried before firing. If insufficiently dried, residual moisture from the clay will vaporize within the vessel walls during heating and cause the vessel to spall, shatter, or warp. Then too, uneven or excessively rapid drying will crack the vessel before it reaches a true greenware state. The drying period may vary because of differences in temperature, humidity, and the water-retention properties of the clay. Most drying is done indoors, usually in a shed or a house.

Firing is a three-stage process. In the first stage, the vessel is warmed (the slower the better), and any moisture remaining is driven from the clay body. If warming proceeds too rapidly, the clay particles fuse before residual moisture escapes, and pockets of steam form within the vessel walls causing them to shatter and spall. During the second stage, organic matter is burned from the clay body, and additional oxygen is introduced through circulation drafts. This oxygen reacts with carbonaceous matter in the clay body and soot from the burning fuel to produce carbon dioxide. As carbon in the clay body is removed, the iron oxides that remain are oxidized producing shades of red, orange, yellow, gray, or brown. Vitrification is the third and final stage. During vitrification, clay constituents soften, stick to each other, and become joined by glass filaments formed from melting and combining silica. If oxidation is incomplete, as it usually is with secondary (residual) clays, the remaining organic matter will form gas at high vitrification temperatures, and the concomitant pressure will cause warping or other forms of wall distortion. Nevertheless, residual clays are usually of low purity and contain natural fluxing agents that produce the beginnings of vitrification at a relatively low temperature (600° to 900° C) thus muting the effects of incomplete oxidation.

Bantu potters, both ancient and modern, normally open-fired their wares using locally available fuels. Potters first cleared grass, sod, earth, or sand from a circular or oval area of suitable dimensions and either smoothed the area to provide a flat surface or dug it out to form a shallow concave surface. Next, potters might prepare a bed of sticks, grass, or bark to lay over the bare soil. The pots to be fired were either placed mouth up or mouth down and nestled into the prepared bed of sticks and grass or arranged on stones or potsherds to allow a draft during the early stages of burning. Potters may also have leaned the vessels together shoulder to shoulder to secure them in an unright position. A mouth-up or mouth-down position may be inferred from the smudge patterns noted on the interior or exterior of pot bottoms, on the exterior and interior of lips and near-lip portions, and on the exterior surface of the shoulder.

Potters then stacked fuel over the pots. It is generally presumed that locally available materials were used. Therefore, it seems reasonable to suppose that wood, grass, and bark were collected from supplies nearby. Firing clouds with a linear configuration and whose size and position indicate the use of sticks or logs may be used to infer fuel composition and stacking techniques. A radial distribution of linear firing clouds indicates the use of a tepeelike frame of sticks or branches. A lattice or dendritic pattern indicates stacking of a different kind. If a wood framework was used, potters most probably covered it with a thatch of grass or bark. If dried dung was also used, potters would have heaped it over the thatch. Potters probably lit the stack on the downwind side (to promote a slower, hotter burn) and added fuel as needed during the burn. Most potters seem to have allowed their wares to cool before pulling them from the dying fire, thus preventing cracking through rapid heat loss.

BIBLIOGRAPHY
Adamson, D. A., J. D. Clark, and M. A. J. Williams. 1987. Pottery tempered with sponge from the White Nile, Sudan. *The African Archaeological Review* 5: 115–127.
Eggert, M. K. H. 1983. Remarks on exploring archaeologically unknown rain forest territory: The case of central Africa. *Beitrage zur Allgemeinen und Vergleichenden Archaeologie* 5: 283–322
Krause, R. A. 1985. *The clay sleeps: An ethnoarchaeological study of three African potters.* Tuscaloosa: The University of Alabama Press.
Kuper, H. 1986. *The Swazi: A South African kingdom.* New York: Holt, Rinehart and Winston.
Laidler, P. W., and F. S. A. Scot. 1936. South African native ceramics: Their characteristics and classification. *Transactions of the Royal Society of South Africa* 26 (2): 93–172.
Oliver, R., and B. M. Fagan. 1975. *Africa in the Iron Age.* Cambridge: Cambridge University Press.
The potters of Buur Heybe, Somalia. 1990. Produced by Tara Belklin. 25 min. Filmakers Library, Inc. Videocassette.
Shinnie, P. L., ed. 1971. *The African Iron Age.* Oxford: Clarendon Press.
Vessels of the spirits. 1990. Produced by N. David. 50 min. University of Calgary, Department of Communications Media. Videocassette.
Vogel, J. O. 1973. The Mosioatunya sequence: The Iron Age cultures in the Victoria Falls region in Zambia. *Zambia Museums Journal* 4: 105–152.

Richard A. Krause

COPPER METALLURGY

Copper in African Prehistory

Copper and its alloys occupied a unique position among metals in the indigenous cultures of sub-Saharan Africa. In many ways, copper played a role similar to that of gold in the Western world. Although copper sometimes served as a means of exchange in the subsistence economy, its greatest importance was in social and ritual contexts where it was a measure of personal wealth and prestige. Unlike iron, few utilitarian objects were made solely of copper, although the metal was often added as a decoration to the handles of tools, particularly those employed on ritual occasions. The history of copper metallurgy south of the Sahara is closely linked to that of iron, and with a possible exception in Niger, there is no evidence for an indigenous Copper or Bronze Age preceding the rapid spread of iron technology between 500 B.C. and A.D. 500.

Africa contains some of the richest copper deposits in the world, but individual ore bodies are localized and not widely distributed over the continent. Major occurrences are often separated by hundreds or even thousands of kilometers. Nevertheless, within geologically favorable areas, outcrops can be numerous, and in almost every known case, exposed copper-carbonate ores were collected or mined by Africans.

In West Africa, copper minerals are restricted to the fringes of the Sahara and the Sahel, with the largest concentrations occurring in Mauritania, central Mali, the Air Massif north of Agadez in Niger, and in the southwestern Sudan. In central Africa, dispersed copper outcrops occur from the Niari River in the Congo Republic south to the hinterland of Benguela in Angola. The largest and richest area of copper mineralization in Africa is the Central African Copperbelt. This geological feature is an arc of rich ore stretching from Kitwe, Zambia, into Shaba Province, Zaire, where it passes through Lubumbashi and ends near Kolwezi. In southern Africa, more limited copper deposits are found in central Zambia, the Zimbabwe Plateau, central Namibia, eastern Botswana, the northern part of the former Transvaal province, and near O'Okiep in the

Western Cape Province. Copper ore is very rare in eastern Africa, and significant deposits are present only at Kilembe in Uganda.

Copper metallurgy was invented in Eurasia and began before 6000 B.C. with the use of native copper followed by the production of metal from ore. Mining and smelting the metal appears to have arisen independently in both the Near East and eastern Europe. The smelting and alloying of copper is thought to have been an outgrowth of the production of kiln-fired ceramics, in which experimentation with powdered copper ores as paints or glazes resulted in the accidental discovery of the smelting process. In Bulgaria, mines more than 10 meters deep and well-crafted ornaments in burials demonstrate a developed metallurgical technology in the Balkans by the 5th millennium B.C. In the Near East, the working of native copper was followed by the development of smelting as early as 3800 B.C. Smelted copper was widespread throughout the area by the mid-4th millennium B.C.

There is no unambiguous evidence for a similar gradual and indigenous invention of copper smelting in sub-Saharan Africa. Metallurgy appears as a fully developed technological repertoire in most areas, although it is no longer considered to form a single techno-complex in association with the origin and spread of agriculture. In almost all cases, iron is either the first metal found in an area or occurs simultaneously with copper. The ultimate source of sub-Saharan metallurgy has not been conclusively identified, but among the most likely source areas are Carthage or southern Morocco via Berber traders crossing the Sahara.

The earliest archaeological evidence for copper mining and smelting south of the tropic of Cancer comes from sites in the central and western Sahel. At Afunfun and Azelik near Agadez, Niger, numerous burned features were initially interpreted as forges and copper-smelting furnaces. Some of these features were radiocarbon-dated to the 2nd millennium B.C. A development from the melting of native copper to the smelting of oxide ores was believed to be represented. Recent analysis of the vitrified contents of these features has established that almost all of the ones dating to earlier than 1000 B.C. were not associated with copper metallurgy, and that all of the early dates from true furnaces may be the result of the use of fossil wood as a source of charcoal. Although the older dates are not accurate, many furnaces at these sites can be dated accurately to between 900 and 300 B.C. These smelters represent the earliest securely dated copper working in West Africa.

Mining and smelting of copper has also been documented at Akjoujt in western Mauritania. Excavations in the Grotte aux Chauves-souris mine produced evidence of the smelting of oxide ores as early as the 5th century B.C. Copper artifacts surface-collected from Neolithic sites in the area include numerous arrow points, spearheads, axes, and a smaller number of bracelets and ornaments. Some of these specimens are stylistically similar to Phoenician artifacts from North Africa and strengthen the case for a trans-Saharan origin for this technology.

Relatively large-scale precolonial mining also took place in two other regions of the Sahel, which have not yet been excavated. These are Nioro-Siracoro on the Mali-Mauritania border, where ethnohistoric evidence suggests mining as early as the 14th century, and Hufrat en-Nahas in the Sudan, where undated mine shafts (ca. A.D. 1000) have been observed.

Although prehistoric copper mines are much more common in central and southern Africa, dating their origins has been made difficult by the lack of archaeological research and because later prehistoric and modern mining activities tend to obliterate evidence of the initial exploitation of a deposit. The earliest direct date for copper smelting south of the equator comes from the Zairean Copperbelt. At the Naviundu Springs near Lubumbashi, charcoal from a copper-smelting furnace was dated to between A.D. 345 and about 375, and additional dates confirm a 4th-century inception for the Iron Age in this area. Other sites near Lubumbashi yielded abundant mounds of copper slag and broken ingots. Based on ceramic comparisons, these sites are thought to range from the 5th to the 18th century. At the Kansanshi mine in Zambia, a large ceramic crucible decorated with Early Iron Age motifs and containing ashes, slag, and droplets of copper was radiocarbon-dated to the 5th century. Concentrations of slag associated with the Kipushi mine

on the Zambia-Zaire border near Lubumbashi yielded dates ranging from the 9th to 12th centuries, and since the entire site could not be studied, earlier exploitation of Kipushi is considered likely. Ancient copper mines are common in Zimbabwe, but only the Umkondo mine has been dated. A 7th-century reading obtained from a digging stick found in a mine shaft certainly reflects the most recent rather than the earliest mining in the area. In South Africa, archaeological research at Phalaborwa has demonstrated that copper mining began perhaps as early as the 8th century and continued until the 19th. Other major prehistoric mines at Messina and O'Okiep in South Africa, Tsumeb and Rehoboth in Namibia, and Tati in Botswana remain undated.

The presence of copper artifacts at archaeological sites provides additional data on the origins and chronology of copper in sub-Saharan Africa. The association of copper artifacts with village sites from the 1st millennium B.C. in the Sahel was noted above. In the Lake Upemba Basin of Zaire, copper is present in Iron Age sites as early as the 7th century as well as in the earlier mining sites near Lubumbashi. In Zambia, copper is found at 4th-century village sites in the copperbelt and northwestern provinces and appears only slightly later in the central and southern provinces. Dates for the appearance of copper at Early Iron Age sites in Zimbabwe begin in the 6th century. At the Broederstroom site 24/73 in the former Transvaal province of South Africa, copper ornaments have been found that date to between the 4th and 7th centuries.

Although copper does not occur at all Early Iron Age sites in sub-Saharan Africa, small quantities of it are found at most sites at or shortly after the appearance of iron technology. The one exception is in East Africa, where copper is conspicuously absent from Early Iron Age sites and very rare at sites dating to the 2nd millennium A.D. In East Africa, the ethnographic record shows that iron was the preferred metal for both utilitarian tools and ornaments. Although the lack of copper ore may have been a contributing factor, the scarcity of indigenous copper ornaments in East African Iron Age sites demonstrates that from the earliest settlements to the present, copper was not as highly valued in this area.

Fig. 14 *Prehistoric mines (•) and archaeological sites (x)*

1	Akjoujt	13	Benguela
2	Nioro-Siracoro	14	Kansanshi
3	Azelik and Afunfun	15	Lubumbashi
4	Agadez	16	Ndola
5	Hufrat en-Nahas	17	Tsumeb
6	Ife	18	Umkondo
7	Benin	19	Great Zimbabwe
8	Kilembe	20	Rehoboth
9	Niari	21	Tati
10	Bembe	22	Messina
11	Kolwezi	23	Phalaborwa,
12	Lake Upemba		Broederstroom
	Basin	25	O'Okiep

Mining, Smelting, and Smithing Techniques

Copper ores can be divided into two types. Sulphide ores are compounds of copper, iron, and sulphur and include the minerals chalcopyrite, chalcocite, and bornite. Sulphide ores are usually the initial contents of copper mineral veins. Oxidized ores result from the decomposition of sulphide ores when exposed to fluids at or near the surface of the earth. The minerals produced by this process of supervenient enrichment include cuprite, malachite, azurite, and chrysocolla. Exposed ore bodies typically form horizons, with an upper layer characterized by oxidized ores superimposed on a sulphide zone. These conditions characterized virtually all outcrops of copper ore in Africa.

Only oxidized ores could be easily smelted by traditional African techniques. Sulphides, which require more complex, multistage treatment before they can be reduced to metal, were generally avoided by African miners. Because oxide ores naturally occur on the exposed surfaces of copper deposits, initial mining probably involved simple collection or the digging of shallow pits. As surface deposits were exhausted, miners employed more elaborate methods such as following concentrations of high-grade ore to the bottom of the oxidized zone, usually less than 50 meters in depth. As a result, the plan of African copper mines was determined by the shape of the ore body.

This influence of the ore body on African mining strategies is evident in both the archaeological and ethnographic record from the Central African Copperbelt. At Kipushi, Zaire, copper minerals had diffused out from a hydrothermal vein to form a large, irregular mass. The ancient mine there took the form of two large open pits with sloping sides. In contrast, the ore body at Kansanshi Hill, Zambia, was a series of vertically oriented fissure veins. These were quarried out to a depth of more than 30 meters using steeply inclined pits that followed the deposits. Exhausted veins took on the appearance of deep trenches with vertical sides. Rubble was used to make ramps to gain access to deeper parts of this mine, and the ramps were sometimes supplemented with wooden ladders. Digging itself was accomplished with modifications of agricultural tools. A narrow-bladed iron ax served as a pick, and a hoe was used to scoop rock into baskets for transport. Ore was carried to the surface and hammered to separate the copper oxides, primarily malachite and chrysocolla, from quartz and other unusable minerals.

The most complete ethnographic account of African copper mining was made at the Dikuluwe mine near Kolwezi in Zaire in the 1920s. The Yeke people who mined Dikuluwe conducted "campaigns" organized by master smelters or chiefs during the dry season. Women and children collected malachite from the surface of the ground, while men, using iron picks, excavated large pits and shafts. Fires were set to crack hard rock, and ore was transported up wooden ladders in bark buckets. Shafts reached an average depth of 10 to 15 meters and connected to tunnels up to 20 meters in length. The deepest shafts were 35 meters and required wooden beams to support the sides. At other sites in the Kolwezi area, it is reported that women did most of the underground mining.

The smelting of oxidized copper ores can be accomplished at temperatures as low as 700° to 800° C in a furnace filled with charcoal. With limited air flow, the charcoal burns to carbon monoxide, and an ore such as malachite, a copper carbonate, is reduced to metallic copper and carbon dioxide. Too much air introduced into the furnace produces carbon dioxide directly and inhibits the reduction process. It is probably for this reason fewer bellows or tuyeres (air pipes) were employed in African copper smelters than in those designed for iron. Temperatures between 800° and 1,083° C result in solid-state reduction of ore that produces a spongy mass of metal. Above that range, copper becomes molten. All known African furnaces were designed to exceed the melting point in order to produce a well-consolidated mass of metal or to facilitate casting.

Copper-smelting furnaces in Africa are less variable in design than iron smelters. In the earliest surviving examples, found near Agadez, Niger, a circular pit, roughly 30 centimeters deep and with a flat bottom was dug, and the walls were plastered with clay. This served as the base of a cylindrical or conical structure with puddled-clay walls extending to an unknown height. In the oldest furnace, the pit was larger than the diameter of the combustion chamber, and a hole was made in the furnace wall to allow for the passage of air from a bellows. Later furnaces were truncated cones between 60 and 80 centimeters in diameter and estimated to have been more than 1 meter in height. Air was supplied by bellows through angled tuyeres mounted at ground level and thus 10 to 40 centimeters above the furnace base. Both types of furnaces had to be destroyed to remove the copper and slag produced by the smelt.

In central Africa, furnaces were often more complex and sometimes designed to allow direct casting. In addition, copper production was often a two-stage process involving initial smelting followed by refining. The process is best illustrated in Zambia, where archaeological and ethnographic research have documented Kaonde copper production from about 1500 to the present. The Kaonde smelting furnace was constructed on level ground and consisted of a shallow, circular depression 50 centimeters in diameter and carefully lined with a paste of fine wood ash to prevent the molten copper from mixing with soil. Around this depression, a conical furnace, probably no more than 1 meter high, was constructed of puddled clay. Two opposed openings in the base of the furnace allowed the entry of a forced draft provided by bellows. The furnace was packed with small pieces of hardwood charcoal, and after ignition, a charge of ore was placed on top of the incandescent fuel. No flux was employed to assist in the separation of slag. Additional charges of fuel and ore were added until the base of the furnace was filled with a pool of metal and slag. The furnace was then allowed to cool and was broken to extract the congealed mass of copper, slag, and charcoal. This was hammered into small pieces to separate the metal, much of which was probably taken to the smelter villages for refining.

The refining furnace was a smaller structure. A crucible consisting of an ordinary clay cooking pot filled with sand and covered with a layer of ash paste was placed on the ground. This was surrounded with carved termite mounds serving as bricks to form a circular structure approximately 60 centimeters high. Spaces between the bricks were plastered with clay. A single tuyere entered the furnace above the mouth of the pot, and draft was supplied by a pair of bag bellows. The furnace was filled with charcoal, and after ignition, pieces of copper were added until the desired amount of molten copper, usually less than 1 kilogram, had accumulated in the crucible. This remelting process separated the last vestiges of slag from the metal. The furnace was then rapidly broken, and the crucible was removed with the aid of wet grass pads. The metal was poured into open ingot mounds.

This basic method is repeated in all other central and southern African copper industries, with differences being primarily in the scale of fur-

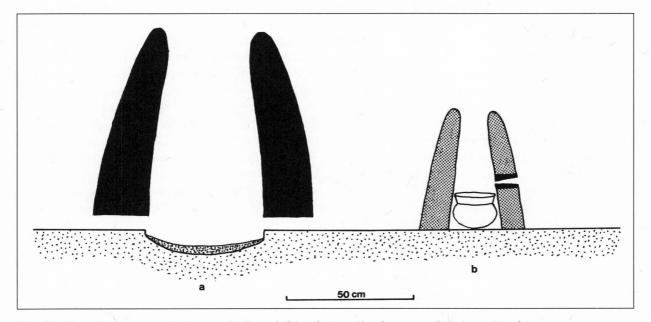

Fig. 15 *Kaonde furnaces for (a) smelting and (b) refining, Northwestern Province, Zambia*

naces or the raw materials available for their construction. The largest furnaces were made by the Sanga people of Zaire and were 1 meter in diameter, 1.75 meters high, and fired by four pairs of bellows. These were permanent structures with large openings at their bases to facilitate the removal of metal and slag. Refining furnaces of the same size were constructed on sloping ground and designed with a tap hole that allowed molten metal to flow down a channel into ingot mounds. Ingots produced by these large furnaces could weigh up to 50 kilograms. Smaller permanent furnaces that allowed direct casting were constructed by the Luba of Zaire. Luba furnaces were built on sloping ground in a beehive shape, 40 to 50 centimeters high and with a chamber diameter of 30 to 40 centimeters. A flux was added to the charge of charcoal and ore to facilitate complete separation of metal from slag and to make the slag flow freely. No tuyeres were employed, but a pair of opposing holes permitted a forced draft. On the downslope side, a small tap hole was bored in the furnace base and plugged with ash paste. A channel led to a flat clay surface, where ingots were cast in shallow mounds made of ashes mixed with clay. When all the metal was extracted, the tap hole was enlarged to empty the furnace of slag.

Alloying copper to other metals was practiced in only a few areas of Africa. Bronze, an alloy of copper and tin, may have been produced as early as the 15th century in the former Transvaal province of South Africa. True bronze is common among the artifacts found at Great Zimbabwe. In central Africa, there is no evidence of intentional production of alloys. In West Africa, the use of brass (an alloy of copper and zinc) was extremely common, and some West African brass has been incorrectly identified as bronze. There is no evidence that brass was produced before the 19th century in Africa, so brass dating from earlier periods must have been imported. Other alloys may have occurred naturally when copper ore was smelted with impurities containing metals such as arsenic.

Casting and annealing (heating and hammering) were the preferred methods of shaping copper in Africa. Casting in an open mold is the simplest method and was employed using a variety of materials ranging from simple templates of the desired shape made in the earth or sand adjacent to the refining furnace or forge to carefully prepared, baked-clay ingot or soapstone mounds with templates on opposing faces. Ingots and ornaments cast in open molds have been dated to as early as the 5th century.

Closed-mold, "lost wax" casting was practiced only in West Africa. In this technique, either a solid wax or latex model of the desired object was prepared, or a model made of clay was covered with a thin layer of wax. This was then encased in clay, with appropriate holes allowing the wax to drain. After drying, the mold was baked, and the wax or latex ran out. While still hot, the mold was filled with molten metal. This technique first appeared in the western Sudan near the end of the 1st millennium and the beginning of the 2nd millennium but reached its height sometime between the 12th and 15th centuries at Ife, Nigeria, and between the 15th and 19th centuries at Benin. Although some of the figures from Ife were cast of pure copper, the majority of later castings were of imported brass, which has a lower melting point and produces less of the gasses that can interfere with closed-mold casting.

The final smithing technique of note was wire drawing. Wire, sometimes produced in extremely fine diameters, was an important component of bracelets and bangles. Wire production was accomplished by hammering a bar of copper into a rod approximately 3 to 5 millimeters in diameter and pointed on one end. The point was forced through a conical hole in an iron ball or elongated drawplate including a graded series of holes. The tip of the bar was grasped with tongs, and often with the aid of a lever, the wire was drawn through the hole, decreasing its diameter. This process was continued using progressively smaller holes until the desired gauge was achieved. This process does not appear in sub-Saharan Africa until the 2nd millennium A.D.

Copper in African Society

Once metallurgy became established in an area, iron became the metal of choice in the subsistence sphere, whereas copper was increasingly restricted to decoration and the prestige sphere of indigenous economies. The earliest copper artifacts in sub-Saharan Africa included a mixture of utilitarian and ornamental forms. In the 1st millennium A.D., however, almost all copper objects were personal adornments or ornaments, with ingots increasing in frequency and becoming more standardized through time. By the 2nd millennium, copper and its alloys not only had become ornamental but also served as a means of exchange, a standard of value, and a symbol of power with important ritual connotations.

This process is best documented in central Africa, where archaeological research in Zambia and Zaire has uncovered widespread but relatively infrequent copper ornaments such as bracelets made of thin copper strip or hammered copper wire in many Early Iron Age sites. By the end of this period, the use of copper as a decorative material intensified. At Sanga and other sites in the Lake Upemba Basin of Zaire, graves dating from the Early to Classic Kisalian (periods of affluent development of complex chiefdoms) of the 8th to 14th centuries contained increasing quantities of copper in a wide variety of forms. It was not until the succeeding Kabambian A and B periods (periods characterized by the metal-rich descendants of the Kisalian chiefdoms) that standardized ingots made their appearance.

The restriction of copper to decorative objects in the archaeological record is indicative of the metal's value. With the exception of East Africa, where many Nilotic pastoralists valued iron ornaments, copper came to symbolize wealth and political power throughout much of sub-Saharan Africa. The use of copper and brass as important elements of chiefly regalia is widely documented in the ethnography of western, central, and southern Africa. Because the symbolic association of copper with political power is so widespread, the documentation of changes over time in the production and distribution of the metal may assist archaeologists in reconstructing the evolution of indigenous African states.

Because of its value, copper was also an important commodity in indigenous trading networks. In the 1st millennium A.D., small quantities passed through intervillage barter along with foodstuffs, iron tools, textiles, pottery, and salt. Although individual exchanges may have covered short distances, the cumulative effect was the movement of copper long distances from its original source. The copper in this early trade was in the form of simple bars and ingots, which were cut in pieces and converted into ornaments. It was in the late 1st and early 2nd millennia that ingots became standardized in form and probably began to function as a currency. The transition from a limited-purpose currency employed on special occasions, such as marriages, to an all-purpose currency used in commercial transactions is illustrated in the dated sequence of graves at Sanga. Beginning in the 14th century, *H*-shaped ingots were rare and relatively large. Over time, the number of cruciform ingots in burials increased as did standardization of form, but the size decreased. The small ingots, probably used in the expanding market economy of the Luba state, disappeared by the 18th century when they were replaced by glass beads in this area.

Other forms of copper currency in widespread use during the 2nd millennium were the bar and ring forms, which appeared as early as the 11th century in West Africa. These were augmented by *manillas,* thick brass bracelets imported in large numbers from the beginning of European contact and still in use in some parts of Nigeria as late as 1948. In the southern Zaire Basin, the flat "hands" form of cross also remained in circulation for social transactions into the 20th century. In Zambia and northern Zimbabwe, large flanged *X*-shaped ingots were used in the prestige sphere, but copper and imported brass wire formed into bracelets or bangles circulated widely in these areas as well as the rest of southern Africa and served for most commercial purposes. The eventual decline of indigenous copper production in Africa may be a consequence of the introduction of large quantities of European copper and brass, which were distributed through preexisting trade networks.

BIBLIOGRAPHY

Bisson, M. S. 1975. Copper currency in central Africa: The archaeological evidence. *World Archaeology* 6: 276–292.

———. 1983. Trade and tribute: Archaeological evidence for the origin of states in south central Africa. *Cahiers d'Etudes Africaines* 22: 343–361.

Cline, W. 1937. *Mining and metallurgy in Negro Africa.* Menasha: George Banta.

de Maret, P. 1977. Sanga, new excavations, more data, and some related problems. *Journal of African History* 18: 321–337.

———. 1985. Archaeology in central Africa. *Journal of African History* 26: 129–148.

Grebenart, D. 1987. Characteristics of the final Neolithic and metal ages in the region of Agadez (Niger). In *Prehistory of arid North Africa: Essays in honor of Fred Wendorf,* ed. A. Close, 287–316. Dallas: Southern Methodist University Press.

Herbert, E. W. 1984. *Red gold of Africa.* Madison: University of Wisconsin Press.

Killick, D., N. J. van der Merwe, R. B. Gordon, and D. Grebenart. 1988. Reassessment of the evidence for early metallurgy in Niger, West Africa. *Journal of Archaeological Science* 15: 367–394.

Posnansky, M. 1977. Brass casting and its antecedents in West Africa. *Journal of African History* 18: 287–300.

Tylecote, R. F. 1976. *A history of metallurgy.* London: Institute of Metals.

Michael S. Bisson

IRONWORKING TECHNOLOGY

Indigenous African metalworking involves two distinct and successive technological activities. The first of these is the chemical process of smelting, in which the elemental metal is separated from its oxide ores in a high-temperature furnace. The second is the physical process of smithing, in which the raw metal is heated and fashioned into useful objects by hammering it into shape. In the indigenous African context, both of these processes, as well as the subsequent use of the metal artifacts, was augmented by nontechnical ritual and symbolism. Forming part of a symbolically meaningful web of daily and seasonal activity, traditional African metal technology incorporated elements of both science and magic and expressed relations of power and influence between the sexes, individuals, and groups.

For approximately the past 2,000 years, African people have been mining iron ore, smelting the metal, and working it into artifacts: jewelry in the form of rings and bangles, tools like hammers and chisels, weapons for hunting and war, and agricultural implements like the hoes indispensable for the efficient production of African crops. Iron ore, the earthy raw material of iron production, occurs plentifully throughout Africa, and a wide diversity of ore types was exploited. Suitable material ranged from low-grade laterite, an iron-rich weathered rock particularly common in the Tropics, to scarcer high-grade magnetite, a dense iron-oxide mineral. To smelt this diversity of ores, a correspondingly wide variety of smelting ovens or furnaces was used, but all operated on essentially the same fundamental principles. The process used for producing iron throughout Africa during this time is known as the *bloomery process.* During the past decade, the last living practitioners of iron smelting have been observed, filmed, and recorded by ethnographers. Today the indigenous bloomery process in Africa is virtually extinct. Nevertheless, the archaeological record is a rich source of information about African ironworking technology because the baked-clay furnaces and air pipes, the silicate waste material known as *slag,* and the metal artifacts themselves are durable and available for study.

The smelting process began with locating and mining suitable ore. This involved excavating laterite from quarry pits, collecting iron-rich river sand and concentrating the heavy iron-ore grains by careful washing, or simply collecting magnetize pebbles from weathered outcrops. Lumps of ore were broken with stone hammers and anvils into small nodules and stockpiled near furnace locations. Another crucial ingredient was charcoal, which was made by the controlled and incomplete burning of stacks of carefully selected hardwood. The furnaces were generally made of clay and varied greatly in shape and size. Documented forms include open, clay-lined pits, low, conical shafts about 1 meter high, and tall, cylindrical shafts more than 3 meters high. The varied details of furnace construction reflected the diversity of ore types, regional specialization, and regional cultural differences in a historically complicated way. Attempts to make sense of the distribution of furnace types (and, where they were used, the bellows types) have not been very successful because of the range of variation and lack of any clear pattern in their distribution. This probably points to a long history of local innovation and development, experimentation, technological borrowing, and movement of individual smelters.

Despite the extreme variation in design, all furnaces were loaded with a mixture of charcoal and crushed ore and fired for many hours or, in some cases, days. Air for the burning charcoal was provided either by pumping it through one or more clay air pipes with bellows or by letting the furnace act as a chimney with the rising column of heated air in the furnace allowing air to flow in passively through air pipes or through holes in the bottom of the furnace wall itself. The final product of the smelt was a bloom, a rough mass containing nodules of metallic iron, bits of the slag waste, partially reacted ore, unburnt charcoal, and often bits of the lining of the furnace. The bloom was removed from the furnace and, when cold, was broken up and the fragments sorted to recover the lumps of metallic iron. These were then worked at the forge or smithy. Here the blacksmith would heat the metal fragments in a forging hearth, usually an open fire with air pumped through a single or double air pipe with bellows, until the metal was red-hot and soft. It was then hammered on a rock or iron anvil to squeeze out the remaining slag and consolidate the metal fragments to a usable size.

The African iron-bloomery furnaces were not simple to operate, nor is it easy to replicate the process experimentally nowadays. By manipulating the air supply and the ratio of ore to fuel, the experienced ironmaster or smelter could control the temperature and composition of the gas in the furnace. This, in turn, affected the chemical reactions taking place in the furnace and, ultimately, allowed the smelter to control the nature of the product. The furnaces produced iron with varying amounts of dissolved carbon, and the final products ranged from soft, nearly pure carbon-free iron to brittle nodules of cast iron with a carbon content in excess of 2 percent. Usually the end product after smithing was steel, a tough but workable alloy of iron and carbon with up to about 0.8 percent carbon content.

The fundamental chemical reactions taking place in the furnace involved removing oxygen from the iron-oxide ores by reaction with either elemental carbon or carbon monoxide produced by the burning charcoal. Basically, the iron ore was reduced according to the sequence: hydrated iron oxides → haematite (Fe_2O_3) → magnetite (Fe_3O_4) → wüstite (FeO) → iron (Fe). Two sets of reactions were involved. The so-called direct reduction involved the removal of oxygen from iron oxides by reaction with solid carbon in the form of fine charcoal or soot according to the following sequence of reactions:

$$6Fe_2O_3 + C \rightarrow 4Fe_3O_4 + CO_2$$
$$2Fe_3O_4 + C \rightarrow 6FeO + CO_2$$
$$2FeO + C \rightarrow 2Fe \text{ (metal)} + CO_2$$

The so-called indirect reduction involved the removal of oxygen from the iron oxides by reaction with gaseous carbon monoxide, produced in the furnace by the burning charcoal, according to the following sequence of reactions:

$$3Fe_2O_3 + CO \rightarrow 2Fe_3O_4 + CO_2$$
$$Fe_3O_4 + CO \rightarrow 3FeO + CO_2$$
$$FeO + CO \rightarrow Fe \text{ (metal)} + CO_2$$

Both direct and indirect reduction may occur in the same furnace, depending on differences in temperature and fluctuations in the ratios of carbon dioxide to carbon monoxide. In theory, smelters could manipulate these reactions to determine the composition of the final bloomery product, but the product was usually a highly variable bloom with a range of carbon composition. Nevertheless, some of the furnace designs took advantage of the flexibility of the process to produce metal of a specific carbon content or to reduce ores of a specifically selected composition.

The Mafa of northern Cameroon, for instance, used a shaft furnace built against a terrace, with a single bellows-driven air pipe hanging down inside the shaft from the top. During the smelt, part of this clay air pipe melted to contribute to the slag, the molten waste that removes unwanted sandy components from the ore. The result, after 10.5 hours of hard pumping at the bellows and the burning of more than 80 kilograms of charcoal, was to reduce 18 kilograms of magnetite ore to a 15-kilogram bloom. About half of this bloom consisted of nodules of cast iron, which later was mixed with the lower carbon steel also present in the bloom and forged into implements with an overall carbon content of less than 0.8 percent. In contrast, the Cewa of Malawi used a furnace 2.5 meters tall, with nine air pipes around the bottom, and no bellows. The furnace was loaded with low-grade laterite ore and charcoal, and after burning for five days and consuming 1,455 kilograms of charcoal, it produced an heterogeneous bloom of low-carbon iron, which was then smelted again in a small conical, bellows-driven furnace. This two-step process was appropriate for the low-grade ore because it allowed the iron-rich initial bloom to be separated from a large amount of the unreacted waste before the final smelting.

Chemical reduction of the iron ore requires temperatures above 800° C and a carbon monoxide to carbon dioxide ratio greater than 3 to 1. Slag production is an unavoidable and necessary part of the reduction process. Quartz (SiO_2) is the most common unwanted mineral in the iron ore, and to remove this and other unwanted silicates from the ore, a slag has to form by reaction of some of the iron oxide in the ore with the unwanted silicate minerals, predominantly quartz (SiO_2), according to the reaction:

$$2FeO + SiO_2 \rightarrow Fe_2SiO_4 \text{ (fayalite)}$$

The melting temperature of fayalite in the slag is about 1,200° C, so in practice smelting has to take place at a temperature higher than this. Essentially, it is the production of a necessary waste product that determines the high temperatures necessary for bloomery smelting. But if the temperature is too high in a highly reducing furnace (that is, one with a high carbon monoxide to carbon dioxide ratio), then a large quantity of very hard and brittle cast iron would form, making the work of the smith very much more difficult. Making carbon steel as African people did by the bloomery process was a tricky business, one that took many years for apprentice ironmasters to learn.

Smithing, by comparison, was relatively less difficult but by no means easy. The smith had to control the carbon content of an implement being forged, because the carbon content determines the working qualities of the metal. The smithing hearth was a small clay shield or open bowl, in which burning charcoal could be maintained at above 900° C by means of air pumped by hand- or foot-operated bellows. One assistant pumped the bellows while another helped the smith hammer the red-hot iron being worked. Most smithing hearths were open and had an oxidizing atmosphere (that is, the ratio of carbon monoxide to carbon dioxide was low), so carbon tended to diffuse out of the high-carbon steel, making the metal softer and more malleable as work progressed. But in some instances, the smithing hearth was an almost closed furnace of its own, with a reducing atmosphere, and low-carbon steel could be "soaked" at a high temperature in the burning charcoal to absorb enough carbon to achieve a hard, durable product.

Whichever system was used, the initial heating of primary bloomery iron in the smithing process had to be high to soften the metal and melt any included fayalite slag. The glowing metal was then removed from the fire with tongs and hammered with a heavy stone hammer on a rock anvil to squeeze out the molten slag and consolidate the iron. Only when the iron was relatively free of slag could the smith lower the temperature of the forge and fabricate the desired object using stone or iron hammers. Repeated heating was necessary to keep the metal soft enough to work without splitting it along lines of weakness caused by residual flattened stringers of slag trapped in the metal.

These slag stringers give bloomery iron a characteristic microstructure, which can be identified in a polished section of metal observed under an incident-light microscope. This is the major research tool of the modern archaeo-metallurgist who studies archaeological metal-processing waste and manufactured metal products in order to reconstruct the processes used, to assess the technological skill of the manufacturers, and to derive a record of the human choices, decisions, and social influences involved in the past production and use of metal. Archaeo-metallurgical studies have shown that African blacksmiths did not employ any heat treatments other than repeated heating to soften the metal while working it. There are no records of intentional quenching and tempering—that is, plunging a red-hot steel object into water to harden it and then reheating it gently to relieve some of the induced brittleness—although African carbon steel would have been very suitable material for such treatment. These techniques were used outside Africa. The fact that quenching and tempering were not employed routinely in Africa is good evidence that, in the details of its practice, African ironworking developed with little or no technological input from outside the continent.

BIBLIOGRAPHY

Childs, S. T., and D. Killick. 1993. Indigenous African metallurgy: Nature and culture. *Annual Review of Anthropology* 22: 317–337.

David, N., R. Heimann, D. Killick, and M. Wayman. 1989. Between bloomery and blast furnace: Mafa iron-smelting technology in North Cameroon. *The African Archaeological Review* 7: 183–208.

Haaland, R., and P. Shinnie, eds. 1985. *African iron working—ancient and traditional.* Oslo: Norwegian University Press.

Miller, D. E., and N. J. van der Merwe. 1994. Early metal working in sub-Saharan Africa: A review of recent research. *Journal of African History* 35: 1–36.

Rowlands, M., and J.-P. Warnier. 1993. The magical production of iron in the Cameroon Grassfields. In *The archaeology of Africa: Food, metals and towns,* eds. T. Shaw, P. Sinclair, B. Andah, and A. Okpoko, 642–651. London: Routledge.

Van der Merwe, N. J., and D. H. Avery. 1987. Science and magic in African technology: Traditional iron smelting in Malawi. *Africa* 57: 143–172.

Duncan Miller

IRONWORKING IN ITS CULTURAL CONTEXT

The advent of ironworking was a dramatic turning point in the history of the Old World, but nowhere was this more true than in sub-Saharan Africa. In much of Europe and Asia, stone-based technology was gradually replaced by a metal-working one focused first on copper and bronze and later on iron. In sub-Saharan Africa, many Stone Age cultures were rapidly brought into the Age of Metals, either by the adoption of ironworking (and copperworking) technology or by iron tools obtained through trade. Scholars hypothesize this led to increased food production through more efficient bush clearing, weeding, and harvesting. Increased food production then resulted in higher population densities, larger and more stable village communities, increased specialization, trade, and social differentiation, and the appearance of a settlement hierarchy and more complex forms of political organization. A regional study of the Bassar ironworking industry of northern Togo has indicated that such demographic, social, and economic changes did in fact occur at the same time as the adoption and growth of iron metallurgy, though the degree of political centralization was relatively modest, involving "big men" or small chiefdoms. Others have stressed the effects of the iron revolution on the African psyche and the difficult challenge posed by the integration of iron production into traditional society. They have suggested that lineage elders who exercised control over people (their juniors) would have resisted the development of a society based on control over production by a specialist class of ironworkers. The raw materials and technology of stone-tool production could not be monopolized, whereas with ironworking, the production of key tools and weapons for food production, warfare, and the use of force was now in the hands of those privileged few who had access to the secrets of iron smelting and smithing. This ultimately led to a complex mosaic of iron-producing, iron-distributing, and iron-using societies.

Mythical Origins

Nothing more dramatically illustrates iron metallurgy's impact than the important role it plays in origin myths. A major theme portrays the ironworker or smith as a divine hero who made civilization possible. In the Dogon (Mali) creation myth, the ancestral blacksmith descends from heaven bringing the raw materials of civilization—fire, iron, and seeds. This primordial being (Nommo) "stole a piece of the sun, carrying it as a lump of red-hot iron down the rainbow to earth." In Bushong (Zaire) creation mythology, Woot is the creator, culture hero, and father of the first divine king. One of the riddles asked of novices during Bushong initiation rites is "Which hoes did Woot forge first?" The answer was "the feet of men." In Yatenga (Burkina Faso), the ironworker was linked to the origin of life: a song relates how the ironworker liberated men from their natural condition but could not eliminate death, how he made the ax for the creation of the village, and how he made the razor that cuts the umbilical cord. The epic oral literature of the Mvet, a subgroup of the Pahouin of southern Cameroon, portrays humanity as emerging from the mother-stone (Nana Ngawgaw), a souvenir of the cosmic stone responsible for the creation of the world. The creation of the world and of life is also represented by the forging stone or anvil (Ngawg-Si) genealogically linked to the mother-stone. Iron provided the basis for civilization by providing hoes and weapons. The Mvet celebrate the superiority of those who have mastered iron metallurgy and portray iron as a symbol of force, power, resistance, and immortality, qualities inculcated during Pahouin initiation rites. Many central African royal dynasties are linked to mythical blacksmiths: the founder of Rwandese kingship, Gihanga, was a hunter and a blacksmith, and the Luba founding myth also involves a hunter and smiths. Finally, the value of iron to Early Iron Age societies has been documented archaeologically in southeastern Africa where caches of unworked lumps of iron bloom have been recovered.

Socioeconomic Context of Ironworking

The advent and integration of iron metallurgy into sub-Saharan African societies provided a major impetus for the development of specialization, trade, and social differentiation and placed the ironworker at the nexus of the majority of socioeconomic circuits. It also made him a man of relative wealth (and often prestige) as iron tools became the center of economic, political, and, often, ritual life. African ironworkers produced and repaired key tools for farming, hunting, fishing, and warfare, including cavalry paraphernalia and guns, tools for woodcarving, boatmaking, leatherworking, weaving, potting, and raffia-

palm tapping, tools for smelting and smithing, and tools for domestic uses, such door locks, lamps, and spoons. They produced slave leg irons, musical instruments, and ornaments of iron; royal regalia, such iron staffs and ceremonial hammers and anvils; iron currency and bride wealth, such as iron bars; circumcision knives for initiation ceremonies; and even iron cache-sexes (coverings for the genitals). However, it was the production of the major implements of farming, hunting, and warfare that made the ironworker an indispensable and respected member of society. It was this economic power, along with the awesome magical power that enabled him to transform ore into metal, that was responsible for his frequently ambivalent social and political status.

The rise of iron metallurgy provided a powerful stimulus for the rise of social differentiation because of the specialization of labor that it frequently entails. Hunting and gathering and even simple horticulture do not require the relatively complex levels of skilled and unskilled labor organization often needed for ironworking, particularly iron smelting. While some societies did not practice ironworking, or practiced only smelting or only smithing, or served as itinerant ironworkers for many groups, and while both smelting and smithing were sometimes performed by the master ironworker and his family, many societies subdivided ironworking into a variety of specialist tasks. Smelting required the prospecting, mining, transport, and preparation of ores; the selection, preparation, and transport of wood charcoal fuel; the extraction, transport, and preparation of the proper clays for furnaces, tuyeres (air pipes), and pot bellows; the construction of furnaces, tuyeres, and bellows; the building of the foundry shelter; and the loading and lighting of the furnace, the operation of bellows, the supervision of the smelt, and the extraction and shingling of the iron bloom. In addition, a number of rituals involving medicines (which had to be gathered), prayers, and sacrifices were necessary along the way to ensure a successful smelt. Workers had to be provided food and water, and music, song, and dance sometimes accompanied the smelting process. After the smelt, the bloom was broken up, reworked, purified, and forged into tool preforms, a task done by the smelter in some societies and by the smith in others. Forging required charcoal preparation; the selection, transport, and installation of a large stone anvil; the making of the smith's stone and iron hammers and other tools; the building of a small bowl or crucible furnace for reworking the bloom; the making of bellows and tuyeres; the construction of the smithy shelter; the actual forging of tools; and the execution of various rituals.

Smelting and smithing were performed only by males. Women and children were often used for labor-intensive tasks not directly associated with ironworking: mining; ore, charcoal, and clay preparation and transport; the construction of pot bellows and crucibles for bloomery refining; and provision of food and drink, sometimes to distant smelting camps. While many unskilled tasks were performed by extended family members, the primary smelting and smithing tasks required years of apprenticeship and were done only by specialists. Skilled specialties also developed for charcoal making, tuyere and bellows construction, furnace building, and even roof thatching. Such specialization was not confined to large-scale producers, such as the Bassar (Togo) and the Babungo chiefdom (Cameroon Grassfields). It also included smaller-scale producers such as the Pahouin of southern Cameroon, the Bagham chiefdom of the Ndop Plain, and the Bassar before A.D. 1000. Finally, those smiths who specialized in the refining of bloomery iron usually produced the heavier tools such as hoes, axes, and bells, whereas those who forged tools from iron preforms made lighter items, such as knives and jewelry. The two types of smiths used different tool assemblages and bellows and were organized differently: cooperative workshop and dispersed individuals, respectively.

Some centers, such as Bassar and Babungo and the Yatenga region of Burkina Faso, became large-scale producers for regional and long-distance trade. This was often accomplished by expanding the lineage labor pool by using slaves and even nonkin freemen in exchange for access to the foundry or smithy. The rise of regional and long-distance trade networks sometimes led to the emergence of specialists in the trade of iron bloom or ironware. These networks included both local smiths who organized trading expeditions, as among the Bassar, and trading specialists or middlemen, as among the Wanga (Lake Victoria region). Several chiefdoms of the Ndop Plain (Cameroon Grassfields) specialized as middlemen in the transport of iron and iron products without performing ironworking themselves.

The efficiency of iron production varied considerably from one society or chiefdom to the next even within a relatively small region such as the Ndop Plain. Babungo's iron production was twice as efficient as Oku's devolved technology based on slag recycling and eight times more efficient than Weh chiefdom's ironworking. It was 40 times more efficient than Bahaya's iron industry in Tanzania. Strikingly, Babungo's efficient technology did not diffuse across political boundaries because its secrets were closely guarded and protected by the chief (Fon) and the ruling advisory council (Tifwan) composed primarily of the heads of smelting lineages.

Iron production was primarily a dry-season activity in most ironworking societies because farming activities were less intensive during this season and because rain and flooding did not interfere with the preparation of charcoal, the collection and transport of ore, the lighting of the furnace, and the movement of clients and specialist trading partners. However, in the Cameroon Grassfields and among the Maa-speaking pastoral societies of northern Kenya, the wet season was preferred, in part because of cooler temperatures. Whether ironworking was a part-time or full-time profession depended upon a number factors: the size of the society, the scale of iron production, and the land's ability to produce food needed by artisans. Most African ironworkers were part-time professionals who devoted some time to farming or other artisanal and societal activities. However, in societies focused on intensive, large-scale production, nearly all able-bodied freemen were involved in either smelting or smithing, and most if not all of the farming was done by the ironworkers' wives, children, and slaves. In addition, some ethnic groups or clans, such as the Tegue (Congo) and the Hungana (Zaire), were trader smiths or itinerant ironworkers who produced and sold their goods to a wide range of ethnic groups, sometimes on a full-time basis. Blacksmiths, living in major cities or towns in the highly centralized polities of Nigeria, such as the Hausa state of Kano, the Nupe, some of the Yoruba city-states, and in Benin, were often full-time specialists organized in guilds or guildlike professional groups under state control. In small-scale acephalous societies (societies that lack a governing head or chief) and in many societies organized under "big men" or village chiefs, iron production was generally under the control of family-compound or lineage heads. However, in relatively centralized polities (complex chiefdoms, kingdoms, and states) with a developed political economy, iron production and distribution inevitably fell under the control of the central power.

The ironworker was generally well rewarded. For example, the Samia blacksmiths of Kenya once could expect to receive a goat or a sack of grain for a single hoe, a bull for three hoes, or a heifer for six hoes. If trading with more distant areas, he might receive three goats for one hoe or a heifer for two hoes. The Songo (Zaire) used to make three to six times more than the average earnings of others during precolonial times. The ironworker and associated specialists (for example, bellow and tuyere makers) working in their native communities generally received much of their pay in food, especially meat or livestock, but could also be paid in metal (bloom or preforms) or special purpose monies (cowrie shells or iron bars) and occasionally by labor in their fields. The ironworker might also barter for such goods as local cotton cloth, arrow poisons, or salt. In many areas, the client provided the ironworker with ore, bloom, or charcoal. In areas such as the Cameroon Grassfields, where most societies were organized in chiefdoms and integrated into both regional and long-distance exchange networks, iron bloom or preforms might be traded for slaves, cowries, palm oil, salt, goats, hoes, camwood, cloth, guns and gunpowder, ivory, and high-value beads, while prestigious double gongs sold for slaves, elite cloth for chiefs, and the most highly valued beads. In areas with well-developed trade circuits, prices were often determined by the law of supply and demand, but in many areas, they were set by tradition, as among the Nande in eastern Zaire. In relatively decentralized pastoral societies like the Endo of

the Kenya Rift Valley, intense competition led to the development of a guildlike professional group, which sought to control prices and restrict competition.

The wealth earned by lineage or compound heads was first used to purchase regional necessities, such as palm oil or salt. Additional sums could then be invested in: (1) bride wealth (cattle, cowrie shells, hoes, and iron bars) for junior members, (2) the political sphere for fees for membership and rank (titles) in male associations, or (3) the purchase of slaves and freeborn dependent males for work in iron production or female slaves to expand the compound's food base through farming and the subsistence-labor base through additional children, as was done in Babungo and Bassar. In Babungo, where smiths' access to political power was blocked by the hereditary dominance of the smelting lineages, wealth was converted into social prestige through public display during festivals, feasts, and funerals organized by private associations or clubs. Finally, wealth accumulated from regional trade could be used to acquire prestige goods through long-distance trade. In short, an ironworking compound or lineage head was often in a position to become a "big man" within his society.

C. Meillassoux in 1978 and Marie-Claude Dupré in 1981 to 1982 wrote about those societies that were unable to come to terms with the full integration of ironworking into their society, particularly once it surpassed a certain production level and had to be organized into specialist activities no longer under the full control of the *maîtres de la terre* (earth priests). The potential for increased production levels leading to export through trade and the concurrent development of a class of "big-men" ironworkers, and ultimately to a more centralized political authority seeking to control this production, were resisted by some societies, like the Téké (Congo), who ultimately rejected iron production that went beyond bare subsistence needs. Dupré's view has strong echoes in the Pahouin Mvet's epic oral literature, which speaks of the struggle between those who wished to get rid of iron (as dangerous) and those who saw the folly of returning men to savagery.

Political Context of Ironworking

The conversion from stone to iron created the potential for centralized control of the production of tools used for surplus food production, warfare, and the use of political force. What was the relationship between the scale of iron production and the degree of political centralization? Did political centralization require centralized control of iron production? What was the relationship between kingship and ironworking in both its political and symbolic aspects? The archaeological, ethnohistorical, and ethnographic records suggest there was not a one-to-one relationship between the intensity of iron production and the degree of political centralization, nor did all centralized polities control their own iron production. The Bassar region was a major West African iron production center from the late 16th to the early 20th centuries. While the archaeological record indicates increases in population density and site size and the appearance of a low-level settlement hierarchy (village and satellite hamlets), political centralization was probably similar to that found in "big-man" societies or those divided into major village chiefdoms. The Bassar chiefdom did not develop until the late 1700s, and it never ruled over the richest and most specialized iron-production centers of Banjeli and Bitchabe. Moreover, there is little evidence that such political centralization was linked to the direct control of iron production and trade. Instead, it apparently evolved to deal with defensive needs and the huge influx of refugees resulting from constant slave raiding by the neighboring Tyokossi and Dagomba (Ghana).

The Cameroon Grassfields contained numerous chiefdoms of all sizes and degrees of political centralization. Babungo, the largest-known iron producer in all of sub-Saharan Africa, was a small chiefdom of fewer than 3,000 people. Iron production was controlled by the chief (Fon) and his advisory council (Tifwan) dominated by the hereditary senior smelters (Voetughau). The Tifwan and the Fon had direct economic power to manage the material-resource base of the chiefdom by setting the conditions of trade and production goals, managing competition between smelting and smithing specialists, and fixing the prices of subsistence foods like maize. Babungo smiths had their own guildlike council (Voetueyoe) but had no political authority in the Tifwan and produced prestige goods (double gongs) for the Fon. Though iron production was centrally controlled, Babungo was neither an autocratic nor an expansionist chiefdom and was dwarfed by much larger, expansionist chiefdoms, such as Bamum (60,000 people). Yet, Bamum imported most of its iron from Babungo in exchange for slaves. To the south, the chiefdoms of Bafanji (smelters) and Bamenyam (smiths) participated in a symbiotic trade relationship. On the Bamenda Plateau, palm-oil-producing chiefdoms, such as Mankon, produced little or no iron and depended upon the sale of palm oil to purchase iron from the Babungo and Oku chiefdoms.

What is clear, however, is that an expansionist polity must directly control either iron production or access to that production if it is going to continue to expand or maintain its superiority. The archaeological and ethnohistorical record clearly shows that the central polities of Ghana (at Mema), Mali (at Niani), and Kongo (at Mbanza Kongo) had important smelting centers adjacent to their capitals or royal palaces or otherwise had control over iron production. E. W. Herbert notes that the Kuba dynasty asserted control over iron production and fought wars with the Luba kingdom over the excellent iron ores near the Mwabe River. P. R. McNaughton, speaking of the Mande (Mali), notes that "four towns of weapon-making blacksmiths are said to have circled the Segou state's capital" and "fields of smelting furnaces are said to have marked the gathering places of Sunjata's and Sumanguru's armies before their final battles." The centralized polities and states of Kanem, Nupe, Benin (Nigeria), Ouahigouya (Burkina Faso), and Nikki (Benin) also exercised direct control over the production of tools for farming and warfare. Those larger, expansionist polities that did not fully control their own iron production often sought to do so by guile or by force. The late 19th-century king of Bamum sent treasures in vain to the Fon of Babungo to try and learn Babungo's iron-smelting secrets in a desperate attempt to reduce Bamum's dependency on Babungo iron. The Kongo kingdom, which had continual difficulty maintaining control over its iron-producing province, sought to diversify its sources of iron with the arrival of the Portuguese. The Dagomba kingdom (Ghana) tried various strategies to ensure access to Bassar iron production: a symbiotic relationship in times of peace, intimidation through slave raiding, and finally a three-year siege of the Bassar chiefdom's capital in the 1870s. However, the conquest of iron-producing regions often had the opposite effect of that intended. When Bamum conquered several iron-producing groups, the ironworkers simply fled after defeat. When the Ngoni conquered the southern Tumbuka (Malawi), they allowed the defeated people to retain much of their social and political organization and iron-trade networks and generally left them alone, because they depended upon their iron production.

A number of authors have emphasized the close, but sometimes ambivalent, ties between ironworkers and dynasts (chiefs and kings) throughout most of sub-Saharan Africa. These ties, which vary in their nature and symbolism, are due to: (1) the ironworker's very real economic power and (2) his perceived abilities as a sorcerer—abilities that allow him to manipulate the power or occult forces (nyama in Mande) that animate the universe, thus permitting him to transform ore into iron (and iron into tools). The elder ironworker controls the means of production of iron tools that are key to food production and warfare and may even subject a group to his curse and refuse to serve them. He is perceived to possess supernatural or magical power that rivals that of the divine king who draws upon the same force to ensure the fertility and well-being of his kingdom. Using the proceeds from the sale of his products to expand his economic power and prestige by investing in wives and even slaves, the elder ironworker has the potential to obtain considerable wealth. He is thus in a position to challenge both the secular and spiritual authority of the king directly if he so chooses. As a result, the founding or expanding dynast must find a way either to subordinate the ironworker or to enter into a symbiotic relationship with him.

In West Africa, Mande leaders over much of the Sudan historically retained ironworkers as advisors and interpreters, and kings whispered their decisions at the royal court to a blacksmith who then stated them to the assembled gathering. The legendary Sundjata Keita, the founder of Mali, arose from his crippled state by leaning on the iron staff he had ordered from a smith. Traditions speak of how Sundjata Keita, not an ironworker himself, relied on the ironworkers as his allies in the wars against the Sosso ruler, Sumanguru Kanté, who was both king and ironworker. Traditions of actual smith-kings have been recorded from the Baguirmi kingdom (Chad), and James H. Vaughan has noted that ironworkers were instrumental in the founding of Gulagu and other royal clans of the Mandara Marghi (Nigeria and Cameroon). According to T. Talmari, some Malinke chiefs married ironworkers' daughters shortly after their rise to power. Intermarriage with the king's clan was also permitted among the Ader Hausa, and Marghi kings were required to marry blacksmiths' daughters, despite prescriptive endogamy (marriage within a specific group) for ironworkers. Similarly, the foreign Wasagari (Mande) princes of the Bariba chiefdom of Nikki (Benin) married daughters of indigenous ironworkers to help create powerful links of friendship. Herbert believes that such marriages reflect the ironworker's control of an indispensable technology and his membership in an indigenous group, as was true for the Bariba, Hausa, and Marghi cases. As Talmari has noted, while foreign dynasties may "deprive another of political and military power, it is generally believed that one may never dispossess a group of its religious or magical prerogatives," such as those associated with indigenous earth priests and ironworkers. Finally, ironworkers played important roles in royal investiture among the Dagomba aristocracy of Ouahigouya (Burkina Faso) and among the Marghi.

Throughout a vast portion of central Africa (Zaire Basin and northern Angola) and the Great Lakes region of eastern Africa, centralized political authority was often well developed, kingship and smithing were hereditary (though not endogamous), and oral traditions speak frequently of the "smith-king." Such smith-kings are known for the Tio and Loango (Congo), Kongo (Angola), Luba and Kuba (Zaire), and the

Rwanda and Burundi kingdoms. In some oral traditions, chiefs state they were once ironworkers, and in others, ironworkers say they were once chiefs because of their wealth. Often the link may be primarily symbolic, reflecting the fusion or alliance of kingship and ironworking. Oral traditions relate how the Baisengobi or Bushbuck people are descended from the Bunyoro king who was a blacksmith by trade, and how they originated the ruling dynasties of numerous pastoral aristocratic states in East Africa. In the highly centralized pastoral societies of the interlacustrine (Great Lakes) region of eastern Africa, the ancient farmers and ironworkers were dominated by intrusive pastoralists. These pastoral leaders maintained direct control over iron technology and developed oral traditions that state their chief invented or brought metallurgy to the region. The development of metallurgy is similarly linked to royalty among the Kuba, Luba, and Kongo. This subordination was symbolized by the use of the smith's hammer and anvil (and other iron weapons, bracelets, or bells) as royal regalia and by the important role the smith often played in royal investiture, funerals, and burials. Pierre de Maret has reported on several excavated central and eastern African royal burials that contained smithing tools (hammers and anvils). The only ruler in West Africa associated with the smith's hammer was the Oba of Benin (Nigeria). Such rituals legitimized royal authority over indigenous metalworkers, while they acknowledged the latter's ancient claims to religious and political authority. Peter Schmidt presents a similar scenario for the intrusive royal dynasties that took control of iron production in two Haya kingdoms near Lake Victoria and legitimized their position through myth, symbolism, and ritual. In some instances, however, dynast and ironworker came to terms of mutual interdependence, rather than subordination, as was the case with the Fipa (Tanzania).

There is a natural symbolic link between kingship and ironworking: both ironworker and king are symbols of the fecundity and transforming ability of magical power. Both ironworker and king must control this power to bring the transformation of ore to iron and iron to tools and to ensure the fertility and well-being of the kingdom. Moreover, the very investiture process represents the transformation of a simple individual into a divine king, a process analogous to the transformations wrought by the ironworker.

Religious and Symbolic Contexts

In 1987, N. J. van der Merwe and D. H. Avery summarized three universal aspects of traditional ironworking in sub-Saharan Africa:

1. Smelters must be technical experts, and a variety of supernatural forces must be conciliated using magical practices
2. Iron smelters, especially those in the chief supervisory role, have mastered both technique and magic and thus have special status, or conversely, they may be avoided or considered members of a caste
3. Smelting is accompanied by sexual symbolism and taboos

Scholars have viewed the magical aspect of ironworking from three perspectives:

1. Magic as superstition without technical impact or as a ritual that helps to maintain a trade monopoly
2. Magic as technology in its own right
3. Magic as an organizational frame of reference for the proper execution of the technological process

Studies of the past two decades have emphasized magic as a technology but in two different ways. Those interested in an analytical (etic) assessment of the role of magic or ritual in the technical and scientific process of transforming ore to iron have concluded that it plays no scientific role. They recognize, however, that African smelters believe it is essential to the process and cannot do without it. Those interested in native categories of thought (emic analysis) emphasize that the African does not make such distinctions, and that both the "technical" and the "magical" are indispensable parts of iron metallurgy.

D. Killick's work in central Malawi found four basic reasons smelters used to explain a failed smelt:

1. A technical error involving the use of improper ores, fuels, or clays or errors in the technical process, such as failing to keep tuyeres free of slag
2. A failure to perform the proper sacrifices to conciliate and honor the ancestors (*mizimu*)
3. A failure to respect sexual taboos, especially regarding sexual abstinence and the presence of fertile and especially menstruating women
4. The smelt was a victim of sorcery due to greed, envy, or spite

Sorcery was usually given as the explanation for the failed smelt when successful technical procedures had been faithfully followed and no known prohibitions or taboos had been violated. The motives for sorcery most frequently noted or suspected involved disputes over property or envy and jealousy of the ironworker's wealthy status. The sorcery disrupted the smelt because the protective medicines placed in a pot below the furnace were not successful in warding off such evil. This fear of sorcery led to considerable variation in furnace design, smelting procedure, and great variety in types of medicines used, because smelters rarely communicated these differences to other smelters.

In 1993, Herbert described how the rituals and taboos associated with ironworking vary considerably in both type, frequency, and extent from culture to culture and how smelting is usually highly ritualized, whereas bloom refining and the act of forging tools are generally far less so. Medicines (vegetal and animal products) are viewed as indispensable throughout sub-Saharan Africa for the successful construction and operation of the smelting furnace and the smith's anvil. In much of Bantu Africa, such medicines are put in a pot that is buried in a hole directly beneath the furnace. Excavations of furnace sites by de Maret (Congo) and Schmidt and S. T. Childs (Tanzania) have uncovered such medicine pits dating to the 1st millennium A.D. Elsewhere medicines are placed at the base of the furnace, incorporated within it, or applied to the structure, as in Bassar and central Malawi, and may be used during other phases of the smelting process, as

among the Ekonda of Zaire. Prayers or sacrifices of animals (chickens, dogs, and goats) may be made to ancestral spirits or ironworking divinities to ensure success during the construction of the furnace and foundry, the placement of the anvil, the forging of the iron hammer, and the prospecting and storage of iron ore. Words (speech or songs), music, and dance also played a role in ensuring a smooth operation by enhancing the morale of the participants and, more importantly, by helping to attract the beneficial spiritual forces that would ensure success. Sometimes diviners were consulted before a smelt was begun to determine whether it would be successful. In general, the medicines, sacrifices, prayers, and so on were designed to prevent any evil spirits or living sorcerers from interfering with the smelt, to ensure that no taboos were violated, and to ensure the production of a high-quality bloom. Some cultures had specific divinities linked to iron production, such as Mosani among the Bariba, Ogun among the Yoruba, and Irungu in the Bacwezi pantheon of East Africa.

Sexual taboos were also widespread. With few exceptions, women were excluded from smelting and smelting rituals, and sexually active females were sometimes forbidden to touch the ore and charcoal that went into the furnace. Women were often allowed to bring food and drink to the smelting camp, but postmenopausal women or young girls were preferable, as fertile, and particularly menstruating, women were considered especially dangerous to a smelt. Male sexual abstinence was almost universally required just before and especially during smelting operations, and sometimes it extended to all phases of smelting, including mining and charcoal preparation. The explanation for these sexual taboos may be seen in the nature of the smelting (and, to a lesser extent, smithing) process itself. The transformation of ore to bloom (and, to a lesser extent, of bloom into tool) is seen as requiring the control of powerful forces (*nyama*) that animate the universe and which are released in massive quantities during smelting. In Africa, sexual activity is often viewed as diminishing one's vital energies, and sexual prohibitions are associated with other important activities besides ironworking (for example, hunting, warfare, and boatbuilding). Most

African societies also make an explicit analogy between the smelting process and the procreative process. The furnace (often with female attributes) is the pregnant woman, who, with the help of her smelter husband, will give birth to bloom (the fetus). Smelters must therefore abstain from sexual relations or they would be committing adultery, which could lead to a failed smelt. Female menstruation was considered to be particularly dangerous as it was viewed as a failed conception. Sexually active women represented a temptation for smelters to break their sexual taboos. This is the main reason why smelting camps were generally located away from the village, though other reasons may have been related to fire safety, the guarding of technological secrets, and access to fuel and ore. However, not all African peoples described the furnace in terms of the procreative process. Some authors believe both procreation and smelting fall under a broader transformational paradigm associated with generally irreversible activities that involve an ambiguous period during which one does not know exactly what is happening and that often require the control of occult forces. Such activities include hunting (killing an animal), farming (the transformation of seeds to plants), circumcision (the transformation of child to adult), funerals (the transformation of person to ancestor), chiefly investiture (the transformation of individual to divine king), pot making (the transformation of clay to pots), and rainmaking.

While smithing also involved the transformation of bloom or preforms to iron tools, it generally was subject to much less ritualization and use of medicines than smelting. Rituals were limited primarily to the creation of a new forge, including the selection and installation of the anvil and the making of the iron hammer. Some societies in central and eastern Africa excluded women from the forge and some did not. In fact, some required the smith to have sexual intercourse with his wife as part of the ritual incorporation of the anvil and hammer into the smithy, welcoming it like a second bride. The prohibition of sexual relations before or during smithing was not common, but menstruating women were still seen as dangerous. The reasons for the lower degree of ritualization is probably due to several fac-

tors, including (1) the public nature of smithing as opposed to the secretive isolation of the smelting camp and (2) the nature of the transformation involved in smithing was perceived to be less dangerous in terms of forces that needed to be controlled and less technically demanding in terms of the complexity and ambiguity of the processes involved, and there was less risk of failure. Smiths were involved in rituals, but they were focused more on protecting the chiefdom or society from foreign witches who might extract life essences and harm fecundity.

Given the importance of magic and ritual in African ironworking, some authors have questioned whether it did not impede technological progress. To the extent that smelters were secretive about their medicines, and to the extent that chiefdoms were secretive about the techniques used by their smelters, new technologies were often slow to diffuse across political boundaries. However, the large-scale production of the Bassar and Babungo iron industries clearly shows that magic or ritual need not be serious impediments. In the Bassar case, much ritual remained despite increased iron-production levels, which were made possible by the use of female, slave, and child labor in work not directly associated with smelting itself. In the Babungo case, smelting rituals, medicines, and taboos were concentrated primarily in two individuals: the foundry owner (Tunaa), who possessed the secret mix of medicines, and the foundry supervisor (Woeniibuu), who was condemned to long periods of sexual abstinence. Except for the creation of the anvil and hammer, smithing in Babungo was relatively devoid of ritual and taboos. The major thrust toward increased iron production was due to innovations in furnace type and fuel sources, the successful recruitment and integration of nonkin labor, and the rise of a complex division of labor in both the production and distribution of iron and ironware. Prohibitions against sexual relations for blacksmiths were probably relaxed for full-time craftsmen. Finally, given stressful conditions, such as the threat of unpredictable attacks from slave-raiding populations or enemy powers, ironworkers moved smelting operations near villages or royal quarters despite the increased danger of violating sexual taboos.

Social Status and Roles

The literature on the status of sub-Saharan African ironworkers has perhaps been overly focused on the concept of caste and on the societies that have true ironworking castes. Early studies focused on emic statements about craftsmen made by noncraftsmen, resulting in a distorted picture of "despised artisan castes" that often did not reflect the reality of daily social relationships. In the Indian Hindu model, a caste system consists of divinely approved, hereditary, endogamous occupational groups, protected by concepts of pollution. A. Tuden and L. Plotnicov provide a similar definition but do not emphasize divine approval. Other criteria, such as residential isolation and caste ranking, are also relevant. Using the Indian model of divine approval, only a few societies in southern Ethiopia and eastern Africa would appear to meet the criteria. If divine approval is dropped but pollution concepts retained, a greater number of societies would perhaps qualify: some in southern Ethiopia, some of the pastoral peoples of the East African grasslands and the Sudan, and some peoples of the Mandara Highlands of Nigeria and Cameroon. The often-described ironworking castes of the West African Sudan, however, would not qualify because pollution concepts are basically absent. Following Vaughan and others, a minimalist definition of caste is used here: "a specialized endogamous group socially differentiated by prescribed behavior and genealogically inherited professional capacities."

In the West African Sudan, ironworkers among the nuclear Mande (for example, the Soninke, Bozo, Bambara, and Malinke), the Tukulor, Wolof, Senufo, Dogon, Songhai, Minianka, and much of the Tuareg, Moorish, and Fulani populations belong to hereditary occupational groups that observe relatively strict rules of endogamy, are seen as a separate race or group, and generally live in their own village quarters or villages. Scholars disagree about caste ranking and whether artisans farmed. McNaughton argues that the old view that Mande artisans are a "despised" caste is not accurate. Ironworkers, in particular, are held in awe because they are seen as sorcerers who possess magical powers

(nyama), partially inherited from their ancestors—powers that allow them to transform ore to bloom and bloom to iron. This, along with the economic importance of the tools (hoes and weapons) they produce, results in their being viewed with an ambivalent mixture of fear and respect by noncraftsmen castes such as nobles (farmers and leaders) and slaves (now an extinct caste). He believes this ambivalent attitude toward ironworkers is analogous to a "joking relationship" and does not constitute ranking, particularly in the absence of divine approval and purity-pollution concepts. He notes that farmers often enjoy the company of smiths. Talmari argues that most West African social scientists believe that social hierarchies are present. Talmari and others agree that artisans have always been allowed to farm, while McNaughton says they did not farm before the colonial period.

According to McNaughton, today's blacksmiths (smelting has ceased) go to great lengths to nourish a belief in their special powers by behaving dramatically, playing with fire in public festivals, and showing fits of public ill temper. This helps maintain their corporate identity and its associated trade monopoly. Moreover, many Mande blacksmiths do much more than ironworking. As craftsmen, they tend to monopolize wood carving, including the sculpting of masks for secret societies. Their perceived magical and transformative powers lead many to develop skills as doctors, priests, rainmakers, diviners, and amulet makers, and they exercise a total monopoly in the practice of male circumcision. They are frequently called upon to act as political and social intermediaries, and the smithy is a place of asylum.

Dolores Richter's 1980 study of the Senufo of Ivory Coast, however, suggests that considerable variation is present from one cultural region to the next. Because Senufo ironworkers once had immigrant status and are relatively few in number, they often violate emic rules of endogamy for economic and political advantage, sometimes becoming village chiefs. Although artisans (fijembele) are emically seen as nonfarmers, most do farm, some exclusively so. Senufo fijembele, including ironworkers, use the threat of supernatural sanctions to prevent Senufo farmers (*senambele*) from entering their professions or even their work areas, thus maintaining their trading monopolies. While they are a distinct social category, ironworkers clearly are not outcasts or of lower status.

To the south, in the coastal Guinean zone, ironworkers generally have high status, and castes are generally absent. Examples include the Bassar (Togo), the Kpelle (Liberia), the Bariba (Benin), and the peoples of the Cameroon Grassfields. The Bassar had no rules of endogamy and master ironworkers often became "big men" by using their wealth to purchase wives, cattle, and slaves. Bassar ironworkers were highly respected and held in awe, and today they are viewed as the most powerful sorcerers in Togo, yet, curiously, they do not serve as diviners, healers, mediators, grave diggers, or ritual leaders outside of ironworking. While all Bassar families, regardless of occupational specialization, participated in farming, master ironworkers left the farming to their younger brothers, wives, and slaves. Among the Bariba (Benin), ironworkers readily took on nonsmith apprentices, and intermarriage between ironworking families was actually forbidden. They had a privileged place in the social hierarchy with chiefly honors and were both feared and respected for their economic, technological, and supernatural powers. Occupational endogamy was only loosely practiced in the Cameroon Grassfields.

The status of ironworkers in the Mandara Highlands varied considerably, including various caste arrangements and the absence of castes. For the Marghi of northeastern Nigeria, Vaughan notes that the nonfarming, endogamous artisan caste (*enkyagu*) includes smiths but not smelters. The relationship between Marghi farmers and smiths is marked by pollution concepts, and they do not eat together or share food. The *enkyagu* are not despised, however—they are simply different—and they do not resent their status. The farmer-smith relationship is seen as symbiotic. The negative emic view of *enkyagu* by Marghi farmers creates a social distance, which the *enkyagu* encourage to help maintain their corporate identity. Among the Mafa of northwestern Cameroon, the nonfarming, artisan class (*ngwazla*) bears a similar relationship to the farmer class (*vavay*). J. Sterner and Nicholas J. David note that, like Marghi *enkyagu*, the Mafa *ngwazla* are viewed as "permissible deviants," people who neither farm nor go to war. They also argue that variations in gender relationships within Mandara Highland societies provide models for intercaste relations. As in the Sudan, *enkyagu* and *ngwazla* both perform other important roles: funeral directors and grave diggers, diviners, doctors, and drummers. Their wives are generally potters. Grave digging is polluting for the Mafa but not for the Marghi.

In southern Ethiopia, J. A. Todd and R. Haaland report that ironworkers often belong to hereditary, strictly endogamous castes that may or may not be ranked or associated with concepts of pollution. Among the Gurage, who practice mixed farming, the Fuga blacksmiths cannot own land, cultivate the staple food crop (ensete), or cross a field with ensete or cattle, for fear their powers of sorcery may damage soil fertility, reduce cattle fecundity, or change the milk of a cow into blood or urine. The Dimi, who are slash-and-burn horticulturists, are divided into seven divinely approved hereditary, endogamous castes, ranked along a purity-pollution continuum as in India, and ironworkers are considered polluted. They are thus avoided and excluded from all farming rituals.

De Maret says there are no true castes in Bantu areas of central and eastern Africa. While ambivalence toward ironworkers is found to some degree all over Africa, Bantu ironworkers are generally highly regarded. They are feared and honored by some (Kikuyu, Kamba, and Chaga of East Africa), or people are indifferent to them (Fang of Gabon). Only Nilotic pastoral peoples have negative attitudes toward Bantu ironworkers. While there are no strict rules of endogamy, ironworkers tend to come from ironworking families, and where ironworking is strictly endogamous (among the Bira, Mbala, and Yaka), ironworkers are not distinct as a social group. Generally speaking, they are viewed primarily for their technological and magical prowess as ironworkers. Some act as dentists and circumcisers, but they generally do serve as healers, diviners, and social intermediaries. Wives are not necessarily potters either.

Most ironworkers are not part of professional associations and most engage in farming.

Another interesting issue concerns ironworkers' wives. In much of West Africa and in many other parts of the continent, they are potters. Even when castes are not present, potters tend to be the wives of ironworkers. Why? Some possible answers suggest themselves. First, knowledge of clay deposits is important for both the potter and the ironworker, for the making of pots, tuyeres, portions of pot bellows, and the furnace itself. Both types of artisans also make use of pyrotechnology to transform clay to pots and to transform ore to bloom and bloom to iron tools. Sterner and David note that the busiest periods of both potters and ironworkers coincide during the dry season, facilitating their cooperation, but often making it difficult to participate effectively in farming. In short, the nature and scheduling of their work make them a natural pair. Finally, at a symbolic level, both are involved in the irreversible transformation of the earth (clay to pot, ore to bloom) using heat.

Until now the discussion has primarily focused on sedentary farming societies. What about pastoral societies? In 1937, W. Cline stated that "despised smith castes and a lack of smelting ritual characterize the northern grasslands of East Africa . . . not so much by peoples who are ruled by pastoral aristocracies as among tribes who conventionally devote themselves to cattle, or who despise all forms of manual labor." Cline described the Maasai ironworker as the "classic example of a despised smith caste," characterized by residential isolation, strict hereditary occupational endogamy, and a polluted status because he makes weapons that can cause bloodshed. He is stigmatized because his need to remain near his furnace or forge separates him from typical Maasai life that involves wandering in search of cattle pasture and periodic warfare. In a more balanced view, J. P. Galaty notes that blacksmiths also keep cattle and are seen as indispensable to Maasai life, because they produce weapons of war and razors for cutting the umbilical cord and for circumcision. Roy Larick notes their role as leaders in the sacred ritual of circumcision. Their combined economic, ritual, and transformative (magical) powers set them apart,

and they are viewed with ambivalence. Galaty notes that Maasai smiths refer to Maasai pastoralists as "despicable and contemptuous," suggesting smiths do not consider themselves inferior.

M. Coy studied blacksmiths (as an apprentice) among Kalenjin-speaking pastoralists of the Kenya Rift Valley who are similar in many ways to the Maasai. His study of the relatively egalitarian Endo and Tugen led him to conclude that the view that smiths are a "despised caste" is the result of past studies focusing on the views of noncraftsmen (pastoralists) about craftsmen, ignoring the latter's major economic role. Among both groups, Coy found strict marital endogamy was not practiced, but marriages between smiths and nonsmiths were restricted for several reasons:

1. The smiths themselves often resisted such marriages because of fear they would lead to craft proliferation and increased competition.
2. Nonsmiths were suspicious of the wealth and magical power of smiths, including their power to curse and withhold production, which might occur in disputes among people related by marriage.
3. The immunity or neutrality of ironworkers during warfare and raiding and their peripheral involvement in generalized reciprocity exchanges (due to their role as both producer and distributor of material goods) made marriage to a blacksmith or his daughter relatively undesirable.

Among the Endo, apprenticeship of nonsmiths did occur but could be restricted if it threatened to extend competition. Moreover, the Endo were organized into a guildlike professional group, which fixed prices, required kinsmen to sell in the local market and not at home, and allowed clan elders to threaten uncooperative craftsmen with their curse. The Tugen allowed apprenticeship under their strict control and forbade apprentices from working within their trade zone. They also used secrecy and taboos to help perpetuate an effective craft monopoly. Coy concludes that ironworkers are feared or disliked and respected, but they are not despised. In short, we see the ambivalent attitude toward smiths prevalent in much of Africa.

Coy's work among the Tugen, who are organized into both pastoral and farming groups according to variations in their mountain and lowland habitat, showed that ironworker status varied as a function of his control over the production of essential versus relatively less essential iron tools. Highland farmers generally feared and respected smiths because they so depended upon their production of agricultural tools, whereas lowland pastoralists depended less upon iron tools for their subsistence and tended to dislike smiths and sometimes harassed them. Finally, Cline himself was aware of peoples similar to those described by Coy. He describes the Chaga (Tanzania) in contrast to the Maasai: smiths are not despised. Rather they are feared and honored. Nonsmiths associate frequently with smiths. Strict endogamy is not practiced, but nonsmiths are ambivalent about marrying their daughters to smiths. Smiths are neutral during warfare, and they hold other important roles, such as diviners and healers.

Coy's work applies primarily to pastoral societies with relatively decentralized polities. The picture is somewhat different for the pastoral aristocracies of the interlacustrine region of East Africa and the Sahel. Although Cline suggests that ironworker status was higher in such societies, both he and J. Roscoe state such pastoral people looked upon farmers and artisans as serfs or slaves, and their manual labor was viewed as low and mean. Roscoe's early 20th-century descriptions of Banyankole and Bakitara (Bunyoro) origin myths, royal investiture and regalia, and funerals make little mention of ironworkers' roles or iron tools. Although Schmidt states the sacred Bacwezi cult linked to ironworking had a role in Bunyoro royal investiture, chiefly authority and divine kingship among the Banyankole and Bakitara were generally mediated by symbolic and concrete links to cattle, not iron. This is not the case in Rwanda and Burundi or with the Babito and Bahinda dynasties among the Bahaya in Tanzania, where the political, economic, and religious importance of indigenous ironworking clans led to their playing important roles in dynastic origin myths and the rituals of royal investiture. The mythical ancestor of the Twanda's royal dynasty, Gihanga, was supposed to have introduced metalworking, fire, cattle, hunting, pottery, and woodworking, as well as kingship. Ironworking, in particular, "mediates the passage from sterility to fecundity" in the Rwandese kingship-origin myth. As elsewhere in central Africa, the iron (or copper) hammer and anvil as royal regalia were the primary symbols of royal power in both Rwanda and Burundi, and the king kept a hammer near his bed. As a member of the Tutsi aristocracy, the Rwandan king could not himself forge, but he did participate symbolically in the forging of the royal hoe. These rituals and regalia emphasized both the king's dominion over the ironworkers and recalled the myths that attribute the introduction of ironworking to the dynasty's founder. Finally, the tomb of the late 17th-century Rwandan Mwami Cyirima Rujugira contained two forged anvil hammers serving as headrests. Hammers are also used during Nyanga investiture in eastern Zaire. Among the Bahaya, whose iron industry began about 500 B.C., oral traditions relate how the Babito and Bahinda pastoral dynasties imposed themselves on local ironworking clans (the Bacwezi) in the 17th century. In short, several pastoral aristocracies in the interlacustrine region reached a political, ritual, and symbolic accommodation with local ironworking clans. It is thus not surprising that the status of ironworkers in such societies was higher than those in which such accommodation did not occur.

Finally, P. Bonte and Galaty note that among some pastoral societies "unequal statuses are codified as 'estates' within a stratified social system," as among the Tswana (Botswana), in Kanem (Chad), and among Saharan Tuareg and Moorish pastoral nomads. In most cases, the hierarchy is based on the superior value of pastoral labor and livestock, and the status of ironworkers is relatively low. However, one must be careful not to confuse the emic view of ironworkers presented by the aristocratic warrior class with the reality of daily social relationships. Among the Tuareg of Niger, ironworkers are linked to chiefly lineages and warrior aristocracies for whom they make and repair arms, jewelry, and objects of daily life. They are part of hereditary, strictly endogamous castes. Their patrons describe them as lazy liars to be held in contempt and disgust, a view that ironworkers have internalized. An important Tuareg folktale, however, stresses how the society would be in bad shape without them. The smiths' sense of corporate identify is very strong, including the use of a secret, pig-latin-like language (tenet). In the stratified, centralized polity of Kanem, ironworkers provided the key tools of hoes and spears. As an imperial Islamic society gradually developed, the local hunter-smiths were politically, maritally, and ritually marginalized. Three social cleavages developed: between cattle-owning warriors of noble descent and inferior hunters and smiths, between freemen and slaves, and between masters and dependents. Barriers to the ownership of cattle by hunters and smiths were rigorously enforced.

Why Castes?

Some scholars have suggested ironworker castes are an adaptation that ensures that societies can retain a group of ironworkers to produce tools critical for survival, that castes help maintain strong technological traditions and stimulate cooperation among ironworkers, and that caste stigmatization helps keep people within the occupation and discourages others from joining. While this seems plausible, it does not explain why many iron-producing societies do not resort to castes and why other non-iron-producing societies simply import needed preforms or iron tools (for example, the Luo, Lugbara, Bagesu, and Busoga). Some have suggested the status of ironworkers primarily reflects whether their clients are farmers or pastoralists. Farmers tend to fear and respect ironworkers who provide the key tools for their survival, whereas pastoralists in relatively decentralized societies generally despise manual labor and are less dependent upon ironworkers' services. As a result, farmers often have an ambivalent attitude toward ironworkers, whereas pastoralists tend to have more negative perceptions of them. Haaland suggests castes are prevalent in societies with a long history of states and a complex civilization with a well-developed specialization of labor as in the Mali Empire and the kingdom of Ethiopia. This explains little, however, about most casted pastoral societies. Hypotheses about Arab influence and the need

to subordinate ironworker authority to chiefly power cannot be generalized to sub-Saharan Africa as a whole.

Another set of hypotheses suggests the introduction of ironworking created a privileged and powerful class (ironworkers) whose economic and transformative (magical) powers incited envy, jealousy, and fear on the part of non-ironworking segments of traditional society. Their wealth threatened traditional lines of power based on kinship and age, as well as chiefly power, and therefore it had to be brought under control. This power could be mitigated by labeling ironworkers as unsavory or polluted and dangerous, by the use of prescriptive endogamy to restrict the power of ironworkers to expand their political and economic control through the acquisition of wives, and by generally assigning them negative status. On the other hand, ironworkers often encourage noncraftsmen to hold them in awe and to view them in a negative light to maintain their corporate monopoly. Together, Sterner and David view it as an "unacknowledged conspiracy" where the noncraftsmen (farmers or pastoralists) get a variety of needed services from the ironworking caste while simultaneously constraining the ironworkers' social and political powers, and where ironworkers maintain their production and trading monopoly. But intriguing as this view may be, it does not allow us to predict when castes will or will not develop. As de Maret cautions, human cultural solutions to similar problems are many, and one cannot always explain cultural variation in terms of deterministic probabilities.

BIBLIOGRAPHY

Clément, P. 1948. Le forgeron en Afrique Noire. *Révue de Géographie Humaine et d'Ethnographie* 2: 35–58.

Cline, W. 1937. *Mining and metallurgy in Negro Africa.* Menasha: George Banta.

Collett, D. P. 1993. Metaphors and representations associated with precolonial iron-smelting in eastern and southern Africa. In *The archaeology of Africa: Food, metals and towns,* eds. T. Shaw, P. Sinclair, B. Andah, and A. Okpoko. 499–511. London: Routledge.

Coy, M. 1989. *Apprenticeship: From theory to method and back.* Albany: State University of New York Press.

de Barros, P. 1988. Societal repercussions of the rise of large-scale traditional iron production: A West African example. *African Archaeological Review* 6: 91–113.

de Maret, P. 1985. The smith's myth and the origin of leadership in central Africa. In *African iron working: Ancient and traditional,* eds. R. Haaland and P. Shinnie, 73–87. Bergen: Norwegian University Press.

Galaty, J. P., and P. Bonte. 1991. *Herders, warriors, and traders: Pastoralism in Africa.* Oxford: Westview Press.

Gibbs, J. L., Jr. 1988. *Peoples of Africa: Cultures of Africa south of the Sahara.* Prospect Heights: Waveland Press.

Haaland, R. 1985. Iron production, its socio-cultural context and ecological implications. In *African iron working: Ancient and traditional,* eds. R. Haaland and P. Shinnie, 50–72. Bergen: Norwegian University Press.

Herbert, E. W. 1993. *Iron, gender, and power: Rituals of transformation in African societies.* Bloomington: Indiana University Press.

McIntosh, S. K. 1994. Changing perceptions of West Africa's past: Archaeological research since 1988. *Journal of Archaeological Research* 2 (2): 165–198.

McNaughton, P. R. 1988. *The Mande blacksmiths.* Bloomington: Indiana University Press.

Miller, D. E., and N. J. van der Merwe. 1994. Early metal working in sub-Saharan Africa: A review of recent research. *Journal of African History* 35: 1–36.

Robertshaw, P., ed. 1990. *A history of African archaeology.* London and Portsmouth: James Currey Ltd. and Heinemann.

Schmidt, P. 1978. *Historical archaeology: A structural approach in an African culture.* Westport: Greenwood Press.

Seldon, D. 1978. *Relations of production: Marxist approaches to economic anthropology.* London: Frank Cass and Co., Ltd.

Tuden, A., and L. Plotnicov. 1970. *Social stratification in Africa.* New York: The Free Press.

Van der Merwe, N. J., and D. H. Avery. 1987. Science and magic in African technology: Traditional iron smelting in Malawi. *Africa* 57 (2): 143–172.

Vansina, J. 1990. *Paths in the rainforests: Toward a history of political tradition in equatorial Africa.* Madison: University of Wisconsin Press.

Philip de Barros

ARCHITECTURE AND SETTLEMENT PATTERNS

The study of settlement organization and architecture belongs within the relatively new discipline of cognitive archaeology, the study of prehistoric ideals, values, and beliefs that constitute a society's worldview. Cognitive archaeologists use the principles of sociocultural anthropology to investigate such diverse things as material symbols, power, and religion, as well as the use of space.

Interest in cognitive aspects of spatial and architectural organization in southern Africa developed more than a decade ago largely as a result of Adam Kuper's work on the symbolic dimensions of the southern Bantu homestead. Following Kuper's structural analysis, archaeologists have identified three spatial patterns associated with Bantu-speaking peoples who lived during the last 2,000 years: a street pattern, suggested by Thomas N. Huffman in 1989 and J. Vansina two years later, a central cattle pattern presented in the work of J. K. Denbow, Huffman, and T. M. O'C. Maggs, and a Zimbabwe pattern defined by Huffman.

Method

These three patterns are normative models—that is, they emphasize the underlying principles that give structure to society. As normative models, these patterns are not primarily concerned with ethnicity. Since ethnicity and culture are not necessarily the same thing, different architectural and spatial forms between different ethnic groups can have the same function. For this reason, the three models have subsumed ethnic variation in order to extract underlying principles.

As normative models, the patterns must be ahistorical, otherwise they would be tied to a specific time and place. If the central cattle pattern, for example, was defined in terms of the Zulu of the Late Iron Age of South Africa, then it could not have occurred among any other group, at any other time, or anywhere else.

As normative models, these three patterns are not designed to investigate daily behavior and dynamics. Dynamic events, such as a change in dynasty, differ from long-term structural changes, such as the transformation from ranked to class-based societies. It is not possible to recognize structural change without a datum for comparison, and normative models are used for this purpose.

In any case, daily behavior and dynamics are not usually random or haphazard. Regardless of the varying ability of individuals and groups to manipulate their culture and spatial organization, they are not free to act in any manner. Human behavior is patterned, and it is cultural norms, values, and attitudes that restrict and make possible the range of behavioral choices. Indeed, the tension between ideal norms and daily behavior is probably a major social dynamic. Most daily behavior, then, can only be fully understood in terms of broader cultural patterns. Structural overviews and historical analyses are both necessary to understand the past.

It is possible to develop spatial and architectural models for the past because of a few well-attested premises of human behavior. First, to create order, human societies everywhere divide their physical environment into discrete locations in each of which only a limited range of activity is permitted. Second, it follows that these spatial locations have social significance and consequences: they provide physical backdrops for social behavior and in many cases help to shape it. The physical boundaries imposed by a building, for instance, force and enable people to replicate standardized behavior. Third, it can be shown that a relatively small set of organizational principles operates on several levels within one society, and these can generate a wide range of features. The spatial principles that determine the organization of a Tswana house, for example, also apply to the households, homestead, and town. Fourth, since spatial order organizes people, spatial and social organizations are different expressions of the same thing, and the underlying structure must be part of a society's worldview. Finally, groups of people sharing the same worldview organize their settlements according to the same principles wherever they live (provided they are free agents).

Although one worldview could hypothetically generate more than one spatial pattern, the re-verse is highly improbable: empirical evidence indicates that the complex internal organization of a settlement is most likely the specific product of a specific worldview.

Although cognitive archaeologists use ethnographic data, settlement models do not suffer from the same problems that hamper formal ethnographic analogies. Simple formal analogies are problematic because the similarity between source (ethnographic data) and subject (archaeological features) is no guarantee of further similarities. Settlement models, however, are a product of the direct historical approach, which involves cross-cultural similarities as well as ethnohistorical continuities. In the direct historical approach, a model is derived first from the ethnography of the descendants. The next step is to apply the model back in time, period by period, to minimize the chronological gap between the ethnographic and archaeological data.

In this second step, the model becomes a hypothesis about the social organization and worldview in the archaeological past. What is therefore important is the relevance and success of the overall interpretation compared to other alternatives. The hypothesis based on the fewest assumptions, covering the most data, and with the greatest coherence and predictive potential is superior. If the ethnographically derived model, rather than any other, is supported by the archaeological evidence, then the same, or essentially the same, social organization that was linked to the spatial model in the ethnographic period (and the same, or essentially the same, worldview that generated them both) must have been present in the older period.

This approach is illustrated in table 9. The main premise of this approach is straightforward: since social and settlement organizations are different aspects of the same view of the world, a continuity in settlement pattern is evidence for continuity in social organization and worldview. Methodically, therefore, where there is identity or at least no crucial difference between settlement patterns in the ethnographic present and archaeological past, we can infer identity in worldview and social organization. The direct historical approach is therefore an argument about sameness, not an argument by analogy.

Table 9 *Settlement pattern and worldview*

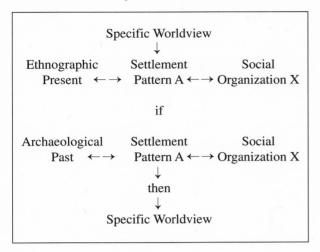

Societies in transition represent a special case. We know from empirical evidence that there can be a gap between a new social organization and the old settlement pattern. Initially, the society believes it is following the old rules while, in fact, new principles are being formulated. Ultimately, the old settlement pattern becomes too awkward for the new rules, and a new pattern evolves to keep in step. Evidently, new patterns evolve in stages, reaffirming that the transformations in social organization, worldview, and settlement organization are all linked processes.

Significantly, this vital relationship between settlement pattern, social organization, and worldview also includes language because language is the major vehicle for thinking about the world and transmitting those thoughts to others. Other than historically determined exceptions, most worldviews correlate with groups of related languages, particularly in small-scale societies, and the Bantu-speaking world is no exception. Settlement models derived from the ethnography of Bantu-speaking people help to establish the macroculture and ethnolinguistic identity of Iron Age archaeological units.

The Street Pattern

Many Bantu linguists recognize a fundamental distinction between Western Bantu (spoken in central Africa) and Eastern Bantu (spoken in eastern and southern Africa). Recent linguistic research shows that this division has great time depth and that Eastern Bantu speakers left their Cameroon homeland well after Neolithic Western Bantu had already inhabited the equatorial forest.

In the recent past, Western Bantu speakers were matrilineal in the sense that they believed people were created through their mother's blood. The majority of Western Bantu arranged marriages by service instead of by payment, and they owned few, if any, cattle. Western Bantu in the equatorial forest incorporated a combination of fishing, hunting, vegeculture, and banana and oil-palm horticulture in their economies. Finally, leadership was achieved through the individual talent of a man, rather than inherited, and so leadership was not normally passed from father to son.

Elements of leadership, economy, marriage patterns, and beliefs about procreation formed part of a worldview that resulted in a group of related settlement patterns. The various spatial organizations of Western Bantu have not been defined to the same degree as the central cattle pattern and the elite Zimbabwe pattern, but it is possible to construct a preliminary model by identifying widespread settlement features found in the recent past among Western Bantu speakers in Angola and Zaire. There, villages characteristically consisted of rectangular houses arranged in a rough rectangle or parallel rows on opposite sides of a street. Whatever the arrangement, status was often expressed through the clustering of houses. In some cases, each side of the village was occupied by a separate generation, and in others, houses were clustered around important men. The rectangular houses often contained separate kitchen, storage, and sleeping rooms.

As a rule, the men's court was at the end of the street or in an open space near the senior leader's house. *V*-shaped pits for processing palm oil were sometimes dug behind the village, and hollows for firing pots could be found near a potter's house. Generally, shrines were placed at the doorway of a house and in front of a headman's house, and they could also be found on top of graves. Although a chief may have been buried in the village center, most graves were dug in communal cemeteries outside the settlement, and corpses were usually interred in extended or seated, rather than flexed, positions.

Metal currency was particularly important, and the status of metalworkers was high. Smiths were often associated with clan origins, and chiefs were often referred to as "master smiths." Consequently, some metalworking tools such as anvils and hammers and objects such as ceremonial axes and iron gongs were symbols of leadership.

These special metal items together with extended burials in mass cemeteries and rectangular houses divided internally in a special way and grouped into streets or rectangles make up the street pattern.

The Central Cattle Pattern

The second model, the central cattle pattern, was found among Eastern Bantu speakers in southern Africa who were predominantly patrilineal, exchanged wives for cattle, and had institutionalized male-hereditary leadership. Among these people, cattle belonged to the domain of men, and the animals were a man's principal form of wealth and the main avenue to his power, success, and status. The center of the settlement was a men's area, and so the cattle were also penned there. Because cattle belonged to the domain of men and were the best sacrifice to ancestor spirits, important people—mostly men—were buried in the central byre (cattle corral). These graves formed a link with the traditional past, and religious ceremonies of a public nature occurred here. Because of these concepts of continuity and community involvement, produce from tribute fields was also stored in this area, sometimes underground, sometimes above. Because the byre was also the focus of male political activity, the central cattle area was used for certain stages of boys' initiation ceremonies and secret meetings of the leader. The leader's court was always nearby, either behind, inside, or in front.

Overall, the residential zone surrounding the central area belonged to the domain of women. This zone contained the houses and grain bins of each married woman. Grain bins were commonly raised up on stone supports, and the bins themselves could be large baskets, unfired clay containers, or miniature houses. The houses among the Sotho-Tswana were rondavels made of pole and *dhaka* (a mixture of mud and cattle dung)

with thatched roofs, while the Nguni built beehive-shaped huts from saplings and thatch.

The front of a settlement was reserved for public, secular, and dangerous activities, while the back was for private, sacred, and life-giving functions. In consequence, the leader lived at the back in the most protected position, and the area behind his residence was reserved for rainmaking rituals. Individual residences were also ordered according to this public-private principle: visitors were received in the front courtyard, facing the cattle byre, and the backyard contained private grain bins and the graves of women and children. In the house itself, the doorway was a focal point for ancestor spirits during group rituals, but they were invoked for private purposes at the back, in the area that was also used for private storage.

In addition to this public-private principle, a settlement was also ordered according to attitudes toward status. A house was often divided into female (left) and male (right) sides, and households were usually arranged on both sides of the senior residence according to some alternating system of status. In large settlements, a similar status principle governed the location of residential units around the chief.

Archaeological Evidence for the Central Cattle Pattern

The distribution of the central cattle pattern back through time has been a contentious issue. For some archaeologists, the central cattle pattern exists in settlements where there is independent ceramic evidence for Eastern Bantu, coupled with the remains of storage pits, cattle byres, and prestige burials in a central zone surrounded by houses and grain bins.

The proper use of the central cattle pattern in the direct historical approach is to apply the model (and compare it to appropriate alternatives) period by period. The pattern is well established for Late Iron Age sites because stone walls make activity areas particularly clear. Proceeding backward, the last stone-walled settlements in southern Africa associated with Sotho-Tswana speakers date to the 16th and 15th centuries. At Ficus near Makapansgat Limeworks, 15th-century ceramics attributed to Sotho-Tswana people characterized a series of homesteads with cattle byres containing pits and a burial and surrounded by a residential zone marked by burned hut floors. Similar ceramics and settlement features have been found at Nylsvley dating to the 14th century. Even though stone walls are absent, these Sotho-Tswana sites conform to the central cattle pattern rather than an alternative pattern. The absence of walling may indicate a change in attitude toward boundaries, but the overall spatial relationships remained constant.

Perhaps the best example of the central cattle pattern dates to the 11th century in Botswana. In large-scale excavations, Denbow uncovered a Toutswe-phase homestead with a central cattle byre containing a single pit in the center and seven male burials, all on their right sides, along the back half of the outer edge. Several female burials, all on their left sides, along with a variety of child burials were found in and among a group of 19 houses spread in an arc around the byre. At least two and possibly four grain bins once stood in this residential arc. Since this Toutswe site has precisely the same kind of evidence as Ficus and Nylsvley, even though the ceramics belong to a different tradition, the central cattle pattern must have also been present. If this conclusion is valid, then the central cattle pattern must also have been in operation at the 5th- to 6th-century site of Broederstroom because the evidence is the same. The presence of the pattern at Broederstroom is significant to gender studies because it shows that bride wealth in cattle already existed in the Early Iron Age. Thus the status of women was determined in relation to men, and gender was a major structuring principle.

The Broederstroom site also suggests that the pattern and its associated social organization and worldview did not originate in southern Africa. Whatever the case, we know it preceded the third model, the Zimbabwe pattern.

The Zimbabwe Pattern

The Zimbabwe pattern has been reconstructed from 16th- to 18th-century Portuguese descriptions of various Shona-speaking kingdoms and from Shona oral history, recent Shona ethnography, and the ethnography of the baVenda, a re-lated people in South Africa. These sources show that one of the principal sociocultural differences between the Zimbabwe culture and the culture of other Eastern Bantu was the existence of an institutionalized bureaucracy. This class distinction is reflected in a dual settlement pattern: small, commoner settlements were organized according to the principles of the central cattle pattern, while royal administrative centers were quite distinct. Some 300 royal centers are on record for an area that includes Zimbabwe, eastern Botswana, northern South Africa, and western Mozambique, a total area about the size of France.

Within these royal settlements, the courts were primarily a place for commoners' disputes, rather than a place to maintain justice between subjects and rulers, and royal disputes were held *in camera* (in private). In consequence, royal herds were not penned in the center near the commoners' court. Although wealth in cattle was important, trade wealth was the foundation of the upper class, and so elite people were not buried in the cattle byre. Instead they were buried on hilltops as part of a metaphorical association between the height of mountains and the high status of leadership.

This mountain imagery and burial location were elements of sacred leadership, a ritualization of leadership that justified the distinction between commoners and royalty. As part of this ritualization, the leader of a royal settlement was secluded in a stone-walled palace on a hill or on a raised stone platform.

These palace walls enclosed *dhaka* structures that were far more substantial than in the street or central cattle patterns. Here solid walls were up to 30 centimeters thick. In addition, the huts of various officials contained unusual features. The leader's audience chamber, for example, was usually divided by a central wall, or it was built as a hut within a hut connected by radiating walls like spokes in a wheel.

This divided audience chamber served to separate the leader from his supplicants. Other features isolated the sacred leader even further. Most of his wives lived outside the palace in their own area, people exaggerated their behavior in his presence, and an island of noise surrounded his procession.

Sacred leaders ruled along with a specially designated sister. A few other officials also stayed inside the palace with him. These included a special messenger and diviner. The front of the palace was surrounded by an entourage of male guards, praisers, and musicians, in accordance with the same public-private dichotomy found in the central cattle pattern, and the back was a national rainmaking center and the residence of a few young wives.

The front and back of a royal settlement, however, were aligned with cardinal directions because of an association of danger and death with the west and security and life with the east. If possible, the front of the palace as well as the settlement faced west, and the rainmaking center faced east.

Besides this life-forces dichotomy, a royal settlement was also ordered by status. The leader and his sister often had separate entrances to the palace, and the quarters of the royal wives were placed to one side of the palace and usually downslope. The leader's first wife lived at the head of this women's area, and since she was in charge of the produce from the tribute fields, this food was stored near her. A confinement area for royal wives giving birth was located at the back, while the leader's mother and the man in charge of female labor lived on opposite sides.

Individual status, class distinction, sacred leadership, and other aspects of the Zimbabwe culture were inculcated in a premarital initiation school for young men and women located on the edge of the royal wives' area. This school, as a means of inculcation, was an integral part of political power, and in some royal settlements, it was the only other stone-walled area besides the palace.

The school, wives' area, and palace were surrounded by commoners living in unwalled residential units. These people formed a protective circle of loyal supporters, and they completed the inner core of a royal settlement. Political competitors who were dangerous to the leader lived in residences outside this core.

One of the visually most impressive aspects of the elite Zimbabwe pattern is its monumental stone architecture. At Great Zimbabwe, some walls are 7.5 meters high and 6 meters thick.

Furthermore, several sites have decorated walls that symbolized various aspects of sacred leadership. The crocodile (check and dentelle designs) in its pool (dark line) referring to the seclusion of the leader was dominant, while the snake of the water (cord design) and snake of the mountain (chevron design) reflected the related themes of control over fertility and rain, respectively. Other stone features such as monoliths (horns and spears) and stone cairns (symbolic grain bins) carried equally charged meanings.

When analyzed together, these designs follow the same structure as the organization of space. Zimbabwe people organized their settlements and symbolic designs according to the dimensions of life forces, status, and security. The palace was private and sacred, and ideally it was placed above, behind, and east of the public and secular area for followers. The public court, on the other hand, was a senior male area to the side of the palace on a separate status axis opposed to the royal wives' compound, the senior women's area. Lastly, the palace and the town were protected from physical and supernatural harm by concentric rings of guards and medicine.

The Zimbabwe pattern incorporates most dimensions of the central cattle pattern, but the elements are arranged differently. Since this arrangement is exclusive to the Zimbabwe culture, the oldest place in the archaeological record with this pattern will be the site of origin.

Archaeological Evidence for the Origins of the Zimbabwe Pattern

The archaeological evidence indicates that the Zimbabwe culture evolved from the central cattle pattern in the Shashi-Limpopo Basin (where the modern countries of Zimbabwe, South Africa, and Botswana meet) at two sites known as K2 and Mapungubwe Hill. K2 (or Bambandyanalo) was first established in about A.D. 980, and an economic change there—namely, participation in the Indian Ocean gold and ivory trade—caused traditional leaders to become incredibly wealthy. This wealth allowed the society to develop class distinctions. The first spatial change was the movement of cattle out of the center of K2 between about 1060 and 1080. When the people abandoned K2 and moved a kilometer away to

Mapungubwe Hill, a cattle kraal (pen) was not reestablished next to the new court, and so the previous shift of cattle away from the center at K2 was a real spatial transformation. This transformation suggests that cattle had become royal property—not a medium to bind ordinary people together—and the central court became the place for unrelated men.

Most people at Mapungubwe lived below the hill in front of the court, but the leader lived on top. This is the first time in the prehistory of southern Africa that a leader was so physically separated from his followers, and it indicates that sacred leadership had evolved.

At first, the leader and a few officials lived on the west end of the hill, but within a few years (the entire town was occupied for only 50 to 70 years), he had moved to the center behind a stone-walled palace. At the same time, stone walls marked the office of the legal expert in charge of the court, passages leading up the hill, the hut platforms of royalty on the hill slopes, and a perimeter wall at the west front of the town. By the middle of the 13th century, then, the elite Zimbabwe pattern had evolved.

Whatever the precise sequence, the broad changes to the central cattle pattern are clear. First, the center-side dichotomy disappeared when the cattle were moved out of the center of K2, and second, the wives were placed together opposite the court. Ritual seclusion, the third major change, was established by moving the great hut onto the hilltop out of the homestead area.

The transformation of the central cattle pattern into the elite Zimbabwe pattern was the single most significant structural change to occur among Iron Age societies in southern Africa. Methodologically, this transformation was recognized by using the two settlement patterns as unitary standards for comparison. Thus, normative, ahistorical models of settlement organization can be useful tools in archaeological analyses.

BIBLIOGRAPHY

Denbow, J. 1986. A new look at the later prehistory of the Kalahari. *Journal of African History* 27: 3–28.

Huffman, T. N., 1986. Iron Age settlement patterns and the origins of class distinction in southern Africa. *Advances in World Archaeology* 5: 291–338.

———. 1989. *Iron Age migrations.* Johannesburg: Witwatersrand University Press.

———. 1996. *Snakes and crocodiles: Power and symbolism in ancient Zimbabwe.* Johannesburg: Witwatersrand University Press.

Kuper, A. 1982. *Wives for cattle: Bridewealth and marriage in southern Africa.* London: Routledge and Kegan Paul.

Maggs, T. O'C. 1976. *Iron Age communities of the southern highveld.* Pietermaritzburg: Natal Museum.

Vansina, J. 1990. *Paths in the rainforests: Toward a history of political tradition in equatorial Africa.* Madison: University of Wisconsin Press.

Thomas N. Huffman

PEOPLE AND CULTURE

Languages

AFRICAN LANGUAGES: A HISTORICAL SURVEY

More than 1,500 languages are spoken in Africa today. Their histories, individually and collectively, reflect an immensely varied human history on the continent. Their genetic relationships and their vocabularies provide us with vast stores of information on that human past.

African Language Families

The great majority of the modern-day African languages belong to just four families: Khoisan, Afro-Asiatic (Afrasian), Nilo-Saharan, and Niger-Congo. A fifth family is represented by a single language, Shabo, spoken by hunter-foragers of far southwestern Ethiopia. Many scholars also separate off Hadza of Tanzania from Khoisan and place it in its own sixth family. The position of another group of languages, Kadu, found in the Nuba Mountains in Sudan, has been disputed. Some scholars include it in the Niger-Congo family, while others propose its membership in Nilo-Saharan. Still others see it as a seventh family.

For two of the families, Afro-Asiatic and Nilo-Saharan, there now exist full phonological reconstructions and extensive dictionaries of the reconstructed root words used in the proto-languages of each, along with provisional subclassifications of each family. A subclassification groups the languages of a family according to the relative closeness of their relationship. It can usually be represented by a family tree diagram, examples of which appear in the tables accompanying this article. The notation *proto-* signifies the ancestral language, spoken long ago, from which all the languages of a family variously descend. We thus call the mother language of the Afro-Asiatic family *proto–Afro-Asiatic,* and the common ancestor of the Nilo-Saharan languages *proto–Nilo-Saharan.*

The historical comparative reconstruction of a third family, Niger-Congo, is less well advanced overall, simply because of its size: it contains perhaps three-quarters of Africa's languages. Interestingly, one major subgroup of Niger-Congo, Bantu, was already put on a solid historical comparative footing early in the 20th century. It was the first genetic grouping of African languages to be so studied. Strong beginnings toward a reconstruction of Niger-Congo as a whole have also been made, and one well-grounded provisional subclassification of the family now exists as well.

For the fourth major family, Khoisan, only tentative proposals on its historical comparative reconstruction have yet been offered. The deepest divisions in the family are clearly among the Sandawe language (spoken, as is Hadza, in Tanzania), the Southern African Khoisan branch, and Hadza, if it also belongs to the family.

Each of the four major language families of Africa has a great historical time depth, far greater than the Indo-European family to which English belongs. The proto–Indo-European speech community existed about 6,000 years ago. In contrast, the protolanguages of the African families were each spoken between 12,000 and 20,000 years ago.

The Khoisan Family

Proto-Khoisan is probably the most ancient of the four protolanguages, dating possibly to 20,000 years ago. The present-day Khoisan-speaking peoples are heirs of a common cultural tradition that once occupied much of the eastern side of the continent, from northern East Africa to the Cape of Good Hope.

Scholars who accept the membership of Hadza in the family usually favor the family tree of Khoisan relationships as shown in table 10. The early stages of Khoisan history, this scheme implies, would have been played out in East Africa, with the spread of the Southern African Khoisan languages into South Africa and Namibia taking place at a later period.

The early Khoisan-speaking communities were perhaps the makers of various versions of an East African Microlithic tradition. Tool assemblages of this broad affiliation appear in the archaeology of East Africa no later than about 17,000 years ago. The Microlithic Age reached south of the Limpopo River only much later, during about the 6th millennium B.C., when Wilton culture, the best-known version of the East African Microlithic tradition, took hold there. Such a history fits well, of course, with the implication of the Khoisan family tree proposed in table 10—that Khoisan languages spread south of the Limpopo only after having long been established farther north.

The Afro-Asiatic Family

Afro-Asiatic is the family of African languages best known to nonspecialists. Along with the more than 200 languages of its Cushitic, Omotic, and Chadic branches, it includes the Berber languages of northern and Saharan Africa, Ancient Egyptian, Semitic, and one subgroup of southwestern Asian languages. Because of the association of Semitic languages with several world religions, the Afro-Asiatic family has long been uncritically presumed by non-Africanist scholars to have originated in southwestern Asian.

But recent studies have determined that the ancestral language, proto–Afro-Asiatic, was spo-

Table 10 *The Khoisan language family*

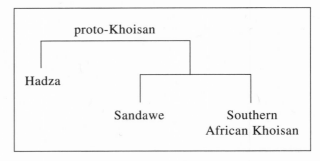

ken in Africa. A family tree of early Afro-Asiatic language history (see table 11) shows us that the first two divergences in the family gave rise to the Omotic branch and the Cushitic branch, both comprising languages spoken no farther north than the southern Red Sea Hills region. Only after the proto-Erythraic stage did the more northerly Afro-Asiatic language groupings come into being.

A second kind of testimony comes from words used in the very early Afro-Asiatic languages. The proto–Afro-Asiatic vocabulary included terms for *flour* (*dzayj-), *grains* (*zar-, * ʕeyl-), and *grindstone* (*baayn-) and also for *donkey* (*kʷer-), but no words at all implying herding or cultivating. By the proto-Erythraic stage, words for *cow* in general (*ɬoʔ-) and *male cattle* (*legʔ-, *yawr-) had been added, showing knowledge of a new animal. But still lacking in proto-Erythraic were any words specifically indicating *cultivation* or *herding*.

These developments in vocabulary show that the proto–Afro-Asiatics gathered wild grains for food and lived within the natural range of the wild donkey. Their proto-Erythraic descendants continued this way of life. To judge from new words for *cattle*, they either moved to areas where the wild cow could be found or experienced a climate shift that allowed the animal to spread into their lands.

This history is strikingly paralleled in the archaeology of northeastern Africa. Wild donkeys ranged the Red Sea Hills and northern edges of the Ethiopian Highlands, just where the proto–Afro-Asiatic language is most probably to be placed. In parts of the same broad region—in Nubia to the west and in the northeastern Ethiopian Highlands—the intensive collection of wild grains took hold before 13,000 B.C. and remained a basic subsistence practice for several thousand years more. The conclusion that the inventors of this way of life were the early Afro-Asiatics seems difficult to avoid.

After the 13th millennium B.C., grain collection spread north to Egypt, and after about 10,000 B.C., to southwestern Asia as well. Peoples who adopted the Afro-Asiatic languages as their own probably extended grain collection at each stage. Wild cattle moved south from the Mediterranean with the beginning of wetter climate in the 11th millennium and so became part of Afro-Asiatic knowledge *after* proto–Afro-Asiatic times, just as the word histories indicate.

The first unmistakable testimony of food production in Afro-Asiatic languages does not appear until the proto-Cushitic, proto-Chadic, and proto-Boreafrasian periods. The proto-Cushitic language contained, for example, nouns for *cultivated field* (*pa?r-) and *cattle pen* (*mawr-) and the verbs for *milking* (*?ilm-) and *cultivating* (*?abr-). Old Cushitic terms for *finger millet* (*dangawc-) and *teff* (*tl'eff-) identify two crops that they cultivated. Similarly, the proto-Chadic people had words for *cultivated field* (*mar) and *sorghum* (*dəwr) and numerous domestic animal terms, such as for *cow* (*ɬa), *sheep* (*tam-k-),

ram (*nzəl), and *goat* (*bəkr). Through archaeological research, these initial moves of Afro-Asiatic peoples toward food production can probably been seen in the spread, beginning around the 9th millennium, of Capsian-related cultures through the northern Sahara and in a nearly contemporaneous spread of proto-Cushitic communities, as yet undiscovered archaeologically, along the northern edges of the Ethiopian Highlands.

The history of the Omotic languages has been little studied as yet. Still, certain broad elements of their history are clear enough. The earliest Omotic speakers were an offshoot of the proto–Afro-Asiatic grain collectors. The early sites of grain collectors found in northeastern Ethiopia may well have been theirs. But their descendants of the last several millennia have been preeminently cultivators, and their staple crop, the ensete plant. The wide occurrence of Omotic loanwords in Cushitic languages reveals that Omotic agricultural societies, as recently as the 5th millennium B.C., occupied most of the Ethiopian Highlands.

One plausible hypothesis implicates environmental change as a major factor in Omotic agricultural invention. First, when the Holocene climatic optimum began around 10,500 B.C., highland areas of grassland were often replaced

Table 11 *The Afro-Asiatic language family*

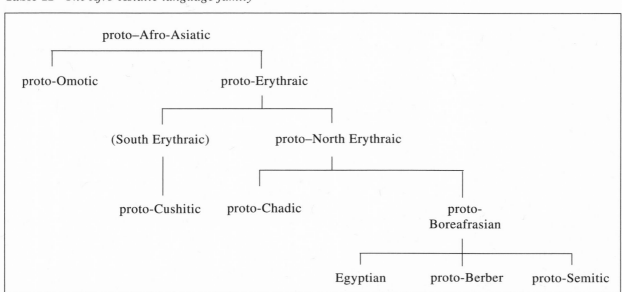

by montane forest, threatening the original Omotic livelihood. In response, it can be proposed, the ancestors of the Omotic peoples of later times created an alternative kind of intensive food collection, using the wild ensete plant. A second transition, in this view, would have come after 6,000 B.C., when climate again became drier, decreasing the availability of wild ensete. To this challenge, some Omotic peoples responded by domesticating the plant. By enhancing their subsistence productivity in this way, these communities became able to expand through large parts of the Ethiopian Highlands.

From 4000 B.C. onward, however, Cushitic peoples began to spread their languages into successively wider areas. Agaw languages in time replaced Omotic tongues in northern and central Ethiopia, and Eastern Cushitic languages came to predominate in most areas around the Rift Valley and the eastern side of the highlands. Only in the southwest and in some areas along the rift have Omotic languages and culture continued to prevail.

One branch of the Cushitic languages, Southern Cushitic, advanced still farther south, first into northern Kenya after 3500 B.C. and then in subsequent centuries into central and southern Kenya and northern Tanzania. There the Cushites encountered Khoisan-speaking peoples of the old East African Microlithic or Cushitic expansions. In East Africa, we can connect the Southern Cushites with the Oldishi and Olmalenge varieties of the Savanna Pastoral Neolithic. These cultures continued to be prominent until the early 1st millennium A.D., and several Southern Cushitic languages are still spoken today in Tanzania and Kenya.

Other expansions of Afro-Asiatic languages took place in western Africa. Proto-Chadic, a member of the North Erythraic branch, was taken by its speakers south from the central Sahara into the eastern Lake Chad Basin in about the 6th millennium B.C. Between the 6th and 4th millennia B.C., descendant languages of proto-Chadic spread over the greater part of today's northern Nigeria and central Chad. Well more than 100 Chadic languages are currently spoken, the best known of which is Hausa.

The Berber languages, another subgroup of the North Erythraic branch, expanded at three different periods. First, in the late 3rd millennium B.C., the speakers of proto-Berber spread across areas extending from the central Maghreb to the borders of Middle Kingdom Egypt. A second Berber expansion covered large parts of North Africa in the last millennium B.C. and gave rise to many of the Berber peoples documented in the Roman records. A final Berber spread took place in the 1st millennium A.D., when the Tuareg, by then possessors of camels, occupied the central Sahara.

Three movements of Semitic languages from Asia back into Africa require mention also. The Ethiopic languages, numbering today about 15 languages, all derive from a dialect of Epigraphic South Arabian carried to Eritrea in about the 6th century B.C. by settlers from Yemen. Because of their central role in commerce and in the rise of early states in the Horn, these immigrants spread their language to many of the indigenous Cushites. The older idea that South Arabian preeminence was caused by their bringing iron or plow agriculture into the region is simply not supported by the evidence. Plow cultivation, in fact, can be shown from Cushitic word histories to antedate the South Arabian arrival by 2,000 or 3,000 years. Today, the most well-known Ethiopian Semitic languages is Amharic.

Another Semitic tongue, Punic, came to be spoken in parts of North Africa in the last millennium B.C. Punic was derived from the language of the Phoenicians, founders of the city of Carthage. By the Roman period, Punic had long been the first language of many urban people in the area of modern-day Tunisia and a language of trade in surrounding regions. It gradually died out after the Arab conquest of North Africa in the 7th century.

Because of this conquest, still another Semitic tongue, Arabic, rapidly took hold all across North Africa, at first in government and commerce, then among townspeople, and eventually in many rural areas. In Egypt, Coptic, the descendant form of Ancient Egyptian, only slowly gave way to Arabic. Coptic finally ceased to be spoken in about the 17th century, although it continues as the scriptural language of Egyptian Christians. In the Maghreb, many Berber languages persist today as speech islands in a sea of Arabic. After

Table 12 *The Nilo-Saharan language family*

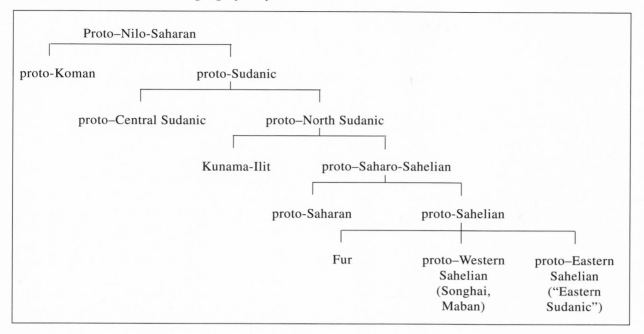

the 11th century, commercial relations, population movements, and the prestige of Islam combined to spread Arabic still farther south, across the western Sahara and a large part of the eastern Sudan.

The Nilo-Saharan Family

The earliest Nilo-Saharan peoples lived in the Middle Nile Basin between about 15,000 and 11,000 B.C. A family tree of Nilo-Saharan helps us picture how these languages came eventually to be spread over a vast expanse, from the bend of the Niger River in Mali to Sudan and Kenya (see table 12).

The first divergence, depicted in table 12, gave rise to the Koman branch, restricted in later times to the east side of the Middle Nile region. From the second divergence emerged the Central Sudanic branch, located in the southwestern parts of the basin, and the North Sudanic branch, originally found in northern areas of the basin. Only with the proto-Saharo-Sahelian period did Nilo-Saharan languages start to spread far west of the Middle Nile.

The evidence of early Nilo-Saharan words reveals two notable early developments: the making of pottery and the domestication of cattle by the proto–North Sudanic communities. Indicative of this history are the reconstructed North Sudanic verbs for *fashioning pottery* (*ted) and for *driving cattle to pasture* (*ṣuk-) and to *water* (ya:ṭ), along with a word for *cow* (*ya:yr). The proto–North Sudanians, it appears, also adopted, probably from their Afro-Asiatic neighbors, something else not known earlier among the Nilo-Saharans—the gathering of wild grains. In the reconstructed vocabulary of proto–North Sudanians are words for *grindstone* (*p'el), *grain* in general (*Way), and *ear of grain* (*ke:n).

By the next period, the proto–Saharo-Sahelian period, the domestication of grains had begun. The evidence includes verbs for *cultivating* ($\hat{*}$ ḍipʰ), *clearing* (tʰaypʰ), and *weeding* (*kʰay) and nouns for *cultivated field* (*ḍomp) and *granary* (*per). Then in the proto-Sahelian period, sheep and goats became known, too, as reflected in the proto-Sahelian adoption of several terms for both animals (for example, *ad for *goat,* *Wer for *sheep,* *g'ent for *he-goat,* and *menkʰ for *ram).

This history closely matches the sequence of changes exemplified in early Neolithic sites of far southern Egypt. There the same three stages appear in the archaeology as in the linguistic record:

Table 13 *The Niger-Congo language family*

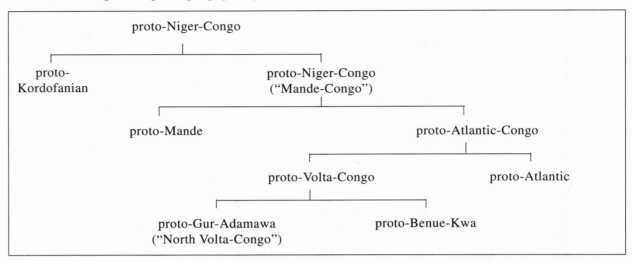

1. Wild grain collection, with grindstones, pottery, and some cattle in the 8th or 9th millennium B.C.
2. Grain cultivation and cattle raising, with granaries, by the late 7th or 8th millennium B.C.
3. The addition of sheep and goats after 5700 B.C. (about the early 7th millennium B.C.)

A wide spreading out of Sahelian peoples brought the proto-Sahelian period to a close. One arm of this expansion moved as far west eventually as Niger. From this settlement came the Songhai society of much later times. Another major direction of expansion passed southward through the Middle Nile Basin. The peoples involved in this set of movements were the speakers of the Eastern Sahelian languages (formerly, Eastern Sudanic). The proposed dating of these movements, to about the 6th millennium B.C., suggests that the drying of the Sahara climate helped push the speakers of these languages into new areas farther south. The Eastern Sahelian expansions probably reached as far as the northern edges of Uganda by the 4th or 3rd millennium B.C. The Nilotic languages, such as Dinka and Maasai, are the best known modern-day languages that descended from these movements.

The Niger-Congo Family

Niger-Congo is another family with a long history. The protolanguage of the family was spoken as early as 15,000 or more years ago. The most widely followed subclassification of the family divides it into a series of branches and subbranches as shown in table 13.

The first expansion of Niger-Congo peoples appears to have stretched from as far east as the Nuba Mountains of Sudan, where proto-Kordofanian would have been spoken, to as far west as Mali, the ancient territory of the Mande branch. The next two branchings depict a growing diversity of Niger-Congo peoples across the regions of the Upper Niger, Senegal, and Volta Rivers.

Two possible archaeological correlations have been proposed for these initial expansions of Niger-Congo. One is with the Aqualithic civilization, which became a prominent way of life, using waterside food resources, between 8000 and 6000 B.C. across 4,000 kilometers of Africa, from Lake Turkana in northern Kenya to the bend of the Niger River in Mali. The other is with the West African Microlithic, a grouping of cultures of the West African savanna areas dating to before that period. For two reasons, the latter attribution is preferred. First of all, the Aquatic adaptation came to prominence too late to be easily identifiable with the earliest Niger-Congo speakers. Second, the evidence of vocabulary shows that the bow (*-ta), a feature in keeping with a microlithic tool kit, was an ancient weapon among them, whereas the Aquatic peoples were principally harpoon and blade-tool users. More likely, the Aquatic adaptation was the work of Nilo-Saharan peoples, including perhaps those of the Central Sudanic branch of the family (see table 12).

The next Niger-Congo divergence, of Volta-Congo into separate Gur-Ubangian and Benue-Congo groups, is best located in the savanna woodland areas that extend from the Volta Basin to central Nigeria. By this time, the beginnings of West African yam-based agriculture were already well underway among these peoples.

The still later spread of Benue-Congo peoples into the rain-forest belt of West Africa is likely to date to the period of full establishment of yam and oil-palm cultivation. The linguistic dating of this spread to the 6th and 5th millennia B.C. correlates well with the archaeologically dated appearance of polished stone axes in the rain-forest archaeology. Yams and oil palms require sunlight to grow, and axes would have been the essential tools of incoming cultivators for clearing forests.

As part of the wider spread of Benue-Congo agriculturists, the speakers of the Bantu languages began moving into the equatorial rain forest of the Zaire Basin as early as the 4th millennium B.C. Over the course of the next 3,000 years, Bantu peoples gradually expanded their settlements through many parts of the forest and into the edges of the woodland savanna just south of it. At the same time, a parallel spread of the Ubangian peoples, an offshoot of the Gur-Adamawa branch, carried the same agricultural way of life eastward, through the woodland savanna zone just north of the equatorial forest.

Then, in the last millennium B.C., one particular set of peoples, the Mashariki (or Eastern) Bantu, moved farther east, into the Great Lakes region of Africa. Around the last three centuries B.C., the Mashariki communities began a relatively rapid expansion that scattered their descendants across eastern Africa from Uganda and Kenya in the north to KwaZulu-Natal in the south. Other Bantu groups spread at about the same time more directly south from the woodland savanna areas of southern Zaire into what is today Angola and Zambia. In all of southern and much of eastern Africa, Bantu expansion proceeded at the expense of Khoisan languages. In Uganda, Kenya, and Tanzania, Southern Cushitic and Eastern

Sahelian languages also were sometimes replaced by Bantu. The overall history of these developments is exceedingly complex, but the outcome is simply stated: because of these population movements, Bantu languages are today spoken across a third of the continent.

The adoption of iron technology in the last millennium B.C. is often credited with setting off the Mashariki expansion. But the history of words for *iron* and *iron tools* shows that the new technology often diffused across the lines of language spread. Instead, we will have to look to other factors, such as the Mashariki development of a new, more adaptive agricultural synthesis, combining Niger-Congo yams with Nilo-Saharan grains, if we are satisfactorily to understand this history.

Austronesian and Indo-European Families in African History

Languages of two other families have become indigenized in some African countries in the past 2,000 years.

Malagasy, an Austronesian language, was brought by Indonesian immigrants to previously uninhabited Madagascar in the early centuries of the 1st millennium A.D. The evidence of loanwords suggests that the Malagasy ancestors settled for a brief period among Bantu peoples along the East African coast before moving on to the island. A great deal of additional Bantu influence appears in the language, brought over from the mainland by different later immigrants from southeastern Africa.

Several Indo-European languages have been spoken in Africa by resident populations at different times. Greek was the language of the townspeople of Cyrene in Cyrenaica from about the 8th century B.C. and may have remained so until the Arab conquest. Portuguese has been a first language of at least small indigenized communities in several Atlantic coastal towns, such as Luanda in Angola, from the 16th century.

A third language, Dutch, taken to South Africa by European settlers in the 17th century, evolved in the interim into Afrikaans, the first language of a large number of people in that country. And because of the colonial era, several other Indo-European languages, among them English,

French, Hindi, and Gujarati, also established footholds on the continent in the 20th century. But none of these offers us evidence on the more ancient eras of African history.

African Language Families in the Longer View

To trace most of the 1,500 languages of Africa back to just four long-ago protolanguages may convey the false impression of a continent once nearly empty of people, but, of course, that was never so. There were probably well more than 1,000 languages spoken in Africa even 20,000 years ago.

Just as more recent Bantu settlements have led to the extinction of languages previously spoken in eastern or southern Africa, so the ancient spread of the Afro-Asiatic, Nilo-Saharan, and Niger-Congo families in West Africa must each have displaced hundreds of languages, members oftentimes of families now wholly extinct. In the Zaire Basin today, the so-called Pygmies speak languages they have adopted at various times over the past four millennia from their Ubangian, Bantu, and even central Sudanic neighbors. But before that, they must have spoken other languages belonging to just such a now wholly extinct family of languages or to more than one such family. The language isolate Shabo, of Ethiopia, may well be the last member of another such family, once widely spread in the Ethiopian Highlands before the arrival of Omotic and other Afro-Asiatic languages.

From a historical perspective, the interesting issue is to explain why one family of languages expands at the expense of others. Sometimes the causes are fairly clear, as when peoples with the advantage of being fully agricultural move into the lands of food collectors. The farmers' social units are larger, and they can support many more people on the same amount of land. The same kind of advantage can be generated by the invention of a new kind of food collecting, as the spread of the Afro-Asiatic languages, tied apparently to the success of wild-grain collection, shows us. Our ability to reconstruct language relationships and the vocabularies of earlier times provides the evidence with which to seek out

cause and effect in language history and to connect that history to the findings of archaeology.

BIBLIOGRAPHY
Bender, M. L., ed. 1976. *The non-Semitic languages of Ethiopia.* East Lansing: Michigan State University.
———. 1989. *Topics in Nilo-Saharan linguistics.* Hamburg: Buske.
Bendor, S. J., and R. Hartell, eds. 1989. *The Niger-Congo languages.* Lanham: University Press of America.
Ehert, C., and M. Posansky, eds. 1982. *The archaeological and linguistic reconstruction of African history.* Berkeley: University of California Press.
Shaw, T., P. Sinclair, B. Andah, and A. Okpoko, eds. 1993. *The archaeology of Africa: Food, metals and towns.* London: Routledge.

Christopher Ehret

LANGUAGES OF EASTERN AND SOUTHERN AFRICA IN HISTORICAL PERSPECTIVE

The purpose of this aricle is threefold. It sets out the language groupings relevant to eastern, southern, and south-central Africa, it outlines linguistic methods and indicates which results are certain and which are less certain, and it sketches possible or likely homelands and dispersal routes of languages to current locations.

Language Groupings

Following J. H. Greenberg's work of the 1960s, four major language groupings (or families) in Africa, with a few isolates, are widely accepted. Only one of these is now entirely based in eastern and southern Africa, the other four being only partly represented there.

The largest grouping in Africa, and specific to Africa, is Niger-Congo. Continentwide, it has nearly 400 million speakers and well more than 1,000 languages. The largest subset of Niger-Congo is Narrow Bantu. Some 250 million people speak as their first languages one of the 300 to 600 Bantu languages today. The exact number of languages, here as in most other groupings, is hard to state firmly, for it depends on the distinction between language and dialect—criteria on which neither native speakers nor linguists agree. Bantu languages predominate in the whole area of sub-Saharan Africa south of a line from western Cameroon to far southern Somalia. The remaining Niger-Congo languages are distributed throughout western Africa and into north-central Africa.

With some 220 million speakers and more than 200 languages, the next biggest grouping in Africa is Afro-Asiatic (or Afrasian), whose best-known members are Arabic and Hebrew in the Middle East. All except 20 or so of these languages are spoken in Africa, which was the main reason for changing the name from older Hamito-Semitic, which emphasized the Middle East connection. Afro-Asiatic is presently divided into six branches, only one of which, Cushitic, is represented in East Africa. More than 200,000 people speak the Southern Cushitic languages of Tanzania, while 7 million speak Eastern Cushitic Somali, and some 25 million Ethiopians speak various Afro-Asiatic languages.

The third grouping is Nilo-Saharan, with perhaps 20 million people and some 60 languages mainly spoken in a band from Chad across Zaire, Sudan, and Uganda, down into Kenya. In East Africa, the largest subset consists of Nilotic speakers, with 6 million people and some 15 languages, concentrated in Uganda and western and northwestern Kenya but tapering down into northern Tanzania. There are a few hundred thousand Sudanic speakers in Uganda.

By far the smallest grouping, with just more than 200,000 speakers and ten languages, is Khoisan. One of these, Sandawe, in western Tanzania, has perhaps 50,000 speakers. Nearby sit perhaps 1,000 Hatsa, the affiliation of whose language is disputed but most often stated to be Khoisan. All the rest are located well more than 1,600 kilometers to the southwest, in Namibia, Botswana, and a smaller but unknown number in Angola.

Finally, it is appropriate to mention the Pygmies (or Pygmoids) of central Africa, most of whom are now, or are assumed once to have been,

hunter-foragers. They live dotted across the Zaire Basin in the area roughly bounded by north- and southeastern Zaire across to the Congo Republic, Gabon, and up to Cameroon. Unlike the Khoisan speakers, they have no single common language and speak local Bantu or Ubangian languages. On the other hand, since they are culturally, physically, genetically, and often economically different from their neighbors, they were also long assumed to have been the autochthons (native peoples with a long cultural development) of the forest. Linguistic work has centered on whether it is possible to extract a common set of words retained from a now lost Pygmy language, or languages, but so far the results are not conclusive. The Pygmies number some 200,000 today.

Methods, Problems, Results, and Reliability

The foregoing draws what appears to be a neat and composite picture, as does the content of the next section. But what is this picture based on? How reliable are its various components? What is not said? This section deals with such questions.

Linguists can be useful to archaeologists and historians in three main ways. The first way is by taking the languages of Africa, assigning them to a number of sets, and then combining these subsets into ever larger sets, until we end up with a few very large groupings. Examination of the geographical extent of groupings at all levels allows hypotheses about early homelands and later movements. This gives nonlinguists a basis for talking about early shared group history instead of having to focus on local and recent ethnic history.

In principle, linguists do this by applying the comparative method. Step one involves taking a collection of languages and trying to establish regular and frequent sound correspondences between each of them. Those for which this is possible are judged to be related, while the others are not. Those so related are said to be members of the same family. When the correspondences are stated, step two consists of positing an original sound for each set of correspondences. The original sound is considered to have once existed in the protolanguage ancestral to the set of languages. In step three, we examine a large set of vocabulary from each related language. We describe as *cognate* each item that has similar or related meaning across the languages and also shows regular sound correspondences, and we assign a form of each of these items to the protolanguage. In step four, we thus build up a vocabulary, a set of sounds, and some grammatical formats for the protolanguage. In the final step, we look at innovations—lexical, phonetic, or other—shared by subsets of related languages. We assume these innovations did not occur separately in each language but occurred just once, in the intermediate protolanguage ancestral to each subset, and this gives us a basis for subdividing families and groups.

In practice, the process is not quite so elegant. More often linguists have an intuition about groupings and announce it: at this point we have a hypothesis of undetermined probability. Sooner or later the comparative method is applied, and we then have a language family of high probability. So far, this text has been careful to use the word *grouping* because not all of our four families are of the same level of probability! As of the time of writing (mid-1995), only the genetic status of Afro-Asiatic has been supported by a reasonable application of the comparative method. Two forthcoming studies of Nilo-Saharan will likely demonstrate its validity. Some form of Niger-Congo is believed to be a family by most comparative linguists, but to date no good application of the comparative method has been mounted. And while some linguists think Khoisan is a genetic unit, no one has yet proved this firmly. Do Khoisan languages form a valid language family, or are they just similar because their speakers lived for many millennia as neighbors?

These difficulties also exist at lower levels within language families. For basic reasons such as lack of data or the daunting complexity of the task, subgroups inside families are often not proved by the method described but by shortcuts such as the use of lexicostatistics, which is based on shared retention rather than on innovation, or on the distribution of loanwords or other methods. Examples of subgroups include Eastern and Western Bantu, the languages of southern Africa (Zone S), and the languages around Lake Victoria (Zone J), Southern Cushitic and Eastern Cushitic,

and Bantu as a part of Niger-Congo. All are tacitly assumed by many but not really proved.

Once a linguistic grouping has been reasonably proved, we can proceed to hypothesize about its original homeland. In general, a homeland is the area in which the greatest concentration of linguistic diversity in the group is located or where its nearest relatives are found. In some cases, a homeland is relatively easy to identify. Since the largest concentration of diversity in Afro-Asiatic is in northeastern Africa, that is probably where a homeland is best sought. Since the greatest concentration of diversity in Nilo-Saharan is not in Kenya or Uganda but to the north and west, that is where its origins are likely to be found. Since all Narrow Bantu's nearest relatives are in the Niger-Cross area of West Africa, that is where we place its cradle.

Khoisan again illustrates the difficulties. When the Dutch settled at the Cape in 1654, Khoisan communities were scattered throughout the whole area south of a line from southern Angola across Zambia and Zimbabwe to a point near the border between South Africa and Mozambique (today they are limited to Namibia, Botswana, and Angola). It did not take Westerners long to realize that these communities could be the earliest identifiable denizens of southern Africa, something their Bantu-speaking neighbors claimed already. A salient feature of these languages is the presence of click speech sounds. In the 19th century came the realization that two Tanzanian languages (Sandawe and Hatsa) also had clicks, and then a third language with clicks (Dahalo) was found in northeastern Kenya. The topological similarities between the southern and eastern languages and the distance between them led to various proposals: the Khoisan homeland had been in the south and the easterners were emigrants, or vice versa, or the whole of eastern and southern Africa had once had a Khoisan population. In fact, the first part of the 20th century saw suggestions that their domain had formerly extended even up into northeastern Africa. For a linguist, the problem here is as it is with Celtic: later intruders had sliced across much of the Khoisan groups' earlier domain, and today's distribution results from that intrusion and is not necessarily diagnostic of the earlier situation.

The second way in which language studies can be helpful to nonlinguists is by the reconstruction of vocabulary for various prehistoric stages of language families, which is, in fact, part of step four of the comparative method, described above. A word does not exist without its referent. On the basis of inherited vocabulary in today's languages, we can reconstruct thousands of words to their referents in protolanguages. Reconstructions of words dealing with economic, social, political, social, and kinship terms, the spiritual world, weapons and tools, and flora and fauna are useful to archaeologists. When linguists state that members of a prehistoric group were pastoralists, or subsistence farmers, or hunter-foragers, or fished, or had iron, or had goats but not cattle, or lived in villages rather than homesteads, these claims are largely based on reconstructions using today's data. The reconstructions are only as good as the data on which they are based. In this sense, evidence of this kind used by linguists is less direct than evidence used by archaeologists, who dig artifacts directly from the ground.

There is a problem not apparent to many nonlinguists. Archaeology journals typically have pages of representations of real artifacts and reconstructions of broken artifacts—that is, they quite rightly want their readers to see the raw materials set out before discussing their topological affinities. The linguistic equivalent would be to show all the raw lexical data on which reconstructions are based. Comparative linguists can rarely do this, partly because there is no tradition of journals that publish this kind of material, partly because it would take up too much space. But without seeing the exact phonetic shapes and geographical distribution of the data on which authors base their reconstructions, no linguist can really pass valid judgment, and accepting the reconstruction is an act of faith, not science.

The third way in which linguists can indicate directions for archaeologists is by uncovering traces of contact with adjacent communities, which might or might not still exist today. Any language consists of a mix of inherited material and new material. Inherited material, especially words, can be determined as outlined above in the discussion of the comparative method. "New"

material can have two sources. It can, in fact, be old, inherited material that is recycled in meaning or shape (for example, the Swahili word for a *head* was originally a metaphorical extension of *anthill),* or it can be absorbed from an outside source. Words are the easiest kind of diagnostic external material to identify, thus works on historical linguistics in Africa and elsewhere are replete with lists of loanwords. Once the transferred material has been listed, the linguist searches for the source and concludes that the words, and usually the referents, have been transferred from the source. There are some simple rules. The more loanwords, the heavier or the longer the contact. The more distant in shape or meaning from the source, the older the transfer. Loans clustering in certain semantic areas indicate heavy influence in those areas. This kind of linguistic detective work has enabled daring claims to be made and has immeasurably widened our horizons.

In recent years, two kinds of advances have been made in contact studies. One is that we have realized that it is not only words that can be transferred, but also sounds, phonological processes, and considerable parts of the grammar. The second is that our transfer models have become more sophisticated. In the past, we assumed that material was mainly transferred from one community to an adjacent one. We now see that material can be transferred under other circumstances. While good, concrete results are only starting to appear, this is a growth area.

No discussion of comparative-linguistic methodology would be complete without some reference to the difficulty of dating. Unless recorded in writing, no linguistic event comes with a date attached. No written records in eastern or southern Africa go back more than a very few centuries. Some linguists have used glottochronology (a method of dating laguages that uses the rate at which the vocabulary of one language is replaced by the vocabulary of another), but others have serious doubts about its use. Suffice it to say here that if the only basis for dating a linguistic event is glottochronology, nonlinguists should beware. To overcome this obstacle, we have had to juxtapose linguistic constructs and dating from archaeology usually based on carbon-14 measurements. If linguistic hypotheses about possible homelands and migrations can be clearly linked to archaeological strata and dates, then we can tentatively accept them, and this takes us a long way to dating protolanguages and reconstructions. Linguistic suggestions about contact and the transfer of material need confirmation by archaeological data that show the communities involved were in the right place at the right time.

There have been striking successes here. The general correlation of linguistic distribution with archaeological profile has worked well for the Bantu advance across Africa, although details remain to be determined. This is also true for early Cushitic and Nilo-Saharan expansion into East Africa. Once again Khoisan can be used to illustrate the pitfalls. Assuming the genetic unity of Khoisan as a working hypothesis, how old are its languages? To answer that, we have to date the communities that speak them by turning to archaeologists and biologists, but they do not agree. Although anatomically modern humans have been in southern Africa for 100,000 years, people morphologically Khoisan have only been demonstrably present for 10,000 years, so we are left currently without an answer to the dating of Khoisan.

A Sketch of Linguistically Based History for Eastern and Southern Africa, 3000 B.C. to A.D. 1000

We know hunter-foragers were the first communities across eastern, central, and southern Africa, and we often assume they spoke Khoisan exclusively. Linguists do not have too much to say about this. The fact that "click" communities exist today in southern and eastern Africa firmly supports the assumption of former Khoisan communities. Loanwords from Khoisan in Bantu languages or groups of Bantu languages where there is no Khoisan presence today suggest early regional contact between the two linguistic communities. It would be nice if we could identify a set of loanwords attributable to contact in northwestern East Africa between early Khoisan and the first Bantu community or communities to emerge from the forest, ancestral to today's Bantu communities, but we cannot. And the difficulties alluded to in the second section of this article do not exclude the possibility of additional hunter-forager communities with linguistic affinities other than Khoisan.

Sometime before 3000 B.C., communities speaking Southern Cushitic languages pressed out of Ethiopia into northern Kenya. By the 2nd millennium B.C., they had reached across central and western (and, possibly, eastern) Kenya and into northern Tanzania, and during the last millennium B.C., they spread through most other parts of Tanzania. They had domestic stock and cultivated grains. Loan material into Bantu suggests contact between Southern Cushitic and early Bantu in the area of the lakes and, thereafter, continued regional contact when Bantu communities fanned out.

A little later came other immigrants speaking various Nilo-Saharan languages, originating mostly in the Sudan. All were cultivators and herders to varying degrees. By the late 2nd millennium B.C., various Sudanic communities had reached the Great Lakes of East Africa and later expanded. At much the same time, Nilotic communities were in the southern Sudan, and Southern Nilotes moved across northern Uganda and into western Kenya during the first millennium B.C. Ironworking seems to have first emerged among these Sudanic communities.

Finally, the first Bantu-speaking peoples started to emerge from the rain forest in about 1000 B.C. and moved east and southeast into the area west of the Great Lakes. Theirs was a mixed late Stone Age economy based on farming, hunting, and fishing. Their only domestic animal seems to have been the goat. During the last millennium B.C., Bantu communities moved as far south as Lake Tanganyika and east to Lake Victoria. Over the same period their economy underwent massive transformations, taking knowledge of ironworking, cattle (and now sheep), and crops and farming techniques from their non-Bantu neighbors and adopting them as they habituated to steppe and savanna. Many of these neighbors must have been assimilated at the same time. Over the last centuries B.C. and the opening centuries of our era, they carried out their final large geographical expansion. Lake Victoria was probably the stepping stone for East Africa, and Lake Tanganyika for southern Africa.

As they expanded, they continued to assimilate non-Bantu neighbors and predecessors and are today by far the largest linguistic presence in eastern and southern Africa. Roughly contemporaneous with the events described in the preceding paragraph, other Bantu-speaking communities worked their way down from Cameroon through Gabon, the Congo Republic, and Zaire into Angola and Namibia.

This modified and expanded picture of the 1990s is largely the work of two scholars, Christopher Ehert and Jan Vansina. Linguistically, both have much in common, and their work captures well what other scholars intuitively felt was amiss with the earlier picture. Both see the Bantu homeland in Cameroon, near its West African relatives. Both see an original Bantu language slowly differentiating and spreading across northern Zaire. Out of this dialectal continuum emerged not only the linguistic ancestors of the language communities still living in that area but also those of the Bantu communities covering the rest of the southern and eastern part of the continent. Both see Bantu communities moving slowly, perhaps a few dozen kilometers per generation, into the areas they now occupy. Neither sees a single huge movement east out of the forest across the savanna to the coast, thence turning south and pushing down into southern Africa. Both reevaluate the archaeological correlation and dating and see eastern and southern Africa as being occupied at much the same time by different subsets of an original eastern Bantu settlement. Both see gradual linguistic differentiation rippling across communities, not bursting forth like a series of fireworks. Both see autochthons absorbed, not pushed aside. With much enlarged linguistic and archaeological knowledge and improved techniques, both have better and more detailed and sophisticated interpretations than we had two decades ago. Just as the last 20 or 30 years have been spent on absorbing and revising the scenario assembled by J. H. Greenberg, M. Guthrie, A. E. Meeussen, R. Oliver, and others, the next years will be spent addressing Ehret and Vansina.

They differ in a number of ways. Their respective historical interpretations rest on different views of how to classify the Bantu languages. While both see the northern languages as occu-pying a special status, Ehret sees the rest as dividing into three (western, central, and eastern) while Vansina has only western and eastern. Underlying this is a difference of technique. Although Vansina treats data in a masterly and creative way, the treatment depends heavily on a new lexicostatistical arrangement of the Bantu languages by Yves Bastin, André Coupez, and Michael Mann. Ehret's division follows the distribution of words, both inherited and borrowed, across Bantu. Not only do words slip quite easily from one language to another, but we are shown only the reconstructions, not the raw data. For linguists, one of the more pressing tasks is to reinvestigate the subclassification of Bantu using techniques other than lexicostatistics or lexical distribution. Until that is done, archaeologists should treat the current hypotheses as the best available, but not as the last, word.

BIBLIOGRAPHY

Ambrose, S. 1982. Archaeology and linguistic reconstructions of history in East Africa. In *The archaeological and linguistic reconstruction of African history,* eds. C. Ehret and M. Posnansky, 104–157. Berkeley: University of California Press.

Vansina, J. 1995. New linguistic evidence and the "Bantu expansion." *Journal of African History* 36: 173–195.

Derek Nurse

WESTERN AFRICAN LANGUAGES IN HISTORICAL PERSPECTIVE

From a historical point of view, it is important to know which languages of a region are related—that is, descended from a common original protolanguage—and how close the relationship is in various cases. Placing related languages on a map enables us to trace migration patterns in the remote past, in periods older than those traceable by oral traditions, and possibly correlate these patterns with archaeological findings.

Classification of the Indigenous Languages and Conclusions about Migration

The indigenous languages of western Africa belong to three of the four phyla of African languages established by J. H. Greenberg in 1963: Afro-Asiatic, Nilo-Saharan, and Niger-Congo. Three of the six families of Afro-Asiatic occur in western Africa: Semitic represented by Arabic, Berber in the northern part of West Africa and extending into North Africa, and Chadic, spoken in central and western Africa.

The Nilo-Saharan phylum is represented by Songhai along the great bend of the Niger River and Saharan in the northeastern part of the area, extending into the Sahara.

Nearest to the Atlantic Coast and occupying by far the greatest area of western Africa is Niger-Congo. All of its families, except Congo, are represented in western Africa, and many of these families are found only there, although Adamawa-Ubangi extends throughout central Africa and Bantu (included within Benue-Congo) spreads through much of central, eastern, and southern Africa. Consequently, the homeland of Niger-Congo is normally placed in western Africa, whereas those of Nilo-Saharan languages and Afro-Asiatic are sought farther to the east and northeast respectively.

From time to time, suggestions have been made that Nilo-Saharan and Niger-Congo are ultimately related. Recently, Roger Blench has proposed that Niger-Congo is simply a branch (or *family,* in the terminology used here) of Nilo-Saharan, most closely related to the Central Sudanic family of Nilo-Saharan, in the center of the African continent. If this view is correct, Niger-Congo would have originated farther east than is usually assumed, perhaps to the northwest of the present-day central Sudan. The Congo family, in Sudan, is assumed to have moved eastward. The other families of Niger-Congo presumably were gradually compressed into West Africa as a result of the desiccation of the Sahara. As western Africa became more crowded, Adamawa-Ubangi and Bantu expanded southward into central Africa and later, in the case of Bantu, into eastern and southern Africa.

The internal divisions of Niger-Congo have been repeatedly revised, particularly by Blench in 1995 (see table 1).

The Mande family, generally thought to be—after Congo—the most distantly related to the rest of Niger-Congo, was probably originally the most northerly. In historical times, Mande languages moved southward and westward to the coast, and this process probably started in prehistoric times. Atlantic (formerly West Atlantic) is also a northerly language but is centered nearer the coast. Its internal divisions are so deep that it has been suggested (but not yet generally accepted) that its three primary branches should be regarded as separate families. Such deep divisions imply a long period of differentiation within its present area.

Two relatively small families, Dogon and Ijoid, are thought to have split off next. Dogon, with little internal differentiation, remained inland, south of the bend in the Niger, while Ijoid, with somewhat more internal differentiation into Defaka and the Ijo group, moved down the Niger to its confluence with the Benue and then either directly along the Niger or via the Benue and the Cross River to the Niger Delta and associated waterways where it is found today.

The remaining families are now collectively known as Volta-Congo. Kru is found close to the coast in present-day Ivory Coast and Liberia. It has been suggested that Kru is most closely related to Gur and Adamawa-Ubangi. The recently reported language Pre is also tentatively classified here. Gur and Adamawa-Ubangi show evidence of having once formed a continuum stretching across the middle of western and central Africa. Similarly, it seems possible that Kwa and Benue-Congo, still forming a continuum south of Gur and Adamawa-Ubangi, moved southward down the Volta and Niger Rivers respectively and reached the Atlantic Coast. Kwa languages stretch along the coast from Ivory Coast to slightly beyond the Nigerian border. Most Nigerian languages that Greenberg classified as (Eastern) Kwa have been reclassified as West Benue-Congo. The Benue-Congo dispersal, centered around the Niger-Benue confluence, expanded in all directions over the greater part of present-day Nigeria, thereby splitting the Gur-Adamawa-Ubangi continuum and absorbing languages that

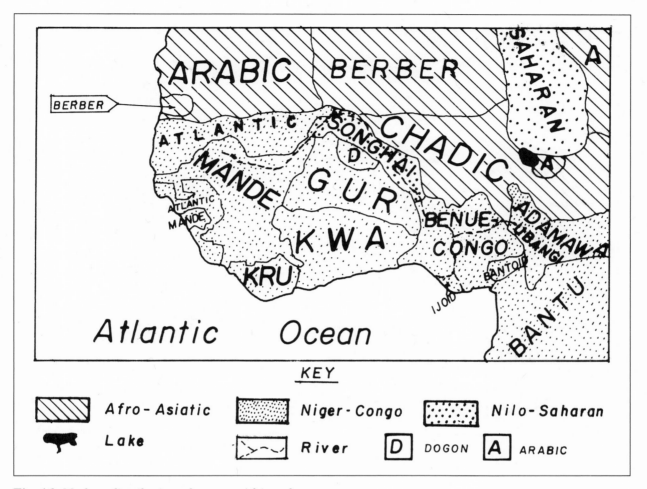

Fig. 16 *Modern distribution of western African languages*

once formed its center. West Benue-Congo comprises Qko (Ogori), Nupoid, Idomoid, Yoruboid, Edoid, Akokoid, and Igboid. Central Benue-Congo includes Ukaan and Akpes. East Benue-Congo comprises Kainji, Platoid (including Jukunoid), Cross River, and Bantoid. Bantoid moved eastward, probably along the Benue, and then expanded to the east and south into areas that, presumably, were relatively less populated, thus forming the Bantu expansion.

While Niger-Congo was expanding in western Africa, other families of Nilo-Saharan were becoming more separated from the main body of Nilo-Saharan languages. Songhai has little internal differentiation and spreads along the middle portion of the Niger. It appears that, at some period, its speakers may have taken refuge near the river from dry conditions farther east before expand-

ing along the river. Saharan occupies a large block of the Sahara and forms a northern extension of Nilo-Saharan languages. Presumably, it expanded north at a time when climatic conditions in the Sahara were favorable, whereas in recent times, there has been a southwestward movement, resulting in the Kanuri presence in present-day northeastern Nigeria.

The homeland of Afro-Asiatic must clearly be placed to the east of the homeland of Nilo-Saharan. Chadic is found in central and western Africa, far to the west of this northeastern homeland. This appears to be the result of an ancient movement westward from near the present-day Omotic or Cushitic area. East Chadic languages are spoken in Chad, Masa Branch languages in Chad and Cameroon, Biu-Mandara (or Central) languages in Chad, Cameroon, Nigeria, and

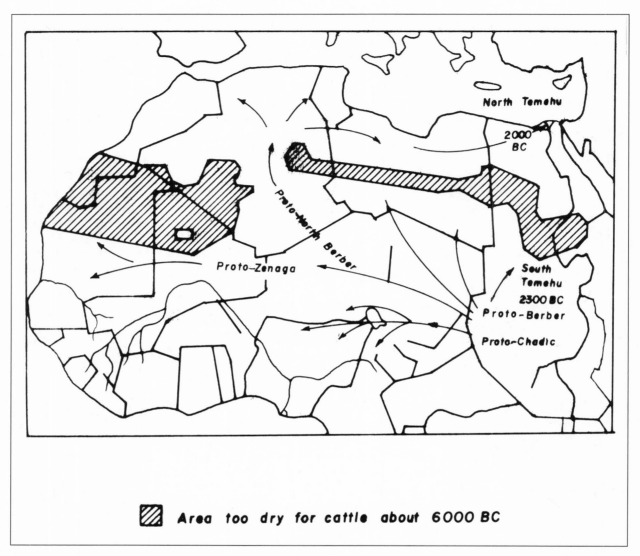

North Temehu

2000
BC

Proto–North Berber

Proto–Zenaga

South
Temehu
2300 BC
Proto–Berber

Proto–Chadic

Area too dry for cattle about 6000 BC

Fig. 17 *Proto-Berber movements and suggested proto-Chadic movements*

Niger, and West Chadic languages in Nigeria and Niger. The largest and best-known Chadic language, Hausa, belongs to West Chadic and has expanded far beyond its original range. The rather deep divisions between West Chadic languages suggest that they had expanded over much of present-day north-central Nigeria before the Benue-Congo languages spread from around the Niger-Benue confluence. Perhaps the incoming West Chadic speakers encountered and absorbed some of the languages of the Gur-Adamawa continuum already suggested to have extended across north-central Nigeria. As Benue-Congo speakers

later differentiated, speakers of its Platoid branch probably, in turn, absorbed some Chadic languages, thus accounting for the heavy substratum influence of Chadic on some Platoid languages. The more recent spread of Hausa has, finally, resulted in the absorption of both Chadic and Benue-Congo languages.

P. Behrens has suggested that Berber had its homeland in western Sudan and, from around 8,000 years ago, moved north toward the Nile, northwest into northern Africa, and also into western Africa to become the rather highly differentiated Zenaga of southern Mauritania. He also suggests that proto-Berber speakers, like proto–Afro-Asiatic speakers, were pastoralists. Modern Berber speakers are adapted to desert conditions and seem to have replaced Niger-Congo, probably Mande, speakers, in parts of their present range. Since Berber has relatively little internal differentiation compared with the deep divisions within Chadic, proto-Chadic speakers must have begun their own move at a much earlier period.

Arabic as a mother-tongue in western Africa is represented by Hassaniya in Mauritania, Senegal, Mali, and Niger, Algerian Arabic in Niger, and Shuwa in the northeastern tip of Nigeria, the northernmost strip of Cameroon, and the Bas Chari region of Chad. The speakers of these languages represent the western tip of the Baggara, the Arabic speakers who keep cattle instead of camels, a practice probably adopted from the Fulɓe (Fulani). Arabic is also a language of religious and scholarly discourse and writing in some of the northern areas of West Africa where Islam is many centuries old.

Some indigenous languages have spread and become important *lingua francas* (a mutually intelligible second language) as a result of the following factors, singly or more often in varying combinations: conquest, political expansion, long-distance trade, the spread of indigenous belief systems, Islam, and Christianity, and modern systems of government and education. Such languages include Songhai, Wolof, Fulfulde, Manding (including Bambara, Jula, and Maninka), Moore, Akan, Yoruba, Igbo, Efik-Ibibio, Jukun, Kanuri, and Hausa.

Languages Due to European Contact

The present-day official languages of countries in western African are, however, in no case indigenous. They are English, French, or Portuguese, depending, in most cases, upon the language of the former colonial power. Liberia, which was never a formal colony, uses English as a result of settlement in the 19th century by Americans of African descent. These languages of European origin represent the most recent linguistic layer in western Africa. Although they are highly prestigious today and have heavily influenced indigenous languages, their presence on the West African coast dates back only a few centuries, and only in the 19th century did they begin to penetrate inland.

While these European languages, together with Spanish, German, Dutch, and Danish, were confined to the coastal regions, they were adopted in a pidginized form as a means of communication in multilingual areas. A number of pidgin and creole languages used vocabularies of largely European origin in idioms and grammatical constructions reflecting those of western African languages. They include English-based ones such as the Krio of Sierra Leone, Gambian Krio, Liberian Creole English, Nigerian Pidgin, and Cameroonian Pidgin. Such French-based languages include West African Pidgin French. The Crioulo language of Guinea Bissau and Cape Verde are based on Portuguese. These languages are important means of interethnic communication and have also influenced indigenous languages. Historically, they testify to complex interactions between European and African languages.

It is therefore clear that the language situation in western Africa is highly complex. It is the norm rather than the exception for western Africans to speak more than one language, and a repertoire of five or six languages, each used in an appropriate setting, is not unusual in multilingual areas. Language shifts among communities are also common as one language expands at the expense of another, which contracts and finally dies.

Linguistic Evidence for Ancient Cultures

Apart from the study of language spread and the patterns of migration, it is possible to use linguistic evidence to trace ancient cultures. By comparing words of a common origin in related languages and understanding the sound changes that have affected their pronunciation, it is possible to reconstruct the form in which they probably occurred in the original protolanguage from which the modern languages have descended. Such reconstructed words often occur in clusters, which indicate the cultural background and way of life of the speakers of the protolanguage. For example, R. G. Armstrong in 1964 noted that a comparison of Idoma and Yoruba shows that, judging by their common protolanguage (in modern terms, West Benue-Congo), which he dates to about 6,000 years ago:

> The original group had pottery, at least in the form of large, open-mouthed pots that may hold beer. They had *rope, bags* and *boxes* and had some idea of time. They could count at least as far as *twenty.* They *hunted,* and they *worshipped* local gods or spirits, including *ancestral spirits.* They dug graves which were in some sense *taboo.* . . . They grew several crops, including *beans, cotton,* and *yams.* They had *markets* and *money* and *bought* (and sold) for *profit.*

It should be noted that this method can only give accurate results when the reconstructed vocabulary has been clearly distinguished from loanwords, which reflect later contacts.

A development of this method is to look at the evolution of culture in a particular area and try to distinguish the different epochs at which particular crops or particular domestic animals, for example, reached the area. An example of this is Blench's history of domestic animals in northern Nigeria. A study of the names for some useful plants in southern Nigeria finds linguistic reasons for distinguishing between indigenous species, those of Southeast Asian origin, and those of more recent origin.

Historical Inferences Based on the Study of Language Interaction

From a historical point of view, there is much to be learned from a close study of languages and their interactions. Words or other features in one group's languages—words that resemble those of another group—may be a clue to the influence of one group upon another. Such influences may be of three types.

Borrowing occurs when speakers of one language adopt words from a second language and use them in their original language, where they are known as *loanwords.* The reason for borrowing is often that the second language has words

for certain items or concepts new to the first language. The word is borrowed along with the thing. When borrowing is extensive, and especially when it is not restricted to items that are completely new to speakers of the original language, it is usually because the second language is socially dominant in some way. If loanwords can be accurately traced, they give information about political, cultural, and religious influences of one language upon another. Sometimes this merely corroborates what is already known from other sources. For example, the Hausa language spoken in Nigeria contains many loanwords from English, whereas that spoken in Niger contains many loanwords from French, reflecting the different colonial experiences of the two countries. At other times, it supplies information about more remote periods. Greenberg observed, for example, that words of Arabic origin in Hausa had in many cases been borrowed through Kanuri, thus suggesting the route by which Islam reached Hausaland. Similarly, S. Reichmuth in 1988 demonstrated that many Islamic terms in Yoruba have been borrowed from Songhai, again suggesting an important direction of influence. Sometimes the study of loanwords contradicts accepted ideas. In a discussion of the names for *maize* in Nigeria, Blench and his colleagues showed that whereas this crop of American origin was generally believed to have been introduced on the coast by the Portuguese and to have worked its way north, only one coastal language, Itsekiri, actually borrowed the Portuguese word. Other languages show clear evidence that maize was introduced from north to south.

Pidginization may be thought of as an incomplete type of language learning, which stops short of mastering the full patterns of the new language. It normally occurs in a multilingual area where speakers of many languages adopt a common language for practical interaction. The common language is most often, in recorded historical instances, a European one. Its basic vocabulary is acquired and slotted into the phonological, grammatical, and idiomatic pattern of the speakers' native languages, which, having been spoken in the same area for an extended period, already have similar patterns to a large extent. The result is a language that is easy to learn. An expanded pidgin, such as the Cameroonian Pidgin, has been developed by the users beyond the minimum needed for practical and commercial interaction. Finally, it becomes a creole language when it acquires a community of native speakers, such as the Krio of Sierra Leone. In this case, language shift has occurred from the indigenous languages to a pidginized one.

Bilingualism is the result of complete language learning, unlike the incomplete type resulting in pidginization. Bilingualism occurs in a community when most members of the community use their ancestral language and some other language, usually a *lingua franca* or otherwise dominant language, with roughly equal facility. Language shift occurs when bilingual speakers of the ancestral language use chiefly or only the *lingua franca* with their children, so that the children grow up with little or no knowledge of the ancestral language. In turn, these children pass on only the *lingua franca* to their children in the next generation, and the ancestral language is lost. Sometimes the process of language shift can be traced. An example is in Opobo Igbo, near the Nigerian coast. Modern Opobo people speak Igbo, but some of their ancestors spoke Ibani, a form of East Ijo. Unlike most Igbo speakers, who live inland and do not generally have words relating to sea fish and sea-fishing techniques, Opobo speakers have such words, which have been retained from the Ibani language of their ancestors. Thus local words for which there are no equivalents in the dominant *lingua franca* may be retained and give a clue to the original language of the area. Place names that cannot be analyzed in the modern language of the area may be of this type. Furthermore, features of pronun-

ciation, vocabulary, and idiomatic patterns may be carried over from the original ancestral language and result in a special dialect of the newly adopted language. These are called *substratum effects.*

BIBLIOGRAPHY

Armstrong, R. G. 1964. The use of linguistic and ethnographic data in the study of Idoma and Yoruba history. In *The historian in tropical Africa,* eds. J. Vansina, R. Mauny, and L. V. Thomas, 127–138. London: Oxford University Press.

Behrens, P. 1984-1985. Wanderungsbewegungen und Sprache der frühen saharanischen Viehzuchter. *Sprache und Geschichte in Afrika* 6: 135–216.

Bendor, S. J. 1989. *The Niger-Congo languages.* Lanham: University Press of America.

Bennett, P. R., and J. P. Sterk. 1977. South-central Niger-Congo: A reclassification. *Studies in African Linguistics* 8: 241–273.

Blench, R. M. 1995. A history of domestic animals in northeastern Nigeria. *Cahiers des Sciences Humaines* 31: 181–237.

Braukämper, U. 1993. Notes on the origin of Baggara Arab culture with special reference to the Shuwa. *Sprache und Geschichte in Afrika* 14: 13–46.

Greenberg, J. H. 1963. *The languages of Africa.* The Hague: Mouton.

Grimes, B. F. 1992. *Ethnologue: Languages of the world.* Austin: Summer Institute of Linguistics.

Reithmuth, S. 1988. Songhai-Lehnworter im Yoruba und ihr historischer kontext. *Sprache und Geschichte in Afrika* 9: 269–299.

Williamson, K. 1993. Linguistic evidence for the use of some tree and tuber food plants in southern Nigeria. In *The archaeology of Africa: Food, metals and towns,* eds. T. Shaw, P. Sinclair, B. Andah, and A. Okpoko, 139–153. London: Routledge.

Kay Williamson

Forager Lifeways

~~~~~~~~~~~~~~~~~~

AFRICAN FORAGERS

Because historical and contemporary hunter-foragers live primarily on marginal stretches of land, environmental constraints and risks impinge on their lifeways and shape their economy and many aspects of their society. In Africa, hunter-foragers are found in deserts and semideserts, such as the Namib and the Kalahari in southern Africa, inhabited by the San and the !Kung or G/wi Bushmen, as well as in subtropical savannas and tropical forests, where the Hadza, Sandawe, Ik (or Teuso), Okiek (or Dorobo), and the various Pygmy groups (Mbuti, Efe, Baka, and Aka) live. With the exception of the latter vegetation zone, drought seasons or cycles are a key environmental risk factor, as is the unpredictable nature of rainfall, which varies from year to year and falls unevenly over the land. As a result, from one year to the next, resources are found unevenly distributed over a band's territory. The land that the semidesert hunter-foragers inhabit is ill-suited for agro-pastoralists. Indeed, for the Bushmen and the Hadza, hunting-foraging is significantly more productive than horticulture. As a mode of production that organizes labor, property, spatial, and social relations, hunting-foraging is an adaptation to the scarcity and risk such environments hold for human inhabitants.

Hunting-foraging is an adaptation that is remarkably efficient, so much so that the lifestyle of subtropical and tropical hunter-foragers has been characterized as affluent. Despite the land's marginal prospects, the people derive quite a rich supply of food from the environment relatively easily. For instance, the Hadza work fewer than two hours a day on subsistence activities, with the women working slightly more than the men, and even fewer hours in the dry season than the wet season. The weekly foraging workload of the !Kung requires between two and three days. Among this group of hunter-foragers, the women work slightly less in order to avoid inducing envy or incurring an obligation to other band members. The Mbuti appear to work even less. Only about half a day of net hunting and gathering brings in enough food for the next day or two. Archery hunting, the people's second hunting technique, is less productive for the Mbuti, and this work is less cooperative and more extensive and intensive.

The subsistence task is divided between men, the hunters, and women, who as gatherers procure the nutritionally more significant food resource, which constitutes from 60 to 80 percent of people's diets. The reason plants are the key item on the menu of hunter-foragers is their relative abundance and their high nutritional quality. Some plant species, for instance the mongongo nut of the !Kung, are staple foods in the people's diet. For hunter-foragers in arid regions, some plant types—wild melons, tubers, and roots—hold significant moisture and provide an alternative source of water in the drought season. Even though—perhaps because—plants are eaten in larger quantities than meat, the latter food resource is the more cherished (by both the stomach and the mind, as animals are salient figures in hunter-forager ritual, myth, and art).

The tool kit with which people exploit the subsistence resources is small and simple, consisting, for the gatherer, of a simple digging stick and various carrying devices, as well as vessels made of natural objects, such as ostrich eggshells, tortoiseshells, or hollowed gourds. Hunting technology is somewhat less simple, consisting of a bow and poisoned arrows, along with a stabbing spear or a gnarled wooden club or throwing stick, and a skinning knife. Snares of various designs may be used (by women as well as by men) to catch small- to medium-sized animals. The hunting net of the Mbuti (and the Biaka, who use the same technique) represents the most elaborate hunting device of this type, involving, in its use, the participation of men and women, old and young. The Ik, who also use nets as one of their hunting methods, and the Mbuti may have obtained this technique from Bantu-speaking neighbors in fairly recent times. The women and girls drive animals into long sections of net stretched in semicircles several hundred meters in length. Another labor-intensive, high-yield group-hunting technique that was practiced in the 19th century by some Bushman groups of the western and eastern Kalahari was to drive herds of large game species down long rows of game fences into staked pits or swamps.

In addition to keeping population density at low levels through a variety of birth-control practices, the two key cultural adaptations that enable hunter-foragers, in such marginal environments and with such simple techniques and technologies, to live the lives of affluence they do are a highly mobile way of life and a loose and flexible social structure. Being mobile and having open groups and territories are adaptations to the unpredictability of resources, the main risk factor, as noted above, of many African hunter-foragers. Mobility enables people readily to move toward areas where food is available or abundant and away from those areas where it is scarce. Open groups with fluid memberships—the bands and camps—are social arrangements that allow members from neighboring groups access to more than one group and resource base. Such open-border policies among neighboring bands and territories are critical risk-management strategies.

The basic pattern of mobility of most hunter-foragers is a transhumant, seasonal movement back and forth between two land stretches and resource bases. Among arid-region hunter-foragers, the primary resource that triggers this relocation is water, which in the dry season is available (if at all) at only some strategic locales, for instance, at permanent water holes. Among such forest hunter-foragers as the Pygmies, the resource that leads people, once each year, to leave one area and move to another is honey, a cherished food item they collect for their own consumption and as a trade item.

The seasonal patterns of resource exploitation are frequently evident in hunter-forager social organization, which alternates between periods of high and low social density. In the first, the period of aggregation, people form relatively large communities, which may consist of dozens or even 100 or more individuals from several camps or bands. This is followed by the dispersal phase, when the multiband unit splits into small camps or subbands, who forage and hunt over a wide area in relative isolation from other camps (although with much visiting among the bands throughout the period). During this time, shelters and campsites are more temporary, makeshift, and haphazardously arranged, and the types of tools used and debris left behind are different in some ways from what it is found at the base camps occupied during the aggregation phase.

There is much regional variation to this pattern, some of it due to microecological diversity within a given area. For example, some Kalahari Bushmen disperse in the wet season and aggregate in the dry season. Others reverse the pattern. Likewise, some Mbuti groups (the archers) concentrate in the honey seasons. Others (the net hunters) disperse while exploiting this coveted resource. What differs as well from group to group is the relative duration of the phases, from two or three months to half a year. For the Mbuti net hunters, whose high-yield hunting technique and resource-rich forest environment allow them to spend most of the year in large groups, the dispersal phase lasts only two months.

This ecologically motivated alternation between spatial and social density and diffuseness significantly affects the social organization of hunter-foragers. This applies especially to the socially charged aggregation phase, which has both negative and positive effects on social interaction. During the period of concentration, staying together in large groupings creates interpersonal tension. The basic social unit, which is best adapted to the resources of the environment on a long-term basis, is the band or camp, made up of the "magic number" of about two dozen people. It is within this familistic social unit that hunter-foragers are probably most comfortable and at ease. Multiband aggregations create a social chemistry that eventually grates on the social sensitivities of people, the more so as, by disposition, hunter-foragers tend to be quite individualistic and individuated. Also, a good number of the people at the aggregation site are, of course, nonkin, from other bands, with whom bonds are less close, notwithstanding the existence of various social mechanisms that establish interband links. For arid-region hunter-foragers, there is an added ecological factor of tension that is especially acute whenever the concentration phase coincides with the period of resource scarcity: anxiety over dwindling resources, both water and food. For the Swung, food becomes less and less available as the drought season progresses. Meat becomes especially scarce, and plant food, in addition to becoming more scarce, also gets progressively less palatable, as only the dry, fibrous, least-appealing plant foods are available toward the latter half of the dry season. The Swung anxiously await the rain and scan the sky each day for signs of rain clouds.

A significant push factor for dispersal, social conflict also complements the ecological pull factor of abundant resources, which appear at the end of the dry season. Among students of African forest hunters whose nonarid environments yield fairly uniform supplies of resources throughout the course of a year, it is a topic of debate whether or not the social factor is a more compelling mechanism for dispersal than the ecological one.

It is primarily during the aggregation phase that hunter-foragers are able to conduct some of the vital social transactions through which the survival of their band society—its capacity for social reproduction—is ensured. There are three such transactions: marriage, exchange, and ritual.

Hunter-forager bands are often exogamous—that is, members marry outside their own bands. Unless a band meets and associates with another band during the dispersal phase, the only chance to court and broker a marriage is when bands get together. A pool of eligible partners is at hand, along with their kin, with whom the conditions of the marriage are negotiated.

Much the same applies to exchange, an important social and economic process in hunter-forager societies in Africa and elsewhere. The exchange referred to here is not the trade between hunter-foragers and their agro-pastoral neighbors, a vital element of the economy of many African foraging groups, but exchange among the people themselves throughout a region's network of individuals, families, and bands. The goods exchanged may be food as well as movable items of property. Among the Bushmen, the ideal items in these two categories are meat and ostrich-eggshell bead necklaces. Such exchange is based on generalized reciprocity (that leaves the question of return unspecified), and it is an extension, beyond the band, of the sharing ethos, which, along with egalitarianism, is one of the basic pillars of hunter-foragers' characters. Individuals are eager to set up exchange relationships with a wide range of partners, within and beyond their own family and band networks. The aggregation phase is one of the optimal social contexts for activating exchange or trade partnerships. Meat, one of the key items of exchange for men, may also be most readily available during parts of the aggregation phase, as it is among the Bushmen of the central Kalahari, where the early winter provides some of the ideal hunting conditions. The availability of large amounts of meat, combined with a gathering of people among whom to divide and share it, allows a man—the "Master of the Meat" whose arrow has brought down the animal—to discharge debts and obligations he may have toward others as well as to bind others to himself (thereby enhancing his "social capital").

Among hunter-foragers, ritual activity consists primarily of shamanic curing and crisis ritual and rites of initiation. While rituals and rites are carried out all year—being, by their nature, ad hoc and triggered by such contingencies as disease, death, hunting failures, or onset of menarche—such activities tend to increase and intensify during the aggregation phase. This applies, for instance, to the Bushman trance curing rite, which tends to be performed more frequently during the aggregation phase, in part to counteract the tension prevailing throughout this period. There is probably a causal link between the exceptionally rich ritual life of the Pygmies, exemplified, for example, by the male *molimo* and the female *bobanda* crisis rituals of the Mbuti and the Biaka respectively, and the exceptionally long periods of time these hunter-foragers spend in the aggregation mode. The former ceremony may draw together all adult men from a territory and last for a full month. The latter rite, like the Bushman trance ritual, is a dance performance, whose dramatic impact is commensurate with the number of participants. It seems as though the hunter-forager practitioners of such rituals are aware of the social anthropological insight about ritual: it is most effective when conducted by a large body of people, whose joint participation in the ritual performance generates a synergetic emergent power, as well as a sense of solidarity, far in excess of what could be achieved through solitary or small-group ritual activity. Such celebratory, dramatic rites of solidarity intensify the social and moral density of the aggregation phase in the hunter-forager's seasonal cycle. Related expressive or ludic (playful) forms of culture that increase in the aggregation phase are storytelling and, perhaps, rock painting (among some Bushman groups), and, among Hadza men, gambling.

What sustains this seasonal pattern of spatial and social oscillation are the openness of hunter-forager social groups and the loose, fluid, flexible organization and institutions of the society. African hunter-foragers are generally not territorial—that is, they do not impose exclusive ownership over their respective band territories. Instead, neighboring bands tend to allow reciprocal right of access to one another's territories. Bands are exogamous and form wide-ranging marriage links with other bands, and postmarital rules of residence tend to be neolocal—that is, individuals were allowed to set up residence with a wide range of different people. The relative ease of divorce is consistent with the gender equality of foragers, as well as with the individualism, the freedom of movement, and lack of commitment to others found among these hunter-foragers. Kin-

ship terminology tends to be classificatory and generational, and kin terms are applied to a wide range of persons. Some are universalistic, extending putative kin designations to either namesakes or friends, as among the !Kung and Mbuti, respectively. Among the former group, this means that virtually everyone within one's social network is classified as kin, at least at the ideological level. Because of its loose and diffuse application, kinship as an institution tends to be somewhat arbitrary. This is consistent with the absence of descent structures (such as lineages) or any other type of corporate kin group beyond the nuclear family. Because of the system's loose and somewhat arbitrary nature, fission and fusion may readily occur both within and between kin.

All this reveals a certain looseness and indeterminacy, which contribute to the organizational ability of hunter-forager societies. The looseness enhances the openness of groups and explains the striking fluidity in the residence patterns of individuals and the composition of camps, whose numbers and membership may change from one month or week to the next, as individuals or family groups come and go in the course of their nomadic lives. The ethos of reciprocity, manifested in sharing and far-ranging exchange, further opens up groups.

Egalitarianism is another key value of hunter-foragers. It is manifested in gender relations as well as in the general absence of craft specialization and status differentiation. Leadership, too, is in tune with the egalitarian ethos, sometimes being absent altogether—as among the net-hunting Mbuti or some Ju/íoansi !Kung, who deem each person to be "headman over himself." Decision making is groupwide and consensual, and conflict resolution operates through indirect sanctions, discreetly and face-savingly imposed. Wherever leaders are set up as headmen (or women), what little authority they do have is based not on their office but on their personal charisma. Ridicule or intentional disregard are two key leveling devices brought against an overly authoritarian or ambitious leader, as well as against any person who is ungenerous and who hoards rather than shares.

In sum, spatial mobility along with loose and open social organization are the key structural elements of the cultural ecology of hunter-foragers. They allow for the dispersal-aggregation dynamic that is so important to the ecological adaptation and social organization of hunter-foragers. Hunter-foragers are thus well adapted to the marginal environment they have come to inhabit in post-Holocene Africa.

Because of the remarkable flexibility and resilience of hunter-forager economic and social organization, foraging groups are found in a wide range of such environments, and their ecological adaptations and social formations have assumed many forms throughout the African continent. It is important to acknowledge that diversity, as it identifies the structural parameters of hunter-forager ecological and social organization. Moreover, it cautions against too ready an employment of the ethnographic analogy by prehistorians—that is, simple and uncritical ethnographic data on extant hunter-forager social organization or symbolic structures derived from one seemingly uniform foraging tribe and applied to extinct hunter-foragers.

Diversity is most striking as one compares hunter-foragers from widely divergent regions, such as different vegetation zones. As seen above, arid and forest hunting-foraging differ in a number of significant ways. Forest-region hunter-foragers enjoy a greater availability of food and water all year-round without marked seasonality. As a result, their degree of affluence is somewhat higher, and the foraging workload is lower. Moreover, the dispersal-aggregation dialectic among forest groups is less polarized and may be dictated less by ecological factors than by social considerations.

However, as seen above, diversity can be found also within one region, such as the Kalahari where differences in the amount of surface water—ranging from nil in the dry season to relatively abundant (for instance, where there are permanent wells in limestone ridges)—have led to the presence of four settlement patterns logically available as options to arid-region hunter-foragers. As shown by Alan Barnard, two of these options are permanent (more or less) dispersal (as followed by the !Xóö) and permanent aggregation (as practiced by the Nharo). The other possibilities are summer dispersal and winter aggregation (followed by the !Kung) and winter dispersal and summer aggregation (practiced by the G/wi).

Sociocultural diversity is even more striking if a single hunter-forager tribe is surveyed in the context of the entire region occupied by its various subgroups. Examples are the various Pygmy groups across central Africa and the many Bushman groups from Angola and Zimbabwe in the north to the Cape in the south. Among these groups, we find an extremely wide spectrum of hunter-forager ecological adaptations and social formations, from loose, widely scattered hunter-gatherer (or grubber) subbands to big-game hunters or Mesolithic-style hunter-forager-fishers. They span the spectrum from small-scale to complex hunter-foragers, with immediate-return and delayed-return economies. Some Bushman groups also own cattle and practice low-level agriculture.

This brings up another factor of diversity among African hunter-foragers: contact with agro-pastoral neighbors. In many cases, the association of hunter-foragers with food-producing neighbors has been long-standing, especially in East Africa, among the Okiek (Dorobo) of Kenya who have traded honey and performed labor services for the herding Maasai for the past 100 to 200 years. This contact, or encapsulation, by Black agro-pastoralists who treated the indigenous hunter-foragers with hostility and contempt has, in a number of instances, undermined the economic self-sufficiency and political independence, as well as the cultural and, at times, linguistic integrity of the hunter-forager enclave. Recent research suggests that the various Pygmy groups of Africa, too, have had extensive and long-term contact with agriculturists, in the form of dependency relationships with various effects on the economic and social organization of the hunter-forager Pygmies. The effects of regional Bantu-speaking agro-pastoral state societies on the Kalahari Bushmen, and the resultant revision of their alleged status as Africa's most isolated, pristine, and archaic hunter-forager people and of their economic and social organization, are hotly debated topics in contemporary Bushman studies.

It is evident, in the face of all this diversity, that the sketch presented here of hunter-forager lifeways is an abstraction. At each place on this continent where such a group is found, and at each time, it deviates, more or less, from this ideal type in response to a range of ecological and social contexts. The foraging band detailed here is a theme that has played itself out over the many millennia in the various regions of the continent. The many variations of this theme attest to the flexibility and adaptability of one of Africa's oldest subsistence modes and societal types.

BIBLIOGRAPHY

Barnard, A. 1992. *Hunters and herders of southern Africa.* Cambridge: Cambridge University Press.

Kelly, R. L. 1995. *The foraging spectrum.* Washington, D.C.: Smithsonian Institution Press.

Kent, S., ed. 1996. *Cultural diversity among hunter-gatherers: An African perspective.* Cambridge: Cambridge University Press.

Lee, R. B., and I. DeVore, eds. 1968. *Man the hunter.* Chicago: Aldine Publishing Company.

Petersen, J., and E. Waehle. 1988. The complexities of residential organization among the Efe Mbuti and the Bgombi Baka: A critical view of the notion of flux in hunter-gatherer societies. In *History, evolution and social change.* Vol. 1 *of Hunters and gatherers,* eds. T. Ingold, D. Riches, and J. Woodburn, 75–90. Oxford: Berg.

Service, E. R. 1973. *The hunters.* Englewood Cliffs: Prentice-Hall, Inc.

Silberbauer, G. 1981. *Hunter and habitat in the central Kalahari Desert.* Cambridge: Cambridge University Press.

Solway, J., and R. B. Lee. 1990. Foragers, genuine or spurious? Situating the Kalahari San in history. *Current Anthropology* 31: 109–146.

Turnbull, C. M. 1965. The Mbuti Pygmies of the Congo. In *Peoples of Africa,* ed. J. L. Gibbs, Jr., 279–318. New York: Holt, Rinehart and Winston, Inc.

———. 1968. The importance of flux in two hunting societies. In *Man the hunter,* eds. R. B. Lee and I. DeVore, 132–137. Chicago: Aldine Publishing Company.

Wilmsen, E. 1989. *Land filled with flies: A political economy of the Kalahari.* Chicago: University of Chicago Press.

Woodburn, J. 1968. An introduction to Hadza ecology. In *Man the hunter,* eds. R. B. Lee and I. DeVore, 49–55. Chicago: Aldine Publishing Company.

———. 1988. African hunter-gatherer social organization: Is it best understood as a product of encapsulation? In *History, evolution and social change.* Vol. 1 of *Hunters and gatherers,* eds. T. Ingold, D. Riches, and J. Woodburn, 31–64. Oxford: Berg.

Mathias G. Guenther

EASTERN AFRICAN FORAGERS

The term *foraging* is used in this article to refer to the organized hunting of wild animals and gathering of wild plants by the later stone tool-using populations of East Africa for purposes of subsistence. These subsistence activities are the oldest and the most enduring in the world. In East Africa, they persisted until quite recent times, when the transition to food production occurred. This change affected the groups living in the region differently: some of them adopted food production and others remained foragers. Indeed, by end of the 19th century, groups like the Waata and Okiek in Kenya and Sandawe and Hadza in Tanzania still lived primarily by foraging. Of these groups, only the Okiek and Hadza still maintain foraging lifeways, but they also consume food crops and meat and other products of domestic animals raised by themselves or obtained from their farming neighbors through trade.

The discussions that follow will focus on the use of natural resources for purposes of subsistence and making stone artifacts. Although the geographic scope of this essay includes Tanzania, Uganda, and Kenya, the discussions will primarily focus on Kenya and northern Tanzania, because the best-studied sites in the region are located in these areas. Further, because of the incomplete nature of the archaeological evidence to be discussed, we will employ ethnographic analogies wherever appropriate. In doing so, we are not suggesting that modern foragers in East Africa or elsewhere have remained unchanged for several thousand years. Rather, our intention is to shed light on the past activities that we know so little about and to identify areas that require further research for a better understanding of the past.

Technology

The technology of making stone tools used by the human populations in question was based on the production of blades and flakes and was widespread in East Africa by 20,000 years ago. The artifacts characteristic of this period were smaller and more formalized and standardized than those of the preceding Middle and Early Stone Age periods, hence their description as *microliths.*

The most common tool types included various forms of scrapers, blades, burins (bevel-pointed tools), and flakes. Some of these artifacts were backed or blunted on one side for two reasons: to ensure they did not cut the users and to provide suitable surfaces for the application of the mastic or binding that held them onto stick handles or hafts. The hafting appears to have facilitated the use of the microliths as composite tools. These included arrows, sickles, adzes, and spears.

It has been suggested that the ecological changes arising from the transition from the arid conditions of the end of the Pleistocene to the wet conditions of the Holocene influenced the reduction in the size of stone tools. The vegetation at the end of the Pleistocene consisted of much grassland mixed with small trees and shrubs. The annual mean temperatures were lower than present-day temperatures by about 5° to 8.8° C. Because of the scarcity of faunal and floral resources during this period, foragers adopted a high-mobility strategy and developed a lighter and more efficient tool kit that would enable them to meet their food requirements. The tool kit may have enabled them to hunt individually and to kill large animals, especially if they used poison-tipped arrows. The standardization and formalization of the artifacts could also suggest emerging specialization in artifact manufacture.

Research on microliths has resulted in the identification of several industries, the best known of which are the Eburran and Elmenteitan in Kenya and the Naseran in Tanzania. The first two industries are best represented in the central Rift Valley in Kenya, and the Naseran in northern Tanzania. The Elmenteitan industry, which was, until recently, thought to be confined to the western side of the Rift Valley, the adjacent Mau Escarpment, and the Loita Plains to the west of the Mau, also occurs in western and southwestern Kenya. That archaeological investigations have been concentrated on sites located in the central Rift Valley in Kenya, thus covering a very small part of East Africa, may explain why the geographic distribution of these industries is still unknown.

The raw materials that were used to make the microliths included locally available material and nonlocal fine-grained materials. Large numbers of the microliths from sites located at Lukenya Hill in central Kenya, for example, are made from obsidian that was imported from the Lake Naivasha area in the central Rift Valley, approximately 150 kilometers away. In contrast, virtually all the artifacts used by the groups that occupied the area during the preceding Middle Stone Age are made of local vein-quartz, chert (or microcrystalline quartz), and obsidian lapilli. Obsidian imports from the Lake Naivasha area have also been identified at sites located in southwestern and western Kenya. In Tanzania, only small quantities of obsidian were imported from the central Rift Valley for use at Nasera. The cost of importing chert from Olduvai Gorge and the Lake Natron area, distances of approximately 30 kilometers and 60 kilometers, respectively, was less than the cost of importing obsidian from the central Rift Valley, a distance of about 250 kilometers.

The extensive use of exotic raw materials appears to have been influenced by human mobility as well as by the mechanical properties of the raw materials and the cost of procuring them. The fine-grained obsidian and chert were certainly suitable for the microlithic technology. The groups that lived at the sites where obsidian was used may have procured the raw material directly from the sources or through exchange with other foraging groups that had direct access to the sources. Direct procurement would have been feasible if the region was sparsely populated and the groups concerned had wide foraging ranges. The feasibility of exchange, on the other hand, would have depended on the existence of elaborate social networks between the groups that had direct access to the sources and those from afar. Be that as it may, reciprocity between the groups concerned may have been crucial in the minimization of direct competition and possible conflict over scarce lithic (stone) raw materials. Further research on past human demographic profiles and on the relationship between humans and their physical and biological environments through time and space is necessary.

Subsistence

The remains of prehistoric wild animals and plants form the obvious direct evidence for the foraging activities of the groups in question. Such evidence is generally lacking at the sites dating to the Late Pleistocene. Where available, animal bones are unidentifiable because of poor preservation. The only identifiable skeletal remains dating to this period come from Lukenya Hill. These belong to Grevy's zebra *(Equus grevyi)* and oryx *(Oryx* spp.), animals that are not represented in the faunal samples of the succeeding Holocene period. Today these animals are found only in arid areas like northern Kenya. Remains of plant foods that may have been exploited during this period are yet to be recovered.

The situation improves considerably at the sites dating to the Holocene. Not only are faunal remains abundant, but a wide variety of species are represented as well. Holocene climatic and environmental conditions, beginning about 12,500 years ago, fostered the appearance of moist forests and grasslands, marshes, and an abundance of surface water. That plant remains are lacking at virtually all the sites dating to the Late Pleistocene and Early Holocene is a consequence of research strategies and can be remedied if deliberate efforts are made to recover them.

Two of the sites that have yielded significant quantities of plant remains, Gogo Falls and Ngenyn in Kenya, also contain skeletal remains of domestic animals. The Gogo Falls site has produced remains of *Eleusine coracana africana*, the wild progenitor of finger millet and fruits of *Abutilon, Ziziphus,* and *Cordia.* Ngenyn, on the other hand, has produced fruits of *Ziziphus,* a plant whose fruit is consumed by the agro-pastoral Tugen and Ilchamus communities in the region.

The paucity of direct evidence of plant use has made some researchers turn to indirect evidence like grinding stones, pestle rubbers, and stone bowls. While these artifacts are widespread in East Africa, it is not clear what their purpose was. They could, for example, have been used to process plant foods (a suggestion that is supported by ethnographic evidence), to pulverize ochre for personal adornment or ritual, or to serve as grave goods. Residue studies planned by the Archaeology Division of the National Museums of Kenya may shed some light on this subject.

Studies of the dietary habits of modern foragers are also likely to be helpful. Approximately 80 percent of the Hadza diet is plant foods, and 20 percent is honey and meat. Okiek diet, on the other hand, comprises 75 percent meat and 30 percent honey and plants. The differences between the two groups could be explained in ecological terms. The plains, where the Hadza live, support a wide variety of wild animals and edible plants and experience a more pronounced seasonality than the forest habitats of the Okiek. Consequently, the Hadza consume tubers, roots, and meat from small-sized animals during the wet season and fruits, nuts, berries, and meat from medium- and large-sized animals in the dry season. On the other hand, the forests have fewer edible wild fruits, nuts, berries, and tubers but support wild animals all year round. Given that men hunt and collect honey and that women and children gather plant foods, it is evident that, traditionally, Okiek men contribute more to their households' food requirements. The opposite is true of the Hadza.

Besides their traditional subsistence activities, the Okiek and Hadza exchange their honey and other products for cereals and domestic animals with their agricultural and pastoral neighbors. In central Kenya, such interactions have taken place between the Okiek and Gikuyu farmers for numerous generations. This kind of coexistence may have started with the inception of food production. The need for research on plant use by prehistoric groups, interactions between foragers and food producers, and the processes of change through space and time can hardly be overemphasized.

Unlike plant remains, faunal remains have been found in association with microliths at numerous Middle and Late Holocene sites in the region. Most of these sites are located in a narrow corridor in the Rift Valley, stretching from northern Kenya to northern Tanzania. Hunting and fishing were the main subsistence activities of the groups that occupied northern and western Kenya. On the other hand, hunting was the main subsistence activity for the groups that occupied southwestern Kenya, central Kenya, and northern Tanzania.

In general, the majority of the species hunted at numerous sites in the region were medium- and large-sized ungulates. These included buffalo *(Syncerus caffer),* common zebra *(Equus burchelli),* eland *(Taurotragus oryx),* giraffe *(Giraffa* sp.), hartebeest *(Alcelaphus buselaphus),* hippopotamus *(Hippopotamus amphibius),* rhinoceros *(Diceros/Ceratotherium* sp.), roan antelope *(Hippotragus equinus),* topi *(Damaliscus lunatus),* and wildebeest *(Connochaetes taurinus).* The exception here is the site of Enkapune ya Muto in the central Rift Valley, where hunters targeted small-sized animals like bush duiker *(Sylvicapra grimmia),* bohor reedbuck *(Redunca redunca),* mountain reedbuck *(Redunca fulvorufula),* and bushbuck *(Tragelaphus scriptus).* The differences may reflect the distribution of animal species in the past or the existence of diverse adaptations.

Relative-age profiles of the animals that were hunted in the region indicate that the hunters concentrated on mature animals rather than juvenile or very old ones. While this preference may have arisen from the fact that mature animals had greater food value than younger ones, it also demonstrates that the people who lived in the region were highly skilled and efficient hunters, an observation that is supported by the fact that they also hunted dangerous animals like buffalo and rhino. The poor representation at archaeological sites of younger and very old animals, both of which are much easier to kill than those at their prime, may be a reflection of the hunters' ethos or preferences. For example, younger animals may have been spared to ensure future supplies and old ones because of their tough meat or possibility of disease. Alternatively, the representation of these age categories in the live herds may have been poor because they are easy prey to carnivores like leopards and lions.

Quantification of the amount of plant foods in the diet of any of these groups cannot be made because direct evidence of plant use is very thin. However, it is likely that some groups may have consumed more plants than meat, as the Hadza do, or less plants and more meat, as the Okiek do. Quantification of the contribution of hunting and fishing to the diet of the groups that lived in western and northern Kenya is problematic largely because of problems associated with identification and quantification of fish remains. This notwithstanding, it is arguable that the contribution of these subsistence activities may have varied through time and space. The existence of such diverse adaptations may have been influenced by a combination of factors, ranging from ecological conditions, to effectiveness and efficiency of the tool kit, to sociocultural factors.

Human groups in the region made appropriate adaptive responses to the climatic and environmental changes like dry spells and the emergence of a bimodal rainfall pattern that occurred during the Middle to Late Holocene. Hunting groups, for example, may have adopted a highly mobile strategy to cope with the effects of the new rainfall pattern on the distribution of faunal and floral resources. This strategy meant following animals as they migrated in search of pasture and water. Success of this strategy depended on efficient gathering and processing of information and probably the existence of reliable and elaborate social networks, similar to those that facilitated the procurement of lithic raw materials. The groups at Lukenya Hill appear to have adopted this strategy.

Other groups may have adopted a strategy that involved less mobility. A restricted foraging range meant the groups subsisted on the resources characteristic of wet conditions in times of plenty. When these resources became scarce, they turned to resources that were locally available instead of migrating to another area. This strategy seems to have been adopted at Nasera, where human groups hunted resident animals during the dry season and migratory species during the wet season. The relatively short distance from the site to the sources of lithic raw material supports the view that the groups in question were relatively sedentary. Such groups may have consumed more plant foods than the highly mobile ones.

That the introduction of food production in East Africa affected different groups in different ways suggests the existence of groups that adopted different foraging strategies. The existence of diverse adaptations may explain why foraging remained attractive and, indeed, continued to contribute significantly to the subsistence of the groups in question. This condition and the apparent coexistence of foragers and food producers may have been made feasible by the manner in which foraging groups obtained their first domestic animals, for example. Their initial supply of domestic stock, which appears to have been fairly small, may have been through trade, probably through mechanisms similar to those by which they procured obsidian.

As mentioned above, food production was not adopted by all the groups that occupied East Africa in the Middle to Late Holocene. That foraging remained an attractive lifeway is best demonstrated by the failures of both colonial administrations and postcolonial governments in the region to compel modern foragers to become food producers. In Tanzania, for example, ideological, religious, and legal pressure on the Hadza to become farmers has been largely unsuccessful, while the Sandawe have become food producers apparently by choice. The initial gradual transition from foraging accelerated in response to population increase and intensified contacts with other farming communities. In Kenya, groups of the Okiek community have been compelled to adopt food production in a piecemeal fashion from the beginning of the 20th century by a combination of several factors: appropriation of their land in the highlands by British colonial authorities, displacement by indigenous farmers and pastoralists, assimilation by farming and pastoral communities, and more recently, politico-legal restrictions on forest life. Although the process of change in these communities has been, and continues to take place, within very different contexts, their attraction to foraging against all odds is a clear indication that the change to food production was more complex than we think.

BIBLIOGRAPHY

Clark, J. D., and S. A. Brandt, eds. 1984. *From hunters to farmers: The causes and consequences of food production in Africa.* Berkeley: University of California Press.

Ehret C., and M. Posnansky, eds. 1982. *The archaeological and linguistic reconstruction of African history.* Berkeley: University of California Press.

Hamilton, A. C. 1982. *Environmental history of East Africa: A study of the Quaternary.* London: Academic Press.

Harris, D. R., and G. C. Hillman. 1989. *Foraging and farming: The evolution of plant exploitation.* London: Unwin Hyman.

Krzyzaniak, L., and M. Kobusiewicz. 1984. *Origin and early development of food-producing cultures in north-eastern Africa.* Poznan: Polish Academy of Sciences.

Leacock, E., and R. Lee. 1982. *Politics and history in band societies.* Cambridge: Cambridge University Press.

Lee, R. B., and I. DeVore, eds. 1968. *Man the hunter.* Chicago: Aldine Publishing Company.

Marean, C. W. 1992. Hunter to herder: Large mammal remains from the hunter-gatherer occupation at Enkapune ya Muto rockshelter, Central Rift, Kenya. *African Archaeological Review* 10: 65–127.

Muriuki, G. 1974. *A history of the Kikuyu, 1500–1900.* Nairobi: Oxford University

Newman, J. L. 1970. *The ecological basis for subsistence change among the Sandawe of Tanzania.* Washington, D.C.: National Academy of Sciences.

Phillipson, D. W. 1977. *The later prehistory of eastern and southern Africa.* London: Heinemann.

Vincent, A. S. 1985. Plant foods in savanna environments: A preliminary report of tubers eaten by the Hadza of northern Tanzania. *World Archaeology* 17: 131–148.

I. Karega-Munene

SOUTHERN AFRICAN FORAGERS

The foraging people of southern Africa have profoundly influenced scholarly thought about hunter-forager lifeways. Beginning with the earliest descriptions of them by European traders in the mid-17th century, southern African groups have been more thoroughly described than any other foraging people, and the sheer volume of material about them has shaped the very definition what it means to be a forager. Landmark ethnographies by L. Marshall and R. B. Lee in the

1970s and G. B. Silberbauer and J. Tanaka in the 1980s of Kalahari Bushmen provide us with rich and compelling portrayals of enviably simple societies with names nearly unpronounceable to Western tongues—Ju/íoansi, G/wi, and !Xóö. Although foragers in southern Africa were once much more widespread than during the 19th and 20th centuries, it is the Bushmen of the Kalahari who are synonymous with southern African hunter-foragers today. They have provided the empirical basis (and, to some, the bias) for many past and current anthropological debates. "Original affluence," mobility and territoriality, trade and exchange, folklore, art, behavioral ecology, and human rights are all issues that have been informed with data from the study of southern African foragers. It is also these people, and in particular the Kua of the eastern Kalahari, who are used here to illustrate details of southern African forager lifeways.

Popular books, magazines, and films about southern African hunter-foragers offer an eager public romantically embellished portrayals of people who, we are told, allow us a captivating glimpse of our common Paleolithic heritage—a lifeway based on sharing and equality. The commercial success of such works reveals both a keen public interest in foraging societies and a romanticism about the past. Whatever the reality, it is undeniable that our convictions about hunter-forager lifeways would be quite different were it not for the numbers of long-range studies that have been conducted with southern African foraging people. Yet we must ask why there has been such a great anthropological interest in foragers in the first place.

Why Study Foragers?

For archaeologists, the importance of studying foragers is axiomatic: nearly all of the human past has been spent in foraging societies. Therefore, uniformitarian logic suggests that to better understand the foraging past we should investigate the foraging present. Yet there is also a nagging unwillingness to believe in such simplistic continuity. It is perhaps not surprising that the validity of this notion has been the subject of a fierce debate in recent years, with the hunter-foragers

of southern Africa at its center. It would be inaccurate to say that the authors, such as R. B. Lee and I. DeVore, of seminal anthropological works on hunter-foragers of southern Africa, believed unyieldingly that their subjects walked unchanged, like living fossils, out of the Pleistocene. Yet, these studies were conducted in the spirit that anthropologists had something important to learn about foraging lifeways and about sociocultural evolution, in general, by investigating them. Recent authors, such as R. J. Gordon, E. N. Wilmsen, and James K. Denbow, have challenged this perspective, but the spirit is still evident in current southern African ethnoarchaeological studies.

R. L. Kelly in 1995 reminded us that "hunter-gatherer is a category we impose on human diversity—it is not itself a causal variable." What Kelly means is that classifying people solely on the basis of their economy is only one of many ways to order cultural variability. Moreover, economic classifications may crosscut other useful categories (for example, language and ethnicity). Because of this, recent attention has focused on documenting flexibility and explaining variability among foraging groups. The fact that interest in foragers has not diminished is surely due in part, as recently argued by R. L. Bettinger, to the efficacy of using foraging people as the acid test of general theory in anthropology. If so, then surely the data provided by the study of southern African groups will be pivotal in evaluating general theory. Thus, what follows is a characterization of a group of people diverse in many aspects of their biology, language, and relations with other groups. They are linked, nonetheless, by at least a part-time pursuit of a foraging economy, as well as by a shared history.

The Ethnographic Present

Our modern characterizations of Bushmen do not capture the social and language diversity that existed historically and prehistorically in southern Africa. By the time of the first synthetic comparative study of southern Africa's hunter-foragers by I. Schapera in 1930, the Bushmen had been eliminated from much of their former territory, and many of their languages had disappeared.

Most southern African foraging people share one or more biological, linguistic, or economic attributes that have been used, in various combinations, to place them into categories with names like *Bushmen, San,* or *Basarwa.* Even more inclusive designations exist. For example, *Khoisan* is a term originally coined as a biological category but is now commonly used to include pastoralists whose languages and biology are closely related to some Bushman groups. Importantly, none of these terms originates in the vocabularies of the people they describe. Rather, they originate in the languages of outsiders. Nonetheless, in acknowledging the political utility of such a name, a number of Namibians, to whom such names would apply, decided at a conference held recently in Windhoek that the most agreeable name would, in fact, be *Bushmen,* although some refer to themselves as *the dispossessed.* Deciding who is a Bushman and who is not has implications beyond academic debate for everything from dispensing aid to granting hunting licenses. Deciding how Bushmen are to be distinguished from other southern African people is challenging. Bringing order to the variability among Bushmen is even more complex.

Ethnicity and Language

Ethnic identity among southern African foragers is complex and flexible. The naming situation has become even muddier because of new names introduced by anthropologists or well-meaning government officials. Compounding the confusion (and likely providing no end of amusement for the informants) is that many people playfully offer anthropologists, government officials, and linguists a host of names for themselves. These terms reflect varying levels of inclusiveness and probably often crosscut one another.

"First languages" or "mother tongues" have been nominated by several authors as the most sensitive identifier of ethnicity and have been used to erect a number of classification schemes. For example, the Kua speak a language belonging to the Tshu-Khwe group of the Khoe family of southern African languages. Wilhelm Bleek's "Central Group" of Bushman languages is a roughly equivalent name for the Khoe language family. The languages of the G/wi, G//ana, and Naron, with whom the Kua share numerous economic and social characteristics, are also part of this family. Rather than restate these complex classification systems here, the reader is referred to the bibliography for details, and in particular to A. Barnard for a regional overview.

Southern African Environments

Understanding the lifeways of modern foragers demands a consideration of the environments to which they adapt. Much of the area from which modern Bushman groups are known is contained within the enormous and ancient Kalahari Desert of southern Africa. Despite the hardships it imposes on its inhabitants and its visitors, the Kalahari has also inspired affectionate descriptions. It has been pointed out many times that the Kalahari would be better characterized as a thirstland or *edaphic desert*, rather than a *true* desert, a place where, as H. J. Cooke noted, "the often almost lush-seeming vegetation contrasts strangely with the total absence of surface water for most of the time."

A variety of plants and animals have great economic importance to the human population. In the Kalahari, where foragers have been best studied, significant fluid-bearing species are found, particularly *Citrullus lanatus* (the tsamma melon) and *Acanthosicyos naudinianus* (the gemsbok cucumber or horned melon). Without these two ubiquitous taxa, human settlement of much of the Kalahari would be impossible.

The mammalian fauna, especially large game, occupy a special place in Bushman perceptions of their environment and figure prominently in daily conversations. Animals commonly hunted include eland, greater kudu, gemsbok, wildebeest, hartebeest, duiker, bat-eared fox, porcupine, and steenbok. At least a dozen more are (or were, in the case of giraffe and some other taxa) taken less frequently. Discussions of hunting are virtually incessant and contribute to the detailed knowledge of animal habits and life histories. Several of the commonly hunted species are gregarious bovids that migrate vast distances in search of water and fresh grass. Some species, notably gemsbok and eland, are able to meet all of their moisture requirements from the consumption of the same fruits and tubers that permit human foragers to live in the region.

Kinship and Social Organization

R. K. Hitchcock has provided a compact summary of Kua kinship and social organization—a summary that describes well many of region's hunter-forager groups. Social units are small and are made up of aggregates of families. These groups are made up of cores of siblings. Groups are flexible in size and composition. Division of labor is along the lines of age and sex. People have reciprocal access to resources in different areas, and the sharing of food and goods is crucial to their adaptive success. The Kua are egalitarian, with decision making being done on the basis of general consensus. There are ties between groups living long distances from one another, some of which are through marriage while others are through trading and exchange links.

The sibling core is usually a group of brothers, their parents, wives, children, and a few more-distant relatives. Kua kinship is reckoned bilaterally. Individual households are typically based upon nuclear families, and residence is usually patrilocal (located in the vicinity of the male's family). During the dispersal phase of the annual cycle, groups that live together at larger camps fragment into units of two or three households. These units themselves may disperse and reunite a few weeks later. Flexibility, once again, is the rule.

Subsistence and Settlement Patterns

Human foragers respond to their environments with numerous strategies and vary their group size, composition, mobility, and subsistence strategies to suit conditions. In much of southern Africa, human adaptations are determined by the distribution of resources, especially water-bearing plants and game. The key to understanding the foraging lifeway in southern Africa is appreciating the secrets to adaptive success in the often hostile habitats of southern Africa: residential mobility and social flexibility. Thus, the settlement patterns evident in the Kalahari today reflect the requirements of subsistence organization, social interaction, and cultural circumscription. For at least the last 2,000 years, an economic spectrum has been evident among the Bushmen of southern Africa. In the "ethnographic present," subsistence adaptations have ranged from sedentary cattle-post living to mobile foraging. Recently, the same individuals may shift from full- or part-time foraging to complete dependence on the cattle-post economy at different times of the year.

Many groups have undergone demonstrable shifts in their seasonal settlement patterns in recent years. For example, from 1985 to 1986, Hitchcock observed some Kua families practicing a different pattern of residential mobility than what was observed from 1975 to 1979. The 1970's pattern led Hitchcock to contrast the Kua residence pattern with the dry-season residence pattern of the !Kung. In the past, the Kua practiced a pattern of dry-season dispersal and wet-season aggregation similar to the pattern noted for the G/wi. The change coincided with the drilling of many new boreholes in the Kua territory of the Kalahari. Until the drilling of boreholes, the absence of surface water during the dry season precluded large aggregations of people. Now their pattern of seasonal settlement is similar to that documented for the Nharo and the !Kung, who, because of permanent water sources, can congregate around these sources during the dry season. To the Kua, the boreholes present an irresistible and previously unavailable alternative for dry-season residence. In general, during the hot portion of the dry season, Bushmen live within "striking distance" of boreholes. Knowing that their fluid requirements will be met with melons, they move to locations farther away from cattle posts to hunt for the latter part of the rainy season and the cool portion of the dry season.

Bushman Hunting and Butchery

Traditional Bushman subsistence technology is highly portable and, in Bleek's terminology, possesses the design characteristics of a "maintainable system." The typical Bushman gathering kit consists of a digging stick, a carrying bag or rope, and perhaps a small metal ax. The basic hunting kit has been illustrated or described by many authors. Because bow hunting is an exclusively male activity, bags and bows are carried only by men. All people carry digging sticks and karosses (carrying bags) made of animal hides.

During the hot dry season, the frequency of kills is relatively high, but the size of the animals obtained is generally small. This is partly explained by the fact that several migratory species (for example, wildebeest and hartebeest) are absent from this part of the Kalahari during this season. During the rainy and cool dry season, the focus is on bow hunting. Animals taken are typically larger bovids such as the eland *(Taurotragus oryx)* and the southern African gemsbok *(Oryx gazella)*. Bushmen employ a variety of hunting methods and technologies, and the methods vary seasonally. These include snaring small prey, walking animals to death (a physically demanding method of pursuit hunting employed only in the hot dry season), the use of dogs and springhare poles to impale spring hares and porcupines in their burrows, and bow and poisoned-arrow hunting. Predictably, hunting is better at the more remote camps. The primary source of Kua arrow poison, the *Diamphidia* sp. larva, becomes available during the first part of the rainy season and can be collected for several months thereafter.

Transport decisions are based on a number of variables. These include distance to the base camp, time of day, number of potential carriers, and size of the carcass obtained. Based on an analysis of each situation, Bushmen select a transport strategy, ranging from carrying the entire intact carcass to moving the camp to the site of the kill. Gun hunting in the Kalahari is rare among Bushmen (probably for economic reasons). More common are biltong (jerky) hunts or expedition hunts. These are logistical tactics used by sedentary cattle-post groups that hunt the increasingly rare eland, giraffe, and hartebeest from horseback with spears.

Camp Variability

Seasonal differences in mobility strategies result in different types of camps. The Kua living in the Kalahari occupy large camps during the hot dry season, but they disperse into smaller camps in the rainy season and cool dry season, when they are sustained by water-bearing melons and tubers. Kua residential mobility produces four distinct types of occupations: (1) base camps, *sensu strictu*, of seasonal variations, (2) transient camps, (3) special-purpose camps, and (4) special-purpose locations, places where the activities performed are similar to those performed at special-purpose camps but do not involve an overnight stay.

DRY SEASON BASE CAMPS. Large base camps occupied during the dry season tend to be relatively large settlement aggregates located near cattle posts operated by Tswana and Herero herders for nonresident owners. They have up to about 75 people and are occupied for a single reason—access to water. These camps are within easy walking distance, usually a kilometer or so, from a drilled borehole with a diesel-driven pump. A particularly unyielding problem posed by cattle-post residence is the local deficiency of economically important fauna and flora. The dilemma is that although the density of wild-food resources increases as a function of distance from the cattle posts, the availability of water decreases. The Kua's desire for access to a reliable water source prompted them to practice the common Kalahari risk-management strategy of minimizing distance to water. Interviews with adult Kua regarding past residence patterns during this season revealed that during their childhood, many moved into the bush in nuclear family units, in much the same way that the G/wi did, as described by Silberbauer, in order to reduce local pressure on water-bearing plants.

CAMPS DURING THE RAINY SEASON AND THE COOL DRY SEASON. With the coming of the rains in January, and acting on reconnaissance information about the abundance of melons and game at specific locations, most Kua move from dry-season cattle-post camps to smaller, rainy-season base camps located at distances of 5 to 40 kilometers from the cattle posts. On the eve of one such move, a Kua informant said it was now time to "sleep near the melons." During this season, the populations of the camps average about ten to 20 individuals, within two to four households. Households are primarily based around nuclear families as they are in the dry-season camps.

Daily foraging trips are made by all camp members to exploit the range of fresh resources. Even the youngest individuals ride along on their mothers' backs, and the oldest individuals forage in areas near camp. As is the case at dry-season camps, some food is consumed in the bush while foraging, but large quantities are returned to camp for consumption by the group. Rainy-season and cool dry-season base camps also form the hub of a network of special-purpose camps. Subgroups spend up to several days at special-purpose camps in order to hunt and butcher game or to collect locally abundant plant foods. Special-purpose camps and locations (no overnight stay, no shelter) most commonly center around the butchery of a large bovid carcass. Activities performed at these camps tend to be restricted in number, and the duration of the occupation generally is a function of the amount of time required to complete the tasks at hand.

The Future of Foraging

Recent changes in the Kalahari habitat have profound implications for the future of Bushmen. Some of these changes are probably driven by cyclical fluctuations in climate, but their occurrence in circumstances changed by other factors gives them increased potency in their effect on the people of the area. From the Bushman perspective, most of these changes are for the worse.

Among the marked environmental changes are the construction of veterinary fencing, increased grazing pressure, and mining. Veterinary fences erected in the Kalahari since the 1950s, combined with an ever-increasing number of cattle, are taking a heavy toll on the ungulate fauna, especially the migratory antelope that depend on much of the same browsing areas and grass. The grass that grows so luxuriantly in remote parts of the Kalahari has drawn a burgeoning population of cattle from areas lacking adequate grazing resources. The ecology of pastoralism in the east-central Kalahari is complex and dynamic, but generally speaking, as the cattle population increases, the yields of economically vital plant and animal species for human foragers decrease. It should be noted that many of the wild species are also important subsistence items for seden-tary cattle-post residents. Mining activities have had a direct impact on only very small areas of the landscape, but the infrastructural changes to support the mines have brought about far-reaching social effects. The world of the Bushmen is rapidly becoming a smaller place.

One Tyua individual from northeastern Botswana described to Hitchcock the last 30 years of change in this way:

> There is too little land for us to continue gathering. Our guns were taken away so we can no longer hunt. We used to take meat, salt, and skins to the Kalanga but the veterinary people will not let us cross the cordon fence with animal parts. Our future lies in having land and cattle, but we cannot get these things. We are being ignored by government. We are being left behind. We are the forgotten people.

BIBLIOGRAPHY

Barnard, A. 1992. *Hunters and herders of southern Africa: A comparative ethnography of the Khoisan peoples.* Cambridge: Cambridge University Press.

Bettinger, R. L. 1991. *Hunter-gatherers: Archaeological and evolutionary theory.* New York: Plenum.

Bicchieri, M. G. 1972. *Hunters and gatherers today.* New York: Holt, Rinehart, and Winston.

Ellen, P. C. B., and R. F. Ellen. 1979. *Social and ecological systems.* London: Academic Press.

Gordon, R. J. 1992. *The Bushman myth: The making of a Namibian underclass.* Boulder: Westview Press.

Kelly, R. L. 1995. *The foraging spectrum: Diversity in hunter-gatherer lifeways.* Washington, D.C.: Smithsonian Institution Press.

Kroll, E. M., and T. D. Price. 1991. *The interpretation of archaeological spatial patterning.* New York: Plenum.

Lee, R. B., and I. DeVore, eds. 1968. *Man the hunter.* Chicago: Aldine Publishing Company.

——. 1976. *Kalahari hunter-gatherers: Studies of the !Kung San and their neighbors.* Cambridge: Harvard University Press.

Marshall, L. 1976. *The !Kung of Nyae Nyae.* Cambridge: Harvard University Press.

Schapera, I. 1930. *The Khoisan peoples of South Africa: Bushmen and Hottentots.* London: George Routledge and Sons Ltd.

Silberbauer, G. B. 1981. *Hunter and habitat in the central Kalahari Desert.* Cambridge: Cambridge University Press.

Tobias, P. V. 1978. *The Bushmen: San hunters and herders of southern Africa.* Cape Town: Human and Rousseau.

Wilmsen, E. N. 1989. *Land filled with flies: A political economy of the Kalahari.* Chicago: University of Chicago Press.

Laurence Bartram, Jr.

FORAGER HUNTING TOOLS AND METHODS

The traditional hunting equipment of modern foragers in southern Africa is well designed to meet the needs of the task. Their tools are effective and sophisticated, yet light and easily transported. Furthermore hunting equipment has a long use-life and is readily made with materials at hand. The primary hunting weapon is the bow and poisoned arrow, but foragers also use spears, clubs, digging sticks, knives, nets, and snares. Most modern hunters-foragers in southern Africa live in or on the edge of the Kalahari Desert. The people living there consist of a number of small, separate independent bands, but collectively they are called Bushmen, San, or Basarwa. Two San groups that have been well studied by anthropologists are the !Kung in the northern Kalahari and the G/wi in the central Kalahari Desert of Botswana.

In the Kalahari Desert, the most common hunting technique of the San using traditional weapons is encounter hunting and stalking with bow and poisoned arrows. The prey taken with bows and arrows ranges from small antelope, such as steenbok, to large animals including giraffes. Kalahari San hunters also snare, take animals from burrows, ambush hunt at night from blinds, chase game with dogs, and scavenge. A hunter on any given day must be prepared to pursue a wide range of animals. Rock art in South Africa also suggests that the San drove antelope into large nets and that hunters used disguises to kill ostriches and other animals. The /Xam, a 19th-century San group in the northern Cape Province of South Africa, had sorcerers who reputedly could lure antelope to hunters waiting in ambush. /Xam Bushmen also tell stories of driving springbok into ambushes. The weapons used for these hunting methods would be the same used in encounter hunting. Today, some Kalahari San hunt on horseback with spears or guns, and 19th-century mountain Bushmen in Lesotho and KwaZulu-Natal did the same. In areas of the Kalahari where fishing is possible, the San use spears or woven-reed traps. Rock art from the Cape Province coast, the Free State, and the Transkei depicts San fishing with spears. On the coast, the San also caught fish with circular rock weirs.

The Kalahari San are traditionally organized in small family groups that often move their residential camps to new localities where food is more plentiful. Even though the Kalahari is a desert, it offers a wide variety of plants and animals for subsistence. Among San groups, the women primarily, but men and children also, collect plant foods and small, slow-moving animals. However, only men hunt, and most hunts are daily sorties by a single hunter or a small group of hunters. Plant foods compose the majority of the food eaten by the San who rely on hunting and gathering, but they value meat highly even though hunters are often not successful.

Availability of food resources in the Kalahari Desert varies greatly between regions and through the seasons. The location of game, primarily antelope, is very difficult to predict. These variations have a significant impact on hunting strategies, methods, and tools. For example, the !Kung depend heavily on nuts from mongongo trees (*Ricinodendron rautanenii*), but these trees are completely absent from the central Kalahari inhabited by the G/wi. The area inhabited by the G/wi lacks any surface water for many months in the year, and they must obtain most of their fluids from plants such as tsamma melons (*Citrullus lanatus*). Among the G/wi, when returns from large- and medium-sized game are low, hunters acquire more meat from snaring small antelope such as steenbok and diukers. The !Kung normally rely on snaring during the winter months. However, when mongongo nut harvests fail, hunters shift their strategies from hunting unpredictable antelope to snaring small game. Snaring requires less energy and results in more consistent returns. Overall, San hunters are reasonably successful, but the strategies they apply toward hunting and tool production can be classified as "time minimization" rather than "resource maximization."

The night before a hunt, men, women, and children in the camp exchange information on the location of game. Men also check and repair their equipment. Hunters straighten arrows, apply fresh poison to arrows, oil bows, check haftings on springbok hooks and spears, sharpen digging sticks, and pack hunting kits for an early departure the next morning. The hunters leave camp soon after sunrise in predetermined directions. Covering up to 25 or 30 kilometers in a day, the men quietly scan the landscape looking for tracks or other signs of game. When the men discover prey, they must stalk within 20 to 30 meters of an animal to have a good chance of striking it with an arrow. Hunters stalk prey rapidly and use the physical landscape to conceal their movements. Usually more than one man attempts to shoot at an animal, thereby increasing the chance for a hit. When an arrow strikes an animal, the poison does not always kill quickly. The hunters attempt to remain undetected to keep the animal from running, so that they will perhaps have another chance to launch an arrow.

After shooting, the hunters retrieve their arrows. If they find a complete arrow, the men know the animal did not get enough poison. If they find only a mainshaft and they saw a solid hit, then the hunters know the animal will probably succumb to the poison and tracking will be worth the effort. If the animal runs, the hunters, hoping it will stop and waiting for the poison to work, track the wounded animal at a distance. When the animal is finally down, the hunters kill it with spears, clubs, or knives. The hunters may butcher the carcass meat, organs, marrow, and fluid depending on the animal's condition, the season, the availability of surface water, and the distance from the residential camp. If the animal is large, often one hunter returns to camp for help, and the others stay to butcher the carcass and protect the meat. If the animal is small, the men butcher the animal on the spot and, depending on its size, carry the whole carcass or split the load between two or more men. Hunters use sticks and spear shafts as carrying yokes. Each hunter can iden-

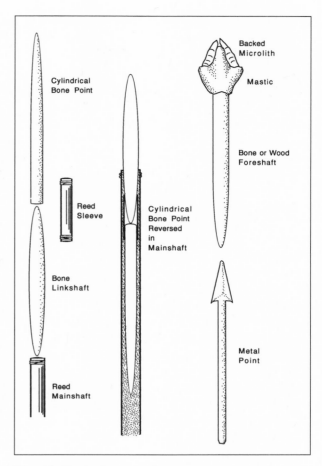

Fig. 18 *Typical projectile points*

tify his own arrows by minor morphological differences, and the hunter whose arrow first struck the animal is responsible for the meat distribution back in camp.

Between March and June, the G/wi mount two to four large biltong (jerky) hunts in the remote sections of their group's territory. Most hunters in a band join the party for one or two weeks at a time. The men approach the hunt with the same methods and strategies used in the daily sorties, but they return their catch to temporary camps where they cut meat into strips and dry it into biltong. Hunters then carry the dried meat back to the main residential camp for consumption by the entire camp over the next few weeks. Only the Nata River groups in the eastern Kalahari, where resource diversity is greater and human population densities are higher, acquire meat and other resources in bulk for long-term storage.

Nineteenth-century /Xam Bushmen in South Africa drove springbok into ambushes. The hunters lined a drive with stations formed by ostrich feathers tied to sticks. An individual stood at one end of the drive line to force the herd to turn toward a group of concealed hunters. Then the men chased springbok down the line toward the hunters. This type of hunting technique is unknown in the Kalahari Desert, but Kalahari San ambush animals from blinds at night.

The equipment carried by San hunters varies slightly by group, but each hunter carries all the necessary equipment to kill and butcher game, rearm himself, and repair his hunting kit. For example, in the central Kalahari Desert, G/wi hunters carry a leather satchel with a shoulder strap. This satchel, which weighs only a few kilograms, holds a bark quiver, eight or ten poisoned arrows, a bow, a club, a digging stick, a spear, and a smaller quiver with a repair kit. The latter contains spare arrow parts such as strands of sinew for bow strings or bindings, a small number of poison cocoons, and binding gum. All hunters wear knives hung in wooden sheaths on belts. The hunting kit is simple, effective, and easily carried. It offers a high degree of reliability and can be easily maintained and repaired. San hunters use bows and poisoned arrows for slowing or stopping game and dispatch slow or injured animals with spears and clubs.

Throughout southern Africa, San men make bows from a single stave of raisin bush *(Grewia flava)*. A hunter carves the wood so that it is tapered at both ends and then binds the ends and the middle with sinew. The sinew binding on the ends holds the bowstring in place, and occasionally a short piece of wood or sinew tab is bound to one end to act as a collar. The string consists of two twisted plies of eland, gemsbok, or springbok sinew. A man often ties the bow string at the base of the bow and then loops it through the sinew or wooden collar to keep it from slipping. The sinew binding in the middle strengthens the wood and helps keep the bow from cracking. San bows are small and light and do not have a great amount of killing power. Men make quivers from *Acacia* sp. roots or boughs of the *Aloe dichotoma* tree. They use a skin cover to seal the bottom of the quiver, sinew to reinforce the sides, and

a leather strap to carry the quiver. Quivers hold ten to 15 finished arrows.

Today, San hunters make arrows with small metal points. Arrows are fairly short (approximately 55 to 60 centimeters) and are usually not fletched (feathered). These arrows have six elements: a *Phragmites* reed mainshaft notched on one end and hollow on the other, a bipointed bone or hardwood linkshaft, a reed sleeve, sinew binding on the mainshaft and the sleeve, a shouldered metal point, and poison. The mainshaft is designed to detach from the point if an animal is hit. This makes it more difficult for the animal to dislodge the point and increases the amount of poison delivered into its bloodstream. Men usually make metal points from fencing wire that they heat and then beat with a stone hammer and anvil into a small, shouldered point with a long, thin tang or stem. The hunters then sharpen the edges of the metal arrow point with a whetstone. Men sharpen spear points and knife blades in a similar fashion. Comparative study demonstrates that the shapes of metal arrow points differ between major groups such as the !Kung and G/wi.

The San also use flat, shouldered bone points or long, narrow, cylindrical bone points with flat bases attached to bone or wood linkshafts. When arrows are not in use, hunters reverse the cylindrical bone points and stick the points into the hollow mainshafts. This protects people from the poison. Arrow makers occasionally lash a quill to the point stem to act as a barb. Hunters then coat the point and quill barb with poison.

Before metal was available, Bushmen made some arrow points with stone microliths. These have two small backed microliths inset into a flat wad of mastic attached to the end of a foreshaft. Mastic is made from pelargonium (geranium) resin or other vegetable gums. Bushmen stuck the blunted backs of the triangular microliths into the mastic so that the points of both microliths protruded slightly to form a sharp point with slicing edges on both sides. Prehistoric microliths have curved backing (called *segments* or *crescents)* or straight backing (called *straight-backed microliths)*. In the Late Holocene, backing became more elaborate, and all faces on a microlith might be retouched with pressure flaking (called *pressure-flaked backed points)*.

For a very short period, San hunters made small, barbed, bifacially flaked stone projectile points. These points may have been imitations of Bantu metal arrowheads. No evidence indicates that the different forms had different functions. Apparently all were used as projectile points or elements of such points. Hunters also manufactured blunt or pointed wooden arrowheads without linkshafts that they used for killing birds or small animals.

Most arrows lack fletching, but all have a limited striking range. When necessary, an arrow maker ties the stems of one or two whole feathers to the lower portion of the mainshaft with sinew. The killing power of the arrows comes from their coating of a potent poison that can kill most animals rather than from force of projection. The San use a wide variety of plant or animal substances for poison. In the Kalahari Desert, the San extract poison from the crushed insides of a chrysomelid beetle larva cocoon. The primary purpose of the arrow is to deliver poison to an animal's bloodstream without causing massive bleeding, which would flush the poison out of the animal. Men dig these cocoons 20 to 30 centimeters below corkwood bushes (*Commiphora* sp.). When hunters need poison, they carefully crush a cocoon between their fingers without breaking the casing. They remove the head and dab the internal juices on the point shaft below the shoulders or barbs. The poison is extremely toxic and is never placed on the point or sharp edges of the arrowhead. When in camp, hunters normally apply poison in seclusion away from communal areas. Men mix poison on a stone or bone cup and apply it to arrows with a stick or bone. Poison on the arrows is dried over a small fire. Men take great care to eliminate any chance of accidents.

Spears are an important component of the hunting kit and an adjunct to bows and arrows. Hunters use spears to kill incapacitated prey, animals chased down by dogs, and animals in burrows. Spears have long, stout wooden shafts tipped with a metal point. The point, similar to the metal knife blade, has a long pointed tang for hafting. Often men bind the wooden shafts with sinew to prevent them from splitting. The San use wooden clubs to kill animals at close range.

They also throw these clubs at small animals and birds. Clubs have a large, heavy knob carved at one end for striking animals.

The San also make metal knife blades. Men mount long-stemmed blades in carved wooden handles. Documents from the 19th century record the use of stone flakes and end-of-blade scrapers as knives. End-of-blade scrapers are long flakes with bluntly trimmed distal ends. The unretouched sharp edges were used for cutting, and the blunted ends provided a safe grip.

Another common hunting technique is snaring. G/wi snare steenbok and duikers, especially during the months when hunted game is difficult to kill because poison supplies are low and during the summer heat when bow-and-arrow hunting is too strenuous. Normally snaring is not as reliable as hunting, but the !Kung rely on snaring when normally dependable plant foods are scarce. Older men who no longer hunt usually do most of the snaring. However, children commonly snare small animals and birds. The snares consist of a *Sansevieria* fiber cord tied to a stout sapling stuck firmly into the ground. Sometimes the hunters build low brush fences to direct animals toward a snare. A trapper ties a cord to the upper end of the pole and ties a noose to the lower portion of the cord. The trapper sets the open noose with a trigger mechanism placed over a small pit, if it is set for steenbok or duikers. The trapper often uses a small bulb, placed within the noose, as bait if the intended prey is small mammals or birds. When an animal springs the trigger mechanism, the noose tightens around it and jerks it into the air. Hunters check snares four or five times daily to keep the trapped animal from escaping and predators from discovering it.

San hunters catch spring hares, a variety of large rodent, in their burrows with poles. These tools consist of multiple long, flexible poles lashed end to end and barbed with metal hooks. Hunters sometimes lash a small antelope horn on the pole to form a hook instead of using a metal hook. San hunters stick the poles deep into the burrows to hook a spring hare. Once hooked, hunters hold the spring hare in place while others excavate to the animal with a wooden digging stick and kill it with a swift hit from a wooden club. Once a spring-hare burrow is found, this method is a reliable, although strenuous, way to obtain meat. The San also take porcupines, anteaters, and warthogs in their burrows. San hunters use a small fire to smoke an animal out of its burrow where they kill it with a spear, or a hunter goes into the burrow with a spear. The latter technique can be very dangerous.

In areas that have enough water to support significant populations of fish, the San use traps or spears. Cape Province, Free State, and Transkei rock art documents spear fishing. Observers of the 19th century described the use of barbed bone points or harpoons. Rock art in the Transkei illustrates hunters spearing fish from small boats. The San also build cylinder reed traps to catch fish. Fish pass through a constricted reed cone set into a larger reed container. Once the fish pass through the cone, they cannot easily escape. On the Cape Province coast, San use circular rock weirs in intertidal zones to capture fish at low tide.

———〰〰〰〰〰———

The hunting equipment of the San represents a highly effective, integrated, and well-designed technological system. Construction materials are common and easily manufactured into a small number of necessary tools. Repair is simple because of modular design. Tools are light in weight and thus easily transported. Most importantly, at any time when the opportunity presents itself, the San are able to kill a wide variety of animals.

BIBLIOGRAPHY

Bleek, W. H. I., and L. C. Lloyd. 1911. *Specimens of Bushman folklore*. London: George Allen and Company Ltd.

Clark, J. D. 1977. Interpretations of prehistoric technology from ancient Egyptian and other sources. Part II: Prehistoric arrow forms in Africa as shown by surviving examples of the traditional arrows of the San Bushmen. *Paleorient 3: 127–150.*

Deacon, J. 1984. *The Later Stone Age of southernmost Africa*. Oxford: British Archaeological Reports.

Goodwin, A. J. H. 1945. Some historic Bushman arrows. *South African Journal of Science* 41: 429–443.

Lee, R. B. 1979. *The !Kung San: Men, women, and work in a foraging society*. Cambridge: Cambridge University Press.

Marshall, L. 1976. *The !Kung of the Nyae Nyae*. Cambridge: Harvard University Press.

Schapera, I. 1930. *The Khoisan peoples of South Africa: Bushmen and Hottentots*. London: George Routledge and Sons Ltd.

Silberbauer, B. G. 1981. *Hunter and habitat in the central Kalahari Desert*. Cambridge: Cambridge University Press.

Van Rippen, B. 1917. Notes on some Bushman implements. *American Anthropological Association* 23: 75–97.

Vinnicombe, P. 1976. *People of the eland*. Pietermaritzburg: Natal University Press.

C. Britt Bousman

Pastoral Lifeways

NORTHEASTERN AFRICAN PASTORALISTS

Pastoral nomads, whether living in the Sahara or in Siberia, generally share certain core characteristics that relate to their livestock, location, mobility, and subsistence strategy.

Pastoralists focus their economic energies on domesticated animals that can be herded. The choice of species and of herd composition is based on a number of interrelated factors: ecology, culture, and economy. In northeastern Africa, the species include camels, sheep, goats, and cattle. Most often the species are combined in various ways to satisfy different needs, so that a particular group of nomadic pastoralists might focus on one or another species but include one or more others.

Ecology is probably the most important selection factor for the primary species. Camels, for example, are dominant in the herds of the Cyrenaican Bedouin in the southern steppes of their territory in Libya and northwestern Sudan. However, camels do not do well on the central savannas of the Sudan, so cattle are found to dominate the herds of the Baggara. Sheep are difficult to manage in the tree-filled mountain regions of Cyrenaica but do well on the plateau foothills. Goats are preferred by the Ma'aza Bedouin in Egypt's Eastern Desert. While vegetation type and availability are important (camels, for example, require salty vegetation), water sources dominate the ecological factors that influence the selection of herd species.

Ecology and cultural and economic factors also influence the strategies for mixing animal species within a herd. While one species of herd animal dominates herd composition, another species may be added as a hedge against disaster. Each species has different characteristics of disease and drought resistance. Among the Baggara, if a cattle herd is decimated by bovine pleuropneumonia, a herder may retain or recover his viability by focusing for a time on sheep or goats, which generally make up a minor part of typical herd composition. In times of drought, cattle are generally least resistant, then sheep, then goats. Again, strategies of mixing herd composition build in flexibility for economic viability.

Economic factors also influence herd composition. Herds of less wealthy families might be composed of larger numbers of small stock as opposed to large stock. Access to markets as well as market demands may influence herd composition. Sheep sell better as meat than goats, for example, so herders near markets might prefer sheep. Farther away from potential meat markets, goats might be favored, as they produce larger amounts of milk, which can be used by the herding households. Among the Hawazma Baggara, an urban demand for milk and milk products encourages herd composition to favor milk-producing animals. Cultural factors also influence herd composition. Among any particular group of nomadic pastoralists, the dominant species holds higher status. The connecting of status to one species leads to a desire to accumulate as large a herd as possible, given the carrying capacity of the ecological zone and the availability of labor. Generally, the dominant herds are regarded as a "walking bank account," and it is considered appropriate to use their products but not to reduce their numbers by massive sales or by everyday consumption of their meat. Baggara herders, for example, raise sheep for sale and for occasional consumption as meat. Their goats are their primary meat sources, and someone in the camp slaughters a goat every seven to ten days to be shared by all camp residents. Cattle are rarely slaughtered and then only for very important social occasions such as marriages or funerals.

Nomadic pastoralists are almost always found in marginal geographic regions where other modes of subsistence cannot easily be practiced (see table 14). While nomadic pastoralists may be found in close proximity or in overlapping zones with horticulturists, the areas they use cannot support either intensive agriculture or sedentary pastoralism on a closed rangeland without the addition of technology such as deep drilled wells, complex irrigation, or the use of high levels of agricultural fertilizers. Rather, the scanty grasslands must be used for short periods and then allowed time to recover. The ecological zones used by nomadic pastoralists may be allocated horizontally between them and farmers or differentiated vertically. In the case of horizontally allocated zones, the grazing lands used by nomadic pastoralists are not necessarily contiguous so that in order to move from one grazing area to another, pastoralists must cross zones used by sedentary farmers. Sometimes, as in central Kordofan in Sudan, the differently used zones were traditionally vertical, with farmers (Nuba) tending fields on hill slopes and nomadic pastoralists (Baggara) grazing their animals on the surrounding plains.

The lifestyle of nomadic pastoralists features a relatively high degree of mobility. The pastoralists may follow an elliptical pattern around a migratory route whose circumnavigation occupies an annual cycle, or they may move along a more-or-less straight line at the beginning and end of a seasonal change. While mobility is key, the patterns follow a great many variations, whether they follow an annual cycle or are based on relatively direct movements back and forth between two sorts of seasonal locations. For ex-

Table 14 *Pastoral nomadic tribes of northeastern Africa*

Baggara	Western Sudan
Batahin	White Nile, Sudan
Beni Selim	White Nile, Sudan
Cyrenaican Bedouin	Libya
Dakhla	Western Egypt
Fezara	North Kordofan, Sudan
Fulani (Ful, Fulɓe, Peul)	Niger, Nigeria, Chad, Sudan
Hamar	Kordofan, Sudan
Howeitat	Eastern Egypt
Kababish	Northwestern Sudan
Ma'aza Bedouin	Egyptian Eastern Desert
Rashaayda Bedouin	Eastern Sudan
Rufaa	Blue Nile, Sudan
Shenabla	North Kordofan, Sudan
Shukria	Northeastern Sudan
Sirticana	Libya
Tuareg	Niger, Chad, Libya

ample, the entire residential unit might make every move together. The movements of the primary unit might be interspersed with movements of a subsidiary herding unit before the primary unit moves on again. In other instances, all members of the primary residential unit might remain at the "home" camping site while only herders make a biannual, unilinear trek during the rainy season. Both natural and cultural ecological factors influence and constrain movements, though grazing and water are the primary constraints. For example, both the Humr Baggara and Hawazma Baggara plan their movements around water availability.

Another characteristic of pastoral nomads is that they are rarely self-sufficient—that is, they exist in a symbiotic relationship to groups (typically agricultural groups) focusing on other subsistence strategies. Nomadic pastoral groups in northeastern Africa require grain, and while they may grow some crops themselves, these are rarely adequate for annual household needs. They also require manufactured products and rely on others, such as urban manufacturers or itinerant blacksmiths, to produce them. In return, nomadic pastoralists provide animal products (milk, meat, hides, and manure) to sedentary peoples. Nomadic pastoralists in this region have also traditionally been involved in providing transportation over long-distance trading routes.

Examples of Nomadic Pastoral Groups

Not surprisingly, each of the three groups serving as examples here, the Bedouin of Cyrenaica, the Ma'aza Bedouin of Egypt's Eastern Desert, and the Baggara of South Kordofan in Sudan, are closely linked to the environmental conditions of their territories. Of the three groups, only the Ma'aza Bedouin are in an ecological zone where all of their lineage segments (complex extended families) are able to focus on the same animal, goats, as the primary herd animal. The Bedouin of Cyrenaica have lineage segments that specialize in camels, sheep, or goats. The Baggara tribes, claiming links to the Bedouin of the Arabian peninsula, are found primarily in the Sudan. While the Baggara are located in sub-Saharan Africa, in zones better suited to cattle, they represent an interesting cultural transition between Arab North Africa and groups representing the East African cattle complex.

The Bedouin of Cyrenaica

The Cyrenaican Bedouin are found in Cyrenaica, a region in eastern Libya along the eastern coast of the Gulf of Sirte. Their area stretches 480 kilometers from west to east. It extends from the coast 40 to 50 kilometers in the southwest, 120 kilometers southward from the coast in the center, and narrows again at the Egyptian border. There are two major natural regions in Cyrenaica: the Jabal (high, mountainous regions in the north) and the Barr (flat, low-lying steppes and floodplains in the south). A less well defined region of undulating plateau foothills lies between the two. R. H. Behnke in 1980 noted that the Bedouin

recognize five ecological zones within these regions. Rainfall is heavy and regular in the north, with marked decreases away from the plateau in all directions, except for the coastal strip in the northwest. Forests and continuous plant cover are found in the north, while the land is mostly barren in the south, except during a good rainy season.

The ecological zones, with their different grazing land, support different species of herd animals. In the Jabal are found primarily cattle, whose herders are semisedentary. There are few sheep as their woolly coats get caught in the underbrush and they prefer the warmer south for lambing. Camels are not suited to the Jabal regions either. Goats may be herded with cattle, but goats are dominant in the zone directly south of the Jabal. The next zone to the south is dominated by sheep herders, while camels predominate only in the southernmost zone.

The Cyrenaican Bedouin designate five seasons. May, June, July, and August are the hot, dry months. The weather begins to cool in autumn, September and October, and the rains begin late in the season. Winter lasts until February. After early spring, February, March, and perhaps April, the pastures begin to dry up and the grain fields ripen. In spring, late April and May, camps are dispersed over a wide area, often as far apart as 3 kilometers. In summer, Bedouin groups converge frequently a short distance from a village or permanent wells for the summer watering period.

Besides several long, seasonal moves, camps move frequently during the summer to maintain cleanliness. If the rains fail, camps may move every ten to 15 days. Even though water is important, movements are also related to intersectional relationships. As soon as the rains start, men begin plowing to prepare for planting barley, which is harvested in early summer.

For sheep-herding groups, one of the most important yearly ceremonies focuses on sheep shearing. All the men of a group work together between April and May to shear each flock. It takes about ten days to shear a large flock. (Camels and goats are sheared by only two or three men working together, and the task is not tied to a celebration.) Sheep wool is very important for bags, tents, and carpets. Women always carry wool with them to spin or wind or may work on looms. Some debts are paid in wool, and relationships are set up through it.

Like other pastoral nomadic groups, the Cyrenaican Bedouin are organized around segmented, patrilineal lineages. Branches on the Cyrenaican genealogy show relationships, not only between groups, but with ecological areas. Sa'ada is the epical ancestress of the Bedouin. The two major divisions descending from Sa'ada represent the eastern and western halves of Cyrenaican Bedouin territory. One group of tribes is found on the plains, while the other is found on the mountain foothills. The different subsections represent ever more parochial ecological boundaries until we arrive at the smallest political unit: a residential group of 150 to 200 people.

Six generations may be ascertained today, though the Bedouin say there are about 12 generations between Sa'ada and the present, a time span of about 250 years. However, historical evidence shows that the Cyrenaican forebears arrived in the mid-11th century, about 900 years or 45 generations ago. On the genealogical chart, 650 years or nearly 33 generations are missing. The named ancestors in the genealogy represent the disposition of tribal sections in a definite pattern. Thus, it is both a genealogical framework of tribal sections and a map showing the territorial distribution of tribes and sections. The genealogy is a model the Bedouin use for conceptualizing their territorial relationships.

Since the genealogical names are markers of blocks of land, the names are as fixed in position as are the landed domains of tribal sections. Ancestral names and the positioning of descent lines from them document landed-property relationships. If a group acquires land by conquest, for example, it necessarily appears on the genealogy as descendant from Sa'ada.

Frequently a reorganization of the population is required when the number of people exceeds the carrying capacity of the land. Displacement is necessary if either the animal or human population increases. Resources also expand and contract with climatic changes, and this affects population growth and decline. The climate in Cyrenaica changes almost whimsically, and small fluctuations in rainfall, for example, greatly affect the carrying capacity of the zone.

E. L. Peters says that in March the Bedouin assess the relationship of groups to resources and decide whether to allow newcomers to join the camp, to keep their existing numbers, or to move some people away. Agnates (relatives whose kinship is traced through male ancestors) cannot order other agnates to move, but there must be some mechanism to shift the population. The authority to command must be vested in one part of the population over another. This authority is found in the relationship of noble groups to client groups. Peters notes that the percentage of client groups moving annually is an index of the general stability of the economy.

Other aspects of intergroup relationships can be seen in movements of people on the landscape. In the open areas of the steppes in the south, there is a great deal of movement between groups, and visiting and hospitality are important aspects of social relationships. In the forested zone of the Jabal, movement around the area is not so free, and travelers are not offered much hospitality. Peters says that the free-wandering Bedouin groups of the south show more cohesion than the more sedentary groups of the north.

Peters supplies some interesting information that archaeologists might use to assess social relationships from physical structures. Both northern and southern regions of Cyrenaica are dotted with saints' tombs, although there are more of them in the Jabal area. Using the tombs as another index of cohesion, Peters correlates the numbers of saints' tombs with solidarity. He says that where there are more tombs, in the Jabal area, cohesion is weak. Compared to the Jabal, the south has few tombs, and cohesion there is high. In the Jabal, cohesion is generated by annual communal pilgrimages to the saints' tombs, carried out by tribal sections. In the south, where there are few saints' tombs, individuals make pilgrimages.

The Ma'aza Bedouin of Egypt's Eastern Desert

The Ma'aza Bedouin are found between the Nile Valley and Egypt's Eastern Desert. They claim to be descendants of Ma'iz ibn al-Jabal, from northwestern Arabia. As their name, meaning "goat people," indicates, goats are the preferred domestic animal.

The Ma'aza are patrilineal and have about 20 lineages. Old men who know tribal history can recite ten to 14 generations. Much of Ma'aza life is linked to segmentary lineages. For example, members of a patrilineal descent group congregate and disperse into camping units according to the availability of water and grass. Cooperation between households within these lineages forms the basis for most economic and social activities. Flexibility in the organization of these units allows them to exploit a wide range of opportunities.

Like the lineages of the Cyrenaican Bedouin, the Ma'aza tribeal lineages are associated with large, jealously guarded territories. Lineage territories are demarcated north to south by boundaries that run east and west, perpendicular to the Red Sea Coast. The population of the Ma'aza is distributed in a ratio of approximately one person to 90 square kilometers.

The Ma'aza raise camels in addition to sheep and goats, though the basis of their economy is the sale of sheep and goats. The Ma'aza say that goats make it possible to live in the desert. The strategy is to have mixed herds of sheep and goats in order to minimize risks and maximize benefits. The animals belong to families and individuals. Women may own some animals in case of divorce, and children also own some. Previously, families had herds of 50 or more camels. Now a family may own only one to four camels to carry baggage or water. While goat milk is important as a symbol of the "good life," meaning health and independence, camel milk is also greatly prized.

Agriculture is not significant for the Ma'aza, but they do take advantage of the opportunity to grow some crops. Garden plots are tended only if rain falls. The Ma'aza plant barley, millet, maize, watermelon, sweet melon, snake cucumber, and okra. Winter crops might include chickpeas, lentils, fava beans, and fenugreek. Rain in Ma'aza territory is spotty, so a particular garden plot may not receive rain for as long as ten years.

The Ma'aza use wool tents arranged in a semicircle, with the opening placed toward the rising sun. Stones are used to hold down the edges. J. J. Hobbs says the Ma'aza examine abandoned camps and can distinguish camps of the Ma'aza from those of the 'Ababda tribe, for example. One indicator is that the 'Ababda use small stones placed in a circle about 20 centimeters across for making bread, while the Ma'aza use a single stone. The Ma'aza build a raised platform of rocks to protect their belongings and food from sand and ants. Stones are also used to prop up cooking pots. Rock enclosures are built to protect small livestock against predators. Cairns of rocks can also communicate information and may mark routes to water.

In addition to using their animals, the Ma'aza also hunt and collect edible or marketable plants. Collected plants may be used for food, medicines, dye, soap, or perfume.

The Baggara of Kordofan, Sudan

Baggara territories extend from the west in what is now the Sudanese province of Darfur to the east along the banks of the White Nile. The southernmost territories of the Baggara are in the region of the Bahr el-Arab River in South Kordofan. From west to east, the five main subtribes of Baggara are the Reizegat, Habbania, Messiriya, Humr, and Hawazma. The tribal name, Baggara, is an umbrella term referring to this group of tribes that claim kinship to each other and to a tribe in the Hijaz. It is likely that a group of Baggara came from the Hijaz at about the same time as the Cyrenaican Bedouin, around A.D. 1100. It is not known how they came to the Sudan—whether directly south through Egypt or via North Africa through Chad.

The Baggara derive their name from the Arabic word for *cattle (bugar)* and are therefore, the "cattle people." Though some of the westernmost Baggara herd camels, most of their savanna territories are better suited to cattle. These zones range from sparse scrub land in the northern areas, through arid and semiarid bushlands and wooded savannas. While the Nuba Mountains are found in the central part of South Kordofan, most of the area is flat savanna. The zone is characterized by a hot, semiarid climate. Annual rainfall varies from about 100 millimeters in the northern areas to about 800 millimeters in the south. Rains occur in a single season, primarily from June to September. Soil types, extending in west to east bands, determine vegetation, which, in turn, influences cattle movement. These bands of soils range from sandy soils (qoz) in the north, to noncracking clays (gardud) in the central areas, to cracking clays (tiin) in the southern Baggara region. For the most part, the Baggara groups move in a north-south direction across these various bands of soil types.

While different Baggara groups tend to be concentrated in particular areas, territories are not as discrete as it might seem. There is overlap and concurrent use of many areas, particularly in the rainy season. Kordofan and Darfur are characterized by great ethnic diversity and interdigitation (interlocking), so that no group is wholly isolated or bounded from other groups. In the various regions, Baggara have close associations with camel nomads (Hamar and Shenabla) and settled agriculturalists (Nuba, Dajut Tungur, Bedayria, Gima'a, Zaghawa, and Dhar Hamid), and camel and sheep nomads (Ma'alia). Symbiotic relationships between herders and farmers are typical wherever pastoralists are found. In Kordofan, the relationship between Hawazma and Nuba farmers is particularly significant. Traditionally, the Nuba were concentrated on and around the hills of the Nuba Mountains, rather than on the plains. The Baggara and the Nuba represent an important example of symbiotic use of the same savanna ecozone. The Nuba are settled farmers who grow sorghum. They provide the Hawazma some manufactured goods and labor for both cropping and herding. The Hawazma sell or exchange animal products such as milk, hides, and manure.

Pastoral Baggara live in camping units called fariqs. The composition and size of the camping units vary seasonally, but generally range from eight to 20 households, with a total camp population of 40 to 100 people. The number of people who can camp together depends partly on factors such as the size of cattle herds and the availability of grazing and water.

Residents in a camp typically belong to one or more patrilines (families defined by the male line of descent) of a lineage. Houses are arranged on the perimeter of a circle. Cattle, brought into the center of the camp at night, mill about the household of their owners. Adult married women own the houses and their housekeeping contents. Dry-season houses are generally larger than rainy-season houses: 3.5 to 4.5 meters in diameter and 3 meters high in the center as compared to 3 meters in diameter and 1.8 to 2.4 meters high. Baggara houses, much more like those found among East African cattle pastoralists than the tents of Cyrenaica and the Eastern Desert, are spherical, built by placing saplings in holes around the perimeter and then bending them over and tying them to form a dome. Smaller branches tied onto the frame horizontally support the structure, which is then covered with thatch in the dry season or mats and tarpaulins during the rains.

Baggara herds are composed primarily of cattle but also include sheep and goats. Camels are kept for riding and pack animals, and oxen are specially trained for riding and carrying loads. Many households also have donkeys. Most pastoral Baggara plant fields of sorghum in their dar (home territory) at the beginning of the rainy season before leaving on their annual trek. Sesame and beans are also sometimes planted. Crops are left unattended, with resulting low yields. Few households can supply all their grain requirements. Hawazma Baggara have significant links between pastoral and agricultural households. Baggara men frequently have one wife who resides in a pastoral camp and another who lives in an agricultural village or a town. Some products and labor are exchanged between the two types of households. This adaptation appears well suited to an area where the Baggara must juggle the exigencies of a precarious environment with social relationships between groups representing pastoralists, farmers, and townsmen.

One common thread between the Bedouin of Cyrenaica, the Ma'aza Bedouin of the Eastern Desert, and the Baggara of South Kordofan and others in northeastern Africa is the link between subsistence activities focused on particular herd animals and environment. Another commonality is the way in which social organization, based on segmentary lineages, provides the mechanism by which groups map their relationships to each other and to the landscape.

BIBLIOGRAPHY

Adamu, M., and A. H. M. Kirk-Greene. 1986. *Pastoralists of the West African savanna.* Manchester: Manchester University Press.

Asad, T. 1970. *The Kababish Arabs: Power, authority and consent in a nomadic tribe.* London: C. Hurst.

Behnke, R. H. 1980. *The herders of Cyrenaica: Ecology, economy and kinship among the Bedouin of eastern Libya.* Urbana: University of Illinois Press.

Cunnison, I. 1966. *The Baggara Arabs.* Oxford: Clarendon Press.

Dupire, M. 1962. *Peuls nomades: Etude descriptive des Wodaabe du Sahel Nigerien.* Paris: Institut d'Ethnologie.

———. 1970. *Organisation sociale des Peul: Etude d'ethnographie comparée.* Paris: Librarie Plon.

Evans Pritchard, E. E. 1949. *The Sanusi of Cyrenaica.* Oxford: Clarendon Press.

Goodman, S. M., and J. J. Hobbs. 1988. The ethnobotany of the Egyptian Eastern Desert: A comparison of common plant usage between two culturally distinct Bedouin groups. *Journal of Ethnopharmacology* 23: 73–89.

Hobbs, J. J. 1989. *Bedouin life in the Egyptian wilderness.* Austin: University of Texas Press.

Johnson, D. L. 1973. *Jabal al Akhdar, Cyrenaica.* Department of Geography Research Paper, no. 148. Chicago: University of Chicago

Keenan, J. 1977. *The Tuareg.* London: Allen Lane.

Michael, B. J. 1987. *Cows, bulls and gender roles: Pastoral strategies for survival and continuity in western Sudan.* Ann Arbor: University Microfilms.

Nomads on the savanna. 1994. Produced by B. J. Michael. Pennsylvania State University Audio-Visual Services. Videocassette.

Murdoch, G. P. 1959. *Africa: Its peoples and their culture history.* New York: McGraw-Hill.

Peters, E. L. 1990. *The Bedouin of Cyrenaica: Studies in personal and corporate power.* Cambridge: Cambridge University Press.

Sadr, K. 1991. *The development of nomadism in ancient Northeast Africa.* Philadelphia: University of Pennsylvania Press.

Stunning, D. J. 1959. *Savannah nomads: A study of the Wodaabe pastoral Fulani of Western Bornu Province, Northern Region, Nigeria.* London: Routledge and Kegan Paul.

Voice of the Whip. 1989. Produced by N. Johnston and L. Wernert. Museum of Modern Art (New York) Circulating Film Library. Videocassette.

Young, W. C. 1996. *The Rashaayda Bedouin: Arab pastoralists of eastern Sudan.* New York: Harcourt Brace.

Barbara J. Michael

EASTERN AFRICAN PASTORALISTS

Pastoralism, a way of life based on keeping herds of domesticated animals, is widely practiced in East Africa, especially in grassland areas where semiarid climates prevail. The image of a herder gripping his spear while gazing at a line of cattle raising clouds of dust is displayed on countless travel posters and picture books that celebrate the geography of the region. In a limited way, such stereotypes of East African pastoralism are quite appropriate, since the prominence of herding in regional economies stems largely from geographic conditions. For example, while substantially less than half of Kenya's land is wet enough to sustain nonirrigation agriculture, most of the country's drier areas support one form of pastoralism or another. However, the stereotype of the East African herder also contains several grossly inappropriate elements, many of which are inextricably linked with an idealized perspective on traditionalism. From this perspective, East African herding cultures are seen as stalwart adherents to a truly indigenous way of life, heroically resisting the blandishments of modernization that have tainted the customs of their nonpastoral neighbors.

One of the chief aims of this article is to replace this traditionalist mystique with a sense of the extraordinary plasticity and adaptability of East African pastoralists by examining the development of pastoral lifeways in the region from earliest times to the present. Thus, while other articles in this volume are concerned with the ecology and ethnology of pastoralism, this article will focus largely on its history. In the present context, "history" includes not only the last few centuries, for which written or oral records of pastoral development are available, but also the preceding three to four millennia during which East African pastoralism is reflected in the archaeological record alone.

But it is difficult to absorb an account of something's development without a basic grasp of its nature. A fundamental understanding of East African pastoralism should include some knowledge of its economic aims, the geographic factors that shape it, and the kinds of relationships that exist between pastoral groups and the cultural and physical space they inhabit. So we are obliged, after all, to examine key attributes of contemporary herding cultures in East Africa, including aspects of their ecology and ethnology that are treated more extensively in other articles.

Livestock can be exploited for a wide range of materials useful to people, including meat, hides, hair, dung, and dairy products. While East African herders often make use of various kinds of animal products, they usually depend primarily on one: milk. For this reason, they can be regarded as dairy pastoralists, for whom the milk yield of their herds is an essential determinant of physical well-being, which in turn is reflected in the maintenance or growth of the human groups that possess herds. Beyond this, livestock (especially large animals, such as cattle and camels) is viewed as wealth and enters into various kinds of social transactions, such as bride-wealth payments. As a result, a herd's composition reflects the web of social relationships within which its owner (typically, the male head of a household, though other individuals also possess livestock) exists, while herd size is indicative of the owner's social status.

The foregoing comments on the economic and social role of livestock in East African pastoral cultures illuminate two salient aspects of the behavior of herd owners. One is a more-or-less boundless striving to enlarge herd size, which leads to increased milk yield and social status. The other is an intense preoccupation with individual animals, each of which is perceived not only as valued property but also as a walking record of social ties and obligations.

This combination of behavioral traits can, in turn, be seen as at least part of the impetus behind the expansionary trend that characterizes pastoral societies in East Africa, a trend so vig-

orous that the pastoral societies often press upon alien cultures and habitats. The likelihood of such encounters is high because of the region's extraordinary geographic diversity. Zonal variation in climate, as illustrated by the contrast between the arid northeastern zone and the exceptionally wet zone centered on Lake Victoria, together with the marked topographic relief associated with the Rift Valley, has created a complex pattern of variation in regional rainfall and vegetation. Variability in these two environmental attributes is particularly relevant to the topic at hand because they are crucial features of pastoral ecology. For example, as rainfall increases to the point where nonirrigation agriculture can be practiced reliably, pastoralism tends to give way to agriculture or agro-pastoralism. On the other hand, declining amounts of rainfall affect the choice of herd animals, with camels replacing cattle toward the low end of the range of variation. As for vegetation, increasing density of tree cover fosters infestation by tsetse flies, the bearers of trypanosomiasis. Since cattle are more vulnerable to this disease than small stock, the varying density of tree cover affects the species composition of pastoral herds.

Such variation in pastoral ecology, together with the remarkably variable character of East African geography, helps to account for the fact that the region contains a greater number and variety of pastoral societies than any other part of the continent. This heterogeneity is expressed not only in differences in herd animals (camels versus cattle, small stock versus large animals) but also in the extent to which subsistence is based on livestock. As regards the latter, there is a continuum of variation from cultures whose economies are so wholly centered on the products of the herd that they can be regarded as specialized pastoralists to cultures whose subsistence regimes are focused more on agricultural production than herding. In fact, this aspect of variation is so finely graded that the distinction between pastoralist and agro-pastoralist cultures is rather arbitrary.

However, such problems in dividing the continuum in pastoral economies toward the agro-pastoral end of the range are less troublesome toward the other extremity of variation. Not only is specialized pastoralism, as practiced for example by the Maasai people, readily distinguishable from other forms in its own right, but it is also easily recognized by the extent to which it exhibits economic symbiosis with neighboring, nonpastoral cultures. Such symbiosis takes many different forms: in some cases, it involves exchanging herd products for wild resources, such as honey (for brewing) collected by foraging cultures. In other cases, it entails the exchange of livestock or livestock products for grain raised by horticultural societies. Exchanges of this kind are, of course, opportunistically practiced by many nonspecialized pastoralists, but they are necessarily practiced by all contemporary specialized pastoralists.

With this brief sketch of East African pastoralism in hand, we may turn to considering its development. In summarizing the preceding observations about herding cultures of the region, it seems fair to say that they exhibit a wide range of variation in habitat, types of animals herded, and degree of economic reliance on livestock. Within this variation, there is a distinct set of cultures that can be identified as specialized pastoralists, all of which depend in varying ways on symbiotic exchange with neighboring, nonpastoral cultures. Thus, the historical problem at hand is to show how, if not why, such patterns of herding emerged.

It is important to note at the outset that pastoralism is not indigenous to East Africa, at least not originally. Since the region's paleontological record contains no wild progenitors for any of the East African domestic species, the livestock must have been introduced from elsewhere. This being the case, it is conceivable that contemporaneous patterns of herding were introduced along with the animals themselves. However, this is not the picture that emerges from the historical record.

The earliest reliably dated occurrences of domestic species in East Africa fall in a range of time between 4,000 and 5,000 radiocarbon years before the present. The animals included both small stock (sheep and goats) and cattle and were introduced from areas to the north, where they are archaeologically evident at sites dating to one millennium or more earlier. Although there is no archaeological evidence that securely identifies

the cultural source of the people who brought the animals into East Africa, linguistic evidence suggests that they spoke a language belonging to the Southern Cushitic family. The southward spread of livestock was probably largely encouraged by a major decline in rainfall throughout northern Africa during the period from about 4,000 to 6,000 years ago, rendering many parts of the region inhospitable to herding.

However, the earliest traces of pastoralism in East Africa reveal an economic regime that differs radically from any ethnographically documented pastoral culture in the same area. For example, food debris from early pastoral sites contains large quantities of wild-animal remains, far in excess of what could be expected to occur in the refuse of modern herders. In general, living pastoral cultures consume modest quantities of wild foods. In fact, some have strong taboos against the flesh of wild animals, and even in the absence of taboos, pastoralists tend to be very selective in their consumption of fish and game. But the early pastoral sites of East Africa contain assemblages of wild fauna that are not only copious but heterogeneous. This points toward subsistence practices that are unmatched by anything that can be observed in living pastoral societies.

There are also striking differences between early East African pastoralists and modern herders in material culture. Some, such as the use of stone instead of metal for tool manufacture, are simply reflections of technological evolution. But others hint at important differences in settlement behavior, especially as regards mobility. For example, while contemporary herders tend to make containers from gourds and other relatively light and portable plant materials, the early pastoralists seem to have relied largely on pottery, which is difficult to transport because of its weight and fragility. Of course, the possession of pottery does not immobilize its owners, as is shown by the fact that some contemporary East African foragers, such as the Okiek who are by no means entirely sedentary, routinely make and use ceramic vessels. Moreover, pastoral sites that date to more than about 3,000 years ago seem to represent ephemeral occupation, suggesting substantial mobility. Yet, the use of pottery implies a greater constraint on movement than is indicated by the types of vessels used by modern herders.

The archaeology of the earliest East African pastoralists is poorly known. Nevertheless, what is known suggests that the introduction of domestic animals gave rise to a way of life that was not only unlike any that has been ethnographically documented in the region but was also remarkably durable, having persisted for at least one millennium (between 3,000 and 4,000 years ago) and perhaps as long as two (between 3,000 and 5,000 years ago). While subsistence seems to have hinged largely on wild fauna, with the flesh of domestic animals composing a very small fraction of the human diet, it is possible that dairy products played an important dietary role, though direct evidence of this is lacking. Thus, although there is no basis for inferring specialized, dairy pastoralism, one may tentatively conclude that the early and highly persistent form of pastoralism that prevailed before 3,000 years ago reflected the same general combination of dietary components evident in the subsistence regimes of modern, specialized pastoralists who rely on obtaining wild foods from neighboring foragers. This does not involve assuming anything about how the early pastoralists obtained wild food, whether by exchange or more directly through their own foraging efforts. The conclusion refers only to the broad character of the diet. In this limited sense, one can argue that the economic foundation for some aspects of modern East African livestock herding may have been established at the outset of pastoralism in the region.

Be that as it may, and the line of reasoning is obviously a very tenuous one, further developments in the history of East African pastoralism do not point toward any sort of continuity from earliest times to the present. In fact, a marked discontinuity in all major aspects of the archaeology of Stone Age pastoralism is evident between about 2,000 and 3,000 years ago. New types of pottery, new techniques of stone-tool manufacture, new subsistence regimes, new settlement practices, and even new breeds of livestock make their appearance during this millennium and more or less abruptly replace the old forms throughout East Africa.

This historical discontinuity is generally attributed to a new episode of pastoral immigration from the north, involving people of different cultural origins than the earliest herders, perhaps speaking languages of the Nilotic family. The new influx of herders may have been triggered by an arid phase throughout northern Africa that peaked about 3,000 years ago. This climatic episode resulted not only in desert expansion, particularly in the Sudan belt that borders East Africa on the north, but also in a precipitous decline of lake levels on the floor of the eastern Rift Valley, which opened vast new areas of rangeland within East Africa. It is also possible that the arid conditions led to a substantial reduction in tree cover in many parts of East Africa that had been infested with tsetse flies, which would have further increased the available rangeland.

The new forms of herding societies are abundantly represented in the late 2nd- to 1st-millennium B.C. archaeological record, comprising a substantial number of sites that are concentrated in the eastern Rift Valley and adjoining areas but are also scattered latitudinally from as far west as the Lake Victoria Basin to east of Mount Kenya. Partly because of the archaeological visibility of this segment of East African pastoral history, it has been reasonably well investigated. It is impossible to summarize adequately the great variety of cultural practices exposed by these investigations in the space available here. Instead, some generalizations about subsistence and settlement practices will be offered, mainly because they seem particularly relevant to our understanding of major features in the development of regional patterns of pastoralism.

The most conspicuous change in subsistence behavior is reflected in the proportions of wild and domestic fauna, which are frequently reversed by comparison with earlier times. The animal remains recovered from many sites dating to between about 2,000 and 3,000 years ago overwhelmingly represent domesticated forms, and wild game is often virtually absent from the food debris. This, together with evidence regarding herd-culling patterns and the dietary importance of various kinds of domestic-animal products (bone marrow, milk, and meat), points toward specialized herding. If so, pastoralism in this period may have depended on the introduction of humped cattle *(Bos indicus),* which is the preferred breed among contemporary pastoralists, having replaced the straight-backed cattle *(Bos taurus)* of earlier times. The humped breed is particularly suited for specialized pastoralism because of its relatively high productivity in hot, arid conditions and its greater resistance to disease and parasites.

But the (presumably) specialized pastoral cultures of the 1st millennium B.C. differed in various crucial ways from living specialists. There is, for example, little evidence of exchange with neighboring farmers or foragers, implying that at least some specialized Stone Age herders of East Africa were economically self-sufficient. In addition, many pastoralist middens of the 1st millennium B.C. contain vast quantities of pottery, grindstones, and other relatively bulky, nonportable artifacts, which are sometimes accompanied by evidence of substantial shelter construction. This suggests a marked reduction in mobility by comparison with both the earliest East African pastoral sites and the settlements of modern specialized pastoralists.

Although the forms of pastoralism established between 2,000 and 3,000 years ago persisted into the 1st millennium A.D., new approaches to herding that are as yet poorly understood emerged during the latter millennium. Toward the end of the millennium, the earliest iron-using pastoral cultures appear in the archaeological record. Within a few centuries, specialized pastoral economies associated with the use of iron tools had become well established in parts of East Africa, especially along the western margin of the eastern Rift Valley. Initially, these herders seem to have subsisted almost entirely on products from their livestock, but eventually they added grain cultivation to their subsistence regime.

By about the middle of the present millennium, East African pastoralism began to experience yet another major realignment that culminated in the 19th century A.D. and persists in modified form into the present. But our knowledge of the circumstances in this case is based on oral traditions and other historical evidence rather than on archaeology. Since historical sources of information are enormously prolific, the sheer mass of data representing the last four or five centuries of pastoral development far outweighs the archaeological data spanning perhaps as many millennia. In the present context, such a massive body of data can only be presented in drastically abbreviated form.

As was true in earlier times, the developments of the historic period were at least partly the result of demographic influx from areas bordering East Africa on the north, this time involving speakers of Eastern Nilotic languages, such as Maa and Turkana. Initially, the new immigrants appear to have pursued the rather eclectic and nonspecialized subsistence regimes practiced by Late Iron Age herders in East Africa. But as societies occupying areas of varying geographic character became increasingly attuned to their ecological possibilities, those who inhabited lands that were best suited for grazing tended to specialize as pastoralists. In so doing, they often established mutually dependent economic relationships with their nonpastoral neighbors. Thus, the emergence of contemporaneous forms of pastoralism in East African can be seen as a coevolutionary process, wherein each particular economic formation was largely the outcome of systemic codevelopment throughout the region.

This process of coevolutionary development has persisted into modern times, when East African pastoral cultures are once again having to adjust to changes in their ecological, social, and political contexts. As in earlier times, the process is likely to generate cultural patterns that are either unprecedented or reconstituted in ways that differ markedly from their past state. Such a dynamic condition is more consistent with East African pastoralist history than the doggedly conservative condition suggested by a traditionalist perspective. It is, moreover, a condition that points toward an essentially unlimited future for a herding way of life in East Africa.

BIBLIOGRAPHY
Bower, J. 1991. The pastoral Neolithic of East Africa. *Journal of World Prehistory* 5: 49–82.
Galaty, J. G. 1993. Maasai expansion and the new East African pastoralism. In *Being Maasai,* eds. T. Spear and R. Waller, 61–86. London: James Currey Ltd.

Marshall, F. 1994. Archaeological perspectives on East African pastoralism. In *African pastoralist systems: An integrated approach,* eds. E. Fratkin, K. A. Galvin, and E. A. Roth, 17–43. Boulder: Lynne Rienner Publishers, Inc.

Robertshaw, P. 1990. *Early pastoralists of southwestern Kenya.* British Institute in Eastern Africa Memoir 11. Nairobi: British Institute in Eastern Africa.

Smith A. B. 1992. *Pastoralism in Africa: Origins and development ecology.* London: Hurst and Company.

Sutton, J. E. G. 1993. Becoming Maasailand. In *Being Maasai,* eds. T. Spear and R. Waller, 38–60. London: James Currey Ltd.

Waller, R., and N. W. Sobania. 1994. Pastoralism in historical perspective. In *African pastoralist systems: An integrated approach,* eds. E. Fratkin, K. A. Galvin, and E. A. Roth, 45–68. Boulder: Lynne Rienner Publishers, Inc.

John R. F. Bower

SOUTHERN AFRICAN PASTORALISTS

In the context of southern Africa, it is important to define the use of the term *pastoralist* since there is a broad continuum of herd use and ownership across the cultural spectrum. In the more arid zones of the Kalahari, modern goat herders may keep up to 400 goats, but their predominant lifestyle revolves around hunting and foraging. Ninety percent of their food comes from wild resources, and rituals revolve around the use of game animals. The goats are used as a cash resource in order to buy processed foods or other consumer items. At the other end of the continuum are agro-pastoralists, who place strong symbolic and economic value on their cattle herds, but whose food is predominantly from domestic grains. Between these two extremes are, or were, pastoral peoples such as the Khoikhoi or Herero, who not only were greatly dependent on their herds for food (primarily milk) but also used them for ritual purposes.

This article discusses the archaeological evidence for the last two groups—agro-pastoralists and pastoralists—since there is considerable overlap between them, but it is important to recognize that any time when there are domestic animals in the landscape, all people of different economic persuasions have access to them, either by exchange or theft.

The Development of the Pastoralist Lifeways of Southern Africa

Even though there are many gaps in the archaeological evidence, modern scholars generally agree that the animals tended by southern African pastoralists had to have come overland from the north, since there are no wild progenitors of any of the domestic animals in southern Africa. How they got to southern Africa and dispersed throughout the subcontinent is more contentious.

The radiocarbon dating of the bones of the earliest domestic animals suggests they arrived around 2,000 years ago and within 200 years were widespread throughout the better-watered grasslands of the Cape at Spoegrivier and Kasteelberg, the former Transvaal province at Silver Leaves, Botswana at Toteng and in Namibia at Geduld. T. N. Huffman believes they came in as part of a package he calls the "central cattle pattern," implying that full-fledged agro-pastoral systems as seen today go back that far in time. E. N. Wilmsen is not convinced and believes the domestic stock were in the hands of Khoisan people before any Bantu-speaking people arrived. He is hesitant, however, to say where the animals came from.

The Spread of Pastoralism

At some time there was a transfer of stock to Khoisan hunting people of southern Africa from whatever source. Presumably some of them spoke a Khoe language as found in northern Botswana today. Since this was the language of the Khoikhoi at the Cape, scholars have developed models of migration by people southward.

By the time of the first European observers at the Cape at the end of the 15th century, the coastal forelands of this part of South Africa were occupied by Khoikhoi herders who used the pasture resources in an annual seasonal round. These people had large herds of cattle and required a coherent strategy of movement in order to maintain their stock in prime condition. This was partially forced upon them by a pasture environment of relatively low nutrient status, in spite of the dependable winter rainfall. Archaeological evidence, however, shows that these cattle herds probably only appeared in significant numbers after 1,000 years ago. The evidence from the site of Kasteelberg on the coast north of Cape Town shows that the earliest stock keepers were sheep herders beginning between 1,600 and 1,800 years ago. Cattle increased in frequency through time, but only after 1,000 years ago did the ratio of large to small stock approach the proportions found in the early records of the Dutch colony of the 17th century.

Agro-pastoralists of southern Africa spread southward to cover most of the well-watered eastern area of the subcontinent. Since the main crops, sorghum and millet, are summer rainfall crops, the spread stopped in the eastern Cape by A.D. 500, and no attempt was made to colonize the western areas, leaving this area open for the Khoikhoi. Interaction on the edges of Khoe-speaking and Bantu-speaking pasture zones, such as along the Orange River and in the eastern Cape, meant there were people of mixed ancestry, demonstrated by Alan Morris's analysis of skeletal material, which showed mixed Khoisan-Negroid morphology along the Orange River.

In the southwestern Cape, similar interactions between Khoikhoi and Soaqua hunters were not on an equal basis so there was much less social mixture. This is highlighted by the difference in frequency of material culture between the two groups. From the open-air site of Kasteelberg, for example, large numbers of sheep bones were excavated along with few formally retouched stone tools (0.02 percent of the total stone assemblage), large numbers of potsherds (up to 700 per cubic meter), grinding equipment, and large ostrich-eggshell beads. By contrast, at the small rock shelter of Witklip only 9 kilometers south of and coeval with Kasteelberg, very few sheep bones (the fauna was dominated by small hunted antelope), few potsherds (ten per cubic meter), small ostrich-eggshell beads, and a continuous use of small microlithic retouched stone tools (40 percent of the stone assemblage) were found before and after the ceramic boundary of 1,800 years ago.

These sites, among others, show separate economic and cultural traditions that mitigate against the assumption of R. Elphick, who would see them as ends of a cyclical continuum. When a person had stock, he was on the "up-cycle" as a herder. Loss of stock through theft, disease, or drought meant a herder could fall back on hunting and be on the "down part" of the cycle.

Such continued separation indicates a formative class structure in the pastoral environment, with hunters at the bottom of the social hierarchy. After 500 years ago, a few large ostrich-eggshell beads appeared at Witklip along with the small ones. This has been interpreted as a firming of the hierarchy as a result of increasing wealth in cattle herds and hunters being brought into the system as clients to perform the needed labor.

The relationships between Khoikhoi and Soaqua can be seen in the following quotation from the journal entry for 16 September 1685 of Simon van der Stel's journey to Namaqualand:

> We find that these Soaquas are just the same as the poor in Europe, each tribe of Hottentots having some of them and employing them to bring news of the approach of a strange tribe. They steal nothing from the kraals of their employers but regularly from other kraals . . . possessing nothing . . . except what they acquire by theft.

The Social Landscape of Pastoralism at the Cape

As shown in the early Dutch records, pastoralists, such as the Khoikhoi, had an annual seasonal round moving between the coast and the interior. Not only did this give their stock food, but the people benefited from milk production, a mainstay in their diet. Meat would have come from the ritual slaughter of their sheep as well as from cattle that died of natural causes. Other meat sources were wild game and marine mammals at the coast. Seal bones constitute the highest percentage of animal remains at Kasteelberg, so the site can properly be considered a sealing camp. Seals were not just a food resource. Seal fat was mixed with ochre and used as body decoration. Shellfish, crayfish, and marine birds were also eaten, but the extremely low numbers of fish bones from the site suggests this was not an important part of the diet. Plant foods included underground bulbs available at the beginning of summer.

Patriclans (groups of related people descending from a male ancestor) communally controlled the pasture territories and constantly raided each other and the Soaqua hunters on the edge of pastoralist society. The area controlled by individual groups varied with the power and fortune of the group. Each territory had to be able to support the pasture and water needs of the animals. Thus as cattle herds grew, the edges of different territories were constantly under pressure. Equally, if a patriclan got too big, it could split. This can be seen at the time of the early Dutch records of the 1650s when the Cochoqua chieftainship was splitting into two groups under Oedesawa and Gonnema. One gets the impression that this was an amicable arrangement, as there appears to have been no fighting between the two groups.

Individual kraals (villages) were made up of related men with their wives chosen exogamously (from outside the kraal), and possibly a few dependents or clients of lower status. The camp population might be more than 100. The composition of the kraals was flexible, as they were constantly on the move. In addition, people could visit relatives in other camps whenever they wanted. This was made easier by the portability of mat hut structures (matjieshuise), which were dismantled and carried on the backs of oxen.

Outsiders were not necessarily excluded from a territory but had to make the appropriate gestures or gifts to the chief for permission to enter a specific territory. This would have been an important consideration where rainfall conditions might have varied from year to year. Thus, if the rains were inadequate in one area, stock could be moved to another (to be reciprocated at some future date). Land was not the property of individuals. In fact, the only individually owned "property" was livestock. All other goods were moved around communally, with people taking what they needed. It was this cavalier attitude to moveable property that the early European travelers did not understand when they accused the Khoikhoi of being thieves. But taking things was not done clandestinely as seen by Sir James Lancaster who wrote in 1601, "They will picke and steale, although you looke on them." In addition, although domestic stock was considered private property, the products of the animals, particularly milk, were communally distributed.

Both sons and daughters could inherit livestock, but that was not the only way the younger generation obtained stock. Animals for individual children were set aside by their father, and even though the animals remained part of the father's herd during his life, they would be transferred on his death to his children.

Sheep were the ritual animals of the Khoikhoi. They were slaughtered for various occasions such as childbirth, puberty, marriages, and funerals. A person, during these transitional periods, was considered !nau, or in a period of danger, which required necessary purification for both the individuals and the group as a whole.

The Social Landscape of Agro-pastoralists

Agro-pastoralists, almost by definition, combine both plant and animal production. If Huffman is correct, and the central cattle kraal existed among the first Iron Age immigrants to southern Africa, then full-fledged agro-pastoralist society entered the subcontinent almost 2,000 years ago. The implications of this are that there was a formative hierarchical society that could easily be structured on a chieftainship basis once the land had been colonized. To the aboriginal hunters already in the landscape, the arrival of food producers would not have initially been a threat. Once the game began to be depleted, the hunters viewed domestic stock as easy game, and the agro-pastoralists viewed them as a threat. However, amicable relations were often set up between hunters and farmers, as seen in the more recent past when the hunters performed services, such as rainmaking. Equally, wives were taken by the polygynous farmers from hunting groups, although this was a one-way exchange, since hunters were not normally able to pay the bride wealth needed to take wives from the farming community. This is called hypergyny or one-way gene flow.

The central cattle pattern meant that the social life of the agro-pastoralists revolved around the cattle enclosure. People might be buried there, and the ancestral graves provided an identifying mark of tenure to the place. Fields for growing sorghum or millet would be in the surrounding area, while cattle were taken out from the central homestead each day.

Once population density reached levels that made access to pasture for the livestock difficult, young men would take the animals away from the homestead to cattle camps. This might mean they were out of touch with their families for days, if not weeks. Such conditions prevailed in larger communities that were becoming villages, with increased centralization of authority.

By the Late Iron Age after A.D. 1000, the social and economic conditions that led to state formation were in place. At Bambandyanalo, in the northern part of the former Transvaal province, large vitrified dung heaps indicate huge cattle kraals. This is immediately followed in the 12th century at nearby Mapungubwe with separation of upper and lower classes, the former living on top of the hill. Such centralization of power ultimately led to the development of the Zimbabwe state in the 13th century, with its power base at Great Zimbabwe, which by the 14th century had a population estimated at 18,000 people.

Contemporaneous descriptions of the BaTlhaping capital, Lattakoe, by William Burchell in 1812 provide some idea of life in a large town with a population estimated at around 16,000:

> In our way we passed through many clusters of houses. . . . Each of these clusters might generally be considered as a village of a different kiwi or chieftains and inhabited for the greater parts by his relations and connections . . . as I passed through . . . the inhabitants ran out to view me. The greater number were women and girls; the men being abroad in the plains, either hunting or attending their cattle.

Cattle were symbols of the power base. Only with cattle could a young man get married, and cattle were crucial in any ritual activities, since they were the link between the living and the ancestral spirits. So important were these animals that among the Zulu there are more than 100 names describing the different characteristics of cattle, such as coat color or horn shape. The Zulu believe that any cattle killed come to life once more as property of the ancestors.

Domestic animals have been central to the lifestyle of most of the traditional societies of southern Africa. The exception might be the aboriginal hunting population, but as we have seen above, they were often intimately involved with stock as well, either as stock thieves or as clients for stock owners. The large herds of cattle belonging to the Khoikhoi at the Cape were the main attraction for the Dutch to set up their refreshment station at Table Bay in the 17th century for the ships plying the East Indian trade—a station that ultimately became the Cape Colony.

BIBLIOGRAPHY

Elphick, R. 1985. *Khoikhoi and the founding of white South Africa.* Johannesburg: Roman Press.

Hall, M. 1990. *The changing past: Farmers, kings and traders in southern African 200–1860.* Cape Town: David Philip.

Huffman, T. N. 1990. Broederstroom and the origins of cattle-keeping in southern Africa. *African Studies* 49: 1–12.

Kinahan, J. 1991. *Pastoral nomads of the central Namib Desert.* Windhoek: New Namibia Books.

Smith, A. 1990. On becoming herders: Khoikhoi and San ethnicity in southern Africa. *African Studies* 49: 51–73.

———. 1992. *Pastoralism in Africa: Origins and development ecology.* London: Hurst and Athens.

———. 1995. *Einiqualand: Studies of the Orange River frontier.* Cape Town: University of Cape Town Press.

Wilmsen, E. N. 1989. *Land filled with flies: A political economy of the Kalahari.* Chicago: Chicago University Press.

Andrew B. Smith

Farming Lifeways

FARMING SOCIETIES IN SUB-SAHARAN AFRICA

Cultural and Social Units

Segmentary farming societies did not form distinctly bounded ethnic and cultural units such as implied by the notion of *tribes*. The tribal unit is to a great extent a creation of colonialism and the nation-states of the 20th century. Instead, we should view communities as forming and dissolving in cultural and economic regions where groups of people organized themselves in the hundreds or thousands without centralized political institutions. Precolonial political organization was dynamic and fluid, and leadership was ephemeral. Chiefdoms often emerged only to collapse again.

Independent communities in large regions shared cultural characteristics such as language, house types, rituals, political structure, and marriage forms, without recognizing any common organization. Culturally related groups could also have different political systems, as did the patrilineal Asu, or Pare, in the South Pare Hills in Tanzania. The eastern side of the mountain was organized into several petty chiefdoms, while the western side consisted of acephalous communities (communities lacking a governing head or chief). Aspects of culture and social organization combined in a multitude of ways. On one hand, people who shared similar political and kinship organization may have spoken different languages and may have had different religious ideas. On the other hand, people sharing a common language and culture may have exhibited differences in kinship and descent systems as among the Bantu-speaking peoples of the Kenyan coastal hinterland.

Political Organization

An important environmental factor that affected social processes in acephalous as well as hierarchical societies in Africa was the relative abundance of land for cultivation and grazing. Population densities were generally low and labor was scarce, which meant that much political maneuvering and economic activities were based on attracting people to local groups.

People organized themselves into communities of varying sizes for daily cooperation and peaceful interaction without recourse to specialized political institutions. Such communities shared common principles and mechanisms for conflict resolution, and the degree to which they cooperated with other like communities depended on distance and the character of extralocal ties. Local order was achieved through a variety of mechanisms. Elders' and eldresses' councils, consisting of senior members of families in the community, mediated disputes and formulated policies for local affairs. Such bodies could be based on a variety of principles such as descent groups, locality, age sets, and secret societies. Policy formulations and dispute settlements were backed up by popular opinion. However, enforcement of decisions in disputes was left to the winning party. While local governing bodies had no ability to apply force, the elders' ultimate weapon was supernatural: they could curse serious offenders.

The norms regulating kinship, age, and gender relationships and the female and male elders' control over resources provided some political cohesion and stability of social forms. However, such stability must be seen as a precarious process in which new resources and circumstances could lead to change. Norms were both constraining and enabling. The same social structure could give rise to more than one form of organization. For example, among the Beti of Cameroon, the same segmentary patrilineal ideology gave rise to different social groups in different regions. Near the coast, vigorous regional and long-distance trade made it possible for individual men to accumulate large amounts of prestige goods for bride-wealth payments. The result was the development of polygynous extended families and patron-client ties. Inland, at the border between the rain forest and the savanna where trade was restricted and polygyny limited, villages consisted of male-lineage mates, their wives, and dependents.

The basic building block of segmentary societies in Africa was the family household, which was part of larger networks of sociopolitical relationships. The most common form of local social organization was the corporate descent group, or lineage, which jointly controlled resources and acted as a unit vis-à-vis other like groups. The majority of the descent group's members lived in contiguous settlements, cooperated in defense and work, recognized the authority of local elders, and participated in common rituals such as ancestral sacrifice. However, the integrity of this group also depended on the principles of recruitment. In patrilineally organized groups, female members were dispersed, leaving a core of males. In matrilineal groups, there was probably a tendency for older men to reside with their sisters on lineage land. Membership was based on descent from a common ancestor or ancestress, usually three to four generations beyond the oldest living members. It is important to note that kinship was a cultural construct not directly based on biological relationships. Indeed, elders and eldresses routinely interpreted and rearranged genealogies to fit current social arrangements.

While 20th-century ethnography often describes corporate groups as unilinear, there was spatial and temporal variation in the degree of linearity. This is especially true for some societies in West Africa where descent groups regularly recruited members through both women and men. Lineages, in turn, were grouped into larger units, which, for reasons of simplicity, we can call *clans*. These groups did usually not act as political or property-holding units. Clan members lived dispersed in different areas, observed exogamy (marriage outside the clan) rules, and, in several societies, gathered for ritual occasions.

As communities grew in size, endemic tensions came to the fore. At the ideological level, their members ultimately held equal rights to the wealth and benefits of the corporation. At the same time, corporations were hierarchically structured according gender, age, and kinship status. Conflicts between young and old, witchcraft accusations, and conflicting aspirations to status positions led to spatial withdrawal and group fission.

Among the Central Ibo and the Tiv in western Africa and, to some extent, the Gusii and Luo of eastern Africa, the lineage idiom provided the dominant principle of social organization. However, in most instances, other principles of social organization operated alongside the lineages. Among many acephalous societies, to varying degrees, age-grade organizations (groups of individuals of like age who establish relationships of mutual obligation or responsibility), locality, secret societies, and wealthy families also provided the bases for corporate groups, political action, and economic cooperation.

Locality

In western Africa, inhabitants of locality-based settlements defined their solidarity in terms of coresidence in an area. Among these people, "original" settlers or "owners of the land" were distinguished from latecomers. "Owners of the land" did not have property rights in land as present in feudal or capitalist societies. Their "ownership" was a mystical link to the land, a connection that gave them special status, reinforced by prevailing ideas about spiritual essence of the earth. The earth-cult priest was an authority figure who represented the group against others and presided to some extent over internal affairs of all the lineages, not just the landowning group. In eastern Africa, a similar distinction was also found among the matrilineal societies of eastern Tanzania. Members of the numerically superior matrilineage in one area were acknowledge as owners of the land and had the authority to allocate land and house sites for all the residents. They also had supernatural links with their ancestresses buried on the land and were responsible for arranging ceremonies for cleansing the land and fertility.

Leadership

Informal, individual leadership based on wealth and political ability occurred in many societies. The majority of such leaders seems to have been men, but there were "big women" as well, especially in matrilineal societies. The local political influence of such people was based on wealth and ability. Political power was achieved through the control over a large family household. "Big men" had many wives and sons, while "big women" controlled daughters, sons, sons-in-law, and daughters-in-law. Such large families also attracted poorer people as clients who contributed to the productive and defensive capabilities of the group. The larger the family, the more wealth it could generate and the more political power the leader wielded, which in turn tended to increase the group's wealth. Such centers of political influence sometimes changed into more permanent organizations with chiefly offices. However, this process is poorly understood. In the archaeological record, it would be difficult to distinguish an acephalous population with achieved leadership from a petty chiefdom.

Descent and Kinship

Descent groups were organized according to different principles of recruitment. The most common rules of affiliation were patrilineal and matrilineal. Cognatic descent groups, recognizing membership both through women and men, seem to have been more prevalent in western than in eastern Africa. Societies operating with double descent, in which both matrilineal and patrilineal descent groups were recognized, were rare.

According to Jack Goody, matrilineal descent systems are found in about 15 percent of societies in present-day Africa, and most are located in the so-called matrilineal belt stretching from eastern Tanzania across the continent to Angola and southern Zaire, and parts of West Africa. Researchers have pointed out that matrilineality is especially prevalent in areas where cattle are scarce. The matrilineal belt overlaps the distribution of tsetse flies, which carry bovine sleeping sickness.

Matrilineal descent groups were reproduced through female links. Men were assigned a secondary role in procreation, and it was only through women that substance, usually expressed as "blood," was transmitted from generation to generation through a line of women to their male and female offspring. Hence, the growth of matrilines (familial allegiances defined through the maternal line) is independent of marriage, and women, not men, controlled the regeneration of the group. In eastern and central Africa, women formed the residential core of the lineage. Men usually lived at their wives' homesteads. Divorce was common, and men strove to return to their natal lineage where they held land. Stable residence on lineage land and control over fertility and human reproduction gave women power and authority in political matters and independent access to economic resources.

During the 20th century, the majority of societies, about 74 percent, have tended toward patrilineality. Membership in social groups was defined according to descent through men only from a common male ancestor. Such systems were found in all ecological zones and economic conditions. There was great variation in the internal structure and the degree to which women were integrated into their husbands' lineages. Women were at a political disadvantage since they were separated from their own kin, were strangers in their husbands' groups, and did not share equal access to lineage resources. They were removed from their natal groups and thus could not exercise full rights in the resources of their own families either.

Marriage Transactions

The establishment and maintenance of socially recognized conjugal unions was accompanied by transfers of wealth or labor from the bridegroom's family and kin group to bride's family and kin group. Such transactions usually took the form of bride wealth, which, during the 20th century, was found in about 82 percent of all societies in sub-Saharan Africa. Cross-culturally, substantial bride wealth is associated with levirate, virilocal marriages (that is, marriages in which the wife's sister becomes part of the household, which is located in the village of the husband). Bride wealth is also related to important patrilines (groups that trace descent through the male line) and the absence of bride service. Low bride wealth and bride service are associated with unstable marriages, high divorce rates, and matriliny. Lineages define one's social and economic locus in society and can be achieved through a culturally acknowledged line or family—whether male or female varies from group to group.

The difference in the value of such payments can be seen in a comparison between the Gusii of Kenya and the Ngulu of Tanzania. The patrilineal Gusii paid up to 18 cows in the 1880s, while the matrilineal Ngulu paid three goats, eight fowls, and metal wire. In patrilineal societies, high bride wealth was primarily a means to obtain rights to a woman's reproductive powers for the husband and his lineage. Bride wealth and bride service also established obligations: a husband must build a house and clear land for his wife, while a wife must cook, brew beer, and care for the children.

Marriage transactions are central to the understanding of the dynamics of precolonial acephalous societies. Bride wealth was the main instrument for building social groups and for establishing relationships of authority over people, for example, junior wives, children, and young men who were dependent on their seniors for access to wealth. Cross-culturally, the assembly and transfer of wealth items involved, to varying degrees, a number of kinfolk and affines (people related by marriage) on the bride's and the groom's sides. Hence, the reception and transfer of bride wealth maintained and defined social relationships outside the immediate families of the spouses.

Throughout the patrilineal regions, the amount of wealth involved was substantial, and political economy was concerned with controlling and obtaining the prestige goods used for marriage payments. The kinds of items that were used varied: livestock, slaves, seashells, and metal objects, especially hoes. Bride service was common in matrilineal societies and was a means to attract the labor of men to local descent groups while not giving up wealth or women. Hence, a woman's husband had to work for her and her family for a number of years to complete the marriage. Sometimes several forms of marriage transactions existed in the same society. Among the Duruma of Kenya, it was possible to choose between a valuable cattle bride wealth, which ensured the affiliation of children to the husband's lineage, and a cheaper cash transfer, which only established marriage and rights of sexual intercourse between the spouses.

Sodalities

Sodalities, prominent in many African cultures, are voluntary associations. The society is organized upon the three legs of a tripod of lineage (association by birth), kinship (association through marriage), and sodalities (association of people not related through birth or kinship). The tripod is the foundation of vital social networks. In probably all African societies, age was an important organizing principle, and advancing age entailed greater personal autonomy and authority over other people. The transition from one social age to another was accompanied by more-or-less elaborate rituals. Age was a major factor in the allocation of roles within the groups pertaining to political authority, production, and consumption. Age grading could be very simple. Among the Gusii of Kenya, every individual passed through different life-course stages from birth to death—child, to young woman or young man, to married woman or married man, to male elder or female elder. However, these grades did not assign any common activity or responsibility to a group of contemporaries. In other cases, all children initiated at a certain time into adulthood con-stituted a named group, which could maintain solidarity and undertake political action. Such a group advanced as a cohort through age grades until reaching elderhood. These grades could be the main vehicles of government overshadowing kinship ties. Although ethnographers have usu-ally focused on men's formal age grades and age sets, ethnohistorical sources reveal that, in many societies, women were also organized into parallel-age organizations.

Another common form of sodality was the secret society, which crosscut lineages and localities and could wield substantial political powers. Men and women had separate societies, guarding ritual knowledge and powerful medi-cines. Access to secret knowledge and organiza-tional capacity made such societies socially influential. These were abundant in West Africa, but isolated examples can also be found in East Africa. Varying in their organization and sociopolitical roles, the societies often entailed initiations into different grades accompanied by payments.

Settlement Pattern

The distribution of people and habitations over the landscape was the outcome of many fac-tors such as defense considerations, different types of land use, exchange objectives, and po-litical and ritual activity. The homes of farmers were usually multifamily homesteads or com-pounds consisting of a cluster of huts or houses. These could be dispersed or located in villages. In western Africa, many people lived in large villages, which were once stockaded and forti-fied, often in a most elaborate and spectacular manner. Compact fortified villages existed also in eastern Africa but were less common, smaller, and clearly related to defense considerations. The size of such villages varied: on the eastern slopes of Mount Kenya, a settlement might contain 500 people, while on the savanna of eastern Tanza-nia, a settlement might contain 100 to 250 people.

In eastern Africa, the fertile highland areas were often densely populated with farmsteads distributed along hillsides at regular distances. Population densities could reach 320 to 480

people per square kilometer in the Gusii High-lands of western Kenya. In such cases, agri-cultural activities and cattle raising forced a division of activities and residence into farming areas with homesteads and grazing areas with cattle camps. Political and economic conditions contributed to differences in settlement forms in restricted regions. Hence, among the Gusii, dis-persed homesteads were found where neighbors maintained peaceful relationships, while forti-fied, multifamily settlements dominated where warfare and raiding were common.

Although political and economic factors may have strongly affected the general dispersal of a population, the particular arrangements of buildings and internal architecture often mirrored social relationships and cultural categories. For example, the outlines of the settlements and ar-chitecture of Bantu-speaking people in eastern and southern Africa were based on common cos-mological and social features.

Production Systems

Cultivation and livestock husbandry, the main production activities, were supplemented by a large variety of crafts and small-scale industries. Iron smelting and blacksmithing were ubiquitous in most areas. Basketry, pottery, medicines, mats, woodcrafts, paints, and salt are examples of other manufactures. West Africa developed the most complex forms of production activities, includ-ing mask makers, wood-carvers, dyers, weavers, and brass casters.

Although the following description is based on 19th-century eastern Africa, many aspects are representative of the social organization of pro-duction in other regions as well. The main spe-cialization in this region was based on a division of labor according to gender and age within the family household as well as in communal labor. Homestead maintenance, cultivation, food pro-cessing, and local marketing were the main responsibilities of women. Men took care of building houses, clearing fields, raising stock, hunting, and long-distance trading in things other than foodstuff. In general terms, the division of labor was not strict, and there were variation and overlap in the concerns of either gender. Among the Nyakyusa of southwestern Tanzania, hoeing and land preparation were men's work, and women were assisted by men in sowing, weeding, and harvesting. Ironworking was usually considered men's work but not always. For example, in Pare, the gathering and smelting of iron ore was also done by women, while only men were blacksmiths. Pots were usually made by women, while wickerwork was done by both genders.

The basic unit of production and consumption was a matrifocal group (a household in which the means of production is maintained within the wife's family holdings) composed of a woman and her unmarried children. To this unit, a man was attached as a whole (monogamous) or partial (polygynous) spouse. While cultivation rights to fields were clearly demarcated according to matrifocal households, cattle were pastured on common grazing grounds controlled by a neighborhood or a descent group. Each woman and her children, consuming or exchanging much of their own products, provided the basic labor force in cultivation. This was the case whether they resided with a woman's own kinship group or gained access to land only through their husbands.

Households related through kinship or marriage cooperated in daily activities, while larger groups such as neighborhoods would mobilize cooperative labor for harvesting and planting. In grain-producing areas, communal work was undertaken mainly in house building and labor-intensive stages of cultivation such as clearing, weeding, harvesting, and threshing.

The degree to which people could control their own labor and products varied according to age, gender, and family structure. Children, young men, and young women had to give up some products to seniors and local political and ritual leaders. Adults maintained a great degree of independence and control over the fruits of their own labor. The degree of economic coordination and the exploitation of family labor by senior members also depended on authority structures. For example, families organized according to the so-called house-property complex in eastern and southern Africa varied with respect to the relative control over livestock and crops by husbands and wives.

The productivity of families or households also varied over time and according to demographic, economic, political, and environmental circumstances. Successful families grew through marriages and births in a developmental cycle beginning with a married couple or a set of siblings, which ideally grew into an extended family under the leadership of a patriarch or matriarch. While exploitation within the family was largely restricted to junior members, there were other mechanisms to enlarge the household labor force as well. It was common to attach clients whose labor could benefit the host family. Such clients were usually men who for some reason had been alienated from their own kin group or had become indebted to a patron.

Exchange and Trade

Sub-Saharan Africa was characterized by a dense web of trade and exchange of goods. Local exchange was connected to regional and extra-regional networks finally linking the continent to Asia and Europe. Although capable of producing the bulk of their own subsistence needs, acephalous farming societies were not isolated self-sufficient communities. Most households routinely planned their production of foodstuffs and crafts for at least some amount of trade. Exchange of products was especially intense at the borders of ecological zones. Variations in natural resources did not have to be profound for local trade to develop. In addition, the presence of raw materials, such as accessible iron ore and clay, created needs for exchange. However, natural differences do not by themselves account for the nature of specialization and exchange. Knowledge of superior production techniques, differences in economic institutions, and relative costs of production in time and effort also affected the patterns of local exchange.

The western part of the continent was the most urbanized and exhibited higher levels of commercial activity than the rest of Africa. One notable exception was coastal East Africa and its immediate hinterland. The coastal urban settlements had permanent markets, and in the hinterlands, regular periodic markets met in such regions as the plains and highlands of northeastern Tanzania and the Kenyan coastal hinterlands of Mombasa and Malindi.

In eastern Africa, the paucity of marketplaces did not exclude a lively traffic in goods and services in other areas. Nonmarket trade and exchange in eastern Africa took the form of "relay trade" where goods moved from hand to hand over short and long distances. There was active trade in livestock and grain in northern Uganda, Kenya, and Tanzania between populations who occupied different ecological niches and specialized to different degrees in crops and livestock production. These regional networks dealt in goods such as iron, pots, and salt. Exchanges were not only utilitarian but also involved prestige goods in the form of cattle, cloth, and metals, thereby linking local production to the wider political economy. Finally, local and regional exchange systems were tied to the international economy through imported goods from Europe and Asia such as cloth, cowrie shells, glass beads, and copper and brass items. In turn, the African economies produced gold, ivory, rock, crystal, and slaves for export.

African economies employed a number of goods in moneylike functions. However, most items used as media of exchange also doubled as prestige goods for social payments and as consumables. Among the various media of exchange were iron, salt, beads, cowrie shells, brass rods, cloth, raffia-palm cloth, gin, gold dust, cattle, goats, sheep, brass bracelets, copper rods, muskets, powder, shot, and slaves. Some of these goods became conventionalized (that is, they attained an established, accepted value), so that in parts of Africa nonfunctional iron hoes, knives, and spear points were manufactured specifically for exchange purposes.

Religion

The supernatural was not compartmentalized from everyday life but was an aspect of all social activities. A sacred aura imbued all African authority. Female and male elders, village heads, chiefs, and kings were all, in some sense, ritual experts or "priests" bound to the group they headed. It was their responsibility to interact with the supernatural for the welfare of the group.

Ancestral cults were central to religious life in most areas. The forebears represented legiti-

mate authority and moral order and might afflict the living if they did not uphold social rules and ritual observances. Male and female elders sometimes performed sacrifices at regular ancestral shrines, burial places, and other locations not associated with actual burials. Among the Tallensi of Ghana, sacrifice in the form of animal blood and beer was offered to the collective ancestors of the segment of the lineage in question. Shrines were associated with some physical feature such as a cone of mud by the grave of the founding ancestor of the Tallensi patriline. Among the many Mijikenda peoples in East Africa, there were several types of ancestral shrines, including wooden markers denoting both male and female ancestors and pots exclusively for the ancestresses.

West African peoples also worshiped a variety of gods, goddesses, and other supernatural agencies. The Idoma of Nigeria propitiated an impersonal god at district shrines. The Ibo believed that God sent rain, controlled fertility, and was the source of the soul. However, offerings were made to lesser gods and goddesses, especially the earth spirit. There was a shrine for her in all villages serviced by special priests.

Cosmologies of Bantu-speaking people included a belief in a high god who usually did not intervene in human affairs. However, in Nilotic religions, God was a formless wind or spirit who took a direct interest in human affairs.

In addition to these aspects of beliefs in the supernatural, there was a plethora of nature spirits, witchcraft, sorcery, mystical forces, and afflictions. Misfortune and afflictions were often seen as the result of the machinations of another person who, through witchcraft and sorcery, attempted to increase his or her vital force at the expense of the victim.

BIBLIOGRAPHY

Baumann, H., ed. 1975 and 1979. *Die volker Afrikas und ihre tradilionellen kulturen: Studien zur kulturkunde.* 2 vols. Wiesbaden: H. Baumann.

Murdock, G. P. 1959. *Africa: Its people and culture history.* New York: McGraw-Hill.

Schneider, H. K. 1981. *The Africans.* Englewood Cliffs: Prentice-Hall.

N. Thomas Hakansson

FARMING METHODS

The native peoples of northern Africa have traditionally looked upon the Sahara as a vast sand sea with the Mediterranean littoral (coast) as the northern shore and the Sahel as the southern. The true desert is exploited only by livestock-herding peoples following the rare or occasional rains. Around the fringes of the desert, rains are heavier and more regular, and desert vegetation is grazed every year in season. Desert forage is of high quality. Animals that graze in the desert gain weight and, when there is enough vegetation, may get fat. When this resource is exhausted, the herders retreat with their flocks to the tall-grass savanna. By this time, the tall grasses have matured and become hard and woody. The animals may lose more weight than they gained on desert range even when the volume of forage is ample. The migration of herds in and out of the desert is a yearly cycle and a part of sub-Saharan agriculture.

There is a considerable interaction between nomads and sedentary farming folk. The herding people milk their animals and prepare various kinds of virtually imperishable dairy products. These are welcomed by the farmers, who find it almost impossible to raise livestock in their villages. A year-long diet of the local tall grass will not sustain a domestic animal. A trip to the desert during the rains or supplemental feed is required. The farmers raise grains and cowpeas, among other crops, but these must be conserved for the people. Sometimes a villager will make a deal with a nomad and entrust one or more, but seldom very many, animals to his care to be slaughtered or sold when the herder comes back on his rounds.

The agriculture of northern Africa is basically the same as that of the Near East with few modifications. Oxen and occasionally donkeys or camels are used for traction, working the land for sowing, trampling out the harvest for thrashing, and transportation. The cereals, mostly wheat and barley, are harvested by sickle and scythe, lentils and chickpeas by uprooting, and sesame by cutting and shocking until the capsules open. This system extends into enclaves south of the Sahara. It is characteristic of the Ethiopian Plateau and limited areas of West Africa and near Lake Chad. Otherwise, indigenous agriculture in sub-Saharan Africa is characterized by the use of a digging stick, hoe, and human labor.

Soil Preparation and Planting

In parts of Cameroon and Chad, a minimum-tillage system is used in which seeds of sorghum, millet, or cowpeas are scattered among the grasses and weeds produced during the rainy season and then hoed-in to kill the vegetation and plant the seed in one operation. More generally, farmers clear the land with hoes after the rains. Using a short-handled scoop hoe, farmers then plant the annual crops. They make a shallow depression by taking out a small scoop of soil, drop a few seeds into the depression, and step on the seeds as they move on to make the next scoop. The work progresses rather rapidly and rhythmically and results in stands that are more or less in rows.

Farmers often take advantage of swales that may stand in water during the rains by burning off the vegetation as soon as it is dry enough and transplanting well-developed seedlings of sorghum or millet into holes made by a large dibble stick, perhaps 1.5 meters in length. The dibble is rammed into the moist claylike soil with considerable force, and the holes made for sorghum may be up to 30 centimeters deep. Farmers pour a little water into each hole from a gourd before inserting the seedlings, which were grown in sandy beds for transplanting. The seedlings must grow and mature on residual moisture since there will be no more rains that growing season. The deeper the holes the better. Mixed crops are common. Cowpeas are often grown under sorghum, millet, sesame, or cotton.

In the wetter zones, drainage, aeration, and fertility pose serious problems to which farmers respond with techniques of mounding, ridging, and using raised beds. Ridges are often formed by taking a scoop of soil from each side of a row and placing them in the center between. This results in three layers of topsoil in the ridge and provides both drainage and aeration. The ridge is then planted with an annual crop. Yams (*Dioscorea*) are usually planted in mounds or ridges, and sweet potatoes in raised beds. The mounds may be 1 meter in height but are usually less. Again, drainage and aeration are the primary objectives, but the piling of topsoil may also improve fertility.

Agricultural regimens in the forest zone always involve some kind of "slashing and burning" or bush fallowing. Farmers in this region chop down the woody vegetation toward the end of the rains and, when it is dry enough, set it on fire. The objective is to produce a hot white-ash burn. The land is, thereby, cleared for planting, weed seeds on or near the surface are killed, and the soil's fertility is improved by the addition of ash. In parts of East Africa, a system called *chitemene* is followed in which additional woody vegetation is cut from a nearby tract and hauled to the field to be planted. This is very laborious, but the added tinder produces a hotter fire and more ash. The heat may have some mineral benefits as well.

Some kind of bush fallowing is practiced in the wet tropics around the world. The systems in Africa are not much different from those in Asia, the South Pacific, and tropical America. After a parcel of land is cleared by slashing and burning, it will support crops for only two to three years and sometimes only one. The scant fertility added by the ash is soon exhausted, weed problems increase, yields decline, and the parcel is abandoned to the regrowth of woody vegetation. Another field is prepared by cutting and burning. Fresh fields are cleared annually, and the abandoned ones are allowed to revert to bush as a sort of fallowing in a rotation. The duration of the bush phase is critical. In the wet tropics of heavy forest, a period of some 15 to 20 years is usually needed to maintain productivity. This requires a great deal of "idle" land, and as human populations increase, the length of the bush-fallowing phase is reduced. Most cultivators are well aware of the value of the bush phase of the rotation. In cases of short rotation, the woody plants are often deliberately cut high in order to get a fast regrowth. In Africa, most of the bush-fallowing regions are overused, and the duration of the bush fallowing is dangerously short. Even a casual study of Food and Agricultural Organization production data shows that per-caput productivity in sub-Saharan Africa is steadily decreasing and is not likely to rise.

Harvesting and Threshing

At harvest time, the first thing a sorghum or millet farmer does is to go though his fields and carefully select single panicles or candles (flower clusters) to supply seed for next year's planting. The farmer dries them and often stores them in the house by hanging them from the *tukel* roof over the kitchen area where smoke from the cooking fires helps reduce insect problems. This attention to planting stock results in very strong human-selection pressure on the plant material. Nothing contributes to the next generation unless it is selected by the farmer. Of course, different farmers have different ideas in mind, and an array of rather well-defined cultivars develop adapted to the region of selection.

After stock seed is selected, the fields are harvested. Individual panicles of sorghum or candles of millet are cut off with knives and piled to be threshed later. In Ethiopia, especially, the stacking of sorghum panicles is almost an art form. A bed of stover (cured stalks of grain) is provided to keep the grain off the soil where it might absorb moisture and mold. Red and white panicles from the same field may be arranged to make decorative patterns. These are, of course, destroyed at threshing time but seem to provide some satisfaction to the farmer for a brief period. There may also be some religious significance to the practice. Millet candles may be stacked between stakes like cordwood. In general, seed keeps better in the unthreshed condition than after it is removed from the inflorescences (flower clusters). Farmers often store unthreshed material even though it takes up much more space than clean grain. A supply is taken out each day to be processed for cooking. Alternatively, the harvest may be threshed out and stored as grain.

Threshing is often a community or village activity. The harvest of several households is combined and processed, usually by flailing. Gangs of men converge on a pile of harvested material and beat it with sticks, usually accompanied by song and drums. Threshing is a social event with singing, dancing, drinking, and general revelry. It is a time to celebrate. In the enclaves where cattle are kept, threshing may be done by trampling, but beating with a stick is the most common procedure in sub-Saharan Africa. Rice, millet, sorghum, cowpeas, and even peanuts are flailed.

After flailing, grain and chaff are separated by winnowing, sometimes aided by screening. In Ethiopia, screens are made of grasses—the mesh woven of a very tough species of eleusine (a goosefoot), the collar woven of pennisetum and straw and edged with leather. The screens are very handsome pieces and are collectible as folk art. Elsewhere, screens are usually made of metal and imported from abroad and sold in the markets.

Granaries take on a great variety of forms from pits in the ground to elevated platforms. The platforms may be some 2 meters high, and the supporting posts are often equipped with collars to keep rats from climbing up to the grain supply. The pits may or may not be plastered. Some granaries are huge ceramic pots, large enough for a man to crawl into. The most common granaries, however, are woven, basketlike containers. Some of these are very handsome pieces, usually on short legs to prevent contact with the soil. Each tribe seems to have its own style. Granaries of the Dogon tribe of Mali are built of stone and plaster or wattle (woven sticks and twigs) and plaster and are noted for their artistically carved wooden doors and wooden locks.

Grain is processed for food by both grinding and pounding in a mortar. In some villages near a rock outcrop, bedrock is used for the lower stone. The women of the village take their grain (and young children) to the rock and, using suitable hand stones, grind against the bedrock. The stationary stone soon becomes pockmarked. More often, the lower stone is kept in the house and grinding is done at home. The woman, often with a baby on her back, does the grinding on her knees. In Muslim villages, where a man is permitted four wives, a workbench is erected with four sleepers (timbers or stones used to support the superstructure or receive floor posts) affixed to it. The women can work together standing up.

Throughout sub-Saharan Africa, the most common sound in the villages morning and evening is the steady plunk-plunk-plunk of pestles pounding grain in mortars, made from hollowed logs or stones. The women and children are the pounders, and usually, more than one person is engaged in the work at one time. The orifice of a tall mortar may be rather small, 30 centimeters or so, and the pestle fairly long, perhaps 1.5 meters or more, but it is common for two or three people to pound at the same time.

Agriculture based on human labor may require an enormous effort at certain times of the year. There are periods when the energy output is greater than the intake, and people are literally working themselves to death. Fortunately, these periods are relatively short, and the toilers of the fields can recover. As populations increase, however, they become more vulnerable. Today, the threat of famine in parts of sub-Saharan Africa is very real and constant. In earlier times with smaller populations, the production system was reasonably adequate both in yield and in storage capacity to carry people through lean times. At the subsistence level, the systems work most of the time but may not generate much surplus.

A strong belief in witchcraft and arcane powers is widespread and tends to influence agricultural practices. This is especially true of the raising of yams and rice. Devices of several sorts, ranging from figurines to mystical symbols, are placed in the fields to guard against witches. If a man in a village gets a good yield and another man gets a poor yield, it is a general consensus that the man with the good yield has "witched" the man with the poor yield, or he has hired a witch to transfer the produce. Variety selection, fertilizers, field rotation, or other practices are considered irrelevant, and yields are in the domain of the occult.

BIBLIOGRAPHY

Allan, W. 1965. *The African husbandman.* London: Oliver and Boyd.

Hall, M. L. 1984. Man's historical and traditional use of fire in southern Africa. In *Ecological effects of fire in South African ecosystems,* eds. P. de V. Booysen and N. M. Tainton, 39–52. Berlin: Springer Verlag.

Harlan, J. R., J. M. J. De Wet, and A. Stemler. 1976. *Origins of African plant domestication.* The Hague: Mouton.

Harris, D. R. 1972. Swidden systems and settlements. In *Settlement and urbanism,* eds. P. J. Ucko, R. Tringham, and G. W. Dimbleby, 245–262. London: Duckworth.

Moran, E. F. 1979. An introduction to African agriculture. *Studies in Third World Societies* 8: 1–14.

Sutton, J. E. G. 1989. History of African agricultural technology and field systems. *Azania* 24: 1–122.

Vogel, J. O. 1986. Subsistence settlements in the prehistory of southwestern Zambia. *Human Ecology* 14: 397–414.

Jack R. Harlan

FOOD CROPS

The most important food crops of sub-Saharan Africa are sorghum, pearl millet, African rice, cowpeas, and yams. Others that are more restricted in use or distribution but are important locally are fonio, black fonio, Guinea millet, Bambara groundnuts, okra, watermelons, yampeas, jute, and oil palm. Crops of the highlands in East Africa include teff, noog, finger millet, and ensete. Other crops are of much less importance to the region.

SORGHUM. On the world scene, sorghum is the most important crop of sub-Saharan African origin. It is said to support some 500 million people worldwide, mostly in India and Africa, although it is gaining in importance in Latin America because it is more drought-resistant than maize. Sorghum ranks fifth among cereals in world production, behind wheat, rice, maize, and barley. An important crop in the United States, nearly all of it grown there is fed to livestock, and human consumption is more or less trivial.

Most likely, the crop was domesticated somewhere in southern Sudan. There, hundreds of square kilometers are covered with massive stands of wild sorghum, and it is a dominant species of a tall-grass acacia (woody leguminous plants) savanna.

PEARL MILLET. Pearl millet is more drought-resistant than sorghum and can be grown around the edges of deserts of warm climates at the dry limits of agriculture. Wild varieties actually penetrate the Sahara in favored locations. It is more palatable than sorghum and lacks the tannins that cause bitterness in some varieties of sorghum. On the whole, the amino-acid profile and nutritional qualities are better, and it is preferred over sorghum where it can be grown. It does not do well under high rainfall, and the pearl-millet belt of Africa is fairly well confined to the Sahel.

The evolution of pearl millet from wild varieties with inflorescences (flower clusters) 1 decimeter long or less to advanced domesticated varieties with false spikes tightly packed with grains and more than 1.5 meters in length is almost as spectacular as the evolution of maize from teosinte (a tall annual grass). It is one of the most remarkable transformations in crop evolution.

FINGER MILLET. Finger millet is a small-grained cereal derived from a weedy goose (or goosefoot) grass. It was taken from Africa to India, where it is grown in the hill country of the north and the south. It was once much used as a food, but today, it is more likely to be malted for beer.

AFRICAN RICE. African rice is a species distinct from Asian rice. The two can be crossed with difficulty and high sterility in the hybrid. The panicle (flower cluster) is more coarse and erect, and the grain is more coarse and less palatable, than those of the better-known Asian rice. The African species is currently being replaced by the Asian species in the rice-growing regions of West Africa.

A genuine rice culture developed in West Africa. For the rice-eating tribes, the crop is not only the staff of life, it is also central to ceremony and ritual. Special figurines are carved of stone and buried in the fields to protect the crop and ensure its increase. A meal without rice is not considered a real meal. For these tribes, rice assumes the same importance in the culture as it holds among some peoples of the Far East. There is a religious and spiritual aspect to the crop that goes far beyond a mere food supply.

YAM. In the United States, the word *yam* is used for the sweet potato, an indigenous American plant. This is unfortunate and causes confusion in understanding what a yam really is. The confusion evidently arose in slavery days when the West African word *nyame* was introduced, but the tuber was not, or at least, if it was introduced, it could not compete with the sweet potato, a domesticate of the American Indian. The two belong to different botanical families.

Yams are mainstays in the diets of many tribes of the forest zone. They are grown in the savanna and in Ethiopia but as an adjunct to the food supply. Among tribes who depend on yams as the major source of food, the plant is revered, and the most important annual ceremonies and festivals are centered on the growth cycle of the plant. There are celebrations at yam-planting and yam-harvesting times with much ritual cleansing and purification. The spiritual and religious concern for yams is matched by or, perhaps, exceeds the concern of rice-eating tribes for their perferred crop. It is interesting to note that along the Bandama River in Ivory Coast, people on the right bank are rice eaters, and people on the left bank are yam eaters.

Although yams are grown in the forest zone and are of primary importance to the people there, the plant is basically of savanna origin. The tuber is an adaptation permitting the plant to survive the annual drought and fires of the dry season. When the rains come, the vine grows very rapidly with the metabolites rushing up into the vine more or less emptying it of food resources. With the onset of the dry season, the process is reversed with the metabolites in the vine rushing downward to the tubers forming below.

FONIO. Fonios belong to the genus *Digitaria,* the same genus as the familiar and not always appreciated crabgrass. Black fonio is restricted to a few rather small localities, but the crop has little significance in African agriculture as a whole. The more widespread fonio has sometimes been called *hungry rice,* a name that is only occasionally appropriate. It is true that because it has a short growing season, it can be raised as a catch crop to tide people over a shortfall of a primary long-season crop (for example, sorghum, pearl millet, or rice) due to drought, disease, insect plague, or other crisis. But, perhaps more importantly, it is a chief's food, a gourmet item. Fonio makes better couscous than wheat. Its importance is somewhat like that of American wild rice. Americans and Canadians do not eat wild rice for survival purposes or because the crop is all that is available to them. Instead they eat it out

of choice. American wild rice commands gourmet prices and is a very profitable commodity.

GROUNDNUT. Bambara groundnuts are legumes that produce seeds underground somewhat like the peanut. The seeds, however, are very large, round, and usually one to a pod. In some plot trials, the plant has produced yields as large as those of peanuts and could well be developed for more wide-scale culture. To date, it is little known outside its African region of production.

COWPEA. The cowpea has had better success as a crop. It is important not only in Africa but in India, the Far East, the United States, and parts of Latin America. It is nutritious, palatable, and lacks the antimetabolites commonly found in other leguminous foods. There is considerable variation in the crop with a range of seed colors including streaked and mottled and pod shapes including the "yard-long" type. A "yard" may be something of an exaggeration, but there are varieties that approach that measure. The wild varieties seem to be small viny plants that climb up understory trees in the forest or forest margins. From these, a weedy, more aggressive vining type evolved and moved into the savanna. This variety is the probable source of the domesticated cowpea. Bush types are a relatively late development.

OKRA. Okra is a plant of the savanna and forest margins from Nigeria westward where it is also known as *ngumbo.*

JUTE. Jute is a fiber crop in Asia, but its seedlings are eaten in Africa. The seedlings are boiled to produce a stringy, slimy dish that is much appreciated by the people.

YAMPEA. The yampea is a minor crop and gets its name because it is a legume (pea) with an underground tuber (yam).

WATERMELON. Watermelons are familiar to people around the world. Wild varieties are adapted to desert margins and may grow in the desert itself in favored locations. Wild varieties can be very bitter, but the juice may make it possible for man and animals to survive in the desert, being the only source of water available in dry season.

OIL PALM. The oil palm is another savanna plant. It is grown commercially today in the forest zone, but it cannot tolerate full shade. It does thrive in the man-made derived savanna (areas of intensive slash-and-burn cultivation where natural vegetation has been so altered that woodlands are reduced to grasslands). Newly developed hybrid cultivars are very high yielding, but the center of oil production has moved to Malaysia. Africans still extract oil for their own culinary uses.

TEFF. Of the Ethiopian complex of domesticates, teff, noog, finger millet, and ensete are the most important food plants. Teff is a lovegrass *(Eragrostis)* with fine, lacy panicles and very small seeds. It is grown more extensively than any other crop in the country. The seeds are ground into flour, mixed with water, and fermented briefly to form a batter that is poured onto a large clay griddle over a fire. The product, *enjera,* resembles a very large pancake. Somewhat spongy and slightly acid because of the fermentation, it is one of the finer breads of the world.

NOOG. Noog is a yellow-flowered composite. An edible oil, extracted from the seeds, is of high quality and the most important cooking oil in the country. As with most crops, there are wild and weedy varieties as well as domesticated ones.

ENSETE. Ensete is a member of the banana genus, but the fruits are not eaten. At harvest, the plant is sacrificed, and the starchy base of the pseudostem is dug up. This is wrapped in leaves of the same plant and buried for a time to ferment. It can then be dried and processed by pounding in a mortar into flour. The flour is used as other flours, to make bread, thicken stews, coat meat, and so forth.

OTHER CROPS. In addition to food plants, there are fatigue-combating and recreational plants, such as coffee, kola, and *chat (khat),* and medicinal plants that can be dangerous if not administered correctly.

———————

Indigenous African food plants either belong to a major savanna complex or a more restricted Ethiopian one. Some, like sorghum and coffee, have had a major impact on the world. Pearl millet supports millions of people in India. Sub-Saharan Africa has made significant contributions to world agriculture and the human food supply.

BIBLIOGRAPHY
Harlan, J. R. 1993. The tropical African cereals. In *The archaeology of Africa: Food, metals and towns,* eds. T. Shaw, P. Sinclair, B. Andah, and A. Opoko, 53–60. London: Routledge.
Harlan, J. R., J. M. J. De Wet, and A. B. L. Stemler. 1976. *Origins of African plant domestication.* The Hague: Mouton.
Harlan, J. R., J. M. J. De Wet, and E. G. Price. 1973. Comparative evolution of cereals. *Evolution* 27: 311–325.
Harris, D. R., and G. C. Hillman. 1989. *Foraging and farming: The evolution of plant exploitation.* London: Unwin Hyman.

Jack R. Harlan

EASTERN AFRICAN TERRACED-IRRIGATION SYSTEMS

A number of occurrences of ancient stone terracing in eastern Africa represent past specialized agricultural systems. The most notable of these are the well-known systems at Engaruka in northern Tanzania, Inyanga in eastern Zimbabwe, and Marateng in the eastern part of the former Transvaal province, for which no published information is yet available. With these may be considered other areas where terracing is still in use or has been abandoned only relatively recently, such as Darfur and Kordofan in the Sudan, Harar in eastern Ethiopia, the Konso area in southern Ethiopia, and minor occurrences such as Elgeyo in the Kenya Rift Valley, Tepeth and Teuso in Uganda, and Pare in northeastern Tanzania. A general survey was given by A. T. Grove and John Sutton in 1989, while Thomas Hakansson in the same year reviewed the social and political aspects of intensive agriculture, including terracing, in eastern Africa.

The building of terraces is a necessary practice wherever farmers wish to cultivate fertile soil on steep slopes. The terraces serve multiple purposes beyond the simple conservation of soils from erosion. One basic function is as a place to move stones when clearing them from the surface and subsoil to provide sufficient soil depth and a suitable surface gradient for cultivation. Another function is to break the slope length, so that rainwater runoff is checked, the maximum amount of water is absorbed, and the capacity of rainwater to carry sediment is reduced. This effect is increased if the terrace wall stands above the soil surface of the upper terrace, but, even so, measures may be required to control excess storm water.

The fact that terrace construction and maintenance requires a major investment of labor implies a powerful stimulus, but such stimuli may be varied and hard to establish archaeologically in the case of ancient systems. External threats or climatic factors, which make more easily worked land unavailable or unsuitable for agriculture, would appear to be appropriate reasons, while population pressure on limited land is less likely in many African contexts. Indeed Hakansson refutes the Boserup thesis (that the impetus toward agricultural production was a response to population growth) with a number of historical cases where intensive agriculture has been abandoned for various reasons in spite of increasing population.

Terracing must also be viewed in its social context, as the organization of labor must be integrated in the whole social system and settlement pattern. In 1989, H. Amborn made the important point that political or social change can disrupt a specialized agricultural system as much or more than climatic or ecological factors. Archaeological study, therefore, cannot be limited to the terraces themselves but must consider the whole cultural context. It is unfortunate that ethnographic descriptions of traditional societies practicing terracing, though offering useful insights, are often silent on vital details that would assist in the interpretation of ancient systems.

Irrigation

Gravity-fed irrigation using small furrows has been used in the recent past and is still practiced by many African societies where topography and water sources allow. Presumably, it was also undertaken in earlier times, though it is difficult to identify archaeologically unless it incorporated stone structures, since erosion probably removed the old furrows or slope wash covered them, except in areas with perennial-grass cover. The Marakwet of the Kerio Valley in Kenya have brought furrow construction to a fine art. They run the furrows for many kilometers through steep rough terrain, use aqueducts to circumvent cliff faces and cross gullies, and bring the water to their fields in the dry valley bottom. The Sonjo of northern Tanzania also have a well-developed irrigation agriculture that requires fewer engineering skills. The Konso, as described by Amborn, irrigate a limited part of their terraces where conditions allow. In gently sloping areas, they rely mostly on terrace walls to trap rainwater for temporary flooding. The maintenance of irrigation furrows and the distribution of the water require well-organized social control, which is achieved without a central authority, often through the kinship system.

To use agricultural plots repeatedly, farmers add manure and use sophisticated practices of intercropping and crop rotation. While these practices are not necessarily required in terrace cultivation, they do serve to prolong fertility. One might expect that accumulating and distributing manure would decrease the number of laborers available to build new terraces, assuming, that is, that new lands were available for terracing. Some ethnographic examples incorporate graduated zones from intensively cultivated plots near the homestead to more extensively worked terraces, which may have fallowing as part of the cycle, farther away.

Among the ancient terrace systems, Engaruka terraces were designed for furrow irrigation; the vast majority of the Nyanga terraces, however, were not leveled for flooding and would not have been accessible to gravity irrigation except on the piedmont slopes. Practices thus vary in different areas with different conditions both in the past and more recently, and any common features appear to reflect similar responses rather than implying any cultural relationship.

Nyanga

The Nyanga ruin complex, as described by R. F. H. Summers in 1958, constitutes the largest and most impressive concentration of terracing in Africa. The main distribution of terracing occurs within an area of about 5,000 square kilometers in the eastern highlands and adjacent lower areas of eastern Zimbabwe. Terracing ranges in altitude from about 900 meters to around 1,700 meters, the present limit for the cultivation of traditional grain crops, such as millet, sorghum, and maize. Terracing is found on the steep flanks of the main highland ridge, on the piedmont slopes and detached foothills, and up to at least 50 kilometers to the west of the base of the escarpment. Terracing is most successful in areas with dolerite rocks and soils of good fertility but also extends into granite areas and to sedimentary argillite rocks in the north.

In the dolerite areas, terrace walls are usually substantial, up to 1 meter or more in thickness and often standing higher than the soil surface above, which is commonly more or less horizontal in profile, though usually sloping laterally. Higher walls may have drains through them. Cultivable surfaces are narrow, commonly 1 to 3 meters wide except on very gentle slopes. Fall between terraces varies with the slope gradient and is usually between 50 and 100 centimeters, occasionally up to 2 meters. The size and spacing of the walls reflect the large amounts of stone to be cleared to leave sufficient soil depth and surface for cultivation. Slope gradients of up to 25° are common, and they may reach 35°. In areas of granite and sedimentary rocks, terraces are generally lower, around 30 to 60 centimeters, and the stonework may consist of little more than a simple revetment, while terrace soil surfaces usually have a sloping profile, at an average angle of around 10°.

The settlement pattern at the Nyanga ruin comprises detached homesteads, often with some spatial grouping. The form of the homesteads varies with altitude and geographical area. Below about 1,400 meters, various types of low-walled enclosures are found near the terracing. These walls enclose house floors and other structures, probably storage huts, with slab floors raised on vertical stones. Many of the homesteads also include a small pit or central walled enclosure, which must have been for livestock. The form of the enclosures varies geographically, implying some cultural difference between the communities of the terrace complex. More substantial, apparently defensive, refuges also occur in some areas. Above 1,400 meters, the general homestead form is the pit structure—a stone-lined pit up to 3 meters deep and 3 to 10 meters in diameter, with a tunnel entrance, and surrounded by house floors and other structures on a stone-revetted platform. The pits were almost certainly for livestock. While these pit structures may be associated with terracing along the base of the escarpment, they appear much more frequently above the terracing at altitudes of 1,700 to 2,000 meters. Groups of up to 25 pits may occur. Average pit size increases sharply above the upper limit of the terracing, suggesting the importance of livestock in the high grasslands. The relationship of the large sites of stone-built ruins on the highest peaks at altitudes of over 2,000 meters to the rest of the complex is unclear.

Old water furrows have thus far been certainly identified only in the high grasslands where they appear to lead from springs and streams to groups of pit structures. No clear evidence has been found for the irrigation of terraces in the form of furrows or distributary works. These features would not be practicable on most of the lowland foothills and were probably unnecessary for the higher terraces. Furrows and distributary works might be expected on the piedmont slopes, however.

In 1950 and 1951, Summers recovered seeds from several lowland enclosures, identified as sorghum, pennisetum, eleusine, cowpea, groundbean, and castor bean, all traditional crops for the region. Faunal samples were small but included cattle and wild animals. It is probable that the farming system integrated agriculture with livestock and included the use of at least some manure accumulated in the pits and walled enclosures.

Dating of the complex is imprecise, but most of it can be bracketed between about A.D. 1500 and 1800. Within this range, the pattern of development of different elements has yet to be established. The historical inhabitants of the area are Shona-speaking groups, some of whose chiefly dynasties have genealogies going back into the 18th century at least, when parts of the complex must still have been occupied. However, there is little information available in oral traditions on the terraces and their use.

The complex is the subject of an ongoing research project, and more information should be available in the near future.

Engaruka

The Engaruka site constitutes a single concentration of stone structures, circumscribed by natural factors of topography, soils, and hydrology. The site lies at the western edge of the East African Rift Valley in northern Tanzania, at the foot of the escarpment of the Crater Highlands, midway between Lakes Natron and Manyara. It was most comprehensively described by John Sutton in 1978 and 1986, and excavations have been carried out by H. Sassoon in the mid-1960s and Peter Robertshaw in the 1980s. Here, the perennial Engaruka River and two seasonal streams descend from the better-watered highlands to debouch on the gently sloping Rift Valley floor where the average annual rainfall is only about 350 millimeters, quite inadequate for any rainfed agriculture. Archaeological remains extend for some 9 kilometers along the foot of the escarpment and up to 3.5 kilometers into the plain, covering a total of around 20 square kilometers.

Except for the upper parts of low foothills not accessible to gravity irrigation and the impossibly rocky areas, the ancient field system is more or less continuous throughout this area. Field plots consist of shallow stone-faced terraces subdivided by stone lines. The plots range from 30 by 12 meters on flatter ground to only about 4 by 1 meters on steeper slopes. Some terrace revetments may reach 1 meter high in the steepest areas but are generally much less.

Double lines of stones 1 meter or less wide wind through the fields with a consistent gradient and form a network of distributary channels. Traces of lesser furrows remain in the plots themselves. The distributary channels can often be traced to their junctions with the main-artery furrows, which were taken off the streams at the highest possible point on the outwash fans and led along the foot of the escarpment. The longest channel is some 3.5 kilometers, and, at one point, it is carried on an artificially banked aqueduct to maintain height across a saddle to one of the foothills. Stone-built sluices control the furrow junc-

tions. The furrows are well engineered to maintain the maximum possible height, with gradients often less than 1°.

Among the fields are stone cairns and walled enclosures. The cairns may be up to 2 meters high and have well-built faces and a rubble core of smaller stones. Their primary purpose would seem to have been as a place to put stones as they were cleared from the fields by cultivation and erosion. They also probably served as bird-scaring platforms. The walled enclosures are up to 20 meters across and 2 meters high and may have been used to pen cattle and sheep or goats, perhaps stall-fed, whose manure would have been used on the fields.

Along the foot of the escarpment, just above the highest terracing, are seven village sites, concentrations of leveled platforms cut into the slope and revetted front and back. The clustering of these village around the Engaruka River implies that the watercourse has always been the only perennial source of water and that the seasonal streams were exploited only during their periods of flow.

Radiocarbon dates support a floruit (period of flourishing) in the 16th and 17th centuries, and there are traces of modifications to the furrows and field plots indicating continuous development over a prolonged period. There are few or no reliable oral traditions concerning the use of the system or the identity of the community responsible for building it. Theories on the latter point vary, with perhaps the most probable being speakers of a Southern Cushitic language, some of whom may have joined the Bantu-speaking Sonjo who still practice irrigation agriculture some 90 kilometers to the north.

Sutton considers that the present discharge of the rivers from the escarpment would be inadequate to water the whole field system and must have been greater in the past. Flow has probably been reduced by changes in the hydrological regime occasioned by a minor reduction in rainfall and perhaps by grazing and deforestation in the highlands. Other reasons for the abandonment of the site were probably inherent in the very specialized nature of the system, which would have made it vulnerable to even minor changes in the environment (including overexploitation) or changes in social and political factors. The community was probably finally finished off by competition from incoming pastoralists.

There are other minor occurrences of apparently related irrigation agriculture in the region, notably at Endamaga and Oldogom at the northern corner of Lake Eyasi. Only at Engaruka, however, did peculiar conditions of topography, hydrology, and soils allow its full development.

BIBLIOGRAPHY

Amborn, H. 1989. Agricultural intensification in the Burji-Konsocluster of south-western Ethiopia. *Azania* 24: 71–83.

Grove, A. T., and J. E. G. Sutton. 1989. Agricultural terracing south of the Sahara. *Azania* 24: 114–122.

Hakansson, T. 1989. Social and political aspects of intensive agriculture in East Africa: Some models from cultural anthropology. *Azania* 24: 12–20.

Hallpike, C. R. 1970. Konso agriculture. *Journal of Ethiopian Studies* 8 (1): 31–43.

Kipkorir, B., Soper, R., and J. Ssennyonga, eds. 1981. *Kerio Valley: Past, present and future.* Nairobi: Institute of African Studies.

Robertshaw, P. 1986. Engaruka revisited: Excavations of 1982. *Azania* 21: 1–20.

Sassoon, H. 1966. Engaruka: Excavations during 1964. *Azania* 1: 79–99.

———. 1967. New views on Engaruka, northern Tanzania. *Journal of African History* 8: 201–217.

Summers, R. 1958. *Inyanga: Prehistoric settlements in southern Rhodesia.* Cambridge: Cambridge University Press.

Sutton, J. E. G. 1978. Engaruka and its waters. *Azania* 13: 37–70.

———. 1986. The irrigation and manuring of the Engaruka field system. *Azania* 21: 27–51.

Robert Soper

STONE-WALLED AGRICULTURAL COMMUNITIES OF SOUTH AFRICA AND BOTSWANA

The 1st millennium A.D. witnessed the spread of iron-using, agricultural communities over most of Africa south of the equator. This initial dispersion of farmers practicing subsistence-level agriculture, often referred to as the *Early Iron Age,* was closely tied to the distribution of the savanna-type vegetation so common to large parts of tropical Africa. By about A.D. 600, virtually all savanna areas that receive sufficient rain to allow for crop production had been settled.

The preference for savanna can best be understood in terms of the resources available to farming communities in these regions. The trees and shrubs yield reliable quantities of wood for building and fuel, while the grassy understory provides good pasture. Savanna soils also tend to be more productive than those of other vegetation types of the subcontinent.

Settlements of this early period were built essentially of poles, thatch, and sun-dried clay. It was not until the 2nd millennium that some southern African agriculturists started to use stone as a major building material. Broadly speaking, two types of communities adopted stone. The Shona-speaking dynasties of the Great Zimbabwe culture developed stone walls for prestige purposes to demarcate areas occupied by the ruling elite. (These are discussed under a separate entry.) Subsistence-agricultural societies in a number of different areas, from the northern savannas of South Africa through Botswana and on into Angola, turned to stone as a substitute for the traditional building materials.

From as early as the 14th century, and particularly from the 16th century onward, a substantial expansion of settlement took place onto regions of grassland neighboring the savannas settled earlier. The reasons for the initial delay in occupying the grasslands and then the large-scale expansion are not well understood, but they appear to relate to the character of the highland environments and resources available there. The grasslands are higher in altitude than neighboring savannas, with cooler, usually, wetter climates. Little or no timber is available, and substitutes would have had to be found both for building and fuel. Soils are more acid, and this would have initially presented problems for both cultivation and the feeding of livestock.

Stone became the main substitute building material, while cattle dung served as the main source of fuel. It is not clear how the agricultural problems were solved, but in the case of grazing, a possibility in some areas was to move the livestock periodically to lower elevations to avoid the poor nutrition of the grasslands in winter.

It was not only in pure grassland areas that stone building became common, though. In some neighboring savannas where high population densities developed in the later centuries, it seems that timber supplies became so depleted that, here too, stone was substituted. Today such areas have reverted to savanna, and the stone ruins of these earlier settlements are often overgrown by thick bush. In contrast, we know from early 19th-century records that such stone towns stood in relatively open grasslands at the time of their occupation.

The early traveler William Burchell, visiting the Tswana town of Dithakong in 1812, described how the trees in a wide area around this town of about 5,000 people had been cut down and reduced to building material and fuel. By moving every few years, this community was able to continue building in timber, whereas some of its neighbors had already converted to stone. There had been an earlier period of stone building at Dithakong, and in fact, the name means "at the ruins."

The use of stone reached a peak in the 17th and 18th centuries over large areas. From an examination of both the settlements and the distinct styles of pottery they contain, as well as from oral tradition, it is clear that several different groups of agriculturists, each with its own distinctive style of settlement pattern, made this transition. For example, several communities from each of the two major linguistic clusters in South Africa, the Nguni and Sotho, took to building in stone. In each case, where there is sufficient archaeological information on the local sequences, it is clear that the traditional form of settlement pattern continued with little change. The softer materials were replaced by stone to a greater or lesser extent, but the types of building and their positioning in relation to one another usually remained constant to the cultural canon.

The greatest effort in building stone walls was not so much the building itself as the process of obtaining the raw material. Loose stone was the main source, but in some cases, extensive quar-

rying was needed to provide sufficient material. Much effort went into collecting the stone and carrying it by hand to the building site. Field research has shown that the availability of suitable rock had a considerable influence on the location of stone settlements. Most were built within 100 meters of a suitable source, although stones serving more specialized requirements, such as rounded river stones used for paving, were sometimes carried much longer distances.

The quality of the walls was also influenced by the nature of the local rock outcrop. The best results were obtained from rock that naturally broke into flat slabs or rectangular blocks. Apart from quarrying, there was no attempt to shape the pieces of stone with the exception of the large blocks selected to form entrances. These blocks often had their sharper edges battered to round them off. This was evidently done to prevent injury to both humans and animals using the entrances.

These communities produced only dry-stone walls, usually constructed in the following way. Larger rocks were selected for the two wall faces, which were built to a batter, the wall being widest at ground level and narrowest at the top. The space remaining between the two faces was filled with smaller rubble as the wall progressed. The largest rocks were usually placed at the base on ground level, there being no foundations.

In some inland areas of KwaZulu-Natal, this technique was adapted for buildings that were more than about 100 meters away from rocky outcrops. Here the core of the wall, 1 meter or more in width, was built of earth, and the stone was used merely to line the two faces of the wall. The outer face sloped inward.

The different communities that built in stone were somewhat closely related to one another, Bantu-speaking, strongly patrilineal, and sharing many other cultural features such as the central symbolic role of the family cattle herd in social and religious life. The importance of cattle was reflected in the central position of the stock pen or pens within the family homestead.

Some archaeologists and anthropologists consider that the underlying similarity between the social systems of southern Bantu-speaking people led to a common structural patterning in their settlements, known as the *central cattle pattern.* The spatial patterning is considered to be a reflection of the social structure in which, among other aspects, status and gender are spatially demarcated and the central cattle pen is a male preserve and a shrine to the ancestors. Brides marrying into the family are exchanged for cattle from the family herd, according to the *lobolo* (bride wealth) system.

In terms of this pattern, it may be significant that in stone-building communities, it was always the stock pen that was constructed of stone, even when other structural elements continued to be built of softer materials. An example may be taken from the interior grasslands of KwaZulu-Natal, which was inhabited by Nguni-speaking people, who were closely related to the Zulu and lived in relatively dispersed homesteads each housing an individual family. These settlements are readily visible today only because of the stone cattle pens. Each homestead consisted of a single, circular pen surrounded by a ring of other structures including huts and granaries. These smaller structures were built of softer materials, which have since disappeared, but huts were sometimes paved with stone, and the granaries were often situated on a stone platform. The survival of these stone features has made it possible to reconstruct much of the homestead plan from the archaeological evidence.

The three structural elements just mentioned, the cattle pen, the domestic hut, and the granary, constitute the primary categories of building on most southern African settlements. All the agricultural communities used the circle as the primary geometrical element of their architecture. The cattle pens, huts, and granaries are therefore almost always circular in plan. Arcuate (bowed) walls may be added to circular structures or placed separate from them to produce secondary enclosed areas. Secondary enclosures, attached internally or externally to cattle pens, served various functions such as calf pens and men's meeting places. Arcuate walls, attached to or partially enclosing huts, defined courtyards, which were used for a variety of domestic purposes.

The Nguni example is a relatively simple pattern and usually has little in the way of secondary buildings. Settlement patterns were often much more complicated among the Sotho-speaking people of the *highveld* plateau and the drier western areas into Botswana where far larger scales of settlement became the norm. Before examining these we should turn to a new source of evidence that throws additional light on these settlements, namely, the rock engravings done by some of their inhabitants.

Unlike the better-known Stone Age rock art of southern Africa, which is dominated by human and animal figures, the great majority of rock engravings done by agricultural communities depict plans of settlements. There is a close correlation between stone buildings and this type of engraving, as the images of the settlements are almost always in close proximity to the actual buildings, sometimes even on rocks incorporated into the walls. By no means all of the stone settlements have engravings nearby. The engravings have been found only in areas where stone walls were used, but not where softer building materials were the norm.

The communities that produced these engravings apparently did not otherwise have a rich heritage of representational art. A few Tswana settlements of the early 19th century had paintings of human and animal figures on walls, while decoration on artifacts, notably knife handles, sometimes took the form of figures. Clay models of animals, particularly cattle, were more common and have been found in several excavations, but aside from these and a few other examples, the stone-building communities evidently produced relatively few images of a representational nature.

The occurrence of the engravings and the predominance of the homestead motif therefore calls for comment. A possible explanation is that the settlement pattern mirrors not only the social structure of the family but also the religious structure of the community. Society is the family writ large. Under these circumstances, the plan of the homestead offers the idealized model for a graphic representation of the community's value system.

Before comparing the engravings with the actual buildings, we should note a few general points about these depictions. Experience has shown that the engraved plans are not representations of specific buildings. Instead, they appear to be simplified and, perhaps, idealized generalizations on the theme of the local settlement style. This is understandable if, as mentioned above, the homestead plan provided a vehicle to depict the social structure of family and community. Another consistent difference between the engraved images and the actual buildings is in the marked emphasis among the former on spatial elements related to cattle (pens and paths) and at the same time a neglect of features associated with women's activities (domestic huts and granaries are seldom depicted, and cultivated fields are never shown). In these societies, cattle were strictly the concern of men and boys, while cultivation was an activity of women. The masculine bias in the art suggests that the engravers were men, and it serves to warn us that the depictions do not fully represent the viewpoint of all sections of the community. On the other hand, the engravings can fill in details, such as the routes taken by cattle paths, which have not survived elsewhere in the archaeological record.

Some of the most extensive stone towns are in the North West Province (western part of the former Transvaal province) close to Botswana. Early 19th-century reports describe such towns of Tswana people numbering up to 20,000 and more. Each was the capital of a chiefdom, which imposed strict sanctions to ensure that most of the community remained resident in the capital except when required to perform economic tasks at a distance. Women, for example, were required to cultivate often distant arable lands, and young men looked after stock at cattle posts.

Settlement was based on wards, each controlled by a headman whose lineage occupied many of the households, though there were often other families present as well. A ring of stone cattle pens opening into a central space formed the core of the ward. Around this was a partial or complete ring of dwellings, each with its hut and courtyards front and back. The arcuate rear courtyard walls of stone, built contiguous to one another, formed a scalloped perimeter to the ward. The huts, constructed of softer materials, featured poles that supported a conical thatch roof and clay curtain walls that define veranda and inner compartments. The latter were typically entered through a sliding wooden door. The larger settlements comprised numbers of these wards built close up against one another but usually with corridors between to permit stock and pedestrian traffic. Engravings of this settlement type, including details of the dwellings, the ring of stock pens, and even the whole ward, have been found, but no engraving of a whole town has ever been recorded.

In other grassland areas between the Vaal and Limpopo Rivers and in the northern Free State, a variety of settlement types can be linked to branches of the Sotho-speaking people on the basis of oral traditions and stylistic characteristics. In some of the treeless parts of the *highveld,* both north and south of the Vaal River, several southern Sotho communities feature a settlement type in which even the huts were built of stone. The hemispherical huts, entered through low doorways with lintels, had corbeled roofs (a projecting stepped arch) made of stone slabs.

Some of the most extensive stone-building projects undertaken in precolonial South Africa occur in a narrow belt along the eastern escarpment. Here not only were the central stock pen and the enclosing walls of the homesteads built of stone, but large extents of hillside were modified for cultivation by the construction of stone terraces. Settlements, up to 3 kilometers in extent on hills and spurs, consisted of as many as 100 homesteads set in terraced-field systems. Roads defined by stone walls linked the homesteads and led through the terraced fields to the open country beyond. Since these terminate at the stock pens at the center of each homestead and control circulation through the terraced areas, the roads clearly functioned as cattle paths, constructed to protect the cultivated fields.

Engravings adjacent to some of these settlements exaggerate the concentric patterning of the homesteads and stress the linking cattle roads. The most elaborate engravings cover a whole boulder with a maze of homesteads and roads. The boulder serves as a model of the hill with its extensive settlement, and the engraved homes and roads follow the model contours as would the actual stone walls of the settlement. Again, the masculine emphasis is apparent, for the agricultural terraces are never depicted.

BIBLIOGRAPHY

Collett, D. P. 1982. Excavations of stone-walled ruins types in the Badfontein Valley, eastern Transvaal. *South African Archaeological Bulletin* 37: 34–44.

———. 1982. Ruin distribution in the stone-walled settlements of the eastern Transvaal, South Africa. *South African Journal of Science* 78: 39–40.

Maggs, T. M. O'C. 1976. *Iron Age communities of the southern* highveld. Pietermaritzburg: The Council of the Natal Museum.

———. 1986. Patterns and perceptions of stone built settlements from the Thukela Valley Late Iron Age. *Annals of the Natal Museum* 29: 417–432.

Taylor, M. O. V. 1984. Southern Transvaal stone walled sites: A spatial consideration. In *Frontiers: Southern African archaeology today,* eds. M. L. Hall, et al. British Archaeological Reports International Series 207, Cambridge Monographs in African Archaeology 10.

Walton, J. 1951. Corbelled stone huts in southern Africa. *Man* 51, article 82.

T. M. O'C. Maggs

Ethnoarchaeology

—∿∿∿∿∿∿∿—

NORTHERN AFRICAN ETHNOARCHAEOLOGY

Northern Africa comprises a vast region of nearly 11.7 million square kilometers and includes the countries of Algeria, Chad, Egypt, Mali, Mauritania, Morocco, Sudan, and Western Sahara, which form the world's largest desert. Within this immense region, surprisingly little ethnoarchaeological research has been conducted, considering its extensive surface area, and the potential for future work is great. It is important to highlight that, for the purposes of this article, northern Africa does not include the important Sahelian zone, which effectively divides Africa into two continents—Saharan and sub-Saharan Africa. The Sahel essentially coincides with the historical Bilad al-Sudan or "land of the Blacks," the name early Arab historians used for the 5.2-million square-kilometer strip that borders the southern Saharan Desert and runs from the Atlantic Coast to the mountain regions of Ethiopia. It was here that the first West African states, such as the Ghana Empire, emerged and that many ethnoarchaeological studies have taken place. Thus, this brief overview concentrates on the Saharan portion of Africa.

Ethnoarchaeology may be defined as the study of contemporary cultures in order to understand human behavior and its relation to the creation of material culture. Thus, ethnoarchaeology provides a framework in which archaeologists can test hypotheses concerning the procurement, production, use, distribution, and discard of material remains and how they interface with human behavior. This can be achieved through the study of the full range of material culture—from simple artifacts to complex settlement and economic systems that leave material residue over a given landscape. Ethnoarchaeology has become an important research endeavor because it provides the most compelling source of data for making analogies between the observable present and past human behaviors, which are unobservable. In a recent ethnoarchaeological study of pastoral nomadic groups south of Lake Chad by Augustin F. C. Holl and T. E. Levy published in 1993, it was possible to generalize four fundamental types of analogies archaeologists rely on for interpreting the archaeological record. These include: (1) simple direct analogy, (2) cautionary tales, (3) processual analogy, and (4) cognitive analogy. In general, ethnoarchaeological research in North Africa has concentrated on simple direct analogies and processual analogies. The three North African ethnoarchaeological projects presented here focus on these two types.

The majority of ethnoarchaeological studies in North Africa have taken place in Egypt as by-products of major archaeological research endeavors. The long technological traditions persisting in the Nile Valley have provided a catalyst for scholars to use ethnoarchaeological research to supplement their studies of ancient Egyptian production systems. These projects are of great general interest because they focus on the full range of material-culture processes such as procurement, processing, consumption, reuse, and discard. By understanding these aspects of present-day material-culture systems, scholars are in a stronger position to interpret the archaeological record.

Dominating ethnoarchaeological research in North Africa, simple analogy falls into two main categories: functional studies and analysis of site-formation processes. Functional studies include "action" or "experimental" archaeology, in which archaeologists reconstruct past technologies. For example, Mark Lerner and his team reconstructed a small pyramid in Egypt to discover the mechanisms by which these ancient monuments may have been constructed more than 4,000 years ago. Alternatively, the replication of use-wear on experimentally manufactured stone tools is another example of simple direct analogy. Functional studies are also characterized by observations on how people used their space (population size versus habitation area), reenactments, or the study of so-called primitive technologies such as metalworking, pottery production, glass-making, basketry, stone-vessel production, and other nonindustrialized means of craft production that may shed light on the organization and techniques of production. To illustrate simple direct analogy, ethnoarchaeological studies of pottery making and stone vessel manufacture are examined.

Pottery Production in Upper Egypt

British archaeologists Paul Nicholson and Helen Patterson designed the Ballas Pottery Project in the 1980s to study the mass production of one ceramic vessel, an amphoralike water jar produced in the region of Qena near Ballas in Upper Egypt. There are a number of factors that made this ethnoarchaeological study attractive:

1. The long tradition of ceramic production in the Qena region since protodynastic times (Nagada I and II, about 5,000 to 6,000 years ago)
2. The relatively simple ceramic technology used by the local potters and perhaps evolving out of ancient traditions
3. The similarity in clay types used in protohistoric and modern ceramics from the Qena region

4. The more complex "industrial" organization of pottery production in the Qena area compared with other ethnoarchaeological studies of pottery production in North Africa

While the majority of ethnoarchaeological studies of pottery production in Africa focus on family-based production systems, the Ballas Pottery Project provides important insights into a more complex "rural nucleated industry" in which a number of individual workshops are nested together to form a "primitive" industrial complex. By studying the organization of this kind of industrial complex, archaeologists are in a stronger position to understand craft production in ancient Egypt, which provided the vast quantities of burial offerings found throughout the Nile Valley.

The present-day Ballas nucleated industry is based on a division of specialist labor. Specialized miners extract clay blocks from huge galleries located about a 40-minute walk from the village production center. These blocks are then brought back to the village on the backs of donkeys or camels. According to the miners, they have a long ("thousands of years") history as a profession separate from the potters.

Once the clay is brought to the industry complex, it is prepared indoors (to prevent drying) for forming by trampling on cobbled floor inside one of the potter's workshops. After the vessels are thrown in the workshop, they are placed in a drying room, the largest room in the potter's workshop. Approximately 500 to 700 vessels are then placed in large outdoor kilns for firing.

Historical sources, some 90 years old, indicate that the Qena vessels were primarily transported by boat as far north as Cairo and south to Aswan. Although the amphora industry at Deir el-Gharbi near Qena is large, produces distinctive artifacts, and has a wide distribution in the Nile Valley, ethnoarchaeologists highlight how difficult it would be for an archaeologist to reconstruct the pottery system without excavating the entire pottery-production complex. However, as a pilot study, the Ballas Pottery Project provides an important case study of ceramic production beyond the domestic mode of production.

Stone-Vase Production in Upper Egypt

The second case study for simple direct analogy was made by T. R. Hester and R. F. Heizer of alabaster vessels and other objects produced in the village of Sheik Abd el Gurna on the western plain of Thebes in Upper Egypt. This small ethnoarchaeological project was undertaken during the course of a larger archaeological investigation of the Colossi of Memnon. The project was aimed at photographing the traditional methods of working with alabaster and undertaking ethnographic interviews and observations to determine the techniques and sequence of producing alabaster vessels and the nature of the alabaster industry in Upper Egypt.

The ethnoarchaeological interest in alabaster stems from its importance as a construction material and mineral source for the production of grave offerings in ancient Egypt. Slabs of alabaster were carefully crafted and used to line passages and rooms in tombs dating to the early dynastic period through New Kingdom period. An indication of the importance of alabaster-vessel manufacture in ancient Egypt is seen in one of the galleries of the 3rd Dynasty step pyramid where more than 30,000 vessels (weighing some 81,000 kilograms) were discovered.

The ethnoarchaeological team assembled all the data on the geologic sources of alabaster in Egypt and the Sinai thereby facilitating both the present-day study of alabaster production and archaeological distribution studies. Unlike pottery production in the Ballas region, the alabaster industry at Gurna does not have a clear lineage. In fact, it seems to have been "reborn" as a result of the growth of the tourist trade in Egypt during the late 19th century. In spite of this questionable pedigree, ethnoarchaeologists have drawn important parallels between the present-day production system and ancient systems recorded in the archaeological record. Metal tools are shown by Hester and Heizer to have counterparts in ancient Egyptian lithic (stone) industries.

Modern Gurna workshops clearly operate under different socioeconomic pressures than those from dynastic times when the production of alabaster vessels was more highly specialized. The ancient system was aimed at mass production of funerary items, whereas today it is aimed at the tourist trade. However, the ethnographic research is most useful in helping archaeologists draw clear analogies on how alabaster vessels were produced.

Ceramic Production and Markets in Complex Societies in Morocco

Exciting processual studies in ethnoarchaeology have been carried out concerning the role of pottery production in market economies in North Africa. In a study by R. Vossen, pottery-manufacturing processes were studied at the six large urban centers in Morocco (Fez, Marrakech, Tetouan, Sidi Kacem, Rabat, Sale, and Safi). Historical records enabled the researcher to trace the lineage of pottery manufacture in urban Morocco as far back as the 11th century. While some traditional means of moving goods to the markets are still used (camels, donkeys, women, and mule- and donkey-drawn carts), today mostly trucks are used. Vossen identified three divisions of labor in the pottery-production process to accommodate its distribution in the traditional market-based system: (1) female production for the family's own needs, (2) male production in urban settings for the market, and (3) the establishment of centers in relatively small towns for the specialized manufacture of cheap utility wares (unglazed casseroles and cooking pots).

The Moroccan study shows how, in a traditional North African setting, the centuries-old system of weekly markets *(souks)* dictates the actual rhythm of ceramic production in the smaller manufacturing centers. The spatial distribution of market towns and pottery-production centers in Morocco is remarkably consistent with an average distance of around 9 to 10 kilometers, or about a two-hour walk. The largest supraregional central markets are visited by people (including pottery producers) from a distance as much as 40 or 50 kilometers (an eight- to ten-hour walk under traditional conditions). The system of weekly markets in Morocco indicates that under "normal" circumstances, a pottery-manufacturing center is required every 20 kilometers to provide the regional population equally with utilitarian pottery. This study is extremely powerful for predicting pottery-production centers because it relies on regional analysis and network analysis used in geography by scholars such as J. G. Christaller, August Losch, P. A. Haggett, and M. G. Smith. For archaeologists, this kind of processual ethnoarchaeological study is of great use for analyzing the interface between regional settlement patterns, systems of production, and the socioeconomic dynamics of ancient societies.

───〜〜〜〜〜〜───

These thumbnail sketches of some of the more significant ethnoarchaeological research projects in North Africa highlight a range of issues germane to archaeologists working the world over. More than other areas of Africa, the Saharan region needs more ethnoarchaeological research to record rapidly disappearing social, economic, and ideological systems that have a present-day material-culture signature.

BIBLIOGRAPHY

Balfet, H. 1966. Ethnographical observations in North Africa and archaeological interpretation. In *Ceramics and man,* ed. F. R. Matson, 161–177. London: Methuen.

Hester, T. R. 1976. Functional analysis of ancient Egyptian stone tools: The potential for future research. *Journal of Field Archaeology* 3: 346–351.

Hester, T. R., and R. F. Heizer. 1980. *Making stone vases: Ethnoarchaeological studies of an alabaster workshop in Upper Egypt.* Malibu: Undena Publications.

Holl, A. F. C., and T. E. Levy. 1993. From the Nile Valley to the Chad Basin: Ethnoarchaeology of Shuwa Arab settlements. *Biblical Archaeology* 56: 166–179.

Lucas, A., and J. R. Harris. 1962. *Ancient Egyptian materials and industries.* London: Edward Arnold.

Nicholson, P., and H. Patterson. 1985. Pottery making in Upper Egypt: An ethnoarchaeological study. *World Archaeology* 17: 222–239.

Peacock, D. 1982. *Pottery in the Roman world.* London: Longmans.

Vossen, R. 1984. Towards building models of traditional trade in ceramics: Case studies from Spain and Morocco. In *The many dimensions of pottery ceramics in archaeology and anthropology,* eds. S. E. van der Leeuw and A. C. Pritchard, 341–496. Amsterdam: University of Amsterdam.

Thomas E. Levy

WESTERN AFRICAN ETHNOARCHAEOLOGY

This article examines the development of ethnoarchaeology in West Africa during the 20th century and its roots in Anglophone and Francophone research traditions.

Ethnoarchaeology is the systematic ethnographic study of present-day communities in order to develop propositions about the cultural contexts of material recovered from archaeological sites. Ethnoarchaeological research in West African differs in a number of ways from that carried out in other parts of the continent. Uniquely, such research in this area has included a vibrant Francophone research tradition, one that is older and has often involved very different methodologies and philosophies than we see in the more prevalent American and British traditions. In other areas of the continent, much ethnoarchaeological research is directed toward the analysis of paleoanthropological problems and toward the study of hunter-foragers. The relative absence in West Africa of sites occupied by our earliest hominid ancestors and of ethnically defined forager groups has meant that these topics are only minimally examined in this region. West African research has, for the most part, involved the study of agricultural and, to a lesser extent, pastoral societies.

Ethnoarchaeological research is a relatively recent pursuit in West Africa. From the beginning of this century, various interested amateurs, including Sir Albert Kitson and Maurice Delafosse, incorporated descriptions of scattered archaeological finds in their accounts of West Africa and its societies, and in some cases they used ethnographic data derived from local communities to interpret these discoveries. In keeping with the dominant paradigms of the time, these works are often heavily diffusionistic, drawing upon groups culturally and geographically remote from West Africa for comparison. They are also extremely unsystematic and are only tangentially relevant to later developments.

French academics, especially Marcel Griaule and Jean-Paul Lebeuf between the late 1930s and the 1950s, were the first to use ethnographic data to interpret archaeological finds in the region. Griaule and Lebeuf participated in the Dakar-Djibouti expedition of the early 1930s. They concentrated upon the ethnographic, historical, and archaeological examination of societies of the southern Lake Chad Basin, primarily in Cameroon and in Chad. It was expected that these various avenues of research would continually inform one another, broadening and enriching interpretations. Analysis of material items was held to be extremely important, because cultures imprint their behaviors and beliefs upon such items. The original goals of this work involved the construction of regional cultural histories and the analysis of the development of complex societies in the region. Active research within this tradition was continued by Lebeuf and his collaborators (including most notably his wife, Anne Lebeuf) until the 1980s.

Less directly influenced by Griaule, and by ethnography, was the work of Raymond Mauny in French West Africa, although his encyclopedic *Tableau Géographique de l'Ouest Africain au Moyen Age* incorporates a considerable amount of ethnographic information. The investigations of Griaule, Lebeuf, and Mauny can only generally be included within the sphere of ethnoarchaeology as presently defined. Systematic explanatory linkages between present-day activities and archaeological residues were rarely made, reliance was placed upon oral and written history rather than upon observation of behavior, and the objective of the work was usually the documentation of cultural continuity in a region over time. Nevertheless, the research-integrated survey, excavation, and fieldwork among living people more closely approached the aims of ethnoarchaeology than did any other studies in West Africa or, indeed, in most other areas of the world at the time.

No equivalent projects were being undertaken in Anglophone West Africa between the 1930s and the early 1960s. Archaeological research in the British colonies (for the most part, in Ghana and Nigeria) was often undertaken as a supplement to other, more salient duties. Very little institutional support was available for such work, although the independence of these colonies, starting with Ghana in 1956, sparked a much

greater interest in local, indigenous cultural histories. Archaeologists working in Anglophone West Africa did incorporate data derived from their observations of contemporary communities in their archaeological reconstructions—archaeologists have always done that. However, the systematic application of such information, and the directed study of living communities to obtain such information, began only in the middle and late 1960s.

These innovations proceeded from two sources. In the first place, from the late 1950s onward, theoretical developments in Europe and North America had raised serious doubts about the utility and applicability of the ethnographic analogies researchers had used to build archaeological interpretations. These concerns, along with calls for more explicit methodologies and with a general dissatisfaction among archaeologists with the ways in which ethnographers treated material culture, led to the development of ethnoarchaeology as a distinct field of research. The first specifically ethnoarchaeological investigations in West Africa in the late 1960s were undertaken by younger researchers and students who had absorbed these attitudes in the course of their work. Thus, Nicholas J. David's investigations at Bé, in northern Cameroon, focused especially upon ceramic production and use and the interpretation of architectural remains in a Fulani community and were carried out in conjunction with archaeological survey and excavation.

The other source contributing to the beginnings of West African ethnoarchaeology at this time was rather different. In 1970, Merrick Posnansky began the West African Trade Project, examining the effects that medieval Sudanic trading relationships had upon Ghanaian societies and focusing especially upon the site of Begho. Posnansky continued his research in the 1980s in Togo. His approach was one of cross-disciplinary syncretism, emphasizing the contributions that archaeological, ethnographic, historical, and artistic data could make to the construction of integrated cultural histories. In this way, his own work resembled the research of Griaule, Lebeuf, and Mauny as much as it did the contemporaneous methods and attitudes of Anglophone "new archaeology." In addition, Posnansky's recognition of the importance of teaching led him to provide a substantial number of students (including, almost uniquely for the time, a number of Africans and women) with an introduction to West African field research. Some of these students would go on to conduct important ethnoarchaeological research on their own through the 1970s and 1980s from a number of different perspectives. These works have included Roderick McIntosh's taphonomic (fossilization) analysis of mud walls at Hani near Begho, Kofi Agorsah's investigations of the social correlates of spatial variability, and Marla Berns's art history study of ceramic production in the Gongola Valley of Nigeria.

After a decrease in the number of ethnoarchaeological projects in West Africa during the late 1970s, the pace of work quickened in the early 1980s, as the initial generation of investigators brought their own students into the field. Thus, the very productive archaeological research by Roderick and Susan McIntosh in the Inland Niger Delta of Mali was the basis for studies of craft specialists by Adria Laviolette. Probably the largest ethnoarchaeological research project in West Africa during this time period was the Mandara Archaeological Project, begun in northern Cameroon by Nicholas J. David in 1984 and continuing (with various offshoots, including Scott MacEachern's Project Mafa-Wandala) through the end of the century. The Mandara project, modeled more-or-less explicitly on the work of Ian Hodder in East Africa, exhibited the same interest in the use of artifacts to determine social relationships across ethnic boundaries and to develop theories of stylistic variation in material culture. Unlike Hodder's work, however, the Mandara project was designed as a broadly based, collaborative undertaking with responsibility for investigations of specific research problems—for the most part different realms of material culture—shared among researchers.

This interchange has been extremely fruitful but has almost inevitably resulted in some divergence of long-term objectives, as different researchers pursue increasingly varied research goals. At the start of this work in 1984, members of the Mandara Archaeological Project had rather optimistic expectations that somewhat straight-

forward relations would be found to exist between artifact variability and social patterning. In fact, these relationships are not at all simple, mediated, as they appear to be, by ideological systems and historical circumstance. Ethnoarchaeological investigations, balanced between archaeology and ethnography, exhibit a tendency to evolve into either more general ethnographic analyses or quite specific technical or experimental approaches designed to provide answers to particular archaeological problems. The Mandara project has displayed this tendency by changing, to some extent, from an ethnoarchaeological project to one primarily concerned with more conventional ethnographic and archaeological analysis.

During the same period, very significant (and different) ethnoarchaeological research was being undertaken in Mali and, to some extent, in Mauritania, by Alain Gallay of the University of Geneva and his associates. This research was tied to the development of "logicist" approaches within Francophone archaeology in western Europe during the 1970s and 1980s. Logicist theory is strongly positivist, and its roots can be traced to very formalist developments in systems theory and computer programming, where meaning is derived from a set of explicit statements proceeding in a sequence. In logicist ethnoarchaeology, the research process depends upon logical relationships between field observations of present-day materials and behaviors and upon propositions made on the basis of these observations. Gallay sought to apply this model of ethnoarchaeological research to a number of field situations with the Mission Archéologique et Ethnoarchéologique Suisse en Afrique de l'Ouest. This work has included the study of ceramic variation among groups in and around the Inland Niger Delta of Mali and the archaeological analysis of the site of Hamdallahi, capital of the empire of Macina in the early to mid-19th century.

The rather rigid logicist method often appears ill adapted to the messy demands of fieldwork. In this, it resembles some of the more doctrinaire developments of "new archaeology" during the 1960s and 1970s, and, as with these latter programs, logicist fieldwork seems sometimes to succeed despite its theoretical underpinnings, rather than because of them. Nevertheless, the ethnoarchaeological and ethnohistorical research associated with Gallay's project has often been successful and high quality, as investigators have developed an important and useful body of data on artifact variation within and between ethnic groups and especially on the role that craft specialization plays in determining the characteristics of artifact assemblages within communities in Mali.

West Africa has seen a profusion of smaller-scale ethnoarchaeological projects being undertaken during the 1980s and 1990s. Perhaps most significant in the long term has been the increasing involvement of local archaeologists in ethnoarchaeological research, in part as a response to the worsening economic situation and to decreasing support of local research. Ethnoarchaeological research is, all other things being equal, cheaper than most equivalent archaeological undertakings. Much ethnoarchaeological work has involved the documentation of technological and economic processes that may disappear under the pressures of modernization in the near future. In addition, the discipline offers local perspectives on West African life—perspectives that can act as valuable correctives and alternatives to prevalent Euro-American archaeological approaches. At least two researchers from West Africa, Kofi Agorsah (Ghana) and Augustin F. C. Holl (Cameroon) have involved themselves in research of broader theoretical applicability. Agorsah began work in the 1970s with Posnansky's West African Trade Project and has continued his earlier research on spatial variability and archaeological and ethnoarchaeological theory. Holl's work has focused upon questions of land use, intrasite variation, and increases in social complexity on the southern plains of the Lake Chad Basin. He is perhaps the primary successor to Lebeuf in this region, although his approaches are very much influenced by Anglophone traditions of processual research.

Other projects undertaken in West Africa over the last 20 years include the work by Robert Netting and Glenn and Priscilla Stone on labor and settlement systems among the Kofyar people of north-central Nigeria. This work illustrates very well the difficulties that can emerge in attempt-

ing a too-rigid definition of ethnoarchaeology, as it has important implications both for archaeological research and for the study of agrarian populations adapting to new economic systems. Other regional studies have included: Olivier Gosselain's exceptionally careful and thorough examination of ceramic-production sequences in southern Cameroon, R. M. A. Bedaux's continued long-term study of ceramics and other items of material culture in and around the territory of the Dogon people of Mali, S. E. Smith's studies of Tuareg environmental adaptations (the first explicit ethnoarchaeological research among pastoral groups in West Africa), C. Descamp's studies of shell middens in Senegal, and A.-M. and P. Pétrequin's study of lakeshore villages in Benin (undertaken to gather data for the interpretation of Neolithic lakeshore sites in Europe). Ethnoarchaeology in this part of the continent obviously remains a diverse field.

By the mid-1990s, the nature of that diversity may have changed somewhat since the beginnings of explicitly ethnoarchaeological research in West Africa in the 1960s. Ethnoarchaeology in this area is still marked by considerable continuity, with research interests—artifact-production sequences, site-formation processes, and land use—remaining rather constant. At the same time, the increased involvement of Africans and of women in this research is an exceptionally important development, since the perspectives of members of these groups have been all too often overlooked in the course of ethnographic work in West Africa. There is also a greater interpenetration of Francophone and Anglophone approaches, due probably to the increasing international nature of the discipline and to an increased willingness on the part of Anglophones (especially North Americans) to consider other research approaches. Finally, the milieu within which West African research is carried out has also changed since the 1960s, often not for the better. The accumulating economic, political, and social crises that exist in a number of West African countries act as a barrier to research within present-day communities, and far more importantly, they remain a great burden upon these nations' citizens, who continue to build decent lives when the research is finished.

BIBLIOGRAPHY

Atherton, J. 1983. Ethnoarchaeology in Africa. *African Archaeological Review* 1: 75–104.

Berns, M. 1993. Art, history and gender: Women and clay in West Africa. *African Archaeological Review* 11: 129–148.

David, N., J. Sterner, and K. Gavua. 1988. Why pots are decorated. *Current Anthropology* 29: 365–389.

de Barros, P. 1990. Changing paradigms, goals and methods in the archaeology of Francophone West Africa. In *A history of African archaeology,* ed. P. Robertshaw, 155–172. London and Portsmouth: James Currey Ltd. and Heinemann.

Gallay, A. 1989. Logicism: A French view of archaeological theory founded in computational perspective. *Antiquity* 63: 27-39.

Gosselain O. 1992. Technology and style: Potters and pottery among Bafia of Cameroon. *Man* 27: 559–586.

Holl, A. F. C. 1987. Mound formation processes and societal transformations: A case study from the Perichadian plain. *Journal of Anthropological Archaeology* 6: 122–158.

Kense, F. 1990. Archaeology in Anglophone West Africa. In *A history of African archaeology,* ed. P. Robertshaw, 135–154. London and Portsmouth: James Currey Ltd. and Heinemann.

Scott MacEachern

PREHISTORY
OF AFRICA

The Emergence of Humanity

HOMINID ORIGINS

Charles Darwin, in his 1871 treatise on human evolution, argued that Africa was the logical cradle of the human species, the place where humankind originated. Of course, Darwin did not base this insightful perspective on fossil evidence because no such evidence existed in his day. Rather, he based it on his conviction that comparative anatomy showed humans were more closely related to living African apes than to Asian apes and thus must have emerged in the former's homeland.

The accuracy of Darwin's insight is demonstrated by several lines of current evidence. Numerous studies on living (extant) hominoids have substantiated that humans share a closer phylogenetic (evolutionary) relationship with African apes than with any other creatures. Studies of fossil apes known from Africa also support this conclusion. Perhaps most importantly, extensive fossil remains of the earliest and most primitive humans known, the australopithecines, now have been recovered from, and only from, Africa.

African Apes and Human Origins

In addition to extensive anatomical evidence, numerous molecular studies have clearly demonstrated that African apes are evolutionarily closer to humans than to Asian apes. Several of these studies, including work by Morris Goodman and colleagues, have also shown that, among African apes, chimpanzees are more similar to humans than to gorillas.

As Milford Wolpoff notes, these molecular studies provide compelling evidence for an African origin of the human line but are playing havoc with traditional approaches to the taxonomy of the hominoids (see table 15).

Fossil apes are known in Africa as far back as the Early Miocene, some 23 million years ago. The earliest apes are placed in the genus *Proconsul*. Peter Andrews, Alan Walker, and several others have documented that proconsuls exhibit cranio-dental similarities to living apes, and the presence of such features as a Y-5 or dryopithecine pattern (the pattern of the cusps is such that the depressed space between them forms a *Y*) on the lower molars establishes them as unequivocal hominoids. Like other hominoids, proconsuls lacked tails, but they also exhibited many primitive (monkeylike) postcranial features. These indicate generalized quadrupedalism rather than the specialized locomotor pattern of the extant African apes, a pattern based on adaptations to brachiation (swinging by the arms) and suspensory (hanging) behavior. Ecological evidence suggests that proconsuls were restricted to the expansive rain forests of the East African Miocene.

African Miocene apes, spreading over a tremendous region, ultimately migrated into Eurasia following the establishment of permanent land contact. Many lineages of the Miocene apes, including the proconsuls, became extinct, but in Africa, the direct line leading to extant apes and humans may be present by 17 to 18 million years ago. The fossil genera *Afropithecus* and *Kenyapithecus,* known from several localities in Kenya, exhibit several cranio-dental characteristics that

Table 15 *Traditional phenetic taxonomy (left) compared to Milford Wolpoff's phylogenetic taxonomy of the extant members of the superfamily Hominoidea*

Phenetic taxonomy	Phylogenetic taxonomy
Family: Hylobatidae Genus: Hylobates (gibbons and siamangs)	Family: Hylobatidae Genus: Hylobates
Family: Pongidae Genera: Pongo (orangutan) Gorilla Pan (chimpanzee)	Family: Pongidae Subfamily: Pongidae Genus: Pongo
Family: Hominidae Genera: Homo (human) Australopithecus*	Subfamily: Anthropithecine Tribe: Gorillini Genus: Gorilla Tribe: Hominini Genera: Pan Homo Australopithecus*
* extinct	

are more similiar than proconsul features to extant apes. Postcranially, however, both Kenyan genera remain primitive, like *Proconsul,* and their exact relationship to living hominoids is unclear.

From the 17- to 18-million-year-old deposits at Moroto in Uganda, a partial face exhibits cranio-dental features similar to those of extant apes—particularly the broadened incisors and premolars documented for the Kenyan genera. Furthermore, a lumbar vertebra indicates a less flexible and more orthograde spine (capable of walking in an upright position), which, according to Carol Ward, conforms to the extant African ape pattern. Dan Gebo and colleagues see evidence of suspensory locomotor capabilities in a newly discovered scapular (shoulder) fragment remains from Moroto. They propose the generic name *Morotopithecus* for the Moroto ape and argue that it represents the first unequivocal member of extant large-bodied hominoids.

By at least 12 million years ago, the line leading to the orangutan, represented by the genus *Sivapithecus,* was established in Asia. *Sivapithecus* and extant orangutans share a number of unique cranio-dental features demonstrating their separation from African apes. Fossils of

African apes are rare and fragmentary at this time, but remains like the 13-million-year-old *Otavipithecus* mandible from Namibia, the approximately 10-million-year-old Samburu Hills maxilla, the 10- to 13-million-year-old Ngorora teeth, and the approximately 6-million-year-old Lukeino molar (all from Kenya) attest to the continued existence of African hominoids. It is from forms like these that extant African apes and humans evolved.

Dart, Darwin, and the First Discoveries of *Australopithecus*

The beginnings of humans as a distinct lineage are found in creatures placed in the genus *Australopithecus.* The first australopithecine specimen to be recognized was described by Raymond Dart in 1925 and came from the site of Taung in South Africa. The fossil consisted of a partial skull, including the face, lower jaw, and endocast (a natural cast of the inside of the brain case) of a child. Dart's assessment of the Taung skull was that it represented an "ape" at or close to the beginning of the human lineage. Dart specifically noted the humanlike form of the canine tooth, indications for bipedalism (as reflected in the perceived position of the brain stem on the endocast), and the site's location in savanna rather than forest as support for his claim. Interestingly, Darwin had speculated in his *Descent of Man* that features such as these would characterize the divergence of humans from the apes and constructed an ecological model involving a shift from arboreal to terrestrial life in less forested habitats as a key to human beginnings.

Dart's interpretation of the Taung child, which he classified as *Australopithecus africanus* (southern ape of Africa), was widely criticized on a number of fronts. Taung was a single specimen, only a child, and did not exhibit the brain enlargement that was expected of even very early humans at this time. In 1936, Robert Broom found the first adult australopithecine at Sterkfontein, and the accumulation of large numbers of australopithecine fossils in South Africa and later in East Africa have demonstrated the accuracy of Dart's interpretation of Taung and of Darwin's insights on the primacy of Africa in the initial phases of human evolution.

Today, australopithecine fossils are known from more than 20 localities in South Africa and along the Rift Valley system of Ethiopia, Kenya, Tanzania, and Malawi. The genus *Australopithecus* is recognized to comprise between four and seven species covering the time frame from at least 4.1 million years (and perhaps as early as 5.6 to 5.8 million years) to about 1.3 million years ago in East Africa and 1 million years ago in South Africa. Despite considerable morphological variability, the genus *Australopithecus* is characterized by a series of distinct features and functional complexes. The major ones are:

1. Numerous features of the axial skeleton and pelvic limb reflecting obligate bipedalism and erect posture
2. Enlarged posterior teeth, massive jaws, and robust facial structure (relative to body size) needed for mastication (chewing)
3. Incipient brain enlargement (encephalization) compared to body size
4. Canine and lower third premolar forms that indicate a nonapelike function for this "canine complex"

These and other features clearly align australopithecines with the human family. Additional features, such as aspects of upper-limb anatomy, dental morphology, and general cranial form, particularly in the earliest australopithecines, unequivocally demonstrate the ape ancestry of humans. Considerable debate still focuses on details of the interpretation of australopithecines' anatomy, phylogeny (evolutionary history), and behavior, but there are no longer any doubts concerning their pivotal role in our evolutionary history.

The Earliest Australopithecines and the African Ape Connection

Since 1978, the earliest and most primitive humans have generally been classified in the taxon *Australopithecus afarensis,* established on the basis of fossil samples from the East African sites of Hadar and Laetoli. The remains from Laetoli were originally assigned to the genus *Homo* by Mary D. Leakey, and three taxa, including *Homo,* were initially identified at Hadar by Don Johanson and colleagues. However, comparative studies by Johanson and especially Tim White demonstrated that the human remains from both sites represented a single primitive and highly variable species. Because of its morphological pattern and early date, White and Johanson argued that *A. afarensis* was the root of two subsequent branches of the human family tree, with one branch leading to *Homo* and the other to later australopithecines.

Since 1994, two earlier, even more primitive human species have been recognized in East Africa. White and his colleagues initially placed the 4.4-million-year-old fragmentary remains from the site of Aramis in Ethiopia into *A. ramidus.* More recently, they have transferred this species to the new genus *Ardipithecus,* which they believe is the sister taxon of *Australopithecus.* This means that the Aramis hominoids are very closely related to, but in a separate line from, the australopithecines. Even more recently, Meave G. Leakey and colleagues have assigned the 3.9- to 4.1-million-year-old specimens from Kanapoi and Allia Bay in Kenya to *A. anamensis* and have argued that this species is more primitive than and possibly ancestral to *A. afarensis*. Whether or not enough differences exist to warrant a new species must await further judgment, but the morphological pattern indicated by the Allia Bay and Kanapoi specimens is commensurate with a slightly earlier representative of the same lineage as seen in the samples from Hadar and Laetoli.

These early humans (A. afarensis including the Allia Bay and Kanapoi sample) have a number of features that are either ape-reminiscent or essentially apelike in expression. Such characteristics are significant because they provide an unequivocal testament of the ape ancestry of the human line and clearly confirm the close phylogenetic relationship of humans and apes.

The canine crowns of these earliest humans, for example, are very large compared to those of later humans. Although these teeth wear down from the tip, as do the teeth of humans, these basal human canines often exhibit a remnant distal cutting blade reminiscent of their ape ancestors. The canine roots are also large and form the facial protrusions (canine jugae) along the side of the nose that are characteristic of apes. The protrusions, combined with the forward regulation and projection of palate (upper jaw), give the lower face of A. afarensis a very apelike appearance. Other ape-reminiscent features of the jaws and teeth include the presence of a space between the upper canine and lateral incisor, expanded medial maxillary central incisors that are much larger than the laterals, and lower third premolars that are elliptical in shape with dominant cheek-side cusps. This last feature is very similar to apes' lower third premolars. In apes, these teeth sharpen (hone) the upper canines, but in early humans, they tend to exhibit more development of the tongue-side cusps and are more rotated in the tooth row.

The contours of the crania, in both lateral and posterior views, are strikingly chimpanzeelike, especially in the region around the mastoid processes (a process of the temporal bone behind the ear). Additionally, the crania of specimens from Hadar (such as the juvenile AL 162-28 and adults AL 333-45 and 444-2) exhibit a lateral compound temporonuchal crest (a bony projection for muscle attachment toward the rear of the skull). Such crests are typical in apes but generally tend to extend across the entire breadth of

the rear of the skull, not just laterally. Crests themselves are not indicative of biological relationships as they are not directly under genetic control. They are, however, reflections of patterns that are phylogenetically significant. In this case, compound temporonuchal crests indicate expansion of the posterior temporalis and nuchal muscles relative to cranial vault size, which in turn reflects ape patterns of anterior tooth (especially canine) use. These early humans no longer use their anterior teeth exactly as apes do, as Wolpoff has demonstrated, but this morphological complex is certainly a remnant from even earlier ancestors who did.

In the postcranial skeleton, A. afarensis exhibits shoulder and upper-limb structures that approach the ape pattern to a considerable extent. These include relatively elongated arms compared to those of later humans, a scapular glenoid (joint for the arm) that is angled cranially, and long, curved fingers and a short thumb. Jack Stern, Randall Susman, and William Jungers argue that these features are climbing and hanging adaptations. It is important to note, however, that all of these features are as close or closer to the human than ape condition, particularly when some are scaled for size. Clearly, for example, there is no evidence of knuckle walking or brachiation in these early humans. Nonetheless, these forms do seem to indicate considerable climbing ability in the earliest human bipeds. Most importantly, they clearly reflect the emergence of early hominids from a body plan like that of extant apes.

Early Australopithecines as Primitive Humans

No other australopithecine fossil is as famous, and few have been as scientifically informative, as Lucy (AL 288-1), the diminutive partial skeleton found at Hadar in 1974. In particular, Lucy's pelvis and femur reveal a creature that was clearly bipedal, despite an estimated size of only about 105 centimeters and 27 kilograms. Owen Lovejoy's assessment of Lucy and other pertinent A. afarensis fossils suggests that they were obligate bipeds with a pelvic and femoral morphology functionally identical to that of more recent humans, except for certain features in which they were even better adapted to bipedalism than present-day humans. For example, Lovejoy notes that the iliac (hip) blades angle out more than in modern people and that femoral necks are relatively longer. He argues that this complex results in a more efficient trunk-balancing system during bipedal locomotion in the australopithecines, because some muscles are in a more biomechanically efficient position relative to the hip joint where this balance takes place. This assessment has been challenged to some degree by Stern and colleagues, who suggest that while early humans were clearly bipeds, some aspects of bipedalism are not fully sophisticated and none represents "superhuman" adaptations. They argue, for instance, that the iliac blade faces posteriorly in *A. afarensis* as in the apes and that the muscles attaching here (the anterior gluteals) could not function like those of a human biped unless the knee and hip were flexed (bent). Regardless of who is more correct regarding this issue, it is clear that *A. afarensis* was an obligate bipedal creature and that bipedalism was developed very early in the human evolutionary story.

Foot bones from Hadar and footprints found on a trail at Laetoli provide further evidence of the essentially human nature of the lower limbs in *A. afarensis*. Studies by Tim White, Gen Suwa, Bruce Latimer, and others have shown that the ankle and foot anatomy of the specimens from Hadar falls within the human range, and Russell Tuttle has shown that the Laetoli footprints are consistent in form with those made by habitually unshod modern humans.

Despite apelike crania, *A. afarensis* already reflects an incipient level of the brain expansion characteristic of later humans. Two specimens (AL 162-28 and 333-45) yield an average cranial capacity of about 430 cubic centimeters. Gorillas have larger cranial capacities, but in mammals, brain size must be considered in relation to body size. The average body weight for *A. afarensis* can be estimated at about 35 kilograms. Gorillas average twice this weight or more, but chimpanzees are a better comparison since the average body size of both sexes combined is about 42 kilograms. Using these figures, a 35-kilogram *A. afarensis* would have a 430-cubic-centimeter

brain, while a slightly bigger (42 kilogram) chimpanzee would have a cranial capacity of only about 385 cubic centimeters. Thus even in the earliest known members of the human family, the brain is beginning to get bigger.

Although there are ape-reminiscent features of the teeth, other dental characteristics align *A. afarensis* with other australopithecines. The pattern of wear on the canines is one significant case in point. Also William Leonard and M. Hegman have demonstrated that the lower third premolars of *A. afarensis* tend to become less primitive and more like those of other australopithecines in the later part of their temporal range. Additionally, these earliest humans exhibit the beginnings of the posterior dental megadontia (an increase in occlusal surface of the back teeth) that typifies subsequent australopithecines. Compared to body size, molars and premolars in *A. afarensis* are large. Relative to later australopithecines, however, these earliest hominids exhibit less posterior dental megadontia. Furthermore, the occlusal enamel on their posterior teeth is very thick, as it is in all subsequent australopithecines and later humans. Enamel thickening and posterior dental megadontia, along with aspects of the jaws, reflect grinding capabilities that are enhanced in later australopithecines.

From the standpoint of paleoecology, these earliest humans are also interesting. From the Miocene into the Pliocene, there was a general climatic trend toward cooling and drying, resulting in the shrinkage and fragmentation of the forested habitats into which most Miocene apes radiated. The expanding open woodlands and savanna would have been a resource-rich niche, which was exploited by some ape lineages toward the end of the Miocene. The lineage leading to humans was undoubtedly one of these, while another leads through *Sivapithecus* to the orangutan and yet another to the giant Plio-Pleistocene ape, *Gigantopithecus*.

A. afarensis appears to have exploited a mosaic of environmental habitats ranging from bush and open woodlands to gallery forest. Its terrestrially focused adaptation to such a wide econiche, particularly the more open areas, certainly reflects an early stage in the emerging adaptive pattern of humans, who exploit an eclectic range of ecological resources. In his model, Darwin implicated hunting as a prime behavioral mover for this shift, and these ideas subsequently influenced Dart's "hunting ape" conception of early humans. There is, however, no indication that these early humans were hunting apes. In fact, we have no archaeological evidence of tools or occupation or activity sites related to them. Nevertheless, *A. afarensis* appears to exhibit an adaptive pattern clearly separate from known apes.

After *A. afarensis*

After 3 million years ago, humans unquestionably diversify phylogenetically, and at least two distinct lineages are evident between 2 and 2.5 million years ago. One of these is represented by *A. africanus*, Dart's original australopithecine taxon, which is traditionally restricted to the South African sites of Taung, Sterkfontein, Gladysvale, and Makapansgat. The other lineage, identified by fossil remains from Lomekwi in Kenya and Omo in Ethiopia, represents the earliest of the robust australopithecines. (See table 16 for other East African sites where human fossils older than 3 million years have been found.)

The South African *A. africanus* sample ranges in age from at least 2.3 million years old to just under 3 million years old. In many ways, *A. africanus* is very similar to *A. afarensis*, and in other ways, it differs in the direction of more recent humans. The postcranial similarities of *A. afarensis* and *A. africanus* are striking. The pelvic region shows the same morphology, the limb proportions and shoulder anatomy are similar, and both had six lumbar vertebrae. Body size also remains roughly the same, with a combined-sex average of about 35 kilograms, but brain size increases slightly to an average of about 470 cubic centimeters. As was also the case with *A. afarensis*, no stone tools or evidence of human activity sites are associated unequivocally with *A. africanus* specimens. Dart's earlier claim of an "osteodontokeratic culture" (a culture using animal bones, teeth, and horns) at Makapansgat has been shown by C. K. Brain to have resulted from carnivore activity.

Marked change is seen in the cranio-dental anatomy and reflects two basic shifts. First, the specifically ape-reminiscent features of *A. afarensis* are gone. Canines and lower third premolars in *A. africanus* are smaller (though still large by modern human standards) and totally humanlike in form. The cranium itself still looks slightly chimpanzeelike, but the compound temporonuchal crests, canine jugae, and apelike anterior palate of *A. afarensis* are largely gone. Second, the trend toward increasing posterior dental megadontia is evident in comparison to *A. afarensis*. The molars and premolars are significantly larger in *A. africanus* compared to body size. Also, the zygomatics (cheeks) are positioned more anteriorly, and the palate is positioned under the upper face to a greater degree in *A. africanus* than in *A. afarensis*. These and other aspects of buttressing in the face creates what Yoel Rak calls the *nasoalveolar triangular frame,* a complex clearly related to powerful mastication in these early humans.

Robust Australopithecines— The Other Guys

About 2.5 million years ago, new and striking forms of early humans begin to appear in the fossil record. Known collectively as robust australopithecines, they have been discovered at numerous sites in both South and East Africa. In East Africa, their earliest occurrences are at the sites of Omo and Lomekwi from around 2.5 million years ago. Subsequently, they are well represented at several sites but seem to disappear about 1.3 million years ago. In South Africa, robust australopithecines are known from Swartkrans (members 1, 2, and 3) and Kromdraai but are less securely dated. One view would place their dates from about 1 to 1.8 million years ago. Based on extensive shifts in the populations of antelope and other bovids, Elisabeth Vrba suggests that the beginnings of these deposits may extend back to the global-cooling event about 2.5 million years ago.

Robust australopithecines share common features, but there are also temporal and geographic differences among them. The shared features generally relate to the presence of a massive mastication (chewing) apparatus. Compared to earlier australopithecines, robusts exhibit signifi-

Table 16 *East African sites with human fossil remains older than 3 million years*

Allia Bay
Kenya (Lake Turkana). Mandible teeth and radius. 3.9 million years old. Placed by M. G. Leakey, A. Walker, and colleagues in *A. anamensis*. Paleoecology: galley forest.

Belohdelie
Ethiopia (Middle Awash Valley). Cranial fragments. Frontal bone similar to Hadar specimens. 3.9 million years old.

Fejej
Ethiopia. Seven teeth. 3.6 to 3.7 million years old.

Hadar
Ethiopia. More than 300 hominid fossils. 2.95 to 3.4 million years old. Largest sample of *A. afarensis*. Considerable size variation. AL 288-1 (the Lucy skeleton), 3.18 million years old. Most specimens, including the AL 333 (the "first family" remains), slightly older. New male skull (AL 444-2), about 3 million years old. Ecological indicators range from bush to woodland grading to gallery forest along lakes and rivers. Olduwan tools from Gona region, 2.6 million years old, younger than hominid deposits.

Kanapoi
Kenya. Maxilla, two mandibles, temporal bone, teeth, distal humerus (found in 1965), and tibia (found in 1994). 4.1 million years old. Placed by M. D. Leakey, A. Walker, and colleagues in *A. anamensis*. Paleoecology: dry, possibly open woodland and bush.

Koobi Fora and West Turkana
Kenya (Lake Turkana). Series of very fragmentary remains with probable affinities to *A. afarensis*. 3.06 to 3.4 million years old.

Laetoli
Tanzania. Jaws, teeth, and a partial juvenile skeleton (LH 21). Human footprint trail at site G. 3.5 to 3.7 million years old. Ecological data suggest open grassland with scattered trees and forest nearby. First hominid finds made in 1935. Recognized as *A. afarensis* in 1981 by T. White.

Lothagam
Kenya. Single mandible fragment. Earliest data for possible hominid. 5.6 to 5.8 million years old.

Mabaget
Kenya (Lake Baringo). Proximal part of humerus. 5.1 million years old.

Maka
Ethiopia (Middle Awash Valley). Humerus, mandibles, teeth, proximal humerus, and bit of ulna. 3.4 to 4 million years old.

Omo
Ethiopia. 23 teeth from Usno formation. 3 million years old.

Silbot Hill
Kenya (Lake Turkana). Radius. 3.8 to 4 million years old.

Tabarin
Kenya. Mandible fragment of possible hominid. 5 million years old.

cantly larger posterior teeth (posterior dental megadontia) and large mandibles. Their faces exhibit wide cheeks to accommodate the large muscles that operate the lower jaw and thus provide the power in chewing. One of these muscles, the temporalis muscle, grows so large that it requires an additional attachment area on the brain case. As a result, sagittal crests (bony ridges developed along the top of the skull to accommodate affixing the muscles that operate the jaws) are formed. In contrast, the anterior teeth (incisors and canines) of robust australopithecines are smaller than those of earlier australopithecines.

Ever since John Robinson suggested that robust australopithecines were specialized herbivores, the generally accepted interpretation has been that their powerful mastication apparatus evolved as an adaptation to a diet of plants. Studies of microwear on posterior teeth of robust australopithecines by Fred Grine, Alan Walker, and colleagues have tended to confirm that small, tough plant remains were certainly a part of the diet of South African robusts but that more fruit and low-quality plant remains were consumed by East African forms. Walker has also noted that microwear can reflect only the diet close to time of death and thus may not reflect the full scope of exploited food resources. Additionally, Andrew Sillen and colleagues show that the chemical analysis of robust australopithecine bones at Swartkrans does not indicate a specialized herbivorous diet but rather a broad omnivorous one. Thus, it appears that the development of robust australopithecine morphology is no longer unequivocally explainable as a relatively narrow dietary specialization.

Robust australopithecines are usually classified into three species. The early East African robusts from Omo and Lomekwi, especially WT 17000 (the "black skull"), are placed in *Australopithecus aethiopicus*. These are the most primitive robusts with apparently very small brains (the cranial capacity estimate for WT 17000 is 415 cubic centimeters), flat cranial bases and marked forward projection of the upper jaws (similar to those of *A. afarensis),* very large sagittal crests, compound temporonuchal crests (also like those of *A. afarensis),* and large anterior teeth. Postcranial remains are rare, but if the very long ulna (a bone of the forearm) from an Omo specimen represents *A. aethiopicus,* the presence of relatively long arms (like earlier australopithecines) is suggested. It also hints that the body size of some of these early robusts was quite large.

Later East African robusts are classified as *Australopithecus boisei* and are well known at Olduvai Gorge, Koobi Fora, Chesowanja, and other localities. These creatures exhibit the most massive faces, jaws, and posterior teeth of any human forms. Unlike earlier australopithecines, their cranial bases are more flexed, as they are in *Homo,* so that the upper jaws do not protrude as far forward as in previous forms. The anterior teeth are very small, and postcranial elements indicate no significant locomotor differences from earlier australopithecines. Body size is comparable to *A. afarensis* and *A. africanus.*

South African robust australopithecines are very similar, but not identical to, their East African cousins. Classified as *Australopithecus robustus,* their crania and jaws conform closely to the *A. boisei* forms. However, their posterior teeth are not as large, nor their anterior teeth as small, as those of *A. boisei.* Their postcranial bones suggest that they have the same body plan and size as other australopithecines. Cranial capacity is somewhat larger with a combined-sex average of 538 cubic centimeters.

The major issues involving the three robust australopithecine species center on their phylogenetic relationship to each other and to other humans. *A. aethiopicus* is often seen as the ancestor of both *A. boisei* and *A. robustus.* In this view, robust australopithecines is a monophyletic group (a group that developed from a single ancestral form). Some scholars see robust morphology as evolving separately, as parallel adaptations to powerful mastication, in two separate early human lineages.

The Appearance of *Homo*

In fossil records dating to just after 2 million years ago appear human remains that most scholars recognize as early members of the genus *Homo.* John Robinson was the first to suggest that some australopithecines were "advanced." The taxon most closely associated with such specimens is *Homo habilis,* established by Louis Leakey and colleagues in 1964. Specimens attributed to early *Homo* are now known from a series of sites in East Africa (including Omo, Olduvai Gorge, and Koobi Fora) and have been claimed at Swartkrans and Sterkfontein in South Africa. The temporal range for these samples is approximately from 1.7 to 2.2 million years ago, although Andrew Hill and Steven Ward argue that the fragmentary temporal bone from Chemeron and dating to 2.4 million years ago also belongs to this group.

The definition of *advanced* in connection with these specimens depends on the presence of one or more of the following features:

1. Relatively large brain (with all presumed early *Homo* crania lumped together, cranium capacity averages 665 cubic centimeters)
2. Craniofacial features similar to those of *Homo erectus*

3. Moderate- to small-sized posterior teeth and anterior teeth that are slightly larger than those of robust australopithecines
4. Postcrania that differ from those of australopithecines and are more like those of *H. erectus* in morphology and limb proportions

Not all specimens exhibit all of these features. In fact, many specimens are placed in *Homo* because they exhibit only one of the characteristics. For example, a 1.9-million-year-old skull (ER 1470) from Koobi Fora has a large cranial capacity (725 cubic centimeters), but its craniofacial anatomy is unlike later *H. erectus*. Another 1.9-million-year-old skull (ER 1813) is very similar to early *H. erectus* in facial form but has a cranial capacity of only 510 cubic centimeters. Other postcrania from Koobi Fora (femora ER 1472 and ER 1481) that are unlike the postcrania of australopithecines cannot be securely associated with any cranial remains. Such differences have led scholars to conclude that more than one taxon is represented in the Koobi Fora sample. Bernard Wood argues that there are two species: *H. habilis* (comprising the smaller specimens— like ER 1813—with "advanced" craniofacial anatomy, relatively smaller brains, and postcrania similar to those of australopithecines) and *H. rudolfensis* (including large-brained specimens— like ER 1470—that tend to have large posterior teeth and skulls similar to those of australopithecines). The "advanced" postcrania may represent *H. rudolfensis,* but this association has never been demonstrated. A two-species scheme was also articulated in the late 1970s by A. C. Walker and Richard F. Leakey. On the other hand, Phillip Tobias, Milford Wolpoff, and others favor maintaining all of the samples from Koobi Fora in a single, variable taxon, *H. habilis.*

Whether or not one recognizes one or two lineages of early *Homo,* the fact is that these humans were clearly a distinct part of the radiation of human lineages during the Late Pliocene and Early Pleistocene. Trying to understand the evolutionary details and adaptive basis for this radiation has been the focus of considerable research and continues to be the subject of lively scientific debate.

Explanations for the Early Human Adaptive Radiation

The root of early human radiation is clearly found in the Pliocene *A. afarensis* sample, regardless of how many taxa it might comprise. It is also evident that at least two distinct human lineages diverged from this species by 2.5 million years ago. One is represented by *A. africanus* and the other by *A. aethiopicus.* These lineages are distinct and cannot be derived from each other. This is because *A. aethiopicus* is too primitive to be a descendent of *A. africanus* and is chronologically too late to be the latter's ancestor. How these two lineages relate phylogenetically to subsequent lineages is a matter of considerable contention.

Precisely what factors lead to the splitting of lineages and adaptive radiation in any organism are almost impossible to identify. Obviously, geographic and ecological factors play significant roles, but exactly what roles they play and how they interact is difficult to glean from the historical record. For example, it is logical to tie the initial emergence of the human lineage to the ecological changes associated with the general cooling and drying trend during the Miocene. There would have certainly been considerable pressure on Miocene apes to exploit expanding open woodlands and savannas, but details of exactly how this unfolded are essentially nonexistent. Noel T. Boaz and Yves Coppens have recently suggested that, during the Miocene, the lineages leading to early humans and the African apes may have been separated by rifting and associated geological phenomena, which also contributed to the formation of the ecological zones into which the early humans radiated.

In a similar vein, Elizabeth Vrba and others have tied a distinct climatic cooling event around 2.5 million years ago to the diversification of human lineages between 2 and 2.5 million years ago. She suggests that this cooling initiated the spread of more arid and open environments in Africa and influenced adaptive diversification of, and species turnover in, humans as well as other organisms. While this is undoubtedly true, it is not clear how humans adapted to the cooler environment. Using paleoecological data,

Tim White has shown that robust australopithecines and early *Homo* did not prefer different habitats. Both tend to be found at the same sites in the same ecological settings. Of course, there may be habitat differences that are simply not extractable from the record, but nonextractable data are useless in the search for empirical explanations.

Adaptive differences have long been sought in the morphology of the australopithecines. For instance, claims of a split between herbivores and omnivores in early humans have been around since John Robinson developed his dietary hypothesis to explain the differences between South Africa robust and "gracile" australopithecines. It continues to be suggested that robust australopithecines were indeed herbivores of one sort or another, while early *Homo* was exploiting a broader dietary niche, including meat. In this scenario, it is often noted that the earliest stone tools at Gona and Omo appear around 2.5 million years ago, at the time of the environmental cooling and just before the appearance of the first identifiable members of *Homo*.

By about 2 million years ago, crude stone tools are known from several sites. Principle among these are Olduvai Gorge and Koobi Fora, where actual activity areas of early humans have been identified. These early indications of human behavior are referred to as the *Olduwan industry,* and it is often implied that this industry is the product of early *Homo*. This may be the case, but the fact is that once tools are present in the archaeological record, they are found with both robust australopithecines and early *Homo*. Thus, there is no objective basis for claiming tool manufacture exclusively for *Homo*. Add to this the indications from chemical analyses that robust australopithecines were not specialized herbivores, and it is clear that the factors underlying the adaptive radiation of early humans are far from simple and clear-cut.

In historical science, it is always easier to document past events than to explain why or how they occurred. The study of early human evolution is no exception. The biological patterns of early human evolution are very well documented as are indications of early human behavior and the broad ecological environment in which these things took place. Trying to understand the details of how these factors interrelate in our evolutionary history is a challenge that will be with us well into the 21st century.

BIBLIOGRAPHY

Aiello, L., and C. Dean. 1990. *An introduction to human evolutionary anatomy.* New York: Academic Press.

Andrews, P. 1992. Evolution and environment in the Hominoidea. *Nature* 360: 641–646.

Boaz, N. 1988. Status of *Australopithecus afarensis. Yearbook of Physical Anthropology* 31: 85–113.

Conroy, G. 1990. *Primate evolution.* New York: W. W. Norton.

Corruccini, R., and R. Ciochon, eds. 1994. *Integrative paths to the past.* Englewood Cliffs: Prentice-Hall.

Fleagle, J. 1988. *Primate adaptation and evolution.* New York: Academic Press.

Grine, F., ed. 1988. *Evolutionary history of the "robust" australopithecines.* New York: Aldine de Gruyter.

Hill, A., and S. Ward. 1988. Origin of the Hominidae: The record of African large hominoid evolution between 14 my and 4 my. *Yearbook of Physical Anthropology* 31: 49–83.

Lovejoy, C. O. 1988. Evolution of human walking. *Scientific American* 259: 118–125.

McHenry, H. 1992. Body size and proportions in early hominids. *American Journal of Physical Anthropology* 87: 407–431.

Rak, Y. 1983. *The australopithecine face.* New York: Academic Press.

Shelton, R. R., and H. McHenry. 1992. Evolutionary relationships among early hominids. *Journal of Human Evolution* 22: 351–366.

Stern, J., and R. Susman. 1983. The locomotor behavior of *Australopithecus afarensis. American Journal of Physical Anthropology* 60: 279–317.

Tattersall, I., E. Delson, and J. Van Couvering, eds. 1988. *Encyclopedia of human evolution and prehistory.* New York: Garland Publishers.

Tuttle, R. 1988. What's new in African paleoanthropology. *Annual Review of Anthropology* 17: 391–426.

Wolpoff, M. 1995. *Human evolution: 1996 edition.* New York: McGraw-Hill.

Wood, B. 1992. Early hominid species and speciation. *Journal of Human Evolution* 22: 351–366.

Fred Smith

MODERN HUMAN ORIGINS

Radiations of closely related species into different adaptive niches or geographic regions are common occurrences in evolutionary history. Human evolutionary history is characterized by at least three and possibly four, five, or six such radiations during the last 12 million years. In all of these, Africa plays a central role. The first was the radiation of African large-bodied hominoids, in the Late Miocene and Early Pliocene, from which the initial human lineage emerged. The second radiation, in the Late Pliocene and Early Pleistocene, resulted in the various australopithecine species, one of which gave rise to the earliest members of *Homo*. While there is basic consensus on the existence of these radiations, there is considerable disagreement regarding the others.

The third radiation is reflected in the evidence for multiple species of early *Homo* around 2 million years ago. These species included *H. habilis, H. rudolfensis,* and early *H. erectus* (sometimes classified as *H. ergaster*). Conventional perspectives view early *H. erectus* as evolving from one of the other two, but there are other opinions. The fourth radiation comprises the spread of early *H. erectus* out of Africa into Eurasia. In this case, there is no doubt about the occurrence of a radiation, but there is considerable debate about whether multiple species are represented in it. The fifth radiation, in the view of some scholars, involved later species of *Homo* and occurred between roughly 100,000 and 500,000 years ago. According to supporters of this view, our own species, *Homo sapiens,* emerged as an African branch of this fifth radiation. Finally, the sixth possible radiation was the spread of *Homo sapiens* (modern humans) out of Africa into Asia, Europe, and ultimately the rest of the world.

Africa is suggested as the source of all of these radiations and is the homeland of the genus *Homo*. Despite recent speculations about certain Asian specimens, the earliest unequivocal dates for *Homo* are from Africa, and there are no plausible ancestors for early *Homo* except in Africa. However, there is anything but consensus concerning the existence of the final two radiations mentioned above. In fact, the argument that modern humans emerged in Africa slightly more than 1 million years ago and spread as a new species out of Africa (the sixth radiation) have ignited one of the most vigorous debates in the recent history of human-evolutionary studies.

The Initial Radiation of *Homo*

The earliest definitive evidence of the genus *Homo* is found at Koobi Fora, Kenya, and dates to less than 2 million years ago. Other contemporaneous material comes from Omo in Ethiopia and, slightly later, from Olduvai Gorge in Tanzania. Some earlier specimens may also represent early *Homo*. The earliest of these is a fragment of a temporal bone from Chemeron in Kenya, dating to 2.4 million years ago. Steven Ward and Andrew Hill have claimed that the position of the mandibular fossa (where the mandible joins the cranium) and other features in this specimen are like those of *Homo* instead of other australopithecines. However, more evidence will be necessary before all doubts are removed about this specimen's affiliations. Otherwise, isolated teeth and lower jaws from Omo, Koobi Fora, and Uraha (Malawi) date to between 2 to 2.4 million years ago and have been claimed to represent *Homo*. The problem is that features unquestionably differentiating early *Homo* have yet to be isolated on mandibles and isolated teeth. Thus, at the present time, secure attribution to early *Homo* can only be made on the basis of reasonably complete crania, particularly the upper face and cranial vault.

The discoveries of early *Homo* remains by Louis and Mary Leakey in the 1960s were placed in the taxon *Homo habilis* in 1964. Although the validity of this taxon was criticized by John Robinson, Loring Brace, Milford Wolpoff, and others in the 1960s and 1970s, almost universal acceptance was gained following the discoveries of more complete early *Homo* specimens by Richard F. Leakey and his team at Koobi Fora in the 1970s. But the Koobi Fora specimens also brought additional problems for *Homo habilis*. The range of variation exhibited in the sample was not a significant issue when only the Olduvai Gorge specimens were known, but the addition

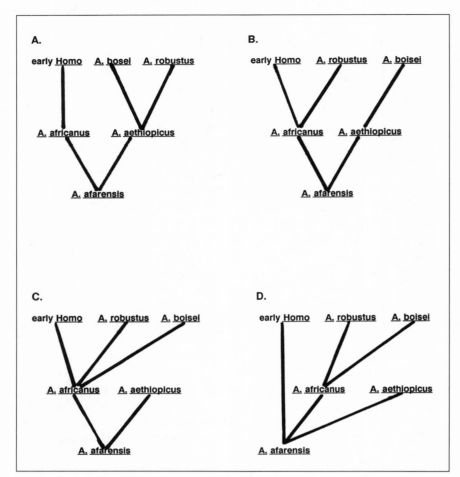

Fig. 19 *Schematic presentations of four interpretations of Plio-Pleistocene human evolutionary history*

ridge), the shape of the cranial vault, and size of the palate are all very similar to those of australopithecines. *H. habilis* is characterized by a smaller brain, smaller teeth, and a face more similar to the face of *H. erectus*, including a distinct supraorbital torus.

While there is general agreement that variation is considerable, there are several difficulties with attempts to partition the known sample into two distinct segments. As Philip Rightmire has noted, there is no completely satisfying way to partition the sample, and no matter how it is done, the resulting groups are more like each other than they are like *H. erectus*.

Recently, Wolpoff has suggested that the earliest remains of *Homo erectus* (which he calls early *Homo sapiens*) were contemporaries of the earliest unequivocal *H. habilis* and *H. rudolfensis* and thus were a part of the earliest radiation of *Homo*. His argument is based on a 1.9-million-year-old occipital bone fragment that exhibits a number of features clearly similar to those of *H. erectus*. Wolpoff also attributes a 1.95-million-year-old hip bone to *H. erectus*, thereby pushing the taxon back in time to almost 2 million years ago. He hypothesizes that early *H. erectus* evolved before the other early *Homo* specimens, making the later forms unrelated to subsequent human evolution. It is not possible, however, to determine conclusively if early *H. erectus* or another early *Homo* species came first. Thus, it is still possible, even accepting the 2-million-year age for the earliest *H. erectus* remains, that this taxon is derived from either *H. habilis* or *H. rudolfensis*.

If *H. erectus* evolved from other early members of *Homo* and if the validity of both *H. habilis* and *H. rudolfensis* as taxa is accepted, the ques-

of the Koobi Fora sample made the range uncomfortably broad for several scientists. In the mid-1980s, Christopher Stringer argued that the range of variation in cranial capacity for the specimens normally placed in *Homo habilis* was too great for a single species. Based on a series of (mostly cranio-dental) features, Alan Walker, Richard F. Leakey, and Bernard Wood advocated separating the early *Homo* sample into two species: *H. habilis* and *H. rudolfensis*. *H. rudolfensis* is larger than *H. habilis* and is characterized by a larger brain and an upper nasal region unlike that of australopithecines. The Koobi Fora specimen ER 1470, for example, has a cranial capacity of more than 750 cubic centimeters. On the other hand, the size and morphology of the rest of the face, the lack of a distinct supraorbital torus (brow

tion then focuses on which taxon is the ancestor of *H. erectus*. *H. rudolfensis* has a brain similar in size to that of *H. erectus* but otherwise is very like the australopithecines. With no clearly associated postcrania, body size and proportions are unknown. *H. habilis* has a small brain, but its face tends to be more like that of *H. erectus*. One presumed *H. habilis* specimen from Koobi Foora has limb proportions like those of australopithecines, and thus its status as an ancestor for later *Homo* is problematic. This is because a 1.6-million-year-old *H. erectus* skeleton from Nariokotome exhibits limb proportions similar to those found among *H. sapiens*. At this point, more cranial-postcranial associations are needed to clarify the beginning of *H. erectus*. Nevertheless, it is clear that, however the variation in humans is partitioned, the root of later evolution of the genus *Homo* is present in Africa at least slightly less than 2 million years ago.

Early *Homo erectus* at Lake Turkana: Koobi Fora and Nariokotome

The earliest unquestionable *Homo erectus* specimen is the ER 3733 cranium, dating to 1.78 million years ago at Koobi Fora. This specimen has a cranial capacity of 848 cubic centimeters and a number of other features that, in addition to its larger brain, differentiate it from earlier humans. Its face is similar to that of *H. habilis* but has a more distinct supraorbital torus, separated from the forehead by a well-developed groove. The nasal opening exhibits everted sides, so that the opening is placed more anteriorly to the eye orbits than in earlier humans. Additionally, in comparison to earlier forms, the foramen magnum (the opening at the base of the skull for the spinal cord) is located more centrally on the cranial base, the well-developed frontal bone (the front of the skull above the eyes) makes the forehead more vertical, and the cranial vault is more expanded relative to the cranial base. Also, while posterior tooth size and morphology are comparable to those of *H. habilis,* the combination of such moderate-sized teeth and so large a brain is unknown in either australopithecines or other early members of *Homo*. Finally, the occipital bone has a well-developed nuchal torus (a bony

growth along the rear of the base of the skull for attachment of neck muscles) that extends across the entire bone, a characteristic feature of *H. erectus*.

Other cranial specimens from the Lake Turkana region of Kenya exhibit a similar morphology and are dated to at least 1.5 million years ago. Prominent among these are a cranial-vault and upper-face specimen and a relatively complete skull associated with a largely complete postcranial skeleton (KNM-WT 15000). The 1.6-million-year old KNM-WT 15000 skeleton (from Nariokotome on the west bank of Lake Turkana) and another 1.7-million-year-old partial skeleton, ER 1808 (from Koobi Fora on the east bank), also provide a picture of the postcranial anatomy of early *H. erectus*. Certain aspects of the morphology of the Koobi Fora specimen are compromised because it is obviously diseased. Also, the Nariokotome remains are of a child approximately 11 years old. Despite the problems, these two specimens, and particularly the one from Nariokotome, are invaluable to a complete picture of early African *H. erectus* morphology and give considerable insight into aspects of their behavior.

The Nariokotome skeleton is amazingly complete, lacking mostly hand and foot bones, and has been analyzed extensively under the general direction of Richard F. Leakey and Alan Walker. It exhibits the same basic cranial features as ER 3733 (the earliest known *H. erectus),* including the association of moderate-sized posterior teeth with a relatively large brain (cranial capacity is 909 cubic centimeters). Postcranially, there are similarities to australopithecines in the possession of six lumbar vertebrae, elongated femoral necks, and perhaps the shape of the pelvic inlet. However, the morphology of most skeletal elements is quite close to more recent humans. Interestingly, the individual was tall (185 centimeters as an adult) and had limb proportions like those of modern humans rather than those of australopithecines. In other words, the overall form and appearance of the skeleton is much more like modern humans than are earlier, relatively complete specimens.

Christopher Ruff has shown that the body build of the Nariokotome specimen is "elongated," with limbs and trunk being lengthened relative to body breadth. He further demonstrates that this pattern is shared with recent humans adapted to hot, relatively open and dry environments like the African savanna grasslands. This contrasts with earlier humans, who were much smaller in stature but had a much broader trunk relative to their height. This body build is similar to that of recent humans living in more closed, tropical forest environments, where limited air movement reduces the effectiveness of sweating as a thermoregulatory process. In such situations, a small body size (which generates less heat) would seem to be the best way to prevent overheating. In more open, dry tropical environments, sweating is much more effective, and larger body size is viable as long as the body build is linear.

Elongated lower limbs and larger body size would be advantageous to early humans, because they lengthen stride length and allow bipedal humans to cover more distance using the same energy. Peter Wheeler argues that elongation and larger body size also places more of the trunk in a "microhabitat" away from the heat of the ground. In the same vein, Robert Franciscus and Erik Trinkaus have shown that the everted lateral borders of the nasal opening, combined with other features around early *H. erectus* noses, indicate a large nasal chamber, which would increase the volume of inhaled air and help retrieve moisture from exhaled air. Both of these make sense for a human adapted to expending considerable muscular activity in a hot, dry environment.

All of this strongly implies that early *H. erectus* inhabited a very different ecological niche than did earlier humans. Ruff argues that australopithecines like Lucy (specimen AL 288-1, found at Hadar in 1974) were adapted to relatively closed, wet environments, while *H. erectus* was adapted to open, dry savannas. Wolpoff believes that this, along with other factors, indicates that *H. erectus* practiced a scavenging-hunting-gathering lifeway quite different from the lives of earlier humans and fundamentally similar to those of later preagricultural *Homo sapiens*.

A final issue concerns what to call the humans represented by specimens like the 1.6-million-year-old skeleton from Nariokotome (KNM-WT 15000) and the 1.78-million-year-old cranium from Koobi Fora (ER 3733). Traditionally, they are referred to as early *H. erectus*, but there are two other possible naming schemes. Bernard Wood, Ian Tattersall, and others suggest that these humans are more primitive than, and lack certain derived features found in, "true" *H. erectus* from East Asia. These scholars classify the African specimens as *Homo ergaster*, an ancestor to the "true" *H. erectus* lineage in Asia and other lineages. However, studies by Günter Bräuer, Ema Mbua, Philip Rightmire, Andrew Kramer, and others have shown there is no basis for separating these early African forms from later *H. erectus* in Asia. Milford Wolpoff, Alan Thorne, Jan Jelinek, and others now classify all *H. erectus*, including the earlier ones, in *H. sapiens*. This is because, in their opinion, *H. erectus* can be neither precisely defined nor unequivocally separated from subsequent humans.

Both claims are consistent with what are two very different theoretical orientations and perspectives on the human-fossil record. Those who support the use of the term *H. ergaster* generally believe that human evolution should have more lineages (species) than are traditionally recognized. Consequently, they focus on the search for morphological features that will support splitting taxonomic units, like *H. erectus*, into such species. Wolpoff, Thorne, and Jelinek see no clear morphological breaks that would identify such splits. They emphasize features that reflect regional morphological continuity, not only in Africa but in Asia and Europe as well. Based on such features, they argue that human populations have been interconnected and have not undergone any speciation events during the last 2 million years. This perspective forms the basis of the multiregional model of human evolution, which holds that humans have been a polytypic single species (that is, a single species represented by many types or subdivisions) ever since the first humans left Africa and inhabited Eurasia.

The Early Spread of *Homo*: Africa and Beyond

H. erectus fossils continue to be found at East Africa sites dating to later than 1.5 million years ago. Perhaps the best known is from Olduvai Gorge—specimen OH9, which Louis Leakey dubbed "Chellean man." Other remains are found in later levels at Olduvai and at sites like Omo, Koobi Fora, and Konso-Gardula and Gombore in Ethiopia. *H. erectus* is also found in South Africa at Swartkrans and spreads into the North African record by about 700,000 years ago, based on the remains from Ternifine (Tighenif), Algeria. Compared to early *H. erectus,* these specimens exhibit fundamental morphological homogeneity. Brain and posterior tooth size remain stable, as do the form of the supraorbital and nuchal tori. These specimens also continue to exhibit considerable variation in size and robustness, probably reflecting sexual dimorphism (physical differences between the sexes). Such patterns underscore the fact that evolutionary change is not continuous or consistent over time but rather is episodic, punctuated by long periods of stasis.

Humans seem to have spread into the Arabian Peninsula by 1.4 million years ago. Here, remains of *H. erectus* are represented at the site of Ubediyeh in Israel. A second specimen, the Dnamnesi mandible from Georgia, also apparently about 1.4 million years old, further documents the initial spread of humans out of Africa.

Recently Carl Swisher and colleagues have dated *H. erectus* remains from Modjekerto and Sangria in Indonesia to 1.81 and 1.65 million years ago respectively, suggesting the appearance of *H. erectus* almost as early in Indonesia as in Africa. The lack of plausible ancestors for *H. erectus* in Asia undermines any challenge to the African origin of the genus *Homo* at the present time.

However, by at least 1 million years ago, *H. erectus* stretched across the Asian tropics to Indonesia, reaching Java when it was connected to mainland Southeast Asia during periods of low sea level in the Pleistocene. The spread into northern China and Europe soon followed. This earliest human radiation from Africa resulted in the initial peopling of Eurasia. According to some, it was followed by two other significant human radiations with African roots. The evidence of the existence for both of these subsequent radiations, however, is far from universally accepted.

After *Homo erectus*

One of the arguments Wolpoff, Thorne, Jelinek, and others make for dropping the taxon

Homo erectus is that, in their opinion, it is impossible to locate a distinct morphological break between late *Homo erectus* and early *Homo sapiens.* While that claim is a point of contention in Asia and Europe, it is certainly true in Africa.

Probably the earliest influential specimen from the time span of 200,000 to 700,000 years ago is a cranium from Bodo in Ethiopia. This large specimen exhibits a massive face and nasal opening, a large supraorbital torus, and long, low frontal bone. The face is moderately prognathic (set forward of the forehead). Also in the face, the inferior margin of the cheek region does not exhibit a distinct notch (maxillary notch) but forms an oblique border from the side of the upper jaw to the lateral part of the cheek. The cheek region has a "puffy" appearance and lacks a well-defined depressed groove (canine fossa) lateral to the nose. While cranial capacity is unknown (but probably larger than 1,300 cubic centimeters), the cranial vault is expanded compared to earlier humans. Overall, the Bodo specimen is advanced compared to early humans, but it exhibits strong similarities to *H. erectus* in aspects of cranial shape and details of its architecture.

Another significant East African specimen is the Ndutu cranium from Tanzania. It appear to be about 35,000 to 40,000 years old. Compared to the Bodo skull, it is much smaller, with a cranial capacity of about 1,100 cubic centimeters. The supraorbital torus is prominent but also much smaller than that of the Bodo specimen. The cranial vault is expanded relative to the cranial base, reflecting larger brain size than in *H. erectus.* Finally, the face is smaller than the Bodo specimen's and appears to exhibit a weak canine fossa and (possibly) a maxillary notch.

A final site that merits some consideration is Kabwe (Broken Hill) in Zambia. A skull found at Kabwe was the first post-*H. erectus,* archaic human discovered outside Europe. Found in 1921, it is often the only specimen from the site discussed, but there are several postcranial specimens and a second maxilla that are also significant. The dating of site is open to debate, but using faunal evidence, Richard Klein and others argue that a date between approximately 200,000 and 400,000 years ago is most appropriate.

The Kabwe cranium is similar to Bodo and Ndutu skulls in most aspects. It has a large face with a very prominent and large supraorbital torus and a long, low frontal bone. The Kabwe cranium also lacks both a canine fossa and a notch in the inferior margin of the cheek region. Although it is less massive than the Bodo specimen in the face and cheek region, the two are fundamentally similar in these areas.

Additionally, the Kabwe cranium, like the Bodo skull, has a large capacity, about 1,300 cubic centimeters. Trinkaus and Wolpoff have shown that, by this time in Africa, brain sizes significantly increase, essentially reaching the size of modern human brains. As was the case from about 700,000 to 1.8 million years ago, brain size again reached a plateau after 200,000 years ago.

The other remains from Kabwe are interesting. An upper-jaw fragment is much smaller than the jaw of the full cranium found there. It seems very similar to the Ndutu specimen, particularly because it appears to exhibit a small canine fossa and maxillary notch. The postcranial remains are large and robust and consist of femora (thigh bone), innominates (the flaring portion of the pelvis), upper-limb remains, and a tibia (hind-leg bone). As in *H. erectus,* limb proportions follow a recent human pattern. The relatively long tibia also suggests limb proportion adapted to the same type of environment as inhabited by *H. erectus,* specifically KNM-WT 15000. The Kabwe postcranial remains also suggest that the body size of these humans is comparable to that of *H. erectus* at Kabwe.

The human sample from this time period (approximately 200,000 to 700,000 years ago) suggests a population of premodern humans who have essentially reached recent human brain size but still exhibit archaic features in their skull anatomy. There is also considerable variation, with males being much larger than females. The females exhibit facial size and morphology, such as maxillary notches and canine fossae, that are characteristic features of the facial anatomy of later humans. It seems clear that this sample of archaic humans is the root of the lineage leading to early-modern Africans and that it also exhibits clear morphological connections to African *H. erectus.*

As is often the case in human paleontology, there is considerable debate on the taxonomy of these archaic Africans, and the debate on taxonomy directly reflects the more significant debate on the pattern of later human evolution. In 1921, Arthur Smith Woodward classified the skull found at Kabwe as *Homo rhodesiensis.* In recent years, the Kabwe group (and specimens from Bodo, Ndutu, other sites) has generally been considered (sometimes uncomfortably) a part of *Homo sapiens,* often as an African Neanderthal variant. In the context of a multiregional evolution model, the Kabwe group, Eurasian Neanderthals, and Asian archaic humans represent earlier phases of *H. sapiens.* A number of researchers, including Tattersall and Stringer, would place this Kabwe group in its own species. Tattersall particularly has argued that there should be several different lineages of *Homo,* and he, Stringer and others have strongly supported restricting *Homo sapiens* to humans fundamentally identical to modern people.

Rightmire has noted the similarity between the Kabwe group and early Europeans. He points out that if these specimens are nonspecific, their proper taxon would be *Homo heidelbergensis,* because that taxonomic name was introduced in 1908, before *H. rhodesiensis.* In Rightmire's scheme, *H. heidelbergensis* subsequently splits into *H. neanderthalensis* in Europe and presumably *H. sapiens* in Africa. In this view, *H. heidelbergensis* also radiated out of Africa at least to Europe. This would constitute the second radiation of human beings from an African root into Eurasia. However, the existence of this radiation, unlike the previous one, is debatable.

The Morphological Transition to Modern Humans in Africa

The transition from humans like those found at Kabwe and Ndutu to modern humans can be seen in a small, but informative sample of remains from sites in Africa. Bräuer was the first to recognize these remains as an "African transitional sample," although several scholars (notably Rightmire) previously had drawn attention to their significance. The dating of many of these specimens is problematic, but they are generally thought to be between 100,000 and 200,000 old.

Two of the specimens, from Eliye Springs in Kenya and Omo in Ethiopia, were surface finds. Others (from Singa in Sudan, for example) have defied attempts at reliable dating. The Singa find also seems diseased and thus cannot be considered a typical representative of this sample. Regardless of these problems, researchers agree that this sample is transitional, evolving in the direction of modern humans.

The crania of the African Transitional Group (ATG) are especially informative. The facial crania from the sites of Florisbad in South Africa, Ngaloba in Tanzania, Jebel Irhoud in Morocco, and Eliye Springs exhibit relatively archaic cranial vaults with low, receding foreheads and supraorbital tori. These tori are reduced in size compared to those found among the Kabwe group but are certainly more marked than would be expected in modern populations. Brain size shows no evidence of having increased in comparison to the Kabwe people. On the other hand, faces of the African Transitional Group are reduced in length and are more lightly built compared to earlier humans. They also exhibit both canine fossae and maxillary notches, making the faces essentially appear quite modern in many respects. Combined with their more archaic cranial vaults, the "progressive" faces of this group give them a distinctly transitional configuration.

Little is known about other aspects of the anatomy in the African Transitional Group. In fact, only one postcranial bone (a humerus) and a juvenile mandible, both from Jebel Irhoud, are known. The humerus is robust and exhibits archaic morphology. The mandible has a distinct chin but also relatively large molars and a more archaic internal aspect of the symphysis (the front of the jaw angles back from the tooth row to the base). Because of its juvenile status, the significance of its symphyseal morphology is difficult to interpret.

Models of Modern Human Origins

Over the last decade, there has been a strong focus on Africa in discussions of the origins of modern people, with several specific models centering on Africa as the point of origin for all modern humans. Although a single origin for modern humans has long been advocated in some circles, just about every place but Africa had been suggested as the source area. Some attention was focused on Africa as a possible center for early-modern people by Louis Leakey in the 1930s. He claimed that fragmentary fossil remains from Kanam and Kanjera in Kenya represented a very early presence of modern humans in East Africa, but this evidence proved unconvincing.

In 1984, Bräuer introduced his Afro-European sapiens hypothesis in which he suggested that modern humans appeared in Africa about 100,000 years ago. Supported with studies on recent African skeletal series and the pertinent fossil record, he argued that modern humans spread initially from Africa into the Near East and later into Europe. He grounded his argument on the evidence of the African Transitional Group and the early presence of modern human morphology in Africa at sites like Border Cave and Omo. He also proposed that the African-derived populations who spread into Eurasia interbred to a limited extent with local archaic populations and thus referred to his model as one that emphasized "replacement with hybridization."

In 1987, Rebecca Cann, Mark Stoneking, and Alan Wilson presented an argument for a recent African origin for modern people based on genetic data. For several years previously, various studies of nuclear DNA (that is, the genetic material associated with chromosomes) suggested that African populations separated from Eurasian populations before the split between European and Asians. This implied to a number of researchers that modern human populations first emerged in Africa. However, because nuclear DNA recombines (there is input from both parents), this pattern could also be the result of greater gene flow between Eurasians. Cann and colleagues worked with mitochondrial DNA (mt DNA), which does not recombine and is inherited from the female parent. Their results, and those of more recent studies, support and strengthen the claim for a recent African origin of modern humans.

Cann, Stoneking, and Wilson noted three aspects of their data suggestive of a recent African origin. First, African populations exhibited more variability in mt DNA types than other populations. Second, statistical analysis of the patterns of relationship among these mt DNA types indicated that the ancestral type was an African one. Third, available evidence demonstrated that mt DNA was selectively neutral and that mt DNA types changed only by mutation. Based on this, they determined a mutation rate (from differences between modern populations whose divergence times were generally known) and calculated that all modern humans shared a common genetic ancestor in Africa about 200,000 years ago. Non-Africans split from Africans, according to this perspective, around 100,000 years ago. This genetic model is referred to as the *African "Eve" model.*

The genetic and skeletal evidence supporting a recent African origin for all modern humans has been skillfully integrated by Christopher Stringer and Peter Andrews into the Recent African Evolution model (RAE). This model states that the only definitive transition to modern humans seen in the fossil record is in Africa. In Europe and Asia, supporters of the Recent African Evolution model note a distinct morphological break between local archaic folk (for example, Neanderthals in Europe and West Asia) and the earliest modern humans in these regions. The model also claims that the earliest morphological evidence of modern humans is in Africa slightly more than 100,000 years ago. Stringer, Andrews, and others note that this fossil evidence is fully commensurate with the genetic evidence presented by Cann and colleagues.

The Multiregional Evolution (MRE) model, unlike the above perspectives, does not focus on Africa as the single source for modern humans. According to this model, the radiation of *Homo erectus* from Africa established regional human lineages throughout much of Eurasia. Rather than positing the forming of different species, the Multiregional Evolution model holds that these regional lineages remained interconnected by gene flow and thus remained regional variants of a single species. Regional differences in morphology are explained as the result of interactions between gene flow, genetic drift, and adaptation to differing environmental conditions. As Wolpoff describes it, the model views the post-australopithecine evolution of humans as a "web of interconnected lineages" representing a highly polytypic species evolving over time as a single

unit. Africa is certainly an important region for the Multiregional Evolution model, but it is not accepted as the source of a radiation of modern humans beginning 100,000 years ago.

Chronology and the Earliest Modern Human Remains in Africa

In addition to the genetic data, marked changes in the chronological framework of several key sites revolutionized perspectives on Africa's role in modern human origins. As recently as the 1970s, it was thought that very archaic humans like those at Kabwe lived in Africa until the beginning of the Middle Stone Age 35,000 to 40,000 years ago. This late date for so primitive a human led J. Desmond Clark to suggest that modern humans must have moved into southern Africa from somewhere else. This view began to change when J. C. Vogel and Peter Beaumont marshaled radiocarbon-dating evidence indicating that the Middle Stone Age had ended, not begun, about 40,000 years ago. Resonance dating has led to even earlier dates for remains critical to establishing the antiquity of modern humans in Africa.

The case for an early presence of modern humans in Africa is based essentially on three sites: Border Cave in South Africa, Omo in Ethiopia, and Klasies River Mouth in South Africa. All of the specimens found at these sites are associated with Middle Stone Age elements. At a few other localities, for example Mumba in Tanzania, isolated teeth showing modern affinities have been found, but isolated teeth do not constitute convincing evidence for modern humans. Dates for the human remains at Border Cave suggest an age of 62,000 to 82,000 years, which is much younger than the 110,000-plus year ages attributed to them earlier. The Omo skull and fragmentary skeleton are associated with a uranium-thorium date of 130,000 years ago. The Klasies River Mouth human remains are mainly from deposits dating to between 88,000 and 94,000 years ago, but two maxillary fragments may be as much as 30,000 years older.

The cranial and mandibular remains from Border Cave and Omo, both heavily reconstructed, are modern in form. One from Border

Cave has a high forehead and an overall cranial contour that would be easily matched in a modern sample. Another from Omo is similar in overall form and also exhibits a cranial vault that is much broader than the cranial base. Both specimens have fragmentary faces, but what is preserved is essentially modern. For example, both probably exhibited maxillary notches, and the Omo specimen exhibits a trace of a canine fossa. Mandibles from Omo and Border Cave have canine fossae and very modern symphyseal regions (junctures of the bones that make up the jaw) with well-developed chins. In fact, all of these specimens, but especially those from Border Cave, could be lost in a modern African (non-Pygmy or Bushman) sample. Fragmentary postcranial remains from both sites also conform to a modern pattern.

If the dates for Border Cave and especially Omo are correct, an early appearance of modern humans in sub-Saharan Africa would be confirmed. Unfortunately, there are problems with the dating of the sites. The uranium-thorium date at Omo is on mollusk shell, which generally provides unreliable dates. Furthermore, the shell was recovered stratigraphically below the specimen, which means that the Omo cranial and mandibular remains are younger than 130,000 years even if the date is correct. Radiocarbon dating from well above the specimen gives a result of less than 30,000 years. The Omo specimen is certainly older than this, but how much older is a matter of great uncertainty. At Border Cave, the dating is probably correct for the archaeological levels, but it is not clear from which levels the human remains came. Andrew Sillen's nitrogen analysis of the human remains suggests they are older than 35,000 years, but again it is not certain how much older than this they are.

The context and dating of the Klasies River Mouth remains are not at issue. Philip Rightmire, Günter Bräuer, Hilary Deacon, and others have interpreted the humans remains as anatomically modern. Studies by Milford Wolpoff, Rachel Caspari, Erik Trinkaus, and others suggest that this is somewhat overstated. The sample is very fragmentary, and some specimens do appear to be quite modern. For example, a frontal bone fragment (with part of a brow ridge) does not exhibit a supraorbital torus, and the most complete mandible has a distinct chin. However, three other mandibles have much less development in the chin area and at least one lacks it completely. Furthermore a zygomatic (cheek) bone is very large (larger than those found at Florisbad or Ngaloba and comparable to a specimen from Kabwe) and has distinct archaic morphological features. An ulna (lower-arm bone) is clearly archaic in form. Thus, the total morphological pattern exhibited by the humans at the Klasies River Mouth site is more archaic than has generally been suggested. It may be premature to consider the sample as representation of fully modern humans.

Considering all these facts, it is not certain that modern humans were present in Africa around 100,000 years ago. Be this as it may, the human remains from Klasies River Mouth do continue a pattern of change reflected in the transition from the Kabwe people to the African Transitional Group. The Klasies River Mouth humans seem to carry these trends somewhat further, and human remains like those at Border Cave and Omo are certainly appropriate as representatives of early modern Africans. It is eminently reasonable to see them as descendants of the Klasies River Mouth humans. However, they are likely to be far more recent in age than some scholars have previously claimed. In any case, this sequence represents perhaps the clearest transition from archaic to modern humans available from any region of the world. Whether it is the only such transition, as those who support the radiation of early *H. erectus* out of Africa into Eurasia claim, is another issue.

Skeletal remains begin to be more common in the African archaeological record after about 30,000 years ago, but reasonably large samples are available only from about 10,000 years ago. Skeletal remains dating to this time, or slightly earlier, exhibit specific morphological affinities with more recent African populations. This indicates that the patterning of morphological diversity evident in African populations today does not have a long time depth. The origin of this modern African morphological diversity is a complex issue, and consideration of it falls out of the purview of this review.

BIBLIOGRAPHY

Bräuer, G. 1992. Africa's place in the evolution of *Homo sapiens*. In *Continuity or replacement: Controversies in* Homo sapiens *evolution,* eds. G. Bräuer and F. H. Smith, 83–98. Rotterdam: A. A. Balkema.

Bräuer, G., and E. Mbua. 1992. *Homo erectus* features used in cladistics and their validity in Asian and African hominids. *Journal of Human Evolution* 22: 79–108.

Cann, R., M. Stoneking, and A. Wilson. 1987. Mitochondrial DNA and human evolution. *Nature* 325: 31–36.

Leakey, L. S. B., P. V. Tobias, and J. R. Napier. 1964. A new species of the genus *Homo* from Olduvai Gorge, Tanzania. *Nature* 202: 308–312.

Rightmire, G. P. 1990. *The evolution of* Homo erectus. Cambridge: Cambridge University Press.

Ruff, C. 1993. Climatic adaptation and hominid evolution: The thermoregulatory imperative. *Evolutionary Anthropology* 2: 53–60.

Smith, F. H. 1992. Models and realities in modern human origins: The African fossil evidence. *Philosophical Transactions of the Royal Society of London, Series B* 337: 243–250.

Smith, F. H., A. B. Falsetti, and S. M. Donnelly. 1989. Modern humans origins. *Yearbook of Physical Anthropology* 32: 35–68.

Stringer, C. B. 1994. Out of Africa: A personal history. In *Origins of anatomically modern humans,* eds. M. H. Nitecki and D. V. Nitecki, 149–174. New York: Plenum.

Stringer, C. B., and P. Andrews. 1988. Genetic and fossil evidence for the origin of modern humans. *Science* 239: 1,263–1,268.

Stoneking, M. 1993. DNA and recent human evolution. *Evolutionary Anthropology* 2: 60–73.

Tattersall, I., E. Delson, and J. Van Couvering. 1988. *Encyclopedia of human evolution and prehistory.* New York: Garland Publishers.

Tobias, P. V. 1991. *The skulls, endocasts and teeth of* Homo habilis. Vol. 4 of *Olduvai Gorge.* Cambridge: Cambridge University Press.

Walker, A., and R. Leakey. 1993. *The Nariokotome* Homo erectus *skeleton.* Cambridge: Harvard University Press.

Wolpoff, M. 1995. *Human evolution: 1996 edition.* New York: McGraw-Hill.

Wood, B. 1991. *Hominid cranial remains.* Vol. 4 in *Koobi Fora research project.* New York: Oxford University Press.

Fred Smith

HUMAN POPULATIONS: THEIR ARCHAEOMETRY

Archaeometry is the application of scientific methods of analysis to archaeological questions. However the scientific study of human remains is a broad field that includes the discipline of physical anthropology—a discipline concentrating on anatomical analysis of human skeletons and not normally associated with archaeometry. In recent years, scientific methods grounded in chemistry rather than anatomy have been applied to human skeletons. Archaeometry of human populations is taken to mean these techniques—that is, the application of scientific methods of analysis to human skeletons, excluding physical anthropology.

Archaeometric techniques, when defined this way, are based on dietary signals that are registered in human and animal skeletons. The techniques include the measurement of stable-isotope ratios and trace elements. While the specific theoretical basis for each method differs, all are based on the demonstration that a chemical signal exists in certain foods and ultimately resides in the skeletons of consumers. Because the techniques are quantitative in nature, they provide proportional information on the relative classes of foods—information that is is otherwise not visible in anatomical and conventional archaeological data.

The use of chemical techniques depends upon a sound understanding of the distribution of the variable in natural environments and the demonstration that chemical changes after interment (known as *diagenesis*) do not obscure or obliterate the signal. Because of diagenesis, chemical signals cannot be universally applied. As a general rule, controls need to be incorporated into chemical studies of archaeological skeletons to ensure that a meaningful biological signal is being retrieved. In spite of this constraint, chemical techniques have become an increasingly indispensable aspect of paleo-dietary analysis. Archaeometric research in sub-Saharan Africa has involved mainly isotopic systems. To date, trace-element techniques have not been successfully applied to recent human populations on the subcontinent.

Applications

Analyses of carbon and nitrogen isotopes have been applied to the study of a number of human and early hominid populations in sub-Saharan Africa. Stanley Ambrose investigated historical populations whose diets were well known. He recognized that isotopic differences should exist in the bone collagen of populations relying mainly on animal products as opposed to plant foods, and the meat of grazing animals as opposed to browsing animals. He analyzed bone collagen in skeletons from a number of different groups, including the Kikuyu farmers of central Kenya, Luyia farmers of western Kenya, Turkana and Dasenesch pastoralists of northern Kenya, highland and lowland Pokot of northwestern Kenya, Nandi and Kipsigis (Kalenjin) farmers and pastoralists of highland western Kenya, and Griqua pastoralists and farmers of the Free State in South Africa.

A clear difference in nitrogen isotopes was seen between groups most dependent upon plant foods (Luyia, Kikuyu, and Kalenjin) and those most dependent on the milk, meat, and blood of domestic animals (Turkana, Dasenesch, Pokot, and Griqua). Differences were also seen in carbon isotopes of the Kalenjin group, who heavily rely on C_4 foods in their diet, and those populations depending on a mix of C_3 and C_4 plants or a mix of products from C_4 grazing and C_3 browsing animals. C_3 plants are temperate and high latitude grasses, all trees, and most shrubs. C_4 plants are tropical and savanna grasses. The two groups of plants are isotopically distinct, and their differences are passed along the food chain to animals eating the plants. As a result, the bone collagen of animals subsisting on the different groups will differ in ways that are measurable. Thus, it was possible, using carbon and nitrogen isotopes, to distinguish pastoralists from farmers, camel pastoralists from capri-bovine (sheep, goats, and cattle) pastoralists, and farmers who grew grain from those who did not. When applied to archaeological specimens, Ambrose demonstrated that, at least with regard to the Kikuyu and Kalenjin, there was close association between the isotopic composition of prehistoric and historic members of the same ethnic groups. He also demonstrated

that people ascribed to the Pastoral Neolithic depended more on animal products than did people from the Elmenteitan Neolithic, who apparently subsisted on a more even mix of plant and animal resources.

More recently, Julia Lee-Thorpe and her colleagues at the University of Cape Town have investigated the carbon and nitrogen isotopic signals in the collagen of Iron Age peoples of southern Africa. Questions they set out to address include the relative importance of stock keeping versus agricultural activities in Iron Age economies of the region and the degree of dietary variation among individuals and groups. Relatively recent Iron Age skeletons (dating to the last few hundred years) were sampled from sites from a variety of biomes, including the moist highland grassland of the Free State through drier mixed savannah woodland to dry *thornveld* in the arid northern region of South Africa.

Not surprisingly, the collagen of Iron Age humans reflects a subsistence base that depended on either on C_4 crops or domestic stock that ate C_4 plants. One unexpected feature, however, was the considerable variability seen both between and within communities, suggesting that Iron Age farmers altered their subsistence strategies substantially according to local conditions. More recently, analysis of an extensive sample of Late Iron Age skeletons from southern Africa, over the period between A.D. 1000 and 1800, has demonstrated that, in all likelihood, maize was introduced in the interior of southern Africa (probably as a result of increased trade with the Portuguese on the east coast).

Carbon isotopes have also been used to examine models for the movement of Late Stone Age peoples in the western Cape. Based on excavated food remains from several archaeological sites in the region, archaeologist John E. Parkington articulated a seasonal-mobility hypothesis, suggesting that hunter-foragers living in the region between 2,000 and 4,000 years ago spent the summer months in the Cape folded-mountain belt, where they exploited temporary abundances of terrestrial plant and animal foods, and spent the winter months at coastal sites such as Eland's Bay Cave. Evidence for this included the presence of large quantities of *Iriaceae* corm casings at inland sites, which are at their largest and most palatable in the summer months. Furthermore, examination of seal mandibles at coastal sites suggest that nearly all excavated mandibles were those of yearlings that died in winter months.

Judith C. Sealy challenged the seasonal-mobility hypothesis by measuring the carbon isotopes in human skeletons from a variety of inland and coastal sites. She reasoned that, if one population was moving back and forth between the two different biomes as part of a seasonal round, there should be little difference in the carbon isotopes of skeletons derived from coastal and inland sites. On the other hand, a difference in carbon isotopes between inland and coastal skeletons would suggest that they were derived from different groups not sharing the same seasonally mobile adaptation. Her results indicated a consistent difference between inland skeletons from the Olifants River Valley and the mountains and coastal skeletons from Eland's Bay. The results suggested that the diet of the inland group was virtually all available terrestrial foods, while coastal people depended quite heavily on marine foods, and that the two groups were, in fact, separate.

More recently, Sealy has examined changes in human diets over time using carbon-isotope measurements in radiometrically dated skeletons. Between 2,000 and 3,000 years ago, people living at coastal sites from Eland's Bay south to the Cape Peninsula relied heavily on marine resources. Sealy found that, after 2,000 years ago, however, coastal people relied less heavily on seafood and consumed a diet with a greater terrestrial component. Moreover, this pattern agrees with the greater variety of food waste found in coastal sites within the last 2,000 years.

Isotopic variation has also been used to study the life histories of individuals from sub-Saharan Africa, based on the principle that different skeletal tissues represent discrete periods of time in the life of an individual. For example, tooth enamel is generally formed when an individual is young, and there is no subsequent calcification of this tissue in adulthood. Moreover, the various teeth calcify at different ages during growth. Bone, on the other hand, is continuously remodeled and thereby incorporates an isoto-

pic signal that represents the diet of adults. By comparing the isotopic signature of the two types of tissues, it is possible to determine whether an individual remained in one area for an entire lifetime or moved into the area from somewhere else.

In addition to the light isotopes discussed above, archaeometric studies also employ the measurement of one heavy isotope ratio: $^{87}Sr/^{86}Sr$, which reflects the ultimate source of strontium in the geological substrate of specific regions.

Such life-history studies have been carried out on a number of historical skeletons, such as an adult female found at Vergelegen, the country estate established at the beginning of the 18th century by the governor of the Cape, Willem Adriaan van der Stel. Recent excavations of a slave lodge on the estate revealed a grave cut through the floor surface. Isotopic analysis of the remains showed that there were striking differences between tissues formed in early adulthood and those in late adulthood. The data suggested that, in early adulthood, this woman consumed C_4 grains in a well-watered environment, probably a tropical or subtropical area. However, in later adulthood, she consumed more seafood. Moreover, strontium analysis of the teeth suggested that she had arrived from somewhere other than the Cape. Taken together, the results suggest her childhood diet was rich in tropical grains and poor in seafood, but in early adulthood, her diet changed radically to include a large amount of seafood. The change is consistent with the interpretation that this woman was a slave brought to the Cape from Indian Ocean colonies. The method has also been used to demonstrate progressive increases in the amount of marine foods in the diets of an individual whose skeleton was buried at the site of Oudepost I, a Dutch East India Company outpost located about 100 kilometers north of the Cape of Good Hope and occupied between 1669 and 1732.

Finally, studies of carbon isotopes have examined the tooth enamel of robust australopithecines from the site of Swartkrans (about 1 to 2 million years ago). These early hominids had conventionally been thought of as specialized herbivores. The data indicated, however, not only consumption of C_3-based foods, but also a surprisingly substantial contribution from C_4 grasses. Although there is no direct isotopic evidence to determine whether the C_4 source was directly from plants or from grazing animals, the scarcity of C_4 plants edible by large primates suggests that the flesh of grazing animals was a more likely source. Thus, the technique has been used to challenge conventional notions of the diet of this species.

In the future, it is anticipated that archaeometric analyses will be extended to other early hominids in the region, particularly early *Homo*. In more recent periods, obvious areas for future work include the expansion of life-history studies to more skeletons from historical sites. Within the Iron Age, it may yet be possible to examine dietary variations related to status. Such studies have been extremely important in examining complex societies in North and South America, and are an obvious next step for archaeometric studies of human populations in sub-Saharan Africa.

BIBLIOGRAPHY

Ambrose, S. H., and M. J. DeNiro.1986. Reconstruction of African human diet using bone collagen carbon and nitrogen isotope ratios. *Nature* 319: 321–324.

Brain, C. K., ed. 1993. *Swartkrans: A cave's chronicle of early man.* Pretoria: Transvaal Museum Monograph No. 8.

Gilbert, C. L. 1995. Diet and subsistence patterns in the Later Iron Age of South Africa: An analysis of stable carbon and nitrogen isotopes and the incidence of caries. Master's thesis, University of Cape Town.

Lambert, J. B., and G. Grupe, eds. *Prehistoric human bone: Archaeology at the molecular level.* Berlin: Springer Verlag.

Sealy, J. C., and N. J. van der Merwe. 1986. Isotope assessment and the seasonal mobility hypothesis in the South-western Cape of South Africa. *Current Anthropology* 27: 135–150.

Sealy, J., R. Armstrong, and C. Schrire. 1995. Beyond lifetime averages: Tracing life histories through isotopic analysis of different calcified tissues form archaeological human skeletons. *Antiquity* 69: 290–300.

Andrew Sillen

EARLY AFRICAN HOMINIDS: BEHAVIOR AND ENVIRONMENTS

Pliocene and Early Pleistocene

Fossils discovered in the last 35 years have led to a new appreciation of the numbers of early species in the family Hominidae. There are now more than 1,300 known Pliocene and Early Pleistocene hominid fossil specimens. The Pliocene spans the period from 1.8 million to 5 million years ago. The Pleistocene, which dates from 10,000 to 1.8 million years ago, is subdivided into Early Pleistocene (750,000 to 1.8 million years ago), Middle Pleistocene (125,000 to 750,000 years ago), and Late Pleistocene (10,000 to 125,000 years ago) periods. The earliest-known hominid genus, *Ardipithecus,* is known from sediments dating to about 4.4 million years ago, and the oldest-known representative of *Australopithecus* dates to about 4.2 million years ago. The genus *Australopithecus* underwent an adaptive radiation in the Late Pliocene and Early Pleistocene. Some scholars place the more robust species of this radiation into a separate genus, *Paranthropus.* The earliest members of our genus, *Homo,* appeared as part of this radiation about 2.5 million years ago. The earliest stone artifacts and archaeological sites date to more than 2.6 million years ago, and the nearly simultaneous appearance of tools and *Homo* suggests to many researchers that members of the genus *Homo* are the makers of the tools. Others point out that the long-lived robust species *Australopithecus boisei* (or *Paranthropus boisei*) also appeared at this time and thus may qualify as the toolmaker.

The period from about 1.6 to 1.8 million years ago is particularly well represented in the fossil record. During this period, there were as many as six different contemporary hominid species in Africa. From our understanding of evolutionary processes, we expect these species to differ from one another not only in their appearance but also in their ways of life. While many details of these unique extinct adaptations are unknown, this article points out what they had in common and, where possible, how they may be expected to have differed.

Our knowledge of early hominids and their behavior depends in large part upon where they have become fossilized and, in the case of archaeological sites, where their living debris has been preserved. Finds of the earliest hominids are confined to the East African Rift Valley. Slightly younger fossils have been found in southern and northern Africa. None are currently known from western Africa, and scholars are uncertain whether early hominids did not inhabit this part of the continent, whether they did not encounter conditions suitable for fossilization, or whether fossils simply have not yet been discovered. The earliest archaeological sites, likewise, are found in the Rift Valley. While hominid fossils are found in caves in southern Africa, the fossils were incorporated in the cave fill through natural means. Hominids seem not to have used the caverns as lairs.

The earliest-known Pliocene hominids inhabited gallery forests surrounding the large Rift Valley riverine system and shared their habitat with the leaf-eating colobus monkey. Fossils of East African hominids of the Late Pliocene and Early Pleistocene have been found in lakeshore environments inhabited by lacustrine (lake) animals such as *Hippopotamus* and woodland animals such as *Giraffa*. The wooded habitat provided shade, food, and refuge from predators, as well as sleeping sites. All hominids are, by definition, bipedal, though each early species may have had its own style of bipedal walking, perhaps differing in gait, speed, and chosen substrate. The curved digits and long upper limbs of a number of early hominid species indicate a preference for life in the trees, and arboreal climbing for feeding, resting, escaping from predators, and sleeping at night may have been a common feature of hominid life until well into the Middle Pleistocene. The habitat away from the water was more open and capable of supporting herbivores (plant eaters) that fed on grass. The parklike appearance of today's East African savanna is maintained by frequent, deliberate burning, and this was not practiced until about 500,000 years ago. The attraction of more open environments for hominids may have been the protein source the

animals provided as well as a different array of plant foods, including underground tubers.

Hominid species no doubt differed in their preferred foods, and we may also expect that there were dietary differences in the same species in separate parts of its geographic range, at successive seasons of the year, and over the tens or hundreds of thousands of years of its life span as a species. Like all primates, hominids are omnivores. They do not rely exclusively upon a single food but consume a mix of plant products, including fruit, leaves, bark, sap, seeds, stems, and roots.

One of the major debates in modern archaeology concerns the degree of reliance upon animal food by early hominids and how these animal products were obtained. Modern primate diet, as well as that of present-day tropical African foraging groups, is primarily vegetarian. Meat composes no more than 25 percent of the diet overall. Food derived from vertebrate animals no doubt included birds, fish, amphibians, and reptiles as well as mammals. Invertebrates, primarily insects, were also an important source of protein and fat.

A characteristic feature of *Australopithecus* and *Paranthropus* is their very large molar and premolar teeth with an extremely thick enamel covering—a feature that distinguishes them from *Homo*. These large rear teeth were probably used to process large quantities of tough, bulky, and perhaps low-quality vegetable food, and these hominids probably spent the major portion of their waking hours feeding. *Homo* is also distinguished from *Australopithecus* and *Paranthropus* on the basis of its relatively larger brain size, a characteristic that provides another argument for the theory that *Homo* was the maker of the earliest stone tools. However, from their anatomy, *Australopithecus* and *Paranthropus* appear potentially as dexterous as early *Homo,* and chimpanzees with brain sizes equivalent to *Australopithecus* or *Paranthropus* are known to use simple tools in the wild.

Animal bones at some of the earliest archaeological sites include those of very large, aggressive animals, including elephants, hippopotamuses, and rhinoceroses, which have exceptionally thick hides. Many archaeologists believe that comparatively small-bodied hominids, with very simple implements, were not capable of killing and butchering these animals. It was argued in the early years of the discipline that the presence of large carcasses at sites implied cooperative hunting, but it has since been observed that modern primates, even those who hunt in groups, do not take animals larger than themselves. For example, at the Tai National Forest, Ivory Coast, the favored prey of the common chimpanzee, with a mean body size for males of 50 kilograms, is the red colobus monkey, which weighs only about 5 to 10 kilograms. From the study of breakage and other damage to bone at early archaeological sites, it has been suggested that scavenging from the kills of contemporary large predators, especially hyenas and large cats, was the major source of animal food in early hominid diet.

The earliest stone tools included flakes, which may have been used to slice meat and tendons from bones, and hammers, which may have been used to smash bones to extract the marrow inside. Early stone hammers were no doubt also used to crack open nuts and hard fruits and to pound tubers and stems to make them palatable and to extract liquid. Some of the most important early inventions were probably made of perishable materials that have not survived. A critical early implement was the digging stick, which enabled hominids to tap important underground resources. Ethnographers have observed that modern human foragers in East Africa are able to obtain as many as 5 kilograms of edible tubers, with a food value of more than 3,000 calories, in a single hour's work with a digging stick. Other important inventions were wooden clubs or spears and trays or containers of bark or wood. Stone tools provided the means to skin animals and prepare hides. While not needed for warmth in much of low-altitude, tropical Africa, hides would have provided welcome protection from sun, rain, rocks, and thorns. There is no direct evidence before the Late Pleistocene for the joining of hides into clothing or footwear, but informal pointed stone tools could have been used to punch holes in hides, which could then be joined with sinew. Carrying slings of hide or skin would also have been particularly important in freeing the hands during the transport of foodstuffs, implements, or offspring, and while there is no

evidence for the manufacture of twine or cord, strips made of grass, sinew, or hide could serve to join objects into bundles.

Two familiar features of modern life, shelter and fire, apparently were not present in the Pliocene or Early Pleistocene. While claims have been made for evidence of the controlled used of fire as early as 1.4 million years ago, such use was probably not routine, and food was consumed uncooked. There is little good evidence for the construction of shelters or the occupation of caves until the Middle Pleistocene, when the use of fire probably allowed hominids to drive predators from their lairs and keep them at bay with burning embers. Concentrations of lava boulders, artifacts, and broken bone at sites in Bed I at Olduvai Gorge were originally interpreted by archaeologists as the remains of huts or windbreaks, but these interpretations are now actively disputed. As foragers, hominid groups were mobile in their search for food, and, to avoid attracting predators, they did not sleep repeatedly in the same place. It does appear that hominids, perhaps attracted to a particular shady spot, fruiting tree, or source of stone for making artifacts, visited some early sites repeatedly over periods of years. However, there is no evidence that they occupied sites for long periods of time or that they altered sites deliberately to suit their needs, though they may well have constructed sleeping nests or other ephemeral structures that have not survived.

While it is conceivable that the largest vegetarian hominids might be nearly solitary, much as the modern orangutan, most early hominids no doubt lived in groups. Group size depends upon a number of factors, including dietary requirements, habitat, and pressure from predators. Considering their body size, it is unlikely that any early hominids lived in groups exceeding 40 or 50 individuals, and daily foraging groups were probably much smaller, perhaps as few as four or five. The amount of landscape with which any individual hominid was acquainted was not large. Small-bodied, more exclusively vegetarian species would have required a smaller territory to support the group, whereas those that depended in part upon hunting or scavenging would have needed a somewhat larger home range, perhaps

250 square kilometers. Sources of stone for tool manufacture at some early sites are known, and before the Middle Pleistocene, there is no evidence that hominids transported tools or the stone used to make them for distances greater than about 10 kilometers.

Hominids needed to drink every day, and without watertight containers, they could not stray more than a day's walk from a potable water source. Since trees provided their main refuge from predators, they would probably hesitate to stray far beyond a patch of woods. Low population densities prohibited the harboring of endemic infectious diseases, and the most common cause of death for early hominids was probably predation. A fairly large number of individuals in arboreal populations would have suffered injuries through falls. Survival would not normally exceed an individual's reproductive years, with a probable maximum life span for most species of about 35 years. Fairly small group sizes and home ranges meant that an individual would probably meet fewer than 200 members of his or her own species in a lifetime, and most of these individuals would be kin.

Physical differences between the sexes (sexual dimorphism) were fairly pronounced among early hominid species, with the most dimorphic in body size probably being the larger forms. Female body weights may have been as little as 60 to 70 percent of male body weight among *Australopithecus boisei (Paranthropus boisei)*, for example. Size differences decreased with the appearance of *Homo erectus,* but pronounced size dimorphism probably remained an important feature of hominid life until the end of the Middle Pleistocene. Dimorphic primate species show sexual differences in foraging behavior that reflect both the animals' size and their individual energy requirements. The largest male apes, for example, may not be able to travel to the ends of smaller branches, where most fruit is found, because the boughs will not bear their weight. A pregnant or lactating female requires greater amounts of high-quality forage, and among some primate species, females range less widely than males, remaining closer to predictable food sources. While male primates are more likely to engage in hunting, it is not an exclusively male

activity, and chimpanzee females have been observed to pursue and capture heavy prey in the forest canopy, even while carrying infants.

The nature of social relations between the sexes among early hominids has been a major source of debate in paleoanthropology. All modern primates species show a lasting social bond between a mother and her offspring, but there is great variety in mating patterns, group size, territoriality, and kin relations among group members. These behaviors no doubt varied among early hominid species. Polygyny is the norm among modern primate species with marked sexual dimorphism in body size and was likely a common form of social organization among early hominid species.

Two nearly universal features of modern human societies are the formalization of sexual relations and the economic cooperation of males and females in the rearing of young. Many paleoanthropologists believe these features to be of prime importance in the evolution of human societies and have attempted to pinpoint when they appeared in evolutionary history. In modern societies, food sharing plays a crucial role in creating lasting economic ties between males and females. Among modern primates, while individuals may occasionally share food or tolerate begging from offspring or potential mates, sharing food is not daily routine, and there is no agreement among paleoanthropologists about when it originated among Hominidae. Some contend that it appeared with the first tools and archaeological sites, while others link it to the appearance of bipedalism, well over 2 million years earlier, and still others postulate that long-term habitual economic cooperation between the sexes did not appear until the Late Pleistocene, more than 2 million years later.

One important clue to early hominid social organization lies in infant brain size. While adult brain size in early *Homo* is greater than those of *Australopithecus* or *Paranthropus,* the early *Homo* pelvis was still quite narrow. A small birth canal means a small brain size for the newborn and suggests a period of accelerated growth in early infancy to achieve large adult brain size. The modern human infant undergoes such a period of rapid postnatal brain growth, during which it is helpless and utterly dependent upon its mother.

This prolonged infant dependency has profound implications for maternal behavior and provides much of the glue that binds modern human society together.

If culture, taken to mean a society's shared set of symbols, beliefs, and ideas about appropriate behavior, existed in the Early or Middle Pleistocene, it has left no tangible sign, and whether early hominids could convey their thoughts to one another through spoken language is hotly debated by paleoanthropologists. Speech required enlargement and reorganization of the primate brain and alteration of the larynx, tongue, jaw, and resonating cavities in the palate and cranium. These developments, together with the invention of a series of complex linguistic devices including syntax, may have occurred in a series of steps over a long period of time. Modern nonhuman primates communicate not only vocally but also through gesture, posture, and facial expression. It is quite possible that a rudimentary form of speech, perhaps incorporating many of these elements, was practiced by early *Homo*. Divergent trajectories among groups in the evolution of speech would have provided a strong mechanism isolating different early hominid species.

Middle Pleistocene

The Middle Pleistocene (125,000 to 750,000 years ago) is important in the development of human behavior because it saw the beginnings of behavioral modernity. With the extinction of *Australopithecus* and *Paranthropus* by about 1.4 million years ago, species diversity within the Hominidae was substantially reduced. Early members of the genus *Homo,* such as *Homo ergaster,* may have survived into the Middle Pleistocene, and *Homo erectus* became firmly established. Climatic change, technological innovation, or population pressure probably provided the impetus for a number of expansions of hominid populations out of Africa.

There is a possibility that *Homo erectus* found its way to Asia as early as 1.8 million years ago, but it was clearly present there by 1 million years ago. By about 500,000 years ago, archaic members of our own species, *Homo sapiens,* had appeared in Africa, Europe, and Asia. African archaic

Homo sapiens populations probably gave rise to the first modern humans, *Homo sapiens sapiens.* Fossilized remains of these earliest modern humans have been found in South Africa and Ethiopia, and date to as much as 130,000 years ago. A rapid expansion of this modern human population out of Africa in the Late Pleistocene seems to have resulted in the displacement or extinction of archaic hominid populations in Eurasia, though some paleoanthropologists argue for an independent or parallel origin of modern humans elsewhere.

Homo erectus and archaic *Homo sapiens* had body proportions similar to modern humans, and their arboreal adaptation had probably become a thing of the past. Male adult height in some cases reached as much as 180 centimeters, which is in the range of the tallest populations of modern humans. Postcranial skeletons were very robust, indicating that these hominids had a high level of endurance for a strenuous and demanding way of life. There are no examples of very aged individuals from this period, and the maximum life span was probably about 40 years. The increased numbers of fossils and archaeological sites indicate that hominids existed in greater numbers, but population densities were still low enough to discourage endemic disease, and the common cause of death was probably traumatic injury or predation. However, one female *Homo erectus* (KNM-ER 1808) is known to have perished through a severe infection or dietary disorder, and a male archaic *Homo sapiens* (from a site at Kabwe) shows signs of serious periodontal disease.

Homo erectus seems to have occupied the entire African continent, with the possible exception of the portions of western and central Africa that are now forested (however, artifacts and fossilized remains of *Homo erectus* may yet be found there). The African geographic range of archaic *Homo sapiens* appears to have been broader still. A tolerance for a wider range of habitats may be due to the advanced nature of Middle Pleistocene technology over that of the preceding period. Perhaps manufacture of watertight containers freed hominids at this time to forage farther from a water source.

About 1.5 million years ago, the ad hoc stone-fracturing techniques of the Oluwan industry gave way to the Acheulian, whose hand axes and cleavers are characterized by standardized tool forms and often careful, bifacial workmanship. Flakes were produced by more formalized methods, including the Levallois technique. By about 200,000 years ago, Middle Stone Age technology had replaced the Acheulian in Africa. Hand axes and cleavers ceased to be made, and smaller tools made on flakes produced by the Levallois and other formal techniques became the norm. Stone tools do not seem to have been designed for particular uses, but individual tools were used for multiple tasks. The use of stone tools to make other artifacts in perishable materials, such as wood, skin, or grass, was probably common. In the later Middle Stone Age, scrapers and points made on flakes show clear signs of hafting onto handles or spears.

Some Middle Pleistocene populations appear to have practiced a new type of foraging, with repeated, perhaps seasonal, reoccupation of favored sites. With the possible exception of circular hut foundations at Middle Stone Age sites in the Orange River Valley in South Africa, signs of occupation structures are still rare and their interpretation problematic. While most sites are found in the open, the occupation of caves became more frequent. The disturbance and damage to bone debris in Acheulian cave occupations indicates that competition with predators was still a serious problem, but living in caves seems to have become more routine for some Middle Stone Age populations. Instrumental in this development was the controlled use of fire, and deliberately fashioned hearths are known from both Acheulian and Middle Stone Age contexts.

The importance of the use of fire cannot be overemphasized. While there is no indication of the use of cooking vessels, tuberous vegetables and meat were probably roasted, rendering a wider array of foods edible and nutritious. Chewing cooked food places substantially less stress on the teeth and jaws, and natural selection for a reduced dentition and masticatory musculature strongly affected the shape of the hominid face.

Charring and scraping is an important technique in woodworking, and a club, spear, and tray apparently made by this method have been recovered at the Acheulian site of Kalambo Falls,

Zambia. The use of fire also had an important impact on the African landscape. Repeated, perhaps seasonal, burnings cleared dense brush and encouraged the growth of fire-resistant tree species and grass. It is not known whether the fires escaped from hominid control, or whether the burning was deliberate, in the manner of some modern foragers and pastoralists, but the process made possible the open landscape that supports the large ungulate herds of today's African savanna.

Homo erectus is thought by many to have consumed more meat than its predecessors and to have practiced cooperative hunting. It is also frequently argued that cooperative hunting or learning to manufacture the standardized and more technically demanding tool forms of the Acheulian and Middle Stone Age required speech. It should be remembered, however, that lions, hyenas, and wolves hunt cooperatively and that birds and insects construct intricate and standardized nests, all without benefit of the spoken word. Nonetheless, with its larger body size, with a brain from one-half to two-thirds the size of a modern human brain, and armed with fire and an improved tool kit, *Homo erectus* seems well matched to its quarry. Examination of faunal remains shows that competition with predators was still a serious issue and that scavenging may have been common at both Acheulian and Middle Stone Age sites. Longer-term occupation of sites and the use of fire indicate that Acheulian hunters had established more secure territorial claims and had moved up in the carnivore hierarchy, but it may not have been until the early part of the Late Pleistocene that Middle Stone Age peoples routinely hunted dangerous game animals.

While sexual dimorphism was reduced in *Homo erectus* and archaic *Homo sapiens,* it seems to have been greater than among modern human populations. Brow ridge development, in particular, was far greater among males than females, and this characteristic feature of the hominid face reached its apogee in the Middle Pleistocene, perhaps maintained by sexual selection. Hominid social organization remains nearly as enigmatic as for earlier periods. There is no unambiguous evidence for symbolic behavior or ritual in African *Homo erectus.* Cut marks made by stone tools on a cranium of archaic *Homo sapiens* from

Bodo, Ethiopia, however, can be interpreted as evidence for either cannibalism or ritual defleshing. Clear signs of cannibalism can be seen on the charred and broken early-modern human bones from the Middle Stone Age context at the Klasies River Mouth, South Africa, connoting either symbolic behavior or an all too familiar pattern of interpersonal or intergroup violence. A number of deliberate early-modern human burials are known from the Middle Stone Age levels at Border Cave, South Africa, though it is possible that these are intrusive from a later level.

From the archaeological record of the African Middle Stone Age, there are additional hints of modern behavior dating to many tens of thousands of years before such behavior appears outside Africa. Definite regional styles of artifact manufacture in the Middle Stone Age suggest the beginnings of ethnic identity. Blades occur in the Kapthurin Formation, Kenya, dating to about 240,000 years ago, and sophisticated bone harpoons, dating to 90,000 years ago, have been found at Katanda, Zaire. Faunal remains and projectile points from the Middle Stone Age site at /=Gi, Botswana, dating to about 77,000 years ago, indicate hunting of dangerous game animals and a deliberate, scheduled use of resources at different seasons of the year. The Middle Stone Age also sees the first extensive use of marine resources by coastal populations. Obsidian that was traded or transported from a source 190 kilometers away has been found in a Middle Stone Age level at the site of Muguruk, Kenya, implying either widespread trade among neighboring groups or acquaintance with distant landscapes or populations, both quite unknown in previous periods. Traces of similar modern behaviors appear quite suddenly in Eurasia about 40,000 years ago, when modern humans apparently arrived from Africa.

BIBLIOGRAPHY

Brooks, A. S., D. M. Helgren, J. S. Cramer, A. Franklin, W. Hornyak, J. M. Heating, R. G. Klein, W. J. Rink, H. Schwarcz, J. N. Leith Smith, K. Stewart, N. E. Todd, J. Verniers, and J. E. Yellen. 1995. Dating and context of three Middle Stone Age sites with bone points in the Upper Semliki Valley, Zaire. *Science* 268: 548–553.

Campbell, B. 1966. *Human evolution.* New York: Aldine Publishing Company.

Clark, J. D. 1970. *The prehistory of Africa.* New York: Praeger.

———. 1988. The Middle Stone Age of East Africa and the beginnings of regional identity. *Journal of World Prehistory* 2: 235–303

———. 1992. African and Asian perspectives on the origins of modern humans. *Philosophical Transactions of the Royal Society of London Series B* 337: 201–215.

Fleagle, J. G. 1988. *Primate adaptation and evolution.* San Diego: Academic Press.

Foley, R. 1984. *Another unique species.* London: Longman.

Isaac, G. Ll. 1982. The earliest archaeological traces. In *The Cambridge history of Africa, vol. 1: From the earliest times to 500 B.C.,* ed. J. D. Clark, 157–247. Cambridge: Cambridge University Press.

Klein, R. G. 1989. *The human career.* Chicago: Chicago University Press.

McBrearty, S. 1989. Cutlery and carnivory. *Journal of Human Evolution* 18: 277–282.

Toth, N., and K. Schick. 1986. The first million years: The archaeology of protohuman culture. *Advances in Archaeological Method and Theory* 9: 1–96.

Volman, T. P. 1984. Early prehistory of southern Africa. In *Southern African prehistory and paleoenvironments,* ed. R. G. Klein, 169–395. Rotterdam: A. A. Balkema.

Yellen, J. E., A. S. Brooks, E. Cornelissen, M. H. Mehlman, and K. Stewart. 1995. A Middle Stone Age worked bone assemblage from Katanda, Upper Semliki Valley, Zaire. *Science* 268: 553–556.

Sally McBrearty

PRIMATE BEHAVIOR AS A PRECURSOR OF HUMAN BEHAVIOR

The original impetus for primate field studies, during the late 1950s, was an explicit intention to employ humanity's nearest biological relatives as models for the evolutionary and behavioral development of earlier hominids. A progressive increase in data and understanding of primate behavior and ecology has led to perceptions of similarities between the nonhuman and human primates. A common view among primatologists is that the nonhuman members of the order differ not in kind but only in degree from the human members. This applies not only to the anatomical similarities but to the ecological, behavioral, social structural, psychological, intellectual, and cognitive patterns.

The initial models derived from primate field studies emphasized social structure, male dominance, and ecological similarity. These analogies focused upon the terrestrial, savanna-dwelling baboons (both the common yellow and olive baboons and *Theropithecus gelada,* the grass- and seed-eating highland gelada baboon) and naturally relied upon features of male hierarchies, power structures, and activities such as group defense. Beginning in the late 1960s and early 1970s, modeling moved toward a chimpanzee analog with an increased emphasis on female roles and tool use for the gathering of vegetative foodstuffs. Eventually, a model based upon the bonobo *(Pan paniscus,* often referred to as the *pygmy chimpanzee)* was formulated. From a theoretical perspective, all of these models are considered to be preferential in that they are based extensively upon the actual behaviors and patterns of social structures among particular living species of cercopithecoids and hominoids. During the 1980s, a preference for conceptual models derived from studies of behavioral ecology came to the fore. Essentially, this revised mode of modeling involved extracting principles and patterns from the field data and applying these to early hominid behavior in an attempt to divorce the modeling effort from any particular "referent" species. However, these attempts were strongly criticized in the 1990s as remaining intimately linked to referential material. The latest attempts at behavioral reconstructions employ the methods of cladistic analysis and ignore the controversy over referential versus conceptual models.

Among the most significant variations on the baboon model were I. DeVore and S. L. Washburn's view that modified and emphasized the "man the hunter" perspective originally proposed by Charles Darwin. Another significant variation was offered by C. J. Jolly who modeled a seed-eating hominid based upon studies of the gelada baboon. All versions of the baboon model placed substantial emphasis upon the organization and roles of males within the society. Since these models were generated on the basis of data collected with a biased methodology—one that did not equalize the balances between the sexes and the different age categories—they naturally reflected a biased, male-dominated perspective. The shift toward a chimpanzee model was driven in part by the inadequacies of the baboon analogies, the accumulation of data that contradicted many of the assumptions (both implicit and explicit) upon which they were based, and data collected by female field researchers. The "woman the gatherer" concept first put forward by S. Linton as a more comprehensive analogy served as the stimulus for the series of papers by N. Tanner, A. Zihlman, and F. Dahlberg. These researchers proposed the gathering hypothesis based explicitly on chimpanzee and bonobo analogies. These models emphasized the gathering of vegetative material through tool use and suggested a significant role for sexual selection in early hominids.

A significant point in the development of primate-derived models for early hominids came with the 1987 publication of the volume edited by W. G. Kinzey, based on a symposium at the 1983 meeting of the American Anthropological Association. Referential models were criticized as being inadequate and inappropriate to the uniqueness of hominid evolution by J. Tooby and I. DeVore in a summary article prepared well after the symposium. It was their preference that modeling hominid behavior should be performed using conceptual models that incorporate hominid morphology and integrate it with information found in behavioral ecology, evolutionary ecology, and sociobiology. An important step toward that aim was provided by R. A. Foley and P. C. Lee in an attempt at reconstructing the sequence of evolutionary pathways leading to hominid behavior. However, as C. B. Stanford and J. S. Allen clearly indicate, conceptual models are not distinct from referential models. Concepts or models of behavior or behavioral ecology are necessarily abstractions from the data of field studies and are intended to generalize principles of order and structure. However, these principles must be tested, and modified as needed, against other preferential species and data. Thus there is a feedback loop linking referent and concept. Stanford and Allen went on to criticize Tanner, Tooby and DeVore, and Foley and Lee as defeating their own principles and presenting "either implicitly chimpanzee-referent models or restatements, updated and improved of the 'man the hunter' hypotheses of the 1950s and '60s."

During the 1990s, behavioral modeling incorporated a new tool, the classificatory techniques of cladistics, along with the use of computer-generated cladograms (branching diagrams that represent the distribution and evolution of characters within a set of species). While the techniques and technology of cladistic analysis are based upon the techniques of cluster analysis and are still developing, they have proven to be very effective in the traditional realm of morphology, and the central operating assumptions can be and have been carried into models of behavior and social structure. R. W. Wrangham made important contributions in reconstructing social organization in early hominids, B. Sillén-Tullborg and A. Mueller examined the evolution of concealed ovulation in relation to mating systems, and D. W. Cameron modeled the "behavioral morphotype" of the common ancestor of hominids and panics (chimpanzees). An advantage of the cladistic methodology for modeling is that it can be focused upon behavioral characteristics and social structural features that display a strong phylogenetic (evolutionary) component. As a consequence, cladistic arguments exclude learned behaviors, traditions, and cultural phenomena. Evaluation of characteristics as to their generalized or specialized states is the first step in the process. This involves a careful consideration of the developmental sequence of forms or variations of the characteristic. Some states are early in the sequence and are most frequently generalized or "primitive," while others occur later in an evolutionary sequence and are usually derived or "advanced" to some extent. An advantage of the phylogenetic-cladistic approach is that it allows the separation of individual behavior patterns from features of social structure. Separate analyses can be performed, and the resultant diagrams compared.

Table 17 presents a summary of the social structural features obtained from several reconstruction models and the methods employed. Authors have specified "early," "earliest," or "late" hominids as well as the "common ancestor" in these models, so the consensus column can only be regarded as a crude approximation or probable case. There is substantial similarity in the set of predictions even though the methods of investigation differ greatly. The consensus column suggests that early hominids lived in a closed social network, one that was reluctant to admit, or rarely able to accept, unknown or new individuals, even though the network fragmented into smaller parties of variable composition. In the terminology of primate studies, this is a fission-fusion society, which allows individual members to travel independently away from the group. In reproductive pattern, African hominids practiced female exogamy and male endogamy by retaining males as the long-term group core, while females dispersed from their natal group. Cameron, however, suggests on the basis of some bonobo field data that the common ancestor was likely to disperse both sexes, a pattern that is actually very rare in primates. Most of the data suggests that hominid males were not restricted to a single mate, nor were females. This also applies to the "variable" status reported by Cameron, since he notes that mating systems in humans are culturally patterned rather than being species specific. In comparisons across the hominids, the probable pattern suggested for mating in the hominid lineage is one of short duration. In terms of intergroup relationships, hostility and male aggression during encounters appear to be most probable, yet related activities—stalking and attacking of members of other groups and territorial behavior—cannot be evaluated, largely because they have not been considered in these studies.

Table 18 presents a comparison of behaviors (categorized under five headings) of activities considered to be important components of hominid patterns. These are surveyed across the African great apes, with modern humans *(Homo)* and a reconstructed common ancestor of the *Pan* and *Homo* lineages on the right. Political maneuvering was recognized as a component in primate behavior with the pioneering work of

Frans de Waal on the chimpanzee population in the Arnhem Zoo and with the compilation of tactical deception and deceitful actions (now referred to as *Machiavellian intelligence*) by R. Byrne and A. Whiten. Primates were recognized to engage in such machinations in the first field studies, where observers made note of "alliances," redirection of aggression, and shifting of power structures. These "political" behaviors are another area in which the behavior of non-human primates approaches that of humans. Similarly, the recognition and acceptance that both homosexual sexual behavior and the existence of face-to-face copulatory patterns have moved the behavior of the chimpanzees closer to the human forms. The existence of predatory

Table 17 *Reconstructions of the social organization of early hominids according to R. W. Wrangham*

Reference	Tanner 1981	McGrew 1981	Baer & McEachron 1982	Lovejoy 1981	Wrangham 1987	Cameron 1993	Consensus of Probable Pattern
Method	Chimp Model	Chimp Model	Behavioral Ecology	Behavioral Ecology	Phylogeny	Cladistic	
Reconstruction of	Late Hominid	Earliest Hominid	Earliest Hominid	Early Hominid	Common Ancestor	Common Ancestor	Common Ancestor to Early Hominid
Closed social network	--	Yes	Yes	--	Yes	Yes	Yes
Party composition	Unstable	Unstable	Stable	Unstable	?	Unstable	Unstable
Females sometimes alone	Yes	Yes	No	Yes	?	Yes	Yes
Males sometimes alone	Yes	Yes	No	Yes	Yes	Yes	Yes
Female exogamy	--	Yes	No	--	Yes	Variable	Yes
Female alliances	--	No	Yes	--	Rare	?	?
Male exogamy	Often	Yes	No	Yes	?	Variable	Yes
Male alliances	--	Yes	--	--	?	?	?
Males with single mate	No	No	No	Yes	No	Variable	No
Length of sexual relationship	Short	Short	Short	Long	?	--	Short
Hostile relations between groups	No	Yes	--	--	Yes	Yes	Yes
Males active in intergroup encounters	--	Yes	--	--	Yes	Yes	Yes
Stalking and attacking	--	--	--	--	Yes	--	?
Territorial defense	--	?	--	--	?	--	?

Key: -- = Variable not considered
? = No decision possible

Table 18 *Comparisons of behavior patterns in African hominoids and a common ancestor*

Behavior Pattern	Gorilla	*P. troglodytes* (Common chimpanzee)	*P. paniscus* (Bonobo)	*Homo*	Common Ancestor
Political					
Manipulation of others	Some	Common	?	Common	Common
Use of deception	Some	Yes	?	Yes	Yes
Misinformation	Yes	Yes	?	Yes	Yes
Sexual					
Homosexual mounting	No	Yes	Yes	Yes	Yes
Face-to-face copulation	Some	Some	Yes	Yes	Yes
Animal consumption					
Male vertebrate hunting	No	Yes	Yes	Yes	Yes
Female vertebrate hunting	No	Yes	No?	Yes	Yes?
Male animal consumption	No	Yes	Yes	Yes	Yes
Female animal consumption	No	Yes	?	Yes	Yes
Aggression					
"Murder" (deliberate killing)	No	Yes	No	Yes	?
"Warfare" (group killing)	No	Yes	No	Yes	?
Miscellaneous					
Tool use	No	Yes	Yes	Yes	Yes
Tool transport	No	Yes	?	Yes	Yes?
Cannibalism	No	Yes	No	Yes	Yes?
Infanticide	Yes	Yes	No	Yes	Yes?

Key: ? = Unknown, data unavailable
No? = Possibly not present
Yes? = Possibly present

Data synthesized from original field studies by Fossey (1983), Goodall (1986), Kuroda (1980), Nishida (1979), McGrew et al. (1981), and HRAF files.

behavior has long been a focus in such human-chimpanzee comparisons, but the recognition of differences in the patterns of male and female hunting activities and in consumption of meat has made the common ancestor less of a "killer ape." One of the more interesting observations in this area is that male chimpanzees have been seen to share meat with estrus (sexually active) females in order to copulate with them. Observers have found that common chimpanzees are much like humans in their propensity to engage in deliberate killing and warfare, but that the bonobo or pygmy chimpanzee is much more inclined to "make love not war," using sexual activity as a mechanism to relieve tension within groups. Bonobo studies have not yet indicated any activity comparable to the warfare and deliberate killing seen in chimpanzees and humans. The use of simple tools, most commonly modified vegetative structures employed as sponges, towels, and termite-fishing sticks, has been noted for all panic and hominid species. Tool transport reaches a high point for the panics with the observations by C. Boesch of the Tai Forest chimpanzees carrying and storing the stone anvils and hammers they use for cracking nuts. There is a lack of information on tool carriage in bonobos, even though they also engage in termite fishing. Cannibalism, primarily of newborn infants, has been observed in chimpanzees, but not in gorillas, and data are lacking for the bonobo. Similarly, infanticide has been noted for all but the bonobo. If this comparison is accepted as a basis upon which to reconstruct the behavior of a common ancestor, it is apparent that this population would be expected to show political behavior involving manipulation, deceit, and the transmission of misinformation. The common ancestor would likely engage in both heterosexual and homosexual behaviors and to do so at least part of the time in the face-to-face position. The ancestor is likely to have engaged in some hunting behavior and to have developed some taste for meat consumption in both sexes. It is impossible to describe the aggressive behaviors of the ancestor since there is no uniform agreement. It should be noted that the consensus of a large number of evolution studies place the bonobo as an offshoot of the main chimpanzee lineage separating 2.5 million years ago. Thus, either the absence of murder and warfare is a newly evolved feature of the line, or these patterns evolved independently in both common chimpanzees and hominids. Finally, tool use, tool transport, cannibalism, and infanticide are all likely to be behaviors of the common ancestor.

There will always be difficulty in constructing detailed, explicit models of early hominid behavior on the basis of either referential or conceptual analogies. Yet either technique (certainly when aided by the constraints of a phylogenetic or cladistic method) can yield reasonable approximations of the behavior and social structure of hominids. Tables 17 and 18 provide a view of the social structures and behaviors likely to be observed in the common ancestor of panics and hominids and perhaps more interestingly indicate that hominids—early, late, or modern—share a large number of common characteristics with

their fellow primates. The viewpoint that humans do not differ in kind, but only in degree, from their nearest primate relatives, remains a viable and useful thesis.

BIBLIOGRAPHY

Boesch, C. 1993. Cultural learning: Towards a new image of culture in wild chimpanzees? *Behavioral and Brain Sciences* 16 (3): 514–515.

Byrne, R., and A. Whiten, 1984. Tactical deception of familiar individuals in baboons. *Animal Behavior* 33: 2.

Cameron, D. W. 1993. The Pliocene hominid and protochimpanzee behavioral morphotypes. *Journal of Anthropological Archaeology* 12: 386–414.

Dahlberg, F., ed. 1981. *Woman the gatherer.* New Haven: Yale University Press.

Darwin, C. 1871. *The descent of man and selection in relation to sex.* New York: Random House.

de Waal, F. 1982. *Chimpanzee politics.* London: Jonathan Cape.

DeVore, I., and S. L. Washburn. 1963. Baboon ecology and human evolution. In *African ecology and human evolution,* eds. F. C. Howell and F. Bourliere, 335–367. Chicago: Aldine Publishing Company.

Foley, R. A., and P. C. Lee. 1989. Finite social space, evolutionary pathways, and reconstructing hominid behavior. *Science* 243: 901–906.

Fossey, D. 1983. *Gorillas in the mist.* Boston: Houghton Mifflin.

Goodall, J. 1986. *The chimpanzees of Gombe: Patterns of behavior.* Cambridge: Belknap Press.

Jolly, C. J. 1970. The seed-eaters: A new model of hominid differentiation based on a baboon analogy. *Man* 5: 6–26.

Kinzey, W. G., ed. 1987. *The evolution of human behavior: Primate models.* New York: State University of New York Press.

Kuroda, S. 1980. Social behavior of the pygmy chimpanzees. *Primates* 21: 181–197.

Linton, S. 1971. Woman the gatherer: Male bias in anthropology. In *Women in cross-cultural perspective: A preliminary sourcebook,* ed. S. E. Jacobs, 9–21. Urbana: University of Illinois Press.

McGrew, W., C. I. G. Tutin, and P. J. Baldwin. 1981. Chimpanzees in a hot, dry and open habitat: Mt. Assirik, Senegal, West Africa. *Journal of Human Evolution* 10: 227–244.

Nishida, T. 1979. The social structure of the chimpanzees of the Mahale Mountains. In *The great apes: Perspectives on human evolution,* vol. 5, eds.

D. A. Hamburg and E. R. McCown, 72–121. Menlo Park: Benjamin/Cummings.

Sillén-Tullborg, B., and A. Mueller. 1993. The relationship between concealed ovulation and mating systems in anthropoid primates: A phylogenetic analysis. *American Naturalist* 141 (1): 1–25.

Stanford, C. B., and J. S. Allen. 1991. On strategic storytelling: Current models of human behavioral evolution. *Current Anthropology* 32 (1): 58–61.

Tanner, N. 1981. *On becoming human: A model of the transition from ape to human and the reconstruction of early human social life.* Cambridge: Cambridge University Press.

Tanner, N. 1983. Hunters, gatherers, and sex roles in space and time. *American Anthropologist* 85 (2): 335–341.

———. 1987. Gathering by females: The chimpanzee model revisited and the gathering hypothesis. In *The evolution of human behavior: Primate models,* ed. W. G. Kinzey, 3–27. New York: State University of New York Press.

Tooby, J., and I. DeVore. 1987. The reconstruction of hominid behavioral evolution through strategic modeling. In *The evolution of human behavior: Primate models,* ed. W. G. Kinzey, 183–238. New York: State University of New York Press.

Wrangham, R. W. 1987. African apes: The significance of African apes for reconstructing human social evolution. In *The evolution of human behavior: Primate models,* ed. W. G. Kinzey, 51–71. New York: State University of New York Press.

Zihlman, A. 1981. Women as shapers of the human adaptation. In *Woman the gatherer,* ed. F. Dahlberg, 77–120. New Haven: Yale University Press.

———. 1983. A behavioral reconstruction of *Australopithecus.* In *Hominid origins,* ed. K. J. Reichs, 207–238. Washington, D.C.: University Press of America.

James D. Paterson

HUMAN BEHAVIOR: ITS EVOLUTION

When anthropologists want to reconstruct the evolution of human behavior, they can use the following comparative approach. First, they can compare characteristics of modern humans with those of our closest living relatives, the great apes. Second, they can compare characteristics of the great apes to those of their more distant relatives, the Old World monkeys. This allows them to see which characteristics are shared with great apes and which are unique to humans. Third, they can compare human characteristics with the characteristics of fossil hominids. This allows them to determine which features are shared with other hominids and which are unique to humans.

After they have identified these patterns of inheritance, they can map characteristics onto a cladogram, a family tree that represents the branching points among related species without regard to the length of time elapsed between branches. Figure 20 provides is a typical example of a cladogram.

Note that each branching point represents an evolutionary divergence or speciation event in which one species split into two. The node at each branching point represents the common ancestor of the two (or more) resulting species (known as *sister species).* Generally speaking, new species form when a small portion of an existing species becomes reproductively isolated from the main portion after prolonged geographic separation. Members of this new, smaller branch usually display characteristics that differentiate them from members of the original species. So, for example, early hominids probably were distinguished from their great ape sister species by bipedal locomotion. It is customary to mark the origin of a new characteristic by drawing a horizontal line across the cladogram just below the node for the common ancestor.

Tracing the Evolution of Bipedalism

Bipedalism is a mode of locomotion that is probably unique to our family, Hominidae. It distinguishes us from our closest living relatives, the African apes, who use a mode of terrestrial locomotion known as *knuckle walking.* (When they are in the trees, the African apes brachiate (swing by their arms) as do the lesser apes, the gibbons.) Figure 20 shows the branching relations among living apes and hominids. The horizontal line (A) represents fully terrestrial bipedalism

(FTB) on this cladogram. The location of this line indicates that FTB probably arose in the common ancestor of *Homo erectus* and *Homo sapiens*. Line B represents semi-arboreal bipedalism and indicates that this mode of locomotion arose in the common ancestor of hominids after hominids split from great apes. Line C represents knuckle walking, which probably arose in the common ancestor of African apes and hominids. Line D represents a sloppy form of knuckle walking known as *fist walking,* which probably arose in the common ancestor of all the living great apes. Line E indicates brachiation (swinging by the arms). Its location indicates that it arose in the common ancestor of all living apes. This cladogram shows that bipedalism evolved in at least two steps: semi-arboreal bipedalism of the australopithecines and the fully terrestrial bipedalism of *Homo erectus.*

When anthropologists already know the evolutionary relationships among species, as among anthropoid primates, they can map the characteristics they choose onto the existing cladogram of their focal group. They do this to illustrate the

ancestry of particular characteristics (as shown in figure 20). These mappings reflect three different kinds of characteristics:

1. Shared characteristics present in the focal group (known as the *ingroup)* and in the next most distantly related group (known as the *outgroup)* and possibly other still more distantly related outgroups
2. Uniquely derived characteristics that have changed from those of the ancestor and are present only in one species
3. Shared-derived characteristics present in two or more sister species with a common ancestor but not present in the outgroup species

In the example given in figure 20, hominids are the ingroup. Bipedalism is a shared-derived characteristic of hominids because it is present in all hominid species and none of the outgroups. Knuckle walking (specialized semi-upright quadrupedal walking on flat feet and flexed knuckles) is a probably a shared-derived characteristic of the African apes and hominids because it is

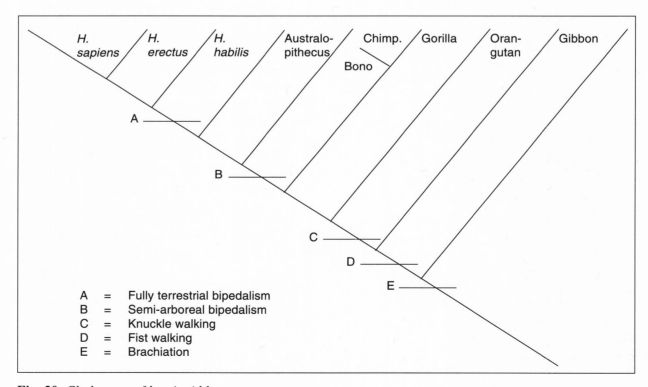

Fig. 20 *Cladogram of hominoid locomotor patterns*

present in all African apes. Alternatively, it may have evolved independently in the African apes after they diverged from each other. Brachiation is a shared characteristic of all living apes because it is present not only in hominids and great apes but also in lesser apes, but not in Old World monkeys. (If the ingroup included all the living apes, then brachiation would be a shared-derived characteristic because it is present in all the apes but not in their outgroup, Old World monkeys.)

Criteria for Selecting Characteristics

Anthropologists can use the comparative cladistic method of reconstruction to determine the ancestry of any characteristics they choose. The validity of the results will depend upon how well they choose the characteristics to compare. If they want their results to be evolutionarily valid, they must choose features that are genetically stable and consistent within their ingroup. They must avoid those that vary significantly (either developmentally or genetically) under different circumstances. The reason is that the taxonomic distribution of these characteristics does not reflect common ancestry. Which ones are stable and which are not?

Generally, locomotion, life-history features, brain size, and intelligence are stable characters within genera and families of monkeys and apes. In contrast, hair patterns, diet, sexual behaviors, and social organization are unstable characteristics that often differ among closely related species of Old World monkeys and apes. These characteristics differ because they can change rapidly during adaptive radiation into new niches. Use of these or other unstable characteristics produces a confusing picture of behavioral evolution.

Choosing valid characteristics depends upon recognizing anatomical or behavioral features that work together to achieve a particular function. These so-called functional complexes reflect a total morphological pattern. It is this pattern, rather than isolated features of a single bone, that changes during evolution. Bipedalism, for example, is a functional complex that involves a set of related features in the backbone, pelvis, knees, ankles, and feet. These features work together to transmit the body weight efficiently

onto the two feet and to move the body forward in a straight line without allowing it to fall. Similarly, the brachiation complex involves a set of related features in the trunk, shoulders, elbows, wrists, and hands. These features work together to allow suspensory locomotion under branches. It is important for anthropologists to recognize the interrelated elements of a functional complex. If they failed to recognize them, they might measure ten correlated features of a complex and interpret them as ten uncorrelated adaptations.

The Evolution of Human Life-History Characteristics

Life-history characteristics are fairly stable in anthropoid primates. The term *life history* refers to dimensions of the life cycle: the length of gestation, infancy, childhood, juvenile period, age at first reproduction, number of offspring per reproduction, birth interval, and life span. Life-history characteristics are fairly similar among monkeys in the same genus and among apes in the same family.

Like functional complexes, life-history features are products of natural selection operating within phylogenetically determined developmental constraints. Such constraints on the evolution of life-history features in primates include continuous determinate growth, placental birth, and lactation. Evolutionary "trade-offs" among various life-history features also constrain their evolution. Early maturation yields shorter generations and higher survival to maturity. Later maturation yields higher initial fecundity owing to greater body size. Shorter generation time yields higher population growth rates. The measurement of life span is tempered by the possibility of some individuals dying in "youth," while others reach "extreme" old age.

Most large primates give birth to a single infant that is well developed—that is, the infant can see, hear, and walk or cling at birth. Such neonates are called *precocial infants*. In contrast, very small primates and many other mammals give birth to large litters of small infants who cannot see, hear, or walk at birth. These neonates, called *altricial infants,* are generally born in large litters in protected nests or dens. Precocial infants generally can follow or cling to their mothers within an hour of birth. The altricial adaptation allows females to bear many young in a single litter of tiny, immature infants. In contrast, the precocial adaptation allows females to nurture a single offspring until it is mature enough to move around on its own. Most primates give birth to precocial young capable of clinging at birth.

We humans are large, slow-developing primates. We take even longer than great apes do to mature. Our maximum life span is about 30 years longer than that of the great apes, and our childhood is about five years longer. Surprisingly, however, our infants are born more helpless than ape infants. Consequently, they require greater parental care than ape infants do. The human pattern of secondary altriciality was probably necessitated by the enlargement of the brain. *Secondary altriciality* means that human infants are born at an immature, helpless stage and require a long period of nurturing (five years or longer). Since the small birth canals favored by bipedalism cannot deliver an infant whose brain is more than about 300 cubic centimeters, the human baby has to come out when it is immature.

When did this shift to secondary altriciality occur? We can reconstruct this event by examining the brain sizes of fossil hominids. Australopithecine species all have brain sizes only slightly larger those of the great apes—that is, around 300 to 500 cubic centimeters. Early *Homo* has brain sizes ranging from 600 to 700 cubic centimeters, and *Homo erectus* has brain sizes ranging from 800 to 1,000 cubic centimeters. If, as seems likely, their infants were born with brains about one-third the size of their parents, *Homo erectus* babies must have been born in a semi-altricial state. Given their brain size and their molar-eruption pattern, it seems likely that children of

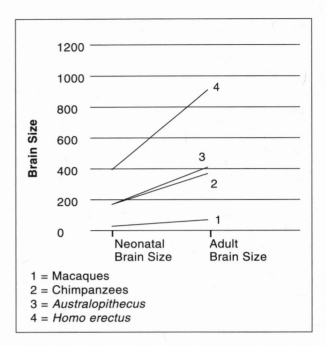

Fig. 21 *Depiction of increase in hominid brain size*

this species developed more slowly than great apes do, but more rapidly than modern humans do. They probably reached adulthood at about 14 years as measured by the eruption of their third molars. See table 19 for a comparison of molar-eruption times in great apes and hominids and figure 21 for a depiction of the evolution of brain size in hominids.

The Evolution of Mother-Infant Communication and Protolanguage

Locomotor and life-history data imply that *Homo erectus* infants could no longer cling to their mothers as australopithecine infants may have done. As hominid infants lost their ability

Table 19 *Molar-eruption sequences for selected anthropoid primate species*

	Macaques	**Chimpanzees**	*Homo erectus*	*Homo sapiens*
Molar 1	1.36 years	3.5 years	4.5 years	6.36 years
Molar 2	3.2 years	6.5 years	9.5 years	12.0 years
Molar 3	5.5 years	10.5 years	14.5 years	18.0 years

to cling, they must have become more dependent on their mothers' motivation to care for them. Consequently, infants must have depended more on visual and vocal communication rather than tactile communication to attract care-taking. This dependence implies the emergence of new humanlike facial signals. Particularly salient in human faces are everted lips capable of both smiling and vocalizations. Also salient are whites of the eyes, which indicate direction of gaze. Both of these features are absent in great apes.

Smiling is an important signal in human mother-infant relations. It expresses pleasure and, thereby, motivates continuing interaction. Interestingly, this signal seems to be absent from great ape mother-infant interactions. Great apes (and some Old World monkeys) do display a facial expression called the *silent-bared-teeth face* or the *grin* similar in form to the human smile. Grin faces (from fully open to fully closed mouths) express attitudes of appeasement blended with varying degrees of fear or friendly approach. These expressions may have evolved into the human smile. Likewise, the *relaxed open-mouth face* or the *play face* expression, which occurs during play, may have evolved into the human laugh.

The infants of humans and great apes display significant developmental differences. Human infants begin walking between nine and 16 months of age, while great ape infants begin walking between four and eight months of age. Infants of both groups are weaned around the third or fourth year (under preindustrial conditions). Infant apes cling to their mothers and spend most of their early months on their mothers' bodies. Human infants, in contrast, are unable to cling and must be carried by their caretakers or left in protected locations. Consequently, communication between great ape mothers and infants is primarily tactile, while communication between human infants and caretakers is primarily visual (focused on the face) and vocal.

The shift from primary dependence on tactile communication to visual and auditory communication implies early development of contingent social interactions (responsive face-to-face interactions including imitation) between infants and

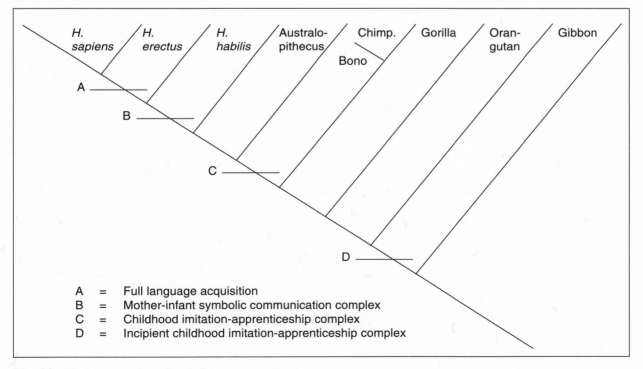

A = Full language acquisition
B = Mother-infant symbolic communication complex
C = Childhood imitation-apprenticeship complex
D = Incipient childhood imitation-apprenticeship complex

Fig. 22 *Cladogram of mother-infant communication patterns*

caretakers. Human infants begin to engage in contingent social interactions as early as three months of age, and in social imitation of novel behaviors as early as nine months of age. In contrast, great ape infants begin to imitate later and do so mainly after they are three or four years of age. Human infants also imitate more behaviors and do so much more often than great ape infants do. It is important to note that human mothers imitate their infants from the time their infants are about three months old, while great ape mothers rarely imitate their offspring of any age. Also, human mothers and infants engage in vocal imitation while great ape mothers and infants do not. Great ape infants are remarkably silent except when they chuckle during play or whimper when they are lost. This unique package of signals and interactions in humans may be called the *mother-infant imitation complex.*

This complex is an important precursor to language development in human infants. The reciprocal facial and vocal games they play are precursors to the verbal turn-taking that occurs during conversation. The imitation of gestures and vocal sounds is closely associated with the emergence of language in modern human infants. Its association with language acquisition lends particular importance to the evolution of imitation.

Great apes are able to learn rudimentary sign language and other symbol systems. Similarities between the abilities of great apes and young children lead anthropologists and others to believe that the earliest form of language was gestural. Neuroanatomists argue that the brains of early *Homo* show certain characteristics indicative of the emergence of language. Judging from their brain size and brain morphology, protolanguage was probably well developed in *Homo erectus.*

Unlike great ape children, young human children engage in prolonged bouts of pretend play. Pretend play usually focuses on practicing simple adult domestic and work roles. Great ape children do imitate some adult behaviors, especially tool-using behaviors as part of their apprenticeship for foraging. While they rarely engage in anything like pretend play, they do exhibit some imitation behaviors. The childhood behaviors of great apes may be called the *incipient childhood imitation-apprenticeship complex.* It seems likely that pretend play became increasingly important as the complexity of adult roles increased. This transition had probably begun by the time of *Homo erectus.* Figure 22 depicts the probable evolution of mother-infant communication in great apes and hominids.

The Evolution of the Capacity for Intelligent Use of Tools

Anthropologists used to call humans the "tool-using animal" until Jane Goodall in 1968 reported that chimpanzees in the wild use tools to fish for termites. Subsequent studies have revealed that chimpanzees use tools to drink fluids from natural bowls, fish for ants, crack open nuts, clean their bodies, and other activities. Following these discoveries, anthropologists called humans the "toolmaking animal." When it became clear that chimpanzees modify the sticks they use in fishing for ants and termites, this distinction also fell.

Anthropologists now emphasize the distinction between worked stone tools and unworked stones and modified wooden tools. The earliest archaeological evidence for worked stone tools comes around 2.4 million years ago. The earliest worked stone tools, Olduwan tools, may have been made only by early *Homo* or by both early *Homo* and *Australopithecus.* The next earliest stone tools, the bifaced Acheulian tools, were made by *Homo erectus* beginning about 1.6 million years ago. More complex stone tools, the Mousterian complex characterized by the prepared-core technique, are associated with archaic *Homo sapiens* beginning about 200,000 years ago. Upper Paleolithic tool complexes characterized by finely worked blades, appear in conjunction with modern *Homo sapiens* some time before 35,000 years ago. These tools are highly variable regionally and undergo rapid historical changes.

Anthropologists have focused on tool use because it is one of the major expressions of the superior intelligence of our large-brained genus *Homo.* Many of the scenarios anthropologists have proposed to explain the origins of bipedalism and the origins of enlarged brains have focused on tool use in hunting and other activities. Clearly, the capacity for the intelligent use of tools evolved through a series of stages over several million years. Current data suggest that these stages of complexity correspond roughly to the stages of evolution of the brain.

The stages of intellectual development in human children (as developed by Jean Piaget) provide a useful framework for classifying the levels of intelligence involved in different kinds of tool use. Piaget describes four major periods of intellectual development in human children from birth through adolescence. Although his model covers both physical and logical-mathematical reasoning, his work on spatial and causal understanding is the most relevant to the analysis of tool use. Tool use in great apes corresponds in complexity to that of two-year-old children at the end of the sensorimotor period or the beginning of the preoperations period. Tool use in early *Homo (Homo habilis)* depended upon spatial understanding similar to that of three- to five-year-old children in the preoperations period. Tool use in late *Homo erectus* depended on spatial intelligence similar to that of six- or seven-year-old children in the concrete operations period.

Figure 23 depicts the probable stages of evolution of tool use in great apes and hominids.

———∿∿∿∿∿∿∿∿∿———

Anthropologists who want to reconstruct the evolution of behavior can use the comparative cladistic method. First, they can identify taxonomically relevant complexes of characteristics. Second, they can use the cladistic method to classify them into shared, shared-derived, and derived complexes. Then, they can map these characteristics onto existing cladograms to show their probable ancestry.

Application of cladistic methodology reveals that key hominid behavioral complexes probably evolved through at least four stages:

1. Bipedalism evolved through a semi-arboreal stage into a fully terrestrial stage.
2. Life history evolved through a semi-precocial into a secondarily atricial stage.
3. Mother-infant communication evolved from a primarily tactile interaction into a visual and vocal mode of symbolic interaction.

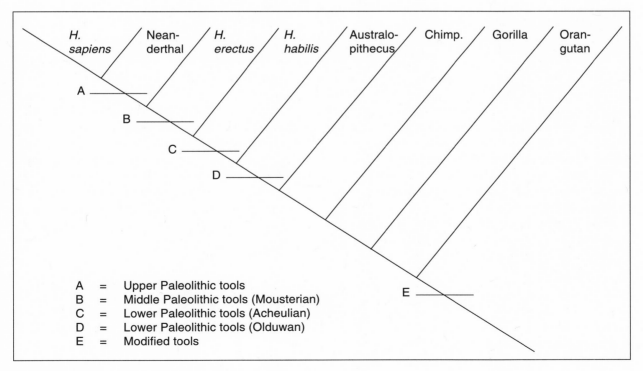

Fig. 23 *Cladogram of kinds of tool-use capacity*

4. The capacity for tool use evolved through a modification into a manufacture stage, followed by four substages of manufacture.

Each transition occurred by the time of *Homo erectus* and was apparently tied directly or indirectly to increased brain size.

BIBLIOGRAPHY

Armstrong, D. F., W. Stoke, and S. Wilcox. 1995. *Gesture and the nature of language.* Cambridge: Cambridge University Press.

Bates, E. 1979. *The emergence of symbols.* New York: Academic Press.

Brooks, D. R., and D. R. McLennan. 1993. *Phylogeny: Ecology and behavior.* Chicago: University of Chicago Press.

Falk, D. 1992. *Braindance.* New York: Holt, Rinehart and Winston.

Fleagle, J. 1988. *Primate adaptation and evolution.* New York: Academic Press.

Gardner, R. C. A., B. A. T. Gardner, and T. van Canffort. 1989. *Teaching sign language to chimpanzees.* Albany: State University of New York Press.

Goodall, J. 1968. Behaviour of free-living chimpanzees of the Gombe Stream area. *Animal Behaviour Monographs* 1: 163–311.

———. 1986. *The chimpanzees of the Gombe.* Cambridge: Harvard University Press.

Harvey, P., L. Martin, L. and J. Clutton–Brock. 1986. Life histories in comparative perspective. In *Primate societies,* eds. B. Smuts, D. Cheney, R. Seyfarth, R. Wrangham, and T. Struhsaker, 181–196. Chicago: University of Chicago Press.

Hunt, K. D. 1994. The evolution of human bipedality: Ecology and functional morphology. *Journal of Human Evolution* 26: 183–202.

Klein, R. 1989. *The human career.* Chicago: University of Chicago Press.

Maple, T., and M. Hoff. 1982. *Gorilla behavior.* New York: Van Nostrand Reinhold.

Martin, L. 1994. Primate reproduction. In *The Cambridge encyclopedia of human evolution,* eds. S. Jones, R. Martin, and D. Pilbeam, 87–90. Cambridge: Cambridge University Press.

McGraw, W. 1992. *Chimpanzee material culture.* Cambridge: Cambridge University Press.

Meltzoff, A. 1990. Foundations for developing a concept of self: The role of imitation in relating self to others and the value of social mirroring, social modeling, and self practice in infancy. In *The self in transition,* eds. D. Chicchetti and M. Beeghly, 28–37. Chicago: University of Chicago Press.

Parker, S. T. 1985. A social-technological model for the evolution of language. *Current Anthropology* 26: 617–639.

———. 1993. Imitation and circular reactions as evolved mechanisms for cognitive construction. *Human Development* 36: 309–323.

Piaget, J. 1962. *Play, dreams and imitation in children.* New York: Norton.

Piaget, J., and B. Inhelder. 1967. *The child's conception of space.* New York: Norton.

———. 1969. *The psychology of the child.* New York: Basic Books.

Richards, A. 1985. *Primates in nature.* New York: Freeman.

Savage-Rumbaugh, S., J. Murphy, R. Sevcik, K. Brakke, S. Williams, and D. Rumbaugh. 1993. Language comprehension in ape and child. *Monographs for the Society for Research in Child Development* 58: 3–4.

Smith, B. H. 1992. Life history and the evolution of human maturation. *Evolutionary Anthropology* 1 (4): 134–142.

Stanley, S. M. 1992. An ecological theory for the origins of *Homo. Paleobiology* 18: 237–259.

Stearns, S. C. 1992. *The evolution of life histories.* New York: Oxford University Press.

Stem, D. 1977. T*he first relationship.* Cambridge: Harvard University Press.

Van Hooff, J. R. A. M. 1972. A comparative approach to the phylogeny of laughter and smiling. In *Nonverbal communication,* ed. R. Hinde, 209–237. Cambridge: Cambridge University Press.

Watson, J. S. 1972. Smiling, cooing and "the game." *Merrill–Palmer Quarterly* 18: 323–339.

Wiley, E. O. 1981. *Phylogenetics: The theory and practice of phylogenetic systematics.* New York: Wiley.

Wynn, T. 1989. *The evolution of spatial competence.* Urbana: University of Illinois Press.

Sue Taylor Parker

First Footsteps in Africa

EARLY HUMAN DIETS

Reconstructions of the diet, subsistence strategies, and overall adaptations of ancient hominids rely on diverse evidence. Sources of evidence include:

1. Hominid fossils
2. Stone artifacts and fossil bones of other animals concentrated at archaeological sites and distributed in lower densities across paleo-landscapes
3. The geological record indicative of ancient habitats, of the processes of site formation, and of temporal relationships of the evidence
4. Analogies based on the behavior of modern animals and the dynamics of modern ecosystems

The challenge to researchers is how best to combine the diverse evidence into testable hypotheses that contribute to the understanding of hominid adaptations.

The hominid fossil record in Africa extends back at least 5 million years and includes from one to several species in each of three or four genera. Because the entire first half of hominid evolutionary history lacks any archaeological evidence, reconstructions of the diet and behavioral adaptations of the earliest hominids must be based on the other sources of evidence listed above. Fossil evidence indicates that the earliest hominids of the genera *Ardipithecus* and *Australopithecus*, unlike apes, were bipedal but were more generally apelike in other significant features such as brain size, dentition, limb proportions, and marked sexual dimorphism (physical differences between the sexes). Based on the fossils and analogies with modern higher primates, it is probable, therefore, that the earliest hominids living in savanna woodland habitats along the East African Rift Valley were generally apelike in diet (predominantly plant-based), in foraging strategies (food consumption at point of acquisition without significant sharing), and in social organization (groups of multiple males and females for efficient exploitation of patchy food resources in mixed to open habitats).

The apparent absence of an archaeological record associated with the earliest hominids is consistent with the inferences of generally apelike adaptations. None of the australopithecines, not even the younger robust australopithecines, can be linked conclusively to the production of an archaeological record indicative of more humanlike behavior and diet, such as the making and use of flaked-stone tools, the increased consumption of meat from large animals, and the transport and sharing of food. On the other hand, fossil and bone chemical evidence from geologically complex cave deposits in South Africa may indicate that *Australopithecus robustus*, commonly regarded as specialized vegetarians, had hands specifically adapted for making and using stone tools and diets that included a significant proportion of animal tissue.

There is also disagreement over the number of species of early *Homo* before 1.8 million years ago. One view is that a single species, *Homo habilis*, represented the beginning of the genus *Homo*. If so, then fossil evidence indicates that early *Homo* exhibited marked sexual dimorphism comparable to modern forest-dwelling apes with smaller females and retained apelike limb proportions and digits for arboreal (tree) locomotion. This suggests that, in diet and behavioral capabilities, early *Homo* was relatively apelike and far removed from the adaptations of modern humanity.

An alternative view is that multiple species characterized the beginning and early evolutionary history of the genus *Homo*. There are two variants to this view. In the first variant, *Homo* before 1.8 million years ago consisted of two species, a large-bodied, terrestrially adapted species, *Homo rudolfensis,* and a small-bodied, more arboreally adapted species, *Homo habilis*. After 1.8 million years ago, early *Homo erectus* (also termed *Homo ergaster)* continued the evolutionary trend toward even larger body size and increased encephalization (brain development), while the small-bodied and more australopithecine-like *Homo habilis* became extinct. In the second variant of the multiple-species view, early *Homo erectus* may be represented in the fossil record as early as 2 million years ago, which would mean the coexistence of two large-bodied and one small-bodied species of *Homo,* along with the robust australopithecines.

While the hominid fossil record provides diverse evidence for defining some of the adaptations and behavioral ecology of the different hominids, the archaeological record offers more detailed evidence of specific behavioral events and aspects of foraging strategies and diet. The earliest archaeological sites in East Africa, dating to approximately 1.6 to 2.4 million years ago, are found along the shores of lakes and streams in the Rift Valley in Ethiopia, Kenya, and Tanzania. The evidence at individual sites consists of:

1. Flaked- and unflaked-stone cobbles and the sharp-edged flakes knocked from the cobbles, which collectively would have enabled the hominid toolmakers to pound, cut, scrape, and saw food items and other raw materials
2. The fossilized bones of diverse animals ranging from small rodents to elephants with a predominance of medium to large

bovids (mainly of the antelope family), which, if shown to be a by-product of hominid activity, would indicate a marked increase in meat consumption as compared to what is known about the diets of australopithecines and other higher primates

Excavated sites, ranging in size from several square meters to more than 300 square meters, have yielded stone-artifact samples ranging from several dozen to several thousand pieces and bone samples ranging from zero to more than 40,000 pieces representing at least several dozen large animals. The largest and most thoroughly studied assemblages of artifacts and bones come from deposits slightly less than 2 million years old at two field areas, Koobi Fora in the Turkana Basin of Kenya and Olduvai Gorge in Tanzania. While not the very oldest archaeological sites, they are used in the following discussion to reveal examples of the major interpretive challenge posed by the early archaeological evidence.

Which hominid species, for example, made and used stone tools and for what purposes? How did the fossil bones of diverse and often quite large animals found buried with the stone tools relate to hominid foraging and diet? What did the large sites with dense accumulations of stone and bone represent in the lives of the hominids? And finally, what is the behavioral meaning of the low-density scatters of archaeological remains across paleo-landscapes away from large sites? All of these issues pose major ongoing questions for archaeologists to address. The following discussion summarizes some of the key evidence and the most likely alternative interpretations of it.

First, it is probably more than mere coincidence that the oldest hominid fossils assigned to the genus *Homo* and the oldest stone artifacts both appear approximately 2.4 million years ago. Although it is plausible that some of the australopithecines made or used tools of stone or other materials, as is documented among modern chimpanzees, it is very likely that the larger brained early *Homo,* the hominid lineage leading to modern humanity, was the principal maker of flaked-stone tools in the early archaeological record. As discussed below, a firmly documented use of sharp-edged stone flakes was the butch-

ery of animal carcasses, which would have provided early *Homo* with the very high-quality dietary component of animal tissues that their meta-
bolically expensive brains required.

In the 1970s, Glynn Isaac developed the influential home-base model, which synthesized
known archaeological evidence from Koobi Fora
and Olduvai Gorge with relevant modern analogs
to account for the behavior of early toolmaking
hominids. Because the stone-artifact and bone
accumulations at early archaeological sites resembled the material remains at the campsites of
modern human hunter-foragers, Isaac reasoned
that the behaviors characteristic of modern
hunter-foragers existed at least 2 million years
ago in the hominids who formed the early archaeological sites. Thus, early *Homo* practiced a
cooperative, gender-based division of labor in
which daily subsistence involved females' foraging for plant foods, males' hunting and scavenging for animals, and the transport of acquired
foods to a prearranged home-base locality for
sharing and other activities.

The home-base model was easy to criticize
because of several inherent assumptions. First,
it is reasonable to assume that early *Homo* consumed significant amounts of plant foods, even
in the absence of preserved plant-food remains
at early sites, but it is problematic to assume the
humanlike transport of plant foods for delayed
consumption and sharing by early *Homo,* rather
than the more apelike individual consumption of
plants at points of acquisition. Second, the initial assumption was that the bone assemblages
were transported by-products of hominid meat
eating simply because they were buried in physical
proximity to stone artifacts. Third, the interpretation of humanlike sharing of food is problematic because of the questionable assumptions
regarding the foraging for plant and animal foods.
Some archaeologists rejected any involvement by
hominids in processing and consuming large animals, while others creatively reinterpreted the
sites as geological mixtures of unrelated stones
and bones or as sites of large carnivore kills at
which hominids obtained scraps of animal tissue
abandoned by the carnivores. Either way, such criti-
cisms cast doubt on the presence of much human-
ness in the behavior and diet of early *Homo.*

In the late 1970s, taphonomic analyses (studies of the processes that affect plant and animal
remains as they fossilize) of the bone assemblages from key early sites at Koobi Fora and
Olduvai Gorge, dating to approximately 1.6 to
1.9 million years ago, provided fresh evidence
for evaluating the home-base model and alternatives to it. While aspects of independent analyses
and interpretations are still debated, fundamental
interpretations of three informative classes of
evidence—taxonomic representation, skeletal-
element proportions, and bone modifications—
are commonly accepted. The bone assemblages
are diverse, with a predominance of medium to
large grazing and browsing animals, indicating
their derivation from both closed and especially
more open habitats. Because some of the best-
preserved sites, such as the *Zinjanthropus* locality FLK at Olduvai Gorge and locality FxJj 50 at
Koobi Fora, are found in dynamic, low-energy
geological contexts near lake and stream margins,
respectively, it is unlikely that geological processes concentrated the bones or that prolonged
periods of site formation produced the large bone
assemblages through attritional, natural mortality
on the sites. Rather, it is probable that hominids
or carnivores repeatedly transported carcasses or
portions thereof to particular sites within restricted, short time periods of several months to
several decades.

The proportions of different skeletal elements
at most of the early home-base sites with large
bone assemblages reveal that limb elements
and mandibles are disproportionately abundant
relative to whole skeletons, while cranial and
other axial (head and trunk) elements are under-
represented. This pattern provides another indication that the carcasses were transported to the
sites. Although various taphonomic factors
may have reduced the proportions of some
less-durable axial elements, such as vertebrae,
the abundance of nutritious limb elements
documents both their availability and repeated
transport to the sites.

Bone modifications, including stone-tool
butchery marks and both rodent and carnivore
gnaw marks, provide the most direct and reveal-
ing evidence of how the bones were transported
to the sites and the sequence in which they were

modified during site formation. Stone-tool butchery marks, including cut marks from skinning, dismembering, and defleshing carcasses and hammer-stone percussion notches and flakes from breaking limb bones and mandibles for marrow fat, are common at sites with excellent bone preservation. At the FLK *Zinjanthropus* site, for example, more than 200 bone specimens out of approximately 3,500 skeletally identifiable bone specimens retain cut marks. At FxJj 50, where bone preservation is not as good and some bone surfaces are consequently obscured, approximately 14 of 762 identifiable bones retain cut marks. Those cut-mark ratios and patterns are comparable to those documented at younger archaeological sites and in ethnoarchaeological and experimental butchery analogs where access to and use of meat are not in doubt. Along with hammer-stone percussion notches, the cut marks and skeletal proportions thus document thorough, systematic use of large carcasses by early *Homo*.

Small-rodent gnaw marks occur on approximately 100 identifiable bones from the FLK *Zinjanthropus* site, including some of the same bones with hominid-induced butchery marks, and in all probability, they were inflicted after hominids transported, used, and abandoned the bones at the site. Similarly, carnivore gnaw marks occur on several hundred identifiable bones from the FLK *Zinjanthropus* site, leading some to suggest, based on studies of modern spotted hyenas, that bones were defleshed and gnawed by carnivores before hominids had access to them. The documented abundance of defleshing cut marks on many of the same bones, however, contradicts this view. In addition, many of the gnaw marks occur on the internal, medullary surfaces of marrow cavities of bones broken by hammer stones—surfaces that would only have been accessible for gnawing after hominids used and abandoned the bones. Finally, most of the gnaw marks are smaller than those inflicted by hyenas and, as with the rodent gnawing, more likely relate to the marginal scavenging activity of small carnivores after hominids used and discarded the bones. It is even plausible that some of the gnaw marks were inflicted by the hominids themselves.

Because modern carnivores are known to consume carcasses in a regular sequence (beginning with the abdominal organs, followed by the upper hind limbs and upper forelimbs, and ending with the cranium), it is possible to use the combined evidence of skeletal proportions and cut marks to clarify how hominids acquired and used carcasses. The very skeletal elements that large carnivores deflesh and consume first at kill sites, specifically the upper hind limb and upper forelimb bones, are abundant at the FLK *Zinjanthropus* site and other areas and retain many defleshing cut marks. This indicates that hominids regularly acquired intact or nearly intact carcasses, selectively transported the most nutritious portions to so-called home-base sites, and used them thoroughly for meat and fat. Based on comparisons to modern primates, including human foragers and chimpanzees, and modern African carnivores, it is probable that carcass acquisition by early *Homo* similarly involved a broad spectrum of hunting and scavenging behavior.

Whatever future research reveals about these topics and related ones, such as the control of fire for cooking, it is clear that by almost 2 million years ago, a marked shift in diet to a significantly increased proportion of large-animal meat and in subsistence behavior to the transport of meat for delayed consumption and probably sharing both occurred in human evolution and that some fundamental elements of diets and subsistence behaviors of modern human foragers were thus present in early *Homo*.

BIBLIOGRAPHY

Bunn, H. T., and J. A. Ezzo. 1993. Hunting and scavenging by Plio-Pleistocene hominids: Nutritional constraints, archaeological patterns, and behavioral implications. *Journal of Archaeological Science* 20: 365–398.

Bunn, H. T., and E. M. Kroll. 1986. Systematic butchery by Plio-Pleistocene hominids at Olduvai Gorge, Tanzania. *Current Anthropology* 27: 431–452.

Foley, R. A. 1989. The evolution of hominid social behavior. In *Comparative socioecology: The behavioural ecology of humans and other mammals,* eds. V. Standen and R. A. Foley, 473–494. Oxford: Blackwell Scientific Publications.

Isaac, G. Ll. 1978. The food-sharing behavior of proto-human hominids. *Scientific American* 238: 90–108.

———. 1996. *Koobi Fora research project, vol. 5: Archaeology.* Oxford: Clarendon Press.

Leakey, M. D. 1971. *Olduvai Gorge, vol. 3: Excavations in beds I and II, 1960-63.* Cambridge: Cambridge University Press.

Lieberman, D. E., B. A. Wood, and D. R. Pilbeam. 1996. Homoplasy and early *Homo:* An analysis of the evolutionary relationships of *H. habilis sensu strictu* and *H. rudolfensis. Journal of Human Evolution* 30: 97–120.

Oliver, J. S., N. E. Sikes, and K. M. Stewart. 1994. *Early hominid behavioural ecology.* London: Academic Press.

Henry T. Bunn

EARLY HOMINID FORAGING STRATEGIES

The strategies used by early hominids to acquire food underwent marked evolutionary change along with the types of plant and animal foods they sought and the amount of equipment and planning the food quest required. Modern hunter-foragers acquire wild edible plants and animals in a corporate manner—that is, males and females practice an economic division of labor to pursue animal prey and plants separately for later pooling and shared consumption at the home base. Their foraging relies on equipment such as projectile weapons, butchery tools, and carrying bags. While plant foods compose the major portion of most foraging peoples' diet, calorically dense foods such as honey and carcasses of large mammals, either hunted or scavenged, are highly prized. The earliest hominids, on the other hand, were probably closer to other higher primates in their foraging strategies. Typically, foraging in nonhuman primates is an individualistic pursuit, involving little or no sharing of foods. Food is usually eaten when and where it is found and, with rare exceptions, is acquired and consumed without the benefit of equipment. Nonhuman primates consume a variety of animal foods, from insects and fledgling birds to hare, monkeys, and infant antelope. The earliest hominids, like all nonhuman primates, were probably unable to ac-

quire and process carcasses of animals larger than 10 kilograms.

Paleoanthropologists are uncertain when and in how many stages these changes occurred. Much research into the issue, however, has focused around the earliest archaeological record of the Late Pliocene and Early Pleistocene. At this time, we find flaked-stone artifacts interspersed with fragmented bones of a wide size range of mammal species at sites in Olduvai Gorge, along Lake Turkana, and elsewhere. The artifacts and bones suggest that hominids, for the first time, were butchering and eating flesh and marrow from animals significantly larger than the prey of nonhuman primates. The interpretation is bolstered by experiments that show the effectiveness of even simple, unmodified flakes to butcher animals as large as elephants and by damage patterns to the fossil bones indicative of slicing meat from bones and smashing long bones to extract fat-rich marrow. These innovations in diet and food processing coincide roughly with the appearance of the genus *Homo,* the first hominid to show significant encephalization (brain development), and are thought by some researchers to signal the origin of the novel human-type foraging strategy.

Glynn Isaac was the strongest advocate of this view. In 1978, he postulated that early hominid lifestyles centered on the sharing of gathered plant foods and hunted or scavenged animal foods. Hominids would collect these foods in surplus quantities and transport them for sharing to a place common to the whole group, the so-called home base. The association between stone artifacts and animal bones at the earliest archaeological sites signaled the existence of home bases. Among the behaviors conducted at the ancient home bases, sharing was, to Isaac, the central feature of hominid foraging, and sharing behavior, coupled with the later evolution of language and complex cultural systems, led to the origin of modern behavior.

Isaac's food-sharing model received its major challenge from Lewis Binford, who emphasized apparent patterns of intense damage to bones inflicted by large carnivores at the early archaeological sites. Binford suggested that hominids were inferior competitors to carnivores for carcass foods and that hominids acquired far too little meat to provide a surplus needed to sustain food sharing. According to Binford, hominids briefly visited the early archaeological sites where bones had been left by carnivores to remove inconsequential scraps of food before continuing on to the next feeding locale. This "routed" pattern of foraging is akin to what Isaac referred to as the "individualistic, feed-as-you-go" strategy of nonhuman primates.

Partly in response to Binford's critique, Isaac softened his stand on the food-sharing model. Feeling that he had made 2-million-year-old hominids appear too human, he replaced the term *home base* with the more neutral zoological term, *central place*. He also admitted that an economic division of labor was not evident and that the need to seek refuge from large carnivores was possibly a more important motivation for the transport of foods than was sharing. In this revised central-place foraging model, Isaac pointed out that food sharing may still have been an unintended consequence of food transport and a precursor to systematic food reciprocity of the type practiced universally today.

Rick Potts proposed yet another scenario for activities at the early archaeological sites. Assuming that hominid possession of carcass parts attracted dangerous predators, Potts saw the excavated occurrences as carcass-processing sites where hominids had stockpiled stone for the manufacture of butchery tools in anticipation of finding a nearby carcass. Although hominids transported carcasses to these "stone caches," the presence at the sites of some unbroken bones retaining food and evidence of carnivore damage to many other bones suggested to Potts that competing large carnivores limited the time hominids spent at the sites to brief feeding bouts. Sharing could not be conducted at such dangerous locales, and other "living" activities were conducted elsewhere.

A key to evaluating these models of carcass consumption by hominids is the ability to infer the amount of food hominids acquired from the carcasses of larger mammals. As a starting point, paleoanthropologists today generally assume that nonhuman primates represent the primitive condition—that is, animal foods formed a minor component of the diet of our earliest direct an-

cestors, with the amount gradually increasing to modern levels throughout human evolution. Most nonhuman primates are omnivorous to some degree, but they supplement a largely vegetarian diet with insects, larvae, and a variety of small vertebrate prey. Consumption of mammal carcasses is common only among chimpanzees and baboons, and here, the carcasses are always from animals smaller than themselves. Baboons focus on hare and newborn gazelles, while chimpanzees are known to hunt a variety of prey, from young bushpigs to colobus monkeys and young baboons. Even for the most carnivorous individuals, however, the contribution of these prey to the overall diet is rarely estimated to exceed 5 percent of net weight or of feeding time. Modern hunting and gathering peoples are substantially more carnivorous. Groups inhabiting tropical areas typically have a diet of about 20 percent animals foods. Hunting and gathering peoples living in high arctic and sub-arctic latitudes, where plant foods are scarce, are almost completely dependent on large marine and terrestrial animal prey for most of the year. The overall greater degree of carnivorousness in humans is, in part, attributable to our use of weapons and other technology to capture and kill animals and the availability of tools to butcher animals too large to be processed manually or orally.

Not all paleoanthropologists have assumed a gradual increase in carnivorous propensities in the evolving hominid lineage. Raymond Dart, discoverer in 1924 of *Australopithecus africanus* from the South African site of Taung, characterized this ancient, pre-*Homo* hominid as a regular carnivore who consumed large quantities of meat and other tissues from a variety of animals substantially bigger than nonhuman primate prey. Dart's evidence lay in the thousands of animal bones accompanying *A. africanus* at another South African cave named Makapansgat that he and coworkers later found. Although they uncovered no stone artifacts at the site, Dart found some parts of antelope skeletons more frequently than one would expect if whole carcasses had been introduced into the cave. Further, many of these common bones bore regular fracture patterns and other damage, suggesting to Dart purposeful modification and use as tools for stabbing, slicing, pounding, scooping, prying, and chopping. Dart referred to this tool kit as the osteodonto-keratic (or bone, tooth, and horn) "culture" and ascribed it to *A. africanus*. The source of the bones was large animals hunted and aggressively dispatched and consumed by australopithecines. In 1953, Dart characterized *Australopithecus* as "carnivorous creatures that seized living quarries by violence, battered them to death, tore apart their broken bodies, dismembered them limb from limb, slaking their ravenous thirst with the hot blood of victims and greedily devouring livid writhing flesh."

In the late 1960s, taphonomic studies (studies relating to the processes that affect animal and plant remains as they fossilize) by C. K. Brain would show that the bones at Makapansgat were more likely accumulated and modified by large, bone-crunching carnivores such as hyenas than by *A. africanus*. While many paleoanthropologists were already skeptical of Dart's behavioral claims, they still viewed *A. africanus* as highly omnivorous, especially in comparison to another hominid species known from the South African Plio-Pleistocene caves, *A. robustus*. The latter australopithecine possesses a number of cranial and dental features, such as large molars and premolars and a sagittal crest (a ridge of bone developed along the top of the skull to attach chewing muscles), which, in the 1950s, paleontologist John Robinson attributed to reliance on a coarse, vegetarian diet. *A. africanus* lacks these specialized mastication features and possesses instead a more generalized dentition and chewing apparatus capable of dealing with a variety of plant and animal foods.

Robinson's dietary-niche distinction between species of South African *Australopithecus* is known as the *dietary hypothesis*. This would come to typify paleoanthropologists' views of the major adaptive difference between two other hominids, *Homo habilis* and *Australopithecus boisei,* discovered in the late 1950s and early 1960s at the East African locality of Olduvai Gorge. *A. boisei* displays a more-developed version of the dental and facial adaptations of *A. robustus* and hence was viewed as even more of a dietary specialist of coarse plant foods. In comparison, *Homo habilis* not only has a more-

generalized dentition than *A. africanus* but also may have manufactured the stone tools and broken the animal bones found at Olduvai Gorge in association with both hominids.

These dietary distinctions now appear to be directly testable through chemical analyses of the trace elements and stable-carbon isotopes in hominid bones and teeth. Strontium is a trace element whose concentration is reduced as one proceeds up the food chain. Recent analyses of the strontium content of *A. robustus* bones conducted by Andrew Sillen indicate that this previously assumed vegetarian was at least as omnivorous as the fossil baboon species with which it is associated at the South African site of Swartkrans. Supporting evidence has more recently been provided by Julia Lee-Thorpe and colleagues, who analyzed the the ratios of stable-carbon isotopes in *A. robustus* tooth enamel. Carbon-13 (^{13}C) is found in different proportions in tropical grasses and trees, and the values found for *A. robustus* tooth enamel are more similar to those in tropical grasses. Since there is no dental evidence that this hominid consumed grasses or their seeds directly, Lee-Thorpe infers that *A. robustus* was consuming grass eaters. Currently, neither chemical technique can show what kinds of animal foods were consumed, whether insect or small or large vertebrate, but the results do show that *A. robustus* was an omnivore like most primates.

Since reconstructing hominid foraging strategies depends in large part on the specific types of animal foods consumed, we must return to the archaeological evidence, specifically the animal bones associated with stone artifacts at the early sites. Understanding how the carcasses of large animals were obtained is particularly important to defining further the unique aspects of the foraging strategies of hominids.

Foods from larger mammals can be acquired in two basic ways. Live prey, either healthy or incapacitated, can be hunted and killed by the consumer. Scavenging occurs when a consumer encounters an animal already dead, whether by old age, starvation, or disease or by a predator of a different species. Scavengers can usurp carcasses from predators (confrontational scavenging) or exploit the often substantial foods remaining on abandoned kills (passive scavenging).

While early hominids are widely accepted to have hunted small vertebrate prey similar in size to prey taken by chimpanzees and baboons, paleoanthropologists debate the dominant mode of carcass acquisition used by the hominids who created the early archaeological sites. Some researchers point out that hominids must have hunted and scavenged large animals since most mammalian carnivores do. This reasoning, however, ignores hominds' unique large-mammal carnivorousness, which is a tool-driven option. Humans have developed a variety of tools and behaviors that facilitate a carnivorous diet, rather than specialized anatomical features (fangs, strong jaws, or claws) or digestive systems found in carnivores. Primatologists often point out that hominids are unlikely to have scavenged because nonhuman primates do so only rarely. This reasoning ignores the uniqueness of early hominid carnivorousness, where the capture, killing, and carcass-processing techniques of nonhuman primates are unlikely to have been effective on the substantially larger and fleeter animals that hominids hunted and processed with stone tools. Finally, studies of modern hunter-foragers have traditionally been heavily biased toward the hunting aspect of subsistence. Even though it was always clear that hunting success of modern humans is dependent on sophisticated weaponry and capture devices not possessed by early hominids who used stone tools, the pervasiveness of hunting throughout all aspects of hunter-forager society and belief systems was seen to reflect deep evolutionary roots for the activity. The association of stone tools with fragmented bones of larger animals at the early sites seemed to provide all the evidence necessary to proclaim a deep ancestry for a hunting way of life.

Widespread views promoting hunting as the glue of modern human society and the dominant subsistence mode of early hominids were merged in the mid-1960s into the influential "man the hunter" paradigm. Hunting was even seen to be the early evolutionary trigger for many unique human traits. Sherwood Washburn argued that the demands of hunting large animals led to a natural selection among early hominids for technically skillful, intelligent, and cooperative individuals with strong planning abilities. Hence, an ancestral hunting way of life could explain the origin and dramatic evolutionary development of hominid technology, brain size, complex social relationships, and even language. Such was the power of "man the hunter" that scavenging was rarely entertained as an alternative strategy of early hominids and was completely neglected in reports of modern hunter-forager behavior for more than 20 years. It was not until the late 1980s that avid scavenging was reported among the Kalahari San and the Hadza of Tanzania, two of the best-studied hunter-forager groups.

When scavenging was entertained as an early hominid foraging tactic during the heyday of "man the hunter," it was usually dismissed as dangerous, unhealthy, nutritionally trivial, rare, and opportunistic. As such, scavenging could not account for the animal bones at early archaeological sites. Nor could it rival hunting's status as a potent evolutionary elixir that favored novel human traits. Only a handful of researchers considered scavenging to be a realistic ecological alternative to hunting, and Louis Leakey was alone in postulating a distinct scavenger phase that preceded large-animal predation in human evolution.

The influence of "man the hunter" began to wane during the early 1980s as archaeologists became more critical of the fossil evidence for hunting. Lewis Binford characterized early stone-tool-using hominids not only as incapable of hunting large animals but also as the most marginal of scavengers. As in his efforts to refute sharing by early hominids, Binford used evidence of carnivore damage to bones at early archaeological sites to infer that hominids scavenged small morsels of marrow and flesh from very thoroughly consumed predator kills. He similarly criticized interpretations of large game hunting by later hominids. He reinterpreted published accounts of Acheulian and Middle Stone Age bone assemblages to overturn the common characterization of *Homo erectus* as a cooperative hunter of very large game and to argue that hunting of large animals and food sharing did not emerge the until the Late Stone Age.

Studies of the scale and characteristics of scavenging opportunities in modern savanna and woodland ecosystems have established a range of possibilities encountered by early hominids.

Robert Blumenschine and colleagues have shown that predictable and safe scavenging opportunities for a diurnal (having a daily cycle), stone-tool user are found in woodlands bordering rivers and lakes. Here, kills abandoned by flesh-eating lions would not provide much meat but, on most carcasses, would offer substantial quantities of fat from bone marrow and brain tissue. Tree-stored kills abandoned by leopards could provide large quantities of flesh for a hominid scavenger in riparian (river or water course) woodlands, as could have the kills of very large animals abandoned by saber-toothed cats. These ecological studies show that many of the scavenging opportunities hominids encountered were nutritionally substantial and that some could even sustain a system of food sharing. These studies also show that scavenging could be a predictable, low-risk, and high-yield activity for hominids, an activity that required sophisticated cognitive skills to locate abandoned kills ahead of other scavengers, while avoiding becoming meals themselves.

The latest analyses of bone assemblages at the early archaeological sites support inferences that hominids scavenged flesh, marrow, and brain tissue from the kills of large carnivores. While there is still debate over whether hominids relied on abandoned kills or usurped carcasses, it seems clear that large-mammal hunting has relatively recent origins. Richard Klein, while positing hunting by Middle Stone Age hominids, still sees them as less effective predators than Late Stone Age hunters. It may not have been until the last 40,000 to 50,000 years that weaponry, planning abilities, and social organization became sufficiently advanced to spawn the types of foraging strategies we see among modern humans.

BIBLIOGRAPHY
Binford, L. R. 1981. *Bones: Ancient men and modern myths.* New York: Academic Press.
Blumenschine, R. J. 1995. Percussion marks, tooth marks, and experimental determinations of the timing of hominid and carnivore access to long bones at FLK *Zinjanthropus,* Olduvai Gorge, Tanzania. *Journal of Human Evolution* 29: 21–51.
Blumenschine, R. J., and J. A. Cavallo. 1992. Scavenging and human evolution. *Scientific American:* 247: 90–96.
Brain, C. K. 1981. *The hunters or the hunted: An introduction to African cave taphonomy.* Chicago: University of Chicago Press.
Dart, R. A. 1953. The predatory transition from ape to man. *International Anthropological and Linguistic Review* 1: 201–219.
Isaac, B., ed. 1989. *The archaeology of human origins: Papers by Glynn Isaac.* Cambridge: Cambridge University Press.
Lee, R. B., and I. DeVore, eds. 1968. *Man the hunter.* Chicago: Aldine Publishing Company.
Lee-Thorpe, J. A., N. J. van der Merwe, and C. K. Brain. 1994. Diet of *Australopithecus robustus* from stable carbon isotopic analysis. *Journal of Human Evolution* 27: 361–372.
Potts, R. 1988. *Early hominid activities at Olduvai Gorge.* New York: Aldine de Gruyter.
Sillen, A. 1992. Strontium-calcium ratios (Sr/Ca) of *Australopithecus robustus* and associated fauna from Swartkrans. *Journal of Human Evolution* 23: 495–516.

Robert J. Blumenschine

EARLIEST AFRICAN CULTURES

At one time, prehistorians measured human development by an established ability to use and reproduce tools or the ability to make and control fire. By these measures, significant numbers of the hominids alive in eastern Africa more than 1.5 million years ago qualified as full-fledged humans. Fire was certainly made, controlled, and used in southern Ethiopia, on the Gadeb Plain and at the Karari site, and in Kenya at Chesowanja by that distant time. At the same time, archaeological sites in the Hadar Basin, in northern Ethiopia, dating to nearly 2.6 million years ago, have produced a number of flaked cobbles, which surely represent some kind of recurrent industrial activity.

Surveys in the Omo Valley of southern Ethiopia have also discovered assemblages of simple flakes struck from small quartz nodules. In Kenya, researchers have found among the consolidated volcanic debris known as *KBS tuff* (dating to 1.8 million years ago) nearly 500 small stone artifacts, as well as a collection of animal bones drawn from a variety of nearby environments, suggesting that the toolmakers had consistently ventured out to bring meat to their home base.

These discoveries of stone artifacts, along with other worked stone collected in Kenya, in the Koobi Fora vicinity, resemble the flaked-stone artifacts collected from the lower portions of the Olduvai Gorge site of southern Tanzania. Along with the apparent butchery sites—where early humans cut up animals they had hunted and killed—in the vicinity of the Koobi Fora locality and in Bed I of Olduvai Gorge, we have substantial evidence of recurrent human cultural activities, from which we can posit a pattern of hunting and foraging in eastern Africa more than 1.5 million years ago.

The Nature of the Earliest Cultures

This genre of physical evidence conforms to an archaeologist's conception of culture: the refuse remnant from replicative industrial or subsistence activities. These are a powerful evidence of an established set of behaviors that would define humanity for many millennia and aid the organization of a very successful way of life throughout the period of the Pleistocene and beyond into recent times—a lifeway that would successfully adapt humanity to the colonization of the globe. Man, a toolmaking, transhumant (seasonally moving) forager, scheduling an annual round of activities to exploit seasonally available resources, evolved on the African continent and crafted a complex instrument—culture—that would eventually permit him to dominate new environments, even as he moved into them.

An anthropologist, on the other hand, sees culture as an interrelated set of learned behaviors, passed down from generation to generation and defining a worldview beyond subsistence and toolmaking. (Elsewhere, we explore the habits and worldview of living people in Africa, who persist in a mode of life we associate with foragers, or hunter-gatherers.) Sometime nearly 2 million years ago, small groups of individuals first explored the possibilities of a lifeway dependent upon shared information—information relating to the cycles of nature, opportunities to exploit these cycles, and the means of enhancing this exploitation through improved technologies.

Simply put, these early humans began to craft culture. The culture they created is one that we can recognize today, not because present-day foragers are "primitive" relics of the prehistoric past, but because foraging in the proper environment can be an energy-efficient means of production, permitting a small number of people a quite adequate level of subsistence at very low cost.

As technical and social means of providing for larger populations developed during the Pleistocene, the human community grew, spreading first out of its homeland in eastern Africa and creating subsistence patterns, which generated greater amounts of energy and required larger population cohorts to maintain them. The earliest cultures in Africa, converting very small amounts of energy from their environment, supported a number of small bandlike formations with a substantial ability to reap the natural harvests—plant as well as animal—of the region.

Before we explore individual archaeological sites or examples of early lifeways, we can reconstruct the mode of life of these early human communities. The critical idea, here, is the persistence of organized communities, groups of allied people congregating toward some mutually beneficial goal. What the mechanism of congregation or belief system supporting their coalescence as a mutually supporting group might have been is beyond our present ability to suggest. What we can suggest, though, were groups of people who had developed the ability to anticipate the seasonally changing nature of their environment. Using this knowledge, they moved from place to place seeking out water sources for their own needs and because of the certainty that game animals and water fowl, as well as edible plants and smaller game and birds in nearby fields, would be found. The earliest cultures organized vital bits of environmental information. Any group subtle enough to assemble this body of data, use it, share it with colleagues, and pass it on to succeeding generations prospered.

Sometime in the past, human evolution became a tale of the attractiveness of different cultural capabilities, the honing of an extensive extrasomatic repertoire (behaviors such as toolmaking and transfers of information or communal networks, which expand the capabilites and potential of the human organism), crafted from increasingly refined industrial abilities, knowledge, and communication and social skills.

Somehow these earliest cultures—the Olduwan, often represented by so-called pebble tools, and the Acheulian, usually characterized by the occurrence of bifacial hand axes and cleavers—must have developed social affinities greater than those implicit in a family band, the nuclear family and its immediate hangers-on. In present-day band societies, the optimum number seems to about two dozen people of differing sexes and ages linked into social networks with each other and neighboring band members, who regularly cross their path. The basis of most social networks derives from the recurrent need to mobilize manpower cohorts greater than those supplied solely by the participants in a single family band. The size of each band is constrained by the resources available in the leanest part of the year: band size cannot usually exceed the number supportable during the dry months or other periods when subsistence resources are inadequate. During more florescent times—as plants ripen following the rains, or as abundant game move into a band's foraging compass—other, larger labor cohorts may be required, and a prime role of society is to supply this requirement adequately in the form of relatives, in-laws, friends, or associates. Though we have no way of knowing how these earliest societies organized themselves, we can suggest that they must have been successful in allying bands, that their social behaviors were ones we would recognize as human, since we have suggestions of groups of humans living together, engaged in hunting activities and frequently reoccupying the same campsites, in the company of other bands, on an annual basis. The KBS faunal data even suggest that, once established, encampments, though transient in principle, served as bases from which parties were dispatched to exploit the potential of other nearby environments.

Some Archaeological Method and Theory

It is evident that the first tools used by humans in the distant past may have been very crude in manufacture or purely the product of casual, if repeated use. Early in this century, E. J. Wayland, of the Uganda Geological Department, argued that the first tools were simple, unifacially flaked cobbles. Though he and others developed an elaborate seriation of such tools, this Kafuan culture was proven untenable. After World War II, Raymond Dart, of the University of Witwatersrand in South Africa, proposed the attractive idea that the human industry was made of bits of worked bone, tooth, and horn. His concept of an osteodontokeratic culture was, however, not supportable by archaeology. The concept of an Olduwan culture, posited by L. S. B. Leakey, as a logical, bifacially flaked extension of Wayland's unifacial tools has stood the test of time and subsequent research, although many published attributions to this culture have not.

Simply put, a crude technology dependent upon a simple token of use, such as use-wear on a broken bone or one or two flaking blows, can easily be reproduced by nature—for example, by the action of gravity dislodging a stone or a cobble rolled in a river or in the jaws of animal scavengers. In the early days of exploration, archaeologists in Africa were often dependent upon finds discovered on the terraced gravels of rivers or lakes. These rolled specimens, rearranged or transported by river action, often had no sure provenance or accurate associations. Only in the 1960s, following the pioneering work of J. Desmond Clark at the Kalambo Falls Prehistoric Site, did archaeology's full attention pass from the investigation of disturbed river gravels to the location of "living floors," the actual ancient living surfaces left by the extended or repeated use of a surface as a campsite, factory, or butchery. At the same time, it became apparent that what we casually refer to as *sites* are, in fact, very complex localities embracing a great many individual encampments. A single surface may have a number of contemporaneous or near-contemporaneous camps, and each of these may have been used repeatedly, creating a complex pattern of horizontal, as well as vertical, stratig-raphy. The layout of these camps became a sub-ject of investigation, as did the types of tools left in them, when folk moved on to their next camp. At the same time, the research of Glynn Issac pointed out the importance, to each encamped com-munity, of the resources of the immediate sur-roundings and of the terrain between the settlement localities, the terrain traversed during the progress of the transhumant annual round.

As Maxine R. Kleindeinst demonstrated in the 1950s, the camps associated with the Acheulian occupation of eastern Africa display significant industrial differences. The differences in the types and kinds of artifacts present at each encamp-ment arose not from different cultural populations but from a single population engaged in trans-humant exploitation of a variety of natural re-sources, manufacturing and using a different tool kit in each situation. Stone may have been transported some distance, or local material used, depending on the kind of tool required. The fin-ished tools were then left behind for future use. They had no function in another circumstance. This argument was complemented by the field research of Isaac, who also observed that the pro-portions of smaller edged tools relative to the numbers of hand axes available was discrete—that is, either one or the other dominated the assemblage, but at no site were they close to equal in numbers. It was obvious that the heavy tools were intended for one kind of activity and the light tools for another. In this way, by measuring the kinds of tools manufactured and positing their function, the different economic and industrial operations of an early transhumant community could be observed.

The localities most attractive to early foragers were along watercourses. The reasons for this are obvious: both humans and their prey were drawn to lakes and rivers. By the same token, passage from eastern Africa to the interior and points farther south was, then as now, constrained by the Great Lakes of the Rift Valley. To pass into Zambia from Tanzania, one has to travel south of Lake Tanganyika or proceed farther south to pass around the southern end of Lake Malawi. Similarly, the various Pleistocene lakes of east-ern Africa presented barriers to east-west passage

and produced, at their northern and southern ends, choke points that concentrated migrating herds. This kind of environmental detail informs archaeologists of the possibilities of an ancient encampment, as it informed early foragers of the economic potential of these places. For this rea-son, many of the site areas discussed here possess a set of similar characteristics, in that they are near water or stone sources in places likely to concentrate game.

The First Toolmakers

The very earliest stone tools reported by Glynn Isaac and Y. Coppens from southern Ethiopia are crude in the extreme. They have the virtue of recovery from acknowledged occupation sites—from living floors within a repeatedly oc-cupied locality. Otherwise, the earliest organized toolmaking industry is that first located at Olduvai Gorge in Tanzania and therefore labeled *Olduwan.*

Olduvai Gorge

The Olduvai locality falls with the broad char-acterization noted above. Throughout most of its history, it was a *playa,* draining a broad area southwest of the Ngorongoro volcanic crater. The history of the mountain affected the history of the lake, causing occasional outlets and, now and then, interfering with its flow. As a result, the shoreline varied from time to time, exposing old surfaces and drowning others with silts or volca-nic debris. This geological complex, explored since before World War I, presents a wide array of hominid fossils as well as the detritus of early transhumant foragers and the game they stalked.

The most famous of the living surfaces un-covered there were Floor FLK and Floor DK in Bed I, the lowest section of the geological stratigraphy. Each represents an almost complete campsite, with oblong central areas, nearly 3 meters across and consisting of concentrated stone and bone fragments. To the lakeward side—the apparent windward side—a break in the array of litter seems to suggest the erection of some kind of thorn fence or windbreak of branches. Two similar circular areas containing artifacts and animal bones were found at a por-tion of the site labeled FLK North I. The early visitors to this area can be seen to have established substantial encampments.

What attracted them to this lakeside was game. There is still an open debate as to whether humans were scavengers, retrieving animal parts from predators, before they became hunters in their own right. The first argument was put forward by Lewis Binford following his intensive examination of faunal remains recovered in southern Africa. His investigation seemed to indicate that a sequence of bite marks produced by animal predators and tool marks made by sharp-edged stone tools could be determined. Since his analyses suggested that the tool marks overlay the animal-produced ones, it was likely that the animal had been killed by an nonhuman predator and that a portion of the kill had been expropriated by human scavengers. Others, examining other faunal collections, have arrived at different results. Whatever the case elsewhere, the predators at Olduvai were undoubtedly human. Here and there along the muddy track to open water, archaeologists have found traces of early hunting activity. Apparently, the favored method was to wait until an animal began to wade into the water and got its hoofs caught in the sticky mud. Then the hunters, safe from retaliation, could descend on it to kill it, apparently by blows between the eyes at close quarters. It is posited that some of the spherical stones found in the Olduvai deposit would have been appropriate weapons for such a task. Then the animal was butchered with lighter, sharply edged flake tools. Portions of the skeleton and the occasional artifact were left behind to be replaced by material close at hand at the next campsite. Confirmation of this set of behaviors was found in East Turkana where a skeleton of a butchered hippopotamus along with three heavy core implements and a number of smaller-edged flake cutting tools were found.

It should be further noted the anatomist Alan Walker, after microscopic analyses of the teeth of robust australopithecines, concluded that they displayed a wear pattern consonant with a fruit and vegetable diet. (Meat eaters show a characteristic wear pattern caused by small splinters of bone.) He argued further that, since faunal assemblages were usual in sites containing the tools needed to prepare meat, that the makers of tools were meat eaters who butchered carcasses. It follows that diet choice and the impulse to manufacture cutting tools may be viewed as self-reinforcing activities, which profoundly influenced early cultural development.

Other Olduwan Sites

Besides Olduvai Gorge, we should take note of other sites that seem to represent a technology similar to the simple bifacial flaking characteristic of the Olduwan culture. The most important of these is Sidi Abderrahmen, a cave worn into a fossil sand dune by sea action on the Atlantic Coast near Casablanca. This locality, like later ones on the Mediterranean Coast of Europe, was probably part of a transhumant pattern by which people exploited coastal resources for a portion of the year. The cave remained attractive to foragers for a long time, for the pebble-tool horizons were superimposed by later occupations of hand-ax-using people.

Farther south in Angola, the Baia Farta site has a similar stratigraphy in which unrolled Acheulian hand axes were found above some rolled pebble tools. Even farther south in South Africa, the caves of Kromdraai and Swartkrans have produced pebble-tool-like implements, described by Mary Leakey as being in the Olduwan tradition. These few sites are our surest contact with mankind's toolmakers.

Acheulian Hunter-Foragers

By the Middle Pleistocene, bands of an advanced form of hominid, *Homo erectus,* using a more economical stoneworking technology, dominated the African landscape. Archaeologists describe this period with reference to the transformation of simply flaked pebble choppers of the Olduwan kind to hand axes and cleavers of the Acheulian type. Mary Leakey, who produced a stratigraphy-linked seriation of Olduwan at the site, posited another 11-stage chronological seriation of the hand-axe assemblages found at Olduvai Gorge. Though obviously not a developmental sequence, it does suggest the changes in style of these implements through time and raises questions about their varying functions. We assume that they were multifunctional, but we are hard put to suggest an enhanced purpose to tools with a sinuous edge as opposed to ones with high dorsal ridges, carefully sharpened around the full extent of their margin. We do know that a higher degree of craftsmanship was executed as hand axes developed. A typical Olduwan tool was crafted by a few percussive blows to its sides producing a pointed, sharp-edged outline. As technique improved, blows were struck alternately on one side and then the other to make a bifacially sharpened edge. Something approaching this transition may be posited for the early Acheulian materials recovered in the Peninj area, west of Lake Natron in Tanzania, where crudely made hand axes and cleavers have been classified as Lower Acheulian.

With even more care, toolmakers used soft hammers to make light blows on the flat surfaces in order to produce finely wrought Acheulian tools, on which little evidence of the weathered pebble surface was visible. At the same time, the use of prepared cores permitted stone knappers to produce a number of similar tools from a minimum of raw material. In fact, we may characterize the subsequent development of stone-based technologies as a search to produce a large amount of edge—the working part of a tool—from a minimum of raw stone.

Changes in material culture permit us to make convenient divisions in the archaeological nomenclature. In reality, though, we are viewing continuities, the refinement of habits already exhibited in the transhumant activities of the very earliest cultures. From the Middle Pleistocene on, we observe human populations expanding as they become more comfortable in a variety of environments. We observe people adapting, culturally, to varied economic opportunities.

Besides the seasonal and functional differences found in the archaeological debris of Acheulian encampments, we can distinguish at least three different assemblages, each determined by the economic activities implicit in the area. Some sites are marked by an abundance of large cutting tools and have been labeled *processing* or *butchery sites* where game was slaughtered and cut up. Beyond sharpening debris, there is little evidence of tool manufacture at these sites,

suggesting that the tools were made elsewhere and brought to the camp. The places where implements were made—factory sites—have few large tools but many smaller implements and an abundance of waste material, relics of the knapping process. On the other hand, heavy-duty tools, such as core scrapers, picks, and choppers, seem to mark the camps, which housed the bulk of the band and where women and children were engaged in the processing animal products—hides, fat, bone—as well as in foraging the vicinity for plants and small game.

Humans, having adapted efficiently to the transhumant seasonal round, anticipated natural harvests of game and vegetation. The sites of this time suggest a pattern better understood from research in Europe, where contemporary groups living in the Pyrenees scattered into family bands for part of the year before coalescing into larger units necessary to extensive hunting of herds passing through natural choke points.

Kalambo Falls Prehistoric Site

A classic example of an intensively, seasonally occupied locality is the Kalambo Falls Prehistoric Site, explored by J. Desmond Clark. The locality is dramatic. It rests on the edge of the Rift Valley and looks out toward Lake Tanganyika, some 40 kilometers to the north and 300 meters below. The site itself is cut by the Kalambo River in its passage to the Kalambo Falls, which tumble more than 220 meters to the valley floor. In Pleistocene times, the river was periodically blocked, causing it to swell its banks and flood its basin. At other times, drainage over the precipice was restored, opening extensive mud flats. These flats were occupied by foraging bands who anticipated the arrival of migrating herds. In time, these encampments were covered by the sediments of the swelling river, preserving a vital record of Acheulian and subsequent visitors. In fact, the site has an almost continuous occupation history from Acheulian into modern times.

Not only do we have an accurate record of the layout of early forager camps and their tools, but the waterlogged conditions of the place have preserved evidence of wood shaped with the aid of fire and seeds, fruits, and nuts collected and consumed. The highly acidic nature of the soil, which preserved the vegetable matter, has destroyed all the bone—animal as well as human. Nevertheless, the careful examination of this site has uncovered arcs of stone (apparently remnants of windbreaks or shelters), shallow pits (filled with vegetable matter and appearing to be bedding pits where people slept), and stone tools (made of stone quarried, formed, and imported from elsewhere). It would appear that only very small tools were made on the spot.

Kalambo's Contemporaries

In characterizing Kalambo as a typical Acheulian period hunter-forager camp, we also describe the other encampments of that time. We understand that each of the major sites of this period was a station in a complex settlement pattern, one investing group effort in harvesting a region on a seasonal basis. As the rains passed from north to south and back, the game moved to fresh pastures stalked by human hunters. We have no idea how hunting methods were improved over the ambush technique described for earlier hunters. Nor have we any need to posit intensive hunting to support the small bands then inhabiting the open highlands of eastern Africa. As populations grew, new bands moved into unoccupied space, creating another seasonally constrained round of periodically inhabited camps.

Typical of the camps these early foragers left behind are Olorgesailie in the Kenyan Rift Valley; Isimilia, a lakeside camp in southern Tanzania; Kanjera on the Kavirondo Gulf of Lake Victoria; and the later phases of Chesowanja on the eastern flank of the Kenyan Rift. Each of these has characteristics already described as necessary for an Acheulian camp: proximity to a watercourse and access to game trails.

Olorgesailie

Visitors to Olorgesailie camped along the watercourses leading to the floodplain silts of a fluctuating lakeshore. The extensive locality covering an area of more than 104 square kilometers has been repeatedly investigated since its discovery by J. W. Gregory in the 1930s. The individual campsites are small, adequate for transient bands, who left behind a large number of hand axes and animal bone. In addition to typical Acheulian implements, investigators have found suggestions of stone weirs constructed in the shallow streams for the trapping of fish and groups of three spheriods—round ball-like stones—that may have been part of a bolalike device used to entangle the legs of large prey. As at Kalambo, there are signs of windbreaks.

Glynn Isaac, who reinvestigated the Olorgesailie locality in the 1970s, found at site DE/89 an unusually large number of baboon bones among the faunal remains. This led him to suggest that the baboons were being hunted by men, who may have herded them together onto killing ground, as later hunters are known to have done with herd animals. Other suggestions for this unusual concentration of primate bones are possible: the bones may have been brought together by water action that eroded the deposit and sorted objects of similar weight and density, though the damage noted on the bones seems similar to damage produced by a heavy stone tool. In any event, the suggestion was reminiscent of an idea put forth by Raymond Dart and popularized in the press of the 1950s. C. K. Brain, though, demonstrated that reported collections of baboon remains in South African caves were not caused by the predations of australopithecines on bands of baboons but most likely were accumulations around the lairs of leopards or bone-eating scavengers.

Isimilia and Kilombe

Isimilia, a riverside site in southern Tanzania, is known for its large, heavy hand axes. The implements seem to have been manufactured elsewhere and imported. Once again, Isimilia is not a single large site but a complex of encampments spread over space and time until uncovered and mapped by archaeologists.

Kilombe in Kenya, on the other hand, has been excavated and described as single, extensive living surface littered with heavy implements. It has been suggested that the large numbers of hand axes gathered there were the result of a factory operation.

Whatever the exact function of these sites, the imported tools found at Isimilia and the interpretation of Kilombe as a factory site suggest that certain sites, like some of the major hunting encampments, drew groups from far and wide to join in coordinated activities, including "social" events that enhanced the vital networks by which help was solicited and information passed from group to group. The progressive standardization of the Acheulian tool kit and modes of manufacture was, no doubt, a function of shared experiences, passed from group to group during these periods of coalescence.

Sites in Western, Northern, and Southern Africa

The Acheulian is best represented on the high, dry grasslands of East Africa. It is nevertheless found in West Africa and the Zaire Basin, though it does not seem to have been a strong presence in either place. The North African occupations, which include the latest horizons at Sidi Abderrahmen in Morocco and Ain Hanech in Algeria, are properly an extension of those in Europe, a fact that leaves open the question of the expansion of *H. erectus* and his culture out of Africa and onto the Eurasian continent, where he is found in continuous series from western France to Beijing.

The movement of *H. erectus* and Acheulian culture to the southern half of the continent is attested to in the gravels of the Luangwa, Zambezi, and Vaal Valleys, at the Cave of Hearths in the former Transvaal province of northern South Africa, and at Montagu Cave in the Cape. In Africa, generally, Acheulian culture was associated with the dry savanna of the east, where it originated.

Post-Acheulian Adaptations

Sometime in the last 50,000 to 60,000 years, a clearly defined Acheulian culture passed from the archaeological record. The distinctive tool types became outmoded and therefore passé, but not the hunter-forager lifeway the Acheulian stoneworkers had refined or many of the industrial practices they had pioneered. Two trends define the demise of characteristic Acheulian industries:

1. The economies implicit in the tendency to maximize the amount of edge relative to the quantity of stone used placed a greater emphasis on lighter implements made on flakes struck from specialized cores. This trait, as seen in toolmakers' use of Levallois tortoise cores, permitted the production of specialized cutting or scraping implements.

2. The drift, already established in the migration of humans out of East Africa, toward regional specialization deemphasized much of the uniformity that informed the Acheulian period, rendering much of the tool kit obsolete.

As people adapted to the forests forming in the river valleys of the interior and western Africa, they replaced the Acheulian tool kit, which so suited the needs of the stalkers of big game on the East African plains. Smaller Sangoan hand axes and later tools adapted to exploiting a forested environment soon dominated the tool kits of people in the Zaire Basin. In central and southern Africa, implements based on large core-struck flakes became prevalent.

Everywhere, growing populations explored new or altered environmental opportunities, creating cultural-ecological arrangements different from those establishing the earliest cultures on the African continent. The first significant stage of human cultural development was past.

BIBLIOGRAPHY

Bishop, W. W. 1978. *Geological background to fossil man.* Edinburgh: Scottish Academic Press.

Butzer, K. W., and G. Ll. Isaac. 1975. *After the australopithecines.* The Hague: Mouton.

Clark, J. D. 1974. *Kalambo Falls prehistoric site,* vol. 2. Cambridge: Cambridge University Press.

———. 1982. *The Cambridge history of Africa: vol. 1, From the earliest times to c. 500 B.C.* Cambridge: Cambridge University Press.

Coppens, Y., F. C. Howells, G. Ll. Isaac, and R. E. F. Leakey. 1976. *Earliest man and environments in the East Rudolf Basin.* Chicago: University of Chicago Press.

Leakey, M. D. 1971. *Olduvai Gorge,* vol. 3. Cambridge: Cambridge University Press.

Phillipson, D. W. 1985. *African archaeology.* Cambridge: Cambridge University Press.

Joseph O. Vogel

WESTERN AFRICA: THE PREHISTORIC SEQUENCE

Some important parts of the prehistoric sequence in western African are still mostly unknown, poorly documented, and even beyond systematic investigation. For the sake of clarity, the western African prehistoric sequence presented here will be divided into three parts based on the standard system of an Early, Middle, and Late Stone Age.

The Early Stone Age

In a strict sense, if we were to limit ourselves to consideration of living surfaces, there are no Early Stone Age sites in western Africa. The chief commentators on African prehistory such as J. Desmond Clark in 1970 and 1982 as well as the contributors to Thurstan Shaw's *Pastoralism in Africa* and D. W. Phillipson in the 1990s are all in agreement on the paucity of evidence of early human settlement in western Africa. Com-

pared to eastern or southern Africa, there is, in truth, very little reliable evidence. Archaeological survey has been carried out by different investigators in Ghana, Senegal, Nigeria, Cameroon, Ivory Coast, Mali, and Niger. The product of these efforts consists of a few isolated discoveries of choppers, chopping tools, crude flakes, hand axes, and other bifaces from the surface or in heavily disturbed fluviatile (river-lain) sediments. Here and there, finds of lightly reworked stone found in some river drainages have suggested the presence of an Early Stone Age site in the vicinity, but no real site with a demonstrable living surface has been found. Glynn Isaac suggested three possible explanations for the scant early evidence in western Africa:

1. The region may have been uninhabited during the greater part of the Pleistocene or only sparsely and sporadically occupied.
2. Early stone tools may have been manufactured so crudely that they are difficult to detect.

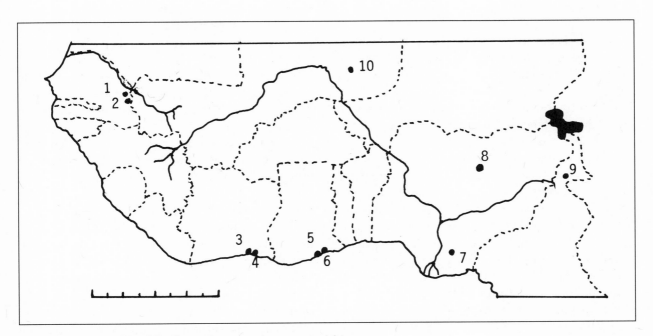

Fig. 24 *Early and Middle Stone Age sites in western Africa*

1 Djita	4 Tema West	6 Anyama	8 Jos Plateau site cluster
2 Sansandé	5 Attinguié	7 Ugwuele-Uturu	9 Figuil-Louti
3 Asokrochona			10 Lagreich

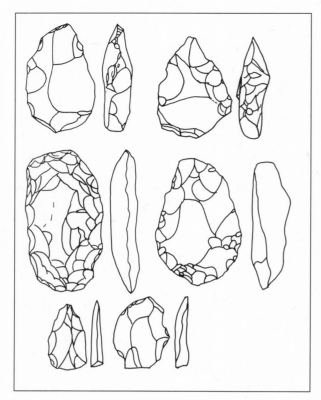

Fig. 25 *Late Acheulian tools from Sansandé*

3. Persistent erosion, deposition, and weathering may have destroyed most of the earliest evidence.

In all likelihood, all of these factors combined to erase the evidence of the early peoples of the western regions of the continent.

Even so, this picture is changing somewhat. As a result of recent research, a few places with fairly large Early Stone Age assemblages of Acheulian tools (such as bifaces, cleavers, heavy scrapers, and unretouched flakes) in more-or-less loose stratigraphic contexts have been investigated at Maiidon Toro, Nok, and Pingell on the Jos Plateau in north-central Nigeria, at Asokrochona and Tema-West on the Atlantic Coast in Ghana, at Sansandé and Djita in the Lower Faleme Valley of eastern Senegal, and at Ugwuele-Uturu, a quarry site in southeastern Nigeria. It is now possible to say that some parts of western Africa, particularly the Lower Faleme Valley in Senegal, where 13 finds have been recorded, the Atlantic Coast in Ghana, Lagreich in

Mali, and the Jos Plateau and Ugwuele-Uturu in Nigeria, were settled by Late Acheulian foragers sometime between nearly 200,000 to 300,000 years ago. Burned flint bifaces from Lagreich also suggest that some of people had a knowledge of fire. (See table 20 for a list of sites in the Lower Faleme Valley in Senegal.)

The Middle Stone Age

Following O. Davies's research and surveys in Ghana in the 1960s, the term *Sangoan* has been used to characterize a cultural period of western African prehistory marked by the recurrent presence of heavy post-Acheulian tools. While the accuracy and relevance of such an attribution is still debated, the material used to support this construct was collected from mixed and disturbed surface assemblages. The transfer of the Sangoan label from its eastern African cradle, where it was formerly considered to have resulted from an adaptation to forested environments, to western Africa is based on an oversimplified view of technological change among prehistoric societies, but the archaeological data from western Africa are still too sketchy and the context of finds too doubtful to assign a precise label without more rigorous research.

As characterized by Clark in 1982, the Middle Stone Age is marked by the general reduction in heavy-duty equipment and an increase in the number of smaller flake tools. It is also a time when regional stone-knapping traditions may have begun. The Middle Stone Age should be thought of as a *techno-complex,* a group of cultures characterized by assemblages sharing a common range of functional activities but with differing specific types of the same general families of artifacts. A techno-complex assemblage was a widely diffused and interlinked response to common factors in environment, economy, and technology. As such, depending on time, place, available raw materials, task to be performed, and other factors, variation can be seen as the rule and homogeneity as the exception.

There is a real dearth of information on Middle Stone Age sites, and no habitation site with a living surface is known. Nevertheless, investigations have been carried out during the past

Table 20 *The Lower Faleme Valley in Senegal: Prehistoric, geological, and paleo-climatological sequences*

Sedimentary Unit	Isotopic Stage	Climatic Trends	Prehistoric Culture	Age (inferred)
Naye Member	9	Humid	Few stones	300,000–345,000 years ago
Erosion Phase II	8	Aird		250,000–300,000
Sansandé Member	7	Humid	Late Acheulian	180,000–250,000
Erosion Phase III	6	Arid		130,000–180,000
Djita Member	6–5	Humid	Later Acheulian	71,000–130,000
Erosion Phase IV	4	Arid		60,000–70,000
Fanira Member	3	Humid	Mousteroid	32,000–58,000
Sehoudebou Member	2	Semiarid	Late Paleolithic	18,000–32,000

couple of decades at Asokrochona and Tema-West in Ghana, Attingue and Anyama in Ivory Coast, on the Jos Plateau in Nigeria, Figuil-Louti in northern Cameroon and the Lower Faleme Valley in Senegal. These sites have given us some insight into the range of variation of Middle Stone Age cultural assemblages. The tool inventories vary from one place to another and comprise many different types. Heavy-duty tools are represented by picks, choppers, and spheroids, tools on flakes (mostly scrapers prepared from Levallois cores), and many unmodified quartz, rhyolite, silexite, and fine-grained sandstone flakes.

The Late Stone Age

In contrast to the Early and Middle Stone Age periods, the Late Stone Age is well documented. Many of the investigated sites contain stratified deposits. Several syntheses have already been published characterizing the major features of the lithic (stone) assemblages of this period, which is epitomized by the presence, in varying proportions, of small stone implements (microliths) with or without geometric shapes. These miniature stone pieces were elements of composite tools, which may have been used to perform various tasks including hunting, fishing, collecting, food processing, and craft making. Considered in this context of a broad range of cultural activity, the presence of microliths in a stone-tool assemblage should not be used solely to suggest an adaptive shift toward a "specialized" hunting way of life as has been the case heretofore. The pres-

ence of a microlithic industry suggests a more complex range of behaviors than has hitherto been postulated.

Though still plagued with problems of definition and identification, we may agree that the Late Stone Age in western African is a phenomenon of the end of the Pleistocene, which, depending on the area, started sometime in the 20th millennium B.C. and lasted until the advent of iron metallurgy. This broad characterization encompasses groups of highly mobile foragers as well as less mobile and settled village-based food-producers. The analytical query, however, is one of positively identifying significant differences between these different kinds of subsistence and socio-economic systems and discriminating between Late Stone Age hunting-gathering societies in a strict sense from food-producing societies, which are sometimes termed *Neolithic*.

The debate on the relevance of the term *Neolithic* in western Africa results, in part, from this difficulty in distinguishing early food producers if their subsistence system was based on the cultivation of oil palms and tubers like yams. This issue will not be considered here. Our focus will be limited to a broadly defined Late Stone Age.

Its earliest manifestation, the Lower Late Stone Age emerged during the dry and arid Ogolian-Kanemian climatic phase, which began 20,000 years ago and ended 10,000 years ago. Such climatic circumstances created an important modification of the western African vegetation belts. The Saharan Desert, the Sahel, and the

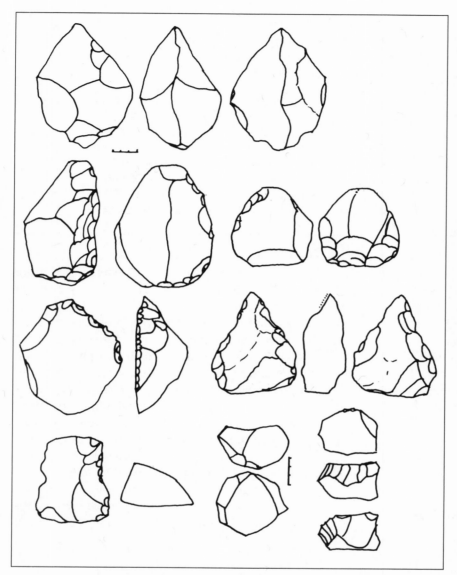

Fig. 26 *Middle Stone Age specimens from Anyama, Ivory Coast*

(beginning about 5,000 years ago and ending 2,000 years ago) is characterized by cultural innovations, notably the advent and expansion of pottery manufacture and probably a sustained drift toward food production. At this time, climatic patterns fluctuated from a relatively arid Middle Holocene phase to wetter, shorter periods. As for settlement types, the most striking feature of the Late Stone Age, generally, was the occupation of rock shelters and shallow caves, in which no Early and Middle Stone Ages material has been recorded.

The development of this new site-location strategy and settlement system cannot be fully understood without more accurate analysis of some well-known local and regional settlement patterns. These, theoretically at least, should demonstrate a system of base camps connected to a series of smaller special-purpose sites spread throughout their immediate vicinity. The distribution of these secondary camps would be regulated by the location of needed resources and the ranging territories of neighboring social groups, if any.

The Lower Late Stone Age sequence is demonstrated at a few sites, presumably at Badoye in the Gambia River Valley and certainly at Mbi Crater in the Cameroon Grassfields, the Bingerville Highway site in Ivory Coast, and Iwo Eleru I in south-central Nigeria. Middle Late Stone Age sites of about 6,000 to 10,000 years ago are far more numerous and widespread than those of the previous stage.

In general, the Middle Late Stone Age instituted a shift in the relative frequencies of micro-

savanna expanded southward, while the rain forest virtually disappeared with some of its relicts (survivors) confined to restricted areas like the southwestern Cameroon Mountains and the Nimba Plateau in Guinea. The Middle Late Stone Age (beginning about 10,000 or 11,000 years ago and ending 6,000 years ago) occurred during the Early Holocene climatic optimum, when a general increase in rainfall produced more humid conditions causing a northward drift of the vegetation belts. The Upper Late Stone Age

Table 21 *Tentative chronology of some West African Late Stone Age sites*

	Lower Late Stone Age	Middle Late Stone Age	Upper Late Stone Age	Undetermined
Open-air settlements	Badoye (?) Bingerville Highway	Tiémassas Obobogo Rim I Ntyebougou Giré-West Giré-East Zampia-North	Kawara Obobogo Thies Rim II-E Asejire Kedama Aribindat	Ugwuele Legon New Todzi Adwuku
Rock shelters and shallow cave settlements	Mbi Crater Iwo Eleru	Mbi Crater Iwo Eleru Dutsen Kongba Bosumpra Shum Laka Abéké Maadaga Rop Yengema Kamabai Yagala Kakimbon	Ugwuagu Iwo Eleru Dutsen Kongba Bosumpra Ukpa Abéké Maadaga (?) Manianbougou Blande	Apreku Achimota Tetewabou Akyekyema Buor Mejiro Sindou Korounkorokalé
Shell middens		Tiémassas (?) Cap Manuel Kpone-West Tchotchoral Tiebiessou Songon Dagbe Ehoussou Nyamwan	Rao	

liths, large flake tools, heavy-duty implements, and cutting tools in the stratigraphic sequence. In the western Cameroon Grassfields, in the earliest level of the Shum Laka sequence (Level III), a microlithic quartz industry was found and dated to about 9,000 years ago. It was replaced in Levels II and I by assemblages with Levallois flakes and large basalt or trachyte flakes. Bifacially retouched tools of the hoe and ax category appear as early as the first half of the 7th millennium B.C. A similar pattern is attested to at the nearby rock-shelter sites of Abéké (Levels III-I) and Mbi Crater (Levels V-I). Faunal remains show that most of the hunted preys were forest species.

Bones of dwarf buffalo and giant forest hogs are the most frequent, with duikers, gorillas, chimpanzees, and cane rats also recorded. A different pattern, with early occupation levels containing relatively large Levallois flakes superseded by a flint microlithic industry, has been recorded at Maadaga shelter in southeastern Burkina Faso. Quarry sites and settlements from the Vallée du Serpent in Mali present another facet of the Middle Late Stone Age's intricate pattern of technocomplexes. These sites produced rather large flakes from prepared cores and are conventionally termed *macrolithic* to contrast them with conventional microlithic industries. Five sites

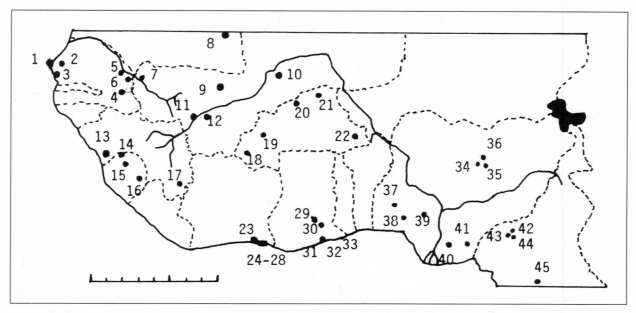

Fig. 27 *Late Stone Age sites in western Africa*

1 Cap Manuel	12 Manianbougou	24 Tchotchoraf	35 Rop
2 Thiès	13 Kakimbon	25 Ehoussou	36 Zenebi
3 Tiémassas	14 Yagala	26 Tiebiessou	37 Mejiro
4 Badoye	15 Kamabai	27 Nyamwan	38 Asejiré
5 Diboli	16 Yengema	28 Songon Dagbe	39 Iwo Eleru
6 Ouboi	17 Blandé	29 Bosumpa	40 Ugwuele-Uturu
7 Kayes	18 Sindiou	30 Adwuku	41 Afikpo
8 Kedama	19 Kawara	31 Achimota	42 Shum Laka
9 Vallée du Serpent cluster	20 Rim	32 Legon Botanical Garden	43 Mbi Crater
10 Zampia-North	21 Aribindat	33 Kpone-West	44 Abéké
11 Korounkorokalé	22 Maadaga	34 Dutsen Kongba	
	23 Bingerville Highway site		

have been sampled (Sirakoro-Ancien, Ntyebougou, Giré-West, Giré-East, and Zampia-North) and dated to between 6,000 and 12,000 years ago. Microliths in varying proportions have been recorded at many other sites broadly spread throughout the area: New Todzi, Achimota, Bosumpra, Apreku, Tetewabou, Akyekyema Buor, and Legon in Ghana; Tiémassas in Senegal; Korounkorokalé in Mali; Rim and Maadaga in Burkina Faso; Obobogo in southern Cameroon; and Mejiro, Rop, Dutsen Kongba, Iwo Eleru, Ukpa, Ugwuagu, and Asejiré in Nigeria. None of these is dated with any certainty. In general, however, in those with a well-defined stratigraphic sequence, earlier microlithic levels and levels lacking ceramics are overlain by deposits containing microliths and pottery. The earliest occurrences of pottery are dated to the 4th and 5th millennia B.C.

The tested sites are widely distributed throughout western Africa. In the easternmost part, the village site of Obobogo in southern Cameroon, where a localized lower level was uncovered at the base of Trench A and dated to about 6,000 years ago, contained a quartz microlithic industry. And in the westernmost portion in Senegal, the site of Tiémassas, a poorly studied large lagoon settlement with exposures extending over several kilometers, has microliths as well as large backed blades, crude crescents, and bifacially flaked foliate (leaf-shaped) projectile points.

The classes of stone tools change in frequency at Iwo Eleru II-IV (about 7,000 to 10,000 years ago), where the relative proportion of microliths decreases from 40 percent to 11.6 percent, the proportion of scrapers rises from 14 percent to 22 percent, and the proportion of chisels rises from 24 percent to 41 percent, with the appearance of core tools in Iwo Eleru III. This suggests that variability of lithic inventories at the regional and local levels seems to be a major characteristic of the Middle Late Stone Age. However, a dominant trend—a relative but sustained decrease in microliths complemented by increasing proportions of large flaked, heavy-duty, and core tools—appears to characterize a socio-technological evolution during the later part of the Late Stone Age (about 2,000 to 5,000 years ago).

During the Upper Late Stone Age, almost all major biomes (ecological communities) of western Africa seem to have been settled. Most of the ceramic microlithic assemblages (from Rop, Dutsen Kongba, and Iwo Eleru in Nigeria; Maadaga, Rim, and Kawara in Burkina Faso; Sindou and Kakimbon in Guinea; Koroun-korokalé in Mali; Yengema, Kamabai, and Yagala in Sierra Leone; and Bosumpra in Ghana) contain larger proportions of choppers, hammer stones, axes, adzelike tools, and scrapers and points. A few shell middens have also been tested along the Atlantic, in Senegal at Rao and Cap Manuel, in Ghana at Kpone, and in Ivory Coast at Tchotchoraf, Tiebiessou, Songon Dagbe, Ehoussou, and Nyamwan on the northern shore of Ebrie Lagoon.

Genuine village life may have existed during this period, as suggested by later evidence from Karkarichinkat in Mali, Dhar Tichitt in Mauritania, the Kintampo culture complex in Ghana and Ivory Coast, firki mound sites in northeastern Nigeria and northern Cameroon, and Obobogo in southern Cameroon. There is evidence of substantial habitation features, numerous pits, extensive domestic and grinding equipment, animal husbandry of sheep, goats, and cattle, and cereal cultivation and horticulture. In the forested and more humid areas, subsistence systems may have been based on hunting; fishing; collecting wild fruits, tubers, and plant leaves; selectively exploiting and protecting oil plants such as *Canarium schweifurthii* and oil palms; and cultivating domesticated varieties of yams. All the components of horticultural systems are highly biodegradable. It is, therefore, not surprising that positive evidence in support of early agricultural practices in humid, tropical western Africa has not yet been found.

BIBLIOGRAPHY

Allsworth-Jones, P. 1981. The Middle Stone Age of the Jos Plateau: A preliminary report. *West African Journal of Archaeology* 11: 1–24.

Andah, B. 1979. The Later Stone Age and Neolithic of Upper Volta viewed in a West African context. *West African Journal of Archaeology* 9: 87–110.

Asombang, R. 1991. Cameroun: Late Stone Age. In *Aux origines de l'Afrique centrale*, eds. R. Lanfranchi and B. Clist, 98–101. Libreville-Paris: Centre International des Civilisations Bantu-Sépia.

Chenorkian, R. 1983. Ivory Coast prehistory: Recent developments. *African Archaeological Review* 1: 127–142.

Clark, J. D. 1970. *The prehistory of Africa.* New York: Praeger.

———, ed. 1982. *The Cambridge history of Africa, vol. 1: From the earliest times to c. 500 B.C.* Cambridge: Cambridge University Press.

Connah, G. 1981. *Three thousand years in Africa.* Cambridge: Cambridge University Press.

Holl, A. 1986. *Economie et société Néolithique du Dhar Tichitt (Mauritanie).* Paris: Editions Recherches sur les Civilisations.

MacDonald, K., and P. Allsworth-Jones. 1994. A reconsideration of the West African macrolithic conundrum: New factory sites and an associated settlement in the Vallée du Serpent, Mali. *African Archaeological Review* 12: 73–104.

McIntosh, S. K., and R. McIntosh. 1988. From stone to metal: New perspectives on the later prehistory of West Africa. *Journal of World Prehistory* 2: 89–133.

———. 1993. Current directions in West African prehistory. *Annual Review of Anthropology* 12: 215–258.

Phillipson, D. W. 1985. *African archaeology.* 2d ed. Cambridge: Cambridge University Press.

Shaw, T. 1978. *Nigeria: Its archaeology and early history.* London: Thames and Hudson.

Shaw, T., P. Sinclair, B. Andah, and A. Okpoko, eds. 1993. *The archaeology of Africa: Food, metals and towns.* London: Routledge.

Smith, A. 1992. *Pastoralism in Africa: Origins and development ecology*. London: Hurst and Co.

Augustin F. C. Holl

CENTRAL AFRICAN TRANSITIONAL CULTURES

The central part of Africa has challenged archaeological research in many regards. Thick forest vegetation is an obstacle to large-scale surveys, so that prehistoric occupation patterns tend to coincide with modern settlement and mining areas. Because acid soils destroy plant and faunal remains, there is a lack of datable organic material and data for reconstructing the environment and subsistence economy. Important erosion phases in some areas are responsible for a hiatus in the post-Acheulian succession of cultural stages. These suffer from a poor definition of industries due to problems of site integrity.

The available data for reconstructing west-central African Quaternary environments were summarized by D. Schwartz and R. Lanfranchi in 1990. In 1991, a compendium followed, presenting the sites of Zaire, the Congo Republic, the Central African Republic, Gabon, Cameroon, Angola, and Equatorial Guinea, edited by R. Lanfranchi and B. Clist. A substantial report on the renewed research in the Semliki Valley in Zaire appeared in 1990 in the volume edited by N. T. Boaz, and a complete survey of archaeological sites in Gabon was published by B. Clist in 1995. This short list reveals that despite fieldwork difficulties, central Africa continues to intrigue archaeologists and that some areas have witnessed intensive archaeological research. For a historical account of the archaeological research, the reader is referred to P. de Maret's "Phases and Facies in the Archaeology of Central Africa" in *A History of African Archaeology*.

Given the nature of the archaeological record available, the southwest, southeast, and northern half of central Africa will be discussed separately. The definition of technological contents and chro-nological position remains a fundamental problem for Sangoan and Lupemban artifacts in the southwestern part. Except for the later Holocene Tshitolian industry, evidence for reconstructing environment and subsistence economy is entirely lacking here. In the southeastern part, only two sites were extensively excavated. For the northeastern and northwestern part, data on microlithic industries have increased over the last few years thanks to excavations on the Atlantic Coast of Gabon, as well as site-specific research in the Semliki Valley in eastern Zaire and in rock shelters in the Northwestern Province of Cameroon. These data permit us to address questions of chronology, evolution in technological contents of industries, and land-use patterns.

Southwestern Central Africa

The Problem of Sangoan and Lupemban Industries

Most of the Sangoan and Lupemban sites found in lower Zaire, the Congo Republic, Kwango, Kasai, and northeastern Angola appear either in fluviatile (river-lain) terraces or in exposures generated by mining operations and road-construction works. Bifacial flaking is a prominent technological feature of these assemblages. The original definitions of Sangoan and Lupemban industries were, however, based on poorly illustrated surface collections and disturbed sites, which resulted in a confusing application of the terms to any occurrence of bifacially flaked implements. As a consequence, a series of revisions of Sangoan and Lupemban artifacts has been proposed. J. Desmond Clark in 1971 offered an excellent review of the pre-1970 historical background of Sangoan and Lupemban. Sangoan would represent an older industry, and Lupemban a more recent one. Sangoan is found on top of, or in the upper part of stone lines (contemporaneous associated materials deposited on terraces at peak flood stages). The formation of stone lines is open to discussion, as noted by D. Schwartz in 1990, but has important implications for the interpretation of the associated archaeological material. This brief survey presents the two main hypotheses arising from the work of D. Cahen and J. Moeyersons in Zaire and from

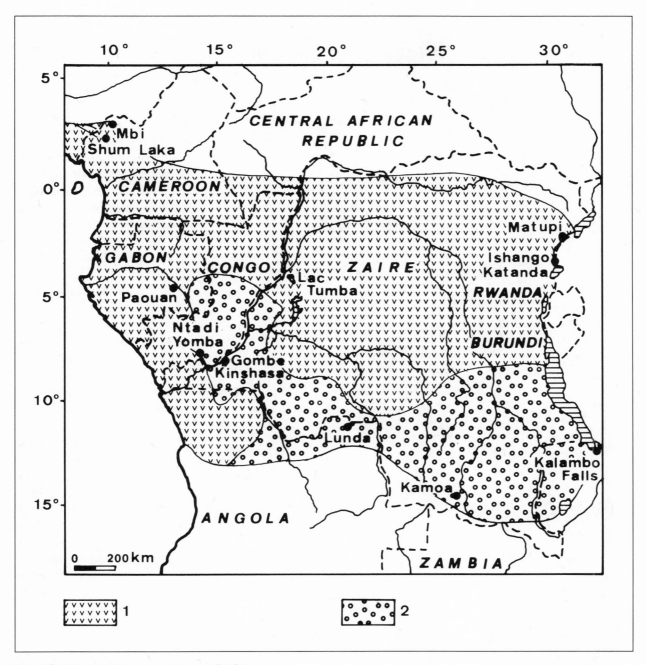

Fig. 28 *Physical features of central Africa*

  1 The present extent of the tropical forest
  2 The area of Kalahari and related sands

the research in progress of R. Lanfranchi and D. Schwartz in west-central Africa.

Cahen resumed excavations at the reference site of Gombe Point in 1973 and 1974 in order to complete and date the sequence. The stratigra-

phy is representative for the area of the Kalahari Sand Belt. Several meters of sand deposits lacking clear sedimentation structures overlay a base of gravel or stone line. Artifacts are not found in clear-cut horizons but in the top of the stone line

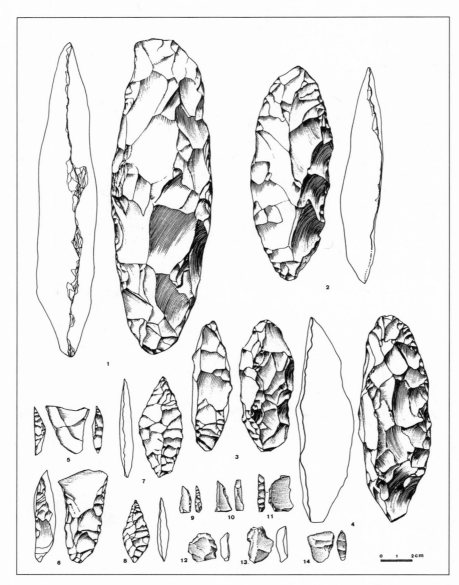

Fig. 29 *Tool types associated with central African (transitional) Pleistocene and Holocene industries*

logical horizons and casts doubt on the association between industries and carbon-14 dates. Such a catastrophic scenario, assumed to have taken place at other sites displaying a similar stratigraphy, led Cahen to consider the apparently mixed assemblages of Sangoan, Lupemban, and even Tshitolian as one large central African post-Acheulian complex.

In a more optimistic approach, Schwartz and Lanfranchi explain stone lines as old erosion surfaces. Erosion presumes a thin vegetation cover and a certain amount of precipitation to enhance the process. Both of these factors imply that stone lines were formed at the end of dry periods. The makers of the Sangoan artifacts would have exploited the stone line as a source of raw material and would have left part of their material culture on top of it. In associating the Sangoan industry with dry climatic conditions and an open savanna environment, this scenario goes against the older interpretation of Sangoan implements as woodworking tools for forest clearing.

If stone lines are stable, old erosion surfaces instead of completely reworked deposits, the question of their age can be addressed. The overlying sands include later industries of Holocene age, which would set the formation of the stone lines in the last dry period of the Leopoldvillian period (12,000 to 30,000 years ago) with maximum aridity around 18,000 years ago. The absence of recent Holocene assemblages near the base of the sands, however, would situate the formation of the stone lines at the end of the previous Pleistocene dry period, the Maluekian.

and throughout the sands, concentrating at various depths. Refitting of artifacts from the new excavations at Gombe Point revealed serious post-depositional perturbations (disturbances of stratigraphic relationships due to events that occurred after the deposit was laid down). Both natural and cultural material had moved progressively downward and accumulated near the base of the sequence, resulting in the formation of stone lines. The process, "catalysed by biogenic activity," probably blurred the original archaeo-

This dry phase is tentatively dated between 40,000 and 70,000 years ago. An age of at least 40,000 years is supported to some extent by the carbon-14 dates for materials situated above the top of stone lines in Gabon (but not associated with Sangoan or Lupemban artifacts). The dating evidence from Kalambo Falls in northeastern Zambia, the only site to have yielded Sangoan artifacts in an archaeological level without apparent disturbances, and carbon-14 dates from the Kinshasa Plain and the Lunda area do not contradict the age of at least 40,000 years.

A detailed analysis of the carbon-14 dates by D. Cahen, J. Moeyersons, and W. G. Mook in 1983 reveals a gap of approximately 10,000 years between 15,000 and 25,000 years ago. The chronological hiatus is not confined to Gombe Point but occurs also in the Lunda region in northeastern Angola, on the sites of the Kinshasa Plain, and at Kalambo Falls in Zambia. Dates between more than 25,000 and 40,000 years ago, some of which are probably beyond the range of carbon-14 dating, are associated with the top of the stone lines. The dates after 15,000 years ago come from the base of the sands. This chronological gap corresponds in the Kalahari Sand Belt with a gap in sedimentation. Cahen, Moeyersons, and Mook propose several explanations, such as a cease in sedimentation under a dense vegetation cover or an erosional phase under savanna vegetation. Lupemban affinities (Sangoan-Lupemban, Lower Lupemban, and Lupembo-Tshitolian) are found on either side of the gap in the Kinshasa Plain and in the Lunda area. The bifacial tradition and size reduction of the artifacts continue as if nothing ever happened. The authors assume it unlikely that the artisans would have left the area to occupy another territory, used a different technology, and then returned and resumed their previous technological tradition. They conclude, therefore, that this period of occupation is presently invisible in the archaeological record of southwestern central Africa.

The perturbations at the reference site of Gombe Point and the context of Sangoan industries in stone lines do not erase the emerging picture of a continuing bifacial tradition and reduction in the size of the artifacts in southwestern central Africa. Subdividing the tradition into several phases seems premature, given the available archaeological record. However, the bifacial tradition has an older phase, Sangoan, and a recent phase, Tshitolian. From a chronological point of view, Sangoan is linked to the Middle Stone Age, for it succeeds the Acheulian and precedes Holocene industries containing microliths. From a technological point of view, the persistence of the bifacial technique is not typical of Middle Stone Age industries, which are generally characterized by a gradual decrease of bifacially flaked implements in favor of flake and blade tools. The lower visibility of debitage ("industrial" wastes left from the knapping process) and smaller flake material on the surface and in stone lines may explain the low frequency in Sangoan and Lupemban collections from this kind of site, compared to the few excavated assemblages in the southeastern part of central Africa. What happened between the Sangoan industries of at least 40,000 years ago and the Tshitolian industries of 13,000 years ago remains an open question, since sites or horizons belonging to this intermediate period are absent. The descriptions of Sangoan-Lupemban, Lower or Upper Lupemban, and Lupembo-Tshitolian may indeed correspond to transitional cultures, but they may also reflect an admixture of old and recent material.

Aside from problems of site integrity and chronological position, the standard typological definition of Sangoan emphasizes the presence of large and heavy picks and bifacially flaked core axes. Lupemban is mostly identified by the presence of long, impressive bifacially flaked lanceolates (tapering lancelike points) and core axes. In the Kalahari Sand Belt, a fine-grained *grès polymorphe* (a kind of metamorphosed sandstone) is used as raw material. Outside this area, quartzites are the basic raw material.

The Tshitolian Industry

The Tshitolian industry has been identified in dated and stratified assemblages from open-air sites in southwestern Zaire, northeastern Angola, and southeastern and central Gabon. Tshitolian artifacts have also been found in rock shelters in the Congo Republic and Gabon. A substantial number of carbon-14 dates situated the Tshitolian in the Holocene, between about 3,000 and 13,000 years ago. From a technological point of view, the Tshitolian lithic industry consists of *petit tranchets* (small triangular points), arrowheads, and small bifacial or unifacial core axes, together with a small number of geometric microliths and a heavy-duty component. Flaking techniques are rather unspecialized. Local raw materials such as chert, quartzite, sandstone, *grès polymorphe,* and quartz are used. Bifacial flaking remains a component of the industry as in the preceding Sangoan and Lupemban, but the general size reduction of artifacts, the use of a blunting technique, and the Holocene age place the Tshitolian in the Late Stone Age.

The cave of Ntadi Yomba in the Congo Republic yielded a faunal assemblage dating to 7,000 years ago. The occupants of the cave exploited a slightly more forested environment than is present in the region today, fished in marshy swamps, and collected large land snails. In the Paouan Cave near Lastourville in Gabon, the lower levels have been described as Tshitolian and were dated to about 5,600 years ago. A detailed analysis of the charcoal yielded only four species. This suggests a highly selective use of resources considering the diversity of woody plants available in the surrounding area.

Southeastern Central Africa

Surface and undated sites in Shaba (southeastern Zaire) have yielded core axes with Levallois debitage, described as Middle Stone Age, and assemblages with microlithic debitage, interpreted as Late Stone Age.

Kamoa in Shaba (Zaire) and Kalambo Falls in northeastern Zambia are the two extensively excavated and dated sites in the southeastern area. Both revealed a sequence from Acheulian times into the Holocene. The lower post-Acheulian industry of Kamoa contains bifacially flaked implements or core axes and a substantial amount of flake production. Unfortunately, only the upper part of the succession has been dated. It has yielded microlithic assemblages dating between 2,000 and 6,000 years ago.

The Sangoan industry of Kalambo Falls, stratified above the Acheulian, dates to between 38,000 and more than 40,000 years ago. Post-Sangoan artifacts are dispersed through the overlying sands and were tentatively ascribed to the Lupemban. The upper microlithic levels were dated to 9,000 years ago. The technological composition of the older industries at Kalambo Falls has not been published in detail yet.

A similar tendency appears at Kamoa and Kalambo Falls. Bifacially flaked tools gradually disappear, and in the Holocene phases, microlithic Late Stone Age industries appear, comparable to the microlithic complex in Zambia.

Northeastern and Northwestern Central Africa

Various finds and surface sites dating to the period between the Acheulian and the Late Stone Age are reported from southern Cameroon, northern and eastern Zaire, the Central African Republic, and stone-line sites from Gabon. These undated assemblages are assigned to Sangoan, and sometimes Lupemban, on the basis of typological comparisons. Collections made in stratigraphic exposures in northern Cameroon reveal the presence of Middle Stone Age industries, characterized by radial and prepared cores. The only dated and excavated Middle Stone Age occurrences come from the Semliki Valley, where a minimum age of 90,000 years is suggested for the open-air Katanda sites. The sites provided evidence of an informal Middle Stone Age industry using local quartzite and quartz and allochthonous chert (flintlike cystalline stone), fish and mammal remains, and the oldest bone points known from a Middle Stone Age context. Bifacial implements of Sangoan or Lupemban affinity were not recovered from the three Katanda sites.

The archaeological record on the microlithic industries of the Late Stone Age, with geometric microliths and backed pieces, includes excavated and dated sequences from the eastern part of central Africa (Matupi Cave and Ishango). The previously virtually blank interior basin of the Zaire River has been intensively surveyed east of Lac Tumba. The western part of this area yielded surface assemblages reminiscent of the more southern Tshitolian industry, whereas microlithic surface sites were located in the eastern part.

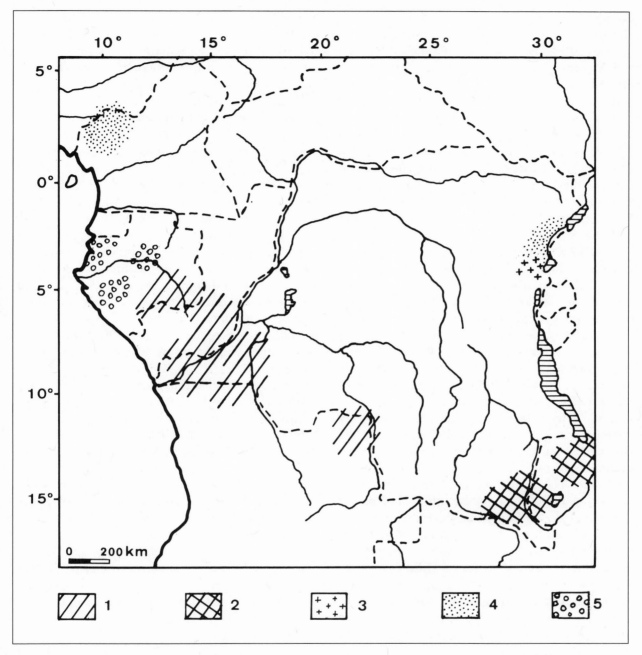

Fig. 30 *Suggested areas of Middle and Late Stone Age occupations*

1 Bifacial tradition of the Sangoan, Lupemban, and Tshitolian industries
2 Middle Stone Age occupations with, and Holocene microlithic industries without, bifacially flaked implements
3 Middle Stone Age occupations without bifacially flaked implements
4 Pre-Holocene microlithic industries
5 Holocene microlithic industries without a bifacial component

From northern Zaire, the Central African Republic, and Equatorial Guinea, surface sites with microlithic assemblages made of quartz were reported. At the western edge, Late Stone Age sites were excavated and dated on the Atlantic Coast of Gabon and in the Northwestern Province of

Cameroon. A large number of carbon-14 dates confirm the establishment of the microlithic industries during the Holocene. The sites of Ishango and Matupi Cave on the eastern edge and the Shum Laka rock shelter to the west reveal a pre-Holocene or late Pleistocene age for the oldest microlithic industries using quartz (Matupi Cave, beyond 40,000 years ago; Shum Laka, about 30,000 years ago; and Ishango, about 18,000 years ago). Because of the pre-Holocene age and because the lower part of the sequences did not yield many formal microliths, the industries could be considered as transitional between Middle and Late Stone Age. In the more recent Holocene layers, however, the proportion of standard microliths remains small. In fact, the sequences show little variation in technological composition and appear as one single microlithic tradition. Another suggestion is that quartz may have been the only raw material accessible to these groups. As a raw material, quartz shatters into small fragments, which explains the microlithic appearance of these industries. At the site of Shum Laka, welded tuff (rock formed of fine volcanic detritus fused together by heat) was only exploited as a raw material during the Middle Holocene occupation but was accessible to the occupants of the rock shelter beginning 30,000 years ago. The use of quartz as basic raw material seems, therefore, to be a cultural choice. The older dates do not imply that the Late Stone Age has no chronological dimension, and the pre-Holocene age is not exceptional in a broader African context. A coexistence of Middle and Late Stone Age technological traditions is not shown in the present archaeological record. On the contrary, the dates derived for artifacts at Katanda suggest that Middle Stone Age would predate by far the old microlithic industries.

The three sites also contained faunal remains. Matupi Cave is presently situated in the Ituri Forest, but the prehistoric occupants relied on the hunting of savanna bovids and occasional forest animals. This indicates that, throughout the Late Stone Age sequence, the environment was more open with gallery forest at a short distance. J. Peters studied the fauna of the three stages of occupation at Ishango. Environmental changes throughout the last 20,000 years apparently did not affect the land-use patterns of hunting in the open grasslands and fishing in the lakes and rivers. Although the faunal remains of the lower levels at Shum Laka in Cameroon have not yet been analyzed in detail, preliminary results indicate the same pattern of environmental exploitation as during the Holocene occupation of the shelter—hunting of forest species. The plant remains consist of burned savanna shrubs. Fauna and charcoal are indicative of a combination of forest and more open vegetation during the occupation of the shelter, a situation that is similar to Matupi Cave and at Mbi Crater, a nearby rock shelter.

Bone industries from Late Stone Age contexts are preserved at the sites of Mbi Crater, Ishango, and Matupi Cave. Fishing equipment has been found only at Ishango. At Mbi Crater, bone needles and points occur as early as about 9,000 years ago. The upper levels at Matupi Cave, dating to between 3,000 and 12,000 years ago, yielded a few fragments of awls or bone points.

Human remains from Late Stone Age contexts were discovered at the three sites. At Ishango, fragmentary human remains were recovered from the level dating to approximately 18,000 years ago and from the base of the overlying level. The single burial in the rock shelter of Mbi Crater was dated to about 7,000 years ago. In the rock shelter of Shum Laka, 19 skeletons of adults and children were unearthed. Two burial phases were identified, the first around 7,000 years ago and the second around 3,000 years ago. Burial modes vary from inhumation to cremation and from single to multiple inhumations. None of the Late Stone Age skeletons shows direct affinities with modern populations.

⎯⎯⎯∿∿∿∿∿∿∿⎯⎯⎯

Despite the typical problems of integrity at central African sites and lack of technological consistency in definitions of industries, sites at Matupi Cave, Semliki Valley, and Shum Laka and the series of Tshitolian and Late Stone Age sites reveal the region's archaeological potential for assessing local changes in technologies and subsistence patterns from Pleistocene to Holocene times. The evidence on environment, subsistence economy, bone industries, human remains, and chronology comes essentially from rock shelters and caves. Given that preservation conditions are more favorable in this type of site, a bias may be introduced to the interpretation of prehistoric settlement patterns. The open-air sites in the Semliki Valley are an exception, but their stratigraphic position on the western ridge of the western Rift Valley is not representative of central African sites. In the south and west, sites yielding Sangoan and Lupemban artifacts are found in stone lines and in the overlying sands, so the definition and chronological position of Sangoan and Lupemban remain problematic.

Although the archaeological record in the different parts of central Africa is unequal, the available data permit a rough chronological and cultural outline.

The dating evidence from stone lines in the southwestern region, corroborated by both the pre-Holocene dates of Late Stone Age assemblages in the northwestern and eastern parts of central Africa and the date of 90,000 years ago from the Katanda sites, suggests that the Middle Stone Age artifacts, including Sangoan, are older than 40,000 years.

In the northern part, microlithic Late Stone Age industries start around 40,000 years ago, whereas in the southern part, they date from the Holocene. As for the southern Holocene industries, two traditions are identified: the western Tshitolian and the eastern microlithic industries. The age of the southern Late Stone Age occupations may predate the Holocene as well. This is neither refuted nor supported by the available dating evidence, because the chronological record presents a gap between about 15,000 and 25,000 years ago. The hiatus, together with the poor finding circumstances, also hampers a more precise assessment of the existence of a Lupemban industry.

In the southwestern region of central Africa, a continuum of Pleistocene and Holocene industries with a strong bifacial component is present throughout the post-Acheulian times. The Sangoan assemblages mark the beginning, whereas the Holocene Tshitolian sites are of the Late Stone Age tradition. Between these, transitional assemblages represent variations on the same bifacial theme and reflect the general tendencies of decreasing artifact size and increasing use of blunting-retouch methods.

In the southeastern part, assemblages containing bifacially flaked implements bearing a resemblance to the southwestern Sangoan and Lupemban artifacts succeed the Acheulian. After the chronological gap, a completely different Holocene Late Stone Age complex appears without bifacial techniques but with geometric microliths and backed pieces, similar to the microlithic industries of southern African and the northern part of central Africa. The sequences of microlithic industries using quartz in the north have pre-Holocene origins. An assessment of whether they are a further development of Middle Stone Age industries is impossible because of a lack of dated or stratified Middle Stone Age sites in the northern part of central Africa.

The number of excavated and dated sites remains desperately low compared to the total surface of central Africa. Every new excavation and date will continue to invite revisions of even the fundamentals of the "established" framework of the central African Pleistocene and Holocene industries or cultures.

BIBLIOGRAPHY

Boaz, N. T., ed. 1990. *Evolution of environments and Hominidae in the African western Rift Valley.* Virginia Museum of Natural History Memoir No. 1. Martinsville: Virginia Museum of Natural History.

Brooks, A. S., D. M. Helgren, J. S. Cramer, A. Franklin, W. Hornyak, J. M. Keating, R. G. Klein, W. J. Rink, H. Schwarcz, J. N. Leith Smith, K. Stewart, K., N. E. Todd, J. Verniers, and J. E. Yellen. 1995. Dating and context of three Middle Stone Age sites with bone points in the Upper Semliki Valley, Zaire. *Science* 268: 548–552.

Brooks, A. S., and P. Robertshaw. 1990. The Glacial Maximum in tropical Africa: 20,000–12,000 B.P. In *Low Latitudes.* 121–169. Vol. 2 of *The world at 18000 B.P.,* eds. C. Gamble and O. Soffer. London: Unwin Hyman.

Clark, J. D. 1971. Problems of archaeological nomenclature and definition in the Congo Basin. *South African Archaeological Bulletin* 26: 67–78.

Clist, B. 1995. *Gabon: 100,000 ans d'histoire.* Paris: Sépia.

Clist, B., and R. Lanfranchi, eds. 1990. *Aux origines de l'Afrique centrale.* Paris: Sépia.

de Maret, P. 1990. Phases and facies in the archaeology of central Africa. In *A history of African archaeology,* ed. P. Robertshaw, 109–134. London and Portsmouth: James Currey Ltd. and Heinemann.

de Maret, P., R. Asombang, E. Cornelissen, P. Lavachery, and J. Moeyersons. 1995. Continuing research at Shum Laka rock shelter, Cameroon (1993–1994 field season). *Nyame Akuma* 43: 2–3.

de Maret, P., and W. Van Neer. 1993. Preliminary results of the 1991–1992 field season at Shum Laka, Northwestern Province, Cameroon. *Nyame Akuma* 39: 13–15.

Lanfranchi, R., and D. Schwartz, eds. 1990. *Paysages quaternaires de l'Afrique centrale atlantique.* Paris: O.R.S.T.O.M.

Oslisly, R., M. Pickford, R. Dechamps, and M. Fontugne. 1994. Ancient rituals in Gabon. *Nature* 367: 25.

Peters, J. 1990. Late Pleistocene hunter-gatherers at Ishango (eastern Zaire): The faunal evidence. *Revue de Paléobiologie* 9: 73–112.

Van Neer, W. 1989. *Contribution to the archaeozoology of central Africa.* Tervuren: Annales sciences zoologiques du Musée Royal de l'Afrique Centrale, no. 259.

Van Noten, F. 1982. *The archaeology of central Africa.* Graz: Akademische Druck und Verlagstalt.

Yellen, J. E., A. S. Brooks, E. Cornelissen, M. J. Mehlman, and K. Stewart. 1995. A Middle Stone Age worked bone industry from Katanda, Upper Semliki Valley, Zaire. *Science* 268: 553–557.

Els Cornelissen

AFRICAN CULTURES IN TRANSITION AND ADAPTATION

Investigations into the emergence of modern peoples have encouraged an interest in the Middle Stone Age of the later Middle and the Late Pleistocene in sub-Saharan Africa. Containing perhaps half the population of the inhabited world until as recently as 50,000 years ago, sub-Saharan Africa was an important center for human evolution. Population fluctuations may have occurred on a local subregional level due to environmental forcing, but there was no major population replacement as has been suggested in Eurasia. Archaeological exploration is uneven, but with the aid of new dating, field, and laboratory techniques, research is producing insights into the lifeways of these broad-spectrum foragers. As more is learned about their lifeways, there is a growing appreciation of the continuities in behavior with later foragers. Whether the behavior of Middle Stone Age foragers should be categorized as near-modern or fully modern is debated, but it is accepted that these people were the direct ancestors of contemporary populations in sub-Saharan Africa if not populations everywhere.

Some 200,000 years ago, the tradition of making large bifacial Acheulian artifacts—a tradition that had lasted 1 million years—was replaced by a technology based on regularly formed stone flakes, half as large. This revolutionary change in technology marked the progression from using hand tools to using stone flakes fixed to handles by binding or gluing with plant gum. Mounting stone flakes as inserts on handles and shafts gave added leverage, and this may account for the spread of flake-dominated industries throughout Africa and in parts of Eurasia from about this time. These artifact industries are conventionally grouped as the Middle Paleolithic and, more specifically in sub-Saharan Africa, as the Middle Stone Age. They represent a period of transition from ancient to modern lifeways.

The term *Middle Stone Age* was proposed in the 1920s to aid in the ordering of museum and field collections of artifacts. In examinations of stratified deposits in caves, characteristic Middle Stone Age flake artifacts were found in layers above those containing Acheulian bifaces and below layers containing the miniaturized Late Stone Age tools. Thus a relative age was given to the stage. (This was before the development of scientific dating methods that make age estimates more precise.) The oldest dated Middle Stone Age sites, at 180,000 years old, are in Ethiopia, but it is thought that Middle Stone Age technology was practiced everywhere in Africa even before then. Radiocarbon dates are available for the younger sites and for the end of the stage. From sites in eastern and southern Africa, the transition to the following Late Stone Age stage and technology associated with bow-and-arrow hunting has been estimated to have occurred around 23,000 years ago. Because many Middle Stone Age sites date to beyond the range of radiocarbon, alternative dating techniques, such as uranium-disequilibrium, luminescence, and amino-acid dating, have to be used to provide a chronological framework for understanding the archaeological evidence.

In southern Africa, where there are a number of well-studied stratified rock-shelter sequences, the main deposits from Middle Stone Age occupation date to between 60,000 and 130,000 years ago. While some occurrences are inferred to be older, none has been dated directly. Sites ranging over a wide area from Zimbabwe to the Cape were either not occupied or occupied very sporadically from 60,000 years ago until they were reoccupied in the Late Stone Age after 20,000 years ago and mainly in the last 10,000 years. This demographic pattern reflects population densities that were higher under favorable environmental conditions and much reduced under conditions of aridity.

Sequences are neither as well known nor as accurately dated in other parts of sub-Saharan Africa. As these areas are affected by tropical rather than subtropical regimes, the timing and scale of any population changes due to environmental forcing are not the same as in southern Africa. Having populations distributed between different environmental zones may explain why contemporary African populations show more genetic diversity than populations in other parts of the world.

Diversity is dependent on population size, and until the relatively recent expansion of world populations, more people lived in sub-Saharan Africa than elsewhere. In spite of regional fluctuations, African population densities remained above a critical minimum to retain a measure of diversity. The large sub-Saharan population pool was important in ensuring the survival of humankind in these times.

Middle Stone Age sites are distributed in a wide range of landscapes. The earlier Acheulian sites were concentrated along watercourses and in wetland areas, suggesting adaptation to re-stricted habitat conditions. Sangoan sites, named after typical artifacts originally found at Sango Bay on Lake Victoria, may represent an intermediate stage between the Acheulian and the Middle Stone Age. In addition to more regular flakes, assemblages of Sangoan-type artifacts, including picklike bifaces and core axes, which are thought to be heavy-duty woodworking tools, indicate an adaptation to woodland environments. Sangoan sites have been described in eastern and central Africa, and the Charaman industry (formerly the Proto-Stillbay) in Zimbabwe may be a more southerly expression. The Fauresmith industry, reported in Kenya and South Africa, is suggested as an adaptation to open habitats. This latter industry is noteworthy for small hand axes and cleavers in the Acheulian tradition associated with flake tools similar to those of the Middle Stone Age.

The dating of Sangoan and Fauresmith industries is not exact. For the present, the artifacts from these industries remain poorly defined archaeological entities. A better case can be made for broad regional differentiation of artifact industries in the Middle Stone Age. The evidence, however, indicates broad-spectrum foraging rather than specialization in the resources of either the savanna or woodland. The Middle Stone Age sites have a similar distribution to those of the Late Stone Age, and frequently the same localities were occupied. No longer restricted to limited habitats, foragers used a wide range of resources, and with the passage of time, these resources were used ever more intensively.

Although the artifacts that have survived from earlier time ranges are often limited to imperishable stone artifacts, those from the Middle Stone Age include animal and plant remains. Some Middle Stone Age sites provide direct evidence of the food resources used. One of the best-studied fauna assemblages is from the Klasies River Mouth site on the southernmost coast of the continent. This site is a 20-meter pile of deposits built up against a cliff face and in cave openings in the face. The deposits, which began to accumulate 120,000 years ago, are made up of many layers representing discrete occupations of short duration. The layers contain artifacts with residues of animal bone and shell food. The carbonized surrounds to the hearths in these layers are all that survive of plant foods that were gathered. Coastal resources were important in this region, and the site provides the earliest evidence for the systematic use of seafoods. The inhabitants of this region harvested shellfish along the rocky shore, caught penguins, and dismembered and ate the carcasses of seals, probably washed up from rookeries offshore. Apart from plant foods, the terrestrial resources included large bovids such as eland, buffalo, extinct large buffalo, and medium- and small-sized antelope. Detailed studies of these faunal remains indicate that the animals were obtained by active hunting.

The absence of the remains of fish and less easily caught but common coastal birds, like cormorants, and the higher representation of the prime adults of more docile game animals may indicate that the Middle Stone Age foragers less intensively exploited available food sources than did the most recent foragers living in the same environment. The intensification of foraging activities in later times may have much to do with the progressively degrading environment and increasing numbers of foragers.

Evidence from other sites in this same time range underscores the ability of Middle Stone Age foragers to hunt animals of all body sizes and to adapt to changes in the availability of prey species. At the Florisbad Spring site, north of Bloemfontein, a 90,000-year-old open-air campsite provides evidence of the hunting of plains fauna including zebras, wildebeests, blesbok, and springbok. Evidence also exists for more selective hunting of a blesbok-sized grazer in sites on the Athi Plains outside Nairobi, Kenya, in the same time range. In the Border Cave sequence, the faunal remains are alternatively dominated by plains game and species from woodland habitats.

The small, dry Strathalan Cave, in the foothills of the Drakensberg Mountains of the eastern Cape region of South Africa, provides an opportunity to learn about the plants gathered in Middle Stone Age times. The main edible plants were bulbs and grasses, which were collected and packed as bedding heaps at the back and sides of the cave. In shrub lands and grasslands of the southern continent, plants with underground organs for food storage were the main collectible

plant foods, but in the tropical woodlands farther north, fruiting trees were an important resource.

The collecting of fruits of the marula (Sclerocarya birrea) is well evidenced from sites in the southern tropics. The endocarps (shells) were roasted to remove the embryos (nuts). Such roasting increased the chances of preservation through carbonization. Fruits, when and where available, remain high-quality items in the diets of foragers, and contemporary traditional communities still invest considerable effort in extracting marula embryos.

The equipment to harvest these resources is reflected only in stone artifacts. Rare artifacts in bone or shell and a single example in wood are preserved. Spears, traps, and bark-and-skin containers may have been used. Retouched points, which may have served to tip spears, are more common in artifact assemblages from eastern African than in equivalent assemblages from southern Africa, reflecting the differences in importance of hunting and the relative richness of the large-mammal faunas. Notching on the sides of flakes suggests working hard material like wood for shafts, possibly for digging sticks and spears. Formal scrapers, used in the preparation of skins for garments, are rare or absent, and no elaborate dress styles can be discerned.

The production of very standard flakes and flake blades, 50 millimeters or more in length, often from prepared cores, tends to characterize all Middle Stone Age industries. It was a ready-to-use technology because the effort put into preparing the cores meant that a flake or flakes struck off were of the predetermined proportions. Most types of stone used for cores were hard, and the robust edges did not need strengthening by secondary trimming. Such trimming or retouch was rare, and modification of the edges of the flakes was frequently the result of damage caused by use. Retouch was used to shape some pieces that had a formal design and, notably, points and backed tools.

Points may show fine invasive retouch on one or both faces. The Lupemban industry of the Middle Stone Age in Zaire and surrounding countries includes elongated, thick-sectioned, bifacial points. These are stylistically different from the short, triangular bifacial points from eastern

African sites, which in turn are different from the point forms found in southern Africa.

In southern African sequences, styles of points changed over time. The spatial and temporal patterning of styles of points indicates the existence of regional networks of shared information, in this case of what form a point should take. The inference is that information exchange had become an essential part of the existence of foragers in southern Africa. A cache of points from a small shelter on the Cape peninsula is evidence that some of the points were specially crafted and probably traded. Goods as well as information were exchanged.

The manufacture of backed tools in the Howieson's Poort substage of the Middle Stone Age is another example of the use of retouch for formal designs. The Howieson's Poort industry, named after a small cave near Grahamstown in South Africa, is a distinctive horizon in sites south of the Zambezi River. Dating to some 70,000 years ago with a duration of 10,000 years or more, this industry represents a period when geometrical crescent- and trapeze-shaped tools, blunted on one side with steep retouch, much as on the blade of a penknife, were fashioned. The mean length was 40 millimeters, and the pieces were made to be inserts on shafts. In the Late Stone Age Wilton industries, dating to the last 8,000 years, there are identical tool forms, but about one-third the size.

The Wilton backed tools are thought to be armatures for arrows. The larger Howieson's Poort examples may also have been hunting equipment, possibly for arming spears. The Howieson's Poort industry shows not only an innovation in tool design but also in technology. Some of the flakes are properly considered to be blades, struck from the core by using a punch. The aim appears to have been to produce thin blades as blanks for backed tools. Outside sub-Saharan Africa, backed tools and blade technology become prominent in industries that are perhaps half as old.

At the main Klasies River Mouth site, there is an increase in the use of nonlocal stone for making backed tools. This suggests the tools were given added value through the effort entailed in obtaining exotic materials. A plausible explana-

tion is that these tools were parts of items that were exchanged. Among contemporary Kalahari foragers, hunting equipment is exchanged between males, a form of reciprocity that reduces social tensions, and it is possible that Middle Stone Age peoples practiced similar forms of exchange for the same purpose.

The Howieson's Poort industry was of limited duration. The backed tools are sufficiently elaborate to have played a role beyond simple function and may have been used in social display. That backed tools became redundant may be best explained in social terms—other means for displaying status or carrying social information replaced the tools.

An industry known from the cave of Mumba near Lake Eyasi may be an East African equivalent of the Howieson's Poort. The Mumba Cave site, which may be as early as the southern Africa site, is interesting because there the making of backed tools appears to have continued until the end of the Middle Stone Age. There, in a different social context, backed tools did not become redundant. Mumba also is of interest because it shows some stone for toolmaking was imported from a source more than 300 kilometers away. This is good evidence for extensive social networks. Artifacts like points and backed tools were important in maintaining these networks.

Hearths, common in all well-preserved sequences, show the ability to make fire at will. They take the form of simple ash-filled hollows, 300 millimeters in diameter, and give structure to occupation areas. The presence of burned bone, shells, or carbonized plant remains underscores their primary domestic function. Hearths repeatedly laid in similar positions suggest formal use of space, and the dumps of shells as at the main Klasies River Mouth site show rules of cleanliness were followed. At Strathalan Cave, the hearth area is in the center toward the front of the cave. The sleeping areas are toward the back and against the sides. The organization of space parallels that found at the campsites of contemporary San foragers where each family unit has its own hearth.

There are very few personal ornaments recovered from sites in this time range, although ornaments in shell and bone are abundant in later times. Personal ornamentation, possibly body painting, seems to be indicated in the widespread occurrence of red ochre, with evidence for the mining of the high-grade iron pigment, specularite, in Swaziland. Red ochre is a color symbol in contemporary traditional societies throughout sub-Saharan Africa, and it is reasonable to suggest that ochre had similar symbolic significance in these earlier times. Evidence for symbolism is important because it indicates an ability to communicate abstract ideas.

The human skeletal remains from sites like Mumba, Border Cave, and Klasies River Mouth have been suggested to be morphologically modern. The remains from Klasies River are the best dated, and most come from two layers dating from 90,000 to 120,000 years ago. The bones, mixed with other discarded food waste, are fragmentary. Some are burned, and cut marks and impact fractures are present. This is more consistent with dietary or ritual cannibalism than with a burial practice. Apart from a possible burial at Border Cave, there are no known formal burials in this region older than 20,000 years.

BIBLIOGRAPHY

Allsworth-Jones, P. 1993. The archaeology of archaic and early modern *Homo sapiens:* An African perspective. *Cambridge Archaeological Journal* 3 (1): 21–39.

Clark, J. D. 1992. African and Asian perspectives on the origins of modern humans. *Philosophical Transactions of the Royal Society of London* Series B 337: 201–215.

Deacon, H. J. 1992. Southern Africa and modern human origin. *Philosophical Transactions of the Royal Society of London* Series B 337: 177–183.

Klein, R. G. 1989. *The human career: Human biological and cultural origins.* Chicago: Chicago University Press.

Mehlman, M. J. 1991. Context for the emergence of modern man in eastern Africa: Some new Tanzanian evidence. In *Cultural beginnings: Approaches to understanding early hominid lifeways in the African savanna,* ed. J. D. Clark, 177–196. Mainz: Romisch-Germanisches Zentral-Museum.

Opperman, H., and B. Heydenrych. 1990. A 22,000 year-old Middle Stone Age camp site with plant food remains from the north-eastern Cape, South Africa. *South African Archaeological Bulletin* 45: 93–99.

Phillipson, D. W. 1993. *African archaeology.* Cambridge: Cambridge University Press.

Hilary John Deacon

Advanced Foragers
~~~~~~~~~~~~~~~~~~~~~~

NORTHERN AFRICAN ADVANCED FORAGERS

The later prehistory of Northern Africa (here restricted to the Maghreb—modern Morocco, Algeria, and Tunisia, and the coastal region of Libya called Cyrenaica) is known primarily from a series of blade and bladelet industries (Ibero-maurusian, Oranian, Capsian) and some very interesting subsistence adaptations (intensive hunting of certain ungulates and very heavy use of land snails) that are not yet well understood. Interpretations of the patterns represented have changed over the years, but the basic outline is widely accepted. The northern part of this area (the coast, coastal ranges, and interior plateaus) today falls under a Mediterranean climatic regime (short, cold, wet winters and long, hot, dry summers), and vegetation associations are a complex mix of *Stipa* and *Artemisia* steppe and semidesert, with evergreen oak, pine, and cedar forests at higher elevations and Mediterranean *maquis* (scrubby underbrush) along the coast. The southern area is part of the Sahara. Here the vegetation associations are widely spread (often ephemeral) areas of Cape evergreen trees and *maquis* at higher elevations within a general pattern of desert shrub. The extent to which these modern patterns reflect the Late Pleistocene and Early Holocene vegetation patterns is as yet unresolved, as is the effect of anthropogenic factors (the impact of man on nature) during the past 20,000 years.

The framework for Northern African cultural history during the past 20,000 years is well es-tablished. The sequence begins with the Ibero-maurusian (beginning about 20,000 years ago and ending about 10,000 years ago), a blade and bladelet industry with a predominance of backed artifacts, found primarily at sites (often caves) along the present Mediterranean Coast, although a few late sites are known from the interior plateaus. There is no confirmed connection between the Iberomaurusian and the earlier Aterian, a Middle Paleolithic industry characterized by the use of Levallois technology and the presence of pedunculated (stemmed) lithic artifacts and widespread throughout the region from the Atlantic Coast of Morocco to the Nile Valley. The single possible candidate for continuity is the Dabban, known only from Cyrenaica. In the Early Holocene (about 6,000 to 10,000 years ago), a number of geographically distinct backed-blade and bladelet industries (Capsian, Columnatian, Keremian, Elassolithic, and Libyco-Capsian) appear at sites throughout the region. The best known is the Capsian, with two facies (*typique* and *supérieur,* referred to hereafter as Typical and Upper, respectively). Capsian sites are almost always large middens of land-snail shells (*escargotières),* fire-cracked rock, ash, bone, and lithic artifacts. The Neolithic of Capsian tradition (which flourished from about 6,000 years ago to 4,000 years ago) is characterized primarily by the presence of bifacial points and some pottery. It has much the same distribution as the Capsian and is distinguished from the Mediterranean Neolithic. There is some evidence from Grotte Capéletti (Neolithic of Capsian tradition) for the introduction of domestic ovicaprids (sheep and goats) and, from A. A. Gilman's reanalysis of several Mediterranean Neolithic sites in northern Morocco, for controlled exploitation of suids (wild pigs).

The wealth of data on Iberomaurusian and Capsian artifacts fueled a debate in the 20th century over the origins of the Aurignacian industry and the relationship between European and North African prehistoric sequences. Development of radiometric dating and a sophisticated typological scheme for comparing assemblages of lithic artifacts put an end to the debate and made it possible to develop syntheses and space-time models and to investigate hypotheses of origins and relationships between industries. Reconstructions of paleo-environments, diet, settlement patterns, and variation within sites are still uncommon.

The Iberomaurusian Industry

Although the Iberomaurusian industry appears to have no connection to the earlier Aterian, there are strong similarities to slightly earlier as well as contemporaneous industries in the Nile Valley. Iberomaurusian assemblages are characterized by very high percentages of backed bladelets. While there is geographical variation (hence the use of the terms *Oranian* and *Eastern Oranian* for some Iberomaurusian assemblages), the data from two stratified sequences suggest very long-term continuity of occupation. At Tamar Hat in Algeria and Haua Fteah in Cyrenaica, where the relevant deposits span periods of about 5,000 years, there is evidence for both technological and stylistic continuity in the lithic artifacts.

The Iberomaurusian system of subsistence and settlement has been a matter of debate. It is unclear whether or not sites were occupied seasonally or year-round (the latter is perhaps more likely given the evidence from oxygen-isotope analyses of marine shells and the continuity in the lithic assemblages). Although E. C. Saxon and colleagues interpreted the evidence from Tamar Hat as indicating the herding of Barbary sheep, reinterpretations of the data all posit specialized hunting. It is also interesting that land snails are actually the most numerous faunal element at Tamar Hat, suggesting perhaps some continuity in basic subsistence practices with the succeeding Capsian.

The Capsian Industry

Three questions have dominated the study of the post-Iberomaurusian prehistory of the Maghreb:

1. What is the origin of the Capsian?
2. What is the relationship between the Capsian and contemporaneous industries to the west and east of its main distribution?
3. What is the meaning of assemblage variation in the Capsian as expressed by the two facies, *typique* and *supèrieur?*

Diffusion and migration have traditionally been used to explain change in the Maghreb, but the data now available suggest that the change from Iberomaurusian to Capsian is better explained by local continuity and adaptation.

Human skeletal data provide the primary evidence suggesting migration and population replacement or assimilation. Such data have been used to construct typologies and to argue that the Capsian culture was introduced from the east by new populations belonging to a robust proto-Mediterranean type, which supposedly differed from the Mechta-Afalou type (an anatomically modern *Homo sapiens sapiens)* associated with the Iberomaurusian. However, analysis of the published data suggests that:

1. There is no basis for creating types based on a sample of 68 skulls from 90,000 square kilometers and scattered over 16,000 years, when there is considerable heterogeneity within samples.
2. Capsian and Iberomaurusian females can not be distinguished from each other.
3. The present pattern can be explained by a decrease in sexual dimorphism (physical differences between the sexes) from the Iberomaurusian to the Capsian combined with increasing geographical isolation and reduced gene flow during the Early Holocene.

The other lines of evidence that could be used to argue for the introduction of the Capsian from the east and a major break in continuity from the Iberomaurusian are: chronology, spatial distribution, technological change, and similarities with industries to the east.

The youngest Iberomaurusian dates overlap the oldest Capsian dates, and it has been argued that there was interaction between Iberomaurusian and Capsian groups.

The Iberomaurusian and Capsian are now known to have overlapping spatial distributions. Late Iberomaurusian sites have been found inland, and while the archaeological record in the interior for the period from 10,000 to 20,000 years ago may have been largely destroyed by erosion, it could equally be argued that cold and arid conditions there were inhospitable to hunter-foragers. There is debate over the nature of the Early Holocene climate of the Maghreb, but there seems to be little doubt that climatic conditions generally improved to some extent north of the Sahara during this time. At the end of the Last Glacial Maximum, as sea levels rose and reduced the area of the coastal plain, populations may have moved inland to increasingly hospitable areas.

The Capsian industry has traditionally been viewed as an introduced technology. However, there is evidence for continuity between late Iberomaurusian and early Capsian assemblages. Chronological seriation suggests a decrease in the number of backed bladelets in the late Iberomaurusian (especially at inland sites) and an increase in the number of geometrics, burins (graving tools), notches, and denticulates (retouched tools with jagged toothlike edges). These trends give a general configuration to the late Iberomaurusian reminiscent of the early Capsian, and late Iberomaurusian geometrics, although few in number, tend to be segments similar to those dominating early Capsian assemblages. There is little difference between the blade and bladelet technology of the Iberomaurusian and early Capsian. Change in the Capsian occurred after 8,000 years ago, at which time finely made, thin, parallel-sided bladelets were used in the manufacture of backed bladelets and geometrics. This later industry looks very different from the Iberomaurusian. However, before 8,000 years ago, Capsian geometrics and backed bladelets are made from thicker, less-standardized blanks, unidirectional retouch is more common, and the gen-

eral character of the industry is much more like the Iberomaurusian. The one major difference between the late Iberomaurusian and early Capsian is the predominance of blades in the early Capsian of the Tébessa-Gafsa region, but this is better explained by the abundance of large flint nodules in that area compared to the more limited lithic resources of the coast and the Constantine Plain.

If the Capsian derived from the east, one would expect to see similar assemblages in that region. Ideally, comparison between Maghreb assemblages and others from the postulated source region should be based on stylistic attributes. A. Close has suggested limited stylistic similarities between the Iberomaurusian, the Eastern Oranian, the Libyco-Capsian, and a number of industries from the Nile Valley, most of which date to before 10,000 years ago. Close notes a strong continuity between the Libyco-Capsian and Eastern Oranian at Haua Fteah, implying local development, and has suggested closer correspondence between the Libyco-Capsian and Algerian Iberomaurusian than between Libyco-Capsian and the Capsian. P. J. Sheppard has also shown little stylistic similarity between the Libyco-Capsian and Maghreb Capsian industries. The only Nilotic assemblages to have been described as similar to the Capsian are the Shamarkian and the Arkinian. However, both are at best contemporaneous if not younger than the earliest Capsian, making them unlikely candidates for a precursor. At present, there is no evidence supporting the development or derivation of the Capsian from outside the Maghreb.

With the emphasis on typology, chronology, and possible source regions, little attention was given to understanding the unique Capsian system of subsistence and settlement. Innovative work in the 1930s was almost completely ignored until the 1970s when several projects began to investigate the Capsian system. The animal protein component of the Capsian diet was provided by collection of several species of land snails and the hunting or trapping of a variety of mammals including rabbits, gazelles, hartebeests, zebras, and wild cattle. Land-snail shells are the most visible element in most Capsian sites, thus their designation as *escargotières*. Calculations have shown that it is unlikely that land snails actually contributed the bulk of the animal protein in the Capsian diet and, furthermore, that gathered plant foods (nuts, fruits, and perhaps wild cereals—but this is much more problematic) must have been important. Land snails would only have been safe to eat during spring and autumn when they were not aestivating (passing the summer in a torpid state), and it therefore seems likely that the majority of Capsian sites represent short-term seasonal camps, most probably on a transhumant (seasonal) route between winter ranges in the northern Sahara and summer occupations in the cooler plateaus of eastern Algerian and southern Tunisia.

In summary, the various lines of evidence used to argue for derivation of the Capsian from the east suggest continuity between the Iberomaurusian and Capsian. In the Early Holocene, as Iberomaurusian populations moved inland to take advantage of improved climatic conditions, they brought with them a knowledge of how to exploit a diversity of resources (some of which—for example, land snails—they had long used for food), and an adaptive divergence occurred resulting in interregional variability.

Eastern and Western Traditions

If we accept the argument for local continuity from the Late Pleistocene through the Early Holocene, we must explain the development of a relatively large number of industries defined for the Early Holocene (Typical and Upper Capsian, Columnatian, Keremian, and Elassolithic). It is possible to group the five industries into two major regional traditions: Eastern and Western. The divergence of these industries was a result of relative geographic isolation and a history of development from regional Iberomaurusian populations who had slightly dissimilar lithic and bone industries. These earlier differences were amplified by the effects of increased isolation and adaptations to new local conditions. The transition zone between this east-west continuum was in the western part of the Constantine High Plains, southwest of Constantine. Movement between these zones was also constrained by the Saharan Atlas, the desert south of the Hodna Basin, and the broken uplands of western Algeria.

The Western Tradition includes the Columnatian, Keremian, and Elassolithic. Although each has distinctive characteristics, the traditions also have a number of traits in common: microbladelets and very small tools made with them, geometrics dominated by segments, trapezes with three retouched sides, microsegments, oblique bevel-edged bone knives (found also in the Iberomaurusian), and high frequencies of endscrapers.

The Eastern Tradition includes Typical and Upper Capsian, which coexisted in the eastern region. Differences between these industries are found primarily in the frequencies of tool types. Examination of roughly contemporary assemblages from geographically restricted areas has shown that there is little stylistic difference between the two industries suggesting activity rather than ethnic distinctions. The major difference between the Western and Eastern Traditions is found in the abundance of geometric forms (primarily triangles before 8,000 years ago) in the east. Another distinction is found in the abundance of endscrapers in the Keremian versus burins in the Typical Capsian. These edge tools were most likely used in manufacturing tasks, suggesting the hypothesis of similar activity-related facies in each region using different tool forms.

The divergence of the Eastern and Western Traditions is related to (1) relative geographic isolation, (2) development from distinct Iberomaurusian traditions, and (3) adaption to local conditions. It is generally agreed that many of the industries grouped in the Western Tradition are related in some way to the Iberomaurusian. Continuity with the Iberomaurusian in the west is shown by the presence of the oblique bevel-edged bone knife in both Western Iberomaurusian (to which it is restricted) and the Western Tradition. In the east, geometric forms (triangles and scalene-backed bladelets) are much more common in the late Iberomaurusian, and we suggest that the importance of geometrics in the Eastern Tradition relates to its history of development from Eastern Iberomaurusian and the Iberomaurusian-like industries diverging from the Western Iberomaurusian during the Late Pleistocene and Early Holocene.

Technological Change in the Eastern Tradition

Traditionally, the Capsian has been divided into Typical and Upper Capsian *(Capsien typique* and *Capsien supérieur).* Since this division reflects important variation in tool frequencies related to activity variation, it should be retained as a facies difference in the Eastern Tradition. In addition, we see a phase distinction based on technological change. Using a metrical analysis of a number of assemblages with long sequences, Sheppard has demonstrated a change in blank production sometime between 7,600 and 8,000 years ago. Bladelets produced after the technological change are thinner and narrower with parallel sides and are generally much more standardized in form. These blanks are struck from conical cores often with a fluted *(cannelé)* core face produced by the removal of a series of standardized bladelets. It is possible that this technological change involved the use of a pressure technique.

The effect of this development in blank production is seen in a dramatic improvement in the standardization of geometric and backed-bladelet forms, an increase in the quantity of trapezes, and the development of elongated scalene triangles. Once this new technique was developed, it appears to have rapidly spread throughout both the Eastern and Western Traditions, and we have argued that this is responsible for the development of apparent homogeneity across the region as has been noted by G. Camps. It is possible that this event also occurred during a period of increased aridity when interregional contact may have intensified as a result of a widening of social networks by hunter-foragers attempting to cope with increased environmental stress. Examination of this hypothesis using what are apparently "stylistic" attributes has shown, however, increased intersite variability at this time. Therefore, although at a technological level there is definite increase in similarity throughout the eastern Maghreb (Tunisia and Algeria), at the stylistic level there is apparently increased social differentiation (that is, stylistic heterogeneity). At this time, it is not possible to state whether this is related to increasing isolation of social units in areas of higher resource productivity or to a de-velopment of ethnicity as a means of formalizing contacts between regions. Postglacial climatic change may have promoted the formation of "no-man's lands" or zones of comparative environmental richness. These zones were still large enough to support a viable risk-minimizing population (one large enough to maintain an effective social safety net). Physiography and climate may need to be combined to predict the social landscape of prehistory. Unfortunately, the available data are still insufficient for a full investigation, but these are certainly hypotheses that warrant further investigation.

BIBLIOGRAPHY

Balout, L. 1955. *Préhistoire de l'Afrique du nord.* Paris: Arts et Métiers Graphiques.

Camps, G. 1974. *Les civilisations préhistoriques de l'Afrique du nord et du Sahara.* Paris: Doin.

Close, A. 1980–1981. The Iberomaurusian sequence at Tamar Hat. *Libyca* 28–29: 69–104.

————. 1986. The place of the Haua Fteah in the Late Palaeolithic of North Africa. In *Stone Age prehistory,* eds. G. N. Bailey and P. Callow, 169–180. Cambridge: Cambridge University Press.

Close, A., and F. Wendorf. 1990. North Africa at 18,000 BP. In *The world at 18,000 b.p.,* eds. O. Soffer and C. Gamble, 41-57. London: Unwin Hyman.

Lubell, D. 1992. Following Alonzo's trail: Paleoeconomic research in Algeria since 1930. In *Alonzo Pond and the Logan Museum Expedition to North Africa: The 1985 Beloit College Symposium,* ed. L. B. Breitborde. *Logan Museum Bulletin 1* (1): 49–57.

Lubell, D. , P. Sheppard, and A. Gilman. 1992. The Maghreb: 20,000 to 4,000 B.P. In *Chronologies in Old World archaeology,* 3d ed., ed. R. W. Ehrich, vol. 1, 305–308, and vol. 2, 257–267. Chicago: University of Chicago Press.

Lubell, D., P. J. Sheppard, and M. Jackes. 1984. Continuity in the Epipaleolithic of Northern Africa with emphasis on the Maghreb. *Advances in World Archaeology* 3: 143–191.

McBurney, C. B. M. 1967. *The Haua Fteah Cyrenaica and the Stone Age of the South-East Mediterranean.* Cambridge: Cambridge University Press.

Roubet, C. 1979. *Economie pastorale pré-agricole en Algérie orientale: Le Néolithique de tradition Capsienne, exemple de l'aurès.* Paris: Centre National de la Recherche Scientifique.

Sheppard, P. J. 1987. *The Capsian of North Africa: Stylistic variation in stone tool assemblages.* B.A.R. International Series. No. 353. Oxford: British Archaeological Reports.

Sheppard, P. J., and D. Lubell. 1990. Early Holocene Maghreb prehistory: An evolutionary approach. *Sahara* 3: 63–69.

David Lubell and Peter J. Sheppard

WESTERN AFRICAN AND SOUTHERN SAHARAN ADVANCED FORAGERS

The Stone Age record of western Africa has long remained a poor relation to those of southern, eastern, and northern Africa. This is not due to a paucity of early hominid or later human activity in the area, but rather to a comparative scarcity of un-reworked Pleistocene sediment outcrops and adequate research programs in the region. Stone Age studies in western Africa have long been hampered by a plenitude of poorly provenanced surface collections of larger artifact types (for example, picks and cleavers), hastily classified on the basis of typology into an idealized schema of cultural succession. The excavation and dating of *in situ* Pleistocene assemblages have remained rare. Organic materials associated with industries predating the Late Stone Age are virtually unrecorded. This is not to say, however, that sufficient well-provenanced artifacts to trace an outline of Stone Age technological developments in western Africa are lacking.

Unfortunately, the chronological control of Pleistocene contexts in western Africa also remains a consistent difficulty. Organic remains and campsites, with their associated hearths, are virtually absent. Industries have thus often been tied in with better-dated "relations" elsewhere in Africa, perhaps obscuring regional differences. Alternatively, artifacts have been tied into hypothetically or relatively dated geological successions that offer no concrete comparison to sequences elsewhere in the late Pleistocene. Radiocarbon dating has been of some assistance,

although on some occasions, dates for industries seem far too recent when compared to dates for similar industries elsewhere in Africa. Thus, the dating of the western African Stone Age industries presented here is often very tentative.

The Acheulian Industry

The Acheulian industry is best known in western Africa from the southern edge of the Sahara. There, surface finds of hand axes are common, and a few *in situ* cultural accumulations are known. One such site, Lagereich (located roughly 100 kilometers northeast of Gao and the Niger Bend), has been dated using the thermo-luminescence technique on two burned flint bifaces, with a resulting possible age range of 226,000 to 338,000 years. This range agrees well with P. Allsworth-Jones's typologically derived attribution of "Late Middle Acheulian" for this site. Other major occurrences in the southern Sahara rely entirely on typology of hand-ax forms for their "dating." The most important of these include the Blaka Kallia workshop site of eastern Niger (Middle Acheulian), several lake bed scatters in the El Beyed Basin of southern Mauritania (mostly Evolved or Late Acheulian), and various concentrations of Evolved Acheulian in the Malian Sahara from the region of Foum el Alba to the Taoudenni Basin. The dominant tool types at all of these sites are bifaces, with varying quantities of cleavers, choppers, and retouched flakes. The Evolved Acheulian sites of the Malian Sahara are particularly notable for the small size of their bifaces, between 60 and 140 millimeters long. None of these sites had associated organic remains, but all seem to have been situated on the shores or within the catchments of substantial freshwater bodies.

In the modern savanna and forest belts, the Acheulian industry is comparatively scarce. There are only a few universally recognized assemblages, all of which are likely to have been deposited by sheet-wash erosion onto river terraces. One such locality, the Sansandé terrace above the Faleme River in eastern Senegal, has been shown, by A. Camara and B. Duboscq, to have a biface and cleaver industry associated with two definite Levallois cores and a number of

Levallois flakes. If one is optimistic, this may be seen as a Final Acheulian or a transitional industry. Alternatively, it may be viewed as yet another sequence from tropical Africa reworked by later hydrological activity. A similar juxtaposition of typical Early Stone Age and Middle Stone Age technologies comes from the site of Pingell in the Jos Plateau of Nigeria, where Levallois materials have been shown to be in a less-abraded state than associated hand axes and cleavers. None of the sub-Saharan sites has any definite chronological markers, although a rough date of from 180,000 to 250,000 years ago has been suggested for Sansandé on the basis of correlations between down-cutting episodes on the terrace and the marine oxygen-isotope sequence.

The Sangoan-Lupemban Techno-Complex in West Africa

The presence of the vexing Sangoan-Lupemban techno-complex in western Africa has long been the subject of debate. Numerous finds of large picks and lanceolates (lancelike blades with tapering points) during the colonial era are now known to be of Holocene age, and thus the number of "true" Sangoan-Lupemban finds has been greatly reduced. The Sangoan industry, first known from Uganda, was initially considered part of the now dismissed First Intermediate Period (between the Early and Middle Stone Ages) and conceived of as a "forest-adapted" contemporary of the Fauresmith or Evolved Acheulian. In recent years, the Sangoan's initial ill-definition and evidence for technological continuity with subsequent industries have led to its amalgamation at a techno-complex level with the "later" Lupemban industry (often distinguished by the presence of lanceolates). Temporally, this techno-complex may still be seen as a "transitional" Early Stone Age to Middle Stone Age industry, but its continuance in some parts of central Africa into the end of the Pleistocene makes the assignment of any specific time range to the Sangoan-Lupemban difficult.

In western Africa, the Sangoan-Lupemban is best documented from the sites of Asokrochona and Tema-West in southern Ghana. Located on a rise between the Mokwe and Sakumo Lagoons,

the Asokrochona locality was first discovered in the 1950s during the cutting of a railway line. Other localities having the same geological succession as Asokrochona have subsequently been found in other estuary areas to the east and west, between Accra and Kpone. From the lower-most Asokrochona formations, an industry with predominantly of light-duty tools (composing between 40 and 60 percent of the assemblage and including scrapers, "knives," and notches) and with smaller, if significant, quantities of heavy-duty tools (composing between 20 and 40 percent and including picks, bifaces, core axes, and choppers) have been excavated from a series of large exposures made behind the cutting. Above the Asokrochona formation lies the Nungua formation, which presents evidence of a more "developed" Asokrochona industry featuring smaller tool forms, more often made from flakes than from cores, imported chert raw materials, and possible Levallois flakes and cores. Characteristically for "true" western African Sangoan-Lupemban sites, no lanceolates are known from either assemblage. Sites within the formations appear to be *in situ* workshop concentrations, with unweathered lithic assemblages and in close proximity to raw-material sources. No traces of structures, hearths, or organic materials have been found. The materials from both formations have been attributed to a local industry of the Sangoan-Lupemban techno-complex, the Asokrochona industry.

The earlier assemblage appears in the upper part of the Asokrochona formation at the top of degraded lateritic (decayed rock with a high iron content) gravel beds. The transition of these gravel beds to the overlying sands of the Nungua formation is thought to be a demarcation between more humid environmental conditions with dense vegetation cover (under which laterite beds form) and a more arid period characterized by erosion and a build-up of aeolian (wind-blown) sand. While neither of these formations has been directly dated, the Nungua formation is thought to represent a Late Pleistocene arid phase, and the Asokrochona formation is attributed to an earlier humid phase. The change in the Asokrochona and Nungua assemblages—a decline of heavy duty tools, a rise in prepared-core flake technology, and the introduction of exotic raw materials—

may thus be partially attributable to a more open landscape with greater group mobility.

Other promising Sangoan-Lupemban localities are known, particularly from Ivory Coast. However, the importance of these industries to African Stone Age archaeology in a broader sense will only be considerably enhanced when they are absolutely dated or organic remains are recovered.

Flake Industries Featuring Levallois Technique: The Middle Stone Age

The Middle Stone Age industries of western Africa have a great deal more in common with the Middle Palaeolithic of northern Africa than the Middle Stone Age of southern Africa. "True" Levallois cores, flakes, and points are common in the Middle Stone Age industries of tropical western Africa, in contrast to those of southern Africa. Additionally, the distinctive Aterian industry of northern Africa has some of its most important sites in northern Mali and Niger. Interestingly, later elements—including ephemeral, non-Levallois prepared-core industries of the end of the Pleistocene and the aforementioned Sangoan-Lupemban techno-complex—are idiosyncratic or more typically sub-Saharan.

As in other periods, some of the best-dated Middle Stone Age material in western Africa comes from the southern Sahara. The chronologically contentious Aterian industry would appear to be distributed only as far south as the edge of the modern Sahara, despite occasional reports of tanged artifacts resembling Aterian ones in the savanna-forest belt. The Aterian localities in Mali, Niger, and Mauritania have no claim on typological or other grounds to an early date. However, they may be among the most recent occurrences of this industry. In particular, Evolved or Upper Aterian industries featuring bifacially retouched pieces are common in the region. Francophone researchers have traditionally claimed a rather recent denouement for the Aterian, positing Aterian refuges in the Saharan Highlands as recently as 20,000 years ago. Indeed, in the Taoudenni Basin, Upper Aterian assemblages have been found associated with a lacustrine event whose carbonates have been dated to as recent as approximately 21,000 years ago, and in the Air Massif of Niger, a travertine (layered calcium carbonate) overlying an Aterian assemblage has been dated to about 18,600 years ago. F. Wendorf and R. Schild have attempted to push back the date for the end of the Aterian to 40,000 years ago or even 70,000 years ago on the basis of the Bir Tarfawi and Bir Sahara East sequences of the Egyptian desert and a recent uranium-series dating program on Saharan paleolakes. Their findings would indicate a permanently arid Sahara between 12,000 and 70,000 years ago incapable of supporting human life. However, other researchers disagree, noting secure dates for Saharan lacustrine events at 60,000 years ago and between 20,000 and 40,000 years ago. They argue that such a long arid period is not in keeping with climatic variability during that same period in Europe.

South of the Sahara, the Middle Stone Age of western African is best represented by assemblages made on igneous materials from the Jos Plateau of Nigeria and from northern Cameroon. There, the Mai Lumba facies, characterized by a high Levallois index and a frequent incidence (around 50 percent of the assemblage) of flakes with dihedral (angle formed by two intersecting planes) or faceted striking platforms, has been defined by Allsworth-Jones. Artifacts from Mai Lumba (Nigeria) and Mayo Louti (Cameroon), the best-documented sites of this expression, both appear to derive from lateritic gravels, making their association with a dry phase likely. A minimum age for the facies is provided by a radiocarbon date of 15,320 years ago from calcareous (chalky) nodules overlying the artifact-bearing gravels at Mayo Louti.

Another facies, perhaps temporally distinct from that of Mai Lumba, is known from the Jos Plateau. This is the Zenabi expression, itself characterized by a lower Levallois index, greater amounts of side scrapers, and a predominance of plain striking platforms on flakes. The two type sites, Zenabi and Tibchi, are poorly dated. A radiocarbon date of 5,440 (±1,110) years ago on a log associated with the older tin- (and artifact-) bearing alluvium at Zenabi appears to demonstrate that these materials had been redeposited during the Holocene wet phase.

Other Middle Stone Age assemblages from western Africa tend to be more diffuse and poorly provenanced than those mentioned. Exceptions are the Mousteroid and Tiémassassian industries of Senegal, which appear on geological grounds to predate 30,000 years ago. Unfortunately, they are largely unpublished.

Microlithic and Macrolithic Industries: The Beginnings of the Late Stone Age

It is becoming increasingly evident that the later Pleistocene of sub-Saharan western Africa witnessed a great diversity of lithic industries. In addition to potential late or remnant Mousteroid industries, there are precocious microlithic industries and ambiguous macrolithic industries. In the southern Sahara, things are more straightforward. The universally agreed upon period of extreme aridity 12,000 to 20,000 years ago seems to have cleared the region of human occupation, thus excluding Late Stone Age industries from the Sahara until the threshold of the Holocene.

At the end of the Pleistocene in the southern Sahara, there are consistent, if sparse, indications of a preceramic Epi-Paleolithic industry dating from the onset of the postglacial wet phase (about 10,000 to 12,000 years ago). Most of these occurrences have been placed within the overarching Ounanian industry, characterized by the presence of shouldered or tanged points made on blades (Ounanian points) and an accompanying nongeometric blade-based assemblage. The primary distribution of these sites falls within the Sahara of Mali, Mauritania, and Niger. Recently, the Epi-Paleolithic nature of this industry has been questioned by J. P. Roset, who has found composite lakeshore assemblages of geometric microliths, Ounanian points, and ceramics dating to about 8,500 to 9,500 years ago beside the Air Massif of Niger. Andrew Smith has defended the preceramic Epi-Paleolithic nature of the Ounanian industry by positing a process of deposition, deflation, and subsequent deposition to account for this technological "mixing." Interestingly, contemporaneous early ceramic sites in the Air region, such as Tagalagal, lack Ounanian elements entirely. If the Ounanian indeed lacked ceramics and if it dates to earlier than the lacustrine phase after 10,000 years ago, then it may be taken to represent the initial recolonization of the Sahara by arid-adapted foragers already living at its margins around 12,000 years ago.

In sub-Saharan western Africa, ceramics appear widely after 6,000 years ago. Before this time, a variety of microlithic and macrolithic industries appear to have coexisted. Broadly speaking, the savanna-forest zone seems to have contained microlithic and mixed microlithic-macrolithic industries, while the later Pleistocene Sahel displays traces of unique macroflake and prepared-core industries.

The industries at the end of the Pleistocene in the Sahel of western Africa are typified by large, plain platform flakes and flake blades (between 40 and 160 millimeters long and between 80 and 160 millimeters wide), occasional prepared-core flakes (which seem "Levallois" but appear to have been struck from non-Levallois cores), and a tool kit consisting of large single- and double-sided scrapers and denticulates. Sites that may be attributed to this unnamed techno-complex include Sirakoro-Ancien and Zampia-North (Mali), Badoye (Senegal), and the quartzite industries of the Central African Republic. The site of Sirakoro-Ancien features large knapping-workshop concentrations and four laterite (decayed rock) cobble rings, which appear to be the foundation of windbreaks or huts. In the absence of organic remains, a date later than 14,000 years ago has been attributed to this site, as it rests atop a stabilized Ogolian red dune from the extremely arid period of 13,000 to 20,000 years ago.

In the savanna and forest, preceramic microlithic industries, characterized by tools made of quartz, are known from several well-documented sites. The only dated open-air site is that of Bingerville Highway (Ivory Coast), where a nongeometric industry has been dated to about 13,050 years ago on associated charcoal. Rockshelter sites at Bosumpra (Ghana) and Korounkorokalé (Mali) possess early Holocene preceramic microlithic phases, and the rock shelters at Iwo Eleru (Nigeria) provide evidence of a geometric microlithic industry (with triangles and backed blades) dating to about 11,200 years ago on associated charcoal. The Iwo Eleru sequence has long remained one of the best in western Africa. It includes the earliest human remains from sub-Saharan western Africa (dating to around 11,000 to 12,000 years ago) and a 12,000-year occupational sequence. However, it lacks good faunal and floral preservation and pre-Holocene deposits, both of which may be found at the recently excavated rock shelter of Shum Laka in Cameroon.

Data from the unique Shum Laka sequence have only been partially published, but the initial results are tantalizing. Below a ceramic-bearing upper ash member is a horizon containing four inhumations (burials) dating to nearly 7,000 years ago and a 2-meter-thick lower member dating to nearly 30,000 years ago. The lower member contains a sequence of at least three microlithic quartz industries, now placed among the earliest in Africa. The orange horizon contains both microlithic quartz and macrolithic basalt elements (including large blades and bifacially retouched pieces), while in the upper ash member, the basalt implements increase in number relative to the quartz microliths and feature some "Levallois" tendencies. This curious microlithic-macrolithic combination has also been documented in Holocene contexts at Mbi Crater and Abéké (Cameroon). Faunal and floral preservation at the site is comparatively good, and the results of recent faunal and floral analyses are eagerly awaited. Earlier analyses of the upper ash member and horizon with inhumations showed a forest fauna dominated by giant forest hogs, dwarf forest buffalo, and duikers. This projected forest environment is surprising given the site's grassland location today, and future studies may provide more important evidence on the economy of early African forest dwellers.

Some unmixed macrolithic occurrences in the savanna and forest, generally core-tool (ax) workshop concentrations, were originally thought to be Sangoan or Middle Stone Age. They are now known to be very recent and associated with the ceramic Late Stone Age–Neolithic of nearly 2,000 to 3,000 years ago. Whether the ax preforms found at these sites were subsequently polished or used unpolished is not yet entirely clear. Such sites include Manianbougou (Mali), Maroua-CFDT (Cameroon), Rim factory and quarry sites (Burkina Faso), Cap Manuel (Senegal), and Blandé rock shelter (Guinea).

BIBLIOGRAPHY

Allsworth-Jones, P. 1986. Middle Stone Age and Middle Palaeolithic: The evidence from Nigeria and Cameroun. In *Stone Age prehistory: Studies in memory of Charles McBurney,* eds. G. N. Bailey and P. Callow, 153–168. Cambridge: Cambridge University Press.

————. 1987. The earliest human settlement in West Africa and the Sahara. *West African Journal of Archaeology* 17: 87–129.

Chenorkian, R. 1983. Ivory Coast prehistory: Recent developments. *African Archaeological Review* 1: 127–142.

de Maret, P., R. Asombang, E. Cornelissen, P. Lavachery, and J. Moeyersons. 1995. Continuing research at Shum Laka rock shelter, Cameroun, 1993–1994 field season. *Nyame Akuma* 43: 2-3.

de Maret, P., B. Clist, and W. Van Neer. 1987. Résultats des premières fouilles dans l'abris de Shum Laka et d'Abéké au nord-ouest du Cameroun. *L'Anthropologie* 91: 559–584.

MacDonald, K. C., and P. Allsworth-Jones. 1994. A reconsideration of the West African macrolithic conundrum: New factory sites and an associated settlement in the Vallée du Serpent, Mali. *African Archaeological Review* 12: 73–104.

Nygaard, S. E., and M. Talbot. 1984. Stone Age archaeology and environment on the southern Accra Plains, Ghana. *Norwegian Archaeological Review* 17: 19–38.

Raimbault, M. 1988. Pour une approche du Paléolithique du Sahara Malien. *Travaux du LAPMO* (1988): 57–88.

Shaw, T., and S. G. H. Daniels. 1984. Excavations at Iwo Eleru, Ondo State, Nigeria. *West African Journal of Archaeology* 14: 1-269.

Smith, A. B. 1993. Terminal Palaeolithic industries of the Sahara: A discussion of new data. In *Environmental change and human culture in the Nile Basin and northern Africa until the second millennium B.C.,* eds. L. Krzyzaniak, M. Kobusiewicz, and J. Alexander, 69–75. Poznan: Poznan Archaeological Museum.

Wendorf, F., and R. Schild. 1992. The Middle Palaeolithic of North Africa: A status report. In *New light on the Northeast African past,* eds. F. Klees and R. Kuper, 39–78. Koln: Heinrich-Barth-Institut.

Kevin MacDonald

EASTERN AFRICAN ADVANCED FORAGERS

The hunting and foraging peoples who lived in eastern Africa between approximately 4,500 and 35,000 years ago, during the main part of the Late Stone Age, were anatomically modern humans *(Homo sapiens sapiens)* with fully developed language and behavioral capabilities. Although there are significant gaps in the record during this time span, there are some very informative archaeological sequences available, especially at key rock shelters.

Some of the better-known rock shelters or caves include Nasera in northern Tanzania, Munyama Cave in Uganda, Matupi Cave in eastern Zaire, the Lukenya Hill shelters southeast of Nairobi in Kenya, and Enkapune ya Muto, or Twilight Cave, on the Mau Escarpment in Kenya. Further afield from the equatorial region, there are shelters such Gogoshiis Qabe in southern Somalia and Nachikufu Cave in Zambia. Some of these shelters are deeply stratified with Late Stone Age deposits overlying Middle Stone Age levels. Although these sites contain long sequences of occupation, the majority of them were probably occupied on a repeated basis for short-term or seasonal visits. The occupation layers reflect the activities of relatively small groups of people who periodically moved about the landscape in response to the availability of food resources and water and possibly for social factors.

In addition to the shelters, there are well-known open-air sites that have been excavated, including some extensive freshwater fishing settlements such as Lothagam and Lowasera, both situated along the Early Holocene beaches of Lake Turkana in northwestern Kenya. Some of the fishing settlements are quite large and may indicate longer-term or more sedentary occupations where people relied on a relatively stable food supply. Smaller open-air sites that indicate very brief occupations are also known.

Comparative studies of the artifacts from the different sites, especially the rock shelters, have led to the recognition of a number of distinctive eastern African Late Stone Age traditions, or industries, such as the Nachikufan of Zambia, the Naseran and Lemutan of northern Tanzania, the Eburran of Kenya (formerly known as the Kenya Capstan), and the Doian/Eibian and Bardaale from Somalia. Each industry has its own set of characteristic tools and specific time span.

The archaeological record of eastern Africa for the period under review is marked by some very significant changes, such as the widespread use of the bow and arrow, along with evidence of numerous well-made bone tools such as spear points and barbed harpoon points. Other notable characteristics include extensive use of ostrich-eggshell beads that were worn as necklaces, intentional burial of the dead, and rock paintings of animals. These very first rock paintings and burials known in eastern Africa provide the first definite signs of ritual in the region. The earliest clay pottery also appears between approximately 6,000 and 8,000 years ago, but it is generally concentrated in the Lake Turkana Basin and farther to the north along the Middle Nile Valley.

Paleo-environmental Changes

Studies of sediments, pollen, lake deposits, and faunal remains have demonstrated that the period between approximately 4,500 and 35,000 years ago was marked by substantial paleo-environmental changes. Fossil pollen recovered from Burundi reveals that it was about 2° to 6° C. cooler during the last part of the Pleistocene, between 13,000 and 30,000 years ago. During the coolest periods, the tree lines on the higher eastern African mountains were between 1,000 and 1,500 meters lower. During the maximum extent of the European ice sheets 18,000 years ago, conditions were exceptionally arid in eastern Africa. In fact, late in the Pleistocene, conditions were so dry that the water level of Lake Victoria, the major source of the White Nile, became so low that there was no overflow into the Nile. When this happened, the tropical forests that had thrived around the lake were replaced by grasslands.

In contrast, the Early Holocene, between approximately 8,000 and 10,000 years ago, was exceptionally wet due to increased precipitation. As a result, the Rift Valley lakes were considerably larger than they are at present. The physical evidence for the large lakes is very compelling.

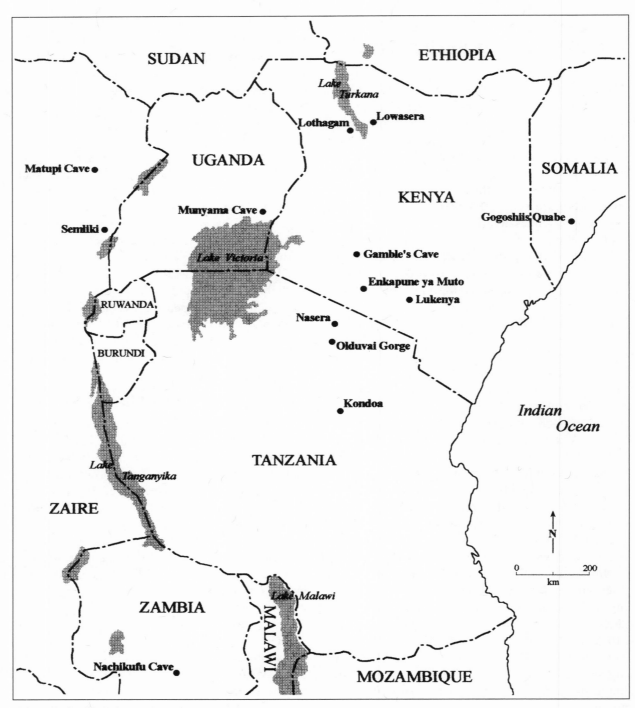

Fig. 31 *Distribution of Late Stone Age sites in eastern Africa*

In the Lake Turkana desert, there are vast exposures of ancient lake beds and beach ridges rich in fossil mollusks and fish bones, as well as artifacts, located between approximately 11 to 16 kilometers to the west of the current lakeshore.

These beds were deposited when the water in the lake rose to a height above 80 meters. The lake overflowed and was, at that time, another source of the White Nile. To the south in the Kenya Rift Valley, Lakes Nakuru and Elmenteita overflowed and became a single large lake, while Lake Naivasha doubled in size.

Late Stone Age People

Who were the Late Stone Age people living in eastern Africa before the arrival of Early Iron Age Bantu-speaking peoples? Early claims by L. S. B. Leakey that Caucasoid peoples once lived in eastern Africa have been shown to be wrong. It has been demonstrated that the early eastern Africans of Late Stone Age times were Negroids who probably would have physically resembled peoples living in the southern Sudan at present. Other research aimed at reconstructing linguistic prehistory has argued that there is a good fit between some of the eastern African skeletal populations, especially those of northwestern Kenya, and the likely remote ancestors of Nilotic- and Cushitic-speaking peoples who live in eastern Africa at present. Other evidence has suggested that some of the people, especially in Tanzania, may have been related to the Khoisan hunting and foraging peoples of southern Africa. However, the Khoisan linkage has recently been criticized by L. A. Schepartz.

Main Features of the Technology

During the Late Stone Age, there was a major shift toward the use of very small stone tools known as *microliths.* Many of these geometrically shaped artifacts, such as crescents, are less than 4 centimeters long. Such artifacts were typically used as parts of composite tools such as arrow barbs where the sharp-edged microliths were inserted in rows along the edges of the arrow immediately adjacent to the tip.

The widespread use of microliths, a sign of a major change in emphasis in stone technology, indicates more efficient hunting abilities through the use of the bow. A range of other highly efficient microlithic tools were in use, such as small backed drills used for making holes in ostrich-eggshell beads, adzes for working in wood, and small scrapers for preparing clothing and other items made from animal skins. Most of these tools are believed to have been hafted (set) into wooden and bone handles.

The use of these small tools opened the door to using a wide variety of high-quality raw materials that were most often naturally found in small pieces such as chert and chalcedony. Whereas people generally obtained material from the nearby area, there is evidence of either exchange of exotic raw materials between groups or long-distance travel to obtain highly desirable raw materials such as obsidian. For example, at the Olduvai Gorge Naisiusiu beds, eight Late Stone Age obsidian artifacts dating to about 17,000 years ago were recovered. The obsidian has been traced by X-ray fluorescence analysis to an area around Lake Naivasha in Kenya about 250 kilometers away from Olduvai.

The oldest-known microliths have been found in Africa. Such information has added significantly to the growing body of evidence documenting the early contributions of prehistoric peoples in Africa to the overall development of technology. In eastern Africa, microliths are present by as early as 35,000 years ago in the deeper levels of a number of sites such as Mumba-Hohle in northern Tanzania and Matupi Cave located near the Ituri Forest in Zaire. At Matupi, the deepest microlithic tool was recovered from deposits radiocarbon-dated to between 22,000 and 32,000 years ago, but there is evidence of the microlithic technique of producing small flakes and platelets from cores that dates back to at least 40,000 years ago. More abundant evidence of microliths is found in sites that are dated to between 10,000 and 17,000 years ago, and it can be said that microliths were in general use after about 9,000 years ago.

While microliths are prevalent, there is considerable variability in the artifact assemblages. Larger stone tools, such backed blades or knives, scrapers on blades, and heavy-duty flake and core scrapers, are also present at many sites, and they may predominate in some sites. There are also many casual or informal tools, such as flakes that have been notched or serrated. In addition, Late Stone Age people used heavy-duty tools such as hammer stones, anvils, and small grinding stones. Bored stones served as digging-stick weights, where the stick could be used to obtain plant foods and small animals from the ground. Clearly such artifacts bear witness to extensive use of tubers, nuts, fruits, and other plant foods available on the savannas and in the woodlands.

Subsistence

In recent and historic times, the eastern African savannas held some of the largest concentrations of wild game known with vast migratory herds of animals such as wildebeests and zebras. It is, therefore, not surprising that the faunal remains found at Late Stone Age sites frequently contain an abundance of animal bones, especially the bones of bovids (cattle). It is clear from the large numbers of animal-bone fragments found at sites that the people were effective hunters throughout most areas during the period under consideration. A great variety of animals are evident, ranging from rhinoceros, elephant, and hippopotamus to buffalo, giraffe, zebra, numerous species of antelope, warthog, bush pig, birds, freshwater fish, and, in a few cases, shellfish. Each site has its own specific record of animal species, reflecting variables such as the nature of the local ecology, season of the year, food preferences, and other factors.

For example, the Lukenya Hill sites are situated in the savannas to the southeast of Nairobi. Here, the evidence is especially interesting during the arid period of the Last Glacial Maximum 18,000 years ago. In this area, people concentrated on hunting an extinct form of small antelope, which was adapted to arid conditions. Further evidence of the dry grassland habitat is provided by Grevy's zebra and oryx. Evidence cited by C. W. Marean and D. Gifford-Gonzalez has demonstrated that dry grassland animals extended as far south as northern Tanzania during the very arid period of the Last Glacial Maximum.

A contrast in setting is provided by the highland site of Enkapune ya Muto located on the approximately 2,400-meter Mau Escarpment. In this deeply stratified shelter, a study of the Early Holocene levels has shown that people were selective in hunting small bovids, such as two species of reedbuck, bushbuck, and duiker.

Another interesting example of subsistence centers on the exploitation of Late Stone Age aquatic resources and the use of barbed spear and harpoon points made from bone. Sometimes these points are associated with pottery decorated with wavy lines. Such points are concentrated at Early

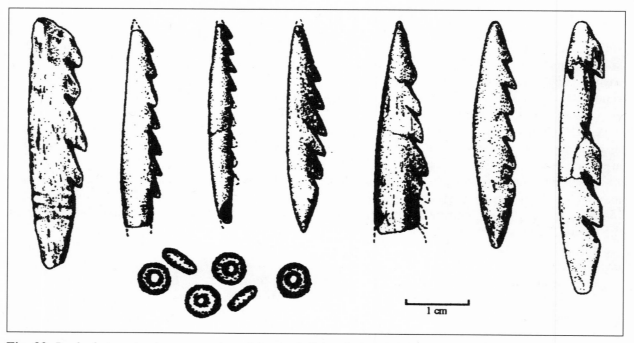

Fig. 32 *Barbed stone implements and ostrich-eggshell beads from Lothagam, Kenya*

Holocene sites along the eastern and western shores of Lake Turkana. Key sites are Lothagam and Lowasera. There are also numerous Early Holocene sites with barbed bone points and wavy-line pottery along the Middle Nile Valley in Sudan, Egypt, and the Sahara. Other earlier examples of barbed bone points are from the Semliki Valley in Zaire. Early suggestions that there was a single cultural pattern or aquatic-based civilization associated with these finds should be modified because of the significant amount of variability in finds at the sites.

It will be recalled that the Early Holocene in eastern Africa was very wet, leading to a substantial rise in the lake levels. K. M. Stewart noted in 1989 that in the case of Lake Turkana, the establishment of a connection with the White Nile improved the conditions of the lake and resulted in a large and diverse fish population. At that time, the site of Lothagam, now situated in a desert area on the western side of the lake, was an island or, perhaps, a peninsula that projected into the lake. More than 200 barbed bone points were recovered at this site including some finds from offshore lake-bottom deposits, suggesting that boats were probably used. Harpoons or spears were used to procure fish, centering on Nile perch that were sometimes more than 1.5 meters in length and weighed more than 45 kilograms. Lake Turkana also contained varieties of large and small catfish, cichlids (perchlike fish), and other fish, along with soft-shelled turtles, Nile crocodiles, and hippopotamuses. While the lake afforded an abundance of aquatic foods, people also foraged and hunted zebras, buffalo, warthogs, giraffes, gazelles, hartebeests, and other animals.

A detailed comparative study of the use of fish at archaeological sites at Lake Turkana done by Stewart reveals that only a few kinds of fish were exploited during the initial high-water phase of the Early Holocene, mainly large Nile perch and cichlids. Subsequently, when the lake level retreated and increased pressures on the subsistence economy, a greater range of fish, including smaller species, were exploited. The taking of a greater variety of fish probably corresponds with new methods of fishing such as the use of plunge baskets.

Burial of the Dead

Three of the better-known burial localities are Gogoshiis Qabe, Lothagam, and Jebel Sahaba, each of which contain specific burial areas, or cemeteries, that were used on a repeated basis. At Lothagam, for example, several burials actually intruded on previous burials. It has been suggested that such specific burial areas, or cemeteries, are associated with comparatively sedentary hunter-forager societies.

The rock shelter of Gogoshiis Qabe in Somalia excavated by S. A. Brandt is an especially interesting burial site dating to the Early Holocene. One person, or perhaps several people, had been buried with 13 pairs of kudu horns, as well as a number of single horns. Brandt reasoned that the dead had been given special ceremonial treatment because of status that was achieved during life, perhaps in regard to exceptional hunting abilities. No other burials at the site or at any other sites in eastern Africa included kudu horns in a similar way. It is also interesting to observe that some of the Gogoshiis Qabe people were buried under small mounds of rocks, while others were not. Such differences in burial treatment may reflect differences within the social group. There is also an example of what anthropologists term a *secondary burial.* In this case, the individual most likely died at some other location, and the remains of the person were subsequently reburied at the rock shelter. In short, this person may have been buried twice.

At Lothagam, in the southeast burial concentration, almost all of the Early Holocene people were buried in a flexed position on their left sides facing east. The tendency to inter people in a specific position may be indicative of religious practices centering on facing the dead toward the rising sun, and the positioning on the left side may also have been symbolically important. While most of the people at Lothagam were not buried with grave goods, one woman was buried with a necklace made from ostrich-eggshell beads, and two other individuals were found with obsidian microliths. The obsidian may well have been an important nonlocal raw material and was, therefore, placed in the grave for use in an afterlife. In another case, a person appears to have died by violence because microliths were found embedded in the foot.

The Late Paleolithic Jebel Sahaba cemetery in northern Sudan is located near Wadi Halfa, about a kilometer from the east bank of the Nile. While this site is outside of the main area of eastern Africa, it is exceptionally interesting. The remains of 58 individuals buried in shallow pits that were typically covered with sandstone slabs were recovered. The site has been dated to between 12,000 and 10,000 B.C. The skeletons were generally in a flexed position on their left sides with the skulls to the east. As in the case of Lothagam, the burial position may indicate ritual beliefs. There are both single and multiple burials at Jebel Sahaba. In one case, a grave contained an old man and three women, while another one may have contained as many as eight people. This cemetery is unusual in that nearly half of the people, including men, women, and children, appear to have died by violence. Numerous stone flakes that were probably parts of arrows or spears were found embedded in the skeletons. They were found in the abdomen and chest as well as inside of the skull in a few cases. Bones also showed evidence of cut marks. Such violence is unusual among hunter-foragers. It may have resulted from competition between groups for the food resources that were concentrated along a limited area of the Nile Valley at a time when climatic conditions at the end of the Pleistocene were becoming increasingly arid and when the surrounding desert had little to offer.

Rock Art

While eastern Africa is not as rich as southern Africa in prehistoric rock art, paintings are known from a number of regions, particularly in Ethiopia, Somalia, Tanzania, Uganda, and Zambia. In some cases, rock engravings are also evident. Although much of the rock art was done by Pastoral Neolithic and Iron Age peoples, there are paintings that are attributed to Late Stone Age foragers, most notably along the base of the Rift Valley in the Kondoa area of central Tanzania.

Several hundred sites near Kondoa contain numerous paintings depicting wild animals and humans and executed in red outline. The specific age of the Kondoa paintings is uncertain, but the best overall cultural association is with the Late Stone Age. For example, at the site of Kisese II, several pieces of rock with traces of paint had broken from the wall and were recovered from Late Stone Age levels, one of which may be about 1,500 years old. Other painted rock fragments are older, but the specific ages cannot be determined, except to estimate that they are not older than the 8,000-year-old levels that underlie the deposits in question. Based on the discovery of pigment in the deeper levels, it is also possible that some of the paintings could be significantly older. Used ochre coloring pencils were found in many levels at Kisese II, including one that is at least 19,000 years old. Whether these early pencils were used for rock painting, and hence document very old paintings, or were used for some other type of activity such as body painting is uncertain.

On the whole, the Kondoa art depicts a wide variety of animals. L. S. B. and Mary Leakey's pioneering study showed that giraffes were very frequently represented, as were eland, elephants, and carnivores, including lions and hyenas. There were also reedbuck, kudu, hartebeests, zebras, rhinoceroses, snakes, and other animals, including domesticated dogs. Although the age of the earliest eastern African dogs is not known, the paintings of dogs are assumed to be comparatively recent. Stylized humans with very round heads and thin bodies are frequently depicted. While most of the paintings of people do not depict them with items of material culture, a composite view of those that do have such items reveals bows and arrows, a form of musical instrument resembling a flute, cloaks, aprons, bracelets, and carrying containers.

The comparative abundance of eland in the Kondoa art is also evident in southern African art. Eland have been shown to have great ritual significance among Khoisan hunter-foragers. Recent studies by David Lewis-Williams have shown that much of the rock art in South Africa relates to the trance experience of medicine people, who engage in curing, rainmaking, and other supernatural activities. Some of the Kondoa art could also fit into this same pattern.

BIBLIOGRAPHY

Anderson, J. E. 1968. Late Paleolithic skeletal remains from Nubia. In *The prehistory of Nubia,* vol. 2. of *Southern Methodist University Contributions in Anthropology,* 996–1,040.

Brandt, S. A. 1988. Early Holocene mortuary practices and hunter-gatherer adaptations in southern Somalia. *World Archaeology* 20: 40–56.

Gamble, C., and O. Soffer, eds. *The world at 18,000 B.P.* Boston and London: Unwin Hyman.

Leakey, M. D. 1983. *Africa's vanishing art: The rock paintings of Tanzania.* New York: Doubleday and Co.

Marean, C. W. 1992. Hunter to herder: Large mammal remains from the hunter-gatherer occupation at Enkapune ya Muto rock shelter, Central Rift, Kenya. *The African Archaeological Review* 10: 65–127.

Merrick H. V., and F. H. Brown. 1984. Obsidian sources and patterns of source utilization in Kenya and northern Tanzania: Some initial findings. *The African Archaeological Review* 2: 129–152.

Schepartz, L. A. 1987. From hunters to herders: Subsistence pattern and morphological change in eastern Africa. Ph.D. diss., University of Michigan, Ann Arbor.

Stewart, K. M. 1989. Environmental change and human adaptation in Late Pleistocene and Holocene African fishing sites. Ph.D. diss., University of Toronto.

Yellen, J. E., A. S. Brooks, E. Cornelissen, M. J. Mehlman, and K. Stewart. 1995. A Middle Stone Age worked bone industry from Katanda, Upper Semliki Valley, Zaire. *Science* 268: 553–556.

Lawrence H. Robbins

SOUTHERN AFRICAN ADVANCED FORAGERS

Southern Africa's hunter-forager cultures occupy a position within the disciplines of archaeology and anthropology that exceeds any intrinsic interest. Often used as archetypal examples of mobile hunter-forager societies, these cultures are now the focus of a major debate on the effects on them of two millennia of interaction with indigenous pastoralists and farmers. Southern African archaeology can make extensive use of ethnographic analogies derived from their study and investigate how these recent lifeways have come to be. Additionally, southern Africa's paintings and engravings form one of the best-understood rock-art traditions anywhere in the world. The oldest fossils of anatomically modern human so far discovered also come from this region, indicating its significance to our understanding of the biological evolution of *Homo sapiens sapiens.*

Southern Africa's foragers are highly diverse but share several characteristics. All speak languages that make extensive use of click sounds and belong to the Khoisan language family. They also share an emphasis on sharing and reciprocity and a generally egalitarian social organization, have similar kinds of kinship classification, and have a related set of religious beliefs and practices. Ethnographic studies of groups such as the Zhu/toãsi (!Kung) and G/wi provide detail on a wide range of cultural phenomena. Historical writings going back to the 17th century and oral traditions preserved by these peoples and other indigenous groups complement this information. Archaeological data for the study of past hunter-foragers are equally diverse. Numerous regional research projects have examined evidence from excavations, landscape surveys, and the study of rock art.

Archaeologists have traditionally emphasized stone-tool technology as a means of ordering southern Africa's past, since stone artifacts are both numerous and well preserved. Archaeologists recognize four broadly successive artifact traditions within the last 20,000 years: Robberg, Oakhurst, Wilton, and Smithfield. All are grouped within the Late Stone Age, partly on the basis of an often-shared pattern of microlithic stone tools. More importantly, many of the artifacts found in these assemblages have clear parallels in the material culture of recent southern African hunter-foragers. Examples include bone arrow points and link shafts, ostrich-eggshell beads and containers, and wooden digging sticks. Although southern African foragers no longer employ flaked-stone artifacts, experiments, microwear studies, and 19th-century accounts provide information on the activities in which they were used.

The Middle Stone Age lacks these clear links to the material culture of the ethnographic present

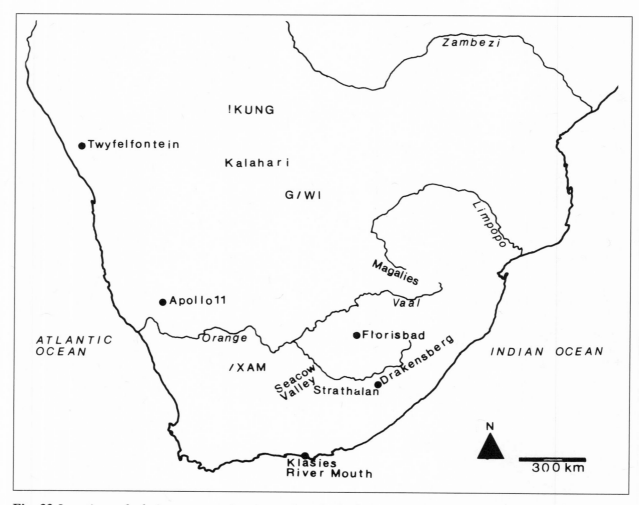

Fig. 33 *Locations of ethnic groups and major archaeological sites in southern Africa*

and is associated with a quite different tradition of artifact manufacture. The transition between the two lies between 20,000 and 60,000 years ago but is not completely understood. However, fossil evidence, notably from the mouth of the Klasies River, demonstrates that Middle Stone Age tools were made by people who were already, in an anatomical sense, little different from those of today. At issue is the extent to which this anatomical modernity necessarily implies similarities in cultural behavior and potential. Moving further back in time, stone-tool assemblages of early Middle Stone Age or Early Stone Age character are associated with more archaic hominids, whose behavior probably differed significantly from that of modern people. It seems unlikely that any direct parallels exist between contemporary hunter-foragers and these Middle and Early Pleistocene human ancestors.

Characteristic of most hunter-foragers, including those of southern Africa, is a seasonal pattern of social aggregation and dispersal. In the central Kalahari, for example, G/wi bands split up in winter (the dry season) into smaller family units that regroup only in summer when there is sufficient surface water to sustain a large group of people. Different subsistence strategies and activities characterize each phase. Ritual activity (including communal healing dances), the exchange and manufacture of objects, travel, and a marked separation of gender roles all characterize times of social aggregation but are absent or rare in the dispersal phase. This aggregation-dispersal model is a powerful tool for understanding the archaeological record, though distinct aggregation and dispersal sites are not yet recognizable before 12,000 years ago. As aggregation and dispersal are fundamental to recent San social organization, perhaps other features—such as kinship systems—were also structured quite differently before this time.

Southern Africa is rich in rock paintings and engravings. In the Lesotho Highlands and the Drakensberg Mountains, the seasonal variation in resource availability suggests that this region was occupied by large numbers of people in summer. Some of the imagery in the art of southern Africa (for example, family groups of eland and roebuck) implies that paintings were executed in summer—in other words, at times of social aggregation appropriate for the rituals with which painting was associated. Interpretations of the art based on 19th- and 20th-century ethnography of the /Xam and Zhu/toãsi Bushmen respectively show that a communal healing dance was foremost among these rituals. Through this dance, medicine people enter a trance state and then cure people of sickness, drive away evil, and heal social tensions. While on these out-of-body travels, shamans can also make rain and control the movements of game animals. For the San, the trance dance is thus a central arena in which they reproduce shared social values and ensure the physical well-being of society. Paintings depict various aspects of the trance experience, either directly or through metaphors, and may have had a critical role in guiding, shaping, and legitimizing what shamans saw and did.

In Lesotho and the Drakensberg Mountains, surviving paintings may be only a few centuries old. Where the rock surface used is more stable (for example, in the western Cape), they may date to 2,000 or more years ago. However, the art has a much greater antiquity, since archaeologists have found painted stone slabs in datable deposits in several rock shelters. The oldest examples, from Apollo 11 Cave in Namibia, are dated to about 27,000 years ago. Where paintable surfaces are rare, rock engravings often occur on boulders and rocky outcrops. Though the technique and medium are different, the content of the art and its underlying meaning are much the same. In both cases, similarities between the rare examples of Pleistocene and Early to Middle Holocene art and more recent art or ethnographically recorded beliefs raise the possibility of long-standing ideological continuities among southern Africa's forager societies. Observations on which to base such a claim are still few, however, and problems in dating paintings on shelter walls or engravings often make it difficult to link the rock art to other aspects of the archaeological record.

Rock-art research has been central to a recent shift in southern African archaeology toward studying social change from a previous emphasis on examining how people adapted to the environments in which they lived. Studies of gift exchange, often known by the !Kung word *hxaro,* are particularly important here. Variation in the frequency of *hxaro* items, such as ostrich-eggshell beads, may be one indicator of whether people used a site as an aggregation- or a dispersal-phase camp. The intensity of *hxaro* also varied over time. For example, the high frequency of beads and bone work in some Wilton contexts may show that people intensified *hxaro* to strengthen ties between individuals and groups in the face of increasing aridity and declining resource availability during the Middle Holocene. One of the reasons people engage in *hxaro* today is precisely to build such ties so that under adverse conditions they can gain access to resources in areas inhabited by other groups. Interestingly, the frequency of *hxaro* items in the archaeological record is very low before 12,000 years ago, suggesting that either Late Pleistocene people practiced quite different forms of gift exchange or that they organized their societies on a different basis from those of more recent hunter-foragers.

Movement of seashells and other exchanged items helps delimit areas of interaction and may point to social alliances between different groups. Archaeologists also infer these "social regions" from the spatial distributions of particular artifact types and the sharing of common raw-material preferences for making stone artifacts. A general trend is for such areas to become smaller and better defined during the last 12,000 years. This was probably linked to a growing importance of more formally structured relations within and between groups as population densities rose and people developed closer ties to particular

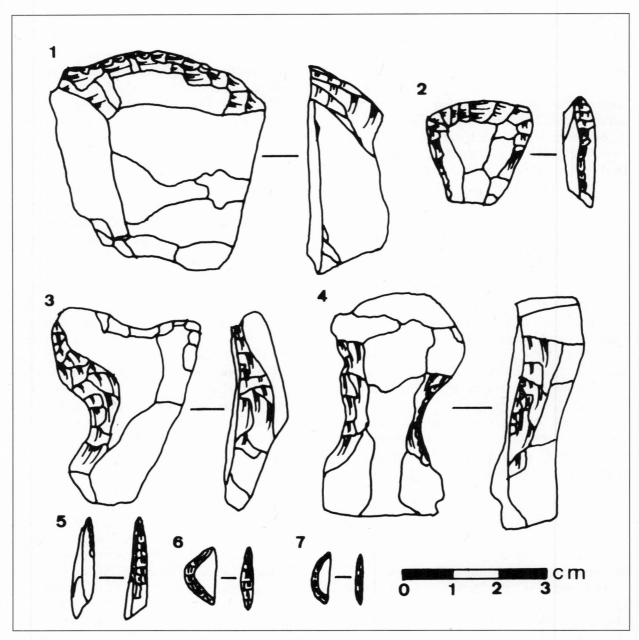

Fig. 34 *Late Stone Age artifacts from southern Africa*

1   Scraper   4   Spoke shaver   6   Segment tied on   7   Segment tied on
2   Scraper   5   Back blade   arrows   arrows
3   Spoke shaver

parts of the southern African landscape. Interpretations of this kind, which stress the possibility that people chose to make and use artifacts of a given kind as statements of their cultural identity, seem less relevant to the Middle Stone Age. Analyses of changes in stone artifacts from several sites also suggest that, on the whole, the Middle Stone Age was marked by much slower rates of change in artifact attributes and a more expedient approach to artifact manufacture (that is, people made and used tools as needed with little intention to conserve them for long-term use).

This raises the question of whether Middle Stone Age people were capable of the same range of cultural behavior as that of more recent hunter-foragers. Analyses of plant and animal remains from archaeological excavations are central to this debate. Contrary to a minimalist view that they only hunted small antelope, scavenged the rest of the meat they ate, and did not share food, faunal analyses at the mouth of the Klasies River and Florisbad show that they hunted a wide variety of game, including small herds of eland. They also collected shellfish in large numbers (presumably to share) and scavenged for seals and penguins. Comparison of their subsistence strategies suggests, however, that Middle Stone Age people did not target dangerous animals, such as bush pigs and buffalo, to the same extent as Late Stone Age hunter-foragers, nor did they fish or take flying birds. Differences in technology or lower population pressure on resources may help explain these contrasts, but it seems likely that Middle Stone Age people also perceived resources differently from their Late Stone Age successors. Interestingly, surveys in the Seacow Valley and Lesotho show that their settlement patterns and use of the landscape were also quite different.

Although large migratory grazing animals such as zebras and wildebeests dominate many Late Pleistocene archaeological faunal assemblages, especially in the Cape, the shift toward the Holocene pattern of small, territorial browsing antelope is not as sharp as once thought and is still more variable across southern Africa as a whole. People may have exploited plant foods less intensively before 12,000 years ago, but sites like Strathalan Cave indicate that plants certainly did not go unused in earlier times. The collecting and use of many plant foods required little more than digging sticks, bored stones commonly used to weigh down the digging sticks and give them added force, and grindstones. More sophisticated implements were characteristic of obtaining many animal foods. Though the bow and poisoned arrow are the classic Bushman weapons, we have little direct information on their antiquity. Other

hunting techniques included the use of snares and a variety of traps, but more important than artifacts for both hunting and gathering was the information people had on resources and animal behavior. The detailed ecological information possessed by modern Bushmen has often astonished Western scientists.

Taking their cue from ethnographic work, many studies of subsistence emphasize models based on seasonal changes in resource availability and the annual round. In the western Cape, for example, people may have scheduled coastal resources such as shellfish, for use in winter, when the coastal forelands are relatively hospitable. They may have moved inland to exploit geophytic plants (perennial plants that, during the winter, bear their buds below the surface of the soil) and ground game (for example, the tortoise and hyrax) during summer. Though some biological indicators, such as hyrax tooth-eruption patterns, substantiate this pattern between 2,000 and 4,000 years ago, different settlement strategies prevailed both before and since. However, isotopic analysis of human skeletons in the same region, suggesting that inland and coastal populations had quite different diets, indicates a lack of seasonal movement. Debate continues on how to reconcile these data with the broader archaeological picture.

In many parts of southern Africa during the Late Holocene, people increasingly made use of foods that, while plentiful, occur in small package sizes. Examples include ground game, fish, freshwater shellfish, and underground plant foods. This is one aspect of a general process of economic intensification (storage of seeds and, perhaps, meat being another) that was accompanied by changes in social organization. Alongside the growing regionalization of material culture already mentioned, formal burial in cemeteries appeared in the southern Cape, perhaps as a means of expressing claims to particular segments of the landscape. The emergence of a tradition of painting on rock-shelter walls (and thus, perhaps, more complex forms of ritual activity) may be a comparable phenomenon. In both the southwestern and southeastern parts of the subcontinent, pottery seems to have been adopted several centuries before any local pastoralist or farming presence. This both expanded the range of edible foods and the potential for storing them. Separating the origins of ceramics from the establishment of local food-producing communities in both the Cape and the southeastern part of southern Africa encourages us to consider whether hunter-foragers played an active role in the development of pastoralist and farming societies.

Nevertheless, linguistics strongly suggests that the ultimate origin of the Khoikhoi pastoralists of the Cape and Namibia was in northern Botswana, where they presumably obtained sheep from Iron Age farmers farther north. The establishment of pastoralism in the Cape resulted in major changes in settlement pattern, subsistence, and social organization among the area's indigenous hunter-foragers. While some archaeologists argue that the two groups remained largely separate and can be identified as such archaeologically, others emphasize their relationship within a single socioeconomic system in which individuals and communities moved from a position of wealth (having livestock) to poverty (depending solely on hunting and gathering) and back again. Observations in the Kalahari indicate that hunter-foragers there have alternated between different subsistence strategies in the recent past but also show that Bushman groups retain a strong cultural identity of their own, despite centuries of interaction with other societies. Over much of southern Africa, this interaction has been with Iron Age farming peoples and has involved relatively equal relations of exchange and intermarriage as well as more exploitative clientship situations in which hunter-foragers herd livestock or hunt for their patrons. Conflict, however, appears to have been relatively rare into the 19th century, with hunter-foragers often recognized as ritually important "owners of the land" for such purposes as rainmaking. In the Drakensberg Mountains, shamans may have assumed a socially more prominent role through distributing livestock acquired as payment for these services, ultimately leading to a qualitative shift in social relations. Though interaction with Europeans contributed to this process by encouraging the emergence of leaders who could organize raids, defense, exchange, and the disposal of booty, it eventually provoked greater disruption of hunter-forager lifeways and led, through a combination of warfare and acculturation, to the disappearance of San communities except in Namibia and Botswana.

BIBLIOGRAPHY

Barnard, A. 1993. *Hunters and herders in Southern Africa.* Oxford: Berg.

Deacon, J. 1984. Later Stone Age people and their descendants in southern Africa. In *Southern African prehistory and palaeoenvironments,* ed. R. Klein, 221–328. Rotterdam: Balkema.

Inskeep, R. R. 1978. *The peopling of southern Africa.* Cape Town: David Philip.

Lee, R., and I. DeVore, eds. 1976. *Kalahari hunter-gatherers.* Cambridge: Harvard University Press.

Lewis-Williams, D., and T. Dowson. 1989. *Images of power.* Johannesburg: Southern Books.

Mazel, A. 1989. People making history: Ten thousand years of hunter-forager history in the Thukela Basin. *Natal Museum Journal of Humanities* 1: 1–189.

Parkington, J., and M. Hall, eds. 1987. *Papers in the prehistory of the western Cape.* Oxford: British Archaeological Reports.

Thackeray. A. 1990. The Middle Stone Age south of the Limpopo River. *Journal of World Prehistory* 6: 385–440.

Wadley, L. 1987. *The Later Stone Age of the southern Transvaal: Social and ecological interpretations.* Oxford: British Archaeological Reports.

Wadley, L. 1993. The Pleistocene Later Stone Age south of the Limpopo River. *Journal of World Prehistory* 7: 243–296.

Peter J. Mitchell

Rock Art

SAHARAN ROCK ART

The evolution of Saharan rock art is a particularly intriguing subject, because for the recent millennia, within the Holocene of northern Africa, such an evolution reflects fairly well the history of Saharan populations viewed on a long-term basis.

The Sahara has not always been the harsh desert we know today. Climates change, and in some periods, the Sahara turned, if not into a prairie, at least into a steppe, which allowed extensive exploitation by man. This was the case during the Neolithic wet period (about 5500 to 3000 B.C.), a favorable period in which the first pastoral societies with cattle herds were developing throughout the whole Sahara. A severe post-Neolithic arid period (about 3000 to 1000 B.C.) interrupted this development. There followed a short and last wet episode around 1000 B.C. and an "actual" arid period, during which populations concentrated only in oases.

Saharan rock art includes both engravings and paintings and is very abundant in many regions. We observe different artistic schools, defined through production techniques, patinas, and styles. Their distributions vary, but none stretches across the entire region.

The Early Period
(about 5000 to 3000 B.C.)

Saharan rock art begins with an early period contemporaneous to the Neolithic wet period. It shows no trace of an initial phase of tentative experiments, no "archaic phase." Since the beginning, we notice an important school of engravings found in a vast area mainly including the Saharan Atlas Mountains, northern Tassili, and Fezzan. They are in dark patina, very carefully incised, with a deep and nearly always polished outline. This school, the Naturalistic Bubaline, is named for an extinct species, *Bubalus antiquus,* the giant or ancient buffalo. It is termed *Naturalistic* because of its very realistic style, despite some conventional features such as animals invariably drawn in profile but with their horns in front view. In addition to wild fauna and very numerous cattle, men are represented as well, although less realistically. Men are often depicted in scenes with mysterious images: masked men, horned "goddesses," theranthropes (a man with an animal head or body), "open women" (with legs wide apart and sex marked with a cupule), hunters armed with inefficient, probably symbolic, weapons, and so on.

The earliest date for the Naturalistic Bubaline is still controversial. The traditional thesis, mainly popularized by H. Lhote, P. Huard, T. Monod, and F. Mori, asserts that this school represents only wild fauna, the so-called Ethiopian fauna (elephants, rhinoceroses, hippopotamuses, aurochs, buffalo, giraffes, and antelope). Hence it is claimed to predate the beginning of animal domestication. However this thesis is questionable, for it was in keeping only with the restricted evidence known in the 1930s. In fact, documents accumulated since then show that the Naturalistic Bubaline school also includes, as all other schools do, depictions of domestic cattle wearing collars, carrying people, or held on a long rein. There is even a milking scene. Moreover in

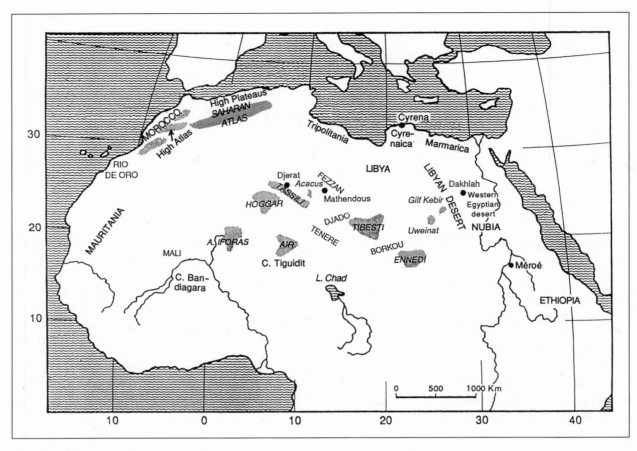

Fig. 35 *Saharan rock-art sites*

the Saharan Atlas Mountains we find pictures of about 60 adorned rams wearing spheroids on their heads and sometimes decorated collars on their necks. Morphological features—long tails, pendulous ears, Roman noses, small horns—bear witness to the fact that they are domestic sheep. Contrary to accepted opinions that set the Naturalistic Bubaline school toward the beginning of the Holocene, or even in the Upper Paleolithic, these depictions of domestic cattle and sheep provide evidence that this school, and therefore the beginning of Saharan rock art, cannot be dated back earlier than the Neolithic wet period. In fact, archaeo-zoologists have been able to prove that animal domestication in northern Africa began during the Neolithic wet period and not earlier (except for a controversial case at a site in the Western Desert of Egypt).

The early period also includes paintings. A well-known group known from Tassili and Acacus, the "Round Heads," mainly depict figures and two animals (Barbary sheep and roan antelope) apparently invested with sacred values. Their style is semischematic and seminaturalistic. The earliest phase, that of the "Primitive Martians," shows schematic figures painted in thick ochre outline. A taboo seems to forbid the artists from painting sexual organs. The "Round Head" paintings reflect an obviously structured spiritual world. Animal masks on human figures are frequently found in exotic contexts. Processions, horned "goddesses," "great gods" surrounded by adorers, and mysterious ceremonies are depicted.

The naturalistic paintings are grouped into a unit called *Bovidian*. But this is a mere artificial grouping of several unrelated units. Its older subgroup, the Early Bovidian, shows figures with clearly Negroid types. Central Saharan rock art usually presents figures with European-type features.

Tibesti and Ennedi also include engravings and paintings of the same early age, and though they are often naturalistic as well, their schools are not the same as those of the central Sahara. In the south (Air and Adrar des Idoras) and east (Djebel Uweinat and Gilf El-Kebir), the massifs were inhabited but contain no rock pictures for this early period.

The Post-Neolithic Arid Period (about 2000 B.C.)

The break caused by the drastic arid episode, well-marked from the Red Sea up to the Atlantic, seems to have emptied the central Sahara. In the Saharan Atlas Mountains, southern Morocco, the Rio de Oro, and Fezzan, where aridity was less severe, a very original school of engravings appeared—the Tazina school. Engravings were still very carefully incised with a polished outline, but now the style was markedly schematic, including fantastic details and excessively elongated extremities of animal legs. These engravings also depict numerous oryx, antelope of semi-desert borders, testifying to an increased aridity.

The Recent Period (from about 1000 B.C.)

After the post-Neolithic arid period, Tassili and Acacus were reoccupied by populations of the earliest Berber communities, of protohistoric then historic age, uninterrupted up to the current Tuaregs. The paintings of the Final Bovidian are executed in polychrome with a fine brush. Their style is very naturalistic and elegant. They mainly depict activities around the campsite, pastoral scenes, and hunting for Barbary sheep and lions.

Later, the fine naturalistic style was abandoned, and depictions of figures were executed in a schematic, rigid, conventional style. A theme was appearing frequently—that of a dignitary with his weapons or a row of dignitaries posing in front view. The bow, until then the usual weapon, was gradually replaced by "modern" weapons, such as throwing sticks (for hunting), thrusting spears, throwing spears, and slightly later on daggers, swords, and shields.

During the next period, the Horse Period, first horses and then chariots drawn by horses were depicted. Both were introduced not earlier than 700 B.C. probably from Cyrena, a city founded in 631 B.C. by the Greeks. These chariots are either engraved, crudely pictured, schematic forms or painted "flying gallop chariots," always represented with a finely executed team of two, three, or four horses. The chariot depictions are traditionally attributed to the Garamantes, an ancient people of Fezzan, however this is only ill-grounded speculation. As for the horse mounted by a rider, it became usual only later, around the beginning of the Christian era.

A few centuries before the Christian era, the camel was also introduced into the Maghreb and the central Sahara. In the paintings of the Camel Period, the schematism became still cruder. Meanwhile, with the camel, a form of writing was introduced through unknown channels up to the central Sahara. It belongs to family of script originating from the Phoenician linear alphabet. These Saharan writings are named *Libyco-Berber* or *Tifinagh*. Inscriptions, always very short, now frequently appeared on rocks. This writing was never used for another function.

During the same period, around the 1st millennium B.C., rock pictures also were carved for the first time in the southern massifs, Air and Adrar des Idoras. They are exclusively engravings, those of the Libyan Warrior school. They mainly show dignitaries—almost exclusively men—drawn in front view, in a very schematic or even geometric style. They often hold, on a long rein, a small and short stereotyped horse.

In Tibesti, Ennedi, and Uweinat, the mounted horse and the camel appeared only later, and no chariots are depicted.

Relations with Foreign Countries

The origin of Saharan rock art, which was already highly developed at its first appearance, is unknown. The Capsian groups of the Maghreb have been proposed as an origin, but only very few crude, small sculptures or drawings have been found in Capsian layers at archaeological sites. A link with the fine engravings of the Naturalistic Bubaline school does not seem obvious.

In the Maghreb, rock pictures are rarely found north of the Saharan Atlas or the Moroccan High Atlas. To the east, some are found in Tripolitania. On the other hand, clearly pharaonic themes and hieroglyphic inscriptions appear in the engravings of the Eastern Desert of Egypt and Nubia, but they totally disappear westward beyond Dakhlah Oasis. Indeed Egyptian or Egypt-influenced objects are absolutely lacking in the finds from excavations in Uweinat, Tibesti, Ennedi, and the central and western Sahara. Even Cyrenaica and the region known as Garamantic (Fezzan) initiated relations with pharaonic Egypt only in the early dynastic period, and we perceive no echo of them in rock pictures. Farther southward, no traces or influence of the Napata or Meröe kingdoms or their Nilotic successors (the X-Group and the Christian kingdom of Nubia) are found west of the Nile Valley.

For the Sahel, on the other hand, the recent phases of the Libyan Warrior school in Air and Adrar des Idoras signal the settling of Berber populations, belonging to the Tuareg confederations. The Berbers steadily pushed southward, creating insecurity along the northern borders of the Ghana and Mali Empires. In Air, Adrar des Idoras, Djado, Tibesti, and Ennedi, the rock pictures of Saharan types come to a stop in the last

Table 22 *The chronology of Saharan rock art*

Approximate Dates (B.C.)		4000	3000	2000	1000	0
Atlas	E	———— Naturalistic Bubaline School ————				
				———— Tazina Style ————		
Fezzan	E	———— Naturalistic Bubaline School ————				
					Tazina Style	Camel Period
Tassili/ Acacus	E	– Naturalistic Bubaline School –		POST-NEOLITHIC ARID PHASE	Abaniora Group	
	P	— Sefar Ozanearé Group — ("Early Bovidian")			Iheren-Tahilahi Group ("Final Bovidian")	Horse Period
		Round Heads			(?)	
Air/ Adrar des Idoras	E	———————— No Rock Pictures ————————			Semi-naturalistic engrs. (Pseudo-Bubline) (Rare)	—— Libyan —— Warrior School

Table 23 *The chronology of Saharan rock art as advanced by Theodore Monod and Henri Lhote*

Approx-imate Dates (B.C.)	6000	5000	4000	3000	2000	1000	0
	Round Head Paintings				Bovidian	Horse Period	Camel Period
	Engravings of the Bubaline School						
	Monumental	Tazina	Decadent				

southern foothills of these massifs. The limit between steppe and savanna is often marked by a cliff line (as at Bandiagara and Tiguidit), south of which we enter another world. The latter sometimes includes rock pictures, but they have no relation at all with the Saharan ones. Moreover, the linguistic and perceptual universes of people living of the steppe significantly differ from those of people of the savannas.

In short, Saharan rock art bloomed during the early period within a world that remained closed on itself for a long time. Only in the very recent protohistoric period, objects (throwing spears, chariots, swords, and shields), the Libyco-Berber writing, and depictions of horses and then camels signal undeniable contacts with Mediterranean coasts. More distant contacts, with Crete, Andalusia, and southern Africa, such as those posited when the diffusionist theses were in fashion in Abbé H. Breuil's day, are merely unsustainable speculations.

As for Egypt, it had perhaps shared with the people of the Sahara a very ancient common dawning, toward the beginning of the Holocene or even before, in some Nilotic region near the homeland of the Afro-Asiatics. This pristine community is mainly surmised by linguists. It left some traces, gradually eroded and eventually difficult to perceive, in myths common to both regions: the jackal-headed theranthropes, the horned goddesses, and maybe a common Nilotic prototype of both the god Amun and the adorned rams of the Atlas Mountains. In addition, people of the Nilo-Saharan linguistic block settled very early in Ennedi and Tibesti, probably as soon as the beginning of the Holocene according to some linguists. They were coming from some region between the Chadic Plain and the Ethiopian Plateau. However, in the following millennia during the Middle Holocene, the Nilotic regions were forever separated from the central Sahara by an almost impassable desert, the terrifying Libyan Desert.

In the west, Christianity conquered the Romanized Maghreb but did not go beyond the fortified limes running through the high plateaus. The Saharan rock pictures show no trace of it either. Even Islam took many centuries to set up in the Saharan central massifs. In the meantime, the "actual" arid period had fragmented the Saharan populations so much that tradition could not be maintained. Saharan rock art died out, without leaving any descent except for some crude graffiti of the later phases of the Camel Period.

The Symbolism of the Rock Pictures

Researchers have tried to retrieve the symbolic meaning of this lost tradition. The pictures of the early period obviously include evidence of a very rich spiritual world. The interpretations first used all the possibilities afforded by ethnographic comparison—hunting magic, fertility or fecundity cults, and so forth. More recently, Gal Huard, after undertaking extensive surveys of material or symbolic features common to wide regions, attributed these features to a unique hunters culture *(culture des chasseurs)*. However all these readings lack proof.

A famous interpretative essay was written by Hampaté Ba and Mrs. G. Dieterlen in 1966. They advanced an explanation of some Tassilian frescoes based on myths and legends of the modern Fulani. Since then, however, despite endless enthusiastic statements about the importance of this conceptual "breakthrough," not a single researcher has ever tried to use this model to interpret another fresco. Indeed, no historical derivation between the Tassilians of 5,000 years ago and current Fulani has been proved.

A more original proposal recently advanced by J.-L. Le Quellec in 1993 attempted to retrieve from a deep level a universal element of *Homo sapiens,* the symbolic function.

As for the recent period of Saharan rock pictures after the post-Neolithic arid period, things are clearer. Ideology had changed, and the scenes with symbolic connotations were becoming rare. What appears now is a stereotype marked out for a brilliant future, that of the warrior or the dignitary, lavishly glorified, represented frontally and in full length, clothed in ceremonial garments and arms. Women are from now on relegated to second place and by some schools even ignored. The sexual scenes reflecting a hierogamy (priestess), the horned goddesses, and the theranthropes disappear. It is now a widely secularized world marching toward history. The so-called primitive symbolic universe, only rich in spirituality, fades away, and the world of harsh, brutal material values and the weight of arms and conquests, the "modern world"—our world—is setting up, for better or worse.

BIBLIOGRAPHY

Calegari, G., ed. 1993. L'arte e l'ambiente del Sahara preistorico: Dati e interpretazioni. *Memorie, Soc. Ital. Scienze Naturali e Museo Civico Storia Naturale Milano* 26 (2) (Actes Congrés Milan 1990).

Jelinek, J. M. 1984. In Galgien, two important Fezzanese rock art sites, Part I, Mathrndush East, Mathrndush Main Gallery; Part II, In Galgien, Comparative Analysis. *Anthropologie Brno* 22: 117-170 and 22: 237–266.

———. 1985. Tilizahren, the key site of Fezzanese rock art, Part I, Tilizahren West Galleries; Part II, Tilizahren East, analyses, discussion, conclusions. *Anthropologie Brno* 23 (2): 125–165 and 23 (3): 223–275.

Le Quellec, J.-L. 1993. *Symbolisme et art rupestre au Sahara.* Paris: l'Harmattan.

Lhote, H. 1970. Les gravures rupestres du Sud-Oranais. *C.R.A.P.E. Mém.* 16.

———. 1973. *A la découverte des fresques du Tassili.* Paris: Arthaud.

———. (vol.1, 1975; vol. 2, 1976). Les gravures rupestres de l'Oued Djerat (Tassili-n-Ajjer). *C.R.A.P.E. Mém* 25.

Mori, F. 1965. *Tadrart Acacus.* Turin: Einaudi.

Muzzolini, A. 1995. *Les images rupestres du Sahara.* Toulouse: the author.

Alfred Muzzolini

WESTERN AFRICAN ROCK ART

Research on rock art in the region south of the Sahara and west of Nigeria has been scarce and irregular and, as a result, much less known than that of the Saharan zones.

The rock art of this part of sub-Saharan Africa was first mentioned in 1907 in the pioneer work of Augustin-Marie-Louis Desplagnes, who surveyed the central plateau of Nigeria as an ethnologist and archaeologist. In 1954, Raymond Mauny published an inventory, together with a brief synthesis, of the rock-art sites then known in western Africa—including the Sahara. In 1979, following a number of limited surveys carried out by various researchers, Eric Huysecom launched his own research program on the Neolithic tradition west of Mali and the rock art associated to it. As a result, a number of homogeneous stylistic groups distributed throughout western Africa were revealed. Séverine Marchi has been studying western African rock art since 1994. Her research has been centered on the Aïré Soroba rock shelter, a site found in the Inland Niger Delta on the boundary of the Sahara and sub-Saharan Africa. The art here represents superimposed paintings of different styles.

This synthesis attempts to establish stylistic groups and takes into account clues of relative chronology, independently of the geographical zones. We have considered only the most characteristic sites, thus leaving aside subjects such as cupped stones and polishers.

THE DOTTED ENGRAVINGS FROM THE BAOULÉ REGION. The engravings in the Baoulé region are characteristic of the art in rock shelters in the national park in Mali and include the popular Fanfannyégèné I and II engravings.

They are often very eroded and constitute one of the most ancient periods of the relative chronology established for rock art in this region. This phase is younger than the characteristic phase of polished grooves but underlies all the paintings on the same site. In all likelihood, the engravings must be related to Baoulé's Neolithic facies (expressions), which date to the end of the 2nd and the beginning of the 1st millennium B.C.

The engravings are covered in dots whose points of impact are more or less dense. The patterns are recurrent and simple and represent bovid figures where the head, the horns, and sometimes the ears are shown. A few schematic drawings have been interpreted as being giraffes by hunters of the region. In one case, a complete figure of a bovid is illustrated in profile with its head facing forward. Other representations include patterns in the shape of flowers, snakes, and radiating circles. As far as we know, such representations seem to be unique in western Africa.

NATURALISTIC PAINTINGS IN NIGERIA. South of the Sahara, the rock shelters in the region of Birnin Kudu, Bauchi, and Igbetti in Nigeria are the only ones to include paintings of a naturalistic type. These figures are still poorly dated, but they can be compared the art found in rock shelters from the same region and occupied during the Neolithic.

The representations are painted in red and white and, rarely, in black. They illustrate bovids (antelope, sheep, and goats) outlined in red or colored in red or white. Other animals, such as antelope, horses, and monkeys are also represented. In Geji, one can observe human figures.

The origin and significance of these paintings, close to certain Saharan representations, are unknown. However, they are very frequently associated with rock gongs (monoliths that produce particular resonances and are used as percussion instruments).

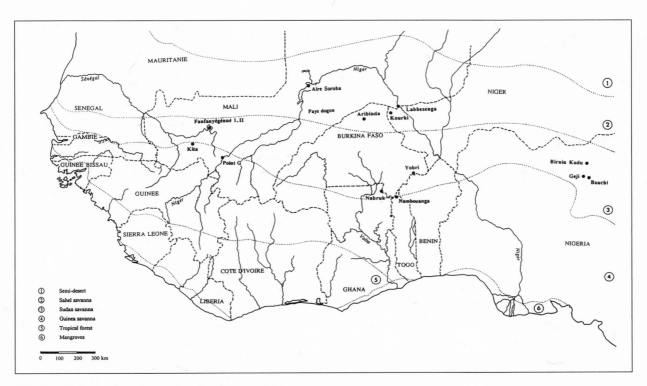

Fig. 36 *Principal rock-art sites in western Africa*

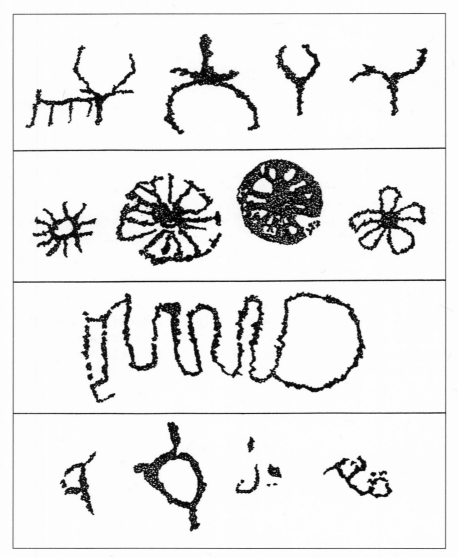

Fig. 37 *Engravings from Fanfannyégèné II in Mali*

The representations are always painted in hematite of a reddish-brown color and are characterized by horses with geometrical bodies—that is, two triangles joined by their summits. These animals are generally mounted by characters armed with spears and shields. They are often illustrated hunting ostriches or giraffes. Their heads are sometimes decorated with elements that recall a headdress of ostrich feathers.

These compositions illustrating hunting are known in Saharan rock art, as well as in the regions of the Sahel and the savanna, in particular in Niger and northern Mali.

HORSES WITH LINEAR BODIES. The group of painted horses with linear bodies proves to be homogeneous from the point of view of style. It is to be found in Mali (Aïré Soroba, Niodougou, Point G, and Fanfannyégèné II), north of Burkina Faso (Nabruk and Aribinda), south of the Niger (Kourki), and north of Togo (Nambouanga).

Only the shelters in Aïré Soroba and Fanfannyégèné II provide information on relative chronology. The facies with linear horses is superimposed over the representations of geometrical horses and the dotted engravings. It is covered with Tifinagh and Arab inscriptions.

The figures are painted or more rarely engraved. They also illustrate riders sitting or standing on horses and hunting ostriches, giraffes, antelope, and, in one case, man. Unlike the horses with geometrical bodies from Aïré Soroba, the animals of this group present simplified forms. There are no more geometrical features, but linear silhouettes illustrate different parts of the body. In

PAINTED HORSES WITH GEOMETRICAL BODIES. A very particular stylistic group was recently discovered in a rock shelter in Aïré Soroba, a rocky islet overlooking the southern bank of Lake Débo, in the Inland Delta of the Niger. As far as we know, this style is unique in sub-Saharan Africa, but it has been used to illustrate characters and horses not only in the Adrar des Idoras north of Mali but also the Tagant in the south of Mauritania.

Presently, it is difficult to date this group, classified as Arabo-Berber in the Sahara. It is, however, the oldest period of rock art in Aïré Soroba.

most cases, the rider is armed with a spear and shield. Other designs are to be noted, such as geometrical figures and isolated animals. Finally, in Aïré Soroba, highly stylized representations of boats carrying schematic human characters and animals seem to be contemporaneous with this style.

Analogous representations of riders are common in the Saharan region. On the other hand, the representations of boats are comparable only to art in the Nile Valley.

PAINTED DROMEDARIES. Three paintings of camels in Aïré Soroba postdate the figures representing horses with geometrical bodies. The dromedaries are in profile and are painted in red and brown. Two of them are driven.

ENGRAVINGS OF CARTS. In Tondia, Mali, two engravings of carts can be compared to those discovered in the Mauritanian Adrar or in Aïré Soroba and remind us directly of the Saharan context. They are extremely stylized and the draft animals (whose species is difficult to determine)

are represented flat with their four legs shown on the side. These two examples are the only ones presently known south of the Sahara and could constitute the first elements of a southern group of Saharan carts.

THE MANDING PAINTINGS. Found principally in Mali, in a region occupied by the Malinké and Bambara people as well as in the region of Bandiagara where the Dogon presently live, the Manding paintings are older than those mentioned above. The sites of Sourkoundingueyé and Takoutala, in northern Mali, and Nabruk and Yobri, in southeastern Burkina Faso, also belong to this group.

From a technical point of view, the figures in the Manding group are always painted in red, white, or black. Highly schematic geometrical representations constitute their main features. One can distinguish abstract signs, isolated human characters, and zoomorphic figures, including saurian (reptilian) motifs. According to ethnological information, a number of these paintings

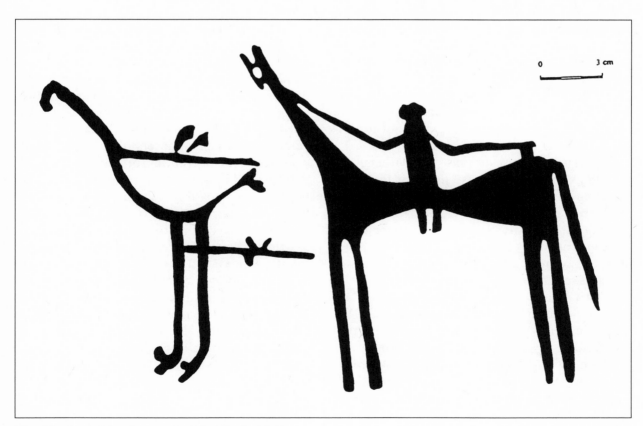

Fig. 38 *Ostrich hunting in Aïré Soroba in Mali*

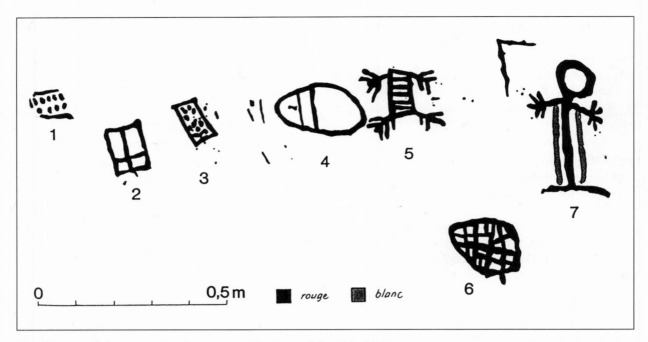

Fig. 39 *Manding geometrical paintings, Fanfannyégèné I in Mali*

seem to be linked to initiation rites, in particular circumcision ceremonies carried out by populations belonging to the Manding group.

THE FISH ENGRAVING OF BAMAKO-SOTUBA. An engraving of a unique style represents a fish. Discovered in Bamako-Sotuba on the right bank of the Niger, it is most probably associated with traces of polishers and polishing and is the sole illustration of a fish yet known south of the Sahara. We have no record of its dating.

THE TIFINAGH INSCRIPTIONS. The Tifinagh inscriptions are to be found essentially in the north, covering the semidesertic and Sahelian zones. The sites are in Mali (Zamgoï, Ouatagouna, Gao, Niangaye, and Aïré Soroba) and Niger (Labbezenga) and are often situated along the Niger River. They are painted in a reddish-orange color or engraved.

The Tifinagh features in the Aïré Soroba are superimposed on depictions of geometrical and linear horses. However, they cannot be classified chronologically with the Arab inscriptions.

Tifinagh is the written transcription of the language used by the Tuaregs, but it is very difficult to situate these inscriptions chronologically. In the Niger region, Arab sources date the arrival of Tuareg camel-rider populations to the 8th century A.D. The Tifinagh inscriptions could be in agreement with this period.

THE ARAB INSCRIPTIONS. Inscriptions in Arab characters are scarce south of the Sahara. One engraving can be found in Diara, Mali, and a number of paintings—of great interest on a chronological basis—in Aïré Soroba. The words found in the Aïré Soroba shelter are painted in red and record a pilgrimage to Mecca in the 11th century A.D. Such an observation constitutes an excellent starting point for the Aïré Soroba paintings and thus confirms the presence of Arab populations—possibly tradesmen—in the Inland Niger Delta during this period.

THE SCHEMATIC PAINTINGS IN MARGHI COUNTRY. Schematic paintings were discovered in a traditional context, still present today, in eastern Nigeria in Marghi country. These paintings are done in red or white and represent armed men with shields and sometimes mounting a horse. They can also be seen with various quadrupeds. They are finger paintings, some of which have been freshened up. Nowadays, young men paint them before their wedding ceremonies, and the paintings are often associated with agrarian rites. This seems to coincide with the passage from adolescence to adulthood.

The rock-art sites of western Africa are all found in the Sahelian and savanna zones. The absence of locations more to the south may well be the consequence of insufficient surveys, possibly because of the forested environment.

From a chronological point of view, the first manifestations seem to stretch back to the arrival of Neolithic populations from Saharan and sub-Saharan regions. The same axis of distribution of rock art could also be found in more recent times. For a number of representations of horse hunters, it could be linked to the intrusion of northern populations looking for slaves or more favorable territories. From the 8th century A.D., the inscriptions indicate commercial relationships with the Islamic populations.

Conversely, a distinctive artistic trend, classified here as the Manding group, seems to have spread in multiple directions, from the regions of northern Guinea and southern Republic of Mali, at the time of the fall of empire of Mali in the 15th century A.D. One of the outcomes of this seems to be the rock art of Dogon country.

In the rock art of present-day populations, such as the Dogon or people from Marghi country, one observes geometrical signs and human characters sometimes mounting horses, respectively. This is evidence of the persistence of ancient themes.

BIBLIOGRAPHY

Bourlard, A. 1989. *Projet d'étude sur "l'abri-sous-roche du Point G" à Bamako (république du Mali).* Bruxelles: Université Libre de Bruxelles, Mémoire de Licence en Histoire de l'Art et Archéologie.

Carter, P. L., and Carter P. J. 1964. Rock paintings from northern Ghana. *Transactions of the Gold Coast and Togoland Historical Society* 7: 1–3.

Desplagnes, A.-M.-L. 1907. *Le plateau central Nigérien: Une mission archéologique et ethnographique au Soudan Français.* Paris: E. Larose.

Fagg, B. E. B. 1957. The cave painting and rock gong of Birnin Kudu. In *Proceedings of the 3rd Pan-African Congress on prehistory,* ed. J. D. Clark, 306–312. London: Chatto & Windus.

Huysecom, E. 1993. L'art rupestre et le "faciès néolithique de Baoulé" (Mali). In *L'arte e l'ambiante des Sahara preistorico: Dati e interpretazioni,* ed. Giulio Calegari, 283–292.

Milano: Società Italiana di Scienze Naturali e del Museo Civico di Storia Naturale di Milano.

Huysecom, E., and Mayor, A. 1991–1992. Etude stylistique de l'art rupestre de la boucle du Baoulé Mali. *Bulletin du Centre Genevois d'Anthropologie* 3: 160–162.

Mauny, R. 1954. *Gravures, peintures et inscriptions rupestres de l'Ouest Africain.* Dakar: Institut Français d'Afrique Noire, Initiations africaines 11.

Rouch, J. 1949. Gravures rupestres de Kourki Niger. *Bulletin de l'Institut Français d'Afrique Noire* 11: 340–353.

———. 1961. Restes anciens et gravures rupestres d'Aribinda Haute-Volta. *Etudes Voltaïques* 2: 61–70.

Shaw, T. 1978. *Nigeria: Its archaeology and early history.* London: Thames and Hudson.

Zeltner, F. de 1911. Les grottes à peintures du Soudan français. *L'Anthropologie* 22: 1–12.

Eric Huysecom and Séverine Marchi

ETHIOPIA AND THE HORN: ROCK ART

Distribution and Thematic Content

Rock art is distributed throughout much of the Horn (Djibouti, Eritrea, Ethiopia, and Somalia), although the largest concentration is in Eritrea and eastern Ethiopia. Rock art is also found in southern and northern Ethiopia, Djibouti, and northern and southern Somalia.

Rock art of the Horn can be divided into two broad categories: engravings or carvings (petroglyphs) and paintings (pictographs). *Paintings* refer to any symbol or representation using a paint (or pigment), while *engraving* is pecking outlines of symbols or representations. A *rock carving* is a form of engraving where a feature is carved to form a relief. The term r*ock art* encompasses all of these.

Another distinction that is widely made by investigators is *parietal art* (art on rock walls) and *art mobilier* (or "movable" art). Due to the paucity of the latter form in the Horn, the following discussion focuses on parietal art.

Fig. 40 *Paintings from Karin Heegan rock shelter in Somalia*

Rock paintings and engravings in the Horn are found on the walls of suitable rock shelters and caves and to a lesser extent on exposed rock surfaces. While a few of the sites contain pictures of wild fauna such elephants and lions, most display images of domestic animals (humpless and humped cattle, goats, sheep, and camels). The extensive depiction of domestic animals (particularly cattle) and the near exclusion of wild animals from the rock art has compelled investigators to describe the rock art of the Horn as "pastoral."

Humans are also represented in the parietal art. They are depicted milking cattle, and sometimes they are armed with bows, arrows, spears, or shields or are shown playing a lyrelike musical instrument. Domestic scenes such as plowing and abstract figures on the ceilings of the shelters are also frequently observed.

The paintings are executed in either outline or flat wash, although at least at one site, paintings are drawn in dotted lines. Various pigments—black, red, reddish-brown, and white—were used to execute the paintings.

History of Investigation

Professional rock-art documentation in the Horn began in the 1930s with the Abbé H. Breuil's work in eastern Ethiopia. Breuil recognized eight main styles in the development of prehistoric rock

art in the Horn, and his work became the basis for later investigations.

The next two decades saw the discovery of many more rock-art sites in the Horn. Studies focused on describing the art and on cautious speculation of the "identity" of the artists. Investigators sought stylistic affinities of the art with other parts of Africa and Europe. Because it was felt that the rock art of the Horn was similar to the later phases of engravings in the Sahara, racial and economic similarities between the two regions were proposed. Scholars also speculated on population movements from the Sahara into the Horn.

The first major synthesis of rock art in the Horn was undertaken by J. Desmond Clark in his pioneering publication, *The Prehistoric Cultures of the Horn of Africa.* In addition to looking for economic and racial similarities between the makers of the art of the Horn with those of the Sahara, Clark also proposed three main stages in the evolution of the rock art: (1) the earliest naturalistic series, (2) conventionalized paintings and engravings, and (3) the most recent schematic series of figures.

Paolo Graziosi and others made new discoveries in Eritrea and Ethiopia during the 1950s and 1960s. Besides arguing for an early age of the rock art, Graziosi also saw similarities of the rock paintings of Eritrea and Ethiopia with those of

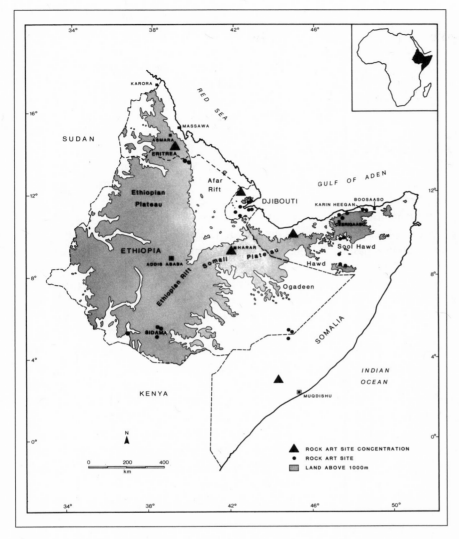

Fig. 41 *Distribution of rock-art sites in the Horn*

recent reconnaissance has resulted in the discovery of new rock-art sites in northern Ethiopia and Eritrea.

In the 1960s and 1970s, rock-art research expanded elsewhere in the Horn. Investigators documented more rock-art sites in southern Ethiopia, although the presence of rock art here was noted as early as the early 1940s. A few sites in southern Ethiopia contain relief carvings of humpless cattle. More sites were discovered in eastern Ethiopia. In the early 1980s, Roger Joussaume synthesized these sites, together with those of other parts of the Horn.

Investigations in the 1980s revealed the presence of new rock-art sites in Somalia and Djibouti. Steven Brandt and Nanny Carder's work, dealing with the relationship of the art of the Horn to the evolution of pastoralism, appeared in the second half of the 1980s. New finds of the 1980s in Somalia and Djibouti as well as most of the previously known sites of the Horn were compiled by Carder in a master's thesis seeking behavioral correlates of the art. Recent archaeological surveys of the 1990s have also documented new rock-art sites in Ethiopia and Eritrea.

Style and Chronology

Stylistically, the rock art of the Horn of Africa is suggested to belong to the Ethiopian-Arabian style. This style, as characterized by Cervicek in 1979:

. . . shows the body and the legs of the cattle in profile, the fore-legs and the hind-legs are each pooled to one thick line;

the Iberian Peninsula, as well as with rock art in northern and southern Africa. Comparing the results of his investigations in Eritrea to the art of eastern Ethiopia, he recognized distinct "Ethiopian" art styles (Eritrea was then part of Ethiopia). In the 1970s, Pavel Cervicek published descriptions of previously discovered engraving sites in Eritrea's Hamasen region—sites that contained bovid and ovine bucrania (sculptured ornaments representing ox and sheep skull, respectively). Cervicek also recognized a distinct art style peculiar to the rock art of the Horn and Arabia and named this style *Ethiopian-Arabian*. After a long hiatus in archaeological research, the hoofs are sometimes stylized to resemble pincers but more often the legs have rounded ends dismissing the hoofs entirely. The head, neck and the horns of the animal are shown from the back like with a bovid which turns its head from the on-looker.

Cervicek distinguishes two main stages in development of the Ethiopian-Arabian style. The first, the Surre-Hanakiya stage, is named after Surre in the Hararghe region of eastern Ethiopia. This stage contains naturalistic and seminaturalistic paintings and engravings dominated by pastoral motifs. The earliest paintings of the Horn are believed to belong to this stage. Based on paleo-environmental and archaeological data, this early phase of the Ethiopian-Arabian style is tentatively dated to between 3,000 and 5,000 years ago. Investigators have also relied heavily on the nature and content of the paintings. The earliest series of paintings are believed to be the naturalistic paintings of cattle, sheep, and humans. Investigators assume that these paintings were succeeded by much larger and "poorly" drawn paintings. The latest paintings included much more schematic designs, and in addition to cattle, they contained representations of camels as well.

The second stylistic stage, Dahthami style proper, which is divided into early and late phases, shows wider geographic distribution and stylistic diversity. In the early phase, the horns of the bovids sometimes "degenerate" into formless stumps, and in the more schematic representations, the heads of the bovids are omitted. In the later phase, humpless cattle are replaced with humped cattle and camels. Paintings belonging to this stage are widely distributed in the Horn.

There is a suggestion that the early phase of the Dahthami style proper might coincide with the return to the more humid conditions that occurred around 2,000 years ago. The increased humidity associated with significant rains seems to have been a widespread phenomenon across the Horn. The stylistic diversity of the Dahthami style proper has, therefore, been suggested as showing a greater emphasis on ritual participation by larger populations on an intra-regional scale in comparison to the preceding Surre-Hanakiya stage.

The later phase of the Dahthami style proper, where humpless bovids are replaced by zebu cattle and camels, may represent the beginning of the Christian era. Brandt and Carder suggested in 1987 that this period "broadly coincides with the return of arid conditions in the Horn of Africa and may reflect behavioral responses to a period of heightened socioeconomic stress."

As seen from the preceding discussion, relative dates recovered through indirect means have been employed in the rock-art studies of the Horn. These dates were inferred from the excavated deposits of the shelters and the recovery of associated artifacts, from the hypothesized movement of pastoral populations from the Sahara into the Horn, and from the artistic styles of the paintings themselves. In some paintings where there is superimpositioning, older figures can be distinguished from the newer ones, although it could have been a few years, a few centuries, or even a few millennia before the artists drew new paintings over the older ones.

Although there have been recent advances in the chronometric dating of rock art, the Horn of Africa has not shared in these advances. However, the use of organic materials in paintings has been noted in ethnohistorical literature elsewhere. If this is the case in the Horn, then chronometric dates would free researchers from the sole preoccupation of reconstructing chronology and permit them focus on the behavioral significance of the art.

Interpretation

Rock art is very susceptible to idiosyncratic interpretations and has been explained in many ways. Sometimes the same rock-art sites have been interpreted differently. The usual interpretations include art for art's sake, aesthetics, representational art, and art as hunting and fertility magic, as a manifestation of rituals, and as a pastime.

Ever since its beginning, rock-art research in the Horn was centered mainly on description, stylistic distribution, and affinity with other sites and on developing a relative chronology or cultural history. Workers focused on documenting rock-art sites, assigning them with tentative dates and looking for stylistic similarities elsewhere—be it in Arabia or the Sahara. Similar rock-art styles that were assumed to be contemporaneous were lumped together into groups. These groups were in turn used to construct chronological stages based on the assumption that the art styles changed (*degeneration* is the word often used) from naturalistic and realistic to schematic. Workers also used the presence or absence of domestic animals in the archaeological record to give credence to these chronologies.

The preoccupation with these aspects of rock art precluded any attempt at gleaning any information on their behavioral significance. Perhaps the only published exception to this is the work of Brandt and Carder, published in 1987. These researchers suggest a relationship between rock art and transhumant mobility patterns of pastoralists from the lowlands to the highlands, depending on the seasonal and or temporal availability of resources and as a response to ecological stress. Having synthesized investigations of prehistoric food production and describing a typical pastoral rock-art site, Brandt and Carder hypothesize that environmental fluctuations of the Middle Holocene in the Sahara caused populations to move into the Horn. Pastoralists soon established patterns of seasonal rounds from the highlands to the lowlands and vice versa in search of pastures. As population densities increased over time, pastoralists came in direct competition with farming communities in the highlands. This may have resulted in risk-minimization strategies including critical interregional information-exchange systems and the institution of rituals. Rock art might have played an important role in these rituals.

The ameliorating environmental conditions around 2,000 years ago would have allowed an increased concentration of populations and may have resulted in an enhanced distribution of rock-art occurrences within the region, which may be exemplified by the frequency of stylistically diversified rock art. With the return of arid conditions in the 4th century A.D., populations would have altered their subsistence base to include drought-resistant livestock (accompanied by their depiction in the rock art) and horticulture. This study, which awaits testing, is a departure from traditional rock-art studies of the Horn.

———~~~~~~~~———

So far, more than 100 rock-art sites are known in the Horn. In light of the recent discoveries of new rock-art sites, the region has demonstrated its potential, and no doubt many more sites are awaiting further investigation. However, as in many aspects of the archaeology in the Horn, rock-art studies have been dominated by a framework of cultural history. Moreover, because few Neolithic sites have been excavated, we know very little about the socioeconomic context of the producers of the art. Regional investigation of rock-art sites—their differences and interrelationships as well as their correlation with the general ecological and cultural remains—must therefore be established. Future research should thus focus on the systematic retrieval of such information.

The rock art in the Horn is in danger of disappearing. Both natural and cultural factors are involved in their destruction. Paintings are being flaked away by natural processes, and contemporary people are drawing all kinds of designs on top of them. Unless this is stopped, the art (at least at some of the sites) that has withstood natural weathering for millennia may disappear forever.

BIBLIOGRAPHY

Brandt, S. A., and N. Carder. 1987. Pastoral rock art in the Horn of Africa: Making sense of udder chaos. *World Archaeology* 19: 173–213.

Breuil, H. 1934. Peintures rupestres prehistoriques du Harar (Abyssinie). *L'Anthropologie* 14: 473–483.

Carder, N. 1988. Modeling the evolution of pastoral rock art in the Horn of Africa. Master's thesis, University of Georgia, Athens.

Cervicek, P. 1979. Some African affinities of Arabian rock art. *Rassegna di Studi Etiopici* 27: 5-12.

Clark, J. D. 1954. *Prehistoric cultures of the Horn of Africa*. Cambridge: Cambridge University Press.

Graziosi, P. 1964. New discoveries of rock paintings in Ethiopia. *Antiquity* 38, part I: 91–98 and part II: 187–194.

Joussaume, R. 1981. L'art rupestre de l'Ethiopie. In *Prehistoire Africaine: Melanzes offerts au doyen Lionel Balout,* eds. C. Boubet, H. J. Hugot, and G. Souville, 159–175. Paris: Editions APDF.

Agazi Negash

EASTERN AFRICAN ROCK ART

Rock art can be either of two forms: painted or engraved (pecked) figures. In both cases, the "canvas" for the art is a rock surface. Engravings tend to be on boulders whereas paintings are found in a variety of rock shelters, from straight-faced to well-defined overhangs to those providing a cavelike setting. The art itself depicts a range of motifs from anthropomorphic to abstract or geometric. In eastern Africa (Tanzania, Kenya, and Uganda), rock art has two loci: around Lake Victoria and the central region of Tanzania (Kondoa and Singida Districts).

Although there has been much interest in rock art worldwide, in eastern Africa the study has not seen the florescence as it has in southern Africa where research units at the Universities of Witwatersrand and Cape Town have provided much of the impetus. This will hopefully change with the East African Rock Art Research Association at the University of Dar Es Salaam in Tanzania. The majority of published works date from the 1960s and 1970s, and there is no one standard work for the whole area. Eastern African rock art tends to be identified with Tanzania where a more substantial body of research exists. E. Anati, in 1986, provided one of the most extensive bibliographies for eastern Africa, primarily on Tanzania. Because of J. H. Chaplin's focus on the Lake Victoria region, his bibliography includes references to sites in all three countries. Generally, eastern African rock art is known by the work in Tanzania of Mary and L. S. B. Leakey. In 1983, Mary Leakey produced a well-illustrated book on sites documented in the 1950s in central Tanzania. It is an excellent companion volume to the articles, including one by L. S. B. Leakey, presented in *Tanganyika Rock Paintings: A Guide and Record* edited by H. A. and J. Fosbrooke, L. S. B. Leakey, and P. Ginner in 1950. Both these latter references focus on an area of rock painting at Kolo, north of the town of Kondoa. For those interested in the rock art of central Tanzania, the most current bibliography is Imogene L. Lim's work produced in 1992. Since there is no one comprehensive reference

to the rock art of eastern Africa, researchers are advised to peruse the journals *Azania, Tanzania Notes and Records,* and *Uganda Journal.* Some of the earliest works are in *Journal of the Royal Anthropological Institute* and *Man.* In addition, scholars who find themselves in these countries should visit the respective national archives. Many of the early colonial administrators and officials provided the first documentation of rock art in their areas. This is the case for A. T. Culwick's 1929 note and another by William Aitken in 1948 in the *Kondoa District Book* on microfilm in the National Archives, Dar Es Salaam.

In any discussion of rock art, the questions of "when," "who," and "why" arise. The answers are neither simple nor easily revealed. In eastern Africa, painted representations are much more common than engraved ones. Unlike the paintings found in southern Africa, they are monochromatic—that is, various hues and values of red, black, and white. Researchers have classified paintings on the basis of color and style in order to establish relative chronologies. F. T. Masao recently attempted to place the art in a general chronological relationship with other African sites. He did this by correlating known archaeological data with that of the paintings to produce four broad phases:

1. Red conventionalized schematic human figures and naturalistic filled-in animals
2. Naturalistic animals painted in outline with in-filling of various motifs
3. White seminaturalistic silhouettes
4. Abstract and geometric styles

Other researchers have dismissed the use of style in linking the art of sub-Saharan areas. In southern and eastern Africa, the art shows similar categories of subject matter, but as David Lewis-Williams notes, the careful selection of features can show almost any two artistic styles to be similar or dissimilar.

In such stylistic chronologies, there is a tendency toward site-specificity. Their utility is, therefore, limited. The database in eastern Africa is comparatively small, and there are noticeable differences in the rock art from area to area. The chronology established is relative to other sites, so the precise age of any particular site is still

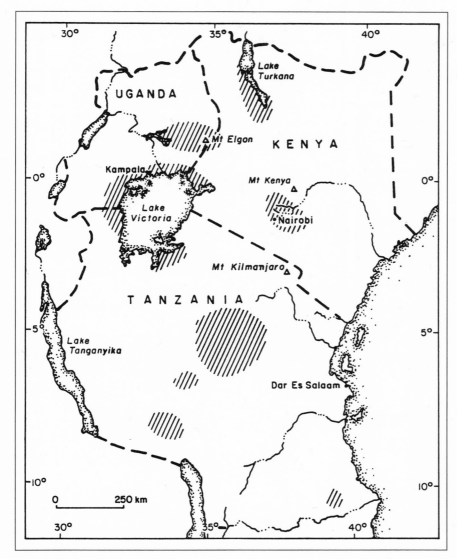

Fig. 42 *Distribution of rock-art sites in eastern Africa*

accelerator mass spectrometry illustrates the fallacy of the assumption that paintings using the same color (and style) are from the same time. This question was discussed by L. Dayton and M. McDonald in 1993.

The dating of engravings is equally difficult. Ascribing age according to the kind of motif depicted is a method used for both engravings and paintings. Anati used this method in his analysis of eastern African rock art. Suggesting that rock art is a reflection of the regional distribution of economies, he describes four horizons that illustrate a chronological succession from the oldest to more recent times: (1) early hunting and gathering, (2) classical and late hunting and gathering, (3) pastoral, and (4) farming and mixed economy. This evolutionary perspective is based on the migration of Bantu, Cushitic, and Nilotic speakers into eastern Africa. In 1982, R. Soper discussed the issue of whether the artists of the engravings found at two sites west of Lake Turkana were Cushitic or Nilotic speakers. Art attributed to pastoralists is based on the identification of motifs associated with meat feasting and cattle brands.

This discussion of dating returns us to a primary question of researchers: who are the artists? It is one that has created much debate. Given the extensive rock-art findings in southern Africa, Anati's characterization of one horizon as hunters and gatherers is well founded. The art in southern Africa has been attributed to the click-speaking San Bushmen. In eastern Africa, there are also extant click-speaking populations: the Hadza of Lake Eyasi and the Sandawe of southwestern

unknown. The oldest date associated with rock paintings comes from the excavation of Kisese II rock shelter in Tanzania by Ray Inskeep. Ochre pencils were found in deposits dating to 19,000 years ago. Unfortunately, no geophysical nor chemical dating has been done on the paintings themselves, as has been the case in North America, Europe, and Australia. Another issue affecting the devising of relative chronologies is color. Since there are a number of variables (natural and cultural) that affect the paint, judging its "freshness" is difficult. Radiocarbon dating by

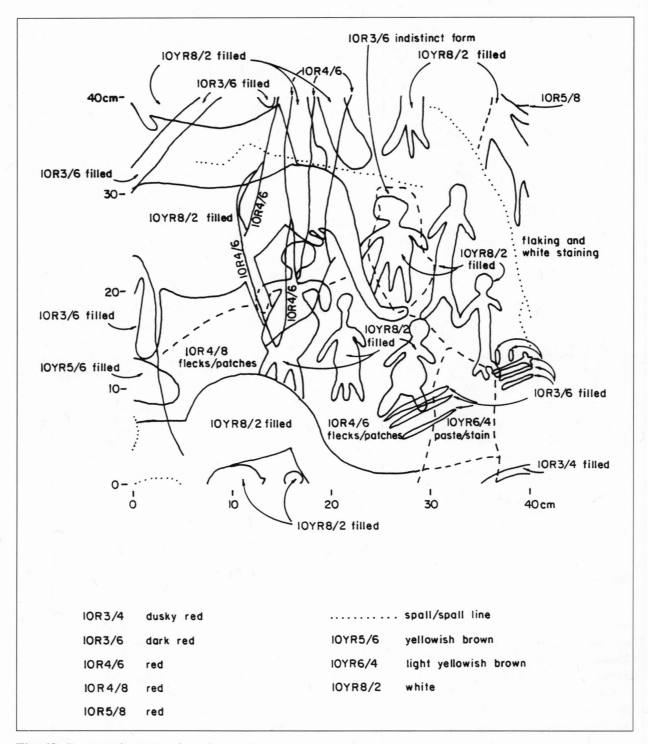

Fig. 43 *Section of painting from Baseto I*

Kondoa District. Both have been identified as sharing linguistic and physical similarities with the San Bushmen. They are also hunter-foragers.

Whether there is any historical or cultural relationship between these southern and eastern African populations is unclear, but researchers agree that the rock art located in the vicinity of both the Hadza and the Sandawe resembles the art of southern Africa more than that of the Sahara.

In exploring the meaning behind the act of painting, some early researchers in Tanzania were progressive in their methodology. In particular, A. T. Culwick, a British colonial administrator, recognized that local peoples might have some knowledge of rock paintings even if they no longer painted. He did what has become common practice—seeking the knowledge of local informants. In this case, he noted their current and prehistoric cultural affiliation. For the latter, he sought out archaeological remains associated with known prehistoric industries. In a 1931 investigation of a site at Bahi, he questioned a local chief about the site's use. The chief provided information on how the current peoples (the Gogo) maintain the site's sacredness by repainting images formerly created by the Wamia. By tracing the genealogy of the Gogo's arrival in Bahi (12 generations), Culwick estimated a minimum age for the paintings. Such use of ethnography did not continue until several decades later.

Since much of the early documentation of rock art was conducted in the process of German and British colonization, information accumulated gradually without any specific plan. Only in 1950 was there an effort to consolidate and make accessible this information as in previously mentioned guide produced by the Tanganyika Society.

Fig. 44 *Portion of red-colored paintings at Tambase II*

This was the first time that rock-art sites within one area were presented as a cohesive work. It provided the closest approximation of a survey, since all other documented efforts were of sites located in a piecemeal fashion within a larger region. As noted by L. S. B. Leakey, this was the beginning of the study of rock art in Tanzania. *The Guide* offered few answers to the "who," "when," and "why" of rock art, but it did provide the best descriptive information then available. H. A. Fosbrooke provided three motives for rock art: paintings as commemorative acts, doodling, and sympathetic magic. The last was interpreted on the basis of figures identified as the object and means of the hunt, followed by anthropomorphs (stylized human shapes) adorned with paraphernalia associated with magic and ritual.

More recent rock-art interpretations are by F. T. Masao, Mary Leakey, and Imogene L. Lim. Except for Lim's work, the interpretations offered are basically identical to those mentioned above. Leakey's perspective, though, is influenced by the work of southern African researchers—that is, she applies ethnographic evidence to her interpretation. Masao, purely speculative on his part, offers one other interpretive possibility for figures that defy description—that they are communicative signs to indicate economic resources. Research in northwestern Spain suggests that this is indeed a plausible explanation, as explained by R. Bradley, F. Criado Boado, and R. Fábregas Valcarce in 1994. Landscape archaeology is another perspective to explore by considering the relationship of rock art to its natural surroundings. The test is to catalog these indeterminate figures to establish their locations and their relationship to sites of economic pursuits. Masao submits that these signs might be band- or tribe-specific. If this is the case, these figures will appear as regional clusters. Research in this direction requires intensive, systematic regional survey and sampling strategies rather than the stumbling upon sites as in the early days.

After a lull of decades in the use of ethnography, Eric Ten Raa once again sought the knowledge of local informants in 1960. In this case,

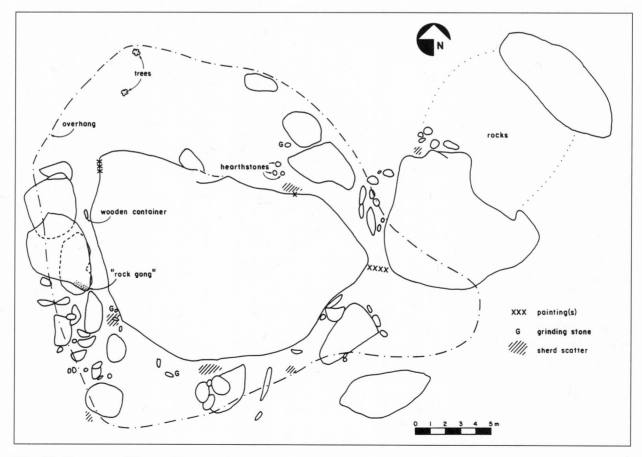

Fig. 45 *Site map of Kimau IA (note the painted areas and the rock gong)*

the Sandawe acknowledged that their ancestors had painted. As a full participant in Sandawe life, Ten Raa witnessed a hunter paint a giraffe on a rock before a group of hunters continued on their trip. The focus of Ten Raa's work was to provide the social context and significance, where possible, of painted sites. He outlined a number of linkages between Sandawe activities and rock-art sites, including hunting and ritual sacrifices (clan spirits and exorcism). For Ten Raa, the essence of rock art was the underlying belief system of the Sandawe. This aspect of his position anticipated that of David Lewis-Williams in southern Africa. Ten Raa also suggested that the art indicated not only multiple motives but possibly multiple uses of sites as well, a position advocated by Lim.

Ten Raa's work is important because through his recording and analysis of Sandawe texts, he demonstrated the historical continuity of the Sandawe to the painters of rock art and the antiquity of the Sandawe in the region. Although he discusses the social context, nothing is mentioned about the context of the physical site or sites that Sandawe use but do not paint.

Lim builds on this foundation of Sandawe ethnography and takes the next step in understanding the rock art by considering the relationship of the paintings to the site and the site within its natural and cultural landscape. She distinguishes two types of paintings: mural and nonmural. The latter is notable for its lack of superposition or overlap. Figures tend to be singular. Mural painting, as the name suggests, is a "canvas" of multiple images overlapping one another. Lim believes the foundation for understanding mural paintings lies in the analysis of ritual behavior, specifically, in *iyari,* the dance of twin births. *Iyari* is one painting tradition still practiced among the Sandawe. It embodies the complexity of meaning found in objects, actions, and the landscape. In Usandawe ("the land of the Sandawe"), meaning and potency of the place is reproduced through ritual—that is, the meaning is in the doing (the process), not in the object (the painted figure). For the Sandawe, rock shelters and baobab trees are metaphors for the "aboriginal womb" where all life, human and animal, was created. These meanings are found in Sandawe cosmology and

rain rites. This suggests that further work in Usandawe will reveal more mural-type paintings directly associated with rain sacrifice. Lim believes that nonmural paintings have multiple associations similar to the motives described by earlier researchers.

With Ten Raa's and Lim's work, caution must be taken in drawing comparisons between hunters and gatherers of eastern and southern Africa and the art of these regions. Lewis-Williams undertook one such comparison before Lim's research. If comparisons are to be made, Lim's study should be the focus. Ten Raa's study was a by-product of his research into the oral traditions of the Sandawe, while Lim's investigation concentrated directly on the meaning of rock art. Lewis-Williams selected illustrations from both Mary Leakey's and Ten Raa's work and incorporated Sandawe ethnography to support his perspective of trance and shamanism as the motive behind rock art. The Kondoa paintings studied by Mary Leakey lie outside the modern boundaries of the Sandawe and differ in their depiction of animals and humans. While the Sandawe admit that their ancestors were painters, more importantly, they note that they were but one among many hunter-forager groups in the region. To assume that all hunting and gathering people painted for the same reasons or that the Sandawe occupied the whole of this central region is presumptuous.

Given the earlier discussion of viewing rock-painting sites within their physical context, this article should mention rock gongs. Rock gongs are natural occurrences that produce a metallic sound when struck. Some are so well defined that there are cup marks or indentations where the rock is to be struck. Gongs have been documented at eastern African sites with rock art, as well as in southern Africa and Nigeria. In some cases, they are also associated with rock slides or chutes and are distinguished by their polished or grooved surfaces. The suggestion is that rock paintings, gongs, and slides are parts of a cultural complex. Rock slides are found in the Lake Victoria region, while none is recorded for the central region of Tanzania.

In many respects, the study of rock art in eastern Africa is still in its infancy. The emphasis here on Tanzanian rock art is indicative of this. In view of the methodologies and analyses touched upon in this essay, eastern Africa is primed to advance the next wave of rock-art research. Ethnographic studies indicate the strength of people's ties to the past and offer new perspectives on the meaning of rock art. As such, rock-art research is a means of exploring the complexity and dynamic nature of human society in eastern Africa.

BIBLIOGRAPHY

Anati, E. 1986. The rock art of Tanzania and the East African sequence. *Bollettino del Centro Camuno di Studi Preistoriei* 23: 15–68.

Bradley, R., F. Criado Boado, and R. Fábregas Valcarce. 1994. Rock art research as landscape archaeology: A pilot study in Galicia, North-West Spain. *World Archaeology* 25 (3): 374–390.

Chaplin, J. H. 1974. The prehistoric rock art of the Lake Victoria region. *Azania* 9: 1–50.

Culwick, A.T. 1931. Ritual use of rock paintings at Bahi. *Man* 31 (41): 33–36.

Dayton, L., and M. McDonald. 1993. The atomic age of cave art. *New Scientist* 137 (1862): 34–37.

Fosbrooke, H. A., P. Ginner, L. S. B. Leakey, and J. Fosbrooke. 1950. Tanganyika rock paintings: A guide and record. *Tanganyika Notes and Records* 29: 1–61.

Leakey, M. D. 1983. *Africa's vanishing art: The rock paintings of Tanzania*. London: Hamish Hamilton Limited.

Lewis-Williams, J. D. 1986. Beyond style and portrait: A comparison of Tanzanian and southern African rock art. In *Contemporary studies on Khoisan, Part 2*, eds. R. Vossen and K. Keuthmann, 95–139. Hamburg: Helmut Buske Verlag.

Lim, Imogene L. 1992. A site-oriented approach to rock art: A study from Usandawe, Central Tanzania. Ph.D. diss., Brown University.

Masao, F. T. 1982. The rock art of Kondoa and Singida: A comparative description. National Museums of Tanzania Occasional Paper No. 5. Dar Es Salaam: National Museums of Tanzania.

Soper, R. 1982. Archaeo-astronomical Cushites: Some comments. *Azania* 17: 145–162.

Ten Raa, E. 1971. Dead art and living society: A study of rock paintings in a social context. *Mankind* 8: 42-58.

Imogene L. Lim

CENTRAL AFRICAN ROCK ART

The rock art in central Africa is not visually spectacular, and given the lack of suitable ethnographies, most early studies were largely descriptive. Various stylistic analyses have been undertaken, but as with many rock-art studies worldwide, these prove to be rather meaningless without an understanding of the social context within which the art was produced and consumed. Recently Peter Garlake has extended and developed the interpretative framework used in southern Africa for the rock paintings of Zimbabwe, and Nic Walker has linked the rock art of the Matopos (southwestern Zimbabwe) to other archaeological results in the region in an attempt to flesh out the social context of rock-painting production. Together these two researchers have moved the study of rock art in central Africa beyond description and misguided notions of style.

The study of rock art in central Africa has been somewhat eclipsed by studies of Saharan and southern African rock art. However, the rock art

Fig. 46 *Red schematic painting from northern Zambia*

of central Africa is no less intriguing. While there are both rock paintings and rock engravings in central Africa, rock-engraving sites are not as common as painted sites. Throughout most of Malawi and Zambia and the adjacent areas of Angola, Mozambique, Tanzania, and Zimbabwe, there are two well-defined kinds of paintings: naturalistic representations and schematic designs. Naturalistic representations are usually monochrome red depictions of animals in lateral view. In some areas, the eland is the most commonly depicted animal. Human figures with bows or spears were also painted. There are very few examples of human or animal figures painted in groups or "scenes," but one example seemingly represents a human figure attempting to drive a feline away from an injured cow.

At some sites, these naturalistic paintings are superimposed by red geometric patterns. These include grid shapes, sets of parallel lines, concentric circles, and elaborate designs made up of finger dots. These are, in turn, superimposed by paintings executed in a thick, greasy white paint, the so-called late whites. This class of painting comprises complex geometric patterns as well as crude representations of stylized animal and human figures. There are also depictions of metal tools. These late whites and the red geometric patterns make up the schematic paintings of central Africa.

It is generally accepted that the naturalistic paintings were made by hunter-foragers, while the later schematic art was made by Bantu-speaking farmers. More specifically, the red schematic paintings are attributed to the Early Iron Age, and the late whites to Late Iron Age communities. David W. Phillipson argues that the late whites are associated with initiation and rainmaking rituals and suggests that the schematic red paintings were associated with similar rituals for earlier Iron Age groups.

In Zimbabwe, the naturalistic-painting traditions are much more developed than in other areas of central Africa. Here, there is a greater variety of subjects depicted and artistic techniques and conventions used that produce often large, complex, and elaborate panels. As done in many early rock-art studies, initially these paintings were simply ordered and classified according to for-

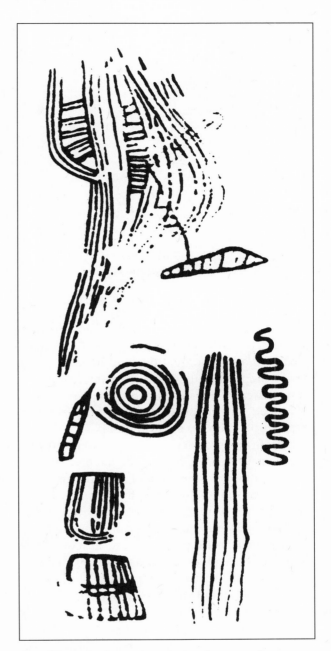

Fig. 47 *Red schematic painting from northern Malawi*

mal qualities of the depictions. Early sequences were based on the artists' use of color, whereas later sequences relied on the various painting techniques the prehistoric artists used and developed an evolution of artistic styles for this region. But the significance of these variations and how they relate to the development of rock art over time cannot be imposed on the art. We

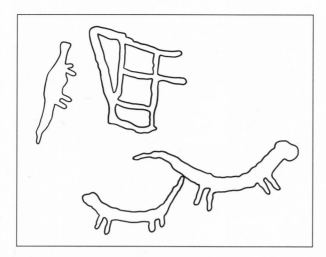

Fig. 48 *White schematic paintings from northern Zambia*

need to understand the motivation and meaning of the art before we can grasp how artists manipulated aesthetic qualities and hence how the art developed through time. Two interesting and quite different approaches to this question have advanced our understanding of the prehistoric rock art in Zimbabwe considerably.

The first approach involves extending the interpretation used in South Africa to the rock paintings of Zimbabwe. With reference to 19th- and 20th-century Bushman ethnography from the Northern Cape Province of South Africa and the Kalahari, Garlake and others have shown that Zimbabwean rock paintings are associated, to some extent, with rituals and beliefs of shamans.

There are no explicit paintings of trance dances, as one finds in southern Africa, but other features show that the rock art is unequivocally associated with the same ritual. For example, human figures holding whisks or wearing rattles definitely indicate a trance context, as these objects are only used during a trance dance. Many postures in which the human figures are painted represent postures shamans adopt during a trance, such as the hand raised to the nose. Shamans are reported to bleed at the nose during a trance ritual. They then collect this blood in their hands and smear it on sick members of their group as part of the curing process. There are the obvious indications of visual and somatic hallucinations, perhaps the most obvious

being extremely elongated human figures. And there are metaphors of trance performance, fight and flight being common. Therianthropes, or half-human–half-animal figures, that represent shamans turning into the animals from which they obtain their supernatural potency are also frequently depicted.

At first, this extending of temporally and regionally specific ethnography from southern Africa to the rock art of Zimbabwe might appear to downplay regional differences. Garlake, however, has carefully explored both the conceptual similarities and the conceptual differences expressed in the available ethnographies and the rock paintings and has produced nuance interpretations that highlight the diversity of shamanistic experience and its artistic expression in southern and central Africa. This can be demonstrated with reference to paintings of dots and flecks.

Painted dots and flecks occur in a wide variety of panels. In one such example, flecks appear to be coming out of the armpits and distended abdomens of female human figures. The Bushmen believe that supernatural potency becomes activated in the stomach. From there, it boils up the spine during the trance ritual. In its activated state, potency is thought to be released from the shaman's body. The distended abdomen is thus a graphic metaphor, or an artistic convention, for this "boiling" supernatural energy, while the emanating flecks represent its release by the shaman in a trance state.

Fig. 49 *Human figures with elongated bodies*

In other painted panels, clusters of flecks occur around human and animal figures as well as trees. In some cases, the human figures are clearly in a trance context because they have dance rattles and whisks—accoutrements of a trance dance. When in an altered state of consciousness, shamans experience visual hallucinations, including dots and flecks. Further, Bushmen believe that the atmosphere at a dance is redolent with supernatural potency, something that only trancing shamans can see. It stands to reason then that the flecks shamans hallucinate during their performance are interpreted as being the supernatural potency that only they can see during the ritual. Painting trance "scenes" with clusters of flecks is just one way of portraying the trance ritual and its attendant shamanistic beliefs for the rest of the community, to make belief in their religious work possible. Analyzing paintings of dots and flecks in Zimbabwe together with Bushman depictions of supernatural potency, Garlake has demonstrated that, while these paintings share a common essence, they differ in the sort of potency they represent.

By examining the conventions and attributes artists use, Garlake has shown that the prehistoric art of Zimbabwe is not as exclusively shamanistic as appears to be the case for the rock art of the southeastern mountains of southern Africa. Rather, by manipulating various conventions, prehistoric artists in Zimbabwe made reference to the many other aspects of their community and its values, or what Garlake terms "the essence of the human condition."

Our understanding of the meaning of Zimbabwean rock art has been greatly improved by cautiously using southern African hunter-forager ethnographies. While these ethnographies cannot shed light on every aspect of Zimbabwean rock art, this approach is by far superior to previous approaches that were posited on the assumption that any guess is as good as the next. This ethnographic approach has provided a framework within which to explore further the meaning and motivation behind the art. Other lines of evidence, including the art itself, can now be used to take these initial interpretations further.

The second approach that attempts to place rock-painting production within a social context explores archaeological evidence for ritual in the Matopos over the last 13,000 years. The rock art in this southwestern region of Zimbabwe is also associated with shamanistic religious beliefs. The paintings themselves then are evidence that some form of trance ritual was being performed during the Late Stone Age in the Matopos. Walker has investigated the nature of ritual activity and artistic production by analyzing the occurrence of rock shelters.

Ochre is the main pigment used in the production of rock paintings. There is indirect evidence for its use as body paint because it appears that some paintings depict men and women with body paint. Ochre is not local. It was always brought into the region in large quantities, but 9,800 years ago, ochre use increased considerably. There was a marked decline by 7,600 years ago, and around 2,200 years ago, there was a brief increase in its use again. There are also noticeable differences of occurrence between sites. Small sites, which appear to be living camps or specialist workstations, have less ochre in their deposits than the much larger sites with many rock paintings.

These periods of increased ochre use correlate with greater population densities in the Matopos. During these times, hunter-foragers appear to have stayed in the Matopos for longer periods. The fact that larger populations exerted more pressure on resources and for much longer periods would almost certainly have had an adverse effect on inter- and intragroup relations. When greater numbers of people come together in the Kalahari, trance dances are held more frequently. But, more importantly, at times of increased social tensions, communities turn more frequently to shamans to resolve tensions within and between groups.

It is highly probable, therefore, that the increased population in the Matopos and the obvious drain on economic and social resources resulted in inter- and intragroup tensions. Trance activities may very well have increased in an attempt to resolve these tensions. Because the production of rock paintings is so intricately linked to trance activities, serving to reinforce the beliefs in shamans' activities, it follows that the periods of greater population densities may

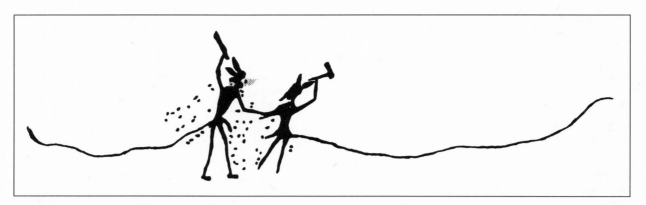

Fig. 50 *Fighting therianthropes*

also have resulted in greater artistic activity. The occurrence of greater volumes of ochre pigments in the deposits that relate to these times supports Walker's hypothesis. Further, Walker suggests that the larger sites with greater quantities of ochre recovered may in fact be ceremonial centers where large groups of people came together for ritual purposes.

In this study, Walker uses material recovered from archaeological deposits to give artistic activity in the Matopos a temporal dimension. This temporal framework may be used to investigate other issues, such as the shift in emphasis from animal to human representations. Did the shift in subject matter occur during times when maintaining group cohesion and social networks was of primary importance to shamans? Although quite different from Garlake's interpretative investigations, Walker's interpretation adds another dimension. Together Garlake's and Walker's studies lay an important and necessary foundation on which future research can develop.

The petroglyphs of central Africa, as with many of the other African regions, have received little attention, particularly in more recent studies. This is partly because the paintings, especially the naturalistic ones, have more seemingly recognizable "scenes." The engraved depictions are almost exclusively geometric patterns and are strikingly similar to engraved geometric patterns found in southern Africa.

Unfortunately, we know very little about who made the engravings, what they could mean, or how they relate to other, similar engraved-art traditions in Africa. New approaches that go beyond

the simple descriptions and meaningless stylistic sequences are required for the study of these enigmatic engravings. In the same way that our understanding of the prehistoric rock paintings in Zimbabwe advanced immeasurably, there is enormous potential for the study of rock engravings.

BIBLIOGRAPHY
Cooke, C. K. 1969. *Rock art of southern Africa.* Cape Town: Books of Africa.
Garlake, P. 1987. *The painted caves: An introduction to the prehistoric art of Zimbabwe.* Harare: Modus Publications.
———. 1990. Symbols of potency in the paintings of Zimbabwe. *South African Archaeological Bulletin* 45: 17–27.
———. 1994. Archetypes and attributes: Rock paintings in Zimbabwe. *World Archaeology* 25: 346–355.
———. 1995. *The hunter's vision: The prehistoric art of Zimbabwe.* Harare: Zimbabwe Publishing House.
Phillipson, D. W. 1972. Zambian rock paintings. *World Archaeology* 3: 313–327.
Summers, R. 1959. *Prehistoric rock art of the Federation of Rhodesia and Nyasaland.* London: Chatto & Windus.
Walker, N. J. 1994. Painting and ceremonial activity in the Later Stone Age of the Matopos, Zimbabwe. In *Contested images: Diversity in southern African rock art research,* eds. T. Dowson and D. Lewis-Williams, 119–130. Johannesburg: Witwatersrand University Press.
———. 1995. Later Pleistocene and Holocene hunter-gatherers of the Matopos. *Studies in African Archaeology,* vol. 10. Uppsala: Uppsala University.

Thomas A. Dowson

SOUTHERN AFRICAN ROCK ART

Rock art is found in most areas of southern Africa and has survived for centuries and, in some instances, millennia. The oldest example is about 27,000 years old. One of the richest areas is the southeastern mountains, or the land in and around Lesotho. In this region, rock paintings rank among the most elaborately done and detailed. The frequently illustrated shaded, polychrome eland is just one example. It has long been accepted that shaded, polychrome paintings were restricted to the southeastern mountains, but recently such depictions of eland were found in the southwestern Cape. Detail in the paintings is often literally pinhead in size. The rock engravings, on the other hand, are less detailed. These images were created by pecking, scraping, or cutting through outer patinated rock surfaces. Although not as finely detailed as rock paintings, rock engravings are as strikingly beautiful.

It is easy then to treat rock art as creations made to pass time or simply to decorate the rock surfaces where Bushmen lived. Due to the pioneering work of Patricia Vinnicombe and David Lewis-Williams in the 1970s, we know that these depictions were not the product of "idle hours," nor were they done for their aesthetic qualities alone, with a kind of art-for-art's-sake mentality. Working with the rich artistic traditions of the southeastern mountains, Vinnicombe and Lewis-Williams proposed that any interpretation of Bushman rock art should be based on authentic Bushman beliefs. By exploring these beliefs, the most convincing interpretative framework, and certainly the one that has lasted, emerged for the study of rock art. Both rock paintings and rock engravings are associated in numerous and diverse ways with beliefs surrounding the trance experiences of medicine peoples (shamans, who are both men and women).

In the 1970s, it was obvious that to counter the racist attitudes concerning Bushman rock art, one had to look to Bushman beliefs. Vinnicombe and Lewis-Williams led rock-art research into a more socially acceptable era, but that was only the beginning of a new line of inquiry. At this time, archaeologists, anthropologists, and historians were grappling with the social dynamics of southern Africa's past, particularly the last 2,000 years. It soon became apparent that historical research had been somewhat segregationalist—the diverse groups of people were seen as living in social isolation. Evidence from a wide variety of fields and sources showed that the different groups were, in fact, in close contact with one another and that there was a great deal of economic and sociopolitical interchange between them.

Fig. 51 *Pecked engraving from the northern Cape, South Africa, interpreted as representing the spirit on out-of-body travel*

Fig. 52 *Complex panel from KwaZulu-Natal Province, South Africa, depicting the death metaphor of a trance experience*

The implications of this were immense, but for rock-art research it meant that we could no longer see the art as being produced and consumed by pristine Bushman communities. By the end of the 1980s, many researchers were drawing on beliefs and concepts from groups other than Bushmen to get a better handle on the meaning and function of rock art in southern African society. Rock art is still seen as a "Bushman thing," something they did as opposed to other groups. By drawing on their beliefs, as well as those on of surrounding communities, researchers began to view the production of rock art as essentially a political statement about the place of the Bushman artist's communities in southern Africa. These beliefs then were resources that artists manipulated in creating their material culture.

A central ritual for all Bushman groups was, and still is among the Kalahari groups, the trance dance. During a trance dance, women clap and sing medicine songs named after things that are

Fig. 53 *Typical trance dance*

Fig. 54 *Three shaman figures*

said to be powerful (such as the eland or giraffe), while men dance in a rhythmic fashion around the women. The Bushmen believe that this dancing and clapping activates supernatural potency, called *n/om* in the Kalahari. The powerful animals contain this potency, and so in the Kalahari, Bushmen say, "We are dancing eland *n/om*," or "giraffe *n/om*."

It is the task of the shamans in the group to harness this potency and enter a trance state or, for the Bushmen, the spirit world. Once in the spirit world, shamans are said to cure the sick and resolve social conflict. A shaman would lay his or her hands on a sick person, and the sickness would flow into the shaman's body. The shaman would then expel the sickness through a hole in the nape of the neck, the *n//au* spot, with a loud shriek. In some Bushman groups, shamans also controlled the game as well as the rain animal that brought rain. One Bushman, Dia!kwain, told Wilhelm Bleek in 1874:

> Then the people who are at home see the rain clouds and they say to each other, "The medicine men really seem to have their hands upon the rain-bull, for you see the rain clouds come gliding."

Curing the sick and controlling the rain and the game can be seen as the shamans' "symbolic work." And it is this symbolic work that guaranteed the existence of Bushman society.

Shamans entering the spirit world experience a wide variety of physical and visual hallucinations. One of the most common physical sensations is the feeling of attenuation. The trance experience is so overwhelming and difficult to describe that shamans compare it with more familiar experiences that others can understand. In many Western societies today, drug-induced trances are commonly called *trips*. The Bushman commonly use *death* and *underwater* as metaphors for trance experience. The Bushman see a similarity between a shaman entering trance and an antelope, particularly an eland, dying. Both bleed at the nose, froth at the mouth, stumble about, and eventually collapse unconscious. The dying eland's hair stands on end, while shamans experience a tingling sensation all over their bodies that they interpret as hair standing on end. And it is for this reason that shamans refer to the entering of a trance as *half-death* or *little death*. Further, going into trance and going underwater share certain physical sensations such as altered vision, affected hearing, and a sense of weightlessness. And shamans often talk of diving into water holes when they enter the spirit world.

In the Kalahari, after the dance, shamans spend time sharing their experiences with each other and the rest of the group. They describe their journeys to the spirit world in great detail, and each shaman's experience, no matter how contradictory to the story of another, is accepted as an authentic revelation of the spirit world.

Fig. 55 *Typical depiction of a trance dance from the Eastern Cape Province of South Africa*

Farther to the south, Bushmen painted and engraved depictions of their trance experiences. The rock art includes representations of these dances—the women clapping, men and shamans dancing, and the powerful symbols of supernatural potency, the most common and important of which is the eland. There are also representations of curing and rain animals and depictions of the various visual and physical hallucinations shamans experience as well as the graphic metaphors shamans used to convey the wide variety of experiences to the rest of the group. Shamans, with their dancing paraphernalia, are often juxtaposed with fish, underwater snakes, and sometimes even turtles to communicate the trance feeling of being underwater. Shamans are also frequently shown alongside a dying eland or other antelope.

Just as discussions about shamans' encounters with the spirit world serve to communicate their experiences and make a belief in their symbolic work possible for the whole group in the Kalahari today, farther to the south paintings and engravings graphically communicated experiences of the spirit world. More importantly, engraved and painted on rock surfaces that surrounded habitation areas, the images provided a permanent backdrop to the beliefs that guaranteed the group's existence.

Although the paintings and engravings depict shamanistic experiences and concepts, there are differences that result from more than varying styles of execution. The nature of the differences can be best understood with reference to shamanistic beliefs. The artists making engravings tended to concentrate on imagery that results from hallucinations experienced in earlier stages of trance. The paintings, on the other hand, appear to derive from deeper stages of trance with more bizarre hallucinations. We do not believe, however, that the rock art was done while in a trance because an artist could not control himself or herself enough to produce the images. It is more likely that they were made after the trance dance. But, in the Eastern Cape Province, an interview with a woman who, in all probability, is the last surviving descendant of a Bushman artist has shed some new light on the possible ritual use of the paintings specifically and rock art in general.

This woman's father was a shaman who painted, and her sister was a rainmaker. Although the woman, referred to as "M," was in her 80s and her recollections were imperfect, she nonetheless gave information that confirmed earlier findings and suggestions about the art. For example, she confirmed that eland blood was used to make paint. She took researchers to a nearby cave in a small valley where she pointed out paintings her father made. Here, she also described how the production of the paintings was incorporated into trance rituals, a description that, if one accepts her account, has far-reaching implications for rock-art studies.

M told how, in her father's time, eland would be driven into the valley and killed at a spot beneath the cave. Blood was carried up to the cave where it was used as an ingredient in paint. The eland's potency was thus transferred from the body to the paint and then to the paintings themselves. When dancing in the cave in front of the freshly executed paintings, the shamans, wanting to increase the level of "spiritual power" in their bodies, would turn to face the paintings so that the latent energy in the paintings would then flow into them. M demonstrated this while singing in a low monotone. Through the use of blood from highly potent animals, such as eland, shaman-artists infused their paint with a spiritual energy. For the Bushmen, potency flowed from the animal, via its blood, to the paintings where it was stored and then from the paintings to trancing shamans.

Different but similar concepts applied to the engravings. Many large engraved panels in Namibia, for example, suggest they were executed in prominent positions around habitation areas where trance rituals took place for specific purposes.

Rock-art panels, then, are not just symbolic traces of supernatural power and the experiences of the spirit world. They are also powerful things themselves. Rock-art sites were storehouses of the potency that made contact with the spirit world possible. The art was produced to create a spiritually powerful landscape.

But it was this spirituality that provided resources for shaman artists to make political statements. Particularly during the last 2,000 years of

Bushman occupation of the southeastern mountains, major and escalating changes were taking place. For many hundreds of years, Bushmen had interacted in various ways with Bantu-speaking farmers. These, for the most part, amicable exchanges were disrupted by expanding European colonialism. New social relations began to develop. Shamans, paid with cattle and a share of the crops by the farmers for whom they made rain, found that they had access to new resources. As European colonists killed off the game and the Bushman territories became restricted, interaction with farmers increased in importance, and struggles developed between competing shamans and between shamans and ordinary people. The "egalitarian" values that held that shamans should not develop political power were eroded.

The social practice of rock painting was certainly implicated in these changes. One type of painting shows groups of people, some of whom are identifiable as shamans, in which no one is larger or more elaborately painted than another. A second type shows groups of people in which two or three shaman figures are more elaborately and individually depicted. The third type shows a single, elaborately painted central shaman with facial features, surrounded by "lesser" figures. The historical record from the Kalahari combines with these three types of paintings to suggest that the art became a site of struggle. As social circumstances changed, shamans translated their potency into political power and vied with one another for control of resources that were, in the final decades, increasingly derived from rainmaking for farmers. As shamans became political leaders, the manner in which they were painted became more personalized.

The artists who made these types of paintings were not merely painting historical events or chronicling social changes. Such an understanding would be related to the close-to-nature stereotype—simple people painting what was around them. Rather, the making of each painting was a sociopolitical intervention that furthered the artist's political status. The art did not simply reflect social relations; it transformed social relations. Each painting was more than an image of the way things were, or even of the way the artist wished they would become. Because the images were themselves things with power that mediated the levels of the cosmos, they had a coercive, persuasive function that was founded in their factuality.

The artists, moreover, invoked this coercive function in dealing with European colonial invasion. Unlike the Bantu-speaking farmers, the colonists were not intended to be among the viewers of the art, but their threatening presence implicated them in the social production of the art nonetheless. For centuries, as the shamans had battled in the spiritual realm with marauding shamans of illness (who often took feline forms), so, the art suggests, did they battle in the spiritual realm with European colonists. The shamans tried to deploy their powers in such a way as to thwart the advance of the settlers. As we know, their efforts were fruitless. The settlers' rifles were, in the end, invincible. At times following a policy of calculated genocide, at other times mounting ad hoc but nevertheless vicious "retaliatory" commandos, the colonists all but wiped out the Bushman communities south of the Orange River. Many Bushmen, it is true, intermarried with farmers, and others went to live with them, but all in all, the unpalatable truth of the matter is that genocide was the finality.

A "history" of any part of southern Africa that ignores the artistic traditions of the Bushmen, silencing the only significant Bushman voice we have left in some areas, merely perpetuates prejudices of the past. Through such emotionally charged images of Bushmen being killed by Europeans, rock art continues to challenge the prejudices of the past. By creating spiritually and politically powerful images, shaman-artists also contributed to creating the politically charged southern African landscape. Rock art can contribute to the making of history, despite, and simultaneously because of, the genocide that brought the traditions to an end.

BIBLIOGRAPHY
Campbell, C. 1986. Images of war: A problem in San rock art research. *World Archaeology* 18: 255–268
Dowson, T. 1992. *Rock engravings of southern Africa*. Johannesburg: Witwatersrand University Press.

———. 1994. Reading art, writing history: Rock art and social change in southern Africa. *World Archaeology* 25: 332–344.

Dowson, T., and D. Lewis-Williams, eds. 1994. *Contested images: Diversity in southern African rock art research.* Johannesburg: Witwatersrand University Press.

Lewis-Williams, D. 1981. *Believing and seeing: Symbolic meanings in southern San rock paintings.* London: Academic Press.

———. 1990. *Discovering southern African rock art.* Cape Town: David Philip.

Lewis-Williams, D., and T. Dowson. 1989. *Images of power: Understanding Bushman rock art.* Johannesburg: Southern Books.

Vinnicombe, P. 1976. *People of the eland: Rock paintings of the Drakensberg Bushmen as a reflection of their life and thought.* Pietermaritzburg: University of Natal Press.

Yates, R., and A. Manhire. 1991. Shamanism and rock paintings: Aspects of the use of rock art in the south-west Cape, South Africa. *South African Archaeological Bulletin* 46: 3–11.

Thomas A. Dowson

The Ceramic Late Stone Age

AFRICAN NEOLITHIC

Geographic Scope

The antecedents of several Neolithic cultures of sub-Saharan Africa are found in North Africa and the Sahara, and many of the cultures' defining characteristics, including exploitation of domestic plants and animals, ground stone, pottery vessels, and settled village organization, occurred first in these northern regions. Thus for the purposes of this article, the division of Africa into parts north and south of the Sahara seems irrelevant. Indeed, during the early Neolithic era, the ecological boundary of sub-Saharan Africa, defined by the Sahel-Sahara ecotone (the transition between two adjacent ecological communities), was located far north of its present location. Some of the earliest Saharan Neolithic sites, located in the western desert at the Sudan-Egypt border, have rich Sahelian flora. The term *Neolithic* has never been systematically used south of the equatorial forest and woodland savanna, and Stone Age food production is poorly documented.

Definitions, Uses, and Alternatives

The term *Neolithic* has a diversity of meanings and uses among scholars both outside and inside Africa. Controversy over the utility and relevance of the term for African archaeology has continued for several decades, so it is appropriate and necessary to discuss its definitions and alternative terminologies. A comprehensive and eloquent discussion of Neolithic terminology was presented by P. Sinclair, Thurstan Shaw, and Bassey Andah in 1993.

Neolithic literally means *New Stone Age*. The term was initially applied to Early Holocene sites in Europe and sites dating to the end of the Pleistocene in western Asia—localities that succeeded Mesolithic (literally, *Middle Stone Age)* sites and contained ground- and polished-stone axes, grindstones, or pottery. The Neolithic was considered an advanced and more sophisticated stage in the evolution of technology and culture that set the stage for metal-using cultures and the rise of civilizations. During the 1920s and 1930s, the relationships among technology, economy, and society became an important focus of investigation. Neolithic cultures were increasingly characterized by food production, large permanent settlements, and more complex social formations. The use of the term thus shifted from a description based on polished-stone and ceramic technology to one based on food-producing economies, in other words, on subsistence modes involving farming or herding. This economic definition is now most widely used by English-speaking archaeologists in Africa. The term has also been used to refer to modern and prehistoric cultures in the New World and Eurasia at the tribe and chiefdom stages of social complexity, with settlement systems ranging from small permanent villages to more complicated hierarchical groupings of settlements of different sizes and functions, including ceremonial centers. This broad use of the term for modern and Stone Age cultures in both the Old and New Worlds has not been widely accepted. Indeed, the term is now becoming increasingly restricted to Europe, western Asia, and North Africa, where it has the longest history of use.

Terminology developed for prehistoric sequences in one region accumulates a heavy burden of connotations that may be irrelevant to the unique characteristics of another region or even obscure them. Grahame Clark suggested a semantically neutral classification system for stages of the Stone Age comprising six modes, which he hoped would carry less regional historical baggage. The first five cultural modes of the Stone Age were, in part, applied to African archaeology by several authors in the first volume of the *Cambridge History of Africa* and by D. W. Phillipson in his 1993 synthesis of *African Archaeology.* Clark's technological modes have the following approximate equivalents in African industrial complexes:

Mode 1	Olduwan
Mode 2	Acheulian
Mode 3	Middle Stone Age
Mode 4	Pleistocene large-blade tool, Late Stone Age
Mode 5	Holocene microlithic, Late Stone Age
Mode 6	Neolithic

Mode 6, which basically described the European and West Asian Neolithic, was never transferred to Africa.

Among French-speaking archaeologists, the term *Neolithic* has frequently been applied to archaeological sites that had microlithic technologies, dated to the Holocene, and had pottery or ground-stone tools. These include archaeological cultures with no direct evidence for economic mode because of poor faunal and floral preservation, as well as those that demonstrably represent settlements occupied by broad-spectrum hunters, foragers, and fishers who did not use domestic plants and animals. For example, G. Camps, in 1982, included sites in the Sahara occupied by people with a hunter-fisher-gatherer economy in his survey of Neolithic herders and farmers of northwestern Africa. They made pottery, ground-stone implements, and bone harpoons, but there is no evidence that they exploited domestic plants and animals. Occasionally, such sites have been assigned to a Mesolithic stage, as at Khartoum on the Nile in northern Sudan,

but this label and the more recently coined term *Aqualithic* for such sites have not been widely accepted.

Manfred Eggert has critically examined the use of the presence of ground-stone axes, hoes, and pottery at archaeological sites to define a Neolithic stage in central Africa. Some occurrences are clearly associated with Early Holocene forest and woodland hunter-foragers using a flaked-stone tool technology. Most sites have no direct evidence of food production, though carbonized seeds of oil palm and other forest-tree species may be present. Nor do many have evidence of flaked-stone technology that would place them in the Stone Age. Indeed, ground-stone axes are sometimes associated with traces of ironworking, which stretches the definition of the Neolithic far beyond its originally intended application to final Stone Age cultures. Based on finds from the Shum Laka rock shelter and other sites in the equatorial forest of west-central Africa that contain pottery or ground-stone tools dating to the last two millennia B.C., Pierre de Maret has proposed the term *from Stone to Metal Age* or SMA. This seems less than satisfactory because it is partly defined on the basis of what follows rather than on its own characteristics and because it may subsume a diversity of archaeological cultures.

In highland East Africa (Kenya and Tanzania), the use of the term *Neolithic* has been particularly problematic. Several discrete archaeological traditions have been subsumed under the Stone Bowl Neolithic cultures. This characteristic artifact type is often recovered from burial sites but rarely from occupation sites. Ground-stone axes, hoes, and grindstones are also rarely recovered from habitation sites. This archaeological tradition was renamed *Pastoral Neolithic,* which was defined as occurrences with Late Stone Age lithic technology, domestic animals, and pottery. This begs the question of the degree to which these cultures relied upon domestic plants. Late Stone Age sites with pottery have been called *Pastoral Neolithic* without demonstrating an association with domesticates. This is problematic because the assumption that sites with pottery or stone bowls also have a food-producing economy is sometimes unwarranted. For example, the

Eburran industry in the central Rift Valley of Kenya can be traced back to preceramic Early Holocene hunter-foragers. At the Enkapune ya Muto rock shelter, the Middle Holocene Eburran levels, dating to 4,900 years ago, are associated with a wild fauna but contain small amounts of pottery types known to be associated with domestic animals in northern lowland Kenya in the 3rd millennium B.C. In this case, Pastoral Neolithic pottery is not associated with a typical Neolithic lifestyle. The first domestic stock appeared at Enkapune ya Muto 900 years after Pastoral Neolithic pottery, and domestics did not dominate Eburran faunal assemblages until 3,400 years ago. Sites characterized as Pastoral Neolithic on the basis of an artifact class or the rare find of domestic stock may thus reveal a distinctly non-Neolithic way of life when thoroughly examined.

The complexities of the archaeological record in highland East Africa pose additional problems for the term *Pastoral Neolithic*. At least three distinct contemporaneous archaeological cultures are known in this region, all of which relied to greater or lesser degrees on domestic animals. After 3,300 years ago, the Eburran was contemporary with the Elmenteitan Neolithic and Savanna Pastoral Neolithic traditions, both of which appear to have developed elsewhere, possibly in the Sudan and Ethiopia, respectively, and then to have been imported into the region. The diversity of ceramic "wares" associated with the provisionally named *Savanna Pastoral Neolithic* may warrant the naming of additional traditions. Some Eburran groups apparently adopted a pastoral lifestyle, while others may have maintained a hunting and gathering lifestyle and interacted with food producers. Historical hunter-foragers, farmers, and herders in the East African highlands provide a useful source of models for prehistoric interaction patterns.

Subsuming three or more discrete cultural traditions with different histories under the blanket terms *Neolithic* or *Pastoral Neolithic* obscures this diversity and impedes the conceptualization of the patterns and processes of adaptation and interaction between cultures. Food production was undoubtedly the most significant cultural change in the closing millennia of the Late Stone Age, but it did not affect all populations in the same ways, and some did not become herders or farmers. It is probably better, therefore, to refer to the period of the Late Stone Age during which food production appeared as the *Neolithic era* and use more specific designations such as *Elmenteitan* or *Eburran* for archaeological traditions during this era. To ignore the cultural and economic diversity of this era by subsuming it under labels such as *Stone Bowl Cultures, Pastoral Neolithic,* or *Stone Age Food Producers* is to reduce archaeology to the study of pottery, stone bowls, and domestic animals rather than of prehistoric human cultures.

In the forest and savanna zones of West Africa, pottery and ground stone were used by Late Stone Age hunter-foragers before the advent of food production. This phase and the succeeding Kintampo industry, in which domestic animals were added to the fauna of the preceding culture, are now conventionally subsumed under the more neutral term *Ceramic Late Stone Age* in order to avoid the problematic connotations of the term *Neolithic.*

In southern Africa, the term *Neolithic* is rarely applied, in part because this region is sufficiently distant and distinct from adjacent continents to have been relatively insulated from developments in the north and to have followed its own trajectory, thus warranting a separate terminology for stages of the prehistoric record, as produced by A. H. J. Goodwin and C. van Riet Lowe in 1929. Also, until recently, the archaeological record provided scant evidence of Stone Age food production, and formal terms for this era have not yet been proposed.

In 1993, Sinclair, Shaw, and Andah recommend abandoning the term *Neolithic* because of its outmoded Eurocentric bias and because it remains an obstacle to communication between researchers. There is another, perhaps more compelling, reason for abandoning the term in Africa: when first applied in Africa, prehistorians assumed that pottery, ground-stone tools, all domestic animals, and the concept of domestication of plants originated outside of Africa and were introduced by immigrants or by the diffusion of ideas from western Asia via the Nile Valley. It is now abundantly evident that these features of material culture and technology, and most aspects of economy, were independent inventions by Late Pleistocene and Early Holocene African hunter-foragers, who adaptively responded to changing natural and social environments.

The Origin and Spread of Neolithic Domestic Plants and Animals

Our understanding of the origin and spread of food production has been radically revised in the last two decades. In 1965, all participants in the Burg-Wartenstein symposium on the African Later Tertiary and Quaternary assumed that the idea of domestication, as well as most species of domestic animals, diffused from western Asia to Africa via the Nile Valley. We now know that food production appeared in the Lower (northern) Nile Valley later than in the desert west of the Nile in Upper (southern) Egypt.

Cattle, sheep, and goats were herded during the Neolithic era. Sheep and goats have no wild progenitors in Africa and were clearly introduced from western Asia. They appeared in North Africa by 6,500 years ago. Cattle were also thought to be non-African domesticates, but there is substantial paleontological evidence for Pleistocene wild cattle in North Africa and somewhat circumstantial archaeological evidence that they were independently domesticated in northeastern Africa as early as 10,000 years ago. Genetic analysis now conclusively demonstrates that humpless African cattle have been distinct from European breeds for more than 20,000 years, thus confirming an independent origin for African domestic cattle.

Most African domestic crops have wild progenitors in the Ethiopian Highlands, Sahel, savanna, and West African savanna-forest ecotone north of the equator. These regional crop complexes and reconstruction of the processes of domestication in each region have been investigated by Jack Harlan. Regrettably, few of the crops have been clearly identified in Early Holocene incipient agricultural sites or even later Neolithic era sites. One significant exception is Nabta Playa, located in the Western Desert of far southern Egypt and dating to 8,000 years ago. The site is a village of small huts, many of which contained dozens of small potholes surrounded by ashy sediments rich in carbonized plants. All belong to the Sudanic floral zone. Many grains of morphologically wild sorghum were recovered. The site also contains storage pits, pottery, and grindstones. Future research may reveal equally early evidence of the incipient stages of domestication of other African grains by indigenous hunter-foragers of the arid savanna-Sahel zone all across Africa.

The spread of food production can occur in two ways. The transfer of concepts, methods, and products of Neolithic food production can take place by a process known as *stimulus diffusion*—that is, indigenous populations adopt aspects of new technologies and economies. This is clearly evident in most regions of Africa. New features are incorporated into the material repertoires of Early Holocene hunter-foragers, implying population continuity. In some cases, food production spread by population movements. This process, known as *demic diffusion,* is reflected by the replacement of indigenous Late Stone Age hunter-forager cultures by Neolithic cultures with new lithic and ceramic industries. Both processes have been identified in the highlands of East Africa. Some Eburran hunter-foragers became pastoralists, and others apparently remained hunter-foragers living alongside intrusive Elmenteitan and other Neolithic food producers. Linguistic evidence can be used to identify areas from which prehistoric populations came as their numbers swelled in response to increased food supplies and the need for new pastures and farmlands.

As discussed above, experiments in cattle and grain domestication were underway 8,000 years ago in the ancient Sahel zone, when it stretched as far north as southern Egypt. During the Early Holocene, the climate was obviously much wetter than it is today but became drier than at present during the Middle Holocene, between 3,000 and 4,500 years ago. As aridity increased, Neolithic food producers or the concepts and methods of food production moved south along with their savanna habitat. Domestic animals appear in the northern fringes of modern sub-Saharan Africa only after 4,000 years ago, possibly because the savanna-woodland zone of tsetse-fly infestation was a barrier to movement before it retreated south during the arid phase of the Middle Holocene. Pastoralism was established in the highlands of East Africa only after 3,400 years ago, near the end of the Middle Holocene arid phase. Domestic sheep crossed the final ecological barrier of the woodland savannas of east-central Africa to arrive in arid southwestern Africa 2,000 years ago. Cattle are not securely documented in the Cape until 1,300 years ago.

The chronology of West African forest root- and tree-crop domestication and that of the Ethiopian highland teff and ensete complex are unknown. It is uncertain whether they were independently invented in response to internal social and demographic forces, climate change, stimulus diffusion, or demic diffusion.

The Neolithic era in Africa encompasses a broad range of human adaptations and cultures. Although the term *Neolithic* carries a heavy load of implicit assumptions about economy and technology and connotations of Eurocentric origins, it has served as a more-or-less convenient label for food-producing cultures, mainly north of the equator, but it has also obscured substantial cultural and adaptive diversity. Mounting evidence for the independent origins of ceramic and ground-stone technology and domestication of plants and cattle in Africa provide ample justification for abandoning the term in Africa. It should now be replaced with more specific and appropriate terms reflecting the unique configurations of economy and technology at the end of the Stone Age in different regions of Africa.

BIBLIOGRAPHY

Ambrose, S. H. 1986. Hunter-gatherer adaptations to non-marginal environments: An ecological and archaeological assessment of the Dorobo model. *Sprache und Geschichte in Afrika* 7: 11–42.

Arkell, A. J. 1949. *Early Khartoum.* Oxford: Oxford University Press.

Bishop, W. W., and J. D. Clark. 1967. *Background to evolution in Africa.* Chicago: University of Chicago Press.

Bower, J. R. F., Nelson, C. M., Waibel, A. F., and S. Wandibba. 1977. The University of Massachusetts' Later Stone Age/Pastoral Neolithic comparative study in central Kenya: An overview. *Azania* 12: 119–143.

Bower, J. R. F., and C. M. Nelson. 1978. Early pottery and pastoral cultures of the central Rift Valley. *Man* 13: 554–566.

Clark, G. 1970. *Aspects of prehistory.* Berkeley: University of California Press.

Clark, J. D. 1959. *The prehistory of southern Africa.* Hammondsworth: Penguin.

———. 1982. *The Cambridge history of Africa,* vol. 1. Cambridge: Cambridge University Press.

Clark, J. D., and S. A. Brandt. 1984. *From hunters to farmers: The causes and consequences of food production in Africa.* Berkeley: University of California Press.

de Maret, P. 1994–95. Pits, pots and the far-west streams. *Azania* 29/30: 318–323.

Ehret, C., and M. Posnansky. 1982. *The archaeological and linguistic reconstruction of African history.* Berkeley: University of California Press.

Goodwin, A. J. H., and C. van Riet Lowe. 1929. The Stone Age cultures of South Africa. *Annals of the South African Museum* 27.

Klein, R. G., and K. Cruz-Uribe. 1989. Faunal evidence for prehistoric herder-forager activities at Kasteelberg, Western Cape Province, South Africa. *South African Archaeological Bulletin* 44: 82–97.

Marean, C. W. 1992. Hunter to herder: Large mammal remains from the hunter-gatherer occupation at Enkapune ya Muto rockshelter, central Rift Valley, Kenya. *African Archaeological Review* 10: 65–127.

Phillipson, D. W. 1993. *African archaeology.* Cambridge: Cambridge University Press.

Robertshaw, P., and D. Collett. 1983. The identification of pastoral peoples in the archaeological record: An example from East Africa. *World Archaeology* 15: 67–78.

Sealy, J., and R. Yates. 1994. The chronology of the introduction of pastoralism to the Cape, South Africa. *Antiquity* 68: 58–67.

Shaw, T., P. Sinclair, B. Andah, and A. Okpoko. 1993. *The archaeology of Africa: Food, metals and towns.* London: Routledge.

Sutton, J. E. G. 1974. The aquatic civilisation of middle Africa. *Journal of African History* 15: 527–546.

Wendorf, F., and R. Schild. 1994. Are the Early Holocene cattle in the eastern Sahara domestic or wild? *Evolutionary Anthropology* 3: 118–128.

Stanley H. Ambrose

NILE VALLEY: PRE-AGRICULTURAL CULTURES

The last hunter-forager people of the Nile Valley lived from 10,000 to 5,000 B.C., just before the introduction of agriculture into this region. They occupy a pivotal position in Nile Valley prehistory as they were a transitional people between Paleolithic hunter-foragers and Neolithic farmers.

They lived in the era following the glaciers when the world experienced sometimes massive environmental and climatic changes. In North Africa and the Nile Valley, dry and wet phases alternated throughout this period. In some parts of the world, farming and herding began during this time and gradually spread to surrounding areas, including the Nile Valley. The archaeological record of preagricultural peoples and the evidence of their adaptations may offer insights into why Nile Valley dwellers began farming. The taking up of farming was a transition that occurred throughout much of the world and is arguably the most significant change in human life on earth. The lifeways of these people are also of interest as the most developed and sophisticated hunter-forager adaptations in this region.

Unfortunately the archaeological record of preagricultural people is meager, consisting of a small number of encampments and work stations scattered spottily along the Nile Valley and in the Fayum. There is no continuous sequence in one area that could offer insights into how these cultures evolved and changed over time. The known sites are scattered, few and far between in time and space, with vast areas of the Nile Valley and chunks of time not represented.

Nonetheless, a sketchy picture of the preagricultural peoples' lifeways can be patched together from the archaeological record and material extrapolated from earlier periods. In the Nile Valley, the most complete record of hunter-forager adaptations, which can provide a model for understanding the preagricultural people, comes from a series of 18,000-year-old camps located in Wadi Kubbaniya near Aswan. These sites indicate that for much of the year, hunter-

foragers relied on a few productive, reliable foods supplemented with a broad range of other seasonally available foods. Their staples were catfish, caught in shallow waters during spawning and dried and stored, and wetland plants, especially root foods and particularly the tubers of *Cyperus rotundus*. These were supplemented with migratory waterfowl, hartebeests, aurochs, and dorcas gazelles, as well as a wide assortment of plant foods. Archaeological data from later preagricultural communities, though very incomplete, suggest similar subsistence patterns with adaptations to changing conditions and technologies.

The oldest known preagricultural cultures of the postglacial era date from nearly 9,000 to 11,000 years ago and were excavated in Nubia on the west bank of the Nile as part of a salvage campaign before the Aswan High Dam flooded the region. These are small camps represented mainly by scatters of microlithic stone tools, a hallmark of this preagricultural period. The microlithic tool industry from the earliest of these Nubian sites, dating to 10,580 years ago, is referred to as the *Arkinian*. The later sites, dating to about 8,860 years ago, produced a somewhat different tool assemblage called the *Shamarkian* industry.

The Nubian sites, consisting mainly of concentrations of stone tools, suggest seasonal encampments by small groups. At one of the Arkinian sites, there were three mounds covered by large quantities of burned stones and stone tools, scattered in 12 very dense concentrations, along with remnants of three fireplaces. Each concentration probably represents a separate seasonal encampment by a small group. This location, like the others used repeatedly, may have been favored for fishing or collecting roots and tubers. Unfortunately, plant remains were not collected during excavations, but it is likely that these Nubian peoples focused on the same abundant, reliable wetland plants collected at Wadi Kubbaniya. The location of the sites along embayments would have supported large marshes and been would have ideal for collecting these plants.

Faunal remains from the sites are similar to those from Wadi Kubbaniya—catfish, hartebeests, aurochs, and gazelles. But there was also evidence of an innovation in Nilotic foraging—fishing in the main Nile channel. While there are rare, scattered finds of deep-water fish in earlier periods, Nile perch and two other deep-water fish appear consistently from the time of the occupation of the Arkinian sites. The new microlithic technology may have facilitated this fishing technique. Microlithic blades could have been hafted (fitted) on a spear to make a harpoon. Fishing the main Nile channel may have been a way to broaden the resource base and find food during periods of scarcity. During the late spring and summer, the poorest time of the year, the Nile was at its lowest point, making it an ideal time to fish the main channel.

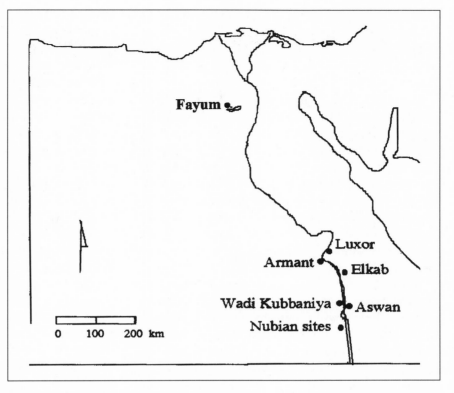

Fig. 56 *Neolithic localities in the Nile Valley*

The next known preagricultural site, dating from 7,885 to 8,340 years ago, is located within the walls of the pharaonic temple at Elkab, 120 kilometers downstream from Aswan. Consisting of eight small concentrations of cultural debris, the site appears to have been a specialized fishing and hunting camp used repeatedly in the fall. Deep-water species predominated among the fish remains, probably because the floodplain here is extremely narrow and offers very little opportunity for shallow water fishing. The mammalian fauna included aurochs, dorcas gazelles, hartebeests, porcupines, hippopotamuses, and possibly Barbary sheep. The stone-tool industry, named for the temple, is the *Elkabian*.

A more extensive record of preagricultural people is known from about 7100 to 6000 B.C. in the northern and southwestern Fayum Depression. A number of teams in the 1920s, 1970s, and 1980s have investigated a variety of small camps, scattered along what was once the lush lakeshore of ancient Lake Moeris. A freshwater lake, it was sustained by Nile flood waters and fluctuated with the Nile inundation. For several millennia,

however, this region of the Fayum has been dry desert, leaving the archaeological record relatively unscathed by farming and settlement. While the sites span about 1,000 years, they all share the same tool industry, referred to as the *Qarunian*. The sites are small, often overlapping encampments that show extensive, repeated occupation. Most have hearths and pits in addition to scatters of stone tools.

Plant remains were extensively collected at one Qarunian site and yielded vegetation of marshes and wet ground, especially seeds of the sedges *Cyperus* and *Scirpus*. Other common seeds came from *Polygonum*, *Rumex*, and *Chenopodium*. The seeds may have been prepared by cooking as a porridge or grinding them into a flour. Some of the plants may have been collected for their young leaves and eaten as greens or cooked like spinach. There was no evidence of the *Cyperus* tubers that were a mainstay of the people at Wadi Kubbaniya, but this is probably not a sign that they were ignored. These highly starchy foods often do not preserve well at archaeological sites, while hard seeds more often do. Most likely the Qarunians did collect *Cyperus* tubers along with other root foods from the marshes. They would surely not have ignored these foods since they were a rich source of carbohydrates, easy to harvest, and abundant for several months of the year.

The faunal remains from the Qarunian site were predominantly fish—catfish, taken from shallow waters along the shore and Nile perch and *Synodontis* caught in deep lake waters. Waterfowl and turtles were very abundant as well. Other fauna included gazelles, hartebeests, and aurochs, common throughout the other preagricultural sites, as well as small quantities of hare, jackals or dogs, and ostriches.

In addition to hunting and gathering, the Qarunian people may also have attempted to manipulate their environment by selectively burning wetlands. Fire would have stimulated plant growth, which in turn would have improved the root harvests and attracted game. The evidence consists of burned areas in some of the swamp sediments exposed in trench profiles at one Qarunian site. Evidence of burning has also been found at other sites dating from the postglacial period, including a number of areas dating to about 12,000 years ago in the Nile Valley. While these burns might have been the result of natural fires, it is likely that they were caused by human activity. Selective burning has been a common practice among recent hunter-foragers in a variety of environments including wetlands.

The last preagricultural sites date from about 1,000 years before the advent of agriculture in Egypt. A single radiocarbon date from one of these sites was about 6,120 to 6,480 years ago (or approximately 5365 to 5065 B.C.). Located between Luxor and Armant, the sites diverge from the earlier preagricultural sites in several significant ways. Including a few very small shards, these sites provide the first evidence of ceramics in the Egyptian Nile Valley. They also yielded evidence of a lithic industry, called the *Tarifian,* which is intermediate between the preagricultural microlithic tools and flake tools of the late farmers. The subsistence patterns of the Tarifian sites are unknown as no floral or faunal remains were recovered. The sites, however,

suggest a lifestyle no different from that of earlier preagricultural communities. They consist of little more than artifact scatters with one site yielding a small, shallow pit and a hearth. Still the worked stone and traces of ceramics suggest that change was underway in the Nile Valley—change that may have laid the groundwork for the transition to food production.

How and why this transition occurred is not understood. The meager archaeological record now available shows that the Nile Valley's preagricultural people followed a generalized hunting-gathering strategy like that practiced in the Late Paleolithic. But they were also improving upon old methods and adapting to new conditions. Such flexibility may have been a crucial factor when the last foragers adopted crops and livestock, thereby becoming the first farmers.

BIBLIOGRAPHY

Brewer, D. 1989. *Fishermen, hunters, and herders: Zooarchaeology in the Fayum, Egypt (ca. 8200–5000).* Oxford: British Archaeological Reports, International Series 478.

Ginter, B., J. K. Kozlowski, and M. Pawlikowski. 1985. Field report from the survey conducted in Upper Egypt in 1983. In *Mitteilungen des Deutschen Archaeologischen Institut-Abteilung Kairo,* 9–23.

van Neer, W. 1989. Fishing along the prehistoric Nile. In *Late prehistory of the Nile Basin and the Sahara,* eds. L. Kryzaniak and M. Kobusiewicz, 49–56. Poznan: Poznan Archaeology Museum.

Wenke, R. J., J. E. Long, and P. E. Buck. 1988. Epi-Paleolithic and Neolithic subsistence and settlement in the Fayum Oasis of Egypt. *Journal of Field Archaeology* 15: 29–51.

Wendorf, F. 1968. *The prehistory of Nubia,* 2 vols. Dallas: Fort Burgwin Research Center and Southern Methodist University Press.

Wendorf, F., and R. Schild. 1989. Summary and synthesis. In *Prehistory of Wadi Kubbaniya, vol 3: Late Paleolithic archaeology,* ed. A. E. Close, 768–824. Dallas: Southern Methodist University Press.

Wetterstrom, W. 1993. Foraging and farming in Egypt: The transition from hunting and gathering to horticulture in the Nile Valley. In *The archaeology of Africa: Food, metal and towns,* eds. T. Shaw, P. Sinclair, B. Andah, and A. Okpoko, 165–226. London: Routledge.

Wilma Wetterstrom

SAHARAN NEOLITHIC

The Neolithic of the Sahara, a complex of cultural traits, flourished approximately between 5,000 and 10,000 years ago in the central Saharan belt situated between 15° and 25° north latitude. Among the novel aspects characterizing these cultures—a set of specific technologies, settlement patterns, and rock art—the appearance of pottery and the beginnings of food production in the form of a pastoral economy are surely the most important phenomena. There is no certain proof of actual cultivation other than the use of wild species belonging to millet and sorghum taxa, nor is there evidence of true permanent settlements. For this reason, debate still reigns as to whether or not these cultures should be referred to as *Neolithic*. Following the arguments of V. Gordon Childe and the functionalist school, there is substantial agreement that the term *Neolithic* defines a complex of correlated changes that deeply modified the socioeconomic structure of society in the Near East and paved the way to complex urban civilizations.

In order to answer the various questions about the nature of the economic context, it is necessary to analyze the Saharan region's cultural development for the whole chronological span corresponding to the Early and Middle Holocene. This seems to be a better approach than the chronotypological perspective, which is limited to acknowledging subsequent phases (Early, Middle, Late Saharan Neolithic) based on the material culture's characteristics.

The beginning of the lifestyle transformation coincided with the return of rains to these territories and the reoccupation of the Sahara, practically abandoned during the severe dry phase that started around 20,000 years ago. Modern paleoclimatic studies support the picture of the Saharan occupation at the Pleistocene-Holocene boundaries. A complex of similar situations resulted, all strongly based on the exploitation of aquatic resources, a lifestyle that inspired J. Sutton's definition of an *Aqualithic* culture. The term received criticism at the time but today still seems quite appropriate. In Mali, a lacustrine phase, placed between 6,900 and 8,500 years ago, was shown by datable stratigraphic sections in

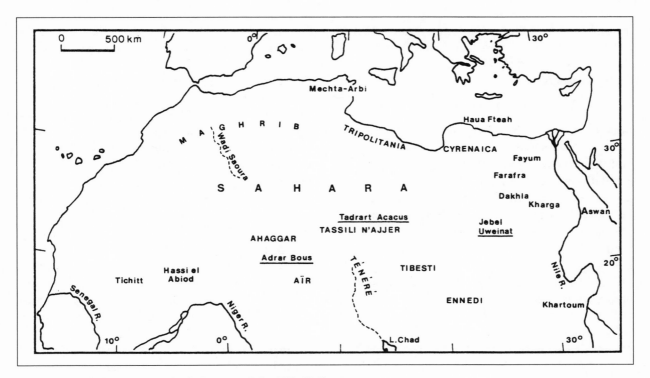

Fig. 57 *Neolithic sites in the Sahara and the Nile Valley*

the ancient lakes bordering on the Erg. Laminate sediments (layered deposits on the lake bottom) and the discovery of shells, aquatic faunal bones, and diatoms (minute colonial algae) indicated the former presence of permanent lakes. The extensive cemeteries recorded in the Taoudenni area were very important to the recognition of paleo-anthropological features. In Algeria, investigations by G. Camps and G. Aumassip at the Amekni and Ti-n-Hanakaten sites revealed an important cultural sequence. During the 1970s, further centers of human occupation, dating to the Early and Middle Holocene, were brought to light by fieldwork carried out in Chad and Tibesti by the French and Germans.

The most firmly established sequences in Nigeria, Libya, and Egypt have placed the first human settlements, after the resumption of the monsoon circulation, at the very beginning of the Holocene.

Niger

The first discoveries in the Air region of Niger were made by J. Desmond Clark in the 1970s. His research in the Wadi Greboun and on the ancient lakeshores in the Adrar Bous area convinced him of the presence of a fully Epipaleolithic horizon, because of the technological traits (backed bladelets, Ounanian and Bou Saada points) and the lifestyle model. During the 1980s, J. P. Roset's research provided stratigraphic data valid enough to permit reconstructing the regional sequence. The more-or-less contemporary sites of Temet 1 (dating to between 9,450 and 9,650 years ago), Ti-n-Ouaffadene (dating to between 9,080 and 9,360 years ago), and Adrar Bous Gisement 10 (dating to between 8,840 and 9,220 years ago) are linked to a humid expansion of an ancient lake during a high rainfall period. The tool assortment of these assemblages is well exemplified by Temet 1, the oldest site. It is an Epipaleolithic assemblage of the type already recognized by Clark. Here, however, it is associated with a ceramic tradition that, although it is still in an incipient phase, shows undoubted richness in its decorative motifs. In the Bagzanes Mountains, south of the Greboun Massif, the Tagalagal site produced another set of early dates for a stratum with ceramics: between 9,200 and

9,460 years ago and between 9,240 and 9,500 years ago. The Tagalagal pottery offers various shapes and well-developed decorations. Among these, the presence of the dotted, wavy line motif is of great interest as it is widely diffused among the ancient Saharan societies. Faunal remains indicate wild animals with an abundance of fish, while the substantial amount of grinding equipment gives evidence of wild-plant gathering. If Roset, on the whole, tends to exclude the presence of an Epipaleolithic horizon, the paleo-hydrological data that C. Dubar offered suggest two main lacustrine phases. The oldest occupations probably occurred at the end of the Pleistocene with a presumed date of 13,000 years ago. The second phase (about 9500 years ago) was brought to light by Roset. The first phase could represent an even more ancient occupation, still featuring a full hunting economy as suggested by Clark.

Libya

The Tadrart Acacus sequence in Libya confirms the settlement chronology of Niger. Along with the bigger Tassili-n-Ajjer, the Tadrart Acacus occupations make up the most important rock-art complex in the Sahara. Since the early 1970s, Barbara Barich has conducted research on the Neolithic occupations. An exemplary sequence has been brought to light in the Wadi Ti-n-Torha, through three settlements that together show a local development starting from the end of the Paleolithic age. Ti-n-Torha East is a true protovillage with a series of hut foundations against the rock-shelter back wall. The faunal list, including wild mammals (Barbary sheep, gazelles, and hare), fish remains (*Clarias* sp. and *Tilapia*), and birds, gives evidence of an economy based on hunting and fishing. However, the presence of poorly preserved specimens of a large bovid, tentatively identified as cattle, has to be emphasized. Also, the practice of gathering wild plants, including several taxa belonging to the millet group, is important. The stratigraphic sequence resulting from the three sites extends throughout the whole Early and Middle Holocene. Thanks to this characteristic, Barich suggested a model of autochthonous transition (a locally derived cultural development uninflu-

Fig. 58 *Ceramic vessel from Ti-n-Torha East*

enced by outside sources) from a predomestic status to aspects of incipient domestication. Trying to explain such a transition inside the geographical context, she pointed out a peculiar relationship that developed between the society and the natural environment in the Late Holocene, a relationship that generated a reorganization of the group during a phase of resource diminishing.

Egypt

In the Egyptian Western Desert, the Nabta and Bir Kiseiba sequences began at the end of the long period of aridity following the Aterian wet phase. The earliest phase at Bir Kiseiba (el Adam phase: 8,200 to 10,000 years ago) is important for having yielded *Bos* remains (dating to between 604 and 1,364 years ago at site E-79-8), which A. Gautier considered to be domestic. Although this hypothesis was challenged, it has been fundamental for correctly evaluating the Saharan Neolithic. Other evidence of wet conditions at the beginning of the Holocene comes from the Selima, Siwa, and Kharga Oases. The Nabta

Neolithic (dating to 7,900 to 8,000 years ago) appears to be a recolonization of the same region after a period of extreme aridity and at the very onset of a new wet phase (dating to 7,900 to 8,200 years ago at Playa II). Grinding stones are now very numerous, and actual grains of wild cereals (millet and sorghum) have been found during the new excavations. More regular rains favored a more permanent settlement system and even the establishment of a true permanent village. Nabta E-75-6 has two parallel rows of structures—houses, hearths, and storage pits—a layout that resembles that of Ti-n-Torha East in the Acacus Mountains. Many comparisons have been made between the lithic industry found here and that of other sites in the Western Desert, such as Wadi Bakht in the Gilf Kebir, Abu Ballas and Lobo in front of the Great Sand Sea, the Masara B horizon at Dachla, and the Early Holocene horizon at Farafra.

Cattle bones are rare at Site E-75-6, while sheep or goats appear late in the Nabta sequence. They were recorded at site E-75-8 only around 7,000 years ago, which is one of the earliest dates known in Africa. A wide chronological gap ex-

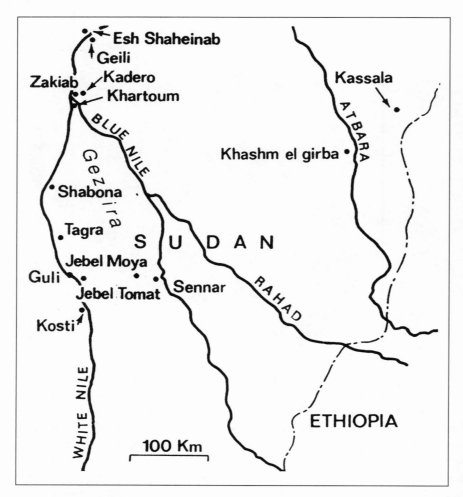

Fig. 59 *Neolithic sites in the Sudan*

Given the chronological gap between the earliest remains of cattle and the actual explosion of pastoralism during the Middle Holocene, some researchers still resist accepting the classification of the ancient bovids of Kiseiba and Nabta as domestic. More likely, one can suppose the existence of an intensive use of wild-animal resources. The situation verified in the Libyan Sahara and, in particular, in the Uan Muhuggiag rock shelter can offer some valid explanations. The economic pattern at Uan Muhuggiag indicates a combination of pastoralism with hunting and gathering of wild plants. This is exactly the aspect that makes this site particularly strategic for understanding the transition toward the pastoral economy.

Although the site's faunal composition still includes wild species (hare, dassies, cats, warthogs, gazelles, and Barbary sheep), their frequency is very low (4.2 percent) in comparison to domestic animals (92.4 percent). The presence of cattle begins from the layers dating to nearly 10,000 years ago. Both technology and environmental data at Uan Muhuggiag provide clear evidence of an independent development of pastoralism that basically occurred locally or, at least, took place completely within the Saharan system. Such changes in lifeways have not been interpreted as an effect of intrusion from the outside. Or, as said earlier, they can be explained as an effect of an improved interaction between human groups and environment.

The florescence of pastoralists seems to have been an independent phenomenon in the Sahara. Between 5,000 and 6,000 years ago, the pastoralist culture spread all over the central Saharan

ists between the ancient findings of the Bir Kiseiba putative domestic cattle in the Western Desert and those in other Saharan and North African regions. In Niger, the settlements of Dogoxmboulo in the Fachi sector (dating to between 6,600 and 7,100 years ago) and Rocher Toubeau (dating to between 5,515 and 5,665 years ago) are the earliest examples of a Middle Holocene occupation based mainly on herding. The tool assemblage of this facies (the Tenerian) is characterized by large bifacial tools such as gouges, discs, arrowheads, and axes. An almost complete skeleton of domestic cattle *(Bos taurus)* recovered at Agorass n'Tast was dated to between 5,260 and 6,260 years ago. In the same area, evidence of plant gathering is suggested by the appearance of brachiaria and sorghum impressions on pottery.

territories. Everywhere, the herders' presence is associated with admirable rock paintings, which seem to act as territorial landmarks where particular ceremonies were performed.

Sudan

The Upper Nile cultures reveal a profound affinity with the Saharan aquatic societies. The first description of this cultural area as *Neolithic of Sudanese Tradition,* given by A. J. Arkell, in which both wavy lines and dotted, wavy lines were the most indicative motifs on the pottery, was based on these resemblances. Arkell placed the most ancient aspect, the Khartoum Mesolithic in the last half of the 8th millennium B.C. Some extensive centers (Tagra and Shabona in the southern region and the Khartoum Hospital site and Saggai in the north) appear to be more permanent settlements, where fishing activities could be carried out extensively, even during the river's meager periods. Indeed, during the annual flooding of the Nile, small centers of the group spread toward the edges of the desert where they practiced hunting, gathering, and herding.

The earliest evidence of food production comes from the Khartoum Neolithic culture, whose type site was first recognized at Es Shaheinab by Arkell in 1949. Investigations during the 1980s provided further clarification of the chronology. However, no confirmation has been given for the gradual transition of the region from a Mesolithic food-extracting economy to a Neolithic food-producing one in the form suggested by Arkell—that is, as a substantially autochthonous process, or one that developed locally without outside influence. Today, the economic transition in central Sudan is attributed to the arrival of external groups that owned domesticates. The Nabta Playa region to the north has been suggested as one of the origin zones, via the Nile Valley, for such species.

The late Neolithic in the Sudan featured the presence of a pastoral lifeway along with a change in the settlement pattern, characterized by camps, fireplaces, and rest stops. The cemeteries in the area of Dongola (Kadruka), Kadada, and Kadero I give evidence of the process of concentration of power by an elite group. While

in the preceding period of mainly riverine exploitation the distribution of cultures was limited to the banks of the Nile, the late Pastoral Neolithic rapidly spread over large territories.

In summary, under the label *Saharan Neolithic,* we can include two main aspects of subsistence organization, which, on the whole, represent the process of the socioeconomic structuring in the Sahara during the Holocene. The initial phase, during the Early Holocene, features aquatic exploitation, semisedentary settlements, planned use of the environment, and a broad resource-exploitation model with fishing, hunting, intensive use of wild cereals, and, probably, of proto-domestic items. Following this (during the Middle and Late Holocene), one can see the progressive decline of generalized exploitation and the increase of a pastoral-based (cattle, sheep, and goats) subsistence model. The settlement pattern becomes more sporadic, consisting of transhumance (seasonal movement) practice, parallel to the emergence of a social structuring in which herd ownership took on a strong ideological value.

BIBLIOGRAPHY

Arkell, A. J. 1949. *Early Khartoum.* London: Oxford University Press.

Barich, B. E., ed. 1987. *Archaeology and environment in the Libyan Sahara: The excavations in the Tadrart Acacus, 1978–1983.* Oxford: British Archaeological Reports, International Series 368.

Camps, G. 1969. *Amekni: Neolithique ancien du Hoggar.* Paris: Arts et Metiers Graphiques.

Close, A. E., ed. 1984. *Cattle-keepers of the eastern Sahara: The Neolithic of Bir Kiseiba.* Dallas: Southern Methodist University Press.

———. 1987. *Prehistory of arid North Africa: Essays in honor of Fred Wendorf.* Dallas: Southern Methodist University Press.

Dutour, O. 1989. *Hommes fossiles du Sahara.* Paris: CNRS.

Haaland, R., and A. A. Hagid. 1995. *Aqualithic sites along the Rivers Nile and Atbara, Sudan.* Bergen: Alma Mater Forlag.

Kuper, R., and F. Klees, eds. 1982. *New light on the northeast African past.* Koln: Heinrich Barth Institut.

Petit-Maire, N., and J. Riser, eds. *Sahara ou Sahel?: Quaternaire recent du Bassin de Taoudenni (Mali).* Paris: CNRS.

Wendorf, F., and R. Schild. 1980. *Prehistory of the eastern Sahara.* New York: Academic Press.

Barbara Barich

THE LATE STONE AGE AND NEOLITHIC CULTURES OF WEST AFRICA AND THE SAHARA

Hunter-Foragers and the Beginnings of Food Production

The temporal demarcation of *Late Stone Age* (or hunter-forager economies) and *Neolithic* (or food-producing economies) is not possible until relatively recently in West Africa. Indeed, both ways of life continued there, sometimes side by side, until the advent of metallurgy. This long economic transition began around 7,000 years ago in the Sahara and slowly spread into the savanna and forest between 3,000 and 4,000 years ago. Throughout this period, West Africa displayed striking cultural diversity and variability in subsistence practices.

One factor that has long confused arguments concerning economic change in the Sahara is the appearance of ceramics there around 9,500 years ago. This development followed closely behind the recolonization of the Sahara due to the favorable wetter climate of the Early Holocene. Most early pottery finds west of the Nile are concentrated in northern Niger, in the Air Highlands at sites such as the Tagalagal rock shelter and Adrar Bous 10. The radiocarbon dates thus far available do not allow us to imply any direction of the spread of early ceramic technology within Africa. Ceramics may have been invented in the southern Sahara and spread to the Nile Valley or vice versa. What is certain is that these early ceramics are among the oldest in the world. The unfortunate archaeological consequence of such a long presence of ceramics is that prehistorians have been unable to agree on how to interpret their economic significance. For Francophone scholars, their mere presence necessitates the use of the term *Néolithique* to describe the societies possessing them—even if they are not coupled with direct evidence for agriculture, they are seen as harbingers of *Néolithisation*. For Anglophone scholars, the fact that most early ceramics are not associated with evidence of food production has disallowed any use of the term *Neolithic* to describe them. Instead they are seen as part of the Late Stone Age, albeit within a phase of wider resource exploitation, especially in terms of riverine and lacustrine resources. All of this underscores the inherent impracticability of the definitions *Neolithic* and *Late Stone Age*—terms that are neither chronologically absolute nor culturally precise.

Our earliest evidence of food production in the Sahara west of Lake Chad is in a pastoral context, with several incidences of domestic cattle remains from sites dating to about 6,000 to 6,500 years ago in northern Niger (Adrar-n-Kiffi) and southwestern Libya (Uan Mulluggiag and Wadi Ti-n-Torha). By 4,000 years ago, societies with large and small livestock stretched across the southern Sahara, from the Air Mountains of Niger to the Mauritanian coast.

Direct evidence for cereal agriculture is scarce in West Africa until after 2,500 years ago. Identifications from before this date are limited to grain and stem impressions of domesticated millet (*Pennisetum* sp.) on pottery. These finds are associated with charcoal carbon-14 dates of 3,200 to 3,420 years ago at Karkarichinkat Sud (Tilemsi Valley, Mali) and 2,995 to 3,215 years ago at Seyyid Ouinquil (Dhar Tichitt, Mauritania). Recent pollen studies in Burkina Faso support a relatively recent date for cereal agriculture in the West African Sahel and savanna. There, pollen profiles indicative of human agricultural activities do not commence until after 3,000 years ago.

On the edge of the West African forest, it would appear that yam and oil-palm cultivation is of long duration. However, the slow process of yam domestication, which would have accompanied the clearing of forests and the maintenance of plots, has thus far evaded direct documentation. Some form of starch analysis, like that undertaken with success in New Guinea, may eventually shed light on this subject. Oil-palm kernels have been recovered in great quantities at the rock shelters of Kintampo and Bosumpra in Ghana, although as yet they have not been associated with known cultivated semiwild or wild varieties. One fragment of definite evidence for the intensification of vegeculture in the West African forest zone is the pollen sequence of Lake Bosumtwi (Ghana). This sequence indicates an increase in oil-palm pollen between 3,000 and 3,500 years ago, dates that may provide a good minimum estimate for their systematic exploitation.

Meanwhile nonfood-producing societies, both riverine and pelagic (ocean) fishers and savanna hunter-foragers, continued more traditional lifestyles. In some regions, extensive research has allowed the examination of economic transitions and symbiosis between agricultural and hunter-forager populations. Three important case studies of regional research include those of the Taoudenni Basin by N. Petit-Maire and J. Riser, the Middle Niger by K. C. MacDonald and W. van Neer, and the Ghanaian wooded savanna by A. Stahl.

Early Fishers and Pastoralists of the Malian Sahara

From 1980 to 1982, research teams led by Petit-Maire and Riser executed the first substantial archaeological and geomorphological survey of the Malian Sahara. Their work allowed the outline of a human occupational sequence for this vast region during the Holocene. In particular, two lacustrine phases were defined, corresponding respectively to the Early Neolithic and the Middle Neolithic. For the Early Lacustrine phase (between 6,400 and 9,500 years ago) three archaeological facies were documented.

The Early Lacustrine Phase

THE OUNANIAN FACIES. A long-known and ill-defined industry, occurring with or without ceramics, grinding stones, and microliths, the Ounanian industry is always associated with large numbers of scrapers and is distinguished by the presence of the distinctive Ounanian point (a pointed blade with a long unilateral tang). In the Taoudenni Basin, grinders and ceramics are usually present, although microliths and faunal remains

are rare. It has long been assumed that this ephemeral tradition represents one of the earliest reoccupations of the Sahara by hunter-forager groups that had adapted to arid conditions. Later, it seems they may have retained their discrete identity and high level of mobility, despite adding ceramics and aquatic resources to their economy.

THE HASSI-EL-ABIOD FACIES. An emphatically aquatic-resource–based economy, the Hassi-el-Abiod facies is characeried by sites usually taking the form of large bone and shell middens containing the remains of lacustrine fishes, aquatic mammals, and crocodiles. The material culture of this facies is equally distinctive. It comprises globular pottery decorated with pivoted-stylus motifs, numerous bone points and harpoons, polished stone axes, and a microlithic industry featuring unusually large crescents.

THE OUM-EL-ASSEL FACIES. A geometric microlithic industry, the Oum-el-Assel facies has some concave based projectile points, usually lacks grinding stones, but is associated with stylus- and comb-decorated pottery. Settlements are on ancient lakeshores, with the circular stone borders of huts or windbreaks visible, but no "kitchen-middens." The economy is assumed to be generalized hunter-forager.

The Late Lacustrine Phase

In the Late Lacustrine phase (between 4,000 and 6,400 years ago), the Hassi-el-Abiod facies appears to have continued with the addition of two new facies:

THE INE-SAKHANE FACIES. This facies seems to have had a pastoral element to its economy, because of the domestic cattle remains associated with it. The hunting of wild bovids and fishing are, however, also indicated by the faunal remains from several assemblages. The lithic (stone) industry is informal and flake-based, featuring a few bifacial projectile points. Polished stone axes and pottery are common. Sites take the form of localized knapping scatters or large settlements beside lake beds with numerous stone-lined hearths.

THE PAYS ROUGE FACIES. This facies is characterized by a population of apparently highly mobile people, occupying the region at the end of the Late Lacustrine phase, when the ancient lakes were reduced to seasonal ponds. There is no evidence for structures. Geometric microliths and points are absent, and scrapers dominate the lithic assemblage. The pottery is often plain and burnished, and grinding stones are present. The people of the Pays Rouge facies may have been pastoralists or hunter-foragers who had adapted to arid conditions.

Although somewhat geographically specific, the Taoudenni sequence serves to illustrate the cultural and economic diversity that existed in the Sahara during the Early to Middle Holocene. Undoubtedly, there was a good deal of trade and interaction between these neighboring groups.

The Holocene Settlement of the Middle Niger

When the last great desiccation of the Sahara began around 4,500 years ago, societies that had existed beside this arid region's lakes and wadis (stream beds in a desert region) were pushed southward. The story of the settlement of the modern Inland Niger Delta begins around 4,000 years ago, when fishing peoples associated with the Hassi-el-Abiod facies entered the region. Before this time, it is assumed that the Inland Delta was perpetually inundated swampland, impenetrable to surrounding pastoral cultures due to the problems of waterborne disease. If specialized fishing peoples entered the area at an earlier date, we have not yet found evidence for their presence. This Hassi-el-Abiod derivative, termed the *Kobadi facies,* rapidly spread out across the Middle Niger, from the Méma region to Gao at the Niger Bend. It appears that these people were specialized fishers without domestic livestock or cereals.

Between 3,000 and 3,500 years ago, increased desiccation forced Saharan populations into the Niger Basin and allowed the region's waterways to shrink enough to facilitate colonization. It appears that there were two primary population movements: one from the Mauritanian Escarpment into the northwestern Inland Delta (the Méma) and another from the Tilemsi Valley into the eastern Inland Delta and environs (the Gourma). Both movements consisted of the incursion, initially seasonal, of agro-pastoral peoples into the ancient floodplain where they met fishing peoples. At sometime, it would seem that groups were assimilated or displaced, although even today specialized fishing groups ply the Middle Niger (for example, the Bozo and the Sorko).

One of these incursion zones, the Méma, deserves closer examination. There, the immigrants leaving the Mauritanian Escarpment were part of one of West Africa's earliest complex societies at Dhar Tichitt. The Dhar Tichitt civilization, developed out of local pastoral populations, flourished, and collapsed between 2,500 and 3,500 years ago. By 3,100 years ago, substantial villages with dry-stone masonry architecture had formed along the escarpment. One of these, Dakhlet el Atrouss, was 90 hectares and contained numerous walled compounds surrounded by large corral areas and stone tumuli (mound graves). It appears that millet agriculture came into being shortly before the growth of the architectural settlements. The Tichitt civilization appears to have been a pristine "chiefdom," developing out of the control of both local resources (cattle, arable land, and ponding areas) and regional trade (particularly in semiprecious stones). Around 3,000 years ago, the civilization expanded eastward along the Mauritanian Escarpment and carried with it distinctive pottery decorated with cord-wrapped sticks and cord roulettes and a lithic industry primarily devoted to the manufacture of fine projectile points. At this time, elements of the Tichitt tradition begin to be visible in the Méma region. There the Tichitt tradition, referred to as the *Ndondi-Tossokel facies,* occurs in ephemeral settlements located along the edge of the floodplain and featuring the distinctive pottery and lithics, as well as axes and stone rings made of imported Mauritanian materials (principally phthanite). Tichitt pottery as well as terracotta figurines of livestock also begin to show up at this time in the middens of the local fishers along with cattle and ovicaprine remains. It is believed that this situation might represent seasonal visits of a pastoral component of the Tichitt tradition into the Méma region where they may have traded with and even lived side by side with local fishing populations of the Kobadi facies. By about 2,500 years ago, continued environmental deterioration and Berber raids led to the abandonment of the last of the Tichitt settlements in Mauritania, bringing further immigrants into Mali. At this time, the Kobadi and Ndondi-Tossokel facies disappear in the Méma region and are replaced with a unified material culture (the Faita facies). Data currently available do not answer the question of whether the disappearance of the facies was the result of assimilation or of population displacement, although Soninke oral traditions hint at the former.

Agricultural Beginnings at the Forest's Edge

Eventually, the abandonment of the Sahara resulted in the interaction of northern populations with those of the West African forest and the forest's edge. There, since the Late Pleistocene, populations employing both microliths and heavy-duty tools had made their living by hunting forest game and through harvesting (and possibly cultivating) tubers and tree products. By 5,000 years ago, most of these peoples appear to have added ceramics to their material culture. Ceramics have been found from around this date at the rock shelters of Korounkorokalé (Mali), Bosumpra (Ghana), and Shum Laka (Cameroon). For the most part, the ceramics show little influence from the Sahara and appear to have been indigenously developed, if not indigenously invented. Rough axes, usually polished only along the blades, also make their appearance at or before this time over most of West Africa. This would all seem to be part of a regional intensification process, described by A. Stahl as being one of "decreasing residential mobility; probable involvement in exchange networks; increased accumulation of material culture; increased investment in food processing, and . . . a degree of food production."

Shortly after 4,000 years ago, however, in the midst of this intensification process, more extensive contacts began with northern populations. These are best chronicled in northern and central Ghana, where 40 years of work by researchers such as O. Davies, C. Flight, F. J. Kense, and A. Stahl has constructed a vivid picture of what is known as the *Kintampo industry*. Although claims of "invasion from the Sahara" have been toned down substantially in recent years, a case for the physical presence of northern peoples and resultant cultural change remains.

Materially, the Kintampo industry appears to be a fusion of Saharan and forest cultures. The former includes small, polished greenstone axes, biconically perforated stone beads, bifacially retouched arrowheads, polished-stone arm rings, a ceramic industry characterized by everted rims, slip, and comb-stamping, and pastoralism (including, at least, sheep and goats). The forest culture components include quartz microliths and an element of forest vegeculture. More ambivalent characteristics include thatched, rectangular wattle-and-daub dwellings that occur at open-air sites (such as Bonoase and Ntereso) and scored, soft stone raps, or grinders (often described inaccurately as "terra-cotta cigars"). A good sequence of cultural interchange comes from Kintampo K6 rock shelter in central Ghana, where the local forest culture (termed here the *Punpun phase*) is transformed rapidly around 3,500 years ago into the Kintampo industry. *Transformed* is the operative term, since many elements of original Punpun culture (including unique mat-and-cord–impressed pottery and quartz microliths) continue side by side with the full set of Kintampo material culture (including livestock remains) in the latter part of the sequence. The view one takes about the nature of relations between peoples of the Punpun phase and those of the Kintampo industry depends greatly upon individual assumptions concerning the origins of modern West African populations, but one thing is clear: forest peoples were not replaced by incoming Saharan populations—they were, at best, acculturated. The finer aspects of this transition, like so many others in West Africa's complex ancient landscape, await future generations of focused research.

BIBLIOGRAPHY

Ballouche, A., and K. Neumann. 1995. A new contribution to the Holocene vegetation history of the West African Sahel. *Vegetation History and Archaeobotany* 4: 31–39.

Close, A. E. 1995. Few and far between: Early ceramics in North Africa. In *The emergence of pottery: Technology and innovation in ancient societies,* eds. W. K. Barnett and J. W. Hoopes, 230–237. Washington, D.C.: Smithsonian Press.

Gautier, A. 1987. Prehistoric men and cattle in North Africa: A dearth of data and a surfeit of models. In *Prehistory of arid North Africa: Essays in honor of Fred Wendorf,* ed. A. E. Close, 163–187. Dallas: Southern Methodist University Press.

Harlan, J. R., J. M. J. De Wet, and A. B. L. Stemmler, eds. 1976. *Origins of African plant domestication.* The Hague: Mouton.

Holl, A. 1993. Late Neolithic cultural landscape in southeastern Mauritania: An essay in spatiometrics. In *Spatial boundaries and social dynamics: Case studies from food-producing societies,* eds. A. Holl and T. E. Levy, 95–133. Ann Arbor: International Monographs in Prehistory.

MacDonald, K. C., and W. van Neer. 1994. Specialised fishing peoples in the Later Holocene of the Méma region (Mali). In *Fish exploitation in the past,* ed. W. van Neer, 243–251. Tervuren: Musée Royal de l'Afrique Centrale.

Petit-Maire, N., and J. Riser. 1983. *Sahara ou Sahel? Quaternaire récent de Bassin de Taoudenni (Mali).* Paris: CNRS.

Raimbault, M. 1990. Pour une approche du Néolithique du Sahara Malien. *Travaux de LAPMO* (1990): 67–81.

Smith, A. B. 1992. *Pastoralism in Africa: Origins and development ecology.* London: C. Hurst and Co.

Stahl, A. 1993. Intensification in the West African Late Stone Age: A view from central Ghana. In *The archaeology of Africa: Food, metals and towns,* eds. T. Shaw, P. Sinclair, B. Andah, and A. Okpoko, 261–273. London: Routledge.

Kevin MacDonald

FORAGERS AND FARMERS: THEIR INTERACTION

Serious studies of foragers in sub-Saharan Africa began in the early 1930s and culminated in the publication of *Man the Hunter* by R. Lee and I. DeVore in 1968, among many other monographs detailing the lifeways of band societies. Our understanding of the forager way of life and foragers' relations with other people in their neighborhood was very limited. With the recent attention of ethnoarchaeological research, there has been a substantial increase in our comprehension of the interactions between foragers and farmers. The results of these investigations suggest the existence of complex social and economic relationships.

Up until now, the relationships between foragers and farmers were characterized as "client-patron." In southern Africa, they were often described as a kind of symbiosis—that is, they were considered to be a kind of patronage from which foragers became the beneficiaries of the goodwill of well-to-do farmers. This view is no longer tenable, as there is sufficient evidence to show that both foragers and farmers accrue benefits from their relations.

Background of Forager-Farmer Interactions

Generally, the first appearance of food producers in sub-Saharan Africa is associated with the Iron Age. This was a time when a new food-getting technology appeared. This new subsistence strategy included the production of items made from iron, a sedentary pattern, and food production. There is sufficient evidence to show that the techniques of food production found in the southern subcontinent were first developed elsewhere and that before the appearance of ironworking, no other form of metallurgy was practiced. There is general consensus that ironworking and cultivation were introduced at the same time and that, in most parts of the subcontinent, peoples practicing these technologies coexisted amicably with foragers.

Recently, discussions of the interactions between foragers and farmers have focused on how such interactions work and what drives them. There is an attempt to comprehend them through a perspective of change, over time, in the manner in which these communities related to one another. Such an approach suggests that these interactions be viewed as responses to various factors such as changes in the environment, nutrition, demography, and other social and economic factors. Archaeological research in southern Africa suggests that the first contacts between foragers and farmers were not an established routine but occurred in answer to some need on the part of the foragers. Even among the foragers of the Ituri Forest in Zaire, foragers interact with their neighbors in order to obtain such products as meat, honey, tobacco, and the like, as well as to obtain food to sustain their protein intake when stressed by environmental circumstances.

Studies of present-day Pygmies in Zaire, the Hadza in Tanzania, and the San in Botswana suggest that their contacts with neighboring farmers are not a result of political or economic dominance alone but relate as well to nutritional stress caused by environmental factors. At some times, the carbohydrate and fat components of the foragers' diets are limited, leading them to be attracted to foodstuffs produced by farmers. During seasons when game is lean and vegetable resources dwindle, the decline in food availability acts as the driving force behind the establishment of relations between foragers and farmers. This situation manifests itself in the Ituri Forest among the Efe Pygmies, who seasonally become dependent on the neighboring Lese agriculturists for about two-thirds of their calories.

For any meaningful interaction to take place, certain factors must be fulfilled first. For example, the availability of food in one place rather another may influence the size of forager bands and regulate their range and frequency of movement—that is, the organization of such bands is regulated by food availability and water supply. In such a scenario, mobility is an important strategy that may be instrumental in any interactions with farmers.

Equally important is the consideration that contact between foragers and farmers could not have been identical in all areas, although there may have been regular patterns in which cultural contacts occurred. P. S. Wells observed in 1980 that in no instance do identical processes operate in two different situations in the same way since all the factors involved can never be precisely the same. This view is supported by archaeological investigations. In eastern Botswana, foragers were either absorbed or displaced by farmers and not necessarily eliminated. The situation was different in the western Botswana,

where social and cultural autonomy was encouraged or permitted. This behavior subsequently led to the incorporation of both foragers and farmers into a regionally integrated system of mutually supportive forms of production and exchange. A consideration of all factors at play suggests that differences between the two areas in the processes of interactions reflect differences in resources. In central Zambia, processes of interaction have been demonstrated and attributed to differences in food-procurement strategies and modes of subsistence.

Earliest Evidence of Forager-Farmer Interaction in Sub-Saharan Africa

To gain a better understanding of the processes of interaction between foragers and the earliest farmers in sub-Saharan Africa, the region will be divided into west, east, and south. While the picture may be clear in some areas as a result of archaeological investigations, others are not yet well documented. This makes the survey difficult as we have to rely on evidence from sites and areas at some distance from one another.

In the rain-forest belt of West Africa, archaeological evidence relating to an early farming population is not yet well documented. Despite the presence of thick forests, the difficulty in locating sites, and the paucity of archaeologists working in the area, investigations carried out in the 1960s and 1970s have revealed the presence of forager and farming communities in the rain-forest belt by the 2nd millennium B.C.

The onset of desiccation in the Sahara before the 2nd millennium B.C. triggered a southward movement of food producers into some areas of West Africa. This undoubtedly brought them into contact with foragers who inhabited the forest fringes. There is no evidence to indicate that at the time of these movements foragers practiced food production. But after food producers entered the region, dwarf cows, cereals—millet and sorghum—and a very distinctive lithic (stone) technology appeared in most parts of the forest fringes. The most popular explanation concerning these movements is that these groups integrated with the exiting societies in varying degrees—a process that is reflected in the regional variations in the Kintampo industry. Unfortunately, this explanation does not indicate how the integration took place or what the driving force behind it was.

The Kintampo industry, found along the forest fringes of Ghana, made its first appearance around 1400 B.C. It was essentially a village farming economy that preceded the Punpun phase associated with foragers. The Punpun phase represents a microlithic industry associated with small quantities of pottery dated to between 1700 and 1400 B.C. Pottery of the Kintampo industry is strikingly different from that found associated with the Punpun phase and yet similar to that from southern Saharan sites. Due to a lack of corroborative evidence in other parts of the region, the processes of interaction between the foraging and farming communities remain poorly understood.

The desiccation of the Sahara also introduced food producers into eastern Africa. Before their arrival, the region was occupied by foragers who practiced a stone-tool technology that had no pottery component. The arrival of food producers was accompanied by a rapid and widespread introduction of pottery. Interestingly, the manufacture and use of stone-based industries continued unabated while the manufacture and use of pottery became widespread. The lack of discernible typological changes in the lithic technology after the appearance of farmers in the region suggests that contact between the foragers and farmers was not of a critical nature during this early period of contact.

Archaeological investigations along the Atlantic Coast in West Africa have revealed the existence of pottery, polished-stone axes, ironworking, and sedentary communities during the 1st millennium B.C. Despite the presence of strong evidence of intensive oil-palm exploitation at Tchissanga, there is little indication of food production at this time. This inhibits our ability to determine the kind and intensity of interaction between the two communities.

In southern Africa, there is an abundant literature on this subject. D. W. Phillipson surveyed early contacts in the 1970s and concluded that the two populations maintained, to a large extent, their separate identities throughout the pe-

riod of coexistence. Investigations have revealed that the most satisfactory interpretation of the occasional interactions is that of temporary "client relationships." Results of investigations in the former Transvaal province have shown that sometime before 2000 B.C., there was a period of mutual and peaceful coexistence of foragers and farmers at many localities and that later contacts between them resulted in the absorption of the former.

Contrary to widely held views, it has been demonstrated that it took more than four centuries of isolation before the Early Iron Age pottery in most parts of Zambia appeared at forager sites. No later Stone Age site suggests a clear boundary between the Early Iron Age and the Late Iron Age pottery found commingled in them. This is an indication that interactions during the initial period of contact were very minimal and that the presence of Early Iron Age pottery at forager sites was more the result of casual collecting of shards from abandoned villages and transporting them home than the result of exchange or other face-to-face interaction between the two communities. Initial contacts between them seem to have been more in the form of encounters between individuals or small groups while foraging than some kind of formal relationship.

This conclusion is supported by accounts of the Tswana of Botswana. In their descriptions of their earliest contacts with the San, the Tswana mentioned the Sans' fear of meeting them. According to the Tswana accounts collected by Lee:

> they were very afraid of us and would hide whenever we came around. We found their villages, but they were always empty because as soon as they saw strangers coming they would scatter and hide in the bush.

Modern Forager-Farmer Interactions

A survey of modern foragers suggests that they occupy diverse environments that are marginal in economic productivity and that farmers have come to occupy some of the former territories of foragers, thus bringing them into contact with each other. Oral traditions of the Tswana, who until recently were pastoralists, attest that they entered the San territory during the later decades of the 19th century. In the Ituri Forest, the Bantu-speaking Babila migrated into the area within the last 200 years. Linguistic evidence from the western part of southern Africa suggests that foragers and cattle herders speaking Khoisan languages lived there before the Bantu migrations some 2,000 years ago. Given the envidence from archaeological investigations in the eastern part of the Kalahari region, Bantu speakers colonized the area occupied by indigenous Khoisan foragers sometime between A.D. 600 and 1000, whereas in the western part, Bantu speakers did not establish themselves until the mid-19th century. Evidence of trade relations between the San and their Bantu neighbors may be observed at Late Stone Age sites in form of iron-tipped weapons, pottery, and smoking pipes.

Since the 1970s, many researchers have studied the relations between foragers and farmers. The research has mostly been focused on specific issues, such as the politics of traditional land practices or land tenure. In Botswana, the establishment of the Bushmen Development Programme in 1975, which later became the Remote Area Dwellers Programme, encouraged investigation of the relations of the San with their Bantu neighbors. These studies established that contacts between these two communities have most often involved the Sans' exchange of furs, hides, honey, and ostrich-eggshell beadwork for Bantu speakers' tobacco, clay pots, iron implements, European goods, and dairy products. Some very interesting evidence relating to trade networks during the 1st millennium A.D. has been found at the Divuyu Iron Age site in the northern Kalahari. Two marine shells of Atlantic Coast origin *(Cerithiidae),* fish bones, river mussel shells, and two iron pendants identical to those from the Shaba Province of Zaire have been recovered. These date to around A.D. 500 and suggest an extensive trade with coastal as well as interior areas.

The Mbuti Pygmies have very elaborate social and economic relations with their Bantu neighbors. In 1991, R. C. Bailey demonstrated how the Efe Pygmies make frequent day trips to Bantu villages to trade honey, game meat, and carbohydrate-rich foods as well as to assist in the harvesting and processing of peanuts. The Efe Pygmies depend on cultivated foods from farmers for roughly two-thirds of their calories, and many of their activities are oriented toward the villages.

Interactions between foragers and farmers go beyond the exchange of goods. Foragers also provide labor. The San are often engaged as herdsmen by villagers in exchange for meal and milk, while in the Ituri Forest, farmers provide Pygmies with food, tobacco, and marijuana in exchange for labor. The Pygmies have been observed to assist in clearing a new garden or helping to plant or harvest crops as well as in collecting building materials for farmers. These tasks are mostly performed by men, although women are often involved in the planting, harvesting, and processing cultivated food.

In addition to garden-related tasks, many other activities are performed by the Efe in their continued social relations with farmers. Men have been observed to climb oil palms to collect nuts, build and repair leaf roofs and mud walls of villagers' houses, dig pit latrines, carry messages between villages, and even prepare and apply medicines for villagers.

These relations play a very important role in the village economy of cultivators. Both the forager and farmer are recipients of some form of benefit for services rendered. The fact that foragers rely so heavily on farmers' foodstuffs and spend so much time idling in villages should not be interpreted to mean that they are parasites and beggars. They offer a service that is highly appreciated by both parties.

Other forms of interactions between foragers and farmers include intermarriages. During famine years, Isanzu cultivators in Tanzania leave their villages to search for food in the same way that the Hadza do until the famine eases and they can return to cultivation. Some of the Isanzu stay on and intermarry with the Hadza. In southern Africa, such relations have produced a spectrum of effects on the land-use patterns, including fragmentation and sedentism in some groups and consolidation and increased mobility in others.

The presence of pastoralists in the San territories towards the end of the 19th century influenced the spatial organization of the San. The pastoralists introduced semipermanent settlements to which the San were attracted. This situation changed their pattern of living as they began to spend more time in a sedentary fashion as opposed to the transhumance (seasonal movement) they had previously employed.

The use of linguistics to understand relations between foragers and farmers introduces an interesting aspect to the subject. It has long been assumed that as farming communities migrated southward, their languages were altered through their contact with foragers. It has also been assumed that, with increases in the population of farming communities, the number of foragers diminished through absorption, elimination, or other means and their territories shrank as a result with a corresponding loss of languages. This pattern emerges in the Ituri Forest where the Pygmy languages have completely disappeared among the Pygmy populations as Bantu languages took root. On the other hand, the San continue to speak Khoisan.

The importance of languages in interactions between foragers and farmers was noted by C. Ehret, who pointed out that when Bantu-speaking people procured cattle from Khoisan herders, they also borrowed a cattle-keeping vocabulary. J. K. Denbow also noted the presence of linguistic terms for cattle, milking, and other elements among populations of the savanna woodlands south of the equatorial forest. The presence of these terms implies a close and sustained contact among foragers, pastoralists, and farmers.

This survey of the interactions between foragers and farmers has considered evidence that is basic to the conventionally held view that sometime after the 1st millennium Iron Age agro-pastoralists gained a dominance over foragers in their vicinity and ultimately absorbed or eliminated them. The evidence suggests, to the contrary, that the process of contact was very slow and that different processes of interaction were operating in different places. The interactions between them were not of a critical nature during the early encounters. This view is supported by studies

of Pygmies and the San and their agricultural neighbors—studies that suggest that, while there is archaeological evidence from the Kalahari linking the San to their Bantu neighbors, no such evidence can be demonstrated for Pygmy-Bantu relations.

Every instance of interaction between foragers and farmers is best understood as a process through time and space, a process in which each contact situation demanded the operation of a different set of processes. There is little evidence to suggest that, despite the existence of relations between foragers and farmers, social processes in either community changed drastically. Rather, there was continuity in social life with no significant innovations. While some people consider such relations to have been critical to determining biological variability in some populations, such as the Khoisan, others attribute cultural variability among these communities to a local process of economic development involving the shift from hunting and gathering to nomadic pastoralism 2,000 years ago.

The first contacts between these different communities were probably very minimal and inconsequential. Over a significant period of time, however, they developed to recognizable levels in which both groups reaped benefits.

BIBLIOGRAPHY

Bailey, R. C. 1991. The behavioral ecology of Efe Pygmy men in the Ituri Forest, Zaire. *Anthropological Papers of the University of Michigan Museum of Anthropology* 86.

Clist, B. 1988. Un nouvelle ensemble Néolithique en Afrique Centrale: Le groupe d'Okala au Gabon. *NSI* 88: 43–51

Denbow, J. 1990. Congo to Kalahari: Data and hypotheses about the political economy of the western stream of the Early Iron Age. *African Archaeological Review* 8: 139–176.

Dreyer, T. F, and A. J. D. Meiring. 1952. The Hottentots. *Research Papers of the Bloemfontein Museum* 1: 19–22.

Ehret, C. 1967. Cattlekeeping and milking in eastern and southern African history: The linguistic evidence. *Journal of African History* 8: 1–17.

Hausman, A. J. 1984. Holocene human evolution in southern Africa. In *From hunters to farmers: The causes and consequences of food production in*

Africa, eds. J. D. Clark and S. A. Brandt, 164–271. Berkeley: University of California Press.

Lee, R. 1979. *The !Kung San: Men, women and work in a foraging society.* Cambridge: Cambridge University Press.

Lee, R, and I. DeVore, eds. 1968. *Man the hunter.* Chicago: Aldine Publishing Company.

de Maret, P. 1986. The Ngovo group: An industry with polished stone tools and pottery in the lower Zaire. *African Archaeological Review* 4: 103–133.

Phillipson, D. W. 1977. *The later prehistory of eastern and southern Africa.* London: Heinemann.

Tobias, P. V. 1955. Physical anthropology and somatic origins of the Hottentots. *African Studies* 14: 1–15.

Francis Musonda

Beginnings of Food Production

EGYPT: BEGINNINGS OF AGRICULTURE

Farming in the Nile Valley dates to the 7th millennium B.C. Systematic investigations over the last three decades have not disclosed any firm evidence of earlier food-producing activities. It would be prudent, therefore, to regard the emergence of food production in the Nile Valley (including the delta) as an event postdating the transition to agriculture in southwestern Asia, beyond the desert areas of the Sinai and Negev, where wheat, barley, and legumes were cultivated and where sheep, goats, pigs, and cattle were domesticated.

Cattle, however, were independently domesticated in the southern part of what is presently the Egyptian Sahara (Western Desert). Although conclusive identification of the bones of domestic cattle before 7,000 years ago is lacking, there is some evidence to suggest that management of cattle may date to 9,000 years ago, if not somewhat earlier, especially because the environmental conditions in the Egyptian Saharan, where scanty remains of cattle were found, were far too dry to have supported cattle without human intervention. Foragers and hunters of small game, such as gazelles and hare, who managed to keep small herds of cattle likely occupied the region during the Early Holocene (a geologic epoch beginning 10,000 years ago). It is not clear where and when the first steps toward cattle domestication were undertaken. It seems likely that cattle were first domesticated in the Sahara in a transitional zone similar to that of the Sahel, a zone between the desert and the steppe. Sheep, goats, wheat, and barley were introduced from southwestern Asia.

The belated emergence of agriculture in the Nile Valley by comparison to the Near East and the likelihood of the domestication of cattle independently in the Sahara beg for an explanation. One possible explanation resides in the climatic-geographic peculiarities of each region and the interregional responses to the climatic events marking the transition from the last major advance of glaciers to the warmer (postglacial) Holocene climate. Although this climatic transition is arbitrarily designated at 10,000 years ago, global climatic oscillations in the Near East and the Nile Valley predate this arbitrary boundary.

One such oscillation, 12,000 to 12,500 years ago, was responsible for exceptionally high Nile floods. At this time, the inhabitants of the Nile Valley were hunters and foragers, who practiced fishing and fowling as indicated by faunal remains. Their activities were in tandem with the ebb and rise of seasonal annual floods. Wild cattle, rich aquatic resources, and plants in the floodplain were intensively exploited following the recession of summer Nile floods. The submergence of the floodplain for most of the year by water during excessively high floods implies certain human responses, such as greater reliance on fish. While reducing the availability of wild cattle, the prolonged inundation of the floodplain afforded exceptional opportunities to catch fish from abundant flood pools. This subsistence shift is indicated by an abundance of fish bones from sites dating to between the 12th and 8th millennium B.C. These sites also show that the change in subsistence was associated with a change in settlement patterns. It is likely that exploitation of abundant fish resources led hunter-foragers to become territorial and perhaps to camp repeatedly in more-or-less the same locale. This is indicated by very large sites consisting of many overlapping concentrations of archaeological debris, mostly stone artifacts. There are also numerous hearths that might have been used for processing fish.

The interment of the deceased in a cemetery in Egyptian Nubia at this time suggests a sense of territorial residency. The presence of projectile points embedded in the skeletons of many individuals suggests violent encounters, which might have been related to intergroup conflicts. Such conflicts might have resulted from territorial disputes or from the breakdown of cultural norms following the traumatic events that attended the catastrophic flooding of the valley. However, the reliability of fish gathered from fish pools after the flood receded and aquatic resources associated with flood ponds, especially during the Early Holocene when flood levels were characteristically high, might not have favored a shift to cultivate cereals or domesticate cattle.

West of the Nile, the desert, totally desiccated during the last glacial episode, was turning green. A shift of monsoonal rain brought about 200 millimeters of annual rainfall to southwestern Egypt and decreased the annual rainfall in northern Egypt to between 25 and 50 millimeters. Rainfall was seasonal. The vegetation was an *Acacia* desert shrub, with a predominance of acacia trees, *Tamarix* bushes, and open vegetation, mostly grasses. After the rain, no fewer than 100 ephemeral species appear in the desert. Wild cattle requiring about 400 millimeters of rain were likely to be present farther south in northern Sudan.

The deglaciation that began 12,500 years ago, bringing rain to the desert and floods to the Nile Valley, was interrupted by an abrupt cooling event 11,000 to 11,700 years ago. This event led to frequent failures of the monsoonal rains and, in the northern fringe of the monsoonal rain area (the paleo-Sahel), increasing aridity and periodic droughts. It was at this time that the management of cattle might have been initiated. Where rainfall is reduced to 200 millimeters, cattle can sur-

vive, but they require artificial means to secure water during the dry season. Faced with reduction in the number of cattle, some people might have started to control the movement of cattle by herding them to permanent water holes and pastures. In special localities where there is marked relief and deep basins to catch and hold rain, lakes were formed. The early pastoralists favored these spots both for gaining a supply of water and for having access to shrubs, grass, and reeds. Sediments deposited in these lakes now exist as desiccated ancient lake beds (known as *playa deposits* from the Spanish word for *beach*). It is mostly in association with such playa sediments that archaeological sites are often located.

The return of wetter conditions during the 10th millennium B.C. (perhaps about 9,500 years ago), associated with a broadening of the rain belt northward, might have brought cattle "herders" into northwestern Egypt. However, the return of arid conditions about 8,200 years ago necessitated digging walk-in wells, now familiar in the drought-stricken African Sahel. At the Nabta Playa in southwestern Egypt, such walk-in wells provide evidence for the return of wetter conditions about 8,000 years ago. Moreover, the evidence shows organized villages with rows of houses and storage pits dating to between 7,900 and 8,100 years ago. Food remains recovered from ash in cooking holes are dominated by stones of the fruits of zizyphys trees, grass grains (including sorghum and millet), and seeds of legumes as well as tubers of some plants. *Tamarix* and *Acacia* species are represented in wood charcoal used for fuel. The sorghum and millet are morphologically wild.

The onset of a short episode of severe droughts after 7,200 years ago was followed by an episode of wetter climate between about 6,200 and 6,900 years ago. Severe aridity was resumed again for one to three centuries. The intensity of the abrupt, severe droughts during these last two episodes was apparently sufficient to drive many desert dwellers into the Nile Valley. Successions of droughts reduced the herds and seriously diminished water availability as the water table declined. Accordingly, the Nile Valley became an attractive alternative to some of the surrounding deserts.

Agro-pastoralists responded to the aridity of these intervals by intensively using local resources around specific favored areas, a pattern that might have started already during the 9th millennium B.C. At present, such locations are associated with numerous depressions in the Siwa, Baharia, Farafra, Dakhla, and Kharga Oases. Here, surface water is more available because of the marked difference in relief between the desert plateau and the deep floors of the oases and because of the capacity of localized depressions to catch rainfall.

Others opted for a continuation of a nomadic lifestyle, traveling for long distances in pursuit of water and pastures in the Sahara. This ushered in a pastoralist mode of subsistence, a lifeway that left behind numerous small campsites with fireplaces all over the desert. Herds of small cattle were most likely of limited size. Animals were probably used mostly for milk and only rarely for meat. Farming is not practical when the annual rainfall is between 250 and 500 millimeters because of marked variability from one year to the next (interannual variability). For example, the yield of barley in northern Egypt where rainfall averages 160 millimeters per year can vary from a maximum of 360 kilograms per acre to nothing, with an average of 147 kilograms. In this region, the 82 percent interannual variability creates a great deal of uncertainty. Accordingly, if cultivation was ever practiced in the desert, it was most likely as a supplement to herding, foraging, and hunting. The herders mostly followed a mode of life similar to that of hunter-foragers, living in small social units of five to 15 families with a diversified diet and a great deal of seasonal as well as intraseasonal mobility. The groups most likely responded to frequent environmental changes, including unpredictable rainfall, from year to year, by altering their composition and character. The nomadic herding units contracted, expanded, or combined as necessary. This feature was a major element in the spread of pastoralism in the Sahara and in the frequent movements of nomads farther away from the desert core and toward refuge areas during centuries of severe droughts. The survival of hunter-foragers in the deserts of Libya until recently suggests that either some groups might never have been in-clined to become herders or that some herders might have reverted to foraging when conditions became too severe to keep herds.

The small groups of herders roaming the desert were probably tied together in tribal associations. The tribal groups, likely sharing a common dialect, split and recombined with a constant exchange of partners through marriage. The sparseness of desert resources regulated the number of such groups. It is unlikely that the population density of pastoralists was greater than 0.1 person per square kilometer in favored areas. The size of tribes was perhaps in the range of 350 to 400 people. The total population of herders in the Western Desert of Egypt was perhaps around 5,000.

By 7,000 years ago, herders had supplemented their cattle with sheep and goats. In fact, as environmental conditions worsened, a shift to a greater reliance on sheep and goats become more practical. Unlike cattle, which have been shown, through DNA analysis, to have been domesticated from an African stock, sheep and goats were clearly introduced into North Africa from the Near East, perhaps during the later part of the 8th millennium B.C. Sheep and goat herding spread rapidly across the Nile Delta along the Mediterranean Coast, southward into the Eastern Desert of Egypt, and from there into the interior of the deserts of North Africa. Sheep and goat herders moved into the Negev and the Sinai from other parts of the Near East following the emergence of farming and herding in a broad belt from Palestine to Anatolia. The droughts by the end of the 8th millennium B.C. provide a likely cause for further movements by such nomadic herders eastward and eventually into the Nile Valley.

At present, the earliest occupations in the Nile Valley with evidence for domesticated animals and wheat and barley are from Merimda Beni Salama in the East Delta dating to 5,900 years ago (about 4800 B.C.). The earliest so-called Neolithic sites in the Fayum dating to 6,350 years ago are considered to be culturally affiliated to those in Merimda because of the similarities in the style of stone tools and pottery and the methods used to manufacture them.

Sites with pottery date to 6,300 years ago (5200 B.C.) in El-Tarif near Luxor, and 5,500 years ago (4400 B.C.) in the Badari region. The Badarian settlements, consisting initially of small encampments, include a special variety of pottery with a shiny, burnished surface and a distinct appearance of ripples. This rippled pottery is produced from very fine, untempered Nile silt. The pots were fired, mostly in an open fire, to primarily brown, but also red, and occasionally all black. Other pots were manufactured from coarser Nile silt with organic temper (straw). This rough ware was mostly brown and was often blackened by smoke.

The Badarian pottery is a variant of a burnished pottery present in late Neolithic sites of the eastern Sahara. Before 6,200 years ago, the pottery, often labeled *Saharo-Sudanese* or *Khartoum,* was usually almost completely decorated with a comb-impressed design. However, sometime before 6,000 years ago, burnished, smoothed, or smudged pottery, often undecorated or with occasional geometric incisions limited to bands, appeared. This pottery is known from Gilf El-Kebir and Dakhla Oasis. It may be thus assumed that shortly after 6,000 years ago, as the rainy period in the Sahara was coming to an end, a novel type of pottery emerged and spread rapidly (within, say, 500 years or less) in the southern Nile Valley and the eastern Sahara. Badarian rippled pottery dating to 5,100 years ago is recorded south of the Badari region near Qena (Mahgar Canal 2), at Nag el Gizariya, in the Nagada region, and at Armant.

Sometime between 4000 and 3800 B.C., new forms of vessels emerge as the popularity of rippled ware declined. The new smooth, polished red- and black-rimmed pottery marks a ceramic-assemblage zone referred to as *Nagada I* or *Amratian* after the name of sites in the Nagada region near Luxor and Al-Amrah farther north.

In the Badari region, as revealed in a stratigraphic sequence at Hemamieh, the transition from Badarian to Nagada I (Amratian) is gradual. Lithic assemblages from the Badarian and the Amratian sites are almost indistinguishable. It is accordingly evident that Amratian pottery is a local Nilotic offshoot from Badarian pottery since they share a number of stylistic traits, suggesting that one developed out of the other. Amratian pottery developed in southern Egypt in a span of

200 years at the beginning of the 4th millennium B.C. In the Nagada region, south of Badari, Nagada I sites are firmly dated to 3750 B.C. At Hemamieh, in the Badari region, an early Amratian assemblage dates to between 3827 and 3620 B.C. We may thus be fairly confident that the emergence of Amratian pottery was not much earlier than 3900 B.C. In Nubia, burnished ware resembling Badarian pottery is recorded at sites located between Wadi Kubanniya, north of Aswan, and Melik en Nasir, south of the Second Cataract. The pieces are collectively designated as manifestations of *Group-A* culture. The northern sites from Shellal to Metardul exhibit ceramics with close affinities to Nagada I assemblages (Nagada-Ic-IIb). To the south, the sites are affiliated with younger Nagada assemblages (Nagada IIb-IIIb). The radiocarbon chronology of the so-called A-Group sites is not well established, but terminal A-Group sites are dated roughly to 3200 B.C. The northern A-Group sites may be coeval with Nagada II (Gerzean), dating to 3550 B.C. (4,750 years ago). All Nagada I and Nagada II sites in the Nile Valley show an almost complete reliance on plain food from cultivated barley and wheat as well as meat from domesticated cattle, sheep, goats, and pigs.

Fishing followed preagricultural practices, suggesting that the fishers and foragers of the Nile Valley were culturally and most probably demographically and biologically fused with the newcomers from the surrounding desert. Villages became numerous during the Amratian period, when a relatively rapid increase in population followed the introduction of agriculture in the Nile Valley. If we assume that the Badarian culture began about 4300 B.C. with a few settlers in hamlets in Middle and Upper Egypt, it took about 20 generations (400 years) to achieve the transition to Nagada I marked not only by a new kind of pottery but, more importantly, by an elaboration of social organization and religious ideology manifest in funerary practices (more specialized and selected grave goods and certain body orientation). Within about 200 years (from 3900 to 3700 B.C.) or ten generations, the changes were leading to the founding of small towns, clearly manifest by 3650 to 3500 B.C. The changes also entailed transformations in social organization and religious ideology that led eventually to the rise of regional states by about 3200 B.C. and a cementing of a unified state society encompassing all of Egypt about 3000 B.C.

BIBLIOGRAPHY

Bard, K. 1994. *From farmers to pharaohs.* Sheffield: Sheffield Academic Press.

Friedman, R., and B. Adams, eds. 1992. *Followers of Horus.* Oxford: Egyptian Studies Publication No. 2, Oxbow Monograph 20.

Hassan, F. A. 1988. The predynastic of Egypt. *Journal of World Prehistory* 2 (2): 135–85.

Wetterstrom, W. 1993. Foraging and farming in Egypt: The transition from hunting and gathering to horticulture in the Egyptian Nile Valley. In *The archaeology of Africa: Food, metals and towns,* eds. T. Shaw, P. Sinclair, B. Andah, and A. Okpoko, 165–226. London: Routledge.

Fekri A. Hassan

AGRICULTURAL BEGINNINGS IN SUB-SAHARAN AFRICA

Africa represents one of the world's most innovative theaters of plant domestication. We find at least three distinct domains of species transformation through intensive exploitation of local wild resources: the semiarid Sahara-dry savanna; the elevated Ethiopian Highlands, and the humid forest and its wooded-savanna margin. Research in Africa has pioneered thinking about the implications of a pastoral precedent to agriculture (particularly cattle in the Sahara). Similarly, research here points to the possibility of a preagricultural landscape of generalized, regional economies made up of increasingly specialized hunters, fishers, pastoralists, and plant gatherers, all linked together by traditions of surplus exchange. This Late Stone Age subsistence specialization may have been a response to climatic variability that encouraged intense collection and manipulation of local plants. We also find in Africa that sedentarism can be a precursor to agriculture. Early cultigens can serve long careers as simple supplements to stable, long-enduring wild foodstuffs. But the greatest contribution of the continent to global theory is the idea of a noncentric process of agricultural beginnings (that is, that multiple local experiments in agriculture occurred over a vast area). However, before prehistorians can appreciate the true innovative role of Africa in the global experience of humans' use and domestication of plants, archaeologists must redress the current lack of data, which leaves us overreliant upon genetic and linguistic reconstructions and far too tied to arguments from negative evidence.

The Lack of Data

It would, perhaps, be going too far to speak of an Africanization of current theory about the origins of agriculture in lands beyond Africa. It is, however, very true that the Near Eastern birthplace of research on this topic has been swept by three paradigms pioneered in Africa:

1. The appearance of plant domesticates is preceded by a long and stable period of use of a wide array of wild cereals and other plants. Domestication must be seen, therefore, not as a revolution, but rather as an intensification of interests in a subset of the wild plants. In the (often protracted) transition from full hunting-fishing-collecting, the new cultigens are supplements to existing diets. Indeed, even in the late twentieth century, fully domesticated cultigens are heavily complemented in local diets by wild plants.

2. Agriculture comes about through multiple experiments. It is the classic noncentric process in prehistory.

3. Experimentation is often most successful or earliest in locations where abundant resources or other unrelated opportunities (such as trade) encouraged permanent or semipermanent settlements. Often sedentarism appears to be linked first with pastoralism, in which case, the intensified manipulation of highly productive and

easily stored cereals takes on, again, a supplementary role.

An acknowledgment of Africa's pioneering position in developing these paradigms is a palliative to some other not-so-good news from the continent as a whole. Fundamental field research on the origins of African agriculture is, with a very few notable exceptions, virtually moribund.

The few exceptions to this statement south of the Sahara only underscore the neglect of basic recovery of archaeological botanical remains and of field paleo-ethnobotany. Expatriate researchers repeatedly fail to include wet and dry sieving and flotation in their excavation tasks, when such lapses would be indefensible in their home countries. These recovery technologies and the craft of low-magnification macrobotanical and dung-constituent identification are low-tech and inexpensive (if tedious). African researchers, too, must share the blame for the continent's growing marginality in the minds of those thinking comparatively and globally about the origins of food production.

After a strong start in the 1970s, there has been a mere trickle of data from the field during the last 15 years. Consequently, researchers studying the origins of agriculture in Africa have had to rely to an extraordinary degree upon proxy measures. One class of proxy, or indirect, information about agricultural origins is derived from the study of the genetic makeup of present-day wild and domesticated plants. We continue to rely heavily upon classic reconstructions of this genre for sorghum and millet. Interpretations are made, for example, on the basis of genetic generality or specificity of different stocks of sorghum and on their relative phylogenetic distance from wild sorghum or from the most primitive (generalized) domestic form, *Sorghum bicolor*. After domestication in the broad, semiarid Chadic-Sudan belt, the ancestral *S. bicolor* spread to India and diversified into regional West African *(S. guinea)* and southern *(S. kaffir)* stocks, probably before 3,000 years ago. This exercise in "botanochronology" is, of course, akin to glottochronology. The exercise is subject to all the cautions attendant upon that linguistic discipline, which archaeologists learned to ignore

during the dabates over Bantu expansion. These interpretations from genetics are only as good as the hard, confirming archaeological data, of which we have very little.

Linguistic reconstruction (with an inevitable glottochronological component) is, in fact, the second class of indirect information about the dates and circumstances of humans' use of plants (and animals). Some linguistic reconstructions fit reasonably well with the scarce archaeological data. As an example, the early appearance of pastoralism in the West African Sahara might fit with a linguist's recent statement that Nilo-Saharan speakers already had cattle as they began to expand into West Africa not later than 7000 B.C. (The initiation of pastoralism was a central event in humans' use of plants in the Sahara.) Unfortunately, the linguist's dates are several millennia too early, and ultimately, we will never know what language the first pastoralists spoke. On the other hand, the 30 years of lexico-statistics work on 250 Bantu languages by the Tervuren Group at the Musée Royal in Belgium has significantly advanced our thinking about the foundation diet and food-production practices of the so-called proto-Bantu of southeastern Nigeria and Cameroon in the earlier part of the 2nd millennium B.C. Interpretations and provisional dating from lexico-statistics stimulated a dedicated exploration of the proto-Bantu homeland in the late 1980s and 1990s by teams from Cameroon, Britain, Belgium, France, and the United States (happily, including flotation for macrobotanical remains of rock-shelter deposits).

As encouraging as these interpretations from language or modern plant genetics might be, they only complement the highly laborious collection of archaeo-botanical (and archaeo-faunal) data at well-dated and well-excavated sites. Here Africa is falling behind.

The consequences of this constriction in the data pipeline are several:

1. Nowhere do we have even a preliminary assessment of the full array of wild plants and animals exploited in immediate preagricultural times.
2. We are unable to assess the changes in the proportion and composition of the ex-

ploited food as farmers responded to the new demands of surplus accumulation, new social hierarchies, urbanization, or climate variability and surprises.

3. Africa has not benefited from the new paleo-ethnobotanical observation and recovery methods that allow straightforward determination of issues such as field size, mix of cultigens, and even degree of domestication of the crops from weeds collected in the harvest.

4. Parts of semiarid, lowland Africa boast an unmatched archaeological and geomorphological record of adaptations to rapid and dramatic climate change. However, the reluctance of researchers systematically to collect faunal, floral, and pollen samples prevents us from attempting the same microenvironmental reconstructions that have proved so stimulating in other parts of the globe. Again the exceptions prove the rule, and this is nowhere more the case than the data for the pastoral precedent to agriculture in the Sahara.

Saharan-Dry Savanna Complex

To understand plant domestication in the Sahara and preequatorial grass savannas, one must confront the implications of a solitary pastoralism, that is pastoralism without a companion agricultural lifeway.

There may be a vestigial allegiance to an older conception (advanced by V. G. Childe) of the "Neolithic Revolution" at play in the reluctance of Near Eastern prehistorians to give credit to the critical contribution of small stock (especially goats) to the process of plant domestication. Most prehistorians were trained to consider early agriculture as revolutionary. When farmers had successfully domesticated grains (or tubers), a community would inevitably undergo radical social transformations, leading ultimately to civilization. Pastoralism was considered a later, marginal pursuit. While not universal, evidence from the early Near Eastern pre-Neolithic sites (dating to earlier than 8500 B.C.) such as Nahal Oren, Beidha, and Zawi Chemi now shows that experiments with sheep and goat (and even gazelle)

herding and with genetic manipulation of these grazers made more rapid progress than experiments with local plants.

By the end of the millennium-long arid period (from about 9000 to 8000 B.C.), small stock were firmly a part of the Near Eastern economy. From that point on, cereals that had luxuriated in a long period of experimentation became intensively exploited. People no longer reverted to a mobile, low-density, hunting-and-collecting way of life at the onset of each subsequent drought, as they apparently had done during earlier climatic fluctuations. These people inhabited permanent or semipermanent communities long before the final domestication (when species become dependent upon humans for reproduction and protection) of wheat, barley, pulsanes (edible seeds such as peas, beans, and lentils), sheep, cattle, pigs, and goats that compose the classic constellation of Near Eastern food production.

The purpose of lingering on the Near Eastern pattern is to show the contrast with Africa. It was, after all, prior Near Eastern research that supplied the expectations of what the African pattern should look like. If (contrary to those older expectations) livestock provided the food-on-the-hoof that allowed the intensification and spread of agriculture and ensured permanence to sedentary village life, why have prehistorians been ambivalent about the contribution of "humble" sheep and goats to the success of "noble" wheat and barley? Africanist prehistorians do not have the luxury of ambivalence on this issue. From the Eastern Sahara of Egypt and the northern regions of the Sudan Republic to the Sahara's Atlantic margin, the evidence of pastoralism as a precursor to agriculture is unassailable. The evidence also has profound implications for the ways archaeologists derive interpretations from their data.

Nowhere in the world today, nor in any ethnohistorical account, do we find pastoralism without agriculture. Pastoralists always have client-patron relations of one form or another with farming communities. Or, they themselves grow grain seasonally. Hence, the precedence of Saharan pastoral lifeways (and possibly the jump start goats give to Near Eastern agriculture) flies in the face of reasoning by uniformitarianism. Archaeologists infer past peoples' behavior from the highly fragmentary evidence they dig up from the ground by making analogies to practices they see today. Conditions in the past were as they are today—this is the ultimate uniformitarianist position. Some archaeologists take a further step by making the argument that we cannot recognize, much less analyze, prehistoric behavior that lacks parallels in today's world. Yet, even the most obdurate has to acknowledge this curious fact about the Saharan and dry grassland-margin homeland of the principal indigenous African grains: cattle are domesticated and cattle pastoralism spreads explosively, often leading to stable village life, millennia before cereal collection and plant manipulation intensify to a degree that we can even begin to speak of true agricultural beginnings.

The best and earliest evidence for this pastoral precedence comes from the Western Desert of Egypt. In about 7500 B.C., at sites such as Bir Kiseiba and Nabta, local inhabitants of a dry, drought-prone steppe began to manipulate herds of wild cattle. Soon they were purposefully moving the cattle into more arid environments, which required the digging of wells and management of herd composition. They subsisted on the milk and blood of their beasts. Apparently, they regarded their animals as food-on-the-hoof, as insurance against climatic surprise, and as a critical element in their strategy for expanding throughout the Middle Holocene Sahara. Pastoralism apparently began as a human-grazer symbiosis. Animals and humans were attracted to the same restricted water holes. In time, people learned to manipulate the wild longhorn's movements to ensure their own access to water and to prevent their food from fleeing. Noticeably missing in this scenario are plants.

What were the tens of thousands of grinding stones found at sites in Egypt's Western Desert used for? Based on the materials recovered from Early and Middle Neolithic sites around Nabta, researchers concluded that the inhabitants exploited a variety of wild grasses (including wild millet and sorghum), legumes, and other plants. These would have satisfied the need of pastoralists for supplemental plant components. Plants add nutrition to a milk diet and are espe-

cially important for sustaining the fragment of the community left behind with the milk cows and calves when the herd is split during a long-range transhumance season. There is no evidence during this time of determined experiments in plant domestication, nor is there evidence of such experiments in the records from the succeeding several millennia as pastoralism spread south and west across the vast Sahara. These Saharan folk did not display any particular desire to rush to embrace Southwest Asian cereals after their arrival at the Nile Delta and Fayum around 4000 B.C.

One Near Eastern prehistorian has claimed that people manipulated plant materials during the period before domestication only when it suited them. It apparently did not suit local Saharan peoples, until quite late, to push the process of gathering wild plants to the point at which we can recognize even the initial stages of agriculture. Significantly, it did very much please them to lavish time and creativity upon their herds. Thousands of intricate rock-art scenes of herds, portraits of prized cows or bulls, domestic tableaux with cattle, and so forth from the Middle Holocene Sahara attest to the reigning obsession of the groups spreading west to the Atlantic Coast and south to the tsetse barrier at roughly 18° north latitude after about 5500 B.C.

The spread of pastoralists—and a possible reason for the nonchalance with which Saharan peoples approached plant domestication—was partially due to climate change. The desiccation of the far northern Sahara began in earnest about 6000 B.C. and, elsewhere by 4500 B.C. Pastoralists progressively colonized a region that had essentially been depopulated since the late glacial period of extreme aridity (except for the central highlands of the Sahara). Many sites appear to have been fully equipped for the collecting, processing, and storing plants. Some, like Foum el Alba in the Malian Sahara, may even have been specialized camps for processing grain. However, various early claims for domesticated grain (pearl millet at Amekni, Algeria, between 6000 and 4500 B.C. and *Brachiaria* and sorghum at Adrar Bous, Niger, between 4000 and 2000 B.C.) have now been discarded. The only trustworthy identifications of domesticated plants are quite late. These are not many: bulrush millet at Dhar Tichitt

(Mauritania) and Karkarichinkat (Mali) at the turn of the 1st millennium B.C. and millet, sorghum and African rice at Jenne-jeno (Mali) at about 200 B.C. The archaeo-botanical data lag significantly behind the paleo-ethnobotanical theory that predicted the widespread success of fully domesticated *Sorghum bicolor* at least by 2000 B.C. However, a lack of archaeo-botanical evidence is negative evidence and carries with it all the cautions attendant upon any reasoning from negative evidence in archaeology. All it takes is one counter, positive case (entirely possible, given the present low density of floral recovery efforts) to bury the case for late domestication. Saharan plant domestication may be genuinely late. On the other hand, prehistorians infer from other evidence, such as the nature of sedentary sites and possible specialization and interconnectedness of communities, that the picture is much more complicated. This preagricultural complication might also be viewed as long-term, multiple experimentation, perhaps by precocious specialists.

Hypothesis: Preagricultural Specialists

In a seminal 1971 article, Jack Harlan, the doyen of Africanist plant domestication, introduced to the paleo-ethnobotanical world the idea of indigenous experimentation with plants in noncentric zones spread over an extensive area. The idea has since become much the fashion in, for example, the Levant and greater Near East. It has, however, languished for lack of confirming data in the region in which Harlan first applied the concept of noncenters, namely, the southern Saharan regions (below 18° north latitude) to savanna grasslands most conducive to wild sorghum, millet, African rice, and fonio.

Now, however, two changes in archaeological perspective have begun a revival of the noncentric idea:

1. Prehistorians once looked upon all Late Stone Age communities of the southern Sahara as representative of an essentially homogeneous "aquatic" way of life (adapted to hunting, fishing, harpooning large water beasts such as hippopotamuses or crocodiles along the banks of the

streams and lakes still in evidence until as late as 1500 to 1000 B.C.). Now, however, there is a much greater appreciation of the fact that, within broad lithic (stone) traditions, there is enormous diversity in the stone tools and in the remains of prey and domestic animals in the sites' refuse. Archaeologists assume that variability in tool kits has some relationship to the variety of tasks undertaken during different seasons and at different sites.

2. In those few places where thorough, systematic survey led to the recording of all sites of all kinds (for example Méma and Douentza), apparently contemporaneous communities of aquatic mammal hunters, fishers, herders, shellfish collectors, and hunter-foragers lived in proximity and possibly even congregated together seasonally.

By adding one last southern Saharan innovation to the equation, a distinctive pattern of adaptation to climatic variability after 4500 B.C. becomes possible indeed. Many Late Stone Age communities are permanently in place. If primarily pastoral in pursuit, they stop their haphazard wandering and substitute a true transhumance pattern. Part of the herd and its tenders many leave for a long-distance seasonal foraging round, but they always return to the home hamlet.

From the size of villages examined, it seems likely that population is growing. That growth may reflect, to a degree, the current theory in the Near East on the shift to intensive exploitation (including genetic manipulation) of local plants and animals. For example, there are more than 400 permanent or semipermanent stone-built villages, dating to between 1800 and 800 B.C., along the cliffs at Dhar Tichitt in Mauritania. One of these villages, Dakhlet, boasts 600 compounds and may have had between 3,000 and 10,000 inhabitants. The Dhar Tichitt people subsisted on their herds and collected wild plants from a vast playa lake nearby. There, millet domestication appears to be genuinely late (1000 to 900 B.C.)—a last-ditch response to the final drought that eliminated the lake.

It has become less and less supportable for prehistorians to interpret the remains of the lakeshore plant-collecting and fishing camps at Dhar Tichitt, the transhumance stations, and stone-built cliff villages as evidence for different peoples, exploiting different resources in the same vicinity, yet little influenced by their neighbors. What are the alternatives to this 19th-century view of how cultures interact?

Some prehistorians interpret the diverse sites as evidence of seasonal rounds. In this view, the same community moves from one set of resources to another as they become available in different months of the year. The tool kit and food debris left behind at each stage in the seasonal round reflect the activities of the moment. Undoubtedly, some sites will eventually be shown to support this model. However, there are often obvious style and form differences in the ceramics and stone tools at these different, nearby sites. The archaeologists who conducted the systematic surveys in the Méma and Douentza (Mali) argue strongly that the sites reflect contemporaneous, articulated specialist communities.

Are we seeing in the Late Holocene Sahara an emerging landscape of interacting specialists? If so, we can hypothesize a generalized regional economy based on a kind of reciprocity among specialists. Reciprocity, or regular rules ensuring confidence in the future repayment of past services, would have buffered any one community from the effects of the temporary ecological disasters befalling their particular niche. Such climatic surprise was a common feature of arid tropical lowlands during the Late Holocene. So buffered, the hypothesis continues, the gatherers in this system would have been encouraged to experiment and to intensify their interest in certain high-yield, high-nutrition species. Specialization (as we possibly see at sites such as Foum el Alba) preceded agriculture but eventually led to grain domestication. In this scenario, the preagricultural specialists' exchanges of grain (collected wild or incipiently cultivated) for the pastoralists' meat, milk, hide, horns, and so forth (and for hunters' meat and hides and fishers' smoked fish and oil) were the glue that bound these communities together.

The beauty of this hypothesis is that it provides a rationale for multiple experiments with multiple local plants, a rationale that is not overly dependent upon passive reaction to climate deterioration. These experiments would be equally, or more, encouraged during short pluvial (rainy) conditions. But, whatever the specific path to agricultural beginnings, in each of the perhaps 1,000 or 10,000 local experiments with the plants at hand, one final attribute appears to characterize the Saharan-dry savanna complexes (whether based on low-rainfall millet, decrue or receding-flood sorghum, or paddy African rice) from their inception to full maturity—a strong tendency to mix domesticated grains with a broad spectrum of wild plants.

When domesticated millet appeared at Karkarichinkat and Dhar Tichitt, it was added to a continuing system of broad wild-resource exploitation. Hunting and the collection of wild plants form the pattern also after domestic species appear at the wooded-savanna site of Kintampo in Ghana between 1600 and 1000 B.C. The best sequence, to date, is provided by the systematic flotation of macrobotanical material from all phases of the 1,600-year, uninterrupted sequence at Jenne-jeno in Mali's Middle Niger. Occupation began about 250 B.C. From the very beginning, Jenne-jeno's inhabitants grew domestic sorghum, millet, and abundant African rice. Domesticated fonio appeared later. But throughout the occupation, the inhabitants happily collected wild cereals—rice (*Oryza barthii*), *Brachiaria ramosa, Panicum laetum, Echinocloa stagnina,* and *E. colona* as well as other legumes and garnish plants (for example, purslane). In fact, so strong was the wild component of the Jenne-jeno sequence that the Malian ethnobotanist who assisted with the identifications made a special collecting expedition to the Middle Niger floodplain to expand his comparative collection. In the process, he confirmed that the practice of supplementing the diet with collected wild species is still very much alive today, unexpectedly right in the midst of one of Africa's granaries. The wild species are not collected as famine foods. They form part of a stable complex of domesticated (or partially domesticated) and wild-plant foods. A similar complex and intricate experimental mix of wild and manipulable crops presumably characterized the beginning of agriculture in the Africa humid savanna and forest. Before we turn to the very different conditions and array of foods there, however, we must briefly review evidence from another dry (if higher altitude) botanical domain—Ethiopia.

The Ethiopian Highlands

The Ethiopian Highlands are another classic case of botanical and linguistic inference running dangerously ahead of data. The debates here turn upon the issues of what plants composed the indigenously domesticated constellation and how (and at what date) this constellation was modified after the introduction of Near Eastern grains.

The genetic theorist N. I. Vavilov considered the Ethiopian Highlands to be one of eight world centers of domestication. Now we know that several of his candidate crops (for example, oats) arrived from elsewhere. Still, at least six important domesticates almost certainly have their origin here, including cereal grains (finger millet and teff), the edible oil plant called *noog,* stimulants (coffee and chat), and the important starch source, ensete.

Some researchers have presumed that the core Ethiopian constellation (especially finger millet and teff) must have been in place and widely cultivated before the arrival of the Near Eastern wheats and barleys sometime between 7000 and 4000 B.C. Their reasoning is that the higher-yield, introduced plants would have forestalled local domestication or would have aborted indigenous domestication already under way, had teff and finger millet not long been mainstays of Ethiopian diets. This view has some support from linguistics. Cushitic is the oldest of the several Ethiopian languages, and many terms for foods and cultivation practices entered into Omotic or Semitic languages from that source. Some linguists believe that the oldest Cushitic languages developed in northeasternmost Africa, near the Red Sea, about 15,000 years ago and that intensive wild-cereal exploitation was already an ancient habit of the people living there. Using language parallels and borrowings, these scholars place a date of around 5000 B.C. as the minimum date for the presence of cereal cultivation (probably for the use of ensete, too) and herding.

In Ethiopia, too, archaeologists sing what is by now a familiar refrain. The evidence from the few sites from which botanical remains have been recovered does not, at present, support claims of great antiquity for any form of cultivation. Finger millet at Gobedra (near Aksum) was once thought to date to the 3rd or 4th millennium B.C. but, upon reexamination, is now thought to be only 1,000 years old. Cereal harvesting in the mid-2nd millennium B.C. has been inferred from silica sheen on microliths from Laga Oda. Of course, it is impossible to know if the Laga Oda harvest was of wild or cultivated cereals or what cereals were involved. At Lalibela Cave (east Lake Tana), there is evidence of barley, chickpea, and legumes at about 500 B.C. Lastly, the very first teff comes not from Africa, but from Hajar bin Humeid (100 B.C. to A.D. 100) in southern Yemen.

Humid, Intertropical Africa

If the lag of archaeological data behind linguistic and ethnobotanical inference frustrates us in the Ethiopian Highlands, the situation is doubly aggravating in the forest-margin savannas and deep forests of western and equatorial Africa. Here preservation is a double curse. First, many of the yams and tubers that certainly were indigenously domesticated here would preserve poorly under even the driest of conditions. Second, the forest and its humid margins are even less populated by archaeologists than the Sahara and its southern fringe.

As is the case with Southeast Asia and (less well documented) the Amazonian Basin, the forest and savanna-forest transition of western and central Africa formed another independent, vast experimentation zone. Due to preservation considerations, it is not surprising that the best-known set of sites here, the 2nd-millennium B.C. Kintampo complex of central Ghana, is located at the dry, wooded savanna frontier.

Kintampo continues a tradition seen earlier (just after 3000 B.C.) at the Ghanaian forest site of Bosumpra—a shift from heavy reliance upon collecting the oily seed of *Canarium schweinfurthii* to intensive interest in oil palm (which was perhaps tended and semidomesticated). At the

Kintampo rock shelters and open-air sites, the sequence begins with heavy use of collected *Celtis* and *Canarium* as well as snails and various hunted animals. Then, mobility decreases, and community size and the number of sedentary villages increase at the time when the sites provide the earliest unquestioned domesticates in West Africa. These include sheep or goats, possible cattle and guinea fowl, and cowpea (perhaps transitional to full domesticate) and abundant oil palm. While these domesticates are growing in dietary importance, the Kintampo folk lost no interest in the hunted animals, collected snails and rodents, and gathered wild plants (still including *Canarium* and hackberry). These well-excavated sites show no signs of new population infusions at the beginning of agriculture. Kintampo provides some of our best evidence of the process of in-place experimentation and intensification of local resources, perhaps encouraged by the ancillary circumstances or pressures that encouraged sedentarism.

The Kintampo sites are exceptional. At others in the forest, such as the 5th-millennium B.C. Iwo Eleru in Nigeria, some prehistorians have inferred a degree of food production (based on yams) from the appearance of sedentarism, pottery, and ground-stone hoes. There is no proof, however, that the Iwo Eleru tubers were not morphologically wild. The data situation is not much better, with a similarly unsatisfactory use of proxy evidence for the beginnings of agriculture, at sites of those part of southeastern Nigeria and Cameroon reckoned to represent the heartland of the Bantu spread. Very recent work at shelter sites with better preservation, such as Shum Laka in Cameroon, promises a dramatic improvement in data. But we still rely too heavily upon botanical and, especially, lexico-statistical reconstructions to determine the structure of the earliest Bantu economies.

The spread of the Bantu languages from their heartland to the Republic of South Africa, beginning in 3000 B.C. (at the latest), ranks as one of the great language migrations of all times. It is not surprising that such a dramatic process should have been the engine for much of the later prehistoric archaeology of eastern, central, and southern Africa. Several questions lay behind this research. What where the technological (iron, food-processing equipment) or social innovations that made the Bantu-speakers so successful? Was the spread stimulated by a population rise, or was the Bantu expansion linked to an ability to exploit new territories, an ability that came into being with forest-adapted food production? Recently, the sophisticated lexico-statistics of the Tervuren Group have revealed the true genetic linkages of core vocabularies hidden beneath more than 3,000 years of loanwords and convergences. Many of these words relate to foods or to farming tools and techniques.

Excavations in the so-called proto-Bantu heartland northwest of the central African forest are beginning to confirm that by 3000 B.C. (and from evidence from Shum Laka, perhaps as early as three millennia earlier) sedentary, ceramic-producing, stone-tool-using villagers practiced a mixed economy that included domesticated yams, oil palm, *Canarium* fruit, gourds, dogs, goats, and fishing and hunting. When the forest began to retreat in response to climate change by the middle of the 2nd millennium B.C., descendant groups were able to shift and massage elements of this variegated economy to adapt quite rapidly and successfully to changing conditions and to various microhabitats within the humid, open woods and dense forests. They had spread to eastern Cameroon by that date. They then quickly spread through the forest to the southeast, due south along the Zaire Basin littoral, and traversed some 2,000 kilometers of savannas north of the forest to reach the East African interlacustrine region (western Kenya, northwestern Tanzania, Uganda, Rwanda, and Burundi) by about 1500 B.C. The great mystery is where, when, and from whom did they adopt grain (millet and sorghum) agriculture while on this northern savanna traverse. Their route led them to skirt the Chadic-Sudan belt proposed by Harlan as the prime zone for *Sorghum bicolor* domestication.

By the time iron was adopted in the later half of the last millennium B.C., Bantu speakers had spread well south of the forest. Even with iron, they maintained a pattern of expanding, low-density, sedentary, mixed farming and small-stock raising. They appeared to coexist for centuries with autochthonous hunter-foragers who had a long previous history there and developed their lifeway before the entrance of the Bantu speakers and, in East Africa, with pastoralists who migrated in from the north centuries earlier. Sorghum and millet agriculture and local adaptation of Asian imports, especially the banana, eventually became the economic base for a rise in population densities in the late 1st millennium A.D.

———~~~~~~~~~———

Always with the proviso that Africanist archaeologists must accept no excuses from their colleagues who do not include the basic techniques of macrobotanical recovery in their field programs, what major themes can we perceive at this very halting stage in our knowledge of African agricultural beginnings? The first theme is that it would be a fool's errand to look for *the* center, or *the* first instance of African plant domestication. The process was dispersed over a large area, locally variable, and supremely noncentric. One should speak more properly of 1,000, or 10,000, local experiments.

Future research will likely show that some of these experiments were very early. Some may even anticipate the first appearance of cattle pastoralism or the first impulses to a more sedentary existence. However, on present evidence, it seems likely that Africa will indeed prove that we must go beyond the limitations of standard uniformitarian inference. We cannot use ethnographic experience to make sense of the presence, for millennia, of prosperous, permanent communities based largely upon cattle pastoralism and lacking any appreciable domesticated grain component. As population grew at these sites, the inhabitants simply exploited wild plants more intensively. This is a pattern that may have continued on into theoretical infinity were it not for two additional factors.

The first was climate. After 4500 B.C., the Sahara alternates between good, pluvial times and droughts that could last a century or more. The Sahara reached its present state at the end of the Late Stone Age. Few of the continent's inhabitants escaped the effects of precipitation fluctuations during the latter half of the Holocene. Those suffering the most were people who lived in the marginally stable subarid and arid zones where

wild predecessors of sorghum, millet, and African rice were found. How did the communities respond? Some responded by moving south or to anomalous aquatic environments such as the Middle Niger. Some tried to hold onto an older way of life by intensifying their use of local grains to the point that those grains were domesticated.

The second (and perhaps equally important) factor for change leading to the beginnings of agriculture was the possible emergence of a generalized, multiple-component economy in the Late Stone Age. Cattle (and small stock) as food-on-the-hoof is one form of insurance against an unpredictable environment. Another is to enter into predictable exchange relations with neighbors who become increasingly adept (specialized) at exploiting one or another resource of the shared region. A good year for you may be your neighbor's year of misery and want. If you satisfy that want, however, rules of reciprocity ensure that you can call upon your neighbor in your own time of want. It is virtually a natural law in regions with a highly tenuous climatic pattern that just such a year of want for you will surely come for your neighbor. This mutual reinforcement of specialization and incipient surplus production for exchange does not have to result in a focus on just one or two species. The lingering appeal of wild plants in the West African diet demonstrates the wisdom of maintaining a degree of diversification. But an articulated regional economy and nascent specialization can encourage other social innovations. The most important of these innovations will contribute to the emergence of food production. These innovations are sedentarism, the relaxation of social injunctions against population rise, and new forms of social ranking—especially if accompanied by new demands for disposable surpluses for prestige and status reasons. Such innovations, in Africa as in the other better-understood parts of the prehistoric Old World, may have contributed importantly to the kinds of experiments with wild plants that led to the beginnings of agriculture.

BIBLIOGRAPHY

Clark, J. D., and S. A. Brandt, eds. 1984. *From hunters to farmers.* Berkeley: University of California Press.

Close, A. E., and F. Wendorf. 1992. The beginnings of food production in the eastern Sahara. In *Transitions to agriculture in prehistory,* eds. A. B. Gebauer and T. D. Price, 63–72. Madison: Prehistory Press.

Harlan, J. R. 1992. Indigenous African agriculture. In *The origins of agriculture: An international perspective,* eds. C. W. Cowan and P. J. Watson, 59–70. Washington, D.C.: Smithsonian Institution Press.

Harlan, J. R., J. M. J. De Wet, and A. B. L. Stemler, eds. 1976. *Origins of African plant domestication.* The Hague: Mouton.

Hassan, F. A. 1986. Desert environment and origins of agriculture in Egypt. *Norwegian Archaeological Review* 19: 63–76.

McIntosh, S. K., and R. J. McIntosh. 1988. From stone to metal: New perspectives on the later prehistory of West Africa. *Journal of World Prehistory* 2: 89–133.

Muzzolini, A. 1993. The emergence of a food producing economy in the Sahara. In *The archaeology of Africa: Food, metals and towns,* eds. T. Shaw, P. Sinclair, B. Andah, and A. Okpoko, 227–239. London: Routledge.

Phillipson, D. W. 1993. The antiquity of cultivation and herding in Ethiopia. In *The archaeology of Africa: Food, metals and towns,* eds. T. Shaw, P. Sinclair, B. Andah, and A. Okpoko, 334–357. London: Routledge.

Roderick J. McIntosh

ANIMAL DOMESTICATION IN AFRICA

Until recently, there has been little research on the history of domestic animals south of the Sahara, and the only major work on the subject, by H. Epstein, was published in 1971. Within the last decade, however, there has been a large number of publications on pastoralism and the development in Africa of prehistoric food-producing economies, and the analysis of animal remains from archaeological sites all over the continent is becoming a rapidly expanding field of research.

Notable among these studies are publications by J. D. Clark and S. A. Brandt in 1984, J. Clutton-Brock in 1993, E. A. Voigt and I. Plug in 1981, M. Hall and A. B. Smith in 1986, A. B. Smith in 1992, and T. Shaw, P. Sinclair, B. Andah, and A. Okpoko in 1993.

The archaeology and ancient fauna, both wild and domestic, of ancient Egypt have been studied in such detail and are now so well known that it is natural for there to be a general assumption that all domestic animals in Africa derive from this civilization. The archaeological record is beginning to indicate, however, that there may have been several different routes by which livestock reached the Sahel and then the equatorial and savanna regions of the south.

Africa has been a center for the local domestication of endemic food plants, which have become important worldwide. In contrast, only one domestic animal, the guinea fowl, had a wild progenitor that occurred only in Africa, and there is slender evidence for the local domestication of only three mammals: the ass, the cat, and North African cattle. Many other species of African ungulates have been systematically exploited over thousands of years—for example, the elephant and several species of antelope and gazelle—but these animals have never undergone the process of domestication whereby they have been bred in captivity and become the personal property of humans. There is one exception, however—the special relationship in southern Africa between the San and the eland. While this antelope was never domesticated, the San did regard the wild herds as personal possessions.

Domestication involves both culture and biology. The cultural process of domestication begins when animals are incorporated into the social structure of a human community and become objects of ownership, inheritance, purchase, and exchange. The morphological changes that occur in domestic animals come second in this integration into human society. The biological process resembles evolution and begins when a small number of parent animals are separated from the wild species. These animals form a founder group, which is changed over successive generations, in response to natural selection under the new regime imposed by the human community and its environment and by artificial selection for economic, cultural, or aesthetic reasons. In the wild, the evolution of a subspecies occurs when a segment of a species becomes reproductively isolated by a geographical barrier. With domestic animals, this separation leads to the development of different breeds, which, under human ownership, may continue to be bred in isolated groups but are not restricted geographically.

Around half of the world's species of wild ungulates, including 87 species of artiodactyls (members of an order of ungulates with an even number of functional toes on each foot), inhabit the continent of Africa, and this raises several questions. Why were none of these species domesticated? Why did the iron-using people who moved south with domestic herds choose to own cattle, sheep, and goats rather than, say, buffalo, impalas, and gazelles? Why did these people not learn how to ride zebras? The answers for Africa are no different from anywhere else in the world, for sheep and goats are just as much immigrants to Europe as they are to Africa. There are remarkably few domestic species of animals worldwide in comparison to the numbers that, in theory, were available for domestication in the prehistoric period. The reasons for this must have to do with human culture and behavior as well as with the biology and behavior of the domesticates, as discussed, for example, by Clutton-Brock in 1987 and Smith in 1992.

Summaries are given below of the archaeozoology of the domestic species in sub-Saharan Africa.

GUINEA FOWL, *NUMIDA MELEAGRIS* AND *NUMIDA PTILORHYNCA.* The guinea fowl is the only domestic animal that certainly originated in Africa. In modern times, two of the four wild species of *Numida* are bred as domestic fowl. These are the helmeted guinea fowl *(N. meleagris),* which is found wild today in West Africa, and *N. ptilorhynca,* which is endemic to East Africa. It was the helmeted guinea fowl that was first domesticated.

There appear to be no references in Europe to the guinea fowl in the Middle Ages until the Portuguese travelers to the African coast gave the bird its present name in the 16th century. At the few archaeological sites in Africa where guinea fowl has been recorded, for example Jebel Shaqadud in Sudan, there is no indication that the birds were reared in captivity.

DOMESTIC FOWL, *GALLUS GALLUS.* Chickens were domesticated sometime before the 6th millennium B.C. in India and Southeast Asia from the red jungle fowl, *Gallus gallus.* It is possible that domestic chickens reached the coast of East Africa in a direct route from Malaysia during the 1st millennium A.D., and from there they rapidly spread across the continent.

In West Africa, chickens have been recently identified at the Iron Age site of Jenne-jeno in Mali, dating to between A.D. 500 and 800. In East Africa, domestic fowl has been recorded at Manekeni and Chibuene, Iron Age sites in Mozambique. In South Africa, the remains of chickens have been recorded at the 8th-century Iron Age site of Ndondondwane in KwaZulu-Natal.

RODENTS. The three most common rodent pests worldwide are the black rat *(Rattus rattus),* the Norway rat *(Rattus norvegicus),* and the house mouse *(Mus domesticus).* Strains of the Norway rat and the house mouse are today bred as laboratory animals and pets, but historically, their association with humans has been only as unwanted commensals, which have traveled everywhere with their hosts. Apart from the presumed association of the black rat with early epidemics of plague in ancient Egypt, little is known of the history or distribution of these rodents in Africa. Remains of black rats have been recorded at Iron Age sites in Zambia and from the 12th-century site of Pont Drift in the northern part of the former Transvaal province. Black rats have also been identified at the 8th-century site of Ndondondwane in KwaZulu-Natal.

The grasscutter or cane rat *(Thryonomys swinderianus),* found in many forest and savanna areas south of the Sahara, is a very large rodent that is a valuable source of meat. In recent years, both the grasscutter and the African giant rat *(Cricetomys gambianus)* have been domesticated in West Africa. Remains of grasscutters, identified from the early Khartoum site in Sudan as a new species, *Thryonomys arkelli,* are now referred to as *Thryonomys swinderianus.*

THE CAT, *FELIS CATUS.* The cat may have been first domesticated by the ancient Egyptians, as tradition holds, but there is no direct evidence for this. Cats are represented in Egyptian art from the Middle Kingdom (from 1991 B.C.), but by this time, there are records of domestic cat remains at a scattering of archaeological sites in western Asia and Europe. The wild progenitor of the domestic cat was most probably *Felis silvestris libyca,* which is the southern form of the widespread species *Felis silvestris. F. s. libyca* is the common wild cat of Africa, and it is found over most of the continent from the Mediterranean to the Cape, except in the tropical rain-forest belt.

There is no information on the history of the domestic cat in Africa, outside Egypt. Unless there was some cultural evidence to suggest domestication, it would not be possible to distinguish the remains of domestic cats from those of wild cats in an archaeological context. At the present in Africa, wild cats will interbreed with feral and house cats, which makes difficult the separation of even the living cats into wild and domestic forms.

THE DOG, *CANIS FAMILIARIS.* Finds of canid remains that can be assumed to be at least tamed wolves, if not fully domestic dogs, indicate that domestication probably occurred first in western Asia, around 12,000 years ago, and that the progenitor of the dog was the small indigenous wolf, *Canis lupus arabs* or *C. l. pallipes.*

Today, the dog is ubiquitous throughout Africa, but as with all other domestic animals, it was a latecomer south of the Sahara. In Africa, the differentiation of fragmentary bones and teeth found at archaeological sites as dog or wild canid is more difficult than in other parts of the world because of the presence everywhere of a species of jackals, whose size is similar to that of some dogs. In reports on faunal remains, it is usual, therefore, to record merely the presence of *Canis* sp. On the other hand, it is clear that there were dogs in North Africa from at least 4000 B.C., and innumerable depictions from ancient Egypt show that there were separate breeds from predynastic times.

How far dogs moved south in the prehistoric period is difficult to ascertain, as there are very few records from early prehistoric sites. One find has been reported from the ancient city of Kerma, in northern Sudan, dating to the 2nd millennium B.C. Domestic dogs have also been identified at Esh Shaheinab (about 3300 B.C.) and at the predynastic site of Toukh in Upper Egypt.

The most recently discovered find is a nearly complete skull and skeleton of a small female dog, excavated from Mound K at the Iron Age site at Ntusi in western Uganda. Bone from this skeleton has yielded an AMS radiocarbon age of 990 to 1,120 years. This age falls at the early end of the range of radiocarbon datings of the Ntusi settlement and of this mound in particular. The dog was between two and four years old when it died, and it stood about 35 centimeters at the shoulders.

No certain identifications of dog remains, south of the equator, are known until the 1st millennium A.D. At Iron Age excavations in the 1960s, at Isamu Pati Mound, Kalomo in Zambia, the remains of seven domestic dogs were dated to about A.D. 950 to 1000. More recently, dog remains have been dated to the late 1st millennium at a number of Iron Age sites in southern Africa, including Mapungubwe, Schroda, and Ndondondwane. There is as yet no evidence for dogs south of the Limpopo River before the 6th century.

As in other parts of the world, the dog in Africa has filled many roles since the prehistoric period. It is a scavenger that helps to keep villages clean. It can be a companion, bed warmer, hunter, and retriever. Dogs are also eaten for food and in ritual ceremonies. Their skins are used, their teeth are made into necklaces, and their bones are employed in medicine and witchcraft.

THE DONKEY, *EQUUS ASINUS.* Like the cat, the donkey is traditionally assumed to have been first domesticated by the ancient Egyptians. However, the osteological evidence shows that there were donkeys in use not only in Egypt but also in western Asia by 2500 B.C. In Egypt, the earliest evidence for donkey comes from a skull, buried in the tomb of Tarkhan and excavated by W. M. Flinders Petrie in 1914. A radiocarbon accelerator age of 4,260 to 4,520 years has been obtained from this skull.

The ancestor of the domestic donkey was the wild ass of North Africa and Arabia, *Equus africanus.* Future research in molecular biology may enable the progenitor of the domestic donkey to be pinpointed from the several subspecies that have been identified from North Africa and western Asia, but at present this is not possible.

Although not part of the pastoral tradition of East African Bantu-speaking people, donkeys extend, through the whole length of greater Maasailand and the neighboring areas, from Kikuyu in the highlands to the northern Swahili coast. Maasailand donkeys seem to represent an old part of the northeastern African distribution. A single donkey bone has been recorded at the early 2nd-millennium A.D. Sirik assemblage at Hyrax Hill.

THE HORSE, *EQUUS CABALLUS*. The Hyksos are considered to be responsible for bringing the first horses into ancient Egypt, and the earliest recorded remains are from the palace of Buhen, where the skeleton of a horse has been dated to about 1675 B.C. From this time onward, the horse was an animal associated with high status and the ceremonial chariot, as so frequently shown in ancient Egyptian art.

Although many breeds of horses and ponies have been developed throughout Africa, it seems likely that until very recently, they were unable to survive in the equatorial region. As Epstein maintained, it is improbable, therefore, that there were horses south of the Sahara until the time of European contact. There is no evidence, for example, that the breed of Basuto ponies originated with the Bantu-speaking people. Epstein claimed that horses were first landed at the Cape in 1653.

THE CAMEL, *CAMELUS DROMEDARIUS*. The dromedary, or one-humped camel, is perfectly adapted to life in hot, arid deserts where it migrates over huge areas, browses on the sparsest vegetation, and survives without water for longer than any other mammal. There are no wild dromedaries in existence, and it is not known when they became extinct. Neither is it known where or when the one-humped camel was first domesticated. An age of 2,600 to 2,780 years ago has been obtained by radiocarbon dating of camel dung from Napatan levels at Qasr Ibrim.

The camel herders of the Sahara exemplify the nomadic way of life, which, for hundreds of years, has enabled people to survive in one of the most inhospitable regions of the world. Following their herds of camels and using water from ancient wells, the desert nomads have exploited a

huge region that cannot be used for traditional agriculture. Dromedaries are decreasing in numbers everywhere. They are rarely found south of the Sahel, for their movement south is prevented by their susceptibility to trypanosomiasis.

THE PIG, *SUS DOMESTICUS*. Domestic pigs are all descended from the wild boar, *Sus scrofa*, which was formerly widespread over Europe, Asia, and North Africa. Remains of the earliest domestic pigs have been found at Neolithic sites in western Asia. They were present in ancient Egypt from the late 3rd millennium B.C.

There has long been a tradition of pig breeding in the equatorial region of West Africa, but it is not known whether these pigs are descendants of ancient North African stock or whether they were introduced by the Portuguese. All the pigs present in southern Africa are descended from swine that were introduced by Europeans.

DOMESTIC CATTLE, *BOS TAURUS* AND *BOS INDICUS*. The history of cattle in Africa is better known than that of any other domestic species. It is also very complicated because, for at least 3,000 years, the continent has been a melting pot for unhumped cattle *(Bos taurus)* brought in from Eurasia and humped cattle *(Bos indicus)* brought in from Asia and, in particular, India. In addition, it is possible that cattle were locally domesticated in North Africa from the endemic wild aurochs *(Bos primigenius)*. Based on examinations of the remains of cattle identified at early Neolithic sites (dating to 7,000 years ago) in the eastern Sahara, F. Wendorf has argued that domestication occurred in this region from the local wild *Bos primigenius*.

By 6,000 years ago, it is probable that cattle pastoralism was well established throughout North Africa and that with the increasing desertification of the Sahara, people began to move south with their cattle, only to meet the tsetse-fly belt. The classic story, following the work of Epstein, is that these cattle were long-horned and humpless. Later they were replaced and crossed with short-horned, humpless cattle, which followed the same routes. At the next stage, both long- and short-horned cattle moved up the Nile Valley and were interbred with humped cattle. Humped cattle can be distinguished in the archaeological record only by the shape of the skull or by the posterior thoracic vertebrae, which, in the zebu, have bifurcated spines.

Epstein divided the humped cattle of Africa into two kinds, cervico-thoracic-humped and thoracic-humped, or true zebu. He hypothesized that cattle with cervico-thoracic humps (humps on their necks) were first introduced by sea into the Horn of Africa. The cattle then spread west and, by interbreeding with the long-horned cattle of West Africa, developed into the Fulani breed. In eastern and southern Africa, humped cattle (at first neck-humped, but later replaced by thoracic-humped) were crossbred with the local humpless cattle to produce the mixed breeds called *Sanga,* which spread all around the Sahel and southward as far as the Cape.

With recent studies of the mitochondrial DNA of humped and unhumped cattle in West Africa, the story is beginning to look different. Molecular analyses have shown that three "indigenous" humped African breeds, the Butana, Kenana, and the White Fulani, are quite separate from the true zebus of recent Indian origin, and they are closer in their mitochondrial DNA to the unhumped European breeds. Two suggestions have been made for the origins of these West African breeds. The first is that these humped cattle may have originated from separate domestication of the truly indigenous wild cattle of North Africa—that is, from *Bos primigenius,* whose fossil remains have been found at archaeological sites along the Mediterranean. The second suggestion is that only zebu bulls were brought into Africa from Asia in early times, which would mean that their genetic lineage in modern cattle would be masked, as mtDNA is present only in the female line.

Despite the spread of the tsetse-fly belt across equatorial Africa, there is a great diversity of cattle breeds over the whole area, with a concentration of Sanga breeds in eastern Africa, which provides sound evidence for their long history of domestication on the continent. Further evidence for the presence of cattle in West Africa for a very long time and their continuity to the present day is provided by the small humpless N'Dama breed and the Borgou, which have evolved a natural immunity to trypanosomiasis, the disease carried by tsetse flies.

In South Africa, there is a different picture, and there are far fewer breeds, despite the general lack of tsetse flies. This may reflect, in part, the shorter history of cattle in the south, but it is also because many breeds have become extinct as a result of so-called European improvement. For nearly 2,000 years, the Bantu-speaking peoples of the east and south as well as the Khoikhoi depended on cattle for many facets of their economic well-being, including riding. The movement of cattle into South Africa began in the early Iron Age, during the 1st millennium A.D. Cattle spread south, together with sheep, and their remains are found at nearly all archaeological sites of this period. Sheep probably moved south along the west coast of southern Africa arriving in the western Cape around 2,000 years ago, while cattle were introduced along the east coast by Iron Age farmers who moved into the eastern Cape several hundred years later. The animal remains from Iron Age sites in southern Africa show that the meat obtained from livestock was combined with that from hunted animals. This is to be expected in an environment where long periods of drought may decimate herds of cattle that are also subject to lethal diseases, parasite infestations, and stock raiders.

Throughout Africa, cattle have played a crucial role in the social, economic, and religious lives of the Bantu-speaking peoples. Cattle have provided meat, hides, and manure and have been used for plowing, as draft oxen, and as a source of blood and milk, although the existence of lactose intolerance among some Bantu-speaking peoples argues against a widespread ancient tradition of milk drinking.

THE GOAT, *CAPRA HIRCUS.* Domestic goats are all descended from the scimitar-horned goat of western Asia, *Capra aegagrus.* This wild goat has never inhabited any part of Africa, so all domestic goats in Africa can be claimed with certainty to have been introduced from abroad. The only species of goat or sheep indigenous to Africa is the Walia ibex, *Capra ibex walie,* which today is an endangered species in the mountains of Ethiopia. The ibex has never been domesticated. Another more distantly related caprine is the wild Barbary sheep, or aoudad, *Ammotragus lervia,* which inhabits the mountains of North Africa.

Epstein divided the domestic goats of Africa into four broad categories, dwarf goats of the equatorial belt, savanna goats, Nubian goats, and Maltese goats of the Atlas countries. There is little or no evidence from the archaeological record for the early history of these animals. An age of about 6,500 years has been cited for goats from the Neolithic Capsian sites in eastern Algeria. The presence of dwarf goats has been recorded at the 2nd-millennium B.C. sites of Ntereso and Kintampo in Ghana.

South of the equator, it seems that goats were much less important livestock animals than sheep, and there are very few records of goat remains. There appear to be no depictions of goats in rock paintings.

Goat remains have been identified with those of sheep at the 4th-century A.D. Iron Age site of The Happy Rest in the former Transvaal province, while at the 8th-century site of Ndondondwane in KwaZulu-Natal, 47 elements were identified as goats and 459 as sheep.

SHEEP, *OVIS ARIES*. All domestic sheep of Africa are descended from introduced stock from Asia. Domestic sheep are descended from the Asiatic mouflon, *Ovis orientalis*.

The earliest evidence for domestic caprines (sheep and goats) in Africa comes from the 5th-millennium site of Haua Fteah north of Cyrenaica, Libya. It is evident that well-defined breeds of domestic sheep were common in ancient Egypt as long ago as 3000 B.C. During the Early Dynastic period (3100 to 2613 B.C.) screw-horned sheep with lop ears were developed, and fat-tailed sheep began to appear during the Middle Kingdom (1991 to 1633 B.C.).

Recently, large numbers of sheep remains, ranging from 2400 to 1500 B.C., have been excavated from the tombs at Kerma in northern Sudan. Analyses of the complete skeletons of 55 sheep and 62 separate bones have shown that they came from a long-legged, thin-tailed breed without the Roman nose of modern desert sheep. Many of the skeletons were mummified so that the skins were preserved. The sheep were hairy and most were single-colored black or white, but there were some black-and-white piebald sheep.

Caprine remains have not been separated into sheep and goats at many of the early archaeological sites in West and East Africa, but there is enough material for the claim that pottery and sheep were spreading down the western side of southern Africa from Angola to the Cape by about 200 B.C.

In East Africa, the presence of domestic caprines has been recorded at 3rd-millennium B.C. sites in the northeastern sector of the Lake Turkana Basin. From here, domestic caprines with cattle can be traced, from the archaeological record, moving slowly southward. In Kenya, their earliest record is from the 1st-millennium B.C. site of Prolonged Drift. Domestic caprines do not appear in the record again until the pre-10th centuries A.D. Caprine remains have been retrieved from a number of early Iron Age sites north and south of the Zambezi River. Sheep reached the eastern Cape together with cattle by the 4th century and are recorded at many Iron Age sites. There is well-documented evidence for the presence of sheep in the western and southern Cape 2,000 years ago. Goats are quite unknown from these early sites, and cattle occur with only very low frequency.

The best evidence for the kinds of livestock owned by pastoralists throughout Africa comes from the rock art, which is often extremely detailed although difficult to date. Both fat- and thin-tailed sheep are seen on rock paintings in Zimbabwe, while fat-tailed sheep are portrayed at 11 sites in the western Cape.

The fat tail of the sheep was an extremely valuable source of fat for pastoralists throughout the continent as it was to the early European immigrants. Early descriptions of the Cape sheep stated that the tail weighed from 13 to 26 kilograms. The fat was semi-fluid and was frequently used for oil and for butter.

———〰〰〰〰〰———

The diffusion of domestic animals throughout Africa took a long time, perhaps because it became essential to keep a store of livestock only when the Bantu-speaking people, who lived in settlements and had the use of iron, began to expand beyond the numbers that could be supplied with hunted meat.

The most important factor in the history of domestic animals in Africa, as everywhere else, was the combination of natural and artificial selection, which led to the evolution of distinctive breeds that were perfectly adapted to their environment but, at the same time, developed some unique characteristics, such as the vast horns of the ankole of East Africa.

With the abundance and diversity of wild animals to be exploited, it is no wonder that domestic animals have played a relatively small part in the ancient history of African peoples. If wild meat is always available, why keep domestic stock? The husbanding of livestock is very troublesome. The animals have to be protected from predators, which, again, are abundant in Africa, and they have to be provided with food and water, but above all they have to be owned. And the ownership of much property, whether it is goods and chattels or livestock, entails settlement and an entirely different social and economic basis to that of the nomadic hunter and gatherer of wild foods. There are many cultural, ritual, and social reasons why people keep large herds of domestic animals, but they become essential for food only when the human population expands beyond the numbers that can be fed from hunted meat, as must have happened at many Iron Age settlements throughout Africa. Even so, the resources supplied by livestock were always supplemented by hunted animals, and the association between pastoralists and their cattle is a very much more complicated matter than the mere provision of food.

BIBLIOGRAPHY

Clark, J. D. and S. A. Brandt, eds. 1984. *From hunter to farmers: The causes and consequences of food production.* Berkeley: University of California Press.

Clutton-Brock, J. 1987. *A natural history of domesticated animals.* Cambridge: Cambridge University Press.

———, ed. 1989. *The walking larder: Patterns of domestication, pastoralism, and predation.* London: Unwin Hyman.

Epstein, H. 1971. *The origin of domestic animals in Africa.* New York: Africana Publishing Company.

Hall, M., and A. B. Smith, eds. 1986. *Prehistoric pastoralism in southern Africa,* Goodwin Series no. 5. Vlaeberg: The South African Archaeological Society.

Shaw, T., P. Sinclair, B. Andah, and A. Okpoko, eds. 1993. *The archaeology of Africa: Food, metals and towns.* London: Routledge.

Smith, A. B. 1992. *Pastoralism in Africa.* London: G. Hurst and the University of Witwatersrand Press.

Voight, E. A., and I. Plug, eds. 1991. *Early Iron Age herders of the Limpopo Valley.* Pretoria: Transvaal Museum.

Wendorf, F., and R. Schild. 1980. *The prehistory of the eastern Sahara.* New York: Academic Press.

Juliet Clutton-Brock

Iron Age

~~~~~~~~~~~~~~~~~~~~~~~~~

WESTERN AFRICAN IRON AGE

This article examines the beginnings of iron use in West Africa in the middle of the 1st millennium B.C. and its subsequent adoption by small-scale societies in the 1st and early 2nd millennia A.D.

No comprehensive, up-to-date study of the West African Iron Age exists today, although there are valuable chapters in *African Civilizations,* by Graham Connah and *The Archaeology of Africa: Foods, Metals and Towns,* edited by Thurstan Shaw, Paul Sinclair, Bassey Andah, and Alex Okpoko. Many of the most important surveys of regional prehistory done during the 1980s and 1990s have been published in various journals by Susan and Roderick McIntosh. Some of these are listed in the bibliography. Most of the material available on this topic exists only in the form of journal articles.

As in other areas of Africa, archaeological investigations of iron-using peoples in West Africa involve questions of data availability and reliability, and the intensity of research has varied a great deal from country to country. The legacy of Eurocentric views of the "Dark Continent" persists, and the question of whether iron technologies were invented in sub-Saharan Africa or introduced from outside has dominated research to a greater extent than would be the case in other parts of the world. We know little about the mechanisms through which iron use spread among West African communities after it was introduced to the area. Archaeologists have more recently begun to examine questions that are probably of greater significance than technological origins: the degree of cultural continuity between Neolithic and Iron Age peoples, changes in the cultures of iron-using peoples over the last 2,000 years, and the ways in which use of iron technologies has affected West African societies and the natural environments that they exist in.

Knowledge of ironworking was probably first introduced into West Africa from the Mediterranean Coast, via Berber peoples of the central Sahara. Copper metallurgy in the Akjoujt region of Mauritania and around Agadez in Niger provides the only instance of extensive pre-Iron Age metalworking in sub-Saharan Africa, but this low-temperature technology was most likely not the basis of the higher-temperature iron-production processes. Sites in Niger (Do Dimi and the Agadez sites), Nigeria (Taruga and Ghwa Kiva) and Cameroon (Doulo) have yielded iron tools, slag, and the remains of smelting furnaces in contexts dating to the middle of the 1st millennium B.C., and today these are the earliest reasonably well attested occurrences of iron use in West Africa. The ranges of uncertainty inherent in radiocarbon dates from these different sites overlap, and we cannot assign preference to any one as the earliest on this part of the continent. The antiquity of some of these dates may derive from the use of old, dead wood as fuels. In this case, radiocarbon determinations would be dating the death of a tree perhaps some centuries earlier than its use by humans. This is potentially a serious problem, but the agreement in dates from sites in three countries indicates that real technological

425

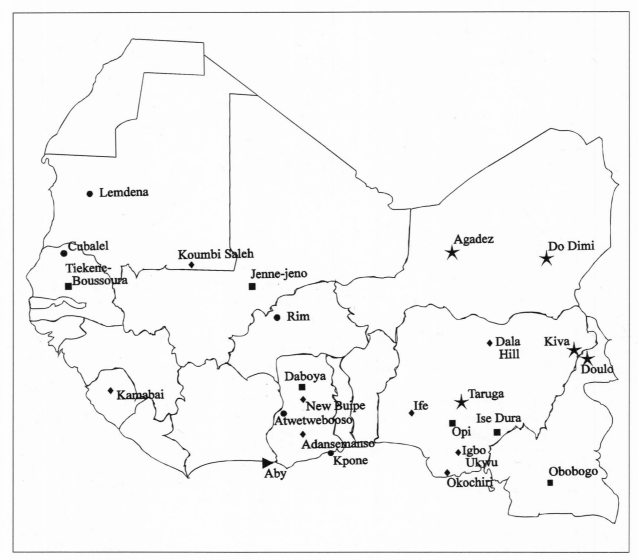

Fig. 60 *Some West African Iron Age sites*

Sites with first occupations:

★ *Before 500 B.C.*

■ *500 B.C. to A.D. 1*

● *A.D. 1 to 500*

◆ *500 to 1000*

▲ *After 1000*

change took place around the middle of the 1st millennium B.C.

Early Iron Age sites are found in quite different environments, from the Sahelian grasslands of Agadez and Do Dimi to the woodlands around Taruga. Climates during the Iron Age were probably similar to those of the present, although most areas would have had more trees than today. The appearance of iron in communities occupying such different environments may indicate that a

period of local adaptation of the technology had already occurred. There is some evidence for continuity between the material culture of earlier Neolithic peoples and these first Iron Age communities. Some stone tools and ceramics with Neolithic motifs continued to be used at the Niger sites and at Doulo. There is no evidence for drastic economic changes, and early Iron Age peoples were almost certainly engaged in the same exploitation of wild and domesticated plant and animal resources as were their Neolithic predecessors. However, iron tools probably made possible the increased use of heavy clay soils in areas like the Lake Chad Basin, they facilitated the water-control techniques used in various regions, and they probably made more feasible the mud construction that remains a feature of West African architecture today. Iron production also requires large amounts of charcoal from particular tree species. Over the last 2,500 years, this demand has probably contributed to environmental degradation and even deforestation in some regions, although this effect has been studied only for more recent periods.

The uneven distribution of archaeological survey and excavation in West Africa means that we do not know whether very early Iron Age sites in Nigeria, Niger, and Cameroon are part of a broader pattern of regional iron use or whether they were isolated occurrences within a Neolithic matrix. After initial development, the use of iron may have spread westward along the grassland and wooded-grassland belt that lies between the Sahara and the tropical forest to the south. Alternatively, a second trans-Saharan transmission of iron technology from Morocco to Senegambia or the Inland Niger Delta may have taken place, but to date no evidence exists for that. The first iron-using site in Mali, at Jenne-jeno, was occupied at the end of the 3rd century B.C., and at the same time, there is unambiguous evidence of iron use at Daboya in northern Ghana, already occupied by Neolithic Kintampo peoples for more than 1,000 years. The evidence for Iron Age occupation in Senegambia is more equivocal. The megalithic site of Tiékène Bassoura has yielded one date in the 2nd century B.C., but evidence from the Casamance and from the Middle Senegal Valley indicates occupation by iron-using peoples only by the first centuries A.D.

The 400- to 600-year delay between adoption of iron technologies in the east and the first use of these technologies farther to the west and southwest cannot be explained at this point. The inundation of parts of the Inland Niger Delta until late in the 1st millennium B.C. may have hampered the movement of people, material, and ideas along the east-west corridor of Sahelian and Sudanic grasslands, a movement that has been a

Table 24 *West African Iron Age sites*

Site	Earliest Radiocarbon Date (Uncalibrated)
Do Dimi	678 ±120 B.C.
Aselik (Agadez)	540 ± 90 B.C.
Doulo	550 ±60 B.C.
Shwa Kiva	680 ±160 B.C.
Taruga	591 ±104 B.C.

feature of West African history until modern times. This east-west corridor is matched by the north-south links that have often been vital for the movement of goods derived from different environmental zones—the coast, forest, grassland, and desert. The initial spread of iron technologies likely took place along preexisting regional trade routes and no doubt contributed to the further development of these routes, as iron ore was imported and finished tools exported around areas like the Inland Niger Delta and the firki (lacustrine clay soil) plains south of Lake Chad.

In Nigeria, Ise Dura and Opi, both in forest-mosaic environments, have yielded radiocarbon dates from the 4th century B.C. Both areas are relatively close to Taruga. Kpone-West, on the coastal savanna of southeast Ghana, is dated to the 2nd century A.D., contemporaneous with Atwetwebooso, at the edge of the present-day tropical forest zone in west-central Ghana. Penetration of iron technologies into the coastal forest of West Africa happened more slowly, with no reliable evidence for occupation before A.D. 500. This lack of early Iron Age forest sites is puzzling and contrasts strongly with data from forested regions of Gabon and the Congo Republic, where the earliest use of iron is dated to the 4th century B.C. It may be ascribed, in part, to the difficulties of doing archaeological survey work in these forested environments and to changes in settlement patterns.

The use of iron had important economic and cultural effects on West African societies, but we should not assume that societies were totally transformed. *Use of iron* may mean different things: the acquisition of rare iron objects as status symbols, the everyday use for tools and weapons, or the focusing of economic activity upon iron production for trade and export. In many cases, the initial adoption of iron may have had a smaller impact upon West African societies than did later events. Thus, in northern Nigeria and Cameroon, the early Iron Age occurrences at Ghwa Kiva and Doulo are literally overshadowed by the remains of cultural developments after A.D. 300, when more intensive occupation or changes in construction techniques led to the formation of more numerous and larger mound sites. There is also evidence for more intensive occupation of Jenne-jeno and the surrounding territory at A.D. 300, and this is close to the time of the increase in occupation intensity identified by Graham Connah in the Daima II stage at this site.

These increases in intensity of exploitation and ensuing social and political developments may be related to a climatic amelioration in West Africa starting at this time. These development were arguably as important as the adoption of iron some hundreds of years earlier. The plains west of Lake Chad, the Inland Niger Delta, and parts of Senegambia seem to have seen especially significant occupation through the middle of the 1st millennium A.D. An important factor in a number of these cases was probably location on or at the margins of floodplains, with floodwaters used through various forms of falling-water agriculture and, in some cases, irrigation. Savanna sites located outside of such favored regions were settled by people involved in dry-land cereal agriculture using sorghum and millet, probably at lower regional population densities. Intensity of occupation led to the development of more complex social and political systems over this time period, as manifested in the evidence for urbanization and site hierarchy around Jenne-jeno in the Inland Niger Delta and by the rich tumuli (mound graves)and megalithic constructions found in Senegal and Gambia from the 1st millennium A.D. onward.

Between 500 and 1000, iron-using communities occupied significant areas of the tropical forest. Some of the evidence for this is inferential. The intensity and complexity of settlement in regions like southern Nigeria—at the time of first European contact in the 15th century the most densely settled area of Africa—demand a significant period of prior development. The extraordinary burial and caches at Igbo Ukwu in southeastern Nigeria, with their magnificent bronze artifacts, most likely date to the 9th century and demonstrate the existence of complex ritual or political institutions, technological specialization, and intercontinental trade. In southwestern Nigeria, the roots of settlement at Ife and the beginning of construction of the Benin earthworks probably date to about the same period. Investigation of these large, spectacular (and difficult) sites has come at the expense of their more modest predecessors. We now know something about cultural florescence in southern Nigeria but virtually nothing about its roots earlier in the 1st millennium.

In Ghana, the savanna sites of Daboya and New Buipe, along with the forest-edge sites of Begho, Abam, and Bonoso, testify to late 1st-millennium and early 2nd-millennium occupation of Iron Age sites, which would eventually dominate the trade routes from the gold fields of the forest to the trading entrepots of the Middle Niger Delta. Within the forest, excavations at Adansemanso, Asantemanso, and related sites demonstrate the local antecedents of the Asante state in Iron Age occupations of the 10th century—and disprove assertions that the forest was unoccupied before the 2nd millennium. If southern Nigerian archaeology has been overly focused upon states and state artwork, Iron Age archaeology in Ghana has often concentrated upon trade, to the north with Muslim states and later to the south with Europeans on the Atlantic Coast. This has, in some cases, obscured the local origins of cultural innovations.

Data on the forest zone west of Ghana are extremely limited. The shell middens of Aby Lagoon in Ivory Coast yielded only unreliable dates between 600 B.C. and A.D. 1825, while deposits at the Kamabai site in Sierra Leone, with 7th- and 8th-century dates on iron fragments, may be mixed. Excavations at these two sites were not particularly informative about cultural affiliations, economies, or regional interactions. They are supplemented only by small-scale excavations of Iron Age sites in areas west of Ghana.

There is often a change in the focus of investigations of archaeological sites toward the end of the 1st millennium. Researchers studying earlier periods have conceptualized their work as the study of small agricultural communities, but much of the research in West Africa over the last 1,500 years has focused upon the processes of urbanization, the development of political complexity, and the intensification and elaboration of trade systems. In West Africa, these questions have been closely related historically, since it has been assumed that state development and urbanization were responses to contact with the Islamic states of North Africa after the beginning of widespread trans-Saharan trade in the late 1st millennium. This assumption has been turned on its head over the last 20 years with the recognition that urbanization and complex societies were developing in West Africa some centuries before that time.

This concentration upon urban centers and trade ignores the fact that, until the colonial period, a great number of West Africans were living in small, noncentralized societies, while even within states only a minority of the population lived in the capitals and urban centers that were the main objects of archaeological research until the 1980s. This fascination has resulted in a lack of regional archaeological studies, especially in the tropical forest zone, and a view of population centers as decontextualized urban agglomerations, existing through trade with North Africa and Europe. Capitals are not states, nor are they societies. Archaeologists must seek to establish the degree of cultural continuity between Iron Age populations of the 1st millennium and historically known peoples, whether within or external to states, and they must also seek to recognize the ways in which societies have changed over the same time period. This work is only beginning in West Africa.

BIBLIOGRAPHY

Connah, G. 1981. *Three thousand years in Africa: Man and his environment in the Lake Chad region of Nigeria.* Cambridge: Cambridge University Press.

Holl, A. 1993. Transition from Late Stone Age to Iron Age in the Sudano-Sahelian zone: A case study from the Perichadian plain. In *The archaeology of Africa: Foods, metals and towns,* eds. T. Shaw, P. Sinclair, B. Andah, and A. Okpoko, 330–343. London: Routledge.

McIntosh, S. K., and McIntosh, R. J. 1980. *Prehistoric investigations in the region of Jenne, Mali.* Cambridge Monographs in African Archaeology 2. Oxford: British Archaeological Reports.

———. 1982. The early city in West Africa: Toward an understanding. *The African Archaeological Review* 2: 73–98.

———. 1988. From stone to metal: New perspectives on the later prehistory of West Africa. *Journal of World Prehistory* 2: 89–133.

Shaw, T. 1977. *Unearthing Igbo-Ukwu.* Ibadan: Oxford University Press.

Stahl, A. B. 1994. Innovation, diffusion and culture contact: The Holocene archaeology of Ghana. *Journal of World Prehistory* 8: 51–112.

Scott MacEachern

EQUATORIAL AFRICAN IRON AGE

In the well-known compilation *Atlas of African Prehistory,* J. Desmond Clark's "Sketch map to show intensity of prehistoric research in Africa" effectively portrays the dismal state of equatorial rain-forest archaeology as it prevailed until well into the 1970s. On this map, the inner Zaire Basin—that is, the middle region of the central African rain forest—appeared as one of the few blank areas and by far the largest one at that. Within a decade, a research program that came to be named the River Reconnaissance Project drastically changed this extremely unfavorable situation. Implemented between 1977 and 1987, this waterborne project led to an archaeological exploration of major rivers within the so-called *Cuvette centrale.* It resulted in a large body of ceramic evidence, which was then used by M. Eggert and H.-P. Wotzka to construct an age-area scheme comprising the first cultural sequences of the equatorial forest.

Thus, systematic archaeological research in the rain forest is a very recent phenomenon. It would be interesting to find out why this part of

Africa has been neglected by archaeologists for so long. Its neglect is all the more surprising since its importance for the linguistic and cultural history of the southern half of the continent has long been recognized. The much-discussed and still quite controversial "problem of the Bantu expansion," to employ the title of a well-known 1966 paper by Roland Oliver, will certainly not be solved without clarifying the role of the equatorial rain forest in early Bantu history. One major reason for the remarkable reserve of archaeologists in this respect might be that because of the forest's reputed hostility to human penetration and settlement, nobody put much faith in its archaeological potential. Rather, archaeologists, anthropologists, and historians of Africa accepted the belief of contemporary forest farmers that Pygmies were the original inhabitants of the forest. This view has only recently been challenged on the basis of the substantial eco-anthropological studies in the Ituri Forest of eastern Zaire by J. A. and T. B. Hart, R. C. Bailey, N. R. Peacock, P. K. Townsend, T. N. Headland, P. A. Colinvaux, and M. B. Bush. The evidence, however, appears to be inconclusive to some anthropologists and archaeologists, such as S. Bahuchet, D. McKey, I. de Garine, and M. Eggert, who think that the empirical basis of the Ituri case is by far too weak to support the wide-reaching conclusion that Pygmies or, for that matter, pygmoids could not survive in the forest independently of farmers. As the remains of Pygmy culture are not easily detected archaeologically and the settlement of the forest by farming populations was considered a very recent phenomenon (assigned by Oliver, for example, to the present millennium), one might conclude that archaeological research in the forest did not appear a very promising endeavor.

The very successful campaigns of the River Reconnaissance Project proved all skeptics wrong. With regard to the role of the equatorial rain forest in the peopling of southern Africa, it is to be lamented that, for political and economic reasons within central Africa and beyond, we have been unable to continue and extend our research program in the inner Zaire Basin. So far, fieldwork has concentrated on the following rivers and river systems: Ruki-Tshuapa-Momboyo, Ikelemba, Lulonga-Lopori-Maringa, Zaire,

Ubangi, Sangha-Ngoko, and Likwala-aux-Herbes. Although necessarily river-centered with only some few explorations of the hinterland, the strategy of waterborne-reconnaissance proved a very effective means of archaeologically exploring large portions of unknown rain-forest territory within a remarkably short time. While interpretation of the data relating to the settlement process in the forest has to take the river-related-strategy bias into account, there are some rather striking implications of the ubiquity of waterways in the forest. For people entering this biotope (a region uniform in its environmental conditions and in its populations of animals and plants), the innumerable rivers and minor watercourses offer a natural network of communication routes, a network that could hardly be more elaborate. As soon as these people disposed of dugouts or rafts, they were able to venture deep into the reputedly impenetrable forest in a very short time. Up to the present day, the river systems of the rain forest constitute a major factor in the regional and interregional traffic network. It is hard to imagine that the early settlers of the central African forest did not take advantage of the important possibilities this biotope offered. Therefore, it seems highly probable that the forest was settled by waterborne settlers who first established settlement nuclei on the riverbanks. Only then was the hinterland successively drawn into the orbit of these river-based food- and pottery-producing populations. There is every reason, then, to suppose that the archaeology of riverbanks is ideally suited as a means of exploring the rain forest on both technical as well as historical grounds.

Settlement and Ceramics: The Current State of Rain-Forest Archaeology

The large body of ceramics brought together by means of systematic excavation, surface-collecting, and ethnoarchaeological studies of contemporary potters' villages encompasses the whole range of rain-forest pottery from the very beginning up to the present. From the start of systematic archaeological fieldwork in the forest, this evidence was integrated by applying a somewhat modified version of the concept of

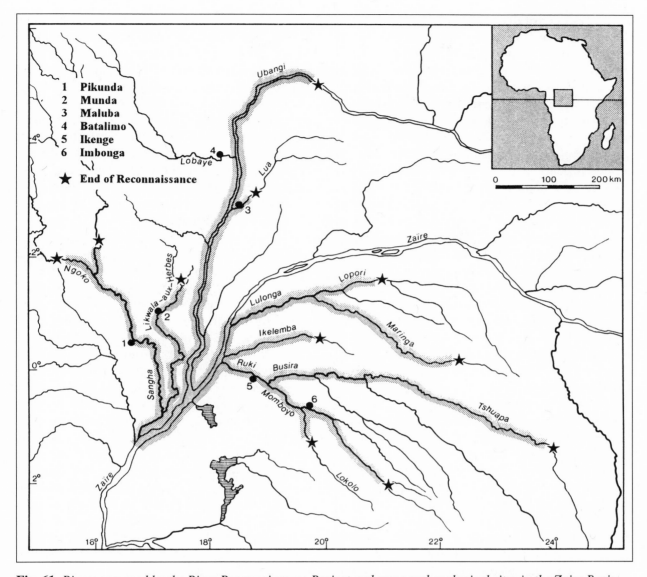

Fig. 61 *Rivers surveyed by the River Reconnaissance Project and some archaeological sites in the Zaire Basin*

horizon style formulated by G. R. Willey in 1945 in the context of Peruvian archaeology. In our context, *horizon* means a specific ceramic group characterized by a particular style and distributed across a particular area. In H.-P. Wotzka's seminal 1995 synthesis of all the ceramic evidence obtained to the south of the Zaire River, this concept of *horizon* or, in his terminology, *style group* (or, for short, *style*) was supplemented by what W. C. Bennett and I. Rouse had earlier, in an American context, called a *co-tradition* and *area co-tradition,* respectively. While a horizon or style group is mainly a phenomenon limited to a specific time and place, a ceramic tradition can be conceptualized as a chain of modifications of a specific horizon or style group through time. The concept of *ceramic co-traditions,* then, denotes at least two ceramic traditions that developed out of either a common stylistic basis, an *ancestor style,* or a number of more-or-less contemporaneous, genealogically related styles. Therefore, a system of ceramic co-traditions consists of several regional sequences of ceramic styles. These coexisting sequences may follow a general pattern of divergence or convergence. In the latter case, different traditions may even merge to form a single new tradition.

Building on this conceptual basis, Wotzka differentiated 34 ceramic style groups and six co-traditions. His West tradition, which integrates the majority of the ceramic evidence at his disposal, is by far the most complex. Beginning with the Imbonga horizon in the last half of the 1st millennium B.C. and ending with the Ikenge horizon represented by pots made in A.D. 1977 and 1982, the West tradition encompasses 21 ceramic style groups. The empirical basis for these groups is not uniform, but rather of uneven quality. While most of the groups are quite firmly established, some need reconsideration at a more advanced level of research. In the same vein, some are radiocarbon-dated while others lack a fixed position on the absolute time scale. The important point, however, is that Wotzka positioned his horizons or stylistic groups in a continuing sequence. He established this sequence or relative chronology by systematically evaluating the variation of form and decoration of the ceramic evidence at his disposal. Wotzka employed a sorting principle that assumed styles that appeared most similar were probably somehow closely related in space or time, while those with little or no similarity were less likely to be contemporaneous. The assumption is that certain styles are fashionable within a given time and space and are shared within a common cultural sphere. Wherever possible, he checked his analyses by observing whether similar styles were found clustered in specific provenances and whether dissimilar ones were separated within stratified deposits.

Wotzka's area of research concerned the territory to the south of the Zaire River. He did not analyze the ceramic material from the River Reconnaissance Project's survey of the Ubangi, the Sangha-Ngoko, and the Likwala-aux-Herbes Rivers, the analysis of which is almost completed now. Thus, his six co-traditions will have to be supplemented in due time by a North (Ubangi) and Northeast tradition (Sangha-Ngoko and Likwala-aux-Herbes). The important point here is that the earliest pottery of both the Northeast tradition (designated as the *Pikunda-Munda ho-rizon* after two type sites on the Sangha and Likwala-aux-Herbes rivers respectively) and the North tradition (designated as the *Batalimo-Maluba horizon* after Batalimo on the Lobaye and Maluba on the Lua) differs from that of the southern regions. According to the radiocarbon dates currently available, Pikunda-Munda pottery dates to around the birth of Christ while Batalimo-Maluba ware seems to be somewhat younger, belonging mainly to the first three centuries of the 1st millennium A.D.

One of the most important results of the River Reconnaissance Project concerns the first occurrence of pottery-producing populations in the central part of the equatorial rain forest. Contrary to what counted as a sort of evident truth until well into the 1970s, it has now been firmly established that the settlement of the inner Zaire Basin by people possessing the knowledge of pottery and, by implication, of food production is much older than the present millennium. At this stage of research, the oldest pottery belongs to the Imbonga horizon, which is radiocarbon-dated to between about 400 and 100 B.C. Thus, the earliest ceramic groups of the north and northeast are definitely younger than the Imbonga horizon of the south.

Even a cursory study of the early ceramics of the central part of the equatorial forest will immediately reveal that it is both highly complex and very elaborate with regard to shape and decoration. Considering its conspicuous degree of differentiation, it is all the more surprising that each of the three earliest ceramic styles seem to have appeared out of nowhere. Despite constant and prolonged efforts, the River Reconnaissance Project has not been successful in linking them with ceramic groups outside their own area. In fact, the planning of the different campaigns of the project was, to a considerable extent, conditioned by the desire to solve the enigma of the origin of the earliest ceramics. As yet this question is still open, although there are at least some vague indications that point toward pottery recently excavated in the western part of central Africa—in southern Cameroon and Gabon. It has to be stressed, however, that the similarities in question are of a very general nature and do not provide a strong case for establishing a straight "genetic" relationship between any of the early ceramic groups and those from outside equatorial Africa.

Subsisting in the Forest: Early Settlers and the Question of Food Plants

During limited excavations, the River Reconnaissance Project obtained evidence for the association of early ceramics with the oil palm (*Elaeis guineensis*) and the fruits of the wild tree *Canarium schweinfurthii*. This association has also been documented elsewhere in central Africa by M. Eggert and P. de Maret. Contrary to some archaeologists who interpret the occurrence of palm nuts in early ceramic contexts as indicating "some sort of sedentary food producers," it has to be emphasized that because of the morphology and physiology of the oil palm, the occurrence can not be taken as a direct indicator of a farming complex. Nevertheless, there is little doubt that the oil palm was of considerable importance for the early forest settlers, who ate it either raw, boiled, or roasted and used its oil. It may have served as the main source of dietary fat.

We still know little about how the early settlers managed to take care of their carbohydrate requirements. Cassava (*Manihot utilissima*), which nowadays serves as the principal staple, was brought from South America to the Atlantic Coast of central Africa only in the 17th century. A possible candidate as main source for carbohydrates is the plantain (*Musa* spp.), which in some areas of the forest continued as the main staple at the time of European colonization. The traditional view that the presence of this plant on the African continent is not as old as the earliest pottery in the rain forest has to be reconsidered in the light of arguments presented by botanists E. de Langhe and his colleagues and G. Rossel in 1996. However, due to the perishable nature of all of its parts, the presence of plantain in archaeological contexts is extremely difficult to establish. This applies as well to wild yams (*Dioscorea* spp.), another very likely candidate for the supply of carbohydrates. Certain species of *Dioscorea* are native to western and central Africa, and their potential importance in this respect (as that of other wild plants of forest set-

tings) has recently been emphasized by S. Bahuchet, D. McKey, and I. de Garine.

As regards hard evidence for early staples, there is much hope put nowadays in the systematic study of phytoliths (stony structures formed by plant activity) of edible plants that otherwise do not leave any traces. In this respect, three instances of phytoliths of *Musaceae* on very early ceramics from the site of Nkang in Cameroon, which has just been studied exhaustively by C. Mbida, are of extreme importance. It is to be hoped that this will be confirmed by further studies and that in general the advancement and application of the technique of phytolith analysis will enjoy all the support it so badly needs. It seems quite obvious that this particular technique offers an avenue of botanical research, the potential of which could hardly be overestimated.

Early Pottery-Producing Settlers in the Forest: The Question of Ironworking

In recent years, considerable effort has been directed at the archaeology of early African iron production. This has led to a very marked progress, especially in the forests and forest edges of Gabon and Cameroon as well as in the savannas of the southeastern part of the Congo Republic. From Gabon alone, about ten sites with pre-Christian ironworking are now known. Seven of the samples dated were obtained from furnaces for which, unfortunately, no details were presented. The other samples were found associated with iron slag. Most of these dates fall between the 10th century B.C. and the 1st century A.D. Thus, it is now quite firmly established that the process of converting iron ore into bloom iron was already known around the middle of the 1st millennium B.C. in west-central Africa.

It is interesting to note that the earliest dates for ironworking in the savannas of the traditional Téké country in the Congo Republic are not as early as those from the forest. The Téké series begins in the 1st century and ends in this century. In this context, mention must be made of a bowl-like, slag-containing feature partly excavated at Munda on the Likwala-aux-Herbes River. This site lies in the immense swamp area of the Sangha River to the northeast of the Téké region.

The bowl feature was partly lined with clay and showed unmistakable signs of intense burning. It contained elements of classical Pikunda-Munda pottery and was superimposed on a shaft containing the same pottery. For these two features, we have four radiocarbon dates, three of which fall within the time bracket of 106 B.C. to A.D. 420.

We do not hesitate to interpret the bowl feature of Munda as a bloomery furnace. Its dating fits well with the earliest dates from the Téké region. At any rate, it is as yet the oldest iron-producing installation from the inner Zaire Basin. In contrast, we do not dispose of any direct or indirect evidence concerning the use of stone or iron for the populations belonging to the Imbonga horizon south of the Zaire River.

Equatorial Rain Forest Archaeology: The Future of the Past

This article has dealt with selected aspects of the archaeology of the equatorial rain forest. Most of what has been reported here was accomplished during a decade of archaeological fieldwork split into five seasons of about six months each. The River Reconnaissance Project has not undertaken a field trip since 1987. The 1990s have brought no progress whatsoever in terms of new or additional fieldwork in the inner Zaire Basin. This is a very sad note on which to conclude a paper on the history of a biotope whose potential has been underestimated and neglected for so long. And it is by no means the potential of the forest for the forest's sake alone that is at stake here. Rather, as has been emphasized above, a profound understanding of the history of rain-forest settlement is an essential precondition for adequately evaluating this biotope's role in the dispersal of speakers of Bantu languages over most of the southern half of Africa.

It is obvious, then, that archaeological research in the central African rain forest must continue under all circumstances. The further exploration of man's history in the forest, which constitutes one of the least-known parts of all of Africa, is a most pressing concern for archaeologists, historians, and historical linguists of Africa. The current tide of anthropological research in its broadest sense is at about its lowest level,

not only in central Africa but also well beyond. Still, we are called up to use every possible means to promote our understanding of what once symbolized the ingrained age-old European anxiety toward the forest. In this sense, we might well conclude this article by proclaiming that the future of "The Heart of Darkness" is its past.

BIBLIOGRAPHY

Bahuchet, S. 1988. Food supply uncertainty among the Aka Pygmies (Lobaye, Central African Republic). In *Coping with uncertainty in food supply,* eds, I. de Garine and G. A. Harrison, 118–149. Oxford: Clarendon Press.

Bahuchet, S., D. McKey, and I. de Garine. 1991. Wild yams revisited: Is independence from agriculture possible for rain forest hunter-gatherers? *Human Ecology* 19: 213–243.

Bailey, R. C. 1990. Exciting opportunities in tropical rain forests: A reply to Townsend. *American Anthropologist* 92: 747–748.

Bailey, R. C., and T. N. Headland. 1991. The tropical rain forest: Is it a productive environment for human foragers? *Human Ecology* 19: 261–285.

Bailey, R. C., and N. R. Peacock. 1988. Efe Pygmies of northeast Zaire: Subsistence strategies in the Ituri Forest. In *Coping with uncertainty in food supply,* eds, I. de Garine and G. A. Harrison, 88–117. Oxford: Clarendon Press.

Bailey, R. C., G. Head, M. Jenike, B. Owen, R. Rechtman, and E. Zechenter. 1989. Hunting and gathering in tropical rain forests: Is it possible? *American Anthropologist* 91: 59–82.

Clist, B. 1989. Archaeology in Gabon (1886–1988). *African Archaeological Review* 7: 59–95.

Colinvaux, P. A., and M. B. Bush. 1991. The rain-forest ecosystem as a resource for hunting and gathering. *American Anthropologist* 93: 153–160.

de Langhe, E., R. Swennen, and D. VuylsTéké. 1996. Plantain in the early Bantu world. *Azania* 29/30: 147–160.

de Maret, P. 1982. New survey of archaeological research and dates for west-central Africa and north-central Africa. *Journal of African History* 23: 1–15.

———. 1986. The Ngovo group: An industry with polished stone tools and pottery in Lower Zaire. *African Archaeological Review* 4: 103–133.

———. 1992. Sédentarisation, agriculture et métallurgie du Sud-Cameroun: Synthèse des recherches depuis (1978). In *L'archéologie au Cameroun: Actes du premier colloque international de Yaoundé (6–9 janvier 1986),* ed. J.-M. Essomba, 247–260. Paris: Editions Karthala.

Eggert, M. K. H. 1983. Remarks on exploring archaeologically unknown rain forest territory: The case of central Africa. *Beitraege zur Allgemeinen und Vergleichenden Archaeologie* 5: 283–322.

———. 1984. Imbonga und Lingonda: Zur frühesten Besiedlung des zentralafrikanischen Regenwaldes. *Beitaege zur Allgemeinen und Vergleichenden Archaeologie* 6: 247–288.

———. 1992. The central African rain forest: Historical speculation and archaeological facts. *World Archaeology* 24: 1–24.

———. 1993. Central Africa and the archaeology of the equatorial rain forest: Reflections on some major topics. In *The archaeology of Africa: Food, metals and towns,* eds. T. Shaw, P. Sinclair, B. Andah, and A. Okpoko, 289–329. London: Routledge.

———. 1996. Pots, farming and analogy: Early ceramics in the equatorial rainforest. *Azania* 29/30: 332–338.

Essomba, J.-M. 1989. Dix ans de recherches archéologiques au Cameroun méridional (1979–1989). *NSI* 6: 33–57.

———. 1992. *Civilisation du fer et sociètiés en Afrique centrale: Le cas du Cameroun méridional (Histoire ancienne et archéologie).* Paris: Editions l'Harmattan.

Hart, T. B., and J. A. Hart. 1986. The ecological basis of hunter-gatherer subsistence in African rain forests: The Mbuti of Eastern Zaire. *Human Ecology* 14: 29–55.

Headland, T. N., and R. C. Bailey. 1991. Introduction: Have hunter-gatherers ever lived in tropical rain forest independently of agriculture? *Human Ecology* 19: 115–122.

Oslisly, R. 1993. *Préhistoire de la moyenne vallée de l'Ogooué (Gabon),* 2 vols. Travaux et Documents Microédités 96. Paris: Editions de l'ORSTOM.

Oslisly, R., and B. Peyrot. 1992. L'arrivée des premiers métallurgistes sur l'Ogooué, Gabon. *African Archaeological Review* 10: 129–138.

Townsend, P. K. 1990. On the possibility/impossibility of tropical forest hunting and gathering. *American Anthropologist* 92: 745–747.

Wotzka, H.-P. 1995. *Studien zur archaeologie des zentralafrikanischen regenwaldes: Die keramik des inneren Zaire-Beckens und ihre Stellung im kontext der Bantu-expansion.* Africa Praehistorica. Köln: Heinrich-Barth Institut.

Manfred K. H. Eggert

BANTU EXPANSION

Throughout most of central, eastern, and southern Africa, people speak some form of Bantu, a closely related family of languages associated, for the most part, with agricultural populations, who first appeared in the southern subcontinent early in the 1st millennium A.D. This family of languages may be further divided into a western group found generally in forested central Africa and regions to the southwest and an eastern one found on the savannas of the east and southeast. Though dialects and vocabulary vary from place to place, many words and grammars are comparable over a wide area. These many similarities suggest that the Bantu speakers are a fairly recent dispersal and that their languages have not had sufficient time to differentiate. As a result, investigators have attempted to trace the roots of this Bantu family of languages in an effort to clarify not only the geographical origins of the people who speak them and when they originated but how they came to be so widely spoken.

This effort has concentrated, for the most part, on the study of the languages themselves and the identification of associated material culture, two of the more durable and useful remnants of the past available to archaeology. In particular, investigators have stressed finding a solution to the question of why the Bantu family of languages came to be so widely distributed from their "homeland" in western Africa. T. N. Huffman has suggested that researchers have created three hypotheses explaining the present distribution of the Bantu-languages:

1. Bantu-speaking foragers were already in the subcontinent since the Late Stone Age.
2. The earliest Bantu were root-crop agriculturists who were situated in the tropical forests of West Africa and who only later acquired cereals, metals, and cattle from sources in eastern Africa.
3. Bantu speakers migrated around the forests into eastern and southern Africa as metal-using mixed-farmers.

It would appear that the spread of the Bantu speakers occurred as groups of farmers spread into empty areas, or ones heretofore the domain of foragers, and created new settlements supported by slash-and-burn cultivation. Joseph O. Vogel has used the earliest settlement of southwestern Zambia to demonstrate the movement of early swidden-based cultivators from one suitable micro-environment to another similar one in the near vicinity, settling each for a while and exhausting its latent productivity before moving on. Only later was the full potential of a region settled more-or-less permanently. A fairly rapid geographical progress could thereby be made without the need to suggest large-scale population movements or "overpopulation" beyond the exhaustion of local carrying capacity. The sequence of early "pioneer" settlements may be tracked by reference to their distinct kinds of pottery and study of the sequence of changes within their distinct decorative styles.

Huffman also demonstrated that it is reasonable to use pottery styles as a means of identifying "ethnic" groups. He has noted that ceramics in southern Africa are both stylistically variable and widespread but are not part of any "cult" or special institution other than "ethnic" groups identifiable by language. Since pottery does not appear to have ever been involved, to any great extent, in exchanges outside the local community, it remains a useful means of identifying localized "ethnic" entities, while providing a marker for retracing the movements of its makers.

The earliest presence of pottery makers, presumed ancestral to later Bantu-speaking populations, occurred in western Africa sometime in the 3rd millennium B.C. By the 7th century A.D., related people had spread throughout subequatorial Africa. Since these later occurrences coincide with an introduction of agricultural economies, new forms of society and metallurgy, and domesticated plants and animals previously unknown, even in wild form, in the subcontinent, it is safe to conjecture that this constellation of traits was brought into the region by people who had not previously lived there. Since these early settlements are all found in regions now populated by Bantu speakers, it is also reasonable to believe that the arrivals of agricultural societies and Bantu speakers are synonymous. It is best to suppose that these early farmers were drawn toward the south by the prospect of suitable tillage.

Though the intermediate stages are still only dimly perceived, it would appear that a case, drawn chiefly from linguistic studies, can be made for placing a "core" area somewhere in the Cross River Valley of present-day Cameroon. This is near the northern limit of spoken Bantu and a region with the most dissimilar modern Bantu languages. Since our reconstruction of the earliest Bantu vocabularies suggests that they already had words related to pottery manufacture and the cultivation of root crops in fields, it is posited that the first outward dispersal of Bantu speakers occurred shortly after the practices of pottery manufacture and farming had taken root in the purported "core" area sometime during the 3rd millennium B.C., but before metallurgy and stock keeping were practiced.

On the basis of this linguistic evidence, J. Vansina has suggested three main phases of Bantu dispersal. In the beginning, Bantu speakers moved eastward out of this "core" area toward the Great Lakes of East Africa, while a second movement headed toward the lower Ogooué River. Succeeding phases saw the differentiation and spread of the western and eastern groups of Bantu languages. A western Bantu "core" area may be ascribed to the northern Congo Republic, while eastern Bantu took shape in the rain forests somewhere east of the Ubangi-Zaire confluence. Vansina suggested further that these "core" areas originated, not in a single stream of Bantu immigrants, but in a succession of waves, southward, advancing through river valleys and along the sea coasts.

There were no words for *metals* or *smelting* in any of the reconstructed protoforms of Bantu, and the first signs of metallurgy appear in the Great Lakes region around 800 B.C. This probably postdates the expansion of the earliest Bantu speakers into the east and west core areas. The Bantu in the east were apparently already familiar with pottery, cereal agriculture, and even small stock. They seem to have acquired the practices of herding cattle and smelting metals somewhere in East Africa, which already had a population of Cushitic-speaking pastoralists with cultural roots in the Nile Valley.

The western Bantu, moving through forested zones unsuited to cereals and domestic stock, other than goats, created a different set of vocabularies stressing root crops, oil palms, and fishing, the mainstays of their economies.

As farmers searching for adequate tillage or pasturage, the Bantu speakers spread to places suitable to their specific agricultural activities. In the west, root cultivation and palm oil were significant, while in the east, emphasis was placed on cereals and herd management. In any event, the Kei River, in South Africa, the southern limit for summer rainfall capable of supporting cereal cultivation, is also the southern limit of the Bantu expansion. Otherwise, with little competition from any preexisting populations, there were relatively few constraints upon the spread of the earliest Bantu-speaking farmers.

The Western Stream

Considerably less evidence exists for the western Bantu migration stream than for the eastern one. Sites, dating to the late 1st millennium B.C., along the Atlantic Coast of Gabon still contain stone implements, as well as stone hoes or axes, and ceramics. The two localities of the Tchissanga site, dating respectively to the 6th and 4th centuries B.C., offer the earliest signs for pottery making anywhere along the Atlantic Coast. The 4th-century B.C. site (Tchissanga East) even has evidence of metallurgy in the form of iron fragments, though it is unclear whether it was manufactured locally. A nearby location, Madingo-Kayes, dating to the 2nd century A.D., has both iron artifacts and iron slag, a waste product of the smelting process and a strong suggestion of local iron production.

The ceramics at Madingo-Kayes are said to resemble those found at Early Iron Age sites in Botswana and South Africa. This has led James K. Denbow to suggest the Congo Republic region as a reasonable epitome of early western Bantu culture north of the Cunene-Okavango in Angola. This western stream did not restrict its movement south solely to the coast though, as it moved inland to follow river courses toward the Okavango Delta region of Botswana.

Divuyu, in northern Botswana, dating to between A.D. 550 and 730, is the earliest example of a full-fledged agricultural settlement in the southwest. Its ceramics resemble those of the Congo

Republic sites, as do barbed and tanged arrowheads, which are found in both places. In common with other sites found to the northwest of the Okavango Delta, Divuyu's material culture bears a strong resemblance to that at other western stream sites in Angola and northwestern Zambia.

Sites to the south and east of the Okavango Delta, on the other hand, contain artifacts more representative of the eastern stream, particularly those of the Gokomere tradition found throughout Zimbabwe, southwest Zambia. and the northern part of the former Transvaal province. It is in the Okavango Delta, however, that we have evidence for the convergence of the two main streams of Bantu settlement, as well as their meeting representatives of preexisting pastoralist-forager peoples.

The Eastern Stream

In contrast to our sketchy knowledge of the western stream, the movements of the eastern Bantu group have been extensively researched. The earliest definitive eastern Bantu complex is characterized by the occurrence of Urewe pottery, named for a type site in the Lake Victoria region. The makers of this pottery seem to have first settled this region around 2,500 years ago. Apparently, they were already ironworkers, since evidence of this practice has been found in Rwanda and eastern Zaire. At the same time, analyses of pollen deposited in the sediments of Lake Victoria indicate a substantial reduction of the forest cover. This, along with the pottery, used to store and process cereals, suggests that they were already accomplished slash-and-burn cultivators—an advantage in marginal savanna soils.

By the 2nd century A.D., Bantu settlements, associated with the Kwale-style of pottery design, were located in the coastal regions of southeastern Kenya and northwestern Tanzania. It may be assumed that this branch continued down the coast toward Mozambique and KwaZulu-Natal. By the 4th century, other eastern Bantu farmers extended their range southward beyond the southernmost of the Great Lakes, where they soon colonized Malawi, eastern Zambia, and Zimbabwe and crossed the Zambezi River around the 4th century. Soon thereafter, they moved across the Limpopo River to populate open country in the former Transvaal province and regions farther south. At the same time, early Bantu communities formed in the Kafue and Zambezi Valleys. In the interior of south-central Africa, the Victoria Falls region had a flourishing agricultural community by the 6th century, though sandhills south of the Sioma Falls in the Upper Zambezi Valley were certainly being farmed a century or so earlier.

D. W. Phillipson divides this eastern stream further into eastern and western facies. The eastern one follows the course set out here. The origins of his western one are still poorly understood but would appear to be a result of a commingling of traits originating in the "main streams" of the eastern and western migrations. Given the situation noted in the Okavango Delta, the time span encompassed, and distances covered by Bantu-speaking people, it makes sense to imagine that here and there in the interior we should find styles neither purely of one tradition nor the other but the result of a commingling of neighboring styles, as marriages or other social interactions brought pottery makers taught in "foreign" areas into one group or another.

Huffman divides the eastern stream into three facies: an eastern one appearing about 200 A.D., a central one dating to around 250, and a western one dating to between 360 and 590. His divisions, like those of Phillipson, are based on perceived differences in ceramic typology and associations of shared traits. These are minimal academic differences of opinion between two of the leading students of the Bantu expansion. There is more general agreement that the tracing of the movements of these early farming populations from generation to generation and from place to place is often difficult to discern from the data now available.

Though there may be an ongoing debate over specific routes or individual cultural components, there is, as we have seen, some basic agreement regarding the direction and time period encompassed by the flow of the eastern stream of Bantu speakers into southern Africa. These movements began in western Africa during the latter centuries B.C. and culminated during the first four centuries of the present era, when Bantu farmers reached southern Africa and the limits of summer rainfall capable of supporting cereal cultivation.

As Vansina has suggested, the earliest Bantu speakers originated in areas north of the rain forests. The subsequent progress of "pioneer" swidden farmers underwrote the creation of extended, segmentary societies supporting the movement of households into new settlement areas, forming new districts, which became "jumping-off" points for further territorial extension. This is the pattern of early settlement we described in the Victoria Falls region. There is no reason to suppose that the expansion of the Bantu speakers required a more complex cause, or that there was a migration with a definite purpose and destination. When one area was exhausted beyond some level of carrying capacity, the group segmented to colonize new locations. As they moved to new areas, they sought out the closest vacant places suitable to their methods of agriculture. The ties of relocated segments to the parent groups created a complex of relationships linking distant settlements into economic combines. Thus, Bantu-speaking agriculturists moved into a vast subcontinent thinly populated by bands of roving foragers, leaving behind the confused and confusing archaeological record we attempt to read today.

BIBLIOGRAPHY
Denbow, J. 1990. Congo to Kalahari: Data and hypothesis about the political economy of the western stream of the Early Iron Age. *African Archaeological Review* 8: 139–176.
Eggert, M. K. H. 1992. The central African rain forest: Historical speculation and archaeological facts. *World Archaeology* 24: 1–24.
Huffman, T. N. 1982. Archaeology and ethnohistory of the African Iron Age. *Annual Reviews in Anthropology* 11: 133–150.
Phillipson, D. W. 1977. The spread of the Bantu language. *Scientific American* 236: 106–114.
Vansina, J. 1995. New linguistic evidence and "the Bantu Expansion." *Journal of African History* 36: 173–195.
Vogel, J. O. 1986. Microenvironments, swidden, and the Early Iron Age settlement of southwestern Zambia. *Azania* 22: 85–97.

Joseph O. Vogel

EASTERN AND SOUTH-CENTRAL AFRICAN IRON AGE

For many thousands of years, the fertile highlands and open savanna grasslands of eastern and southern Africa were sparsely populated by bands of transhumant stone-using foragers pursuing a way of life that had originated in the dawn of humanity's experiments with culture nearly 2 million years earlier. This well-adapted and familiar ecosystem was penetrated, more than 2,000 years ago, by groups of newcomers using a different lifeway that depended less on the anticipation of natural harvests than on the creation of an artificially enhanced ecosystem.

Transforming the Ecosystem

The Bantu-speaking populations filtering into the subcontinent used novel food-producing economies and managed substantial inputs of human labor organized within extensive social systems. These new societies, with the economic means to sustain the larger populations needed to maintain consistent production within an agricultural regimen, soon came not only to occupy the most productive areas, but to dominate culturally the life of the southern African subcontinent to the present day.

The eastern and southern African world the foragers had occupied was punctuated by a transient pursuit of seasonally available economic opportunities. The farmers prepared gardens, constructed permanent settlements, and managed the strategic stores needed to sustain their labor cohorts through the periods between harvests. This way of life entailed an ideological investment in the maintenance of property rights through genealogical lines and an adherence to territorially affiliated animistic beliefs and ancestor cults associated with an attachment to place.

While genealogical affinity established land tenure in these new societies, extended families supplied the labor needed to sustain production in what is essentially a very labor-intensive means of production. The interleaving of extended families through marriage created a means of managing some of the risk of marginal savanna farming and access to resources found at some distance from a group's primary area of exploitation. The lifeway of the savanna farmers was inherently more productive than that of the forager bands they had displaced, but it was also inherently more risky, due to the narrow range of food sources grown in the marginal soils and uncertain tropical rainfall patterns. These farmers needed complex social arrangements more intricate than those that sustained the hunter-foragers over so many millennia.

The Early Iron Age

The intricacies of the food-producing economies and the societies the farmers spawned ultimately gave rise to complex tribal and statelike arrangements throughout the subcontinent. These matters, as well as the origins of food production on the continent, the pattern of migrations that brought it south, the forager lifeway, and a general picture of the organization of traditional farming societies, are dealt with elsewhere. Here we need to consider only the evidence for that period of time archaeologists sometimes refer to as the *Early Iron Age* and which D. W. Phillipson has suggested could be encompassed within the portmanteau term, *Chifumbaze complex,* associated with the dispersion of Bantu-speaking populations throughout the subcontinent.

In contrast to the foragers who preceded them, the farmers used technology based on the smelting of iron from native ores into blooms worked into metal by their smiths to produce a tool kit useful to field preparation (axes and hoes), hunting (arrow and spear points), food preparation (knives), other useful domestic items (razors), and jewelry (rings, bangles, and necklaces). Along with the smelting of ores into copper, which was widely traded and used as a marker of status and wealth, iron-based metallurgy was introduced to the southern subcontinent by the earliest farmers and helps to mark them archaeologically.

The Investigation of the Iron Age

The complex later stages of the Iron Age have been closely examined since the end of the 19th century. At that time, investigators were intrigued by the stone-built enclosures of southeastern Africa and the elaborate terracing extending from northeastern Zimbabwe and Mozambique north to the terraced hillsides of Uganda. Although these researchers erroneously attributed the enclosures and terraces to "foreign" builders or a spurious race of "advanced" Africans, they laid a groundwork upon which later investigators established the later prehistory of eastern and southern Africa.

During the first half of the 20th century, there was little interest in the archaeological investigation of the remains of village life. Many authorities believed that the Bantu-speaking peoples of eastern and southern Africa were fairly recent arrivals, with a scant record of change or achievement. With the advent of political independence in the 1960s, scientific interest shifted to the question of the antecedents of the traditional cultures of the subcontinent. In so doing, individuals such as Brian Fagan and John Sutton in eastern Africa, K. R. Robinson in Malawi, and Ray Inskeep, Robert Soper, David W. Phillipson, Joseph Vogel, and Thomas Huffman in south-central Africa created a central core of information about the earliest manifestations of the Iron Age way of life. In later years, the area of vital research expanded to include most of the land mass of the subcontinent from the Great Lakes to the coast of Mozambique, the fringes of the Kalahari and southward to the Cape, including the research of many of those who have contributed to the summaries in this volume.

This long period of intensive research has left the Iron Age of the subcontinent one of the better-researched subdisciplines of Africanist archaeology. We will outline the archaeology of the Chifumbaze complex and suggest some of its descendants, the more settled farming populations of the region, some of whom participated in the florescent cultural developments of the mid- to later 2nd millennium.

In addition to the prominent appearance of metals in farming settlements is the evidence of pottery manufacture. Archaeologists have found it convenient to describe the various styles of pottery manufacture and ascribe them to particular times and locales. In this way, they can not only depict the complex passage of farming populations across otherwise trackless landscapes in time but also signify their progressive adaptation through time to particular regions.

The Beginnings and Staples of the Iron Age Lifeway

The present evidence, predominantly remains dated by radiocarbon techniques and associated with sparse finds of pottery recognized as the progenitor of other, later styles, suggests that the earliest manifestations of the Chifumbaze complex appeared on the west side of Lake Victoria nearly 2,500 years ago. From there, diverse clusters of people spread eastward and southward along multiple routes, paralleling the river courses of the subcontinent, for the most part, to search out tillable soils. They established themselves throughout southeastern Africa by the 3rd century.

The staples of this dispersion were the raising of native food crops (essentially drought-resistant grains like pennisetum, millet, and sorghum grown in gardens managed in a slash-and-burn regimen near the farmers' permanent villages of sun-dried clay houses), the mining and smelting of iron for implements, the manufacture of clay pottery, and the smelting and working of copper. These activities provide the paramount archaeological evidences as well. The search for Iron Age sites entails seeking out likely soils once cleared for cultivation and habitation and the physical evidence of pottery shards and bits of rusted iron, once a tool. At many Iron Age sites, copper and other materials, gained locally or through trade, are part of the remains. It is all these things that entice an archaeologist to further research. But it is the pottery, with its characteristic style, shape, or embellishments, that often gives us clues to the affinity of the occupants of one site with those of another. Changes in these pottery traits might suggest a temporal progression. Since pottery is so often the only thing found, or reported, in abundance at early settlements, much of the following discussion relates the changes and affinities of pottery in the archaeological record in order to outline how early Iron Age settlers and their descendants carried a food-producing way of life to the subcontinent.

In most places, given the marginal fertility of thin tropical African soils, early farming communities depended upon a slash-and-burn regimen based on cereal cultivation. The cereals they grew were drought-resistant enough to do well in the chancy climates of the southern savanna, but the nutrient-poor soils could be tilled only by clearing and burning vegetation to obtain their nutrient-filled ash. These fields could be profitably cropped for three to five years before they needed to be allowed to fallow, while another field was cultivated. Consequently, farmers needed access to many garden plots and a total acreage three to four times that needed to sustain the village. Shifting slash-and-burn cultivation produced adequate yields, but it forced thin population densities and little latitude to increase production.

Slash-and-burn cultivators first came to the southern savanna 1,700 years ago as small-scale farmers searching out arable land and adequate pasturage for their cattle. Their settlements of a few sun-dried clay-walled houses, set in forest openings created by their gardens, transformed the landscape into a mosaic of gardens on freshly cut fields amid spent clearings regenerating under secondary growth.

Few of the very earliest settlements retain more than a suggestion of village layout or the multitude of activities we attribute to these communities. The 7th- and 8th-century settlements at Kumadzulo and Kabondo Kumbo in the Victoria Falls region of southern Zambia are probably fairly typical of the early farming hamlets in southern Africa.

Each village consisted of a group of small houses built of sun-dried clay on a frame of thin poles and withies (slender, flexible branches) topped by a roof of thatched grass. The houses were arranged in concentric circles around a central open area. At Kabondo Kumbo, the center is filled with ash-filled pits once used to smelt iron, the remnants of the clay tubes used to pump fresh air into the heart of the furnace, and slag. Though in later times round huts are common, the earliest villagers in southern Zambia, at least, made square ones.

The smallish square post-hole wall houses were nearly 3 meters to a side, with floors prepared from sun-dried clay. Wall posts were sunk into the ground and woven together with withies (slender, flexible branches) and grass, before being covered with puddled clay and topped with a thatched-grass roof. Such structures, common even today in many parts of rural Africa, are inherently cool, resistant to insect invasions, and economically constructed with materials close at hand.

Upon establishing a new village, farmers solicited labor from within the extended family, who felt obliged to aid in the construction of new houses and the clearing of fields. In southern Zambia, gardens, fallowing fields, and a grassy clearing for cattle lie outside the settlement. This appears to be the case in the ancient settlements as well, though elsewhere in the subcontinent, space within the village confines is preserved for housing cattle as well.

In addition to the usual manufactured objects, such as iron hoes, axes, and spear- and arrowheads, these hamlets had copper, glass, and cowrie shells, probably obtained through long-distance trade. Since there was no local copper, Vogel surmised that it came into the Zambezi Valley along the same trade routes that carried ostrich-eggshell beads into these out-of-the-way settlements. Their closest source of ostrich eggshell was south of the Zambezi River, in Zimbabwe or Botswana. In addition, an analysis of the early pottery in the region suggests ethnic ties to people who lived farther south and produced a coherent pattern of decorated pottery, the Gokomere tradition.

Gokomere tradition pottery is distributed throughout the early settlements of Zimbabwe, southwestern Zambia, eastern Botswana, and the northern portions of the former Transvaal province in South Africa. A piece of glass, found at the 6th-century village at Kumadzulo, and cowrie shells, found with burials at the 7th-century cemetery at Chundu, probably came indirectly from Indian Ocean traders. A couple of centuries later, foreign traders and trade goods penetrated the Limpopo Basin in sufficient numbers to encourage the growth of complex, socially stratified towns.

The burial furnishings, village layout, and the general distribution of "elite" copper ornaments in settlements in the Victoria Falls region do not suggest a very profound level of social differentiation. For the most part, southwestern Zambia remained apart from the social and economic changes occurring farther south and retained the basic fabric of the savanna farming lifeway.

In eastern Botswana, on the other hand, as part of the local Toutswe tradition, there is evidence both of personal prestige based upon cattle ownership and the development of a hierarchical social system, in which an emerging class of "elite" individuals segregated their abodes upon hilltops, separated from the villages of the commoners. Cattle provided the mainstay of the local economy, imparting a particular layout to the villages of southern Africa, in which the houses were grouped around the central cattle kraal. Broederstroom, a well-researched locality in the former Transvaal province, near Johannesburg, displays equally strong evidence of cattle management and ironworking within the context of permanent agricultural settlements.

The evidence from eastern and southern Africa strongly supports the idea that from the period of the earliest farming settlements, there existed a stable, well-developed economy, using well-founded technologies, within a society capable of adaptation as conditions or opportunities presented themselves.

Whereas metals, or metal objects, were a primary means of accumulating and displaying wealth and prestige in many places in Africa, cattle often fulfilled this function in south-central and southern Africa. Cattle were traded and loaned between men to form political alliances, and cattle were reckoned prominently in the valuation of bride wealth and blood wealth, by which marriages were sealed and grievances were alleviated between families. The first archaeological evidence of these practices, which form a prominent part of later African societies and played a significant role in the emergence of statelike systems in southern Africa, is dated to the 7th century as part of the Toutswe tradition of Botswana.

Contemporaneous with the settlement of the Victoria Falls region and the first stirring of social complexity along the Kalahari's margins was the situation in the southern and central parts of the former Transvaal province characterized by the large 6th-century complex of agricultural

hamlets at Broederstroom. There iron was worked, though no iron implements have been recovered, and a few cattle may have been kept. At the 5th-century mixed-farming settlements near Lydenburg, a number of human heads modeled in terra-cotta have been recovered. It is presumed that these terra-cotta heads represent a ritual context, suggesting that in the middle centuries of the 1st millennium, communities throughout eastern and southern Africa already demonstrated a wide variety of technical, social, and ritual behaviors and that these behaviors would dominate lifeways in the subcontinent up until the present day.

Settlement of the Southern Subcontinent

The progress of the first farming populations in the subcontinent has been studied by archaeologists since the early 1960s. The first iron-using food-producing people in eastern Africa appeared in the Lake Victoria area in the last centuries B.C. Their communities are characterized by pottery attributed to the Urewe group. Pottery of this kind has been found in Rwanda, Zaire, southern Uganda, northwestern Tanzania, and southwestern Kenya. In Buhaya, on the southern shore of Lake Victoria, P. Schmidt has reported extensive iron-using settlements and advanced iron-making capabilities at village sites like Katuruka, dating to the early centuries A.D. F. Van Noten has suggested that these people kept domestic cattle and grew grains, like finger millet and sorghum.

By the 2nd century A.D., the coastal regions of northeastern Tanzania and southeastern Kenya were populated by people manufacturing Kwale ware pottery. These people apparently formed a later radiation eastward of the Urewe-affiliated populations. R. Soper has noted that settlements of the Kwale-affiliated people were in well-watered, hilly country, similar to land favored by modern-day subsistence agriculturists in the region, suggesting that they were themselves seeking farmland. This is bolstered by the fact that the more arid territory in the vicinity remained the domain of stone-using pastoralists, whose lifeway predates the arrival of the farmers.

At the same time iron-using, food-producing people were establishing themselves along the east coast, other groups affiliated with the Urewe and Kwale pottery traditions were migrating into the interior and spreading southward along the line of the Great Lakes. From their point of initial settlement on the shores of Lake Victoria, two substreams radiated southward, first along the east side of Lake Tanganyika to the Kalambo Falls, where the streams split into one carrying food-producing people toward Lake Bangweulu (as at the Samfya site investigated by D. Derricourt) and one moving to the Copperbelt sites studied by D. W. Phillipson. Apparently, this stream was equally responsible for early settlement as far south as Lusaka, the Kafue Valley, and the Batoka Plateau in southern Zambia.

Contemporaneous settlements on the Upper Zambezi—at Sioma, Senanga, and Lubusi—appear to be the product of a totally different stream of people penetrating western Zambia and adjacent Angola from the northwest. Otherwise the history of the middle reaches of the Zambezi Valley and the southern plateaus reaching southward to the Limpopo River and beyond were the product of people affiliated with the Urewe and Kwale pottery traditions. Moving from north to south along the shores of Lake Malawi, their settlements were identified by K. R. Robinson at Mwabulambo and Nkope in Malawi in the 1970s and earlier at the Gokomere and Ziwa sites in northeastern Zimbabwe. From northeastern Zimbabwe, the stream spread south toward the former Transvaal province and eastward toward Botswana and into southwestern Zambia and the Victoria Falls region, where numerous small farming settlements, many iron implements, and two prominent smelting sites have been located. The related settlements in Botswana, investigated by J. K. Denbow, disclose the importance of cattle ranging in these communities and the early institution of a "rank society" leading to the complex chiefdoms we identify with Great Zimbabwe.

By the end of the 1st millennium, the southern savanna was marked by many small farming hamlets woven into intricate social webs and engaged in long-distance and local exchanges of products and services. In the Limpopo Valley, in the copper-producing regions of central Africa, and along the shores of Lake Victoria, small communities were experimenting with emergent social complexity.

Elsewhere, smaller, less-complex societies took root. The earliest Kafue Valley communities gave birth to a cultural complex, first identified by B. M. Fagan at Kangila and Sebanzi as ancestral to the Tonga-speaking people of southern Zambia, who by the 11th century spread into the Zambezi Valley and supplanted a culture rooted in the first farming communities of the Victoria Falls region.

The sequence of early farming communities, investigated by Vogel, in the Victoria Falls region apparently originated in settlements founded in the Upper Zambezi Valley of southwestern Zambia. Pottery, located at Lusu and other 5th-century hilltop sites bordering the western edges of the Zambezi Valley, is affiliated with similar wares from the Zimbabwe Highlands south of the river. Having exploited the fertility of the sandy soils of western Zambia for a generation or so, farmers shifted to the *miombo* patches (areas of distinctive forest whose soils are capable of supporting crops) of the Victoria Falls region periodically transferring the locus of their activities in a common shifting agricultural pattern. By the 11th century, their smallish settlements had achieved a kind of stability, until they were absorbed into those of the folk moving southward out of the Kafue Valley.

In Botswana, as we have seen, the earliest communities grew into hierarchical systems supporting an emerging elite. The first manifestation of this growing social complexity in South Africa is detectable at the town of Bambandyanalo in the Limpopo Valley. Meanwhile, the populations associated with the Leopard's Kopje culture, described by T. N. Huffman, from the Bulawayo area formed a base upon which later societies would elaborate. Though Leopard's Kopje culture, itself, may have originated somewhere south of the Limpopo, it was well established around the Bulawayo area by the beginning of the 2nd millennium. In sites associated with the Leopard's Kopje culture, people lived in circular-pole, sun-dried clay huts, grew grains, kept cattle, and manufactured implements of iron and objects of personal adornment of copper. They participated in trade, which extended all the way to the east coast. By the 13th century, the people of the Bulawayo area had access to locally manufactured cotton cloth and had begun the construction dry-stone walls.

Similarly, in the eastern highlands of Zimbabwe, populations founded in the early Iron Age and affiliated with the Gokomere and Ziwa pottery styles combined their agricultural production with an annual pastoral round, allowing them to maintain sizable herds within the shifting rainfall patterns of the plateau. Eventually, as at Maxon Farm, Great Zimbabwe, and elsewhere, dry-stone walled sites made their appearance as well.

Along the coast of Mozambique, a diagnostic kind of pottery, affiliated with the Kwale ware found farther north, is known as *Matola ware,* after a site investigated by T. da Cruz y Silva near Maputo. It has been recognized that nearly 40 small, apparently short-lived settlements were spread along the Mozambique coast, KwaZulu-Natal, and inland to the eastern part of the former Transvaal province, at sites like Tzaneen. In common with the other sites settled during the 1st millennium, they occur on soils congenial to the cultivation of grains, though many of the coastal villages seem to have exploited marine resources as well.

———～～～～～———

By the middle of the 2nd millennium, the pattern of life in the subcontinent was well established. Here and there, in the shadow of the prominent lacustrine and savanna states, small confederations of subsistence or otherwise small-scale farmers practiced stable agricultural regimens, adjusted to changes in the social environment, and continued their lifeway throughout much of the colonial period until the major transitions afforded by the political upheavals of the mid-20th century.

BIBLIOGRAPHY
Hall, M. L. 1987. *Farmers, kings and traders: The people of southern Africa 200-1860.* Chicago: University of Chicago Press.
Huffman, T. N. 1988. Southern Africa to the south of Zambezi. In *Africa from the seventh to the eleventh century,* eds. M. El Fasi and I. Hrbek, 664–680. Berkeley: Heinemann Educational Books.
Mokhtar, G. 1981. *Ancient civilizations of Africa.* London: Heinemann Educational Books, Ltd.
Oliver, R., and B. M. Fagan. 1975. *Africa in the Iron Age: c. 500 B.C. to A.D. 1400.* Cambridge: Cambridge University Press.
Phillipson, D. W. 1993. *African Archaeology.* New York: Cambridge University Press.
Vogel, J. O. 1994. *Great Zimbabwe: The Iron Age of south central Africa.* New York: Garland Publishing, Inc.

Joseph O. Vogel

SOUTHERN AFRICAN IRON AGE

This article deals with the iron-using agricultural societies of southern Africa, from their first appearance early in the modern era to the 19th century. Written reports of life there before the 16th century are rare. For the most part, therefore, conventional archaeological investigation provides the only means of describing and comprehending the history and richness of agricultural life in southern Africa.

Because ceramics are distinctively decorated and generally the most abundant artifact found in agricultural settlements, archaeologists commonly use ceramic styles to trace the movement of people across space and to delineate their history through time. This is feasible wherever ceramics were not produced for large-scale trade. Throughout this article, we refer to ceramic traditions, usually named after the first or most important site from which particular styles were recovered. These traditions do not always correlate with sociopolitical units. Research in southern Africa suggests they usually correspond with linguistic entities that, in most cases, composed several political units. Thus, it is suggested that makers of related ceramic styles would have spoken related languages. In this article, the archaeology of iron-using agriculturists is essentially the archaeology of Bantu-speaking people.

Urewe ceramics were originally described as "dimple-based" after a distinctive dimplelike depression similar to that on the bottom of a champagne bottle found on the base of many pots. They are named after a site on the northeastern side of Lake Victoria. These ceramics and related iron-smelting remains mark the first appearance of Bantu-speaking agriculturists in the interlacustrine region. In all probability, they reached this area from the west, where linguistic studies place the nucleus of the Bantu languages in the vicinity of Cameroon around the beginning of the 1st millennium A.D. Their movement and subsequent settlement may have been facilitated by drier or more seasonal conditions that created a more open forest there about 3,000 years ago.

The relationship between Urewe and earlier Late Stone Age communities of the region is unclear. The earlier communities produced Kansyore ceramics and may have kept livestock. Dates related to Kansyore settlements are equivocal, however, and it is not certain whether Kansyore communities were extant in the region at the time of the initial Urewe settlement.

Little else is known of Urewe people other than their metallurgy. No Urewe settlements have been excavated, and evidence of their crops and livestock is limited and uncertain. Nevertheless, the variety of Urewe vessel shapes is indicative of a society living, at least, in semipermanent villages. Moreover, detailed survey data from Uganda shows sharp distinctions between Urewe settlement locations and the location of Late Stone Age sites, including those with Kansyore ceramics. Whereas Late Stone Age sites occurred on land with limited agricultural potential, Urewe settlements indicate a marked preference for well-watered or waterside environments with fertile soil and gentle slopes. This is a pattern typical of early agriculturist sites elsewhere in sub-Saharan Africa and is strongly suggestive of a horticultural economy. Urewe agricultural and industrial activities appear to have had a significant impact on the environment for paleo-environmental studies suggest localized clearing of forests beginning 2,200 years ago. Given this data, it is unlikely, and indeed, theoretically improbable that Urewe and Late Stone Age communities were, as some suggest, economically very similar.

Movement into Southern Africa

By the 3rd century, agriculturists had spread eastward, probably south of the arid eastern Rift Valley, toward the East African coast where they settled in well-watered, wooded environments. This expansion is archaeologically recognizable by the presence of Leselu and Kwale ceramics, which are stylistically related to Urewe ware. M. Klapwick has suggested that evidently some people continued moving south, possibly by boat, reaching southern Africa by the 4th century. The rapidity of this movement is evident from the close correlation of associated radiocarbon dates over a broad area and the remarkable similarity between Kwale ware and Silver Leaves ceramics in southern Africa. These and other related ceramic entities are grouped into the Kwale branch of the Urewe tradition, which approximates the lowland facies of D. W. Phillipson's "eastern stream" (Bantu speakers who settled southern Africa along routes east of the Great Lakes). Recent analyses show that several phases of the Kwale branch persisted in South Africa through into the 8th century at least.

There is clear evidence that Silver Leaves people were mixed agriculturists. Pottery shards found at Silver Leaves contained carbonized seeds of bulrush millet *(Pennisetum typhoides),* while another South African site of the same phase yielded cattle remains. Deep pits, at least some of which were used for storing grain, occur at many Kwale branch sites in southern Africa. Site locations reflect a concern for adequate summer rainfall, and in KwaZulu-Natal, settlement during the 5th and early 6th centuries was restricted to coastal areas by arid conditions farther inland. Sites close to the coast in Mozambique and South Africa show that early agriculturists exploited marine resources, particularly the brown mussel, *Perna perna,* and a range of wild fauna and flora was probably used. There is clear evidence of iron production at many early sites, and these first agriculturists may have been actively seeking ore sources.

Evidence of Kwale branch social organization comes from the 7th-century site of Broederstroom in South Africa, where excavations have revealed a village settlement layout known as the *central*

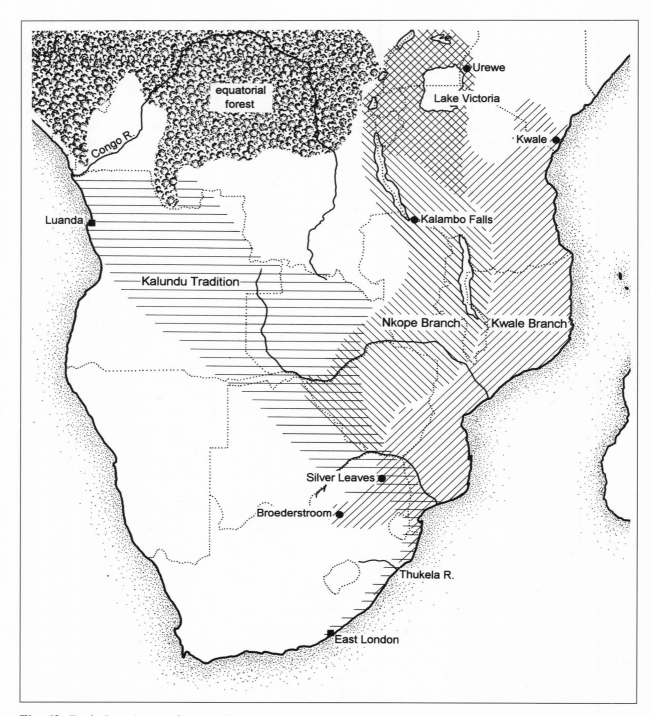

Fig. 62 *Early Iron Age traditions of eastern and southern Africa*

cattle pattern. This concept, derived from the observations of anthropologists of present-day people in southern Africa, has been traced back through the archaeological record to the middle of the 1st millennium and is regarded as evidence of a patrilineal society in which cattle were the favored bride wealth. There is some suggestion from the first two Kwale branch phases in South Africa, however, that at this time at least, the scale of organization of society was fairly small.

Inland of the Kwale branch, related ceramics from the Nkope branch of the Urewe tradition are roughly equivalent to the highland facies of Phillipson's eastern stream. Sites with Nkope ceramics show that some communities moved more directly southward from the interlacustrine region, reaching modern Zimbabwe by the 6th century. They continued to settle in environments with arable soils. Livestock remains also occur at sites with Nkope ceramics, though in small numbers, and hunting may have been an important subsistence activity.

At the Kalambo Falls sites in northern Zambia, deep pits with pottery, worked stone, burned clay, and ironworking debris were posited as graves, due to the high levels of phosphorous and calcium detected in them. The phosphorous levels may have been derived, however, from dung, and the pits may have been originally located within a livestock enclosure. This would have significant implications for our understanding of early agriculturist economy if shown to be true: first, because of the identification of livestock in the absence of faunal remains and, second, because pits within cattle pens are an important component of the central cattle pattern.

Kalundu Tradition

Not all ceramic facies in southern and south-central Africa are part of the Urewe tradition. Some agriculturists appear to have made their way south through the equatorial forest, perhaps during the same period of aridity that facilitated the settlement of Urewe communities in the interlacustrine region. These people made ceramics that archaeologists place in the Kalundu tradition, which is distinct from yet related to the Urewe tradition. Early Kalundu sites near Luanda date to the 3rd century. In the following 200 to 300 years, agriculturists of the Kalundu tradition spread through Botswana into Zimbabwe, Zambia, and South Africa.

According to some archaeologists, the first phase of this expansion is represented by the presence of Bambata ceramics in Zimbabwe and Botswana. Bambata ceramics, however, occur in rock-shelter deposits as well as open sites and are not universally accepted as the product of

agriculturists. Some archaeologists consider them to have been made by hunter-foragers or pastoralists. This debate over the origin of Bambata ceramics has as much to do with the definition of the Bambata style as with the presence of Bambata shards in Late Stone Age contexts and clearly requires resolution. For those who believe Bambata ceramics were made by Kalundu agriculturists, the shards from rock shelters suggest interaction between agriculturists and Late Stone Age communities, either hunter-foragers or pastoralists and the subsequent dispersal of shards through long-distance exchange networks ahead of the agriculturist expansion.

There is no indication that receipt of Bambata ceramics ahead of actual contact changed the pattern of hunter-forager life in any way. Actual contact, however, had considerable impact. Hunter-foragers were drawn to early agriculturist settlements where they entered into cooperative alliances that possibly encouraged the transfer of economic practices and resources. This is particularly evident in the Thukela Basin in South Africa, where dated deposits and sharp topographical contrasts clearly indicate a movement of hunter-foragers from grassland and montane environments to the savanna *bushveld* occupied by agriculturists in the 1st millennium. The precise nature of the relationship is uncertain, and it may have varied from place to place. The evidence does suggest, however, a closer integration than the client relationships that existed in more recent times. Artifacts at agriculturist sites similar to artifacts from the Late Stone Age reflect hunting and skin dressing, suggesting that hunter-foragers were contributing to this component of the integrated economy. Exchanges between the two groups may have included cultivated foodstuffs, medicinal plants and practices, iron, and wives.

By the late 8th century, Kalundu people had settled in savanna environments to the southernmost limits of the summer rainfall region, near modern East London in South Africa. Sites there yield evidence of bulrush millet, finger millet *(Eleusine corocana),* and sorghum. Wild plants were also exploited for food. Carbonized marula seeds, for example, are common at several sites. For smelting purposes, hardwoods such as wild olive *(Olea africana)* were selected. Faunal samples include the remains of cattle, sheep, goats, chickens, and dogs as well as a range of wild animals, including marine and freshwater fish.

Social Organization

Some archaeologists, like Martin Hall, T. M. O'C. Maggs, and Joseph O. Vogel, for example, suggest that early villages were economically and politically independent, or small in scale with communities dependent upon insecure "close-neighbor relationships." Others, like T. N. Huffman or Gavin Whitelaw, argue that Kalundu

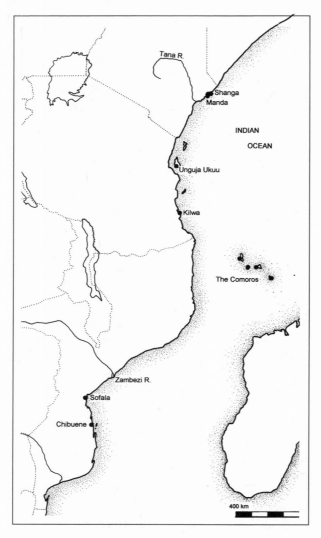

Fig. 63 *Swahili settlements on the East African coast*

sites, like the 7th-century settlement at Broederstroom, have a layout reflecting the central cattle pattern and that Kalundu society was politically complex with several villages organized in up to three hierarchical levels. Recently gathered data from the Congo Republic even suggests that the initial expansion of agriculturists into South Africa originated from hierarchical societies. Such arguments are inconsistent with the popular image of small-scale agriculturists tentatively experimenting with local conditions and resources as they moved slowly southward.

Ritual Activity

There is considerable evidence for ritual activity at 1st millennium sites in southern Africa, including human and animal figurines and hollow ceramic heads. These are invariably broken, strongly suggesting that they were employed in rites of passage, the breaking symbolizing an irreversible change in status. A recent interpretation by J. H. N. Loubser argues that these objects had a didactic function within formalized initiation schools that took place in 1st-millennium villages. Incisions on figurines suggest the practice of cicatrization (production of railed scars as a form of bodily decoration), and there is a growing body of skeletal evidence indicating the practice of dental mutilation. Both practices mark the body irreversibly and, therefore, probably accompanied the initiation of children into the wider community. It is also tempting to link the widespread occurrence of bottomless pots with a rite of passage. These perhaps represented a symbolic defloration of pubescent girls.

Zhiso Tradition

Toward the end of the 1st millennium, agriculturist communities in the extreme south appear to have been increasingly affected by a period of aridity that ultimately forced them to move northward. In contrast, Zhiso agriculturists in the Shashi-Limpopo Basin experienced relatively high rainfall. These favorable conditions, coupled with the presence of large elephant herds, provided the economic foundation for the development of an important Zhiso center, Schroda, near the Shashi-Limpopo confluence. By the middle of the 9th century, the Schroda authorities had entered into a trade relationship with Islamic traders on the east coast, exchanging ivory and carnivore pelts for glass beads. Evidence from Vilanculous Bay indicates that traders landed the imported goods at Chibuene and then distributed the items through one mechanism or another to Schroda and other southern African centers. Items such as glass beads and Persian ceramics, or the shards thereof, reached villages in the vicinity of Durban by the 10th century. It seems most likely that these were transferred through overland exchange networks, though they tempt consideration of how far south the traders may have sailed.

Schroda's burgeoning wealth and the good agricultural potential of the Shashi-Limpopo Basin attracted the attention of Kalundu people farther south who, in the late 10th century, took control of the region and trade resources. This movement is archaeologically recognizable from the abandonment of Schroda and sudden appearance of Leopard's Kopje ceramics throughout the Shashi-Limpopo region. Leopard's Kopje elite established a capital at Bambandyanalo and locked into the Indian Ocean trade network. The enormous wealth they accumulated generated opportunities for a structural transformation of society including the creation of a new class-based system. This social formation was given expression in a new settlement layout at Mapungubwe in the 12th century. Since Mapungubwe ceramics are an early expression of historic Shona society, Mapungubwe people must have spoken an early form of Shona. Zhiso people, on the other hand, probably owed their ancestry to communities derived from the Nkope branch.

Toutswe Chiefdom

A nearly threefold increase in the number of Zhiso-related sites on the margins of the Kalahari suggests that some Zhiso people opted to move away from Leopard's Kopje control. The hilltop settlement of Toutswemogala was first established at roughly this time. Since it subsequently became the center of the Toutswe chiefdom, it is tempting to wonder whether the new arrivals from the east either took control of the Toutswe area or simply maintained a control that they had once exercised from Schroda. Environmental conditions in eastern Botswana at the turn of the millennium were clearly optimal for pastoralism, for there is a dramatic increase in the size of Toutswe cattle herds. These provided the principal source of wealth within the chiefdom and allowed the development of from three to five hierarchical levels.

The Toutswe chiefdom does not appear to have been directly involved with trade on the east coast. Leopard's Kopje ceramics occur at Toutswe, however, and Toutswe ceramics are present in Leopard's Kopje contexts. This suggests some kind of interaction, perhaps marriage transactions, with the Leopard's Kopje complex. A more important exchange system seems to have developed northward across the Kgalagadi. Bosutswe, a hilltop settlement about 100 kilometers northwest of Toutswemogala, is smaller than the Toutswe center. It may have been the headquarters of a regional chief within the Toutswe chiefdom or the center of a smaller related chiefdom. Whatever the case, it appears to have been a key channel through which copper, ivory, and, possibly, pelts flowed from regions north of the Okavango swamps toward Toutswemogala. In return, items from the Indian Ocean trade were channeled through Bosutswe from Toutswemogala to communities in northern Botswana and beyond.

Bosutswe contributed items to the exchange network. The site is located on high-quality chert and agate outcrops, which were quarried apparently for exchange with hunter-foragers in northern Botswana. Agate beads have since been recorded from sites there, while both chert and agate nodules occur at Mapungubwe.

Toutswemogala was abandoned in the 13th century. Elsewhere in Botswana, Toutswe-related communities retained their identity to the 15th century, at least. While occupation of Bosutswe continued after the collapse of Toutswemogala, Mapungubwe shards in the upper levels of the deposit suggest that Bosutswe fell under the Mapungubwe hegemony. A second shift occurred after the rise of Great Zimbabwe when the emphasis of the Kgalagadi trade shifted to salt from the Sowe Pan area, apparently contributing to a reduction in Bosutswe's importance.

Zimbabwean Hegemony and Interaction

Mapungubwe was succeeded near the end of the 13th century by Great Zimbabwe to the northeast, where the new settlement layout, the Zimbabwe culture pattern, was developed more fully. As the capital of an enormous state, the hub of the southern African sector of the Indian Ocean trade system, and the home to up to 18,000 people, Great Zimbabwe was occupied for less than 200 years before internal dissent and complications in subsistence production possibly caused its abandonment and the breakup of the state. Two smaller daughter states emerged: the Torwa state centered on its capital Khami near modern Bulawayo in Zimbabwe and the smaller Mutapa state with its capital, Fura, in northeastern Zimbabwe.

Between the 13th and 15th centuries, new ceramics styles appear south of the Mapungubwe and Zimbabwe states. One of the new styles, Moor Park, is accompanied by a radical change in settlement style and location. Moor Park sites are found on hilltops in grassland areas rather than in savanna environments and are characterized by low stone walls. Some archaeologists, such as J. K. Denbow and T. M. O'C. Maggs, suggest that the changes may be the product of major social and cultural restructuring within existing populations. Others, such as T. N. Huffman, argue that the new styles are evidence of a second large-scale movement of Urewe tradition communities from eastern to southern Africa. All agree, however, that the producers of these

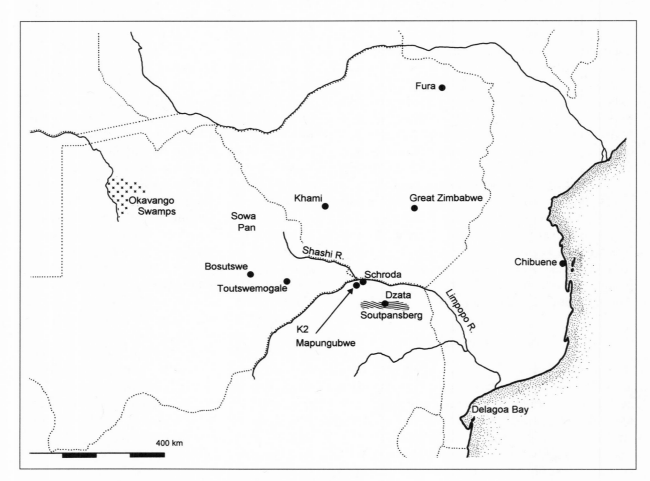

Fig. 64 *Greater Zambezia during the Middle to Late Iron Ages*

new ceramic styles are ancestors of the Nguni and Sotho-Tswana speakers of present-day southern Africa.

Sotho-Tswana Origins

Early Sotho-Tswana sites, marked by the presence of Moloko ceramics, first appear in an environment already occupied by late Kalundu tradition communities, or Eiland settlements. This period is underresearched, but it appears that Eiland and Moloko settlements were contemporaneous for only a short period before the production of Eiland ceramics ceased. Southeastern Botswana is an exception, however, for there Eiland communities retained their identity to the 15th century, at least. Elsewhere, Eiland decorative elements occur on early Moloko vessels, suggesting that Eiland people quickly merged with the new arrivals and became Sotho-Tswana. The reasons for this are uncertain, though it is possible that the Little Ice Age, which caused severe aridity over parts of southern Africa, may be implicated.

Early interaction between Shona and Sotho speakers in the Soutpansberg Range in northern South Africa prompted significant cultural developments in the latter half of the 2nd millennium. These developments have been elucidated through a combination of archaeology, oral history, and documentary sources. The Soutpansberg Range is rich in metal ores, good soils, and pasture and once harbored abundant game, particularly elephants. These resources clearly attracted Mapungubwe people, who continued to live north of the mountains after the collapse of the Mapungubwe state. First Eiland and later Sotho people to the south interacted with the Shona elite across the mountains, which functioned as a relatively rigid ethnic and economic boundary.

Khami ceramics and stone-built Zimbabwe pattern settlements appear in the Soutpansberg area from the middle of the 15th century onward. Khami ceramics replaced the late Mapungubwe style, indicating that at this time, the area fell under the control of Khami dynasties, who possibly required new sources of gold, copper, and ivory. Through the Khami elite, the Soutpansberg

area once again became involved in the Indian Ocean trade. The mountain boundary between Shona and Sotho became increasingly fluid, and Khami ceramics and prestige goods are present at Moloko sites south of the Soutpansberg region. Authority was still clearly vested with the Khami elite, however, since Khami sites occur only in the north and Moloko ceramics are better represented on commoner settlements. Nevertheless, this more intense interaction between Shona and Sotho gave birth to two merged ceramic styles, Tavhatshena and Letaba, in the 16th century. Both styles represent the development of new languages from Sotho and Shona. The Tavhatshena language is not yet identified. Letaba, however, which replaced Khami, Tavhatshena, and Moloko in the mid-16th century, marked the first appearance of Venda. The mixed ancestry of Letaba conforms with linguistic evidence of Venda being essentially an amalgamation of Shona and Sotho. Its development was probably facilitated by the isolation of the Soutpansberg elite from the Torwa state in the north.

Torwa rulers were conquered by the Changamire-Rozvi dynasty around 1680. Following a dispute, the Singo split from the Rozvi and invaded Venda polities in the Soutpansberg area. The Singo established a capital at Dzala, a site built of dark blue stone in a modified Zimbabwe pattern, between 1680 and 1700. The Singo maintained external trade and, interestingly, gradually became Venda and adopted the language of their conquered subjects. From the 18th century onward, however, changing dynamics within the external trade routes gradually reduced Singo control of trade on the east coast. In particular, the growing importance of Delagoa Bay (the site of modern Maputo) and Natal Bay (modern Durban) as points of access to the interior allowed other groups to supplant Venda control. The result was the fragmentation of the Venda polity.

The earliest Sotho-Tswana people apparently rarely used stone as a building material. Sites consist of hut remains surrounding central cattle enclosures (though these are not always preserved), all built of organic materials. A warm, wet period around the 15th century improved the agricultural potential of the southern *highveld* grasslands. This facilitated the expansion of

Fokeng and subsequently Koena communities into the region from north of the Vaal River. In the absence of abundant woody vegetation, they used dung for fuel and constructed substantial parts of their settlements of stone. The visibility of stone-built sites from the air has allowed archaeologists to map the distribution of different settlement types with relative ease using aerial photographs. Sites of this period have a fairly restricted distribution in the eastern *highveld.* They compose large clusters of settlement units or homesteads, and some must have housed more than 1,000 people.

Different settlement patterns dating to the 16th and 17th centuries suggest that new people from north of the Vaal River settled on the southern *highveld* at this time, substantially increasing the population of agriculturists. This second expansion may have been encouraged by developments north of the Vaal River, including political turmoil among the Hurutshe and the westward intrusion of Nguni-speaking Ndebele onto the Pietersburg Plateau from the *lowveld* south of the Olifants River. The military stress of this time is suggested by the occurrence of Sotho-Tswana settlements on defensible hilltop locations.

The settlements of Taung and various Kgatla lineages, in particular the Tioka and Sia, came to replace those of an earlier type and had a more extensive distribution, extending farther to the west, south, and northeast. These settlements vary in size from a few homesteads to more than 100. A somewhat indistinct, but related, settlement type is found in the Caledon Valley along the northwestern border of Lesotho. These settlements were possibly associated with Nguni speakers who had moved west from the Upper Thukela Basin. The more recently identified Doompoort pattern resembles the Caledon Valley sites and may have also been the product of Nguni speakers. All spoke some form of seSotho by the 19th century.

Variations of domed or "beehive" huts were constructed at all these sites. In contrast, cone-on-cylinder huts occur at sites to the west. These settlements date from the 16th to the 19th centuries. Sites vary from a single unit to more than a dozen, and some may have housed more than 1,000 people. They most closely resemble

Tswana settlements to the north and are associated with the Kubung, who are an offshoot of the Rolong, a southern Tswana group. These sites, and their contrasting architectural styles, are of interest because they indicate a cultural distinction between Sotho and Tswana speakers that is of some antiquity.

Below the Drakensberg Escarpment to the southeast, limited archaeological information is available for the 2nd millennium. Moor Park sites dating to the 14th century are the earliest agriculturist settlements in the South African grasslands. Comprising stone-built hut terraces and enclosures, they suggest an emphasis on livestock and possibly represent seasonal cattle posts. Reports of Portuguese sailors shipwrecked in the 16th and 17th centuries indicate a way of life that changed little from this time to the 19th century. From the 17th century onward, and probably earlier given the evidence of Moor Park, communities lived in varied ecological zones. This was significant because it meant that communities had unequal access to key resources, such as iron ore and good grazing land. Compensatory strategies were developed. For example, herding strategies designed to maximize cattle production were implemented, and communities of specialized smiths traded their products for cattle as far afield as the southern *highveld,* or for other prized commodities, such as saltwater fish.

Control of trading networks probably rested with chiefs, particularly where iron was involved. Political entities early in the last half of the 2nd millennium, for the most part, seem to have been small, though this began to change with the increasing use of Delagoa Bay by the Portuguese and other European traders from the 17th century onward. Ivory was the principal export, while slaving may have been a factor in the early 19th century. Key imports were copper, brass, glass beads, cloth, and, of huge significance for subsistence agriculture, maize. Maize is easier to cultivate than sorghum and millet and has a far higher yield. It became a staple crop during the 18th century and allowed for substantial population increases in the grasslands where it was a more suitable crop than the traditional cultigens. Archaeological evidence for this includes the increased number of late 18th-century settle-

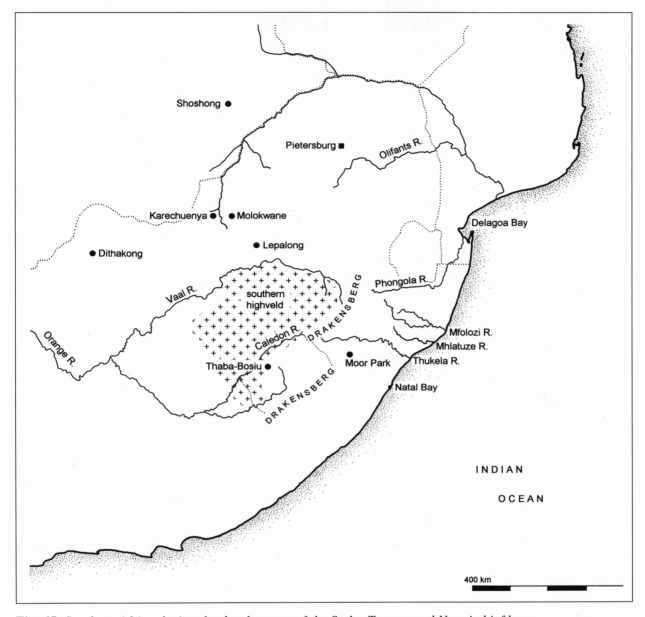

Fig. 65 *Southern Africa during the development of the Sotho-Tswana and Nguni chiefdoms*

ments in the grasslands, carbonized cobs, and characteristic grindstones.

Rise of the Nguni

Efforts to control the interior sector of this trade and the wealth it generated resulted in policies of aggressive expansion and confrontation among northern Nguni polities. In particular, the Ndwandwe, between the Phongolo and Black Mfolozi Rivers, and the Mthethwa, between the Mfolozi and Mhlatuze Rivers, were key players. Their growth prompted important social changes. Among the most significant was the evolution of *amabutho* (age-group sets) into military regiments. In the Zulu state of the 1820s, *amabutho* were housed in a new settlement form, the *amakhanda* (military barracks), though there is no archaeological confirmation of when this new settlement form first developed. Also, access to power was increasingly restricted to core groups who, in effect, became an aristocracy.

By 1816, expansionist policies brought the Ndwandwe under Zwide kaLanga and the Mthethwa under Dingiswayo kaJobe face-to-face on a broad frontier along the Mfolozi River. The frontier erupted the following year when the Ndwandwe defeated the Mthethwa and killed Dingiswayo. The Mthethwa state collapsed, leaving Dingiswayo's ally, Shaka kaSenzangakhona of the Zulu, to face the Ndwandwe. The Zulu survived two attacks. Then, bolstered by the resources of neighboring chiefdoms drawn into a Zulu-dominated alliance through a mixture of rough diplomacy and military intervention, the Zulu repelled a third attack, driving the Ndwandwe northward. By 1820, the Zulu were the dominant political power between the Phongolo and Thukela Rivers.

The aggressive growth of the northern Nguni states had a domino effect on neighboring chiefdoms. Some aggregated to form loose defensive polities. Some leaders led their followers from their home territories to establish dominance over smaller chiefdoms at a distance from the epicenter of the conflict. Others were simply killed, their followers crushed and roughly incorporated into greater powers. A tragic drought that caused the collapse of the maize-based subsistence economy around the end of the 18th century exacerbated the conflict. Archaeological research of this period and subsequent times has concentrated mainly on the Zulu capitals. However, rock shelters throughout the region preserve evidence of occupation by agriculturist refugees. More poignant is evidence for the abandonment of homesteads of local building styles around the 18th century. The subsequent widespread occurrence of homesteads of the lowland Zulu style is indicative of Zulu hegemony in the 19th century, since homestead styles are an expression of male identity.

The Mfecane

The repercussions of the growth of the Zulu and earlier Nguni states were severe. The region south of the Thukela River felt the impact from the late 18th century onward. The Khumalo under Mzilikazi moved to the north and west in the 1820s, reaching modern Zimbabwe where they settled in the area around Bulawayo, once dominated by the Torwa. Some Nguni people under Zwangendaba, having swept aside the Shona chiefdoms of northeastern Zimbabwe, crossed the Zambezi River to settle in Malawi. Other Nguni people reached as far north as southern Tanzania. Nguni invasions of the southern *highveld* scattered local Sotho communities in the 1820s, some of whom, in turn, became destitute raiding groups. After 1824, Moshoeshoe emerged as an unifying force in the vicinity of the Caledon Valley and gathered displaced people under his suzerainty. Based on his mountain fortress of Thaba-Boslu, Moshoeshoe's Sotho successfully defended themselves against numerous attackers, including the British at the battles of Viervoet and Berea. However, growing conflict with the Boers of the Orange Free State Republic forced Moshoeshoe to accept British annexation in 1868, thus ending his fierce resistance to white colonial expansion.

The conventional view blames the turmoil of this time in southern Africa on Nguni, particularly Zulu, aggression. However, Tswana communities on the western *highveld* north of the Vaal River were relatively unaffected by the growth of the Zulu and other Nguni polities. They nevertheless experienced a period of considerable military strife from the middle of the 18th century onward. This was due to a disenchantment among subordinate chiefdoms with the Hurutshe hegemony, which in turn was stimulated by growing competition for resources of both subsistence and export value. Griqua, Korana, Boer, and Ndebele aggression and the drought around the turn of the century further exacerbated the situation. The threat posed by this rising level of conflict forced communities to aggregate for defensive purposes into "towns," such as Molokwane, Dithakong, and Shoshong, which were among the largest single concentrations of people in southern Africa at this time, housing from 10,000 to 16,000 people.

Archaeological evidence complements other historical data. Although some of these settlements were established as early as the 17th century, radiocarbon dates show that they grew in size in the latter half of the 18th century. Furthermore, underground caverns, like rock shelters to the southeast, preserve evidence of occupation. One such cavern, Lepalong, served as a refuge for the baMmatau after they were driven from Molokwane by Mzilikazi in the 1820s. The baMmatau later fled south across the Vaal River, linked up with the Boers under Andries Potgieter, and returned northward with them. The Boers defeated Mzilikazi at the battle of Vegkop in 1836 and drove his people northward.

By the middle of the 19th century, the growing presence of Europeans throughout southern Africa and the establishment of colonial regimes effected the independent development of traditional African lifeways there. The once-great states, independent chiefdoms, and self-sufficient agriculturist communities of the subcontinent passed from contemporary view or were relegated to side-show status in the imperial carnival.

BIBLIOGRAPHY

Denbow, J. 1986. A new look at the later prehistory of the Kalahari. *Journal of African History* 27: 3–28.

———. 1990. Congo to Kalahari: Data and hypotheses about the political economy of the western stream of the Early Iron Age. *The African Archaeological Review* 8: 139-175.

Duminy, A., and W. Guest. 1989. *Natal and Zululand from the earliest times to 1910: A new history.* Pietermaritzburg: University of Natal Press and Shooter and Shuter.

Hall, M. L. 1987. *The changing past: Farmers, kings and traders in southern Africa, 200–1860.* Cape Town: David Phillip.

Hamilton, C. 1995. *The Mfecane aftermath: Reconstructive debates in southern African history.* Johannesburg: Witwatersrand University Press.

Huffman, T. N. 1989. Ceramics, settlements and Late Iron Age migrations. *The African Archaeological Review* 7: 155–182.

———. 1989. *Iron Age migrations.* Johannesburg: Witwatersrand University Press.

Loubser, J. H. N. 1991. The ethnoarchaeology of Venda-speakers in southern Africa. *Navorsinge van die Nasionale Museum Bloemfontein* 7: 145–464.

Maggs, T. M. O'C. 1984. The Iron Age south of the Zambezi. In *Southern African prehistory and paleoenvironments,* ed. R. G. Klein, 329–360. Rotterdam: A. A. Balkema.

Maggs, T. M. O'C., and G. Whitelaw. 1991. A review of recent archaeological research on food-producing communities in southern Africa. *Journal of African History* 32: 3–24.

Phillipson, D. W. 1985. *African archaeology.* Cambridge: Cambridge University Press.

———. 1997. *The later prehistory of eastern and southern Africa.* London: Heinemann Educational Books.

Shaw, T., P. Sinclair, B. Andah, and A. Okpoko, eds. 1993. *The archaeology of Africa: Food, metals and towns.* London: Routledge.

Sutton, J. E. G. 1994–1995. The growth of farming communities in Africa from the equator southwards. *Azania* (special volume) 29-30. Nairobi: British Institute in Eastern Africa.

Vogel, J. O. 1990. The cultural basis, development, and consequences of a socially mediated trading corporation in southern Zambezia. *Journal of Anthropological Archaeology* 9: 105–147.

Gavin Whitelaw

Social Complexity

DEVELOPMENT OF STATES IN SUB-SAHARAN AFRICA

As population densities rose in some parts of tropical Africa during the last few thousand years, the societies involved resorted to strategies that would enable large numbers of people to live relatively close together without continual conflict. One of the most important developments was the emergence, in some cases, of a centralized and specialized governmental organization, what is often called a *state*. As was usually the case in other parts of the world, early African states concentrated authority in a particular individual who nominally or in fact wielded power over everyone else and whose position was reinforced by religious belief. Consequently, scholars of Africa's past have frequently referred to such states as *kingdoms* or *empires,* in the case of some of the larger and ethnically more diverse states. These terms are useful but in some instances misleading because of their European associations. Whatever one calls this form of government, however, its sophistication, complexity, and variability in Africa before the impact of colonialism has led researchers to pay particular attention to its origins and development in the African context. Documentary sources—African, Arabic, and European—as well as extensive oral sources within the societies themselves have enabled historians to throw a great deal of light on this subject, while social anthropologists, ethnologists, political scientists, geographers, and others have

also contributed substantially to its study. Nevertheless, as with so many other aspects of the African past, our knowledge of state development is extraordinarily variable. For some periods and for some areas, the available sources can tell us little or nothing. If we are to escape the tail-biting supposition that can sometimes result from untested theoretical discussion, we need another source of evidence. Archaeology attempts to provide this by investigating material remains that result from the activities of African states. The questions are: how can archaeological research throw light on such matters of political organization and to what extent has it been successful so far in doing so?

Without doubt, the identification of physical evidence relevant to the development of states in sub-Saharan Africa and the interpretation of the evidence are problematical. Assumptions have to be made that in some cases are vulnerable to challenge. Nevertheless, by carefully juxtaposing the archaeological and the historical and other evidence, it is possible in specific instances to demonstrate the association of particular material remains with known former states and to argue by analogy for such an association in the case of states whose existence is otherwise poorly known or unknown. The result is a mosaic of evidence of variable quality, with huge gaps in areas or periods that have had little or no archaeological attention or which, for environmental or cultural reasons, have little apparent evidence available for study. Patchy though the mosaic may be, we can begin to discern the general outline of a picture.

Broad-scale evidence for the previous existence of states can sometimes be discerned in studies of site distribution. A high density of settlement sites, or even of cemeteries, ranging in size from large to small and located in a confined but resource-rich area, may be indicative of past state development. Instances where this seems to be the case can be seen along the Middle Nile in southern Egypt and the Sudan, where there are site clusters associated with the Meroitic state and with the later Christian states of Nubia. Rather less certain in this respect is the high density of settlement sites in the Nigerian rain forest around Benin City. These sites contain evidence that might be interpreted as being related to the former state of Benin, in spite of the existence of similar high densities east of the Niger River, where the Ibo people do not seem to have developed a comparable centralized state. We enter the realms of the hypothetical, however, if we argue for the previous existence of a state of Zimbabwe solely on the basis of elegant computer studies of site distribution. It seems likely that it did exist, but to prove it is another matter.

When we look at the individual settlement sites rather than at a region as a whole, it is often apparent that some sites are bigger than others. Although most appear to be former villages, there are some whose size and density of occupation indicate that they were towns or cities. This does not necessarily imply the existence of a state, because the processes of urbanization and state formation are two different things. Nevertheless, they seem often to have been associated: the precolonial Hausa towns and cities of what is now northern Nigeria, for example, appear to have functioned at times as individual city-states, while the city of Harar in Ethiopia was described during the 19th century as quite separate from the countryside around it. In other cases, a major city became the nerve center from which a surrounding state was controlled. This appears to have been the role of Meroë in the Sudan and Koumbi-Saleh in Mauritania. Perhaps it is reasonable to infer that the archaeologically investigated city of Jenne-jeno, situated in an apparently densely occupied part of the Inland Niger Delta region of Mali, also functioned in one or another of these ways as early as the beginning of the 1st millennium A.D. Similarly, it seems quite possible that the early 2nd-millennium towns and cities

of the East African coastal region, in Kenya and Tanzania, were either governed as individual city-states or, in some cases, served as capitals for the regions in which they were situated. If we are to associate urbanization with the development of states in this way, then the earliest state in tropical Africa is likely to have been one of which Kerma, on the Middle Nile in the Sudan, may already have been the capital by the mid-2nd millennium B.C.

Over the last few thousand years, African settlements of all sizes have enclosed themselves by one means or another, primarily as a means of protection. In the case of towns and cities, stone or mud walls or earthen banks or timber stockades have much to tell us about the community that was thereby contained. First of all, a group of people who erect a barrier around themselves clearly see themselves as having a distinct identity, although they might also retain a close relationship with the surrounding region. This seems to have been the case, for instance, with the Hausa walled cities, and it is interesting to note that the cities of the East African coast were also walled, although in a far less ambitious manner. More importantly, however, the very existence of such defenses implies the presence of centralized direction, or at least of collective effort, in order to marshal labor and other resources to build what were essentially major public works. At Kano in Nigeria, for example, mud walls up to 15 meters high and nearly 18 kilometers in circumference could not have been constructed and maintained without considerable organization. The presence of such city walls is also indicative of political stress and the reality or threat of armed conflict, common enough features in the densely populated areas that were often the scene of state emergence. In addition, changes to the layout of a city-wall system may reflect the growing size and importance of the city itself and, therefore, of the state with which it was associated, as at Kano, Zaria, and Old Oyo, all in Nigeria. The changes may also reflect fluctuating fortunes through time, as at Ife, also in Nigeria. Indeed, in the Benin City area of Nigeria, the extraordinary network of enclosing structures or earthworks is so extensive and so complex that it could provide a direct record of the process of state development in addition to implying the growth of the city itself. Earthworks of this sort probably had more to do with the demarcation of land, for agricultural and other purposes, than with formal defense and (like many other enclosing structures) may also have had a role as status symbols. On the other side of Africa, in Uganda, Bigo and several other extensive earthwork enclosures may be comparable in these latter respects. However, African city walls, in the proper sense of the term, like African cities, have been around for a long time: the Nile city of Qasr Ibrim in the extreme south of Egypt was first walled in the late 11th or early 10th century B.C. and remained occupied until the early 19th century A.D., with its stone and mud-brick defenses being enlarged, strengthened, or repaired during the Ptolemaic, Roman, Christian, and Islamic periods.

City walls are not the only sort of monumental structures that may imply the former existence of a state. In the first half of the 1st millennium, for instance, the people of Aksum in Ethiopia quarried, transported, and erected tall granite obelisks weighing many hundreds of metric tons and constructed elite multistoried stone residences. Both activities indicate the existence of a centralized authority that is confirmed by written sources. Interestingly, the Aksumite cities were not surrounded by city walls, which suggests that this was a state whose power and isolation were sufficient protection. There are several other examples of monumental structures in tropical Africa. A group of buildings at the city of Meroë has been interpreted as a palace complex. There is evidence of elite domestic buildings at Gedi and Kilwa on the East African coast. The Bornu sites of Birnin Gazargamo and Gambaru in Nigeria include the remains of fired-brick structures. And the famous stone walls of Great Zimbabwe appear to have been high-status enclosures for the fine mud-built dwellings of the elite. Like city walls, all these structures imply centralized direction and control of resources, but most of them also show that some societies found it necessary to construct accommodations suitable for a ruling or, at least, a privileged class.

Burials may also provide evidence that suggests that state formation was in progress or that a society was beginning to move in that direction. This evidence can take two different forms. First, in some instances the apparent expenditure of resources on the interment of a particular individual, or on those of several individuals, was so much greater than was the case with other burials of the period that elite status is clearly indicated. Thus, at Meroë, in the early 1st millennium, the rulers and members of their families were placed in rock-cut tombs, whose locations were marked by stone or fired-brick pyramids. In Mali, early in the 2nd millennium, the elite people were buried beneath large earthen mounds such as that at El Qualedji. In Nigeria, at a date perhaps slightly earlier, the massive quantity of bronze and other grave goods associated with a seated burial at Igbo Ukwu could indicate the existence of a state that subsequently disappeared.

The second sort of burial evidence that hints at state development has a more macabre quality. In some instances, indications of large-scale human sacrifice suggest the presence of powerful authority and compelling religion. At Kerma in the 2nd millennium B.C., for instance, more than 300 people were sacrificed to accompany one of the elite burials, while at Ballana in southern Egypt, in the middle of the 1st millennium, sacrificed servants were neatly laid out as part of the grave goods needed by the deceased ruler and his wife in the next world. In Benin City, although human sacrifices are not known to have accompanied elite burials, the sacrifice of more than 40 young women dropped into a deep shaft is nevertheless suggestive of powerful authority by the early 2nd millennium.

Art can be another source of information on state development, both directly through its subject matter and indirectly by the implications of its existence. The best examples of its value in this respect are the remarkable bronzes from Benin City and Ife in Nigeria. In both cases, they include what appear to be portrait heads of precolonial rulers, those from Ife belonging to the first half of the 2nd millennium A.D. and those from Benin City being somewhat later. In Benin City, however, there are also a large number of bronze plaques, which appear to have provided a historical record and clearly depict a hierarchical and militaristic society in action. In addition, both Ife and Benin City bronzes imply the existence of powerful patronage, which was able not only to support the artists who produced them but to provide expensive raw materials that had to be obtained from distant locations, as well. As so often is the case, it was the nature of the patronage that dictated the character of the art.

Apart from artistic items, there are other things that might also be called *artifacts of power.* A number of iron objects, found in northwestern Tanzania, for instance, are known to have been insignia used by the rulers of the state of Karagwe during the 19th century. By analogy, iron bells, anvils, and ceremonial axes from Kisalian and related graves of 1,000 years earlier in southeastern Zaire might also suggest state development, in this case the emergence of the Luba kingdom.

However, some of the archaeological evidence for state development in tropical Africa is more directly informative. From Meroitic sites, for instance, have come actual inscriptions. Although the language in which they are written is still not understood, their very existence, as well as their general character, indicates that Meroitic society had reached a sophisticated level of complexity. Aksumite inscriptions of the early 1st millennium can be properly read and are consequently of even greater value. Several of them are attributable to the 4th-century King Ezana, and through them, an early African state can actually speak to us: "I will rule the people," he claims, "with righteousness and justice, and will not oppress them." Elsewhere and at other times, inscriptions were rare but played a bigger role than is sometimes realized. Greek was used along the Middle Nile until early in the 2nd millennium, and Arabic appeared from the first half of that millennium at East African coastal sites, as well as in the West African savanna and the adjacent Sahara.

Another type of evidence that might be overlooked is the development and use of formal currency. The Aksumite state struck its own coins in gold, silver, and copper, frequently depicting its kings. Some East African coastal cities also produced coins that carried the names of their rulers. In addition, other forms of currency used across large parts of Africa suggest a growing network of political authority. Examples include copper crosses in southeastern Zaire and neighboring areas and cowrie shells over much of West Africa.

The development of a variety of currencies in different parts of tropical Africa is indicative of the growing importance of trade over the last 2,000 years or so. There is abundant archaeological evidence of this growth. Closely related to increasing functional specialization within the societies concerned, trade is an indication that state development was in progress. It is, perhaps, no accident that so many scholars in the past have attributed the rise of African states to the external contacts resulting from long-distance trade, whether through the Sahara, down the Nile, or across the Indian Ocean. From the West African savanna to the East African coast, such trade clearly did have an important impact. Increasingly, however, archaeological evidence is suggesting that complex trading networks within tropical Africa are older than the external routes and that the origins of African state development are probably related to these internal systems rather than to any external influences. It seems likely that trade in certain basic commodities was especially important. Thus it could well have been the monopolization of trade in agricultural products, iron, copper, and salt that provided the economic underpinning of African state development. Once that development had taken place, the way was then clear for large-scale participation in international trade.

Obviously, the types of archaeological evidence for the development of states in sub-Saharan Africa vary greatly in their value. In particular, it would probably be unwise to single out any one of them and claim that it constituted irrefutable evidence that a state existed at a certain place at a certain time in the past. However, in cases where a broad range of such evidence exists, it is perhaps reasonable to make such an assumption. If one does this, it is then appropriate to ask to what extent archaeological evidence has informed us on the overall subject of African state development.

The emerging picture seems to be one in which the earliest states of tropical Africa appeared among societies along the Middle Nile between approximately 1,500 and 3,500 years ago. By the latter part of this period, similar developments had taken place in northern Ethiopia, and there are also indications of state formation in parts of the West African savanna between about 1,000 and 2,000 years ago. In the rain forest of West Africa, however, the first states appeared a little later, very roughly between 500 and 1,000 years ago. States may have formed on the East African coast, on the Zimbabwe Plateau, and in western Uganda and adjacent regions during the same period. This general picture of African state development is still chronologically inadequate and geographically incomplete. In the latter respect, for instance, archaeology has still not contributed anything substantial to our understanding of state development over a huge area of central Africa, where states such as Kongo or Loango appear in the historical record but remain archaeologically unknown. Nevertheless, in spite of these shortcomings, the evidence we do have suggests that states tended to develop in parts of Africa that had a rich resource base and a high-population density. Individuals who were able to take control of some crucial resource, such as well-watered land, cattle, copper, salt, or other trade commodities, thereby acquired power over their own societies, for whom they were able to provide some measure of conflict resolution. Problems inevitably arise, however, in deciding whether particular cases of such developments in the past actually constituted states in the proper sense of the word or were merely chiefdoms. Perhaps the best way of dealing with this difficulty is to recognize the possibility of a "gradient of centralization," as did the social anthropologist Jack Goody many years ago, when he suggested that "the nucleus of state systems can be discerned even among the lineages, age sets, cult associations, and other basic groupings of acephalous societies." By acephalous societies, he meant those that lacked even chiefs. If one follows this line of thought, then the study of state development in tropical Africa becomes less a matter of recognizing presence or absence, but rather a process of identifying points in a continuum.

BIBLIOGRAPHY

Connah, G. 1987. *African civilizations: Precolonial cities and states in tropical Africa.* Cambridge: Cambridge University Press.

Garlake, P. S. 1978. *The kingdoms of Africa.* Oxford: Elsevier-Phaidon.

Goody, J. 1963. Feudalism in Africa? *Journal of African History* 4: 1–18.

Lonsdale, J. 1981. States and social processes in Africa: A historiographical survey. *African Studies Review* 24: 39–225.

Munro-Hay, S. C. 1991. *Aksum: An African civilisation of late antiquity.* Edinburgh: Edinburgh University Press.

Shaw, T., P. Sinclair, B. Andah, and A. Okpoko, eds. 1993. *The archaeology of Africa: Food, metals and towns.* London: Routledge.

Welsby, D. A. 1996. *The Kingdom of Kush: The Napatan and Meroitic empires.* London: British Museum Press.

Graham Connah

URBANISM IN SUB-SAHARAN AFRICA

Our current understanding that urbanism was a phenomenon widespread in both space and time in sub-Saharan Africa dates largely to the postcolonial period.

In the colonial imagination, Africa was predominantly rural in character, composed of small, undifferentiated villages of mud and thatch huts. The idea of an indigenous urban tradition in Black Africa was not seriously considered, even by anthropologists studying the Yoruba of Nigeria, whose habit of living in large, densely populated, nucleated settlements clearly had considerable time depth. One of the main obstacles to the recognition of precolonial African urbanism was that all the conceptual tools available for investigating this topic had been developed with reference to Western sequences of historical development. The bulk of the ideas on what cities are and how they have changed through time dealt with European urban transformations from classical antiquity through the Middle Ages to the Industrial Revolution. Thus, many 19th- and early 20th-century attempts to define *urban* proceeded by constructing ideal types that identified essential features differentiating Western urban society from pre- or nonurban society. These were conceptualized as dichotomies: kin-based versus territorially based societies, *societas* (intimate, traditional village association) versus *civitas* (impersonal, contract-based urban association), mechanical solidarity (through shared common norms) versus organic solidarity (due to functional interdependence of, for example, craft specialists and farmers), and productive (rural, agrarian society) versus parasitic (urban aristocrats, bureaucrats, and military living off of rural production). The problem was that such formulations could not accommodate intermediate situations possessing characteristics of both types. Yoruba towns, for example, were organized strongly along lineage (kin) principles, had very few "parasitic," nonagricultural inhabitants, but had distinct, interdependent groups of craftsmen and merchants. Because they met some criteria but not others of the postulated urban-rural dichotomy, many anthropologists would not recognize even the largest Yoruba settlements as urban. The insistence by some scholars, such as sociologist Gideon Sjoberg and archaeologist V. G. Childe, that the presence of a literate elite was the single-best criterion for distinguishing cities from other types of settlement further excluded much of Black Africa from consideration.

Childe also included monumental architecture on his list for identifying cities, reflecting the long-standing association in the West of cities as centers of despotic power with impressive architecture reflecting such power. Theorists of urbanism were influenced by Old Testament images of the iniquities and oppression visited upon the pastoral Israelites by city-dwelling despots who employed corvée or slave labor to build vast edifices such as the Tower of Babel. It is now recognized that the building of monumental structures, while a strategy commonly employed by rulers of early city-states in Mesoamerica and Mesopotamia (among others), did not necessarily occur at all early urban centers. The Bronze Age cities of China, for example, had no monumental architecture. Despite this knowledge, archaeologists have persisted in their preference for studying sites with monuments, which helps explain the fascination with Great Zimbabwe as one of the relatively few sites with massive stone architecture in Black Africa.

Elsewhere in sub-Saharan Africa, particularly throughout the forest zone, urban sites tend to lack visually impressive monuments and stone-built architecture of any kind. Early sources reported that the capital of Kongo, first visited by the Portuguese in 1491, had a massive population (variously estimated in the 16th century between 50,000 and 100,000 people), all—including the king and his extended family—living in mud and thatch huts. Among the reasons for the lack of investment in stone-built monuments in much of sub-Saharan Africa are lack of suitable materials in some areas and the prevalence of extensive, slash-and-burn agricultural systems that required settlements to relocate after several decades. In many areas, the location of the capital city shifted with every accession of a new ruler. Ecological constraints linked to a value system that conceived of space as a social (rooted in kin groups and genealogical proximity) region, rather than as a particular physical place, produced African urban configurations that looked quite different from the cities of the West.

Because African towns and cities did not conform to concepts of urbanism derived from Western historical sequences, European observers failed to recognize them. This ethnocentric myopia had a deeper, more insidious ideological aspect, however. Europeans had long ago relegated Africans to the realm of the timeless primitive. Georg Wilhlem Friedrich Hegel, the early 19th-century philospher, declared that "Africa is no historical part of the world. It has no movement or development to exhibit. As we see the African peoples at this day, such have they always been. . . ."

A century later, Graham Clark, Disney Professor of Archaeology at Cambridge, echoed this sentiment in his 1969 *World Prehistory,* writing that for the last 10,000 to 15,000 years, much of Africa "remained a kind of cultural museum, without contributing much to the main course of progress."

When we recall that traditional theories of urbanism regarded cities as sources of innovation and social change, as centers from which civilization emerged and spread, it is clear why the possibility of an African urban tradition was denied. In areas where towns conforming to European expectation existed, such as the West African Sudanic zone and along the East African coast, they were attributed entirely to foreign colonization and trade with the Islamic world. It is only in the last 20 years that the dynamic indigenous tradition that helped shape these developments has been identified and appreciated.

The postcolonial period has seen a reorientation of research that has exposed the ethnographic assumptions and ideological underpinnings of many of the earlier theories of urbanism. Emphasis has shifted from what a city is (widely agreed to be a futile pursuit in view of the tremendous range of urban forms) to what a city does. We owe to geographers the important realization that urban centers never exist in isolation—they are always articulated with a regional hinterland. Whatever else a city may be, it is a unit of settlement that performs specialized functions in relation to a broader hinterland. The specialized functions may be of an economic nature, such as production and export of goods and services, or they have a more social aspect, such as the elaboration of power and new social institutions or the exchange of information. Urbanism thus represents a novel kind of relationship among sites in a region and involves the emergence of specialization and functional interdependence. This common structural factor unites in one urban category, for example, the 18-hectare Swahili site of Gedi and the 1,300-hectare site of Ife, holy city of the Yoruba people.

Gedi was tied into a trade network that linked the Indian Ocean and Red Sea to the East African mainland. Much of the agricultural produce that supported the merchant population of Gedi was grown by small hinterland settlements. Ife, like other Yoruba towns, had many kinds of craft specialists, from weavers to ironworkers and brass casters, who provided goods and services to people in the town and the wider region, in addition to the Oni, whose office represents specialized religious and political functions.

The symbiotic character of the urban system emerges out of the circulation of commodities essential to subsistence (food, iron used to produce food). Urban systems are based on exchanges of agricultural surplus. Their characteristic spatial format is a hierarchy of higher- and lower-order settlements. Higher-order sites are larger and more populous and fill a wider range of specialized functions than lower-order settlements.

The Archaeology of Urbanism in Tropical Africa

For reasons already mentioned, the archaeological study of early urban systems in tropical Africa is still in its infancy. Areas with highly visible, stone-built architecture or monuments have the longest histories of exploration, yet the tendencies of earlier archaeologists to focus exclusively on the most spectacular ruins have not answered many questions about the extent and nature of the larger urban system and its early, possibly premonumental, evolution. This is certainly the case for the earliest towns known in tropical Africa—Kerma, Napata, and Meroë—which emerged at successive points during the last two millennia B.C. as important trade centers on the Middle Nile. Excavation at the various Egyptian-inspired tombs, towers, and temples of these Nubian kingdoms began early in the 20th century. The spectacular stone stelae (carved or inscribed stone slabs used for commemorative purposes) of Aksum, located in the Ethiopian Highlands, attracted a German archaeological expedition in 1906. This group documented the monumental residential architecture, granite tombs, and stelae at a series of Aksumite settlements extending east to the Red Sea port of Adulis. Although these sites were generally rather small (20 hectares or less), they have abundant evidence of mercantile and religious specialization, confirmed by the reference to Askum as a *metropolis* by a 1st-century classical source. Despite considerable research in recent decades, the origins and role of foreign influences on the development of this extraordinary civilization are not yet well understood.

Trade was also instrumental in the development of the "Swahili" towns found on the East African coast and offshore islands from Somalia to Mozambique. Attention has shifted recently from the stone-built mosques, tombs, and houses to the "empty" areas that once held mud-and-thatch buildings and meticulous excavation of early levels containing no stone architecture. As a result, the development of these towns, once attributed solely to colonists from the Persian Gulf, now appears to have an important indigenous component due to the close interrelation of towns and villages.

A series of settlements with stone-built enclosures dominated the Zimbabwe Plateau region beginning in the 13th century. The granite in this region tended to exfoliate in thin slabs that could be easily broken into rectangles. This made it possible to create extremely regular walls without mortar. Both the regularity and the size of the walls, particularly at the largest site, Great Zimbabwe, led early explorers and white Rhodesians to suppose that these sites were built by foreign colonists (variously postulated to be Phoenicians or the Queen of Sheba), despite the evidence from numerous scientific excavations showing hut floors and artifacts very similar to those of the Shona people in the area today. Persian bowls and Near Eastern glass dating to the 13th and 14th centuries, as well as Chinese ceramics, have been recovered from Great Zimbabwe, attesting to its involvement in coastal trade networks, likely exchanging ivory and gold from nearby placers. Estimates of the Great Zimbabwe's population range from 1,000 to 18,000 people. Without much more extensive excavations away from the stone enclosures housing the elite, it will be impossible to narrow this range. While it appears likely that Great Zimbabwe was an emerging urban center, research aimed at investigating the functional links between Great Zimbabwe and its hinterland will be necessary to evaluate this more fully.

The elaborate royal enclosures that dominate Great Zimbabwe exemplify a common pattern in African central places throughout the Bantu world and beyond. At the center of these settlements was the king's ritual power and sanctity, symbolized by the prominence of the king's residence, which was often set apart from other compounds by a wall. The central palace was the core feature of the Black African city, in much the same way the central business district was of the 19th-century American city or the temple was to the Near Eastern city. The absence of separate temple complexes in non-Islamic Black Africa is noteworthy. The central-palace principle structured the capitals of the Kongo, the Yoruba, the

Asante, and the interlacustrine kingdoms of Buganda and Rwanda. Much of what is known of these centers comes from historical sources and oral traditions. Very little, if any, of the archaeological research necessary to understand the emergence of urban systems in these areas has yet been undertaken.

In the Sudan of West Africa, archaeological research has overturned earlier assumptions that the installation of North African and Arabo-Berber traders in stone-built trade centers in the southern Sahara (by A.D. 900) provided the necessary stimulus for urban growth to the south. Excavation and survey at the vast mound of Jenne-jeno along the Middle Niger in Mali revealed the site's growth to over 30 hectares as the center of a tight cluster of more than 40 mounds by A.D. 800. The functional interdependence of these mounds was indicated by surface distributions of iron-smithing debris and fishing equipment that were restricted to only a few of the sites within the cluster. Interregional trade in local staples for raw materials such as stone and iron, unavailable on the floodplain, appears to have fueled this growth. The population of the entire urban cluster is estimated to have been between 10,000 and 25,000 people. R. J. McIntosh has suggested that clustered, functionally integrated settlements such as these may have been a common form of early urbanism in Africa, as well as China, in cases where a powerful centralized authority had not yet emerged. This idea flies in the face of the received wisdom that views urbanism as a manifestation of the state. But as we have seen already, many aspects of urbanism that were once claimed to be universal proved to be specific to Western historical experience. Archaeological studies of urbanism in Africa thus hold tremendous promise for broadening our understanding of the forms and circumstances of early urban development.

BIBLIOGRAPHY
Connah, G. 1987. *African civilizations: Pre-colonial cities and states in tropical Africa.* Cambridge: Cambridge University Press.
Coquery-Vidrovitch, C. 1991. The process of urbanization in Africa: From the origins to the beginning of independence. *African Studies Review* 34: 1–98.

Davidson, B. 1959. *The lost cities of Africa.* Boston: Little, Brown.

Hull, R. 1976. *African cities and towns before the European conquest.* New York: Norton.

McIntosh, R. J. 1991. Early urban clusters in China and Africa. *Journal of Field Archaeology* 18: 199–212.

McIntosh, S. K., and R. J. McIntosh. 1984. The early city in Africa: Toward an understanding. *African Archaeological Review* 2: 302–319.

Wheatley, P. 1972. The concept of urbanism. In *Man, settlement and urbanism,* eds. P. J. Ucko, R. Tringham, and G. W. Dimbleby, 601–637. London: Duckworth.

Winters, C. 1983. The classification of traditional African cities. *Journal of Urban History* 10: 3–31.

Susan Keech McIntosh

EGYPT AND SUB-SAHARAN AFRICA: THEIR INTERACTION

The relationship between Egypt and sub-Saharan Africa has been a difficult subject for archaeology and Egyptology. Unlike the cultures of western Asia, which provide a continuous synchronic matrix of interrelated high cultures across the whole region, Egypt, for the period of its ancient greatness (about 4000 B.C. to A.D. 300), was a lonely eminence of concentrated monumentality on the African continent, with the kingdoms of Nubia and Sudan as her only other native companions in scale. In the past, attempts to explore Egypt's involvement with her own continent had to rely on vague, sometimes contradictory, and often fantastic accounts of Greeks or on comparisons with sometimes unreliable reports of current conditions, none of them filling the scholar's perceived need for a dense network of contemporary evidence. As a result, most scholars avoided the subject, and some, noting the lack of evidence, even denied that the relationship was significant. However, in recent decades, political movements gave energy to the question. Major, detailed epigraphic and archaeological exploration of the Sahara, archaeological research in central Africa, and well-documented studies of modern peoples offer new opportunities to examine the relationship between Egypt and sub-Saharan Africa with greater confidence in the results. Nevertheless, there are large gaps in the evidence of all types, and many different opinions will have to be tried and discarded before some prove durable.

Although Egypt is now separated from sub-Saharan Africa geographically by a huge expanse of desert and culturally by large areas dominated by Arabic-speaking peoples, neither condition prevailed throughout ancient times. During Egypt's formative ages, the Sahara was not truly a desert, while the Nile Valley and Red Sea Hills provided well-watered routes for trade and migration at all periods.

The Aqualithic (Early Neolithic) Age

Before the Neolithic era, episodes of extremely hostile climatic conditions left long gaps in Egypt's cultural record. The beginning of continuous occupation was the early Neolithic era. This time period saw the widespread appearance of two cultural types, the multibarbed bone harpoon, which appears in the Paleolithic era in central Africa, and pottery bowls and jars decorated with impressed patterns of dotted, wavy lines. An independent development in Africa, this pottery appeared almost as far west as the Atlantic along the southern fringes of what is now the Sahara and spread north along the Nile. The harpoon spread similarly but much farther north along the Nile and reached into Palestine. It is not always easy to connect deeper cultural life with practical artifacts, but this was also the era when rock drawings in the so-called round-head style first spread across the Sahara, probably reaching the parts of Egypt where sandstone outcrops make rock art possible. The rock art does not give detailed records, but it does clearly indicate that important cultural links spread across the continent.

The Nubian and the Taso-Badarian Cultures

The culture of Egypt as we understand it emerged in Upper (southern) Egypt during the Nagada period. Its cultural forebears actually appeared in Upper Egypt somewhat earlier, in the Tasian and Badarian cultures. In some significant aspects of culture, such as pottery, Egypt maintained important relations with Nubia and Sudan, directly to the south. Vessels with rippled surfaces, produced by burnishing a rocker-incised vessel with a pebble, appear in both places made in related shapes. A distinctive tulip-shaped vessel with incised and white-filled decoration also appeared in Upper Egypt and Sudan. Both of these features could be considered Sudanese. Some other objects, including palettes and the harpoons, were also probably of Sudanese origin, but the culture of Upper Egypt already differed from Sudan. Some differences may have been due to contact with the cultures of northern Egypt and the Libyan Desert (which was not a desert at the time), but others appear to have been due to internal development. Among these are coffin burials and animal representations on ivory spoons and pendants, both significant developments in symbolic life. Nevertheless, Upper Egypt continued to share traditions with Sudan, such as the deposit of rich property in burials, including female figurines, which did not characterize northern Egypt.

The Nagada Period

The Nagada period, called, misleadingly, the *predynastic period,* represented a vast expansion and elaboration of material culture in almost every sphere and was a clear outgrowth of the preceding cultures in Upper Egypt. Internal coherence, sophistication, and wealth in the Nagada period were such that new ideas and influences from the south were often difficult to detect. By the start of the 1st Dynasty, elements appeared that can be traced into specific hieroglyphic form in Egypt. Rock drawings include boats that later appear as the sacred conveyance of Egypt's pharaohs and gods. Humans and animals appear in hunting scenes in Saharan rock art in its earlier hunting or round-head style. Some art in early Egypt included composite figures of animal-headed humans, common images in the Sahara. Some southern pottery types do exist, and some burials with distinctive shell-hook ornaments may belong to persons from Lower Nubia, the region between Aswan and the Second Cataract.

At this time, and until the coming of Islam, the area south of Aswan, at least, may be considered part of sub-Saharan Africa, and it was here that the first influences of Egypt on the south appear. The civilization of Egypt, even in this early phase, can be considered Nilotic, and its specific influence was almost always confined to the valley and adjacent regions. In the early, Nagada I period, Egyptian pottery and objects were deposited in Nubian-style round graves just south of Aswan. These objects are convincingly at home, and they were accompanied, as this culture spread southward, by rock drawings that included ships of the same types as found in Upper Egypt. The culture, the A-Group, became more and more distinct from the Nagada culture as it expanded southward, absorbing ideas from the Sudanese cultures nearby, but it nonetheless participated strongly in the development of Nagada period culture and symbolism. (The cultural labels *A-Group, B-Group,* and so on reflect archaeologists' perception of distinct and discrete cultural assemblages with traits that occur at particular times and places and that distinguish them from other groupings.) Nagada symbolism included the first pharaonic images—images that indicate that the office of pharaoh preceded the 1st Dynasty by some centuries. The earliest evidence of pharaonic figures is rare, but the ships that are a major part of the symbolism are not, and it is no surprise that in the late Nagada period, one of the places where pharaohs were buried was near the southern end of Lower Nubia. Although Qustul shared this distinction with Hierakonpolis, Nagada, Abydos, and probably a few other places in Upper Egypt, there is evidence that the Qustul kingdom was united as far north as Aswan, and perhaps farther, making it the most geographically extensive of the group. It even remains possible that the dynasts (rulers) who ultimately united Egypt were Nubian. There were some Nubian pottery vessels in Upper Egypt at this time, and some A-Group tombs can be identified, one of them of royal type.

The Archaic Period and the Old Kingdom

At the beginning of the 1st Dynasty, Pharaoh Aha claimed the smiting of Ta Seti (Nubia), and settlement all but disappeared in Nubia's northern regions for several centuries. Adopting an apparent antisettlement policy in Sinai and perhaps southern Palestine as well as Nubia, Egypt was effectively isolated, except for overseas contacts with Punt (the Horn of Africa) and the coast of Asia. This did not mean the diminution of Egypt's African substratum, but an elaboration and intense refinement that accompanied the unprecedented concentration of wealth and power in the Egyptian state. When Egypt again confronted its neighbors in Africa directly, it was on dramatically different ground.

At this point, some word about the African substratum is appropriate. As different as a 4th Dynasty pharaoh and a rain king in modern-day southern Sudan might appear, they faced much the same situation. A man who incarnates a god is responsible for maintaining a harmonious relationship between the world of human action and the world of the divine, which controls the forces of nature. As he is more or less successful in this task, so goes his career. His rule is not automatically stable, since it depends, for example, on a productive natural cycle, so success might found a dynasty, while failure would reveal that the incarnation had moved on to others. The latter is sooner or later inevitable. The one great difference between the incarnations of Sudan and Egypt was that in Sudan the incarnations are primarily concerned with rain, while in Egypt the flood was paramount. Some peoples in Sudan have incarnations of spirits that specialize in different types of problems, while in Egypt, the pharaoh was the center of divine activity. To him fell the duty of controlling chaos—relating with the gods through the cult, controlling the animals through mass hunts (the same as campaigns), and defeating enemies and rebels, executing their leaders, hacking up their towns and lands, leading the people off to captivity, and, finally, ensuring the arrival of tribute.

Egypt's historical records of contacts with southern lands before the end of the 5th Dynasty are few, and they mostly mention campaigns or raids in the dry and compact style of early Egyptian annals. The Egyptians must have feared some power in the south, because they substantially fortified their southernmost city, on Elephantine Island. One significant archaeological find, at Buhen near Wadi Halfa, was a group of fortified factories or workshops for working metal. Seal impressions at the site indicate that many items were imported from Egypt, but there was also local pottery, resembling that of the A-Group produced hundreds of years earlier. Still, it is fair to say that the era contemporary with Egypt's archaic and Old Kingdom periods is poorly represented archaeologically in Nubia and even deeper in Sudan. However, this condition can be deceptive, for much archaeological knowledge depends on pottery, which can be abandoned by mobile people in favor of gourds, baskets, and leather containers, which are light, strong, and capable of being impressively decorated.

By the beginning of the 6th Dynasty, possibly as early as the mid-5th, all this changed. Nubia, at least as far as Dongola and possibly as far south as Khartoum, was intensively resettled, most likely from the south and west. Nubians quickly entered Egyptian service, primarily as soldiers, but they also rapidly founded several principalities or kingdoms on the Nile south of Aswan. These polities are readily recognizable as an African cattle culture, for they often represented cattle in a way that indicated special honor, their tombs frequently contain cowhide garments and wrappings, and cattle horns were deposited with burials. Sometimes at Kerma in the Dongola Reach, important persons had the skulls of hundreds of cattle ringing their tumuli (mound-type graves). The culture of this period has other inner-African characteristics, such as tumulus burials surrounded by stone rings, leather garments decorated with geometric patterns of beads, and black polished pottery with incised designs. Important Nubian features, which must have survived without durable expression in tombs and pottery, continued traditions known in the A-Group, and Nubia rapidly became important to Egypt, and vice versa.

Two groups of Egyptian documents are coupled with this rapid archaeological emergence. The more colorful are a series of tomb biographies of the Egyptian governors of Aswan who were charged with control of the southern lands. These record armed caravans that passed through the emerging kingdoms to trade with the most southern countries known, possibly Punt.

They sometimes acted in a high-handed manner, and the princes closest to the Egyptian frontier were sometimes tributary. However, Nubians who went to Egypt became important enough there to be feared, and some 177 of them were cursed in ritual texts. The traffic between Nubia and Egypt already flowed in both directions, but it was in the next period that Nubia's influence became most obvious.

The First Intermediate Period and the Middle Kingdom

By the First Intermediate Period, Nubians deeply penetrated Egyptian life, most prominently as soldiers but also as administrators. At least one Nubian cemetery is known north of Aswan, at Wadi Kubbaniya. Some women rose high in the Theban court during the 11th Dynasty, and the ruler they served, Mentuhotep I, may himself have had a Nubian background. There were some cultural contributions from the south. Women with Nubian-style tattoos were found buried in tombs of good quality and prominent position at Thebes. Chapel paintings at Beni Hasan depict men wrestling in a situation so prominent that a symbolic, rather than merely sporting, purpose is implied, perhaps akin to the wrestling customs of the modern Nuba. These are details, as is the thin man who has a big shock of woolly hair and is shown leading cattle to the owners of tombs at Beni Hasan and Meir. This figure is probably also a Nubian. The difficulty of identifying influences from Nubia, or elsewhere in Africa, is intensified by twin problems: the cultures were closely related enough that innovations from the south appear imperceptibly merged into Egyptian life, and Egypt's vast cultural apparatus rapidly overwhelmed influences from its related neighbors.

The same was not true of Egyptian objects and ideas in the south. Egyptian products had become so distinctive and urbane that they normally stand out from the simpler items produced even by sophisticated cultures elsewhere. Thus beads of Egyptian manufacture appear in large numbers of C-Group tombs in Lower Nubia, and beads of precious metal fashioned into virtually perfect rings appear far more often than in Egypt,

reflecting, perhaps, the high rewards of a military career in the north. In some of the richer Nubian cemeteries, there are more elaborate objects, mostly jewelry, and sometimes even stelae (carved or inscribed stone slabs used for commemorative purposes). These were always associated with C-Group tumuli, but there is evidence of even greater influence. A number of inscriptions carved on the rocks record two pharaohs with names characteristic of the period. A third pharaoh, who once called himself Son of Re, had a Nubian personal name. Since he recorded a battle in the north of his kingdom, he must have fought some Egyptians, but he nevertheless used Egyptian titles in an Egyptian way, which shows he had an Egyptian court.

The bidirectional communication was perhaps emphasized by the birth of the founder of the 12th Dynasty to a woman from Nubia or Aswan. Amenemhat rose to the vizierate under the last pharaoh of the 11th Dynasty, whom he ultimately replaced. For important political reasons, however, he moved the government back from Thebes to Memphis, and the south was, for a time, eclipsed. His successors embarked on a career of expansion in Nubia. Fortresses were built to keep the population of northern Nubia under control and those outside away. Migration into Egypt, which had filled private armies with capable southern soldiers, was severely restricted. All of this took place in part because Egypt wanted ready access to resources in the north. However, more important was the rise of a considerable southern power, Kush (or Cush). The rise of this power and the Egyptians it employed illustrate a major mode by which Egypt influenced its neighbors, in Africa and outside.

As shown in the records or representations of every era, Egyptian administrators used elements of force and exaction. They invited strangers from outside to serve the Egyptian powers in their various projects. At the same time, they encouraged Egyptians to seek their fortunes in freer, but possibly more hazardous, climes. From some records, it is clear that many expatriates had skills confined to cultivation, but others included professionals, such as the soldier Sinuhe, who fled to Asia, and ship captains, who worked at Kerma, the capital of Kush, in Sudan. Also at

Kerma, metalworkers erected a great box-shaped oven with subterranean fire boxes and long flues, part of a large and complex metal factory located in front of the main temple of the city. The skills these metallurgical craftsmen brought from Egypt later provided Kerma with some of its most impressive objects, some of military significance. Late in the Middle Kingdom, this outpouring of skill and population so enhanced the wealth and power of western Asia and Sudan that immigration to Egypt was again common, and ultimately, Egypt fell under the domination of these powers.

The Asiatic invaders of the 17th and 16th centuries B.C., the Hyksos, have received most of the attention, but Kushites, centered on Kerma in Sudan, conquered Lower Nubia as far as Aswan and allied themselves with the Hyksos. Egyptians remained in charge of the old fortress communities in northern Nubia, where they even acknowledged the Kushite ruler as a pharaoh on their monuments. There is reason to believe that the Kermans shared this attitude toward their ruler, for he was otherwise surrounded by attributes of the pharaonic office, although his tomb was a tumulus and his temples were heavy brick towers with small chambers that seem almost to be artificial caves. Other Nubians, the Medjay, entered Egyptian service, and their distinctive pottery and burials are known almost as far north as the Nile Delta. The pottery occurs commonly in all debris of the period. Egypt, dominated politically by Asiatics and Nubians, not surprisingly displayed many new foreign features in the early New Kingdom.

The New Kingdom

The expulsion of the Asiatic invaders of Egypt also entailed the reconquest of northern Nubia by the start of the 18th Dynasty. The rulers of Kush, who had been begged by their Hyksos ally to strike at Egypt, found themselves hard-pressed, for Egypt, reversing a long-standing policy of avoiding far-flung conquest, conquered and absorbed Kush as far as the Fourth Cataract of the Nile. The Egyptians made use of both their own administrators and subordinate local rulers, but they came to impose more and more of the temple-based economy that dominated Upper Egypt. While Kushites went north primarily to present tribute to the Egyptian court or to serve as pages, Egypt entered into its greatest age of direct influence on southern regions. With the temple estates came large temples and temple towns, often dedicated to Nubian aspects of Egyptian deities. Most prominent of these was the Amun-Re of Napata, whose temple was located just before the huge rock of Gebel Barkal, in which he was thought to reside.

Although the people of Nubia hardly disappeared, the Egyptian influence was so strong that burial and religious practices appear Egyptian. On the other hand, there were a number of new influences from Nubia, including, perhaps, even some imagery of the national god Amun-Re, newly prominent after centuries of limited recognition. In addition, early New Kingdom rulers have been connected with Nubia by some scientists, but among the other imports, the famous blue crown of New Kingdom rulers closely resembles a beaded miter crown once used in Cameroon. If it was an import, its symbolic importance would link the pharaonic office with the more recent rulers in southern Sudan. Another detail of symbolic importance from Nubia was the golden fly amulet, which became an Egyptian military decoration. In other cases, Egypt served as a conduit for spreading innovations from outside Africa more widely across the continent. For example, the horse-drawn chariot, a light car with four spoked wheels and pulled by two horses, is first clearly seen on stelae from the shaft graves at Mycenae. It is mentioned by Kamose and depicted in a rock drawing from Lower Nubia with a figure who carries an ax of late 17th Dynasty type. Pictures of the same type of vehicle and showing horses at a flying gallop, spread across the Sahara as far as Tassili-n-Ajjer. The occurrence of chariot tracks confirms the vehicle's prevalence and widespread distribution. This influence rebounded on Egypt when Libyans, in the late New Kingdom, attacked the Nile Delta using chariots of Egyptian type. Such a prominently displayed institution as chariotry must represent some influence on other aspects of life as well. The chariot remained important in the central Sahara, particularly among the

Garamantes of Fezzan down into Roman times when their quadrigae (chariots drawn by four horses abreast) were famous.

The Kushite Centuries

At the end of the 2nd millennium and the beginning of the 1st, new powers rose to the south of the ancient world's fertile regions. Midian and South Arabia to the east, Kush along the Nile, and Garma in Fezzan emerged to mediate trade between the economic powers near the Mediterranean—the Fertile Crescent, Egypt, and Carthage—and regions to the south.

At the beginning of this period, Nubia fell away from Egyptian rule after its last viceroy, himself apparently a Nubian, intervened in the government of the high priest of Amun-Re in Upper Egypt. Although the adjacent regions of Africa are almost unknown in the centuries between 1100 and 900 B.C., once Nubia emerged again culturally and historically, it rose rapidly to lead Egypt to a new era of greatness. The first written records show us Pharaoh Piye on the march north of Thebes to settle the scandalously disordered state of Egypt and restore the proper regime of Amun-Re. Preceded by four generations of rulers interred under Nubian tumuli, he was buried under a pyramid, a type of tomb that was no longer used in Egypt. His burial in this way shows, first, that the Kushites viewed the pyramid as the equivalent of a tumulus and, second, the manner by which Kushites incorporated Egyptian culture into their civilization. Piye and his successors were in many respects Egyptian in dress and religion. They wrote in Egyptian but kept their Kushite names, mode of succession, and elements of dress or regalia. They had an especially high regard for horses, which were sacred to the sun god Re in Kush. Although they set up or restored pharaonic institutions, such as temples and nomes, in Kush, they clearly did so in a spirit of adaptation. In Egypt, they were regarded well enough that most of the country supported them against Assyria, although the Libyan-dominated north was often in revolt. However, the Assyrians prevailed, and Taharqo, the great builder, and his successor, Tanutamani, were finally driven from Egypt.

In their brief century of rule in Egypt, the Kushites had not merely pushed the country toward greatness, they had truly renewed pharaonic culture in Sudan. In a bold geographic initiative, they expanded the culture across a barren desert to the Isle of Meroë. There Kushite civilization blossomed in the last centuries B.C. with monumental cities scattered well away from the Nile. Kushite civilization became the key source of "Egyptian" influence in sub-Saharan Africa at that time.

The greatest city of Kush was Meroë, with a great royal walled compound, temples, pyramid cemeteries, and even a nymphaeum (public fountain and pool) and observatory. It also contained a thriving iron industry, one of the oldest in Africa, which may have played an important role in the spread of ironworking in the continent. The Meroites developed a method of gathering water into reservoirs for irrigation that is used in Sudan to this day. Although Meroitic culture preserved its pharaonic heritage and even imported some new fashions from Egypt, it increasingly went its own way, with new styles in art, local deities, and its own written language. Although its political power seems to have been concentrated along the Nile in the Dongola Reach and near the Nile in the Isle of Meroë just north of Khartoum, Meroitic goods and some influence—in both directions—can be traced at least as far south as Gebel Moya and Senaar in Sudan and as far east as Aksum.

At the end of the Meroitic period, in the 4th century A.D., the Isle of Meroë and the Nile Valley far to the north fell under the control of the Noba-Noubadians, people whose nearest relations are in Darfur. They returned to many non-Egypto-Kushite ideas and practices but used many Meroitic items and elements and adapted crowns and weapons to a new style. At least the weapon, a great, swordlike spear, continued in use, through various modifications, to become the spear of southern Sudan and the lion spear of the Maasai.

General Themes

Relations between Egypt and Africa were mediated on the Nile side by the peoples of Kush.

In the Eastern Desert, the Medjay (Bedja) separated Egypt from inland Punt, while on the Red Sea, the Puntites were the contact point for Egypt with the Horn of Africa and perhaps the coast beyond the Straits of Hormuz. Egypt, despite the contracted circumnavigation of the continent by Phoenician sailors for Psammetichos, pharaoh in the 7th century B.C., did not attempt to reach central Africa until the 1820s, but it initiated wider contacts than most African states before the Middle Ages, and they were certainly more wide ranging than the contacts of such famous entities as the Kongo kingdom, the Asante, and the Zulu.

Scattered through Egyptian history were periods when Egypt had particularly intense contacts with her neighbors in Africa, which included Punt on the Horn. In addition to the phases of contact and individual items of interchange, some objects and representations in Egypt have strong similarities in sub-Saharan Africa. In most cases, it is difficult to decide when the item was exchanged or how. Nevertheless, a number of elements, such as musical instruments, certain weapons, and ritualized contests, are similar enough to postulate that they originated in Egypt, sub-Saharan Africa, or someplace between, but that they could not have had a completely independent origin or one outside the continent. Future research may show that other elements—the composite beings of Saharan and Egyptian art, sacred sites and structures, including tumuli and pyramids, and decorated rock faces or clefts and Egyptian rock stelae and temples—also have a close relationship.

A major problem in tracing the flow of influence between Egypt and sub-Saharan Africa is that despite insistent attempts to prove the identity of some aspects of Egypt with some aspects found far across the continent, the cultural matrices are not mutually coherent. Relationships exist on a relatively diffused level, elements passed through many intermediaries, and some elements derived from traditions of remote origin, possibly in the Neolithic Sahara. Closer at hand, we can see actual relations more convincingly. If we accept the cultures of Neolithic Sudan as sub-Saharan, they played a strong, and possibly decisive, part in the original development of Egypt. In the 3rd mil-

lennium B.C., new cultures of sub-Saharan type came to dominate the Nile from the Fourth Cataract to Aswan and played a significant role in Egypt down to about 1600 B.C. Finally, Kush, in the 1st millennium B.C., may have had an immediate origin near the Nile, but the ancient Sudanese sub-Saharan culture was visible in its early phases and became more pronouced as the center moved to Meroë, which is almost as far south as Tombouctou.

The period when sub-Saharan Africa was most influential in Egypt was a time when neither Egypt, as we understand it culturally, nor the Sahara, as we understand it geographically, existed. Populations and cultures now found south of the desert roamed far to the north. The culture of Upper Egypt, which became dynastic Egyptian civilization, could fairly be called a Sudanese transplant. Egypt rapidly found a method of disciplining the river, the land, and the people to transform the country into a titanic garden. Egypt rapidly developed detailed cultural forms that dwarfed its forebears in urbanity and elaboration. Thus, when new details arrived, they were rapidly adapted to the vast cultural superstructure already present. On the other hand, pharaonic culture was so bound to its place near the Nile that its huge, interlocked religious, administrative, and formal structures could not be readily transferred to relatively mobile cultures of the desert, savanna, and forest. The influence of the mature pharaonic civilizations of Egypt and Kush was almost confined to their sophisticated trade goods and some significant elements of technology. Nevertheless, the religious substratum of Egypt and Kush was so similar to that of many cultures in southern Sudan today that it remains possible that fundamental elements derived from the two high cultures to the north live on.

BIBLIOGRAPHY

Adam, S., with the collaboration of J. Vercoutter. 1981. The importance of Nubia: A link between central Africa and the Mediteranean. In *UNESCO general history of Africa,* vol. 2, ed. G. Mokhtar, 226–244. Berkeley: University of California Press.

Camps, G. 1982. Beginnings of pastoralism and cultivation in north-west Africa and the Sahara: Origins of the Berbers. In *The Cambridge history of Africa,* vol. 1, ed. J. D. Clark, 548–623. Cambridge: Cambridge University Press.

Debono, F. 1981. Prehistory in the Nile Valley. In *UNESCO general history of Africa,* vol. 1, ed. J. Ki-Zerbo, 634–655. Berkeley: University of California Press.

Hakem, A. A., with the collaboration of I. Hrbek and J. Vercoutter. 1981. The civilization of Napata and Meroë. In *UNESCO general history of Africa,* vol. 2, ed. G. Mokhtar, 198–325. Berkeley: University of California Press.

Kemp, B. J. 1982. Old Kingdom, Middle Kingdom and Second Intermediate Period in Egypt. In *The Cambridge history of Africa,* vol. 1. ed. J. D. Clark, 658–769. Cambridge: Cambridge University Press.

Kendall, T. 1989. Ethnoarchaeology in Meroitic studies. *Meroitica* 10: 625–745.

Leclant, J. 1981. The empire of Kush: Napata and Meroë. In *UNESCO general history of Africa,* vol. 2, ed. G. Mokhtar, 278–297. Berkeley: University of California Press.

Mauny, R. 1978. Trans-Saharan contacts and the Iron Age in West Africa. In *The Cambridge history of Africa,* vol. 2, ed. J. D. Fage, 272–341. Cambridge: Cambridge University Press.

O'Connor, D. 1982. Egypt, 1552–664 B.C. In *The Cambridge history of Africa,* vol. 1. ed. J. D. Clark, 830–940. Cambridge: Cambridge University Press.

Sherif, N. M. 1981. Nubia before Napata (- 3100 to - 750). In *UNESCO general history of Africa,* vol. 2, ed. G. Mokhtar, 245–277. Berkeley: University of California Press: 245-77.

Shinnie, P. L. 1978. The Nilotic Sudan and Ethiopia. In *The Cambridge history of Africa,* vol. 2, ed. J. D. Fage, 210–271. Cambridge: Cambridge University Press.

Vercoutter, J. 1981. Discovery and diffusion of metals and development of social systems up to the fifth century before our era. In *UNESCO general history of Africa,* vol. 1, ed. J. Ki-Zerbo, 706–729. Berkeley: University of California Press.

Yoyotte, J. 1981. Pharaonic Egypt: Society, economy and culture. In *UNESCO general history of Africa,* vol. 2, ed. G. Mokhtar, 112–135. Berkeley: University of California Press.

Zayed, A. H., with the collaboration of J. Devisse. 1981. Egypt's relations with the rest of Africa. In *UNESCO general history of Africa,* vol. 2, ed. G. Mokhtar, 136–154. Berkeley: University of California Press

Bruce Williams

EGYPT: EMERGENCE OF STATE SOCIETY

Nation-states are now a dominant feature of the global cultural landscape. They are political units that claim sovereignty and command the allegiance of masses of peoples in the name of nationalism, an ideology of recent origin. Nation-states emerged in the past as unions of peoples from different cultural backgrounds through alliances or conquest. In England and France, the early nation-state dates to the unification by Saxon and Frankish kings, respectively, in the early Middle Ages. Modern nation-states emerged within the context of expanding commerce and industrialization during the 18th century. In Egypt, record of a nation-state dates to about 5,000 years ago. According to an ancient Egyptian tradition, northern Egypt (the Nile Delta or Lower Egypt) and southern Egypt (Upper Egypt) were unified by a warrior king (Narmer). A ceremonial palette showing Narmer smiting an enemy, is often interpreted as a historical document of the unification of Egypt. However, recent investigations reveal that the unification was a protracted process and that parts of the Nile Delta were not under the rule of Narmer. It has also become evident that the course of state formation may be traced back to the herders of the Sahara approximately 2,000 years before unification. There is also new evidence that documents the evolution of several state societies in Upper Egypt from smaller political units or chiefdoms.

In attempting to understand the process of political developments that led to the rise of the state, we ought to keep in mind that we depend on archaeological remains as well as textual and iconographic data. Writing emerged perhaps about 3200 B.C. However, Egyptian records that relate to the rise of the state are not historical documents of actual events. In dealing with both archaeological and textual evidence, we cannot avoid making interpretative inferences. In addition, both archaeological remains and texts have been selectively preserved. Archaeologists also may investigate only certain remains using certain analytical methods. For example, until recently, information on predynastic Egypt was derived from cemeteries. There was very little interest in the economic basis of predynastic societies, and discussions of political evolution were, in general, speculative.

Many scholars have singled out trade, warfare, population pressure, irrigation, or technological developments as the primary causes of the rise of the Egyptian state. In this article, the rise of the Egyptian state, a complex cultural phenomenon, is regarded as a sequential development in successive stages. Different variables, as an ensemble, were influential in each stage. The cultural developments in each stage provided a point of departure for the people who came afterwards. The key variables that influenced the course of state formation were fluctuations in rainfall and Nile floods, farming and herding, political organization, demographic changes, and religion. Although environmental parameters and food production stimulated the earliest forms of political units, the institution of divine kingship, together with its central role in cultural affairs, marked the rise of a unified Egyptian state.

Chronology

The earliest evidence for farming communities in the Nile Valley dates to 4800 B.C. at Merimda Beni Salama in the western Nile Delta. This community was followed at the same sites by components dating to 4600 B.C. and 4400 B.C. In the Fayum Depression, early settlements assigned to the Neolithic era on the basis of similarities with Merimda (although evidence for farming is lacking) date to about 5200 B.C., but Late Neolithic sites there date to 4000 B.C. In Upper Egypt, the earliest farming communities date to slightly earlier than 4000 B.C. The type locality for these settlements is in the Badari region in the neighborhood of Assyut. The sites contain a ceramics sequence referred to as the *Badarian*. Ceramics are also used to identify two successive ceramic-assemblage zones: Nagada I (or Amratian, dating to 3750 B.C. at Nagada near Qena) and Nagada II (or Gerzean, dating to 3425 B.C. at South Town in Nagada and to 3550 B.C. at Hierakonpolis farther south). A final predynastic ceramic-assemblage zone is tentatively dated to between 3300 and 3000 B.C.).

From 3600 to 3300 B.C., the emerging cult and urban centers were probably associated with chiefdoms, principalities, provincial petty states, and village corporate organizations. From 3300 B.C. onward, polities in both Upper Egypt and the Nile Delta were united into regional kingdoms, culminating with the unification of most of Egypt into a single nation-state. The beginning of dynastic Egypt is considered to be coincident with the rule of Narmer, who is sometimes identified with another royal personage—Menes. Other kings, such as the Scorpion King and Sekhen or Ka and most probably many other unidentified kings, preceded Narmer. Between 3300 and 3000 B.C., powerful kingdoms emerged in Lower and Upper Egypt, and it now appears that the unification of several of these kingdoms preceded the final unification. Among these kingdoms were Nekhen (Hierakonpolis), which united with Nagada in Upper Egypt, and Buto, which combined with Saïs in the delta.

Unions between 3100 and 2800 B.C. were perhaps fragile and may not have encompassed a few pockets of resistance. Once the whole country was unified, a period of national achievements prepared Egypt for the age of the pyramids (the Old Kingdom).

By the final decades of the predynastic period and the formative decades of the early dynastic period, the events that had started the process toward unification were many generations old. Without written records, the predynastic past was already in the realm of myth.

From Agriculture to a State Society

The emergence of state societies in Egypt was made possible by the development of an agricultural mode of food production. By 4000 B.C., farming villages and hamlets existed all over Egypt. It now appears that agricultural communities were first established in pockets in the Nile Delta (for example, Merimda Beni Salama) and Upper Egypt (for example, Badari) and then spread outward. Regional variations in pottery and stone artifacts indicate that distinct cultural regions were in place by 3800 B.C.

The cultivation of barley and wheat was mixed with herding cattle, sheep, goats, and pigs. Fishing and fowling were also practiced. The shift from hunting and gathering to farming was most likely a result of the arrival of herders and farmers from the neighboring deserts in the wake of severe droughts during the 6th and 5th millennium B.C. The recent discovery of planned (albeit small) hamlets, megaliths, and tumuli (mound graves) in the Western Desert dating to the 5th millennium B.C. suggests that the nucleus of social complexity in Egypt began among desert communities. There is also clear evidence that the communities in the Badari region near Assyut were organized in village chiefdoms by 4000 B.C., if not before. Social complexity developed in tandem with agriculture as people saw the advantages of living in large cooperative communities.

Agricultural productivity is a risky business. As a community became primarily dependent upon agriculture, unanticipated adverse environmental events (droughts, overflooding, destruction of natural dikes, or untimely dust storms) or shortages in yield (as a result of pest infestations, infectious diseases, weeds, or delayed sowing or seeding) could produce disastrous results. Dependence on agriculture as the primary source of subsistence was achieved by the middle predynastic (Nagada I) period.

From 40 to 100 people may have lived in each of the early settlements, some of which may have experienced rapid growth to a much larger size (as seen in the upper archaeological layers of Merimda Beni Salama). The low productivity of the land newly under cultivation and the acceptable distance of a home range set limits to village size. Very small communities of a few families may have grown close to a size that provides a labor force sufficient to increase return per capita, but at the same time, the communities would have remained fairly small in order not to incur increasing costs and diminishing returns. Daughter hamlets and settlements might have emerged in response to occasional population increase or whenever resources within the vicinity of a village deteriorated.

Neighboring communities were thus bonded by kinship and social ties (marriage alliances, common descent, and ritual celebrations). These ties provided a basis for intercommunity food exchange and defense. Aiding those in need

within the context of kinship obligations and community rituals may be regarded both as an extension of a traditional ethos of sharing and as the first step toward a new strategy of food management, a strategy that would ultimately expand to include neighboring districts. In hunting-gathering and pastoral cultures, people moved as resources declined in one place. In agricultural societies, people were tethered to their fields, and food was moved to even out regional disparities. From this perspective, two of the most important elements in the life of predynastic people were the donkey and the boat. Boats existed in Egypt by the middle of the predynastic period. The donkey may have been domesticated in the Sahara. However, the earliest known bones of a domesticated donkey are reported from Maadi. A single specimen of a small adult equid is reported from Hierakonpolis, a center of trade with Nubia. Previously limited evidence for domesticated asses was reported from Abydos. Donkeys are also depicted on the Tjehenu palette and are also known from an early dynastic cemetery in Tarkha Maadi, a center of trade with the Near East.

The emergence of trade was most likely tied to the rise of a managerial, ritual elite, who acquired status goods from abroad. The use of gold and copper perhaps involved religious-ritual symbolism. Nagada has been linked with gold, as indicated by the name of its temple, Nubt. Location close to temples or trade centers (both probably interrelated) explains the rise of early towns at Nagada, Hierakonpolis, Maadi, and Buto. The towns, with populations in the range of a few thousand, were not big cities. The demand for status goods by the elite stimulated and fostered quarrying and mining activities, as well as artistic and industrial developments. This is clearly indicated by the presence of glazed steatite (soapstone) beads (in the Badarian culture), copper and gold jewelry, stone vases, highly decorated slate palettes, gemstones, and decorated pottery. These items imply the emergence of a cadre of skilled artisans and craft specialists.

Social differentiation is clearly manifest in burial remains. By 3800 B.C., large cemeteries in Nagada and Hierakonpolis included a few tombs with numerous grave goods. There was also marked variations in the size of tombs. The largest tombs become progressively larger through time, a trend that culminated in the building of monumental pyramids. The Decorated Tomb-100 at Hierakonpolis (3600 B.C.) provides an example of the tombs of great chiefs or kings during Nagada II.

The elite had their own separate burial grounds within the main cemeteries during Nagada I. Later, they had their own cemeteries as shown by Cemetery T in Nagada. The depictions of Narmer as a figure larger than others signifies the great position of the king. This iconographic tradition may be traced back to the depiction of a female deity much bigger than other figures.

The emergence of administrative functions associated with early state societies during Nagada II is indicated by clay sealings that were used to seal containers and room doors at South Town, Nagada.

The emergence of religious ideology, mythology, and ritual later synthesized in separate "schools" of Egyptian "theology" are indicated by standard body positions in burials, grave goods, and iconography. As indicated by the Narmer palette, cow goddesses were linked with royalty as well as with the sky as in the palette from Gerza. The depictions of boats and large female figures with raised arms, plants, desert animals, and signs of water most likely reflect belief in a journey to the netherworld and rebirth—precursors to similar beliefs later on. Depictions of shrines also indicate that cult centers probably existed by Nagada II. Religious specialists (evolving later into priests), who performed rituals related to divine rulers, may also date to Nagada II. Writing, for which there is evidence from Abydos during the late predynastic period, probably emerged for designating items intended for the royal house and for inscribing the name of the king so that it could be "read" correctly regardless of differences in dialect or language.

The depictions of fortified settlements and scenes of fighting on palettes at the end of the predynastic period suggest that armed conflict between chiefdoms and kingdoms along the Nile Valley was not uncommon. However, there is no evidence of foreign invasions.

Genetic variations among early Egyptian populations were due to differences in the provenance of the original agrarian founding populations (who came from mixed North African, Mediterranean, Nubian, and Levantine stocks). However, it also seems that the elite might have constituted an inbreeding class as indicated by the study of those buried at the Nagada T cemetery.

Sociopolitical Dynamics of State Formation

Conflicts between neighboring groups were resolved by the formation of a political system that integrated neighboring groups on the basis of a common figure who was related to a family of universal gods. Initially, different groups might have adopted totemic ancestors (such as the falcon or the scorpion), and some totemic icons might have been adopted by the leaders of a political entity (confederate).

Within the confederates, fomed by the union of adjacent communities, kin-based relationships were complemented by the role of a leader as a shepherd who protects and ensures the well-being of his flock. The conceptual schema of a leader, as was clearly the case in dynastic times, combined elements of his role as a warrior smiting the enemies and mediator who ensured good floods and abundant food.

Politics and Cosmogony

Agriculture perpetuated a state of potential conflict and heightened anxiety. Not only were people threatened by crop failures, they also had to worry about assailants from the desert or neighboring communities. In addition, there were the difficulties of living closely in a permanent relationship with others—a shift from the nomadic lifeways of hunters and herders. In such a world, a cosmogony (theory of the origins of the universe) that restored order and deified roles was essential for the formation of a sense of self that was capable of withstanding conflicts and coping with adversities. In ancient Egypt, divine kingship was at the heart of such a cosmogony. In a sense, divine kingship defined Egyptian society in its image. The elaborate theology and ritual in Egyptian religion are indeed an indication of the centrality of divine kingship in Egyptian society. The preoccupation with an afterlife in Egyptian religion is also related to kingship and the cosmic order. The divine king was both a living sign of this order and a mediator between people and the gods. Not only did all the beneficial and creative power flow into the world through him, he was also at the center of supernatural relationships that provided the sacred order of things. Through him, society acquired both meaning and purpose, and people found the prescriptions for a good life and a meaning for their existence.

From Nomes to Nation-State

The integration of villages in territorial political regions (spats or nomes), well known from various historical periods, may have existed in late predynastic times as a survival of the elementary political units of several neighboring villages. It is generally held that at the end of the predynastic period (Dynasty 0 or Nagada III), Egypt consisted of provincial or petty states. The nomes (or provinces) were administrative divisions in which traditional authority was in the hands of a local god. The rule of the god was exercised through that of a chief (nomarch). The nome was also an agricultural tract defined in terms of flood basins. Various nomes in Lower and Upper Egypt were united into provincial kingdoms (consisting of several nomes each).

The unification of the kingdoms of Upper Egypt and the Nile Delta is the subject of great controversy. The Palermo Stone contains the names of predynastic and early dynastic kings. The list was recorded in the 5th Dynasty. Predynastic kings wearing the red crown of Lower Egypt are followed by kings wearing the double crown of a united Egypt.

The insignia of royalty of Upper and Lower Egypt were different. Lower Egypt was represented by a red crown (deshert); Upper Egypt, with a white crown (hedjet). Later the two crowns were combined. A representation of the red crown of Lower Egypt was depicted on a fragment from a pot of the middle predynastic (Nagada I or Amratian) period.

Apparently, the conquest of the Nile Delta took place well before the 1st Dynasty, about 100 to 150 years before King Narmer. Cultural traits from Upper Egypt are clearly evident in the delta during the later part of Nagada II (Nagada IIc) at approximately 3500 B.C. However, the union was not complete, and many parts of the delta remained independent. The representations on the Narmer palette were probably heraldic representations of the victor of the Upper Egyptian king over his enemies and not a depiction of the conquest of foreign enemies or rebels.

The impact of Upper Egypt on the Nile Delta is clear. The elements of the Maadian cultural complex, named for the site of Maadi, which was shared by many societies from Maadi to Buto in the northern delta, were replaced by Nagada II. This is well illustrated by the emergence of burial customs and pottery of Nagada II affinities at Minshat Abu Omar in the eastern delta. However, there is no evidence of military conquests. It is thus likely that the rise of a unified Egyptian state was most likely not the result of a single battle, but the culmination of alliances, as well as fragmentation and reunification, over a period of at least 250 years or about ten to 12 generations. These alliances perhaps began with a few major kingdoms that emerged between 3400 and 3200 B.C., and perhaps as early as 3500 B.C. These included the kingdoms of Nagada and Hierakonpolis in Upper Egypt. Three goddesses, Nekhbet, Wadjet, and Neith, were associated with Hierakonpolis and the adjacent El-Kab. Nagada was identified with Hathor and Seth.

Trade and other cultural relationships during late Nagada II (Gerzean) and the end of the predynastic period, interrupted occasionally or frequently by war, must have been responsible for the dissemination of many cultural traits both up and down the Nile. Contacts with the Near East and Nubia also brought new cultural traits into the region.

The red crown of Lower Egypt might have originally belonged to a kingdom in Upper Egypt (Nagada), where the crown presumably dates to Nagada I. It is also likely that the cult of Horus emerged in the Nile Delta or somewhere else and was adopted by the people of Nekhen. Conversely, it may have appeared in Nekhen (Hierakonpolis) and then spread as a symbol of victory to other nomes in Middle and Lower

Egypt. It is also very likely that the first major political power resulted from the unification of the kingdoms of Hierakonpolis and Nagada. The followers of Horus from Hierakonpolis apparently conquered and annexed the kingdom of Nagada in late predynastic times. The unification of these two kingdoms may have been generated the legend of the Two Lands identified with the gods of Nagada (Seth) and Hierakonpolis (Horus). The standards of King Scorpion, from Hierakonpolis, included two that bore the Seth-animal, suggesting that he ruled over a united kingdom.

The next step in the unification of Egypt may have involved the annexation of the key nomes of Middle Egypt (around Shutub and Abydos) as a result of peaceable negotiations or a brief war. In the next step, further annexation of northern nomes may have followed, perhaps under the generalship of Narmer. Abydos may have then served as a capital midway between Hierakonpolis and the northern territories. It is perhaps for this reason that Abydos was probably the site of royal burials for rulers of both the 1st and late 2nd Dynasties and became identified with the cult of the dead (ancestral) king. This is indicated by the size, orientation, and goods of the funerary enclosures at Abydos.

The polities of Lower Egypt at the end of the predynastic period included Buto (Tell el Faraíain, also called Pe, or Per-Wadjet), presumed to be the capital of Lower Egypt. A temple dating to the 1st Dynasty was discovered at Buto. Recent excavation at this site revealed clay cones, pottery, and other artifacts showing contacts with Amuq F period in northern Syria and Mesopotamia. The clay cones are similar to those of Uruk-Warka used in decorating temples. The earliest pottery from Buto and other Nile Delta sites, such as Tell Aswad and Tell Ibrahim Awad, belong to an indigenous delta pottery tradition.

The Nile Delta is also known for several important predynastic cult centers. Saïs at Sa el Hagar in the western delta was a chief city of the fifth nome. The goddess of the realm was Neith. She was represented by crossbows and arrows and symbolized warfare. The bee was regarded as the state symbol. The king of Saïs assumed the red crown, which later became the crown of all of Lower Egypt. Kings of the first two dynasties also assumed a title that combined the bee (a symbol of Lower Egypt) with the sedge plant of Upper Egypt.

Busiris (originally Djedu, or Per-Usire, literally *House of Osiris)* was a religious center identified with Osiris. The center was originally dedicated to a vegetation god, Andjeti. Historical accounts identify Osiris as the first king and attribute to him the use of a crown combining the two plumes of the kingdom of the eastern delta with the red crown. However, the pyramid texts refer to Osiris solely as a symbol of dead kingship.

Another key religious center was On (Mataryia), where both Osiris and the local deity Atum were recognized. On also became the cult center for the sun god Re. The priests of On were presumably credited with astronomical observations and the recording of the height of Nile floods using a Nilometer. The attribution of the invention of the solar calendar to the priests of On is very unlikely. However, On is credited with the creation of a cosmogony of gods—the Ennead. The Ennead consists of Atum, the god who begot himself and who subsequently fathered Shu (air god) and Tefnut (moisture), who in turn begot Geb (earth god) and Nut (sky goddess), who then begot two couples: Osiris and Isis and Seth and Nephtys.

The cosmogony developed at On was apparently a result of efforts to synthesize a divine (cosmic) genealogy of the king with some of the deities previously recognized, for example, Seth from Nagada in Upper Egypt and Osiris from Busiris in the Nile Delta. The king, as Horus, was identified with the falcon. According to the Osirian myth, the rule of Horus as the legitimate ruler of all of Egypt was the result of a verdict issued by divine judges to settle a dispute between Seth and Horus.

Osiris, the father of Horus, was once a living king and then became the king of the netherworld. Horus, the king, was a god whose presence on earth made him a link between people and the gods. His well-being was identified with the welfare of the people. The king was invigorated by the ceremonies of the Sed festival. During this festival, rooms for the throne and robing were especially built as a part of a recoronation ritual that asserted the sovereignty of the king. Chiefs of Upper and Lower Egypt paid homage to the king and proclaimed allegiance to the throne. A court, the Heb-Sed court, with chapels of the various provinces (nomes) of Upper and Lower Egypt on both sides, was a key feature of the festival. The king ran around a track four times as the ruler for the south and four times as the ruler of the north. The evolution of Egyptian kingship was clearly linked with political unions and religious ideologies that attempted to reconcile and amalgamate elements from different regions within a royal cosmogony.

Political unification depended both on the success of a national ideology and on the ability of the king to maintain a flow of trade goods to reward his court, allies, and subordinates. Minshat Abu Omar, located on the Pelusian branch directly in line with the overland route to Palestine, was apparently a trading post. This also seems to be the case of Kufur Nigm. Maadi in the eastern delta was clearly a trading center containing a commercial zone with stores, magazines, and dwellings. It was also a manufacturing center with artisans specializing in metallurgy and the manufacture of stone tools, pottery, and stone vases.

The appearance of Nagada IIc elements in the Nile Delta coincides with an increase in trade with Palestine and Mesopotamia. It is possible that a trading colony for Upper Egypt was located in the delta and served as a depot and a center for trade between Hierakonpolis and Palestinian centers, especially for copper and turquoise. Settlements in northern Sinai and southern Palestine were clearly those of merchants situated along trade routes. These trade relationships were increased under Narmer and Den. Egyptian trading colonies were established in Palestine where *serekhs* (personal seals) of Narmer were found. In Egypt, Palestinian elements, including copper in association with Narmer's s*erekh,* were found at Kufur Nigm and Tell Ibrahim Awad. A few wavy-handled jars imported from Palestine are found in Upper Egypt. It also appears that local potters in Egypt during Nagada IIc began to produce imitations of the imported wavy-handled pottery. Trade with Mesopotamia explains the presence of cylinder seals and other

items of Mesopotamian origins in Egypt (for example, palace face decorations). However, the fundamental elements and character of Egyptian civilization were deeply rooted indigenous developments in the predynastic past. There are clear continuities from the Badarian culture onward. For example, the lithic (stone) artifacts of Nagada I and II are almost identical. Many hieroglyphic signs may be also traced to signs on decorated pottery. In addition, an interpretation of rock-art symbols and Nagada II (Gerzean) iconography reveals continuities in Egyptian religion.

The rise of a nation-state was associated with the emergence of a royal capital and a royal acropolis. The location of Narmer's capital at Memphis represents the role of the capital at the center of its domain of power. The location of the capital between Upper Egypt and the Nile Delta permitted both political and economic integration of the two regions. It also provided the king with the ability to dispatch troops to subdue rebels or separatists.

The movement of the capital northward may have encouraged the Nubians to attack Upper Egypt or to withhold or interrupt the flow of goods and gold from Nubia and farther south. Aha, Narmer's successor, won a decisive victory over Nubia and established Egyptian hegemony.

———————〰〰〰〰〰———————

Although there are still many gaps in our understanding of the emergence of the early Egyptian state, it is plausible to assume that the beginnings of the political process were a result of the integration of neighboring farming villages in regional chiefdoms to minimize the impact of agricultural failures and to enhance social solidarity. There are no indications that the state formed to oversee major irrigation works. The rise of chiefs marked the beginnings of territoriality, administrative nomes, and cult centers. It also fostered trade to secure prestige goods. The religious ideology of the chiefs was related to burial rituals and practices. Conflicts arising from agricultural failures and alliances formed to secure trade goods from Nubia and the Near East (Syria-Palestine and Mesopotamia) and to aggrandize the power of the chiefs led to a series of political developments, including the rise of petty states and regional kingdoms, which were subsequently fused in yet larger kingdoms. In Lower and Upper Egypt, developments were apparently fairly independent until about 3,500 years ago, when cultural elements from Upper Egypt become predominant in the Nile Delta. There is no evidence of a military conquest. The cultural transition, perhaps marking the ascent to dominance of merchants or trade colonies from Upper Egypt, coincides with an expansion of trade relations with the Near East and Nubia. The transition to a national unit was largely the result of a new ideology of kingship linked to a universal cosmogony to which the king was related. The king, as a god himself descended from cosmic, nonterritorial gods, became the protector and provider of the people. This concept of divine kingship, supported by temples and funerary complexes, rituals, and religious treatise, marked the emergence of the nation-state and provided a fundamental, enduring element of Egyptian civilization in spite of political, sectarian, and economic upheavals. Divine kingship was so powerful as an ideology that it was adopted by foreign invaders. The end of the religious basis of Egyptian kingship with the advent of Christianity undermined the very foundation of Egyptian civilization and transformed its cultural landscape, until the introduction of Islam by Arab invaders. The economic transformations, particularly since the Roman period, also propelled Egypt into a "global" economy that annihilated the pharaonic pattern of economic transactions.

BIBLIOGRAPHY

Friedman, R., and B. Adams. 1992. *The followers of Horus.* Oxford: Egyptian Studies Publication No. 2, Oxbow Monograph 20.

Hassan, F. A. 1988. The predynastic of Egypt. *Journal of World Prehistory* 2 (2): 135–85.

Kemp, B. 1989. *Ancient Egypt: Anatomy of a civilization.* London: Routledge.

Wenke, R. J. 1989. Egypt: Origins of complex societies. *Annual Review of Anthropology* 18: 129–55.

———. 1991. The evolution of early Egyptian civilization: Issues and evidence. *Journal of World Prehistory* 3: 279–329.

Fekri A. Hassan

THE NEAR EAST AND EASTERN AFRICA: THEIR INTERACTION

Scholars usually assume that contacts between the Near East and Africa occurred since prehistoric times along the "Fertile Crescent" connecting Mesopotamia to Egypt through Syria and Israel. It was also assumed that the interaction with East Africa, particularly the Horn of Africa, started in the 1st millennium B.C. when a kingdom with strong South Arabian features arose on the Tigrean Plateau in northern Ethiopia and Eritrea. The origins of this kingdom have been ascribed to a migration of people from Arabia to Africa in late prehistoric times or to a South Arabian colonization of the Tigrean Plateau, in Eritrea and northern Ethiopia, in early historical times.

Archaeological investigations conducted since the early 1980s in Africa and Arabia have revealed a much more complicated pattern of interaction. They have made evident the existence of a Afro-Arabian interregional network of contacts, connecting the Persian Gulf to the Red Sea, since the Early Holocene.

At present, the development of this pattern of contacts can be divided into five stages:

1. The establishment of an interregional exchange circuit from the 7th to the 4th millennia B.C.
2. The consolidation of an Afro-Arabian exchange network and possibly a movement of people from Arabia to Africa in the 3rd and 2nd millennia B.C.
3. The rise of an Ethio-Sabean state on the Tigrean Plateau in the 1st millennium B.C.
4. The commercial expansion of the Ethiopian kingdom of Aksum along the northern Indian Ocean in the 1st millennium A.D.
5. Islamic commercial and political expansion from Arabia to East Africa since the late 1st millennium

An embryonic interchange network, based mainly on the circulation of obsidian between Africa and Arabia, emerged from the 7th to 4th millennia B.C., although the pattern of interaction is not yet well known. The analysis of obsidian finds from different regions in Arabia and north-eastern Africa suggests that an interregional trade of this material, in the form of raw material and artifacts, occurred from the Horn of Africa to southern Arabia since the 7th millennium B.C. Most likely, two or three major obsidian sources in Eritrea or Djibuti were exploited at this time. The occurrence of a lithic (stone) industry comparable to those of the Wilton techno-complex at Dahlak Kebir corroborates the capabilities of the African peoples to cross the Red Sea in Early to Middle Holocene times.

In the 4th millennium B.C., this exchange network included the lower Nile Valley in Egypt. Obsidian coming from the Horn of Africa has been recorded in predynastic burials. A maritime trade along the Red Sea from Mesopotamia or possibly India may have been practiced as well. Square boats similar to vessels represented on Protliterate seals in Mesopotamia are depicted along the valley of the Wadj Hammamat, connecting the Nile Valley to the coast of the Red Sea in Upper Egypt. In turn, a bracelet made with *Xancus pyrum,* a shell with a certain Indian origin, from a Nubian tomb of the late 4th millennium B.C. suggests that products from the Indian Ocean arrived in Lower Nubia at a quite early time.

The interregional exchange circuit between the Horn of Africa and southern Arabia was consolidated from the 3rd to 2nd millennia B.C., as a consequence of the Egyptian commercial expansion toward the southern regions of the Red Sea. However, the obsidian evidence suggests that the earlier trade was still practiced in the 2nd and 1st millennia B.C. and declined by the end of the 1st millennium B.C. In this late phase of obsidian trade, different sources in Arabia and Africa, perhaps as far as Shoa in central Ethiopia, were probably exploited.

A quite regular interchange circuit between Egypt and the southern Red Sea countries (Punt), directly involving Nubia, was established from the late 3rd to mid-2nd millennia B.C. Most likely, the Egyptian economic expansion to the south reinforced the Afro-Arabian interaction and generated a proper trade circuit between southern Arabia and the northern Horn of Africa (the Tigrean Plateau and adjacent lowlands). This is corroborated by the comparison of the ceramics from sites in eastern Sudan, Ethiopia, Djibuti, and Yemen. Such a comparison points to more intense interregional contacts between 2500 and 1500 B.C. At this time, the people living in the western Eritrean-Sudanese lowlands, and particularly in the Gash Delta (Kassala), were the interface between the Egyptian and Afro-Arabian circuits. In fact, the evidence ascribable to the so-called Gash Group culture (which flourished from 2700 to 1500 or 1400 B.C.) from the site of Mahal Teglinos (Kassala) in eastern Sudan suggests that the Eritrean-Sudanese Lowlands were included in a network of contacts with the Horn of Africa and southern Arabia, as well as with Nubia and Egypt.

Pottery with decorations similar to Gash Group embellishments was recorded at Erkowit in the southern Red Sea Hills (eastern Sudan), Lake Besaka in the Afar (Ethiopian Rift Valley), and Asa Koma near Lake Abbe (Djibuti). The decorative patterns and techniques of the Gash Group pottery show also some similarities to those of the Early Bronze Age pottery in Yemen, dating to about 2900 to 1800 B.C. Some shards from the Middle and Classic Gash Group layers (from about 2300 to 1700 B.C.) at Mahal Teglinos are decorated with motifs very similar to those on the contemporary ceramics from northern Yemen. The shards from Mahal Teglinos seem to be exotic and may represent imported pottery.

More intriguing is the evidence of a camel tooth found at the Gobedra rock shelter near Aksum (western Tigray). This tooth was associated with a microlithic industry and the region's earliest evidence of pottery, dating to between the 4th and 2nd millennia B.C., but doubts remain about a possible intrusive origin of the sample. An early date might be corroborated by the find of a domestic camel bone, dating to between the late 4th and mid-2nd millennia B.C., at Ele Bor (northern Kenya). If confirmed, the find at Gobedra might suggest contacts between the western Tigrean Plateau and southern Arabia between the late 3rd and mid-2nd millennia B.C. The archaeological evidence from the Arabian Red Sea Coast suggests that camels were already domesticated in the region in the late 3rd millennium B.C. and were used as transport animals in the first half of the 2nd millennium B.C.

In the mid-2nd millennium B.C., during the New Kingdom, the Egyptian maritime trade to Punt became more intense, and the people of the western lowlands were almost completely cut off from the main commercial route. Apparently, a consequence of this maritime trade was the establishment of a new pattern of interaction, by which the coastal people of Eritrea and southern Arabia traded with the people of the plateau in central Eritrea. At this time, the people of the Hamasien Plateau in Eritrea became the intermediaries between the lowlands and the coast and were possibly involved in the maritime trade. Most likely, they were also affected by some Arabian cultural influence. This population can be identified in the archaeological record with the so-called Ona Group-A culture, which flourished between 1500 and 1000 or 900 B.C.

A stronger interaction between African and Arabian people can be inferred from the rise of a coastal Afro-Arabian cultural complex (Tihama cultural complex) in the mid-2nd millennium B.C. The pottery from the sites ascribable to this complex shows many similarities to the ceramics of Kerma and C-Group in Nubia. Moreover, the lithic tools from the Saudi Tihama sites are comparable to those of the Gash Group in Kassala. Thus, an African background might be suggested for this coastal complex.

Representative sites of the coastal complex have been reported at Sihi (in the southern Saudi coastal plains), Adulis (near the Gulf of Zula in Eritrea), Wadi Urq' (near Hodeida on the Red Sea Coast of Yemen), and Sabir (or Subr, near Aden in the coastal plains of southern Yemen). These sites share enough ceramic features to be regarded as regional variants of one cultural tradition. This complex can be dated to the second half of the 2nd millennium B.C. (about 1500 to 1200 or 1100) on the basis of two radiocarbon determinations from Sihi and Sabir.

A few elements suggest that the people of the western Eritrean-Sudanese Lowlands had some contacts with people of the Arabian Tihama culture. Shards decorated with a burnished linear motif occur in the Terminal Gash Group (about 1500 to 1400 B.C.) at Mahal Teglinos (Kassala) and in sites near Wadi Urq' on the Red Sea Coast of Yemen. The northeastern Tigrean Plateau in

Eritrea was also included in the cultural area of the Tihama complex. The ceramics from the lowest layers at Matara in central Eritrea show some similarities to the pottery from Adulis and include some big jars with a vertical elliptical handle or a deep groove along the rim, features typical of the pottery at Sabir. Moreover, a few shards similar to the earliest ones from Matara were found in the deepest layers at the site of Yeha near Adua in western Tigray (northern Ethiopia). They might suggest that the western Tigrean Plateau was already part of a network of contacts with the coast at this time.

A possibly Arabian influence is noticeable in the Ona Group-A culture, recorded on the Hamasien Plateau near Asmara in Eritrea. This cultural unit is presently dated to the second half of the 2nd millennium B.C. The Ona Group-A culture is characterized by a polished, red, slipped ware, often decorated with impressed or incised rim bands or shoulder bands, polished axes, and small chipped-stone bull heads. The origins of this culture are still uncertain. The ceramics reflect a local tradition, partly comparable to the Tihama. On the contrary, the chipped-stone bull heads could be ascribed to an Arabian influence, as bull crania are a common motif in the rock art of central Arabia.

Indirect evidence suggests that the Ona people were able to sail along the Red Sea. In fact, pots with long necks, reminiscent of the Ona Group-A vessels, are represented as part of the commodities on a cargo boat from Punt in a Theban tomb almost surely dating to the time of Amenophis II (about 1425 to 1401 B.C.).

Finally, an Arabian influence can be observed in some sculptures of human figures with big hands and a long hairdress at Daaro Caulos and Ba'atti Mariam Caves near Asmara. These sculptures are comparable to figures in Arabian rock art, dating to the 2nd or early 1st millennium B.C.

In the 3rd and 2nd millennia B.C., pastoral people sharing a similar rock-art tradition occupied central and southern Arabia as well as the eastern Horn of Africa. Their artistic style is characterized by painted or engraved bovines with the body depicted in profile and the head and horns in plan. It is recorded as Jubba style in northern Saudi Arabia, Dahthamani style in central Arabia, and Ethiopian-Arabian style in the Horn of Africa.

The earliest evidence of this style has been traced in northern Saudi Arabia to the mid-5th millennium B.C. By the mid-3rd millennium B.C., it spread to the southern Hidjaz in Saudi Arabia, northern Hararge in eastern Ethiopia, and along the Ethiopian Rift Valley to Sidamo in southern Ethiopia. Figures dating to the 2nd and early 1st millennia B.C. have been recorded at Jebel Qara in central Arabia, Hararge in eastern Ethiopia, northern Somalia, and Eritrea. By the 1st millennium B.C., this style spread from Eritrea to Nubia, southern Upper Egypt, and the Sahara. This evidence might suggest a movement of people from Arabia to Ethiopia, between the 3rd and 2nd millennia B.C.

Contacts between the peoples of southwestern Arabia and eastern Ethiopia might be also corroborated by some dolmens (monuments of upright stones supporting lintel stones) discovered in the region of Harar (eastern Ethiopia) and dating to the late 2nd millennium B.C. They are comparable to some dolmens recorded at Mosna' in southern Yemen, but the cultural and chronological relationship between these monuments is not yet clear.

After the collapse of the Egyptian trade to Punt in the 12th century B.C., the southern Arabs gained control of the trade between the southern Red Sea and the Mediterranean Sea. In the 1st millennium B.C., some kingdoms arose in southwestern Arabia: Saba, Qataban, Hadramawt, Main, and Himyar. The earliest was the kingdom of Saba (about 800 to 400 B.C.).

The Tigrean Plateau in Eritrea and northern Ethiopia was progressively included into the area of southern Arabian economic and political influence in the early 1st millennium B.C. Eventually, the interaction between the peoples of the opposite shores of the Red Sea culminated with the rise of a Ethio-Sabean state (kingdom of Daamat) on the plateau in central Eritrea and western Tigray. This kingdom is identified in the archaeological record with the pre-Aksumite culture and can be dated to about 700 or 600 to 400 B.C. Major ceremonial centers and probable urban sites were recorded at Kaskasè in central Eritrea and Yeha in western Tigray. The evidence of a possible town was found at Matara as well.

At present, it seems that the southern Arabs were already established on the northeastern edge of the Tigrean Plateau just before the rise of the Ethio-Sabean kingdom. This can be inferred from some rock inscriptions recorded around Cohaito in central Eritrea and dating from the mid-9th to mid-6th centuries B.C. Moreover, the presence of southern Arabian shards in the layers beneath the foundations of a monumental temple at Yeha suggests that western Tigray was also included in a network of contacts with southern Arabia before the consolidation of the state.

The epigraphic evidence in southern Arabia records four kings, two of whom used the Sabean title of *mukarib*. The pre-Aksumite kings worshiped southern Arabian and indigenous gods. Moreover, the inscriptions state that Sabeans were living on the plateau in the mid-1st millennium B.C.

Most scholars assume that the pre-Aksumite kingdom originated from a Sabean colonization of the Tigrean Plateau in the first half of the 1st millennium B.C. Only a few scholars suggest that the kingdom emerged from a contact between a local chiefdom and the Sabeans.

Despite textual evidence pointing to Sabean as the official language of the kingdom, the archaeological evidence does not support a Sabean colonization of the plateau. The material remains suggest that the southern Arabian elements were a superficial, though impressive, component of the pre-Aksumite culture affecting only the elite. The southern Arabian influence is evident in all power manifestations of the elite: monumental architecture, monumental inscriptions, art, votive incense altars, offering tables, bronze seals, and writing. Moreover, most elements—except for the language—can be connected with not only Saba but different southern Arabian regions as well. On the contrary, most of the ceramics have a local origin. Only very few vessels are southern Arabian in style, and these could have been imported. The main component of the pre-Aksumite pottery can be related to the Ona Group-A ware, which can be regarded as the local cultural background to the kingdom. Lithic tools are another local (African) element of the pre-Aksumite culture, as they are quite similar to the late prehistoric tools of the Sudan and the Horn of Africa.

On the whole, the available evidence suggests that different southern Arabian groups, including the Sabeans, mixed with the local population and generated an acculturated elite over people who maintained their indigenous traditions.

By the 4th century B.C., after the decline of the kingdom of Saba in southwestern Arabia, the Ethio-Sabean kingdom of Daamat apparently collapsed, and the Tigrean Plateau was isolated for a few centuries from the main interchange circuit with the Mediterranean Sea. Hellenistic sources state that the African coast of the Red Sea, as far as northern Somalia, was frequented by Ptolemaic ships, but archaeological evidence of such visits is scarce.

A new relevant step in the development of interregional contacts between eastern Africa and the Near East was made with the inclusion of the African coastal regions into the Roman trade circuit from Egypt to the Indian Ocean in the early 1st millennium. In the first centuries A.D., Roman ships were sailing along the African coast up to Rhapta in present-day Tanzania.

A new state, the kingdom of Aksum (about A.D. 100 to 900), arose on the Tigrean Plateau as a consequence of the inclusion of this region in the Roman circuit. Aksum became the main African commercial partner of the Roman Empire and controlled the trade from the Ethiopian and Sudanese hinterland to the Red Sea, where a major port was located at Adulis.

The imported materials, dating to between the 1st or 2nd century and the 4th century, from the royal and elite tombs at the capital city of Aksum include amphoras (pottery vessels with large oval bodies, narrow necks, and handles) and glasses with an Egyptian and Syrian origin. They provide clear evidence that the kingdom had trade contacts with the eastern provinces of the Roman Empire. In turn, the epigraphic evidence from southwestern Arabia suggests that the Aksumites sent military expeditions to this region and probably occupied it for a short time in the 2nd and 3rd centuries, but no archaeological evidence of these events has been found so far.

The most important consequence of the commercial links with the eastern Mediterranean countries, particularly Syria, was the introduction of Christianity as an official religion of the state in the early 4th century.

The contacts with Syria were particularly relevant. They are well corroborated by the monumental evidence. The residences of the Aksumite elite apparently derive from the prototype of the Roman villas in southern Syria. The Christian churches are comparable to northern Syrian models, either with a rounded apse of the 4th century or with a square apse of the 6th century. Both types of Aksumite baptisteries, elliptical or octagonal in shape, have Syrian origins. The construction technique of a possible royal tomb (Enda Caleb) of the 6th century at Aksum is very similar to that of contemporary monuments in Syria. The memory of these contacts also survives in the Ethiopian traditions, which ascribe the eventual diffusion of Christianity in the kingdom of Aksum to nine saints with a Syrian origin.

Aksum reached the peak of its power from the 4th to the 7th centuries. In the 6th century, the Aksumites subjugated southern Arabia for about 50 years. This event is corroborated by a few architectural remains in an Aksumite style in northern Yemen. At this time, Aksum apparently controlled the trade along the Red Sea and northern Indian Ocean. Recent archaeological investigations conducted at the ancient port of Qana on the coast of Hadramawt in southern Arabia have documented the Aksumite commercial expansion in the mid-1st millennium. By the end of the 4th century, objects with a eastern Mediterranean origin dramatically decrease, and Aksumite pottery increases at this site. Moreover, utilitarian pottery of Ethiopian type was found in 5th- and 6th-century layers and may suggest the presence of people from Ethiopia in Qana.

The advent of Islam in the 7th century deeply changed the pattern of interaction between eastern Africa and the Near East. The Arab conquest of Egypt in 647 and the progressive spread of Muslim people along the coast of Eritrea and Somalia isolated the Aksumites more and more and caused the decline and southward shift of the Christian kingdom to Lasta in the region of Wollo.

In the 8th century, Islamic communities were scattered along the African coast of the Red Sea, and a port was established at Badi. The location of Badi is still uncertain. The occurrence of Islamic pottery and buildings on the island of er-Rih, facing the bay of Aqiq at the Eritrean-

Sudanese border, may suggest that this was the original site of Badi. In the 9th century, a sultanate arose also at Dahlak Kebir. The archaeological evidence of this sultanate consists of a cemetery with inscribed stelae (carved or inscribed stone slabs used for commemorative purposes) dating from the 10th to 16th centuries and the remains of monumental domed tombs, similar to the traditional *qubbas* (domed tombs) of northern Africa.

In the late 1st and early 2nd millennia, Islamic communities penetrated the Rift Valley from the coast into the inland regions of Ethiopia, where they established some sultanates that represented threats to the Christian kingdom of the northern plateau. Yet, the archaeological record of this penetration is still almost completely absent. Some coins found in big tumuli near Harar suggest that the plateau in eastern Ethiopia was already included in the area of Islamic trade in the 8th century. Ruins of Islamic fortified villages and towns, dating to the 14th and 15th centuries, have been recorded in the southern Afar region of Ethiopia. These settlements were located on the top of hills, which could be easily defended, and contained imported materials with an Indian origin. Finally, Islamic settlements dated to the 15th and 16th centuries have been recorded in the Ogaden.

BIBLIOGRAPHY

Anfray, F. 1990. *Les anciens Ethiopiens.* Paris: Colin.

Brandt, S. A., and N. Carder 1987. Pastoral rock art in the Horn of Africa: Making sense from udder chaos. *World Archaeology* 19: 195–213.

Cervicek, P. 1979. Some African affinities of Arabian rock art. *Rassegna di Studi Etiopici* 27: 5–12.

de Contenson, H. 1981. Pre-Aksumite culture. In *UNESCO general history of Africa, vol. 2: Ancient civilizations of Africa,* ed. G. Mokhtar, 341–361. Berkeley: University of California Press.

Doe, B. 1971. *Southern Arabia.* London: Thames and Hudson.

Fattovich, R. 1988. Remarks on the late prehistory and early history of northern Ethiopia. In *Proceedings of the Eighth International Conference of Ethiopian Studies,* ed. I. Tadesse Beyene, 85–104. Addis Ababa: Institute of Ethiopian Studies.

———. 1990. Remarks on the pre-Aksumite period in northern Ethiopia. *Journal of Ethiopian Studies* 23: 5 –33.

———. 1991. At the periphery of the empire: The Gash Delta (eastern Sudan). In *Egypt and Africa: Nubia from prehistory to Islam,* ed. W. Vivian Davies, 40–48. London: British Museum.

———. 1993. Punt: The archaeological perspective. In *Atti del VI. Congresso Internazionale di Egiptoloqia,* vol. 2, 399–405. Torino: Societa Italiana per il Gas.

———. 1993. The Gash Group of the Eastern Sudan: An outline. In *Environmental change and human culture in the Nile Basin and northern Africa until the second millennium B.C.,* eds. L. Krzyzaniak, M. Kobusiewicz, and J. Alexander, 439–448. Poznan: Poznan Archaeological Museum.

Joussaume, R. 1980. *Le megalithisme en Ethiopie.* Addis Ababa: Artistic Printers.

Kitchen, K. A. 1993. The land of Punt. In *The archaeology of Africa: Food, metals and towns,* eds. T. Shaw, P. Sinclair, B. Andah, and A. Okpoko, 587–608. London: Routledge.

Phillipson, D. W. 1990. Aksum in Africa. *Journal of Ethiopian Studies* 23: 55–60.

Zarins, J. 1990. Obsidian and the Red Sea trade: Prehistoric aspects. In *South Asian archaeology 1987,* eds I. M. Taddei and P. Cawen, 507–541. Roma: IsMEO.

Rodolfo Fattovich

NORTHEASTERN AFRICAN STATES

Hierarchical societies arose in the regions southeast of the Nile Valley from the 4th to the 2nd millennia B.C. They were the background to the formation of the ancient historical states in northern Ethiopia and Eritrea: the kingdom of Daamat (about mid-1st millennium B.C.) and the kingdom of Aksum (1st millennium A.D.). The rise of complex societies and states in these regions was due to:

1. Egyptian commercial activity along the Nile Valley and the Red Sea from the 4th to the 2nd millennia B.C.
2. Southern Arabian economic and political expansion into Africa in the 1st millennium B.C.

3. Roman trade to the Indian Ocean in the early 1st millennium A.D.

Egyptian Commercial Activity

The Egyptian expansion toward the southern African hinterland, as far as the Horn of Africa, started in the mid-4th millennium B.C. when chiefdoms arose in Upper Egypt and possibly in the Nile Delta. In fact, the emerging elite's desire for prestige goods made the exchanges with Africa, the Near East, and the Middle East more intense.

Quite soon, Lower Nubia (between the First and the Second Cataract of the Nile) was included in a interchange circuit with Upper Egypt, and complex societies arose in this region in the late 4th millennium B.C. Most likely, the Horn of Africa was already connected to the Nubian circuit in the 4th millennium B.C., as obsidian from the Red Sea Coast in Eritrea or Djibuti was found in predynastic tombs in Egypt.

At this time, a hierarchical (rank) society appeared on the plains immediately to the east of the middle Atbara Valley near Khashm el-Girba (eastern Sudan). The evidence of this society is provided by the remains of the so-called Butana Group (which flourished from about 3800 to 2700 B.C.). The Butana Group people were hunters and gatherers, who started to breed cattle and cultivate cereals by the end of the 4th millennium B.C. The occurrence of black-topped pots, similar to pots from the Nile Valley, at Butana Group sites may suggest contacts with the Lower Nile Valley. In turn, some luxury and prestige items (for example, heads for maces, or staffs) made of porphyry from the Eastern Desert suggest a form of social differentiation.

Since the beginning of the 1st Dynasty (from about 3150 to 2925 B.C.), the Egyptians attempted to gain control of Lower Nubia. During the Old Kingdom (from about 2700 to 2200 B.C.), fortified settlements were built along the Nile as far as Buhen, close to the Second Cataract. Because of the Egyptian pressure, Lower Nubia was apparently depopulated in the early 3rd millennium B.C., and a pastoral people, originating from the Western Desert, occupied the region in the late 3rd millennium B.C. They are identified in the

archaeological record with the C-Group culture (which flourished from about 2500 to 1400 B.C.).

In the Old Kingdom, the Egyptians extended their commercial activity to Upper Nubia (from the Second to the Fourth Cataracts) and the Horn of Africa. The earliest record of contacts with the land of Punt, which can be located in eastern Sudan and Eritrea, go back the 6th Dynasty (from about 2460 to 2200 B.C.).

In the mid-3rd millennium B.C., the descendants of the Butana Group people settled in the Gash Delta along the Eritrean-Sudanese Lowlands. The subsistence economy of the Gash Group culture (which flourished from about 2700 to 1400 B.C.) relied on cattle and sheep or goat breeding, as well as on the cultivation of barley. They were surely included in an interchange circuit with Egypt. This is supported by a few Egyptian pottery shards from a layer of the Early Gash Group (about 2700 to 2300 B.C.) at the site of Mahal Teglinos (Kassala). In turn, the presence of shards from Upper Nubia and northern Yemen at the same site suggests that the Early Gash Group people were also part of an exchange network with these regions. A few clay stamp seals, fragments of clay sealing, and tokens from Mahal Teglinos (Kassala) point to a form of social complexity in the Gash Delta in the mid-3rd millennium B.C.

During the First Intermediate Period (from about 2200 to 2040 B.C.), the Egyptian state practically collapsed, and the Egyptians abandoned Lower Nubia. The decline of a strong state in Egypt enabled the Kerma people in Upper Nubia to become the main intermediary in the exchanges between the southern African regions and the Lower Nile Valley. This is evident in the archaeological record from the Middle Gash Group layers (dating to between 2300 and 1900 B.C.) at Kassala, where the Egyptian elements disappear and the Kerma features dramatically increase. As a consequence of Kerma's crucial role as an intermediary in the Nile Basin exchange circuit, the earliest state in sub-Saharan Africa (the kingdom of Kerma) arose in the Middle Nile Valley at the end of the 3rd millennium B.C.

During the Middle Kingdom (from about 2040 to 1785 B.C.), after Egypt was again unified under the rule of a Theban dynasty, the Egyptians gained control of Lower Nubia, and a system of forts was created along the valley as far as the Third Cataract. These forts were built to control the local C-Group peoples and to face with the threat of Kerma. Naval expeditions were also sent along the Red Sea to Punt from a harbor at Wadj Gawasis north of Quseir, most likely in order to bypass Upper Nubia. However, the pharaohs maintained intense commercial contacts with the kingdom of Kerma, as a great quantity of Egyptian materials was found at the site of the capital city.

The kingdom of Kerma was at the peak of its power during the Second Intermediate Period (from about 1785 to 1552 B.C.) in Egypt, when the pharaonic state declined and the Nile Delta was ruled by the foreign Hyksos dynasty (Classic Kerma phase, about 1750 to 1550 B.C.). At this time, Kerma was a major trading partner with the Hyksos kingdom.

In the first half of the 2nd millennium B.C., the Gash Group people were an important trading partner of the kingdom of Kerma, and a chiefdom arose in the Gash Delta (Middle Gash Group phase, about 1900 to 1700 B.C., and Late Gash Group phase, about 1700 to 1500 or 1400 B.C.). This is suggested by the settlement pattern (with a clearly defined settlement hierarchy, dominated by a large residential settlement of about 11 hectares at Mahal Teglinos), the presence of administrative devices (clay stamp seals and tokens) at Mahal Teglinos, and mortuary practices. In the Classic Gash Group phase, contemporary to the Middle Kerma phase, stone monoliths marked the burials, and the number of personal ornaments indicated a differentiation in rank and prestige. The great quantity of faunal remains near the tombs suggests that social differentiation was also made evident by the number of animals killed for the funerary banquets. In the Late Gash Group phase, contemporaneous to the Classic Kerma phase, quite large mud-brick storage rooms were built at Mahal Teglinos. The clay seals and tokens were more differentiated, suggesting a more complex administrative system.

In the mid-2nd millennium B.C., Egypt was reunified, and quite soon the pharaohs gained control of the Nile up to the Fourth Cataract in the Middle Nile Valley. For about 500 years, during the New Kingdom (from about 1552 to 1069 B.C.), all of Nubia was a colony of Egypt. Probably, the sea route to Punt was also more frequently used in this period.

The conquest of Nubia had repercussions on the culture and social organization of the Nubians. In the 18th and 19th Dynasties (about 1552 to 1295 and 1295 to 1188 B.C.), the Egyptians established temple towns in Lower and Upper Nubia, and the local people were increasingly Egyptianized. The kingdom of Kerma vanished, and indigenous complex societies were progressively crushed by the Egyptian dominion, although the indigenous elite did not completely disappear.

In turn, a consequence of the increasing Egyptian Red Sea trade was the impoverishment, albeit not a complete disappearance, of the chiefdoms in the lowlands southeast of the Nile. In the region of Kassala, the Gash Group declined, and the local population was apparently assimilated by northern people, culturally related to the Pan Grave culture of the Eastern Desert (Jebel Mokram Group, which flourished from 1400 to 1000 or 900 B.C.). They were an agro-pastoral people, almost completely excluded from the main trade networks, as exotic materials are limited to a few Nubian potsherds. The settlement pattern still shows a site size hierarchy, with a major center at Jebel Abu Gamal, about 35 kilometers south of Kassala, and suggests that a form of social complexity survived in the region. However, administrative devices are totally absent from the Jebel Mokram sites. This points to a possible regression from a protostate to a tribal chiefdom.

Most likely, the people of the northeastern Tigrean Plateau and Red Sea Coast in Eritrea became the intermediaries between the African hinterland and the coast and participated more directly in the trade with Egypt during the latter half of the 2nd millennium B.C. The pots on a boat coming from Punt depicted in a Theban tomb of the early 18th Dynasty are comparable to the red ware of the so-called Ona Group culture (which flourished between 1500 and 1000 B.C.) in the region of Asmara (Eritrea). This trade may have stimulated an increasing social complexity in the region, but direct archaeological evidence is still very scarce. A large residential village, perhaps up to 25 hectares in size, with some traces of a stone building, was located at Sembel Cuscet near Asmara.

After the end of the 20th Dynasty, in the Third Intermediate Period (from about 1069 to 656 B.C.), the Egyptian state again declined. Nubia was abandoned, and the maritime trade to Punt collapsed. An indigenous Nubian polity arose in the early 1st millennium B.C. in the region of Napata, near Karima in Upper Nubia, and eventually conquered Egypt, where the Nubian kings are known as the 25th Dynasty (from about 747 to 646 B.C.). This was the kingdom of Kush (or Cush), which dominated the Nile Valley south of Egypt up to the 3rd century A.D.

Southern Arabian Economic and Political Expansion

The end of the Egyptian commercial monopoly along the Red Sea opened also the way to the commercial expansion of the southern Arabs. In the first half of the 1st millennium B.C., the kingdom of Saba (which flourished from about 800 to 400 B.C.) in northern Yemen controlled the trade to the Mediterranean Sea and included the Tigrean Plateau in Eritrea and northern Ethiopia in its area of economic and political influence. As a consequence of these inter-regional contacts, the Ethio-Sabean kingdom of Daamat (which flourished from about 700 to 400 B.C.) arose on the plateau. This state quite soon included into its territory most of the Tigrean Plateau from central Eritrea to western Tigray. The material remains of this state are identified in the archaeological record with the so-called pre-Aksumite culture (from 800 or 700 to 400 or 300 B.C.).

At this time, a urban society appeared on the plateau. Large ceremonial centers, with temples of southern Arabian type, appeared at Kaskasè in central Eritrea and Yeha in western Tigray. A town was located at Matara in central Eritrea. Moreover, the presence of monumental temples, a sophisticated art, and elaborated craft of stone carving, and bronze seals, as well as monumental royal inscriptions in a southern Arabian writ-

ing, point to a very complex society. The subsistence economy surely relied on agriculture and cattle breeding. The remains of a dam in masonry of southern Arabian type at Safra in central Eritrea suggest that artificially regulated irrigation was practiced, at least in this region. The pre-Aksumite culture was characterized by a strong southern Arabian influence, but evidence of contacts with the Nubian kingdom of Kush, the Achemenian Empire, and possibly the Greek world can be also recognized. The inscriptions record the names of four kings. The earliest three kings involved their queens in ruling. People of the pre-Askumite culture worshiped either southern Arabian or indigenous gods.

In the late 1st millennium B.C., the kingdom of Daamat apparently disappeared, as there is no royal inscription later than the 4th century B.C. The scarce archaeological evidence dating to this period also suggests a collapse of the urban society, at least in the western Tigray. However, a form of urban society possibly survived in central Eritrea, as a continuity in the occupation of the town from pre-Aksumite to Aksumite times can be observed at Matara.

By the end of the 1st century B.C., the Tigrean Plateau was again included in the Roman interchange circuit of the Red Sea and Indian Ocean, and a new state, the kingdom of Aksum (which flourished from A.D. 50 to 900) arose in the region. Recent archaeological investigations at Bieta Gyorgis, near the capital city at Aksum, have documented the kingdom's emergence from a local complex society, dating from the late 1st century B.C. to the early 1st century A.D. A typical feature of the proto-Aksumite complex society was the construction of a massive stone platform associated with pit graves, excavated in the bedrock, and rough funeral stelae (carved or inscribed stone slabs).

Massive man-made stone platforms with rock-cut tombs and monumental carved stelae, up to 33 meters in height, are also striking features of the Aksumite kingdom in the initial stage of its development (Early Aksumite phase, A.D. 50 or 100 to 400). Particularly relevant are the hewn stelae with an architectural decoration, most likely dating to the 3rd or 4th century. In this period, the Aksumites extended their dominion over the whole Tigrean Plateau and sent military expeditions to southern Arabia. Major urban centers were located at Adulis on the Red Sea Coast, Matara on the plateau in central Eritrea, and Aksum in western Tigray. Coinage was introduced in the 3rd century. The most crucial event in the history of Aksum was the introduction of Christianity in the early 4th century. By then, churches with a basilican plan became the most impressive monuments of the Aksumite culture. Macrobotanical remains, dating to early Aksumite times, from the site of Dicta Gyorgis (Aksum), indicate that the subsistence economy of the Aksumites relied on the cultivation of barley and wheat, along with cattle breeding.

In the mid-1st millennium A.D., Aksum was the capital city of a very powerful kingdom, which controlled the trade routes from the African hinterland to the Mediterranean Sea and Indian Ocean through the port of Adulis (Middle Aksumite phase, about 400 to 700). Copper, bronze, silver, and gold coins of Roman and Byzantine type were used. The archaeological evidence from Matara points to a clear stratification of the urban population. Three main types of buildings have been distinguished: elite residential "palaces" with a square building in the center of a courtyard surrounded by an arrangement of rooms, simple square buildings like those of the elite but without annexed rooms, and ordinary houses. Some seeds of teff, an indigenous Ethiopian crop, from a Middle Aksumite assemblage at Bieta Gyorgis, may suggest that this plant was already cultivated in northern Ethiopia in the mid-1st millennium A.D.

The kingdom started to decline in the 7th century, because of the Islamic expansion along the African coast of the Red Sea, and eventually disappeared in the early 10th century (Late Aksumite phase, about 700 to 900). Aksum decreased dramatically in size, and the capital apparently moved southward. In the 9th century, the capital was located at a place called Ka'bar in the Islamic sources. No archaeological evidence of this site has been found so far. The presence of large dishes similar to the traditional ones used for *injera*, a local bread made of teff, in Late Aksumite assemblages seems to corroborate that the plant was more extensively cultivated at this time.

In the 12th and 13th centuries, a new Christian kingdom arose in the region of Lasta (north-central Ethiopia) under a local dynasty (Zagwè period, from about 1150 to 1270). The territory of this kingdom stretched from western Tigray in northern Ethiopia to northern Shoa in central Ethiopia. Finally, another kingdom replaced the former one under the so-called Solomonic Dynasty, originating from northern Shoa, from the 14th to the 16th centuries. The archaeological evidence of these post-Aksumite states is still very scarce. It consists mainly of rock-hewn churches dating to between the 10th and 15th centuries and scattered through the whole plateau from Tigray to Shoa. These churches corroborate a basic continuity of the Aksumite cultural traditions up to the Zagwè period and indicate the progressive diffusion of Christianity toward central Ethiopia in medieval times. The most impressive rock-hewn churches were carved in the Zagwè period at Lalibela, near the capital of the kingdom, where they form a monumental Christian ceremonial center reproducing the ancient Zion.

Finally, hierarchical societies most likely arose in central and southern Ethiopia from the 10th to the 15th centuries. Their origins are still unknown, but we can quite safely assume that the people relied on the cultivation of ensete or "false banana." Some evidence of these hierarchical societies is provided by a great deal of megalithic stelae recorded mainly in the regions of Guraghe and Soddo in Shoa (central Ethiopia) and in Sidamo (southern Ethiopia).

The stelae of Shoa include four different types of monuments:

1. Those representing the upper part of a human body in a very schematic way
2. Those decorated with carved metal swords and symbols
3. Those decorated with very schematic human figures
4. Those representing schematic dressed human figures

The monuments surely belong to one cultural tradition and can be ascribed to indigenous populations who occupied the region before the Oromo invasion in the 16th century. Excavations conducted at the site of Tiya, to the south of Addis Ababa, have documented the funerary function of these megaliths.

Thousands of stelae were recorded in Sidamo. They can be either isolated or grouped in large stelae fields. Two main types can be distinguished: "phallic" stelae and anthropomorphic stelae. Their age is still uncertain.

BIBLIOGRAPHY

Anfray, F. 1990. *Les anciens Ethiopiens.* Paris: Colin.

Fattovich, R. 1991. At the periphery of the empire: The Gash Delta (eastern Sudan). In *Egypt and Africa: Nubia from prehistory to Islam,* ed. W. Vivian Davies, 40–48. London: British Museum Press.

Marks, A. E., A. M. Ali, and R. Fattovich. 1986. The archaeology of the eastern Sudan: A first look. *Archaeology* 39: 44–50.

Munro-Hay, S. 1991. *Aksum: An African civilization of late antiquity.* Edinburgh: Edinburgh University Press.

O'Connor, D. 1993. *Ancient Nubia: Egypt's rival in Africa.* Philadelphia: University of Pennsylvania Press.

Sadr, K. 1991. *The development of nomadism in ancient Northeast Africa.* Philadelphia: University of Pennsylvania Press.

Zarins, J. 1989. Ancient Egypt and the Red Sea trade: The case for obsidian in the predynastic and archaic periods. In *Essays in ancient civilization presented to Helene J. Kantor,* eds. A. Leonard and B. B. Williams, 339–368. Chicago: Oriental Institute of the University of Chicago.

Rodolfo Fattovich

WESTERN AFRICAN STATES

The medieval states of Ghana, Mali, and Songhai are the earliest-known complex societies in West Africa. At one time or another from the early centuries of the present era to about 1600, they dominated a part of the Sahel region of the western Sudan. Very little fieldwork has been done in these regions. Most of the information we have concerning these societies is from oral traditions and histories written by contemporary Arab travelers.

The Sahel region has always been an important zone for humanity in Africa. Graham Connah has even suggested that it is not too great an exaggeration to say that this was an optimal zone, which fostered increasing complexity of human cultures. It is suitable for both cereal cultivation and livestock rearing. Of greater significance though, it is geographically a flat region with few internal barriers. It is bordered on the north by the Sahara and on the south by tropical forests and the Atlantic Ocean, both major obstacles to movement. Of the two, the Sahara proved easier to breach. Moslems reached the Sahel by the early 8th century.

The Sahel encompasses the steppe and savanna zones. There is a considerable range of ecotones (transition areas between adjacent ecological communities) represented, and a wide variety of raw materials and resources are available. Because different environments possessed some resources but lacked others, both the necessity and the occasion developed for exchange across environmental boundaries. Connah states further that the complexity of the western African environment as a whole provided conditions conducive to the development of complex networks of regional commerce. Cities located in the Sahel region, such as Tombouctou, became the terminus points for the trans-Saharan trade routes—the entrepots where goods were switched from camel to canoe and where the peoples from north of the desert interacted with those from south of the Sahara.

Without some hardships, there is little incentive to develop technology, better agricultural methods, or the mechanisms of society. The Sahel is an environment of constraints. The most limiting is the availability of water. Rainfall is markedly seasonal and decreases both in amount and duration as one moves north toward the Sahara. A second constraint is temperature. This region is hot, which further restricts the availability of water because of evaporation. The margins of perennial rivers and lakes are oases, which encourage population concentrations and agricultural activity. The primary farming technique uses recessional cultivation (involving naturally irrigated areas from which floodwaters have receded). Another general constraint to the region is the prevalence of disease. The major diseases that affect human or animal health are associated with water: sleeping sickness, animal trypanosomiasis, malaria, schistosomiasis, filariasis, river blindness, and several intestinal parasitic diseases. Thus water sites offer both attractions and detractions to settlement.

Jenne-jeno

The beginnings of urbanization and state development in West Africa date to the Jenne-jeno settlement in present-day Mali. It is located within the Inland Delta of the Niger River and was first settled around 250 B.C. The settlement at Jenne-jeno probably first gained local significance as a place where farmers, herders, and fishers brought their produce to exchange. Systematic trade developed on the local level and expanded to include a broader geographical area. No sources of iron, stone, or copper exist in the immediate vicinity, yet all three are found at Jenne-jeno. The site probably developed as the first interregional trade center in western Africa. Of relevance is that trade developed and was well established in this region before any Arab contact or the advent of the great trans-Saharan trade routes.

Ghana

Ghana was the first of three states to rise to power. It was ruled by the Soninke. What little is known of this polity is based on the writings of Arab travelers, such as El Fazari, who described an expedition mounted by Arabs in Morocco around 734 to raid Ghana, reputedly a land of gold. Although Ghana is first mentioned only in the 8th century, it may have been in existence as a power in West Africa from as early as the 4th century.

Gold symbolized Ghanaian royalty. M. Shinnie has pointed out that, as with many other African polities, minerals were the property of the king and that nuggets of gold found in the mines of this empire belonged to him. The king was said to own a gold nugget so large that he could tether his horse to it. Stories of its weight varied from 13 kilograms to 1 metric ton. Gold was probably a staple of local trade for centuries, but its value came to be determined by outside commerce. African markets were the main source of gold in Europe and the Mediterranean world in antiquity. Gold was not mined within Ghana, however, but by people in Wangara, a district southwest of Ghana. The Wangara people needed salt and, having no local supply of it, traded their gold for salt. Slaves, obtained from the forest zone and kola nuts (popular in the desert because chewing them helps quench thirst and stay hunger) also were important trade items.

Al Masudi, the renowned Arab traveler, wrote in 950 about the "silent trade" used in Ghana:

> They have traced a boundary which no one who sets out to them ever crosses. When the merchants reach this boundary, they place their wares and cloth on the ground and then depart, and so the people of the Sudan come bearing gold which they leave beside the merchandise and then depart. The owners of the merchandise then return, and if they are satisfied with what they have found, they take it. If not, they go away again, and the people of the Sudan return and add to the price until the bargain is concluded.

The location of their gold sources, however, remains unidentified to the present time. Nor have great quantities of gold artifacts been located. This may be because they have been lost long ago, or perhaps there never were great quantities of gold to begin with. The latter is unlikely, because there are so many eyewitness accounts of the gold. In addition to regulating the supply of gold, the Ghana royalty imposed a tax on every load of goods entering or leaving the area over which they had political control. Thus, the source of wealth in Ghana was control of all commerce, not just the gold trade.

The capital city of Ghana was located at what is now the site of Koumbi-Saleh, at the northern limits of reliable crop cultivation. It was in an ideal location to control the trade of gold and salt, the two commodities on which its economy was based. The other major city of the kingdom of Ghana was Awdaghast, a market center to which Arabs came to trade for gold judged to be the best in the world. Both cities were situated along major trade routes.

Koumbi-Saleh was actually two cities, although only one has been located. Al Bakri, writing in the middle of the 11th century, described it as two towns: one an Islamic town, in which the merchants resided, and the other the royal town. The royal town, El-Ghaba, was where the king lived and held his court. The royal court consisted of a fortress and several huts with domed roofs enclosed within a wall. This city has not yet been located. The second city—the archaeological site of Koumbi-Saleh—built partially of stone houses and straw-thatched mud houses, was where the Moslem population lived. The finds at this city include multistoried stone houses, extensive cemeteries, and a mixture of Arab and African objects: glass weights for weighing gold, pottery, verses of the Koran painted on stone tablets, scissors, farming tools, and weapons. J. L. Newman estimates that Koumbi-Saleh grew to include 15,000 to 20,000 inhabitants.

Historians dispute the reasons for Ghana's decline, which began in the second half of the 11th century. It was probably due to a combination of factors. The location of its capital in a marginal environment would make it dependent at times on imported food, and perhaps this contributed to the decline of the empire. Newman feels the population of Ghana had been weakened by forced mixing with other cultural groups. In particular, he stresses the loss of internal cohesion, a result of the incorporation, often by force, of many non-Soninke into the population. When strong competitors appeared on the scene, the fragility of Ghana became evident. Additionally, Ghana was attacked by the fanatical Moslems, the Almoravids, who captured Awdaghast in 1054 and Koumbi-Saleh from 1076 to 1077. The Almoravid leader in the Sudan, Abu Bakr, was killed in 1087, and Ghana regained its independence, but the years under Arab rule had weakened its commercial links and political power over surrounding peoples. Ibn Khaldun, the Arab historian, wrote that the Almoravids, in spreading their dominion over the Black African populations, devastated

their territories, imposed poll taxes and tribute, and compelled many to become Muslims. In 1203, Koumbi-Saleh was sacked, and its people were enslaved by the Sosso, a neighboring group that was fervently anti-Islamic.

Mali

The Sosso kingdom had a very short life span and was soon conquered by the Mandingo people who became the rulers of the kingdom of Mali. Specifically, these people were another Malinke clan, the Keita. The Mandingo originally were the rulers of Kangaba, a small state located in the Inland Niger Delta. They were converted to Islam by the Almoravids. In the 13th century, they began to expand their domain. It was at this time that the Sosso, who regarded the Mandingo as rivals, conquered Ghana. Tradition has it that Sumanguru, king of the Sosso, arranged to have 11 brothers, heirs to the throne of Mali, put to death. A sickly 12th brother, Sundiata, was overlooked, however, and the throne passed to him in 1230. He was able to unite his people successfully and defeated and killed Sumanguru in 1235. Over the next five years, he annexed the remaining Sosso territory. In 1240, he established his capital at Niani.

There is now some argument whether Niani was, in fact, the capital of the kingdom of Mali, and if so, whether it was the principal city for only a brief period. D. C. Conrad argues that a ruler would avoid accumulating monumental symbols, not only because he regularly changed capitals, but also because in the risky political climate of the day, there was no particular advantage to nonportable features like elaborate dwellings, funeral tumuli, or other public structures that drew attention to success and tied one down to a location that had to be defended. He further argues that the town of Dakajalan, located on the Upper Niger, was the earliest site of Mali's capital.

By the end of the 13th century, Sundiata had enclosed the gold areas of Wangara and Bambuk within his sphere of control and had made Mali the richest and most powerful state in the western Sudan. He established a standing army and thereby eliminated the need for constant recruitment. Because it was an Islamic state, many merchants, Moslem scholars, and holy men where attracted there. Trade flourished in the towns, and first Walata and then Tombouctou became the main terminus for the Saharan trade routes. Because of raiding by Arab-Maures in the Western Desert, trade routes linking the Sahel and the Sudan with Morocco became less favored over more easterly routes that linked the region with Algeria, Tunisia, and Egypt. Jenne-jeno, Tombouctou, and Gao benefited from the relocation of the trade center.

The most famous Malian king was Mansa Musa (also known as Kankan Musa). He was the grandson of Sundiata and came to power in 1307. During his reign, Mali became known throughout the Mediterranean world and in Europe. The state began to be shown on maps, and its ruler was described as a lord called Musa Mali, Lord of the Negroes of Guinea. The abundance of the gold in his country was also noted. He is particularly remembered for his pilgrimage to Mecca in 1324. Al Omari left a secondhand account of the ruler's progress through Cairo, describing the 500 slaves, each carrying a staff of gold, who accompanied him.

> This man spread upon Cairo the flood of his generosity . . . so much gold was current in Cairo that it ruined the value of money. Let me add that gold in Egypt had enjoyed a high rate of exchange up to the moment of their arrival. But from that day onward, its value dwindled. That is how it has been for twelve years from that time, because of the great amounts of gold they brought to Egypt and spent there.

While their ruler was away on his pilgrimage, the armies continued their expansionist activities and captured Gao, the capital of Songhai. Mansa Musa halted there on his return from Mecca and demanded submission from the ruler of Songhai. To ensure continued homage from this area, Mansa Musa took the Songhain's two sons back to Mali with him as hostages. Ultimately, this would lead to Mali's downfall because these sons later betrayed Mansa Musa and led the Songhai to supremacy in the region.

Mansa Musa is also remembered for his patronage of the arts and scholarly activities in Mali.

He brought back from Mecca a poet and architect named Es-Saheli, who was originally from Andalusia, Spain. Es-Saheli is reputed to be the first to introduce burned brick into the Sudan, and he is known for building the great mosques at Gao and Tombouctou.

Mansa Musa died in 1332, and the kingdom of Mali began its decline. He was succeeded by his son, Maghan, who was a weaker ruler than his father. He lost Tombouctou to the Mossi, who lived along the southern border. He placed his trust in the two Songhai princes, who betrayed him. They returned to Gao and expelled all Mandingo people from Songhai-held territories. The Tuareg then captured Tombouctou, Walata, and much of the northern portion of the Mali domain. Mali was never able to recover. In the 15th and 16th centuries, the Mandingo appealed to the Portuguese for help, but they were unwilling to alienate other clans in the area. Eventually, by the 17th century, the Mandingo retreated to Kangaba, their original state.

Songhai

The last great western Sudan state was that of the Songhai. The origins of these people are not fully known. J. L. Newman posits that they descended from the Late Stone Age aquatic tradition. B. Davidson elaborates on these origins by suggesting that the ancestors of the Songhai were Sorko, who were fishers from the east (perhaps from Lake Chad by way of the Benue River), and the Gow, who were hunters. Another tradition mentioned both by Shinnie and Davidson suggests that a Berber tribe, the Dia, took political control of the Songhai people in the 7th century. In summary, Davidson states:

> One need take neither the dates nor the traditions too seriously. All that comes out as relatively sure is that the Songhay empire of Gao had its organized beginnings in the region of Dendi; that its civilization was the product of native initiative stimulated by migrant incursion; and that, with others, it took its rise in early centuries after the western Sudan had fully entered its Iron Age.

In 1009, King Kossoi of Gao accepted Islam, probably under the influence of merchants or scholars who preceded the Almoravid incursions in the area. Davidson argues that to the African kings of the time, Islam was probably equated with commerce. Islam also provided a unifying structure that crossed tribal gods and ancestor beliefs. At this time, the capital was established at Gao. Songhai then became a tributary state to the kingdom of Mali from 1325 to 1335. Ali Kohlen was the hostage brother who restored freedom to the Songhai. Little is known of the next century other than that it was probably a time of struggle for the Songhai, who were constantly fighting off neighbors: the Tuareg, the Mossi, and the Mandingo.

In 1464, Sonni Ali ascended the throne of Songhai. He was the 18th ruler in the line of kings founded by Kossoi in 1009. Reported to have been a man of unusual courage and strength of purpose, Sonni Ali, though probably not himself a pagan, was sympathetic to the Songhai pagan traditions. Muslim biographers invariably regard him as an enemy of their faith. He was a ruthless ruler. In 1468, he captured Tombouctou and killed most of its inhabitants. He took Jenne-jeno by 1473, and by his death in 1492, he had established a fairly stable area over much of the Middle and Upper Niger. He was not liked by his people because of his cruelty and dictatorial rule. He was succeeded by his son, who only lasted a few months before one of Sonni Ali's generals, with popular support, usurped the crown. This general, Mohammed Toure, was a Moslem, and he became known as Askia Mohammed. His main strength was organization, and he proceeded to divide the state into administered provinces, each with its own governor, often a member of his own family. He created central offices to administer financial, agricultural, and other matters and instituted a tax system. He made all weights and measures uniform within his domain. He was sympathetic to Moslems and encouraged their work. Once again Tombouctou, Jenne-jeno, and Walata flourished as centers of learning and religion. The University of Tombouctou was one of the first in Africa and drew scholars from all over the Moslem world. Trade was based on gold and salt primarily but also included slaves, ivory,

ebony, kola nuts, cotton goods, grains, and ostrich feathers. A cache of hippopotamus ivory, recently discovered at Gao, may have represented a shipment of ivory that was carefully buried and for some reason was not later retrieved. From the north, imported goods included horses, North African and European luxury items, weapons (sword blades came from as far away as Spain and Germany), and cowrie shells. The absence of local salt and the need to import it from Taghaza more than 800 kilometers away is mentioned by Leo Africanus.

Askia Mohammed, too, made a pilgrimage to Mecca, arriving there in 1497. He is said to have given 10,000 gold pieces as alms to the poor and for the establishment and upkeep of a hostel for other pilgrims from the western Sudan. When he returned, he continued the expansion of the state and eventually took all land that had once belonged to Mali. He then attacked the Hausa states to the east, and by 1515, he had successfully defeated the Tuareg and taken their stronghold at Agadez in the Air region. This gave him control over the trade routes leading to Tunis, Tripoli, and Egypt. Askia Mohammed created the largest African state in the western Sudan. It was well administered and probably the most organized of the African states. In addition, with Moslem support, trade, culture, scholarly activities, and religion flourished as never before. Leo Africanus noted that numerous judges, doctors, and clerics in Tombouctou received salaries from the ruler, who was reputed to respect men of learning. Since there was a rich market for books in manuscript, profit was made from the book trade as well.

Songhai continued to flourish, even though Askia Mohammed was deposed by his son in 1528, and there ensued a series of struggles for the crown. Morocco, however, had long been envious of the power of the Songhai, and in 1589, El Mansur set out to attack the Songhai Empire. None of his advisors thought it would be possible to cross the Sahara with an army and all the supplies that would necessarily have to accompany it. A Spaniard, named Judar, was chosen as commander over an army of 4,000 soldiers, mostly Europeans with a few Moroccans. Accompanying the troops were some 9,000 transport animals. It took approximately six months to cross the desert, and news of the army's progress was reported to the Songhai king by travelers. The king, Askia Ishak, faced the Moroccan army at Tondibi, 56 kilometers from Gao, with an army composed of 18,000 cavalry and 9,000 infantry. Judar's army had been reduced to 1,000 men during the arduous desert crossing. But the Moroccans had guns, which the Songhai did not, and given the advantage of gunpowder and firearms over the simple weapons of the Songhai, it is not surprising that Judar won without difficulty. In spite of this victory, a Moroccan province was never established. Songhai resistance continued into the early decades of the 17th century, and disease, particularly malaria and dysentery, took its toll on the mostly European mercenaries fighting for Morocco. The region fragmented into many smaller states and chiefdoms. The cities retained a more international flavor but gradually declined in importance as the trans-Atlantic trade grew.

What is amazing about these states is not that they formed, but that they were able to maintain their control over such large regions and so many diverse peoples. Perhaps they successfully remained in control because they did not try to impose their rule upon subject populations but instead created tributary confederations based on the security created by a powerful polity. Local populations were essentially free to pursue their various agricultural, herding, hunting, and fishing practices as long as they swore loyalty to the ruler. He, in turn, provided a secure environment in which to live and trade.

Mention is frequently made in Arab histories of the armies of the western Sudanese states. Al Bekri wrote in 1067 that the Ghanaian sovereign could put 200,000 warriors in the field. Al Omari wrote in 1336 of a Malian army numbering 100,000, whose officers and soldiers received gifts of land and presents for their service to the king. These great armies were certainly used for conquest and expansion as well as for defense of the kingdom. Nowhere is there any mention of a police role for the military. Its main job seems to be the provision of a secure setting for trade to flourish. Ibn Battuta wrote that the Mandingo

were seldom unjust and that they had a greater dislike of injustice than any other people. In his words, there was complete security in their country, and neither traveler nor inhabitant had anything to fear.

Islam had a great effect on these African states by providing an ecumenical element that unified diverse ethnic groups and traditional belief systems. Commerce, frequently equated with Islam, grew and prospered because the Moslem states to the north were most willing to trade with other Moslem states. Yet the West African states never lost their essentially African character. Ibn Battuta did not approve of the social position and freedom of women in Mali:

> Women go naked into the sultan's presence, too, without even a veil; his daughters also go about naked. On the twenty-seventh night of Ramadhan I saw about a hundred women slaves coming out of the sultan's palace with food, and they were naked. Two daughters of the sultan were with them, and these had no veil either, although they had big breasts.

He was also amazed that succession was matrilineal, a situation unique in the Moslem world, which he had seen nowhere else, except among the heathens of Malabar.

Burial practices remained traditional in nature after the introduction of Islam and were only gradually replaced by Islamic rites. Al-Bakri recorded the burial rites of the kings of Ghana in the middle of the 11th century:

> When the king dies, they build a huge dome of wood over the burial place. Then they bring him on a bed lightly covered, and put him inside the dome. At his side they place his ornaments, his arms and the vessels from which he used to eat and drink, filled with food and beverages. They bring in those men who used to serve his food and drink. Then they close the door of the dome and cover it with mats and other materials. People gather and pile earth over it until it becomes like a large mound. Then they dig a ditch around it so that it can be reached only from one place.

They sacrifice to their dead and make offerings of intoxicating drinks.

Inhumation in a tumulus was a common practice, as was inhumation in large pottery urns in the Inland Niger Delta region. Cemeteries became more common, particularly in the cities, and tombstones, imported from Spain and containing scripture from the Koran, have been excavated at Sane near Gao.

Several Arab writers were most impressed with the courts of the kings and wrote many descriptions of the royal reception areas. The courts are full of pomp and circumstance and royal ritual. Other traditional practices stand out as well. Ibn Battuta wrote of Mansa Musa's court where two saddled and bridled horses were brought, along with two goats, which were held to serve as protection against the evil eye. He further described how the king's subjects entered the royal presence:

> The person summoned takes off his clothes and puts on worn garments, removes his turban and dons a dirty skullcap, and enters with his garments and trousers raised knee-high. He goes forward in an attitude of humility and dejection, and knocks the ground hard with his elbows, then stands with bowed head and bent back listening to what he says. If anyone addresses the king and receives a reply from him, he uncovers his back and throws dust over his head and back.

Ibn Battuta regarded the habit of throwing dust and cinders on their heads, a traditional sign of good manners and respect, as one of the more deplorable African customs (along with the nakedness and freedom of women).

With the growth in trade through these centuries, there was also population growth, although the exact figures are impossible to know. Following the demise of Songhai, population declined to a fairly stagnant point until the 20th century. A figure as high as 40 million to 50 million inhabitants has been proposed for Mali, but it seems unlikely that a population this large could have sustained itself on an agricultural economy dependent on the hoe, human labor, and low-yielding grains.

Yet, three of the continent's most successful states were native to this region. With the exception of Ghana, these kingdoms grew and flourished in regions that encompassed the Inland Niger Delta and the upper and middle zones of the Niger, which probably explains their ability to survive in marginal environments. Ghana controlled the trade routes, and the southern reaches of the state were within the Inland Niger Delta. Trade became a necessity in this region of so many different environments, and it seems that already existing interregional trade routes were the basis for the establishment of large-scale, long-distance exchange and the states that subsequently controlled it. Gold and salt were the two most important commodities. Gold brought this region to the attention of outsiders, especially to the Islamic world, already established in northern Africa. Islam, a proselytizing religion, quickly expanded into the western Sudan and provided a unifying element that transcended tribal rivalries and parochial religious beliefs. Trade grew, and the African kingdoms grew wealthy. At their peak, these states provided stable and secure economic and social environments, noted for their fabled wealth and their centers of commerce, scholarship, and administration at such cities as Tombouctou, Walata, Jenne-jeno, and Gao.

Trade was the driving force of these kingdoms, and once new regions of commerce were discovered, particularly the Americas, the volume and importance of trade declined. Gold could be obtained from the trans-Atlantic trade, and by the middle of the 15th century, the adoption of the lateen sail and the stern-post rudder allowed ships to sail to the West African coast and return to Europe. Previously, the return trip had been nearly impossible. There was no need to cross the desert anymore to trade with West African entities. The discovery about 1440 that a ship could sail several hundred kilometers west into the Atlantic from West Africa and there find winds that would return it to the Mediterranean or Europe effectively opened the West African coast to European sailors. This discovery was made by the Portuguese, who had adopted the maneuverable caravel. As a result, the focus of long-distance trade shifted to the coasts of Africa and away from the Sahelian areas, which were never again to see empires established the likes of Ghana, Mali, and Songhai.

BIBLIOGRAPHY

Connah, G. 1987. *African civilizations.* Cambridge: Cambridge University Press.

Conrad, D. C. 1994. A town called Dakajalan: The Sunjata tradition and the question of ancient Mali's Capital. *Journal of African History* 35: 355–377.

Davidson, B. 1959. *The lost cities of Africa.* Boston: Little, Brown and Company.

———. 1991. *African civilization revisited.* Trenton: Africa World Press.

Gomez, M. A. 1990. Timbuktu under imperial Songhay: A reconsideration of autonomy. *Journal of African History* 31: 5–24.

Insoll, T. 1994. A cache of hippopotamus ivory at Gao, Mali; and a hypothesis of its use. *Antiquity* 69: 327-336.

Mair, L. 1977. *African kingdoms.* Oxford: Clarendon Press.

Newman, J. L. 1995. *The peopling of Africa: A geographic interpretation.* New Haven: Yale University.

Shinnie, M. 1965. *Ancient African kingdoms.* London: Edward Arnold (Publishers) Ltd.

Patricia A. Vaum

SAVANNA STATES

The savanna, stretching just south of the rain forest from the Atlantic Coast to the Great Lakes region of East Africa, saw the progressive emergence of states, in contrast with what happened elsewhere in central Africa. Particularly prominent were the states of the Kongo, Loango, Tio, Mbundu, Kuba, Lunda, Lozi, and Luba, scattered from the coast to the interior. Most of these states ruled vast territories up until the time of colonial conquest. But so far, we have little archaeological evidence to document how these kingdoms arose out of the numerous communities present in the region during the 1st millennium A.D. Written documents exist for the Kongo kingdom from the 16th century onward. For most of the interior, written records improved only after 1880. This lack of documentary sources can be partially compensated for by numerous oral-history accounts, even though in the best of cases, they are limited in time to the couple of centuries before they were collected. The recent investigation successfully combining historical, linguistic, and ethnographic data, the "words and things" technique, has nonetheless allowed for significant advances in our understanding of the political tradition in the rain forests in the region just north of the savanna.

Both areas were progressively colonized several millennia ago by Bantu-speaking farmers, who brought with them an ideological tradition oscillating between praise for "big men" and the maintenance of equality of all. While the latter part of the alternative prevailed in equatorial Africa, the notion of *big men* developed into sacred kingship in several areas on the southern savannas. Deep down, this political tradition may have resulted first due to the influence of the Eastern Bantu, who eventually migrated westward across the savannas, progressively mixing with the older Western Bantu speakers. These newcomers could have brought a more centralized ideology with them, probably under the influence of other East African populations.

In addition to having an ideological influence, the Bantu-speaking people also left a technological imprint. They introduced a new, largely cereal-based food-production system better adapted to the savanna habitat. Over time, this may well have resulted in population growth, especially in zones where there were rich, diversified resources.

Growing population densities provoked the need for a wider range of raw materials, which in turn led to increased trade. Moreover, the uneven distribution of some resources such as copper, salt, or fish and techniques like smelting, as well as demographic factors, may have produced both social inequality and increasing competition. This situation saw the emergence of more complex and centralized polities.

Environmental determinism alone cannot explain the process of state formation. These factors do not always lead to growth of scale and complexity, as amply demonstrated by the Western Bantu inhabitants of the rain forests to the north. Hence the underlying political tradition becomes important.

The need for security and solidarity, combined with the desire for flexibility and autonomy, must have created a state of equilibrium between communities based on kinship and associations. With respect to the latter, witchcraft and diviners played important roles for social control, counteracting the aspirations of "big men." Wars may also have helped maintain the status quo. Trade and economic development alone was not enough to provoke the emergence of large and complex polities. Well into the 1st millennium A.D., the scale of social organization was probably not larger than that of a group of approximately a dozen villages.

A particularly talented warrior or diviner or an enterprising trader or "big man" who grasped new opportunities in the production and distribution of goods would probably have been able to offset this stability. As chiefdoms regrouped, the resulting principalities may well have reached new states of equilibrium. Some of political entities became increasingly successful and started incorporating growing numbers of neighboring principalities. The three main kingdoms of the western savannas, the Loango, Kongo, and Tio, are believed to have originated through this process.

Linguistic evidence relating to a specific fashion of word shortening, to a set of political titles, and to terms designating single and twinned clapperless bells (authority emblems throughout central Africa) indicates that both the Tio and Kongo principalities originated well before A.D.1200.

The notion of the paramount chief living in a village regarded as a "capital," surrounded by a court of title holders who elaborated rituals and emblems, arose within these principalities. This was a further development of the idea that the chief was the master of the land. The copper-rich area at the border between the Congo Republic and Zaire seems to have played a crucial role in these changes, probably due to the copper trade and major commercial routes and marketplaces like the Malebo Pool on the Zaire River.

Unfortunately, from an archaeological point of view, if there are traces of agricultural communities on the coast and in the lower stretches of the Zaire Valley from the 4th century B.C. to the 5th century A.D., there is a surprising gap in the record up to the 11th century. Subsequently, there is evidence of iron and copper metallurgy in the copper deposit of the Boko Songho-Mindouli area, where several furnaces dating to between the 11th and the 14th centuries have been excavated.

Meanwhile, along the Zaire River, from the Malebo Pool to 200 kilometers upstream, numerous sites belonging to an important river-based culture have been surveyed and test excavated. They are likely to correspond to the Tio kingdom. Numerous other sites in the Lower Zaire Valley and on the coast north of the present-day town of Pointe Noire may correspond respectively to the Kongo and Loango states.

The Kongo Kingdom

The emergence of these states probably occurred more-or-less simultaneously. The period of their emergence is generally dated to the 14th century on the basis of the known list of Kongo kings. Judging from the antiquity and the quantity of the archaeological deposits throughout this area, however, as well as the antiquity of the political process in other savanna areas, these kingdoms may be significantly older.

Excavating the site of the Kongo capital, Mbanza Kongo (now Sao Salvador) in Angola, its various provincial capitals, and the capitals and major sites of the other kingdoms will be necessary to test this hypothesis. While doing so has been on the archaeological agenda for more than 20 years, the prolonged political and economic crises endured by Zaire and Angola has made such fieldwork impossible.

Research throughout the lower portion of the Zaire Valley has nonetheless yielded several richly decorated pottery groups from the 17th and 18th centuries. Their distribution up to the Malebo Pool corresponds to the trade routes of the Kongo kingdom. In the pool region, sites like Kingabwa, yielding pottery identified with sources from both upstream and down, confirm that the area was a major commercial center. The cemeteries of two provincial capitals, Mbanza Soyo and Mbanza Mbuta, have also been partially excavated, and some construction work in

Mbanza Kongo has revealed the foundations of various structures. This confirms the great archaeological potential of the site, which presently is at risk due to urbanization.

Visitors to Mbanza Kongo in the 17th century described the city as a large agglomeration of perhaps 40,000 inhabitants. Centered around the royal enclosure and function, it nonetheless continued to resemble a giant village with separate houses surrounded by gardens.

Kongo was considerably more centralized than other states in the region. There were six provinces ruled by governors, who were appointed by the king—and eventually removed by him—as well as many court title holders, who derived their income from tribute, tolls, and fines. Small *nzimbu* shells were used as a national currency. Their source was strictly controlled by the king, who closely supervised commercial, religious, legal, and military matters. He disposed of a permanent praetorian guard but did not maintain a standing army. Kongo gained control over a large territorial expanse and accumulated a large number of slaves.

The Portuguese played an important role in the Kongo kingdom after their arrival in 1483. At the apex of the political structure, the king ruled by virtue of his ancestors. His religious function was essential, but his power was more symbolic than real in areas outside the capital district. While Kongo was much more centralized than, for example, the Tio kingdom, much depended on the adhesion of major village leaders at the local level. This complex symbolic construct was paradoxically fragile because of the king figure himself. Indeed, much depended on his personality, but the absence of clear rules for succession led to many conflicts and civil wars.

The Mbundu Kingdom

Thanks to its control of commercial routes and economic resources, the Mbundu political power emerged in the 16th century, south of the Kongo kingdom, along the middle region of the Kwanza River. The Mbundu used a piece of iron called a *ngola* as the emblem of their authority. By the 1560s, one holder of such an emblem created a major kingdom. Mbundu kings, the Ngola a Kiluanje, played a major role in the slave trade of the following centuries. By the 19th century, the Mbundu had organized, along with Portuguese immigrants, a large commercial network, whose considerable caravans reached the Lozi and Lunda kingdoms far to the east.

Small stone buildings have been noted in the Mbundu area since the 17th century. These tombs, probably dating to the 16th or 17th centuries, have only recently been excavated.

As already demonstrated for the rain forest, it is likely that kingdoms of the savanna also evolved from ideas of political and social structuring resonant within a common Bantu tradition. The concept of *royalty* in an ecumenical sense became well established. Yet, the royal ideology in support of this ideal seems to have developed out of the symbols, beliefs, and practices first used to legitimize the authority of local leaders.

Proceeding farther inland, evidence of the origin and the early development of states becomes even weaker. There is a total absence of traditional and written records or archaeological research.

The Luba Kingdom

At the center of the continent, more than 1,500 kilometers from either ocean coast, the Luba state emerged as a major political structure and ruled a vast area of savanna and woodland of southeastern Zaire. Written descriptions of this part of the continent were not made until the end of the 18th century. These, along with oral traditions, have helped reconstruct the major events that shaped this kingdom from 1700 onward.

Oral traditions here most often recount myths of origin, which are more helpful in understanding Luba's symbolic and cosmological mind-set than any precise historical events. Fortunately, the area is also rich in archaeological sites, recording the continuous development of the first agricultural, iron-using inhabitants of the region.

The Upemba Depression, which now appears to be the Luba heartland, has yielded a wide range of archaeological information providing a 1,500-year-long sequence of continuous human occupation. The vast floodplain of the Lualaba

(Upper Zaire) River is dotted with various lakes, and the Upemba Depression is rich in natural resources.

While more than 50 archaeological sites have been surveyed throughout the depression, the ongoing political crisis in Zaire has hampered intensive research efforts. Only six sites known there have been partially excavated. These are mostly in the northern half of the depression. Sanga is the most famous of these. Little evidence of occupation sites has been preserved, since most of the few places suitable for the establishment of villages have been in continuous use over a long period of time. Most of the data, therefore, come from the more than 300 excavated graves.

The unusual state of preservation of the burial sites, the wealth of the grave goods, and more than 50 radiocarbon dates have led to the identification of four main occupation phases. The most important conclusion here, nonetheless, pertains to the continuity of occupation and the persistence of many objects and customs. This indicates that the population remained much the same over time. The high population density supported by the richness of the ecosystem, appears to have strongly contrasted with neighboring less-populated areas.

At the present, the Luba kingdom of the last three centuries is regarded as the latest development of this long cultural process. The 19th-century capital, however, was located about 100 kilometers to the northwest and was moved after the death of each king. It has recently been suggested that Luba power was not vested in a single king or center but in a constellation of title holders and principalities whose identification with a single nucleus was a means of legitimating their role. The Luba state may well have been, above all else, a construction of the mind, its symbolic reach being more extensive than its practical one. Like many savanna states, it did not really reflect the Western ethnocentric view of *kingdom.* It was the strength of colonial preconceptions and policies that created the image of a highly centralized and powerful empire. In reality, it was very much a symbolic commonwealth.

From an archaeological standpoint, the long cultural continuity linking the present-day Luba to the first food-producing, iron-using commu-nities allows for a credible use of ethnographic data to interpret excavated objects.

There are few such objects for the oldest period, commonly referred to as *Kamilambian.* The pottery of this period is similar to that associated with the Early Iron Age tradition farther south in the Copperbelt along the border between Zaire and Zambia. There is no evidence, however, that copper objects reached the Upemba Depression at that time. It seems that by the 7th century, the relatively sparse Kamilambian population had few trade contacts beyond their immediate sphere of activity.

The subsequent period, the Ancient Kisalian, seems to result from the transformation of the Kamilambian between the 8th and 10th centuries. Judging from the number of burial sites and their dispersion, the Ancient Kisalian population must have remained fairly small and, like its predecessors, scattered widely over the northern half of the depression. By this time, it can be assumed that the people living in the Upemba region had become involved in the copper trade due to the rare presence of some bracelets and necklaces at archaeological sites. Valued for its color and malleability, this metal was probably more in demand than any other commodity at that time. Smoked fish was (and still is) the staple food of people living in the region. It was exported over long distances and bartered for other commodities, such as raffia and beads in recent time, copper and other prestigious products in earlier periods.

Grave goods included vessels and various iron weapons, tools, and ornaments. In two of the wealthiest graves, ceremonial axes were found. What appears to have been their wooden handles were studded with iron nails, and their hollow iron blades were delicately engraved. They remain important symbols of Luba power today. In one grave, such an ax was found along with an iron anvil, another major symbol of authority in traditional Bantu society. This suggests that the buried individuals were local leaders who were manipulating elaborate symbols of power for their own legitimization.

Toward the 10th century, the early Kisalian culture evolved into a large and complex society and eventually gave way to the Classic Kisalian period, which lasted until the end of the 13th century. The size and number of sites from this period, spread both across the northern half of the depression and outside of it to the west, suggest significant demographic growth.

Tools, weapons, food, and other products found in the graves demonstrate the nature and range of local economic activities: fishing, hunting, farming, trading, smithing, and pottery making. Very specialized and skilled artisans made fine pots. Some were crafted specifically as funerary items. Some miniatures were made for interment with children. The exclusive use of copper for ornaments and utilitarian objects testifies to the strong trade links with the copper-producing area to the south. The appearance of a few cowrie shells even suggests some contacts with the coast of the Indian Ocean approximately 1,500 kilometers to the east.

Funeral rites, which took into account age, sex, and rank, were complex. Some of the richest burials, with respect to the number of vessels and the amount of unusual and probably valuable objects, were those of women and children. This suggests that wealth and status were inherited by this time.

It is likely that the highly sophisticated Kisalian society, centered on the Upemba Depression with its 500-year-long tradition in the use of complex symbols of power and rank by its chiefs and notables, was at the origin of the savoir-faire and the great prestige enjoyed by the Luba ever after. For much of this part of the savanna, the Luba kingdom became the epitome of civilized life.

The Luba had a long tradition of secret societies and associations that may have already existed in Kisalian times. Their various rituals indicate how a complex structure could have emerged in the absence of central authority. In Luba language, the word for king is much more recent than the word for chief or notable. By the end of Kisalian times, the old Bantu egalitarian tradition still seems to have been resisting centralization.

At the turn of the 13th century, Kisalian gave way, after a brief transition, to the Kabambian period. This is revealed by changes in pottery style, attendant rituals, and the appearance of cast-copper cross ingots as grave goods. There

seem to have been less cultural homogeneity at this time and fewer grave goods on the average. Evidence also suggests that social stratification had increased, as graves of intermediary wealth apparently disappeared.

Political power may have evolved as well. Status symbols, except for cone-shell disks and a small iron bell, are absent from even the wealthiest Kabambian graves. Such regalia may have been reserved for the most prominent leaders, who were buried separately.

The initial phase of the Kabambian was replaced by the Kabambian B around the 15th century. Grave goods were then reduced to a few vessels, and the large copper crosses, previously placed on the chest, were moved to the hands and hips. At the same time, these crosses became much smaller and more standardized, suggesting a shift from a special-purpose currency to a more general use in a market-oriented economy.

Around the 17th century, graves of the Luba resembled those of more recent people. Bracelets, belts, and anklets alone (usually made of glass beads) came to constitute grave goods.

The capitals of the Luba kingdom after 1700 were located outside of the Upemba Depression, to the northwest—an area for which there is no archaeological data. It can be conjectured, however, that the more recent Luba polity results from some political changes that came into effect by Kabambian times. This is especially so if this polity draws its inspiration from the long Kisalian tradition of manipulating status symbols in what was a complex, but still little-centralized, civilization. It may well be the result of new rulers, who progressively took control as they arrived from the east and likely fused the new hierarchical order with the old Kisalian symbolic political system.

After an initial use of force, the new rulers managed to control a large area through a strategy of intermarriage and through the use of old regalia, which they adopted to emphasize their legitimacy. Similarly, due to the difficulty of maintaining a standing army and to the resurgence of the old Bantu political tradition of autonomy, the modern Luba state relied more on prestige and influence than on authority or force. This is another reason why the Luba made use of a wide array of beautiful memorial objects and performances.

Luba prestige and influence extended widely, as chiefs and kings to the east and south claimed Luba origins. These polities often resulted from various local processes, the elevated Luba notion of *leadership,* and a flexible system of political rule. The Lunda kingdom developed into a very extensive territorial state. By combining political and ritual syncretism with limited control of the military and trade, it established a loose polity over a huge area in the 18th and early 19th centuries.

<hr/>

Archaeological evidence for the origins and history of the savanna states is not widely available—except for Luba. It does provide, however, some interesting examples of political process for the recent past by stressing the importance of old underlying ideological traditions, symbolic and ritual behaviors, and unpredictable occurrences. These examples may help mainstream theoretical archaeologists revise conventional ethnocentric preconceptions about states—preconceptions that are all-too-often based on political, economic, and military factors.

BIBLIOGRAPHY

Birmingham, D., and P. M. Martin. 1983. *History of central Africa.* London: Longmann.

de Maret, P. 1992. *Fouilles archéologiques dans la vallée du Haut-Lualaba, Zaire III: Kamilamba, Kikulu et Malemba-Nkulu, 1975.* Tervuren: Musée Royal de l'Afrique Centrale.

Gutierrez, M., and F. Valentin. 1955. Archéologie et anthropologie des tumulus de Kapanda (Angola). *Journal des Africanistes* 65 (2): 145–169.

Hilton, A. 1985. *The kingdom of Kongo.* Oxford: Oxford University Press.

Lanfranchi, R., and B. Clist. 1991. *Aux origines de l'Afrique centrale.* Paris: Sepia.

Miller, J. 1976. *Kings and kinsmen: Early Mbundu states in Angola.* Oxford: Oxford University Press.

Nooter R., M. Roberts, and A. F. Roberts. 1996. *Memory—Luba art and the making of history.* Unich: Prestel for the Museum for African Art, New York.

Reefe, T. Q. 1981. *The rainbow and the kings: A history of the Luba Empire to 1891.* Berkeley: University of California Press.

Vansina, J. 1966. *Kingdoms of the savanna.* Madison: University of Wisconsin Press.

———. 1990. *Paths in the rainforests: Toward a history of political tradition in equatorial Africa.* Madison: University of Wisconsin Press.

Pierre de Maret

LACUSTRINE STATES

The region of eastern Africa, bordered to the east by Lakes Victoria and Kyoga and to the west by the lakes of the Western Rift (the interlacustrine or Great Lakes region), witnessed the emergence of a number of highly organized societies in the 2nd millennium A.D. Arab traders and European explorers first encountered these kingdoms in the mid-19th century. Their possible origins were immediately a topic of considerable interest to Europeans because, unlike other parts of the continent, the lacustrine states could not obviously be explained by the presence of non-African rulers or traders. This preoccupation with origins has characterized the subsequent archaeological work on the lacustrine states. As will be seen, however, there have been a number of approaches to the archaeological record. These different approaches emphasize the significance of the historiography of archaeological research in the lacustrine states.

In Uganda, early documentation of archaeological sites was dependent on the recreational interests of Protectorate officials. Through their enthusiastic notes and records, writers such as E. J. Wayland and E. C. Lanning are still important primary sources on archaeological sites. In Rwanda and Burundi, by contrast, the major influence appears to have been the location of mission stations. From the early days of the Uganda Protectorate, large archaeological sites were recorded. These were not apparently associated with the 19th-century kingdoms or their dynastic traditions. The sites often featured networks of ditches that extended for several kilometers. On the basis of information from oral traditions and on historical interpretations of these traditions, it was concluded that these sites were capitals of an

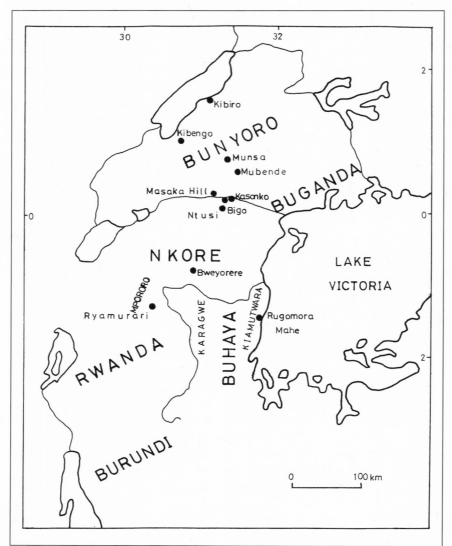

Fig. 66 *The lacustrine states*

empire run by mysterious characters known as Cwezi. The initial concept of state formation in the region was in terms of conquest, imposition of a preformed political system, and subsequent degeneration of this system. It was in this context that archaeologists first investigated sites in the region.

In 1957 and 1960 respectively, P. Shinnie and M. Posnansky excavated Bigo, the foremost of the "earthwork" sites. In 1958, Posnansky also excavated Bweyorere, a site attributed to early rulers of the Nkore kingdom. These various excavations have subsequently been criticized, since they were intended merely to verify his-

tory from oral traditions. With the benefit of hindsight, it is difficult to imagine what might have constituted proof of Cwezi identity. Since then, the focus of archaeological work shifted away from Uganda and its earthworks. In Buhaya in northwestern Tanzania, P. Schmidt undertook a more critical evaluation of oral traditions to investigate the nature of power and authority in regard to ironworking, a process he traced to the very earliest Urewe ironworkers. F. Van Noten and others conducted similar work on ironworking in Rwanda and Burundi. Since 1986, there has been a resumption of archaeological research in Uganda. Interestingly, this has still been based on sites that have been known for many years, reaffirming the quality of early archaeological records. This latest work is largely ongoing and has not yet been fully published.

Archaeological research in its early stages generally focused on sites with either large ditch networks or associated by oral traditions with the Cwezi. Most noteworthy of all the ditch network sites has been Bigo. Situated on a hill overlooking the Katonga River, this site would appear to dominate the Mawogola Grasslands to the south. The identification of two smaller sites, one on either side along the river, added to this impression. The ditches themselves are cut to a depth of up to 4 meters into the subsoil and form an outer line and an inner complex of ditches clustering on the main hilltop. In all, there are some 10 kilometers of ditches representing a considerable feat of labor. Five kilometers down the Katonga River, there is the large network of Kasonko. Munsa, 80 kilometers north of Bigo, features similar outer, middle, and inner ditches focused around a hilltop and with a river to the north. Excavations have shown the ditches to be up to 3.5 meters in depth. Kibengo, near the southern end of Lake Albert, completes the collection of the better-known and larger earthwork sites.

The function of the ditches and of the earthworks as a whole is not yet understood. Those at Bigo and Munsa, in particular, could not have been effective defensively, since the land beyond the outer ditches is higher than that inside, placing potential attackers at an advantage. While archaeological material is present within the inner ditches of most of these sites, the largest area, encircled by the outer ditch, is in all cases devoid of cultural material, suggesting that it was not occupied. The logical alternatives, therefore, would seem to be either land use for agriculture or pasturage. While there are several mounds of archaeological debris, ash, and dung at Bigo, suggesting a concentration of occupation, there is not a single trace of archaeological material or of occupation at Kasonko. At Munsa, moreover, the central area, situated on a hilltop, features a number of burials. The only dating evidence published so far comes from Bigo, with radiocarbon evaluations falling between the 15th and 19th centuries, and Munsa, dating to around the 14th or 15th centuries.

Archaeological sites principally associated with the Cwezi include Mubende Hill and Masaka Hill. Understanding of these sites is complicated by their continued use as shrines. Indeed in the first half of the 1990s, there was a revival in activity at these and other shrines. Excavations have been conducted on several occasions at Mubende Hill. In the 1950s, E. C. Lanning found a collection of five large, well-preserved pots near the tree that forms the shrine. Excavations in 1987 by P. Robertshaw indicated two occupations of the site, the first dating to the 13th and 14th centuries and the second to the 19th and 20th centuries. The earlier phase is conceivably consistent with oral traditions that state that this was the capital of Ndahura, one of the leading Cwezi characters. Archaeologically, there are large amounts of animal bone, dominated by cattle, and a number of pits into which grinding stones were thrown. The

site itself covers a maximum area of 5 hectares. There is little, therefore, in the archaeological record to indicate whether this was a royal center, a ritual center, or an ordinary residential site enhanced by subsequent traditions.

Besides the earthworks, which are restricted to the area of western Uganda between the southern shores of Lake Albert and the middle regions of the Katonga River, and the Cwezi sites, the region's archaeological sites dating to the 2nd millennium appear to have a broad unity. Most obviously, pottery is predominantly decorated by the use of roulette—knotted or twisted plant fiber or patterns carved in wood and rolled over the surface of the wet clay. While superficially uniform, encompassing all sites from the 2nd millennium as well as ethnographic collections from the 19th and 20th centuries, more detailed analyses have tended to indicate that subtle variations do occur in this pottery. Thus, G. Connah's work at Kibiro indicates a preference for carved, wooden roulettes not noticed at other sites. He also established a sequence of changes that have taken place in the Kibiro pottery assemblages between the 13th and 19th centuries. In western Uganda, Robertshaw has produced a pottery sequence on the basis of attribute clusters for sites located by archaeological survey. More ambitiously, C. Desmedts has identified three separate styles of rouletting that she considers to indicate separate waves of migration into the greater lacustrine region beginning in the 8th century. Given the richness of the ethnographic record, the continued production of pottery in the region today, and the success of iron-smelting reconstructions in the region, it is surprising that no analysis has yet adopted an approach to pottery collections based on categories recognized by potters themselves.

Since the mid-1980s, research has attempted to rely on interpretations based purely on excavated data rather than on historical reconstructions. In all cases, work has commenced at previously recognized sites, but research strategies have included surveys to examine sites in a broader, subregional perspective.

The earliest indicators of social complexity come from archaeological work on grasslands of the southern Uganda and at the site of Ntusi.

J. E. G. Sutton and A. Reid encountered occupation horizons at Ntusi dating from the 11th to the 15th century. From its earliest days, this settlement appears to have been predominantly concerned with the production of cattle. Evidence from faunal remains indicate herd-management strategies that exploited large quantities of immature animals. Cultivation of grain crops, such as sorghum and finger millet, was also widespread. By the 14th century, the site of Ntusi had grown to a size of as much as 100 hectares. In its later years, there is evidence for far-reaching trade in the occasional recovery of glass and cowrie-shell beads. Of more local origin, the inhabitants of Ntusi made regular use of ostrich-eggshell and ivory beads. Evidence for the manufacture of the latter was found in the midden of a household.

Central to the Ntusi economy was its control of cattle. Archaeological survey in the surrounding Mawogola area encountered more than 50 sites. Excavations were subsequently conducted at three: Buteraniro, Kakinga, and Kasebwongera. These sites are all small in size (less than 1 hectare) and are characterized at their lower end by long, low banks of ash and dung, suggesting single livestock enclosures. The banks contain abundant pottery and remains of cattle and occasional evidence for agriculture. Mortality patterns at these sites suggest the culling of animals at younger ages than evident at Ntusi. This pattern might be best explained by the removal of more mature animals to Ntusi.

Ntusi quite clearly dominated its hinterland, and its size and comparative artifact diversity imply both its economic and political hegemony. This two-tier settlement hierarchy suggests chiefly power and the maintenance of dominant lineages. Excavations indicate that cattle keeping and agricultural production were conducted within the same household. In later centuries, class divisions within the cattle-keeping states were based on the exclusive production of cattle by elite individuals and agricultural production by commoners. This creation of classes and, therefore, formation of the state, had evidently not occurred at Ntusi.

Elsewhere in the region, other important developments were taking place. From the 12th or 13th centuries, the site of Kibiro on the eastern shores of Lake Albert was first occupied. Connah found that archaeological deposits, more than 2 meters in depth, date from that time through to the 20th century.

Kibiro is significant for its salt production, an activity that continues today. Salt is produced by boiling soil impregnated by salt-rich springs. From historical sources, it is known that Kibiro became an economic asset of the Bunyoro state and was so important that at the end of the 19th century, it was targeted and destroyed several times by British punitive expeditions. Excavations have encountered industrial waste associated with salt working from the inception of the settlement. Kibiro's location at the base and in the rain shadow of a 500-meter escarpment means that it does not receive enough rainfall to make agriculture feasible. Stock rearing is possible but, on the basis of the archaeological faunal remains, does not appear to have been a major concern. It would seem, therefore, that the only viable means of economic activity for the community, besides fishing, would have been salt production. This being the case, the settlement would have been an important center for trade. Possible confirmation of Kibiro's economic significance comes from the recovery of glass beads throughout the archaeological sequence, augmented later by cowrie shells. At present, there is no evidence to suggest when Kibiro came under the direct control of the Bunyoro state, nor indeed is it known when Bunyoro itself came into existence as a state.

In a third area, based around Mubende and Munsa in western Uganda, there is further evidence for change. Robertshaw encountered around 130 sites during his widespread survey. On the basis of pottery collected from the surface, a tentative pottery sequence was created using attribute-data and cluster analysis. This analysis suggested that five distinct pottery facies could be recognized, and it was argued that these represented a chronological sequence. On the basis of this sequence, settlement of the area had begun by the 12th century. Furthermore, there is possible evidence of larger sites, site hierarchies, and defensive locations being created by the 14th century. These latter innovations would suggest increasing pressure and competition for the control of land. Work is currently in progress to generate chronological data with which to evaluate this proposed pottery sequence.

Collectively, the developments at Ntusi and Kibiro and around Mubende are significant. Surveys in all three areas indicate that there had been no prior occupation of these locations by earlier ironworking communities. Such communities, characteristically using Urewe pottery, have been encountered in archaeological sites around the margins of Lake Victoria, along the Nile, and in the highlands of Rwanda and Burundi. All these locations have a good cover of vegetation and high and reliable rainfall regimes. Movement into the much drier grasslands around Ntusi and the arid shoreline of Lake Albert, therefore, represents a significant change. Although little economic evidence exists for these earlier communities, the uniformity of environments suggests a mixed-farming economy as a characteristic feature. The development of large-scale cattle production at Ntusi, the beginnings of salt production at Kibiro, and the settlement of new agricultural lands in western Uganda in the early 2nd millennium, all represent, therefore, considerable diversification and specialization in the regional economy. The power of the regional economy is perhaps best illustrated by the presence of glass trade beads by the 14th century. It is not known from which direction these items came, posing a challenge for archaeologists in neighboring regions. The beads are in small enough quantities to indicate that they were not the product of direct contacts with coastal trade, but their presence suggests that the regional economy was sufficiently vibrant to draw exclusive trade items from distant communities. The development of higher-risk economic activities, like cattle keeping and salt production, would have required the creation of new forms of physical storage and social support (such as clans) extending back into the long-settled lake and forest margins. These economic and social changes were a vital adjunct to political changes that ultimately led to the creation of the kingdoms.

This notion of increasingly sophisticated economies and gradual development of complex societies is consistent with new reconstructions based on oral traditions and on comparative linguistics. In particular, D. Schoenbrun's work on comparative linguistics has highlighted new forms of power from the 8th century onward based on cattle and the control of land. The early stages of this process centered on personal power and charismatic leadership rather than on formal state structures. Archaeological work on the origins of the lacustrine states suggests that political complexity evolved, rather than devolved, during the 2nd millennium.

Archaeological research, therefore, has been largely preoccupied with the origins of the lacustrine states. The little work that has been done on the states that had matured by the latter part of the millennium suggest a valuable resource for general theories regarding the workings of complex societies. For instance, separate studies on different aspects of ironworking in Buhaya, Karagwe, Burundi, Rwanda, and Bunyoro have revealed a wealth of data on the physical and social contexts of iron production. Although much of this work has concentrated on smelting reconstructions in order to assist with the understanding of earlier episodes of ironworking, it is now being realized that these studies produce information of considerable interest for the study of the kingdoms themselves. Most obviously Schmidt's excavations of the 17th-century Kiamutwara capital of Rugamora Mahe (at Katuruka) demonstrated the importance of control over ritual and technology within the kingdoms of the interlacustrine region. At this site on the western edge of Lake Victoria, Schmidt demonstrated the juxtaposition of extensive iron-smelting evidence dating from the 3rd century B.C., a 17th-century royal enclosure, and modern oral traditions and spiritual power.

Unique archaeological work in Rwanda has augmented this interconnectedness of technology and ritual. Van Noten's excavations of the graves of Cyirima Rujugira and Kigeri Rwabugiri, both kings of Rwanda, provided an archaeological insight into the rituals of death. Due to the resurgence of the lacustrine states in the 1990s, such work is unlikely to be repeated in the near future. The graves contained large numbers of artifacts and provide a visible documentation of royal ritual to complement ethnographic information.

Rituals and artifacts involved in royal burials relate to the power of the king in life. Thus burials are important in ensuring the successful transition from king to restful spirit. Failure to follow these rituals results in the spirit wandering across the land causing havoc. Study of a 19th-century iron-producing community in the neighboring kingdom of Karagwe demonstrates the many different levels in which knowledge of iron smelting was interwoven within the state. There, smelters ultimately performed the burial ritual for the dead king.

Excavations have been conducted at two capitals of smaller states dominated by cattle keepers. Bweyorere, a center of the Nkore kingdom, and Ryamurari, a capital of Mpororo, both occupied in the 17th and 18th centuries, consist of central areas surrounded by long, low banks of ash and dung. The central enclosures are, in turn, surrounded by smaller enclosures. Bone recovered in excavations indicates, not surprisingly, the predominance of young cattle at the sites. The results of excavations at Bweyorere, in particular, and the recognition of structures suggest that research designs focused on the organization of complex societies would be very successful. Reconnaissance of other Nkore capitals demonstrated that they are archaeologically insignificant, neither being occupied for a long time, nor covering a large area. These are characteristics that could not be predicted from historical studies. Clearly, further work is required in these areas to explain the lack of material at the majority of sites and its abundance at sites like Bweyorere.

As yet unstudied archaeologically are the capitals of the larger 19th-century kingdoms of Buganda, Bunyoro, and Rwanda. On the basis of extant historical accounts, these are known to have been very large (in terms of both size and population) yet were occupied for periods of less than ten years. They were very different from sites such as Ntusi, with its longevity of occupation, and Bigo, with its ditch network. This suggests that there were significant changes in protourban forms in quite recent times, changes that could be examined archaeologically.

Research into the lacustrine states has been considerably affected by the changing relationship between archaeology and history. Archaeology is now providing a more coherent picture of the early transformations leading to the formation of states in the region. This success, however, merely serves to highlight the considerable gaps in archaeological input toward understanding the lacustrine states. Conspicuously absent from the archaeological reconstructions are the enigmatic earthwork sites, emphasizing the need to tackle these sites with focused, large-scale archaeological projects. Such a comprehensive program is currently being attempted by Robertshaw at the site of Munsa.

Archaeology also needs to recognize its own potential significance in contributing to more recent historical periods. Historians are increasingly aware of contradictions in historical sources and their significance for understanding the structure of the lacustrine states. Archaeologists can make a contribution to these debates, whether in general terms regarding settlement forms, or examining the roles of specific forms of production within the states. Most striking is the complete absence of any archaeological statement on any aspect of Buganda, the largest and, ultimately, the most complex of the kingdoms

Another large gap, particularly by comparison with other regions of incipient state formation, is the absence of sensitive regional and subregional environmental data for the 2nd millennium A.D. The ecological consequences of large-scale cattle production and permanent agricultural settlement must have been considerable. They are certainly acute problems in the present. The absence of environmental data for the region and the lack of understanding of ecological dynamics will hinder the construction of more sophisticated explanations for the creation and elaboration of the lacustrine states over the last 1,000 years.

BIBLIOGRAPHY

Connah, G. 1991. The salt of Bunyoro: Seeking the origins of an African kingdom. *Antiquity* 65: 479–494.

Desmedts, C. 1991. Poteries anciennes décorées à la roulette dans la région des Grands Lacs. *African Archaeological Review* 9: 161–196.

Posnansky, M. 1969. Bigo bya Mugenyi. *Uganda Journal* 33: 125–150.

Reid, A., and R. Maclean. 1995. Symbolism and the social contexts of iron production in Karagwe. *World Archaeology* 27 (1): 144–161.

Robertshaw, P. 1994. Archaeological survey, ceramic analysis, and state formation in western Uganda. *African Archaeological Review* 12: 105–131.

Schmidt, P. 1978. *Historical archaeology: A structural approach in an African culture.* Westport: Greenwood Press.

———. 1990. Oral traditions and archaeology in Africa. In *A history of African archaeology,* ed. P. Robertshaw, 252-270. London and Portsmouth: James Currey Ltd. and Heinemann.

Schoenbrun, D. 1993. Cattle herds and banana gardens: The historical geography of the western Great Lakes region, ca. A.D. 800–1500. *African Archaeological Review* 11: 39–72.

Sutton, J. E. G. 1993. The antecedents of the interlacustrine kingdoms. *Journal of African History* 34: 33–64.

Van Noten, F. 1983. *Histoire archéologique du Rwanda.* Tervuren: Musée Royal de l'Afrique Centrale.

Andrew Reid

SWAHILI AND THE COASTAL CITY-STATES

Anthropologists and historians use the term *Swahili coast* to refer to the East African coast and adjacent islands. The Swahili coast is a 20- to 200-kilometer-wide strip of the East African coast more than 3,000 kilometers long, extending from Mogadishu in Somalia to Cape Delgado in Mozambique. The area includes the Comoro and Lamu Archipelagos and the islands of Mombasa, Pemba, Zanzibar, Mafia, and Kirimba.

The Swahili coast is ecologically diverse and has a wide range of plant and animal resources. The offshore islands, including Lamu, Mombasa, Pemba, Zanzibar, and Mafia, formed out of fossil coral reef. Surrounded by deep harbors, these islands have freshwater and defensive advantages. The coral reefs and littorals bear rich fishing grounds. Inland from the reefs, the islands have poor soils but adequate freshwater supplies from the sand-dune formations close to the seashore.

On the mainland, the coastal swamps contain at least eight species of mangroves, important sources of timber and excellent fish-spawning habitats. The soils in the coastal strip are, in general, well watered and fertile. The lowland, wet forest along the coastal strip supports large animals, including cats, elephants, and rhinoceroses. The riverine woodlands in the Tana and Rufiji Deltas have green, well-watered forests and relatively fertile soils. West of the northern coastal littoral lies the dry rangeland acacia scrub. In contrast, the southern coastal hinterland is relatively well watered by the great Rufiji, Ruvuma, and Lukuledi Rivers.

On the northern coast between the Tana River and Mombasa are cliffs and shallow beaches stretching out to the reef. There are some creeks and countless small inlets rich in mangrove forests and fish. The Mrima coast, extending from the southern Kenya border to the vast delta of the Rufiji, rises in the northwest to the highlands of Shambaa, Pare, and Kilimanjaro. Southward lie the relatively fertile eastern plains of Tanzania.

The ecological diversity of the Swahili coast offered excellent resources for human adaptation. The creeks, lagoons, rivers, and the sea provided marine resources, including fish, coral reef, and mangroves, and allowed important communication networks to develop. Most creeks along the coast are navigable for several kilometers inland. The Lana River is navigable for longer distances, albeit only by canoes and small boats. The Rufiji is navigable for at least 30 kilometers inland and even farther by careful maneuvering. The sea and rivers offered an excellent communication system that could be used for developing and maintaining alliances, connections, and trade networks conducive for exploiting the coast, interior, and islands and indeed the Indian Ocean's vast resources. Soils on the islands are often sandy, heavily leached, and coralline. By contrast, the riverine woodlands and the floodplains of the major rivers flowing into the Indian Ocean, including the Juba, Tana, Ruvuma, Lukuledi, and Rufiji, contained fertile, well-watered soils and forests conducive to agriculture and hunting. Rice, millet, beans, peas, sesame, bananas, pumpkins, maniac, and yams were grown both for local consumption and exchange with island communities.

Fish, wild game, fowls, goats, camels, and domestic zebu cattle supplemented the diet.

In sum, the hot and humid climate of the Swahili coast, the fairly reliable rainfall, the abundant fish resources, the freshwater close to the sea along the beaches on both islands and mainland, the defensive advantages offered by the islands, the mangrove forests providing building timber, and the communication channels provided by the sea, creeks, and rivers, all combined to make the Swahili coast an attractive habitat for human settlement.

A very distinctive feature of this coast up to the early 20th century was remnants of ruined mansions, towns, and mosques built in coral rock. In 1956, Oxford Africanist historian and archaeologist Gervase Mathew described the Swahili coast as:

> a compromise culture, always at least nominally Islamic, influenced from South Arabia, from Western India, and perhaps from Portugal but certainly deeply Africanized and probably integrally African. The ruined towns represent a group of small island states, oligarchic in their social structures, using currency of beads and rolls of cloth, and trading in ivory and slaves.

The first attempt to synthesize the archaeology of the Swahili coast was J. S. Kirkman's *Men and Monuments on the East African Coast,* published in 1964, in which the author treated all the ruined sites from Mogadishu to northern Madagascar as belonging to a single, continuous Muslim civilization of Arab origin. Recent studies by G. H. O. Abungu, J. de V. Allen, M. C. Horton, C. M. Kusimba, A. A. Mazrui, and J. B. Shariff, D. Nurse, and T. Spear, and R. Pouwels have shown that although a dynamic cultural, biological, and technical interaction existed among peoples living along the coast, in the interior, and throughout the wider Indian Ocean region, the resulting culture was African. Thus archaeologists no longer consider the identity of the Swahili coast inhabitants an issue. They have begun to evaluate the coast's archaeology as part of a world economic system delimited by the Indian Ocean.

Archaeological and ethnological research on the Swahili coast during the last 50 years shows that interactions between East Africans and communities traversing the Indian Ocean and the Persian Gulf may predate the development of urban polities on the Swahili coast and littoral islands. Many of the food crops and domestic animals that are now staple foods in much of sub-Saharan Africa were first experimented with and domesticated either in the Middle East, Southeast Asia, or the Americas. Likewise, some food crops that now grow in India and Southeast Asia were first domesticated in Africa. The presence of Asian artifacts (including Islamic, Indian, and Chinese ceramics) at Swahili sites, the widespread use of *dhows* (Arab lanteen-rigged boats), outriggers, and other sailing vessels in the Indian Ocean, the similarity in architectural styles both for settlement sites, and a common adherence to Islam among most of the coast's inhabitants suggest a common cultural base for coastal societies and a relatively close link with cultures inhabiting other parts of the Indian Ocean region. The inhabitants of Swahili towns are now known to have played a prominent role in the triangular mercantile trade linking India, the Persian Gulf, and East Africa. Early writings by Arab travelers that survive from the early 10th century, plus accounts by European authors from the 16th century, show the significance of long-distance maritime trade in the Indian Ocean and the role of East Africans in this trade.

Trade items from the East African coast consigned to foreign markets in India, the Middle East, and China included marine products (such as turtle shell and ambergris), terrestrial animal products (such as ivory, rhinoceros horns, and cat skins), and plant products (such as mangrove poles, incense, and timber). Turtle shells and ambergris were in high demand in India and China. Ivory, rhinoceros horns, and leopard skins were exported to India, China, and the Persian Gulf. African timber for building and aromatic products were needed in the Persian Gulf until relatively recently. Silk was manufactured in Mogadishu and Pate, red cotton was woven in Zanzibar, and the surplus exported. Iron production was an important industrial activity at Malindi and several other Swahili towns. Recent analytical study of iron artifacts from archaeological contexts on the Swahili coast have yielded crucible steel, previously credited only to Indian and Sri Lankan smelters of the 10th century. One crucible sample was dated to the 7th century, making it the earliest reported crucible steel in the world by perhaps as much as 300 years.

Historical Chronology of the Archaeological Record

The traditional method of determining the chronology of sites along the Swahili coast has been the comparative analysis of imported ceramics from known kilns in China and the Middle East. Many archaeologists now recognize the importance of radiometric dates and have begun submitting charcoal samples more regularly. Four broad archaeological periods, each with several phases, are now widely recognized. These periods include: Period I (100 B.C. to A.D. 300), Period II (300 to 1000), Period III (1000 to 1500), and Period IV (1500 to 1950).

Period I (100 B.C. to A.D. 300)

Few archaeological sites are known in Period I. These include Misasa, Kwale, and Ras Hafun located in Tanzania, Kenya, and Somalia respectively. The sites have been linked with the communities of proto–Bantu-speakers whose descendants now inhabit much of eastern and southern Africa. Period I sites have been associated with low-fired pottery, often having beveled, fluted rims and shoulders and decorated with narrow incised and stamped bands. Much of this pottery is dated to the 4th century B.C. in the Great Lakes region of eastern Africa and in southern Africa. Several phases of Period I are known by regional variants including Chifumbaze and Mwitu.

Period II (300 to 1000)

Period II is divided into two phases, characterized by pottery with a general decorative motif of triangular, oblique, and double zigzag incisions. The early phase (300 to 600) is also called the *Azanian period*. The later phase (600 to 1000) is called the *Zanjian period*. Known Azanian sites included Amboni Tanga, Chibuene, Kiwangwa, Limbo, Masuguru, Misasa, Mpiji, and Unguja Ukuu located on the southern Swahili coast. Later Period II sites are more widespread along the length of the coast and include Gezira, Irodo, Kaole, Kilwa, Mahilaka, Manda, Monapo, Pate, and Shanga.

Unlike Period I sites, which are primarily dominated by local finds, Period II sites have yielded nonlocal artifacts including Sassanian pottery, glass, and carnelian beads. The presence of these items suggests that the people living on the Swahili coast had contact with the Persian Gulf. About 40 percent of the decorative motifs exhibited in Period I are retained in Early Period II, indicating continuity of stylistic traditions. Late Period II pottery was largely, though not exclusively, composed of red, burnished, and bag-shaped cooking pots and bowls with thickened rims. The common decorative motifs were graphite finish and trellis-pattern incisions. Archaeologists refer to local pottery by various names including *Kitchenware, Wenje ware, Tana ware,* and *Dembeni ware.* F. A. Chami recently proposed a more neutral, inclusive designation, *triangular incised ware,* to replace the earlier names.

Locally produced iron farming tools and fish and animal bones found at Swahili sites during this period imply a village subsistence economy based largely on the exploitation of local resources with some participation in local and international trade. Communication between Africans, Middle Easterners, and Indians appears to have increased during Late Period II. Much of this communication was primarily motivated by long-distance maritime trade. For example, al Masudi in 915 stressed the importance of ivory and the quest for amber, leopard skins, turtle shells, and gold in the trade between the Zanj and the Persian Gulf. He argued that the Zanj regarded iron and copper an equal to gold and silver as an ornament. Commenting on the technical quality of iron produced in East Africa, al Idrisi (1100–1166) noted that it was an important trade item for southern Indian merchants, who confessed of its superior malleability to Indian iron.

Imported ceramics recovered from Period II sites include Partho Sassanian Islamic wares, tin glazed ware, Chinese Sue ware, Guangdong coastal green ware, Ding ware (800–1150), Gonxian (northern white ware), Indian purple ware, and fragments of Egyptian glass. Domestic structures were characterized by square mud-on-wooden frames with coral foundations. Shell beads, iron and copper artifacts, and shell spoons were locally produced.

Period III (1000–1500)

Period III is largely associated with the emergence of autonomous polities, the Swahili city-states. Settlements founded earlier expanded in size from villages into towns and cities. Many others including Barawa, Jongowe, Kingany, Kisimayu, Lamu, Mafia, Mkumbuu, Mogadishu, Mtambwe Mkuu, and Vohemar, among others, were founded. A marked increase in the quantities of imported material culture occurred. The vast buildings with coral walls appeared, suggesting establishment of a more secure economic base, increasing sociopolitical diversity, and an economy capable of supporting professional craft specialists like masons. The enormous quantities of slag and pottery recovered from Period III excavations at Kilwa, Manda, Shanga, and Ungwana, for example, suggest increased production to satisfy both local and international demand. Some scholars have interpreted the increased volume of debris to have been the result of population expansion due to immigration by coastal, hinterland, and Indian Ocean peoples who sought to benefit from the booming economy of the emerging Swahili coast cosmopolitan cities of Kilwa, Manda, and Mogadishu.

During Period III, Islamic *sgraffiato* pottery, Chinese *qing bai*, and Cizhou ware (dating from 1200 or 1250 to 1400), and chlorite schist (probably from Madagascar) were introduced. Bronze mirrors, kohl sticks, glass beads, and rock crystal (a semiprecious stone from the interior of Kenya) were added to the women's wardrobes. Cooking ovens and crucibles of pottery are found for the first time. Spindle whorls made from local pottery suggest the beginning of weaving and textile production. The appearance of copper and silver coins bearing the name of Ali Ibn al Hasan toward the end of 12th century and the increased use of stone in domestic architecture over much of the Swahili coast have been interpreted by some archaeologists as evidence for immigration by Persians from Shiraz and later by Arabs to East Africa.

Many archaeological sites of the 13th century contain Friday congregation mosques. Because the archaeological sites in Period III have mosques, most built in coral stone, it is safe to conclude that many inhabitants were converted to Islam during this time. For example, when Ibn Batuta visited Kilwa in 1331, he found the town's inhabitants "were engaged in a holy war, for their country lies beside that of Pagan Zanj."

Expansion and extension of trade continued in the 14th century. The use of coral stone in domestic architecture became more standardized among the wealthy elite, who constituted the farmers and traders. Cut coral, called *pyrites,* was used for door jambs, mihrabs (a niche or chamber in a mosque indicating the direction of Mecca), and for decorative purposes in the elite houses to signify socioeconomic status. Moreover, paneled tombs like those at Songo Mnara (Tanzania) and Kingany (Madagascar) first appeared on the Swahili coast to augment the domed tombs that were first introduced at Kilwa in the 12th century.

Chinese celadons, especially Longquan and Tongan (dating to between 1250 and 1500) and Sawankhalok or Sisatchanalai jars (dating to between 1350 and 1450 or 1500), perhaps from Indonesia, dominated the imports. Trade in Islamic pottery and Chinese blue and white wares declined, but Indian beads and Egyptian glass continued to be imported in large volume. The large number of spindle whorls indicated thriving textile industries at Kilwa, Pate, and Mogadishu to supply the increased local and regional demand for clothing. Local copper mints at Kilwa and Mogadishu provide evidence of the dynamic economic climate.

During the 15th century, East Africans continued to maintain trade with cultures around the Persian Gulf, India, and Madagascar. Blue and white Chinese porcelain and Longquan, Tongan, and other varieties of celadon were still imported, having undercut the Islamic ceramics in the preceding century. However, the appearance in considerable quantities of Persian Islamic pottery with a flower motif may indicate renewed attempts by Persian potters to recapture the African market. Indian beads were consistently imported. Innovations in local pottery making included the portable stove and lamps.

Two contrasting processes occurred in Late Period III especially at Kilwa: a marked decline in the volume of locally produced artifacts and a structural expansion and elaboration of public and domestic architecture. The proportion of houses built in coral and lime mortar and dressed in plaster dramatically increased. The volume of imported ceramics, especially Chinese ceramics, also increased. In contrast, the volume of iron slag and the number of spindle whorls decreased and by 1600 almost stopped. It is puzzling that decrease in local production of iron and textiles does not correspond with the inferred level of consumption and demand for these items. In fact, decline in local production industries is accompanied by the highest level of structural expansion at Kilwa, in the form of more elegant and larger houses and public buildings, including mosques and palaces built of squared coral blocks. Decline in local craft enterprises may indicate a shift of elite attention from local crafts to other, perhaps more profitable, concerns provided by the economic boom of the 14th and 15th centuries

Decline in ironworking and textile making marked Kilwa's transition from a local manufacturing center to an international cosmopolitan trading entrepot. The location of Kilwa on the southern Mgao coast and Kerimba coast placed Kilwa's elite in a strategic position to participate, manage, and control much of the African trade between southeastern Africans and others on the northern Swahili coast, Madagascar, the Comoro Islands, southern India, Indonesia, and the Persian Gulf states. Gold, copper, ivory, slaves, and iron from southern Africa came to Kilwa via Sofala. Cloth, glass beads, cowrie shells, shell beads, and other trade items found their way to the interior through Kilwa.

Stylistic changes in local pottery in Period III suggest the professionalization of the craft technologies as well as demographic changes in the cultural and ethnic makeup of coastal societies. As an international trading region, the Swahili coast was an emerging cosmopolitan center that attracted settlement by all communities who wished to benefit from the economic fortunes of the era. Perhaps the cultural diversity of the population pressured the potters to make pots and vessels in response to consumers' tastes. Demand for pottery may have led to the development of full-time professional potters' guilds. Decline in iron production may be attributed to competition for iron bloom brought in possibly from the interior and from Indian Ocean towns having commercial connections with the Swahili coast.

Period IV (1500–1950)

During Period IV, the colonial period, East Africans lost their territory and self-determination to a series of foreign powers. These powers included the Portuguese (from 1500 to 1970), the Omani Arabs (from the 1770s to 1884), the British (from 1884 to 1963), and the Germans (from 1884 to 1918). When the Portuguese arrived in 1495, they found on the Swahili coast a thriving civilization that had developed a complex regional and international trading system. Despite this commercial success, the Swahili coast was not sufficiently united to confront and resist foreign invasion. The Swahili coast was neither homogeneous, nor had it any naval power over the sea. Although the locals often outnumbered the invaders, the foreigners had the technological and military edge of well-equipped and highly sophisticated gunboats and firepower. For example, the Portuguese triple mission of finding the sea route to India, controlling the spice trade, and stopping the Islamic expansion helped them conquer the less-united autonomous polities.

The archaeology of Period IV is not well understood, in part because little research has been conducted on the contact period. Many Swahili sites appear to have been in decline by the 16th century and to have been abandoned soon after. Others diminished to small towns and villages, while some, despite the colonial setback, continued to thrive. Many chronicles of the Swahili towns were written during the colonial period and thus relate events of Swahili great rule. Kirkman's 1974 study of the Portuguese fortress of Fort Jesus in Mombasa remains the most important study of Period IV. Large-scale immigration from the colonial powers to the Swahili coast occurred during these times. The archaeological record of the colonial period needs to be carefully studied in order to understand interactions during the last 500 years. The archaeological rendering of the

Period IV will supplement the largely historical and ethnographic sources currently available.

The Development of the Swahili Coast

The archaeological record indicates that the inhabitants of Period I coastal sites exploited local resources through fishing, farming, and ironworking to meet local needs and for trade with neighboring communities. These people probably developed a canoe and boat technology, which they used to sail along the coast, trade with each other, and colonize new areas. The ecological diversity of the Swahili coast favored the development of local exchange networks between communities to supplement locally unavailable resources. The sea and proper boats provided excellent means of communication.

Socioeconomic and technological transformations were already in motion before the onset of large-scale long-distance trade and also before Islam was fully adopted and adapted as a religion of the locals. By the end of the 1st millennium A.D., a cadre of leaders with greater access to important resources had emerged on the Swahili coast. Qualitative distinctions between those with more access and those with less access is indicated by a greater diversity in domestic structures in Period III than is seen in earlier periods. This marked the emergence of an elite class, which is often associated with complex polities.

Once Islam was adopted by many local inhabitants in Late Period II and Early Period III, it became a major integrative mechanism in Swahili culture. The small size of Period II mosques suggests that Islam was initially the religion of a minority. Once adopted and adapted to local conditions, Islam became a major factor in determining sociopolitical, economic, and ideological relationship between the Swahili coast and other regions.

The archaeology of the Swahili coast, though far from being exhaustively known, shows that the area reached its political floruit in the 14th century and began a slow but steady decline in the 15th century. This path was accelerated by colonization from the early 16th century up to the 1960s. It was a coast composed of autonomous polities that were initially self-reliant in technology and food production but became more and more dependent upon external trade toward the end of Period II. Long-distance trade played a crucial role in the formation of an elite class in Period II. It is possible that overreliance on external trade affected the development of local industries. Consequently, the Swahili coast may have been unable to sustain itself without external trade. This dependence may have led to political instability, thus paving the way for the colonial period, which lasted for the next five centuries.

BIBLIOGRAPHY

Abungu, G. H. O. 1990. Communities on the River Tana, Kenya: An archaeological study of relations between the delta and the river basin. 700–1890 A.D. Ph.D. diss, Cambridge University.

Allen, J. de V. 1993. *Swahili origins.* London: Heinemann.

Champ F. A. 1994. *The coast of East Africa in the first millennium* A.D.: *A study of the iron working farming communities.* Uppsala: Societas Archaeologica Upsaliensis.

Chandra, S. 1987. Introduction. In *The Indian Ocean: Exploration in history, commerce, and politics,* ed. S. Chandra, 11–26. New Delhi: Sage Publications.

Chittick, N. H. 1974. *Kilwa: An Islamic trading city on the East African coast.* Nairobi: British Institute in Eastern Africa.

Davidson, B. 1991. *African civilization revisited: From antiquity to modern times.* Trenton: Africa World Press.

Freeman-Grenville, G. S. P. 1962. *The East African coast: Select documents from the first to the early nineteenth century.* Oxford: Clarendon.

Garlake, P. S. 1966. *Islamic architecture on the East African coast.* Nairobi: The British Institute in Eastern Africa.

Horton, M. C. 1987. The Swahili corridor. *Scientific American* (September 1987): 86–93.

Kindy, H. 1972. *Life and politics in Mombasa.* Nairobi: East African Publishing House.

Kirkman, J. S. 1964. *Men and monuments on the East African coast.* London: Butterworth Press.

———. 1974. *Fort Jesus: A Portuguese fortress on the East African coast.* Oxford: Clarendon Press.

Kusimba. C. M. 1993. *The archaeology and ethnography of iron metallurgy on the Swahili coast.* Ann Arbor: University Microfilm International.

Kusimba, C. M., D. Killick, and R. G. Creswell. 1994. Indigenous and imported metals on Swahili sites of Kenya. *Masca Papers in Science and Archaeology.*

Lewicki, T. 1969. Arabic external sources for the history of Africa to the south of the Sahara. *Oddzial Krakowie Prace Komisji Orientalistycznej,* No. 9. Polska Akademia Nauk, Wroclaw.

Mathew, G. 1956. The culture of the East African coast in the eighteenth and nineteenth centuries in the light of recent archaeological discoveries. *Man* 56: 65–68.

Mazrui, A. A., and I. B. Shariff. 1994. *The Swahili: Idiom and identity of an African people.* Trenton: Africa World Press.

Mbuia-Joao, T. N. 1990. *The revolt of Dom Jeronimo Chingulia of Mombasa, 1590–1637: An African episode in the Portuguese century of decline.* Ann Arbor: University Microfilm International.

Nurse, D., and T. Spear. 1985. *The Swahili: Reconstructing the history and language of an African society, 800–1500.* Philadelphia: University of Pennsylvania Press.

Pouwels, R. 1987. *Horn and crescent: Cultural change and traditional Islam on the East African coast, 800–1900.* Cambridge: Cambridge University Press.

Tolmacheva, M. 1993. *The Pate chronicle.* East Lansing: Michigan State University Press.

Toussaint, A. 1966. *History of the Indian Ocean.* Chicago: University of Chicago Press.

Verin, P. 1986. *The history of civilization in North Madagascar.* Rotterdam: A. A. Balkema.

Villers, A. 1940. *Sons of Sinbad.* New York: Charles Scribner and Sons.

Chapurukha M. Kusimba

ZAMBEZIAN STATES

The ancient Zimbabwe culture was characterized by sacred leadership, a well-defined political hierarchy, and a marked distinction between nobles and commoners. Senior families of different lineages across the cultural area formed a single bureaucratic upper class, concentrating wealth, prestige, and political power to themselves. By virtue of birth, these senior families formed a high-status community with universally recognized rights, duties, and behaviors. This class distinction manifested itself, among other ways, in two settlement patterns: commoner settlements followed the principles of the central cattle pattern, while the elite Zimbabwe pattern characterized political centers.

The elite Zimbabwe pattern was the result of a worldview that included the concept of *sacred leadership.* A noble leader's power was based in part on the claim that his ancestors could intercede directly with God to ensure the fertility of the land and his people. As part of the spatial pattern, this sacred leader was ritually secluded behind a stone-walled palace.

Stone-walled palaces have been recorded over a large area of modern-day Zimbabwe, eastern Botswana, northern South Africa, and parts of Mozambique. Some of these sites were the headquarters of political organizations sufficiently large and complex to be called *states.*

Archaeologists now divide the Zimbabwe culture into three chronological periods named after important state capitals: Mapungubwe (from 1220 to 1290), Great Zimbabwe (from 1290 to 1450), and Khami (from 1450 to 1820). Three other states existed during the Khami period: the Changamire-Rozvi state based at Danangombe (or, more popularly, Dhlo Dhlo), the Mutapa state centered in the northeastern corner of Zimbabwe, and the Thovhela state based at Dzala in the Venda area.

Portuguese eyewitness accounts written during the Khami period make it clear that the Zimbabwe culture was the product of Shona-speaking people. These accounts, along with Shona and Venda oral histories and ethnographic data, help reconstruct the nature and extent of these states.

The Nature of Zambezian Political Hierarchies

In the Zimbabwe cultural area (and indeed throughout southern Africa), every settlement had a place, a court, where men met to discuss political matters and resolve disputes. This court was directly associated with the leader of the settlement, and the extent of this person's jurisdiction

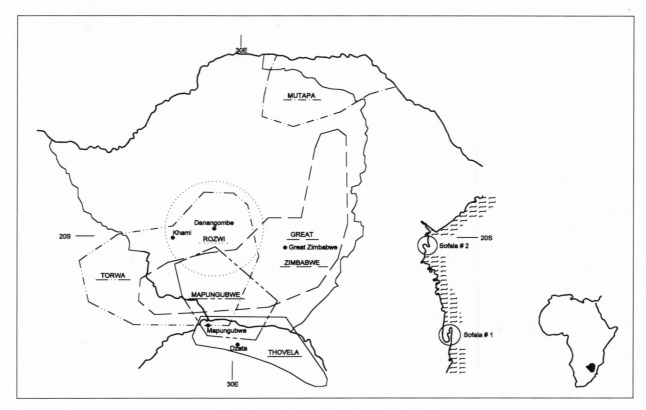

Fig. 67 *Zambezian states*

varied according to his rank and class. The head of a commoner homestead, for example, resolved disputes between members of his family, while disputes between members of separate homesteads went to the court of the ward headman, and then to the court of a chief. The chief was always a sacred leader and member of the ruling class. Each court level received cases from the level below, and the final court of appeal usually reserved for itself the right to administer the death penalty, ordeals of confession that could end in death, and all cases of national importance, such as witchcraft and treason. As part of the dynamics of political life, the status of a court may have been disputed or the system challenged in other ways. Nevertheless, the general principle of a hierarchy remains.

This court hierarchy goes hand in hand with a hierarchy of settlement size because of a systemic relation between political power and the unequal distribution of wealth. As a rule, the senior leader had the largest settlement because he was the most wealthy person in the nation. Within the Zimbabwe culture, cattle were usually the exclusive property of the ruling class, and the leader, accumulating cattle through death dues, court fines, forfeits, tribute, raids, and the high bride price of his daughters, had more than anyone else.

Besides cattle, the Zimbabwe leaders participated in a long-distance trade network that brought glass beads, cloth, and glazed ceramics from locations around the Indian Ocean, as well as from Egypt and China, in return for local ivory, rhinoceros horn, and gold. Zimbabwe people used the wealth they accumulated from trade for bride price and other traditional transactions, and so the wealth augmented the traditional wealth in cattle. The control of this trade was a major dynamic in local politics and the underlying basis of class distinction. Zimbabwe leaders also participated in a regional trade network for such items as salt, tin, and copper.

Leaders used their cattle and trade wealth to establish allegiances (through loans and payments) and political alliances (through the exchange of cattle for wives). Besides formal marriage alliances, a leader received wives as tribute, and he usually had more wives than any of his subjects. One Venda chief was supposed to have had more than 100 wives, and one Mutapa king, more than 1,000.

Partly because of so many wives, the senior leader had more fields around his capital than anyone else. In addition, there were also a number of fields elsewhere, cultivated for him as another form of tribute. In fact, a nation wanted its leader to be wealthy so that he could function properly. As "father of the nation," the leader was expected to feed his people in time of famine, to support those who could not support themselves, to lend cattle to commoners, and to supply refreshment to visitors in the capital.

To help them function, leaders maintained a body of court officials, including guards, messengers, musicians, retainers, and councilors. Usually, the senior leader had more of these officials than his subordinates because the staff in the capital had more to do. The capital was more active than other centers, partly because it was both a district headquarters and a national center, and partly because more people lived in the leader's district than elsewhere. Thus, the capital needed to be large to accommodate all of the district and national activities as well as the relatively high number of family, officials, nobles, and commoners who lived there. In Zimbabwe states, this overall pattern was replicated at the next administrative level because these leaders were the next most wealthy and powerful people.

Because of the intertwined relationship of wealth and political power, the number of court levels in a group was related to the size of its population and territory. Small territories with low populations usually had only a few levels, while large territories with high populations had many.

Ethnographic examples drawn from Sotho-Tswana–speaking people illustrate the differences between levels (in this example Level 1 represents household heads, Level 2 represents ward headmen, Level 3 represents petty chiefs, Level 4 represents senior chiefs, and Level 5 represents paramount chiefs):

	Level-3 Hierarchy	Level-4 Hierarchy	Level-5 Hierarchy
Paramount chiefs	-	-	1
Senior chiefs	-	1	19
Petty chiefs	1	5	316
Ward headmen	4	133	1,006
Total population	1,800	39,000	500,000

In recent examples and in the Zimbabwe states, Level-5 capitals controlled areas ranging from 30,000 to 40,000 square kilometers. Some archaeologists only apply the term *state* to hierarchies of this size because at least three administrative levels existed above the common people: a king and his court at the head of the nation, followed by provincial governors and district chiefs.

In recent historic examples, Level-5 capitals were two to three times larger than capitals of Level-4 hierarchies, and these, in turn, were two to three times the size of Level-3 capitals. In actual numbers, Level-5 capitals had 5,000 to 7,000 people, Level-4 capitals had 1,000 to 2,000 people, and Level-3 captials had from 300 to 600. The majority of people in all hierarchies lived in small settlements close to their agricultural lands.

To estimate the populations of the various Zimbabwe state capitals, archaeologists have used Great Zimbabwe as a datum for comparison because it has been intensively surveyed. First, they extrapolated the densities of huts found in excavations inside and outside the stone enclosures to comparable areas throughout the town. Second, they calculated the number of adults and then children by applying a 19th- and early 20th-century population pyramid to the hut count. Using this procedure, they reached the reasonable estimate of 18,000 people.

This total is three times the number of people in the capitals of historically known Level-5 leaders such as Chaka of the Zulu and Lobengula of the Zimbabwe Ndebele. The king at Great Zimbabwe, therefore, represented a sixth level of authority, and he probably controlled at least 90,000 to 120,000 square kilometers. This is the largest-known indigenous state ever to have existed in southern Africa.

The later capital at Khami, near present-day Bulawayo, was two-thirds the size of Great Zimbabwe. About 13,000 people lived there. Khami is the only other Level-6 capital on record. The remaining state capitals were all at the pinnacle of Level-5 hierarchies, all more-or-less the same size, and each housed about 5,000 people.

Military conquest was one means of increasing the size of a nation, and it must have been present from the beginning. In southern Africa, however, the ideology of sacred leadership was equally important. Ideological unity occurred in three different spheres. First, the ideology of sacred leadership unified ruling families into a single upper class. Second, it brought together the upper and lower classes into a larger social formation. And third, it formed the common basis of sociopolitical organization in different places at lower levels of the political hierarchy.

A brief history of the Zimbabwe culture will help place the importance of ideology, economy, and war into context.

The Origins of the Zambezian States

At one time, Great Zimbabwe was thought to have been the place of origin, but now we know that class distinction and sacred leadership—the cultural essence of all Zimbabwe states—evolved in the basin of the Shashi and Limpopo Rivers, where present-day Zimbabwe, Botswana, and South Africa meet. This evolution took place at a series of sites known as Schroda, Bambandyanalo (K2), and Mapungubwe.

A change in climate to warmer and wetter conditions than present today made it possible for Iron Age cattle-herding agriculturists to occupy the Shashi-Limpopo Basin at about A.D. 900. The first people to inhabit the area are known archaeologically as Zhiso, and their capital was located at Schroda. The Zhizo settlement hierarchy shows that Schroda was a Level-3 capital and housed between 300 and 500 people. The wealth of the capital was partly based on cattle, for it was organized according to the central cattle pattern, and partly on the east coast trade, for Schroda is the earliest Iron Age site in the interior of southern Africa to yield a sub-stantial amount of locally made ivory objects and imported glass beads.

Even today, *mopane* woodland makes the basin prime elephant country. Furthermore, the rivers that drain the western gold reefs of Zimbabwe flow into the Shashi and Limpopo Rivers, and it would have been possible to pan for alluvial gold anywhere in this region. Significantly, a 10th-century Arab document suggests that gold was part of the trade.

Archaeologists in Mozambique have located coastal trading stations, such as Chibuene in the Bazaruto Archipelago, that probably supplied glass beads to Schroda. Stations such as Chibuene can be identified as the Sofala of early Arab documents.

According to the archaeological record, Schroda lost control of this trade at about 1000 to a new group of people, the Leopard's Kopje, who moved into the basin from the south. Among other things, this interpretation is based on the abrupt and massive introduction of Leopard's Kopje ceramics, the simultaneous abandonment of Schroda, and the disappearance of Zhizo ceramics throughout the basin and southwestern Zimbabwe. Furthermore, archaeologists found a threefold increase in Zhizo-derived ceramics (known as *Toutswe*) dating to this time farther west in Botswana, and the largest sites were all located on hilltops in defensive positions. Although the linkage is not straightforward, Leopard's Kopje can be identified with the ancestors of present-day Shona speakers.

The Leopard's Kopje people responsible for the takeover in the Shashi-Limpopo Basin established their capital at Bambandyanalo, a short distance from Schroda. Excavations at Bambandyanalo have produced considerably more ivory objects and glass beads than fieldwork at any other settlement at this time. Few trade goods reached the Toutswe area, and the Leopard's Kopje people had clearly taken over the interior portion of the coastal trade. An enormous midden next to the court and central cattle byre yielded most of these trade items. The size of this midden was due to the amount of activity in the court, and the trade items show that the leader's status had been enhanced by the trade wealth. The coastal trade injected far more wealth into the basin than could be generated locally with cattle, and by the time of its abandonment, Bambandyanalo had reached Level-4 status.

What is more, the local control of this trade resulted in an unprecedented inequality that ultimately led to the evolution of a bureaucratic class.

The evolution of this bureaucratic class and its associated worldview led to the transformation of the central cattle pattern into the elite Zimbabwe pattern. When Bambandyanalo was abandoned in about 1220, the capital shifted to Mapungubwe, less than 1 kilometer away. The leader lived on the hilltop above the court, while the majority of his people lived down below. This is the first time in southern Africa that a leader was so physically separated from his followers. A short while later, the now-sacred leader lived behind a stone-walled palace, and the elite Zimbabwe pattern had evolved.

The famous gold burials on the hilltop show that gold had acquired an indigenous value: it was no longer simply a means to wealth but wealth itself. The continuing coastal trade must have also increased Mapungubwe's power and territorial sovereignty because, by about 1250, it had become the capital of a Level-5 bureaucracy. Mapungubwe was, therefore, the center of southern Africa's first state.

In about 1290, the climate throughout southern Africa was affected by the spread of the Little Ice Age, and it became colder and drier. In many areas, it was no longer possible to cultivate traditional grain crops such as sorghum and millet. As a result, Mapungubwe was abandoned, and the entire basin was depopulated, as was the Toutswe area farther west in Botswana. The state disintegrated, and Great Zimbabwe became Mapungubwe's economic, cultural, and political successor.

The particularly dry conditions at the beginning of the Little Ice Age help explain the rise of Great Zimbabwe. Located along the southeastern escarpment, Great Zimbabwe received whatever rain did fall, and it, therefore, had an ecological advantage over its competitors. With this advantage, Zimbabwe people were able to seize the opportunity presented by the demise of Mapungubwe. Many other Zimbabwe cultural settlements are located along this escarpment, both small

commoner villages and larger chiefly settlements, and grain-bin foundations are common. The settlements were concentrated in this zone because it was one of the few good areas at the time for subsistence agriculture.

Although the people at both Mapungubwe and Great Zimbabwe were probably ancestral Shona speakers, the ceramic evidence indicates that they belonged to related but separate populations. Consequently, the leaders at Great Zimbabwe could not have belonged to the same dynasty that controlled Mapungubwe.

Chronological and stratigraphical evidence shows that Zimbabwe leaders adopted the elite spatial pattern from Mapungubwe at the beginning of their own dramatic increase in wealth and importance. The elite spatial pattern did not evolve independently at Great Zimbabwe. These leaders therefore also adopted sacred leadership and class distinction. It is unclear what processes were involved in these adoptions—perhaps a few Mapungubwe royals moved to Great Zimbabwe. Whatever the case, convincing the common people to accept this new order must have posed a problem. To legitimize their authority, Zimbabwe royalty needed to emphasize the link between God and their ancestors. The famous Zimbabwe bird stones appear to have been one solution.

The soapstone birds are unique. None is known from any other capital. Seven were found in the ritual enclosure of the palace, and one in the lower valley. Each is about 30 centimeters long and perches on the end of a pillar 1 meter high. Although they present a general raptor theme, it is not possible to identify any specific species because the carvings combine human and bird attributes. For example, they all have masculine limbs, and most have four or five toes, or fingers, rather than talons. The role of raptors in relation to royal ancestors explains this combination of human and bird attributes.

Because eagles travel between heaven and earth, they are sometimes seen as messengers of God and mediators between God and man. Royal ancestors are also mediators, and the spirits of former kings are said to travel between earth and heaven as eagles do, interceding with God on behalf of the nation. The bird stones, then, were a sculptural metaphor for the intercessory role of royal ancestors—the prime spiritual duty of sacred leadership.

The bird stones probably did not commemorate actual rulers at Great Zimbabwe, for the style suggest the stones in the palace had been carved at the same time, rather than sequentially. Instead of rulers at Great Zimbabwe, the bird stones probably represented leaders before the rise of Great Zimbabwe. A new sacred leader must glorify his ancestors, not himself.

This ancestral glorification would have been disseminated to the people through an institutionalized premarital school where Zimbabwe values, symbols, and traditions were inculcated to commoners and royals alike. Perhaps this glorification was disseminated further through actual attendance at royal rituals, for the Eastern Enclosure, where most of the bird stones stood, was notably larger than equivalent areas in later capitals.

This new need to legitimate sacred leadership also explains why more bird stones have not been found elsewhere. Great Zimbabwe was the capital of a state for about 150 years, three times longer that Mapungubwe's tenure as a capital. During this time, the state spread over an area three to six times larger than the Mapungubwe polity, and the ruling class expanded accordingly. As a result, virtually every ruling dynasty in the culture was already integrated into a single upper class by the mid-14th century, and there was no need to recreate and reestablish their link with God when Great Zimbabwe declined. Thus, early leaders at Great Zimbabwe used ideology to unify their followers and consolidate their power.

Great Zimbabwe was abandoned between about 1420 and 1450. In the past, scholars believed the abandonment was due to ecological degradation, but this explanation no longer suffices. Cultivated fields vulnerable to degradation would have been an important component in the neighborhood around Great Zimbabwe, but a system of tribute from distant areas provided the main support. These distant fields, as well as other resources, were an important component of the political hinterland of Great Zimbabwe.

A further reason to reject the degradation hypothesis involves the climate. Independent climatic data indicate that the effects of the Little Ice Age began to ameliorate at about 1420, and

southern Africa became warmer and wetter. It would have, therefore, been easier to feed the population at Great Zimbabwe, not more difficult. Had environmental degradation been the cause, Great Zimbabwe would have been abandoned much earlier.

It is more likely that political disruptions caused the hinterland of Great Zimbabwe to fragment. Some scholars associate the origins of the Mutapa state in the northeast with the abandonment of Great Zimbabwe. In this interpretation, the last king at Great Zimbabwe moved north to become the first Mutapa king. The archaeological evidence, however, indicates that the capital at Khami near Bulawayo in the southwest was the successor to Great Zimbabwe. Consequently, it is more likely that a provincial leader in the northeast used the political breakdown of Great Zimbabwe as an opportunity to become independent. Or, possibly, his own bid for independence was part of the political upheavals.

Whatever the case, the Mutapa state was the result of the northward spread of the Zimbabwe culture. Oral traditions suggest that the spread proceeded through a combination of conquest, political assimilation, and ideological unification.

As Zimbabwe people spread north, they moved into a non–Shona-speaking area occupied by the Musengezi and Ingombe Ilede cultures. Scholars have identified the Ingombe Ilede group as the VaMbara noted in 16th-century Portuguese documents. By the late 16th century, they had been incorporated into the Mutapa state, and their descendants today speak Khoikhoi, the northern dialect cluster of Shona. The former Musengezi area is also inside the modern Khoikhoi zone, and these people were also incorporated. Among other mechanisms, some of these non-Shona people would have joined the upper class. Furthermore, some traditional leaders would have been integrated into the new political hierarchy, ruling their own kinsmen on behalf of a Mutapa king. The precise modes of contact and assimilation, however, will remain unclear without further research. Events to the south are better known.

In the 15th century, several Zimbabwe groups moved south of the Limpopo River and established new chiefdoms. Today, this area is the traditional homeland of the Venda. According to

Venda oral traditions, various Level-4 chiefdoms are associated with Zimbabwe settlements in the Khami phase. These royal Zimbabwe settlements all have basal dates around 1450, suggesting the chiefdoms moved south when Great Zimbabwe collapsed.

With the collapse of Great Zimbabwe and fragmentation of the empire, a state arose at Khami about 300 kilometers away. It is not clear if the dynasty at Khami came from Great Zimbabwe or if a new dynasty had taken over. Counterparts to the Khami's rulers competitors in the Mutapa state referred to them as the *Torwa* (stranger or foreigner), and scholars have adopted this name.

The Torwa-Changamire state based at Khami was second in size only to Great Zimbabwe and it must have controlled an area two or three times the size of the Mutapa kingdom. Archaeological evidence indicates that they controlled copper and salt deposits around the Makarikari Pans to the west and that they traded for tin with Rooiberg, 500 kilometers to the south.

Both the Torwa-Changamire and Mutapa states were greatly affected by the European discovery of southern Africa. At the beginning of the 16th century, the Portuguese came into contact with the Mutapa state. The Portuguese pursued a policy of divide-and-rule, introduced guns, and changed the scope of warfare forever. This intervention ultimately proved counterproductive to trade. As civil wars raged, no one could mine gold yet the indigenous armies were paid in trade goods. As the economic and political bases of the Mutapa state were undermined, class distinction and sacred leadership diminished.

In 1644, the Portuguese participated in a civil war in the Khami state and helped to sack Khami. The winner probably ruled from a new capital, Njanja (or Regina), but the size of this capital suggests that the new leader's power was reduced to Level-4 status.

A new royal dynasty, the Rozvi, began a military campaign in the 1680s and 1690s under Changamire Dombolakonchingwango, and for a while, the Rozvi state controlled most of Zimbabwe. After this Changamire's death in 1696, his sons fought over the kingship. Normally in such succession disputes, the losers leave with their followers and establish a chieftainship some-

where else. In the case of the 1696 dispute, one son went to the Wanke area, near Victoria Falls, spreading the Zimbabwe culture into a new region. Settlement data suggest that this chieftainship never grew beyond Level-4 status.

Another son moved south across the Limpopo into Venda. Later known as the Singo, these former Rozvi conquered the area and formed a new Level-5 state based at Dzala. This state can be identified as the Thovhela kingdom mentioned in 1730 by the Dutch in Delagoa Bay. Shortly after this time, the center of trade shifted south from the Portuguese in central Mozambique to the English and Dutch in Delagoa Bay. This important shift coincided with the rise of the Pedi and northern Nguni and with civil war in Venda. At this time, the Thovhela state fragmented into three Level-4 chieftaincies, and these divisions remain today. Thus, the Thovhela state only lasted for about 50 years. It is possible that the trade shift undermined the economic base of the Thovhela kingdom while stimulating others.

The original winner of the Rozvi-Changamire succession dispute maintained his capital at Danangombe where it remained until the early 19th century. Largely independent of Portuguese interference, the state continued until it was defeated through warfare during the *difaqane* (the aftermath of the Zulu and Afrikaner expansion).

The successor to the Rozvi were the Zimbabwe Ndebele under first Mzilikazi and then Lobengula. Although these paramount chiefs ruled a Level-5 hierarchy, the society lacked class distinction and an institutionalized bureaucracy. Instead, it had a military organization like that of the Zulu from whom the Ndebele derived, and trade wealth was no longer fundamental. Their appearance brought an end to the Zimbabwe states.

BIBLIOGRAPHY

Beach, D. N. 1980. *The Shona and Zimbabwe, 900–1850.* Gwelo: Mambo Press.

Caton-Thompson, G. 1931. *The Zimbabwe culture: Ruins and reactions.* Oxford: Clarendon Press.

Garlake, P. S. 1973. *Great Zimbabwe.* London: Thames and Hudson.

Huffman, T. N. 1986. Iron Age settlement patterns and the origins of class distinction in southern Africa. *Advances in World Archaeology* 5: 291–338.

MacIver, D. R. 1906. *Medieval Rhodesia.* London: Macmillan.

Robinson, K. R. 1959. *Khami ruins.* Cambridge: Cambridge University Press.

Summers, R. 1963. *Zimbabwe: A Rhodesian mystery.* Cape Town: Nelson.

Thomas N. Huffman

PRECOLONIAL TOWNS OF ZAMBEZIA

The Zambezian states, over an extended period between the 10th and 19th centuries, were dominant economic and political authorities on the Zimbabwe Plateau. They included the Mapungubwe state in the Limpopo Valley, the Great Zimbabwe state in south-central Zimbabwe, the Mutapa state on the northern plateau margins, and the Torwa-Changamire state in southwestern Zimbabwe. The present evidence suggests that this complex of states occurred as a historically related cultural succession. They share a significant number of cultural traits and should be regarded as serial manifestations of an autochthonous (locally derived) sociopolitical tradition.

Over time, the geographical focus of authority transferred from polities on the plateau margins to ones located farther into the interior. This progression seems to have been dictated by a number of different factors, including environmental and security considerations, as well as the economic potential of the different regions. Each state was organized around a principal lineage associated with a major town. Each town had impressive monumental stone-built architecture, increased specialization in domestic crafts, long-distance trade connected with the east coast and the world beyond, a transfer of settlement loci from valley floors to terraced hillsides and hilltops, and an increasing importance of cattle in the economy.

This system lasted for nearly 1,000 years. The foundation of the Mapungubwe state in the 11th century laid the basis for the state centered at Great Zimbabwe from the 13th century onward to the Mutapa and Torwa-Changamire (Rozvi)

states of historic times. It may be suggested that these states flourished as participants in east coast trade. Although no satisfactory explanation may be posited for the demise of any individual state, observations of present-day land-use and demographic patterns suggest the difficulty of sustaining large populations without seriously upsetting the ecological balance.

The transfers of authority from region to region may be explainable, therefore, within a context of agricultural and ranging potential. This is most evident with respect to the succession of Great Zimbabwe from the Mapungubwe state. Similarly, by the late 15th century, northern Zimbabwe offered better agricultural and commercial opportunities than did areas farther south, while in the southwest, the area of the Torwa-Changamire state seems to have been more capable of supporting the viable pastoral economy necessary to underwriting social complexity.

The Mapungubwe State

The Mapungubwe state managed affairs in the middle Shashi-Limpopo Valley from its principal seat of authority on Mapungubwe Hill. Originating within an indigenous farming community, it soon extended its influence throughout southern Zimbabwe and the northern part of the former Transvaal province.

Bambandyanalo

Bambandyanalo is a massive midden of occupation debris and cattle dung, about 1 kilometer east of Mapungubwe Hill south of the Shashi-Limpopo confluence. It flourished during the early centuries of the 2nd millennium as the principal town in a settlement system, which included Schroda, 6 kilometers to the northeast, and numerous agricultural communities spread along the valley periphery. The productivity of these farms must have been constrained by the hot, dry conditions. Nevertheless, these people prospered, their herds grew, and the richness of the area's natural resources attracted long-distance trade.

Bambandyanalo's inhabitants were adept cattle herders and elephant hunters who worked extensively in ivory and bone. The ivory was carved into bangles and bracelets, and the bone

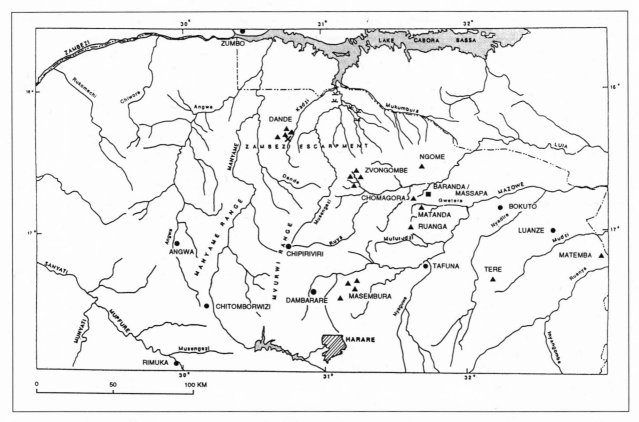

Fig. 68 *Great Zimbabwe tradition sites in northern Zimbabwe*

▲ Stone-walled enclosures
■ Non-stone-walled field sites

● Sites connected with the Portuguese trade in
the 16th and 17th centuries A.D.

was carved into points. These items and some gold from farther north were at first traded locally but later were exchanged for goods brought up the valley from coastal towns, such as Chibuene, in southern Mozambique. Trade goods began arriving in the Shashi-Limpopo Basin as early as the 9th century to be exchanged for ivory and animal skins, an activity mentioned by 10th-century Muslim travelers.

The people at Bambandyanalo lived with little apparent social distinction in houses plastered with sun-dried clay and featuring hardened earth floors. The layout of the town is still unclear, but as the political role of the settlement changed, the traditional cattle byre was moved from the center in order to make room for a more restricted men's assembly area. The primacy of Bambandyanalo was shortlived, however. The house floors and vast amounts of domestic refuse were

all accumulated in the period of a single generation. By the late 11th century, the elite moved to nearby Mapungubwe Hill.

Mapungubwe Hill

Mapungubwe is a high sandstone hill, 3 kilometers south of the Shashi-Limpopo confluence. It has steep sides topped by a settlement of substantial houses enclosed in rough stone walls. Below the hill to the southwest is an extensive settlement originally founded in the 11th century. By the 12th century, the summit was settled, as well.

Like Bambandyanalo, the town sent gold and ivory to the coastal towns of Mozambique and received glass beads, cowrie shells, copper, and iron in return. Mapungubwe produced pottery, iron, and other crafts, such as ivory and bone carving.

The volume of trade and indications of elite management increased under the rule at Mapungubwe. But its time as the paramount power on the plateau was rapidly coming to an end. The town was abandoned in the 13th century, as political and economic power transferred to Great Zimbabwe.

Mapela

Mapela, a satellite of Mapungubwe, shared the florescence and the fate of its paramount. It is a stone-terraced bluff rising above the Shashi, 85 kilometers northwest of Mapungubwe. Its flat summit featured stone-walled enclosures arranged on platforms, similar to those at Mapungubwe. The sides of the hill were terraced. The elite lived on the hill top in well-made, polished, and decorated *dhaka* houses. Those lower down the social ladder lived at the base on the hill in simpler pole-and-*dhaka* huts.

Mapela obtained gold from Matabeleland and many trade items, such as ivory and glass beads, through a network of local exchanges and external trade managed by their kindred at Mapungubwe.

Finally, the prominence of the Shashi-Limpopo Basin declined as the center of trade and authority passed to the Save River and Great Zimbabwe.

The Great Zimbabwe State

Great Zimbabwe

Great Zimbabwe, the capital of the largest and most powerful of the Zambezian states, is 27 kilometers southeast of Masvingo on the eastern edge of plateau. It is surrounded by granite kopjes (small hills) and rock outcrops interspersed with level plains and stream valleys. Its setting is *middleveld,* the hilly country of the Zimbabwean Plateau. The area of moderate temperature receives rain throughout the year and possesses a thick vegetation cover. It has access to both *sourveld* and *sweetveld,* vegetation zones vital to livestock management. *Sweetveld* is nutritious throughout the year.

Great Zimbabwe is a large town covering more than 720 hectares. Its core settlement includes the hill to the north, the Great Enclosure to the south, and the valley to the east, as well as a large open area with no evidence of occupation.

The base of the hill is marked by a north-south perimeter wall. When the settlement grew large enough to include the valley and the Great Enclosure, a new western boundary of the town was marked by a second perimeter wall. Other settlements developed outside this to accommodate the growing population and expanding functions of the town. Population estimates vary from a little as 11,000 to as many as 18,000 people.

The town is built from granite quarried from nearby hills. The famous walls were erected without mortar on earthen or stone foundations. The dressed-stone walls, though unbonded, are abutted firmly against one another in a manner meant to minimize structural weakness and ensure stability. The walls are 4 meters thick in some cases, and some of them are battered with each succeeding course sloping inward to give additional stability.

In 1958, K. R. Robinson described four occupation periods of the town. Period I was a 1st-millennium early farming community, which predated building in stone. Period II marks the appearance of later farming communities of the Gumanye culture, whose people constructed pole-and-*dhaka* houses and participated in long-distance trade for glass beads. During Period III, people constructed substantial *dhaka*-plastered houses and the first stone walls on the hill. The peak of development occurred during Period IV when stone walls were extended beyond the center. The most elaborate walls, for example the Great Enclosure, were built around this time. Following investigations in the Great Enclosure, R. F. H. Summers proposed the existence of Period V, during which the quality of the architecture deteriorated and rough stone walls were erected.

The high point of Great Zimbabwe during Period III occurred between the 12th and early 13th century. Period IV extended into the next century and declined in the 15th century. The life of the town may be said to be mirrored in its monumental stone walls.

The stone walls at Great Zimbabwe were a political expression of the authority and prestige of the builders. The monumental stonework is a natural extension of the granite terrain, uniting man and nature. Here and there were upright monoliths and turrets atop some of the highest walls on the hill and the Great Enclosure. They are thought to represent the power of the leaders as mediators between man and the elements. Inside the walls are well-made *dhaka* houses, with grass roofs supported by timber beams.

Great Zimbabwe was a considerable human achievement. It took nearly 200 years to build it. The town and its freestone walls symbolize a confident and powerful society—a hierarchical society based on elite control of production and an authority to command both a capable, reliable labor force and the wealth needed to maintain the allegiance of its labor reserves.

By the mid-15th century, control of the gold trade and the political confederacy built on it had slipped away from Great Zimbabwe. Other lineages elsewhere on the plateau extended their reach, and the Torwa-Changamire state at Khami and Dhlo-Dhlo and the Mutapa state in northern Zimbabwe grew in prominence. Each was the cultural and political heir to founders of the Great Zimbabwe state. Imports to Great Zimbabwe ceased during the 15th century, while they grew in abundance at Khami and Baranda. By the end of the century, Great Zimbabwe had little commercial significance. The Portuguese reports are rather vague on its status and never refer to it as

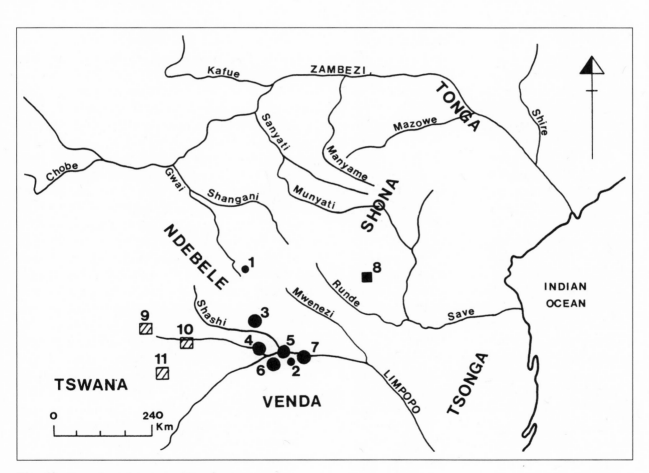

Fig. 69 *Precolonial towns of Zambezia*

- • Leopard's Kopje (A.D. 950–1200)
- ● Mapungubwe (1050–1200)
- ■ Great Zimbabwe (1250–1450)
- ▨ Toutswe tradition (700–1300)

1 Leopard's Kopje
2 Bambandyanalo (K2)
3 Mapela
4 Mmamgwa
5 Mapungubwe

6   Little Muck
7   Skutwater
8   Great Zimbabwe
9   Bosutswe
10 Toutswe
11 Shoshong

a place of commercial interest. Though they were conscious of the place, the chroniclers imply an aura of bygone glories.

Mutapa State

In the late 15th century, as the Portuguese established their trading stations in the Zambezi Valley, the flow of goods to Great Zimbabwe dried up. As a result, authority passed to the chiefs living in northern Zimbabwe. This Mutapa state, well-documented in Portuguese chronicles and studied in detail by historians, dominated political and economic life into the 19th century.

Mount Fura

Mount Fura, a rock-spined peak 1,507 meters above sea level, is located in the Mount Darwin district of northern Zimbabwe. About 150 kilometers from Harare, Mount Fura is part of a mountainous zone stretching to the Mazowe River. On its slopes are stone-built structures, described by the Portuguese in the 17th century. Manuel e Sousa, dos Santos, and Diogo de Couto refer to them as "great stone buildings." Manuel e Sousa commented "in the mountain of Afur near Massapa are seen the ruins of stately buildings supposed to be palaces and castles." Muslim legends even associated the Queen of Sheba and the exploitation of the gold fields of the Mukaradzi River with the construction of these *zimbaoe* (a Portuguese transliteration of a Shona term for elite residences marked by stone-built enclosures).

In the 1980s, Thomas N. Huffman posited Mount Fura as a seat of the Mutapa state and claimed that the presence there of elite enclosures encircling a large palace, court, and a premarital building. His concept of the Mutapa state derived from the historical research of E. Axelson and D. P. Abraham, who identified loopholed stone structures as part of the Great Zimbabwe tradition.

The Portuguese were informed that these buildings were used by the Mutapa, and as a result, Mount Fura became linked with the capitals of the Mutapa state. These secondhand accounts created the impression that the Mutapa courts were built of rough walls—an idea taken up by 20th-century investigators, who posited that the Mutapa capitals were smaller than those of the preceding Great Zimbabwe state. Recent research though has located building in the Great Zimbabwe style of walling and related unwalled sites at Mount Fura. The chronicler may have been referring to these, rather than the cruder architecture of the loopholed structures.

Investigators have recorded 19 of these later structures in the Mount Fura area. Their building style is coarse, and some of the enclosures have loopholes. They are nearly circular in plan but lack the radial walls typically found in enclosures of the Great Zimbabwe style. This suggests a somewhat different building canon from that associated with the earlier states on the plateau. The style of pottery does not compare with any known ceramic assemblage.

The sites have a distinctive linear plan imposed by the lay of the land, as do other enclosures located on nearby spurs or ridges of the mountain. There are no court, premarital building, or other elite enclosures to be found there. If there was a capital on the mountain during the 16th century, the Portuguese would have observed it, but they never mention Mount Fura as the capital of the Mutapa state. In fact, the Portuguese reports make no mention of mountain locations at all. Their only mention of stone walls on Mount Fura is from the early 17th century, and these walls were built in response to wars at that time.

The rugged nature of the mountain, and the difficult access to the settlements there, makes Mount Fura a poor choice as a capital.

Baranda

Baranda, in the Chesa farming area of Mount Darwin, about 165 kilometers northeast of Harare, has more graphite, burnished pottery in the Great Zimbabwe style and imported Chinese, Persian, and Iberian pottery and glass beads than any other 16th- to 17th-century town in northern Zimbabwe. The town is on a granite outcrop in a zone of whitish-gray sandy soils dominated by wooded savanna. There is only a thin grass cover. It is a small settlement with an area of nearly 1.8 square kilometers

Baranda flourished between the early 16th and 17th centuries. It was well placed to exploit the gold fields in the Mukaradzi Valley to the south. As a result, it developed extensive commercial contacts, which brought it locally made pottery and imported ceramics, glassware, glass beads, and copper from the northern copperbelts. Crucibles in the settlement debris attest to the processing of gold ore for exportation. Quantities of slag, as well as finished iron implements, at Baranda suggest a substantial companion ironworking industry.

The location of Baranda coincides with that of the 16th- to 18th-century trading station of Massapa, described by Portuguese as frequented by Swahili traders even before it became an official Portuguese possession after 1580. Joao dos Santos named it as one of three villages in Mukaranga where the Portuguese conducted trade with the local people and located it near Mount Fura. Diogo de Couto described it as a "very extensive and very rich" market, 50 leagues from Tete reached by traveling along the Mazowe River. Antonio Bocarro located it 4 leagues from the Mazowe River, 50 from Tete, and 10 from Bokuto and described it as the principal market in Mukaranga. De Couto reported that the richest gold mines were in Fura, an area near Massapa. A Portuguese official representative to the Mutapa stayed at Massapa to treat with Portuguese traders coming into the state.

In the early 17th century, Massapa is mentioned again in connection with civil strife in the Mutapa state. At some point, it was attacked by Marave, who used the mountain of Chizinga as a stronghold. In 1610, the Portuguese built a fort at Massapa, which was occupied by Mutapa Kapararidze while fighting the Portuguese in November 1628, though he was expelled soon after. About 1631, it is described as a town with a church. But it soon thereafter lost importance following civil war and lawlessness in the Mutapa state. In November 1693, a force led by Changamire Dombolakonchingwango destroyed it, and the Portuguese left for Sena on the Zambezi River. The town was reoccupied briefly in the 18th century.

Massapa was not founded by the Portuguese traders. All the evidence points to Baranda as a prosperous trade center in northern Zimbabwe long before the coming of Europeans. At Baranda, though, we have an opportunity to see the impact of Portuguese merchant capital on the Mutapa state. The settlement reflects socioeconomic transformation, and this change represents an intermediate stage between the Great Zimbabwe and the Mahonje traditions. Baranda was a major center with a dual identity. It was part of the Afro-Portuguese trading network as well as a component of the traditional culture of the region.

Torwa-Changamire (Rozvi) State

At the same time that Great Zimbabwe was declining in importance and the Mutapa state came to dominate affairs along the Zambezi Valley, another state emerged in southwestern Zimbabwe. It developed in an area of grassland, which may be the Guruuswa region called Butua by the Portuguese in the 16th and 17th centuries. The Torwa-Changamire state, which emerged at the decline of Great Zimbabwe, was the peer of Mutapa. It was a highly organized society. Its people had migrated out of the Mutapa core area and settled beyond its borders. The Mupfuri-Munyati River Basin acted as a buffer zone.

Between 1490 and 1547, there was a rebellion in the Mutapa state. According to the Portuguese, it was caused by Torwa-Changamire from the southwest, people outside the chiefly lineages who felt shut out of deliberations of the court. Sometime late in the 15th century, the Torwa-Changamire dynasty broke away from Mutapa and established itself in Guruuswa. The rise of the Torwa-Changamire state led to the eminence of the town at Khami near Bulawayo. We know nothing more about the state until the mid-17th century when the capital was destroyed in a civil war. Further strife within the state occurred in the early 1640s, when a Torwa-Changamire ruler was bested in a power struggle. Forced to flee, he appealed to the Portuguese for help. A small Portuguese army, led by Sismundo Dias Bayao, was sent to the area. These events precipitated the decline of Khami and the loss of the nearby middle plateau lands west of the Bembezi River.

Following the fall of the Torwa-Changamire state in the early 17th century, the principal town in southwestern Zimbabwe, the center of Rozvi authority, was transferred eastward to Danangombe (known popularly as Dhlo Dhlo).

The Rozvi state emerged when the Torwa-Changamire dynasty was replaced by the Karanga under Changamire Dombolakonchingwango and his Rozvi followers. The Rozvi managed to expel the Portuguese from the Zimbabwe Plateau and establish their own state. There is little apparent difference between the Torwa and Changamire states, and much of what transpired in the 17th century was little more than a military reorganization of the society, in a desperate effort to ensure the survival of the state under a strong leader against the growing menace of Portuguese settlers and traders. Historians are not clear who the Rozvi were. What is clear is that after 1680 they ruled the land of the Torwa.

During the early years of this state, the Khami style of stone building was common in southwestern Zimbabwe. This is characterized by retaining walls built with well-shaped rectangular blocks supporting an elevated platform for circular houses. Characteristically, the stone walls were profusely decorated with checkered, herringbone, dentele, and other linear patterns. The Rozvi continued to build in the same style, indicative of a cultural continuity between the two states, and decorated walls retained their significance as displays of wealth and the command of labor.

Khami

Khami, the second largest town on the Zimbabwe Plateau after Great Zimbabwe, is located west of Bulawayo on the banks of the Khami River. It was the principal town of the Torwa-Chagamire state. Although it was a vital town throughout the period covered by Portuguese documents, it was never mentioned in them.

The stone-built structures at Khami are a combination of the building canon inherited from Great Zimbabwe and local invention. The architecture includes the use of terraced-stone platforms, elaborately decorated stone retaining walls, houses erected on top of stone platforms or small hills, and roofed passages plastered with *dhaka*.

At its peak development, the town covered an area of over 40 hectares and accommodated about 7,000 people. The ruling lineages erected ten stone enclosures within the complex. The paramount lived in the largest of these. It was located to the north of the main group and was entered through a secret passage, covered by a *dhaka*-plastered roof supported by timber beams. A hidden room was discovered in 1947 at the top of the passage. In it, the royal regalia was found in a basket, wrapped in cloth. The room also contained iron axes (one with a wooden handle covered in copper), iron spears, copper ingots, ivory carvings of lions and leopards from ceremonial staffs, a set of carved ivory divining dice, and drinking pots marked with red and black patterns.

There are between 80 and 100 zimbabwes (sites with elaborate stone-built architecture) of the Khami type in southwestern Zimbabwe. Many of these are small, with a single stone-faced platform on which the main house is built. Their number and distribution is an indication of the spread of Torwa-Changamire political influence.

Unsettled conditions in the mid-17th century led to the destruction of Khami, and the state center was moved to Danangombe.

Danangombe

Danangombe is located on a granite eminence commanding a wide view of the countryside, 120 kilometers northeast of Bulawayo. The surrounding country is wooded grassland well suited for cattle ranging.

The town spreads outward in a radius of nearly 200 meters. A perimeter wall marks its southern and southeastern limits. On open ground within the town are prominent middens and house mounds. In the vicinity are a number of satellite enclosures, indicative of the attraction of the town as a political and economic center.

Danangombe has a central building complex of two large rectangular rubble platforms, separated by a passage. One platform covers an area of 900 square meters, with a retaining wall of well-fitted stone blocks rising more than 6 meters in places. The other platform is even more impressive and covers an area of 2,800 square meters and rises to a height of 3 meters. The retaining walls are profusely decorated with checkered, cord, herringbone, and chevron patterns. Huffman estimates the population of the town to have been between 5,000 and 6,000 people.

A large open area is enclosed by low, rough, free-standing walls forming a subrectangular enclosure. This enclosure is appended to the central complex which faces to the west. Immediately adjacent to the enclosure and the platform complex is an extensive midden, rising to the height of the platforms.

D. Randall-MacIver posited that Danangombe was a fortress commanding a high ground with strategic advantages. This idea is no longer tenable, since we now understand that the terraced platforms were linked to the most important people in town, while the lower areas belonged to the commoners. Differences in the value of grave offerings confirms this impression of unequal distribution of wealth.

Danangombe is correctly associated with the Changamire state. Though some small additions to the original stone walls were made, the erection of elaborate stone walls ceased sometime in the 18th century, a time of declining gold production, when the state was declining in influence.

Naletale

Naletale is a site of the Khami phase situated about 25 kilometers east of Danangombe in the Insiza District. It is on a kopje commanding a wide view of the countryside. A contemporary of Danangombe, Naletale used ironstone obtained from the nearby gold belt to erect the most elaborately decorated walls in Zimbabwe. The town has an elliptical, neatly coursed outer girdle wall with a maximum diameter of nearly 55 meters. It is decorated with chevron, herringbone, and checkered patterns in varying degrees of elaboration around the entire enclosure. The wall is interrupted to the west by a large circular platform on top of which are well-preserved *dhaka* remains.

The interior is arranged almost symmetrically. The most important part was a platform on the northern half, 2.5 meters high overlooking the top of the girding wall. Three other platforms fill the interior of the enclosure. The main platform, made of large stones layered successively with *dhaka* plaster and wooden posts inserted at regular intervals, is 28 meters across at the bottom and 18 meters at the top, on which sits a circular house. The house has a wall 40 centimeters thick, and some standing wall portions reach 1.7 meters. The floor plaster is 20 centimeters thick. An underground chamber, possibly a latrine, 1.2 meters deep and 50 centimeters at the top, was sunk in the rubble foundation and carefully lined on its sides with stones. This house is divided into four outer rooms from a central room by radial walls.

Radial walls extend from the platform of the main house toward the girdle wall, dividing the town into several enclosures connected by passages in the south. There are no doorways on the northern side, however. The main house is approached only via the entrance to the west. It is here and in parts of the northern section that decoration is most elaborate.

On top of the outer perimeter are nine so-called battlements, on top of which were four monoliths more than 50 centimeters high. Two of these were still standing at the beginning of the 20th century. On the inside of the battlements, the facade wall descends in four tiers to the ground level. A staircase leads to the main house. Outside, the wall is two-tiered. The lower tier rises 1 meter from the ground level, and the other, receding 2.2 meters from it, rises 1.7 meters.

Another house connected to the main platform by a gangway and steps has a circular room 5 meters in diameter, with no partitions. Directly inside is a curb of *dhaka* plaster, built parallel to the outer wall, and a regular line of post holes, dug close to the edges of the floor. Two pits were filled with ivory fragments, remnants of large elephant tusks set into the floor.

Naletale was a center of some importance. Although it was a prominent part of the Torwa-Changamire state, its small size suggests that it served as a secondary center. However, it managed the affairs of a considerable territory with a number of nearby elite towns subservient to it.

BIBLIOGRAPHY
Axelson, E. 1956. Some loopholed forts in the Mt. Darwin district. *Rhodesia Scientific Association, Proceedings and Transactions* 44: 7–12.
Beach, D. N. 1980. *The Shona and Zimbabwe, A.D. 900–1850.* Gweru: Mambo Press.
Caton-Thompson, G. 1931. *The Zimbabwe culture: Ruins and reactions.* Oxford: Clarendon Press.
Eloff, J. F., and A. Meyer. 1981. The Greefswald sites. In *Guide to archaeological sites in the northern Transvaal,* ed. E. A. Voight, 7–22. Pretoria: Southern African Association of Archaeologists.

Garlake, P. S. 1973. *Great Zimbabwe*. London: Thames and Hudson.

Huffman, T. N. 1987. *Symbols in stone: Unravelling the mystery of Great Zimbabwe*. Johannesburg: Witwatersrand University Press.

Pikirayi, I. 1993. *The archaeological identity of the Mutapa state: Towards an historical archaeology of northern Zimbabwe*. Uppsala: Societas Archaeologica Upsaliensis.

Randall-MacIver, D. 1906. *Medieval Rhodesia*. London: Macmillan and Co. Ltd.

Soper, R. 1988. Mt. Fura and Iron Age hierarchies. *Zimbabwe Prehistory* 20: 14–15.

Summers, R. 1971. *Ancient ruins and vanished civilisations of southern Africa*. Cape Town: Bulpin.

Innocent Pikirayi

Trade and Commerce

WESTERN AFRICAN AND WESTERN SAHARAN TRADE

Trade within West Africa and between West Africa and Islamic and European worlds has been significant in sociocultural change in the region, as well as in structuring theoretical approaches to understanding West African development.

Trade and the social contacts engendered by traders have long been important in West Africa. Trade has transported desirable resources across West African ecological zones from their source areas, thereby enabling a richer material life across the region. In addition, trade contacts have been a profound agent of human migration and have promoted long-distance interaction between groups of different linguistic, cultural, and historical affiliations.

Within West Africa, trade has played an important role in societies for thousands of years. This trade probably originated primarily to transport plant products (such as kola, vegetable oils, and malaguetta pepper), minerals (including salt, gold, and iron), and livestock from areas in which they were plentiful or easily obtained or raised to areas where demand was high but environmental or other factors limited their availability. Due to West Africa's climate, with precipitation increasing from north to south, trade patterns tended to cross the broad environmental bands. Traders took products from the forest and coast to the savanna and Sahel and products from the desert and Sahel to the more forested areas to the south. The earliest periods of this trade are not well known archaeologically, as part-time trading left few traces in the archaeological sites of this period that have thus far been investigated.

Within the last 2,000 years or so, the emergence of trade specialists and middlemen who managed or controlled aspects of West African trade permitted a greater understanding of dynamics and operation of the complex trading systems. Towns such as Begho in Ghana and Kong in Ivory Coast grew up at the forest-savanna ecotones (a transition area between two ecological zones). The towns were well placed to take advantage of trade routes and environmentally mandated transshipment points, where burdens were transferred from donkey caravans to the human porters needed in the forest regions affected by trypanosomiasis. Farther to the west in the forest zone, towns did not take on the same controlling role. Instead a far-flung trading network based on strong interpersonal obligations and the shared Mande language was established. Archaeological investigations of trade towns have been conducted at Begho and the surrounding area, where M. Posnansky's research has shown that a Mande quarter, populated by trading professionals, constituted a portion of the town. This archaeological evidence, along with the historical evidence gathered by others, has demonstrated the importance of traders as agents of social change and has provided a key theoretical concept central to much of the archaeological research conducted in West Africa.

Longer-distance trade, first involving peoples from the Mediterranean-focused North African coastal area and later Europeans, has played an important role in West African societies for well

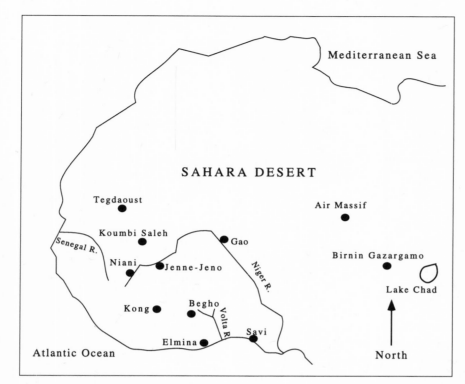

Fig. 70 *Trade towns in western Africa*

more than 1,000 years. West African trade with these two areas used vastly different routes and primarily affected very different societies. The North African trade was conducted across the Sahara by means of caravans, while the European trade was undertaken by coastal groups interacting with seaborne Europeans. Archaeological investigations at important termini of the trans-Saharan trade, such as Jenne-jeno in Mali or Koumbi-Saleh in Mauritania, have demonstrated the antiquity of the trade with North Africa, dating to perhaps as much as 2,000 years ago. Additionally, rock engravings and paintings of horse-drawn chariots or carts recorded in many areas of the Sahara may indicate the routes taken by traders, possibly as early as Phoenician or Roman times.

Recent excavations at Jenne-jeno have indicated that the town was founded more than 2,000 years ago and was engaged in long-distance trade even at the beginning, well before the establishment of Islamic trade. These findings are in contrast to theories that posit the formation of West African trading towns and states as the result of

trade contacts with North Africa during the Islamic era. Regional research conducted by R. J. and S. K. McIntosh in the area surrounding Jenne-jeno has suggested that the town supported itself as an urban center and focused on a regional trading system, based in part on intensive agriculture in the floodplain. Archaeological evidence of trade within West African from Jenne-jeno includes metals such as iron, copper, and gold, all of which were either being worked, as in the case of iron and copper, or used, as with gold, in a region located a considerable distance from the sources of these minerals well before the advent of Islamic trade. Additionally, the biological necessity of salt for human survival suggests that trade networks supplying this mineral may have been present as long as sedentary agriculturists have been settled in interior West Africa. Furthermore, the presence of towns and other settlements in inhospitable desert areas, which depended on the trade for their very existence, demonstrates the importance of trade routes.

While long-distance trade across the Sahara existed in pre-Islamic times, it reached its maximum height after the new religion spread in the region. Archaeological indications are numerous, ranging from the increasing numbers of important trade centers, the sheer volume of trade goods found in the Sahelian towns, and the widespread evidence of materials originating outside West Africa found in sites far from the trade centers. In addition to Jenne-jeno, other significant trade centers have been investigated archaeologically, including Koumbi-Saleh, the presumed capital of ancient Ghana, and Tegdaoust, identified as Awdaghast, an important trading terminus in Mali. These towns have revealed considerable evidence of trans-Saharan trade, including North African objects and structures with

Maghrebian and Islamic influences. Unfortunately, excavations to date at Koumbi-Saleh appear to have been concentrated in the site of the Islamic traders' town, and not in the area of the nearby "royal town" or indigenous settlement, which has yet to be identified. Other important trade centers archaeologically investigated include Gao, where current research has yielded Islamic gravestones imported from Spain, Niani in Mali, Birnin Gazargamo in Nigeria, and the region of the Air Massif in Niger. However, it remains clear that given the importance of trans-Saharan trade for West Africa, it will be more fully understood only with additional archaeological research at many sites.

The era of primary importance for trans-Saharan trade began to close in the years after A.D. 1500. This was occasioned by a gradual refocusing of trade efforts toward the coast, as seaborne European traders began to make contact with the West African shoreline from the middle of the 15th century. European explorers began trading in West Africa for gold, ivory, pepper, and other commodities that had previously only been available via the trans-Saharan trade routes. The Portuguese, as the spearhead of significant European contact, established several permanent trading castles on the West African coast before 1500. The fort at Elmina in Ghana was the Portuguese flagship and headquarters. Over the next several hundred years, virtually every European nation became involved in West African trade, with the French, English, Brandenbergers, Dutch, and Danes, among others establishing permanent trading posts from the mouth of the Senegal River to the mouth of the Niger. As the number of Europeans trading with West Africa increased, the cargoes they sought changed. From the mid-17th century, trade in African slaves became increasingly important.

In contrast to the situation in the Sahel, trade with Europeans proved a considerable stimulant in the increasing political complexity of some regions of the West African coast. States such as Benin existed before the beginning of European trade. Others, however, such as the Fante kingdoms in coastal Ghana, and the kingdoms of Allada and Dahomey in present-day Benin, owed much to their new-found importance as trading states. Archaeological investigations of this area and era are in their infancy, as only a few major projects have been conducted in the coastal areas. Excavations conducted by C. R. DeCorse in the African town (occupied from 1482 to 1873) that grew up outside the Portuguese fort at Elmina and excavations in the palace and town areas of the site of Savi (occupied from 1670 to 1727), capital of the Hueda kingdom, recently conducted by Kenneth G. Kelley, have demonstrated the considerable material impact of European trade but also indicated the continuity of indigenous African systems of thought. Future investigations of African settlements in other areas of coastal West Africa, such as Senegambia or Sierra Leone, may provide a richer understanding of the variety of African adaptations to European trading and its impact on coastal and inland groups.

BIBLIOGRAPHY

Bovill, E. W. 1958. *The golden trade of the Moors.* Oxford: Oxford University Press.

Brooks, G. E. 1993. *Landlords and strangers: Ecology, society, and trade in western Africa, 1000–1630.* Boulder: Westview Press.

Connah, G. 1987. *African civilizations.* Cambridge: Cambridge University Press.

DeCorse, C. R. Culture contact, continuity, and change on the Gold Coast: A.D. 1400–1900. *African Archaeological Review* 10: 163–196.

Kelly, K. G. 1994. Recent excavations at Savi: An eighteenth century West African trade town. *Nyame Akuma* 41: 2–8.

McIntosh, R. J., and S. K. McIntosh. 1988. From *siècles obscurs* to revolutionary centuries on the Middle Niger. *World Archaeology* 20: 141–165.

McIntosh, S. K. 1994. Changing perceptions of West Africa's past: Archaeological research since 1988. *Journal of Archaeological Research* 2: 165–198.

Oliver, R., and A. Atmore. 1981. *The African Middle Ages, 1400–1800.* Cambridge: Cambridge University Press.

Posnansky, M. 1973. Aspects of early West African trade. *World Archaeology* 5: 149–162.

———. 1982. African archaeology comes of age. *World Archaeology* 13: 345–358.

Searing, J. F. 1993. *West African slavery and Atlantic commerce: The Senegal River Valley, 1700–1860.* Cambridge: Cambridge University Press.

Kenneth G. Kelly

SLAVE TRADE IN AFRICA

Despite decades of interest and extensive scholarship, slavery in Africa remains a complex and difficult subject, one that defies simple explanations.

Slavery was present and persisted in many locations over the length and breadth of the continent, from the Mediterranean to the Cape of Good Hope and from Gorée Island to the Horn of Africa. Slavery itself had many different facets. There were many "slave trades" that varied in time and place, and as an institution, slavery was conceived of in different ways, depending on the context. Slavery had a long-standing role in various African societies at different times, and the institution of slavery served many different social purposes. Attitudes toward slavery were very different from those prevailing today. Although the New World consequences of this "forced migration" have been studied extensively by archaeologists, historians, and sociologists, the effects in Africa of this massive trade in people are only now beginning to be the subject of significant historical and archaeological research.

In order to understand the complexity and variability present in the slave trade, this article describes the internal trade serving indigenous needs (including domestic and agricultural slavery), the slave trade with the Eastern Islamic world and beyond (both via the Sahara Desert and the ports of the Swahili coast), and the trans-Atlantic or Western trade (supplying enslaved labor for the plantations, mines, and farms of the Americas). Estimates of the numbers of Africans exported from the continent in the slave trade run from about 10 million to as high as 30 million individuals. These figures reflect actual exports of slaves but do not include the loss of life incurred during the predatory warfare waged to acquire captives, nor the mortality incurred in transporting slaves to the port of embarkation, nor on the ships of the "middle passage" (the time slaves spent cramped in the holds of ships transporting them across the Atlantic Ocean) and other voyages. Although there is little agreement on the toll inflicted by the "middle passage," the mortality rate was considerable. Some researchers estimate losses in excess of 30 percent. The numbers of Africans enslaved in the internal market are harder to arrive at with any reliability but have been estimated to be a number equal to the Eastern and Western trades combined.

Internal Slavery

Slavery within Africa cannot be considered as a monolithic and unchanging institution. Indeed, there is substantial evidence that at least in some areas of Africa, organized slavery has a long history and a varied ideology. Although slavery has meant different things to various social groups at different times, for the enslaved, slavery has always meant the loss of freedom at best and ill-treatment or death at worst. Social dependency was a common factor in African social systems, and it could range from the "pawning" of individuals as security for debts or other obligations (a system that was fairly universal throughout West Africa), through lifetime domestic slavery (where the children of slaves were free), to perpetual bondage in which slaves and their descendants remained slaves and could be sold, with the threat of sale considered a terrible sanction. For example, five grades of servitude were identified among the Asante ranging from slaves under sentence of death to pawned servants whose freedom was only temporarily restricted. Additionally, in Calabar and Dahomey, as well as among the Igbo, there were cult slaves who were outcasts destined as sacrificial victims.

Not only did the status of slaves change but their perceived "value" to owners also varied. Initially, the slave was probably valued for his labor alone, yet in many African societies, the possession of a large number of slaves also endowed the owner with prestige and power. Later, with the advent of the European trade, the slave acquired a trade value, where the slave could be exchanged for goods. This shift in value altered motivations guiding the acquisition of slaves. Influential scholars such as W. Rodney have argued that internal African slavery expanded considerably with the beginning of very high European demand for slaves. Others have pointed to considerable evidence from the Sudan demonstrating that a well-developed slave society was already present before the advent of European trade. States such as Ghana and Mali in the 11th and 14th centuries maintained extensive standing armies that were engaged in jihads (holy wars) and wars of expansion and conquest, in which the enslavement of captives was an expressed goal. While some of these captives were destined for the trans-Saharan slave trade, the majority were probably kept in servitude in the Sudan. For example, when Almoravid troops conquered Awdaghast, then a part of the Ghanaian Empire, from 1054 to 1055, they found "slaves by the thousand." Slavery was also an important institution in Kongo before the arrival of the Portuguese, and on São Tomé, Kongolese nobles ran sugar plantations supported by enslaved labor.

In the internal African market for enslaved people, women and children were preferred. Male captives were often killed out of hand. A man's standing was dependent on the size of his household, and he could marry a slave without paying any bride price, thus increasing his family and his standing in society. Although not preferred for the initial marriage, slave women were frequently an option pursued for subsequent marriages. Females were consistently in higher demand in Africa, as reflected by higher prices, and they were also easily assimilated into existing labor patterns. The European demand, which emphasized male captives for plantation labor, thus dovetailed neatly with indigenous patterns of trade.

The internal slave trade was further stimulated by European demand for agricultural produce required to feed captives awaiting shipment to the New World and the need for provisions for the "middle passage." This demand for foodstuffs was met by the development of African-run, slave-worked plantations.

Ultimately, as the Atlantic slave trade began to wither in the 19th century, the growth in so-called legitimate trade further stimulated internal slavery in Africa as former slave-trading states increasingly relied on slave labor to produce the palm oil, cloves, and other commodities demanded by European trading partners. By the end of the 19th century, the Sokoto Caliphate had more slaves (as many as 2.5 million) within its borders than any other nation, with the exception of the United States at the beginning of the

Civil War in 1860 (about 4 million). During the colonial era, European powers made efforts to prohibit the trade in slaves in their colonies, yet they continued to turn a blind eye to the actual presence of slaves. Indeed, European administrators feared the social disruption the elimination of slavery could have precipitated in the colonies. Although slavery was officially abolished throughout Africa during the 20th century, the reabolition of slavery in Mauritania in 1978 and evidence from other parts of Africa suggest that de facto slavery has continued to be a part of the lives of some Africans up to the present time.

Trans-Saharan and East Coast Trade

The internal demand for slaves was but one aspect of the slave trade in Africa. The Eastern trade with the Islamic world and beyond was certainly the most long-lived of the external trades. Trade to the Islamic world followed two main routes: the trans-Saharan trade to North Africa and the east coast trade via the Swahili coastal towns. Slaves were never a primary item in the trans-Saharan trade, yet they were present throughout its duration. Although slaves were used in the salt mines of the Sahara, the principal use of them in the Islamic world was in the domestic sphere, where enslaved Africans served as concubines, soldiers, administrators, and laborers. The numbers of Africans exported to the Islamic world has been estimated at more than 9 million via the Sahara from 650 to 1900 and about 5 million via the East African routes from 800 to 1890. The Islamic slave trade emphasized the acquisition of women and children, with the most attractive women destined for harems. Boys were traded for military or domestic service, and men were used as laborers. According to Islam, capture and enslavement were accepted means of converting non-Muslims to Islam. In theory, Muslims cannot be enslaved. However, as most children of slaves were assimilated and became Muslims, the demand for slaves continued unabated throughout the Islamic world. The use of slave concubines also permitted wealthy individuals to side-step the Islamic prohibition against a man's marrying more than four wives and thereby increase the size of their families. In the 19th century, increasing demand from the Middle East for slave women and children caused a surplus of men in the Sudan. These men were enslaved in huge numbers. They could be obtained cheaply, since external demand for male slaves was not high. This led to the growth of slave labor on the expanding agricultural plantations that provided cash crops for trade with European nations.

Before the arrival of Islam and in the inland areas of eastern Africa, slavery was not an established part of social structures, except perhaps in areas of the Zambezi Valley and among the Shona of Zimbabwe. Thus the slave trade along the east coast was relatively small until the mid-18th century, when it expanded in response to French demand for labor on sugar plantations in the Mascarene Islands. During the early 19th century, the east coast trade to the New World expanded enormously due to Brazilian demand and the fact that fewer slaves were available from the west coast. At the same time, under the supremacy of the Omani Sultanate, large numbers of female slaves were exported from the east coast to the Persian Gulf and India. Large numbers of male slaves then became available at low prices, and they were rapidly incorporated into the expanding plantation economy of the east coast, the Mascarene Islands, and Zanzibar.

The Trans-Atlantic Trade

Up until the arrival of the Portuguese in the 15th century, coastal Africa had been relatively isolated from external contact. Initially, Portuguese traders transported limited numbers of slaves to Portugal, the islands in the Mediterranean, Cape Verde, Madeira, and the Canary Islands to work on sugar plantations. By the 1470s and 1480s, the Portuguese were actively purchasing slaves in the Bight of Benin and exchanging them for gold on the Gold Coast. These slaves were then put to work in the gold mines. At the beginning of the 16th century, the exportation of slaves increased dramatically due to the inclusion of Kongo in the trading network, along with the development of São Tomé sugar plantations. By the late 16th and early 17th centuries, many European nations had joined the slave trade due to

expanding labor demand in their various colonies. This period witnessed an increase in the numbers of European trading stations spread from Senegal to Angola, via the west coast of Africa including the Gold Coast, the Bight of Benin, and Calabar. The primary source of slaves were the Gold Coast, the Bight of Benin, and Kongo. In the mid- to late 17th century, the trade expanded in response to increased labor demand for the expanding sugar plantations in the New World, especially in the Caribbean. The demand for slaves remained high until the first decade of the 19th century, when Denmark, Britain, the United States, and other nations attempted to abolish the trade. Despite these efforts, the trade continued at significant levels and did not substantially decrease until the abolition of the institution of slavery in the Americas. It is estimated that at least 15 million enslaved Africans were exported to the Americas during the 400 years of the Western slave trade.

While slavery undoubtedly existed in Africa for centuries before the advent of the trans-Atlantic slave trade, it must be recognized that the expanding European and Islamic demand for slaves fundamentally transformed the social, political, and economic life of Africa. The individuals who were enslaved were not the only people affected by this trade, nor was this effect only felt during the period of the trade. The long-term effects of the slave trade also include the population loss due to slave raids, slaving wars, as well as famine, epidemics, and loss of life encountered in the movement of slaves. In West Africa specifically, the short-term effect of the trade was to aid the rise of military states such as Dahomey, Asante, and Oyo in the forest and coastal regions of the Gold Coast and the Bight of Benin. The long-term effects of the massive trade in people are many and complex. They include depopulation of vast areas, stagnation and sometimes reversal of population growth, increased social fragmentation and instability, and expansion of internal slavery. The loss of vast numbers of people, their reproductive capacity, and their skills seriously curtailed economic development in Africa.

BIBLIOGRAPHY

Brooks, G. E. 1993. *Landlords and strangers: Ecology, society, and trade in western Africa, 1000–1630.* Boulder: Westview Press.

Eldredge, E. A., and F. Morton. 1994. *Slavery in South Africa: Captive labor on the Dutch frontier.* Boulder: Westview Press.

Inikori, J. E. 1982. *Forced migration: The impact of the export slave trade on African societies.* New York: Africana Publishing Company.

Inikori, J. E., and S. Engerman. 1992. *The Atlantic slave trade: Effects on economies, societies, and peoples in Africa, the Americas, and Europe.* Durham, N.C.: Duke University Press.

Lovejoy, P. E. 1983. *Transformations in slavery: A history of slavery in Africa.* Cambridge: Cambridge University Press.

Manning, P. 1990. *Slavery and African life: Occidental, oriental, and African slave trades.* Cambridge: Cambridge University Press.

Robertson, C. C., and M. A. Klein. 1983. *Women and slavery in Africa.* Madison: University of Wisconsin Press.

Searing, J. F. 1993. *West African slavery and Atlantic commerce: The Senegal River Valley, 1700–1860.* Cambridge: Cambridge University Press.

Kenneth G. Kelly

SALT PRODUCTION AND THE SALT TRADE

Throughout Africa, as elsewhere, common salt (sodium chloride) is a dietary necessity for human beings, who die in convulsions without it. It is particularly necessary to people living within the tropics whose staple foods are cereals or root crops. Those who live mainly on animal products take in enough salt to avoid the need to supplement their diet, but all others must obtain, usually with considerable effort, salt from the sea or salt lakes, geological deposits, plants, insects, or mollusks. Human knowledge of some of these sources must go back to the beginnings of our species, since salt is necessary to all animals. Natural exposures of salt are regularly visited by many species today and have always made good hunting grounds for predators. Another sodium salt, sodium carbonate or natron, also occurs in natural exposures and has long been used by human communities.

With the development of agriculture in Africa, at least 8,000 years ago, the need for salt must have increased since both crop growers with little access to animal food and herders whose domestic animals needed salt searched for supplementary sources. Additional uses were found for salt in preserving food and skins and more recently in making soap, refining silver, and preserving human bodies. This need for extra salt had important social consequences, including the reduction of agriculturists' self-sufficiency, the undertaking of large-scale salt production, the development of regional and long-distance trade networks, and outbreaks of warfare to control rich salt deposits. As a result, salt came to be an important source of revenue and capital to its controllers and was used as a currency. It was also considered to be a suitable offering to deities and spirit mediums and a much-esteemed medicine.

Traditional methods of production have been increasingly abandoned in recent centuries, as salt produced in Europe and exported to Africa was many times cheaper and purer. Many areas of Africa, however, are still sufficiently isolated to have to rely on local sources of salt and local trading networks, and studies of these regions allow researchers to understand a good deal about how it was produced and traded in the past. Ethnographic evidence has been collected in Africa for many centuries, especially the last five, and also helps our understanding, for little archaeological study has so far been directed to the location and excavation of salt-producing sites. From the few sites that have been dated, production can be shown to have taken place in the last 2,000 years, and literary evidence shows that it was used in Egypt at least 4,000 years ago. The archaeological recognition of salt, except at sites where it was being produced, is difficult, and the recognition of salt trading, unless there are distinctive containers, is virtually impossible, but a combination of literary, ethnographic, and archaeological evidence allows an outline of its use in Africa to be constructed. There are five main sources of salt: animal salt, vegetable salt, sea salt, rock salt, and salty springs along with the salt-impregnated land round them. The methods of obtaining the salt vary with each and can best be considered under the headings of "unprocessed" and "processed."

Unprocessed Salt from Animals

It is possible to obtain sufficient sodium chloride for good health by consuming mainly animal products—flesh, milk, blood, and urine. Such consumption is present today among some hunting communities and would have been prevalent among their stone-using predecessors. Although only the bones of their prey and their weapons can suggest such consumption, hunting must have been the earliest way in which human beings obtained salt.

When the specialized herding of domestic animals began in Africa in the 7th millennium B.C. in what is today the Sahara Desert, the use of urine, milk, and blood (without killing the animals) became another way of acquiring salt. Herding was being practiced in eastern Africa by the 3rd millennium B.C. and in southern Africa by the 1st millennium A.D. Some communities like the Maasai of Kenya still live on this kind of diet and need no salt supplement. Such a diet is difficult to recognize archaeologically, but recently investigations of teeth and bones have provided evidence of this diet in the Middle Nile Valley in the 4th millennium B.C.

Unprocessed Salt from Surface Exposures

Where salt crusts have been formed by solar evaporation on the land surface, salt can be scraped up and used without any processing. These crusts occur where saltwater lakes have dried up, on the soil around brine springs, and on seacoasts where lagoons form and then dry out. Salt is still collected on many African beaches especially in western Africa. The scrapings are usually mixed with earth, a process that gives the salt a gray or red color. This surface-collection leaves no archaeologically detectable remains but may well have been an important source in early, even preagricultural, times.

The collection of salt from surface exposures was described in the 19th century at the salt lakes of Katwe and Kasenyi in Uganda. Here three grades of salt were produced, the best two in the dry season by solar evaporation and the third by breaking slabs of precipitated salt from the lake bed throughout the year.

Sodium carbonate (natron) also occurs in natural exposures and was much used from the 3rd millennium B.C. in Egypt for soap, especially in religious ablutions, and for preserving human bodies. The name *natron* derived from the Ancient Egyptian word for *holy*.

This type of sodium was also used elsewhere in Africa, particularly in Bomu (Nigeria) where there was an important production center distributing widely in the 18th century.

Processed Salt

Salt from most sources in Africa requires preparation before it can be used or traded, and much labor and organization are necessary. Almost all the salt used by ordinary people in the last five centuries was obtained from local sources, and many hundreds of small processing sites have been identified, because the processing leaves archaeologically visible remains. These sites were both on seashores and in the interior of Africa. The ethnographic evidence suggests that these sites served relatively small regions, their salt being bartered at local markets within a radius of 100 kilometers. Only the few, particularly rich sources were more intensively exploited and the product traded over distances of up to 1,000 kilometers. The salt can come from vegetation, from the sea, or from brine springs and their surrounding salty earth.

Vegetable Salt

Plants from which salt can be obtained are known all over Africa. Such knowledge may well have been inherited from humans' stone-using predecessors. Although leaves or roots can be used directly in cooking, salt can only be made by collecting quantities of them, burning them, and filtering water through the ashes to make brine. The brine is then boiled until the salt is precipitated. The process was widely used in Africa but only documented from the 1st millennium, although it is probably very much older. It has been well described in western Africa at Fog'la (Chad) and is still in use there. In the Inland Niger Delta of Nigeria, a more sophisticated version of the process involved burning the wood of red and white mangrove trees and trading the resulting salt inland by canoe. The laborious nature of this process meant that salt from other sources was always welcome. In the forests of Angola, for example, elephant hunters in the 19th century were glad to exchange their ivory for salt from the coast.

Sea (or Bay) Salt

On African coasts wherever or whenever humidity was high and solar evaporation slow, boiling sea water was a common method of processing salt. Many sites along the African coasts have been identified as sites for this technique through archaeological evidence in the form of scatters or even mounds of broken boiling pots *(briqetage),* charcoal fragments, and the burned areas of fires. Boiling sea water requires much time and labor—firewood must be collected, boiling equipment prepared, and a watch kept over the boiling so that the pots are topped-up with more brine as the water evaporates. When full of salt and boiled dry, the pots are broken, and the solid lumps of quite pure salt are ready for transporting.

The best regional study of such salt processing was in Benin (western Africa), where much salt is still produced in this way by women who sell it in local markets. The processing and trade of salt seems to have been going on there for more than 1,000 years, since an excavation at Zounbodje produced carbon-14 dates of A.D. 610 to 790. The trading of sea salt along rivers in western Africa went far inland. In the 17th century in Senegal, it stretched 1,000 kilometers eastward to Tombouctou.

Brine Springs and Salt-Impregnated Earth

In much of inland Africa, a plentiful rainfall dissolves buried deposits of salt and reemerges as springs, which then precipitate their salt in the soil around them and fill shallow depressions in which surface crusts, or pans, form. Long known, they are still important self-renewing sources today and, in the past, were the most common type of salt-rich site. In Zimbabwe, for example, where no other kinds of big salt deposits exist, 32 complexes of brine springs provided for the whole region. The methods used to gather the salt from these sites are similar throughout the continent. The salt crusts are scraped or dug up and turned into brine by filtering water through them. The water is then boiled, with the pots being regularly topped-up, until evaporation leaves them full of salt. The pots are then broken, and the salt used. Archaeological sites that engaged in this type salt processing are characterized by pits, mounds of discarded earth, mounds of *briqetage,* and fireplaces. Several of the sites dating to the 13th and 14th centuries have been excavated. In recent centuries, most of the work has been done by women, who worked part-time and seasonally to provide for their families or who labored as groups to produce salt for distant markets. The method has been well studied in Tanzania at Uvinza, a place to which 20,000 people came in one year in the 19th century to make salt for themselves. During the few weeks in the dry season, the visitors, mainly women, cut their own firewood, made their own boiling pots at the site, and loaded and carried the salt on their head for up to 200 kilometers. Another excavation in Tanzania, at Ivuna, showed a similar method had been in use over a period of 700 years. At Kabiro in Uganda on the shore of Lake Victoria, women still carefully scrape the surface of their "salt gardens" daily. Similar sites have been investigated recently in the Sudan and Zimbabwe.

Rock (or Haline) Salt

Strata of crystalline salt that precipitated on the beds of long-vanished seas and lakes and compressed into rock with perfect cubic cleavage are found at various depths in some parts of Africa. The salt is of great purity, is often available in large quantities, and can be mined, because of its cleavage, in large slabs suitable for immediate transportation. Rock salt has been much sought after as a luxury, and as a result large-scale exploitation has taken place in some areas by teams of male professionals (often slaves or prisoners) serving powerful monopolists. The salt from these centers was then traded over thousands of square kilometers in western, eastern, and southern Africa.

The most famous deposits are in the deserts of Mauritania and Mali. These sites have supplied the savannas to the south with salt for more than 1,000 years. The earliest-known rock salt mine was in Idjil (Mauritania), where laborers exploited the deposits from the 10th to 15th centuries. Taghaza (Mali) was also in full production in the 15th century, when Ibn Batuta reported that the salt was quarried in thick slabs by slaves who lived in huts made of salt. All food was imported, and the salt was taken out by caravans of camels from Tombouctou. After the destruction of Taghaza in the 16th century, Taodeni (Taghaza al Ghizlan) took its place and in 1975 was still producing several thousand tons of salt a year. From 16 square kilometers of salt pans, laborers, mainly convicts, mined the salt in 60-kilogram slabs from shallow trenches. The workers still lived in huts of salt slabs, and camel caravans still exported the slabs to Tombouctou. In southern Africa, the production center of good rock salt in the Kisama region of northern Angola is another example. Europeans arriving in the 15th century noted the mining of salt in Kisama, and for the next 100 years, miners excavated carefully shaped, 60-centimeter-wide blocks, which were taken by canoes and head loads along the Kwanza River to Kabaso, a great salt market and capital of the ruler who had the monopoly of the salt trade. Traders traveled for 27 days to come to Kabaso for salt, which was widely distributed through the Zaire Basin. Another famous source of fine salt seems to have been in use for at least 2,000 years. In the Afar region of Somalia in northeastern Africa, a lava flow cut off an arm of the sea to form a lake. This became the Danakil Salt Pans, covering several hundred square kilometers and lying 60 meters below sea level. Some of the pans, which flood with rainwater annually, are left with thick crusts of salt. These deposits were broken and shaped into 18-centimeter-long bars *(amoleh)*. Other pans were quarried in shallow trenches. Mule caravans transported the bars, long used as currency, into Ethiopia and beyond. The trade is well documented in the 12th century but probably existed in the 4th century since a local (Aksumite) ruler was reported to be obtaining gold nuggets from much farther inland (probably from the Blue Nile Basin) in exchange for bars of salt.

The Trading and Transporting of Salt

The trade of salt occurred at two very different levels. Ordinary people, mostly subsistence farmers, obtained the salt they needed from nearby sources, which often produced poor quality salt and needed much work to exploit. Some might make it for themselves, but most salt was transported by head, animal, or canoe to local markets and bartered for other products. Wealthy people gratified their taste for purer salt through long-distance trade with big production centers. In western and northern Africa, the introduction of the camel from Asia in the 1st millennium B.C. made the rich deposits of the Sahara Desert available, and beginning 1,000 years later, salt in this region was certainly controlled by monopolists, the earliest known being the rulers of the ancient empire of Ghana (in northern Mali). In southern and eastern Africa, similar trading patterns developed, and salt traveled as part of a range of luxuries, which came to include gold, ivory, and slaves, and was interchangeable with them.

Soon after the beginnings of cultivation, whether of cereals or root crops, salt supplements became necessary parts of human diets. Researchers' focus on long-distance trade has tended to obscure the much greater importance of local small-scale production and short-distance trading, which have supplied the bulk of peoples' needs. Because this aspect of prehistoric archaeology has received very little attention, the early history of salt production is not known. Its history over the last 2,000 years is clearer, especially as part of the luxury trade. The African salt trade flourished into the 20th century and only withered away under the competition of cheaper, purer imports from other continents.

BIBLIOGRAPHY

Alexander, J. 1993. The salt industries of West Africa. In *The archaeology of Africa: Food, metal and towns,* eds. T. Shaw, P. Sinclair, B. Andah, and A. Okpoko, 652–657. London: Routledge.

Black, M. 1967. The social influence of salt. *Scientific American* (September 1967): 24–28.

Connah, G. 1995. *The salt industry at Kabiro.* Nairobi: British Institute in Eastern Africa.

de Brisay, K., ed 1975. *Salt: The study of an ancient industry*. Colchester: Colchester Archaeological Society.

Fagan, B., and J. Yellen. 1968. Ivuna: Ancient salt workings in South Tanzania. *Azania* 3: 1–45.

Good, C. M. 1972. Salt, trade and disease in Africa's northern Great Lakes region. *The International Journal of African Historical Studies* 4: 543–587.

Meillasaux, Charles ed. 1971. *The development of indigenous trade and markets in West Africa*. Oxford: Oxford University Press.

Rivaillain, J. 1980. Le sel dans les villages cotiers et lagunaires du Bas Dahomey. *Annales de l'Université de Abidjan* 8: 143–167.

Sutton, J., and Roberts, A. 1968. Uvinza and its salt industry. *Azania* 3: 45-87.

Trench, R. 1978. *Forbidden sands*. London: Routledge.

John Alexander

SOUTHEASTERN AFRICAN GOLD MINING AND TRADE

The numerous, abandoned gold mines on the Zimbabwe Plateau at the end of the 19th century are an important component of the archaeology of southeastern Africa. As early as 947, Masudi recorded the availability of gold for trade on the East African coast. Other Islamic geographers between the 10th and 14th centuries made similar references. Subsequently, from the 16th to the 18th centuries, Portuguese merchants took advantage of the East African gold trade and established trading settlements in northeastern Zimbabwe.

In the late 19th century, European explorers and hunters, such as T. Baines and F. C. Selous, noted large numbers of abandoned gold workings between the Limpopo and Zambezi Rivers. From 1890 onward, European settlers staked thousands of mining claims on the sites of precolonial workings. More than 1,200 20th-century gold mines in Zimbabwe and Botswana trace their origins to precolonial workings. The Zimbabwe Plateau is the only part of southeastern Africa where evidence for large-scale gold mining in prehistory has been found.

Quartz is the principal host of free gold on the plateau. It seems that wherever an outcrop of gold-bearing quartz appeared at the surface a working was started by precolonial miners. The strategy adopted was to remove as little rock as possible, select the richest ore, and extract barely enough surrounding rock to enable access. Some precolonial mines are recorded to have reached more than 30 meters in depth. Tools were iron gads, set into wooden handles, and hammer stones, used together with a chiseling motion. Hoes were sometimes adapted as shovels. Ore was carried out of the workings in wooden buckets or leather satchels. Fire setting helped to break the ore from the parent rock. Footholds were chiseled into the sides of vertical shafts. The few human skeletons found in precolonial mines indicate that the greater proportion of miners were women.

Once the ore was removed from underground, it was crushed and milled to fine sand using stone pestles and mortars. Elliptical and circular crushing and milling hollows are found in numerous rock outcrops in Zimbabwe, particularly close to gold mines or at nearby prehistoric settlements. The milled ore was swilled with water in a wooden pan to separate the lighter, waste material, leaving gold in the bottom of the pan. Gold was exported at this stage in the process, in the form of dust, carried in porcupine quills or feather quills of vultures.

With the development of state-organized societies in the region, first evident at Mapungubwe in the former Transvaal province then at Great Zimbabwe and finally at Khami and related sites, there was local demand for gold for use by elite individuals. Gold ornaments were restricted to elite settlements. Vitrified potsherds with embedded drills of gold, found at some archaeological elite settlements, show that gold was melted and poured into molds. Gold was manufactured into spherical or biconical beads or drawn to make wire, which was then wound into tight spirals to make necklaces or bangles. Gold was also beaten into foil to cover wooden objects. Tiny gold tacks secured the foil in place.

The elites in state societies were apparently able to exact tribute from the commoner population in the form of gold, if not by force then perhaps in terms of a redistribution network. Because of drought, an inherent part of the southeastern African climate, communities were mutually dependent and supplemented production by using alternative, local resources in times of crop failure. Even in modern times, subsistence farmers resort to alluvial gold panning in drought years. In the past, communities took advantage of the demand for gold at east coast markets.

The socioeconomic processes of precolonial trade are not well understood, but the distribution of imported goods in archaeological sites indicates that collection, exchange, and redistribution of trade goods took place at elite centers. Chinese porcelains, for example, were restricted to elite settlements, while imported glass beads were available to all levels of society. In fact, the demand for imported glass beads, as vital status symbols or as bride wealth, may have induced farmers to undertake gold mining in spite of the hard work and hazards involved.

Too few archaeological deposits in precolonial gold workings have been examined scientifically for a detailed chronology of gold mining in southeastern Africa to be established. Evidence exists for trade contact between the Zimbabwe Plateau and the east coast in the 1st millennium A.D. The incentive for coastal merchants to voyage as far south as the present-day Mozambique coast was perhaps copper from the countries now known as Zambia, Zaire, and Zimbabwe and gold from the Zimbabwe region. The earliest gold extraction may have been in the form of alluvial panning. The earliest radiocarbon dates for reef mining calibrate to between the 12th and 14th centuries, coinciding with Great Zimbabwe's floruit and the enriching of east coast settlements, particularly Kilwa in Tanzania. Portuguese merchants of the 16th to 18th centuries complained about the limited amount of gold produced, because mining was the dry-season activity of a farming population. By the late 19th century, underground workings were obsolete, primarily because the payable ore was exhausted or groundwater was reached. Traditional alluvial mining continues today.

BIBLIOGRAPHY

Huffman, T. N. 1974. Ancient mining and Zimbabwe. *Journal of the South African Institute of Mining and Metallurgy* 74: 238–242.

Mennell, F. P., and R. Summers. 1950. The "ancient workings" of southern Rhodesia. *Occasional Papers of the National Museum of Southern Rhodesia* 2 (20): 765–778.

Phimister, I. 1974. Alluvial gold mining and trade in nineteenth century south central Africa. *Journal of African History* 15: 445–456.

Phimister, I. 1976. Pre-colonial gold mining in southern Zambezia: A reassessment. *African Social Research* 21: 1–30.

Schofield, J. F. 1925. The ancient workings of southeast Africa. *The Southern Rhodesia Native Affairs Department Annual* 3: 5–12.

Summers, R. 1969. *Ancient mining in Rhodesia and adjacent areas.* Salisbury: Trustees of the National Museums of Rhodesia.

Swan, L. M. 1994. *Early gold mining on the Zimbabwean Plateau.* Studies in African Archaeology 9. Uppsala: Societas Archaeologica Upsaliensis.

Lorraine Swan

INDIAN OCEAN TRADE

Scholars generally agree that the earliest settled farming communities of southern Africa appeared as a result of gradual population movements from the north and were established in the region by the 3rd century A.D. For the greater part of the 1st millennium A.D., these early iron-using farming populations were organized as nonstratified village communities mainly engaged in cultivating crops, rearing domestic animals, and hunting for subsistence. Among other things, remains of carbonized seeds of domesticated millets and sorghum provide evidence of the agricultural economy, while bones of domestic cattle, sheep, and goats recovered at numerous sites in the region clearly indicate animal husbandry. The evidence suggests that these farming communities were self-sufficient villages with no contact with the outside world. However, evidence from around the 8th century A.D. suggests that the communities had established links with the outside world via the Indian Ocean Coast of East Africa.

Early sites on the Mozambique coast, the most important of which is Chibuene dated to the 8th century A.D., as well as a number in the southern African interior suggest that trading networks between the coast and the interior were established by around A.D. 700. The well-researched site of Schroda in the Shashi-Limpopo Basin, as described by E. O. M. Hanisch in 1981, as well as Makuru on the southern Zimbabwe Plateau, investigated by Thomas N. Huffman, have yielded evidence of external contacts. This evidence has come in the form of glass beads of various types and colors. The most common are blue, green, and yellow segments of blown canes of glass and, later, Indian red beads. By the 10th century A.D., ceramic vessels from Persia and, at a later stage, blue and white porcelain from as far way as China had been introduced as trade items. Although not documented through archaeological finds, cloth was also part of the trade. The evidence for this comes from the early writings of Arab travelers. Of these, the best-known is *Periplus of the Ethyrean Sea,* written during the early part of the Christian era. Later in time are the writings of al Masudi and al Idrisi, who compiled information on the East African coast and referred to some of the products exchanged with African populations.

It is important to note what African populations exchanged for the exotic beads, ceramics, and cloth. The archaeological evidence shows that from around the 8th century, the basic subsistence-oriented economy expanded to include the production of local commodities that had exchange value on the external market. Initially, we see from Schroda, for example, the hunting of elephants for ivory, which was in demand in the Arab world. Here the evidence suggests that while some of the ivory was used locally for the manufacture of ornaments, most of it was destined for the external market. Skins of animals, such as leopards, were also exported. The archaeological evidence for this is in the form of bone remains of such nonsubsistence animals recovered from sites.

During the early part of the 2nd millennium, gold mining also became evident, particularly on the Zimbabwe Plateau where gold fields were abundant and rich. Although not all have been securely dated, the numerous ancient mines identified on the Zimbabwe Plateau reflect the scale and importance of this economic activity. As with ivory, most of the gold mined was destined for the outside market. There are indications that through time, gold replaced ivory as the major export as its value in the outside world increased.

The introduction of external trade in southern Africa represented a new economic force among the populations, and it has generally been thought that this was directly related to the development of more complex forms of sociopolitical organization commonly referred to as *state systems.* It has been argued that participation in the trade transformed the relations of production among the previously nonstratified societies and led to the rise of hierarchically organized societies. A few individuals accumulated a new form of wealth by way of exotic goods and thereby gained a springboard to economic, social, and political power. Exotic goods from a distant source differed from local forms of wealth like cattle herds. Those who participated in the trade and eventually managed to control it used the proceeds to build up a following in society by redistributing trade goods.

The earliest such systems to develop was the Mapungubwe state, with its capital at the site of Mapungubwe just south of the Limpopo River. Dating to the 11th century, Mapungubwe and related sites like Mapela in the Shashi-Limpopo Basin have yielded evidence of large-scale participation in external trade as well as evidence of ivory and gold exploitation. At these sites, the relationship between the development of the state and this new branch of production cannot be denied. The probable entry point of exotic goods into southern Africa at this stage was Chibuene. Local ceramics of the Gokomere-Zhizo tradition provide evidence that Chibuene was contemporary with sites of this tradition in the interior—for example, Schroda. More importantly, glass-bead types recovered by P. Sinclair from the interior sites are similar to those recovered from sites on the coast. Attention should also be drawn to the fact that apart from glass beads, Chibuene has yielded Islamic or Persian ceramic vessels of the Sassanian Islamic ware dating to the 9th century. These vessels are similar to imported ceramics from the early phases of the site of Kilwa, which was to develop into a major coastal trading city on the East African coast during the 2nd millennium. What this suggests is that by the 9th century, a chain of trading sites on the Indian Ocean Coast formed a commercial network with the interior.

The Mapungubwe state went into decline and eventually collapsed during the 13th century. Its decline coincides with the rise of the Zimbabwe state with its capital at the monumental stone-built site of Great Zimbabwe on the southeastern part of the Zimbabwe Plateau. The development of Great Zimbabwe has been directly linked to the decline of Mapungubwe within the context of the importance of the Indian Ocean trade and the growth of sociopolitical complexity in the region. The rise of Zimbabwe is seen as a result of the growing importance of gold on the international market. Political power shifted from Mapungubwe to the Zimbabwe Plateau as gold, abundant on the plateau, became more important in trade than ivory. It is also of interest to note that on the coast, there was a shift of the trading towns from the south to the north. The new coastal settlements later became the important Portuguese port of Sofala.

The Zimbabwe state arose in the 13th century and started to decline sometime around the middle of the 15th century. By the end of the 15th century, Great Zimbabwe had ceased to be an important political or economic center. The rise of the state has been linked to the accumulation of enormous amounts of wealth as a result of participation in the Indian Ocean trade. There is abundant evidence from the site of Great Zimbabwe of large-scale participation in this trade network. Thousands of glass beads have been recovered, in addition to imported ceramics, particularly blue and white Chinese porcelain. The city of Kilwa on the East African coast rose at the same time as Great Zimbabwe. Scholars now generally agree that the two centers were connected and benefited from each other. Kilwa was the coastal entry point of exotic goods into the southern African interior, while the political power at Great Zimbabwe controlled their distribution and also played a role in the procurement of exports, particularly gold. Perhaps the most telling evidence of the connection between the two ancient cities was the recovery at Great Zimbabwe of a 13th-century coin minted at Kilwa. It is of further interest to note that both

Great Zimbabwe and Kilwa went into decline at about the same time during the 15th century. The decline of Great Zimbabwe and its abandonment as a major economic and political center has been interpreted in terms of ecological collapse resulting from high population levels. Its decline may also have been caused by the probable shift in trade routes away from Great Zimbabwe, which implies that the site lost its control of external trade, one of the major elements in its economy.

The Zimbabwe state was succeeded around the middle of the 15th century by the Mutapa state in northern Zimbabwe and the Torwa-Changamire state centered at the site of Khami in southwestern Zimbabwe. Both states continued to construct their capitals in stone similar to Great Zimbabwe, although much smaller in size. From the site of Khami, sizable quantities of trade beads and ceramics have been recovered, clearly showing continued participation in the Indian Ocean trade. The Mutapa site has provided both historical and archaeological information documenting the relationship between state power and long-distance trade and other indigenous branches of production. Recent archaeological research by I. Pikirayi at the site of Baranda near Mount Darwin in northern Zimbabwe has unearthed more than 20,000 imported glass beads and large quantities of imported ceramics. This evidence reflects the extent to which the Mutapa state maintained trading relations with the coast. This is further documented in the early written records of Portuguese travelers in the early part of the 16th century. These records indicate that gold was mined in considerable quantities in the different parts of the Mutapa state and exported in order to satisfy the local demand for exotic goods. In fact, Portuguese ambitions to gain the gold fields in the areas under the control of Mutapa in part caused the state to decline and finally collapse in the 19th century.

So far, this account has concentrated on the Indian Ocean trade in relation to the major social formations of southern Africa. The evidence from many ordinary farming village sites within these major political entities suggests that the products of external trade did find their way to ordinary people and were not an elite monopoly.

The Portuguese records already referred to go on to show us how these ordinary village peasants were integrated into the trade networks. Within the Mutapa state, the rulers distributed cattle to their subjects as payment for mining the gold required on the external market. Some of the proceeds from the trade were also similarly distributed. The rulers no doubt retained the bulk of the exotic items, however. It is probable that this system also operated in the Mapungubwe, Zimbabwe, and Torwa-Changamire states. In this way, external trade goods became an important aspect of social and economic relations and thus are fairly common at archaeological sites throughout the region. This, however, does not imply, as has often been assumed, that external trade necessarily became the backbone of prehistoric state systems in southern Africa.

While external trade was clearly important, it was integrated with several other branches of production to produce an economy sufficiently successful to maintain the systems. These branches include cattle herding, agriculture, and various specialist crafts such as cotton spinning. Stone-built sites of the Great Zimbabwe tradition, and especially Great Zimbabwe itself, have yielded abundant evidence of the pivotal role of cattle herding in the economy of the state. Some scholars now feel that, in fact, cattle herding may best explain the rise and development of the state. Although not as clearly reflected in the archaeological record, agricultural production was an integral part of the state economies. Portuguese records indicate that the subject people of the Mutapa state paid tribute in the form of agricultural produce or agricultural labor. The manufacture of cotton cloth is reflected at many sites by the presence of spindle whorls. What all this evidence shows is that the Indian Ocean trade was just one of several important economic activities that prehistoric populations of southern Africa engaged in during the 2nd millennium A.D.

BIBLIOGRAPHY

Garlake, P. S. 1978. Pastoralism and Zimbabwe. *Journal of African History* 19: 479–498.

Hall, M. 1987. *The changing past: Farmers, kings and traders in southern Africa, 200–1860.* Cape Town and Johannesburg: David Phillip.

Huffman, T. N. 1973. Test excavations at Makuru. *Arnoldia* 5 (39): 1–21.

Phillipson, D. W. 1985. *African archaeology.* Cambridge: Cambridge University Press.

Pikirayi, I. 1993. *The archaeological identity of the Mutapa state: Towards an historical archaeology of northern Zimbabwe.* Uppsala: Societas Archaeologica Upsaliensis.

Sinclair, P. 1987. *Space, time and social formation.* Uppsala: Societas Archaeologica Upsaliensis.

Swan, L. M. 1994. *Early gold mining on the Zimbabwean Plateau.* Studies in African Archaeology 9. Uppsala: Societas Archaeologica Upsaliensis.

Theal, G. M. 1989–1903. *Records of south-eastern Africa.* 9 vols. Cape Town: S. Struik.

Voight, E., ed. 1981. *Guide to archaeological sites in the northern Transvaal.* Pretoria: Southern African Association of Archaeologists.

Gilbert Pwiti

Historical Archaeology

WESTERN AFRICAN HISTORICAL ARCHAEOLOGY

Historical archaeology integrates the study of the archaeological past with written records and oral traditions. In western Africa, the earliest documentary sources date to the late 1st millennium A.D. with Arabic accounts of the savanna and Sudan. European descriptions of the coast and hinterland first appeared in the 15th century. Records such as these, by travelers, traders, and visitors from outside of western Africa, provide the primary written sources on the early past. Indigenous writing systems were invented, notably the Vai script in Liberia and Bamum hieroglyphic writing in Cameroon, but these sources date only to the 19th century and are very limited in scope. The principal indigenous means of preserving and passing on information is through oral traditions. Surveys of all these sources underscore the incomplete record they provide. Outsiders' accounts concentrate on certain regions and time periods and generally offer only marginal insight into African cultures. Oral traditions, on the other hand, frequently have a limited time depth and focus on specific categories of information such as the recounting of ruling lineages or origin myths. Because of the limited and uneven nature of the written and oral sources, the term *protohistoric* has often been used, particularly in the Francophone countries, to describe the western African past during most of the last 1,000 years. Archaeological research

focusing on sites of this time period has typically been holistic in perspective, drawing on all available sources. The specific information used, the areas examined, and the research questions addressed have varied widely, ranging from the early states of the western savanna to the study of European forts and castles on the coast. As is the case with archaeological research on earlier time periods, conclusions and observations are frequently limited by a paucity of excavation, artifact chronologies, and regional syntheses.

The West African Savanna

The earliest Arabic accounts describe indigenous African kingdoms, the trans-Saharan trade, and the renaissance of Islamic learning in the West African Sudan beginning in the late 1st millennium. Historical archaeological research has been aimed at identifying and exploring sites known from documentary accounts, including Tegdaoust and Azugi (Mauritania), Jenne-jeno, Tombouctou, and Gao (present-day Mali), and Azelik and Marandet (Niger).

Koumbi-Saleh, located in southern Mauritania near the Mali border, is of particular interest. It is believed to have been the capital of ancient Ghana, which extended over portions of the present-day countries of Senegal, Mali, and Mauritania. Ghana emerged as the most powerful empire in the Sudan region by 1000. In 1067, the Arab traveler al Bekri described its capital as a large settlement consisting of two towns nearly 10 kilometers apart. One was occupied by Muslim Arab traders and had 12 mosques, while the other was an indigenous African town where the palace of the Ghanaian king was located. The area between the towns was filled with houses. Oral traditions of the Soninke people still speak of an ancient empire whose capital was Koumbi. Excavations at Koumbi-Saleh have revealed the remains of two settlements that seem to match the written and oral descriptions. One has produced evidence of multistoried stone dwellings and Islamic tomb burials. The other settlement, located a short distance to the south, lacks any evidence of stone construction. This may be the royal town of al-Ghala where the non-Muslim Ghanaian king once held court. The size of these settlements suggests a large urban center, which may have had a population of tens of thousands.

A site that perhaps was the capital of ancient Mali has also been investigated. Mali was one of the states that emerged as an important kingdom after the decline of the Ghana Empire. It reached its greatest extent in the 13th and 14th centuries, when its boundaries extended well beyond those of ancient Ghana, covering much of the present-day countries of Mali, Senegal, Gambia, Mauritania, and Guinea. Malian rulers, most notably Mansa Musa, made pilgrimages to Mecca and established Arab scholars at towns like Jenne-jeno (old Jenne) and Tombouctou. The site of Niani, in present-day Guinea, corresponds with some aspects of Mali's capital described in the scant written accounts. Archaeological research, however, suggests Niani was first occupied between 600 and 1000, abandoned, and then reoccupied during the 16th and 17th centuries. Archaeological data would, therefore, seem to suggest Niani was not the capital during Mali's apogee. It is possible that the capital city was located to the north.

Excavations at other sites such as Jenne-jeno and Gao-Sané in the Inland Niger Delta have produced finds—such as Chinese porcelain, European and Islamic beads, and glass from Mameluke Egypt—that underscore external trade connections. Documentary accounts of any kind remain sporadic, though the study of early Gao has benefited from the study of royal epitaphs, some of which may have been commissioned in southern Spain in the 12th century. Significantly, archaeological research in the Inland Niger Delta has been very important in demonstrating the growth of indigenous long-distance trade and socio-political complexity in the Sudan before the advent of the trans-Saharan Arab trade and written records. Features such a increasing evidence of urbanization, trade, and uniformity in pottery styles beginning in the 1st millennium may indicate the increasingly centralized political authority later manifest in the kingdoms of Ghana and Mali.

Arabic accounts afford even less information on the early savanna and forest states south of the Sudan. Settlements in central and northern Ghana—such as Daboya, Bono Manso, Yendi Dabari, and Begho—are primarily known through archaeological research and oral traditions. Begho may have developed as a trade center because of its position near the forest savanna margin, a location that would have facilitated access to the resource areas to the north and the south. Archaeological research revealed evidence of occupation spanning the 11th through 17th centuries. No written descriptions of the town exist, but Arabic accounts and later European sources describe a trade center that may have been Begho. Oral traditions, in contrast, are much more informative. Informants have identified the settlement's quarters that were occupied by the indigenous Brong-speaking people, Muslims (Kramo), and artisans (Twumfour).

European Contact

Europeans arrived on the West African coast in the 15th century and reached the area of Sierra Leone in the 1460s and the Bight of Benin before the end of the 15th century. Although a few outposts were established in the interior, especially in Senegambia, European settlement was mostly confined to small trading enclaves along the coast. Documentary accounts concentrate on African societies that were in direct contact with the European traders. Records are comparatively good in some areas—for example, coastal Ghana—while written sources of any kind remain nonexistent for other parts of the coast and much of the interior until the late 19th and 20th centuries.

European forts, trading posts, and plantations dating between the 15th and 19th centuries are described and illustrated in documentary records. Present-day Ghana, historically known as the Gold Coast, had more European outposts than any other part of Africa. Here, some 60 monuments lie scattered along the 240-kilometer-long coastline. Archaeological work has been principally concerned with the structural history of the buildings and preservation matters. A similar focus is seen in work on European outposts in other countries, such as Gorée Island in Senegal, James Island in Gambia, Bunce Island in Sierra Leone, and the Portuguese fort at Ouidah in the country of Benin.

Excavation has provided important insights into the African settlements and states that emerged in the centuries following the advent of the European trade. Elmina in the central region of present-day Ghana is one of the most thoroughly investigated coastal towns. A sizable African settlement was located at the site when the Portuguese founded Castelo de Sao Jorge da Mina in 1482, the first European outpost in sub-Saharan Africa. The castle was subsequently captured by the Dutch in 1637 and ceded to the British in 1871. The adjacent African town expanded from a village of several hundred inhabitants to a thriving community with a population of 15,000 to 20,000 by the 19th century. With the support of the Portuguese and the Dutch, Elmina gained its independence from the neighboring African polities and became the capital of the Edina state. Research at the town site has uncovered an array of trade items, providing evidence of both the growth of European commerce and the wealth of the town's African merchants. Despite economic and political transformations, archaeological evidence of ritual and burial practices, as well as the use of space within the settlement, attest to the continuity in African belief systems during the past 500 years.

One of the states that developed close trade contacts with Elmina was the kingdom of Asante, which emerged as a powerful state in the forest of southern Ghana during the 18th and 19th centuries. Asante controlled trade routes between the European enclaves on the coast and the hinterland and exacted tribute from neighboring states. European expansion during the 19th century challenged Asante's control of the trade, and the state was drawn into several conflicts with the British. Although Asante is well described in 19th-century European accounts and in more recent ethnographic studies, the early origins of the state are poorly known. Archaeological research shed some insight on its beginnings through the investigation of settlements that oral traditions identify as important during the early history of the state. Some traditions of origin describe how Asantemanso was the place where the first Asante people emerged from the ground, and excavations there have demonstrated initial occupation dating back to the 1st millennium. More recent finds, as well as research at other sites such as Anyinam and Esiease, provided evidence of increasing settlement and the growth of European trade between the 15th and 19th centuries.

Archival research and archaeological excavations have also focused on the coast and hinterland of the country of Benin, located in the portion of West Africa historically known as the Slave Coast. Benin emerged as an important source of slaves for the Atlantic trade between the 16th and the 18th centuries. A number of small states vied for the control of the trade. One of the best-known historically is the kingdom of Dahomey, which reached its apogee in the 18th century. Excavations at Ouidah, the principal port of Dahomey, have been limited by the modern settlement covering the site. The artifacts that have been recovered, however, allow the settlement's history to be related to finds at other sites.

More poorly known in documentary records are the states of Allada and Hueda, also located in coastal Benin. Both were overshadowed by Dahomey, which destroyed Togudo-Awute, the seat of the Allada kingdom, in 1724 and the Hueda capital of Savi in 1727. Allada appears on late 16th-century Portuguese maps, by which time slaves from the area were already reaching Brazil. The ascendancy of the Hueda kingdom dates to the late 17th century, when rebellion along the coast temporarily displaced the trade at Allada. The Hueda king closely regulated the activities of the European traders and prohibited them from fortifying their outposts and warehouses. By around 1700, English, Dutch, and French trading lodges were located within the palace complex. Archaeological research has traced the origins, growth, and destruction of the towns of Savi and Togudo-Awute. As in the case of other trading centers like Elmina, the imported artifacts recovered provide an important means of developing a chronology of the associated African artifacts, especially ceramics.

Farther to the east, another early state described in European accounts was the kingdom of Benin, located in the southern Nigerian rain forest west of the Niger River. In the 16th century, Portuguese writers vividly described Benin as a powerful kingdom ruled by the Oba. Archaeological research at Benin City, the capital of the kingdom, indicates the settlement was occupied by the 13th century and demonstrates that the origins of the settlement, and probably the kingdom, predate the European's arrival. Another striking aspect of the site is the network of walls encircling the town. Written sources, oral traditions, and archaeological research all indicate that the innermost walls date to the mid-15th century.

European accounts and more recent Arabic sources provide increasing insight into the origins and movements of peoples in the West African hinterland over the past few centuries. Nevertheless, oral traditions and ethnographic observations of modern communities remain of important, often providing the principal source of insight into past. Archaeologists can work backward in time, tracing the archaeological records of known populations. This affords a means of evaluating of the variable consequences of indigenous sociopolitical developments, the slave trade, and the advent of colonialism. These studies underscore the complex nature of the changes occurring in populations over the past 500 years.

Throughout West Africa, the consequences of the Atlantic slave trade, including increased conflict, the rise of warrior states, depopulation, and migration, are documented through written sources and oral traditions. Archaeologically, some of these transformations are reflected in a dramatic change in pottery styles and settlement patterns. In Senegambia, for example, pottery dating from after 1600 is different in form, surface finish, decoration, and firing from ceramics produced earlier. In Sierra Leone, Liberia, and Guinea, defensive hilltop sites and walled settlements became common in the 18th century. Similarly, work in southern Ghana has provided evidence of a dramatic change in pottery styles and

the appearance of earthworks beginning in the 15th century. Researchers have suggested that these changes represent responses to increased slave raiding.

In northern Togo, archaeological research has focused on the Bassar region, which had emerged as a center of iron production by the 17th century. Bassar became linked to the Hausa caravan trade and witnessed higher population densities and increased craft specialization. There does not, however, appear to have been a substantial increase in political centralization. Beginning in the late 18th century, the Bassar region was intensively raided by the Dagomba from the west and the Tyokossi from the north, events described in many oral traditions. Archaeological research demonstrates that these conflicts led to the abandonment of many settlements and the cessation of iron production in many centers by 1800. The Bassar area was not described in detail by European officials until incursions by German colonial officials in the 1890s. By that time, the influence of the Bassar chiefdom was reduced to villages centering around the town of Bassar.

In contrast, increasing political centralization and social differentiation is illustrated by archaeological research in the Mandara Highlands of northern Cameroon. Written accounts of this region are also very limited, though Arabic accounts dating back to the 9th century suggest the region was already involved in the trans-Saharan slave trade by that time. The Wandala may have started to consolidate power beginning in the 16th century by dominating the iron trade to the west. Slaves, raided from the neighboring Sao and Mafa communities, further fueled the state's expansion in the following centuries. The growth of the Wandala state and the effects on the societies raided for slaves had dramatic consequences. Refugee populations fled to peripheral areas, less desirable for settlement such as the Mandara Mountains, which were minimally occupied before 500 years ago.

More detailed written and oral traditions also allow a means of examining how the archaeological record represents—or does not represent—cultural and linguistic divisions observed ethnographically. Study of groups such as the Mafa and Bulahay in northern Cameroon indicate that decorative motifs on pottery express cosmological and religious beliefs and hence afford a material record of group identity. Other studies have noted aspects of construction and spatial organization distinctive of certain populations. On the other hand, culture traits ranging from pottery styles to food-preparation practices in many instances crosscut ethnographically perceived cultural boundaries. For, example the material aspects of the Limba, Yalunka, and Kurano in northern Sierra Leone are primarily manifest in small, impermanent ritual structures, which are not readily studied through archaeology. These observations have methodological and interpretive implications for archaeological interpretations in all world areas.

BIBLIOGRAPHY
Connah, G. 1987. *African civilizations: Precolonial cities and states in tropical Africa, an archaeological perspective.* Cambridge: Cambridge University Press.
DeCorse, C. R. 1992. Culture contact, continuity, and change on the Gold Coast, A.D. 1400–1900. *African Archaeological Review* 10: 163–196.
———. 1997. *Historical archaeology in West Africa: Culture contact, continuity and change.* Washington, D. C.: Smithsonian Institution Press.
McIntosh, S. K. 1994. Changing perceptions of West Africa's past: Archaeological research since 1988. *Journal of Archaeological Research* 2 (2): 165–198.

Christopher DeCorse

EASTERN AFRICAN HISTORICAL ARCHAEOLOGY

Historical archaeology can be broadly defined as areas where the material evidence of the past is supplemented by historical sources—both documentary and oral—to provide a linked synthesis. The later archaeology of eastern Africa, especially the coastal strip, and areas influenced by it has this additional dimension through the survival of such sources, which can enable a broader understanding of both social processes and political action beyond that recovered from the archaeological record alone.

Archaeologists have made extensive use of such evidence but have often constructed elaborate hypotheses based on very meager evidence. The historians of the region have on occasions relied heavily upon archaeological material but almost always accept the priority of historical sources, wherever there is disagreement. Historical archaeology remains a methodological minefield, with little consideration given to the proper way of linking of texts and material-culture evidence. The important theoretical contributions made by historical archaeologists in the New World, Australia, and medieval and post-medieval Europe have had little impact on in Africa. In this article, we will examine three areas where historical archaeology has developed—in the archaeology of coastal towns, ethnohistory, and the archaeology of colonialism.

The Swahili Coastal Towns

Historical archaeology has been practiced on the East African coast since the late 1940s, and this was where the term was first applied in African archaeology. A combination of surviving ruins (making site location very simple), a rich legacy of "internal" oral traditions and histories, and "external" descriptions written by foreigners in at least eight languages (Greek, Arabic, Persian, Chinese, Portuguese, Dutch, French, and English) led to the early development of text-aided archaeology.

Archaeology and the "External" Sources

The East African coast can be described within the domain of historical archaeology from the mid-1st century A.D., with the survival of extraordinary accounts of long-distance trade in the Western Indian Ocean. The *Periplus of the Erythrean Sea* (dating to about A.D. 40) contains a passage describing the sea voyage to Rhapta and provides details of the coast and intermediate ports and some ethnographic details of the coastal populations. Claudius Ptolemy's *Geography* (dating to about 150) offers additional place names and positional data. These documents have been scrutinized and reinterpreted on numerous occasions, but none of the key places, south of Ras Hafun (which may have been the classical-era port of Opone), has yet been identified on the ground. This lack of archaeological evidence considerably reduces the usefulness of any information the sources contain about the existence of links between the early coastal traders of the classical sources and the later Swahili communities. We do not even know whether the *Periplus*-period traders were recently arrived Bantu-speaking farmers or earlier, possibly Cushitic-speaking, pastoralists. The recent archaeological surveys in Tanzania, both on the mainland and on Zanzibar, have demonstrated that the origins of the Swahili communities can be placed in the 6th century, when a group, possibly farmers, developed maritime trading connections. These people are identified by their pottery (known as *Tana tradition* or triangular, incised ware). Documentary evidence throws no specific light upon these communities, and while there is some suggestion of a general revival in Indian Ocean commerce in the times of the Byzantine Emperor Justinian, the one source that survives from this period, *The Christian Topography of Cosmas Indicopleustes,* provides only the most general of reference to Zingium, or the East African coast.

Numerous geographical descriptions of the coastal region, mainly written in Arabic, survive from the 9th century. The most important is in al Masudi's *Muruj al-Dhahab,* which was based upon an actual voyage to Qanbalu, an East African port, in 916. Other writers of the time include al Jahiz, al Biruni, and al Idrisi, who exercised some discrimination and critical thought. The works of still others are much less useful, ranging from the ill-informed to fantastic, with tales of sea monsters and bizarre African habits. This was the stuff of encyclopedists, keen to excite a readership with the exotic. A little Persian material dating to the 10th century and remarkable Chinese accounts, probably collected from Arab merchants, are particularly detailed in their ethnographic detail of East African societies.

Archaeologists have used these sources to flesh out the detail from their excavations of coastal towns. Neville Chittick's 1977 synthesis of the East African Coast in the *Cambridge History of Africa* remains the most comprehensive attempt to link texts and archaeology, but the result was an account that is flawed in both fact and interpretation. The reality is that there is a poor match between the results of modern archaeology and the fragmentary historical sources. Three examples can be cited.

Between the 9th and 10th centuries, the most important coastal settlement was Qanbalu, visited by al Masudi and mentioned in many Arabic sources. There is as yet no convincing archaeological information as to its location. A variety of suggestions have been made, including Ras Mkumbuu on Pemba and sites on the Comoro Islands and Madagascar, but at none of these is the archaeological evidence wholly convincing. In comparison, the largest known 9th- and 10th-century site is Manda, in the Lamu Archipelago. Manda was first cited in the early 16th-century accounts and was apparently completely ignored by all the earlier geographers. The other large site of the period, Unguja Ukuu on Zanzibar may be al Jahiz's Languya but remains otherwise unremarked.

By the 12th century, geographical science had developed in the Islamic world, and the Middle East had been in regular trading contact with East Africa for several centuries. One might expect more historical detail from this period to have survived. But most of the places cited by al Idrisi and Ibn Said remain unlocated or the subject of several possibilities. It is only with the early 13th-century *Geographical Dictionary of Yakut* that the towns of Mogadishu, Merca, Barawa, Mombasa, Mkumbuu, Mtambwe, Tumbatu, and Kilwa can be correlated with known archaeological sites. Pate and Lamu, with archaeological sequences going back to the 10th century, are first mentioned in the 15th century. Four sites that have been subject to major excavations—Shanga, Gedi, Jumba la Mtwana, and Songa Mnara—are not mentioned in any contemporary source.

The second example concerns the origins of Islam. According to the sources, only at Qanbalu was there a small community of Muslims. All the geographers—al Masudi, Buzurg, and al Idrisi—are unanimous that the rest of the coast was pagan, and they even included descriptions of the religious practices of the inhabitants. Al Idrisi, writing in about 1150, describes a town that is almost certainly Barawa, where the inhabitants worship and anoint standing stones with oil, yet at Barawa there is a dedicatory inscription to the mosque with a date of 500 H, or A.D. 1104. Even more clear is the evidence from Shanga, a relatively minor trading community in the Lamu Archipelago, where there is a sequence of mosques from around 780 onward. If Shanga had a Muslim community at this date, then it is highly likely that many of the larger sites were Muslim as well.

Direct contradictions remain about the identity of the main trading partners of the Swahili communities. Here, the historical synthesis has again been written from the sources, which originate largely in the Persian Gulf.

The sources refer to ports such as Siraf and Sohar, and later Kish and Hormuz, as the terminus of the dhow (a type of Arab ship) trade. The archaeological evidence suggests a much more complex picture, in which Red Sea, Indian, and Southeast Asian merchants were major traders on the East African coast from the 10th century. Because these activities were not described in writing, their existence is often denied, and a wholly misleading view of trade and connections has emerged.

Perhaps the best example of the use and abuses of text-based archaeology comes from Ibn Battuta, who visited the coastal towns in 1331. In his description of Kilwa, he described the town as "entirely built of wood," but G. S. T. Freeman-Grenville, who was aware of the results of the excavations on the site where stone houses of the 14th century had been found, altered the Arabic to read "with elegance," while leaving the description of (unexcavated) Mombasa as "built of wood." If textual sources can be altered with such flexibility, in the face of archaeological evidence, what is the point in using them at all?

Archaeology and "Internal" Sources

If external sources are problematical, then the use of internal sources—that is, evidence recorded and transmitted by African societies themselves—is even more difficult for archaeologists to use. There is often little control on their chronology, and the dates given cannot be taken at face value. Oral traditions form the bulk of internal evidence,

but much argument centers on their validity beyond a few generations. Histories and chronicles maintain better control on accuracy. In areas of early literacy, such as the Swahili coast, chronicles were written down. One from Kilwa was published in Portuguese by João de Barros in 1552. Another Arabic chronicle of Kilwa dates to the early 19th century. The bulk of surviving histories are accounts written from the late 19th century onward but purporting to give historical information for periods often hundreds of years earlier.

Oral traditions may contain elements relating to the origins of communities. It is claimed that such accounts can survive over millennia, while the more recent traditions are discarded. In the case of the Swahili, particular speculation has surrounded traditions connected with Shungwaya, or Singwaya, a homeland from which the Bajuni Swahili as well as a number of other coastal (non-Islamic) groups derived. The main documentary source is the *Book of Zenj,* a very late compilation of traditions from southern Somalia.

Shungwaya appears on a 17th-century Portuguese map, in the general area between Pate and Barawa. Sir Richard Burton placed Shungwaya on the mainland opposite Pate Island, while there is a Kaya Singwaya close to the Sabaki River. Recently, Justin Willis has shown there to be little pre-19th-century authority for any of the Shungwaya traditions. No site of Shungwaya has been found or excavated.

Notwithstanding these limitations, the Shungwaya traditions have been used as major elements in the historical, linguistic, and archaeological reconstruction of coastal history. Derek Nurse and Tom Spear proposed a model suggesting that the Tana-Sabaki River area produced a Bantu-speaking society around 800. According to these researchers, one component of the society formed the non-Muslim Pokomo and Mijikenda groups, while another became the Muslim Swahili. New archaeological evidence from 6th-century sites in Tanzania has forced scholars to relocate this homeland to south, but the basic model remains widely accepted. James de Vere Allen proposed a very much more extreme hypothesis, using the same basic data. He argued for a Shungwaya state operating in the 1st millennium A.D. around the border of Somalia and Kenya. This state incorporated pastoralists, as well as Bantu-speaking farmers, who traded over much of eastern Africa and spawned a series of successor states. While Allen was keen to cite archaeological evidence, wherever it suited his narrative, his interpretation, which could be easily tested against the archaeological data, remains untenable.

The existence of at least early accounts of Kilwa was the main reason why this town was chosen by the British Institute in Eastern Africa for a major research project in the 1960s. The two versions of the *History of Kilwa* provide lists of rulers who could be linked with the names found on the locally minted copper coins. Researchers hoped to find coins in stratigraphic association with particular buildings and dated deposits, thus correlating the dynastic sequence with the stratigraphic record, in order to write a cultural history not only of Kilwa, but of the whole East African coast.

The Kilwa project was a significant failure in its attempt to write history. One reason for the failure was Chittick's firm conviction that the builders of Kilwa were descendants of Asiatic traders and that the semimythological account of the arrival of brothers from Shiraz (in what is now Iran), provided in the *History of Kilwa*, should be accepted literally. Equally serious was the assumption that the first Shirazi ruler of Kilwa, cited in the history as Ali bin al-Husein, was Ali bin al-Hasan.

Significantly the archaeologist Chittick and the numismatist Freeman-Grenville came to contradictory conclusions about the chronology of the coinage, and these contraditions have still not been fully resolved. The history does not provide a complete list of kings, and the names on the coins themselves may not represent the rulers of Kilwa. The coins are not dated, so the chronology was supplied by stratigraphic association, dated by imported pottery. Not only are the dates of imported pottery, which Chittick used, widely questioned, but the crudeness of the excavation methods led to mixed contexts and poor associations. Further doubt on the Kilwa chronology comes from a hoard of coins, found on Pemba in

1984, at Mtambwe Mkuu. The find raised questions about Ali bin al-Hasan, who Chittick thought was the first of the "Shirazi" rulers of Kilwa, living around 1200, because the coins at Mtambwe are associated with Fatimid gold coins and probably date to around 1000.

Ethnohistory and Archaeology

While the East African coast has the benefit of sources that may be contemporary with archaeological sites, for the interior, the absence of any written sources before the mid-19th century considerably limits the scope of historical archaeology. Indeed, the particular focus of archaeologists in this area has been to work with Stone Age, early pastoralist, and Early Iron Age societies, dating to before 1,500 years ago, rather than with the later Iron Age societies in which the use of oral history and chronicles can be more useful. There has been a marked reluctance to study the archaeology of the last millennium, and there remains a considerable lack of clarity between the archaeological record and historically attested groups, be they Maasai, Kikyu, or Mijikenda. Without such links, the use of oral tradition or historical linguistics to reconstruct the more remote past becomes very difficult.

Peter Schmidt pioneered the use of historical archaeology to study early iron smelting in the Buhaya region of western Tanzania. He used oral tradition to locate sites and ethnography to reconstruct ancient technologies. Historians did not accept that sites, dated by radiocarbon methods to 2,500 years ago, could display such "continuity" to the present day. They posited that any correlations must have been coincidental. Archaeologists, however, still broadly support Schmidt's conclusions.

In another area—the Great Lakes region—it becomes clear that historical archaeology has both potential and pitfalls. European explorers first encountered the states lying between the lakes, such as Buganda, Bunyoro, and Ankole, in the mid-19th century. These states have a rich oral and chronicled history. Only recently, especially with the resumption of fieldwork in Uganda, have there been attempts to link the oral and written sources with the archaeological evidence. One particular group, that is seen as "ancestral," was the semimythical Cwezi. Shrines and holy places are still associated with them, especially at the site of Mubende, which has been the subject of recent excavation by Peter Robertshaw. Other major sites, however, such as Bigo and Ntusi, have much weaker Cwezi associations yet have contemporary occupation levels. The transmission and reworking of historical ideas are a very complex process, in which archaeological methods cannot fully recover.

Archaeological work in other areas of eastern Africa has shown how rapidly the past, remembered as oral tradition, can be lost. At Engaruka, located on the escarpment of the East African Rift Valley, extensive field systems based upon irrigation agriculture operated from the 15th to the early 18th centuries, when they were abandoned. However, the society that managed these fields has been completely forgotten, as have any historical links with other groups such as the Sonjo and Marakwet, who still farm using similar methods in the Rift Valley.

The Archaeology of Colonialism

The process of colonialism in eastern Africa has left behind both extensive material remains, in the form of forts, churches, mosques, and administrative buildings, and an extensive archives. However, unlike Swahili archaeology and the archaeology of the interior, the archaeology of colonial settlements has received little academic attention. The study of these material remains has been viewed as adding little to the documents and, with so much indigenous archaeology to be done, as a waste of scarce resources. Yet, as has been shown in other parts of the world, this material can contribute a particular understanding that cannot be recovered from the documents.

The Portuguese (1498–1698)

Despite 200 years of colonial presence, the Portuguese left relatively little mark on East African societies. Fort Jesus in Mombasa, excavated by James Kirkman, is the outstanding building but dates only to 1593, nearly a century after the first contact. The site provides a range of artifactual and architectural evidence of this later period. The site of a wrecked Portuguese ship, which sank during the siege of Fort Jesus in 1697, has been excavated, but little of the findings have been published.

Otherwise the remains are scanty. At Malindi, a small chapel exists, built in about 1508, but the rest of the site (which probably includes a trading factory and customhouse) has never been investigated and has been built over in modern times. Another possible factory site is the Gereza, in Zanzibar City, where the remains of the church survive in the walls of the fort but only limited excavation has taken place. A Portuguese house may survive at Dondo, in the Lamu Archipelago, and two houses, possibly associated with the Portuguese, have been found in northern Zanzibar, but they were built using Swahili architectural styles. Finally, there are the remains of a fort (encased in a later fort) at Kilwa, probably built in 1506.

Questions that have not yet been properly addressed include how much the arrival of the Portuguese, the scale of contact and trade between the two groups, and the spread of Christianity had an impact on Swahili society and how the economy was affected by the Portuguese presence. The answer is probably "not very much." Sites contemporary with the Portuguese presence, such as Takwa and Gedi, contain few Portuguese artifacts. On Pemba, an island apparently settled by Portuguese farmers, there is no archaeological evidence whatsoever for their presence.

The Omani Arabs (1698–1964)

With the takeover of Fort Jesus, Omani Arabs began a period of settlement, initially in Mombasa and then from the mid-18th century on Zanzibar and Pemba and along the coastal areas between Malindi and Vumba. By the early 19th century, the ascendancy of the Bu'saidi over the Mazrui led to establishment of Sa'id bin Sultan's court on Zanzibar in 1834 and the development of a plantation economy, based upon coconuts and cloves and using slave labor. This process transformed the coastal economy and created links, through the caravan trade, with the far interior.

The archaeological evidence for Omani activity is present in surviving buildings and landscapes, but most of the work so far undertaken has been in the hands of conservation architects, supported by international funds to preserve the architectural heritage of East Africa. On Zanzibar, the royal palaces have been recorded and recently restored, and further work is planned on the forts of Zanzibar and Pemba. Conservation of and research on the Zanzibar Old Town (with many late 19th-century buildings), Bagamoyo (with the remains of the slave-trading settlement and German administrative buildings), Mombasa Old Town, and Lamu Fort have been undertaken with little archaeological input. In some cases, substantial damage has occurred to the archaeological resource. Outside the urban centers, numerous field monuments relating to the Omani occupation have survived, but these have little or no statutory protection.

The European Powers (about 1880–1964)

The establishment of European control in East Africa was rapid and effective and has left remains that are beginning to be appreciated as elements in the cultural landscape. These findings add a particular dimension to the understanding of the African past.

German *bomas,* District Commissioner's offices and courthouses, customhouses, and post offices survive from the early phases of colonization. Many of these buildings are now redundant, and while some have been reused as museums (such as the German *boma* at Arushu or the Lamu Museum), many have fallen into disrepair. The Karen Blixen Museum in Nairobi provides an excellent example of a colonial house that has been restored and furnished.

Serious study of the industrial archaeology of the region has hardly begun. The building of the Uganda Railway from the coast to Kampala was a major feat of Victorian engineering, and elements of the original scheme survive as stations, bridgeworks, and cuttings. Collections relating to the railway's construction are conserved in a small museum in Nairobi. Other examples of industrial archaeology include sisal mills, sugar mills, light railways (such as the Bububu Railway on Zanzibar), and port installations.

BIBLIOGRAPHY

Chittick, N. 1974. *Kilwa.* Nairobi: British Institute in Eastern Africa.

Horton. M. 1996. *Shanga: The archaeology of a Muslim trading settlement on the coast of East Africa.* London: British Institute in Eastern Africa.

Kirkman, J. 1957. Historical archaeology in Kenya, 1948–1956. *Antiquaries Journal* 37: 16–29.

———. 1974. *Fort Jesus: A Portuguese fortress on the East African coast.* Nairobi: British Institute in Eastern Africa.

Oliver, R. 1977. *Cambridge history of Africa,* vol. 3. Berkeley: University of California.

Schmidt, P. 1978. *Historical archaeology: A structural approach to an African culture.* Westport: Greenwood Press.

Sutton, J. 1990. *A thousand years of East Africa.* Nairobi: British Institute in Eastern Africa.

Mark Horton

CENTRAL AND SOUTHERN AFRICAN HISTORICAL ARCHAEOLOGY

Historical archaeology, understood as the study of material culture and concurrent written and oral sources of evidence, has a central role in writing the history of the last 500 years in southern and southeastern Africa. Oral traditions have, in some cases, been traced to the 15th century and have been used in conjunction with archaeological evidence for interpretations as diverse as rock paintings of the southwestern Cape and the stone ruins of the Zimbabwe Plateau. Written sources began with Arabic accounts of merchant adventurers cruising the Indian Ocean coastline and archives left by Portuguese, German, Dutch, and British colonial settlers. Considered together, such material and verbal sources of information are a rich vein of historical understanding.

There is no specific time at which prehistory (a problematic term in itself) can be said to end and historical archaeology to begin. On the Zimbabwe Plateau, the center of the precolonial state founded around Great Zimbabwe, the 16th- to

17th-century state of Mutapa is known from careful reconstruction of oral traditions, while the locations of many of its key settlements are still unknown. But on the southern part of the same upland area, the contemporary state of Torwa is known only from its archaeology. Here, the fragile thread of orally transmitted memory has been broken. Near the southern tip of the continent, the activities of the Dutch East Company's commander at the new garrison that was to become Cape Town are known from the daily logbook. But the ways in which the ordinary people of the new town lived, and the lives of the slaves who were to become one of the most significant sectors of the colonial population, can only be discerned from archaeological evidence. Many were illiterate, and little about their lives was written down.

Rather than an epoch or age, then, historical archaeology is an approach used to discover the past. As such, it is appropriate to review its contribution to understanding the past by following the major themes that have guided research and writing. Some of these themes have been traced in other entries in this volume: for example, rock-art studies using recorded San oral traditions and precolonial states where archaeology and oral evidence come together as sources of evidence. This article concentrates on the historical archaeology of European colonial settlement and penetration, processes that left behind more accumulated archaeological evidence than any other phase in Africa's very long history and which have caused unprecedented destabilization in the subcontinent's social texture and environments.

European colonial settlement in Africa began early in the 15th century with Portuguese enterprises on the continent's Mediterranean shoreline. Over the following decades, Portuguese adventurers pushed southward along the Atlantic Coast, finally rounding the Cape in 1488 and opening up the sea route to the East. They encountered pastoralists and, farther along the Indian Ocean Coast, farmers who practiced a mixed agricultural lifeway. Farther inland (although the crews of the caravels did not know it) were communities with a wide range of social and economic diversity: nomadic herders, agriculturists, hunter-foragers, chiefdoms, and state systems with complex economic arrangements and political hierarchies.

Neither the Portuguese nor the Dutch and British who followed them were much interested in southern Africa, which seemed a barren and inhospitable land with little to offer. Their goal was the East African coastline with its long-established Islamic city-states and, beyond them, the immense profits offered by a successful trade with the East. However, the sea voyage from Europe to Indonesia was long and grueling, and the Cape offered a convenient landfall for the fleets. In 1652, the Dutch East India Company established a scruffy settlement around a small earthen fort at Table Bay, with a vegetable garden to counter the depredations of scurvy. But extensive farming and ranching were more feasible, and over the following decades, the frontier was pushed toward the interior. Meanwhile, a parallel process of expansion had taken hold from the Indian Ocean coastline. Adventurers, many of them convicts with no prospects back home in Portugal, were cut loose from the king's garrisons that had been established at coastal anchorages. Seeking quick profits from trading and raiding, such *prazeros* established vast fiefdoms deep in the interior.

By the middle of the 18th century, the effects of European colonial penetration were firmly imprinted on southern Africa. A traveler arriving at the Cape found vineyards and wheat estates, heavily dependent on slave labor, where there were suitable soils and climate and colonial pastoralists grazing livestock deep into the interior. A visitor to Portuguese Sofala, or to one of the other coastal forts, would have found European settlement most established along the coastline or the river-valley trade routes involving slaves, ivory, and other commodities. Between these colonial regions were Xhosa, Zulu, and Sotho kingdoms and chiefdoms, increasingly involved in conflict with their colonial neighbors.

Given that one of the consistent themes in the history of southern Africa over the last 500 years has been conflict, it is not surprising that there has been emphasis on the frontier in historical archaeological research. For example, excavations at Oudepost, a bleak Dutch East India Company outpost on the southwestern Cape coast, were intended to establish the nature of the relationship between the small garrison of soldiers and local Khoikhoi pastoralists at the very end of the 17th century. Placed near the farthest limits of colonial penetration at the time, Oudepost's occupants traded with indigenous herdsmen and hunted extensively to supplement their meager rations before being massacred.

Other research projects have focused on the impact of the colonial frontier on local communities. For example, extensive research in the Zeekou Valley in the arid interior of the southern Cape has succeeded in mapping the addition of colonial artifacts to Stone Age possessions, suggesting the outline that colonial penetration took on a local basis and using archaeology to extend the limited range of documentary sources.

Frontiers continued to be zones of conflict between European traders and settlers in the 19th century. Long after Khoikhoi resistance had been broken by warfare and disease, groups of San hunter-foragers continued to control mountainous areas and occasionally raided colonial farms for livestock, thus invoking ferocious retaliation. But there was also cooperation—relations of trade and barter that created new patterns in the possession of material culture. Here, the most ubiquitous category of archaeological evidence is glass trade beads, which were imported into southern Africa in vast quantities and have survived in archaeological deposits. The wide geographical dispersal of archaeological sites from which glass beads have been recovered is testimony to the effects of contact with Europe, either through direct interaction or through commodities that entered long-established systems of distribution.

Archaeological studies at Oudepost, at the sites in the Zeekou Valley, and at the village occupations where glass beads have been found trace the consequences of European colonial settlement on the lives of ordinary men and women, whether soldiers at a garrison outpost many months from home or indigenous farmers and hunter-foragers taking advantage of new opportunities or feeling the consequences of a new political and economic order. It is one of the particular aims of historical archaeology to elucidate such ordinary lives, whether these be slaves, servants, or others who constituted the broad "underclass" in southern Africa's colonies.

Slavery was widespread in southern and south-central Africa. The Dutch East India Company imported slaves from the earliest years of the fledgling settlement, and, by the end of the 18th century, slaves formed the majority of Cape Town's population. Similarly, early towns on the eastern coast depended on slaves for a wide range of purposes, and Portuguese adventurers into the interior relied on their slave armies. At the same time, people from Europe whose place was near the bottom of colonial hierarchies lived in conditions that could have been worse than slavery, since these people did not represent a capital investment. Dutch East India Company soldiers who came to Cape Town were drawn from the poorest of the European peasantry, while those who made a life in outlying areas and on the frontier often did so as a last resort. Similarly, the Portuguese colonial enterprise depended heavily on convicts, who were freed on license and had no other prospects. Such people have often left little trace in the documentary record, being enumerated in broad terms or emerging only in court records. But despite archaeology's often-stated claim that it can elucidate such aspects of the past, evidence for material remains left by ordinary people can also be frustratingly difficult to find.

One site at which there does appear to be archaeological evidence for slavery is the Castle in Cape Town. Begun in 1666, this building housed the Dutch East India Company administration in southern Africa (as well as seving as the administrative center for the British colony in the 19th century) and was a microcosm of many aspects of colonial life, with workshops, stores, offices, barracks for the garrison, and houses for leading administrators. Slaves were also housed within the Castle (although not in formally designated areas). Parts of the Castle have been extensively excavated, allowing comparison between the ways in which the local elite lived and aspects of the lives of slaves housed communally in a dark and dank storeroom in the back part of the building. This sort of study adds to understanding the ways in which slaves lived and also the ways in which material culture was used in differentiating people from one another on day-by-day basis.

The archaeology of Cape Town's Castle is complemented by the archaeology of Vergelegen, a slave estate located a day's ride from the port and built at the beginning of the 18th century by a notoriously avaricious governor, who ensured that his needs were met on a palatial scale. Among the excavated buildings at Vergelegen is a slave barracks, in which a vernacular architectural style from northern Europe was adapted to a new colonial purpose. In this case, archaeological traces of the day-by-day debris left by slaves were disappointingly few—a nearby river seems to have claimed much that would otherwise have been the usual rubbish that makes up an archaeological site. However, an unexpected source of evidence was the burial of a middle-aged woman beneath the floor of the slave house. Isotopic analysis of tooth enamel and bone collagen has shown that her childhood diet was dominated by tropical grain crops that do not grow at the Cape, while as an adult slave woman, she ate mostly seafood. Studies such as these open up the possibilities of tracing aspects of life histories and their correlation with broad documentary sources.

In the early 18th century, when the Vergelegen slaves lived and died, Cape Town was still only a small settlement, and the only colonial town in the southeast was the nascent village of Stellenbosch, still a cluster of a few houses around a mill. But as the century unfolded, the distinction between the colonial town and countryside increased. This is reflected in probate inventories of material possessions taken at a person's death (long-established as key documentary source of historical archaeology) and in new patterns of architecture. Early colonial buildings reflected European vernacular traditions or were ad hoc constructions that reflected the needs imposed by the southern African environment and the possibilities offered by available materials. But from the third decade of the 18th century onward, new styles of colonial architecture began to emerge, particularly on the slave-run plantations, in which rigorous attention was given to symmetry in both plan and facade. Owners began to vie with one another for the latest fashions in

gable design. Historical archaeology has a central role in tracking the history of those buildings that still stand, in reconstructing the details of building histories, and in excavating what remains of formative structures.

It is a fair generalization that much of the purpose of this new architecture was the clear and public delimitation of differences standing within the colony, and again archaeology has an important contribution to make in tracking the evidence for the lives of the underclasses. For example, the excavation of well deposits from the 18th and 19th centuries have begun to provide details of the material culture used by people who lived and worked in the yards and alleys behind fashionable town houses in Cape Town and more information about the food people ate. Other important archaeological sites within the city are town dumps, which provide a broader impression of life across several streets or wards. Indeed, it is becoming clear that, in many respects, a city like Cape Town needs to be treated as a single archaeological site, making possible comparison with the archaeology of other towns in southern Africa and, for that matter, contemporary settlements in other parts of the interlinked world forged through European colonial expansion.

Less is known about the archaeology of rural areas, either in the Cape or in the Portuguese hinterland away from the Indian Ocean coastline. Excavations at Paradys, in the forests that backed Table Mountain, have resulted in a sequence that covers much of the 18th century, and artifact assemblages left by woodcutters and slaves. Paradys, however, was a specialized company outpost, and its occupants were not involved in mainstream farming activities. Other farming settlements in the Cape's wine and wheat lands have been partially excavated and sometimes show rich collections of artifacts and food remains. These settlements have potential for widespread research in the future. Even less fieldwork has been carried out in the central and eastern rural areas of the subcontinent, although there has been sufficient pilot research to demonstrate that much has probably survived the passage of time.

One aspect of the early colonial countryside that has attracted attention is vernacular architecture, reasserting the close connection between structuralist studies of buildings and historical archaeology, which has become the trademark of the discipline in the eastern United States. Thus it has been argued that farm buildings in the early colonial Cape conformed to a competence, a set of structural oppositions that constrained the built environment to a set of subconsciously held rules and procedures. This approach continues a line of interpretation that has long been argued for precolonial settlement forms among Bantu-speaking communities over much of southern and southeastern Africa and has, in turn, been continued in explanations of 19th-century colonial architecture in the "British" eastern Cape region. An objection to such structuralist explanations has been that, although they may provide convincing classifications for the built environment, they render their subject matter timeless and therefore "out of history," denying one of the main purposes of archaeological research.

An alternative to structuralist syntheses of the archaeology of colonialism has been a return to rich, particularistic historical description, concentrating on the detail of specific circumstances while remaining aware of general patterns in the ways in which material culture has been used. These sorts of studies tend to concentrate on the dynamics of power in colonial settlement, the ways in which material culture was used to impose authority. An example is the interpretation that has been offered for the moat around Cape Town's Castle. It was certainly intended that the new fortifications should defend the Dutch garrison, and the pace of construction reflected the general state of European politics, with feverish bursts of building when news came of war and temporary abandonment of the project during periods of peace. But at the same time, it is striking that so much attention was given to the moat. It was always clear that the moat could add little to the defense of the Castle in the event of attack, and excavation has shown that its formal specifications were never achieved. The moat was little more than an easily waded ditch. Its greater value was symbolic: a declaration of Dutch colonial authority.

In general, historical archaeology in south-central and southern Africa can be seen as a bridge between our own world and the long millennia of prehistory, which stretches back to the earliest evidence of humanity. There is an immense amount of historical archaeological evidence available for interpretation: midden deposits, building foundations, standing structures, and the very landscape itself, much of which is an artifact of the last few centuries of colonialism. As a discipline, historical archaeology is concerned with themes that make use of this rich body of evidence to address aspects of the history of colonialism, supplement documentary sources, and add perspectives to the interpretation of the past, which cannot be addressed through documentary evidence alone.

BIBLIOGRAPHY
Hall, M. 1996. *Archaeology of Africa.* London: James Currey, Ltd.
Schrire, C. 1995. *Digging through darkness: Chronicles of an archaeologist.* Charlottesville: University of Virginia Press.

Martin Hall

MARITIME ARCHAEOLOGY

Maritime archaeology, essentially a specialization within the field of archaeology, is a study of past people's relations to the sea. These relations can be complex and diverse and are not limited to a specific time period. Since the 1960s, the specialization has contributed in different ways to more complete understanding of past human activity. Focusing on the sea, either as a source of food or as a means of transport and communication, much information has been retrieved from the underwater environment and, in some cases, the adjacent shore. Often incorrectly regarded as a technical specialization, maritime archaeology entails more than underwater excavations and attempts to answer specific research questions using archaeological method and theory.

Maritime archaeology developed relatively recently in Africa. Its main focus is on historical shipwrecks, although the lifeways of indigenous coastal communities and traces of their shore-bound material culture, like shell middens and fish traps, also fall within the sphere of this specialization. In addition, traces of sealing and whaling activities undertaken during historical periods have been found in the southern regions of the continent and warrant further research. Nevertheless, most of the terrestrial work to date has been undertaken by prehistorical archaeologists.

Africa has seen intercontinental shipping traffic along its seaboards for many centuries, resulting in communication and interaction with various nations. In fact, non-Africans' impact, resulting not only in the disruption of indigenous societies through slavery and colonialism but also in a stimulation trade, international contact, and the emergence of people of color and multiracial communities, cannot be seen as separate from developments in the maritime sphere. There are strong indications that sporadic contacts between mariners and merchants from Arabia and India and Africans took place since the 1st century A.D. Although archaeological evidence is scanty, historical records indicate such contacts, which resulted in the exchange of products near the mouth of the Zambezi River and possibly farther south. At Kilwa, on the southern Tanzanian coast, ceramics from the Persian Gulf have been found, whereas at Chibuene in Mozambique, Persian ceramics and glass beads were excavated. Occupation at both places dates to the 8th and 9th centuries, indicating the early beginnings of intercontinental maritime trade. Going back even further in time, an account by Herodotus implies that Phoenicians might have rounded the southern tip of the African continent as early as 600 B.C., but archaeological evidence to support this account has not been found.

With the emergence of the Portuguese seaborne empire during the 15th century, western European nations started exploring the coasts of the African continent. In 1488, the Cape of Good Hope was rounded, but it took until 1497 before the sea route to Asia was discovered. During the 16th and 17th centuries, shipping traffic increased, motivated by the desire for African gold, ivory, and slaves and by trade with Asia. Maritime activities in the region inevitably resulted in shipping disasters. During the

last few decades, many historical shipwrecks were located, but the majority of these have been exploited by commercially motivated salvers or sport divers, resulting in a great loss of valuable historical and archaeological information.

The oldest historical wrecks identified to date are Portuguese. Of these, only very few have been explored scientifically, the best example being the *Santo Antonio de Tanna* 1697) off Mombasa, Kenya. Other Portuguese ships foundered in the Seychelles and around the coast of South Africa, where approximately 13 vessels were wrecked during the period between 1551 and 1647. Survivor camps are associated with some of these wrecks, at least one of which, the campsite of the survivors from the *Sao Gonçalo* 1630), has been excavated by archaeologists. With the emergence of the Dutch East India and English East India Companies during the beginning of the 17th century, shipping traffic along the African coast intensified and more wrecks occurred. One of the oldest examples is the wreck of the Dutch East India Company ship *Mauritius,* which sank during a homeward-bound voyage off Cape Lopez, Gabon, in 1609. Four years later, in 1613, another Dutch vessel was wrecked during an encounter with a Portuguese fleet off the island of St. Helena. Like the *Mauritius,* the shipwreck of the *Witte Leeuw* was explored by a team of archaeologists, and these projects, together with the underwater excavations in Mombasa, have indicated the need for the proper development of maritime archaeology in Africa.

At present, South Africa is playing a leading role in the field. Because of its location at the southernmost tip of the continent and about halfway between Asia and Europe, thousands of ships, many of which foundered, of many different nations passed here before the opening of the Suez Canal. This resulted in a huge concentration of shipwrecks of various types and age and representing approximately 30 different countries. The quantity and diversity of historical shipwrecks in South African waters is quite unique in a global context, and this resource can provide invaluable information on the history and culture of various nations.

Since the late 1980s, an infrastructure has been established to promote maritime archaeological research. Currently, the archaeology department of the University of Cape Town is the only place in Africa offering this specialization as part of its curriculum, and several research projects affilitated with the university have been carried out. These include a survey of historical shipwrecks around Robben Island, as part of a cultural-resource management program, and the first scientific underwater excavation in the southern African region. The ongoing excavation of the Dutch East India Company ship *Oosterland* (1697) in Table Bay not only serves to collect and analyze historical and archaeological information, it is also used as a teaching project where students and interested sport divers are instructed in aspects of fieldwork. In addition, the *Oosterland* project sets a standard for future involvement in the exploration of the nonrenewable resource represented by historical shipwrecks.

Maritime archaeology in Africa is still very much an open field. Although the archaeological potential situated under the sea and on the shores of the continent is tremendous, there is a minimal infrastructure available to promote teaching, research, and conservation. In addition, most African countries do not have adequate legislation or policing systems to protect their maritime heritage, which is under constant threat from indiscriminate salvage activities.

BIBLIOGRAPHY

Avery, G. 1975. Discussion on the age and use of tidal fish-traps *(visvywers)*. *The South African Archaeological Bulletin* 30: 105–113.

Green, J. 1980. East Indiamen wrecks. In *Archaeology under water: An atlas of the world's submerged sites,* ed. K. Muckelroy, 122–129. New York: McGraw-Hill.

L'Hour, M., L. Long, and E. Rieth. 1989. *Le Mauritius: La mémoire engloutée.* Paris: Casterman.

Parkington, J., et al. 1988. Holocene coastal settlement patterns in the western Cape. In *The archaeology of prehistoric coastlines,* eds. G. Bailey and J. Parkington, 22-42. Cambridge: Cambridge University Press.

Smith, A. B. 1986. Excavations at Plettenberg Bay, South Africa of the camp-site of the survivors of the wreck of the *Sao Gonçalo,* 1630. *The International Journal of Nautical Archaeology and Underwater Exploration* 15: 53–63.

Sténuit, R. 1977. *Le Witte Leeuw:* Fouilles sous-marine sur l'épave d'un navire de la V.O.C. coulé en 1613 a l'ile de Sainte Hélène. *Bulletin van het Rijksmuseum* 25: 4.

Werz, Bruno E. J. S. 1992. The excavation of the *Oosterland* in Table Bay: The first systematic exercise in maritime archaeology in southern Africa. *South African Journal of Science* 88: 85–90.

———. 1993. Shipwrecks of Robben Island, South Africa: An exercise in cultural resource management in the underwater environment. *The International Journal of Nautical Archaeology and Underwater Exploration* 22: 245-256.

———. 1993. South African shipwrecks and salvage: The need for improved management. *The International Journal of Nautical Archaeology and Underwater Exploration* 22: 237–244.

Bruno E. J. S. Werz

Index

——⁓⁓⁓⁓⁓⁓⁓——

References to illustrations and tables are printed in italics.

Olduwan industry in, 110
origins of ironworking in, 53
residual mountains in, 32
rock art in, 352, 353, 356
and salt production, 536, 537
Nigerian Pidgin (language), 175
Niki (Benin), ironworking in, 139, 140
Nile Basin, languages of, 163, 164
Nile River
   floodplains, 30
   water overflow into, 37
Nile Valley
   archaeological research in, 54
   civilization in, 56
   Egyptian civilization in, 52, 53
   environment of, 388
   origins of agriculture in, 57
Nilo-Saharan languages, 94–95, *95,* 99, 159, *163,* 163–164,
        166, 167, 168, 170, 172, 208
   culture of speakers of, 163–164
Nilo-Saharan–speaking people, 351
Nilotic languages, 99, 164, 167, 170
Niodougou (Mali), rock art at, 354
Nioro-Siracoro, copperworking at, 126
Njilian phase (of the Pleistocene), 44
Njoro River Cave (Kenya), 83
Nkile pottery horizon, 120, 121
Nkope (Malawi), Urewe and Kwale pottery in, 443
Nkope culture, subsistence patterns of, 447
Nkore kingdom, 502, 506
Nkrumah, K., 60
Noba-Noubadians (people), 470
Nok (Nigeria), 29, 306
noog, 225, 227
   domestication in Ethiopia, 415
north-central Africa, languages of, 167
North Africa, languages of, 160, 162
North Afro-Asiatic languages, 97
North Erythraic languages, 162
North Sudanic languages, 163
northeastern Africa, pastoralists in, 199–204, 200
northern Africa
   industries of, 325–329
   languages of, 172, 174
   See also Late Stone Age, in northern Africa; Neolithic
        Age, in northern Africa
Ntadi Yomba (Congo Republic), Tshitolian industry at, 316
Ntereso (Ghana), 67, 397
   evidence of domestic goats at, 423
Ntusi (Uganda), 503–504, 505
   evidence of domestic dogs at, 420
   historical archaeological research at, 553
Ntyebougou (Mali), Middle Late Stone Age, tools at, 310
Nuba (people), 62
Nubia
   attack on Egypt, 478
   control by Egypt, 485–486, 487
   evidence of early pottery in, 408

and the Indian Ocean trade, 480
influence on Egypt, 465–471
preagricultural cultures in, 386–388
resettlement of, 467
rock art in, 350
and trade with Egypt and the Horn of Africa, 485–487
Nubian C-Group culture, 70
Nubian kingdoms, 463
Nubian states, 458
Nuer (language), 62
Nuer (people), 62
Nungua industry, 331–332
Nupe (Nigeria), ironworking in, 139
Nupe (people), and ironworking, 138
Nupoid (language), 173
Nurse, D., 508, 551
Nyakyusa (people), 220
Nyamulagira (volcanoe), 31
Nyanga. *See* Inyanga (Zimbabwe)
Nyamwan (Ivory Coast), Upper Late Stone Age tools at, 311
Nyiragongo (volcanoe), 31
Nylsvley (South Africa), settlement patterns at, 152, 153
Nyos, Lake, 31

Oakhurst industry, 341
Oakley, K. P., 103
Obobogo (Cameroon)
   evidence of Upper Late Stone Age village life at, 311
   Middle Late Stone Age microliths at, 310
Ogori (language), 173
Oil palm, 33, 41, 226–227, 394–395
   early production of, 415–416
   production, and pottery manufacturing, 433
Okiek, or Dorobo (people), 179, 183, 184, 188, 207
   diet of, 186, 187
Okpoko, A., 418, 425
okra, 225, 226
Oku (chiefdom), and ironworking, 137, 139
Old Kingdom (Egypt), 466–468
Old Oyo (Nigeria), city walls at, 458
Oldogom (Tanzania), agriculture at, 231
Oldoninyo, Lengai (volcanoe), 31–32
Olduvai Developed Olduwan B industry. *See* Developed
        Olduwan industry
Olduvai Gorge (Tanzania), 29, 77, 78, 85, 86, 87, 88
   Australopithecus remains at, 254
   Developed Olduwan industry at, 111
   evidence of hominid diet at, 291–292, 293, 295
   evidence of hunting and forging at, 298, 301
   hominid remains at, 51, 290
   Homo remains at, 254, 257, 260
   huts and windbreaks at, evidence disputed, 271
   lakes at, 32
   obsidian artifacts at, 337
   Olduwan industry at, 110
   physical features of, 300
   as source of stone for tools, 185
   stone tools at, 256, 298, 300

IRON AGE AFRICA

VALLEY

Axum

Jebel Moya

Meroe

Napata

Jebel et Tomat

Nile

River

Koro Toro

BANTU EXPANSION

SAHARA DESERT

Daima

Agadez

Nok

Karkarichinkat

River

Jenne-Jeno

Rim

NIGER BASIN

Kumbi Saleh

Niger

Tegdaoust

Bambuk

Rao